ENCYCLOPEDIA
OF THE
MUSICAL THEATRE

ENCYCLOPEDIA
OF THE
MUSICAL THEATRE

Stanley Green

*An updated reference guide to over 2000 performers,
writers, directors, productions and songs of the
musical stage, both in New York and London.*

A DA CAPO PAPERBACK

Library of Congress Cataloging in Publication Data

Green, Stanley.
    Encyclopedia of the musical theatre.

    (A Da Capo paperback)
    Original title: Encyclopaedia of the musical
theatre.
    Reprint of the ed. published by Dodd, Mead, New York.
    1. Musical revue, comedy, etc. – Dictionaries.
I. Title.
[ML102.M88G7 1980]   782.81'03'21   79-27168
ISBN 0-306-80113-2

This Da Capo Press paperback edition of
Encyclopedia of the Musical Theatre
is an unabridged republication of the
first edition published in New York in 1976,
supplemented with photographs and addenda.
It is reprinted by arrangement
with Dodd, Mead & Company.

Published by Da Capo Press, Inc.
A Subsidiary of Plenum Publishing Corporation
233 Spring Street, New York, New York 10013

PREFACE

This is a ready-reference book containing succinct information regarding the most prominent people, productions, and songs of the musical theatre, both in New York (incl. off-Bway) and London. The term "musical theatre" is used to designate productions generally called musical comedy, musical play, musical farce, musical spectacle, just plain musical, revue, operetta, and, if offered for a regular commercial run, opera. Though there are exceptions, the aim has been to steer clear of vaudeville (or variety), Gilbert and Sullivan, limited engagements, cabaret entertainments, plays with one or two songs, foreign-language musicals, one-man or one-woman shows, one-act musicals, minstrel shows, concert parties, màtinée musicals, midnight musicals, children's musicals, pantomime, ice shows, amateur shows, benefit shows, retrospective revues devoted to one composer's career, and revues that aren't really musical (such as *Beyond the Fringe*).

The people included herein are actors, composers, lyricists, librettists, directors, choreographers, and producers. Each entry contains a year-by-year listing of all the New York or London musical stage productions with which the person was associated. Since only two cities are involved, the designated locales of (NY) and (L) are used only when the show was *not* presented in the city where the individual usually worked. A name in parenthesis preceded by "né" or "née" is the person's real full name; a capitalized name in parenthesis is the person's first or middle name or nickname that is not used professionally.

In the case of an actor or actress, the parts he or she played in book musicals follow the titles of the shows. Roles in major touring companies are also included.

If the entry is that of a composer or lyricist, the name of the collaborator follows the show's title, except when otherwise indicated.

An actor, director, choreographer, or producer who was involved in a musical presented first in New York and then in London—or first in London and then in New York—receives a second listing of that particular show; the composer, lyricist, or librettist, however, is credited only for the original production. Whenever a different title appears in parentheses following the title of a musical, the second one is that of a previously listed musical from which the new one has been adapted.

Under musical productions, only the best-known songs and leading cast members (followed by the roles they played) are listed. Performance numbers follow the theatre where the show played; the absence of a number means that the show was still playing as of January 1, 1976. Books written about specific shows are listed at the end of the entries; printed texts are found in the Addendum. Original-cast and studio-cast record albums are also listed in the Addendum.

Some abbreviations used:

> p. — performances
> r — revival or revision
> repl. — cast replacement
> lyr. — lyricist
> lib. — librettist
> sk. — sketches
> comp. — composer
> chor. — choreographer
> dir. — director

v

prod. — producer
bib. — bibliography

Appreciation is due the following for their interest and help: Bill Borden, Louis Botto, Rita Chambers, Robert Friedman, Vivien Friedman (of Chappell Music), Charles Gaynor, Martin Gross, Edward Jablonski, Miles Kreuger, Dan Langan, Irv Lichtman, Ian MacBey, Alfred Simon, Tilda Stoneburn, Walter Wager (of ASCAP). Special thanks, too, to bibliothecal specialists Paul Myers, Dorothy Swerdlove, Monty Arnold, Rod Bladell, Donald Fowle, Brigitta Keupers, Maxwell Silverman, and Betty Wharton of the Theatre Collection, NY Public Library at Lincoln Center, and Louis A. Rachow and Carl Willers of the Walter Hampden Memorial Library at The Players, NY.

I am also particularly grateful that, as usual, Kay Green, Susan Green, and Rudy David Green were available to read text, make corrections, offer suggestions, provide information, and help decide who goes in and what stays out.

STANLEY GREEN

CONTENTS

Aarons, Alex A., producer; b. Philadelphia, Pa., 1891; d. Beverly Hills, Cal., March 14, 1943. Aarons joined Vinton Freedley in 1923 to form a Bway producing team that presented 11 musicals in 10 years (incl. *Lady, Be Good!, Oh, Kay!, Funny Face, Hold Everything!, Girl Crazy*). Seven Aarons-Freedley shows and two produced by Aarons alone had scores by George and Ira Gershwin. In 1928 the producers built the Alvin Theatre, NY. Fred and Adele Astaire appeared in three Aarons musicals; Gertrude Lawrence was in two. Aarons was the son of Bway producer-composer Alfred E. Aarons.

Asterisk indicates musical co-produced with Mr. Freedley:
1919   La La Lucille
1922   For Goodness Sake
1924   Lady, Be Good! *
1925   Tell Me More
       Tip-Toes *
1926   Oh, Kay! *
1927   Funny Face *
1928   Here's Howe *
       Hold Everything! *
       Treasure Girl *
1929   Spring Is Here *
       Heads Up! *
1930   Girl Crazy *
1933   Pardon My English *

Abbott, George (Francis), director, librettist, producer; b. Forestville, NY. June 25, 1887. One of the most influential Bway directors, Abbott is most closely identified with well-constructed, swiftly-paced musical comedies. He directed five Rodgers and Hart shows between 1935 and 1940 (incl. *On Your Toes, The Boys from Syracuse, Pal Joey*); since then he has worked on musicals with scores by Hugh Martin and Ralph Blane (*Best Foot Forward*), Leonard Bernstein, Betty Comden and Adolph Green (*Wonderful Town*), Jule Styne and Sammy Cahn (*High Button Shoes*), Frank Loesser (*Where's Charley?*), Irving Berlin (*Call Me Madam*), Arthur Schwartz and Dorothy Fields (*A Tree Grows in Brooklyn*), Rodgers and Hammerstein (*Me and Juliet*), Richard Adler and Jerry Ross (*The Pajama Game, Damn Yankees*), Bob Merrill (*New Girl in Town*), Jerry Bock and Sheldon Harnick (*Fiorello!*), Stephen Sondheim (*A Funny Thing Happened on the Way to the Forum*). Ray Bolger, Gwen Verdon, and Carol Burnett each appeared in two shows directed by Abbott; other actors in his musicals: Jimmy Durante, Gene Kelly, Vivienne Segal, Phil Silvers, Ethel Merman, Shirley Booth, Rosalind Russell, John Raitt, Zero Mostel, Liza Minnelli.

Abbott began his Bway career as an actor in 1913, became a playwright in 1925 (*Broadway, Three Men on a Horse*), a director in 1926, a producer in 1934. Bib: *Mister Abbott* by Abbott (Random, NY 1963).

Unless otherwise noted Mr. Abbott was director of following; asterisk indicates he was also librettist or co-librettist:
1935   Jumbo
1936   On Your Toes *
1938   The Boys from Syracuse * (also prod.)
1939   Too Many Girls (also prod.)
1940   Pal Joey (also prod.)
1941   Best Foot Forward (also prod.)
1942   Beat the Band (also prod.)
1944   On the Town
1945   Billion Dollar Baby
1947   Barefoot Boy with Cheek (also prod.)
       High Button Shoes

1948	Look, Ma, I'm Dancin' (also prod.)
	Where's Charley? *
1949	Touch and Go (prod. only)
1950	Call Me Madam
1951	A Tree Grows in Brooklyn * (also prod.)
1953	Wonderful Town
	Me and Juliet
1954	The Pajama Game *
	On Your Toes * (r) (also prod.)
1955	Damn Yankees *
1957	New Girl in Town *
1959	Once Upon a Mattress
	Fiorello! *
1960	Tenderloin *
1962	A Funny Thing Happened on the Way to the Forum
1963	A Funny Thing Happened on the Way to the Forum (L)
1964	Fade Out—Fade In
1965	Flora, the Red Menace *
	Anya *
1967	How Now, Dow Jones
1968	The Education of H*Y*M*A*N K*A*P*L*A*N
1969	The Fig Leaves Are Falling
1973	The Pajama Game* (r)
1976	Music Is*

Adams, Lee, lyricist; b. Mansfield, Ohio, Aug. 14, 1924. With composer Charles Strouse, Adams has written scores for Bway successes *Bye Bye Birdie* ("A Lot of Livin' to Do," "One Boy," "Put on a Happy Face"), *Golden Boy* ("I Want to Be with You"), *Applause* ("Applause"). The team's "Once Upon a Time" was sung in *All American.*

1960	Bye Bye Birdie
1962	All American
1964	Golden Boy
1966	It's a Bird It's a Plane It's Superman
1970	Applausé
1972	I and Albert (L)
1978	A Broadway Musical

"Adelaide's Lament." Music & lyric by Frank Loesser. Soliloquy sung by Vivian Blaine in *Guys and Dolls* (NY 1950; L 1953), revealing psychosomatic ailments as a result of the continual postponements of her marriage. Originally the song was to have been the lament of a strip-tease dancer who catches cold from overexposure, but the lyric was altered once the role was changed to that of a singer.

Adler, Richard, composer, lyricist, producer; b. New York, Aug. 3, 1921. Adler and his partner, Jerry Ross, had two major Bway hits: *The Pajama Game* ("Hey, There," "Hernando's Hideaway," "There Once Was a Man") and *Damn Yankees* ("Heart," "Whatever Lola Wants"). The writers, who were protégés of composer-lyricist Frank Loesser, began their career with songs for *John Murray Anderson's Almanac* (1953). Since Ross's death in 1955, Adler has devoted most of his time to writing commercial jingles and producing. He was once married to actress Sally Ann Howes.

1954	The Pajama Game (Ross)
1955	Damn Yankees (Ross)
1961	Kwamina
1973	The Pajama Game (r) (also coprod.)

Adonis (1884). Music by John Eller & Edward E. Rice; lyrics & book by William F. Gill & Henry E. Dixey.

SONGS: "I'm a Merry Little Mountain Maid," "A Most Romantic Meeting," "The Blushing Bride," "He Would Away," "It's English, You Know" (added).

NEW YORK: Sept. 4, 1884
BIJOU OPERA HOUSE: 603 p.

Presented by William F. Gill; directed by Henry E. Dixey; costumes, P. Godchaux; music director, Henry Sator.

CAST: Henry E. Dixey (*Adonis*), Amelia Summerville (*Rosetta*), George Howard (*Bunion Turke*), Herbert Gresham (*Marquis de Baccarat*), Lillie Grubb (*Talamea*), Carrie Godfrey (*Artea*).

In the theatre program *Adonis* was heralded as "A Spectacular Burlesque Nightmare," its libretto was described as "A Perversion of Common Sense," and the title character was identified as "an accomplished young gentleman of undeniably good family, inasmuch as he can trace his ancestry back through the Genozoic, Mesazoic and Palaeozoic periods, until he finds it resting on the Archaean Time. His family name, by the way, is 'Marble.'" All this self-confessed madness apparently helped put audiences in the right mood to enjoy a story dealing with a Greek sculptress, Talamea, who falls in love with her marble statue of Adonis. When the goddess Artea brings Adonis to life, however, the stone-hearted hero cold-shoulders his creator in favor of the simple country maid, Rosetta. But their love is thwarted by the wicked Marquis de Baccarat, and when Artea allows Adonis to choose between remaining a mortal or returning to limestone, he willingly goes back to his pedestal. Before he does, however, the character has appeared in such guises as "astronomer, dancer, slugger, postmaster, dry-goods clerk, tonsorial artist, drug clerk, and old-clothes man; also Henry Irving, the Country Girl and Paderewski."

The musical made a matinee idol of Henry E. Dixey, thenceforth known as Adonis Dixey, who toured in it extensively, and in 1886 brought it to the Gaiety Theatre, London. Until it was overtaken by *A Trip to China-town*, *Adonis* held the record as Bway's longest-running musical. Its story, of course, was a burlesque of the Pygmalion-Galatea legend that inspired Bernard Shaw and, ultimately, *My Fair Lady*. Another musical about a statue coming to life and eventually returning to stone was *One Touch of Venus* (NY 1943).

Adrian, Max (né Max Bor), actor; b. Enniskillen, Ireland, Nov. 1, 1903; d. London, Jan. 19, 1973. Reedy-voiced, sharp-featured, flamboyant actor who appeared in classical dramas as well as musicals. After his London stage debut in 1927, Adrian won success in Laurier Lister revues for 10 years, creating most of his own material. He was also seen in many films (incl. *Henry V*).

1942	Light and Shade
1947	Tuppence Coloured
1948	Oranges and Lemons
1951	Penny Plain
1953	Airs on a Shoestring
1956	Fresh Airs
	Candide (NY) (*Dr. Pangloss*)
1972	Trelawney (*Sir William Gower*)

"After the Ball." Music & lyric by Charles K. Harris. Interpolated during the run of *A Trip to Chinatown* (NY 1892), in which it was sung by J. Aldrich Libbey. Also sung in *Show Boat* in the 1905 Trocadero New Year's Eve scene by Norma Terris (NY 1927) and Edith Day (L 1928). The use of the song in the Kern and Hammerstein musical is unusual in that the writers chose a genuine old song for the climactic reunion between heroine and her father rather than writing a new "old" one themselves. Purists, too, have noted that since the song was written in 1892, it was a bit dated for the scene, which took place in 1905. Though the lyric of the song's refrain is unspecific, the three stanzas of the verse relate the sad saga of a lovers' breakup during a formal ball as a result of the young man's observing his sweetheart being kissed by a stranger. They are never reconciled, and years later the man discovers that the kissing stranger was the girl's brother.

"After You, Who?" Music & lyric by Cole Porter. Fred Astaire's serenade to an irreplaceable love, sung in *Gay Divorce* both in NY (1932) and London (1933).

"Ah! Sweet Mystery of Life." Music by Victor Herbert; lyric by Rida Johnson Young. Sung by Orville Harrold and Emma Trentini as the final romantic expression in *Naughty Marietta* (NY 1910). The song was used throughout the operetta as an incomplete motif since the coquettish heroine, unable to recall more than fragments of a melody that came to her in a dream (the song was originally called "Dream Melody"), vows to give her heart only to the man who can complete it. (A similar use was made of the song "My Ship" in *Lady in the Dark*, NY 1941.)

"Ain't Misbehavin'." Music by Thomas "Fats" Waller & Harry Brooks; lyric by Andy Razaf. Song of self-repression introduced by Margaret Simms, Paul Bass, and Russell Wooding's Hallelujah Singers in all-Negro revue, *Hot Chocolates* (NY 1929). Six weeks after the opening, Louis Armstrong joined the cast and was featured during intermission playing the music on his trumpet. Later during run, Bass was replaced by Cab (then Cabell) Calloway.

Albert, Eddie (né Edward Albert Heimberger), actor, singer; b. Rock Island, Ill., April 22, 1908. Genial, blond Bway leading man who introduced "This Can't Be Love" in *The Boys from Syracuse* and "Let's Take an Old-Fashioned Walk" in *Miss Liberty*. Albert has also been in nonmusicals (*Brother Rat, Room Service*) and in over 50 films.

> 1938   The Boys from Syracuse (*Antipholus of Syracuse*)
> 1949   Miss Liberty (*Horace Miller*)

> 1960   The Music Man (*Harold Hill,* repl.)

Albery, (Arthur Rolleston) Donald, producer; b. London, June 19, 1914. Albery produced London's biggest musical hit, *Oliver!* Other long-run attractions include *Grab Me a Gondola, Irma la Douce, Fings Ain't Wot They Used t'Be,* and *Blitz!*

> 1956   Grab Me a Gondola
> 1957   Zuleika
> 1958   Irma la Douce
> 1959   Make Me an Offer
> 1960   Fings Ain't Wot They Used t'Be
>   Oliver!
>   The Art of Living
> 1962   Not to Worry?
>   Blitz!
>   Fiorello!
> 1963   Oliver! (NY)
> 1964   Instant Marriage
> 1966   Jorrocks
> 1967   Oliver!(r)
> 1968   Man of La Mancha
> 1970   Mandrake
> 1972   Popkiss
> 1976   Very Good Eddie (r)

"Alice Blue Gown." Music by Harry Tierney; lyric by Joseph McCarthy. Sung by Edith Day in *Irene* (NY 1919, L 1920) in recollection of a gown that a friend had once given her. As she explained, "Mother'll tell you it's the only thing I ever put on a hanger." "Alice Blue" was the name given to a particular shade favored by President Theodore Roosevelt's daughter, Alice.

"All Alone." Music & lyric by Irving Berlin. Though not written specifically for the theatre, this poignant waltz was added to the 1924 *Music Box Revue* after the show's opening. Grace Moore and Oscar Shaw sang it to each other via illuminated telephones as they stood on opposite sides of a bare, darkened stage.

"All Alone Monday." Music by Harry Ruby; lyric by Bert Kalmar. Mutual loneliness covering every day in the week enumerated by Marie Saxon and Jack Whiting in *The Ramblers* (NY 1926).

"All at Once You Love Her." Music by Richard Rodgers; lyric by Oscar Hammerstein II. Latin-flavored ballad about the suddenness of falling in love introduced in last scene of Act I of *Pipe Dream* (NY 1955). In the scene, a beach restaurant, the piece is first sung by a strolling Mexican (Jerry LaZarre) in Spanish; hero (William Johnson) then interprets the lyric to heroine (Judy Tyler), they sing the last part as a duet, and there's no question that the sentiment now applies to them.

"All er Nothin'." Music by Richard Rodgers; lyric by Oscar Hammerstein II. Will Parker's ultimatum to boy-crazy Ado Annie in *Oklahoma!*—which she refuses to accept. Sung by Lee Dixon and Celeste Holm in NY (1943), by Walter Donahue and Dorothea MacFarland in London (1947).

"All for the Best." Music & lyric by Stephen Schwartz. Contrapuntal philosophical duet performed as rapid-fire vaudeville turn by Jesus (Stephen Nathan) and Judas (David Haskell) in *Godspell* (NY 1971). In London version (1971), parts were played by David Essex and Jeremy Irons.

"All I Need Is the Girl." Music by Jule Styne; lyric by Stephen Sondheim. Song-and-dance routine of a would-be Fred Astaire performed by Paul Wallace in *Gypsy* (NY 1959) and joined in the "finale" by Sandra

Church. Andrew Norman and Zan Charisse did it in the show's London production (1973).

"All in Fun." Music by Jerome Kern; lyric by Oscar Hammerstein II. A casual affair in glittering Manhattan becomes surprisingly serious. Frances Mercer and Jack Whiting introduced the song in *Very Warm for May* (NY 1939).

"All of These and More." Music by Jerry Bock; lyric by Sheldon Harnick. Breathless revelation of what a girl and boy feel like when the other is near—all the way from shooting star and a rising tide to a sparkling wine and a sweeping waltz. Introduced by Mindy Carson and Steve Forrest in *The Body Beautiful* (NY 1958).

"All of You." Music & lyric by Cole Porter. Cartographical love song used by Don Ameche, as the irrepressible American, to break down the resistance of Hildegarde Neff, as the repressible Russian, in *Silk Stockings* (NY 1955).

"All the Things You Are." Music by Jerome Kern; lyric by Oscar Hammerstein II. Sung by Hollace Shaw, Frances Mercer, Hiram Sherman, Ralph Stuart in *Very Warm for May* (NY 1939). In a poll conducted by Henry Hewes in the *Saturday Review* in 1964, more composers picked this song as their favorite than any other. Hammerstein, however, was never satisfied with his use of the word "divine" in the line, "Some day I'll know that moment divine," but was unable to find a more appropriate word for the needed rhyme.

"All Through the Night." Music & lyric by Cole Porter. Serenade to an exclusively nocturnal love in *Anything Goes*, sung by William Gaxton (NY 1934) and Jack Whiting (L 1935). The theme is similar to that of the Kern-Hammerstein "In the Heart of the Dark," sung in *Very Warm for May* (NY 1939).

Allegro (1947). Music by Richard Rodgers; lyrics & book by Oscar Hammerstein II.

SONGS: "I Know It Can Happen Again," "One Foot, Other Foot," "A Fellow Needs a Girl," "So Far," "To Have and to Hold," "You Are Never Away," "Money Isn't Everything," "Yatata, Yatata, Yatata," "The Gentleman Is a Dope," "Allegro," "Come Home."

NEW YORK: Oct. 10, 1947
MAJESTIC THEATRE; 315 p.

Presented by The Theatre Guild; directed & choreographed by Agnes de Mille; settings & lighting, Jo Mielziner; costumes, Lucinda Ballard; music director, Salvatore Dell'Isola; orchestrations, Robert Russell Bennett.

CAST: John Battles (*Joseph Taylor Jr.*), Annamary Dickey (*Marjorie Taylor*), William Ching (*Dr. Joseph Taylor*), John Conte (*Charlie Townsend*), Muriel O'Malley (*Grandma Taylor*), Roberta Jonay (*Jennie Brinker*), Lisa Kirk (*Emily West*).

Rodgers and Hammerstein's third collaboration was an ambitious undertaking dealing with the theme of institutional corruption told through the life of a doctor from his birth through his 35th year. The story covers his school days, marriage, success, and disillusionment working in a big Chicago hospital, and eventual return to the small midwestern town whence he came. Along the way his wife proves unfaithful and he falls in love with a nurse. Because of the episodic nature of the story, choreographer Agnes de Mille, to ensure greater fluidity, was given her first chance to direct an entire production. Representational sets were abandoned in favor of bare backdrops with multilevel staging areas designed and lighted by Jo Mielziner. There was also a Greek chorus to comment on the action and speak and sing directly to the actors and audience. Beginning Nov. 1948, the musical toured for six months.

Allen, Fred (né John Florence Sullivan), actor; b. Cambridge, Mass., May 31, 1894; d. New York, March 17, 1956. Heavily pouched eyes, a deadpan expression, and a down-east twang easily identified Fred Allen. Specializing in topical monologues, he was a vaudeville headliner before scoring his biggest Bway hits in *The Little Show* and *Three's a Crowd*. Allen won even greater fame during the 30s and 40s in his own radio series, in which his wife, Portland Hoffa, was a member of the cast. Bib: *Much Ado About Me* by Allen (Little, Brown, Boston, 1956).

1922	The Passing Show	
1924	Vogues of 1924	
1929	Polly (*Addie Stiles*)	
	The Little Show	
1930	Three's a Crowd	

"Almost Like Being in Love." Music by Frederick Loewe; lyric by Alan Jay Lerner. The chief romantic duet for American wanderer David Brooks and Scottish maiden Marion Bell in *Brigadoon* (NY 1947). In London version (1949), it was sung by Philip Hanna and Patricia Hughes.

"Alone Together." Music by Arthur Schwartz; lyric by Howard Dietz. Brooding, minor-key ballad sung by Jean Sargent and danced by Tamara Geva and Clifton Webb in Bway revue, *Flying Colors* (1932). For this number, designer Norman Bel Geddes constructed a receding stage which enabled the two inseparable lovers to disappear after their dance.

Alton, Robert (né Robert Alton Hart), choreographer; b. Bennington, Vt., 1897; d. Hollywood, Cal., June 12, 1957. Bway choreographer of the 30s and 40s who did much to help individualize routines by giving dancers solos and breaking up chorus line into small groups. Also directed dances for Hollywood films.

1919	Take It from Me (dancer only)
1924	Greenwich Village Follies (dancer only)
1933	Hold Your Horses
1934	Ziegfeld Follies
	Life Begins at 8:40
	Anything Goes
	Thumbs Up!
1935	Parade
1936	Ziegfeld Follies
1937	Hooray for What!
	Between the Devil
1938	You Never Know
	Leave It to Me
1939	One for the Money
	The Streets of Paris
	Too Many Girls
	DuBarry Was a Lady
1940	Two for the Show
	Panama Hattie
	Higher and Higher
	Pal Joey
1941	Sons o' Fun
1942	By Jupiter
	Count Me In
1943	Ziegfeld Follies
	Early to Bed (also dir.)
1944	Laffing Room Only
1952	Pal Joey (r) (also dir.)
1953	Hazel Flagg
	Me and Juliet
1955	The Vamp (also dir.)

"Always True to You in My Fashion." Music & lyric by Cole Porter. Qualified view of romantic fidelity sung by Lisa Kirk in *Kiss Me, Kate* (NY 1948), then by Julie Wilson in London production (1951). The title was derived from the line, "I have been faithful to thee, Cynara! in my fashion," from Ernest Dowson's poem *"Nom Sum Qualis Eram Bonae Sub Regno Cynarae."*

Ameche, Don (né Dominic Felix Amici), actor, singer; b. Kenosha, Wis., May 31, 1908. Toothy, mustached romantic lead who first won fame as screen actor, and who introduced "Paris Loves Lovers" and "All of You" in *Silk Stockings*.

1955	Silk Stockings (*Steve Canfield*)
1958	Goldilocks (*Max Grady*)
1961	13 Daughters (*Chun*)
1967	Henry, Sweet Henry (*Henry Orient*)
1972	No, No, Nanette (US tour) (*Jimmy Smith*)

"America." Music by Leonard Bernstein; lyric by Stephen Sondheim. Rhythmic put-down of life in America as seen through the eyes of Puerto Ricans. Sung and danced by Chita Rivera, Marilyn Cooper, and "Shark" girls in *West Side Story* (NY 1957); in London version (1958) by Miss Rivera, Francesca Bell, and "Shark" girls.

"And Her Mother Came Too." Music by Ivor Novello; lyric by Dion Titheradge. Sung by Jack Buchanan in revue *A to Z* (L 1921), and by Clifton Webb in *Jack and Jill* (NY 1923). The confession of a gentleman of leisure who is unable to be alone with his inamorata because of the tenacious presence of the girl's mother.

"And Love Was Born." Music by Jerome Kern; lyric by Oscar Hammerstein II. Poetic images attending the birth described by Reinald Werrenrath in *Music in the Air* (NY 1932) and by Lance Fairfax in London production (1933).

"And This Is My Beloved." Music & lyric by Robert Wright & George Forrest, based on third movement of Aleksandr Borodin's String Quartet in D. Appropriately, the song was introduced by a vocal quartet in *Kismet* (NY 1953). Unable to keep an appointment with her beloved, Doretta Morrow is questioned by her father, Alfred Drake, about the man's appearance. At the same time, on the other side of the stage, Caliph Richard Kiley describes Doretta in answer to questions put to him by his Wazir of Police, Henry Calvin. In London version (1955), the quartet was Miss Morrow, Drake, Peter Grant, and Paul Whitsun-Jones.

Anderson, John Murray, director, lyricist; b. St. John's, Newfoundland, Sept. 20, 1886; d. New York, Jan. 30, 1954. Anderson's coordination of movement, color and design, plus his use of technical innovations such as the revolving stage and treadmills, helped establish him as one of Bway's most innovative directors. His *Greenwich Village Follies* series, his two *Almanacs, Jumbo,* and two post-Ziegfeld *Ziegfeld Follies* were among his notable productions. He also staged circuses, Billy Rose's Aquacades, nightclub revues, and the film *The King of Jazz.* As lyricist, he collaborated with composers A. Baldwin Sloane, Milton Ager ("A Young Man's Fancy" with co-lyricist Jack Yellen), Carey Morgan, Louis Hirsch, Con Conrad. Bib: *Out Without My Rubbers* by Anderson (Library, NY, 1954).

Asterisk indicates Mr. Anderson was also lyricist:

1919	Greenwich Village Follies * (Sloane)
1920	What's in a Name * (Ager) (also sk., prod.)
	Greenwich Village Follies * (Sloane)
1921	League of Notions (L)
	Greenwich Village Follies * (Morgan) (also sk.)
1922	Greenwich Village Follies * (Hirsch)
1923	Jack and Jill
	Greenwich Village Follies * (Hirsch, Conrad)
1924	Greenwich Village Follies (also sk.)
	Music Box Revue
1925	Dearest Enemy
1928	Hello, Daddy
1929	John Murray Anderson's Almanac (also prod.)
1932	Bow Bells (L)
	Fanfare (L)
	Over the Page (Fanfare) (L) (also sk.)
1934	Ziegfeld Follies
	Life Begins at 8:40
	Thumbs Up!
1935	Jumbo
1936	Ziegfeld Follies
1937	Home and Beauty (L)
1939	One for the Money
1940	Two for the Show
1941	Sunny River
1943	Ziegfeld Follies
1944	Laffing Room Only
1945	The Firebrand of Florence
1946	Three to Make Ready
1948	Heaven on Earth
1952	New Faces of 1952
	Two's Company
1953	John Murray Anderson's Almanac

Anderson, Maxwell, librettist, lyricist; b. Atlantic, Pa., Dec. 15, 1888; d. Stamford, Conn., Feb. 28, 1959. Playwright (*What Price Glory, Mary of Scotland, Winterset*) who joined composer Kurt Weill to create two Bway musicals. Their songs include "September Song," "It Never Was You," "Lost in the Stars."

1938	Knickerbocker Holiday
1949	Lost in the Stars

André Charlot's Revue of 1924 (1924). Music by Noël Coward, Philip Braham, Ivor Novello, etc.; lyrics by Coward, Ronald Jeans, Dion Titheradge, Douglas Furber, etc.; sketches by Jeans, Furber, Titheradge, etc. Songs:"Parisian Pierrot" (Coward), "You Were Meant for Me" (Noble Sissle–Eubie Blake), "There's Life in the Old Girl Yet" (Coward), "Limehouse Blues" (Braham-Furber), "March with Me!" (Novello-Furber), "Night May Have Its Sadness" (Novello–Collie Knox).

NEW YORK: Jan. 9, 1924
TIMES SQUARE THEATRE; 298 p.

Presented by The Selwyns; directed by André Charlot; choreographed by David Bennett; settings, Marc Henri & Laverdet; costumes, G. K. Benda, Guy de Gerald, Lenief, Louiseboulanger; music director, Philip Braham.

CAST: Beatrice Lillie, Gertrude Lawrence, Jack Buchanan, Fred Leslie, Herbert Mundin, Douglas Furber, Robert Hobbs, Marjorie Brooks, Jessie Matthews (chorus), Constance Carpenter (chorus).

LONDON: March 30, 1925
PRINCE OF WALES THEATRE; 513 p.

Presented by André Charlot; directed by Charlot & Dion Titheradge; settings, Marc Henri & Laverdet; costumes, G. K. Benda, Guy de Gerald, Lucien Lelong; music director, Philip Braham.

CAST: Beatrice Lillie, Gertrude Lawrence, Robert Hobbs, Herbert Mundin, Peter Haddon, Jessie Matthews, Dorma Ward, Hazel Wynne, Patrick Adair, Marjorie Robertson (Anna Neagle) (chorus).

Made up of material from previous André Charlot London revues—incl. Bran Pie (1919), A to Z (1921), and Noël Coward's London Calling! (1923)—the intimate, witty Bway production was a welcome contrast to the elaborate revues of Ziegfeld, John

Murray Anderson, George White, and Earl Carroll. More important, it served to introduce New York to Beatrice Lillie (whose highlight number was "March with Me!"), Gertrude Lawrence (singing "Parisian Pierrot" and "Limehouse Blues"), and Jack Buchanan (replaced in April 1924 by Nelson Keys).

Capitalizing on the show's transatlantic fame, Charlot offered a London version at the end of a six-month US tour. (It was actually a second edition of a Charlot Revue that had opened at the Prince of Wales Sept. 23, 1924, with Morris Harvey, Maisie Gay, Henry Kendall, and Phyllis Monkman.) For this production Miss Lillie and Miss Lawrence teamed for a "Broadway Medley" of US songs. In July 1925, Miss Lillie left the cast and Jack Buchanan joined it. In Nov. he was replaced by Cyril Ritchard.

On Nov. 10, 1925, The Charlot Revue of 1926 opened at the Selwyn Theatre, NY, with Miss Lillie, Miss Lawrence, Buchanan, Betty Stockfeld, Hugh Sinclair, Douglas Furber, and Constance Carpenter. It ran 140 performances. "March with Me!" was retained ("by request"); other numbers included "Poor Little Rich Girl" and "A Cup of Coffee, a Sandwich and You," and a sketch, "Fallen Babies," with Miss Lillie and Miss Lawrence as two precocious infants in their prams.

A cut-down version of the London revue The Charlot Show of 1926, was added to the then-running Bway revue Earl Carroll Vanities on Jan. 4, 1927. Jessie Matthews, Herbert Mundin, Henry Lytton Jr., and Hazel Wynne were in the cast. In Feb. 1927, the Charlot people extracted themselves from the revue, added some more numbers, and went on a brief US tour as The Charlot Show of 1927.

Andrews, Julie (née Julia Elizabeth Wells), actress, singer; b. Walton-on-Thames, Eng., Oct. 1, 1935. Miss Andrews' air of patrician innocence and her cool, clear voice first attracted notice on Bway in the London import *The Boy Friend.* Her biggest stage success, both in NY'and London, was *My Fair Lady,* in which she introduced "Wouldn't It Be Loverly?," "The Rain in Spain," and "I Could Have Danced All Night." Miss Andrews, who began her stage career in England as a child performer, won international acclaim in films *Mary Poppins* and *The Sound of Music.* Bib: *Julie Andrews: Life Story of a Superstar* by John Cottrell (Barker, L 1968); *Julie Andrews* by Robert Windeler (Putnam, NY 1970).

1947	Starlight Roof (L)	
1954	The Boy Friend (NY) (*Polly Browne*)	
1956	My Fair Lady (NY) (*Eliza Doolittle*)	
1958	My Fair Lady (L) (*Eliza Doolittle*)	
1960	Camelot (NY) (*Queen Guenevere*)	

Annie Get Your Gun (1946). Music & lyrics by Irving Berlin; book by Herbert & Dorothy Fields.

SONGS: "I'm a Bad, Bad Man," "Doin' What Comes Natur'lly," "The Girl That I Marry," "You Can't Get a Man with a Gun," "There's No Business Like Show Business," "They Say It's Wonderful," "Moonshine Lullaby," "My Defenses Are Down," "Who Do You Love, I Hope," "I'm an Indian, Too," "I Got Lost in His Arms," "I Got the Sun in the Morning," "Anything You Can Do."

NEW YORK: May 16, 1946
IMPERIAL THEATRE; 1,147 p.

Presented by Richard Rodgers & Oscar Hammerstein II; directed by Joshua Logan; choreographed by Helen Tamiris; settings & lighting, Jo Mielziner; costumes, Lucinda Ballard; music director, Jay S. Blackton; orchestrations, Philip J. Lang, Robert Russell Bennett, Ted Royal.

CAST: Ethel Merman (*Annie Oakley*), Ray Middleton (*Frank Butler*), Marty May (*Charlie Davenport*), Kenny Bowers (*Tommy Keeler*), Betty Anne Nyman (*Winnie Tate*), William O'Neal (*Buffalo Bill Cody*), Lea Penman (*Dolly Tate*), Ellen Hanley (*Mary*), George Lipton (*Pawnee Bill Lillie*), Warren Berlinger (*Little Boy*), Daniel Nagrin (*Iron Tail*), Lubov Roudenko (*Riding Mistress*), Harry Bellaver (*Sitting Bull*), Leon Bibb (*Waiter*).

LONDON: June 7, 1947
COLISEUM; 1,304 p.

Presented by Prince Littler; restaged & choreographed by Helen Tamiris; settings & lighting, Jo Mielziner; costumes, Physhe; music director, Lew Stone; orchestrations, Philip J. Lang, Robert Russell Bennett, Ted Royal.

CAST: Dolores Gray (*Annie Oakley*), Bill Johnson (*Frank Butler*), Hal Bryan (*Charlie Davenport*), Irving Davies (*Tommy Keeler*), Wendy Toye (*Winnie Tate*), Ellis Irving (*Buffalo Bill Cody*), Barbara Babington (*Dolly Tate*), Edmund Dalby (*Pawnee Bill Lillie*), Paddy Stone (*Iron Tail*), Patricia Garnett (*Riding Mistress*), John Garside (*Sitting Bull*).

The idea of doing a musical based on the life of sharpshooter Annie Oakley originated with Dorothy Fields, who thought it would be a natural for her friend Ethel Merman. She and her brother Herbert offered the show (originally called *Annie Oakley*) to producers Rodgers and Hammerstein, and it became their only musical production for which they did not also write the songs. Initially, the score was to have been written by Miss Fields and Jerome Kern, but the composer died before beginning the project, and the producers then secured Irving Berlin to write both music and lyrics. *Annie Get Your Gun* became the second book musical to run over 1,000 performances on Bway (*Oklahoma!* was the first); it was also the biggest success ever scored by Merman, Berlin, and the Fieldses.

The story tells of the rise of hillbilly Annie Oakley to become the star attraction of Buffalo Bill's Wild West Show, even eclipsing the fame of marksman Frank Butler. Although Annie loves Frank, their rivalry keeps them apart until our heroine realizes the only way to get her man is to let him best her in a shooting contest. The action takes place in the late 1800s and includes such scenes as the Minneapolis Fair Grounds, where Annie displays her marksmanship while riding a motorcycle, and Governor's Island, NY, where the final reconciliation takes place. In Aug. 1948, Ray Middleton was succeeded by Milton Watson; during Miss Merman's six-week vacation in 1948, Mary Jane Walsh played Annie.

Mary Martin and Earl Covert had the leads in the US tour, which began Oct. 1947, and continued for one year, seven months. In July 1948, Miss Martin was succeeded by Joan Edwards, then Billie Worth. The London production, which ran longer than in NY, made a star of Dolores Gray (who got the part after it had been turned down by June Havoc). In 1966, Rodgers revived the musical at the Music Theatre of Lincoln Center with Miss Merman and Bruce Yarnell. For this production, Berlin wrote a new song, "An Old-Fashioned Wedding." The show toured briefly, then played two months at the Broadway Theatre, NY.

FILM VERSION: Betty Hutton and Howard Keel (MGM 1950, George Sidney dir.).

"Another Hundred People." Music & lyric by Stephen Sondheim. Frenetic portrait of life in teeming Manhattan sung by Pamela Myers in *Company* (NY 1970), then by Annie McGreevey in London production (1972).

"Another Op'nin', Another Show." Music & lyric by Cole Porter. Led by Annabelle Hill, the chorus offered this rousing ode to show business in the opening scene of *Kiss Me, Kate* (NY 1948). In London version, it was sung by Adelaide Hall and chorus. Next to Irving Berlin's "There's No Business Like Show Business," it is probably the best-known song about the theatre to emanate from the musical stage.

"Another Time, Another Place." Music & lyric by Richard Adler. Emotional duet of a love that might have been, sung by white nurse Sally Ann Howes and African doctor Terry Carter in *Kwamina* (NY 1961).

"Any Place I Hang My Hat Is Home." Music by Harold Arlen; lyric by Johnny Mercer. Ruby Hill sang this credo of a roaming woman ("Howdy stranger, so long friend") in *St. Louis Woman* (NY 1946).

"Anyone Can Whistle." Music & lyric by Stephen Sondheim. Emotional frustration revealed by Lee Remick in *Anyone Can Whistle* (NY 1964).

"Anyone Would Love You." Music & lyric by Harold Rome. Trying to keep things impersonal, Andy Griffith and Dolores Gray revealed their mutual attraction in *Destry Rides Again* (NY 1959).

Anything Goes (1934). Music & lyrics by Cole Porter; book by Guy Bolton & P. G. Wodehouse, revised by Howard Lindsay & Russel Crouse.

SONGS: "I Get a Kick Out of You," "There'll Always Be a Lady Fair," "All Through the Night," "You're the Top," "Anything Goes," "Blow, Gabriel, Blow," "Be Like the Bluebird," "The Gypsy in Me."

NEW YORK: Nov. 21, 1934
ALVIN THEATRE; 420 p.

Presented by Vinton Freedley; directed by Howard Lindsay; choreographed by Robert Alton; settings, Donald Oenslager; costumes, Jenkins; music director, Earl Busby; orchestrations, Russell Bennett, Hans Spialek.
CAST: Ethel Merman (*Reno Sweeney*), William Gaxton (*Billy Crocker*), Victor Moore (*Moon-Face Mooney*), Bettina Hall (*Hope Harcourt*), Vera Dunn (*Bonnie Latour*), Vivian Vance (*Babe*).

LONDON: June 14, 1935
PALACE THEATRE; 261 p.

Presented by Charles B. Cochran; directed by Frank Collins; choreographed by Buddy Bradley; settings, Alick Johnstone; costumes, Ada Peacock; music director, Francis Collinson.
CAST: Jeanne Aubert (*Reno Lagrange*), Jack Whiting (*Billy Crocker*), Sydney Howard (*Moon-Face Mooney*), Adele Dixon (*Hope Harcourt*), Betty Kean (*Bonnie*).

NEW YORK: May 15, 1962
ORPHEUM THEATRE; 239 p.

Presented by Jane Friedlander, Michael Parver, Gene Andrewski; directed by Lawrence Kasha; choreographed by Ronald Field; settings & lighting, Don Jensen; costumes, Bill Hargate; music director, Ted Simons; orchestrations, Julian Stein.
CAST: Eileen Rodgers (*Reno Sweeney*), Hal Linden (*Billy Crocker*), Mickey Deems (*Moon*), Barbara Lang (*Hope Harcourt*), Margery Gray (*Bonnie Latour*), Kenneth Mars (*Sir Evelyn Oakleigh*).

One of the most successful and durable musicals of the mid-30s was conceived in despair and rewritten in tragedy. Producer Freedley, who had just lost all his money on the musical *Pardon My English,* planned *Anything Goes* (originally titled *Hard to Get,* then *Bon Voyage*) to feature the greatest talent available at the time in the musical theatre: Merman, Gaxton, Moore, Porter, Bolton, and Wodehouse. His idea was a show that would bring together assorted comic characters in a shipwreck, but the sinking of the *S.S. Morro Castle* on Sept. 8, 1934, forced the script to be revised. With neither Wodehouse nor Bolton available, Freedley assigned the writing to his director, Howard Lindsay, and also brought in Russel Crouse as collaborator. The new plot, though still taking place aboard ship, eliminated the shipwreck and had the story revolve around nightclub singer Reno Sweeney, her friend Billy Crocker (who stows aboard to be near Hope Harcourt), and Moon-Face Mooney, alias Rev. Dr. Moon, currently Public Enemy #13. The show made Ethel Merman a star, reinforced Victor Moore's claim as Bway's most endearing funnyman, and was responsible for Cole Porter's most popular score to date. For London version, to suit the French actress playing the role, Reno had a change of nationality. P. G. Wodehouse also contributed local references in dialogue and song lyrics. A 1969 London revival was unsuccessful.

FILM VERSIONS: Bing Crosby, Ethel

Merman, Charles Ruggles (Par. 1936, Lewis Milestone dir.); Bing Crosby, Jeanmaire, Mitzi Gaynor, Donald O'Connor (different story, added songs) (Par. 1956, Robert Lewis dir.).

"Anything Goes." Music & lyric by Cole Porter. Cynical appraisal of 1934 morals and mores introduced by Ethel Merman in Bway musical, *Anything Goes*. Jeanne Aubert gave it a French accent in London version the following year. Included in the lyrics are such catalogued symptoms of decaying civilization as the shortening of women's skirts, authors who use only four-letter words, nudist parties, and grandmamas going out with gigolos.

"Anything You Can Do." Music & lyric by Irving Berlin. Challenge song testing claims to superiority in assorted skills made by Ethel Merman and Ray Middleton in *Annie Get Your Gun* (NY 1946), and by Dolores Gray and Bill Johnson in London production (1947).

Applause (1970). Music by Charles Strouse; lyrics by Lee Adams; book by Betty Comden & Adolph Green, based on film *All About Eve*, by Joseph Mankiewicz, adapted from short story *The Wisdom of Eve*, by Mary Orr.

SONGS: "Think How It's Gonna Be," "But Alive," "The Best Night of My Life," "Who's That Girl?," "Applause," "Fasten Your Seat Belts," "Welcome to the Theater," "One of a Kind," "Something Greater."

NEW YORK: March 30, 1970
PALACE THEATRE; 896 p.

Presented by Joseph Kipness & Lawrence Kasha, with Nederlander Productions & George Steinbrenner III; directed & choreographed by Ron Field; settings, Robert Randolph; costumes, Ray Aghayan; lighting, Tharon Musser; music director, Donald Pippin; orchestrations, Philip J. Lang.

CAST: Lauren Bacall (*Margo Channing*), Len Cariou (*Bill Sampson*), Penny Fuller (*Eve Harrington*), Robert Mandan (*Howard Benedict*), Ann Williams (*Karen Richards*), Brandon Maggart (*Buzz Richards*), Lee Roy Reams (*Duane Fox*), Bonnie Franklin (*Bonnie*).

LONDON: Nov. 16, 1972
HER MAJESTY'S THEATRE; 382 p.

Presented by Bernard Delfont & Alexander H. Cohen; directed & choreographed by Ron Field; settings, Robert Randolph; costumes, Ray Aghayan; lighting, Tharon Musser; music director, Robert Lowe; orchestrations, Philip J. Lang.

CAST: Lauren Bacall (*Margo Channing*), Eric Flynn (*Duane Fox*), Angela Richards (*Eve Harrington*), Basil Hoskins (*Howard Benedict*), Sarah Marshall (*Karen Richards*), Rod McLellan (*Buzz Richards*), Ken Walsh (*Bill Sampson*), Sheila O'Neill (*Sheila*).

In her first musical, Lauren Bacall scored a major success as the tempestuous Bway star Margo Channing, who takes in—and is taken in by—Eve Harrington, a scheming young actress who scratches her way to the top. The musical won applause for its seeming authenticity of backstage life and for the action-filled staging of Ron Field, here directing his first complete Bway production. (One temptation the authors avoided was not turning Margo into a musical-comedy actress in order to show on-stage scenes from her latest production.) During run, Miss Bacall was succeeded by Anne Baxter (7-71), who had played Eve in the movie on which the show had been based, and Arlene Dahl (5-72). Miss Bacall (later succeeded by Eleanor Parker) headed the road company, which opened Oct. 1971 and toured for almost nine months.

"Applause." Music by Charles Strouse; lyric by Lee Adams. The reason anyone becomes an actor was revealed in the musical of the same name by Bonnie Franklin and "Gypsies" (NY 1970) and Sheila O'Neill and "Gypsies" (L 1973). The production number following the song featured thumbnail versions of recent and current stage successes from *Oklahoma!* to *Oh, Calcutta!*

"April in Paris." Music by Vernon Duke; lyric by E. Y. Harburg. Sung by Evelyn Hoey (who was barely heard opening night because she had laryngitis) in Bway revue *Walk a Little Faster* (1932). Duke got the idea for the song one day when a group of friends were sitting at a New York restaurant called Tony's, sipping French wine and dreaming French dreams. "Oh, to be in Paris now that April's there!" exclaimed Monty Woolley. " 'April in Paris'—what a song title!" said Duke—and off he went to find the nearest piano. The lyric was written even before Harburg had ever been to Paris. Two years later, the composer penned a tribute to another city in "Autumn in New York," sung in *Thumbs Up!*

"April Showers." Music by Louis Silvers; lyric by B. G. DeSylva. Interpolated in *Bombo* (NY 1920) by Al Jolson, who sang the number from a runway jutting into the audience.

"Aquarius." Music by Galt MacDermot; lyric by Gerome Ragni & James Rado. This depiction of a world of love and peace was sung by the company in the second act of *Hair* when it

was presented off-Bway in 1967. When the show was rewritten for Bway, the song became the opening number (1968). It was also sung in London version later the same year.

Arcadians, The (1909). Music by Lionel Monckton & Howard Talbot; lyrics by Arthur Wimperis; book by Mark Ambient, A. M. Thompson, Robert Courtneidge.

SONGS: "Bring Me a Rose" (Monckton), "The Girl with the Brogue" (Monckton), "Pipes of Pan" (Monckton), "My Motter" (Talbot), "Arcady Is Ever Young" (Monckton), "Back Your Fancy" (Monckton), "All Down Piccadilly" (Talbot), "Charming Weather" (Monckton), "Half Past Two" (Talbot).

LONDON: April 28, 1909
SHAFTESBURY THEATRE; 809 p.

Presented & directed by Robert Courtneidge; choreographed by Harry Grattan; settings, Conrad Tritschler, etc.; costumes, Wilhelm, Lucile; music director, Arthur Wood.

CAST: Alfred Lester (*Peter Doody*), Phyllis Dare (*Eileen Cavanagh*), Dan Rolyat (*Simplicitas*), Harry Welchman (*Jack Meadows*), Florence Smithson (*Sombra*), Ada Blanche (*Mrs. Smith*), Cicely Courtneidge (*Chrysea*), Nelson Keys (*Bobby*).

NEW YORK: Jan. 17, 1910
LIBERTY THEATRE; 136 p.

Presented by Charles Frohman; directed by Thomas Reynolds; settings, Homer Emens; costumes, Wilhelm, Lord & Taylor; music director, Watty Hydes.

CAST: Percival Knight (*Peter Doody*), Julia Sanderson (*Eileen Cavanagh*), Frank Moulan (*Simplicitas*), Alan Mudie (*Jack Meadows*), Ethel Cadman (*Sombra*), Connie Ediss (*Mrs. Smith*), Audrey Maple (*Chrysea*).

Billed as "A Fantastic Musical

Play," *The Arcadians* was second only to *A Chinese Honeymoon* as London's longest running musical prior to 1910. The production, the most successful ever presented by Robert Courtneidge, was hailed for its imaginative story, broad comedy, and realistic scenic effects. It spun the tale of a mortal, James Smith, who accidentally falls into Arcadia from an airplane. There he regains his youth, adopts the name of Simplicitas, and leads the Arcadians on a mission to convert wicked London to the more idyllic Arcadian life. Simplicitas also meets horse owner Jack Meadows, and rides his horse, The Deuce, to victory at Askwood Racetrack. Cicely Courtneidge, Robert Courtneidge's daughter, made her London debut in the play, and, during run, succeeded Phyllis Dare as Eileen, Jack's beloved. Miss Courtneidge also played the role when *The Arcadians* was revived in London in 1915. The musical was a tremendous success in the provinces and toured for 10 years.

Arden, Eve (née Eunice Quedens), actress; b. Mill Valley, Cal., April 30, 1912. Tall, angular, stylish comedienne noted for deadpan delivery. In addition to Bway appearances, Miss Arden acted in some 60 Hollywood films and had her own tv series.

1934   Ziegfeld Follies
1935   Parade
1936   Ziegfeld Follies
1939   Very Warm for May (*Winnie Spofford*)
1940   Two for the Show
1941   Let's Face It! (*Maggie Watson*)
1966   Hello, Dolly! (US tour) (*Dolly Levi*, repl.)

"Are You Havin' Any Fun?" Music by Sammy Fain; lyric by Jack Yellen. Enjoy life while you can was the advice of Ella Logan, the Kim Loo Sisters, and the Three Stooges in *George*

White's Scandals (NY 1939). The words to the song were printed on the wide-brimmed hats of the chorus girls so that the audience might sing along.

Arlen, Harold (né Hyman Arluck), composer; b. Buffalo, NY, Feb. 15, 1905. Celebrated for his ability to utilize Negro rhythms and blues, Arlen is an innovative composer who has written for cabarets (Cotton Club revues) and Hollywood films (*The Wizard of Oz, A Star Is Born*) as well as Bway. His biggest stage success was *Bloomer Girl* ("Right as the Rain," "Evelina"), lyrics by E. Y. Harburg, with whom he also wrote "Down with Love" and "Moanin' in the Mornin' " for *Hooray for What!* and "Cocoanut Sweet" for *Jamaica*. Other collaborators include Jack Yellen, Ira Gershwin ("Let's Take a Walk Around the Block," lyric with Harburg, for *Life Begins at 8:40*), Johnny Mercer ("Come Rain or Come Shine" for *St. Louis Woman*), Truman Capote ("A Sleepin' Bee" and "I Never Has Seen Snow" for *House of Flowers*). Arlen's first Bway song hits were "Get Happy" (*9:15 Revue*) and "I Gotta Right to Sing the Blues" (*Earl Carroll Vanities*, 1932), both with Ted Koehler. Bib: *Harold Arlen: Happy with the Blues* by Edward Jablonski (Doubleday, NY 1961).

1930   Earl Carroll Vanities (Koehler)
1931   You Said It (Yellen)
1934   Life Begins at 8:40 (Gershwin, Harburg)
1937   Hooray for What! (Harburg)
1944   Bloomer Girl (Harburg)
1946   St. Louis Woman (Mercer)
1954   House of Flowers (Capote, Arlen)
1957   Jamaica (Harburg)
1959   Saratoga (Mercer)

Arthur, Beatrice (née Bernice Frankel), actress, singer; b. New York, May 13. Earthy, sharp-tongued comedienne who won nationwide fame in tv series *Maude*. Miss Arthur is married to director Gene Saks.

1954 The Threepenny Opera (*Lucy Brown*)
1955 Shoestring Revue
     Seventh Heaven (*Mme. Suze*)
1960 Gay Divorce (r) (*Hortense*)
1964 Fiddler on the Roof (*Yente*)
1966 Mame (*Vera Charles*)

"**Artificial Flowers.**" Music by Jerry Bock; lyric by Sheldon Harnick. Mock tearjerker in the fashion of a late nineteenth-century ballad about poor orphan Annie who made artificial flowers until her health slipped away "and wiring and waxing she waned." Introduced in *Tenderloin* (NY 1960) by Ron Husmann and reprised by Margery Grey.

"**As Long as He Needs Me.**" Music & lyric by Lionel Bart. Masochistic tenacity avowed by Georgia Brown in *Oliver!*, both in London (1960) and NY (1963).

As Thousands Cheer (1933). Music & lyrics by Irving Berlin; sketches by Moss Hart.

SONGS: "How's Chances?," "Heat Wave," "Easter Parade," "The Funnies," "Supper Time," "Harlem on My Mind," "Lonely Heart," "Not for All the Rice in China."

NEW YORK: Sept. 30, 1933
MUSIC BOX THEATRE; 400 p.
Presented by Sam H. Harris; directed by Hassard Short; choreographed by Charles Weidman; settings, Albert Johnson; costumes, Irene Sharaff, Varady; music director, Frank Tours; orchestrations, Tours, Adolph Deutsch, Helmy Kresa.
CAST: Marilyn Miller, Clifton Webb, Helen Broderick, Ethel Waters, Leslie Adams, Hal Forde, Jerome Cowan, Harry Stockwell, Hamtree Harrington, Leticia Ide, José Limon, Katherine Litz.

LONDON: Feb. 21, 1935
ADELPHI THEATRE; 148 p.
Presented by Clifford Whitley; directed by Hassard Short; choreographed by LeRoy Prinz; settings & costumes, Doris Zinkeisen; music director, Hyam Greenbaum; added sketches by Greatrex Newman; added songs by Arthur Schwartz & Howard Dietz; retitled *Stop Press*.
CAST: Dorothy Dickson, Phyllis Monkman, Edward Styles, Robert Helpmann, Gordon Little.

As Thousands Cheer, one of the most successful revues of the 30s, was created in the form of a newspaper, with songs and sketches representing various sections. Apart from general news, they included comics, rotogravure, society, theatre, the weather, and advice to the lovelorn. All dealt with their themes in a light, satirical fashion except for the dramatic "Supper Time," introduced by the headline, "UNKNOWN NEGRO LYNCHED BY FRENZIED MOB." Principals in the revue portrayed well-known people of the day: Marilyn Miller was Barbara Hutton and Joan Crawford; Clifton Webb was Prince Mdivani, Douglas Fairbanks Jr., John D. Rockefeller, and Mahatma Gandhi; Helen Broderick was Mrs. Herbert Hoover, Aimee Semple MacPherson, Queen Mary, and The Statue of Liberty; Ethel Waters was Josephine Baker. In July 1934, Miss Miller was succeeded by Dorothy Stone, Webb by Charles Collins.

The London version, which retained four Irving Berlin songs, added others by Dietz and Schwartz from *The Band Wagon* and *Revenge with Music*, and substituted sketches of local news interest.

"As Time Goes By." Music & lyric by Herman Hupfeld. Hupfeld's most durable song was introduced by Frances Williams in *Everybody's Welcome* (NY 1931). The lyric maintains that despite modern inventions and discoveries, the fundamental romantic things still apply.

Asche, Oscar (né John Strange Heiss), actor, singer, librettist, lyricist, director, producer; b. Geelong, Australia, Jan. 16, 1871; d. London, March 23, 1936. Asche was a man of many theatrical talents who began his London career in Shakespearean roles. His biggest hit was *Chu Chin Chow*, in which he appeared with his wife, Lily Brayton. As lyricist, he collaborated with composers Frederick Norton, Grace Torrens, Percy Fletcher. Bib: *Oscar Asche: His Life by Himself* (1929).

Asterisk indicates Mr. Asche was also librettist, lyricist, director, producer:

1916　Chu Chin Chow * (*Abu Hasan*) (Norton)
1917　The Maid of the Mountains (dir. only)
1919　Eastward, Ho! (co-lib., lyr. only) (Torrens)
1920　A Southern Maid (dir. only) Mecca * (NY) (*Ali Shar*) (Fletcher)
1921　Cairo * (Mecca) (*Ali Shar*) (Fletcher)
1925　Frasquita (dir. only) Cleopatra (dir. only) The Good Old Days * (*Earl of Jawleyford*) (Fletcher)
1928　Marjolaine (*Brooke Hoskyn*)
1929　The White Camelia (dir. only)
1930　El Dorado (*Alcide de Barros*) (also dir.)

Astaire, Adele (née Adele Austerlitz), actress, dancer, singer; b. Omaha, Neb., Sept. 10, 1897. Adele Astaire and her brother Fred were musical comedy's most acclaimed dancing cou-

ple during the 20s in both NY and London. Combining impish agility with uncommon grace, the Astaires were vaudeville headliners before making their Bway debuts. They scored first major hit in *For Goodness Sake*, then made an even bigger impression in London where the show was renamed *Stop Flirting*. Other Bway-to-London successes were *Lady, Be Good!* (in which Miss Astaire sang "Fascinating Rhythm") and *Funny Face* ("Funny Face," "He Loves and She Loves," "'S Wonderful," "The Babbitt and the Bromide"). Miss Astaire retired in 1932 after the run of *The Band Wagon* ("Hoops," "I Love Louisa").

1917　Over the Top
1918　The Passing Show
1919　Apple Blossoms (*Molly*)
1921　The Love Letter (*Aline Moray*)
1922　For Goodness Sake (*Suzanne Hayden*)
　　　The Bunch and Judy (*Judy Jordan*)
1923　Stop Flirting (For Goodness Sake) (L) (*Suzanne Hayden*)
1924　Lady, Be Good! (*Suzie Trevor*)
1926　Lady, Be Good! (L) (*Suzie Trevor*)
1927　Funny Face (*Frankie Wynne*)
1928　Funny Face (L) (*Frankie Wynne*)
1930　Smiles (*Dot Hastings*)
1931　The Band Wagon

Astaire, Fred (né Frederick Austerlitz), actor, dancer, singer; b. Omaha, Neb., May 10, 1899. Fred Astaire and his sister Adele were musical comedy's most acclaimed dancing couple during the 20s in both NY and London. Combining impish agility with uncommon grace, the Astaires were vaudeville headliners before making their Bway debuts. They scored first major hit in *For Goodness Sake*, then made an even bigger impression in London, where the show was renamed *Stop Flirting*. Other

Bway-to-London successes were *Lady, Be Good!* (in which Fred sang "Fascinating Rhythm") and *Funny Face* ("Funny Face," "My One and Only," "The Babbitt and the Bromide"). Following the retirement of his sister after the run of *The Band Wagon* ("Hoops," "New Sun in the Sky," "I Love Louisa"), Astaire became a solo star in *Gay Divorce* ("Night and Day"). He appeared in 31 Hollywood musicals (incl. *Top Hat, Easter Parade, Funny Face*), made records, and starred on tv. Bib: *Steps in Time* by Astaire (Harper, NY 1959); *Starring Fred Astaire* by Stanley Green, Burt Goldblatt (Dodd Mead, NY 1973).

1917	Over the Top
1918	The Passing Show
1919	Apple Blossoms (*Johnnie*)
1921	The Love Letter (*Richard Kolner*)
1922	For Goodness Sake (*Teddy Lawrence*)
	The Bunch and Judy (*Gerald Lane*)
1923	Stop Flirting (For Goodness Sake) (L) (*Teddy Lawrence*)
1924	Lady, Be Good! (*Dick Trevor*)
1926	Lady, Be Good! (L) (*Dick Trevor*)
1927	Funny Face (*Jimmie Reeve*)
1928	Funny Face (L) (*Jimmie Reeve*)
1930	Smiles (*Bob Hastings*)
1931	The Band Wagon
1932	Gay Divorce (*Guy Holden*)
1933	Gay Divorce (L) (*Guy Holden*)

"**At Long Last Love.**" Music & lyric by Cole Porter. In which Clifton Webb, in *You Never Know* (NY 1938), wonders whether his new romance will prove to be permanent or transitory ("Will it be Bach I shall hear or just a Cole Porter song?"). The phrase "At long last" had been used by King Edward VIII at the beginning of his abdication speech in 1936.

"**At the Roxy Music Hall.**" Music by Richard Rodgers; lyric by Lorenz Hart. The second-act show-stopper in *I Married an Angel* (NY 1938) was a takeoff on the opulent pretentions of New York's Radio City Music Hall (the "Roxy" referred to the Music Hall's late managing director, "Roxy" Rothafel). An entire row of Rockettes was represented by Vivienne Segal and Audrey Christie, and Vera Zorina performed a "symbolic" dance with a headless dancer. The lyric to the song, sung by Miss Christie, paid tribute to such wonders as the colorful fountains, the plush seats, the naked statues, the super-duper organ, and the palatial size of the ladies' room.

"**Auf Wiedersehn.**" Music by Sigmund Romberg; lyric by Herbert Reynolds (M. E. Rourke). Romberg's first popular song success, a teary expression of leave-taking, was sung by Vivienne Segal in *The Blue Paradise* (NY 1915).

"**Autumn in New York.**" Music & lyric by Vernon Duke. Evocative hymn to Gotham glamour sung by J. Harold Murray before a cyclorama of skyscrapers in the 1934 Bway revue *Thumbs Up!* Duke had previously written the music to another city-praising song, "April in Paris," sung in *Walk a Little Faster*.

"**Avalon.**" Music by Vincent Rose; lyric by B. G. De Sylva & Al Jolson. This memory of a love won and lost on Santa Catalina island was interpolated by Al Jolson after the opening of *Sinbad* (NY 1918). Opera composer Giacomo Puccini sued the song's publisher, accusing the writers of stealing the melody from his "*E lucevan le stelle*" area in *Tosca*. He was awarded $25,000.

B

"Babbitt and the Bromide, The." Music by George Gershwin; lyric by Ira Gershwin. Sung by Fred and Adele Astaire as two "sub-sti-an-tial men" in *Funny Face* (NY 1927, L 1928). The song kidded conversational sterility by depicting three widely spaced meetings between individuals who can speak only in deadpan clichés. Written during the show's out-of-town tryout, the number featured the Astaires' trademark runaround dance routine. "Babbitt" was the leading character in Sinclair Lewis' novel of the same name (1922); "Bromide" originated with Gelett Burgess' *Goops and How to Be Them* (1900) and *Are You A Bromide?* (1907).

Babes in Arms (1937). Music by Richard Rodgers; lyrics by Lorenz Hart; book by Rodgers & Hart.

SONGS: "Where or When," "Babes in Arms," "I Wish I Were in Love Again," "My Funny Valentine," "Johnny One Note," "The Lady Is a Tramp," "You Are So Fair."

NEW YORK: April 14, 1937
SHUBERT THEATRE; 289 p.

Presented by Dwight Deere Wiman; directed by Robert Sinclair; choreographed by George Balanchine; settings, Raymond Sovey; costumes, Helene Pons; music director, Gene Salzer; orchestrations, Hans Spialek.

CAST: Mitzi Green (*Billie Smith*), Ray Heatherton (*Val Lamar*), Duke McHale (*Peter*), Wynn Murray (*Baby Rose*), Harold Nicholas (*Ivor DeQuincy*), Fayard Nicholas (*Irving DeQuincy*), Rolly Pickert (*Gus Fielding*), Grace McDonald (*Dolores Reynolds*), Ray McDonald (*Sam Reynolds*), Alfred Drake (*Marshall Blackstone*), Robert Rounseville (*Bob*), Dan Dailey (*gang member*); Edgar Fairchild & Adam Carroll (duo-pianos).

The accent was on youth in *Babes in Arms*, which had an army of teenagers, no stars, modest settings, and a profitable run. It also has the distinction of offering a larger collection of Rodgers and Hart song hits than any of their other productions. The play's story concerned a group of youngsters who put on a musical show to avoid being sent to a work farm.

FILM VERSION: Judy Garland, Mickey Rooney, Charles Winninger (MGM 1939, Busby Berkeley dir.).

Babes in Toyland (1903). Music by Victor Herbert; lyrics & book by Glen MacDonough.

SONGS: "I Can't Do the Sum," "Go to Sleep, Slumber Deep," "March of the Toys," "Toyland," "Never Mind, Bo-Peep."

NEW YORK: Oct. 13, 1903
MAJESTIC THEATRE; 192 p.

Presented by Fred R. Hamlin & Julian Mitchell; directed by Mitchell; settings, John Young & Homer Emens; music director, Max Hirshfeld.

CAST: William Norris (*Alan*), Mabel Barrison (*Jane*), George W. Denham (*Uncle Barnaby*), Amy Ricard (*Contrary Mary*), Bessie Wynn (*Tom Tom*), Nella Webb (*Bo-Peep*).

This was Victor Herbert's first musical planned for an extended Bway run, rather than for a limited engagement. The idea originated with producers Hamlin and Mitchell, who wanted a successor to their popular children's fantasy, *The Wizard of Oz.* The story, which made use of elaborate scenic effects, was concerned with the adventures of Jane and Alan, who, after being shipwrecked, find themselves in the city of Toyland, where they meet assorted Mother Goose characters. The Herbert-Mac-Donough *Wonderland* (NY 1905) was a successor to *Babes in Toyland.*

FILM VERSIONS: Laurel & Hardy (MGM 1934, Gus Meins & Charles Rogers dirs.); Ray Bolger, Ed Wynn, Tommy Sands (Buena Vista 1961, Jack Donohue dir.).

Bacall, Lauren (née Betty Joan Perske), actress; b. New York, Sept. 16, 1924. Smokey-voiced actress of angular intensity who won acclaim in her first Bway musical. Miss Bacall acted in Hollywood films 1944–1966, and appeared in nonmusical plays (incl. *Cactus Flower*).

1970 Applause (*Margo Channing*)
1972 Applause (L) (*Margo Channing*)

Bacharach, Burt, composer; b. Kansas City, Mo., May 12, 1928. A successful pop and film composer, Bacharach and his lyric-writing partner, Hal David, made a notable Bway debut with *Promises, Promises* ("I'll Never Fall in Love Again," "Whoever You Are").

1968 Promises, Promises

"Bachelor Gay, A." Music by James W. Tate; lyric by F. Clifford Harris & (Arthur) Valentine. Written during the pre-London tryout of *The Maid of the Mountain* (1917), this lilting saga of the bachelor life was introduced by Thorpe Bates. In NY production (1918), it was sung by Carl Gantvoort.

Baddeley, Hermione (Clinton-), actress; b. Broseley, Eng., Nov. 13,

1906. Gravel-voiced comedienne who made London debut in 1918 and has also appeared in dramas (incl. *A Taste of Honey*). She is the sister of actress Angela Baddeley.

1924 The Punch Bowl
     The Co-Optimists
1925 On with the Dance
     Still Dancing!
1926 Cochran's Revue of 1926
     Queen High (*Coddles*)
1929 The Five o'Clock Girl (*Susie Snow*)
1932 After Dinner
     Ballyhoo
1933 Paris Fantasie
1936 To and Fro
1937 Floodlight
1938 Nine Sharp
1939 The Little Revue
1941 Rise Above It
1942 Sky High
1945 The Gaieties
1948 A la Carte
1953 At the Lyric
1954 Going to Town (At the Lyric)
1969 Canterbury Tales (NY) (*Wife of Bath*, etc.)
1972 The Threepenny Opera (r) (*Mrs. Peachum*)

Bagley, Ben, producer; b. Hardwick, Vt., Oct. 18, 1933. Bagley's off-Bway revues introduced Dody Goodman, Chita Rivera, Beatrice Arthur, Dorothy Greener, Tammy Grimes, Joel Grey, and writers Charles Strouse, Lee Adams, Michael Stewart, Sheldon Harnick, Harvey Schmidt, Tom Jones. Bagley has also presented a Cole Porter revue and is a record producer.

1955 Shoestring Revue
1956 The Littlest Revue
     Shoestring '57

Bailey, Pearl (Mae), actress, singer; b. Newport News, Va., March 29, 1918. Originally a pop singer known for her diffident, slurred singing style, Miss

Bailey made her biggest Bway hit in *Hello, Dolly!*, in which she toured. Bib: *The Raw Pearl* by Miss Bailey (1968).

1946 St. Louis Woman (*Butterfly*)
1950 Arms and the Girl (*Connecticut*)
Bless You All
1954 House of Flowers (*Madame Fleur*)
1967 Hello, Dolly! (*Dolly Levi, repl.*)
1975 Hello, Dolly! (r) (*Dolly Levi*)

Balanchine, George (né Gyorgi Melitonovitch Balanchivadze), choreographer, director; b. St. Petersburg, Russia, Jan. 9, 1904. An acknowledged leader in classical ballet, Balanchine was also one of Bway's most innovative choreographers in adapting ballet to the musical stage. His "Slaughter on 10th Avenue" in *On Your Toes* was the first ballet ever conceived as an integral part of a libretto, and his work for three other Rodgers & Hart musicals was also highly influential. Balanchine was first associated with the ballet companies of Diaghilev (1924–1929) and Col. de Basil (1931–1933). He settled in NY in 1934 and founded the School of American Ballet; four years later he organized the NYC Ballet Co., of which he remains as director. Tamara Geva and Vera Zorina were the second and third of his five wives. Bib: *Balanchine* by Bernard Taper (Macmillan, NY 1974).

1929 Wake Up and Dream! (L)
1930 Cochran's 1930 Revue (L)
1936 Ziegfeld Follies
On Your Toes
1937 Babes in Arms
1938 I Married an Angel
The Boys from Syracuse
1940 Keep Off the Grass
Louisiana Purchase
Cabin in the Sky (also co-dir.)
1942 The Lady Comes Across
Rosalinda
1943 What's Up (also co-dir.)

1944 Dream with Music
Song of Norway
1945 Mr. Strauss Goes to Boston
1947 The Chocolate Soldier (r)
1948 Where's Charley?
1951 Courtin' Time

"Bali Ha'i." Music by Richard Rodgers; lyric by Oscar Hammerstein II. Sung by Juanita Hall in *South Pacific* (NY 1949); in London version (1951) by Muriel Smith. In the story, the song is used as an aphrodisiac to lure a naive American lieutenant to a neighboring South Sea island. The writing of the music illustrates the speed of Rodgers' creativity. One afternoon, while Rodgers was dining with Joshua Logan, Hammerstein rushed in with the finished lyric. The composer merely moved the dishes to one side, quickly went over the words that had just been handed to him, turned the paper over, and wrote the music in about the same time it took to jot down the notes.

Ball, Lucille (Desiree), actress; b. Butte, Montana, Aug. 6, 1910. Blonde knockabout comedienne of Hollywood films and tv (*I Love Lucy*), who introduced "Hey, Look Me Over" in her only Bway musical.

1960 Wildcat (*Wildcat Jackson*)

"Ballad for Americans." Music & lyric by Earl Robinson. Patriotic choral piece made famous by Paul Robeson during World War II, which was introduced as "Ballad of Uncle Sam" in the 1939 Bway revue *Sing for Your Supper*. Gordon Clarke led the chorus in the show, the last sponsored by the Federal Theatre under the WPA. The theme of the piece was America's strength through its diversity of ethnic backgrounds, religions, and occupations.

"Ballad of the Sad Young Men." Music by Tommy Wolf; lyric by Fran Landesman. Threnody about the sad young men who escape from reality by going from bar to bar, "drinking up the night, trying not to drown." Introduced by Tani Seitz in *The Nervous Set* (NY 1959).

Ballard, Kaye (née Catherine Gloria Balotta), actress, singer; b. Cleveland, Ohio, Nov. 20, 1926. Miss Ballard made notable Bway appearances in *The Golden Apple* (introducing "Lazy Afternoon") and *Carnival*. She has also appeared in nightclubs and on tv.

1947	Three to Make Ready (US tour)	
1950	Touch and Go (L)	
1952	Top Banana (US tour) (*Betty Dillon*)	
1954	The Golden Apple (*Helen Troy*)	
1961	Carnival (*Rosalie*)	
1973	Molly (*Molly Goldberg*)	

"Bambalina." Music by Vincent Youmans; lyric by Otto Harbach & Oscar Hammerstein II. Sung in *Wildflower* by Edith Day (NY 1923) and Kitty Reidy (L 1926). The perky tune accompanies a lyric that relates the curious antics of a fiddler at a country fair who liked nothing better than to stop playing in the middle of a number just to embarrass the dancers.

Band Wagon, The (1931). Music by Arthur Schwartz; lyrics by Howard Dietz; sketches by George S. Kaufman & Dietz.
SONGS: "It Better Be Good," "Sweet Music," "Hoops," "High and Low," "Confession," "New Sun in the Sky," "Miserable with You," "I Love Louisa," "Dancing in the Dark," "Where Can He Be?," "The Beggar Waltz," "White Heat."

NEW YORK: June 3, 1931
NEW AMSTERDAM THEATRE; 260 p.
Presented by Max Gordon; directed by Hassard Short; choreographed by Albertina Rasch; settings, Albert Johnson; costumes, Kiviette, Constance Ripley; music director, Al Goodman; orchestrations, Robert Russell Bennett.
CAST: Fred & Adele Astaire, Frank Morgan, Helen Broderick, Tilly Losch, Philip Loeb, John Barker.
A follow-up to *Three's a Crowd*, but with a different cast, the revue had the same producer, composer, lyricist, director, choreographer, and designers. Like its predecessor, it was celebrated for its stylish, artistic approach to the revue form. On a technical level, it was the first production to use a double revolving stage as an integral part of the songs and sketches. The most famous sketch, "The Pride of the Claghornes," depicted the consternation of a proud southern patriarch when he discovers his daughter is a virgin. It was after the NY run that Adele Astaire retired from the stage.
FILM VERSION: Fred Astaire, Cyd Charisse, Jack Buchanan, Nanette Fabray (with story) (MGM 1953, Vincente Minnelli dir.).

Barer, Marshall L., lyricist; b. Astoria, NY, Feb. 19, 1923. Barer's best-known score was for the off-Bway musical *Once Upon a Mattress* ("Shy," "In a Little While"). He also wrote songs for *New Faces of 1956*, nightclub acts, industrial shows. Collaborators: Mary Rodgers, Dean Fuller, Duke Ellington.

1955	Once Over Lightly (Fuller)	
1959	Once Upon a Mattress (Rodgers) (also co-lib.)	
1966	The Mad Show (Rodgers) Pousse-Café (Ellington)	

Barry, John, composer; b. Yorkshire, Eng., 1933. Prolific film composer whose London scores were written with lyricist Trevor Peacock ("How

Much of the Dream Comes True?") and Don Black ("Some of Us Belong to the Stars").

1965   Passion Flower Hotel (Peacock)
1974   Billy (Black)

Bart, Lionel (né Lionel Begleiter), composer, lyricist, librettist; b. London, Aug. 1, 1930. Former pop songwriter who achieved greatest London success *Oliver!* ("As Long as He Needs Me," "Consider Yourself," "Who Will Buy?"). Other long-running musicals: *Lock Up Your Daughters* (music by Laurie Johnson), *Fings Ain't Wot They Used t'Be, Blitz!, Maggie May.*

> Unless otherwise noted, Mr. Bart was composer-lyricist of following:
>
> 1959   Lock Up Your Daughters (lyr. only) (Johnson)
> 1960   Fings Ain't Wot They Used t'Be Oliver! (also lib.)
> 1962   Blitz! (also lib.)
> 1964   Maggie May
> 1965   Twang!! (also lib.)
> 1969   La Strada (NY)

Barton, James, actor; b. Gloucester, NJ, Nov. 1, 1890; d. Mineola, NY, Feb. 19, 1962. Gritty-voiced, flat-nosed comic actor, celebrated for his drunk routine, who appeared in vaudeville and stock as well as Bway musicals and dramas (incl. *Tobacco Road, The Iceman Cometh*). Barton introduced "I Still See Elisa" in *Paint Your Wagon.*

1919   The Passing Show
1921   The Last Waltz (*Matt Maltby*)
1922   The Rose of Stamboul (*Bob*)
1923   Dew Drop Inn (*Ananias Washington*)
1924   The Passing Show
1925   Artists and Models
1926   No Foolin'
1930   Sweet and Low
1951   Paint Your Wagon (*Ben Rumson*)

"Baubles, Bangles and Beads." Music & lyric by Robert Wright & George Forrest, based on theme from Alek-sandr Borodin's String Quartet in D. Doretta Morrow introduced the willowy piece in both NY (1953) and London (1955) productions of *Kismet* in the scene at the Baghdad bazaar.

Bayes, Nora (née Dora Goldberg), actress, singer; b. Joliet, Ill., 1880; d. Brooklyn, NY, March 19, 1928. Deep-voiced, dynamic song belter, who won fame both in vaudeville and on Bway. The second of Miss Bayes's five husbands was Jack Norworth, with whom she wrote and introduced "Shine On, Harvest Moon" in Ziegfeld's *Follies of 1908.* She also introduced "Has Anybody Here Seen Kelly?" in *The Jolly Bachelors.*

1901   Rogers Brothers in Washington (*Esther Pace*)
1907   Follies of 1907 (added)
1908   Nearly a Hero (*Angeline de Vere,* repl.)
       Follies of 1908
1909   Follies of 1909
1910   The Jolly Bachelors (*Astarita Vandergould*)
1911   Little Miss Fix-It (*Delia Wendell*) (also co-comp., lyr.)
1912   Roly Poly (*La Frolique*)
1914   The Merry-Go-Round (L)
1915   Maid in America
1917   The Cohan Revue
1918   Ladies First (*Betty Burt*)
1920   Her Family Tree (*Nora Bayes,* etc.)
1921   Snapshots of 1921
1922   Queen o' Hearts (*Elizabeth Bennett*)

"Be Kind to Your Parents." Music & lyric by Harold Rome. A mother's advice to her young son. In *Fanny* (NY 1954) it was sung by Florence Henderson to Lloyd Reese, who joined her in a duet; in London company (1956), by Janet Pavek and Robert Passfield.

"Beat Out Dat Rhythm on a Drum." Music by Georges Bizet; lyric by

Oscar Hammerstein II. Lillas Pastia's tavern in the opera *Carmen* became Billy Pastor's café in the Bway musical *Carmen Jones* (1943), and a song about a tambourine (*"Les tringles des sistres tintaient"*) became a pulsating number about the wild effects of "dat bum-bum-bumpin'" under music" of drummer-man Cosy Cole. June Hawkins led the singers and dancers.

Beaumont, Hugh ("Binkie"), producer; b. Cardiff, Wales, March 27, 1908; d. London, March 22, 1973. See **Tennent Ltd., H.M.**

"Bedelia." Music by Jean Schwartz; lyric by William Jerome. Irish-style ballad that was Blanche Ring's show-stopping interpolation in *The Jersey Lily* (NY 1903). In the lyric, the enamored swain likens himself to Chauncey Olcott, then America's most celebrated Irish tenor.

"Before the Parade Passes By." Music by Jerry Herman & Charles Strouse; lyric by Herman & Lee Adams. After telling her dead husband of her plans to remarry, Dolly Gallagher Levi exultantly proclaims her determination to "go and taste Saturday's high life" as she takes in the 14th Street Parade for the Act I finale of *Hello, Dolly!* (NY 1964). Carol Channing was the original Dolly; Mary Martin played the role in London (1965).

"Begin the Beguine." Music & lyric by Cole Porter. Smoldering ballad of a love lost amid swaying palms, introduced by June Knight in the Café Martinique scene in *Jubilee* (NY 1935), then danced by Miss Knight and Charles Walters (choreography by Tony DeMarco). Porter, who composed most of the show's score while on a worldwide cruise, initially heard the song's basic melody performed as a war dance on the Indonesian island of Kalabahi. Because of its extreme length—105 measures—Moss Hart, *Jubilee's* librettist, once admitted that on first hearing he thought it had ended when Porter had played only about half the song. A persistent myth is that the song went unnoticed when first performed in the musical. Actually, it was singled out by more reviewers than any other number in the score, though it did take an Artie Shaw recording some three years later to turn it into a hit. In 1944, Porter wrote a take-off on the song, "Dancin' to a Jungle Drum (Let's End the Beguine)," which Beatrice Lillie sang in *Seven Lively Arts*. Other parodies: Noël Coward's "Nina," sung by Cyril Ritchard in *Sigh No More* (L 1945); Sheldon Harnick's "Boston Beguine," sung by Alice Ghostley in *New Faces of 1952* (NY); Jim Wise, George Haimsohn, and Robin Miller's "The Beguine," sung by Tamara Long in *Dames at Sea* (NY 1968).

Belle of New York, The (1897). Music by Gustave Kerker; lyrics & book by Hugh Morton (C.M.S. McLellan).

SONGS: "Teach Me How to Kiss," "They All Follow Me," "She Is the Belle of New York," "The Purity Brigade," "La Belle Parisienne," "They Call Me the Belle of New York," "On the Beach at Narragansett," "My Little Baby."

NEW YORK: Sept. 28, 1897
CASINO THEATRE; 56 p.

Presented & directed by George Lederer; settings, Ernest Albert, D. Frank Dodge, E. M. Gros; costumes, Mme. Caroline Siedle; music director, Gustave Kerker.

CAST: Edna May (*Violet Gray*), Harry Davenport (*Harry Bronson*), Dan Daly (*Ichabod Bronson*), David Warfield (*Karl Von Pumpernick*), William Cameron (*Blinky Bill*), Ada Dare (*Cora Angelique*), George K. Fortescue (*Doc Snifkins*).

LONDON: April 12, 1898
SHAFTESBURY THEATRE; 697 p.

Presented & directed by George Lederer; settings, Ernest Albert, D. Frank Dodge, E. M. Gros; costumes, Mme. Caroline Siedle; music ·director, Gustave Kerker.

CAST: Edna May (*Violet Gray*), Harry Davenport (*Harry Bronson*), Dan Daly (*Ichabod Bronson*), J. E. Sullivan (*Karl Von Pumpernick*), Frank Lawton (*Blinky Bill*), Helen Dupont (*Cora Angelique*), George K. Fortescue (*Doc Snifkins*).

The Belle of New York holds the distinction of being the first Bway musical to enjoy an extended run in London. It also provided the means by which Edna May became the first American star to win acclaim in the West End. In the story, wealthy New York playboy Harry Bronson ends an all-night bachelor party in his Riverside Drive apartment just in time for his wedding to Cora Angelique, the Queen of Comic Opera. But Papa Bronson, who heads the Young Men's Rescue League and Anti-Cigarette Society, is so angered at his son marrying an actress that he calls off the marriage and cuts off Harry's allowance. What's more, he decided to leave all his money to Violet Gray, a virtuous Salvation Army lass, whom father and son meet in Chinatown. Because Violet and Harry have fallen in love, the girl purposely shocks her benefactor by singing a naughty French song at a party, thereby assuring that the inheritance once more reverts to Harry. The musical proved so endearing to Londoners that it was revived in 1914, 1916, 1919, 1931, 1933, and 1942.

In 1921 the Shuberts offered a revised version called *The Whirl of New*

York, which played the Winter Garden, NY. The cast was headed by J. Harold Murray (*Harry*), Nancy Gibbs (*Violet*), John T. Murray (*Ichabod*), Joe Smith (*I. Ketchum*), Charlie Dale (*U. Cheatam*), Rosie Green (*Mamie*). The run was 124 performances.

FILM VERSION: Fred Astaire and Vera-Ellen (new songs) (MGM 1952, Charles Walters dir.).

Bells Are Ringing (1956). Music by Jule Styne; lyrics & book by Betty Comden & Adolph Green.

SONGS: "It's a Perfect Relationship," "On My Own," "It's a Simple Little System," "Is It a Crime?" "Hello, Hello There!" "I Met a Girl," "Long Before I Knew You," "Mu-Cha-Cha," "Just in Time," "Drop That Name," "The Party's Over," "I'm Going Back."

NEW YORK: Nov. 29, 1956
SHUBERT THEATRE; 924 p.

Presented by The Theatre Guild; directed by Jerome Robbins; choreographed by Robbins & Bob Fosse; settings & costumes, Raoul Pène du Bois; lighting, Peggy Clark; music director, Milton Rosenstock; orchestrations, Robert Russell Bennett.

CAST: Judy Holliday (*Ella Peterson*), Sydney Chaplin (*Jeff Moss*), Jean Stapleton (*Sue Summers*), Eddie Lawrence (*Sandor*), Dort Clark (*Inspector Barnes*), Frank Aletter (*Blake Barton*), George S. Irving (*Larry Hastings*), Peter Gennaro (*Carl*), Bernie West (*Dr. Kitchell*), Pat Wilkes (*Gwynne Smith*), Jack Weston (*Francis*).

LONDON: Nov. 14, 1957
COLISEUM; 292 p.

Presented by S. A. Gorlinsky; book restaged by Gerald Freedman; dances reproduced by Robert Tucker; settings, Henry Graveney; costumes, Rosemary Carvill, Hilary Virgo.

Maggy Rouff; lighting, Michael Northen; music director, Reginald Burston.

CAST: Janet Blair (*Ella Peterson*), George Gaynes (*Jeff Moss*), Allyn McLerie (*Gwynne Smith*), Eddie Molloy (*Sandor*), Jean St. Clair (*Sue Summers*), Donald Stewart (*Inspector Barnes*), C. Denier Warren (*Francis*), Harry Naughton (*Carl*), Robert Henderson (*Larry Hastings*), Franklin Fox (*Blake Barton*).

Comden and Green wrote the musical especially for their friend Judy Holliday, with whom they had appeared in a nightclub act, The Revuers. In the show, she played a meddlesome switchboard operator at Susanswerphone, a telephone answering service, who falls in love with subscriber Jeff Moss though they have never met. Jeff, a writer, thinks she's just a motherly old lady. Ella's true identity is kept from Jeff long enough for the show to take us—as had Comden and Green's previous *On the Town*—to such New York attractions as the subway, Central Park, a penthouse, and a couple of nightclubs. (In 1928, the Bway musical *The Five o'Clock Girl* was also about a telephone operator who falls in love with a young man sight unseen.) During NY run, Sydney Chaplin (who made his Bway debut in this production) was succeeded by Hal Linden, Jean Stapleton by Alice Pearce. Miss Holliday and Linden headed the touring company, which began its travels in March 1959. *Bells Are Ringing* was the most successful show created by Comden and Green with composer Jule Styne.

FILM VERSION: Judy Holliday and Dean Martin (MGM 1960, Vincente Minnelli dir.).

Bennett, Michael (né Michael DiFiglia), director, choreographer, dancer; b. Buffalo, NY, 1943. Began Bway career as chorus dancer; won first major success with dances for *Promises, Promises*; became solo director with *Seesaw*. Bennett's chief creative achievement to date is *A Chorus Line*.

Unless otherwise noted, Mr. Bennett was choreographer of following:

1961	Subways Are for Sleeping (dancer only)
1963	Here's Love (dancer only)
1964	Bajour (dancer only)
1966	A Joyful Noise
1967	Henry, Sweet Henry
1968	Promises, Promises
1969	Promises, Promises (L)
	Coco
1970	Company
1971	Follies (also co-dir.)
1972	Company (L)
1973	Seesaw (also dir., lib.)
1975	A Chorus Line (also dir.)
1978	Ballroom (also dir.)

Bennett, Wilda, actress, singer; b. Asbury Park, NJ, Dec. 19, 1894; d. Winnemucca, Nev., Dec. 20, 1967. After making Bway debut in 1911, Miss Bennett introduced "When You're Away" in *The Only Girl* and "Say It with Music" in the *Music Box Revue*.

1914	The Only Girl (*Ruth Wilson*)
1917	Sybil (US tour) (*Sybil*)
	The Riviera Girl (*Sylva Vareska*)
1918	The Girl Behind the Gun (*Lucienne Lambrissac*)
1919	Apple Blossoms (*Nancy*)
1921	Music Box Revue
1922	The Lady in Ermine (*Mariana*)
1924	Madame Pompadour (*Mme. Pompadour*)
1928	Lovely Lady (*Folly Watteau*, repl.)

Berkeley, Busby (né William Berkeley Enos), choreographer, actor; b. Los Angeles, Cal., Nov. 29, 1895. Following a decade as a Bway dance director, Berkeley went to Hollywood where he won fame as a creator of elaborate kaleidoscopic routines (*42nd Street, Footlight Parade*, etc.). As actor, he introduced the song "You

Took Advantage of Me" in *Present Arms.*

    1920   Irene (US tour) (also *Mme. Lucy*)
    1925   Holka-Polka
    1926   The Wild Rose
    1927   Lady Do
           A Connecticut Yankee
           The White Eagle
    1928   Present Arms (also *Douglas Atwell*)
           Earl Carroll Vanities
           Good Boy
           Rainbow
           Hello, Daddy
    1929   Pleasure Bound
           A Night in Venice
           Broadway Nights
           The Street Singer (also dir., prod.)
    1930   9:15 Revue
           International Revue
           Sweet and Low
    1971   No, No, Nanette (r) (supervisor)

Berle, Milton (né Milton Berlinger), actor; b. New York, July 12, 1908. Buck-toothed, rapid-fire comedian who appeared in vaudeville, night-clubs, and Hollywood films, and who made biggest success in early days of tv. Bib: *The Autobiography of Milton Berle* (Delacorte, NY 1974).

    1920   Florodora (r) (Boy Sextette)
    1932   Earl Carroll Vanities
    1934   Saluta (*Windy Walker*) (also lyr.)
    1935   Life Begins at 8:40 (US tour)
    1943   Ziegfeld Follies
    1951   Seventeen (co-prod. only)

Berlin, Irving (né Israel Baline), composer, lyricist, producer; b. Temun, Russia, May 11, 1888. In a career spanning more than 50 years, Berlin remains unsurpassed in creating a body of songs that expressed the basic moods and emotions of his countrymen. As Jerome Kern once wrote: "Irving Berlin has no *place* in American music; he *is* American music."

Berlin's parents settled in the US when he was a baby. He began his career as a singing waiter on NY's Lower East Side, then became a lyricist, and eventually a self-taught composer. In 1914 he introduced ragtime into the Bway theatre with his score for *Watch Your Step* ("Play a Simple Melody"). Other early revues: *Stop! Look! Listen!* ("The Girl on the Magazine Cover," "I Love a Piano"), the all-soldier show *Yip, Yip, Yaphank* ("Mandy," "Oh, How I Hate to Get Up in the Morning"), *Ziegfeld Follies* of 1919, 1920, and 1927 ("A Pretty Girl Is Like a Melody," "You'd Be Surprised," "Tell Me, Little Gypsy," "Shaking the Blues Away"). In 1921 Berlin and producer Sam H. Harris built the Music Box Theatre as a showplace for four editions of the *Music Box Revue* ("Say It with Music," "Everybody Step," "Lady of the Evening," "What'll I Do?," "All Alone").

Early in the 30s, Berlin wrote songs for two satirical musicals, *Face the Music* ("Let's Have Another Cup o' Coffee," "Soft Lights and Sweet Music") and *As Thousands Cheer* ("Heat Wave," "Easter Parade," "Not for All the Rice in China"). The next decade he had such long-running attractions as *Louisiana Purchase* ("It's a Lovely Day Tomorrow," "You're Lonely and I'm Lonely," "Fools Fall in Love"), the all-soldier show *This Is the Army* ("This Is the Army, Mr. Jones," "I Left My Heart at the Stage Door Canteen"), and his biggest hit, *Annie Get Your Gun* ("Doin' What Comes Natur'lly," "The Girl That I Marry," "There's No Business Like Show Business," "They Say It's Wonderful," "I Got the Sun in the Morning," "You Can't Get a Man with a Gun"). The most popular latter-day Berlin show was *Call Me Madam* ("You're Just in Love," "It's a Lovely Day Today," "They Like Ike").

Eddie Cantor, Grace Moore, Marilyn Miller, William Gaxton, and Ethel

Merman each appeared in two Berlin musicals. The composer has also written for Hollywood films (incl. *Top Hat, Alexander's Ragtime Band, Holiday Inn*), and has had many song hits unaffiliated with stage or screen productions. Bib: *The Story of Irving Berlin* by Alexander Woollcott (Putnam, NY 1925); *Irving Berlin* by Michael Freedland (Stein & Day, NY 1974).

1910 Up Stage and Down (singer)
1914 Watch Your Step
1915 Stop! Look! Listen!
1916 The Century Girl
1917 The Cohan Revue
1918 Yip, Yip, Yaphank (also singer)
1919 Ziegfeld Follies
1920 Ziegfeld Follies
1921 Music Box Revue (also singer)
1922 Music Box Revue
1923 Music Box Revue
1924 Music Box Revue
1925 The Cocoanuts
1927 Ziegfeld Follies
1932 Face the Music
1933 As Thousands Cheer
1940 Louisiana Purchase (also co-prod.)
1942 This Is the Army (also singer)
1946 Annie Get Your Gun
1949 Miss Liberty (also co-prod.)
1950 Call Me Madam
1962 Mr. President

Bernstein, Leonard, composer, lyricist; b. Lawrence, Mass., Aug. 25, 1918. Bernstein's scores for Bway musicals have displayed both his affinity for life in NY (*On the Town, Wonderful Town, West Side Story*) and his classical background (*Candide*). In addition to writing his own lyrics, he has also collaborated with Betty Comden and Adolph Green ("New York, New York," "Lucky to Be Me," "Ohio," "A Quiet Girl," "It's Love"), Richard Wilbur ("Glitter and Be Gay"), Stephen Sondheim ("Something's Coming," "Tonight," "Maria"). The composer's career has primarily been in the world of concert music as conductor (music director, NY Philharmonic, 1956–1969), piano soloist, composer, lecturer. Bib: *The Joy of Music* by Bernstein (S&S, NY 1959); *Leonard Bernstein* by John Briggs (World, Cleve. 1961).

1944 On the Town (Comden, Green)
1950 Peter Pan (also lyr.)
1953 Wonderful Town (Comden, Green)
1956 Candide (Wilbur, etc.)
1957 West Side Story (Sondheim)
1976 1600 Pennsylvania Ave. (Lerner)

Besoyan, (Richard) Rick, composer, lyricist, librettist; b. Reedley, Cal., July 2, 1924; d. Sayville, NY, March 13, 1970. Besoyan made a notable debut with his long-running off-Bway operetta spoof, *Little Mary Sunshine*. He had formerly been a singing teacher and actor.

1959 Little Mary Sunshine
1963 The Student Gypsy
1964 Babes in the Wood

"Bess, You Is My Woman Now." Music by George Gershwin; lyric by Ira Gershwin & DuBose Heyward. Ardent duet for Todd Duncan and Anne Brown in *Porgy and Bess* (NY 1935). Later sung by William Warfield and Leontyne Price in London (1952).

Best Foot Forward (1941). Music & lyrics by Hugh Martin & Ralph Blane; book by John Cecil Holm.

SONGS: "Three Men on a Date," "That's How I Love the Blues," "Ev'ry Time," "The Guy Who Brought Me," "Shady Lady Bird," "Buckle Down, Winsocki," "My First Promise," "The Three B's," "What Do You Think I Am?," "Just a Little Joint with a Jukebox."

NEW YORK: Oct. 1, 1941
ETHEL BARRYMORE THEATRE; 326 p.

Presented by George Abbott & Richard Rodgers (uncredited); directed by Abbott; choreographed by Gene Kelly; settings, Jo Mielziner; costumes, Miles White; music director, Archie Bleyer; orchestrations, Don Walker, Hans Spialek.

CAST: Rosemary Lane (*Gale Joy*), Marty May (*Jack Haggerty*), Gil Stratton Jr. (*Bud Hooper*), Maureen Cannon (*Helen Schlesinger*), Nancy Walker (*Blind Date*), Jack Jordan Jr. (*Dutch Miller*), June Allyson (*Minerva Brooks*), Kenneth Bowers (*Hunk Hoyt*), Victoria Schools (*Ethel*), Betty Anne Nyman (*Miss Ferguson*), Tommy Dix (*Chuck Green*), Danny Daniels (dancer), Stanley Donen (dancer).

NEW YORK: April 2, 1963
STAGE 73; 224 p.

Presented by Arthur Whitelaw, Buster Davis, Joan D'Incecco, Lawrence Baker Jr.; directed & choreographed by Danny Daniels; settings & costumes, Robert Fletcher; lighting, Jules Fisher; music director, Buster Davis.

CAST: Paula Wayne (*Gale Joy*), Liza Minnelli (*Ethel Hofflinger*), Glenn Walken (*Bud Hooper*), Karin Wolfe (*Helen Schlesinger*), Grant Walden (*Jack Haggerty*), Edmund Gaynes (*Hunk Hoyt*), Kay Cole (*Minerva Brooks*), Ronald Walken (*Dutch Miller*).

George Abbott was particularly attracted to the script of *Best Foot Forward* (originally titled *Young Man's Fancy*) because, since the cast would be mostly composed of teenagers, the young men would not yet be eligible for the draft. For his first musical without a score by Rodgers and Hart (though Rodgers was an uncredited co-producer), Abbott signed the new team of Hugh Martin and Ralph Blane, with each writing songs independently of the other. The setting for the show was Winsocki, a prep

school in Pennsylvania, where all kinds of complications result when movie star Gale Joy, as a publicity gimmick, shows up at the prom. The musical marked the first featured roles for Nancy Walker and June Allyson, and its 1963 revival gave Liza Minnelli her first theatrical break. During run of that production, Paula Wayne was succeeded by Veronica Lake.

FILM VERSION: Lucille Ball, William Gaxton, Nancy Walker, June Allyson (MGM 1943, Eddie Buzzell dir.).

"Best of All Possible Worlds, The." Music by Leonard Bernstein; lyric by Richard Wilbur. The philosophy of Voltaire's optimistic Dr. Pangloss —"All's for the best in this best of all possible worlds"—espoused by Max Adrian in *Candide* (NY 1956) and by Laurence Naismith in London version (1959).

"Best Thing for You, The." Music & lyric by Irving Berlin. Ethel Merman and Paul Lukas expressed their romantic conviction in *Call Me Madam* (NY 1950). In London (1952) the couple was played by Billie Worth and Anton Walbrook.

"Best Things in Life Are Free, The." Music by Ray Henderson; lyric by B. G. DeSylva & Lew Brown. Ode to priceless gifts sung by John Price Jones and Mary Lawlor in *Good News!* (NY 1927). In the story, rich hero leads up to the song by trying to convince poor heroine that "a lot of things make up for the shortage of money." In London version (1928) it was sung by Neil Collins and Evelyn Hoey.

"Bewitched." Music by Richard Rodgers; lyric by Lorenz Hart. A middle-aged woman's jaded, cynical look at falling in love again first sung by Vivienne Segal in *Pal Joey* (NY 1940), later by Carol Bruce in London production (1954). For commercial use, the lines "He's a laugh but I love it/ Because the laugh's on me" were changed to "He can laugh but I love it/ Although the laugh's on me." Song also known as "Bewitched, Bothered and Bewildered."

"Bidin' My Time." Music by George Gershwin; lyric by Ira Gershwin. Ballad of indolence sung in *Girl Crazy* (NY 1930) by a quartet of cowboys known as The Foursome (Marshall Smith, Ray Johnson, Del Porter, Dwight Snyder), who accompanied themselves on the harmonica, jew's harp, ocarina, and tin flute.

"Big Best Shoes." Music & lyric by Sandy Wilson. Bustling number about the joys of dressing up in a silly, frilly frock and wearing "big best shoes that go nicka-nacka-nock, nicka-nacka-nock, nicka-nacka-nock." Introduced in *Valmouth* by Bertice Reading (L 1958), succeeded by Cleo Laine, then sung in NY version by Miss Reading (1960).

"Big D." Music & lyric by Frank Loesser. Bouncy tribute to Dallas, Texas, sung by homesick Susan Johnson and Shorty Long in *The Most Happy Fella* (NY 1956). In London production (1960) it was sung by Libi Staiger and Jack DeLon.

"Big Spender." Music by Cy Coleman; lyric by Dorothy Fields. Lethargic invitation proffered by Helen Gallagher, Thelma Oliver, and hostesses of the Fan-Dango Ballroom while draping themselves in awkwardly seductive poses in *Sweet Charity* (NY 1966). Josephine Blake and Paula Kelly led the girls in London production (1967).

"Bill." Music by Jerome Kern; lyric by P. G. Wodehouse. Sung by Helen Morgan (atop an upright piano) in *Show Boat* (NY 1927), and by Marie Burke in 1928 London version. In the story, though the song is presented at the Trocadero Music Hall during a rehearsal for the floor show, it actually reveals the singer's devotion to a wastrel named not Bill but Steve. Originally, with a somewhat different lyric, the song was to have been sung by Vivienne Segal in *Oh, Lady! Lady!!* (NY 1918), but it was dropped before the opening because the lyric did not exactly apply to the musical's hero, Willoughby "Bill" Finch. Another, more appreciative song, "Do Look at Him"—with almost the same verse as the discarded "Bill"—had to be substituted. A second attempt to have "Bill" sung on Bway—in Marilyn Miller's *Sally*—did not work out either. Eventually, with an altered lyric, it was given to Miss Morgan and quickly became her trademark. For *Show Boat*'s 1946 Bway revival, Oscar Hammerstein included the following disclaimer of authorship in the program: "I am particularly anxious to point out that the lyric for the song 'Bill' was written by P. G. Wodehouse. Although he has always been given credit in the program, it has frequently been assumed that since I wrote all the other lyrics for *Show Boat*, I also wrote this one, and I have had praise for it which belonged to another man." Nevertheless, Hammerstein's name appears as co-lyricist in the vocal score.

"Billie." Music & lyric by George M. Cohan. The heroine of *Billie* (NY 1928), played by Polly Walker, reveals how much she loves her name even though her parents, expecting a boy, had named her after her father. In *George M!* (NY 1968), the waltz was sung by Jill O'Hara. Previous "name" songs by Cohan were "Mary's a Grand Old Name" (*Forty-Five Minutes from Broadway*) and "Ring to the Name of Rose" (*The Rise of Rosie O'Reilly*).

Billy (1974). Music by John Barry; lyrics by Don Black; book by Dick Clement & Ian La Frenais, based on play *Billy Liar* by Keith Waterhouse & Willis Hall & novel by Waterhouse.

SONGS: "Ambrosia," "Some of Us Belong to the Stars," "Lies," "It Were All Green Hills," "Aren't You Billy Fisher?," "Is This Where I Wake Up?," "Billy," "Remembering," "Any Minute Now," "The Lady from L.A.," "I Missed the Last Rainbow."

LONDON: May 1, 1974
DRURY LANE THEATRE; 904 p.

Presented by Peter Witt, with H. M. Tennent Ltd.; directed by Patrick Garland; choreographed by Onna White; settings, Ralph Koltai; costumes, Annena Stubbs; lighting, Jules Fisher; music director, Alfred Ralston; orchestrations, John Barry, Bobby Richards.

CAST: Michael Crawford (*Billy Fisher*), Avis Bunnage (*Alice Fisher*), Bryan Pringle (*Geoffrey Fisher*), Diana Quick (*Liz Benson*), Christopher Hancock (*Mr. Shadrack*), Lockwood West (*Councillor Duxbury*), Gay Soper (*Barbara*), Elaine Paige (*Rita*).

The saga of lying, day-dreaming Billy Fisher, an undertaker's assistant who yearns to break out of his drab, middle-class north-country surroundings, was turned into the most popular British musical in 10 years thanks largely to the winning performance of

Michael Crawford. In Billy's dreams, our hero is wafted to the land of Ambrosia, where he is President, Commander-in-Chief and captain of the Ambrosian World Cup football team. Other fantasies find him as both Gene Kelly *and* Fred Astaire, and also as a rock and roll singing idol. The story is set in Stradhoughton, Yorkshire.

In 1964, an off-Bway musical, *The Secret Life of Walter Mitty* (based on the James Thurber story) was also about a man who escapes from life through improbable daydreams.

Birch, Patricia, choreographer, dancer; b. Scarsdale, NY. Beginning as dancer with Martha Graham and NYC Center Lt. Opera Co., Miss Birch has won praise for her choreography for *Grease* and *Over Here*.

Unless otherwise noted, Miss Birch was choreographer of following:

1958	Goldilocks (dancer only)
1960	West Side Story (*Anybody's*, repl., only)
1962	Fortuna (*Constance* only)
1967	You're a Good Man, Charlie Brown
1968	Up Eden
1970	The Me Nobody Knows
1971	F. Jasmine Addams
1972	Grease
1973	A Little Night Music Grease (L)
1974	Over Here Candide
1975	Diamond Studs
1976	Pacific Overtures

"Birth of the Blues, The." Music by Ray Henderson; lyric by B. G. De-Sylva & Lew Brown. Sung by Harry Richman in the first-act finale of Bway revue *George White's Scandals* (1926). The scene was the Gates of Heaven for a jazz-vs.-classics debate. Richman, to impress "Beethoven" (Willie Howard) and "Liszt" (Eugene

Howard), offered this musical history lesson as evidence that the blues are an important part of music. With his case bolstered by the McCarthy Sisters singing "St. Louis Blues" and "Memphis Blues," and particularly by Gershwin's "Rhapsody in Blue" (with lyrics!), Richman finally got those in charge to open the pearly gates to accept American blues into the musical Valhalla.

Bitter Sweet (1929). Music, lyrics & book by Noël Coward.

SONGS: "The Call of Life," "If You Could Only Come with Me," "I'll See You Again," "Dear Little Café," "If Love Were All," "Ladies of the Town," "Tokay," "Zigeuner," "Green Carnation."

LONDON: July 12, 1929
HIS MAJESTY'S THEATRE; 697 p.

Presented by Charles B. Cochran; directed by Noël Coward; choreographed by Tilly Losch; settings & costumes, G. E. Calthrop; music director, Reginald Burston; orchestrations, Orellana.

CAST: Peggy Wood (*Sarah Millick*), Georges Metaxa (*Carl Linden*), Ivy St. Helier (*Manon*), Billy Milton (*Vincent Howard*), Robert Newton (*Hugh Devon*), Norah Howard (*Gussi*), Alan Napier (*Marquis of Shayne*), Gerald Nodin (*Capt. Schenzi*).

NEW YORK: Nov. 5, 1929
ZIEGFELD THEATRE; 157 p.

Presented by Florenz Ziegfeld & Arch Selwyn; directed by Noël Coward; choreographed by Tilly Losch; settings & costumes, G. E. Calthrop; music director, Arthur Jones.

CAST: Evelyn Laye (*Sarah Millick*), Gerald Nodin (*Carl Linden*), Mireille (*Manon*), Max Kirby (*Vincent Howard*), Tracy Holmes (*Hugh Devon*), Sylvia Leslie (*Gussi*), John Evelyn (*Marquis of Shayne*).

Noël Coward's most successful romantic operetta was originally intended for Gertrude Lawrence, but her vocal limitations forced the author to look elsewhere. Evelyn Laye, because of her antagonism toward producer Charles Cochran at the time, refused the part, which went to the American actress Peggy Wood. (Miss Laye later made up with Cochran, headed the NY company, and then replaced Miss Wood for two months.) Told in flashback, the sentimental tale is concerned with headstrong Sarah Millick, who in 1875 leaves her intended bridegroom in London and elopes to Vienna with music teacher Carl Linden. Five years later, her happiness is shattered when Carl is killed in a duel, but she goes on to become a prima donna and marry the faithful Marquis of Shayne.

Coward, who got the idea for the Viennese setting while listening to a recording of *Die Fledermaus*, was motivated to write *Bitter Sweet* because he felt the time was ripe for a romantic renaissance in the theatre. For NY production, an Italian tenor had been chosen for the role of Carl, but a language problem forced his replacement during the Boston tryout by Gerald Nodin, Georges Metaxa's London understudy. In 1938, Coward and Peggy Wood were reunited for the London operetta *Operette*.

The 1947 London hit *Bless the Bride*, set in the same general period, told a similar tale but with a happier ending.

FILM VERSIONS: Anna Neagle and Ferdinand Graavey (Brit. & Dom. 1933, Herbert Wilcox dir.); Jeanette MacDonald and Nelson Eddy (MGM 1941, W. S. Van Dyke dir.).

"Black Bottom." Music by Ray Henderson; lyric by B. G. DeSylva & Lew Brown. Dance inspired by the mud flats of the Suwanee River, calling for participants to squirm like a worm. Introduced as first-act finale of *George White's Scandals* (NY 1926) by Ann Pennington, the McCarthy Sisters, Frances Williams, and Tom Patricola.

Black Crook, The (1866). Music by Thomas Baker, etc.; lyrics by miscellaneous writers; book by Charles M. Barras.

SONGS: "You Naughty, Naughty Men," (G. Bicknell–T. Kennick) "March of the Amazons," "The Political Whip," "Dare I Tell?", "Kissing."

NEW YORK: Sept. 12, 1866
NIBLO'S GARDEN; 474 p.

Presented by William Wheatley & Henry C. Jarrett; choreographed by David Costa; settings, Richard Marston.

CAST: Milly Cavendish *(Carline)*, Annie Bowler *(Stalacta)*, C. H. Morton *(Hertzog)*, J. W. Blaisdell *(Count Wolfenstein)*, George Atkins *(Greppo)*, Rose Morton *(Amina)*, also ballerinas Rita Sangalli, Betty Rigl, Emily Rigl, Marie Bonfanti.

Though there were previous dramatic productions with songs, *The Black Crook* has enjoyed the legendary distinction of being the first American musical. Its creation was entirely by accident. A French ballet troupe had been booked into NY's Academy of Music, but the theatre burned down shortly before the scheduled opening. At the same time, *The Black Crook*, a preposterous melodrama based loosely on the Faustian theme of a man selling his soul to the devil, was set to open at Niblo's Garden. Because he had little faith in the play's success, William Wheatley, the manager of Niblo's, hired the ballet company and its scenery for those sequences that required the participation of dancing demons and spirits.

The first-night performance began at 7:45 P.M. and ended at 1:15, but no one seemed to mind. The sight of some 100 bare-limbed dancing girls (Marie Bonfanti was premiere ballerina) was enough to ensure a lasting run for this "magical and spectacular" production. It toured extensively throughout the US and returned to NY in 1869, 1871, 1873, 1879, 1881, 1884, 1889, and 1903. A revival was presented in Hoboken, NJ, in 1929, with Agnes de Mille and with lyrics by Christopher Morley.

A production of *The Black Crook* opened at the Alhambra Theatre in London, on Dec. 23, 1874, with an adaptation by Harry Paulton. It ran for 204 performances. A sequel to *The Black Crook*, called *The White Fawn*, with book by James Mortimer, was presented in NY in 1868. In 1954 the Broadway musical *The Girl in Pink Tights* was based on the circumstances surrounding the original production of *The Black Crook*. It had a book by Jerome Chodorov and Joseph Fields, a score by composer Sigmund Romberg (who died before the production) and lyricist Leo Robin, and starred Jeanmaire and Charles Goldner. It ran for 115 performances.

Black, George, producer; b. Birmingham, Eng., April 20, 1890; d. London, March 4, 1945. After serving as managing director, Moss' Empires Ltd., Black became independent producer with series of Crazy Gang shows at the London Palladium. He was also associated with director Robert Nesbitt in creating a number of colorful, nightclub-style revues. His sons, George and Alfred Black, were also London producers.

1936   Okay for Sound
1937   Swing Is in the Air
         London Rhapsody
         Hide and Seek

Blackbirds of 1928. Music by Jimmy McHugh; lyrics by Dorothy Fields.

SONGS: "Diga Diga Doo," "I Can't Give You Anything but Love," "Porgy," "Doin' the New Low-Down," "Magnolia's Wedding Day," "I Must Have That Man," "Bandanna Babies," "Shuffle Your Feet."

NEW YORK: May 9, 1928
LIBERTY THEATRE; 518 p.

Presented & directed by Lew Leslie; setting, Premier Scenic Studios; costumes, Kiviette; music director, Allie Ross; orchestrations, Will Vodery, Ken MacComber, Arthur Goodman.

CAST: Adelaide Hall, Bill Robinson, Aida Ward, Tim Moore, Mantan Moreland, Elisabeth Welch, Hall Johnson Choir.

This was the most successful *Blackbirds* production and became the longest running all-black revue in Bway history. Leslie had produced and staged his first *Blackbirds* in London in 1926. He had planned to star the sensation of that production, Florence Mills, in the 1928 Bway edition, but Miss Mills died before preparations began and Leslie signed Aida Ward as replacement. Bill Robinson was hired during the out-of-town tryout and appeared in only one number in the second act, "Doin' the New Low-Down." Besides Robinson and Miss Ward, the show benefited from the talents of Adelaide Hall and Tim Moore, the well-paced direction, and the score by McHugh and Fields (making their Bway debut).

Leslie had far less success with subsequent Bway *Blackbirds*. Despite the presence of Ethel Waters, Buck and Bubbles, and Flournoy Miller, the 1930 edition ran only 26 performances. The 1933 edition, with Bill Robinson, ran 25, and the one in 1939, with Lena Horne, lasted nine. The producer's luck was better in London. The 1934 *Blackbirds* remained for 123 performances, and the 1936 edition, with the Nicholas Brothers, lasted 124. As a racial variation, Leslie offered *Whitebirds* in London in 1927. It starred Maurice Chevalier and José Collins, and continued for 80 performances.

Blaine, Vivian (née Vivian Stapleton), actress, singer; b. Newark, NJ, Nov. 21, 1921. Vivacious blonde actress who also appeared in vaudeville and nonmusical plays as well as Hollywood films. Miss Blaine's greatest Bway success was in *Guys and Dolls* (introducing "Adelaide's Lament," "Sue Me," "A Bushel and a Peck").

1950 Guys and Dolls (*Miss Adelaide*)
1953 Guys and Dolls (L) (*Miss Adelaide*)
1958 Say, Darling (*Irene Lovelle*)
1971 Company (*Joanne*, repl.)

Blake, (James Hubert) Eubie, composer, singer; b. Baltimore, Md., Feb. 7, 1883. Blake teamed with lyricist Noble Sissle to write the score for *Shuffle Along* ("I'm Just Wild About Harry," "Love Will Find a Way"), Bway's first long-run all-Negro musical. With Sissle he also wrote "You

Were Meant for Me" (*André Charlot's Revue of 1924*) and with Andy Razaf "Memories of You" (*Blackbirds*). Other collaborators were Cecil Mack and Milton Reddie. Blake appeared as singer and pianist in most of his shows and has also made many records. Bib: *Reminiscing with Sissle and Blake* by Robert Kimball and William Bolcom (Viking, NY 1973).

1921 Shuffle Along (Sissle)
1923 Elsie (Sissle)
1924 Chocolate Dandies (Sissle)
1930 Blackbirds (Razaf)
1932 Shuffle Along of 1933 (Sissle)
1937 Swing It (Mack, Reddie)
1952 Shuffle Along (Sissle)

Blane, Ralph (né Ralph Uriah Hunsecker), composer, lyricist, singer; b. Broken Arrow, Okla., July 26, 1914. Blane's most celebrated Bway score was for *Best Foot Forward* ("Buckle Down, Winsocki," "Ev'ry Time," "Just a Little Joint with a Jukebox"), which he wrote with composer-lyricist Hugh Martin. After beginning theatre career as a vocal arranger, Blane organized a quartet with Martin called The Martins (1940–1942). The team also wrote Hollywood film scores, incl. *Meet Me in St. Louis.*

1936 New Faces of 1936 (singer only)
1937 Hooray for What! (singer only)
1940 Louisiana Purchase (singer only)
1941 Best Foot Forward (Martin)
1942 The Lady Comes Across (singer only)
1952 Three Wishes for Jamie

Bless the Bride (1947). Music by Vivian Ellis; lyrics & book by A. P. Herbert.

SONGS: "Ma Belle Marguerite," "This Is My Lovely Day," "I Was Never Kissed Before," "Table for Two," "Come Dance, My Dear," "The Silent Heart," "Bless the Bride," "My Big Moment."

LONDON: April 26, 1947
ADELPHI THEATRE; 886 p.
Presented by Charles B. Cochran; directed & choreographed by Wendy Toye; settings & costumes, Tanya Moiseiwitsch; music director, Michael Collins.

CAST: Lizbeth Webb (*Lucy Veracity Willow*), Georges Guetary (*Pierre Fontaine*), Brian Reece (*Thomas Trout*), Betty Paul (*Suzanne Valois*).

London's most popular home-grown product of 1947 was a refuge for those resisting the American invasion led by *Oklahoma!* and *Annie Get Your Gun*, both produced the same year. Taking place in 1870, it was a romance of the Franco-Prussian war involving an English girl, Lucy, who elopes, *Bitter Sweet* fashion, to France with the dashing actor Pierre Fontaine. Though they are separated when war breaks out, the two are eventually reunited in England. The musical, Cochran's penultimate, was the producer's longest-running attraction.

Blitzstein, Marc, composer, lyricist, librettist; b. Philadelphia, Pa., March 2, 1905; d. Martinique, WI, Jan. 22, 1964. Classically trained composer whose works include symphonies, concerti, sonatas, string quartets, ballets, cantatas. Best known for off-Bway English adaptation of Kurt Weill–Bert Brecht *Threepenny Opera* ("The Ballad of Mack the Knife," "Pirate Jenny").

1937 The Cradle Will Rock
1949 Regina
1954 The Threepenny Opera (lib., lyr. only) (Weill)
1959 Juno (comp., lyr. only)

Bloomer Girl (1944). Music by Harold Arlen; lyrics by E. Y. Harburg; book by Sig Herzig & Fred Saidy, based on an unproduced play by Lilith & Dan James.

SONGS: "When the Boys Come Home," "Welcome Hinges," "The Eagle and Me," "Right as the Rain," "Sunday in Cicero Falls," "Evelina," "The Rakish Young Man with the Whiskers," "I Got a Song," "T'morra, T'morra," "It Was Good Enough for Grandma," "I Never Was Born."

NEW YORK: Oct. 5, 1944
SHUBERT THEATRE; 654 p.

Presented by John C. Wilson, with Nat Goldstone; directed by Harburg & William Schorr; choreographed by Agnes de Mille; settings & lighting, Lemuel Ayers; costumes, Miles White; music director, Leon Leonardi; orchestrations, Robert Russell Bennett.

CAST: Celeste Holm (*Evelina Applegate*), David Brooks (*Jeff Calhoun*), Dooley Wilson (*Pompey*), Joan McCracken (*Daisy*), Richard Huey (*Alexander*), Mabel Taliaferro (*Serena Applegate*), Matt Briggs (*Horatio Applegate*), Toni Hart (*Julia*), Margaret Douglass (*Dolly Bloomer*).

A slice of Civil War Americana, *Bloomer Girl* combined themes involving women's rights and civil rights. Set in Cicero Falls, NY, in 1861, it relates the rebellion of Evelina Applegate against her father, Horatio Applegate, a manufacturer of hoop skirts, who wishes her to marry a hoop-skirt salesman. Evelina even joins her radical Aunt Dolly in advocating pantalettes for women and also in her abolitionist activities, though the latter is complicated when she falls in love with a southern slaveholder, Jeff Calhoun. The second act highlight was an Agnes de Mille ballet interpreting the longing of women who must wait at home while their men are at war. During run, Miss Holm was succeeded by Nanette Fabray.

Other musicals dealing with the Civil War: *The Girl from Dixie* (NY 1903); *Caroline* (NY 1923); *My Maryland* (NY 1927); *My Darlin' Aida* (NY 1952); *Gone with the Wind* (L 1972); *Shenandoah* (NY 1975).

Blossom, Henry, Jr., lyricist, librettist; b. St. Louis, Mo., May 6, 1866; d. New York, March 23, 1919. Blossom wrote eight Bway musicals with composer Victor Herbert, including *Mlle. Modiste* ("Kiss Me Again," "I Want What I Want When I Want It"), *The Red Mill* ("When You're Pretty and the World Is Fair," "Moonbeams," "Every Day Is Ladies' Day with Me," "The Streets of New York"), *The Only Girl* ("When You're Away"), *The Princess Pat*, and *Eileen* ("Thine Alone"). Other composers with whom he collaborated were Alfred Robyn, Paul Rubens, Leslie Stuart, Raymond Hubbell, Zoel Paranteau.

1904	The Yankee Consul (Robyn)
1905	Mlle. Modiste (Herbert)
1906	The Red Mill (Herbert)
1907	The Hoyden (lyr. only) (Rubens)
1908	The Prima Donna (Herbert)
1911	The Slim Princess (Stuart)
1912	Baron Trenck (lib. only)
	The Man from Cook's (Hubbell)
	All for the Ladies (Robyn)
1913	A Glimpse of the Great White Way (Robyn)
1914	The Only Girl (Herbert)
1915	The Princess Pat (Herbert)
1916	The Century Girl (lyr. only) (Herbert)
1917	Eileen (Herbert)
1918	Follow the Girl (Paranteau)
1919	The Velvet Lady (lyr. only) (Herbert)

Blossom Time (1921). Music by Franz Schubert arranged by Sigmund Romberg; lyrics & book by Dorothy Donnelly, based on Viennese operetta *Das Dreimäderlhaus*, by A. M. Wilner & Heinz Reichert, music arranged by Heinrich Berté, adapted from novel *Schwammerl,* by Dr. R. H. Bartsch.

SONGS: "This Is an Old Vienna Town," "Serenade," "Song of Love," "Tell Me, Daisy," "My Springtime Thou Art," "Three Little Maids," "Let Me Awake," "Peace to My Lonely Heart."

NEW YORK: Sept. 29, 1921
AMBASSADOR THEATRE; 592 p.

Presented by Messrs. Shubert; directed by J. C. Huffman; choreographed by F. M. Gillespie; settings, Watson Barratt; costumes, Mode Costume Co.; music director, Oscar Radin.

CAST: Bertram Peacock (*Franz Schubert*), Olga Cook (*Mitzi Kranz*), Howard Marsh (*Franz Von Schober*), William Danforth (*Kranz*), Roy Cropper (*Vogl*), Perry Askam (*Erkmann*), Zoe Barrett (*Bellabruna*).

As staff composer for Messrs. Shubert, Sigmund Romberg was assigned to write new arrangements for Schubert melodies to be used in a Bway version of a five-year-old operetta. The plot, something of a reverse twist on *Cyrano de Bergerac*, concerns the composer's love for Mitzi, which, because of shyness, he is afraid to express. Unfortunately, when he has his friend Baron Von Schober sing his songs to his beloved, Schubert ends up with neither sweetheart nor friend. But the experience does get him to compose the "Unfinished Symphony." The production, the second longest running musical of the 20s, became a nationwide success when four road companies were dispatched soon after the NY opening. Subsequent Bway reappearances took place in 1939 and 1943.

London has never seen the Romberg-Donnelly version. The 1922 West End adaptation, called *Lilac Time*, used arrangements by Heinrich Berté and G. H. Clutsam and book and lyrics by Adrian Ross. In 1942 a London version by Rodney Ackland, also called *Blossom Time*, was specially written for Richard Tauber. This story had Schubert in love with Vicki (Leueen McGrath), Vicki in love with Peter (Neal Arden), and Mitzi (Hella Kurty) in love with Schubert.

Other composers whose works were adapted as Bway musical scores include Offenbach (*The Love Song*, 1925); Tschaikowsky (*Nadja*, 1925); Chopin (*White Lilacs*, 1928); Johann Strauss Jr. and Sr. (*The Great Waltz*, 1934); Strauss Jr. and Sr. and Oscar Straus (*Three Waltzes*, 1937); Grieg (*Song of Norway*, 1944); Fritz Kreisler (*Rhapsody*, 1944); Chopin (*Polonaise*, 1945); Johann Strauss Jr. (*Mr. Strauss Goes to Boston*, 1945); Tschaikowsky (*Music in My Heart*, 1947); Villa Lobos (*Magdalena*, 1948); Borodin (*Kismet*, 1953); Offenbach (*The Happiest Girl in the World*, 1961).

"Blow, Gabriel, Blow." Music & lyric by Cole Porter. Revivalistic exhortation trumpeted by Ethel Merman during a ship's party in *Anything Goes* (NY 1934), then by Jeanne Aubert in London version (1935).

"Blue Room, The." Music by Richard Rodgers; lyric by Lorenz Hart. Sammy White and Eva Puck sang this tribute to romantic seclusion in *The Girl Friend* (NY 1926). Roy Royston and Louise Brown sang it in London musical with different story but also called *The Girl Friend* (1927). Though original sheet music includes the definite article in the title, it is not sung in the lyric, and the song is generally known as "Blue Room."

"Blue Skies." Music & lyric by Irving Berlin. Love's power to turn gray skies to blue was demonstrated by Belle Baker in *Betsy* (NY 1926). Note that each of the song's three main sections begins with a "blue" variation: "Blue skies smiling," "Bluebirds singing" and "Blue days, all of them gone." Though Rodgers and Hart wrote all the other songs for the musical, producer Florenz Ziegfeld had the Berlin ballad interpolated in the score. It was the biggest hit of the show and on opening night Miss Baker scored so notably with it that the composer was called on to take a spotlighted bow.

Bock, (Jerrold Lewis) Jerry, composer; b. New Haven, Conn., Nov. 23, 1928. With lyricist Sheldon Harnick, Bock has created Bway scores that are noted for capturing the locale and color of their subjects, ranging from NY of the 20s & 30s in *Fiorello!* ("Little Tin Box") to Mitteleuropa in the 30s in *She Loves Me* ("Will He Like Me?," "She Loves Me") to a Jewish village in czarist Russia in his biggest hit, *Fiddler on the Roof* ("Matchmaker, Matchmaker," "If I Were a Rich Man," "Sunrise, Sunset," "Miracle of Miracles"). Bock has also collaborated with Larry Holofcener and George Weiss on the score for *Mr. Wonderful* ("Mr. Wonderful," "Too Close for Comfort").

Unless otherwise noted, the following were written with Mr. Harnick:
1956 Mr. Wonderful (Holofcener, Weiss)
1958 The Body Beautiful
1959 Fiorello!
1960 Tenderloin
1963 She Loves Me
1964 Fiddler on the Roof
1966 The Apple Tree
1970 The Rothschilds

"Body and Soul." Music by Johnny Green; lyric by Edward Heyman, Robert Sour, Frank Eyton. The misery of romantic slavery revealed by Libby Holman in the revue *Three's a Crowd* (NY 1930). Originally written for an unproduced Bway musical, the song was given to Gertrude Lawrence, who then got British bandleader Jack Hylton to make a recording of it. This proved so popular that Howard Dietz bought the piece for *Three's a Crowd*. Initially, however, it did not make any impression, but once Ralph Rainger (composer of "Moanin' Low") made a new arrangement, the torch ballad became the hit of the show. Because of incendiary lines such as "You know I'm yours for just the taking," Dietz wrote a special lyric that was briefly used over the air. Co-lyricist Eyton's contribution was in making only a few minor changes for the British market.

Boland, Mary, actress; b. Philadelphia, Pa., Jan. 28, 1880; d. New York, June 23, 1965. Fluttery, grand-dame comedienne who made Bway debut in 1905 and appeared in over 40 Hollywood films.
1932 Face the Music (*Mrs. Martin Van Buren Meshbesher*)
1935 Jubilee (*The Queen*)

Boles, John, actor, singer; b. Greenville, Texas, Oct. 28, 1895; d. San Angelo, Texas, Feb. 27, 1969. Strongjawed Bway leading man in Hollywood during 30s.
1923 Little Jessie James (*Paul Revere,* repl.)
1925 Mercenary Mary (*Lyman Webster*)
1926 Kitty's Kisses (*Robert Mason*)
1943 One Touch of Venus (*Whitelaw Savory*)
1948 Sky High (L)

Bolger, (Raymond Wallace) Ray, actor, dancer; b. Dorchester, Mass., Jan. 10, 1904. Nimble, rubber-legged dancing comedian who scored biggest Bway successes in *On Your Toes* (singing "There's a Small Hotel," "On Your Toes"), *By Jupiter, Three to Make Ready* ("The Old Soft Shoe"), *Where's*

Charley? ("Once in Love with Amy," "Make a Miracle"). Bolger has also appeared in nightclubs and films (incl. *The Wizard of Oz*).

1926 The Merry World
1929 Heads Up! *(Georgie)*
1931 George White's Scandals
1934 Life Begins at 8:40
1936 On Your Toes *(Phil Dolan)*
1940 Keep Off the Grass
1942 By Jupiter *(Sapiens)*
1946 Three to Make Ready
1948 Where's Charley? *(Charley Wykeham)*
1962 All American *(Prof. Fodorski)*
1969 Come Summer *(Phineas Sharp)*

Bolton, Guy (Reginald), librettist; b. Broxbourne, Eng., Nov. 23, 1884 (American parents). A former architect, Bolton became one of the musical theatre's most prolific librettists in both NY and London. Writing almost always in collaboration, he was co-author with P. G. Wodehouse of 13 librettos, with Fred Thompson of 15. Bolton achieved his first Bway successes with the Princess Theatre musicals (*Very Good Eddie, Oh, Boy!, Oh, Lady! Lady!!*) and *Leave It to Jane,* written with composer Jerome Kern and—except for the first—Wodehouse. Other Bway hits: *Sally, Tangerine, Lady, Be Good!, Tip-Toes, The Ramblers, Oh, Kay!, Rio Rita, Rosalie, Girl Crazy, Anything Goes, Follow the Girls*. Bib: *Bring on the Girls!* by Wodehouse and Bolton (S&S, NY 1953). *(D. London, Sept. 5, 1979.)*

One asterisk indicates libretto written with Mr. Wodehouse; two indicate libretto with Mr. Thompson:

1915 90 in the Shade
Nobody Home
Very Good Eddie
1916 Miss Springtime
1917 Have a Heart *
Oh, Boy! *
Leave It to Jane *
The Riviera Girl *
Miss 1917 *

1918 Oh, Lady! Lady!! *
The Girl Behind the Gun *
Oh, My Dear! *
1919 The Rose of China *
1920 Sally
1921 Tangerine
1922 The Hotel Mouse
Daffy Dill
1924 Sitting Pretty *
Primrose (L)
Lady, Be Good! **
1925 The Bamboula (L)
Tip-Toes **
1926 The Ramblers
Oh, Kay! *
1927 The Nightingale *
Rio Rita **
The Five o'Clock Girl **
1928 She's My Baby
Rosalie
Blue Eyes (L)
1929 Polly
Top Speed
1930 Simple Simon
Girl Crazy
1931 Song of the Drum ** (L)
1933 Give Me a Ring (L)
1934 Anything Goes *
1935 Seeing Stars ** (L)
1936 At the Silver Swan (L)
Swing Along ** (L)
This'll Make You Whistle ** (L)
Going Places ** (L)
1937 Going Greek ** (L)
Hide and Seek ** (L)
1938 The Fleet's Lit Up ** (L)
Running Riot (L)
Bobby Get Your Gun ** (L)
1939 Magyar Melody ** (L)
1940 Walk with Music
Hold on to Your Hats
1944 Jackpot
Follow the Girls **
1947 The Chocolate Soldier (r)
1950 Music at Midnight (L)
1951 Rainbow Square (L)
1955 Ankles Aweigh
1965 Anya

Booth, Shirley (née Thelma Ford), actress, singer; b. New York, Aug. 30, 1907. Versatile actress who had most notable Bway musical-comedy successes in earthy, wise-cracking roles (incl. *A Tree Grows in Brooklyn*, in which she introduced "Love Is the Reason" and "Look Who's Dancing"). Miss Booth, who made her debut in 1925, also appeared in nonmusicals (*My Sister Eileen*, *Come Back, Little Sheba*), and has acted on radio and tv, and in films.

1945 Hollywood Pinafore (*Louhedda Hopsons*)
1951 A Tree Grows in Brooklyn (*Cissy*)
1954 By the Beautiful Sea (*Lottie Gibson*)
1959 Juno (*Juno Boyle*)
1970 Look to the Lilies (*Mother Maria*)

Bordoni, Irene, actress, singer; b. Corsica, Jan 16, 1895; d. New York, March 19, 1953. Eye-rolling, coquettish Irene Bordoni was the successor to Anna Held as Bway's epitome of Parisian oo-la-la. She first appeared on the French stage in 1907 and made her NY debut in 1912. She introduced "Do It Again" in *The French Doll*, "Let's Do It" in *Paris*, "It's a Lovely Day Tomorrow" in *Louisiana Purchase*. Miss Bordoni was married to and divorced from producer E. Ray Goetz (who produced three of her Bway shows).

1912 Broadway to Paris
1915 Miss Information (*Elaine Foazane*)
1917 Hitchy-Koo
1918 Hitchy-Koo
1920 As You Were (*Gervaise, Ninon, Cleopatra, Helen*)
1922 The French Doll (*Georgine Mazulier*)
1928 Paris (*Vivienne Rolland*)
1938 Great Lady (*Mme. Colette*)
1940 Louisiana Purchase (*Mme. Bordelaise*)
1951 South Pacific (US tour) (*Bloody Mary*, repl.)

"Boston Beguine." Music & lyric by Sheldon Harnick. In his first Bway song, Harnick used the restrictive confines of Boston as the setting for a takeoff on Cole Porter's smoldering lament "Begin the Beguine." It was Alice Ghostley's big hit in *New Faces of 1952*.

"Bowery, The." Music by William Gaunt; lyric by Charles Hoyt. Sung by Harry Conor in *A Trip to Chinatown* (NY 1892). Even though the play was set in San Francisco, the song's lyric tells of a series of misadventures that befall a rube visiting NY's Bowery. Because it became such a popular success, the number is credited with turning the production into a hit, despite the protests of the merchants of the area who felt they were being maligned.

Boy Friend, The (1954). Music, lyrics & book by Sandy Wilson.
SONGS: "Perfect Young Ladies," "The Boy Friend," "Won't You Charleston with Me?," "Fancy Forgetting," "I Could Be Happy with You," "Sur le Plage," "A Room in Bloomsbury," "You Don't Want to Play with Me Blues," "The Riviera," "It's Never Too Late to Fall in Love," "Poor Little Pierrette."

LONDON: Jan. 14, 1954
WYNDHAM'S THEATRE; 2,084 p.
Presented by The Players Theatre; directed by Vida Hope; choreographed by John Heawood; settings & costumes, Reginald Woolley; music director, Stan Edwards; orchestrations, Phil Cardew.
CAST: Anne Rogers (*Polly Browne*), Anthony Hayes (*Tony*), Hugh Paddick (*Percival Browne*), Joan Sterndale Bennett (*Mme. Dubonnet*), Larry Drew (*Bobby Van Husen*), John Rutland (*Lord Brockhurst*), Beryl Cooke (*Lady Brockhurst*), Denise Hirst (*Maisie*), Violetta (*Hortense*), Marie Charles (*Dulcie*).

NEW YORK: Sept. 30, 1954
ROYALE THEATRE; 485 p.

Presented by Cy Feuer & Ernest Martin; directed by Vida Hope; choreographed by John Heawood; settings & costumes, Reginald Woolley; lighting, Feder; music director, Anton Coppola; orchestrations, Ted Royal, Charles Cooke.

CAST: Julie Andrews (*Polly Browne*), John Hewer (*Tony*), Eric Berry (*Percival Browne*), Ruth Altman (*Mme. Dubonnet*), Bob Scheerer (*Bobby Van Husen*), Geoffrey Hibbert (*Lord Brockhurst*), Moyna MacGill (*Lady Brockhurst*), Ann Wakefield (*Maisie*), Paulette Girard (*Hortense*), Dilys Lay (*Dulcie*), Millicent Martin (*Nancy*), Buddy Schwab (*Alphonse*).

NEW YORK: Jan. 25, 1958
DOWNTOWN THEATRE; 763 p.

Presented by New Princess Co.; directed by Gus Schirmer; choreographed by Buddy Schwab; settings & lighting, Charles Brandon; costumes, Joe Crosby; music director, Natalie Charlson.

CAST: Ellen McCown (*Polly Browne*), Bill Mullikin (*Tony*), Leon Shaw (*Percival Browne*), Evelyn Page (*Mme. Dubonnet*), Peter Conlow (*Bobby Van Husen*), David Vaughan (*Lord Brockhurst*), Phoebe Mackay (*Lady Brockhurst*), Gerrianne Raphael (*Maisie*), Adele Aron (*Hortense*), June Squibb (*Dulcie*), Neal Kenyon (*Pierre*).

LONDON: Nov. 29, 1967
COMEDY THEATRE; 365 p.

Presented by Michael Codron; directed by Sandy Wilson; settings & costumes, Andrew & Margaret Brownfoot; music director, Grant Hossack.

CAST: Cheryl Kennedy (*Polly Browne*), Tony Adams (*Tony*), Jeremy Hawk (*Percival Browne*), Marion Grimaldi (*Mme. Dubonnet*), Nicholas Bennett (*Bobby Van Husen*), Geoffrey Hibbert (*Lord Brockhurst*), Celia Hilda (*Lady Brockhurst*), Frances Barlow (*Maisie*), Ann Beach (*Hortense*), Jacqueline Clarke (*Dulcie*).

Sandy Wilson's affectionate spoof of flapper-era musical comedy began life at the Players Club, London, on April 14, 1953, as part of the club's "Late Joys" program. Its duration was about an hour and a half and it had a three-week run. Because of its success, it was expanded to a three-act production, which reopened at the club Oct. 13 and ran six weeks. Though considered a questionable prospect for the West End, the musical was eventually transferred to Wyndham's Theatre, where its 2,084-performance run has made it currently the seventh longest running musical in London history. Set on the Riviera, each act—as per most musicals of the 20s—had a different locale: the Villa Caprice (Mme. Dubonnet's Finishing School), the Plage, and the Terrasse of the Café Cataplon. Polly, an English heiress at the school, and Tony, the son of Lord Brockhurst posing as a delivery boy, fall in love, and have a misunderstanding in time for the second-act curtain. Ultimately, costumed as Pierrette and Pierrot, they are reunited at the Carnival Ball. To help capture the period flavor, most of the songs deliberately recalled specific popular tunes of the day.

Playing her first leading role, Julie Andrews scored a major success in the initial Bway version; she was succeeded Oct. 1955 by Jean Bayless. A second Bway version in 1970 was staged and choreographed by those responsible for the 1958 off-Bway production, and its sets and costumes were designed by those who did the 1967 London production. The cast was headed by Judy Carne (*Polly*), Sandy Duncan (*Maisie*), Ronald Young (*Tony*), and Harvey Evans

(*Bobby*), and the run lasted 119 performances.

In 1964, Wilson wrote a parody of 30s musicals, *Divorce Me, Darling!*, in which the original *Boy Friend* characters were seen 10 years later. In the cast were Patricia Michael (*Polly*), Philip Gilbert (*Tony*), Anna Sharkey (*Maisie*), Cy Young (*Bobby*), Joan Heal (*Madame K.*). Originally presented at the Players Club, the show was transferred to the Globe, Feb. 1, 1965. It had a 91-performance run.

A prior spoof of 20s musicals was seen on Bway in 1948 as the first-act finale of the revue *Lend an Ear*. Written by Charles Gaynor, this minimusical, called *The Gladiola Girl*, contained six songs and a cast headed by Gloria Hamilton, William Eythe, Yvonne Adair, and, in the chorus, Carol Channing.

FILM VERSION: Twiggy, Christopher Gable, Max Adrian, Tommy Tune (MGM 1972, Ken Russell dir.).

Boys from Syracuse, The (1938). Music by Richard Rodgers; lyrics by Lorenz Hart; book by George Abbott, based on Shakespeare's *The Comedy of Errors*, adapted from Plautus' *Menaechmi.*

SONGS: "Dear Old Syracuse," "Falling in Love with Love," "The Shortest Day of the Year," "This Can't Be Love," "You Have Cast Your Shadow on the Sea," "Sing for Your Supper," "Oh, Diogenes," "He and She," "What Can You Do With a Man?"

NEW YORK: Nov. 23, 1938
ALVIN THEATRE; 235 p.

Presented & directed by George Abbott; choreographed by George Balanchine; settings, Jo Mielziner; costumes, Irene Sharaff; music director, Harry Levant; orchestrations, Hans Spialek.

CAST: Jimmy Savo (*Dromio of Syra-* cuse), Wynn Murray (*Luce*), Eddie Albert (*Antipholus of Syracuse*), Muriel Angelus (*Adriana*), Teddy Hart (*Dromio of Ephesus*), Marcy Westcott (*Luciana*), Ronald Graham (*Antipholus of Ephesus*), Betty Bruce (*Courtesan*), Burl Ives (*Tailor's Apprentice*).

NEW YORK: April 15, 1963
THEATRE FOUR; 502 p.

Presented by Richard York; directed by Christopher Hewett; choreographed by Bob Herget; settings, Herbert Senn & Helen Pond; costumes, Guy Kent; music director, Rene Wiegert; orchestrations, Larry Wilcox.

CAST: Ellen Hanley (*Adriana*), Danny Carroll (*Dromio of Syracuse*), Cathryn Damon (*Courtesan*), Stuart Damon (*Antipholus of Syracuse*), Clifford David (*Antipholus of Ephesus*), Julienne Marie (*Luciana*), Karen Morrow (*Luce*), Rudy Tronto (*Dromio of Ephesus*).

LONDON: Nov. 7, 1963
DRURY LANE THEATRE; 100 p.

Presented by Williamson Music Ltd.; directed by Christopher Hewett; choreographed by Bob Herget; settings, Herbert Senn & Helen Pond; costumes, Irene Sharaff; music director, Robert Lowe; orchestrations, Ralph Burns; supervisor, Jerome Whyte.

CAST: Bob Monkhouse (*Antipholus of Syracuse*), Maggie Fitzgibbon (*Luce*), Lynn Kennington (*Adriana*), Paula Hendrix (*Luciana*), Pat Turner (*Courtesan*), Ronnie Corbett (*Dromio of Syracuse*), Sonny Farrar (*Dromio of Ephesus*), Denis Quilley (*Antipholus of Ephesus*).

The fact that no one had ever before thought of basing a musical on a play by Shakespeare made the idea all the more appealing to Rodgers and Hart. They chose *The Comedy of Errors* primarily because it offered the chance to bring together Jimmy Savo and Teddy Hart (Lorenz's brother), who were often mistaken for each other. Set in Ephesus, in ancient Greece, the tale involves the attempt of Antipholus and Dromio of Syracuse to find their long-lost twins. Complications arise when Adriana and Luce, wives of the Ephesian Antipholus and Dromio, mistake the boys from Syracuse for their husbands. The 1963 off-Bway revival enjoyed an even longer run than the original, though the attempt to restage it in the vastness of London's Drury Lane proved unsuccessful.

Other Shakespeare plays that inspired or were adapted as musicals: *A Midsummer Night's Dream* (*Swingin' the Dream*, NY 1939 and *Babes in the Wood*, NY 1964); *The Taming of the Shrew* (*Kiss Me, Kate*, NY 1948); *Romeo and Juliet* (*West Side Story*, NY 1957); *Twelfth Night* (*Love and Let Love*, NY 1968 and *Your Own Thing*, NY 1968); *Othello* (*Catch My Soul*, L 1970); *The Two Gentlemen of Verona* (NY 1971).

FILM VERSION: Allan Jones, Joe Penner, Martha Raye (RKO 1940, A. Edward Sutherland dir.).

Brian, Donald, actor, dancer, singer; b. St. John's, Newfoundland, Feb. 17, 1877; d. Great Neck, NY, Dec. 22, 1948. After being in two George M. Cohan musicals (*Little Johnny Jones, Forty-Five Minutes from Broadway*), round-faced, wavy-haired, dimpled Donald Brian achieved Bway matinée-idol status in *The Merry Widow*. He also co-starred with Julia Sanderson in three musicals, incl. *The Girl from Utah* (introducing "They Didn't Believe Me").

1901 The Supper Club (*Castor Beane*)
1902 Florodora (r) (*Arthur Donegal*)
     The Belle of Broadway (*Tom Finch*)

1904 Little Johnny Jones (*Henry Hapgood*)
1906 Forty-Five Minutes from Broadway (*Tom Bennet*)
1907 The Merry Widow (*Prince Danilo*)
1909 The Dollar Princess (*Freddy Smythe*)
1911 The Siren (*Marquis de Ravaillac*)
1913 The Marriage Market (*Jack Fleetwood*)
1914 The Girl from Utah (*Sandy Blair*)
1916 Sybil (*Grand Duke*)
1917 Her Regiment (*André de Courcy*)
1918 The Girl Behind the Gun (*Robert Lambrissac*)
1919 Buddies (*Sonny*)
1921 The Chocolate Soldier (r) (*Bumerli*)
1922 Up She Goes (*Albert Bennett*)
1926 No, No, Nanette (US tour) (*Billy Early*)
1927 Castles in the Air (*John Brown*, repl.)
     Yes, Yes, Yvette (*Robert Bennett*, repl.)
1933 Music in the Air (*Bruno Mahler*, repl.)
1939 Very Warm for May (*William Graham*)

Brice, Fanny (née Fanny Borach), actress, singer; b. New York, Oct. 29, 1891; d. Hollywood, Cal., May 29, 1951. Miss Brice was noted for three main characterizations: a raucous, Jewish-accented clown, a heart-tearing ballad singer of the streets, and a mischievous child named Baby Snooks (which brought her fame on radio). The actress appeared in burlesque and vaudeville before Ziegfeld cast her in the first of nine *Follies* (latter two produced by Shuberts). Among songs she introduced: "My Man," "Rose of Washington Square," "Second Hand Rose," "I'm an Indian," "Overnight," "I Found a Million-Dollar Baby in a Five and Ten Cent Store." She was married to and divorced from producer Billy Rose, and was the subject of the 1964 Bway musical *Funny Girl.* Bib: *The Fabulous Fanny* by Norman Katkov (Knopf, NY 1953).

1910	Follies of 1910
1911	Follies of 1911
1913	The Honeymoon Express (*Marcelle*)
1915	Nobody Home (*Tony Miller,* repl.)
1916	Ziegfeld Follies
1917	Ziegfeld Follies
1920	Ziegfeld Follies
1921	Ziegfeld Follies
1923	Ziegfeld Follies
1924	Music Box Revue
1929	Fioretta (*Marchesa Vera di Livio*)
1930	Sweet and Low
1931	Crazy Quilt
1934	Ziegfeld Follies
1936	Ziegfeld Follies

Bricusse, Leslie, composer, lyricist, librettist; b. London, Jan. 29, 1931. Collaborator with Anthony Newley on "morality" musicals dealing with downtrodden little man bucking the system. Best known songs: "What Kind of Fool Am I?," "Gonna Build a Mountain," "Once in a Lifetime" (all from *Stop the World—I Want to Get Off*); "A Wonderful Day Like Today," "Who Can I Turn To?," "Nothing Can Stop Me Now" (all from *The Roar of the Greasepaint—The Smell of the Crowd*). Bricusse has also written with Robin Beaumont and for films.

Unless otherwise noted, Mr. Bricusse wrote the following with Mr. Newley:

1958	Lady at the Wheel (L) (Beaumont)
1961	Stop the World—I Want to Get Off (L)
1965	The Roar of the Greasepaint—The Smell of the Crowd (NY)
1972	The Good Old Bad Old Days! (L)

Brigadoon (1947). Music by Frederick Loewe; lyrics & book by Alan Jay Lerner.

SONGS: "Brigadoon," "Waitin' for My Dearie," "I'll Go Home with Bonnie Jean," "The Heather on the Hill," "The Love of My Life," "Come to Me, Bend to Me," "Almost Like Being in Love," "There but for You Go I," "My Mother's Wedding Day," "From This Day On."

NEW YORK: March 13, 1947
ZIEGFELD THEATRE; 581 p.

Presented by Cheryl Crawford; directed by Robert Lewis; choreographed by Agnes de Mille; settings, Oliver Smith; costumes, David Ffolkes; music director, Franz Allers; orchestrations, Ted Royal.

CAST: David Brooks (*Tommy Albright*), Marion Bell (*Fiona MacLaren*), Pamela Britton (*Meg Brockie*), Lee Sullivan (*Charlie Dalrymple*), George Keane (*Jeff Douglas*), James Mitchell (*Harry Beaton*), Helen Gallagher (dancer).

LONDON: April 14, 1949
HIS MAJESTY'S THEATRE; 685 p.

Presented by Prince Littler; directed by Robert Lewis; dances reproduced by James MacGregor Jamieson; settings, Alick Johnstone; costumes, Mae Rogers, Morris Angel; music director, Charles Prentice.

CAST: Philip Hanna (*Tommy Albright*), Patricia Hughes (*Fiona MacKeith*), Noele Gordon (*Meg Brockie*), Hiram Sherman (*Jeff Douglas*), James Jamieson (*Harry Ritchie*), Bill O'Connor (*Charlie Cameron*).

Lerner and Loewe's third Bway musical and first hit was a fantasy about a Scottish town that reawakens for one day every century. On that particular day in the twentieth century, Brigadoon is discovered by two Americans, Tommy and Jeff. Tommy soon falls in love with Fiona, but when he learns the town's secret he returns to New York. His love, however, proves so strong that he goes back to the highlands to join the somnolent community. Lerner claimed that the story was motivated by his fondness for the works of James M. Barrie and his desire to write a musical with a Scottish setting. Critic George Jean Nathan, however, claimed that the plot was lifted from a German story, *Germelshausen*, by Wilhelm Friedrich Gerstacker, the main difference being that in the ending of the original the hero is unable to be reunited with his beloved. The production won praise for its atmospheric charm, its heather-scented score, and its choreography by Agnes de Mille (including a sword dance, a chase through the forest, and a funeral dance).

Note that some characters' names changed in London and that production had longer run than in NY.

FILM VERSION: Gene Kelly, Cyd Charisse, Van Johnson (MGM 1954, Vincente Minnelli dir.).

Brisson, Carl (né Carl Pederson), actor, dancer, singer; b. Copenhagen, Denmark, Dec. 24, 1895; d. Copenhagen, Sept. 26, 1958. Dimpled, top-hatted entertainer who scored biggest hits in London in *The Merry Widow* and *The Wonder Bar*. Brisson, who also appeared in screen musicals, was the father of producer Frederick Brisson and father-in-law of actress Rosalind Russell.

  1923 The Merry Widow (r) (*Prince Danilo*)
  1925 The Dollar Princess (r) (*Harry Conder*)
          Cleopatra (special dancer, added)
  1927 The Apache (*Romaine Tierce*)
  1930 The Wonder Bar (*Harry*)
  1936 Forbidden Melody (NY) (*Gregor Florescu*)

Broderick, Helen, actress; b. Philadelphia, Pa., 1891; d. Beverly Hills, Cal., Sept. 25, 1959. Caustic, wise-cracking, deadpan comedienne whose major Bway roles were in *Fifty Million Frenchmen, The Band Wagon,* and *As*

Thousands Cheer. Miss Broderick appeared in vaudeville with husband Lester Crawford and made many Hollywood films (incl. *Top Hat, Swing Time*).

  1907 Follies of 1907 (chorus)
  1908 The Girl Question (chorus)
          Algeria (chorus)
  1911 Jumping Jupiter (*Miss Winston*)
  1913 The Honeymoon Express (chorus)
  1923 Nifties of 1923
  1925 Puzzles of 1925
  1926 Oh, Please! (*Emma Bliss*)
  1929 Fifty Million Frenchmen (*Violet Hildegarde*)
  1931 The Band Wagon
  1932 Earl Carroll Vanities
  1933 As Thousands Cheer

"Brother, Can You Spare a Dime?" Music by Jay Gorney; lyric by E. Y. Harburg. Sung by Rex Weber waiting in a breadline in a scene in *New Americana* (NY 1932). Originally the melody had been intended for a romantic torch ballad, but Harburg was determined to write a lyric about the economic condition of the country at the time. "This man isn't bitter," the lyricist has said. "He's bewildered. Here is a man who has built his faith and hope in this country. He was able to take advantages of its opportunities and make his fortune. Then came the crash. Now he can't accept the fact that his bubble has burst. He still believes. He still has his faith. He just doesn't understand what could have gone wrong." Though the song soon became the theme of the country's Depression years, producer J. J. Shubert never liked it. He said it was too "sorbid."

Brown, (Joseph Evans) Joe E., actor; b. Holgate, Ohio, July 28, 1892; d. Hollywood, Cal., July 6, 1973. Wide-mouthed, quizzical-looking comedian who appeared in circuses and vaudeville before Bway debut. Celebrated for his pantomime baseball routine, Brown toured in nonmusicals, incl. *Elmer the Great* and *Harvey*, and acted in Hollywood films, 1929–1963. Bib: *Laughter Is a Wonderful Thing* by Brown (1959).

1919   Listen, Lester (US tour) (*Lester Lite*)
1920   Jim Jam Jems (*Philip Quack*)
1921   Greenwich Village Follies
1924   Betty Lee (*Lawrence Glass*)
1925   Captain Jinks (*Hap Jones*)
1926   Twinkle Twinkle (*Peachy Robinson*)
1951   Courtin' Time (*Samuel Rilling*)

Brown, Lew (né Louis Brownstein), lyricist, librettist, producer; b. Odessa, Russia, Dec. 10, 1893; d. New York, Feb. 5, 1958. With co-lyricist B. G. DeSylva and composer Ray Henderson, Brown wrote scores for Bway musical comedies that reflected the youthful, carefree spirit of the Flapper Age. The trio's first song was "It All Depends on You" for *Big Boy*, and their first score was for *George White's Scandals* of 1925. For the next year's edition, they had two hits: "Lucky Day" and "The Birth of the Blues." Their biggest stage successes were *Good News!* ("The Best Things in Life Are Free," "Lucky in Love," "The Varsity Drag"), *Hold Everything!* ("You're the Cream in My Coffee"), *Follow Thru* ("Button Up Your Overcoat"), *Flying High* ("Thank Your Father"). After DeSylva left the team, Brown and Henderson created songs for the 1931 *Scandals* ("Life Is Just a Bowl of Cherries," "This Is the Missus," "The Thrill Is Gone," "My Song"). Brown also wrote with composers Cliff Friend, Harry Akst, and Sam Stept, and with lyricist Charles Tobias ("Comes Love"). Willie and Eugene Howard and Bert Lahr were each in three Brown musicals, Harry Richman and Ann Pennington were in two.

Unless otherwise noted, the following were written with Messrs. DeSylva and Henderson or with Mr. Henderson alone; asterisk indicates Mr. Brown was also co-librettist, director, and producer:

1925   George White's Scandals
1926   George White's Scandals
1927   Piggy (Friend)
        Good News!
        Manhattan Mary
1928   George White's Scandals
        Hold Everything!
1929   Follow Thru
1930   Flying High (also co-lib.)
1931   George White's Scandals
1932   Hot-Cha! (also co-lib.)
1933   Strike Me Pink *
1934   Calling All Stars * (Akst)
1939   Yokel Boy * (Tobias, Stept)

Bruce, Carol, actress, singer; b. Great Neck, NY, Nov. 15, 1919. Dark-haired, throaty-voiced singing actress who made impressive Bway debut in *Louisiana Purchase*, and was a memorable Julie in *Show Boat* revival.

1940   George White's Scandals (US tour)
        Louisiana Purchase (*Beatrice*)
1946   Show Boat (r) (*Julie LaVerne*)
1949   Along Fifth Avenue
1953   Pal Joey (US tour) (*Vera Simpson*)
1954   Pal Joey (L) (*Vera Simpson*)
1962   A Family Affair (*Tilly Siegel,* repl.)
1965   Do I Hear a Waltz? (*Signora Fioria*)
1967   Henry, Sweet Henry (*Mrs. Boyd*)

"Brush Up Your Shakespeare." Music & lyric by Cole Porter. Romantic advice—in which "embessida" rhymes with "Cressida" and "flatter 'er" with "Cleopatterer"—offered by two stage-struck thugs, Harry Clark and Jack Diamond, in *Kiss Me, Kate* (NY 1948). In London version (1951), the singers were Danny Green and Sydney James.

Bryan, Dora (née Dora Broadbent), actress, singer; b. Southport, Eng., Feb. 7, 1924. Tiny, round-faced comic actress, who made London debut in 1947 and has also appeared in dramatic roles. First won notice in revues; scored major hit in *Hello, Dolly!*

1951	The Lyric Revue
1952	The Globe Revue
1953	At the Lyric
1954	Going to Town (At the Lyric)
1955	The Water Gipsies (*Lily Belle*)
1958	Living for Pleasure
1962	Gentlemen Prefer Blondes (*Lorelei Lee*)
1963	Six of One
1966	Hello, Dolly! (*Dolly Levi*, repl.)

Brynner, Yul (né Youl Bryner), actor; b. Sakhalin, Russia, July 11, 1915. Bald, bold Oriental-looking actor who won stardom as the King in *The King and I.* Since 1956, Brynner has divided his time with film acting.

1946	Lute Song (*Tsai-Yong*)
1948	Lute Song (L) (*Tsai-Yong*)
1951	The King and I (*King*)
1975	Home Sweet Homer (*Odysseus*)
1977	The King and I (r) (*King*)

Buchanan, Jack, actor, singer, dancer, director, choreographer, producer; b. Helensburgh, Scotland, April 2, 1891; d. London, Oct. 20, 1957. A dapper, reedy-voiced song-and-dance man, Buchanan scored early London success in *Bubbly,* made even bigger hit on Bway in *André Charlot's Revue* (with Beatrice Lillie and Gertrude Lawrence), then spent most of career in West End musicals (incl. *Sunny, That's a Good Girl, Stand Up and Sing*). Among songs he introduced: "And Her Mother Came Too," "Fancy Our Meeting," "There's Always Tomorrow," "Oceans of Time," "I'm in a Dancing Mood," "A Cup of Coffee, a Sandwich and You," "By Myself." Buchanan also acted in films, incl. *The Band Wagon.*

Asterisk indicates Mr. Buchanan was also producer and/or director:

1912	The Grass Widows (*M. Deschamps*)
1913	All the Winners
1914	A Mixed Grill
1915	Tonight's the Night (UK tour)
1917	Bubbly
	Round the Map
1918	Tails Up
1920	Wild Geese (*Hon. Bill Malcolm*)
	Bran Pie (repl.)
	Jumble Sale (chor. only)
1921	Faust on Toast (*Faust*)
	A to Z
1922	Battling Butler * (*Alfred Butler*)
1924	André Charlot's Revue * (NY)
	Toni * (*Toni Prince*)
1925	Boodle * (*Algernon Kenilworth*)
	The Charlot Revue of 1926 * (NY)
1926	Sunny * (*Jim Deming*)
1928	Lady Mary (co-prod. only)
	That's a Good Girl * (*Bill Barrow*)
1929	Wake Up and Dream! (NY)
1931	Stand Up and Sing * (*Rockingham Smith*) (also co-lib.)
1934	Mr. Whittington * (*Dick Whittington*)
1935	The Flying Trapeze * (*Rene*)
1936	This'll Make You Whistle * (*Bill Hopping*)
1937	Between the Devil (NY) (*Peter Anthony*)
1942	Waltz Without End (prod., dir. only)
1943	It's Time to Dance * (*Wilmott Brown*)
1945	Fine Feathers
1948	The King's Jesters (co-prod. only)
1951	King's Rhapsody (*Nikki*, repl.)

Buck, (Edward Eugene) Gene, lyricist, sketch writer, director; b. Detroit, Mich., Aug. 8, 1885; d. Great Neck, NY, Feb. 25, 1957. Buck began writing lyrics for the *Ziegfeld Follies* in 1912, then became Ziegfeld's assistant. From 1924 to 1941, he was also president of ASCAP (US performing rights society). His most frequent collaborator was composer David Stamper; others with whom he wrote:

Louis Hirsch ("Hello, Frisco"), Jerome Kern, Victor Herbert, Raymond Hubbell, Rudolf Friml, James F. Hanley.

1916 Ziegfeld Follies (Stamper, Kern, Hirsch)
1917 Zig-Zag (L) (Stamper)
Ziegfeld Follies (Stamper, Hubbell)
1918 Ziegfeld Follies (Stamper, Hirsch)
1922 Ziegfeld Follies (Stamper, Hirsch)
1923 Ziegfeld Follies (Stamper, Herbert)
1924 Ziegfeld Follies (Stamper, Hubbell)
1926 No Foolin' (Friml, Hanley)
1927 Yours Truly (prod., dir. only)
Take the Air (Stamper) (also prod., dir.)
1931 Ziegfeld Follies (dir. only)

"Buckle Down, Winsocki." Music & lyrics by Ralph Blane & Hugh Martin. Marching song to rally prep-school football team sung by Tommy Dix, Stuart Langley, and company in *Best Foot Forward* (NY 1941). At the time the song was written, the name of the school had not yet been determined, and the dummy lyric bore the name "Wisconsin." Then for the audition it was sung as "Buckle down, Tioga," but no one liked the name. "What we need," said co-producer George Abbott, "is a name that has something to do with winning with a lot of sock in it." "That's it!" said co-producer Richard Rodgers. "That's our school—Winsocki!"

Burnett, Carol (Creighton), actress, singer; b. San Antonio, Texas, April 26, 1933. Gawky comedienne who has won greatest fame in tv comedy series.

1959 Once Upon a Mattress (*Princess Winifred*)

1964 Fade Out—Fade In (*Hope Springfield*)

Burns, David, actor; b. New York, June 22, 1902; d. Philadelphia, Pa., March 12, 1971. Round-faced, snarling David Burns achieved his greatest Bway success in the long-running *Hello, Dolly!* Other hits included *The Music Man, Do Re Mi, A Funny Thing Happened on the Way to the Forum.*

1932 Face the Music (*Louie*)
1933 Nymph Errant (L) (*Constantine*)
1936 Laughter Over London (L)
1937 Big Business (L) (*Spike Morgan*)
Hide and Seek (L) (*Bennie*)
1938 Bobby Get Your Gun (L) (*Flash Tomkins*)
1941 Pal Joey (*Ludlow Lowell*, repl.)
1943 My Dear Public (*Walters*)
Oklahoma! (US tour) (*Ali Hakim*)
1945 Billion Dollar Baby (*Dapper Welch*)
1946 Oklahoma! (*Ali Hakim*, repl.)
1948 Make Mine Manhattan
Heaven on Earth (*H.H. Hutton*)
1950 Alive and Kicking
Out of This World (*Niki Skolianos*)
1951 South Pacific (US tour) (*Luther Billis*, repl.)
1952 Two's Company
1955 Catch a Star!
1957 The Music Man (*Mayor Shinn*)
1960 Do Re Mi (*Brains Berman*)
1962 A Funny Thing Happened on the Way to the Forum (*Senex*)
1964 Hello, Dolly! (*Horace Vandergelder*)
1970 Lovely Ladies, Kind Gentlemen (*Col. Purdy*)

Burnside, R(ichard) H. director, lyricist, librettist; b. Glasgow, Scotland, Aug. 13, 1870; d. Metuchen, NJ, Sept. 14, 1952. Burnside was chiefly identified with 11 spectacular musicals he directed at the NY Hippodrome between 1908 and 1922. As lyricist, he wrote songs with composers A. Baldwin Sloane, Gustave Kerker, Manuel

Klein, Raymond Hubbell, Milton Lusk, Ivan Caryll, Silvio Hein.

Asterisk indicates Mr. Burnside was also librettist and/or lyricist:

1895 Thrilby
1902 The Emerald Isle
     The Mocking Bird
1903 The Runaways
1904 Sergeant Kitty * (Sloane)
     Lady Teazle
1905 Fantana
     The Earl and the Girl
     The Babes and the Baron
1906 Mexicana
     The Social Whirl
     The Tourists * (Kerker)
     My Lady's Maid *
1907 The Belle of London Town
     Fascinating Flora * (Kerker)
     The Gay White Way
1908 Sporting Days
     The Pied Piper * (Klein)
1909 A Trip to Japan (also prod.)
1910 The International Cup
1911 The Red Rose
     When Sweet Sixteen
     The Three Romeos * (Hubbell)
1912 Over the River
     The Lady of the Slipper
1914 The Beauty Shop
     The Dancing Duchess * (Lusk)
     Chin-Chin *
     Watch Your Step
1915 Watch Your Step (L)
     Hip-Hip-Hooray!
     Stop! Look! Listen!
1916 The Big Show
1917 When Johnny Comes Marching Home
     Cheer Up
     Jack o' Lantern * (Caryll)
1918 Everything
1919 Happy Days * (Hubbell)
     Miss Millions * (Hubbell)
1920 The Girl from Home
     Good Times * (Hubbell)
     Tip Top * (Caryll)
1921 Get Together
1922 Some Party * (Hein)
     Better Times * (Hubbell)
1923 Nifties of 1923
     Stepping Stones *

1924 Madame Pompadour
1925 China Rose
     The City Chap
     The Blue Kitten (L)
1926 Criss-Cross
1927 The Girl from Cook's * (L) (Hubbell)
1928 Three Cheers *
1929 Great Day
1932 Smiling Faces
1933 Hold Your Horses
1940 Walk with Music

Burrows, Abe (né Abram Solman Borowitz), librettist, director; b. New York, Dec. 18, 1910. Burrows' most celebrated Bway musicals were the raffish *Guys and Dolls* and the satirical *How to Succeed in Business Without Really Trying*, both with scores by Frank Loesser and both produced by Cy Feuer and Ernest Martin. Two other hits for the same producers, *Can-Can* and *Silk Stockings*, had songs by Cole Porter. Burrows has also written and directed nonmusicals (incl. *Cactus Flower, Forty Carats*).

Unless otherwise noted, Mr. Burrows was librettist or co-librettist of following; asterisk indicates he was also director:

1950 Guys and Dolls
1951 Make a Wish
     Two on the Aisle (dir. only)
1952 Three Wishes for Jamie *
1953 Can-Can *
1955 Silk Stockings
1956 Happy Hunting (dir. only)
1958 Say, Darling *
1959 First Impressions *
1961 How to Succeed in Business Without Really Trying *
1963 How to Succeed in Business Without Really Trying * (L)
1964 What Makes Sammy Run? (dir. only)

Burton, Richard, actor; b. Pontrhydfen, South Wales, Nov. 10, 1925. A commanding actor with a rich, resonant voice, Burton is primarily known for dramatic roles on both stage and screen. On Bway, he introduced "Camelot" and "How to Handle a Woman."

    1960   Camelot (*King Arthur*)

"Bushel and a Peck, A." Music & lyric by Frank Loesser. Satirical number squealed by Vivian Blaine and Farmerette chorus as part of the Hot Box nighclub floorshow in *Guys and Dolls* (NY 1950, L 1953).

"But Not for Me." Music by George Gershwin; lyric by Ira Gershwin. Torch ballad for dejected heroine Ginger Rogers in *Girl Crazy* (NY 1930), also sung by Willie Howard.

Butt, Alfred, producer; b. London, March 20, 1878; d. Dec. 8, 1962. Knighted 1918, baronet 1929. Sir Alfred managed London theatres incl. the Palace, Gaiety, Empire, Adelphi, Victoria. He was joint managing director of Drury Lane, 1919–1925; chairman and managing director, 1925–1931. During latter period he inaugurated successful policy of importing Bway operettas. He introduced Fred and Adele Astaire to London and produced all three of their West End shows.

1914	The Passing Show
	The Merry-Go-Round
	By Jingo, If We Do—!
1915	The Passing Show
	Watch Your Step
	Bric-a-brac
1916	Follow the Crowd
	Vanity Fair
1917	Airs and Graces
	The Boy
	Cash on Delivery
	Pamela
	The Beauty Spot
1918	Hullo, America!
1919	Who's Hooper?
	The Kiss Call
	The Red Mill
1920	The Shop Girl (r)

1923	Stop Flirting
1925	Rose-Marie
1926	Lady, Be Good!
	Queen High
1927	The Desert Song
	Peggy-Ann
1928	Show Boat
	Funny Face
1929	The New Moon
1930	The Three Musketeers
1931	Song of the Drum
	Viktoria and Her Hussar

"Button Up Your Overcoat." Music by Ray Henderson; lyric by B. G. DeSylva & Lew Brown. Sung by Zelma O'Neal and Jack Haley in *Follow Thru* (NY 1928), and by Ada May and Leslie Henson in London version (1929). A prescription for physical well-being that includes, besides the titular admonition, warnings about eating the proper food, crossing the streets, getting to bed by three, and avoiding bootleg hootch.

By Jupiter (1942). Music by Richard Rodgers; lyrics by Lorenz Hart; book by Rodgers & Hart, based on play *The Warrior's Husband*, by Julian Thompson.

    Songs: "Jupiter Forbid," "Life With Father," "Nobody's Heart," "The Gateway to the Temple of Minerva," "Here's a Hand," "Ev'rything I've Got," "Careless Rhapsody," "Wait Till You See Her," "Now That I've Got My Strength."

New York: June 2, 1942
Shubert Theatre; 427 p.
    Presented by Dwight Deere Wiman & Richard Rodgers, with Richard Kollmar; directed by Joshua Logan; choreographed by Robert Alton; settings & lighting, Jo Mielziner; costumes, Irene Sharaff; music director, Johnny Green; orchestrations, Don Walker.
    Cast: Ray Bolger (*Sapiens*), Con-

stance Moore (*Antiope*), Benay Venuta (*Hippolyta*), Ronald Graham (*Theseus*), Bertha Belmore (*Pomposia*), Margaret Bannerman (*Heroica*), Berni Gould (*Homer*), Vera-Ellen (*Minerva*), Ralph Dumke (*Hercules*).

Rodgers and Hart's last original musical, something of a successor to *The Boys from Syracuse*, was their longest running Bway show. Its run, in fact, could have been longer had not Ray Bolger (playing his first starring part) quit the show to entertain US troops in the Far East. The lavishly mounted production was concerned with the war between the Greeks and the Amazons on the island of Pontus, with the humor derived from the Amazonian reversal of sexes in which men are dominated by women. After the Amazons have been defeated, however, they assume roles subordinate to their conquerors. During the pre-Bway tryout, the show was called *All's Fair* and the role of Theseus was played by Richard Ainley. Eight months after the Bway opening Miss Moore was succeeded by Nanette Fabray.

Prompted by the successful 1963 off-Bway revival of *The Boys from Syracuse*, *By Jupiter* was revived in 1967 at the same theatre (Theatre Four) with the same director (Christopher Hewett). Fred Ebb wrote additional dialogue and in the cast were Bob Dishy (*Sapiens*), Sheila Sullivan (*Antiope*), Jackie Alloway (*Hippolyta*), Robert R. Kaye (*Theseus*). The run was 118 performances.

"By Myself." Music by Arthur Schwartz; lyric by Howard Dietz. Rueful song of solitude sung by bigamist Jack Buchanan while being shadowed by the police in *Between the Devil* (NY 1937).

"By Strauss." Music by George Gershwin; lyric by Ira Gershwin. Take-off on the Viennese waltz sung by Gracie Barrie and Robert Shafer, and danced by Mitzi Mayfair and chorus, as the second-act opening of *The Show Is On* (NY 1936).

"By the Light of the Silvery Moon." Music by Gus Edwards; lyric by Edward Madden. Sung by Lillian Lorraine in the *Follies of 1909* (NY), though originally introduced by Georgie Price in vaudeville sketch, *School Boys and Girls*. Save for "beams" and "dreams," the lyric to the song has a rhyme scheme limited exclusively to the "oon" sound.

"Bye and Bye." Music by Richard Rodgers; lyric by Lorenz Hart. Ballad of postponed romantic bliss introduced in *Dearest Enemy* (NY 1925) by Helen Ford and Charles Purcell.

"Bye, Bye, Baby." Music by Jule Styne; lyric by Leo Robin. Jaunty farewell—with a reminder to be faithful—sung by Jack McCauley to Carol Channing (as Lorelei Lee) as the lady is about to embark on a transatlantic voyage in *Gentlemen Prefer Blondes* (NY 1949). In London production (1962) it was sung by Donald Stewart to Dora Bryan.

Bye Bye Birdie (1960). Music by Charles Strouse; lyrics by Lee Adams; book by Michael Stewart.

SONGS: "An English Teacher," "The Telephone Hour," "How Lovely to Be a Woman," "Put on a Happy Face," "One Boy," "Honestly Sincere," "One Last Kiss," "A Lot of Livin' to Do," "Kids," "Baby, Talk to Me."

NEW YORK: April 14, 1960
MARTIN BECK THEATRE; 607 p.

Presented by Edward Padula, with L. Slade Brown; directed & choreographed by Gower Champion; settings, Robert Randolph; costumes, Miles White; lighting, Peggy Clark; music director, Elliott Lawrence; orchestrations, Robert Ginzler.

CAST: Dick Van Dyke (*Albert Peterson*), Chita Rivera (*Rose Grant*), Kay Medford (*Mae Peterson*), Paul Lynde (*Mr. MacAfee*), Dick Gautier (*Conrad Birdie*), Michael J. Pollard (*Hugo Peabody*), Susan Watson (*Kim MacAfee*), Charles Nelson Reilly (*Mr. Hinkle*), Karin Wolfe (*Helen*), Jerry Dodge (*Karl*), Marijane Maricle (*Mrs. MacAfee*).

LONDON: June 15, 1961
HER MAJESTY'S THEATRE; 268 p.

Presented by H. M. Tennent Ltd, with L. Slade Brown; directed & choreographed by Gower Champion; settings, Robert Randolph; costumes, Miles White; lighting, Joe Davis; music director, Alyn Ainsworth; orchestrations, Robert Ginzler.

CAST: Peter Marshall (*Albert Peterson*), Chita Rivera (*Rose Grant*), Angela Baddeley (*Mae Peterson*), Robert Nichols (*Mr. MacAfee*), Marty Wilde (*Conrad Birdie*), Clive Endersby (*Hugo Peabody*), Sylvia Tysick (*Kim MacAfee*), Mary Laura Wood (*Mrs. MacAfee*).

The first hit musical about the rock-and-roll craze among teenagers had an original story dealing with the effect of one Conrad Birdie—read Elvis Presley or Conway Twitty—upon the all-American town of Sweet Apple, Ohio. The show, though satirical, offered a basically sunny view of modern youth as something of a contrast to *West Side Story*. Among the highlights were "The Telephone Hour," performed in a honeycomb-type setting, and Chita Rivera's madcap dance at a Shriners' convention. The production marked the Bway debuts of composer Strouse, lyricist Adams, librettist Stewart, and producer Padula. It was also the first book musical directed by Gower Champion. In April 1961, Dick Van Dyke was succeeded by Gene Rayburn, Miss Rivera by Gretchen Wyler. The US tour, which opened April 1961, lasted 10 months. The cast was headed by Bill Hayes (*Albert*), Elaine Dunn (*Rose*), Joan Blondell (*Mae*), Jesse Pearson (*Conrad*), Karin Wolfe (*Kim*).

FILM VERSION: Ann-Margret, Janet Leigh, Dick Van Dyke (Col. 1963, George Sidney dir.).

Byng, Douglas, actor, singer; b. Nottinghamshire, Eng., March 17, 1893. Byng was noted for his grand-dame characterizations in seven Cochran revues in London. He also sang "Miss Otis Regrets" in *Hi-Diddle-Diddle* and appeared in pantomimes and nightclubs. Bib: *As You Were* by Byng (Duckworth, L 1970).

1917	Theodore & Co. (*Blissett*, repl.)
	Yes, Uncle!
1920	A Night Out
1925	On with the Dance
	Still Dancing!
1926	Cochran's Revue of 1926
1927	One Dam Thing After Another
1928	This Year of Grace!
1929	Wake Up and Dream!
1930	Cochran's 1930 Revue
1933	How D'You Do?
1934	Hi-Diddle-Diddle
1935	Stop—Go!
1938	Maritza (*Prince Keloman*)
1941	Strike Up the Music
1942	Fine and Dandy
1943	Flying Colours
1946	The Shephard Show
1950	Sauce Piquante
1952	The Bells of St. Martin's
1959	The Love Doctor (*Polidor Argan*)
1963	House of Cards (*Gen. Kruititsky*)

C

Cabaret (1966). Music by John Kander; lyrics by Fred Ebb; book by Joe Masteroff, based on Christopher Isherwood's *Berlin Stories* & John Van Druten's play *I Am a Camera*.

SONGS: "Willkommen," "So What," "Don't Tell Mama," "Perfectly Marvelous," "Tomorrow Belongs to Me," "Two Ladies," "Why Should I Wake Up?," "If You Could See Her Through My Eyes," "Married," "Meeskite," "Cabaret," "The Money Song," "What Would You Do?"

NEW YORK: Nov. 20, 1966
BROADHURST THEATRE; 1,165 p.

Presented by Harold Prince, with Ruth Mitchell; directed by Prince; choreographed by Ron Field; settings, Boris Aronson; costumes, Patricia Zipprodt; lighting, Jean Rosenthal; music director, Harold Hastings; orchestrations, Don Walker.

CAST: Jill Haworth (*Sally Bowles*), Jack Gilford (*Herr Schultz*), Bert Convy (*Clifford Bradshaw*), Lotte Lenya (*Fräulein Schneider*), Joel Grey (*Master of Ceremonies*), Peg Murray (*Fräulein Kost*), Edward Winter (*Ernst Ludwig*).

LONDON: Feb. 28, 1968
PALACE THEATRE; 336 p.

Presented by Harold Prince & Richard Pilbrow, with Ruth Mitchell; directed by Prince; choreographed by Ron Field; settings, Boris Aronson; costumes, Patricia Zipprodt; lighting, Jean Rosenthal; music director, Gareth Davies; orchestrations, Don Walker.

CAST: Judi Dench (*Sally Bowles*), Lila Kedrova (*Fräulein Schneider*), Peter Sallis (*Herr Schultz*), Kevin Colson (*Clifford Bradshaw*), Barry Dennen (*Master of Ceremonies*), Pamela Strong (*Fräulein Kost*), Richard Owens (*Ernst Ludwig*).

Cabaret (originally called *Welcome to Berlin*) was a bitter evocation of the tawdry life in Berlin just before the Nazis took over, with the settings suggesting George Grosz and the music recalling Kurt Weill. The story—about a hedonistic English girl and her doomed romance with an English writer—is told in tandem with performances at the Kit Kat Klub, presided over by a leering, epicene Master of Ceremonies. To heighten the cabaret atmosphere, the curtain is up as theatregoers arrive, with their distorted images reflected on a slanted mirror above the stage. Joel Grey, who scored a personal success, was succeeded by Martin Ross (1-68); Jill Haworth by Anita Gillette (11-68), Melissa Hart (6-69), Tandy Cronyn (6-69). The US touring company opened Dec. 1967 and continued for one year, seven months. The cast was headed by Melissa Hart (*Sally*), Signe Hasso (*Fräulein*), Leo Fuchs (*Schultz*), Gene Rupert (*Clifford*), Robert Salvio (*MC*).

FILM VERSION: Liza Minnelli, Michael York, Joel Grey (altered story) (Allied 1972, Bob Fosse dir.).

"Cabaret." Music by John Kander; lyric by Fred Ebb. Insinuating, then sardonic invitation presented as part of the Kit Kat Klub floor show in *Cabaret* by Jill Haworth (NY 1966) and Judi Dench (L 1968). The melody is slightly reminiscent of "Won't You Come Home, Bill Bailey?"

Cabin in the Sky (1940). Music by Vernon Duke; lyrics by John Latouche; book by Lynn Root.

SONGS: "Takin' a Chance on Love" (lyric with Ted Fetter), "Cabin in the Sky," "Love Turned the Light Out," "Honey in the Honeycomb," "In My Old Virginia Home," "Do What You Wanna Do," "Savannah."

NEW YORK: Oct. 25, 1940
MARTIN BECK THEATRE; 156 p.

Presented by Albert Lewis, with Vinton Freedley; directed by George Balanchine & Lewis; choreographed by Balanchine; settings & costumes, Boris Aronson; music director, Max Meth; orchestrations, Domenico Savino, Charles Cooke, Nathan Van Cleve.

CAST: Ethel Waters (*Petunia Jackson*), Dooley Wilson (*Joe Jackson*), Todd Duncan (*Lawd's General*), Rex Ingram (*Lucifer Jr.*), Katherine Dunham (*Georgia Brown*), J. Rosamond Johnson (*Brother Green*), Talley Beattey (dancer).

A parable of Negro life in the South, this musical was Vernon Duke's major contribution to the Bway theatre. It was also Balanchine's first assignment as director of an entire production, and was a triumph for Ethel Waters in her only book musical. The story, echoing both *The Green Pastures* and *Liliom*, is concerned with the battle between the Lawd's General and Lucifer Jr. for the soul of Little Joe Jackson. Eventually, helped by his wife, Petunia, Joe makes it to the Pearly Gates. An off-Bway revival in 1963, with Rosetta LeNoire as Petunia, was unsuccessful.

FILM VERSION: Ethel Waters, Eddie Anderson, Lena Horne (MGM 1944, Vincente Minnelli dir.).

"**Cabin in the Sky.**" Music by Vernon Duke; lyric by John Latouche. The Heavenly life as pictured by Ethel Waters in *Cabin in the Sky* (NY 1940).

Caesar, (Isidore) Irving, lyricist; b. New York, July 4, 1895. Caesar's biggest Bway hit was *No, No, Nanette* ("Tea for Two," "I Want to Be Happy"), written with composer Vincent Youmans. In addition to scores, he wrote interpolated songs for revues and book musicals, incl. *George White's Scandals* and *Hit the Deck* ("Sometimes I'm Happy"). His collaborators include Louis Hirsch, Con Conrad, Albert Sirmay, Rudolf Friml, James Hanley, Harold Orlob, Phil Charig, Roger Wolfe Kahn and Joseph Meyer ("Crazy Rhythm"), Oscar Levant, Sigmund Romberg, Robert Katscher, Ralph Benatzky, Ray Henderson, Gerald Marks.

1922	Greenwich Village Follies (Hirsch)
1923	Greenwich Village Follies (Hirsch, Conrad)
1924	Betty Lee (Hirsch, Conrad)
1925	The Bamboula (L) (Sirmay)
	No, No, Nanette (Youmans)
1926	Sweetheart Time (Meyer)
	No Foolin' (Hanley, Friml)
	Betsy (co-lib. only)
1927	Talk About Girls (Orlob)
	Yes, Yes, Yvette (Charig)
1928	Here's Howe (Kahn, Meyer)
	Americana (Kahn)
1929	Polly (Charig)
1930	Ripples (Levant, Sirmay)
	Nina Rosa (Romberg)
1931	The Wonder Bar (also lib.) (Katscher)
1933	Melody (Romberg)
1936	White Horse Inn (Benatzky)
	Transatlantic Rhythm (L) (Henderson)
1943	My Dear Public (also co-lib., prod.) (Marks)

Caesar, (Isaac Sidney) Sid, actor; b. Yonkers, NY, Sept. 8, 1922. A satirical comedian who specializes in variety of accents and comic types, Caesar won his greatest fame in tv. On Bway, he introduced "Real Live Girl" in *Little Me*.

1948 Make Mine Manhattan
1962 Little Me (*Noble Eggleston*, etc.)

Cahill, Marie, actress, singer; b. Brooklyn, NY, Feb. 7, 1870; d. New York, Aug. 23, 1933. Miss Cahill was a plump, pugnacious comedienne who introduced "Under the Bamboo Tree" in *Sally in Our Alley* and starred in six Bway musicals produced by her husband, Daniel V. Arthur.

1894 Morocco Bound (L) (repl.)
1895 Excelsior Jr. (*Blanche Calvé Santootsie*)
1896 Excelsior Jr. (US tour) (*H. W. Excelsior Jr.*)
     The Gold Bug (*Lady Patty Larceny*)
1897 A Runaway Girl (repl.)
1898 Monte Carlo (*Gertie Gelatine*)
1899 Three Little Lambs (*Phyllis Argyle*)
1900 Star and Garter (*Mme. Piquet*)
1902 The Wild Rose (*Vera Von Lahn*)
     Sally in Our Alley (*Sally*)
1903 Nancy Brown (*Nancy Brown*)
1904 It Happened in Nordland (*Katherine Poopfogle*)
1905 Moonshine (*Molly Moonshine*)
1906 Marrying Mary (*Mary Montgomery*)
1908 The Boys and Betty (*Betty Barbeau*)
1910 Judy Forgot (*Judy Evans*)
1912 The Opera Ball (*Celeste Deremy*)
1915 90 in the Shade (*Polly Bainbridge*)
1927 Merry-Go-Round
1930 The New Yorkers (*Gloria Wentworth*)

Cahn, Sammy (né Samuel Cohen), lyricist; b. New York, June 18, 1913. Cahn's longest-running Bway musical was *High Button Shoes* ("Papa, Won't You Dance with Me?," "I Still Get Jealous"), music by Jule Styne. He has also written scores with James Van Heusen and songs for revues with Vernon Duke (incl. *Two's Company*). Cahn, who spent most of his career in Hollywood, appeared on Bway in collection of his songs, *Words and Music* (1974). Bib: *I Should Care* by Cahn (Arbor, NY 1974).

1947 High Button Shoes (Styne)
1965 Skyscraper (Van Heusen)
1966 Walking Happy (Van Heusen)
1970 Look to the Lilies (Styne)

Caldwell, Anne, lyricist, librettist; b. Boston, Mass., Aug. 30, 1867; d. Beverly Hills, Cal., Oct. 22, 1936. Began career as singer; married lyricist James O'Dea. Collaborated with following Bway composers: Jean Schwartz, Ivan Caryll ("Wait Till the Cows Come Home"), Hugo Felix, A. Baldwin Sloane, Jerome Kern ("Ka-lu-a"), Robert Winterberg, Harold Levey, Vincent Youmans ("I Know That You Know"), Raymond Hubbell. Miss Caldwell also wrote with librettist-lyricist Otto Harbach.

Unless otherwise noted, Miss Caldwell was lyricist-librettist of following:

1907 Top o' the World (sk. only)
1912 The Lady of the Slipper (co-lib. only)
1914 When Claudia Smiles (Schwartz)
     Chin-Chin (Caryll)
1916 Pom-Pom (Felix)
     Go to It! (Sloane)
1917 Jack o' Lantern (Caryll)
1918 The Canary (lyr. only) (Caryll)
1919 She's a Good Fellow (Kern)
     The Lady in Red (Winterberg)
1920 The Night Boat (Kern)
     The Sweetheart Shop (Felix)
     Tip Top (Caryll)
     Hitchy-Koo (Kern)
1921 Good Morning Dearie (Kern)
1922 The Bunch and Judy (Kern)
1923 Stepping Stones (Kern)
1924 Peg o' My Dreams (lyr. only) (Felix)
     The Magnolia Lady (Levey)
1925 The City Chap (lyr. only) (Kern)

1926 Criss-Cross (Kern, Harbach)
 Oh, Please! (Youmans)
1927 Yours Truly (lyr. only) (Hubbell)
 Take the Air (co-lib. only)
1928 Three Cheers (Hubbell)

"California, Here I Come." Music by Joseph Meyer; lyric by B. G. DeSylva. Assertive declaration of homecoming—transferred from the usual South to the far West—interpolated by Al Jolson in *Bombo* (NY 1923).

Call Me Madam (1950). Music & lyrics by Irving Berlin; book by Howard Lindsay & Russel Crouse.

SONGS: "The Hostess with the Mostes' on the Ball," "Marrying for Love," "Lichtenburg," "Can You Use Any Money Today?," "It's a Lovely Day Today," "They Like Ike," "The Ocarina," "You're Just in Love," "The Best Thing for You," "Something to Dance About."

NEW YORK: Oct. 12, 1950
IMPERIAL THEATRE; 644 p.

Presented by Leland Hayward; directed by George Abbott; choreographed by Jerome Robbins; settings & costumes, Raoul Pène du Bois; Miss Merman's clothes by Main Bocher; music director, Jay S. Blackton; orchestrations, Don Walker.

CAST: Ethel Merman (*Sally Adams*), Paul Lukas (*Cosmo Constantine*), Russell Nype (*Ken Gibson*), Pat Harrington (*Congressman Wilkins*), Alan Hewitt (*Pemberton Maxwell*), Henry Lascoe (*Sebastian Sebastian*), Galina Talva (*Princess Maria*), Tommy Rall (dancer), Muriel Bentley (dancer).

LONDON: March 15, 1952
COLISEUM; 485 p.

Presented by Jack Hylton; directed by Richard Bird; choreographed by George Carden; settings & costumes, Raoul Pène du Bois; music director, Cyril Ornadel.

CAST: Billie Worth (*Sally Adams*), Anton Walbrook (*Cosmo Constantine*), Jeff Warren (*Ken Gibson*), Sidney Keith (*Congressman Wilkins*), Donald Burr (*Pemberton Maxwell*), Stanley Van Beers (*Sebastian Sebastian*), Shani Wallis (*Princess Maria*), George Carden (dancer), Olga Roberts (dancer).

According to the program, "The play is laid in two mythical countries. One is called Lichtenburg, the other the United States of America." The idea for this political satire was sparked when President Harry Truman appointed Washington party-giver Perle Mesta as ambassador to Liechtenstein. In her second musical singing Irving Berlin songs, Ethel Merman, as party-giver Sally Adams, was an endearingly brash and forthright representative who loses her heart to Lichtenburg's foreign minister, Cosmo Constantine, while also helping the romance of young attaché Ken Gibson and Princess Maria. (Victor Herbert's *It Happened in Nordland* also had to do with a woman ambassador, but the story was entirely different.) One of the show's highlights was the nightly appearance of Truman look-alike Irving Fisher, a former musical-comedy juvenile, who showed up just to take a bow with Miss Merman. The US touring company began its travels May 1952, and continued for 11 months. Elaine Stritch (*Sally*), Kent Smith (*Cosmo*), David Daniels (*Ken*), and Galina Talva (*Maria*) headed the cast.

FILM VERSION: Ethel Merman, George Sanders, Donald O'Connor, Vera-Ellen (20th Cent. 1953, Walter Lang dir.).

Camelot (1960). Music by Frederick Loewe; lyrics & book by Alan Jay Lerner, based on T. H. White's novel, *The Once and Future King*.

SONGS: "I Wonder What the King Is Doing Tonight," "The Simple Joys of Maidenhood," "Camelot," "C'est Moi," "The Lusty Month of May," "If Ever I Would Leave You," "Before I Gaze on You Again," "What Do the Simple Folk Do?," "Follow Me," "I Loved You Once in Silence," "How to Handle a Woman," "Guenevere."

NEW YORK: Dec. 3. 1960
MAJESTIC THEATRE; 873 p.
Presented by Frederick Loewe, Alan Jay Lerner, & Moss Hart; directed by Hart; choreographed by Hanya Holm; settings, Oliver Smith; costumes, Adrian, Tony Duquette; lighting, Feder; music director, Franz Allers; orchestrations, Robert Russell Bennett, Philip J. Lang.
CAST: Julie Andrews (Queen Guenevere), Richard Burton (King Arthur), Robert Goulet (Sir Lancelot), Roddy McDowall (Mordred), Robert Coote (King Pellinore), M'el Dowd (Morgan LeFay), Bruce Yarnell (Sir Lionel), John Cullum (Sir Dinadan), David Hurst (Merlyn).

LONDON: Aug. 19, 1964
DRURY LANE THEATRE; 518 p.
Presented by Jack Hylton; directed & choreographed by Robert Helpmann; settings & costumes, John Truscott; lighting, Richard Pilbrow; music director, Kenneth Alwyn; orchestrations, Robert Russell Bennett, Philip J. Lang.
CAST: Laurence Harvey (King Arthur), Elizabeth Larner (Queen Guenevere), Miles Malleson (Merlyn), Moyra Fraser (Morgan LeFay), Barry Kent (Sir Lancelot), Nicky Henson (Mordred), Cardew Robinson (King Pellinore), Raymond Edwards (Sir Lionel), Victor Flattery (Sir Dinadan).
A visually stunning retelling of the Arthurian legend, Camelot centers on the destruction of the idyllic world of knighthood as a result of the tragic tri-

angular relationship of the King, his Queen, and Sir Lancelot. The musical reunited most of those responsible for My Fair Lady: Lerner, Loewe, Hart, Hanya Holm, Oliver Smith, Franz Allers, plus actors Julie Andrews and Robert Coote. During pre-Bway tryouts, Lerner was hospitalized and Hart had a heart attack. Though the opening-night critics were mostly unenthusiastic, the show had a large advance ticket sale. Once he recovered sufficiently, Hart redirected many scenes, including the ending, which—at the suggestion of critic John Chapman—was made more optimistic. A previous Bway view of King Arthur's court was Rodgers and Hart's 1927 musical satire A Connecticut Yankee.

During Bway run, Richard Burton was succeeded by William Squire (9-61); Miss Andrews by Patricia Bredin (4-62), Janet Pavek (7-62), Kathryn Grayson (10-62); Robert Goulet by Robert Peterson (10-62); Roddy McDowall by John Cullum (5-61); Robert Coote by Arthur Treacher (10-62); M'el Dowd by Madeleine Sherwood (3-62), Tani Seitz (7-62). The US road company opened Jan. 1963, and toured for a year and a half. The cast was headed by Kathryn Grayson (then Anne Jeffreys), William Squire (then Louis Hayward and George Wallace), Robert Peterson, Arthur Treacher.

FILM VERSION: Vanessa Redgrave and Richard Harris (Warner 1967, Joshua Logan dir.).

"Camelot." Music by Frederick Loewe; lyric by Alan Jay Lerner. In wooing the fair Guenevere, King Arthur stoutly maintains that in Camelot "we have far and away the most equitable climate in all the world. Ordained by decree! Extremely uncommon." In the song that follows, he offers examples of its extraordinary weather conditions, and when Guenevere tenderly repeats his words we know she has accepted his proposal. Richard Burton and Julie Andrews were Arthur and Guenevere in NY (1960); Laurence Harvey and Elizabeth Larner played the roles in London (1964).

"Can This Be Love?" Music by Kay Swift; lyric by Paul James (James Paul Warburg). Romantic quandary voiced by Alice Boulden in *Fine and Dandy* (NY 1930).

Can-Can (1953). Music & lyrics by Cole Porter; book by Abe Burrows.

SONGS: "C'est Magnifique," "I Am in Love," "Allez-vous-en," "Never Give Anything Away," "Maidens Typical of France," "It's All Right with Me," "I Love Paris," "Come Along with Me," "Montmart'."

NEW YORK: May 7, 1953
SHUBERT THEATRE; 892 p.
Presented by Cy Feuer & Ernest Martin; directed by Abe Burrows; choreographed by Michael Kidd; settings & lighting, Jo Mielziner; costumes, Motley; music director, Milton Rosenstock; orchestrations, Philip J. Lang.
CAST: Lilo (*La Mome Pistache*), Peter Cookson (*Aristide Forestier*), Hans Conried (*Boris Adzinidzinadze*), Gwen Verdon (*Claudine*), Erik Rhodes (*Hilaire Jussac*), Phil Leeds (*Theophile*), Richard Purdy (*Étienne*), Deedee Wood (*Jailer*), Dania Krupska (*Mimi*), Ralph Beaumont (dancer), Tom Panko (dancer).

LONDON: Oct. 14, 1954
COLISEUM; 394 p.
Presented by Prince Littler & Williamson Music Ltd; restaged by Jerome Whyte; dances reproduced by Deidre Vivian; settings & lighting, Jo Mielziner; costumes, Motley; music

director, Charles Prentice; orchestrations, Philip J. Lang.
CAST: Irene Hilda (*La Mome Pistache*), Edmund Hockridge (*Aristide Forestier*), Alfred Marks (*Boris Adzinidzinadze*), Gillian Lynne (*Claudine*), George Gee (*Hilaire Jussac*), Warren Mitchell (*Theophile*), Alan Gilbert (*Étienne*).

Next to *Kiss Me, Kate*, *Can-Can* was Cole Porter's most successful Bway musical. To devise the story, librettist Burrows went to Paris, where he researched records of the police and Chamber of Deputies, and studied the arguments and trials of the late 1800s. The tale was concerned with the introduction of the scandalous dance known as the can-can, and the way Pastiche, owner of the Bal du Paradis, breaks down the resistance of the stern judge Aristide Forestier, who has been sent to investigate. Eventually the judge himself defends Pastiche and her can-can dancers and wins acquittal. Though Lilo was the star of the musical, it was Gwen Verdon, in her first major Bway role, who attracted the most notice, especially with her "Garden of Eden" ballet and Apache dance. In 1955 Lilo was succeeded by Rita Dimitri, Peter Cookson by Norwood Smith and John Tyers, Hans Conried by George S. Irving, Miss Verdon by Joan Holloway and Ronnie Cunningham. Dimitri, Tyers, Irving, and Cunningham headed the touring company, which began its travels in June 1955.

FILM VERSION: Frank Sinatra, Maurice Chevalier, Shirley MacLaine (new story) (20th Cent. 1960, Walter Lang dir.).

Candide (1956). Music by Leonard Bernstein; lyrics by Richard Wilbur, etc.; book by Lillian Hellman, based on Voltaire's novel.

SONGS: "The Best of All Possible

Worlds," "Oh, Happy We," "It Must Be So," "Glitter and Be Gay," "You Were Dead, You Know" (lyric with John Latouche), "I Am Easily Assimilated" (lyric, Bernstein), "Quiet," "Eldorado" (lyric, Hellman), "Bon Voyage," "What's the Use?," "Make Our Garden Grow."

NEW YORK: Dec. 1, 1956
MARTIN BECK THEATRE; 73 p.

Presented by Ethel Linder Reiner, with Lester Osterman Jr.; directed by Tyrone Guthrie; settings, Oliver Smith; costumes, Irene Sharaff; lighting, Paul Morrison; music director, Samuel Krachmalnick; orchestrations, Leonard Bernstein, Hershy Kay.

CAST: Max Adrian (*Dr. Pangloss, Martin*), Robert Rounseville (*Candide*), Barbara Cook (*Cunegonde*), Irra Petina (*Old Lady*), William Olvis (*Governor of Buenos Aires*), Boris Aplon (*Marquis*), William Chapman (*Lawyer*), Louis Edmonds (*Maximilian*), Joseph Bernard (*Sultan*), Conrad Bain (*King of Hesse*).

LONDON: April 30, 1959
SAVILLE THEATRE; 60 p.

Presented by Linnit & Dunfee Ltd.; directed by Robert Lewis; choreographed by Jack Cole; settings & costumes, Osbert Lancaster; lighting, Michael Northen; music director, Alexander Faris.

CAST: Laurence Naismith (*Dr. Pangloss, Martin*), Denis Quilley (*Candide*), Mary Costa (*Cunegonde*), Edith Coates (*Old Lady*), Ron Moody (*Governor of Buenos Aires*), Victor Spinetti (*Marquis*), James Cairncross (*Sultan*), Dennis Stephenson (*Maximilian*), Vincent Charles (*King of Hesse*).

NEW YORK: March 8, 1974
BROADWAY THEATRE; 740 p.

Presented by Chelsea Theatre Center of Brooklyn, with Harold Prince & Ruth Mitchell; directed by Prince; choreographed by Patricia Birch; settings & costumes, Eugene & Franne Lee; lighting, Tharon Musser; music director, John Mauceri; orchestrations, Hershy Kay; new book by Hugh Wheeler; added lyrics by Stephen Sondheim.

CAST: Lewis J. Stadlen (*Dr. Pangloss, Governor of Buenos Aires*), Mark Baker (*Candide*), Maureen Brennan (*Cunegonde*), June Gable (*Old Lady*), Sam Freed (*Maximilian*), Deborah St. Darr (*Paquette*).

Originally designated "A Comic Operetta," the Voltaire satire failed to attract audiences in NY or London when it was first presented, despite the highly praised score and visual production. Hewing faithfully to the novel's outline, the story was concerned with the multiple adventures of Candide and his beloved Cunegonde, who, under the tutelage of their philosophy professor, believe this to be "the best of all possible worlds." Their gullible idealism is maintained despite banishment, rape, the Spanish Inquisition, and betrayal while whirling around the world to Lisbon, Paris, Buenos Aires, Venice, and back home to Westphalia. Eventually they accept the fact that wisdom is not to be found striving for perfection but in making the best of reality. (In this regard, Candide shares basically the same discovery as the hero in *Pippin*.) The original production marked the only Bway appearance of Max Adrian, and the only musical directed by Tyrone Guthrie. John Latouche, the intended lyricist, died during the early stages of the preparation.

With a new book, additional lyrics, and Harold Prince's imaginative staging, the musical was revived Dec. 19, 1973, for a limited run at the Chelsea Theatre Center in the Brooklyn Academy of Music. Among the changes:

the character of the pessimist Martin was eliminated and Paquette was added. After winning favorable notices, the musical reopened on Bway. For this occasion, the Broadway Theatre was reconstructed, with 10 different acting areas linked by ramps, bridges, platforms, and trap doors. To emphasize the "environmental" nature of the staging, spectators sat in bleachers or on stools with the action surrounding them.

"Can't Help Lovin' Dat Man." Music by Jerome Kern; lyric by Oscar Hammerstein II. Unreasoned devotion expressed by Helen Morgan, Aunt Jemima (Tess Gardella), Norma Terris, Jules Bledsoe, and Arthur Campbell in *Show Boat* (NY 1927); later reprised by Miss Terris for audition at Trocadero Music Hall. In London production (1928) it was sung by Marie Burke, Alberta Hunter, Edith Day, Paul Robeson, and Jack Martin; reprised by Miss Day. As presented in the musical, the ballad is supposed to be a traditional song only "colored folks" know. When, at the audition, the Trocadero manager objects to it as being too sad, the heroine gets the job by jazzing it up.

"Can't We Be Friends?" Music by Kay Swift; lyric by Paul James (James P. Warburg). Torchy end of a romance suffered by Libby Holman in *The Little Show* (NY 1929).

Canterbury Tales (1968). Music by Richard Hill & John Hawkins; lyrics by Nevill Coghill; book by Coghill & Martin Starkie, based on Coghill's version of Chaucer's narrative poem.

SONGS: "I Have a Noble Cock," "There's the Moon," "Some Call It Love," "Fill Your Glass," "Come on and Marry Me, Honey," "I'll Give My Love a Ring," "Love Will Conquer All," "If She Has Never Loved Before," "April Song."

LONDON: March 21, 1968
PHOENIX THEATRE; 2,082 p.
Presented by Chanticleer Prod. Ltd. & Classic Presentations Ltd.; directed by Martin Starkie & Vlado Habunek; choreographed by David Drew; settings, Derek Cousins; costumes, Loudon Sainthill; lighting, Michael Northen; music director, Gordon Rose; orchestrations, Richard Hill & John Hawkins.

CAST: Wilfrid Brambell (*Steward, Carpenter, January*), Jessie Evans (*Wife of Bath, Old Woman*), Kenneth J. Warren (*Miller, Gervase, Pluto*), Nicky Henson (*Squire, Nicholas, Alan, Damian*), Billy Boyle (*Clerk of Oxford*), Pamela Charles (*Prioress, Prosperina*), Gay Soper (*Alison*), James Ottaway (*Chaucer*).

NEW YORK: Feb. 3, 1969
EUGENE O'NEILL THEATRE; 121 p.
Presented by Management III Prod. & Frank Prod.; directed by Martin Starkie; choreographed by Sammy Bayes; setting, Derek Cousins; costumes, Loudon Sainthill; lighting, Jules Fisher; music director, Oscar Kosarin; orchestrations, Richard Hill & John Hawkins.

CAST: Martyn Green (*Chaucer*), Hermione Baddeley (*Wife of Bath, Old Woman*), George Rose (*Steward, Carpenter, January*), Roy Cooper (*Miller, Gervase, Pluto*), Ed Evanko (*Squire, Nicholas, Alan, Damian*), Sandy Duncan (*Alison*), Ann Gardner (*Prioress, Prosperina*), Bruce Hyde (*Clerk of Oxford*).

Martin Starkie first directed Prof. Coghill's dramatization of *Canterbury Tales* at the Oxford Playhouse, 1964, where it was presented to celebrate the 650th anniversary of Oxford's Exeter College. Starkie and Coghill then revised the play to emphasize stories dealing with love and marriage and the battle of the sexes: "The Miller's Tale" (two students vie for the carpenter's wife), "The Steward's Tale" (multiple bed-hopping in the miller's menage), "The Merchant's Tale" (wife of rich old man deceives him with Squire), and "The Wife of Bath's Tale" (witch turns into beautiful young girl to please amorous Knight). Composers Hill and Hawkins, who had been working separately on a musical suite based on the Chaucer characters, first met Starkie when they provided the music for a recording he made of the Coghill translation. This led to the decision that the four combine their efforts into a stage musical. *Canterbury Tales* is currently the eighth longest running London musical.

Cantor, Eddie (né Isidore Itzkowitz), actor, singer; b. New York, Jan. 31, 1892; d. Hollywood, Cal., Oct. 10, 1964. Eye-popping, eye-rolling comedian whose characterization was usually that of the energetic but mousy little man who eventually triumphs over his bullying adversaries. In delivering a song, Cantor would jump up and down clapping his hands and end the number prancing offstage waving a handkerchief. He appeared frequently in blackface and was a vaudeville headliner before making his Bway bow. His most popular shows were *Kid Boots* ("Alabamy Bound," "If You Knew Susie") and *Whoopee* ("Makin' Whoopee"). Other songs he introduced: "You'd Be Surprised" (*Ziegfeld Follies*, 1919) and "We're Having a Baby" (*Banjo Eyes*). Cantor also starred in Hollywood films (*Roman Scandals, Kid Millions*), appeared on radio, and made

records. Bib: *My Life Is in Your Hands* (Harper, NY 1928), *Take My Life* (Doubleday, NY 1957), both by Cantor.

1914	Not Likely (L)
1916	Canary Cottage (US tour) (*Sam Beverly*)
1917	Ziegfeld Follies
1918	Ziegfeld Follies
1919	Ziegfeld Follies
1920	Broadway Brevities
1922	Make It Snappy
1923	Ziegfeld Follies (added)
	Kid Boots (*Kid Boots*)
1927	Ziegfeld Follies
1928	Whoopee (*Henry Williams*)
1929	Earl Carroll Sketch Book (sk. only)
1941	Banjo Eyes (*Erwin Trowbridge*)
1946	Nellie Bly (co-prod. only)

Carlisle, Kitty, actress, singer; b. New Orleans, La., Sept. 3, 1914. A classically trained singer, Miss Carlisle rose to stardom after her first Bway appearance. In addition to musicals, she has sung in opera (*Fledermaus, The Rape of Lucretia*) and acted in plays (*Anniversary Waltz*) and films (*A Night at the Opera*). She was married to librettist Moss Hart.

1933	Champagne, Sec (*Prince Orlovsky*)
1936	White Horse Inn (*Katarina*)
1937	Three Waltzes (*Marie, Charlotte, Franzi*)
1940	Walk with Music (*Pamela Gibson*)

Carmen Jones (1943). Music by Georges Bizet; lyrics & book by Oscar Hammerstein II, based on Henri Meilhac & Ludovic Halevy's opera libretto adapted from Prosper Merimée's novel *Carmen*.

SONGS: "Dat's Love," "You Talk Just Like My Maw," "Dere's a Café on de Corner," "Beat Out dat Rhythm on a Drum," "Stan' Up and Fight," "Whizzin' Away Along de Track," "Dis Flower," "My Joe."

NEW YORK: Dec. 2, 1943
BROADWAY THEATRE; 502 p.

Presented by Billy Rose; directed by Hassard Short & Charles Friedman; choreographed by Eugene Loring; settings, Howard Bay; costumes, Raoul Pène du Bois; lighting, Short; music director, Joseph Littau; orchestrations, Robert Russell Bennett.

CAST: Muriel Smith or Muriel Rahn (*Carmen Jones*), Luther Saxon or Napoleon Reed (*Joe*), Carlotta Franzell or Elton J. Warren (*Cindy Lou*), Glenn Bryant (*Husky Miller*), June Hawkins (*Frankie*), Cosy Cole (*Drummer*).

Oscar Hammerstein updated the libretto of Bizet's opera *Carmen* by making the characters Negro workers in a southern parachute factory during World War II. As closely as possible, however, he adhered to the original form, with almost all the pieces sung in their accustomed order. The tale recounts the love of Joe, an army corporal, for temptress Carmen Jones, which ends with his stabbing her to death after she leaves him for boxer Husky Miller. The decor of the production was particularly striking, with a different basic color used for each scene. After the Bway run, the show toured for one year, seven months.

Other operas adapted as Bway musicals: Rossini's *The Barber of Seville* (*Once Over Lightly*, 1942) and Verdi's *Aida* (*My Darlin' Aida*, 1952).

FILM VERSION: Dorothy Dandridge, Harry Belafonte, Diahann Carroll, Pearl Bailey (20th Cent. 1954, Otto Preminger dir.).

Carmichael, Ian, actor, singer; b. Hull, Eng., June 18, 1920. Boyishly befuddled comic actor best known for appearances in British films and tv (as Lord Peter Wimsey).

1940 Nine Sharp (UK tour)
1951 The Lyric Revue
1952 The Globe Revue
1953 High Spirits
      At the Lyric
1954 Going to Town (At the Lyric)
1959 The Love Doctor (*Tramp*)
1968 I Do! I Do! (*Michael*)

Carnival (1961). Music & lyrics by Bob Merrill; book by Michael Stewart, based on film *Lili* by Helen Deutsch, adapted from story by Paul Gallico.

SONGS: "Direct from Vienna," "A Very Nice Man," "I've Got to Find a Reason," "Mira," "A Sword and a Rose and a Cape," "Humming," "Yes, My Heart," "Everybody Likes You," "Love Makes the World Go Round," "Yum Ticky-Ticky," "The Rich," "Beautiful Candy," "Her Face," "Grand Imperial Cirque de Paris," "Always Always You," "She's My Love."

NEW YORK: April 13, 1961
IMPERIAL THEATRE; 719 p.

Presented by David Merrick; directed & choreographed by Gower Champion; settings & lighting, Will Steven Armstrong; costumes, Freddy Wittop; music director, Saul Schechtman; orchestrations, Philip J. Lang.

CAST: Anna Maria Alberghetti (*Lili*), James Mitchell (*Marco*), Jerry Orbach (*Paul Berthalet*), Kaye Ballard (*Rosalie*), Pierre Olaf (*Jacquot*), Henry Lascoe (*Schlegel*), Anita Gillette (*Gypsy*), Luba Lisa (*Princess Olga*).

LONDON: Feb. 8, 1963
LYRIC THEATRE; 34 p.

Presented by H. M. Tennent Ltd.; restaged by Lucia Victor; dances reproduced by Doria Avila; settings, Will Steven Armstrong; costumes, Freddy Wittop; lighting, Joe Davis; music director, Jan Cervenka; orchestrations, Philip J. Lang.

CAST: Sally Logan (*Lili*), James Mitchell (*Marco*), Michael Maurel

(*Paul Berthalet*), Shirley Sands (*Rosalie*), Bob Harris (*Jacquot*), Peter Bayliss (*Schlegel*).

Carnival, the first Bway musical adapted from a screen musical (*Lili*), reunited librettist Stewart with director Champion for their initial effort following *Bye Bye Birdie.* The production was noted primarily for Champion's skill in creating the atmosphere of a seedy European carnival and for two dramatically effective scenes: the opening (without an overture) in which the roustabouts set up the carnival tents at dawn, and the dance in which the sleeping company suddenly awakes and imagines itself once again the Grand Imperial Cirque de Paris. In the story, Lilo, an orphaned waif from a town called Mira, joins the carnival and falls in love with magician Marco the Magnificent. She makes friends with the puppets in the show, then realizes that her heart belongs to Paul, the lame puppeteer. During Bway run, Anna Maria Alberghetti (who had a well-publicized feud with producer David Merrick) was succeeded by Susan Watson and Carla Alberghetti (her sister), and Jerry Orbach was succeeded by Ed Ames. The US tour began Dec. 1961, with Miss Watson (later Anna Maria Alberghetti) and Ames in the leading roles.

Carousel (1945). Music by Richard Rodgers; lyrics & book by Oscar Hammerstein II, based on Ferenc Molnar's play *Liliom.*

SONGS: "Carousel Waltz," "You're a Queer One, Julie Jordan," "Mister Snow," "If I Loved You," "Blow High, Blow Low," "June Is Bustin' Out All Over," "Soliloquy," "When the Children Are Asleep," "A Real Nice Clambake," "What's the Use of Wond'rin'?," "There's Nothin' So Bad for a Woman," "You'll Never Walk Alone," "The Highest Judge of All."

NEW YORK: April 19, 1945
MAJESTIC THEATRE; 890 p.

Presented by The Theatre Guild; directed by Rouben Mamoulian; choreographed by Agnes de Mille; settings & lighting, Jo Mielziner; costumes, Miles White; music director, Joseph Littau; orchestrations, Don Walker.

CAST: John Raitt (*Billy Bigelow*), Jan Clayton (*Julie Jordan*), Jean Darling (*Carrie Pipperidge*), Eric Mattson (*Enoch Snow*), Christine Johnson (*Nettie Fowler*), Murvyn Vye (*Jigger Craigin*), Russell Collins (*Starkeeper*), Bambi Linn (*Louise Bigelow*), Jean Casto (*Mrs. Mullin*), Pearl Lang (*June Girl*), Iva Withers (chorus).

LONDON: June 7, 1950
DRURY LANE THEATRE; 566 p.

Presented by Prince Littler, with The Theatre Guild; production restaged by Jerome Whyte; choreographed by Agnes de Mille; settings, Jo Mielziner; costumes, Miles White; music director, Frederick Dvonch; orchestrations, Don Walker.

CAST: Stephen Douglass (*Billy Bigelow*), Iva Withers (*Julie Jordan*), Margot Moser (*Carrie Pipperidge*), Eric Mattson (*Enoch Snow*), Marion Ross (*Nettie Fowler*), Morgan Davies (*Jigger Craigin*), William Sherwood (*Starkeeper*), Bambi Linn (*Louise Bigelow*), Marjorie Mars (*Mrs. Mullin*), Mavis Ray (*June Girl*).

Molnar's tough-tender fantasy *Liliom,* about a carnival barker who marries a local factory girl, is killed in an attempted robbery, and then briefly returns to earth, provided the basis for Rodgers and Hammerstein's second collaboration. Though at first the writers thought the story unsuitable, everything fell into place once they shifted the locale from Budapest to

New England and added a more optimistic ending.

The production reunited the team with their associates of *Oklahoma!*—Theresa Helburn and Lawrence Langner of the Theatre Guild, director Mamoulian, choreographer de Mille, designer White. For almost two years *Carousel*, at the Majestic Theatre, and *Oklahoma!*, at the St. James, played across the street from each other. During NY run, John Raitt (who made his Bway debut in this production) was succeeded by Henry Michel (1-47), Jan Clayton by Iva Withers (12-45), Murvyn Vye by John Conte (1-46), Jean Darling by Connie Baxter (4-47). Beginning May 1947, the musical toured one year, nine months. During tour, Michel succeeded by Stephen Douglass, Miss Baxter by Ann Crowley. In London, Douglass was succeeded by Edmund Hockridge, Miss Withers by LaVerne Burden.

FILM VERSION: Gordon MacRae and Shirley Jones (20th Cent. 1956, Henry King dir.).

"Carousel Waltz." Music by Richard Rodgers. Waltz used instead of an overture to establish the mood and main characters in the musical *Carousel* (NY 1945). The scene is an amusement park on the New England coast in 1873 and, in pantomime, we see the barker for the carousel (John Raitt) flirt with the innocent factory girl (Jan Clayton), much to the anger of the carousel's proprietress (Jean Casto). Others who take part in the scene are a juggler, "Three Beauties of Europe," a dancing bear, a ballerina, a clown, plus the fairgoers. In London production (1950), the main characters were played by Stephen Douglass, Iva Withers, and Marjorie Mars.

Carroll, Diahann (née Carol Diahann Johnson), actress, singer; b. New York, July 17, 1935. Stylish performer who sang "A Sleepin' Bee" in *House of Flowers* and starred in *No Strings* (in which she introduced "The Sweetest Sounds"). Besides Bway, Miss Carroll has also had a successful career on tv, in nightclubs, and in films.

1954 House of Flowers (*Ottilie*)
1962 No Strings (*Barbara Woodruff*)

Carroll, Earl, producer, director, composer, lyricist; b. Pittsburgh, Pa., Sept. 16, 1893; d. plane crash, Mt. Carmel, Pa., June 17, 1948. Carroll's series of 10 *Vanities* (plus two *Sketch Books*), which rivaled the *Ziegfeld Follies* and *George White's Scandals,* were distinguished by lavish spectacle, undraped girls, and censorable humor. He settled in NY in 1912 to become a songwriter (besides himself, his collaborators were composers Alfred Robyn and Alfred Francis), and began producing revues in 1923. Among performers who appeared in the *Vanities* were Joe Cook (three), Sophie Tucker, Ted Healy, Jessie Matthews, W. C. Fields, Jimmy Savo, Jack Benny, Patsy Kelly, Milton Berle, Helen Broderick.

Unless otherwise noted, Mr. Carroll was producer-director of following:

1914 Pretty Mrs. Smith (lyr. only)
     (Robyn)
1916 So Long, Letty (lyr., comp. only)
     Canary Cottage (lyr., comp. only)
1918 The Love Mill (lib., lyr. only)
     (Francis)
1923 Earl Carroll Vanities (also lyr., comp.)
1924 Earl Carroll Vanities (also lyr., comp.)
1925 Earl Carroll Vanities
1926 Earl Carroll Vanities
1928 Earl Carroll Vanities
1929 Fioretta (also co-lib.)
     Earl Carroll Sketch Book
1930 Earl Carroll Vanities
1931 Earl Carroll Vanities
1932 Earl Carroll Vanities

1933 Murder at the Vanities (also co-lib.)
1935 Earl Carroll Sketch Book
1940 Earl Carroll Vanities

Carter, Desmond, lyricist, librettist; b. Bristol, Eng., d. London, Feb. 3, 1939. Carter's biggest London song hits: "The Wind in the Willows" (*Cochran's 1930 Revue*), "I'm on a See-Saw" (*Jill Darling*). Among his collaborators: George Gershwin, Jack Strachey, H. B. Hedley, Hal Brody, Harry Acres, Jack Clarke, Maurice Yvain, Joseph Meyer, Herman Finck, Oscar Straus, Vernon Duke, Vivian Ellis, Arthur Schwartz, Ralph Benatzky, Johann Strauss, Noel Gay, Henry Sullivan, Robert Stolz, Billy Mayerl, Kurt Weill, Jack Waller, Joseph Tunbridge.

Unless otherwise noted, Mr. Carter was lyricist of following:
1924 Primrose (Gershwin)
1925 Dear Little Billie (Hedley, Strachey)
1926 Just a Kiss (Yvain)
      Merely Molly (Meyer, Finck)
      My Son John (Straus)
1927 Lady Luck (Hedley, Strachey)
      Shake Your Feet (Hedley, Strachey)
1928 The Yellow Mask (Duke)
      So This Is Love (Brody)
1929 Love Lies (Brody)
1930 Darling, I Love You (Hedley, Acres)
      Here Comes the Bride (Schwartz)
      The Love Race (Clarke)
      Little Tommy Tucker (Ellis) (also co-lib.)
      Chelsea Follies (Charles)
1931 Song of the Drum (Ellis, Finck)
      Blue Roses (Ellis) (also co-lib.)
      My Sister and I (Benatzky)
      Waltzes from Vienna (Strauss) (also co-lib.)
      Hold My Hand (Gay)
1932 Bow Bells (Sullivan)
      The DuBarry (co-lib. only)
      Fanfare (Sullivan)

Rhyme and Rhythm (Clarke)
      Wild Violets (Stolz) (also co-lib.)
1933 Ballerina (Sullivan)
      That's a Pretty Thing (Gay)
1934 Sporting Love (Mayerl)
      Jill Darling (Ellis) (also co-lib.)
1935 The Flying Trapeze (Benatzky)
      Love Laughs—! (Gay)
      A Kingdom for a Cow (Weill)
1936 Follow the Sun (Schwartz)
      Rise and Shine (Stolz) (also co-lib.)
      Over She Goes (Mayerl)
1937 Big Business (Waller, Tunbridge) (also co-lib.)
      Crazy Days (Mayerl)
1938 Bobby Get Your Gun (Waller, Tunbridge)

Caryll, Ivan (né Felix Tilken), composer; b. Liège, Belgium, 1860; d. New York, Nov. 29, 1921. Between 1894 and 1909, Caryll was one of the most prominent composers for the London stage, with five musicals (*The Shop Girl, A Runaway Girl, The Toreador, The Orchid, Our Miss Gibbs*) running over 500 performances. In 1911 he settled in NY, where his biggest hits were *The Pink Lady* ("My Beautiful Lady"), *Chin-Chin, Jack o' Lantern* ("Wait Till the Cows Come Home"). His most frequent lyric-writing partners were Adrian Ross, Percy Greenbank, and C. M. S. McLellan; others were George Dance, George Sims, H. J. W. Dam, Harry Greenbank, Audrey Hopwood, Claude Aveling, Owen Hall, W. H. Risque, Basil Hood, P. G. Wodehouse, Anne Caldwell, Harry B. Smith, R. H. Burnside, Clifford Grey, Philander Johnson.
1890 La Cigale (Burnand)
1892 Ma Mie Rosette (Dance)
1893 Little Christopher Columbus (Sims)
1894 The Shop Girl (Dam)
1895 Dandy Dick Whittington (Sims)
1896 The Gay Parisienne (Dance)
      The Circus Girl (H. Greenbank, Ross)

1898 A Runaway Girl (Hopwood, H. Greenbank)
1900 The Messenger Boy (P. Greenbank, Ross)
1901 The Toreador (P. Greenbank, Ross)
      The Ladies' Paradise (NY) (Dance)
1902 The Girl from Kay's (Ross, Aveling)
1903 The Duchess of Dantzic (Hamilton)
      The Orchid (P. Greenbank, Ross)
      The Earl and the Girl (P. Greenbank)
      The Cherry Girl (Hopwood)
1905 The Spring Chicken (P. Greenbank, Ross)
1906 The Little Cherub (Hall)
      The New Aladdin (Risque)
1907 Nelly Neil (McLellan)
      The Girls of Gottenberg (Ross, Hood)
1909 Our Miss Gibbs (P. Greenbank, Ross)
1911 Marriage à la Carte (NY) (McLellan)
      The Pink Lady (NY) (McLellan)
1912 Oh! Oh! Delphine (NY) (McLellan)
1913 The Little Café (NY) (McLellan)
1914 The Belle of Bond Street (NY) (The Girl from Kay's) (Ross, Aveling)
      Chin-Chin (NY) (Caldwell, O'Dea)
      Papa's Darling (NY) (Smith)
1917 Jack o' Lantern (NY) (Caldwell)
1918 The Girl Behind the Gun (NY) (Wodehouse)
      The Canary (NY) (Wodehouse, Caldwell)
1919 The Kiss Call (P. Greenbank, Ross, Grey)
1920 Tip Top (NY) (Caldwell, Burnside)
      Kissing Time (NY) (Johnson)
1922 The Hotel Mouse (NY) (Grey)

Cassidy, (John) Jack, actor, singer; b. Richmond Hills, NY, March 5, 1925. Blond, dimpled juvenile who first at-tracted notice in *Wish You Were Here* (singing title song and "Where Did the Night Go?"), later turned to comedy and dramatic roles. Divorced from actress Shirley Jones. (*D. Dec. 12, 1976.*)

1943 Something for the Boys (chorus)
1944 Sadie Thompson (chorus)
1945 The Firebrand of Florence (chorus)
1946 Around the World (chorus)
1947 Music in My Heart (chorus)
1948 Inside USA (chorus)
      Small Wonder
1950 Alive and Kicking
1952 South Pacific (*Richard West*, repl.)
      Wish You Were Here (*Chick Miller*)
1954 Sandhog (*Johnny O'Sullivan*)
1956 Shangri-la (*Charles Mallinson*)
1963 She Loves Me (*Steven Kodaly*)
1964 Fade Out—Fade In (*Byron Prong*)
1966 It's a Bird It's a Plane It's Superman (*Max Mencken*)
1968 Maggie Flynn (*Phineas Flynn*)

Castle, Irene (née Irene Foote), actress, dancer; b. New Rochelle, NY, April 7, 1893; d. Eureka Springs, Ark., Jan. 25, 1969. With husband, Vernon Castle, she became the most influential ballroom dancer in the world, introducing or popularizing such steps as the Castle Walk, the Turkey Trot, the Maxixe, the tango, and the polka. The Castles scored their first success in Paris in 1912, and appeared together on Bway in *Watch Your Step*. Bib: *Modern Dancing* by the Castles (World Synd., NY 1914); *Castles in the Air* by Mrs. Castle (Doubleday, NY 1958).

1910 The Summer Widowers (dancer, repl.)
1911 The Hen-Pecks (dancer, repl.)
1913 The Sunshine Girl (dancer)
1914 Watch Your Step (*Mrs. Vernon Castle*)
1917 Miss 1917

Castle, Vernon (né Vernon Blyth), actor, dancer; b. Norwich, Eng., May 2, 1887; d. airplane crash, Houston, Texas, Feb. 15, 1918. With wife, Irene Castle, he became the most influential ballroom dancer in the world, introducing or popularizing such steps as the Castle Walk, the Turkey Trot, the Maxixe, the tango, and the polka. Castle began his Bway career as a comic stooge for Lew Fields in seven productions. He and his wife scored their first success as dancers in Paris in 1912, and appeared together on Bway in *Watch Your Step*. Bib: *Modern Dancing* by the Castles (World Synd., NY 1914); *Castles in the Air* by Mrs. Castle (Doubleday, NY 1958).

1906   About Town
1907   The Girl Behind the Counter
       (*Hon. Aubrey Battersea*)
1908   The Mimic World
1909   The Midnight Sons (*Souseberry Lushmore*)
       Old Dutch (*Hon. Algy Clymber*)
1910   The Summer Widowers (*Oxford Tighe*)
1911   The Hen-Pecks (*Zowie*)
1912   The Lady of the Slipper (*Atzel*)
1913   The Sunshine Girl (*Lord Bingo Bicester*)
1914   Watch Your Step (*Joseph Lilyburn*)

Cat and the Fiddle, The (1931). Music by Jerome Kern; lyrics & book by Otto Harbach.

SONGS: "The Night Was Made for Love," "I Watch the Love Parade," "Try to Forget," "She Didn't Say 'Yes'," "A New Love Is Old," "One Moment Alone," "Poor Pierrot."

NEW YORK: Oct. 15, 1931
GLOBE THEATRE; 395 p.

Presented by Max Gordon; directed by José Ruben; choreographed by Albertina Rasch; settings, Henry Dreyfuss; costumes, Constance Ripley, Kiviette; music director, Victor Baravalle; orchestrations, Robert Russell Bennett.

CAST: Georges Metaxa (*Victor Florescu*), Bettina Hall (*Shirley Sheridan*), Odette Myrtil (*Odette*), Eddie Foy, Jr. (*Alexander Sheridan*), José Ruben (*Clement Daudet*), Lawrence Grossmith (*Sir George Chatterly*), Doris Carson (*Angie Sheridan*), George Meader (*Pompineau*), Flora LeBreton (*Maizie Gripps*).

LONDON: March 4, 1932
PALACE THEATRE; 219 p.

Presented by Charles B. Cochran; directed by William Mollison; choreographed by Buddy Bradley; settings, Henry Dreyfuss; costumes, Kay Norton, Becannes, etc.; music director, Hyam Greenbaum.

CAST: Francis Lederer (*Victor Florescu*), Peggy Wood (*Shirley Sheridan*), Alice Delysia (*Alice*), Fred Conyngham (*Alexander Sheridan*), Austin Trevor (*Clement Daudet*), Martin Walker (*Sir George Chatterly*), Gina Malo (*Angie Sheridan*), Henri Leoni (*Pompineau*), Babs Valerie (*Maizie Gripps*).

The Cat and the Fiddle was a pioneering effort to adapt the operetta tradition to a more intimate, contemporary setting. Victor and Shirley, both music students in Brussels, are attracted to each other—though not to each other's music. Victor's operetta, *The Passionate Pilgrim*, is considered pretty heavy going by the producer, who interpolates some of Shirley's jazzier numbers into the score. Victor is furious, but true love eventually has hero and heroine singing in harmony. (It should be noted that when Jerome Kern was getting started in the Bway theatre, he first won notice for his interpolated songs in imported operettas.) This production preceded Kern and Hammerstein's *Music in the Air* by about a year. Both had modern European settings, both were concerned with the production of a musical play, and both took pains to integrate the music as an important part of the story. During Bway run, Eddie Foy Jr. was succeeded by Bobby Jarvis (7-32), Lawrence Grossmith by Arthur Treacher (7-32), Georges Metaxa by Michael Bartlett (8-32).

FILM VERSION: Jeanette MacDonald, Ramon Novarro, Vivienne Segal (MGM 1934, William K. Howard dir.).

Catch of the Season, The (1904). Music by Herbert E. Haines & Evelyn Baker; lyrics by Charles H. Taylor; book by Seymour Hicks & Cosmo Hamilton.

SONGS: "Rainbow," "Teasing," "A Wise Old Owl," "Cigarette."

LONDON: Sept. 9, 1904
VAUDEVILLE THEATRE; 621 p.

Presented by A. & S. Gatti & Charles Frohman; directed by Seymour Hicks; choreographed by Edward Royce; settings, W. Harford; costumes, Lucile; music director, Carl Kiefert.

CAST: Zena Dare (*Angela Crystal*), Seymour Hicks (*Duke of St. Jermyns*), Compton Coutts (*William Gibson*), Olive Morrell (*Sophia Crystal*), Hilda Jacobson (*Honoria Crystal*), Mollie Lowell (*Lady Crystal*), Rosina Filippi (*Lady Caterham*), Camille Clifford (*Sylvia Gibson*).

NEW YORK: Aug. 28, 1905
DALY'S THEATRE; 104 p.

Presented by Charles Frohman; directed by Ben Teal; settings, Ernest Gros; costumes, Ward; music director, William T. Francis; revised version with added songs by William T. Francis, Jerome Kern, etc.

CAST: Edna May (*Angela Crystal*), Farren Soutar (*Duke of St. Jermyns*), Fred Wright, Jr. (*William Gibson*),

Fred Kaye (*Lord Bagdad Monteagle*), Jane May (*Sophia Crystal*), Margaret Fraser (*Honoria Crystal*), Lillian Burns (*Lady Louise Dorsay*), Annie Esmond (*Lady Crystal*).

Seymour Hicks's first musical for producer Charles Frohman, following the actor's break with George Edwardes, was an undisguised modern retelling of the Cinderella story, complete with two haughty sisters and a ball at which our heroine wins the catch of the season. In the leading role, Zena Dare was succeeded by Ellaline Terriss (Mrs. Hicks) and Phyllis Dare (her sister). The show won fame by introducing the bare shoulders, padded hips, and upswept hairdo of the Gibson Girl, inspired by artist Charles Dana Gibson and personified by Camille Clifford. Hicks, however, was less fashionably influential when he tried to change male formal attire to knee britches and silk stockings.

Catlett, Walter, actor; b. San Francisco, Cal., Feb. 4, 1889; d. Los Angeles, Cal., Nov. 4, 1960. Catlett usually played the affable, derby-wearing, cigar-chomping blusterer, and scored his biggest Bway hits in *Sally* and *Lady, Be Good!* (introducing "Oh, Lady, Be Good!"). He began film career in 1929.

1910 The Prince of Pilsen (*Artie*)
1916 So Long, Letty (*Harry Miller*)
1917 Ziegfeld Follies
1918 Follow the Girl (*Buck Sweeney*)
      Little Simplicity (*Prof. Erasmus Duckworth*)
1919 Baby Bunting (L) (*William Pye*)
1920 Sally (*Otis Hooper*)
1924 Dear Sir (*Andrew Bloxom*)
      Lady, Be Good! (*J. Watterson Watkins*)
1927 Lucky (*Charley Simpson*)
      Rio Rita (*Ed Lovett*, repl.)
1928 Here's Howe (*Basil Carroway*, repl.)
      Treasure Girl (*Larry Hopkins*)

Cawthorn, Joseph, actor; b. New York, March 29, 1867; d. Beverly Hills, Cal., Jan. 21, 1949. Character comedian known for German dialect parts, Cawthorn is best remembered on Bway for the five musicals in which he costarred with Julia Sanderson (1913–1918). The actor began career in minstrel shows and British music halls, later appeared in many Hollywood films. He was married to actress Queenie Vassar.

1897	Nature (*Hans Schultz*)
	Miss Philadelphia (*William Penn Jr.*)
1898	The Fortune Teller (*Boris*)
1899	The Rounders (*Siegfried Gotterdammerung*)
	The Singing Girl (*Aufpassen*)
1901	The Fortune Teller (L) (*Boris*)
	The Sleeping Beauty (*Lena*)
1903	Mother Goose (*Mother Goose*)
1905	Fritz in Tammany Hall (*Fritz von Swobenfritz*)
1906	The Free Lance (*Siegmund Lump*)
1907	The Hoyden (*Baron Hugo Weybach*)
1908	Little Nemo (*Dr. Pill*)
1910	Girlies (*Oscar Spiel*)
1911	The Slim Princess (*Louis Von Schloppenhauer*)
1913	The Sunshine Girl (*Schlump*)
1914	The Girl from Utah (*Trimpel*)
1916	Sybil (*Otto Spreckels*)
1917	The Rambler Rose (*Joseph Guppy*)
1918	The Canary (*Timothy*)
1920	The Half Moon (*Hon. Hudson Hobson*)
1922	The Blue Kitten (*Theodore Vanderpop*)
1925	Sunny (*Siegfried Peters*)

"C'est Magnifique." Music & lyric by Cole Porter. Macaronic appreciation of a new love sung by Lilo to a resisting Peter Cookson in *Can-Can* (NY 1953). In London version (1954) the singers were Irene Hilda and Edmund Hockridge.

Champion Gower, director, choreographer, dancer; b. Geneva, Ill., June 22, 1920. Stage and screen dancer who became one of Bway's most acclaimed directors, noted for large-scale, imaginatively mounted productions. His biggest hits: *Bye Bye Birdie, Carnival, Hello, Dolly!* Champion was a professional dancer at 15, later teamed with wife, Marge (now divorced).

Unless otherwise noted, Mr. Champion was director-choreographer of following:

1939	The Streets of Paris (dancer only)
1942	Count Me In (dancer only)
1948	Small Wonder (chor. only)
	Lend an Ear
1951	Make a Wish (chor. only)
1955	Three for Tonight (also dancer)
1960	Bye Bye Birdie
1961	Carnival
	Bye Bye Birdie (L)
1964	Hello, Dolly!
1965	Hello, Dolly! (L)
1966	I Do! I Do!
1968	The Happy Time
1972	Sugar
1973	Irene
1974	Mack & Mabel

Channing, Carol (Elaine), actress, singer; b. Seattle, Wash., Jan. 31, 1921. Blonde, wide-eyed, long-legged comedienne with squeal-to-growl voice who won Bway stardom in *Gentlemen Prefer Blondes* (introducing "Diamonds Are a Girl's Best Friend" and "A Little Girl from Little Rock"). Miss Channing, who has also appeared in nightclubs, made her biggest hit in *Hello, Dolly!* ("Hello, Dolly," "Before the Parade Passes By").

1948	Lend an Ear
1949	Gentlemen Prefer Blondes (*Lorelei Lee*)
1954	Wonderful Town (*Ruth Sherwood*, repl.)
1955	The Vamp (*Flora Weems*)
1961	Show Girl

1964 Hello, Dolly! (*Dolly Levi*)
1974 Lorelei (Gentlemen Prefer Blondes) (*Lorelei Lee*)
1978 Hello, Dolly! (r) (*Dolly Levi*)

Chaplin, Sydney, actor, singer; b. Los Angeles, Cal., March 31, 1926. Deep-voiced dependable Bway leading man who introduced "Just in Time," "Long Before I Knew You" (both in *Bells Are Ringing*) and "Comes Once in a Lifetime" (*Subways Are for Sleeping*). The son of Charlie Chaplin, he also appeared in *Sweet Charity* in Paris.

1956 Bells Are Ringing (*Jeff Moss*)
1961 Subways Are for Sleeping (*Tom Bailey*)
1964 Funny Girl (*Nick Arnstein*)

Chappell, William, director, choreographer, dancer; b. Wolverhampton, Staffs, Eng., Sept. 27, 1908. Chappell has been a ballet dancer, costume and scenic designer, and director of London revues (*The Lyric Revue, Living for Pleasure*) and book musicals (*Where's Charley?, Expresso Bongo*).

Unless otherwise noted, Mr. Chappell was director of following; asterisk indicates he was also choreographer:

1932 Helen! (dancer only)
A Kiss in Spring (dancer only)
1933 Beau Brummell (*Stranger*, only)
1948 A la Carte (chor. only)
1951 The Lyric Revue *
1952 The Globe Revue *
1953 High Spirits *
At the Lyric *
1954 Going to Town (At the Lyric) *
1955 The Buccaneer
1958 Where's Charley?
Expresso Bongo *
Living for Pleasure *
1960 Joie de Vivre
1961 On the Avenue *
1963 So Much to Remember *
Six of One
1965 Passion Flower Hotel
1973 Cockie
1974 Oh, Kay! (r)

Charig, Philip, composer; b. New York, Aug. 31, 1902; d. New York, July 21, 1960. Charig's biggest Bway hit was *Follow the Girls* ("I Wanna Get Married"). He also contributed songs for revues ("Sunny Disposish") and composed two London scores for Jack Buchanan: *That's a Good Girl* ("Fancy Our Meeting") and *Stand Up and Sing* ("There's Always Tomorrow"). He wrote with composer Joseph Meyer and with lyricists Irving Caesar, Leo Robin, Ira Gershwin, Douglas Furber, Dan Shapiro, Milton Pascal.

1927 Yes, Yes, Yvette (Caesar)
Just Fancy (Meyer-Robin)
1928 That's a Good Girl (L) (Meyer-Furber, Gershwin)
1929 Polly (Caesar)
1931 Stand Up and Sing (L) (Furber)
1943 Artists and Models (Shapiro, Pascal)
1944 Follow the Girls (Shapiro, Pascal)

"Charleston." Music & lyrics by Jimmy Johnson & Cecil Mack. Elisabeth Welch sang and danced the number in the all-Negro *Runnin' Wild* (NY 1923). As a result of the song's popularity, the high-kicking Charleston replaced the Shimmy as the latest dance-floor gyration of the 20s.

Charlie Girl (1965). Music & lyrics by David Heneker & John Taylor; book by Hugh & Margaret Williams, with Ray Cooney, based on story by Ross Taylor.

SONGS: "Charlie Girl," "Lets Do a Deal," "My Favorite Occupation" (Taylor alone), "I Was Young," "The Party of a Lifetime," "What's the Magic?" (Taylor alone).

LONDON: Dec. 15, 1965
ADELPHI THEATRE; 2,202 p.

Presented by Harold Fielding; directed by Wallace Douglas; choreographed by Alfred Rodrigues; settings, Tod Kingman; costumes, Cynthia Tingey; lighting, Michael Northen; music director, Kenneth Alwyn; orchestrations, Arthur Wilkinson.

CAST: Joe Brown (*Joe Studholme*), Anna Neagle (*Lady Hadwell*), Hy Hazell (*Kay Connor*), Christine Holmes (*Charlie*), Derek Nimmo (*Nicholas Wainwright*), Stuart Damon (*Jack Connor*).

Currently the sixth longest running musical in London theatre history, *Charlie Girl* spread its appeal to include those who were attracted by the return of Anna Neagle (her first musical in 12 years) and those who were attracted by young pop singing star Joe Brown. The story, set in the stately home of Hadwell Hall, now a tourist attraction, concerns hoydenish Lady Charlotte Hadwell, known as Charlie, and her brief fling with rich American playboy Jack Connor. By the time the final curtain falls, she is happy to settle down with the local lad, Joe Studholme. During run, Miss Neagle succeeded by Evelyn Laye, Miss Holmes by Stephanie Voss.

Charlot, André, producer, director; b. Paris, France, July 26, 1882; d. Woodland, Cal., May 20, 1956. Charlot won his fame as producer of smart, intimate revues that flourished in London during the 1910s and 1920s. In 1924 *André Charlot's Revue* introduced New York to Beatrice Lillie, Gertrude Lawrence and Jack Buchanan. Others who appeared in Charlot productions were George Grossmith, Noël Coward, Jack Hulbert, Gertie Millar, June, Binnie Hale, Jessie Matthews. In 1937 the producer went to Hollywood to work in films.

1912 Kill That Fly!
1913 Eightpence a Mile
     Keep Smiling

1914 Not Likely!
1915 5064 Gerrard
     Now's the Time!
     Samples
1916 Some
     This and That
     See-Saw
     Three Cheers
1917 Cheep
     Bubbly
1918 Flora
     Tabs
     Very Good Eddie
     Tails Up
     The Officer's Mess
     Buzz-Buzz
1919 Bran-Pie
1920 Just Fancy
     Jumble Sale
1921 Puss-Puss
     Now and Then
     A to Z
     Pot Luck
1922 Snap
     Dé-Dé
1923 Rats
     London Calling!
     Yes!
1924 Puppets
     André Charlot's Revue (NY)
     Charlot's Revue
1925 The Charlot Revue of 1926 (NY)
1926 The Charlot Show of 1926
1928 Charlot, 1928
1930 Charlot's Masquerade
     The Wonder Bar
1933 How D'You Do?
     Please
1934 Hi-Diddle-Diddle
1935 Charlot's Char-a-Bang
     Dancing City
     Shall We Reverse?
     Stop . . . Go!
1936 The Town Talks
1937 Red, Bright and Blue
     Charlot's Non-Stop Revue

Chinese Honeymoon, A (1901). Music by Howard Talbot; lyrics & book by George Dance.

SONGS: "The à la Girl," "Daisie with the Dimple on Her Chin," "A Paper Fan," "Martha Spank the Grand

Pianner," "I Want to Be a Lidy," "Mister Dooley" (Jean Schwartz-William Jerome) (added in NY).

LONDON: Oct. 5, 1901
STRAND THEATRE; 1,075 p.

Presented by Frank Curzon; directed by Charles Wilson; choreographed by Will Bishop & Fred Farren; settings, Philip Howden & Walter Hann; costumes, Comelli; music director, Ernest Vousden.

CAST: Lily Elsie (*Princess Soo-Soo*), Louie Freear (*Fi-Fi*), Lionel Rignold (*Samuel Pineapple*), Marie Dainton (*Mrs. Pineapple*), Leslie Stiles (*Tom Hatherton*), Percy Clifton (*Adm. Hi Lung*), M. A. Victor (*Mrs. Brown*).

NEW YORK: June 2, 1902
CASINO THEATRE; 376 p.

Presented by Sam S. Shubert, Sam Nixon & J. F. Zimmerman; directed by Gerald Coventry; settings, D. Frank Dodge; costumes, Mme. Caroline Siedle; music director, Herman Perlet.

CAST: Amelia Stone (*Princess Soo-Soo*), Katie Barry (*Fi-Fi*), Thomas Q. Seabrooke (*Samuel Pineapple*), Adele Ritchie (*Mrs. Pineapple*), Van Rensselaer Wheeler (*Tom Hatherton*), William Pruette (*Adm. Hi Lung*), Annie Yeamans (*Mrs. Brown*), Julia Sanderson (chorus).

The first London musical to run over 1,000 performances, *A Chinese Honeymoon* held the endurance record until overtaken by another oriental attraction, *Chu Chin Chow*, in 1916. In the story, Samuel Pineapple and his bride spend their honeymoon in the mythical Chinese locale of Yiang Yiang. Both Pineapples come afoul of local custom, which holds that a kiss automatically makes the kisser the spouse of the kissee. Since Pineapple has kissed a local princess and his wife has kissed the emperor, it takes a new law to straighten things

out. The NY engagement was Sam Shubert's second production and his first hit.

Chocolate Soldier, The (1909). Music by Oscar Straus; lyrics & book by Stanislaus Stange, based on Viennese operetta *Der Tapfere Soldat*, by Rudolph Bernauer & Leopold Jacobson, adapted from Bernard Shaw's play *Arms and the Man*.

SONGS: "My Hero," "Sympathy," "Seek the Spy," "Alexius the Heroic," "Never Was There Such a Lover," "The Tale of a Coat," "That Would Be Lovely," "Falling in Love," "The Letter Song."

NEW YORK: Sept. 13, 1909
LYRIC THEATRE; 296 p.

Presented by Fred C. Whitney; directed by Stanislaus Stange; choreographed by A. L. Holbrook; settings, Unitt & Wickes; costumes, Hugo Baruch; music director, A. DeNovellis.

CAST: J. E. Gardner (*Lt. Bumerli*), Ida Brooks Hunt (*Nadina Popoff*), Flavia Arcaro (*Aurelia Popoff*), William Pruette (*Col. Kasimir Popoff*), George Tallman (*Major Alexius Spiridoff*).

LONDON: Sept. 10, 1910
LYRIC THEATRE; 500 p.

Presented by Fred C. Whitney; directed by Stanislaus Stange; choreographed by A. L. Holbrook; settings & costumes, Hugo Baruch; lighting, Digby; music director, Jacques Heuvel.

CAST: C. H. Workman (*Lt. Bumerli*), Constance Drever (*Nadina Popoff*), Amy Augarde (*Aurelia Popoff*), John Dunsmure (*Col. Kasimir Popoff*), Roland Cunningham (*Major Alexius Spiridoff*).

The first musical adapted from a play by Bernard Shaw (the second was *My Fair Lady*), *The Chocolate Soldier* was originally presented in Vienna in 1908. Possibly because it took a satirical look at traditional operetta heroics, the production was not an initial success. Lt. Bumerli, the chocolate-eating soldier, was more interested in saving his neck than in performing valorous deeds on the battlefield, while the genuine military hero, Major Alexius Spiridoff, was a ridiculously pompous character. In the story, Bumerli, fighting with the Serbs in Bulgaria, escapes capture by hiding in the home of Col. Popoff, where he falls asleep in Nadina Popoff's bed. Though Nadina's hero is Alexius, the girl soon falls in love with Bumerli, not knowing who he is. After his identity is revealed, love conquers an obstinate papa.

Even before the Viennese opening, producer Whitney had secured the English-language rights. In London it had an even bigger success than in NY, possibly because of Bernard Shaw's well-publicized jibes. Though he had given permission for the musical version of his *Arms and the Man*, he insisted that the program carry the following disclaimer: "With apologies to Mr. Bernard Shaw for an unauthorized parody of one of his comedies."

In the original NY production, Thomas G. Richards succeeded J. E. Gardner within a month after the opening. The first Bway revival was in 1921, when the Messrs. Shubert offered it at the Century Theatre for 83 performances. The cast was headed by Donald Brian and Tessa Kosta. It also had limited NY runs in 1930 and 1931. In 1947 Guy Bolton's revised version was presented for 70 performances at the New Century Theatre. In the cast were Keith Andes (*Bumerli*), Frances McCann (*Nadina*), and Billy Gilbert (*Popoff*). London saw revivals in 1914, 1932, and 1940.

FILM VERSION: Risë Stevens and Nelson Eddy (different story) (MGM 1941, Roy Del Ruth dir.).

Chorus Line, A (1975). Music by Marvin Hamlisch; lyrics by Edward Kleban; book by James Kirkwood & Nicholas Dante, from concept by Michael Bennett.

SONGS: "I Hope I Get It," "I Can Do That," "At the Ballet," "Sing!," "Hello, Twelve, Hello Thirteen, Hello Love," "Nothing," "The Music and the Mirror," "Dance: Ten; Looks: Three," "One," "What I Did for Love."

NEW YORK: May 21, 1975
PUBLIC THEATRE (NEWMAN THEATRE)

Presented by the New York Shakespeare Festival Public Theatre, Joseph Papp producer; directed & choreographed by Michael Bennett; co-choreographer, Bob Avian; settings, Robin Wagner; costumes, Theoni V. Aldredge; lighting, Tharon Musser; music director, Don Pippin; orchestrations, Bill Byers, Hershy Kay, Jonathan Tunick.

CAST: Renee Baughman (*Kristine*), Carole Bishop (*Sheila*), Pamela Blair (*Val*), Wayne Cilento (*Mike*), Clive Clerk (*Larry*), Kay Cole (*Maggie*), Baayork Lee (*Connie*), Priscilla Lopéz (*Diane*), Robert LuPone (*Zach*), Donna McKechnie (*Cassie*), Don Percassi (*Al*), Sammy Williams (*Paul*).

Acknowledged to be a major breakthrough in structure and theme, *A Chorus Line* was first performed as a workshop production at Joseph Papp's Public Theatre, then mounted as a full-scale musical at the Newman Theatre (a part of the Public Theatre complex). Less than two months after its highly acclaimed opening, the show moved to the Shubert Theatre.

The musical's genesis began when Michael Bennett met with some 24 dancers for two marathon tape-recorded sessions intended to probe their backgrounds and motivations. The tapes were turned over to Nicholas Dante, one of the dancers present, to fashion into a play with the collaboration of playwright James Kirkwood. It was only after the first runthrough that Marvin Hamlisch and Edward Kleban were brought in to create the score. The story takes place on the bare stage of a theatre during an audition for eight chorus dancers. One by one, as they are prodded from the back of the auditorium by Zach (Robert LuPone), the show's director, the dancers reveal who they are and why they are there. The main story deals with Cassie (Donna McKechnie), who is trying to start over again after a brief success, and her relationship with Zach, her former lover, who opposes the move. "The show is dedicated to anyone who has ever danced in a chorus or marched in step . . . anywhere."

Chu Chin Chow (1916). Music by Frederic Norton; lyrics & book by Oscar Asche.

SONGS: "I Am Chu Chin Chow," "Serenade," "I'll Sing and Dance," "Any Time's Kissing Time," "The Cobbler's Song," "Song of the Scimitar," "I Long for the Sun," "I Love Thee So," "Behold!," "I Built a Fairy Palace in the Sky."

LONDON: Aug. 31, 1916
HIS MAJESTY'S THEATRE; 2,238 p.
Presented by Oscar Asche & Lily Brayton; directed by Asche; choreographed by Espinosa; settings, Joseph & Phil Harker; costumes, Percy Anderson; music director, Percy Fletcher; orchestrations, Fletcher.
CAST: Oscar Asche (*Abu Hasan*), Lily Brayton (*Zahrat Al-Kulub*), Violet Essex (*Marjanah*), Courtice Pounds

(*Ali Baba*), J. V. Bryant (*Nur Al-Huda*), Frank Cochrane (*Kasim Baba*), Aileen d'Orme (*Alcolom*), Sydney Fairbrother (*Mahbubah*).

NEW YORK: Oct. 22, 1917
MANHATTAN OPERA HOUSE; 208 p.
Presented by William Elliott, F. Ray Comstock, Morris Gest; directed by E. Lyall Swete; choreographed by Alexis Kosloff; settings, Joseph & Phil Harker; costumes, Percy Anderson; music director, Gustave Ferrari; orchestrations, Percy Fletcher.
CAST: Tyrone Power (*Abu Hasan*), Florence Reed (*Zahrat Al-Kulub*), Tessa Kosta (*Marjanah*), Henry E. Dixey (*Ali Baba*), George Rasely (*Nur Al-Huda*), Kate Condon (*Alcolom*), Albert Howson (*Kasim Baba*), Lucy Beaumont (*Mahbubah*).

The great London hit of World War I—subtitled "A Musical Tale of the East"—had a record-breaking run that was not surpassed until *Salad Days*, almost 40 years later (it is still the fifth longest-running West End musical). A lavish production loosely based on the tale of "Ali Baba and the 40 Thieves," it made a star of Oscar Asche and remains the production for which he is best remembered. In the colorful story, set in and around Baghdad, the bandit chief Abu Hasan of Khorasan disguises himself as Chinese merchant Chu Chin Chow to gain access to the palace of Kasim Baba. But his identity is revealed by his slave, Zahrat, and his hideout under a rock—opened only by the passwords "Open sesame"— is discovered by Kasim Baba's slave, Marjanah, her lover Nur Al-Huda, and Nur's father, Ali Baba. After killing Kasim, Abu Hasan attends the wedding of Marjanah and Nur disguised as an oil merchant with 40 jars supposedly filled with oil. In reality, there's a thief in every jar, but they are all killed when Zahrat has boiled oil poured over them. She then finishes the job by stabbing Abu Hasan to death.

FILM VERSION: Fritz Kortner, George Robey, Anna May Wong (Gaumont-Brit. 1934, Walter Forde dir.).

City Center Light Opera Co. Organized in 1954 at the NY City Center to offer limited-run revivals of established musicals at moderate prices. William Hammerstein served as general director 1954–1956 and was responsible for nine productions; Jean Dalrymple served 1957–1968 and presented 47. In all, 30 different musicals were mounted over the 15-year period, with the most frequent repeaters being *Brigadoon* (5), *South Pacific* (4), *The King and I* (4), *Carousel* (3), *Finian's Rainbow* (3), *Guys and Dolls* (3), *Oklahoma!* (3), and *Wonderful Town* (3). John Fearnley (with 16 shows) and Gus Schirmer Jr. (with 13) were the most frequently employed directors.

"Civilization (Bongo, Bongo, Bongo)." Music by Carl Sigman; lyric by Sigman & Bob Hilliard. Despite a missionary's entreaties, one African native has no intention of trading his happy, simple life for the "bright lights, false teeth, door bells, landlords" of "civilization." First sung by Elaine Stritch in revue *Angel in the Wings* (NY 1947).

Claire, Ina (née Ina Fagan), actress, singer; b. Washington, DC, Oct. 15, 1892. Stylish light comedienne, primarily known for appearances in Bway nonmusical comedies (*The Gold Diggers, Biography*) Began career in vaudeville, and introduced "Hello, Frisco" in *Ziegfeld Follies* of 1915.

1911 Jumping Jupiter (*Molly Pebbleford*)
The Quaker Girl (*Prudence Pym*)

1913 The Honeymoon Express (*Marcelle*, repl.)
The Girl from Utah (L) (*Una Trance*)
1914 The Belle of Bond Street (L) (*Winnie Harborough*)
Lady Luxury (*Eloise Van Cuyler*)
1915 Ziegfeld Follies
1916 Ziegfeld Follies

"Clap Yo' Hands." Music by George Gershwin; lyric by Ira Gershwin. Revivalistic-type number sung by Harland Dixon, Betty Compton, Constance Carpenter, Paulette Winsten, Janette Gilmore, and chorus in *Oh, Kay!* (NY 1926). In London production (1927) sung by Claude Hulbert, danced by Hulbert and Rita McLean. The lyric to the verse of the song was written by Howard Dietz.

Clark, (Robert Edwin) Bobby, actor; b. Springfield, Ohio, June 16, 1888; d. New York, Feb. 12, 1960. A leering, stubby clown with a guttural growl and painted-on glasses, Clark, along with his partner, Paul McCullough, was a vaudeville headliner before appearing in Bway musicals. The two joined up in 1905, and the partnership lasted 27 years. Clark, a master at manipulating props, usually played a shady but likable operator who rises to such heights as presidential adviser (*Strike Up the Band*) and presidential husband (*As the Girls Go*).

1922 Chuckles of 1922 (L)
Music Box Revue
1924 Music Box Revue
1926 The Ramblers (*Prof. Cunningham*)
1930 Strike Up the Band (*Col. Holmes*)
1931 Cochran's 1931 Revue (L)
Here Goes the Bride (*Hives*)
1932 Walk a Little Faster
1934 Thumbs Up!
1936 Ziegfeld Follies
1939 The Streets of Paris
1942 Star and Garter

1944 Mexican Hayride (*Joe Bascom*)
1947 Sweethearts (*Mikel Mikeloviz*)
1948 As the Girls Go (*Waldo Wellington*)
1950 Michael Todd's Peep Show (dir. only)
1956 Damn Yankees (US tour) (*Mr. Applegate*)

Clayton, (Jane Byral) Jan, actress, singer; b. Alamogordo, N. Mex., Aug. 26, 1917. Slim blonde actress who introduced "If I Loved You" and "What's the Use of Wond'rin'?" in *Carousel*. Has appeared on tv in *Lassie* series.

1945 Carousel (*Julie Jordan*)
1946 Show Boat (r) (*Magnolia Hawks*)
1951 Guys and Dolls (US tour) (*Sarah Brown*)
1972 Follies (*Christine Crane*, repl.)

Cliff, Laddie (née Clifford Albyn Perry), actor, producer, director, choreographer; b. Bristol, Eng., Sept. 3, 1891; d. Montana, Switzerland, Dec. 8, 1937. Bespectacled London comic who began career in US vaudeville (1907–1917). As producer, Cliff was associated with actor Stanley Lupino in five musicals between 1928 and 1936.

Asterisk indicates Mr. Cliff was also producer:
1911 Folies Bergère (NY)
1917 The Bing Girls Are There
1919 His Little Widows (*Peter Lloyd*)
1920 Wild Geese (chor. only)
     Jig-Saw
1921 Pins and Needles (chor. only)
     The Co-Optimists
     Fantasia (sk. only)
1923 Katinka (*Thaddeus T. Hopper*, repl.)
     Brighter London (repl.)
1924 Leap Year
     The Co-Optimists
     Primrose (chor. only)
1925 Dear Little Billie (*Sir Frederick Fotheringay*) (also dir.)
1926 Tip-Toes (*Al Kaye*)

1927 Lady Luck * (*Biff Morton*)
     Shake Your Feet (prod. only)
     The Bow-Wows (prod. only)
1928 The Yellow Mask (prod. only)
     So This Is Love * (*Hap. J. Haggard*)
1929 Love Lies * (*Rolly Ryder*)
     The Co-Optimists (also dir.)
1930 Darling! I Love You (prod., dir. only)
     Frederica (prod. only)
     The Love Race * (*Bobby Mostyne*)
1931 Red Roses (prod. only)
     The Millionaire Kid * (*Albert Skinner*) (also dir.)
1932 Rhyme and Rhythm * (also dir.)
1934 Sporting Love * (*Peter Brace*) (also chor.)
1935 Love Laughs—! (*Gus Burns*)
1936 Over She Goes * (*Billy Bowler*) (also chor.)
1937 Crazy Days (prod. only)

"Climb Ev'ry Mountain." Music by Richard Rodgers; lyric by Oscar Hammerstein II. Mother Abbess Patricia Neway sang this song of inspiration to Postulant Mary Martin as she was about to leave Nonnberg Abbey in *The Sound of Music* (NY 1959). The song was also reprised by Miss Neway and nuns at play's end as the Trapp family began their climb over the mountains to Switzerland. In London production (1961) it was sung by Constance Shacklock to Jean Bayless.

"Close as Pages in a Book." Music by Sigmund Romberg; lyric by Dorothy Fields. Romantic propinquity expressed in *Up in Central Park* (NY 1945) by Maureen Cannon and Wilbur Evans.

Coca, Imogene (Fernandez y), actress; b. Philadelphia, Pa., Nov. 18, 1908. Wide-eyed, elfin comedienne who scored first Bway hit in Leonard Sillman's *New Faces*. Has appeared in dramas and on tv, most successfully in Sid Caesar programs.

1925 When You Smile (dancer)
1926 Bunk of 1926
1930 The Garrick Gaieties
1931 Shoot the Works!
1932 Flying Colors
1934 New Faces
     Fools Rush In
1936 New Faces of 1936
1938 Who's Who
1939 The Straw Hat Revue
1940 All in Fun
1978 On the 20th Century (*Letitia*)

Cochran, Charles B(lake), producer; b. Sussex, Eng., Sept. 25, 1872; d. London, Jan. 31, 1951. Knighted 1948. Known as Britain's Greatest Showman, Cochran was the most prolific London producer of the 20s and 30s, sponsoring, in addition to revues and book musicals, such diverse entertainments as dramas, Wild West shows, ballets, and prizefights. He produced five musicals by Noël Coward (*On with the Dance, This Year of Grace!, Bitter Sweet, Words and Music, Conversation Piece*), two by Rodgers and Hart (*One Dam Thing After Another, Ever Green*), two by Cole Porter (*Wake Up and Dream!, Nymph Errant*). Cochran's productions were opulent and inventive, and famed for the beauty of the chorus girls, known as "Mr. Cochran's Young Ladies." Alice Delysia was in 11 of his shows, Evelyn Laye in six, Binnie Hale and Jessie Matthews in three each, Peggy Wood and Beatrice Lillie in two each. Bib: *Secrets of a Showman* (Heinemann, L 1925), *I Had Almost Forgotten* (Hutchinson, L 1932), *Cock-a-Doodle-Doo* (Dent, L 1941), *Showman Looks On* (Dent, L 1945), all by Cochran; *The Cochran Story* by Charles Graves (Allen, L 1951); *"Cockie"* by Sam Heppner (Frewin, L 1969).

1914 Odds and Ends
1915 More
1916 Half-Past Eight
     Pell-Mell
     Houp-La!
1917 150 Pound Revue
     The Better 'Ole
     Carminetta
1918 As You Were
     Jolly Jack Tar
1919 Afgar
     Maggie
1920 Pretty Peggy
     Cherry
     London, Paris and New York
1921 League of Notions
     The Fun of the Fayre
1922 Mayfair and Montmartre
     Chuckles of 1922
     Phi-Phi
1923 Music Box Revue
     Dover Street to Dixie
     Little Nellie Kelly
1925 On with the Dance
     Still Dancing!
1926 Turned Up
     Cochran's Revue of 1926
     Blackbirds
1927 One Dam Thing After Another
     Castles in the Air
1928 This Year of Grace!
1929 Wake Up and Dream!
     Bitter Sweet
1930 Cochran's 1930 Revue
     Ever Green
1931 Cochran's 1931 Revue
1932 Helen!
     The Cat and the Fiddle
     Words and Music
1933 Mother of Pearl
     Music in the Air
     Nymph Errant
1934 Conversation Piece
     Streamline
1935 Anything Goes
1936 Follow the Sun
     Blackbirds of 1936
1937 Home and Beauty
     Paganini
1938 Happy Returns
1940 Lights Up
1942 Big Top
1946 Big Ben
1947 Bless the Bride
1949 Tough at the Top

"**Cockeyed Optimist, A.**" Music by Richard Rodgers; lyric by Oscar Hammerstein II. Mary Martin, as the immature and incurably green Nellie Forbush of *South Pacific* (NY 1949, L 1951), expresses the philosophy of one who's "stuck like a dope with a thing called hope."

"**Cocoanut Sweet.**" Music by Harold Arlen; lyric by E. Y. Harburg. Evocative lullaby introduced by Adelaide Hall and Lena Horne in *Jamaica* (NY 1957).

Cohan, George M(ichael), actor, composer, lyricist, librettist, director, producer; b. Providence, RI, July 4, 1878; d. New York, Nov. 5, 1942. Bway's most multiply talented theatre man was the embodiment of American aggression, brashness, vigor, and naivité at the beginning of the century. His shows were fast-paced, colloquial, and flag-waving, giving him ample opportunity to display his gifts as actor, dancer, and talk-singer. Cohan began in vaudeville, in act The Four Cohans, with parents Jerry and Nellie and sister Josie. In addition to writing, acting, and directing, he was also a producer, initially in partnership with Sam H. Harris (1904–1920).

Among Cohan's songs: "The Yankee Doodle Boy," "Give My Regards to Broadway" (*Little Johnny Jones*); "Mary's a Grand Old Name," "So Long, Mary," "Forty-Five Minutes from Broadway" (*Forty-Five Minutes from Broadway*); "You're a Grand Old Flag," "I Was Born in Virginia" (*George Washington, Jr.*); "Harrigan" (*Fifty Miles from Boston*); "The Man Who Owns Broadway" (*The Man Who Owns Broadway*); "Nellie Kelly, I Love You" (*Little Nellie Kelly*); "Billie" (*Billie*). In addition to musicals, Cohan wrote 20 nonmusical plays (incl. *Seven Keys to Baldpate, The Tavern*), many of which he acted in himself. The only productions in which he appeared that he did not write were O'Neill's *Ah, Wilderness!* and the musical *I'd Rather Be Right*. Cohan's first of two wives was singer Ethel Levey. He was the subject of the 1968 Bway musical *George M!*
Bib: *Twenty Years on Broadway* by Cohan (Harper, NY 1925); *George M. Cohan: Prince of the American Theatre* by Ward Morehouse (Lippincott, Phila. 1943); *George M. Cohan; The Man Who Owned Broadway* by John McCabe (Doubleday, NY 1973).

Unless otherwise noted, Mr. Cohan was composer-lyricist-librettist of following; asterisk indicates Cohan and Harris production directed by Mr. Cohan:

1901	The Governor's Son (also *Algy Wheelock*)
1903	Running for Office (also *Augie Wright*)
1904	Little Johnny Jones (also *Johnny Jones, dir.*)
1906	Forty-Five Minutes from Broadway (also dir.)
	George Washington, Jr. (also *George Belgrave, dir.*)
1907	The Honeymooners * (Running for Office) (also *Augie Wright*)
	The Talk of New York*
1908	Fifty Miles from Boston*
	The Yankee Prince* (also *Percy Springer*)
	The American Idea*
1909	The Man Who Owns Broadway*
1911	The Little Millionaire * (also *Robert Spencer*)
	The Red Widow (co-prod. only)
1912	Forty-Five Minutes from Broadway * (r) (also *Kid Burns*)
1914	The Beauty Shop (co-prod. only)
	Hello, Broadway! * (also actor)
1916	The Cohan Revue*
1917	Going Up (co-prod. only)
	The Cohan Revue*
1918	The Voice of McConnell*
1919	The Royal Vagabond*
1920	Mary (co-dir., prod. only)
1921	The O'Brien Girl (prod. only)
1922	Little Nellie Kelly (also prod.)

1923	The Rise of Rosie O'Reilly (also dir., prod.)
1927	The Merry Malones (also *John Malone*, prod.)
1928	Billie (also prod.)
1937	I'd Rather Be Right (*Franklin D. Roosevelt* only)

Cohen, Alexander H., producer; b. New York, July 24, 1920. Began Bway career as co-producer of *Angel Street* (1941), and has since produced over 50 attractions, incl. musicals, dramas, and appearances by Nichols and May, Yves Montand, Maurice Chevalier, Marlene Dietrich, Victor Borge, Flanders and Swann.

1942	Of V We Sing
1951	Make a Wish
	Courtin' Time
1965	Baker Street
1966	A Time for Singing
1969	Dear World
1970	1776 (L)
1972	Applause (L)
1979	I Remember Mama

Cole, Jack, choreographer, director, dancer; b. New Brunswick, NJ, April 27, 1914; d. Los Angeles, Cal., Feb. 16, 1974. Cole began as dancer with the Denishawn company, then formed own group specializing in dances of the orient. As Bway choreographer, he developed jazz-influenced style and trained Gwen Verdon (his assistant for seven years) and Carol Haney. His most notable work was for *Kismet* and *Man of La Mancha.*

Unless otherwise noted, Mr. Cole was choreographer of following:

1934	Caviar (dancer only)
	Thumbs Up! (dancer only)
1935	May Wine (dancer only)
1942	Something for the Boys
1943	Ziegfeld Follies (also dancer)
1944	Allah Be Praised!
1948	Magdalena
1950	Alive and Kicking (also dancer)
1953	Kismet
1955	Kismet (L)
1957	Jamaica

1959	Candide (L)
1961	Donnybrook (also dir.)
	Kean (also dir.)
1962	A Funny Thing Happened on the Way to the Forum
1964	Foxy
1965	Man of La Mancha

Coleman, Cy, composer; b. New York, June 14, 1929. Coleman is a classically trained, jazz-influenced Bway composer who has also had a career as supper-club pianist. With lyricist Carolyn Leigh he wrote "Hey, Look Me Over" (*Wildcat*), "Real Live Girl" and "I've Got Your Number" (both for *Little Me*); with lyricist Dorothy Fields, "Big Spender," "If My Friends Could See Me Now," and "Where Am I Going?" (all for *Sweet Charity*).

1960	Wildcat (Leigh)
1962	Little Me (Leigh)
1966	Sweet Charity (Fields)
1973	Seesaw (Fields)

Collins, José, actress, singer; b. London, May 23, 1887; d. London, Dec. 6, 1958. Raven-haired, tempestuous singing actress who won success in Bway musicals (1911–1915), then returned to London to be acclaimed as *The Maid of the Mountains* (in which she sang "Love Will Find a Way"). Miss Collins was the daughter of music-hall singer Lottie Collins, and stepdaughter of composer James W. Tate. Bib: *The Maid of the Mountains* by Miss Collins (1932).

1908	The Antelope (*Iris Fenton*)
1911	Vera Violetta (NY) (*Vera Violetta*)
1912	The Whirl of Society (NY)
	The Merry Countess (NY)
	(*Countess Rosalinde Cliquot*)
1913	Ziegfeld Follies (NY)
1914	The Passing Show (NY)
	Suzi (NY) (*Suzi*)
1915	Alone at Last (NY) (*Tilly Dachau*)
1916	The Happy Day (*Camille*)
1917	The Maid of the Mountains (*Theresa*)

1920 The Southern Maid (*Dolores*)
1921 Sybil (*Sybil*)
1922 The Last Waltz (*Countess Vera Lisaveta*)
1923 Catherine (*Catherine*)
1924 Our Nell (*Nell Gwynne*)
1925 Frasquita (*Frasquita*)
1927 Whitebirds

Comden, Betty, lyricist, librettist; b. New York, May 3, 1915. Miss Comden and her partner, Adolph Green, have been together longer than any writing team in the history of the Bway musical theatre. Their librettos and/or lyrics have shown special affinity for the varied faces of New York, particularly in such musicals as *On the Town* ("New York, New York," "Lucky to Be Me"), *Wonderful Town* ("Ohio," "A Quiet Girl," "It's Love"), *Bells Are Ringing* ("Just in Time," "The Party's Over"), *Do Re Mi* ("Make Someone Happy"), *Subways Are for Sleeping* ("Comes Once in a Lifetime"), *Applause*. Their most frequent composer collaborator has been Jule Styne, with whom they wrote eight scores plus additional songs for *Lorelei*. Others: Leonard Bernstein and Morton Gould. Bert Lahr, Dolores Gray, Rosalind Russell, Mary Martin, Cyril Ritchard, Judy Holliday, Phil Silvers, Carol Burnett, Lauren Bacall have appeared in Comden and Green musicals. The team has also written film scripts incl. *Singin' in the Rain*.

Unless otherwise noted, Comden and Green wrote librettos and lyrics for following:

1944 On the Town (Bernstein) (also *Claire de Loon*)
1945 Billion Dollar Baby (Gould)
1951 Two on the Aisle (Styne)
1953 Wonderful Town (lyr. only) (Bernstein)
1954 Peter Pan (lyr. only) (Styne)
1956 Bells Are Ringing (Styne)
1958 Say, Darling (lyr. only) (Styne)
1960 Do Re Mi (lyr. only) (Styne)
1961 Subways Are for Sleeping (Styne)
1964 Fade Out—Fade In (Styne)
1967 Hallelujah, Baby! (lyr. only) (Styne)
1970 Applause (lib. only)
1978 On the 20th Century (Coleman)

"Come Back to Me." Music by Burton Lane; lyric by Alan Jay Lerner. John Cullum's urgent plea to Barbara Harris in *On a Clear Day You Can See Forever* (NY 1965).

"Come Down, Ma Evenin' Star." Music by John Stromberg; lyric by Robert B. Smith. Sung by Lillian Russell in *Twirly Whirly* (NY 1902), a Weber and Fields burlesque. Though the song became one of Miss Russell's most successful numbers, composer Stromberg, fearing that the singer's voice was unsuitable, refused to let her have the music and planned to write a different melody for her. It was only after Stromberg's death four days before rehearsals that the manuscript was discovered in his house.

"Come Rain or Come Shine." Music by Harold Arlen; lyric by Johnny Mercer. Love duet in *St. Louis Woman* (NY 1946), sung by Ruby Hill and Harold Nicholas as the opening number in Act II. Upon hearing the melody for the first time, lyricist Mercer quickly came up with an opening line, "I'm gonna love you, like nobody's loved you," to which composer Arlen added jokingly, "Come hell or high water." Mercer promptly changed that to "Come rain or come shine," and the rest of it followed easily.

"Come to Me, Bend to Me." Music by Frederick Loewe; lyric by Alan Jay Lerner. Lee Sullivan's tenderly affectionate song to his bride-to-be in *Brigadoon* (NY 1947). Bill O'Connor sang it in London version (1949).

"**Come to the Ball.**" Music by Lionel Monckton; lyric by Adrian Ross. Sung by George Carvey, as Prince Carlo, in *The Quaker Girl* (London 1910), as an invitation to the play's heroine, Gertie Millar. In NY production (1911) it was sung by Lawrence Rea.

"**Comedy Tonight.**" Music & lyric by Stephen Sondheim. The opening number of *A Funny Thing Happened on the Way to the Forum*, sung by Zero Mostel and company (NY 1962) and Frankie Howerd and company (L 1963). Originally, Mostel, as Prologus, and the Proteans opened the show with an airy soft shoe called "Love Is in the Air," but during the Washington tryout Jerome Robbins, who had been called in to help in the direction, objected because it didn't tell the audience what the show was about. Sondheim wanted to substitute "Invocation," which he had written before rehearsals, but "Comedy Tonight" was even more effective in setting the raucous tone of the evening. The song is generally credited as the single most important factor in assuring the musical's success. Sondheim once admitted to composer Harold Arlen that the song's melody had been "inspired" by Arlen's "Cakewalk Your Lady" from *St. Louis Woman*. Arlen, however, confessed that he had never noticed the similarity.

"**Comes Love.**" Music by Sammy Stept; lyric by Lew Brown & Charles Tobias. The incurability of love, first propounded by Judy Canova in *Yokel Boy* (NY 1939), in which it was danced by Dixie Dunbar.

"**Comes Once in a Lifetime.**" Music by Jule Styne; lyric by Betty Comden & Adolph Green. Lilting advice to live each day to the limit, offered by Carol Lawrence and Sydney Chaplin in *Subways Are for Sleeping* (NY 1961).

Company (1970). Music & lyrics by Stephen Sondheim; book by George Furth.

SONGS: "Company," "The Little Things You Do Together," "You Could Drive a Person Crazy," "Someone Is Waiting," "Another Hundred People," "Getting Married Today," "What Would We Do Without You?," "Barcelona," "The Ladies Who Lunch," "Being Alive."

NEW YORK: April 26, 1970
ALVIN THEATRE; 705 p.

Presented by Harold Prince, with Ruth Mitchell; directed by Prince; choreographed by Michael Bennett; settings, Boris Aronson; costumes, D. D. Ryan; lighting, Robert Ornbo; music director, Harold Hastings; orchestrations, Jonathan Tunick.

CAST: Dean Jones (*Robert*), Elaine Stritch (*Joanne*), Barbara Barrie (*Sarah*), George Coe (*David*), John Cunningham (*Peter*), Teri Ralston (*Jenny*), Charles Kimbrough (*Harry*), Donna McKechnie (*Kathy*), Charles Braswell (*Larry*), Susan Browning (*April*), Steve Elmore (*Paul*), Beth Howland (*Amy*), Pamela Myers (*Marta*), Merle Louise (*Susan*).

LONDON: Jan. 8, 1972
HER MAJESTY'S THEATRE; 344 p.

Presented by Harold Prince & Richard Pilbrow, with Ruth Mitchell; directed by Prince; choreographed by Michael Bennett; settings, Boris Aronson; costumes, D. D. Ryan; lighting, Robert Ornbo; music director, Gareth Davies; orchestrations, Jonathan Tunick.

CAST: Larry Kert (*Robert*), Elaine Stritch (*Joanne*), Marti Stevens (*Sarah*), Lee Goodman (*David*), J. T. Cromwell (*Peter*), Teri Ralston (*Jenny*), Kenneth Kimmins (*Harry*),

Donna McKechnie (*Kathy*), Robert Goss (*Larry*), Carol Richards (*April*), Steve Elmore (*Paul*), Beth Howland (*Amy*), Annie McGreevey (*Marta*), Joy Franz (*Susan*).

Though the story was originally written as a play without songs, *Company* developed into a tightly coordinated "conceptual" musical, utilizing music and dance not only as part of the action but also to comment on the situations and characters. It was particularly applauded for the way director Prince and composer-lyricist Sondheim fused their talents to achieve a seemingly seamless production that was almost as much a revue with a theme as it was a book musical. That theme was marriage, focusing on the relationship between five married couples and a bachelor named Robert whom they dote upon and want to see end his bachelor life. At the end he's ready to do it. In a larger sense, the musical also dealt with social mores as they affect an affluent segment of New Yorkers. To help achieve the desired stylized effect, *Company* made use of skeletal sets, elevators, stairways, and projections.

During Bway run, Dean Jones (in a role originally intended for Anthony Perkins) was succeeded by Larry Kert (5-70), Gary Krawford (12-71); Elaine Stritch by Jane Russell (5-71), Vivian Blaine (11-71). The US tour, which ran for a year, opened in May 1971, with Robert played by George Chakiris (then Allen Case, Gary Krawford), Joanne by Miss Stritch (then Julie Wilson), Sarah by Marti Stevens. In London, Kert was succeeded by Eric Flynn (7-72), Miss Stritch by Marti Stevens (7-72).

"Company Way, The." Music & lyric by Frank Loesser. The importance of conformity and servility in the world of big business. Lustily expounded by Sammy Smith and Robert Morse in *How to Succeed in Business Without Really Trying* (NY 1961), and by Bernard Spear and Warren Berlinger in London company (1963).

Comstock, F. Ray, producer; b. Buffalo, NY, 1880; d. Boston, Mass., Oct. 15, 1949. Comstock is best remembered for co-sponsoring a series of influential intimate musicals at the Princess Theatre, NY, that introduced the trio of Guy Bolton, P. G. Wodehouse and Jerome Kern.

Asterisk indicates Princess Theatre production:

1908	Bandanna Land
1909	Mr. Lode of Koal
1915	Nobody Home*
	Very Good Eddie *
1916	Go to It*
1917	Oh, Boy!*
	Leave It to Jane
	Chu Chin Chow
	Kitty Darlin'
1918	Oh, Lady! Lady!!*
	The Maid of the Mountains
	Oh, My Dear!*
1920	Mecca

Connecticut Yankee, A (1927). Music by Richard Rodgers; lyrics by Lorenz Hart; book by Herbert Fields, based on Mark Twain's novel *A Connecticut Yankee in King Arthur's Court.*

SONGS: "My Heart Stood Still," "Thou Swell," "On a Desert Island with Thee," "Someone Should Tell Them," "I Feel at Home with You," "Can't You Do a Friend a Favor?" (added 1943), "To Keep My Love Alive" (added 1943).

NEW YORK: Nov. 3, 1927
VANDERBILT THEATRE; 418 p.

Presented by Lew Fields & Lyle D. Andrews; directed by Alexander Leftwich; choreographed by Busby Berkeley; settings & costumes, John Hawkins Jr.; music director, Roy Webb.

CAST: William Gaxton (*Martin*), Constance Carpenter (*Alice Carter*), Nana Bryant (*Fay Morgan*), William Norris (*Merlin*), Jack Thompson (*Gerald Lake*), June Cochrane (*Evelyn*), Paul Everton (*Arthur Pendragos*).

LONDON: Oct. 10, 1929
DALY'S THEATRE; 43 p.
Presented by British Amalgamated Theatres Ltd.; directed by David Miller; choreographed by Fred Leslie & Charles Brooks; settings, F. L. Lyndhurst: retitled *A Yankee at the Court of King Arthur.*
CAST: Harry Fox (*Martin*), Constance Carpenter (*Alice Carter*), Norah Robinson (*Fay Morgan*), J. G. Taylor (*Merlin*), Billy Holland (*Gerald Lake*), Gladys Cruickshank (*Evelyn*), Sam Livesey (*Arthur Pendragos*).

NEW YORK: Nov. 17, 1943
MARTIN BECK THEATRE; 135 p.
Presented by Richard Rodgers; directed by John C. Wilson; choreographed by William Holbrook & Al White Jr.; settings & costumes, Nat Karson; lighting, Peggy Clark; music director, George Hirst; orchestrations, Don Walker.
CAST: Dick Foran (*Lt. Martin Barrett*), Vivienne Segal (*Lt. Fay Merrill*), Julie Warren (*Corp. Alice Courtleigh*), Chester Stratton (*Ens. Gerald Lake*), Robert Chisholm (*Adm. Arthur K. Arthur*).
Though it took Rodgers, Hart and Fields over five years to get permission from the Mark Twain estate to turn the novel into a musical comedy, the wait was apparently worth it since the show became the trio's biggest hit of the 20s. The story told in flashback how, on the eve of his wedding in Hartford, Conn., Martin gets bopped on the head by his fiancée and dreams he is back in the days of King Arthur. At first suspected as an outsider, he soon wins the confidence of the king by industrializing the country. The dream also made Martin realize he is engaged to the wrong girl and he straightens things out when he wakes up. The 1943 version, which retained five songs and added six new ones, made the present-day scenes conform to the current wartime situation by putting all the characters in the armed forces. The revival, remembered primarily for Vivienne Segal singing "To Keep My Love Alive," was Lorenz Hart's final work for the theatre. He died five days after the opening.

Connolly, (Robert) Bobby, choreographer, director; b. 1895; d. Encino, Cal., Feb. 29, 1944. Connolly staged dances for seven musicals produced by Schwab and Mandel, three by Aarons and Freedley, three by Ziegfeld.

Asterisk indicates Mr. Connolly was also director:

1920	Hitchy-Koo (dancer only)
1926	Kitty's Kisses
	Honeymoon Lane
	The Desert Song
1927	Judy
	Good News!
	Funny Face
1928	The New Moon
	Treasure Girl
1929	Follow Thru
	Spring Is Here
	Show Girl
	Sons o' Guns *
1930	Flying High
	Princess Charming *
1931	America's Sweetheart
	Ziegfeld Follies
	Free for All
	East Wind
1932	Hot-Cha!
	Ballyhoo of 1932 *
	Take a Chance
1933	Melody
1934	Ziegfeld Follies *

"Consider Yourself." Music & lyric by Lionel Bart. Oliver Twist's rollicking introduction to the world of Fagin and his gang of youthful pickpockets in *Oliver!* Martin Horsey and Keith Hamshere led the singing in London (1960); David Jones and Bruce Prochnik did it in NY (1963).

Conversation Piece (1934). Music, lyrics & book by Noël Coward.
SONGS: "I'll Follow My Secret Heart," "Regency Rakes," "Charming, Charming," "Dear Little Soldiers," "English Lesson," "There's Always Something Fishy About the French," "Nevermore."

LONDON: Feb. 16, 1934
HIS MAJESTY'S THEATRE; 177 p.
Presented by Charles B. Cochran; directed by Noël Coward; settings & costumes, G. E. Calthrop; music director, Reginald Burston; orchestrations, Charles Prentice.
CAST: Yvonne Printemps (*Melanie*), Noël Coward (*Paul, Duc de Chaucigny-Varennes*), Irene Browne (*Lady Julia Charteris*), Athole Stewart (*Duke of Beneden*), Louis Hayward (*Marquis of Sheere*), Heather Thatcher (*Sophie Otford*), Moya Nugent (*Martha James*), George Sanders (*Earl of Harringford*).

NEW YORK: Oct. 23, 1934
44TH ST. THEATRE; 55 p.
Presented by Arch Selwyn & Harold Franklin, with Charles B. Cochran; directed by Noël Coward; settings & costumes, G. E. Calthrop; music director, Victor Baravalle; orchestrations, Charles Prentice.
CAST: Yvonne Printemps (*Melanie*), Pierre Fresnay (*Paul, duc de Chaucigny-Varennes*), Irene Browne (*Lady Julia Charteris*), Athole Stewart (*Duke of Beneden*), Carl Harbord (*Marquis of Sheere*), Sylvia Leslie (*Sophie Otford*), Moya Nugent (*Martha James*), George Sanders (*Earl of Harringford*).

For his second costume operetta (the first was *Bitter Sweet*), Coward created a story and score specifically for the talents of Yvonne Printemps. Set in Regency England, the stylish tale concerned a down-at-the-heels French nobleman who accompanies his ward, Melanie, to Brighton with the aim of getting her a rich husband. They find one but ultimately also find they are in love with each other. Pierre Fresnay, who inherited Coward's role in NY, substituted for Coward during London engagement.

Cook, Barbara (Nell), actress, singer; b. Atlanta, Ga., Oct. 25, 1927. Blonde, doll-faced Bway leading lady whose lyric soprano introduced "Glitter and Be Gay" in *Candide*, "Till There Was You" and "Goodnight, My Someone" in *The Music Man*, "Magic Moment" in *The Gay Life*, "Ice Cream" in *She Loves Me*. In the 70s Miss Cook became a concert and nightclub singer.
1951   Flahooley (*Sandy*)
1953   Oklahoma! (US tour) (*Ado Annie, repl.*)
1955   Plain and Fancy (*Hilda Miller*)
1956   Candide (*Cunegonde*)
1957   The Music Man (*Marian Paroo*)
1961   The Gay Life (*Liesl Brandel*)
1963   She Loves Me (*Amalia Balash*)
1964   Something More! (*Carol Deems*)
1971   The Grass Harp (*Dolly Talbo*)

Cook, Joe (né Joseph Lopez), actor; b. Evansville, Ind., 1890; d. Clinton Hollow, NY, May 16, 1959. Widemouthed, innocent-looking clown, famed for his juggling, his "Rube Goldberg" inventions, and his routine called "The Four Hawaiians." After joining a traveling show at 12, Cook began his vaudeville career in 1907. His two biggest Bway successes were *Rain or Shine* and *Fine and Dandy* (in which he introduced the title song).
1919   Hitchy-Koo

1923 Earl Carroll Vanities
1924 Earl Carroll Vanities
1925 Earl Carroll Vanities (added)
1928 Rain or Shine (*Smiling Johnson*)
1930 Fine and Dandy (*Joe Squibb*)
1932 Fanfare (L)
1933 Hold Your Horses (*Broadway Joe*)

Co-Optimists, The (1921). Music & lyrics by Melville Gideon, etc.; sketches by the company.

SONGS: "When the Sun Goes Down," "Coal Black Mammy," "If Winter Comes," "Tampa Bay," "Down Love Lane."

LONDON: June 27, 1921
ROYALTY THEATRE; 500 p.

Presented by Archibald De Bear; directed by Laddie Cliff; settings, Hugh Willoughby; music director, Melville Gideon.

CAST: Davy Burnaby, Phyllis Monkman, Melville Gideon, Laddie Cliff, Stanley Holloway, Gilbert Childs, H. B. Hedley, Betty Chester, Babs Valerie, Elsa Macfarlane.

The most successful revue series on the London stage was an informal, inexpensive (the first production cost £950) show that grew out of British seaside resort concert parties. Billed as "A Pierrotic Entertainment," the cast of 10 wore purple and gold Pierrot and Pierrette costumes, used few props, and soon became a national institution. The originators of the first production were Stanley Holloway, Davy Burnaby, Laddie Cliff, and Archibald De Bear, who conceived of a show in which all the members of the cast would have musical specialties and engage in satirical, clownish sketches.

None of the subsequent five annual productions had runs equaling the first, but all were successful. In 1922, *The Co-Optimists* played the Prince of Wales Theatre and lasted 232 per-formances; in 1923 it lasted 210. The following year it played the Palace for 207 performances; in 1925 His Majesty's Theatre for 203, the next year for 216. Though the casts were basically the same, replacements through the years included Austin Melford, Hermione Baddeley, Mary Leigh, and Doris Bentley. Gideon, Holloway, Burnaby, and Childs were in all six editions.

After an absence of three years, *The Co-Optimists* returned at the Vaudeville Theatre and remained 133 performances. The cast included Holloway, Monkman, Gideon, Burnaby, Chester, and Macfarlane, plus newcomers Sydney Howard and Charles Collins. In 1930, with Arthur Schwartz music and Leslie Henson directing, it had a brief run at the London Hippodrome. For this edition, Cyril Ritchard, Mimi Crawford, Elsie Randolph, and Herbert Mundin joined Burnaby, Holloway, and Monkman. The last edition—and the least successful—was presented in 1935 at the Palace. In addition to Burnaby, the cast included Marriott Edgar, Ivy Tresmand, and Harry Milton.

In 1928 a Bway version of the revue, called *The Optimists*, opened at the Casino de Paris. Gideon, the only member of the original company in it, was joined by Luella Gear, Eleanor Powell, George Hassell, Bobby Watson, and Flora Le Breton. It lasted 24 performances.

FILM VERSION: Laddie Cliff, Melville Gideon, Phyllis Monkman, Davy Burnaby, Stanley Holloway (New Era 1930, Edwin Greenwood dir.).

Coots, J(ohn) Fred, composer; b. Brooklyn, NY, May 2, 1897. Coots's biggest Bway hits were *Sally, Irene and Mary* and *Sons o' Guns* ("Why?"). His lyric-writing collaborators: Raymond Klages, Clifford Grey, Sam Coslow, McElbert Moore, Al Dubin, Benny Davis, Arthur Swanstrom. He also wrote with composer Maurie Rubens.

1922 Sally, Irene and Mary (Klages)
1924 Artists and Models (Grey, Coslow)
1925 Artists and Models (Grey)
June Days (Grey)
Gay Paree (Grey)
1926 The Merry World (Grey)
A Night in Paris (Grey, Moore-Rubens)
1927 White Lights (Dubin)
1929 Sons o' Guns (Davis, Swanstrom)

"Corner of the Sky." Music & lyric by Stephen Schwartz. Youth's determination to find meaning in his life sung in *Pippin* by John Rubinstein (NY 1972) and by Paul Jones (L 1973).

Courtneidge, (Esmerelda) Cicely, actress, singer; b. Sydney, Australia, April 1, 1893. Dame British Empire 1972. Though they had appeared together on the London musical stage as early as 1913, the elegantly knockabout comedienne Cicely Courtneidge and her husband, Jack Hulbert, did not become a team until 1923. Since then, with only two exceptions, Hulbert directed all of Miss Courtneidge's musicals (incl. *Under the Counter, Gay's the Word*) and appeared with her in nine (incl. *By the Way, Clowns in Clover, Under Your Hat*). Among songs the actress introduced: "The King's Horses" in *Folly to Be Wise* and "Vitality" in *Gay's the Word*. She and her husband acted in many British films in the 30s. Miss Courtneidge is the daughter of producer Robert Courtneidge. Bib: *Cicely* by Miss Courtneidge (Hutchinson, L 1953).

Asterisk indicates appearance with Mr. Hulbert:
1909 The Arcadians (*Chrysea; Eileen Cavanagh,* repl.)

1911 The Mousmé (*Miyo Ko San*)
1912 Princess Caprice (*Princess Clementine*)
1913 The Pearl Girl * (*Lady Betty Biddulph*)
1914 The Cinema Star * (*Phyllis*)
1915 The Arcadians *(r) (*Eileen Cavanagh*)
1916 The Light Blues * (*Cynthia Petrie*)
1921 Ring Up *
1923 The Little Revue Starts at 9 *
1925 By the Way *
By the Way * (NY)
1926 Lido Lady * (*Peggy Bassett*)
1927 Clowns in Clover *
1929 The House That Jack Built *
1931 Folly to Be Wise
1937 Hide and Seek (*Sally*)
1938 Under Your Hat * (*Kay Porter*)
1942 Full Swing * (*Kay Porter*)
1943 Something in the Air * (*Terry Potter*)
1945 Under the Counter (*Jo Fox*)
1947 Under the Counter (NY) (*Jo Fox*)
1949 Her Excellency (*Lady Frances Maxwell*)
1951 Gay's the Word (*Gay Daventry*)
1953 Over the Moon
1964 High Spirits (*Mme. Arcati*)

Courtneidge, Robert, producer, director, librettist; b. Glasgow, Scotland, June 29, 1859; d. Brighton, Eng., April 6, 1939. Courtneidge was a dramatic actor before turning to production and direction. He was the father of Cicely Courtneidge (who appeared in seven of her father's London musicals, incl. his biggest hit, *The Arcadians*) and the father-in-law of Jack Hulbert (who was in three). Bib: *I Was an Actor Once* by Courtneidge (Hutchinson, L 1930).

Unless otherwise noted, Mr. Courtneidge was producer-director of following:
1903 The Duchess of Dantzic (dir. only)
1905 The Blue Moon
The Babes and the Baron (NY) (co-lib. only)

1906   The Dairymaids (also co-lib.)
1907   Tom Jones (also co-lib.)
1909   The Arcadians (also co-lib.)
1911   The Mousmé (also co-lib.)
1912   Princess Caprice (prod. only)
1913   Oh! Oh!! Delphine!!!
       The Pearl Girl
1914   The Cinema Star
1916   My Lady Frayle
       The Light Blues
       Young England
1917   The Boy (dir. only)
1927   The Blue Mazurka
1930   The Damask Rose (also co-lib.)

Coward, Noël (Pierce), composer, lyricist, librettist, actor, director; b. Teddington, Eng., Dec. 16, 1899; d. Jamaica, BWI, March 26, 1973. Knighted 1970. Coward was the most successful multitalented writer in British theatre history. In the musical theatre field, he was a distinctive creator of smart, satrical revues and musical comedies (*London Calling!*, *This Year of Grace!*, *Words and Music*) as well as sentimental, stylized operettas (*Bitter Sweet*, *Conversation Piece*). In all, he was responsible for 25 non-musical plays (incl. *The Vortex*, *Hay Fever*, *Private Lives*, *Cavalcade*, *Design for Living*, *Blithe Spirit*), plus a collection of nine one-act plays, *Tonight at 8:30*, which included three musicals (*Red Peppers*, *Shadow Play*, *Family Album*). Coward, who began as a child actor in 1911, appeared in many of these productions himself. He also acted in and wrote for films (incl. *In Which We Serve*), sang in nightclubs, and made records of his own compositions.

Coward's songs are notable for their urbanity and lapidary wit, yet some of his most enduring pieces are strongly emotional and melodic. Among his best known: "Parisian Pierrot," "Poor Little Rich Girl," "A Room with a View," "Dance Little Lady," "I'll See You Again," "Zigeuner," "If Love Were All," "Mad Dogs and Englishmen," "Mad About the Boy," "The Party's Over Now," "I'll Follow My Secret Heart," "Has Anybody Seen Our Ship?," "Dearest Love," "The Stately Homes of England," "I Went to a Marvellous Party," "London Pride," "Matelot," "Sail Away," "Why Do the Wrong People Travel?" Coward appeared in three productions with Gertrude Lawrence, one with Beatrice Lillie. His songs have also been introduced by Jessie Matthews, Alice Delysia, Peggy Wood, Evelyn Laye, Mary Martin, Yvonne Printemps.

Bib: *The Amazing Mr. Noël Coward* by Patrick Braybrooke (Archer, L 1933); *Present Indicative* (1937), *Future Indefinite* (1954), both by Coward (Heinemann, L); *The Art of Noël Coward* by Robert Greacen (Hand & Flower, Eng. 1953); *Noël Coward Song Book* (Joseph, L 1953); *Theatrical Companion to Noël Coward* by Joe Mander & Raymond Mitchenson (Rockliff, L 1957); *The Lyrics of Noël Coward* (Heinemann, L 1965); *The Wit of Noël Coward* (Frewin, L 1968); *A Talent to Amuse* by Sheridan Morley (Heinemann, L 1969); *Noël* by Charles Castle (Allen, L 1973); *A Last Encore* (Little Brown, Boston 1973).

Unless otherwise noted, Mr. Coward was composer-lyricist-librettist (or sketch writer) of following; asterisk indicates he was also director:

1916   The Light Blues (*Basil Pyecroft* only)
1923   London Calling! (also actor)
1925   On with the Dance
1928   This Year of Grace!
       This Year of Grace! *(NY) (also actor)
1929   Bitter Sweet *
       Bitter Sweet * (NY)
1932   Words and Music *
1934   Conversation Piece * (also *Paul duc de Chaucigny-Varennes*)
       Conversation Piece * (NY)

1936 Tonight at 8:30 * (also *George Pepper, Simon Gayforth, Jasper Featherways*)
Tonight at 8:30 * (NY) (also *George Pepper, Simon Gayforth, Jasper Featherways*)
1938 Operette *
1939 Set to Music * (NY)
1945 Sigh No More *
1946 Pacific 1860 *
1950 Ace of Clubs *
1954 After the Ball
1961 Sail Away * (NY)
1962 Sail Away *
1963 The Girl Who Came to Supper (NY) (comp., lyr. only)
1964 High Spirits (NY) (dir. only)

Coyne, Joseph, actor; b. New York, March 27, 1867; d. Virginia Water, Surrey, Eng., Feb. 17, 1941. Heavy-lidded, light-footed Joe Coyne settled in London in 1907, where he soon appeared in his most celebrated role, Prince Danilo in the first English-language *Merry Widow* (introducing "Maxim's" and "The Merry Widow Waltz"). Other West End hits: *The Dollar Princess, The Quaker Girl, No, No, Nanette* ("I Want to Be Happy").

1897 The Good Mr. Best (NY) (*Marmaduke Mush*)
1899 The Girl in the Barracks (NY) (*Paul Roland*)
1900 Star and Garter (NY) (*Willett Work*)
1901 The Night of the 4th (NY) (*Keenan Swift*)
The Girl from Up There (*Bertie Tappertit*)
1902 The Toreador (NY) (*Francis Wilson*)
1903 Rogers Brothers in London (NY)
1904 In Newport (NY) (*Percy Van Alstyne*)
1905 The Rollicking Girl (NY) (*Panagl*)
1906 The Social Whirl (NY) (*Artie Endicott*)
My Lady's Maid (NY) (*Croya Brown*)
1907 Nelly Neil (*Billy Ricketts*)

The Merry Widow (*Prince Danilo*)
1909 The Dollar Princess (*Harry Q. Condor*)
1910 The Quaker Girl (*Tony Chute*)
1912 The Dancing Mistress (*Teddy Cavanaugh*)
1913 The Girl from Utah (*Sandy Blair*)
1915 Watch Your Step (*Joseph Lilyburn*)
1916 Follow the Crowd
1917 The Bing Girls Are There
Arlette (*Prince Paul*)
1918 Going Up (*Robert Street*)
1922 Dé-Dé (*André*)
1923 Katinka (*Thaddeus T. Hopper*)
1925 No, No, Nanette (*Jimmy Smith*)
1926 Queen High (*T. Boggs Johns*)
1931 My Sister and I (*Filosel*)

Crawford, Cheryl, producer; b. Akron, Ohio, Sept. 24, 1902. Miss Crawford's most successful Bway musicals were *Porgy and Bess, One Touch of Venus,* and *Brigadoon.*

1942 Porgy and Bess (r)
1943 One Touch of Venus
1947 Brigadoon
1948 Love Life
1949 Regina
1951 Flahooley
Paint Your Wagon
1963 Jennie
1969 Celebration

Crazy Gang, The. See **Flanagan, Bud.**

"Crazy Rhythm." Music by Roger Wolfe Kahn & Joseph Meyer; lyric by Irving Caesar. Staccato follow-up to "Fascinating Rhythm," sung by Ben Bernie, Peggy Chamberlain, and June O'Dea in *Here's Howe* (NY 1928).

"Crinoline Days." Music & lyric by Irving Berlin. Canorous tribute to the dear old days of 1874 when "rosy complexions weren't bought in a store." Introduced in *Music Box Revue of 1922* by Grace LaRue, who, as she sang, was slowly propelled upward by a stage elevator until her gathered hoopskirt covered the entire stage.

Crouse, Russel, librettist; b. Findlay, Ohio, Feb. 20, 1893; d. New York, April 3, 1966. A former newspaperman and Theatre Guild publicist, Crouse became a librettist in 1931. In collaboration with Howard Lindsay, he wrote seven musicals, including the team's biggest hit, *The Sound of Music*. Lindsay and Crouse wrote four librettos for Ethel Merman, and were associated with composers Cole Porter and Irving Berlin on two shows each. The partners were also responsible for eight nonmusical plays, among them *Life with Father, State of the Union*.

Asterisk indicates production written with Mr. Lindsay:

1931　The Gang's All Here
1933　Hold Your Horses
1934　Anything Goes *
1936　Red, Hot and Blue! *
1937　Hooray for What! *
1950　Call Me Madam *
1956　Happy Hunting *
1959　The Sound of Music *
1962　Mr. President *

Crumit, Frank, actor, singer; b. Jackson, Ohio, Sept. 26, 1889; d. Longmeadow, Mass., Sept. 7, 1943. Vaudeville headliner who married Julia Sanderson, with whom he appeared in five musicals (incl. biggest hit, *Tangerine*). After retiring from the Bway stage, Crumit and Sanderson became a radio team, 1929–1943.

1920　Betty, Be Good (*Sam Kirby*)
　　　Greenwich Village Follies
1921　Tangerine (*Dick Owens*)
1923　Nifties of 1923

1924　Moonlight (*Brooks*, repl.)
1925　No, No, Nanette (US tour) (*Jimmy Smith*)
1927　Oh, Kay! (US tour) (*Jimmy Winters*)
　　　Queen High (US tour) (*T. Boggs Johns*)

"Cry for Us All." Music by Mitch Leigh; lyric by William Alfred & Phyllis Robinson. Robust threnody introduced by Steve Arlen in *Cry for Us All* (NY 1970).

"Cuddle Up a Little Closer, Lovey Mine." Music by Karl Hoschna; lyric by Otto Hauerbach (Harbach). Insinuating invitation proferred by Alice Yorke in *Three Twins* (NY 1908). The writers had first created the song for a vaudeville sketch but added it to the score of the musical when they didn't get paid.

Cullum, John, actor, singer; b. Knoxville, Tenn., March 2, 1930. Tawny-haired, sharp-featured Bway singing actor who introduced "On a Clear Day" and "Come Back to Me" in *On a Clear Day You Can See Forever*.

1960　Camelot (*Sir Dinadan*)
1965　On a Clear Day You Can See Forever (*Dr. Mark Bruckner*)
1967　Man of La Mancha (*Don Quixote*, repl.)
1970　1776 (*Edward Rutledge*, repl.)
1975　Shenandoah (*Charlie Anderson*)
1978　On the 20th Century (*Oscar*)

"Cup of Coffee, a Sandwich and You, A." Music by Joseph Meyer; lyric by Al Dubin & Billy Rose. Romantic duet of simple pleasures sung and danced by Gertrude Lawrence and Jack Buchanan in *The Charlot Revue of 1926* (NY 1925).

D

Dalrymple, Jean, producer; b. Morristown, NJ, Sept. 2, 1910. Bib: *September Child* by Miss Dalrymple (Dodd Mead, NY 1963). See **City Center Light Opera Co***,*

Damn Yankees (1955). Music & lyrics by Richard Adler & Jerry Ross; book by George Abbott & Douglass Wallop, based on Wallop's novel *The Day the Yankees Lost the Pennant*.

SONGS: "Goodbye, Old Girl," "Heart," "Shoeless Joe from Hannibal, Mo.," "A Man Doesn't Know," "A Little Brains—a Little Talent," "Whatever Lola Wants (Lola Gets)," "The Game," "Who's Got the Pain?," "Near to You," "Those Were the Good Old Days," "Two Lost Souls."

NEW YORK: May 5, 1955
46TH ST. THEATRE; 1,019 p.

Presented by Frederick Brisson, Robert E. Griffith, & Harold S. Prince; directed by George Abbott; choreographed by Bob Fosse; settings & costumes, William & Jean Eckart; music director, Harold Hastings; orchestrations, Don Walker.

CAST: Gwen Verdon (*Lola*), Stephen Douglass (*Joe Hardy*), Ray Walston (*Mr. Applegate*), Russ Brown (*Van Buren*), Shannon Bolin (*Meg Boyd*), Jimmy Komack (*Rocky*), Rae Allen (*Gloria*), Robert Shafer (*Joe Boyd*), Nathaniel Frey (*Smokey*), Eddie Phillips (*Sohovik*), Jean Stapleton (*Sister*).

LONDON: March 28, 1957
COLISEUM; 258 p.

Presented by Williamson Music Ltd.; restaged by James Hammerstein; dances reproduced by Zoya Leporska; settings & costumes, William & Jean Eckart; music director, Robert Lowe; orchestrations, Don Walker; supervisor, Jerome Whyte.

CAST: Belita (*Lola*), Ivor Emmanuel (*Joe Hardy*), Bill Kerr (*Mr. Applegate*), Donald Stewart (*Van Buren*), Betty Paul (*Meg Boyd*), Robin Hunter (*Rocky*), Judy Bruce (*Gloria*), Phil Vickers (*Joe Boyd*), Edward Devereaux (*Smokey*), Bob Stevenson (*Sohovik*).

The most successful musical ever to deal with a sport subject was a variant on the Faust legend, which had been around since *The Black Crook*. In this tale, a baseball enthusiast sells his soul to the devil—or Mr. Applegate— just for the chance to play ball with the Washington Senators. There is, fortunately, an escape clause, and Applegate, even aided by temptress Lola, must eventually let Joe Hardy return to his long-suffering spouse. Gwen Verdon, as Lola (a part first offered to Mitzi Gaynor), scored so resoundingly that she was elevated to stardom during the run. She was succeeded by Gretchen Wyler (11-56), Stephen Douglass by Allen Case (8-57), Ray Walston by Nathaniel Frey (3-57). The US touring company, headed by Bobby Clark (*Applegate*), Sherry O'Neil (*Lola*), and Case, began its two-year, four-month tour in Jan. 1955. In London, Elizabeth Seal succeeded Belita soon after the opening. Except for director Robbins and designer Ayers, *Damn Yankees* was put together by the same people responsible for the previous season's success, *The Pajama Game* (incl. uncredited co-librettist Richard Bissell).

FILM VERSION: Gwen Verdon, Tab Hunter, Ray Walston (Warner 1958, George Abbott dir.).

"Dance Little Lady." Music & lyric by Noël Coward. Pulsating number sung by Sonnie Hale to fast-living Lauri Devine in the revue *This Year of Grace!* (L 1928). Later the same year it was sung by Mr. Coward to Florence Desmond in the NY version of the show. In both productions, the singer was surrounded by dancers wearing grotesque, grinning masks. According to Coward, "The high tone of moral indignation implicit in the lyric impressed a number of people, including Aimee Semple MacPherson."

"Dancing in the Dark." Music by Arthur Schwartz; lyric by Howard Dietz. Introduced in the revue *The Band Wagon* (NY 1931), in which it was sung by John Barker and danced by Tilly Losch on a slanted, mirrored stage illuminated by constantly changing lights. During the writing of the score, composer Schwartz was in need of a slow, sultry melody for the Tilly Losch dance sequence. For days he couldn't think of anything that pleased him. One morning he suddenly awoke with the entire melody in his head; all that was needed was to go to his piano and jot down the notes. Though lyric contains line, "We're waltzing in the wonder of why we're here," note that melody is in 4/4 time.

"Dancing on the Ceiling." Music by Richard Rodgers; lyric by Lorenz Hart. Sung by Jessie Matthews and Sonnie Hale in a dream sequence in *Ever Green* (1930), in which, surrounded by the chorus, the couple danced all around a huge, inverted chandelier that looked like an illuminated brass willow. The song had been intended for the Broadway musical *Simple Simon* earlier the same year, but producer Florenz Ziegfeld disliked it and insisted it be taken out. It was also featured in the London revue *Happy Returns* (1938), in which it was sung by Constance Carpenter.

Dancing Years, The (1939). Music & book by Ivor Novello; lyrics by Christopher Hassall.

SONGS: "Waltz of My Heart," "My Life Belongs to You," "I Can Give You the Starlight," "My Dearest Dear," "Primrose," "Leap Year Waltz," "Lorelei," "Rainbow in the Fountain," "Wings of Sleep."

LONDON: March 23, 1939
DRURY LANE THEATRE; 187 p.

Presented by Tom Arnold; directed by Leontine Sagan; choreographed by Freddie Carpenter, Suria Magito; settings, Joseph Carl, Edward Delaney, Alick Johnstone; costumes, Frederick Dineson, Louis Brooks; music director, Charles Prentice; orchestrations, Prentice, Harry Acres.

CAST: Ivor Novello (*Rudi Kleber*), Mary Ellis (*Maria Zeigler*), Roma Beaumont (*Grete Schone*), Olive Gilbert (*Cäcilie Kurt*), Peter Graves (*Franzl*), Anthony Nicholls (*Prince Charles Metternich*).

Ivor Novello's fourth successive and successful production at Drury Lane was forced to close when the outbreak of World War II caused an abrupt drop in attendance. One year later it began an 18-month tour with basically the same cast, except for the replacement of Peter Graves by Barry Sinclair. The musical returned to London on March 14, 1942, at the Adelphi Theatre; its run of 969 performances made it the most popular musical presented in London during the war, and the termination of its run was due only to the increase in the number of German air raids. (In April 1944 Novello was jailed for a month for illegally purchasing petrol; his return to the cast was the occasion for a tumultuous reception.) After the London run, *The Dancing Years* again toured the provinces with Sinclair succeeding Novello, and Jessica James replacing Mary Ellis. The company played a return engagement in London in March 1947, then resumed its tour. In all, the operetta played almost consecutively for 10 years. In 1968, it was revived at the Saville Theatre, London, with June Bronhill and David Knight.

Although *The Dancing Years* was in the tradition of bittersweet romances associated with Novello (as in his previous *Perchance to Dream,* he again played the part of a composer), it did aim for a certain topicality by voicing opposition to Nazi dictatorship. The story begins in 1911 at an inn outside Vienna where poor Rudi Kleber and operetta star Maria Ziegler meet and fall in love. Three years later their bliss is shattered when, as a result of a misunderstanding, Maria leaves Rudi to marry Prince Charles. After another 12 years Rudi and Maria meet again, discover they are still in love, but part for the sake of their son, who thinks the prince is his father. In 1938, following the German conquest of Austria, Rudi is arrested for opposing the new regime but Maria manages to get him released.

Another musical that also dealt with the Nazi invasion of Austria was *The Sound of Music* (NY 1959).

FILM VERSION: Dennis Price and Giselle Preville (Assoc. Brit. 1950, Harold French dir.).

Dare, Phyllis (née Phyllis Dones), actress, singer; b. London, Aug. 15, 1890; d. Brighton, Eng., April 27, 1975. Durable West End leading lady whose successes included *The Arcadians, Miss Hook of Holland,* and *Lido Lady.* She was the sister of actress Zena Dare. Bib: *Phyllis Dare by Herself* (1921).

1901	Bluebell in Fairyland (*Mab*)
1905	The Catch of the Season (*Lady Angela,* repl.)
1906	The Belle of Mayfair (*Julia Chaldicott,* repl.)
1909	The Arcadians (*Eileen Cavanagh*)
1910	The Girl in the Train (*Gonda Van der Loo*)
1911	Peggy (*Peggy Barrison*)
1912	The Sunshine Girl (*Delia Dale*)
1913	The Dancing Mistress (*Nancy Joyce,* repl.)
	The Girl from Utah (*Dora Manners*)
1914	Miss Hook of Holland (*Sally Hook*)
1915	Tina (*Tina*)
1917	Hanky-Panky
1919	Kissing Time (*Lucienne Touquet*)
1921	Ring Up
1922	The Lady of the Rose (*Mariana*)
1924	The Street Singer (*Yvette*)
1926	Lido Lady (*Fay Blake*)
1928	The Yellow Mask (*Mary Bannister*)
1932	Words and Music (repl.)
1934	Music in the Air (UK tour) (*Frieda Hatzfeld*)
1949	King's Rhapsody (*Marta Karillos*)

Darion, Joe, lyricist; b. New York, Jan. 30, 1917. With composer Mitch Leigh, Darion had his greatest Bway success with the score for *Man of La Mancha* ("The Impossible Dream," "To Each His Dulcinea"). Other collaborators: George Kleinsinger, Manos Hadjidakis ("Never on Sunday"), Dov Seltzer.

1957	Shinbone Alley (Kleinsinger)
1965	Man of La Mancha (Leigh)
1967	Illya Darling (Hadjidakis)

1968 The Megilla of Itzik Manger
(Seltzer)

Da Silva, Howard (né Howard Silverblatt), actor, singer; b. Cleveland, Ohio, May 4, 1909. Rugged, garglevoiced character actor who sang "Pore Jud" in *Oklahoma!* and "Little Tin Box" in *Fiorello!* Da Silva has also appeared in nonmusical plays and films.

1937 The Cradle Will Rock (*Larry Foreman*)
1943 Oklahoma! (*Jud Fry*)
1954 Sandhog (dir. only)
1959 Fiorello! (*Ben Marino*)
1964 The Cradle Will Rock (r) (dir. only)
1965 The Zulu and the Zayda (co-lib. only)
1969 1776 (*Ben Franklin*)

"Dat's Love." Music by Georges Bizet; lyric by Oscar Hammerstein II. Bizet's "Habanera" in his opera *Carmen* became "Dat's Love" in Hammerstein's adaptation called *Carmen Jones* (NY 1943). It was sung by Muriel Smith (who alternated the title role with Muriel Rahn). According to the lyricist, "The score of *Carmen* is a Frenchman's version of Spanish music. Do not forget, however, that Spanish music was deeply influenced by the Moors from Africa. The rhythm of the 'Habanera' is even closer to the home of Carmen Jones."

David, Hal, lyricist; b. New York, May 25, 1921. A successful pop and film lyricist, David and his composer partner, Burt Bacharach, made a notable Bway debut with *Promises, Promises* ("I'll Never Fall in Love Again," "Whoever You Are").

1968 Promises, Promises

Davis, (Ruth Elizabeth) Bette, actress; b. Lowell, Mass., April 5, 1908. Actress of flaming intensity best known for succession of screen portrayals of neurotic heroines.

1952 Two's Company

Davis, Sammy, Jr., actor, singer, dancer; b. New York, Dec. 8, 1925. Versatile entertainer, primarily in nightclubs and on records, who introduced "Mr. Wonderful" and "Too Close for Comfort" in *Mr. Wonderful,* "I Want to Be with You" in *Golden Boy.* Bib: *Yes I Can* by Davis, Jane and Burt Boyar (Farrar, NY 1965).

1956 Mr. Wonderful (*Charlie Welch*)
1964 Golden Boy (*Joe Wellington*)
1968 Golden Boy (L) (*Joe Wellington*)

Dawn, Hazel (née Hazel Dawn La Tout), actress, singer; b. Ogden, Utah, March 23, 1891. Dewy-eyed blonde charmer who scored biggest Bway success as violinist in *The Pink Lady* (introducing "My Beautiful Lady"). Also sang "Valencia" in *The Great Temptations.*

1909 Dear Little Denmark (L) (*Xandra*)
1910 The Balkan Princess (L) (*Olga*)
The Dollar Princess (L) (*Dulcie DuCros*)
1911 The Pink Lady (*Claudine*)
1912 The Pink Lady (L) (*Claudine*)
1913 The Little Café (*Gaby Gaufrette*)
1914 The Débutante (*Elaine*)
1916 The Century Girl
1923 Ziegfeld Follies (US tour)
Nifties of 1923
1924 Keep Kool
1926 The Great Temptations

"Day After Tomorrow, The." Music & lyric by Lionel Bart. During World War II, British singer Vera Lynn was closely identified with the sentimental ballad "We'll Meet Again," by Ross Parker and Hughie Charles. In his score for *Blitz!* (L 1962), which took place during the war, Bart deliberately wrote "The Day After Tomorrow" to suggest the previous song, even having it introduced as a Vera Lynn recording heard over the radio.

"Day by Day." Music by Stephen Schwartz; lyric by St. Richard of Chichester. Adapted from a 12th-century prayer, the song was introduced in *Godspell* (NY 1971) by Robin Lamont and company. In London production (1971), it was sung by Verity-Anne Meldrum and company.

Day, Edith, actress, singer, dancer; b. Minneapolis, Minn., April 10, 1896; d. London, May 2, 1971. Miss Day was a dark-haired, round-faced, slightly pop-eyed singer and dancer who first won fame in NY in *Irene* (introducing "Irene," "Alice Blue Gown"), and also scored successes in *Orange Blossoms* ("A Kiss in the Dark") and *Wildflower* ("Bambalina"). Settling in London in 1925, she became known as the Queen of Drury Lane for her four-year reign in *Rose-Marie, The Desert Song,* and *Show Boat.* The actress was married to and divorced from producer Carle Carlton and actor Pat Somerset.

1915	Dancing Around (US tour)
1916	Pom-Pom (NY) (*Evelyn*)
	Follow Me (NY) (*Denise*)
1917	His Little Widows (NY) (*Murilla,* repl.)
	Going Up (NY) (*Grace Douglas*)
1919	Irene (NY) (*Irene O'Dare*)
1920	Irene (*Irene O'Dare*)
1922	Jenny (*Jenny*)
	Orange Blossoms (NY) (*Kitty*)
1923	Wildflower (NY) (*Nina Benedetto*)
1925	Rose-Marie (*Rose-Marie La Flamme*)
1927	The Desert Song (*Margot Bonvalet*)
1928	Show Boat (*Magnolia Hawks*)
1929	Rose-Marie (r) (*Rose-Marie La Flamme*)
1930	Rio Rita (*Rita Ferguson*)
1936	The Desert Song (r) (*Margot Bonvalet*)
1943	Sunny River (*Lolita*)
1962	Sail Away (*Mrs. Sweeney*)

Day, Frances (née Frances Victoria Schenk), actress, singer; b. East Orange, NJ, Dec. 16, 1908. Tall, blonde song belter who first sang in nightclubs, NY and London, then became a London musical-comedy star in *Jill Darling,* and introduced "He Wears a Pair of Silver Wings" in *Black Vanities.*

1932	Out of the Bottle (*Molly Harper*)
1933	How D'You Do?
1934	Jill Darling (*Jill Sonning*)
1937	Floodlight
1938	The Fleet's Lit Up (*Polly Brown*)
1939	Black and Blue
1941	Black Vanities
1942	DuBarry Was a Lady (*Jenny Daly*)
1946	Evangeline (*Evangeline Edwards*) (also co-dir.)
1949	Latin Quarter

"Dear Friend." Music by Jerry Bock; lyric by Sheldon Harnick. At the Café Imperiale, a romantic rendezvous in *She Loves Me* (NY 1963), Barbara Cook sits alone with her rose and her book and pours her heart out at being stood up on her first date with an unknown correspondent. Anne Rogers played the part in the London production (1964). Bock and Harnick had previously written a different song with the same title for the 1960 Bway musical *Tenderloin.*

"Dear World." Music & lyric by Jerry Herman. The first-act finale of the musical of the same name (NY 1968) found Angela Lansbury leading the cast in a robust get-well message to a sick world.

Dearest Enemy (1925). Music by Richard Rodgers; lyrics by Lorenz Hart; book by Herbert Fields.

SONGS: "War Is War," "I Beg Your Pardon," "Cheerio," "Here in My Arms," "The Hermits," "I'd Like to Hide It," "Where the Hudson River Flows," "Bye and Bye," "Old Enough to Love," "Sweet Peter," "Here's a Kiss."

NEW YORK: Sept. 18, 1925
KNICKERBOCKER THEATRE; 286 p.
Presented by George Ford; directed by John Murray Anderson, Charles Sinclair, Harry Ford; choreographed by Carl Hemmer; settings, Clark Robinson; costumes, Mark Mooring, Hubert Davis, James Reynolds; music director, Richard Rodgers; orchestrations, Emil Gerstenberger.

CAST: Helen Ford (Betsy Burke), Charles Purcell (Capt. Sir John Copeland), Flavia Arcaro (Mrs. Robert Murray), Detmar Poppen (Gen. John Tryon), Harold Crane (Gen. Sir William Howe).

Rodgers, Hart and Fields' first book musical was based on an incident in the American Revolution, which in itself was considered somewhat revolutionary for the Broadway musical stage. The incident was the one in which Mrs. Robert Murray, of the Murray Hill Murrays, detained the British troops long enough to let Gen. Putnam's forces join Gen. Washington's. Romance was provided by American patriot Betsy Burke and British officer Sir John Copeland (who meet when Betsy, after a nude swim, is clad only in a barrel). The musical, originally tried out under the title Dear Enemy, opened during the same seven-day period as No, No, Nanette, The Vagabond King, and Sunny. Other Bway musicals dealing with the American Revolution: A Daughter of the Revolution (1895), Virginia (1937), Arms and the Girl (1950), Ben Franklin in Paris (1964), 1776 (1969).

"Dearest Love." Music & lyric by Noël Coward. In Operette (L 1938), this waltzing love duet was sung by Max Oldaker and Muriel Barron in a scene from a 1905 musical comedy called The Model Maid. It was later reprised by Peggy Wood. The song was also sung by Eva Ortega and Hugh French in Set to Music (NY 1938).

"Deep in My Heart, Dear." Music by Sigmund Romberg; lyric by Dorothy Donnelly. Ardent duet for Howard Marsh and Ilse Marvenga in The Student Prince in Heidelberg (NY 1924). In London production (1926) it was sung by Allan Prior and Miss Marvenga.

De Koven, (Henry Louis) Reginald, composer; b. Middleton, Conn., April 3, 1861; d. Chicago, Ill., Jan. 15, 1920. Composer of romantic Bway operettas whose greatest fame rests on Robin Hood ("Oh, Promise Me"). De Koven wrote 17 scores with lyricist Harry B. Smith; other collaborators: George V. Hobart, Charles Emerson Cook, Frederick Ranken, Stanislaus Stange, Joseph Herbert, Channing Pollock, Rennald Wolf. Bib: A Musician and His Wife by Anna De Koven (1926).

Asterisk indicates score written with Mr. Smith:

1887	The Begum *
1889	Don Quixote *
1890	Robin Hood *
1892	The Knickerbockers *
1893	The Algerian *
	The Fencing Master *
1894	Rob Roy *
1895	The Tzigane *
1896	The Mandarin *
1897	The Highwayman *
1899	The Three Dragoons *
	Papa's Wife *
1900	Foxy Quiller *
1901	The Little Duchess *
1902	Maid Marian *
1903	The Jersey Lily (Hobart)
	The Red Feather (Cook)
1905	Happyland (Ranken)
1906	The Student King (Stange)
1907	The Girls of Holland (Stange)

1908	The Golden Butterfly *
1909	The Beauty Spot (Herbert)
1911	The Wedding Trip *
1913	Her Little Highness (Pollock, Wolf)

Delfont, Bernard (né Barnet Winogradsky), producer; b. Tokmak, Russia, Sept. 5, 1909. Knighted 1974. Delfont's biggest London successes: *Pickwick, Maggie May, Stop the World—I Want to Get Off, Sweet Charity*. He has also presented variety-type revues at the Prince of Wales, Palace and Palladium.

1944	Something for the Boys
1945	Gay Rosalinda
	Big Boy
1946	Here Come the Boys
1949	Her Excellency
1950	Touch and Go
1952	Paris to Piccadilly
1957	We're Having a Ball
1958	Large as Life
1961	Stop the World—I Want to Get Off
1963	Pickwick
1964	Maggie May
	Little Me
	Our Man Crichton
1966	Funny Girl
	Joey, Joey
	Way Out in Piccadilly
1967	Queenie
	Sweet Charity
	The Four Musketeers!
1968	You're a Good Man, Charlie Brown
1969	Mame
1970	The Great Waltz (r)
1972	Stand and Deliver
	Applause
	The Good Old Bad Old Days!
1974	The Good Companions

Delroy, Irene (née Josephine Sanders), actress, dancer, singer; b. Bloomington, Ill., 1898. Blonde ingenue who began as toe dancer and also appeared in vaudeville. Biggest hits: *Greenwich Village Follies, Ziegfeld Follies, Follow Thru*.

1920	Frivolities of 1920
1923	Greenwich Village Follies
1924	Vogues of 1924
	'Round the Town
1925	Greenwich Village Follies
	Hitchy-Koo (US tour)
1927	Ziegfeld Follies
1928	Here's Howe (*Joyce Baxter*)
1929	Follow Thru (*Lora Moore*)
	Top Speed (*Virginia Rollins*)
1935	Anything Goes (*Hope Harcourt*, repl.)

Delysia, Alice (née Alice Lapize), actress, singer; b. Paris, France, March 3, 1888. Amply proportioned prognathous entertainer who wore daring backless costumes and appeared in 11 London musicals produced by Charles B. Cochran. She introduced "If You Could Care" in *As You Were*.

1914	Odds and Ends
1915	More
1916	Pell-Mell
1917	Carminetta (*Carminetta*)
1918	As You Were (*Gervaise, Ninon, Cleopatra, Helen*)
1919	Afgar (*Zaydee*)
1920	Afgar (NY) (*Zaydee*)
1922	Mayfair and Montmartre
1923	Topics of 1923 (NY)
1925	On with the Dance
	Still Dancing!
1926	Princess Charming (*Wanda Navaro*)
1932	The Cat and the Fiddle (*Alice*)
1933	Mother of Pearl (*Josephine Pavani*)
1936	At the Silver Swan (*Alice Brevanne*)

de Mille, Agnes (George), choreographer, director; b. New York, 1905. Ballet choreographer who had great impact on Bway musicals in expanding the scope of dancing, especially with *Oklahoma!* (its dream ballet started a trend), *One Touch of Venus, Bloomer Girl* (the Civil War ballet), *Carousel*, and *Brigadoon*. Miss de Mille began career as a ballet dancer, making her

NY debut in 1927. Her early work, "Three Virgins and a Devil," was first performed in London revue, *Why Not Tonight?* Bib: *Dance to the Piper* (1952), *And Promenade Home* (1958), *Speak to Me, Dance with Me* (1973), all by Miss de Mille (Atlantic, Boston).

Unless otherwise noted, Miss de Mille was choreographer of following:
1928 Grand Street Follies (dancer only)
1933 Nymph Errant (L)
1934 Why Not Tonight? (L)
1937 Hooray for What!
1939 Swingin' the Dream
1943 Oklahoma!
      One Touch of Venus
1944 Bloomer Girl
1945 Carousel
1947 Brigadoon
      Allegro (also dir.)
1949 Gentlemen Prefer Blondes
1950 Carousel (L)
      Out of This World (dir. only)
1951 Paint Your Wagon
1954 The Girl in Pink Tights
1958 Goldilocks
1959 Juno
1961 Kwamina
1963 110 in the Shade
1969 Come Summer (also dir.)

"Den of Iniquity." Music by Richard Rodgers; lyric by Lorenz Hart. Wealthy socialite Vera Simpson (Vivienne Segal) and paramour Joey Evans (Gene Kelly) express innocent delight in describing their loving room in *Pal Joey* NY 1940). In London (1954), the parts were played by Carol Bruce and Harold Lang.

Desert Song, The (1926). Music by Sigmund Romberg; lyrics by Otto Harbach & Oscar Hammerstein II; book by Harbach, Hammerstein & Frank Mandel.
SONGS: "The Riff Song," "Margot," "Romance," "French Marching Song," "Then You Will Know," "I Want a Kiss," "It," "The Desert Song," "Let Love Go," "One Flower Grows Alone in Your Garden," "One Alone," "The Sabre Song."

NEW YORK: Nov. 30, 1926
CASINO THEATRE; 471 p.
Presented by Laurence Schwab & Frank Mandel; directed by Arthur Hurley; choreographed by Bobby Connolly; settings, Woodman Thompson; costumes, Vyvyan Donner, Mark Mooring; music director, Oscar Bradley.
CAST: Vivienne Segal (*Margot Bonvalet*), Robert Halliday (*Pierre Birabeau*), Eddie Buzzell (*Bennie Kidd*), Pearl Regay (*Azuri*), William O'Neal (*Sid El Kar*), Glen Dale (*Capt. Paul Fontaine*), Margaret Irving (*Clementina*), Nellie Breen (*Susan*).

LONDON: April 7, 1927
DRURY LANE THEATRE; 432 p.
Presented by Alfred Butt, with Lee Ephraim; directed by Laurence Schwab; choreographed by Bobby Connolly; settings, Joseph & Phil Harker; costumes, Robert Groves; music director, Herman Finck.
CAST: Edith Day (*Margot Bonvalet*), Harry Welchman (*Pierre Birabeau*), Gene Gerrard (*Bennie Kidd*), Phebe Brune (*Azuri*), Sidney Pointer (*Sid El Kar*), Barry Mackaye (*Capt. Paul Fontaine*), Maria Minetti (*Clementina*), Clarice Hardwicke (*Susan*), Marjorie Robertson (Anna Neagle) (chorus).
The Desert Song has long been considered the most durable of all Bway operettas, particularly as a summer-theatre attraction. In writing the story, the authors attempted to combine the old fashioned operetta form with such modern news and literary events as the Riff uprising in Morocco, the exploits of Lawrence of Arabia, and the novel called *The Sheik*, which had recently been filmed with Rudolph Val-

entino. That story was concerned with an English lady's adventures after being abducted into the desert by an Arab chieftain—who turns out to be a titled Englishman. In the musical, the authors dealt with the situation of a French girl being abducted into the desert by the Red Shadow, the masked leader of the warring Riffs, who is really the son of the French governor of Morocco.

Before the Bway opening, when the show was called *Lady Fair*, the actress playing the lead was replaced by Vivienne Segal. During run, Miss Segal was succeeded by Charlotte Lansing (6-27), Ethel Louise Wright (8-27); Robert Halliday by Leonard Ceeley (11-27). The US touring company, headed by Miss Lansing and John Ehrly, began its travels Aug. 1927, and continued for one year, nine months. During original London run, Harry Welchman was succeeded by Howett Worster. Other London productions were in 1931, 1936 (with Edith Day and Harry Welchman), 1939, 1943, and 1967 (John Hanson and Patricia Michael). The last ran for 383 performances at the Palace Theatre. A NY revival in 1973, with Chris Callan and Stanley Grover, was unsuccessful.

FILM VERSIONS: John Boles, Carlotta King, Myrna Loy (Warner 1929, Roy Del Ruth dir.); Dennis Morgan and Irene Manning (Warner 1943, Robert Florey dir.); Kathryn Grayson and Gordon MacRae (Warner 1953, Bruce Humberstone dir.).

"Desert Song, The." Music by Sigmund Romberg; lyric by Otto Harbach & Oscar Hammerstein II. When, at the end of Act I of *The Desert Song* (NY 1926), the Red Shadow (Robert Halliday) comes to sweep Margot (Vivienne Segal) away with him into the desert, he first—literally—sweeps her

off her feet with this heady and impassioned aria. Later Miss Segal gets a chance to sing it, too. In London production (1927) it was sung by Harry Welchman and Edith Day.

Desmond, Florence (née Florence Dawson), actress, singer, dancer; b. London, May 31, 1907. A leading impressionist in London revues, Miss Desmond began her career as a dancer in pantomimes in 1916. Bib: *Florence Desmond* by Herself (Harrap, L 1953).

1925	On with the Dance
1926	Cochran's Revue of 1926
1928	This Year of Grace!
	This Year of Grace! (NY)
1930	Charlot's Masquerade
1932	Savoy Follies
1934	Why Not Tonight?
	Streamline
1935	Seeing Stars (*Poldi*)
1936	Let's Raise the Curtain
1937	Wonderful World
1940	Funny Side Up
	Apple Sauce
1943	Hi-De-Hi
1946	Under the Counter (*Jo Fox*, repl.)
	If the Shoe Fits (NY) (*Lady Eve*)

DeSylva, (George Gard) B. G. ("Buddy"), lyricist, librettist, producer; b. New York, Jan. 27, 1895; d. Los Angeles, Cal., July 11, 1950. With co-lyricist Lew Brown and composer Ray Henderson, DeSylva wrote scores for Bway musicals that reflected the youthful, carefree spirit of the Flapper Age. His first songs— "Avalon," "April Showers," "California, Here I Come"—were sung by Al Jolson in *Sinbad* and *Bombo*. Other early numbers were written with composers Jerome Kern ("Look for the Silver Lining" in *Sally*), Victor Herbert ("A Kiss in the Dark" in *Orange Blossoms*), Emmerich Kalman, George Gershwin ("I'll Build a Stairway to Paradise," "Somebody Loves

Me" in the 1922 and 1924 *George White's Scandals*), Joseph Meyer ("If You Knew Susie" in *Big Boy*), James Hanley, Lewis Gensler; also with lyricist Ira Gershwin.

The first DeSylva–Brown–Henderson song was "It All Depends on You" for *Big Boy*, and their first score was for *George White's Scandals* of 1925. For the next year's edition, they had two hits: "Lucky Day" and "The Birth of the Blues." Their biggest stage successes were *Good News!* ("The Best Things in Life Are Free," "Lucky in Love," "The Varsity Drag"), *Hold Everything!* ("You're the Cream in My Coffee"), *Follow Thru* ("Button Up Your Overcoat"), *Flying High* "(Thank Your Father"). After leaving the team, DeSylva became a Hollywood film executive and also produced four successful Bway musicals (for *Take a Chance* he collaborated on "You're an Old Smoothie," "Eadie Was a Lady," and "Rise 'n Shine" with composers Richard Whiting, Nacio Herb Brown, and Vincent Youmans). Al Jolson, Ethel Merman, and Bert Lahr were each in three DeSylva musicals; Willie and Eugene Howard, Harry Richman, and Ann Pennington were in two.

Unless otherwise noted, the following were written with Messrs. Brown and Henderson; asterisk indicates Mr. DeSylva was also co-librettist:

1919 La La Lucille (Gershwin)
1922 George White's Scandals (Gershwin)
 Orange Blossoms (Herbert)
 The Yankee Princess (Kalman)
1923 George White's Scandals (Gershwin)
1924 Sweet Little Devil (Gershwin)
 George White's Scandals (Gershwin)
1925 Big Boy (Meyer, Hanley)
 Tell Me More! (Gershwin, Gershwin)
 George White's Scandals

 Captain Jinks (Gensler)
1926 George White's Scandals
 Queen High * (Gensler)
1927 Good News! *
 Manhattan Mary
1928 George White's Scandals
 Hold Everything! *
1929 Follow Thru *
1930 Flying High *
1932 Take a Chance (N. H. Brown, Whiting, Youmans) (also prod.)
1939 DuBarry Was a Lady (co-lib., prod. only)
1940 Louisiana Purchase (co-prod. only)
 Panama Hattie (co-lib., prod. only)

"Diamonds Are a Girl's Best Friend." Music by Jule Styne; lyric by Leo Robin. Materialistic philosophy propounded by Carol Channing in *Gentlemen Prefer Blondes* (NY 1949). It was the show's show-stopper. In London production (1962), the number was sung by Dora Bryan; in revised version, *Lorelei* (NY 1974), it was again Miss Channing's turn.

Dickson, Dorothy, actress, dancer; b. Kansas City, Mo., July 26, 1896. The blonde, delicate featured Miss Dickson made her first appearance as a dancer on Bway in partnership with Carl Hyson, then her husband. After settling in London in 1921, she won her greatest fame in West End versions of *Sally*, *Tip-Toes*, and *Peggy-Ann*. She also introduced "These Foolish Things" in *Spread It Abroad*.

1917 Oh, Boy! (NY) (dancer)
 Ziegfeld Follies (NY) (dancer)
1918 Girl o' Mine (NY) (*Betty*)
 Rock-a-bye Baby (NY) (*Dorothy Manners*)
 Ziegfeld Follies (NY)
1919 The Royal Vagabond (NY) (*Carlotta*)
1920 Lassie (NY) (*Lady Gwendolyn Spencer-Hill*)

1921	London, Paris and New York
	Sally (*Sally Green*)
1922	The Cabaret Girl (*Marilynn Morgan*)
1923	The Beauty Prize (*Carol Stuart*)
1924	Patricia (*Patricia*)
1925	Charlot's Revue
1926	Tip-Toes (*Tip-Toes Kaye*)
1927	Peggy-Ann (*Peggy-Ann*)
1929	Coo-ee!
	Hold Everything (*Sue O'Keefe*, repl.)
1930	The Wonder Bar (*Liane*)
1932	Casanova (*Princess Potomska*)
1935	Stop Press
1936	Spread It Abroad
	Careless Rapture (*Penelope Lee*)
1937	Crest of the Wave (*Honey Wortle*)
1942	Fine and Dandy

Diener, Joan, actress, singer; b. Cleveland, Ohio, Feb. 24, 1934. Blonde singer with wide-range voice whose major Bway successes were *Kismet* and *Man of La Mancha*, both directed by husband, Albert Marre.

1948	Small Wonder
1953	Kismet (*Lalume*)
1955	Kismet (L) (*Lalume*)
1965	Man of La Mancha (*Aldonza*)
1968	Man of La Mancha (L) (*Aldonza*)
1970	Cry for Us All (*Kathleen Stanton*)
1975	Home Sweet Homer (*Penelope*)

Dietz, Howard, lyricist, librettist; b. New York, Sept. 8, 1896. Worldly, witty lyricist whose collaborations with composer Arthur Schwartz were heard in some of the most acclaimed Bway revues of the 30s. Among the team's songs: "I Guess I'll Have to Change My Plan" (*The Little Show*); "Something to Remember You By" (*Three's a Crowd*); "Dancing in the Dark," "I Love Louisa," "New Sun in the Sky" (*The Band Wagon*); "A Shine on Your Shoes," "Alone Together," "Louisiana Hayride" (*Flying Colors*); "You and the Night and the Music," "If There Is Someone Lovelier Than You" (*Revenge with Music*); "Paree," "Get Yourself a Geisha" (*At Home Abroad*); "I See Your Face Before Me," "By Myself" (*Between the Devil*); "Haunted Heart" (*Inside USA*). Dietz has also written with composers Jerome Kern, Henry Souvaine, Jay Gorney, Ralph Rainger ("Moanin' Low" in *The Little Show*), Vernon Duke. Libby Holman and Clifton Webb both appeared in three Dietz musicals, Beatrice Lillie was in two. Dietz, who was director of publicity for MGM for over 30 years, is married to designer Lucinda Ballard. Bib: *Dancing in the Dark* by Dietz (Quadrangle, NY 1974).

Unless otherwise noted, following were written with Mr. Schwartz; asterisk indicates Mr. Dietz was also sketch writer or librettist:

1924	Dear Sir (Kern)
1927	Merry-Go-Round * (Souvaine, Gorney)
1929	The Little Show *
1930	Here Comes the Bride (L)
	The Second Little Show
	Three's a Crowd *
1931	The Band Wagon *
1932	Flying Colors * (also dir.)
1934	Revenge with Music * (also dir.)
1935	At Home Abroad *
1937	Between the Devil *
1944	Jackpot (Duke)
	Sadie Thompson * (Duke)
1948	Inside USA
1961	The Gay Life
1963	Jennie

"Diga Diga Doo." Music by Jimmy McHugh; lyric by Dorothy Fields. Adelaide Hall and chorus offered this pseudo-African number in the Jungleland scene in the Bway revue *Blackbirds of 1928*. The title has also been spelled "Digga-Digga-Do."

Dillingham, Charles B(ancroft), producer; b. Hartford, Conn., May 30, 1868; d. New York, Aug. 30, 1934. Dillingham's biggest Bway hits were

Mlle. Modiste, The Red Mill, Watch Your Step, Stepping Stones, and *Sunny,* plus eight spectacular revues at the Hippodrome. Victor Herbert and Jerome Kern each wrote nine scores for Dillingham, who produced nine musicals with Fred Stone, seven with Elsie Janis, five with Fritzi Scheff, three with Fred and Adele Astaire.

1903	The Office Boy
	Babette
1904	The Madcap Princess
	The Two Roses
1905	Sergeant Brue
	Miss Dolly Dollars
	Mlle. Modiste
1906	The Red Mill
1907	The Tattooed Man
	The Hoyden
1908	The Prima Donna
1909	The Fair Coed
	The Candy Shop
1910	The Old Town
	The Echo
	The Girl on the Train
1911	The Slim Princess
1912	Over the River
	The Lady of the Slipper
1914	Chin-Chin
	Watch Your Step
1915	Hip-Hip-Hooray!
	Miss Information
	Stop! Look! Listen!
1916	The Big Show
	Betty
	The Century Girl
1917	Cheer Up
	Jack o' Lantern
	Miss 1917
	A Night in Spain
1918	Everything
	The Canary
1919	She's a Good Fellow
	Happy Days
	Apple Blossoms
1920	The Night Boat
	The Girl from Home
	Good Times
	Tip Top
	The Half Moon
1921	Get Together
	The Love Letter
	Good Morning Dearie
1922	Better Times
	The Bunch and Judy
1923	Nifties of 1923
	Stepping Stones
	One Kiss
1924	Madame Pompadour
1925	China Rose
	Puzzles of 1925
	The City Chap
	Sunny
1926	Criss-Cross
	Oh, Please!
1927	Lucky
	Sidewalks of New York
1928	She's My Baby
	Three Cheers
1930	Ripples
1934	New Faces

Dixey, Henry E., actor, singer; b. Boston, Mass., Jan. 6, 1859; d. Atlantic City, NJ, Feb. 25, 1943. Began as actor in Boston, 1875–1879; became Bway matinee idol in title role in *Adonis* which he wrote with composer Edward Rice. He became so identified with this role that he thenceforth was known as Adonis Dixey.

1877	Evangeline (r) (*Redsnake*)
1879	Babes in the Woods (*Physician*)
1880	Fatinitza (*Mustapha*)
	Billee Taylor (*Sir Mincing Lane*)
	New Evangeline (*Peter Papyrus*)
	Hiawatha (*Romulus Smith*)
1883	The Mascot (*Laurent*)
	The Merry Duchess (*Brabazon Sykes*)
1884	Adonis (*Adonis*) (also lib., lyr.) (Rice)
1886	Adonis (L) (*Adonis*)
1888	Pearl of Pekin (co-prod. only)
1897	Gayest Manhattan
1898	Erminie (r) (*Ravennes*)
1900	The Burgomaster (*Peter Stuyvesant*)
1917	Chu Chin Chow (*Ali Baba*)
1928	The Merry Malones (*John Malone*, repl.)

"Do Do Do." Music by George Gershwin; lyric by Ira Gershwin. Lighthearted romantic duet sung by Gertrude Lawrence and Oscar Shaw in

Oh, Kay! (NY 1926), and by Miss Lawrence and Harold French in London version (1927). Ira Gershwin has written that he had an idea for a lyric using the sounds of "do, do, do" and "done, done, done," and together the brothers wrote the entire refrain in half an hour. The lyricist also insists that all the girl and boy want to do do do is kiss kiss kiss.

"Do I Hear a Waltz?" Music by Richard Rodgers; lyric by Stephen Sondheim. Believing that she will know true love only when she hears a waltz, Elizabeth Allen, the heroine of *Do I Hear a Waltz?* (NY 1965), hears it and sings.

"Do I Love You?" Music & lyric by Cole Porter. The main romantic duet in *DuBarry Was a Lady* (NY 1939) was asked and affirmatively answered by Ronald Graham and Ethel Merman. In London it was sung by Frances Day in both *Black Vanities* (1941) and *DuBarry Was a Lady* (1942) (the latter with Bruce Trent).

"Do It Again." Music by George Gershwin; lyric by B. G. DeSylva. Coquettishly implored by Irene Bordoni in *The French Doll* (NY 1922) and by Alice Delysia in *Mayfair and Montmartre* (L 1922). The "It" of the title refers to osculation.

"Do You Love Me?" Music by Jerry Bock; lyric by Sheldon Harnick. In which Tevye (Zero Mostel) and Golde (Maria Karnilova) in *Fiddler on the Roof* (NY 1964) awkwardly express affection for each other after being married 25 years. Topol and Miriam Karlin sang it in the London version (1967).

"Doin' What Comes Natur'lly." Music & lyric by Irving Berlin. Comic ode to the uneducated life sung in *Annie Get Your Gun* (NY 1946) by Ethel Merman, and in London version (1947) by Dolores Gray.

Dolly Sisters, dancers, actresses. Jennie (née Janszieka Deutsch), b. Budapest, Hungary, Oct. 25, 1892; d. Hollywood, Cal., June 1, 1941. Rosie (née Roszika Deutsch), b. Budapest, Hungary, Oct. 25, 1892; d. New York, Feb. 1, 1970. Jennie and Rosie were dancing headliners in US vaudeville before scoring first Bway hit in *Ziegfeld Follies,* 1911. Between 1913 and 1915 the girls temporarily split up when Jennie married singer Harry Fox and Rosie married composer Jean Schwartz.

One asterisk indicates Jennie without Rosie; two indicate Rosie without Jennie:

1910	The Echo (*Dorothy; Edith*)
1911	Ziegfeld Follies
1912	A Winsome Widow (*Jennie; Rosie*)
	The Merry Countess (*Adele; Felice*)
1913	The Honeymoon Express * (*Marguerite*)
	Lieber Augustin ** (*Clementine*)
1914	The Whirl of the World **
	Hello, Broadway! **
	Maid in America * (*Gaby*)
1916	Her Bridal Night (*Tiny; Vi*)
1919	Oh, Look! (US tour) (*Genevieve; Grace*)
1920	Jig-Saw (L)
1921	League of Notions (L)
	The Fun of the Fayre (L)
1924	Greenwich Village Follies

Donahue, Jack, actor, dancer, singer, librettist; b. Charlestown, Mass., 1892; d. New York, Oct. 1, 1930. Loose-limbed dancer who rose to Bway fame with Marilyn Miller in *Sunny* and *Rosalie,* then won stardom in *Sons o' Guns.*

1919	Angel Face (*Slooch*)
1920	Ziegfeld Follies

1922	Molly Darling (*Chick Jiggs*)
1924	Be Yourself (*Matt McLean*)
1925	Sunny (*Jim Deming*)
1928	Rosalie (*Bill Delroy*)
1929	Sons o' Guns (*Jimmy Canfield*) (also co-lib.)
1930	Princess Charming (lib. only)

Donaldson, Walter, composer; b. Brooklyn, NY, Feb. 15, 1893; d. Santa Monica, Cal., July 15, 1947. Pop song writer whose Bway hit *Whoopee* included "Makin' Whoopee" and "I'm Bringing a Red Red Rose." Lyric-writing collaborators: Ballard Macdonald, Gus Kahn.

1926	Sweetheart Time (Macdonald)
1928	Whoopee (Kahn)

Donnelly, Dorothy, librettist, lyricist; b. New York, Jan. 28, 1880; d. New York, Jan. 3, 1928. Miss Donnelly began her career as an actress, creating role of Shaw's Candida in US. She was most noted for operettas written with composer Sigmund Romberg: *Blossom Time* ("Song of Love"), *The Student Prince* ("Golden Days," "Drinking Song," "Deep in My Heart, Dear," "Serenade"), *My Maryland* ("Your Land and My Land"). Other collaborators: Stephen Jones, William Kernell.

1916	Flora Bella (co-lib. only)
1918	Fancy Free (co-lib. only)
1921	Blossom Time (Romberg)
1923	Poppy (Jones)
1924	The Student Prince in Heidelberg (Romberg)
1926	Hello, Lola (Kernell)
1927	My Maryland (Romberg)
	My Princess (Romberg)

"Don't Ever Leave Me." Music by Jerome Kern; lyric by Oscar Hammerstein II. Romantic plea sung as the chief duet in *Sweet Adeline* (NY 1929) by Helen Morgan and Robert Chisholm.

"Don't Let It Get You Down." Music by Burton Lane; lyric by E. Y. Harburg. Breezy advice to avoid taking love seriously. Introduced by Jack Whiting, Eunice Healey, Russ Brown, Gil Lamb, Margaret Irving, Radio Aces, and Tanner Sisters in *Hold on to Your Hats* (NY 1940). The song was distinguished by a blaring brass figure that interrupted the main melodic theme.

"Don't Rain on My Parade." Music by Jule Styne; lyric by Bob Merrill. Knock-'em-dead avowal of dauntless determination belted out by Barbra Streisand as the first-act finale of *Funny Girl* (NY 1964, L 1966).

Dooley, (Rachel Rice) Ray, actress; b. Glasgow, Scotland, Oct. 30, 1896. Hoydenish comedienne married to Eddie Dowling, with whom she appeared in four Bway musicals and in vaudeville. Her specialty was playing bratty kid parts.

1917	Words and Music
1918	Hitchy-Koo
1919	Ziegfeld Follies
1920	Ziegfeld Follies
1921	Ziegfeld Follies
1922	The Bunch and Judy (*Evie Dallas*)
1923	Nifties of 1923
1925	Ziegfeld Follies (added)
1926	No Foolin'
1927	Sidewalks of New York (*Gertie*)
1928	Earl Carroll Vanities
1934	Thumbs Up!

"Do-Re-Mi." Music by Richard Rodgers; lyric by Oscar Hammerstein II. Sung by Mary Martin and children (Lauri Peters, William Snowden, Kathy Dunn, Joseph Stewart, Marilyn Rogers, Mary Susan Locke, Evanna Lien) in *The Sound of Music* (NY 1959). In London production (1961), sung by Jean Bayless with Barbara Brown, John Coxall, Janet Ware, John

Bosch, Susan Whitnell, Ann Dyer, and Melanie Parr. In the play, this elementary introduction to the notes of the diatonic scale was the means through which Miss Martin, as a young governess, ingratiates herself with her new charges.

Dowling, Eddie (né Joseph Nelson Goucher), actor, lyricist, librettist; b. Woonsocket, RI, Dec. 11, 1894. Genial Bway song-and-dance man who later became dramatic actor and producer (*The Time of Your Life, The Glass Menagerie*). Dowling made his biggest musical-comedy successes in *Sally, Irene and Mary* and *Honeymoon Lane* (singing "The Little White House," which he wrote with James Hanley). He is married to actress Ray Dooley, with whom he appeared in four Bway musicals. (*D. Feb. 18, 1976.*)

Asterisk indicates Mr. Dowling was also librettist:

1919 The Velvet Lady (*Mooney*)
    Ziegfeld Follies
1920 Ziegfeld Follies
1922 Sally, Irene and Mary * (*Jimmie Dugan*)
1926 Honeymoon Lane * (*Tim Murphy*) (also lyr.) (Hanley)
1927 Sidewalks of New York (lib., lyr. only) (Hanley)
1934 Thumbs Up! (also prod.)

"Down in the Depths (on the Ninetieth Floor)." Music & lyric by Cole Porter. In her regal eagle nest, wearing her pet pailletted gown, Ethel Merman sits alone above the town and imagines the fun people are having at all the night spots. The composer wrote the song during the Boston tryout of *Red, Hot and Blue* (NY 1936) and it was in the show two days later.

"Down with Love." Music by Harold Arlen; lyric by E. Y. Harburg. Rhythmic rejection of all things romantic—

including "songs that moan about 'Night and Day' "—introduced by Jack Whiting, June Clyde, and Vivian Vance in *Hooray for What!* (NY 1937).

Drake, Alfred (né Alfredo Capurro), actor, singer; b. New York, Oct. 7, 1914. Drake was Bway's most dashing and robust musical comedy star during the 40s and 50s. His most famous roles were in *Oklahoma!* (in which he introduced "Oh, What a Beautiful Mornin'," "People Will Say We're in Love," "The Surrey with the Fringe on Top," "Oklahoma"), *Kiss Me, Kate* ("Wunderbar," "So in Love," "Where Is the Life That Late I Led?"), and *Kismet* ("And This Is My Beloved"). He also sang "How High the Moon" in *Two for the Show*. Drake has appeared in nonmusicals, incl. Shakespeare.

1936 White Horse Inn (chorus)
1937 Babes in Arms (*Marshall Blackstone*)
1938 The Two Bouquets (*Albert Porter*)
1939 One for the Money
    The Straw Hat Revue
1940 Two for the Show
1943 Oklahoma! (*Curly McLain*)
1944 Sing Out, Sweet Land (*Barnaby Goodchild*)
1946 The Beggar's Holiday (*Macheath*)
1947 The Cradle Will Rock (r) (*Larry Foreman*)
1948 Kiss Me, Kate (*Fred Graham*)
1950 The Liar (co-lib., dir. only)
1951 Courtin' Time (dir. only)
1953 The King and I (*King*, temp. repl.)
    Kismet (*Hajj*)
1955 Kismet (L) (*Hajj*)
1961 Kean (*Edmund Kean*)
1973 Gigi (*Honore Lachailles*)

Dressler, Marie (née Leila Marie Koerber), actress, singer; b. Coburg, Canada, Nov. 9, 1869; d. Santa Barbara, Cal., July 28, 1934. A buxom, bulldog-faced comedienne, Miss Dressler introduced "Heaven Will

Protect the Working Girl" in *Tillie's Nightmare*. She began film career in 1914 and achieved greatest fame during early 30s. Bib: *Life Story of an Ugly Duckling* (McBride, NY 1925), *My Own Story* (Little Brown, Boston 1934), both by Miss Dressler.

1892	The Robber of the Rhine (*Cunigonde*)
1893	Princess Nicotine (*Duchess*)
1894	Giroflé-Giroflá (*Aurore*)
1895	Madeleine (*Mary Douclee*)
	A Stag Party (*Georgia West*)
1896	The Lady Slavey (*Flo Honeydew*)
1898	Hotel Topsy-Turvy (*Flora*)
1899	The Man in the Moon (*Viola*)
1900	Miss Prinnt (*Helen Prinnt*)
1901	The King's Carnival (*Queen Anne*)
1902	The Hall of Fame (*Lady Oblivion*)
	King Highball (*Queen Tarantula*)
1904	Higgledy Piggledy (*Philopena Schnitz*)
1906	Twiddle Twaddle (*Matilda Grabfelder*)
1909	The Boy and the Girl (*Gladys Divine*)
	Philopoena (L) (*Philopoena*)
1910	Tillie's Nightmare (*Tillie Blobbs*)
1912	Roly Poly (*Bijou Fitzsimmons*)
1913	Marie Dressler's All-Star Gambol
1916	The Century Girl
1920	The Passing Show
1921	Cinderella on Broadway (US tour)
1923	The Dancing Girl (*Gloria Seabright*)

"Drinking Song." Music by Sigmund Romberg; lyric by Dorothy Donnelly. Sung by Raymond Marlowe and bibulous student chorus in *The Student Prince in Heidelberg* (NY 1924). Mr. Marlowe also led the roisterers in the London production (1926).

"Drums in My Heart." Music by Vincent Youmans; lyric by Edward Heyman. Percussive, militaristic number, bearing scant relationship to the plot, sung in *Through the Years* (NY 1932) by Gregory Gaye.

DuBarry Was a Lady (1939). Music & lyrics by Cole Porter; book by Herbert Fields & B. G. DeSylva.

SONGS: "It Ain't Etiquette," "When Love Beckoned (in 52nd Street)," "Come on In," "But in the Morning, No," "Do I Love You?," "Give Him the Oo-la-la," "Well Did You Evah!," "It Was Written in the Stars," "Katie Went to Haiti," "Friendship."

NEW YORK: Dec. 6, 1939
46TH ST. THEATRE; 408 p.

Presented by B. G. DeSylva; directed by Edgar MacGregor; choreographed by Robert Alton; settings & costumes, Raoul Pène duBois; music director, Gene Salzer; orchestrations, Hans Spialek.

CAST: Bert Lahr (*Louis Blore*), Ethel Merman (*May Daly*), Betty Grable (*Alice Barton*), Benny Baker (*Charley*), Ronald Graham (*Alex Barton*), Charles Walters (*Harry Norton*).

LONDON: Oct. 22, 1942
HIS MAJESTY'S THEATRE; 178 p.

Presented by Tom Arnold & Harry Foster; directed by Richard Bird; choreographed by Joan Davis; settings, Clifford Pember; costumes, Berkeley Sutcliffe; music director, Harry Collins.

CAST: Arthur Riscoe (*Louis Blore*), Frances Day (*May Daly*), Frances Marsden (*Alice Barton*), Jackie Hunter (*Charley*), Bruce Trent (*Alex Barton*), Teddy Beaumont (*Harry Norton*).

Louis Blore, washroom attendant at the Club Petite in NY, loves May Daly, star of the nightclub's floor show. After winning $75,000 in the Irish Sweepstakes, he also hopes to win May. In the washroom, mistakenly taking a mickey finn he had intended for May's sweetheart, Louis dreams that he is Louis XV and May is DuBarry. Still no soap. The story emerged from the merging of two basic concepts: co-librettist Fields (who had previously used the dream flashback in *A Connecticut Yankee*) wanted to do a show with Mae West as DuBarry, and co-librettist DeSylva had an idea about a nightclub washroom attendant who yearns for the likes of debutante Brenda Frazier. What resulted—with the help of Bert Lahr and Ethel Merman—was the third longest-running Bway book musical of the 30s. During tryout, Ronald Graham replaced Phil Regan in the romantic lead. During Bway run, Miss Merman was succeeded by Betty Allen (8-40), Gypsy Rose Lee (10-40), Frances Williams (11-40). In June, Betty Grable's legs took her off to a Hollywood film career.

FILM VERSION: Lucille Ball, Gene Kelly, Red Skelton (MGM 1943, Roy Del Ruth dir.).

Duke, Vernon (né Vladimir Dukelsky), composer; b. Parafianovo, Russia, Oct. 10, 1903; d. Santa Monica, Cal., Jan. 16, 1969. Duke was a classically trained composer whose highly polished melodies graced Bway revues of the 30s (incl. *The Garrick Gaieties, Ziegfeld Follies, The Show Is On*). With E. Y. Harburg he wrote "April in Paris" and "I Like the Likes of You;" with Ira Gershwin "I Can't Get Started." He also wrote his own lyric to "Autumn in New York." Duke's first book show was *Cabin in the Sky* ("Cabin in the Sky," "Taking a Chance on Love"), lyrics by John Latouche. Other collaborators: Percy Greenbank, Desmond Carter, Collie Knox, Harold Adamson, Howard Dietz, Ogden Nash, Sammy Cahn. Duke, who also composed symphonic and ballet music, first wrote for the London musical theatre in 1926, settled in US in 1929. Bib: *Passport to Paris* by Duke (Little Brown, Boston 1955).

1926	Yvonne (L) (Greenbank)
1928	The Yellow Mask (L) (Carter)
1930	Open Your Eyes (L) (Knox)
1932	Walk a Little Faster Harburg)
1934	Ziegfeld Follies (Harburg)
1936	Ziegfeld Follies (Gershwin)
1940	Cabin in the Sky (Latouche)
1941	Banjo Eyes (Latouche, Adamson)
1942	The Lady Comes Across (Latouche)
1944	Jackpot (Dietz)
	Sadie Thompson (Dietz)
1952	Two's Company (Nash, Cahn)
1956	The Littlest Revue (Nash)

Duncan, Sandy, actress, singer; b. Henderson, Texas, Feb. 20, 1946. The perky, squeaky-voiced, teeth-flashing Miss Duncan acted in NY City Center musical revivals before making Bway debut. Has appeared frequently on tv.

1968	Your Own Thing (*Viola*, repl.)
1969	Canterbury Tales (*Alison*, etc.)
1970	The Boy Friend (r) (*Maisie*)
1979	Peter Pan (r) (*Peter Pan*)

Duncan Sisters, actresses, singers. Rosetta, b. Los Angeles, Cal., Nov. 23, 1900; d. Chicago, Ill., Dec. 4, 1959. Vivian, b. Los Angeles, Cal., June 17, 1902. Vaudeville headliners, originally with Gus Edwards, who won Bway fame writing and starring in *Topsy and Eva*.

1917	Doing Our Bit
1919	She's a Good Fellow (*Mazie Moore; Betty Blair*)
1920	Tip Top
1921	Pins and Needles (L) (added)
1924	Topsy and Eva (*Topsy; Eva*) (also comp., lyr.)
1928	Clowns in Clover (L) (added)
	Topsy and Eva (L) (*Topsy; Eva*) (also comp., lyr.)
1936	New Faces (added)

Duncan, (Robert) Todd, actor, singer; b. Danville, Ky., Feb. 12, 1900. Primarily identified with role in *Porgy and Bess*, in which he introduced "I Got Plenty o' Nuttin'," "Bess, You Is

My Woman Now," "I Loves You, Porgy." Also sang "Lost in the Stars" in musical of that name.

1935 Porgy and Bess (*Porgy*)
1940 Cabin in the Sky (*Lawd's General*)
1942 Porgy and Bess (r) (*Porgy*)
1949 Lost in the Stars (*Stephen Kumalo*)

Dunne Irene, actress, singer; b. Louisville, Ky., Dec. 20, 1901. Bway ingenue with trained soprano voice who became patrician leading lady of film musicals (*Roberta, Show Boat*) and comedies.

1920 Irene (US tour) (*Irene O'Dare*)
1922 The Clinging Vine (*Tessie*)
1924 Lollipop (*Virginia,* repl.)
1925 The City Chap (*Grace Bartlett*)
1926 Sweetheart Time (*Violet,* repl.)
1927 Yours Truly (*Diana*)
1928 She's My Baby (*Polly*)
     Luckee Girl (*Arlette*)
1929 Show Boat (US tour) (*Magnolia Hawks*)

Durante, (James Francis) Jimmy, actor; b. New York, Feb. 10, 1893. Rough-and-tumble clown, famed for his "schnozzola," his stiff-kneed strut, and his "hachacha." Originally a member of the vaudeville trio Clayton, Jackson and Durante, he was joined by his partners for his first two Bway musicals. Durante also appeared in Hollywood films, nightclubs, and on tv. Bib: *Schnozzola* by Gene Fowler (Viking, NY 1951).

1929 Show Girl (*Snozzle*)
1930 The New Yorkers (*Jimmie Deegan*)
1933 Strike Me Pink
1935 Jumbo (*Claudius Bowers*)
1936 Red, Hot and Blue! (*Policy Pinkle*)
1939 Stars in Your Eyes (*Bill*)
1940 Keep Off the Grass

Dussault, Nancy, actress, singer; b. Pensacola, Fla., June 30, 1936. Slim, blonde leading lady who made notable Bway debut in *Do Re Mi* (introducing "Cry Like the Wind"). Has also appeared in opera and NY City Center revivals.

1958 Diversions
1960 Do Re Mi (*Tilda Mullen*)
1962 The Sound of Music (*Maria Rainer,* repl.)
1964 Bajour (*Emily Kirsten*)
1970 Whispers on the Wind (*First Woman*)

E

"Eadie Was a Lady." Music by Richard A. Whiting; lyric by B. G. DeSylva. Narrative number celebrating a deceased lady of sin who had "Klass with a Capital K." It was introduced in *Take a Chance* (NY 1932) by Ethel Merman as part of a show within a show called *Humpty Dumpty,* in which the setting was a New Orleans levee saloon during the Spanish-American War. The number had been written in the style of "The Man on the Flying Trapeze" because Walter O'Keefe, who was identified with that song, had been signed for the show. When he withdrew before rehearsals, "Eadie" was dropped but was later reinstated for the production number.

"Eagle and Me, The." Music by Harold Arlen; lyric by E. Y. Harburg. Playing the role of a slave, Dooley Wilson expressed this yearning for freedom in *Bloomer Girl* (NY 1944).

Earl Carroll Vanities (1931). Music by Burton Lane, etc.; lyrics by Harold Adamson, etc.; sketches by Ralph Spence, Eddie Welch.

SONGS: "Have a Heart," "Heigh-Ho, the Gang's All Here," "Goodnight, Sweetheart" (Ray Noble, Jimmy Campbell, Reg Connelly), "Bolero" (Maurice Ravel), "Tonight or Never" (Vincent Rose-Ray Klages, Jack Meskill).

NEW YORK: Aug. 27, 1931
EARL CARROLL THEATRE; 278 p.

Presented by Earl Carroll; directed by Carroll & Edgar MacGregor; choreographed by George Hale, Gluck Sandor; settings, Vincente Minelli, Hugh Willoughby; costumes, Minnelli, Charles LeMaire; music director, Ray Kavanaugh; orchestrations, Domenico Savino.

CAST: Will Mahoney, Lillian Roth, William Demarest, Frank Mitchell, Jack Durant, Milton Watson, Lucille Page, Woods Miller, Slate Brothers, Helen Lynd, Beryl Wallace, Irene Ahlberg.

With the 1931 edition of his annual Bway revue series, impressario Earl Carroll also opened a new theatre, built on the same site, 7th Ave. and 50th St., as the previous Earl Carroll Theatre. The 3,000-seat house was hailed as the most sumptuous in New York, and it cost $4.5 million to open both theatre and show. Because of its size, Carroll was able to scale down the orchestra ticket price to $3.30. The show itself offered the customary Carroll blend of tastelessness, nudity, and overpowering spectacle. Among the attractions were a tom-tommed "Bolero," a "living curtain" offering showgirls as "prehistoric" allegorical figures, and a parasol parade with the girls as wicked ladies of history.

Firm in his conviction that nothing succeeds like excess, Carroll began his *Vanities* in 1923 as an obvious rival to *Ziegfeld Follies,* and at times his obviousness got him in trouble with the police (which of course, only helped the box office). In all, Carroll offered 11 *Vanities* (there were two in 1925), plus two editions, 1929 and 1935, designated as *Sketch Books.* All revues were presented at the two Earl Carroll Theatres, except for those offered in 1924 (Music Box), 1932 (Broadway), 1935 (Winter Garden), 1940 (St. James). The longest-running production was the 1929 *Sketch Book,* which lasted 400 performances.

The best-known slogan of the *Vanities* was the sign over the stage door: "Through These Portals Pass the Most Beautiful Girls in the World." For the 1930 edition, Carroll used the phrase "Meeting America's Demand for Sophisticated Entertainment" and called the show "The World's Greatest Revue." The following year he scaled down the claim to "America's Greatest Revue."

Among performers who appeared in *Vanities* and *Sketch Book* editions: Joe Cook (3), Patsy Kelly (3), Lillian Roth (3), Peggy Hopkins Joyce, Jessica Dragonette, Smith and Dale, Frank Tinney, Jessie Matthews (in an abbreviated *Charlot's Revue* offered as part of the 1927 *Vanities'* "International Edition"), W. C. Fields, Ray Dooley, Jimmy Savo, Jack Benny, Herb Williams, Milton Berle, Helen Broderick, and Will Fyffe. Though the series was not noted for its music, such writers as Harold Arlen, E. Y. Harburg, Ted Koehler, and Jay Gorney wrote songs for the *Vanities,* with the most durable number being "I Gotta Right to Sing the Blues."

In 1933 Carroll tried a variation on the revue by offering a revue with a plot called *Murder at the Vanities.* It ran 207 performances.

FILM VERSIONS (both with plots,

new songs): Dennis O'Keefe and Constance Moore (Rep. 1945, Joseph Santley dir.); Constance Moore and William Marshall (Rep. 1946, Albert Rogell dir.).

"Easter Parade." Music & lyric by Irving Berlin. Sung by Clifton Webb and Marilyn Miller as they lead a stylish parade down 5th Avenue in the first-act finale of the revue *As Thousands Cheer* (NY 1933). Since the entire show was created in the form of a newspaper, the justification for the number was a rotogravure section showing the parade as it might have looked in 1883. As Irving Berlin recalls: "I'd written a couple of old-fashioned-type songs but they were lousy. So I reached back to something I'd written in 1917. It went, 'Smile and show your dimple, you'll find it's very simple . . .' It was a poor imitation of the cheer-up kind of songs of the day, like 'Pack Up Your Troubles in Your Old Kit Bag.' But I'd always liked the main four-bar theme. So for *As Thousands Cheer*, instead of trying to write a new old-fashioned melody I simply used a real old-fashioned melody. Except that now, of course, I made the words apply to an Easter parade." In a much-revised London edition of the revue, called *Stop Press* (1935), the song was used for the finale and was sung by Dorothy Dickson and Gordon Little. For this version, reference in the lyric to Fifth Avenue was altered to apply to Hyde Park's Rotten Row.

"Easy to Be Hard." Music by Galt MacDermot; lyric by Gerome Ragni & James Rado. People's indifference to people. Introduced in *Hair* (NY 1967) by Suzannah Evans, Linda Compton, Paul Jabara, and company, and by Annabel Leventon in London transplant (1968).

Eaton, Mary, dancer, singer, actress; b. Norfolk, Va., 1902; d. Hollywood, Cal., Oct. 10, 1948. Blonde dancer who was Ziegfeld's replacement for Marilyn Miller. Miss Eaton's biggest Bway hit was *The Five o'Clock Girl* (introducing "Thinking of You").

1916	Follow Me (chorus)
1917	Over the Top
1919	The Royal Vagabond (*Rozello*)
1920	Ziegfeld Follies
1921	Ziegfeld Follies
1922	Ziegfeld Follies
1923	Kid Boots (*Polly Pendleton*)
1927	Lucky (*Lucky*)
	The Five o'Clock Girl (*Patricia Brown*)
1931	Folly to Be Wise (L)

Ebb, Fred, lyricist; b. New York, April 8, 1932. Ebb and his partner, composer John Kander, have written three Bway scores for producer Harold Prince incl. their biggest hit, *Cabaret* ("Willkommen," "Tomorrow Belongs to Me," "Married," "Cabaret"). The lyricist has also contributed songs to revues with Paul Klein.

Unless otherwise noted, following written with Mr. Kander:

1963	Morning Sun (Klein)
1965	Flora, the Red Menace
1966	Cabaret
1968	The Happy Time
	Zorbá
1971	70, Girls, 70
1975	Chicago (also co-lib.)
1977	The Act

Ebsen, (Christian Rudolf) Buddy, actor, dancer; b. Orlando, Fla., April 2, 1908. Lanky, contortionistic dancer with hayseed personality, Ebsen was teamed with sister Vilma until mid-30s. On Bway they danced to "A Shine on Your Shoes" in *Flying Colors* and "I Like the Likes of You" in *Ziegfeld Follies*. Ebsen appeared in Hollywood films (*Born to Dance*), then won new popularity in tv series *The Beverly Hillbillies* and *Barnaby Jones*.

1928 Whoopee (chorus)
1932 Flying Colors
1934 Ziegfeld Follies
1939 Yokel Boy (*Elmer Whipple*)
1946 Show Boat (r) (*Frank Schultz*)

"Edelweiss." Music by Richard Rodgers; lyric by Oscar Hammerstein II. Tender ode to the Alpine flower sung in *The Sound of Music* (NY 1959) by Capt. Von Trapp and his family to show their love of their homeland just before escaping to Switzerland. Theodore Bikel played Von Trapp in NY, Roger Dann in London (1961). This was the last lyric written by Oscar Hammerstein.

Edwardes, George (né George Edwardes), producer; b. Clee, Eng., Oct. 14, 1855; d. London, Oct. 4, 1915. Edwardes, London's most renowned theatre manager from the late 19th through the early years of the 20th century, is credited with having introduced the form of entertainment known as musical comedy with his productions of *In Town* and *A Gaiety Girl*. The success of the latter persuaded him to abandon the musical burlesques he had been presenting and concentrate on original comic stories with songs. Among Edwardes' greatest hits—all running over 500 performances—were *The Shop Girl, The Geisha, La Poupée, A Runaway Girl, San Toy, The Toreador, A Country Girl, The Orchid, The Merry Widow, Our Miss Gibbs, The Quaker Girl*. George Grossmith appeared in 12 Edwardes musicals, Gertie Millar was in nine, Lily Elsie in eight, Joseph Coyne and Ellaline Terriss in five each, Seymour Hicks and Edna May in three each. Composers and lyricists who wrote scores for the producer included Sidney Jones, Ivan Caryll, Lionel Monckton, Harry and Percy Greenbank, Adrian Ross, Howard Talbot, Paul Rubens, Owen Hall.

Bib: *Curtain Call for the Guv'nor* by Ursula Bloom (Hutchinson, L 1954).

1885 Little Jack Sheppard
1886 Adonis
     Monte Cristo Jr.
1887 Miss Esmerelda
     Frankenstein
1888 Faust Up to Date
1889 Ruy Blas and the Blasé Roué
1890 Carmen Up to Date
1891 Joan of Arc
     Cinder-Ellen Up Too Late
1892 In Town
1893 A Gaiety Girl
     Don Juan
1894 His Excellency
     The Shop Girl
1895 An Artist's Model
     Gentleman Joe
1896 The Geisha
     My Girl
     The Circus Girl
1897 La Poupée
1898 A Runaway Girl
     A Greek Slave
     The Royal Star
1899 The Coquette
     San Toy
1900 The Messenger Boy
1901 The Toreador
     Kitty Grey
1902 A Country Girl
     Three Little Maids
     The Girl from Kay's
1903 The School Girl
     The Duchess of Dantsic
     The Orchid
     The Earl and the Girl
     The Cherry Girl
     Madame Sherry
1904 The Cingalee
     Veronique
     Lady Madcap
1905 The Little Michus
     The Spring Chicken
     Rogues and Vagabonds
1906 The Naughty Boys
     The Little Cherub
     The Girl on the Stage
     See-See
     The New Aladdin
     The Merveilleuses
     The Vicar of Wakefield
1907 The Girls of Gottenberg

The Merry Widow
1908 A Waltz Dream
Havana
1909 Our Miss Gibbs
The Dollar Princess
1910 The Girl on the Train
The Quaker Girl
1911 Peggy
By George!
The Count of Luxembourg
1912 The Sunshine Girl
Autumn Manoeuvres
Gipsy Love
The Dancing Mistress
1913 The Girl on the Film
The Marriage Market
The Girl from Utah
1914 After the Girl
Adèle

Edwards, Sherman, composer, lyricist; b. New York, April 4, 1919. Edwards, a former dance-band pianist and pop song writer, has had one Bway musical and one Bway hit.
1969 1776

"El Capitan's Song." Music & lyric by John Philip Sousa. DeWolf Hopper's swaggering self-introduction in *El Capitan* (NY 1896, L 1899), in which he announced: "Behold El Capitan;/ Gaze on his misanthropic stare,/ Notice his penetrating glare,/ Come match him if you can./ He is the champion beyond compare." Sousa later adapted this melody as part of his *El Capitan March.*

Ellis, Mary (née Mary Elsas), actress, singer; b. New York, June 15, 1900. Before settling in London in 1930, Miss Ellis scored Bway success in *Rose-Marie,* in which she introduced "Indian Love Call." In London she was the heroine of three Ivor Novello operettas, *Glamorous Night* ("Fold Your Wings," "Glamorous Night"), *The Dancing Years* ("Waltz of My Heart," "I Can Give You the Starlight"), and *Arc de Triomphe.* She began career as singer with the Metropolitan Opera (1918), and has also acted in nonmusicals.
1924 Rose-Marie (NY) (*Rose-Marie La Flamme*)
1933 Music in the Air (*Frieda Hatzfeld*)
1935 Glamorous Night (*Militza Hajos*)
1939 The Dancing Years (*Maria Ziegler*)
1943 Arc de Triomphe (*Marie Foret*)
1954 After the Ball (*Mrs. Erlynne*)

Ellis, Vivian, composer, lyricist; b. Hemstead, Eng., Oct. 29, 1904. Began career as concert pianist, then wrote songs for London revues. His biggest success was *Bless the Bride* ("This Is My Lovely Day," "Ma Belle Marguerite"), lyrics by A. P. Herbert. Ellis also wrote his own lyrics ("She's My Lovely") and collaborated with Graham John, Greatrex Newman, Ronald Jeans, Donovan Parsons, Clifford Grey ("Spread a Little Happiness"), Beverley Nichols, Douglas Furber, Desmond Carter ("The Wind in the Willows," "I'm on a See-Saw"). Among those who introduced Ellis' songs: Bobby Howes, Binnie Hale, John Mills, Frances Day, Cicely Courtneidge, Jack Hulbert. Bib: *I'm on a See-Saw* by Ellis (Joseph, L 1953).
1925 ·By the Way (John)
1926 Palladium Pleasures (Newman, Jeans)
Just a Kiss (Carter)
1928 Will o' the Whispers (Parsons)
1929 Mr. Cinders (Grey, Newman)
1930 Cochran's 1930 Revue (Nichols)
Follow a Star (Furber)
Little Tommy Tucker (Carter)
1931 Song of the Drum (Carter)
Blue Roses (Carter)
Stand Up and Sing (Furber)
1932 Out of the Bottle (Grey)
Over the Page
1934 Streamline (Herbert)
Jill Darling (Carter)
1936 The Town Talks

Going Places
1937 Hide and Seek
1938 The Fleet's Lit Up
Running Riot
Under Your Hat
1946 Big Ben (Herbert)
1947 Bless the Bride (Herbert)
1949 Tough at the Top (Herbert)
1951 And So to Bed
1953 Over the Moon
1955 The Water Gipsies (Herbert)
1961 Four to the Bar

Elsie, Lily (née Lily Elsie Cotton), actress, singer; b. Wortley, Eng., April 8, 1886; d. London, Dec. 16, 1962. Slim, elegant, graceful prima donna with cameo profile who scored her greatest London triumph in the first English-language *Merry Widow* (introducing "Vilia," "The Merry Widow Waltz"). Other successes were *The Dollar Princess* and *The Count of Luxembourg.*

1901 A Chinese Honeymoon (*Princess Soo-Soo*)
1904 Lady Madcap (*Gwenny Holden*)
The Cingalee (UK tour) (*Lady Patricia Vereker*)
1905 The Little Michus (*Mme. duTertre*)
1906 The Little Cherub (*Lady Agnes Congress*)
See-See (*Humming Bird*)
The New Aladdin (*Lally*)
1907 The Merry Widow (*Sonia Sadoya*)
1909 The Dollar Princess (*Alice Couder*)
1911 A Waltz Dream (r) (*Franzi Steingruber*)
The Count of Luxembourg (*Angèle Didier*)
1917 Pamela (*Pamela*)
1927 The Blue Train (*Eileen Mayne*)

"Embraceable You." Music by George Gershwin; lyric by Ira Gershwin. Romantic duet for Ginger Rogers and Allen Kearns in *Girl Crazy* (NY 1930). The number, which was staged by Fred Astaire, had originally been written in 1929 for an unproduced musical version of *East Is West* called *Ming Toy*, and was intended for Marilyn Miller.

Englander, Ludwig, composer; b. Vienna, Austria, 1853; d. Far Rockaway, NY, Sept. 13, 1914. To US 1882. Englander's Bway hits were *The Passing Show* (first NY revue), *The Rich Mr. Hoggenheimer* and *Miss Innocence.* Collaborators: Sydney Rosenfeld, J. Cheever Goodwin, Harry B. Smith, Grant Stewart, Stanislaus Stange, George V. Hobart, Edward Paulton.

1894 The Passing Show (Rosenfeld)
1895 The 20th Century Girl (Rosenfeld)
A Daughter of the Revolution (Goodwin)
1896 The Caliph (Smith)
1897 Gayest Manhattan (Smith)
A Round of Pleasure (Rosenfeld)
1898 The Little Corporal (Smith)
1899 In Gay Paree (Stewart)
The Man in the Moon (Stange)
The Rounders (Smith)
1900 The Casino Girl (Smith)
The Monks of Malabar (Goodwin)
The Cadet Girl (Smith)
The Belle of Bohemia (Smith)
1901 The Strollers (Smith)
The New Yorkers (Hobart)
1902 The Wild Rose (Smith, Hobart)
Sally in Our Alley (Hobart)
1903 The Jewel of Asia (Smith)
The Office Boy (Smith)
1904 A Madcap Princess (Smith)
The Two Roses (Stange)
1905 The White Cat (Smith)
1906 The Rich Mr. Hoggenheimer (Smith)
1907 The Gay White Way (Rosenfeld)
1908 Miss Innocence (Smith)
1914 Madame Moselle (Paulton)

Erlanger, A(braham) L(incoln), producer; b. Buffalo, NY, May 4, 1860; d. New York, March 7, 1930. With partner Marc Klaw, Erlanger became the most powerful American booking agent, controlling at one time some 700 theatres. As Bway producer (he broke with Klaw in 1919), Erlanger had such successes as *The Ham Tree, Forty-Five Minutes from Broadway, The Pink Lady, The Perfect Fool, Honeymoon Lane.*

1894 The Brownies
1896 Jack and the Beanstalk
1897 A Round of Pleasure
1898 The Bride-Elect
1900 Rogers Brothers in Central Park
     Foxy Quiller
1901 Rogers Brothers in Washington
     The Liberty Belles
     Sleeping Beauty
1902 Rogers Brothers in Harvard
     The Billionaire
1903 Mr. Bluebeard
     Rogers Brothers in London
     Mother Goose
1904 A Little Bit of Everything
     Rogers Brothers in Paris
     Humpty Dumpty
     In Newport
1905 Lifting the Lid
     The Pearl and the Pumpkin
     The Ham Tree
     Rogers Brothers in Ireland
     Fritz in Tammany Hall
     Veronique
     The White Cat
1906 Forty-Five Minutes from Broadway
     The Free Lance
     The Spring Chicken
1907 The Grand Mogul
     Rogers Brothers in Panama
     Lola from Berlin
1908 Little Nemo
1909 The Mascot
     In Hayti
     The Silver Star
1910 The Young Turk
     The Bachelor Belles
1911 The Pink Lady
1912 The Count of Luxembourg
     Oh! Oh! Delphine
     Eva
1913 The Little Café
1914 Papa's Darling
1915 Fads and Fancies
     Around the Map
1916 Miss Springtime
1917 The Riviera Girl
1918 The Rainbow Girl
     The Girl Behind the Gun
1919 The Velvet Lady
1921 Two Little Girls in Blue
     The Perfect Fool
1922 The Yankee Princess
1925 By the Way
1926 Honeymoon Lane
     Happy Go Lucky
1927 Ziegfeld Follies

Errol, Leon, actor, director; b. Sydney, Australia, July 3, 1881; d. Hollywood, Cal., Oct. 12, 1951. Errol was a bandy-legged, sour-faced comic who rose to Bway fame in the *Ziegfeld Follies* and became star in *Sally.* He also appeared in vaudeville and in Hollywood films.

1910 Follies of 1910
1911 Ziegfeld Follies
1912 A Winsome Widow (*Ben Gay*)
     Ziegfeld Follies
1913 Ziegfeld Follies
1914 Ziegfeld Follies (also dir.)
1915 Ziegfeld Follies (also dir.)
1916 The Century Girl (also co-dir.)
1917 Hitchy-Koo
     Words and Music (dir. only)
1918 Hitchy-Koo
1919 Joy-Bells (L)
1920 Sally (*Connie*)
1922 The Blue Kitten (dir. only)
1925 Louie the 14th (*Louie Ketchup*)
1927 Yours Truly (*Truly*)
1929 Fioretta (*Julio Pepoli*)

Etting, Ruth, actress, singer; b. David City, Neb., Nov. 23, 1907. Slim, blonde torch singer who made greatest success in nightclubs. On Bway, introduced "Shaking the Blues Away" (*Ziegfeld Follies of 1927*), "Love Me or Leave Me" (*Whoopee*), "Get Happy" (*9:15 Revue*), "Ten Cents a Dance" (*Simple Simon*); reintroduced "Shine on Harvest Moon" (*Ziegfeld Follies of 1931*). (D. Sept. 24, 1978.)

1927 Ziegfeld Follies
1928 Whoopee (*Leslie Daw*)
1930 Ruth Selwyn's 9:15 Revue
      Simple Simon (*Sal*)
1931 Ziegfeld Follies
1936 Transatlantic Rhythm (L)

Evangeline (1874). Music by Edward E. Rice; lyrics by J. Cheever Goodwin; book by Rice & Goodwin, based on Longfellow's poem.

SONGS: "Evangeline March," "Thinking, Love, of Thee," "Sweet Evangeline," "Sweet the Song of Birds," "We Are Off to Seek for Eva," "Where Art Thou Now, My Beloved?," "Fie Upon You, Fie," "My Best Beloved," "I Don't—Do You?" (added).

NEW YORK: July 27, 1874
NIBLO'S GARDEN; 2 weeks.

Presented & directed by Edward E. Rice; settings, George Heister; costumes, Harry Seymour; music director, John T. Braham.

CAST: Ione Burke (*Evangeline*), James Dunn (*Basil*), W. H. Crane (*LeBlanc*), J. W. Thoman (*Lone Fisherman*), Connie Thompson (*Gabriel*), Louis Mestayer (*Catherine*).

After seeing the English dancer Lydia Thomson perform with her troupe of high-kicking blondes, composer Rice and librettist Goodwin decided to write an "American extravaganza" that would feature similar bare-legged dancing. They settled on Longfellow's poem *Evangeline* for general inspiration and created a travesty that was among the first American musicals with a completely original score. Subtitled *The Belle of Acadia*, it was initially offered as a two-week interim booking at Niblo's Garden, but it scored such a hit that it went on tour and then returned to NY in a more elaborate production at Daly's Theatre, June 4, 1877. Lizzie Harold

played the title role, N. C. Goodwin was Le Blanc, and Henry E. Dixey made his Bway debut as Redsnake. The show was revived periodically for some 30 years.

To reveal their legs, some of the female members of the cast—including Connie Thompson (later Elizabeth Weathersby) as Gabriel—appeared in tights playing male roles. A man, Louis Mestayer (later George K. Fortescue), played the leading female comic. One of the major attractions, beside a two-man dancing cow, was The Lone Fisherman, who had little to do with the story but sat on the stage isolated and mute (J. W. Thoman, who originated the role, was succeeded by James S. Maffitt). What plot the show had bore scant resemblance to Longfellow, as it took our heroine from Acadia to Africa to Arizona. A major revival was mounted in NY in 1885, with a revised book by John J. McNally and Fay Templeton as Gabriel. This production ran 251 performances. For many of its appearances on the road, the musical was billed as *Rice's Beautiful Evangeline*.

Rice also wrote and produced two other musicals based on Longfellow poems: *Hiawatha* (1880) and *Excelsior Jr.* (1895).

Evans, Maurice, actor; b. Dorchester, Eng., June 3, 1901. Shakespearean actor famed for his Bway productions of *Richard II, Hamlet,* and *Henry IV, Part 1*.

1933 Ball at the Savoy (L) (*Aristide*)
1960 Tenderloin (NY) (*Dr. Brock*)

"Evelina." Music by Harold Arlen; lyric by E. Y. Harburg. Jaunty marriage proposal—with asides by the proposee—sung by David Brooks and Celeste Holm in *Bloomer Girl* (NY 1944).

Ever Green (1930). Music by Richard Rodgers; lyrics by Lorenz Hart; book by Benn W. Levy, based on idea by Rodgers & Hart.

SONGS: "Dear, Dear," "No Place but Home," "In the Cool of the Evening," "Dancing on the Ceiling," "If I Give in to You."

LONDON: Dec. 3, 1930
ADELPHI THEATRE; 254 p.

Presented by Charles B. Cochran; directed by Frank Collins; choreographed by Buddy Bradley & Billy Pierce; settings, Ernst Stern; costumes, Reville, Ltd.; music director, Richard Crean; orchestrations, Robert Russell Bennett.

CAST: Jessie Matthews (*Harriet Green*), Sonnie Hale (*Tommy Thompson*), Joyce Barbour (*Mary Tucket*), Jean Cadell (*Mrs. Platter*), Albert Burdon (*Eric Merivale*), Kay Hammond (*Dolly*).

Jessie Matthews' greatest stage success (her fourth opposite Sonnie Hale) cast her as a young girl who, to advance her career, hits upon the idea of claiming to be 60 years old, miraculously preserved by cosmetology. After eventually admitting her deception, she wins over both leading man Tommy Thompson and loyal public. The production was excessively lavish—it introduced the revolving stage to London—and was set in such varied locales as the Albert Hall, the Neuilly Fair outside Paris, the Casino des Folies in Paris, and a religious festival in Catalonia, Spain. This was the first attraction at the renovated Adelphi Theatre and was the last of three musicals Rodgers and Hart wrote in London.

FILM VERSION: Jessie Matthews and Sonnie Hale (title spelled as one word, with story altered and new songs added) (Gaumont Brit. 1934, Victor Saville dir.).

"Every Day Is Ladies' Day with Me." Music by Victor Herbert; lyric by Henry Blossom. Sung by Neal McCay as the roguish governor of Zeeland in *The Red Mill* (NY 1906), and by Gus Sharland in London version (1919).

"Every Little Movement." Music by Karl Hoschna; lyric by Otto Hauerbach (Harbach). Slightly suggestive song hit of *Madame Sherry* (NY 1910), in which it was sung by Frances Demarest and John Reinhard.

"Ev'ry Street's a Boulevard in Old New York." Music by Jule Styne; lyric by Bob Hilliard. Show-stopping, hammy ode to the city in *Hazel Flagg* (NY 1952), sung and soft-shoed by Jimmy Walkerish mayor Jack Whiting.

"Ev'ry Time." Music & lyrics by Hugh Martin & Ralph Blane. Torchy lament of a born loser introduced by Maureen Cannon in *Best Foot Forward* (NY 1941). In final eight bars of the second chorus, the lyric includes the titles of two Bway musicals of the previous season, *Cabin in the Sky* and *Lady in the Dark*.

"Ev'ry Time We Say Goodbye." Music & lyric by Cole Porter. Brooding song of farewell introduced by Nan Wynn and Jere MacMahon in *Seven Lively Arts* (NY 1944). Note that at the end of the song, the melody, as prescribed by the lyric, goes from major to minor.

"Everybody Has the Right to Be Wrong." Music by James Van Heusen; lyric by Sammy Cahn. Human fallibility defended by Peter L. Marshall in *Skyscraper* (NY 1965), later concurred in by Julie Harris.

"Everybody Step." Music & lyric by Irving Berlin. Syncopated invitation to the dance introduced as the first-act finale of the *Music Box Revue* by the Brox Sisters and company (NY 1921, L 1923).

"Ev'rybody's Got a Home but Me." Music by Richard Rodgers; lyric by Oscar Hammerstein II. Lament of a homeless girl sung by Judy Tyler in *Pipe Dream* (NY 1955).

"Ev'rything I Love." Music & lyric by Cole Porter. Danny Kaye and Mary Jane Walsh pledged their total devotion in *Let's Face It* (NY 1941). In London version (1942), it was Bobby Howes and Pat Kirkwood.

"Ev'rything I've Got." Music by Richard Rodgers; lyric by Lorenz Hart. Comic duet of verbal and physical threats sung by Benay Venuta and Ray Bolger in *By Jupiter* (NY 1942).

"Everything's Coming Up Roses." Music by Jule Styne; lyric by Stephen Sondheim. Song of indestructibility sung by Ethel Merman, alone on a midwestern railway platform, as the first-act finale of *Gypsy* (NY 1959). In London production (1973), sung by Angela Lansbury. The same music, but with a different lyric and called "Betwixt and Between," had been cut from the score of *High Button Shoes.*

"Exactly Like You." Music by Jimmy McHugh; lyric by Dorothy Fields. Mutual praise exchanged by Gertrude Lawrence and Harry Richman in Lew Leslie's *International Revue* (NY 1930).

"Experiment." Music & lyric by Cole Porter. Didactic advice offered as theme song of *Nymph Errant* (L 1933) by Moya Nugent, reprised by Gertrude Lawrence.

F

Fabray, Nanette (née Nanette Theresa Fabares), actress, singer; b. San Diego, Cal., Oct. 27, 1922. A vivacious, snub-nosed singing actress, Miss Fabray first attracted notice on Bway in *Meet the People*. After replacing the leads in two Bway successes she won major roles in *High Button Shoes* (introducing "Papa, Won't You Dance with Me?" and "I Still Get Jealous") and *Love Life* ("Green-up Time" and "Here I'll Stay"). Miss Fabray has also acted in films (incl. *The Band Wagon*) and on tv.

1940 Meet the People
1941 Let's Face It! (*Jean Blanchard*)
1943 By Jupiter (*Antiope*, repl.)
     My Dear Public (*Jean*)
1944 Jackpot (*Sally Madison*)
1945 Bloomer Girl (*Evelina*, repl.)
1947 High Button Shoes (*Sara Longstreet*)
1948 Love Life (*Susan Cooper*)
1950 Arms and the Girl (*Jo Kirkland*)
1951 Make a Wish (*Janette*)
1962 Mr. President (*Nell Henderson*)

Fain, Sammy (né Samuel Feinberg), composer; b. New York, June 17, 1902. On Bway, Fain wrote songs for the long-running Olsen and Johnson hits, *Hellzapoppin* and *Sons o' Fun* ("Happy in Love"). Less successful productions contained such durable numbers as "I'll Be Seeing You," "I Can Dream, Can't I?," "Are You Havin' Any Fun?," "Here's to Your

Illusions," "The World Is Your Balloon," "He's Only Wonderful," and "The Springtime Cometh" (the last four from *Flahooley*). A Hollywood writer for many years, Fain has collaborated with lyricists Irving Kahal, Charles Tobias, Jack Yellen, George Marion Jr., E. Y. Harburg, Dan Shapiro, Paul Francis Webster, Alan and Marilyn Bergman.

1931 Everybody's Welcome (Kahal)
1938 Right This Way (Kahal)
      Hellzapoppin (Tobias)
1939 George White's Scandals (Yellen)
1940 Boys and Girls Together (Kahal, Yellen)
1941 Sons o' Fun (Yellen)
1946 Toplitzky of Notre Dame (Marion)
1951 Flahooley (Harburg)
1955 Ankles Aweigh (Shapiro)
1960 Christine (Webster)
1964 Something More! (Bergmans)

"Falling in Love with Love." Music by Richard Rodgers; lyric by Lorenz Hart. Rueful waltz introduced by Muriel Angelus and her maids as they weave a tapestry in *The Boys from Syracuse* (NY 1938). In London revival (1963), Lynn Kennington did the singing and weaving. The ballad was also sung by Binnie Hale in *Up and Doing* (L 1940).

"Fancy Our Meeting." Music by Philip Charig & Joseph Meyer; lyric by Douglas Furber. Casual song-and-dance number occasioned by a chance encounter between Jack Buchanan and Elsie Randolph in *That's a Good Girl* (L 1928). The song, which was responsible for establishing Buchanan and Randolph as a London team, was also performed by Buchanan—this time with Jessie Matthews—in *Wake Up and Dream!* (NY 1929). The melody of the Walter Donaldson–Harold Adamson song "Did I Remember?" is similar to that of "Fancy Our Meeting."

Fanny (1954). Music & lyrics by Harold Rome; book by S. N. Behrman and Joshua Logan, based on Marcel Pagnol's trilogy, *Marius, César* and *Fanny*.

SONGS: "Never Too Late for Love," "Restless Heart," "Why Be Afraid to Dance?," "Welcome Home," "I Have to Tell You," "Fanny," "Love Is a Very Light Thing," "I Like You."

NEW YORK: Nov. 4, 1954
MAJESTIC THEATRE; 888 p.
Presented by David Merrick & Joshua Logan; directed by Logan; choreographed by Helen Tamiris; settings & lighting, Jo Mielziner; costumes, Alvin Colt; music director, Lehman Engel; orchestrations, Philip J. Lang.
CAST: Ezio Pinza (*César*), Walter Slezak (*Panisse*), Florence Henderson (*Fanny*), William Tabbert (*Marius*), Nejla Ates (*Dancing Girl*), Gerald Price (*The Admiral*), Alan Carney (*Escartifique*), Tani Seitz (*Claudine*), Dran Seitz (*Claudette*), Mohammed el Bakkar (*Rug Dealer*), Edna Preston (*Honorine*).

LONDON: Nov. 15, 1956
DRURY LANE THEATRE; 347 p.
Presented by S. A. Gorlinsky; directed by William Hammerstein; choreographed by Onna White; settings & costumes, Georges Wakhevitch; lighting, Michael Northen; music director, Michael Collins; orchestrations, Philip J. Lang.
CAST: Ian Wallace (*César*), Robert Morley (*Panisse*), Janet Pavek (*Fanny*), Kevin Scott (*Marius*), Hameda (*Dancing Girl*), Michael Gough (*The Admiral*), C. Denier Warren (*Escartifique*), Leander Fedden (*Claudette*), Eira Heath (*Claudine*), Alan Gabriel (*Rug Dealer*), Mona Washbourne (*Honorine*).
Producer David Merrick worked three years with various librettists

until he brought in Joshua Logan to write the adaptation with S. N. Behrman. Because of his recent association with the musical Wish You Were Here, Logan then added composer Harold Rome. The story of Fanny, condensed from the film trilogy, is set on the waterfront of Marseilles. César's son, Marius, loves Fanny but goes away to sea. Fanny, who is pregnant, accepts the marriage proposal of César's friend, middle-aged Panisse. During Bway run, Ezio Pinza was succeeded by Lawrence Tibbett, Walter Slezak by Billy Gilbert. Beginning Dec. 1956, the show toured five months with Italo Tajo and Gilbert. The London Fanny marked the musical stage debut of Robert Morley.

FILM VERSION: Leslie Caron, Maurice Chevalier, Charles Boyer (no songs) (Warner 1960, Joshua Logan dir.).

"Fanny." Music & lyric by Harold Rome. Impassioned aria sung by William Tabbert to Florence Henderson in Fanny (NY 1954) to explain that his love for the sea was even stronger than his love for her. In London production (1956), it was sung by Kevin Scott to Janet Pavek.

Fantasticks, The (1960). Music by Harvey Schmidt; lyrics & book by Tom Jones, based on Edmund Rostand's play Les Romanesques.

SONGS: "Try to Remember," "Much More," "It Depends on What You Pay," "Soon It's Gonna Rain," "I Can See It," "Plant a Radish," "Round and Round," "They Were You."

NEW YORK: May 3, 1960
SULLIVAN ST. PLAYHOUSE
Presented by Lore Noto; directed by Word Baker; settings & costumes, Ed Wittstein; music director, Julian Stein; orchestrations, Stein.

CAST: Jerry Orbach (El Gallo), Kenneth Nelson (Matt Hucklebee), Rita Gardner (Luisa Bellamy), William Larsen (Hucklebee), Hugh Thomas (Amos Babcock Bellamy), Thomas Bruce (Tom Jones) (Henry Albertson), George Curley (Mortimer).

LONDON: Sept. 7, 1961
APOLLO THEATRE; 44 p.
Presented by Toby Rowland Ltd. & Frank Productions; directed by Word Baker; settings & costumes, Ed Wittstein; music director, Raymond Holder.

CAST: Terence Cooper (El Gallo), Peter Gilmore (Matt Hucklebee), Stephanie Voss (Luisa Bellamy), Michael Barrington (Hucklebee), Timothy Bateson (Amos Babcock Bellamy), John Wood (Henry Albertson), John Caton (Mortimer).

At this writing, The Fantasticks is still playing in NY, thus making it the musical with the greatest number of consecutive performances ever to run either in NY or London (the theatre, however, seats only 150). The work, which is much concerned with the theme of seasonal rebirth, spins the fanciful tale of two young people whose fathers express disapproval to ensure their falling in love. The fathers even hire El Gallo to perform a mock rape scene with two actors so that the hero may prove his valor and pave the way for parental approval. The lovers, however, learn of the hoax and quarrel. After the boy runs away and suffers numerous indignities, he returns to the waiting girl. Through disillusionment, they have both found love and maturity.

Harvey Schmidt and Tom Jones (who originated the role of the old actor) initially wrote the musical under the title of Joy Comes to Deadhorse, with the story about Mexican and Anglo families living on adjoining ranches in the US Southwest. But the concept was too elaborate, and the writers then scaled the project down to its essentials, running no longer than an hour. This version, called *The Fantasticks* (the title of the first English-language translation of the Rostand play), was presented at Barnard College in 1959. Producer Lore Noto saw it and offered to present it off-Bway, provided that it was extended to a full evening's entertainment. Despite a mixed press and shaky start, the show soon found its apparently inexhaustible audience. To date, 23 actors have appeared as El Gallo (incl. Bert Convy, David Cryer, Keith Charles), 19 as Matt, 16 as Luisa. *The Fantasticks* has been performed extensively throughout the world, particularly at colleges. Beginning Sept. 1966, David Cryer (also doubling as El Gallo) and Albert Poland sponsored three tours, each lasting three months.

Schmidt and Jones also used the theme of seasonal rebirth in their 1960 Bway musical, *Celebration*.

"Faraway Boy." Music & lyric by Frank Loesser. Though she has found a new love, the heroine (Ellen McCown) in *Greenwillow* (NY 1960) still yearns wistfully for that faraway boy "who first wakened my heart."

Farjeon, Herbert, lyricist, sketch writer, director, producer, b. South Hempstead, Eng., March 5, 1887; d. London, May 3, 1945. Farjeon is best remembered for his two long-running intimate London revues, *Nine Sharp* and *The Little Revue*, both with music by Walter Leigh. Other composer collaborators: Harold Scott, Arthur Swanstrom, Ord Hamilton, William Walker, Clifton Parker. Farjeon, who also wrote with his sister Eleanor, was a grandson of American actor Joseph Jefferson.

Asterisk indicates Mr. Farjeon was also producer:
1928	Many Happy Returns (Scott)
1934	Yours Sincerely (misc.)
	Why Not Tonight? (Hamilton)
1936	Spread It Abroad (Walker)
	The Two Bouquets (misc.)
1938	Nine Sharp * (Leigh)
	An Elephant in Arcady * (misc.)
1939	The Little Revue * (Leigh)
1940	In Town Again * (Leigh)
1942	Big Top (misc.)
	Light and Shade * (Parker)

"Fascinating Rhythm." Music by George Gershwin; lyric by Ira Gershwin. This prime example of Gershwin's brand of sophisticated syncopation was sung and danced by Fred and Adele Astaire and Cliff Edwards in *Lady, Be Good!* (NY 1924), and by the Astaires and Buddy Lee in London facsimile (1926).

Fay, Frank, actor; b. San Francisco, Cal., Nov. 17, 1897; d. Santa Monica, Cal., Sept. 25, 1961. Red-haired monologuist noted for his expert timing, who also made success in nonmusical plays, especially *Harvey*. He was once married to actress Barbara Stanwyck.
1918	Girl o' Mine (*Jack*)
	The Passing Show
1919	Oh, What a Girl! (*Bill Corcoran*)
1920	Jim Jam Jems (*Johnny Case*)
1922	Frank Fay's Fables (also sk., dir.)
	Raymond Hitchcock's Pinwheel
1923	Artists and Models
1927	Harry Delmar's Revels
1933	Tattle Tales (also prod.)

"FDR Jones." Music & lyric by Harold Rome. Rhythmic tribute to President Roosevelt sung by Rex Ingram and Harlem citizens (including Hazel Scott) at a christening in the Bway revue *Sing Out the News* (1938). It was also sung by Bud Flanagan and Chesney Allen in London revue *The Little Dog Laughed* (1939), and by Flanagan in *Clown Jewels* (1959).

"Feeling Good." Music & lyric by Leslie Bricusse & Anthony Newley. "Birds flying high—you know how I feel" begins this booming song of emancipation. Gilbert Price, as The Negro, won an ovation singing it in *The Roar of the Greasepaint-The Smell of the Crowd* (NY 1965).

"A Fellow Needs a Girl." Music by Richard Rodgers; lyric by Oscar Hammerstein II. Sung by William Ching and Annamary Dickey in *Allegro* (NY 1947) as they think about the kind of girl their son will marry.

Ferrer, José (Vicente), actor, singer, director; b. Santurce, PR, Jan. 8, 1912. Resonant-voiced Bway actor famed for his dramatic *Cyrano de Bergerac* and his comic *Charley's Aunt.* Ferrer also has appeared in films.

- 1943 Let's Face It! (*Jerry Walker*, repl.)
- 1958 Oh, Captain! (co-lib., dir. only)
- 1959 Juno (dir. only)
- 1963 The Girl Who Came to Supper (*Grand Duke Charles*)
- 1966 Man of La Mancha (*Don Quixote*, repl.)
  Man of La Mancha (US tour) (*Don Quixote*)
- 1979 Carmelina (dir. only)

"Feudin' and Fightin'." Music by Burton Lane; lyric by Al Dubin & Lane. Comic hillbilly number sung by Pat Brewster in the Bway revue *Laffing Room Only* (1944).

Feuer, Cy, producer, director; b. New York, Jan. 15, 1911. All of Feuer's Bway musicals—incl. three with scores by Frank Loesser, two by Cole Porter—were presented in partnership with Ernest Martin.

Asterisk indicates Mr. Feuer was also director or co-director:

- 1948 Where's Charley?
- 1950 Guys and Dolls
- 1953 Can-Can
- 1954 The Boy Friend
- 1955 Silk Stockings *
- 1958 Whoop-Up! * (also co-lib.)
- 1961 How to Succeed in Business Without Really Trying
- 1962 Little Me *
- 1965 Skyscraper *
- 1966 Walking Happy *

Fiddler on the Roof (1964). Music by Jerry Bock; lyrics by Sheldon Harnick; book by Joseph Stein, based on stories by Sholom Aleichem incl. "Tevye's Daughters."

SONGS: "Tradition," "Matchmaker, Matchmaker," "If I Were a Rich Man," "To Life," "Sunrise, Sunset," "Miracle of Miracles," "Now I Have Everything," "Do You Love Me?," "Anatevka."

NEW YORK: Sept. 22, 1964
IMPERIAL THEATRE; 3,242 p.

Presented by Harold Prince; directed & choreographed by Jerome Robbins; settings, Boris Aronson; costumes, Patricia Zipprodt; lighting, Jean Rosenthal; music director, Milton Greene; orchestrations, Don Walker.

CAST: Zero Mostel (*Tevye*), Maria Karnilova (*Golde*), Beatrice Arthur (*Yente*), Joanna Merlin (*Tzeitel*), Austin Pendleton (*Motel*), Bert Convy (*Perchik*), Julia Migenes (*Hodel*), Michael Granger (*Lazar Wolf*), Tanya Everett (*Chava*).

LONDON: Feb. 16, 1967
HER MAJESTY'S THEATRE; 2,030 p.

Presented by Harold Prince & Richard Pilbrow; directed & choreographed by Jerome Robbins; settings, Boris Aronson; costumes, Patricia Zipprodt; lighting, Richard Pilbrow;

music director, Gareth Davies; orchestrations, Don Walker.

CAST: Topol (*Tevye*), Miriam Karlin (*Golde*), Cynthia Grenville (*Yente*), Paul Whitsun-Jones (*Lazar Wolf*), Sandor Eles (*Perchik*), Rosemary Nicols (*Tzeitel*), Linda Gardner (*Hodel*), Jonathan Lynn (*Motel*), Caryl Little (*Chava*).

The longest-running Bway production (incl. nonmusicals) and the ninth longest running London musical was concerned with persecution and the problems of parenthood and had neither attractive costumes nor scenery. Yet its theme of a people vainly trying to preserve tradition in an alien, hostile and changing world turned out to be one with which large numbers could readily identify. Set in 1905 in czarist Russia, the story focused on Tevye, the dairyman, and his family in the Jewish village of Anatevka. Oldest daughter Tzeitel marries a poor tailor after Tevye had promised her to a rich, middle-aged butcher; second daughter Hodel marries a revolutionary who is sent to Siberia; third daughter Chava marries out of her faith. At the play's end, the police destroy the village during a pogrom and Tevye and what's left of his family are forced to begin a new life in America.

The idea for the musical began in 1960. Composer Bock, lyricist Harnick, and librettist Stein had worked together on the Bway musical *The Body Beautiful* (Bock and Stein had also been associated with *Mr. Wonderful*). A friend suggested they read Sholom Aleichem's *Wandering Star*; though they didn't think it suitable, they became intrigued by other Aleichem works and settled on the stories about Tevye and his daughters. They took the first draft to producer Harold Prince (he had sponsored Bock and Harnick's *Fiorello!* and *Tenderloin*),

but Prince turned it down because he was planning to direct his next musical and he didn't think the story was right for him. He did, however, tell the writers that the only director who could give *Tevye* (the original title) the universality it required was Jerome Robbins. Eventually they got Robbins, and, after two other producers had to abandon the musical because of money problems, they also got Prince.

Since the original concept of Tevye was that of a thin, gaunt man, the first actor they tried to get for the lead was Danny Kaye. Others considered were Tom Bosley, Howard Da Silva, Danny Thomas, and Alan King. The ultimate selection, Zero Mostel, scored a triumph, though the musical was strong enough to continue successfully with replacements Luther Adler (8-65), Herschel Bernardi (11-65), Harry Goz (11-67), Paul Lipson (1-70), Jan Peerce (12-71). Jerry Jarrett substituted for both Goz and Lipson (who, because of appearances in the touring company, played the role of Tevye more often than any other actor). During Bway run, Maria Karnilova was succeeded by Martha Schlamme (4-68), Dolores Wilson (7-68), Rae Allen (7-68), Peg Murray (6-69), with Mimi Randolph and Laura Stuart substituting for Miss Murray. Bette Midler played Tzeitel between Feb. 1967 and Feb. 1970. The US tour, which began April 1966, continued for two years, three months. Luther Adler (succeeded by Lipson, Theodore Bikel, and Goz) played Tevye, and Dolores Wilson (followed by Mimi Randolph) was Golde. In London, Topol was succeeded by Alfie Bass (2-68) (temporarily replaced by Lex Goudsmit) and Miriam Karlin by Avis Bunnage (2-68) and Hy Hazell (8-69) (Miss Bunnage returned to the cast at the death of Miss Hazell). Bib: *The Making of a Musical* by Richard Altman and Mervyn Kaufman (Crown, NY 1971).

FILM VERSION: Topol, Norma Crane, Molly Picon (UA 1971, Norman Jewison dir.).

Field, (Ronald) Ron, director, choreographer, dancer; b. Queens, NY, 1934. Field first attracted notice with his dances for *Cabaret;* he became a director with *Applause.*

Unless otherwise noted, Mr. Field was choreographer of following; asterisk indicates he was also director:

1941 Lady in the Dark (dancer only)
1949 Gentlemen Prefer Blondes (dancer only)
1953 Carnival in Flanders (dancer only)
1954 Kismet (dancer only)
1955 The Boy Friend (*Pepe* only)
1962 Anything Goes (r)
     Nowhere to Go but Up
1964 Café Crown
1966 Cabaret
1968 Cabaret (L)
     Zorbá
1970 Applause *
1971 On the Town * (r)
1972 Applause * (L)
1978 King of Hearts*

Fielding, Harold, producer; b. Woking, Eng. Has presented concerts and tours throughout UK. Biggest London hits: *Half a Sixpence, Charlie Girl, Show Boat.*

1960 Billy Barnes Revue
1961 The Music Man
1962 Sail Away
1963 Half a Sixpence
     Round Leicester Square
1965 Charlie Girl
1966 Man of Magic
1967 Sweet Charity
1968 You're a Good Man, Charlie Brown
1969 Mame
     Phil the Fluter
1970 The Great Waltz (r)
1971 Show Boat (r)

1972 Gone with the Wind
     Hulla-Balou
1973 The King and I (r)
1974 Hans Andersen

Fields, Dorothy, lyricist, librettist; b. Allenhurst, NJ, July 15, 1904; d. New York, March 28, 1974. In a career spanning over 45 years, Dorothy Fields was among the most durable lyricists to write for the Bway musical stage. The daughter of comedian-producer Lew Fields and sister of librettists Herbert and Joseph Fields, she began as a writer of nightclub material with composer Jimmy McHugh. On Bway, the team wrote "I Can't Give You Anything but Love," "I Must Have that Man," and "Diga Diga Doo" for *Blackbirds of 1928,* "Exactly Like You" and "On the Sunny Side of the Street" for Lew Leslie's *International Revue.* Other composers with whom Miss Fields collaborated incl. Arthur Schwartz ("Look Who's Dancing" and "I'll Buy You a Star" in *A Tree Grows in Brooklyn*), Sigmund Romberg ("Close as Pages in a Book" in *Up in Central Park*), Morton Gould, Albert Hague ("Merely Marvelous" in *Redhead*), Cy Coleman ("Big Spender," "If My Friends Could See Me Now," and "Where Am I Going?" in *Sweet Charity*).

As librettist, Miss Fields collaborated with her brother Herbert on eight musicals, incl. *Let's Face It!* and *Mexican Hayride* (both scores by Cole Porter), and their biggest hit, *Annie Get Your Gun* (Irving Berlin score). Ethel Merman starred in three Dorothy Fields musicals, Shirley Booth and Gwen Verdon were in two each. Miss Fields also wrote songs for Hollywood films (incl. *Swing Time*).

Asterisk indicates libretto written with Herbert Fields:

1928	Blackbirds of 1928 (McHugh)
	Hello, Daddy (McHugh)
1930	International Revue (McHugh)
1939	Stars in Your Eyes (Schwartz)
1941	Let's Face It! *
1943	Something for the Boys *
1944	Mexican Hayride *
1945	Up in Central Park * (Romberg)
1946	Annie Get Your Gun *
1950	Arms and the Girl * (Gould)
1951	A Tree Grows in Brooklyn (Schwartz)
1954	By the Beautiful Sea * (Schwartz)
1959	Redhead * (Hague)
1966	Sweet Charity (Coleman)
1973	Seesaw (Coleman)

Fields, Herbert, librettist; b. New York, July 26, 1897; d. New York, March 24, 1958. Fields began his career as the libretto-writing collaborator of songwriters Richard Rodgers and Lorenz Hart, with whom he wrote seven Bway musicals (incl. *Dearest Enemy, Peggy-Ann, A Connecticut Yankee*). Between 1929 and 1944 he was primarily associated with composer Cole Porter, with whom he also did seven shows (incl. *Fifty Million Frenchmen, DuBarry Was a Lady, Panama Hattie, Let's Face It!, Mexican Hayride*). Fields also worked with Vincent Youmans (*Hit the Deck*), George and Ira Gershwin, Sigmund Romberg (*Up in Central Park*), and Arthur Schwartz. The son of comedian-producer Lew Fields and the brother of librettist Joseph Fields, he collaborated on eight musicals with his sister Dorothy Fields, the most successful being *Annie Get Your Gun* (songs by Irving Berlin). Ethel Merman starred in four Herbert Fields musicals, Helen Ford and Charles King were in three each.

Asterisk indicates libretto written with Dorothy Fields:

1925	The Garrick Gaieties (chor. only)
	Dearest Enemy
1926	The Girl Friend
	The Garrick Gaieties (chor. only)

	Peggy-Ann
1927	Hit the Deck
	A Connecticut Yankee
1928	Present Arms
	Chee-Chee
	Hello, Daddy
1929	Fifty Million Frenchmen
1930	The New Yorkers
1931	America's Sweetheart
1933	Pardon My English
1939	DuBarry Was a Lady
1940	Panama Hattie
1941	Let's Face It! *
1943	Something for the Boys * (also dir.)
	A Connecticut Yankee
1944	Mexican Hayride *
1945	Up in Central Park *
1946	Annie Get Your Gun *
1950	Arms and the Girl *
1954	By the Beautiful Sea *
1959	Redhead *

Fields, Joseph (Albert), librettist; b. New York, Feb. 21, 1895; d. Beverly Hills, Cal., March 3, 1966. On Bway Fields collaborated with librettists Anita Loos, Jerome Chodorov (with whom he also wrote the plays *My Sister Eileen* and *Junior Miss*), and Oscar Hammerstein II. His father was comedian-producer Lew Fields, his sister lyricist-librettist Dorothy Fields, his brother librettist Herbert Fields.

1949	Gentlemen Prefer Blondes (Loos)
1953	Wonderful Town (Chodorov)
1954	The Girl in Pink Tights (Chodorov)
1958	Flower Drum Song (Hammerstein)

Fields, Lew (né Lewis Schanfield), actor, producer, director; b. New York, Jan. 1, 1867; d. Beverly Hills, Cal., July 20, 1941. Fields won his greatest fame with his partner, Joe Weber, as "Dutch" comics in a series of burlesque musicals they presented for eight years at the Weber & Fields Broadway Music Hall. In the act, both men usually wore chin whiskers, tiny derbies, and garishly checkered suits, with Fields towering over his diminutive, well-padded partner. The act broke up in 1904, but, beginning in 1912, the men were occasionally reunited. From 1920 to 1928, Fields produced six musicals with scores by Rodgers and Hart and librettos by his son, Herbert Fields (incl. *Dearest Enemy, Peggy-Ann, A Connecticut Yankee*). He was also the father of librettist-lyricist Dorothy Fields and librettist Joseph Fields. Vernon Castle appeared in seven Fields productions, Lillian Russell in six, Fay Templeton in five, DeWolf Hopper, Nora Bayes, Marie Dressler, and Helen Hayes in three each. Bib: *Weber and Fields* by Felix Isman (Boni & Liveright, NY 1924).

Unless otherwise noted, Mr. Fields was producer or co-producer of following; asterisk indicates appearance and/or production with Mr. Weber:

1896 The Art of Maryland *
The Geezer *
1897 Under the Red Globe *
The Glad Hand (*Augustus Miller*)
Pousse-Cafe * (*Herr Bierheister*)
1898 The Con-Curers *
Hurly Burly * (*Herr Bierheister*)
Cyranose de Bricabrac *
1899 Helter Skelter *
Catherine * (*Frederick*)
Whirl-i-Gig * (*Wilhelm Hochderkaiser*)
1900 Fiddle-Dee-Dee * (*Rudolf Bungstarter*)
1901 Hoity Toity * (*Herman Kaffelkuchen*)
1902 Twirly Whirly * (*Meyer Ausgaaben*)
1903 Whoop-Dee-Doo * (*Meyer Schmartzgeezer*)
1904 An English Daisy *
It Happened in Nordland (also *Hubert Peepfogle*)
1906 About Town (also actor)
1907 The Girl Behind the Counter (also *Herman Schniff*)
1908 The Mimic World

1909 The Midnight Sons
The Rose of Algeria
Old Dutch (also *Ludwig Streusand*)
1910 The Jolly Bachelors
The Prince of Bohemia
The Yankee Girl
Tillie's Nightmare
The Summer Widowers (also *Otto Ott*)
1911 The Hen-Pecks (also *Henderson Peck*)
The Never Homes
The Wife Hunters
1912 Hokey Pokey * (*Meyer Bockheister*)
Hanky Panky
Roly Poly * (*Meyer Talzmann*)
The Sun Dodgers
1913 Marie Dressler's All-Star Gambol *
All Aboard (also actor)
A Glimpse of the Great White Way
1914 Suzi
1916 Step This Way (The Girl Behind the Counter) (also *Herman Schniff*)
1917 Miss 1917 (actor only)
1919 A Lonely Romeo (also *Augustus Tripp*)
1920 Poor Little Ritz Girl
1921 Blue Eyes (*Peter Van Dam* only)
Snapshots of 1921 (also actor)
1923 Jack and Jill (*Daniel Malone*, repl., only)
Greenwich Village Follies (dir. only)
1924 Greenwich Village Follies (dir. only)
1926 The Girl Friend
Peggy-Ann
1927 Hit the Deck
Peggy-Ann (L) (also dir.)
A Connecticut Yankee
1928 Present Arms
Chee-Chee
1929 Hello, Daddy (also *Henry Block*)
1930 Vanderbilt Revue (also dir.)

Fields, W. C. (né William Claude Dukinfield), actor; b. Philadelphia, Pa.,

April 9, 1879; d. Pasadena, Cal., Dec. 25, 1946. Bulbous-nosed comic who personified the unsentimentalized con man, ever disdainful of suckers, pets, and children. Fields, who began as a juggler in vaudeville in 1897, scored his greatest Bway success in *Poppy*. He began his screen career in 1925, appearing in such films as *David Copperfield* and *The Bank Dick*. Bib: W. C. *Fields: His Follies and Fortunes* by Robert Lewis Taylor (Doubleday, NY 1949); W. C. *Fields by Himself* ed. by Ronald Fields (Prentice-Hall, NJ 1972).

1905	The Ham Tree (*Sherlock Baffles*)
1915	Ziegfeld Follies
1916	Ziegfeld Follies
1917	Ziegfeld Follies
1918	Ziegfeld Follies
1920	Ziegfeld Follies
1921	Ziegfeld Follies
1922	George White's Scandals
1923	Poppy (*Prof. Eustace McGargle*)
1925	Ziegfeld Follies (added)
1928	Earl Carroll Vanities
1930	Ballyhoo (*Q.Q. Quayle*)

Fifty Million Frenchmen (1929). Music & lyrics by Cole Porter; book by Herbert Fields.

SONGS: "You Do Something to Me," "You've Got That Thing," "Find Me a Primitive Man," "You Don't Know Paree," "Paree, What Did You Do to Me?," "The Tale of an Oyster."

NEW YORK: Nov. 27, 1929
LYRIC THEATRE; 254 p.

Presented by E. Ray Goetz; directed by Edgar M. (Monty) Woolley; choreographed by Larry Ceballos; settings, Norman Bel Geddes; costumes, James Reynolds; music director, Gene Salzer.

CAST: William Gaxton (*Peter Forbes*), Genevieve Tobin (*Looloo Carroll*), Helen Broderick (*Violet Hildegarde*), Jack Thompson (*Michael Cummins*), Evelyn Hoey (*May De-*

Vere), Betty Compton (*Joyce Wheeler*), Thurston Hall (*Emmitt Carroll*).

This "Musical Comedy Tour of Paris" was Cole Porter's first major success and his first (of seven) musicals with librettist Herbert Fields. In the story, wealthy Peter Forbes, smitten with tourist Looloo Carroll, bets his friend Michael Cummins that they will be engaged within a month. To win the bet, Peter takes a job as a guide and woos his inamorata with the aid of such romantic locales as the Ritz Bar, the Café de la Paix, the Longchamps Racetrack, and Les Halles.

FILM VERSION: Olsen & Johnson, William Gaxton, Helen Broderick (no songs) (Warner 1931, Lloyd Bacon dir.).

"Finding Words for Spring." Music & lyric by Marian Grudeff & Raymond Jessel. Lofty aria in which Inga Swenson in *Baker Street* (NY 1965) admitted the impossibility of finding the proper words to explain "love's sweet splendor."

"Fine and Dandy." Music by Kay Swift; lyric by Paul James (James Paul Warburg). Jaunty revelation of mutual happiness sung by Joe Cook and Alice Boulden (and reprised by Nell O'Day) in *Fine and Dandy* (NY 1930). Added lyrics in the song dealt with the radio popularity of Amos 'n Andy, the romance between Napoleon and Josephine, and the recent Max Schmeling–Jack Sharkey heavyweight title fight.

Fings Ain't Wot They Used t'Be (1960). Music & lyrics by Lionel Bart; book by Frank Norman.

SONGS: "Fings Ain't Wot They

Used t'Be," "Contempery," "Big Time," "Where Do Little Birds Go?," "Where It's Hot," "Cop a Bit of Pride."

LONDON: Feb. 11, 1960
GARRICK THEATRE; 886 p.

Presented by Donald Albery & Audley Sq. Playwrights Ltd; directed by Joan Littlewood; settings, John Bury; costumes, Margaret Bury; music director, Ronnie Franklin.

CAST: Miriam Karlin (*Lily Smith*), James Booth (*Tosher*), Wallas Eaton (*Horace Seaton*), Glynn Edwards (*Fred Cochran*), Barbara Windsor (*Rosie*), Toni Palmer (*Betty*), Tom Chatto (*Sgt. Collins*), Paddy Joyce (*Paddy*).

Part of a new wave of British musicals (*Expresso Bongo, The Crooked Mile*) dealing with the more sordid aspects of London life, *Fings Ain't Wot They Used t'Be* was celebrated for its realistic depiction of such Soho institutions as brasses (prostitutes), ponces (pimps), and spielers (gambling dens). Author Frank Norman, a former member of Soho's underworld, originally wrote the story as a play without music and sent the first draft to Joan Littlewood of the Theatre Workshop. Miss Littlewood then called in Lionel Bart, who had previously written only lyrics, and the three turned it into a musical. It was first presented at the Theatre Royal, Stratford, Feb. 17, 1959, with the cast improvising much of the dialogue and situations. Its Guys-and-Dollsish story is concerned with Fred Cochran, who runs a grubby spieler, and his ambition to become a bigshot again. After winning a huge bet on a horse race, Fred has his place redecorated, but the opening-night party is ruined when Fred is beaten up for failing to pay off the police. Eventually he marries his longtime girlfriend, Lily. During run, Glynn Edwards was succeeded by Bryan Pringle, James Booth by Maurice Kaufmann.

"Fings Ain't Wot They Used t'Be." Music & lyric by Lionel Bart. The decline of vice lamented by Miriam Karlin and Glynn Edwards in the London musical of the same name (1960). Because the show was written by ex-gambler Frank Norman and produced by Joan Littlewood, the song contained the lines, "Big hoods now are little hoods,/Gamblers now do Littlewoods." Melodically the number is reminiscent of Rodgers and Hart's "Mountain Greenery."

Finian's Rainbow (1947). Music by Burton Lane; lyrics by E. Y. Harburg; book by Harburg & Fred Saidy.

SONGS: "How Are Things in Glocca Morra?," "If This Isn't Love," "Look to the Rainbow," "Old Devil Moon," "Something Sort of Grandish," "Necessity," "When the Idle Poor Become the Idle Rich," "When I'm Not Near the Girl I Love," "That Great Come-and-Get-It Day," "The Begat."

NEW YORK: Jan. 10, 1947
46th ST. THEATRE; 725 p.

Presented by Lee Sabinson & William Katzell; directed by Bretaigne Windust; choreographed by Michael Kidd; settings & lighting, Jo Mielziner; costumes, Eleanor Goldsmith; music director, Milton Rosenstock; orchestrations, Robert Russell Bennett, Don Walker.

CAST: Ella Logan (*Sharon McLonergan*), Albert Sharpe (*Finian McLonergan*), Donald Richards (*Woody Mahoney*), David Wayne (*Og*), Anita Alvarez (*Susan Mahoney*), Robert Pitkin (*Sen. Billboard Rawkins*).

LONDON: Oct. 21, 1947
PALACE THEATRE; 55 p.

Presented by Emile Littler; re-staged & lighted by James Gelb; choreographed by Michael Kidd; settings, Jo Mielziner; costumes, Eleanor Goldsmith; music director, Phil Green.

CAST: Beryl Seton (*Sharon McLonergan*), Patrick J. Kelly (*Finian McLonergan*), Alan Gilbert (*Woody Mahoney*), Alfie Bass (*Og*), Beryl Kaye (*Susan Mahoney*), Frank Royde (*Sen. Billboard Rawkins*).

Finian's Rainbow, a fantasy with social commentary, evolved out of co-librettist Yip Harburg's desire to satirize an economic system dependent upon keeping gold reserves buried in the ground. This led to his thinking of a pot of gold, which reminded him of leprechauns and their crock of gold that was good for three wishes. The story concerns a simple-minded Irish immigrant who believes that since the US became rich by burying gold at Fort Knox, he could get rich by burying a crock of gold he had stolen from a leprechaun. Og, a leprechaun who has followed Finian to Rainbow Valley, Missitucky, tries to retrieve the crock. He has also fallen in love with Finian's daughter, Sharon, who much prefers Woody, the union organizer. Harburg also combined another story, about a bigoted Southern senator who miraculously turns black, by making the transformation one of the three wishes. The main philosophical point: people find riches not in gold but in trusting one another. During Bway run, Ella Logan was succeeded by Dorothy Claire and Nan Wynn, Albert Sharpe by James O'Neill, Patrick J. Kelly, and Ian Martin, Anita Alvarez by Beryl Kaye.

In 1960 a City Center revival was transferred briefly to the 46th St.

Theatre. The cast included Jeannie Carson (*Sharon*), Bobby Howes (*Finian*), Biff McGuire (*Woody*), Howard Morris (*Og*), Anita Alvarez (*Susan*), Carol Brice (*Maude*), Sorrell Booke (*Senator*).

FILM VERSION: Fred Astaire, Petula Clark, Tommy Steele (Warner 1968, Francis Ford Coppola dir.).

Fiorello! (1959). Music by Jerry Bock; lyrics by Sheldon Harnick; book by Jerome Weidman & George Abbott.

SONGS: "On the Side of the Angels," "Politics and Poker," "The Name's LaGuardia," "I Love a Cop," "'Til Tomorrow," "Home Again," "When Did I Fall in Love?," "Gentleman Jimmy," "Little Tin Box," "The Very Next Man."

NEW YORK: Nov. 23, 1949
BROADHURST THEATRE; 795 p.

Presented by Robert Griffith & Harold Prince; directed by George Abbott; choreographed by Peter Gennaro; settings, costumes, & lighting, William & Jean Eckart; music director, Harold Hastings; orchestrations, Irwin Kostal.

CAST: Tom Bosley (*Fiorello LaGuardia*), Patricia Wilson (*Marie Fischer*), Ellen Hanley (*Thea LaGuardia*), Howard Da Silva (*Ben Marino*), Mark Dawson (*Floyd Macduff*), Nathaniel Frey (*Morris Cohen*), Eileen Rodgers (*Mitzi Travers*), Pat Stanley (*Dora*), Bob Holiday (*Neil*), Ron Husmann (*Fourth Hack*).

LONDON: Oct. 8, 1962
PICCADILLY THEATRE; 56 p.

Presented by Donald Albery, with Oscar Lewenstein; directed by Val May; choreographed by Peter Wright; settings, Graham Barlow; costumes, Alan Barrett & Audrey Price; lighting, Ian Albery; music director, Marcus

Dods; orchestrations, Eric Rodgers, Burt Rhodes.

CAST: Derek Smith (*Fiorello LaGuardia*), Nicolette Roig (*Marie Fischer*), Marian Grimaldi (*Thea LaGuardia*), Peter Reeves (*Ben Marino*), Simon Oates (*Floyd Macduff*), David Lander (*Morris Cohen*), Patricia Michael (*Mitzi Travers*), Bridget Armstrong (*Dora*).

Pugnacious, volatile Fiorello LaGuardia, the former mayor of New York, was the kind of larger-than-life political leader whose personality and career lend themselves to theatrical treatment. The musical based on his life covers a 10-year period, beginning shortly before World War I and ending with LaGuardia's election as mayor. Along the way, it shows our hero as a pilot in the US Air Force, a reform congressman, and an initially unsuccessful mayoralty candidate. One of the problems was in casting someone to fit LaGuardia's squat appearance and aggressive personality. Many actors, from Mickey Rooney to Eli Wallach, were tested until the producers settled on Tom Bosley, who had never before appeared on Bway. The London version was played by an all-English cast. *Tenderloin* (1960), involving the same writers, producers, and director, was something of a sequel, as it covered NY corruption during an even earlier period. In 1969 the Bway musical *Jimmy* was based on the life of James J. Walker (played by Frank Gorshin), who defeated LaGuardia in his first try for mayor.

Firefly, The (1912). Music by Rudolf Friml; lyrics & book by Otto Hauerbach (Harbach).

SONGS: "Giannina Mia," "When a Maid Comes Knocking at Your Heart," "Love Is Like a Firefly,"

"Sympathy," "In Sapphire Seas," "An American Beauty Rose."

NEW YORK: Dec. 2, 1912
LYRIC THEATRE; 120 p.

Presented by Arthur Hammerstein; directed by Fred G. Latham; choreographed by Signor Albertieri, Sammy Lee; settings, Reisig-Dove, P. Dodd Ackerman; costumes, W. Matthews; music director, Gaetano Merola.

CAST: Emma Trentini (*Nina*), Craig Campbell (*Jack Travers*), Roy Atwell (*Jenkins*), Sammy Lee (*Pietro*), Audrey Maple (*Geraldine Vandare*), Melville Stewart (*John Thornton*), Ruby Norton (*Suzette*).

For his first Bway production, Arthur Hammerstein commissioned Rudolf Friml to write his first Bway score. Friml got the assignment because Victor Herbert, the original composer, had had a row with Signorina Trentini during the run of *Naughty Marietta* and refused to have anything further to do with the diva. The story concerns an Italian street singer in NY who, to be near wealthy Jack Travers, disguises herself as a cabin boy on his yacht. A music teacher is impressed with her voice and within three years she becomes both prima donna and Mrs. Jack Travers.

FILM VERSION: Jeanette MacDonald and Allan Jones (different story) (MGM 1937, Robert Z. Leonard dir.).

Flanagan, Bud (né Robert Winthrop), actor; b. 1896; d. Oct. 20, 1968. Slapstick British comic who teamed with Chesney Allen for 20 years (1924–1944). In 1936 they joined two other double acts, Charlie Naughton and Jimmy Gold and Jimmy Nervo and Teddy Knox, for a series of music-hall–type revues at the Palladium that were known as the Crazy Gang shows.

After Allen's retirement, Flanagan continued appearing with the other two teams in revues presented virtually without interruption at the Victoria Palace from 1947 to 1962.

Asterisk indicates Crazy Gang show:

1933 Give Me a Ring (*Bill Marks*)
1936 Okay for Sound *
1937 Swing Is in the Air *
       London Rhapsody *
1938 Happy Returns
       These Foolish Things *
1939 The Little Dog Laughed *
1941 Black Vanities
1943 Hi-De-Hi
1946 The Night and the Laughter
1947 Together Again *
1950 Knights of Madness *
1952 Ring Out the Bells *
1954 Jokers Wild *
1956 These Foolish Kings *
1959 Clown Jewels *
1960 Young in Heart *

Florodora (1899). Music by Leslie Stuart; lyrics by Ernest Boyd-Jones, Paul Rubens & Stuart; book by Owen Hall.

SONGS: "The Silver Star of Love" (Stuart), "When I Leave Town" (Rubens), "The Shade of the Palm" (Stuart), "Tact" (Rubens), "When You're a Millionaire" (Boyd-Jones), "Tell Me Pretty Maiden" (Stuart), "The Island of Love" (Ivan Caryll–Aubrey Hopwood), "I Want to Be a Military Man" (lyric, Frank Clement).

LONDON: Nov. 11, 1899
LYRIC THEATRE; 455 p.

Presented by Tom B. Davis; directed by Sydney Ellison; settings, Julian Hicks; costumes, Comelli; music director, Carl Kiefert.

CAST: Ada Reeve (*Lady Holyrood*), Evie Greene (*Dolores*), Melville Stewart (*Frank Abercoed*), Willie Edouin (*Anthony Tweedlepunch*), Charles E. Stevens (*Cyrus Gilfain*), Kate Cutler (*Angela Gilfain*), Edgar

Stevens (*Arthur Donegal*), also Nancy Girling, Lydia West, Lily McIntyre, Fanny Dango, Blanche Carlow, Beatrice Grenville (*Sextette*).

NEW YORK: Nov. 12, 1900
CASINO THEATRE; 553 p.

Presented by Tom Ryley & John C. Fisher; directed by Lewis Hooper & Willie Edouin; settings, Moses & Hamilton; music director, Arthur Weld; book revised by Frank Pixley.

CAST: Edna Wallace Hopper (*Lady Holyrood*), Fannie Johnston (*Dolores*), Sydney Deane (*Frank Abercoed*), Willie Edouin (*Anthony Tweedlepunch*), R. E. Graham (*Cyrus Gilfain*), May Edouin (*Angela Gilfain*), Cyril Scott (*Arthur Donegal*), also Daisy Greene, Marjorie Relyea, Vaughn Texsmith, Margaret Walker, Agnes Wayburn, Marie L. Wilson (*Sextette*).

NEW YORK: April 5, 1920
CENTURY THEATRE; 150 p.

Presented by J. J. Shubert; directed by Lewis Morton; choreographed by Allan K. Foster; settings, Watson Barratt; costumes, Cora MacGeachy; music director, Oscar Radin.

CAST: Christie MacDonald (*Lady Holyrood*), Eleanor Painter (*Dolores*), George Hassell (*Anthony Tweedlepunch*), Walter Woolf (*Frank Abercoed*), John T. Murray (*Cyrus Gilfain*), Harry Fender (*Arthur Donegal*), Margot Kelly (*Angela Gilfain*), also Dama Sykes, Dorothy Leeds, Fay Evelyn, Beatrice Swanson, Marcella Swanson, Muriel Lodge (*Sextette*), Milton Berle, Ben Grauer (both in *Boy Sextette*).

The epitome of turn-of-the-century musical comedy, *Florodora* became the rage of both London and NY partly because of the fame of the dainty Florodora Sextette and their song, "Tell Me Pretty Maiden." Florodora was not the name of the heroine; it was an island in the Philippines owned by wealthy American Cyrus Gilfain, who manufactures a perfume also called Florodora. The island, however, really belongs to Dolores, whose father was cheated by Gilfain. Gilfain wants to marry Dolores, Dolores wants to marry Gilfain's manager, Frank Abercoed, whom Gilfain wants for his daughter, Angela, who loves Arthur Donegal. Dolores and Frank leave the Philippines for Wales (Abercoed has come into a title), and Gilfain, accompanied by Lady Holyrood, follows them and buys himself a castle. Eventually investigator Anthony Tweedlepunch exposes Gilfain, who gives Florodora to Dolores and the lovers are properly paired off. New York saw a revival in 1902, London in 1915 and 1931.

Flower Drum Song (1958). Music by Richard Rodgers; lyrics by Oscar Hammerstein II; book by Hammerstein & Joseph Fields, based on Chin Y. Lee's novel.

SONGS: "You Are Beautiful," "I Am Going to Like It Here," "A Hundred Million Miracles," "I Enjoy Being a Girl," "Don't Marry Me," "Grant Avenue," "Chop Suey," "Love, Look Away," "Sunday."

NEW YORK: Dec. 1, 1958
ST. JAMES THEATRE; 600 p.
Presented by Richard Rodgers & Oscar Hammerstein II, with Joseph Fields; directed by Gene Kelly; choreographed by Carol Haney; settings, Oliver Smith; costumes, Irene Sharaff; lighting, Peggy Clark; music director, Salvatore Dell'Isola; orchestrations, Robert Russell Bennett.
CAST: Miyoshi Umeki (Mei Li), Pat Suzuki (Linda Low), Larry Blyden (Sammy Fong), Juanita Hall (Madam Liang), Ed Kenney (Wang Ta), Keye Luke (Wang Chi Yang), Arabella

Hong (Helen Chao), Anita Ellis (nightclub singer), Jack Soo (Frankie Wing).

LONDON: March 24, 1960
PALACE THEATRE; 464 p.
Presented by Williamson Music Ltd.; restaged by Jerome Whyte; dances reproduced by Dierdre Vivian; settings, Oliver Smith; costumes, Irene Sharaff; music director, Robert Lowe; orchestrations, Robert Russell Bennett.
CAST: Yau Shan Tung (Mei Li), Yama Saki (Linda Low), Tim Herbert (Sammy Fong), Ida Shepley (Madam Liang), Kevin Scott (Wang Ta), George Pastell (Wang Chi Yang), Joan Pethers (Helen Chao), Ruth Silvestre (nightclub singer), Leon Thau (Frankie Wing).

Co-librettist Joseph Fields first secured the rights to the novel on which the musical was based, and then approached Rodgers and Hammerstein to collaborate with him. The theme was the conflict between the traditions of older Chinese-Americans in San Francisco and their younger, more Americanized offspring. In the story, Mei Li, a "picture bride" from China, arrives in San Francisco to marry nightclub owner Sammy Fong. Sammy, however, loves Linda Low, a stripper in his club, and he eventually prevails upon his friend Wang Ta, who also loves Linda, to marry Mei Li. The problems in casting the musical, the first ever written about Chinese living in the US, led to the signing of Japanese Miyoshi Umeki and Japanese-American Pat Suzuki for the leading roles.

FILM VERSION: Nancy Kwan and Miyoshi Umeki (Univ. 1961, Henry Koster dir.).

Flying High (1930). Music by Ray Henderson; lyrics by B. G. DeSylva and Lew Brown; book by John McGowan, DeSylva, and Brown.

SONGS: "I'll Know Him," "Thank Your Father," "Good for You—Bad for Me," "Red Hot Chicago," "Without Love," "Mrs. Krause's Blue-Eyed Baby Boy," "Wasn't It Beautiful While It Lasted?," "I'll Get My Man."

NEW YORK: March 3, 1930
APOLLO THEATRE; 357 p.

Presented by George White; directed by White & Edward Clark Lilley; choreographed by Bobby Connolly; settings, Joseph Urban; costumes, Charles LeMaire; music director, Al Goodman.

CAST: Bert Lahr (*Rusty Krause*), Oscar Shaw (*Tod Addison*), Grace Brinkley (*Eileen Cassidy*), Kate Smith (*Pansy Sparks*), Russ Brown (*Sport Wardell*), Pearl Osgood (*Bunny McHugh*).

Mechanic Rusty Krause mistakenly takes off in pilot Tod Addison's plane and sets a world record for hours in the air—because he doesn't know how to get the plane down. Romance is provided by Tod and Eileen, on whose roof Tod makes a parachuted entrance. *Flying High*, in which Bert Lahr scored a major hit, was the fourth and final DeSylva, Brown, and Henderson musical comedy based on current fads and sports (the others: *Good News!*, *Hold Everything!*, *Follow Thru*). The show was a success despite the fact that the story was not completed until rehearsals were about to begin.

FILM VERSION: Bert Lahr, Charlotte Greenwood, Pat O'Brien (MGM 1931, Charles F. Reisner dir.).

"**Fold Your Wings.**" Music by Ivor Novello; lyric by Christopher Hassall. Soaring duet for voluntarily enslaved lovers Mary Ellis and Trefor Jones appearing in operetta-within-operetta,

both called *Glamorous Night* (L 1935).

"**Follow Me.**" Music by Frederick Loewe; lyric by Alan Jay Lerner. Willowy siren song heard in *Camelot* (NY 1960), as the voice of Nimue (Marjorie Smith) beckons Merlyn to his cavernous destiny. In London production (1964), the voice belonged to Josephine Gordon.

Follow the Girls (1944). Music by Phil Charig; lyrics by Dan Shapiro & Milton Pascal; book by Guy Bolton, Eddie Davis & Fred Thompson.

SONGS "You're Perf," "Twelve o'Clock and All's Well," "Follow the Girls," "I Wanna Get Married," "I'm Gonna Hang My Hat," "Out for No Good," "Today Will Be Yesterday Tomorrow."

NEW YORK: April 8, 1944
NEW CENTURY THEATRE; 882 p.

Presented by Dave Wolper, with Albert Borde; directed by Harry Delmar & Fred Thompson; choreographed by Catherine Littlefield; settings & lighting, Howard Bay; costumes, Lou Eisele; music director, Will Irwin; orchestrations, Joe Glover, Charles Cooke, etc.

CAST: Gertrude Niesen (*Bubbles LaMarr*), Jackie Gleason (*Goofy Gale*), Buster West (*Dinky Riley*), Tim Herbert (*Spud Doolittle*), Val Valentinoff (*Val*), Irina Baronova (*Anna Viskinova*), Frank Parker (*Bob Monroe*), William Tabbert (*Yokel*).

LONDON: Oct. 25, 1945
HIS MAJESTY'S THEATRE; 572 p.

Presented by Jack Hylton; directed by Walter Forde; choreographed by Jack Billings & Wendy Toye; settings, Alick Johnstone; costumes, Slade Lucas, Colin Becke; lighting, Alec Shanks; music director, Freddie Bretherton.

CAST: Arthur Askey (*Goofy Gale*), Evelyn Dall (*Bubbles LaMarr*), Jack Billings (*Dinky Riley*), Vic Marlowe (*Spud Doolittle*), Hugh French (*Bob Monroe*), Wendy Toye (*Betty Deleaninnion*), Charles Peters (*Felix*).

All but forgotten today, *Follow the Girls* was one of the major wartime hits in both NY and London. Its story—something about a burlesque strip-tease dancer who becomes the leading attraction of a servicemen's canteen called the Spotlight—was simply a peg on which to throw assorted dance routines and comic specialties, the latter chiefly by Jackie Gleason in NY and Arthur Askey in London. Torch singer Gertrude Niesen made a strong impression in her only book musical. During run, Albert Borde became the show's sole producer.

Follow Thru (1929). Music by Ray Henderson; lyrics by B. G. DeSylva & Lew Brown; book by Laurence Schwab & DeSylva.

SONGS: "My Lucky Star," "Button Up Your Overcoat," "You Wouldn't Fool Me, Would You?," "I Want to Be Bad," "Then I'll Have Time for You."

NEW YORK: Jan. 9, 1929
46th ST. THEATRE; 403 p.

Presented by Laurence Schwab & Frank Mandel; directed by Edgar MacGregor; choreographed by Bobby Connolly; settings, Donald Oenslager; costumes, Kiviette; music director, Al Goodman.

CAST: Jack Haley (*Jack Martin*), Irene Delroy (*Lora Moore*), Zelma O'Neal (*Angie Howard*), Madeline Cameron (*Ruth Van Horn*), John Barker (*Jerry Downs*), Eleanor Powell (*Molly*), Margaret Lee (*Babs Bascomb*).

LONDON: Oct. 3, 1929
DOMINION THEATRE; 148 p.

Presented by Firth Shephard & Leslie Henson; directed by Henson; choreographed by Arthur Apell; settings, Joseph & Phil Harker; music director, Percival Mackey.

CAST: Leslie Henson (*Jack Martin*), Ivy Tresmand (*Lora Moore*), Ada May (*Angie Howard*), Elsie Randolph (*Ruth Vanning*), Bernard Clifton (*Jerry Downs*), Rita Page (*Babs Bascomb*).

Dubbed "A Musical Slice of Country Club Life," *Follow Thru* was a follow-up to *Good News!* (about football) and *Hold Everything!* (about boxing), with DeSylva, Brown and Henderson providing all three scores. In the story, Lora and Ruth keep their eyes on both the club championship and golfing ace Jerry Downs. Lora wins both prizes. The show gave Jack Haley his first major comic role.

FILM VERSION: Jack Haley, Zelma O'Neal, Nancy Carroll, Charles "Buddy" Rogers (Par. 1930, Laurence Schwab & Lloyd Corrigan dirs.).

"Fools Fall in Love." Music & lyric by Irving Berlin. Though they knew only idiots take a chance, William Gaxton and Vera Zorina were unable to keep from falling in love in *Louisiana Purchase* (NY 1940).

Ford, Helen (née Helen Isabel Barnett), actress, singer; b. Troy, NY, June 6. Dainty Miss Ford scored her biggest Bway successes in *Helen of Troy, New York*, *Dearest Enemy* (singing "Here in My Arms"), and *Peggy-Ann* ("A Tree in the Park," "Where's That Rainbow?").

    1919   Sometime (*Enid Vaughan*, repl.)
    1920   Always You (*Toinette Fontaine*)
           The Sweetheart Shop (*Natalie Blythe*)

1922	For Goodness Sake (*Marjorie Leeds*)
	The Gingham Girl (*Mary Thompson*)
1923	Helen of Troy, New York (*Helen McGuffy*)
1924	No Other Girl (*Hope Franklin*)
1925	Dearest Enemy (*Betsy Burke*)
1926	Peggy-Ann (*Peggy-Ann*)
1928	Chee-Chee (*Chee-Chee*)
1933	Champagne, Sec (*Adele*)
1938	Great Lady (*Freelove Clark*)

"Forever and a Day." Music & lyric by Hugh Martin & Timothy Gray. Pledge of love everlasting made in *High Spirits* by Tammy Grimes and Edward Woodward (NY 1964), and by Marti Stevens and Denis Quilley (L 1964). In the scene the piece was also heard on a recording featuring the voice of co-writer Timothy Gray.

Forrest, George ("Chet") (né George Forrest Chichester Jr.), lyricist, composer; b. Brooklyn, NY, July 31, 1915. Forrest has worked exclusively with Robert Wright, primarily in the field of adapting classics into Bway scores. They also combined the scores of Victor Herbert's *The Fortune Teller* and *The Serenade* to create *Gypsy Lady*. The team's biggest hits: *Song of Norway* ("Strange Music," "I Love You"), *Kismet* ("Baubles, Bangles and Beads," "And This Is My Beloved," "Stranger in Paradise").

1944	Song of Norway (Grieg)
1946	Gypsy Lady (Herbert)
1948	Magdalena (Villa-Lobos)
1953	Kismet (Borodin)
1959	The Love Doctor (L) (also co-lib.)
1961	Kean
1965	Anya (Rachmaninoff)
1970	The Great Waltz (L) (r) (Strauss)

Fortune Teller, The (1898). Music by Victor Herbert; lyrics & book by Harry B. Smith.

SONGS: "Always Do as People Say You Should," "Romany Life," "Gypsy Love Song," "Czardas," "Ho! Ye Townsmen," "Only in the Play."

NEW YORK: Sept. 26, 1898
WALLACK'S THEATRE; 40 p.

Presented by Frank L. Perley; directed by Julian Mitchell; settings, Josef Physioc; costumes, Mme. Caroline Siedle; music director, Paul Steindorff; orchestrations, Victor Herbert.

CAST: Alice Nielsen (*Musette, Irma*), Eugene Cowles (*Sandor*), Frank Rushworth (*Capt. Ladislas*), Marguerite Sylva (*Mlle. Pompon*), Joseph Herbert (*Count Berezowski*), Joseph Cawthorn (*Boris*), May Boley (*Etelka*).

The Fortune Teller was the second of three operettas Victor Herbert and Harry B. Smith wrote for Alice Nielsen (the others were *The Serenade* and *The Singing Girl*), and the first commissioned for the newly formed Alice Nielsen Opera Co. The work is full of spectacle and gypsy fire as it relates the tale of two girls, Hungarian heiress Irma and gypsy fortune teller Musette, whose identical appearance makes for a good deal of romantic confusion. Eventually—somehow aided by a Hungarian military victory—each ends up with her appropriate inamorato.

The Bway run was short because the company was organized as a touring unit and was booked in other cities. Beginning April 9, 1901, the operetta was presented in London at the Shaftesbury Theatre, with the main cast change being Viola Gillette for Marguerite Sylva. The engagement was terminated after three months because of Miss Nielsen's illness, which also caused the company to break up. In 1946 a Bway musical called *Gypsy Lady* combined the scores of both *The*

Fortune Teller and *The Serenade.* Though it had an original plot, three of the leading characters were called Musetta, Sandor, and Boris.

Forty-Five Minutes from Broadway (1906). Music, lyrics, & book by George M. Cohan.
SONGS: "Gentlemen of the Press," "I Want to Be a Popular Millionaire," "Mary's a Grand Old Name," "So Long, Mary," "Forty-Five Minutes from Broadway."
NEW YORK: Jan. 1, 1906
NEW AMSTERDAM THEATRE; 90 p.
Presented by Marc Klaw & A. L. Erlanger; directed by George M. Cohan; settings, John Young, Ernest Albert, Frank Marsden; costumes, F. Richard Anderson; music director, Frederic Solomon.
CAST: Fay Templeton (*Mary Jane Jenkins*), Victor Moore (*Kid Burns*), Donald Brian (*Tom Bennet*), Lois Ewell (*Flora Dora Dean*).

NEW YORK: March 14, 1912
COHAN THEATRE; 36 p.
Presented by George M. Cohan & Sam H. Harris; directed by Cohan; settings, Unitt & Wickes; costumes, Schneider-Anderson; music director, Charles J. Gebest.
CAST: George M. Cohan (*Kid Burns*), Sallie Fisher (*Mary Jane Jenkins*), Lawrence Wheat (*Tom Bennet*), Louise Aichel (*Flora Dora Dean*).
Cohan wrote this comedy with music (there were only five songs) for Fay Templeton, but Victor Moore, in his first Bway musical, almost stole the notices. The story is set in New Rochelle—45 minutes from Bway— and has to do with a missing will left by a deceased millionaire. Kid Burns discovers the will, which leaves everything to the man's housekeeper, Mary Jane Jenkins, but this only makes things worse. The proud

"square-sporting man" is in love with Mary and simply refuses to marry anyone with so much money. The only solution: Mary tears up the will. Though the Bway run lasted only three months, the show was a hit throughout the country (four months in Chicago before NY, four months after). Cohan originally called the play *Mary* but changed the name to what the producers felt was a more commercial title. In 1907 Cohan again cast Victor Moore as Kid Burns in the musical *The Talk of New York*, and in 1912 Cohan himself appeared in the part in a revival of *Forty-Five Minutes from Broadway.*

"Forty-Five Minutes from Broadway." Music & lyric by George M. Cohan. Victor Moore and chorus introduced the number in the 1906 Bway musical of the same name. Though it sang the praises of New Rochelle, the local chamber of commerce took strong exception to having its citizens called "Reubens" and described as having "whiskers like hay." The song was also sung by Joel Grey and Loni Ackerman in *George M!* (NY 1968).

Fosse, (Robert Louis) Bob, director, choreographer, actor, dancer; b. Chicago, Ill., June 23, 1927. Fosse's razzle-dazzle choreography, musical staging, and overall direction has helped to create an almost unbroken succession of Bway hits. A professional dancer at 13, he appeared on Bway and in Hollywood films (incl. *Kiss Me, Kate*), and has also directed films (*Cabaret*). Fosse was married to dancers Mary Ann Niles (his first partner), Joan McCracken, and Gwen Verdon (who has been in five of his shows).
Unless otherwise noted, Mr. Fosse was choreographer of following; asterisk indicates he was also director:

1948	Call Me Mister (US tour) (dancer only)
	Make Mine Manhattan (US tour) (dancer only)
1950	Dance Me a Song (dancer only)
1954	The Pajama Game
1955	Damn Yankees
1956	Bells Are Ringing
1957	New Girl in Town
1959	Redhead *
1961	How to Succeed in Business Without Really Trying
1962	Little Me *
1963	How to Succeed in Business Without Really Trying (L)
1966	Sweet Charity *
1972	Pippin *
1973	Pippin * (L)
1975	Chicago * (also co-lib.)
1978	Dancin'*

Foy, Eddie (né Edwin Fitzgerald), actor, dancer; b. New York, March 9, 1854; d. Kansas City, Mo., Feb. 16, 1928. Puckish comic with pointed nose and wide V-shaped mouth, noted for his slurred way of speaking and his acrobatic dancing. Began in vaudeville 1869 and returned to vaudeville in 1912 with act, Eddie Foy and the Seven Little Foys. His only son to continue as actor is Eddie Foy, Jr. Bib: *Clowning Through Life* by Foy (1928).

1895	Off the Earth (*Cluster*)
1898	Hotel Topsy-Turvy (*Lebeau*)
1899	An Arabian Girl (*Cassim D'Artagnan*)
1901	The Strollers (*Kamfer*)
1902	The Wild Rose (*Paracelsus Noodle*)
1903	Mr. Bluebeard (*Sister Anne*)
1904	Piff! Paff!! Pouf!!! (*Peter Pouffle*)
1905	The Earl and the Girl (*Jim Cheese*)
1907	The Orchid (*Artie Choke*)
1908	Mr. Hamlet of Broadway (*Joey Wheeze*)
1910	Up and Down Broadway
1912	Over the River (*Madison Parke*)

Foy, Eddie, Jr. (né Edwin Fitzgerald Jr.), actor; b. New Rochelle, NY, Feb.

4, 1905. This spry, needle-nosed son of comedian Eddie Foy scored his biggest Bway hits in *The Red Mill* and *The Pajama Game*. He began career in vaudeville act, Eddie Foy and the Seven Little Foys (1912–1929).

1929	Show Girl (*Denny Kerrigan*)
1930	Ripples (*Cpl. Jack Sterling*)
	Smiles (*Gilbert Stone*)
1931	The Cat and the Fiddle (*Alexander Sheridan*)
1935	At Home Abroad
	Orchids Preferred (*Bubbles Wilson*)
1945	The Red Mill (r) (*Kid Connor*)
1948	High Button Shoes (US tour) (*Harrison Floy*)
1954	The Pajama Game (*Hines*)
1957	Rumple (*Rumple*)
1961	Donnybrook (*Mikeen Flynn*)

"Freddy, My Love." Music & lyric by Jim Jacobs & Warren Casey. Rock and roll love letter—two syllables on word "love"—harmonized by Katie Hanley, Garn Stephens, Marya Small, and Adrienne Barbeau in *Grease* (NY 1972). In London version (1973) the quartet consisted of Hilary Labow, Colette Kelly, Felicity Harrison, and Jacquie-Ann Carr.

Freedley, Vinton, producer; b. Philadelphia, Pa., Nov. 5, 1891; d. New York, June 5, 1969. Freedley began his career as an actor, then joined Alex A. Aarons in 1923 to form Bway producing team that presented 11 musicals in 10 years (incl. *Lady, Be Good!, Oh, Kay!, Funny Face, Hold Everything!, Girl Crazy*). Seven Aarons-Freedley shows had scores by George and Ira Gershwin; four produced by Freedley alone had scores by Cole Porter (*Anything Goes, Red, Hot and Blue!, Leave It to Me!, Let's Face It!*). In 1928, Aarons and Freedley built the Alvin Theatre, NY. Ethel Merman appeared in three Freedley musicals, Fred and Adele Astaire, Gertrude

Lawrence, William Gaxton, and Victor Moore were in two each.

> Unless otherwise noted, Mr. Freedley was producer of following; asterisk indicates he was co-producer with Mr. Aarons:
>
> 1922 For Goodness Sake (*Jefferson Dangerfield* only)
> 1923 Elsie (*Harry Hammond* only)
> 1924 Lady, Be Good! *
> 1925 Tip-Toes *
> 1926 Oh, Kay! *
> 1927 Funny Face *
> 1928 Here's Howe *
> Hold Everything! *
> Treasure Girl *
> 1929 Spring Is Here *
> Heads Up! *
> 1930 Girl Crazy *
> 1933 Pardon My English *
> 1934 Anything Goes
> 1936 Red, Hot and Blue!
> 1938 Leave It to Me!
> 1940 Cabin in the Sky
> 1941 Let's Face It!
> 1944 Jackpot
> 1945 Memphis Bound
> 1950 Great to Be Alive!

"Friendliest Thing, The." Music & lyric by Ervin Drake. Bernice Massi's seductive offer to Steve Lawrence in *What Makes Sammy Run?* (NY 1964) to do the friendliest thing two people can do. The song—along with Cole Porter's "Love for Sale"—is a rare instance in the musical theatre of a direct invitation to sexual intercourse.

"Friendship." Music & lyric by Cole Porter. Sung by Ethel Merman and Bert Lahr in *DuBarry Was a Lady* (NY 1939) in mock-hillbilly style, this show-stopping number catalogues all the self-sacrificing acts that reinforce the singers' mutual friendship. In London version (1942) Frances Day and Arthur Riscoe exchanged pledges.

Friml, Rudolf, composer; b. Prague, Bohemia, Dec. 8, 1879; d. Hollywood, Cal., Nov. 12, 1972. Like composer Sigmund Romberg, Friml helped continue the tradition of romantic operetta first popularized on Bway by Victor Herbert. His initial assignment, *The Firefly* ("Giannina Mia," "Sympathy"), was, in fact, originally slated for Herbert. Friml's most durable hits (all starring Dennis King): *Rose-Marie* ("Rose-Marie," "The Mounties," "Indian Love Call"), *The Vagabond King* ("Only a Rose," "Song of the Vagabonds," "Some Day"), *The Three Musketeers* ("March of the Musketeers," "Ma Belle"). The composer wrote 10 scores with lyricist Otto Harbach (two of them also with Oscar Hammerstein II). Others with whom he wrote: Herbert Reynolds, Harold Atteridge, P. G. Wodehouse, Rida Johnson Young, Catherine Chisholm Cushing, Brian Hooker, Edward Clark, Clifford Grey, J. Keirn Brennan, Rowland Leigh, John Shubert.

> 1912 The Firefly (Harbach)
> 1913 High Jinks (Harbach)
> 1915 The Peasant Girl, (Reynolds, Atteridge)
> Katinka (Harbach)
> 1917 You're in Love (Harbach)
> Kitty Darlin' (Harbach, Wodehouse)
> 1918 Sometime (Young)
> Glorianna (Cushing)
> 1919 Tumble In (Harbach)
> The Little Whopper (Harbach)
> 1921 June Love (Hooker)
> 1922 The Blue Kitten (Harbach)
> 1923 Cinders (Clark)
> 1924 Rose-Marie (Harbach, Hammerstein)
> 1925 The Vagabond King (Hooker)
> 1926 The Wild Rose (Harbach, Hammerstein)
> 1927 The White Eagle (Hooker)
> 1928 The Three Musketeers (Grey, Wodehouse)
> 1930 Luana (Brennan)
> 1934 Music Hath Charms (Leigh, Shubert)

Frohman, Charles, producer; b. Sandusky, Ohio, June 17, 1860; d. *Lusi-*

tania sinking, May 7, 1915. Though primarily a Bway producer, with such hits as *The Girl from Kay's* and *The Dollar Princess*, Frohman was also a manager in London, where he built the Aldwych and Hicks Theatres for Seymour Hicks, and where he also presented *Three Little Maids*, *My Lady Molly*, and *The Catch of the Season*. Julia Sanderson and Edna May both appeared in six Frohman musicals. Bib: *Charles Frohman: Manager and Man* by Isaac Marcosson and Daniel Frohman (his brother, also a producer) (Harper, NY 1916).

1895 His Excellency
     The Shop Girl
     An Artist's Model
1897 In Town
1898 Hotel Topsy-Turvy
1901 The Girl from Up There
     The Girl from Up There (L)
     Bluebell in Fairyland (L)
1902 Three Little Maids (L)
1903 My Lady Molly (L)
     The School Girl (L)
     Three Little Maids
     The Girl from Kay's
     Madame Sherry (L)
1904 My Lady Molly
     The School Girl
     The Catch of the Season (L)
1905 The Rollicking Girl
     The Catch of the Season
1906 The Beauty of Bath (L)
     The Little Cherub
     The Rich Mr. Hoggenheimer
1907 Nelly Neil (L)
     My Darling (L)
     The Dairymaids
     The Gay Gordons (L)
     The Hoyden
     Miss Hook of Holland
1908 A Waltz Dream (L)
     The Girls of Gottenberg
     Fluffy Ruffles
1909 Kitty Grey
     The Dollar Princess
1910 The Arcadians
     Our Miss Gibbs
1911 The Siren
1912 The Pink Lady (L)
     The Girl from Montmartre

1913 The Sunshine Girl
     The Doll Girl
     The Marriage Market
1914 The Laughing Husband
     The Girl from Utah

"From Now On." Music & lyric by Cole Porter. In *Leave It to Me!* (NY 1938), William Gaxton and Tamara decide the time has come to settle down.

Fryer, Robert, producer; b. Washington, DC, Nov. 18, 1920. Fryer's major Bway productions were *A Tree Grows in Brooklyn, Wonderful Town, Redhead, Sweet Charity, Mame,* and *Chicago*. Six of his musicals were offered in partnership with Lawrence Carr. Gwen Verdon appeared in three Fryer productions; Shirley Booth in two.

1951 A Tree Grows in Brooklyn
1953 Wonderful Town
1954 By the Beautiful Sea
1956 Shangri-la
1959 Redhead
     Saratoga
1963 Hot Spot
1966 Sweet Charity
     Mame
1975 Chicago

"Fugue for Tinhorns." Music & lyric by Frank Loesser. As three Bway horse players in *Guys and Dolls* (NY 1950), Stubby Kaye, Johnny Silver, and Douglas Deane offered a fugal debate on the merits of horses named Paul Revere, Valentine, and Epitaph. In London production (1953), the trio was Kaye, Silver, and Robert Arden. Originally called "Three Cornered Tune," the song had a different lyric and a slower tempo, and was intended for Isabel Bigley, Sam Levene, and Robert Alda. It was dropped during *Guys and Dolls'* pre-Bway tour and then rewritten in its present form.

"Fun to Be Fooled." Music by Harold Arlen; lyric by Ira Gershwin & E. Y.

Harburg. Romantic self-deception revealed by Frances Williams in *Life Begins at 8:40* (NY 1934).

Funny Face (1927). Music by George Gershwin; lyrics by Ira Gershwin; book by Paul Gerard Smith & Fred Thompson.

SONGS: "Funny Face," "High Hat," "He Loves and She Loves," "Let's Kiss and Make Up," " 'S Wonderful," "Tell the Doc," "My One and Only," "The Babbitt and the Bromide."

NEW YORK: Nov. 22, 1927
ALVIN THEATRE; 250 p.

Presented by Alex A. Aarons & Vinton Freedley; directed by Edgar Mac-Gregor; choreographed by Bobby Connolly; settings, John Wenger; costumes, Kiviette; music director, Alfred Newman.

CAST: Fred Astaire (*Jimmie Reeve*), Adele Astaire (*Frankie Wynne*), Victor Moore (*Herbert*), William Kent (*Dugsie Gibbs*), Allen Kearns (*Peter Thurston*), Betty Compton (*Dora Wynne*), Gertrude McDonald (*June Wynne*); Phil Ohman & Vic Arden (duo-pianos).

LONDON: Nov. 8, 1928
PRINCES THEATRE; 263 p.

Presented by Alfred Butt & Lee Ephraim, with Aarons & Freedley; directed by Felix Edwardes; choreographed by Bobby Connolly; settings, Joseph & Phil Harker; costumes, Jenny, Reville; music director, Julian Jones.

CAST: Fred Astaire (*Jimmie Reeve*), Adele Astaire (*Frankie Wynne*), Leslie Henson (*Dugsie Gibbs*), Sydney Howard (*Herbert*), Bernard Clifton (*Peter Thurston*), Rita Page (*Dora Wynne*), Eileen Hatton (*June Wynne*); Jacques Frey & Mario Braggiotti (duo-pianos).

Funny Face started out under the title *Smarty*, with a book co-authored by Robert Benchley. During tryout tour, the name was changed, Benchley was replaced by Fred Thompson, Victor Moore joined the cast, Allen Kearns took over Stanley Ridges' part, seven numbers (incl. "How Long Has This Been Going On?") were dropped and five were added. The alterations apparently helped, because *Funny Face*, the first attraction at NY's Alvin Theatre, was hailed as a fitting successor to *Lady, Be Good!*, the previous effort of Fred and Adele, George and Ira, and Aarons and Freedley. In the plot, Jimmie's ward, Frankie, feels so restricted she induces beau Peter to help her steal back her diary which Jimmie had hidden in his safe. Everyone—incl. Dugsie and Herbert, a comic burglar masquerading as a butler—goes in pursuit of a bracelet that Peter took instead of the diary, a quest that takes the cast to Canoe Inn, Lake Wapatog, NJ, the Paymore Hotel, Atlantic City, and the Two-Million-Dollar Pier. The Astaires and the songs were the main attraction both in NY and London.

FILM VERSION: Fred Astaire and Audrey Hepburn (new story, added songs) (Par. 1957, Stanley Donen dir.).

"Funny Face." Music by George Gershwin; lyric by Ira Gershwin. Sung by Fred and Adele Astaire in *Funny Face* (NY 1927, L 1928), while Fred was pulling Adele around the stage in a toy wagon. The affectionate put-down of physical appearance is similar in intent to the Rodgers and Hart "My Funny Valentine."

Funny Girl (1964). Music by Jule Styne; lyrics by Bob Merrill; book by Isobel Lennart.

SONGS: "I'm the Greatest Star," "Cornet Man," "People," "You Are Woman," "Don't Rain on My Parade," "Sadie, Sadie," "Who Are You

Now?," "The Music That Makes Me Dance."

NEW YORK: March 26, 1964
WINTER GARDEN; 1,348 p.

Presented by Ray Stark; directed by Garson Kanin, Jerome Robbins; choreographed by Carol Haney; settings & lighting, Robert Randolph; costumes, Irene Sharaff; music director, Milton Rosenstock; orchestrations, Ralph Burns.

CAST: Barbra Streisand (*Fanny Brice*), Sydney Chaplin (*Nick Arnstein*), Danny Meehan (*Eddie Ryan*), Kay Medford (*Mrs. Brice*), Jean Stapleton (*Mrs. Strakosh*), Reginald De Koven (*Florenz Ziegfeld*), Lainie Kazan (*Vera*).

LONDON: April 13, 1966
PRINCE OF WALES THEATRE; 112 p.

Presented by Bernard Delfont & Arthur Lewis; restaged by Lawrence Kasha; dances reproduced by Larry Fuller; settings & lighting, Robert Randolph; costumes, Irene Sharaff; music director, Marcus Dods; orchestrations, Ralph Burns.

CAST: Barbra Streisand (*Fanny Brice*), Michael Craig (*Nick Arnstein*), Lee Allen (*Eddie Ryan*), Kay Medford (*Mrs. Brice*), Stella Moray (*Mrs. Strakosh*), Ronald Leigh-Hunt (*Florenz Ziegfeld*).

The saga of Fanny Brice covers her discovery by Ziegfeld, her stage triumph in the *Follies*, her marriage to gambler Nick Arnstein, and the breakup of the marriage after Arnstein gets out of jail for stock swindling. The musical was produced by Ray Stark, Miss Brice's son-in-law, who first planned it for the screen, but Isobel Lennart's original draft convinced him it would be better on the stage. Writing took a year and a half, and at various times three directors (Robbins, Bob Fosse, Kanin) were used. Five opening-night postponements

were required before all was ready. The reception accorded Barbra Streisand, in her first major role, quickly established her as a star. During run, Miss Streisand was succeeded by Mimi Hines (12-65), Sydney Chaplin by Johnny Desmond (7-65), Danny Meehan by Lee Allen (3-64) and Phil Ford (12-65). The US tour, which began Oct. 1965, lasted one year, one month. The cast was headed by Marilyn Michaels (*Fanny*), Anthony George (*Nick*), Danny Carroll (*Eddie*), Lillian Roth (*Mrs. Brice*). The London facsimile was forced to close because of Miss Streisand's impending motherhood.

Other Bway stage performers whose lives provided librettos for musicals: Gypsy Rose Lee (Sandra Church in *Gypsy*, 1959); Sophie Tucker (Libi Staiger in *Sophie*, 1963); George M. Cohan (Joel Grey in *George M!*, 1968); the Marx Brothers (Lewis J. Stadlen, Irwin Pearl, Daniel Fortus, Alvin Kupperman in *Minnie's Boys*, 1970).

FILM VERSION: Barbra Streisand and Omar Sharif (Col. 1968, William Wyler dir.).

Funny Thing Happened on the Way to the Forum, A (1962). Music & lyrics by Stephen Sondheim; book by Burt Shevelove & Larry Gelbart, based on plays by Titus Maccius Plautus.

SONGS: "Comedy Tonight," "Love, I Hear," "Free," "Lovely," "Everybody Ought to Have a Maid," "I'm Calm," "Impossible," "Pretty Little Picture."

NEW YORK: May 8, 1962
ALVIN THEATRE; 964 p.

Presented by Harold Prince; directed by George Abbott; choreographed by Jack Cole; settings & costumes, Tony Walton; lighting, Jean Rosenthal; music director, Harold

Hastings; orchestrations, Irwin Kostal & Sid Ramin.

CAST: Zero Mostel (*Pseudolus*), Jack Gilford (*Hysterium*), David Burns (*Senex*), Raymond Walburn (*Erronius*), John Carradine (*Lycus*), Ruth Kobart (*Domina*), Brian Davies (*Hero*), Preshy Marker (*Philia*), Ronald Holgate (*Miles Gloriosus*).

LONDON: Oct. 3, 1963
STRAND THEATRE; 762 p.

Presented by Harold Prince, Tony Walton, & Richard Pilbrow; directed by George Abbott; dances reproduced by George Martin; settings & costumes, Tony Walton; lighting, Jean Rosenthal; music director, Alyn Ainsworth; orchestrations, Irwin Kostal & Sid Ramin.

CAST: Frankie Howerd (*Pseudolus*), Kenneth Connor (*Hysterium*), "Monsewer" Eddie Gray (*Senex*), Robertson Hare (*Erronius*), Jon Pertwee (*Lycus*), Linda Gray (*Domina*), John Rye (*Hero*), Isla Blair (*Philia*), Leon Greene (*Miles Gloriosus*).

NEW YORK: March 30, 1972
LUNT-FONTANNE THEATRE; 156 p.

Presented by David Black, with Seymour Vail & Henry Honeckman; directed by Burt Shevelove; choreographed by Ralph Beaumont; settings, James Trittipo; costumes, Noel Taylor; lighting, H. R. Poindexter; music director, Milton Rosenstock; orchestrations, Irwin Kostal & Sid Ramin.

CAST: Phil Silvers (*Pseudolus*), Larry Blyden (*Hysterium*), Jack Collins (*Senex*), Carl Ballantine (*Lycus*), Reginald Owen (*Erronius*), Lizabeth Pritchett (*Domina*), Pamela Hall (*Philia*), John Hansen (*Hero*), Carl Lindstrom (*Miles Gloriosus*).

A bawdy, farcical musical full of sight gags, pratfalls, mistaken identity, and other familiar vaudeville ingredients (the printed text includes the Authors' Note, "This is a scenario for vaudevillians"). Though originally slated for Phil Silvers, then Milton Berle, the role of Pseudolus was played by Zero Mostel, whose looming presence dominated the proceedings. Last-minute—and uncredited—direction by Jerome Robbins helped turn the production, which had floundered during its tryout tour, into a major success. The most important addition: the song "Comedy Tonight," which opened the show and set the proper tone.

To come up with a proper script, the authors researched all 21 surviving comedies by Plautus, then decided to write an original libretto incorporating characters and situations found in the plays. (Miles Gloriosus' line "I am a parade" was the only line they retained from Plautus.) The situation in the musical involving a doddering old man who is kept from entering a house he thinks is haunted, was originally in a play called *Mostellaria*. The show contained the standard Plautus characters: the conniving servants, the lascivious master, the domineering mistress, the self-centered warrior, the simple-minded hero (called Hero) and heroine, the senile old man. During original Bway run, Mostel was succeeded by Dick Shawn (2-64) and Danny Dayton (8-64); David Burns by Frank McHugh (10-63); John Carradine by Erik Rhodes (9-63). During London version, Frankie Howerd was succeeded by Dave King. The run of the 1972 revival was curtailed by the illness of Phil Silvers, who was succeeded by John Bentley and Tom Poston.

FILM VERSION: Zero Mostel, Phil Silvers, Buster Keaton, Jack Gilford (UA 1966, Richard Lester dir.).

Furber, Douglas, lyricist, librettist, actor; b. London, May 13, 1885; d. London, Feb. 19, 1961. Furber's most durable song was "Limehouse Blues," written with composer Philip Braham, first sung in London in *A to Z* but popularized in NY in *André Charlot's Revue of 1924*. Other successes: "March with Me!," "Fancy Our Meeting," "Oceans of Time," "The Lambeth Walk" (in Furber's longest-running London show, *Me and My Girl*). Composers with whom he worked include Emmett Adams, Charles Cuvillier, Edward Kunneke, Herman Finck, Hugo Hirsch, Max Darewski, Albert Sirmay, Franz Lehar, Joseph Meyer, Phil Charig, Ivor Novello, Jack Waller and Joseph Tunbridge, Vivian Ellis, Arthur Schwartz, Johnny Green, Harry Archer, Ralph Benatzky, Noel Gay, Manning Sherwin, Carroll Gibbons.

Asterisk indicates libretto or sketches also written by Mr. Furber:

1917 150 Pounds Revue (Adams) (also actor)
  Carminetta (Lassaily)
1919 Afgar (Cuvillier)
1920 Pretty Peggy (Adams)
1921 Ring Up (actor, added)
1922 A to Z (actor, added)
  Battling Butler (Braham) (also *Ted Spink*)
1923 The Cousin from Nowhere (Kunneke)
  Yes! * (Blaney)
  The Little Revue Starts at 9 * (Finck)
1924 Toni * (Hirsch)
1925 Boodle (Braham, Darewski) (also *Dixon*)

The Bamboula (Sirmay)
Clo-Clo (Lehar)
Charlot Revue of 1926 * (NY) (misc.) (also actor, repl.)
1927 Up with the Lark * (Braham)
1928 That's a Good Girl * (Charig)
  Lucky Girl * (Charig)
1929 The House That Jack Built * (Novello)
1930 Silver Wings * (Waller, Tunbridge)
  Follow a Star * (Ellis)
1931 Stand Up and Sing * (Charig, Ellis)
1933 Nice Goings On * (Schwartz)
1934 Mr. Whittington * (Green, Waller, Tunbridge)
  Lucky Break * (Archer)
1935 The Flying Trapeze * (Benatzky)
1936 Swing Along (co-lib. only)
  Let's Raise the Curtain (lib. only)
1937 And on We Go (sk. only)
  Going Greek (co-lib. only)
  Hide and Seek (co-lib. only)
  Me and My Girl * (Gay)
1938 Wild Oats * (Gay)
  Running Riot (lib. only)
1939 Sitting Pretty * (Sherwin)
  Black Velvet (sk. only)
  Shephard's Pie * (Sherwin) (also dir.)
1940 Up and Doing * (Sherwin)
1941 Fun and Games * (Sherwin) (also dir.)
1943 It's Foolish but It's Fun * (misc.) (also dir.)
  The Magic Carpet (co-lib. only)
1945 The Gaieties * (Gibbons)
  Big Boy * (Gibbons)

❦ G ❧

Gaiety Girl, A (1893). Music by Sidney Jones; lyrics by Harry Greenbank; book by Owen Hall.
SONGS: "Private Tommy Atkins" (Potter-Hamilton), "Sunshine Above," "Beneath the Skies," "It Seems to Me," "When Your Pride Has a Tumble."

LONDON: Oct. 14, 1893
PRINCE OF WALES THEATRE; 413 p.
Presented by George Edwardes; directed by J. A. E. Malone; settings, Walter Hann, William Telbin; costumes, Edel & Redfern; music director, Sidney Jones.
CAST: Lottie Venne (*Lady Virginia*

Forest), C. Hayden Coffin (Capt. Charles Goldfield), Maud Hobson (Alma Somerset), Harry Monkhouse (Rev. Montague Brierly), Louie Pounds (Daisy Ormsbury), Marie Studholme (Gladys Stourton), Leedham Bantock (Harry Fitzwarren), Kate Cutler (Lady Edytha Aldwyn), Fred Kaye (Major Barclay), W. Louis Bradfield (Bobbie Rivers).

NEW YORK: Sept. 17, 1894
DALY'S THEATRE; 81 p.
   Presented by George Edwardes; directed by J. A. E. Malone; settings, Reid; costumes, Edel & Redfern; music director, Granville Bantock.
   CAST: Maud Hobson (Lady Virginia Forest), W. Louis Bradfield (Capt. Charles Goldfield), Blanche Massey (Alma Somerset), Harry Monkhouse (Rev. Montague Brierly), Ethel Selwyn (Daisy Ormsbury), Sophie Elliott (Gladys Stourton), E. G. Woodhouse (Harry Fitzwarren), Marie Yorke (Lady Edytha Aldwyn), Fred Kaye (Major Barclay), Cecil Hope (Bobbie Rivers).

   The first musical comedy to be designated a "musical comedy," A Gaiety Girl also celebrated London's leading theatre for musical entertainment. Four young ladies from the Gaiety Theatre attend a garden party in Windsor as guests of Major Barclay, and, at the urging of Lady Virginia, sing and dance for the other guests. Alma, one of the girls, is admired by Capt. Goldfield, but true love must wait because poor Alma has been falsely accused of stealing a diamond comb that had been maliciously put into her purse. Once they all go to the Riviera, however, Alma's innocence is proved.
   During the run producer Edwardes wanted to transfer the musical to the more appropriate Gaiety Theatre, but a previous booking forced him to set-

tle for Daly's. It also played Daly's in 1899. The idea for the musical came about when Owen Hall, who had never before written for the stage, rashly told the producer that he could write a better plot than In Town, then playing at the Gaiety. Apparently he did, since the success of A Gaiety Girl persuaded Edwardes to specialize in musical comedies.

Gallagher, Helen, actress, dancer, singer; b. Brooklyn, NY, 1926. Slim, dark-haired dancer-singer who scored biggest Bway success in the revival of No, No, Nanette. Also introduced "Big Spender" in Sweet Charity.

1944	Seven Lively Arts (dancer)
1945	Mr. Strauss Goes to Boston (dancer)
	Billion Dollar Baby (dancer)
1947	Brigadoon (dancer)
	High Button Shoes (Nancy)
1949	Touch and Go
1950	Touch and Go (L)
1951	Make a Wish (Poupette)
1952	Pal Joey (r) (Gladys Bumps)
1953	Hazel Flagg (Hazel Flagg)
1955	The Pajama Game (Gladys, repl.)
1958	Portofino (Kitty)
1966	Sweet Charity (Nickie; Charity, repl.)
1968	Mame (Agnes Gooch, repl.)
1970	Cry for Us All (Bessie Legg)
1971	No, No, Nanette (r) (Lucille Early)
1977	The Misanthrope (Arsinoe)

"Game of Poker." Music by Harold Arlen; lyric by Johnny Mercer. Love as a hit-or-miss proposition. Introduced by Howard Keel in Saratoga (NY 1959), then reprised by Keel and Carol Lawrence as a countermelody to Odette Myrtil's delicate "Love Held Lightly."

Garrick Gaieties, The (1925). Music by Richard Rodgers; lyrics by Lorenz Hart; sketches by Benjamin Kaye, Arthur Sullivan, Morrie Ryskind, Louis Sorin, Sam Jaffe, Howard Green, Edith Meiser.

SONGS: "The Butcher, the Baker, the Candle-Stick Maker" (Mana Zucca, Benjamin Kaye), "An Old-Fashioned Girl" (lyric, Edith Meiser), "April Fool," "Manhattan," "The Three Musketeers," "Do You Love Me?," "On with the Dance," "Sentimental Me."

NEW YORK: June 8, 1925
GARRICK THEATRE; 211 p.

Presented by the Theatre Guild; directed by Philip Loeb; choreographed by Herbert Fields; settings & costumes, Carolyn Hancock; music director, Richard Rodgers.

CAST: Sterling Holloway, Romney Brent, Betty Starbuck, Philip Loeb, Elisabeth (Libby) Holman, James Norris, June Cochrane, Edith Meiser, Hildegarde Halliday, Eleanor Shaler, Rose Rolando, House Jamieson, Alvah Bessie, Sanford Meisner, Lee Strasberg.

The Garrick Gaieties, with its hit song, "Manhattan," was the first Bway success by Rodgers and Hart. The show was a youthful, modest, impertinent revue organized by "The Theatre Guild Junior Players," a group of young Theatre Guild actors. It was originally presented for two special Sunday performances on May 17, 1925, to help the Guild raise funds for tapestries at the new Guild Theatre. After catching on with the public, the revue was offered for a regular commercial run. Most songs and sketches satirized the theatre in general and the Theatre Guild in particular, with special aim taken at anything arty or pretentious. For the first-act finale, Rodgers and Hart contributed "An American Jazz Opera" called *The Joy Spreader*, an early attempt to include an abbreviated but complete

musical production within a revue (it was, however, cut in June).

A second edition, involving most of the same people, was mounted the following year on May 10, and ran 174 performances. Though lacking the novelty of the original, it included such popular attractions as Rodgers and Hart's "Mountain Greenery" and their operetta spoof "The Rose of Arizona."

A third *Gaieties* opened in 1930 and ran 158 performances. Again sponsored by the Theatre Guild (but at the Guild Theatre, not the Garrick), it was directed by Philip Loeb with a cast including such *Gaieties* veterans as Sterling Holloway, Edith Meiser, Loeb, Hildegarde Halliday, and James Norris. Newcomers were Albert Carroll, Nan Blackstone, Imogene Coca, Ray Heatherton, and Ted Fetter. Rosalind Russell was in the cast when the revue returned for a limited pre-tour engagement. "The Three Musketeers" and "The Rose of Arizona" were retained, with new material written by Carroll Carroll, Benjamin Kaye, Newman Levy, Johnny Mercer, Ira Gershwin, E. Y. Harburg, Vernon Duke, Kay Swift, James P. Warburg, Marc Blitzstein, and Ronald Jeans.

Gaxton, William (né Arturo Antonio Gaxiola), actor, singer; b. San Francisco, Cal., Dec. 2, 1893; d. New York, Feb. 12, 1963. In the 30s and early 40s, the sight of the brash, nervously aggressive Gaxton offered sharp contrast to bumbling Victor Moore, his co-star in seven Bway musicals. Among them: *Of Thee I Sing* (in which Gaxton sang "Of Thee I Sing, Baby" and "Who Cares?"), *Anything Goes* ("You're the Top," "All Through the Night"), *Leave It to Me!* ("From Now On"), *Louisiana Purchase*

("Fools Fall in Love"). Gaxton also introduced "My Heart Stood Still" and "Thou Swell" in *A Connecticut Yankee,* "You Do Something to Me" in *Fifty Million Frenchmen,* and "Mine" in *Let 'Em Eat Cake.*

Asterisk indicates appearance with Mr. Moore:

1922 Music Box Revue
1925 Betty Lee (US tour) (*Wallingford Speed*)
1927 A Connecticut Yankee (*Martin*)
1929 Fifty Million Frenchmen (*Peter Forbes*)
1931 Of Thee I Sing * (*John P. Wintergreen*)
1933 Let 'Em Eat Cake * (*John P. Wintergreen*)
1934 Anything Goes * (*Billy Crocker*)
1936 White Horse Inn (*Leopold*)
1938 Leave It to Me! * (*Buckley Joyce Thomas*)
1940 Louisiana Purchase * (*Jim Taylor*)
1945 Hollywood Pinafore * (*Dick Live-Eye*)
1946 Nellie Bly * (*Frank Jordan*)

Gay Divorce (1932). Music & lyrics by Cole Porter; book by Kenneth Webb & Samuel Hoffenstein, based on play by Dwight Taylor adapted from unproduced play *An Adorable Adventure,* by J. Hartley Manners.

SONGS: "After You, Who?," "I Still Love the Red, White and Blue," "Night and Day," "How's Your Romance?," "I've Got You on My Mind," "Mister and Missus Fitch," "You're in Love."

NEW YORK: Nov. 29, 1932
ETHEL BARRYMORE THEATRE; 248 p.

Presented by Dwight Deere Wiman & Tom Weatherly; directed by Howard Lindsay; choreographed by Carl Randall & Barbara Newberry; settings, Jo Mielziner; costumes, Raymond Sovey; music director, Gene Salzer; orchestrations, Hans Spialek, Robert Russell Bennett.

CAST: Fred Astaire (*Guy Holden*),
Claire Luce (*Mimi*), Luella Gear (*Hortense*), G.P. Huntley, Jr. (*Teddy*), Betty Starbuck (*Barbara Wray*), Erik Rhodes (*Tonetti*), Eric Blore (*Waiter*), Roland Bottomley (*Pratt*).

LONDON: Nov. 2, 1933
PALACE THEATRE; 180 p.

Presented by Lee Ephraim; directed by Felix Edwardes; choreographed by Carl Randall & Barbara Newberry; settings, Joseph & Phil Harker; costumes, Betty Boor; music director, Percival Mackey; orchestrations, Hans Spialek, Robert Russell Bennett.

CAST: Fred Astaire (*Guy Holden*), Claire Luce (*Mimi*), Olive Blakeney (*Gertrude Howard*), Claud Allister (*Teddy*), Joan Gardner (*Barbara Wray*), Erik Rhodes (*Tonetti*), Eric Blore (*Waiter*), Fred Hearne (*Octavius Mann*)

Fred Astaire's only stage vehicle without his sister, Adele, was not welcomed too enthusiastically by the reviewers, but thanks to the star's dancing and Cole Porter's songs, particularly "Night and Day," it managed to have a respectable run. The story concerns novelist Guy Holden, who is mistaken for a professional corespondent in Mimi's divorce case. Once the misunderstanding is cleared up, Guy and Mimi prepare to spend all their nights and days together.

During NY run, Astaire was succeeded by Joseph Santley (6-33), Claire Luce by Dorothy Stone (5-33). During tour, Miss Gear succeeded by Fay Bainter. In 1960, an off-Bway revival had a brief run. Its cast was headed by Frank Aletter (*Guy*), Judy Johnson (*Mimi*), Beatrice Arthur (*Hortense*).

FILM VERSION: Fred Astaire and Ginger Rogers (called *The Gay Divorcee,* with mostly new songs) (RKO 1934, Mark Sandrich dir.).

Gay, Maisie (née Maisie Munro-Noble), actress, singer; b. London, Jan. 7, 1883; d. London, Sept. 13, 1945. Well-rounded comedienne noted for her appearances in London revue sketches, especially Noël Coward's *London Calling!* and *This Year of Grace.* Introduced "March With Me!" in *A to Z.* Bib: *Laughing Through Life* by Miss Gay (1931).

1904	A Country Girl (UK tour) (*Nan*)
1908	A Waltz Dream (*Fifi*, repl.)
	The Girls of Gottenberg (*Clementine*, repl.)
1909	Our Miss Gibbs (*Mrs. Farquhar*)
1911	The Quaker Girl (*Mme. Blum*, repl.)
	The Quaker Girl (NY) (*Mme. Blum*)
1913	The Girl on the Film (*Euphemia Knox*, repl.)
1914	High Jinks (US tour) (*Adelaide Fontaine*)
1916	Sybil (NY) (*Margot*)
1917	The Boy (*Millicent Meebles*)
	The Beauty Spot (*Josephine Bramble*)
1918	Soldier Boy (*Amy Lee*)
1919	The Whirligig
1920	Jig-Saw
1921	Faust-on-Toast (*Martha*)
	Pins and Needles
1922	Pins and Needles (NY)
	A to Z (repl.)
	Snap
1923	London Calling!
1924	Charlot's Revue
1925	Better Days
	Charlot's Revue (added)
1926	Wildflower (*Lucrezia Larotta*)
1927	Whitebirds
	Peggy-Ann (*Mrs. Frost*)
1928	This Year of Grace!
1930	Cochran's 1930 Revue
	Follow a Star (*Georgia Madison*, repl.)

Gay, Noel (né Reginald Moxon Armitage), composer; b. Wakefield, Eng., July 15, 1898; d. London, March 4, 1954. London's leading creator of novelty songs, Gay wrote the score for the hugely successful *Me and My Girl*, including "The Lambeth Walk." Other hits: *Clowns in Clover, Folly to Be Wise* ("The King's Horses"). Among his collaborators were Donovan Parsons, Dion Titheradge, Harry Graham, Desmond Carter, Clifford Grey, Douglas Furber, Frank Eyton, Ian Grant.

1927	Clowns in Clover (Parsons)
1931	Folly to Be Wise (Titheradge, Graham)
	Hold My Hand (Carter)
1933	That's a Pretty Thing (Carter)
1935	Jack o' Diamonds (Grey)
	Love Laughs—! (Grey)
1937	Me and My Girl (Furber)
1938	Wild Oats (Furber)
1940	Lights Up (Eyton, Grant)
	Present Arms (Eyton)
1943	La-De-Da-De-Da (Eyton)
	The Love Racket (Eyton)
1944	Meet Me, Victoria (Eyton)
1946	Sweetheart Mine (Eyton)
1948	Bob's Your Uncle (Eyton)

Gaynor, Charles (Beauclerk), composer, lyricist; b. Boston, Mass., April 3, 1909. Gaynor's *Lend an Ear* (featuring "The Gladiola Girl") was one of the notable revues of the 40s. The composer also contributed songs to revues and musicals, incl. *Sweeter and Lower* (L) and the 1973 revival of *Irene* (NY). (*D. Dec. 18, 1975.*)

1948	Lend an Ear
1961	Show Girl

Gay's the Word (1951). Music & book by Ivor Novello; lyrics by Alan Melville.

SONGS: "Vitality," "It's Bound to Be Right on the Night," "Sweet Thames," "On Such a Night as This," "Bees Are Buzzin'," "Finder, Please Return."

LONDON: Feb. 16, 1951
SAVILLE THEATRE; 502 p.

Presented by Tom Arnold & Ivor Novello; directed by Jack Hulbert;

settings, Edward Delaney; costumes, Berkeley Sutcliffe; music director, Robert Probst.

CAST: Cicely Courtneidge (*Gay Daventry*), Lizbeth Webb (*Rosetta*), Thorley Walters (*Peter Lynton*), Maidie Andrews (*Monica Stevens*), Elizabeth Seal (dancer).

The final work of· Ivor Novello before his death, this was, in part, something of a spoof of the composer's own Ruritanian operettas. Written especially for Cicely Courtneidge (from an idea suggested by Jack Hulbert), it provided the star with one of her longest-running hits. In the story, Gay Daventry, an aging operetta prima donna, opens an acting school with the financial aid of a student named Peter Lynton. The school fails, but Peter's father backs Gay in a new, modern musical, which, of course, succeeds.

Gear, Luella (Gardner van Nort), actress; b. New York, Sept. 5, 1897. Miss Gear was primarily known for her roles as a sharp-tongued, worldly-wise comedienne. She also appeared in many nonmusical productions on Bway.

1917 Love o' Mike (*Luella*)
1923 Elsie (*Margery Hammond*)
     Poppy (*Mary Delafield*)
1924 Poppy (L) (*Mary Delafield*)
1926 Queen High (*Florence Cole*)
1928 The Optimists
     Ups-a-Daisy (*Ethel Billings*)
1932 Gay Divorce (*Hortense*)
1934 Life Begins at 8:40
1936 On Your Toes (*Peggy Porterfield*)
1939 The Streets of Paris
1941 Crazy with the Heat
1942 Count Me In (*Mama*)
1948 My Romance (*Octavia Fotheringham*)

Geisha, The (1896). Music by Sidney Jones; lyrics by Harry Greenbank; book by Owen Hall.

SONGS: "Chin-Chin-Chinaman," "The Toy Monkey" (music, Lionel Monckton), "The Amorous Goldfish," "The Jewel of Asia" (music, James Philp), "Jack's the Boy" (music, Monckton), "Chon Kina," "Star of My Soul."

LONDON: April 25, 1896
DALY'S THEATRE; 760 p.

Presented by George Edwardes; directed by J. A. E. Malone; choreographed by Willie Warde; settings, William Telbin; costumes, Percy Anderson; music director, Ernest Ford.

CAST: Marie Tempest (*O Mimosa San*), C. Hayden Coffin (*Reginald Fairfax*), Huntley Wright (*Wun-Hi*), Letty Lind (*Molly Seamore*), Harry Monkhouse (*Marquis Imari*), Juliette Nesville (*Juliette Diamant*), Maud Hobson (*Lady Constance Wynne*), Louis Bradfield (*Dick Cunningham*), Leedham Bantock (*Lt. Arthur Cuddy*), William Philp (*Capt. Katana*).

NEW YORK: Sept. 9, 1896
DALY'S THEATRE; 161 p.

Presented by Augustin Daly; directed by Herbert Gresham; settings, Henry E. Hoyt, William Telbin; costumes, Percy Anderson; music director, William Withers.

CAST: Dorothy Morton (*O Mimosa San*), Van Rensselaer Wheeler (*Reginald Fairfax*), William Sampson (*Wun Hi*), Violet Lloyd (*Molly Seamore*), Edwin Stevens (*Marquis Imari*), Helma Nelson (*Juliette Diamant*), Marie St. John (*Lady Constance Wynne*), Herbert Gresham (*Dick Cunningham*), George Lesoir (*Lt. Arthur Cuddy*), Neil McCay (*Capt. Katana*), Isadora Duncan (dancer).

Influenced by Gilbert and Sullivan's *The Mikado, The Geisha* (or *A Story of a Teahouse*) was the first production designated a "musical play," indicating an attempt at a more substantial romantic plot than "musical farce" or "musical comedy." Molly Seamore, visiting the Teahouse of 10 Thousand Joys, tries on a geisha costume and is mistaken for the real thing. It's only through the efforts of Reginald Fairfax, an officer aboard HMS *Turtle,* and O Mimosa San, a real geisha, that she is saved from marrying a Japanese marquis. During NY run, Dorothy Morton was succeeded by Nancy McIntosh, Violet Lloyd by Virginia Earle, William Sampson by James T. Powers. *The Geezer,* the first Weber and Fields musical-comedy burlesque, opened just one month after *The Geisha* at a theatre next door. The musical was revived in London in 1906, 1931, 1934.

San Toy (1899), though set in China, was George Edwardes' successor to *The Geisha.* It also had a score by Sidney Jones and Harry Greenbank, starred Marie Tempest, and ran over 700 performances.

Gennaro, Peter, choreographer, dancer; b. Metairie, La. Gennaro, who began career as a dancer with the San Carlo Opera Co., won his greatest Bway success with his choreography for *Fiorello!, The Unsinkable Molly Brown,* and *Irene.*

Unless otherwise noted, Mr. Gennaro was choreographer of following:

1948 Make Mine Manhattan (dancer only)
Kiss Me, Kate (dancer only)
1950 Arms and the Girl (dancer only)
Guys and Dolls (dancer only)
1954 The Pajama Game (dancer only)
1955 Seventh Heaven
1956 Bells Are Ringing (Carl only)
1957 West Side Story (co-chor.)
1959 Fiorello!
1960 The Unsinkable Molly Brown
1962 Mr. President
1964 Bajour
1969 Jimmy
1973 Irene

"Gentleman Is a Dope, The." Music by Richard Rodgers; lyric by Oscar Hammerstein II. Sung by Lisa Kirk in *Allegro* (NY 1947). The scene in the musical depicts a street in Chicago during a rainstorm. The girl tries vainly to hail a taxi while mumbling about the way her boss, a doctor, is being led around by his wife. As the monologue turns into song, she reveals how much she loves him even while itemizing all the gentleman's faults. At the end of the song, still trying to hail a taxi, she suddenly caps the scene with, "Oh, hell, I'll walk!"—and stamps off.

Gentlemen Prefer Blondes (1949). Music by Jule Styne; lyrics by Leo Robin; book by Anita Loos & Joseph Fields, based on Miss Loos's novel.

SONGS: "Bye, Bye, Baby," "A Little Girl from Little Rock," "I Love What I'm Doing," "Just a Kiss Apart," "It's Delightful Down in Chile," "You Say You Care," "Mamie Is Mimi," "Diamonds Are a Girl's Best Friend," "Gentlemen Prefer Blondes," "Homesick Blues."

NEW YORK: Dec. 8, 1949
ZIEGFELD THEATRE; 740 p.

Presented by Herman Levin & Oliver Smith; directed by John C. Wilson; choreographed by Agnes de Mille; settings, Smith; costumes, Miles White; music director, Milton Rosenstock; orchestrations, Don Walker.

CAST: Carol Channing (*Lorelei Lee*), Yvonne Adair (*Dorothy Shaw*), Jack McCauley (*Gus Esmond*), Eric Brotherson (*Henry Spofford*), Alice Pearce (*Ella Spofford*), Rex Evans (*Sir Francis Beekman*), Anita Alvarez (*Gloria Stark*), George S. Irving (*Josephus Gage*), Reta Shaw (*Lady Phyllis Beekman*), Howard Morris (*Louis Lemanteur*), Mort Marshall (*Robert Lemanteur*).

LONDON: Aug. 20, 1962
PRINCES THEATRE; 223 p.

Presented by Kenneth Wagg & Addey, Owen & Hollerith Ltd.;

directed by Henry Kaplan; choreographed by Ralph Beaumont; settings, Hutchinson Scott; costumes, Hilary Virgo, Rosemary Carvill; lighting, William Bundy; music director, Alyn Ainsworth.

CAST: Dora Bryan (*Lorelei Lee*), Anne Hart (*Dorothy Shaw*), Donald Stewart (*Gus Esmond*), Robin Palmer (*Henry Spofford*), Bessie Love (*Ella Spofford*), Guy Middleton (*Sir Francis Beekman*), Valerie Walsh (*Gloria Stark*), Michael Malnick (*Josephus Gage*), Totti Truman Taylor (*Lady Phyllis Beekman*), Michael Ashlin (*Louis Lemanteur*), John Heawood (*Robert Lemanteur*).

NEW YORK: Jan. 27, 1974
PALACE THEATRE; 320 p.

Presented by Lee Guber & Shelly Gross; directed by Robert Moore; choreographed by Ernest Flatt; settings, John Conklin; costumes, Alvin Colt; Miss Channing's costumes, Ray Aghayan, Bob Mackie; lighting, John Gleason; music director, Milton Rosenstock; orchestrations, Philip J. Lang, Don Walker; added music by Jule Styne; added lyrics by Betty Comden & Adolph Green; new book by Kenny Solms & Gail Parent; retitled *Lorelei*.

CAST: Carol Channing (*Lorelei Lee*), Dody Goodman (*Ella Spofford*), Tamara Long (*Dorothy Shaw*), Peter Palmer (*Gus Esmond*), Lee Roy Reams (*Henry Spofford*), Brandon Maggart (*Josephus Gage*), Jack Fletcher (*Sir Francis Beekman*), Jean Bruno (*Lady Phyllis Beekman*), Bob Fitch (*Robert Lemanteur*), Ian Tucker (*Louis Lemanteur*).

The saga of gold-digging Lorelei Lee in the hedonistic 20s propelled Carol Channing's career so meteorically that she was elevated to stardom during the run. Lorelei, engaged to button tycoon Gus Es-

mond, sails aboard the *Ile de France* with her chum Dorothy Shaw. Along the way she discovers enough rich gentlemen to make sure she has a good time both on ship and in various spots throughout Paris. As for the less predatory Dorothy, she finds true romance with Philadelphian Henry Spofford.

The 1974 version, subtitled *Gentlemen Still Prefer Blondes*, still starred Carol Channing. The major change was adding a prologue and epilogue in which Lorelei, now Gus's widow, reminisces about her madcap youth. Five songs were added, with 10 retained from the original score. This production toured 11 months before opening on Bway.

FILM VERSION: Marilyn Monroe and Jane Russell (new score) (20th Cent. 1953, Howard Hawks dir.).

George White's Scandals (1926). Music by Ray Henderson; lyrics by B. G. DeSylva & Lew Brown; sketches by George White & William K. Wells.

SONGS: "Lucky Day," "Tweet-Tweet," "The Birth of the Blues," "Black Bottom," "The Girl Is You and the Boy Is Me," "Rhapsody in Blue" (music, George Gershwin).

NEW YORK: June 14, 1926
APOLLO THEATRE; 424 p.

Presented, directed & choreographed by George White; settings, Gustave Weidhaus; costumes, Erté; music director, William Daly.

CAST: Ann Pennington, Willie and Eugene Howard, Tom Patricola, Harry Richman, Buster West, Frances Williams, McCarthy Sisters, Fairbanks Twins, Fowler and Tamara, Lloyd Garrett, Rose Perfect, John Wells, Portland Hoffa (chorus).

The eighth annual edition of *George White's Scandals* had the longest run and is generally conceded to be the outstanding revue in the series. It was the second to have a score by DeSylva, Brown and Henderson, and it marked the *Scandals* debuts of Harry Richman, Willie and Eugene Howard, and Frances Williams. White was so confident of the show's success that he charged $55 per ticket for the first nine rows on opening night.

Though the *Scandals* were an obvious offshoot of the annual *Ziegfeld Follies*, they had a more youthful look, were faster paced, and put greater accent on dancing. They also differed by having one song-writing team responsible for an entire score. White began his series in 1919 and offered 11 editions in 13 years. He produced, directed, and choreographed all of them and also had a hand in the sketches and songs.

The song-writing teams involved with the *Scandals* were Richard A. Whiting, Arthur Jackson and White (1919); George Gershwin and Jackson (1920–1921); Gershwin and B. G. DeSylva (1922–1924); DeSylva, Brown and Henderson (1925–1926, 1928); Cliff Friend and White (1929); Brown and Henderson (1931); Jack Yellen and Henderson (1935); Yellen and Sammy Fain (1939). Among the songs: "Drifting Along with the Tide" (1921), "I'll Build a Stairway to Paradise" (1922), "Somebody Loves Me" (1924), "Life Is Just a Bowl of Cherries" (1931), "This Is the Missus" (1931), "That's Why Darkies Were Born" (1931), "My Song" (1931), "The Thrill Is Gone" (1931).

Those who appeared in multiple editions include Willie and Eugene Howard (6), Ann Pennington (5), George White (5), Tom Patricola (4), Lou Holtz (3), Winnie Lightner (3), Frances Williams (3), Harry Richman (2), Rudy Vallée (2). Ethel Merman,

the Howard brothers, Vallée, and Ray Bolger were all in the 1931 edition, which rivaled the 1926 *Scandals* in quality and ran 202 performances.

The revue played the following theatres: Liberty (1919, 1921), Globe (1920, 1922–1923), Apollo (1924–1931), New Amsterdam (1935), Alvin (1939).

Although there was no *Scandals* in 1927, the almost bookless "book" musical, *Manhattan Mary*, with a DeSylva-Brown-Henderson score, ended by having the heroine (Ona Munson) become a star of the *Scandals*. In 1932 White offered a more economic variation called *George White's Music Hall Varieties*. It was presented at the Casino Theatre with Harry Richman, Bert Lahr, Eleanor Powell, Lily Damita.

FILM VERSIONS (all with plots, new songs): Rudy Vallée, Jimmy Durante, Alice Faye (20th Cent. 1934, George White, Thornton Freeland dirs.); Alice Faye, James Dunn, Eleanor Powell (20th Cent. 1935, George White dir.); Joan Davis and Jack Haley (RKO 1945, Felix Feist dir.).

Gershwin, George (né Jacob Gershvin), composer; b. Brooklyn, NY, Sept. 26, 1898; d. Beverly Hills, Cal., July 11, 1937. With his brisk, athletic rhythms and plaintive melodies, Gershwin brought a fresh vitality to the Bway musical stage during the 20s and early 30s. Moreover, his career showed an almost steady progression of widening horizons—from revue (five *George White's Scandals*) to musical comedy (*Lady, Be Good!*, *Oh, Kay!*, *Funny Face*, *Girl Crazy*) to comic opera (*Strike Up the Band*, *Of Thee I Sing*) to "folk" opera (*Porgy and Bess*).

The composer's first Bway lyric-writing partners were Arthur Jackson, B. G. DeSylva ("I'll Build a Stairway to Paradise," "Somebody Loves Me" in the 1922 and 1924 *George White's Scandals*), John Henry Mears, E. Ray Goetz, Brian Hooker, Clifford Grey, Desmond Carter. Beginning in 1924, he worked almost exclusively with his brother, Ira Gershwin. Among their songs: "Fascinating Rhythm," "Oh, Lady, Be Good!" (*Lady, Be Good!*); "That Certain Feeling," "Looking for a Boy," (*Tip-Toes*); "Maybe," "Clap Yo' Hands" "Do Do Do," "Someone to Watch Over Me" (*Oh, Kay!*); "Funny Face," "'S Wonderful," "The Babbitt and the Bromide," "He Loves and She Loves" (*Funny Face*); "How Long Has This Been Going On?" (*Rosalie*); "I've Got a Crush on You" (*Treasure Girl*); "Liza," with Gus Kahn (*Show Girl*); "Soon," "Strike Up the Band" (*Strike Up the Band*); "Embraceable You," "I Got Rhythm," "But Not for Me" (*Girl Crazy*); "Wintergreen for President," "Love Is Sweeping the Country," "Of Thee I Sing, Baby," "Who Cares?" (*Of Thee I Sing*); "Isn't It a Pity?" (*Pardon My English*); "Mine" (*Let 'Em Eat Cake*); "Bess, You Is My Woman Now," "I Loves You, Porgy," "I Got Plenty o' Nuttin'," "It Ain't Necessarily So," "There's a Boat Dat's Leavin' Soon for New York" (*Porgy and Bess*). DuBose Heyward, co-lyricist of the last three, was lyricist for "Summertime." Gershwin also wrote with Otto Harbach and Oscar Hammerstein II and composer Herbert Stothart.

Fred and Adele Astaire, Gertrude Lawrence, William Gaxton, and Victor Moore were each in two Gershwin musicals. In addition to songs, the composer also wrote concert pieces (*Rhapsody in Blue, An American in Paris, Piano Concerto in F*) and Hollywood film scores (*Shall We Dance, The Goldwyn Follies*). Bib: *George Gershwin: A Study in American Music* by Isaac Goldberg, Edith Gar-

son (S&S, NY 1931; Ungar, NY 1958); *George Gershwin*, Merle Armitage ed. (Longmans, NY 1938); *George Gershwin: Man and Legend* by Merle Armitage (Duell Sloan, NY 1958); *Gershwin* by Robert Payne (Pyramid, NY 1960); *George Gershwin: His Journey to Greatness* by David Ewen (Prentice-Hall, NJ 1970); *The Gershwin Years* by Edward Jablonski & Lawrence Stewart (Doubleday, NY 1973); *The Gershwins* by Robert Kimball & Alfred Simon (Atheneum, NY 1973); *Gershwin: His Life and Music* by Charles Schwartz (Bobbs-Merrill, Ind. 1973).

Unless otherwise noted, following were written with Ira Gershwin:

1919	La La Lucille (Jackson, DeSylva)
1920	George White's Scandals (Jackson)
1921	George White's Scandals (Jackson)
1922	George White's Scandals (DeSylva, Goetz)
	Our Nell (Hooker)
1923	The Rainbow (L) (Grey)
	George White's Scandals (DeSylva, Goetz)
1924	Sweet Little Devil (DeSylva)
	George White's Scandals (DeSylva)
	Primrose (L) (Carter)
	Lady, Be Good!
1925	Tell Me More! (also DeSylva)
	Tip-Toes
	Song of the Flame (Harbach, Hammerstein-Stothart)
1926	Oh, Kay!
1927	Funny Face
1928	Rosalie
	Treasure Girl
1929	Show Girl (also Kahn)
1930	Strike Up the Band
	Girl Crazy
1931	Of Thee I Sing
1933	Pardon My English
	Let 'Em Eat Cake
1935	Porgy and Bess (also Heyward)

Gershwin, Ira (né Israel Gershvin), lyricist; b. New York, Dec. 6, 1896.

Gershwin's agile wit, originality of phrase, and rhyming ingenuity greatly enhanced the appeal of the music written by his brother, George Gershwin. Among their songs: "Fascinating Rhythm," "Oh, Lady, Be Good!" *(Lady, Be Good!)*; "That Certain Feeling," "Looking for a Boy," *(Tip-Toes)*; "Maybe," "Clap Yo' Hands," "Do Do Do," "Someone to Watch Over Me"*(Oh, Kay!)*; "Funny Face," "'S Wonderful," "The Babbitt and the Bromide," "He Loves and She Loves" *Funny Face)*; "How Long Has This Been Going On?" *(Rosalie)*; "I've Got a Crush on You" *(Treasure Girl)*; "Liza," with Gus Kahn *(Show Girl)*; "Soon," "Strike Up the Band" *(Strike Up the Band)*; "Embraceable You," "I Got Rhythm," "But Not for Me" *(Girl Crazy)*; "Wintergreen for President," "Love Is Sweeping the Country," "Of Thee I Sing, Baby," "Who Cares?" *(Of Thee I Sing)*; "Isn't It a Pity?" *(Pardon My English)*; "Mine" *(Let 'Em Eat Cake)*; "Bess, You Is My Woman Now," "I Loves You, Porgy," "I Got Plenty o' Nuttin'," "It Ain't Necessarily So," "There's a Boat Dat's Leavin' Soon for New York" *(Porgy and Bess)*, the first three written with DuBose Heyward.

Ira also collaborated with lyricists B. G. DeSylva, Gus Kahn, and E. Y. Harburg, and with composers Vincent Youmans, Joseph Meyer, Philip Charig ("Sunny Disposish"), Harold Arlen ("Let's Take a Walk Around the Block"), Vernon Duke ("I Can't Get Started"), Kurt Weill ("This Is New," "Jenny," "Tschaikowsky" in *Lady in the Dark*), and Arthur Schwartz. Gertrude Lawrence was in three Ira Gershwin musicals; Fred and Adele Astaire, William Gaxton, and Victor Moore were in two each. Bib: *The Gershwin Years* by Edward Jablonski & Lawrence Stewart (Doubleday, NY 1958, 1973); *Lyrics on Several Occasions* by Gershwin (Knopf, NY 1959); *The George and Ira Gershwin Song Book* (S&S, NY 1960); *The Gershwins* by Robert Kimball & Alfred Simon (Atheneum, NY 1973).

Unless otherwise noted, following were written with George Gershwin:
1921 Two Little Girls in Blue (Youmans)
1924 Lady, Be Good!
1925 Tell Me More! (also DeSylva)
Tip-Toes
1926 Oh, Kay!
1927 Funny Face
1928 Rosalie
That's a Good Girl (L) (Meyer, Charig)
Treasure Girl
1929 Show Girl (also Kahn)
1930 Strike Up the Band
Girl Crazy
1931 Of Thee I Sing
1933 Pardon My English
Let 'Em Eat Cake
1934 Life Begins at 8:40 (Arlen, Harburg)
1935 Porgy and Bess (also Heyward)
1936 Ziegfeld Follies (Duke)
1941 Lady in the Dark (Weill)
1945 The Firebrand of Florence (Weill)
1946 Park Avenue (Schwartz)

Gesner, Clark, composer, lyricist; b. Augusta, Me., March 27, 1938. In addition to writing his *Peanuts* musical, *You're a Good Man, Charlie Brown*, Gesner has also contributed special material to tv, Bway, and nightclub revues.
1967 You're a Good Man, Charlie Brown

"Get Happy." Music by Harold Arlen; lyric by Ted Koehler. Rousing exhortation delivered by Ruth Etting in the first-act finale—a beach scene with the cast in bathing suits and the stage covered with sand—of Ruth Selwyn's *9:15 Revue* (NY 1930). Though the show lasted only one week, the song became Arlen's first hit.

"Get Me to the Church on Time." Music by Frederick Loewe; lyric by Alan Jay Lerner. Alfred Doolittle's final fling before succumbing to "middle-class morality" was turned into a bouncing music-hall turn by Stanley Holloway and well-wishers (NY 1956, L 1958).

"Get Out of Town." Music & lyric by Cole Porter. Throbbing torch ballad sung by Tamara during a temporary estrangement in *Leave It to Me!* (NY 1938).

"Get Yourself a Geisha." Music by Arthur Schwartz; lyric by Howard Dietz. Practical advice for coping with oriental living ("It's better with your shoes off"), offered by Beatrice Lillie in *At Home Abroad* (NY 1935) and *Happy Returns* (L 1938).

"Getting to Know You." Music by Richard Rodgers; lyric by Oscar Hammerstein II. In the schoolroom scene early in *The King and I* (NY 1950), Gertrude Lawrence, playing the English teacher, introduced the song to the royal Siamese children as her way of showing how much she liked them. During the Boston tryout of the musical, Miss Lawrence had suggested to Rodgers and Hammerstein that a number with the children would give the first act a needed lift, and they obliged by matching a new lyric to a melody once intended for *South Pacific* but discarded in favor of "Younger than Springtime." In London production (1953), Valerie Hobson played the teacher.

Geva, Tamara (née Sheversheieva Gevergeva), actress, dancer; b. St. Petersburg, Russia, 1907. Appeared as ballet dancer with George Balanchine (her first husband) in Europe, then with Diaghilev's Monte Carlo Ballet. Her initial Bway appearance was in the Russian revue *Chauve Souris*, and her most famous role was in *On Your Toes*. Bib: *Split Seconds* by Miss Geva (Doubleday, NY 1972).

1928 Whoopee (*Yolandi*) (also co-chor.)
1930 Three's a Crowd
1932 Flying Colors
1936 On Your Toes (*Vera Barnova*)

"Giannina Mia." Music by Rudolf Friml; lyric by Otto Hauerbach (Harbach). Sung by Emma Trentini in Friml's first Bway production, *The Firefly* (1912). The song was something of a sequel to Srta. Trentini's "Italian Street Song" in *Naughty Marietta*.

"Gilbert the Filbert." Music by Herman Finck; lyric by Arthur Wimperis. In top hat, white tie and tails, Basil Hallam sang of the elegant dude, "the pride of Piccadilly, the blasé roué," in *The Passing Show* (L 1914). In NY, Donald Brian described him in *The Girl from Utah* (1914).

Gilford, Jack (né Jacob Gellman), actor; b. New York, July 25, 1913. Meek, sad-eyed comic actor who began career in vaudeville (1934), and has also appeared in Bway non-musicals (incl. *The Diary of Anne Frank*).

1940 Meet the People
1950 Alive and Kicking
1955 Once Over Lightly
1959 Once Upon a Mattress (*King Sextimus*)
1962 A Funny Thing Happened on the Way to the Forum (*Hysterium*)
1966 Cabaret (*Herr Schultz*)
1971 No, No, Nanette (r) (*Jimmy Smith*)

Gingold, Hermione (Ferdinanda), actress, singer; b. London, Dec. 9, 1897. Miss Gingold, who appeared in London revues before NY debut in 1953, is best known for her slightly shady grande-dame roles that combine regality with raffishness. She has appeared in films (incl. *Gigi*) and was once married to lyricist Eric Maschwitz. Bib: *The World Is Square* by Miss Gingold (Athene, NY 1958).

1908 Pinkie and the Fairies (*Herald*)
1936 Spread It Abroad
1938 The Gate Revue
1940 Swinging the Gate
1941 Rise Above It
1942 Sky High
1943 Sweet and Low
1944 Sweeter and Lower
1945 Sweetest and Lowest
1948 Slings and Arrows (also sk.)
1953 John Murray Anderson's Almanac (NY)
1959 First Impressions (NY) (*Mrs. Bennet*)
1960 From A to Z (NY)
1962 Milk and Honey (NY) (*Clara Weiss*, repl.)
1973 A Little Night Music (NY) (*Mme. Armfeldt*)
1975 A Little Night Music (*Mme. Armfeldt*)

Girl Crazy (1930). Music by George Gershwin; lyrics by Ira Gershwin; book by Guy Bolton & John McGowan.

SONGS: "Bidin' My Time," "Could You Use Me?," "Embraceable You," "Sam and Delilah," "I Got Rhythm," "But Not for Me," "Treat Me Rough," "Boy! What Love Has Done to Me!"

NEW YORK: Oct. 14, 1930
ALVIN THEATRE; 272 p.

Presented by Alex A. Aarons & Vinton Freedley; directed by Alexander Leftwich; choreographed by George Hale; settings, Donald Oenslager; costumes, Kiviette; music director, Earl Busby; orchestrations, Robert Russell Bennett.

CAST. Willie Howard (*Gieber Goldfarb*), Allen Kearns (*Danny Churchill*), Ginger Rogers (*Molly Gray*), William Kent (*Slick Fothergill*), Ethel Merman (*Kate Fothergill*), Eunice Healey (*Flora James*), Lew Parker (*Jake Howell*), Antonio & Renée De Marco (dancers), The Foursome, Red Nichols Orch. (incl. Benny Goodman, Glenn Miller, Jimmy Dorsey, Gene Krupa, Jack Teagarden).

Celebrated as the Bway debut of Ethel Merman, *Girl Crazy* was the seventh and penultimate musical comedy the brothers Gershwin wrote for producers Aarons and Freedley. It was also one of the rare Bway appearances of Willie Howard (in a role intended for Bert Lahr) minus brother Eugene, and it marked the second stage musical for Ginger Rogers. The story, set in and around Custerville, Ariz., was about Danny Churchill, a wealthy NY playboy, whose father sends him west to get away from bootleggers and gold diggers. Danny finds true love in postmistress Molly Gray and ends up running a dude ranch. Howard's role was that of a taxi driver who drives Danny to Arizona and becomes the sheriff; Merman played the wife of the local saloonkeeper.

FILM VERSIONS: Bert Wheeler and Robert Woolsey (RKO 1932, William A. Seiter dir.); Judy Garland, Mickey Rooney, June Allyson (MGM 1943, Norman Taurog dir.); Harve Presnell and Connie Francis (called *When the Boys Meet the Girls*) (altered story) (MGM 1965, Alvin Ganzer dir.).

"Girl Friend, The." Music by Richard Rodgers; lyric by Lorenz Hart. Hopping panegyric ("She's knockout, she's regal, her beauty's illegal") sung in the musical of the same name (NY 1926) by Sammy White to Eva Puck, who then returned the compliment. In 1928 London musical with same title—though based on a different source—the number was sung by George Gee and Emma Haig. The song was the model for Sandy Wilson's pastiche, "The Boy Friend" (1953).

"Girl on the Magazine Cover, The." Music & lyric by Irving Berlin. Ardent tribute introduced by Joseph Santley in *Stop! Look! Listen!* (NY 1915).

"Girl That I Marry, The." Music & lyric by Irving Berlin. Sung by Ray Middleton in *Annie Get Your Gun* (NY 1946) to impress hoydenish Ethel Merman (as Annie Oakley) that she wasn't the dainty kind of girl for him. In London production (1947), it was sung by Bill Johnson.

"Girls That Boys Dream About, The." Music by Ron Grainer; lyric by Ronald Millar. In *Robert and Elizabeth* (L 1964), the six sons of Edward Moulton-Barrett, accompanied by their two sisters, express whispery affection for imaginary sweethearts.

"Give It Back to the Indians." Music by Richard Rodgers; lyric by Lorenz Hart. Sung by Mary Jane Walsh and danced by Hal LeRoy in *Too Many Girls* (NY 1939). An itemized catalogue of some of the more unbearable aspects of living in New York (i.e., cost of cigarettes, traffic congestion, street excavations, the decline of Bway), the song was a humorous antidote to the affection previously shown in the writers' "Manhattan."

"Give My Regards to Broadway." Music & lyric by George M. Cohan. Cohan sang the number in *Little Johnny Jones* (NY 1904), in which he played an American jockey in London. Accused of throwing a race, he is at the Southampton pier waiting for a signal—a flare from a ship—that will clear his name. At first he sings the song plaintively, then, once he sees the signal, he does an exultant song-and-dance version. In *George M!* (NY 1968), the number was sung and danced by Joel Grey in a recreation of the original scene.

"Glad to Be Unhappy." Music by Richard Rodgers; lyric by Lorenz Hart. A torch song following a lovers' quarrel sung by Doris Carson and David Morris in *On Your Toes* (NY 1936). In London production (1937) it was sung by Gina Malo and Eddie Pola.

"Gladiola Girl, The." Music & lyric by Charles Gaynor. The first-act finale of the Bway revue *Lend an Ear* (1948) was a satire on musical comedies of the 20s. Performed in two parts, the mini-musical had six songs: "Join Us in a Cup of Tea," "Where Is the She for Me?," "I'll Be True to You," "Doin' the Old Yahoo Step," "A Little Game of Tennis," "In Our Teeny Little Weeny Nest." Gloria Hamilton played Rosalie ("The Gladiola Girl"), William Eythe was Larry Van Patten, Yvonne Adair was Ginger O'Toole, and Carol Channing was a highly visible member of the chorus.

"Glamorous Night." Music by Ivor Novello; lyric by Christopher Hassall. Whipped-cream aria in the musical of the same name (L 1935), in which Mary Ellis recalled moments of love on a magical, glamorous night.

Gleason, (Herbert John) Jackie, actor; b. Brooklyn, NY, Feb. 26, 1916. Pugnacious, rotund comic actor who scored his greatest success in tv series. On Bway, he introduced "Take Me Along" in *Take Me Along*. Bib: *The Golden Ham* by Jim Bishop (S&S, NY 1956).

    1940   Keep Off the Grass
    1943   Artists and Models

1944 Follow the Girls (*Goofy Gale*)
1949 Along Fifth Avenue
1959 Take Me Along (*Uncle Sid*)

"Glitter and Be Gay." Music by Leonard Bernstein; lyric by Richard Wilbur. Coloratura confession of a demimondaine who, despite the sordidness of her life, admits to relishing such compensations as champagne, expensive clothes, and jewels. Sung in *Candide* by Barbara Cook (NY 1956) and Mary Costa (L 1959) while covering themselves with diamond bracelets and necklaces.

"God's Country." Music by Harold Arlen; lyric by E. Y. Harburg. Lighthearted flag-waver (in which Popeye and Gypsy Rose Lee are viewed as preferable to Mussolini and Mosley), introduced by Jack Whiting and the Five Reillys in *Hooray for What!* (NY 1937).

Godspell (1971). Music & lyrics by Stephen Schwartz; book by John-Michael Tebelak, based on the Gospel According to St. Matthew.
SONGS: "Prepare Ye the Way of the Lord," "Save the People," "Day by Day" (lyric, St. Richard of Chichester), "Bless the Lord," "All for the Best," "Light of the World," "Turn Back, O Man," "We Beseech Thee."

NEW YORK: May 17, 1971
CHERRY LANE THEATRE; 2,124 p.
Presented by Edgar Lansbury, Stuart Duncan, Joseph Beruh; directed by John-Michael Tebelak; costumes, Susan Tsu; lighting, Lowell Atchziger.
CAST: Stephen Nathan (*Jesus*), David Haskell (*Judas*), Herb Simon, Sonia Manzano, Robin Lamont.

LONDON: Nov. 17, 1971
WYNDHAM'S THEATRE; 1,128 p.
Presented by H. M. Tennent Ltd.; directed by John-Michael Tebelak; costumes, Susan Tsu; lighting, Lowell Atchziger.
CAST: David Essex (*Jesus*), Jeremy Irons (*Judas*), Verity-Anne Meldrum, Julie Covington, Marti Webb.
A semi-rock musical, loose in design, dealing with the last days of Christ and containing dramatized parables taken from St. Matthew—the Prodigal Son, the Good Samaritan, the Pharisee and the Tax Collector. The work, which originated as librettist Tebelak's master's degree thesis at Carnegie Tech, was first presented at La Mama. It moved to the Promenade Theatre, Aug. 1971. At one time, seven companies were performing it throughout the US. The more elaborate *Jesus Christ Superstar* (NY 1971) also dealt with the last days of Christ.
FILM VERSION: Victor Garber and David Haskell (Col. 1973, David Greene dir.).

Goetz, E. Ray, lyricist, composer, producer; b. Buffalo, NY, June 12, 1886; d. Greenwich, Conn., June 12, 1954. Goetz had some song hits as a lyricist, but on Bway he is primarily remembered for starring his wife, Irene Bordoni, in three musicals, including *Paris*, one of three Cole Porter musicals Goetz produced. Goetz's songwriting collaborators included A. Baldwin Sloane, Silvio Hein, George Gershwin, Sigmund Romberg.
Unless otherwise noted, Mr. Goetz was lyricist of following; asterisk indicates he was also producer:
1910 The Prince of Bohemia (Sloane)
     A Matinee Idol (Hein)
1911 The Hen Pecks (Sloane)
     The Never Homes (Sloane)
1912 Hokey Pokey (Sloane)
     Hanky Panky (Sloane)
     Roly Poly (Sloane)
     The Sun Dodgers (Sloane)
1913 All Aboard (also comp.)
     The Pleasure Seekers (also comp.)

1915 Hands Up (also comp. with Romberg)
1916 Step This Way (also comp.)
1917 Hitchy-Koo * (also comp.)
    Words and Music * (also comp.)
1918 Follow the Girl (co-prod. only)
1920 As You Were * (also comp.)
1922 The French Doll (prod. only)
    George White's Scandals (Gershwin)
1928 Paris * (also comp.)
1929 Fifty Million Frenchmen (prod. only)
1930 The New Yorkers (prod. only)

Golden Apple, The (1954). Music by Jerome Moross; lyrics & book by John Latouche, based on Homer's *Odyssey* & *Iliad*.

SONGS: "My Love Is on the Way," "Come Along, Boys," "It's the Going Home Together," "Helen Is Always Willing," "Lazy Afternoon," "My Picture in the Papers," "Store-Bought Suit," "Scylla and Charybdis," "Goona-Goona."

NEW YORK: March 11, 1954
PHOENIX THEATRE; 125 p.

Presented by the Phoenix Theatre (T. Edward Hambledon & Norris Houghton); directed by Norman Lloyd; choreographed by Hanya Holm; settings, William & Jean Eckart; costumes, Alvin Colt; lighting, Klaus Holm; music director, Hugh Ross; orchestrations, Jerome Moross & Hershy Kay.

CAST: Priscilla Gillette (*Penelope*), Stephen Douglass (*Ulysses*), Kaye Ballard (*Helen*), Jack Whiting (*Hector Charybdis*), Bibi Osterwald (*Lovey Mars*), Jonathan Lucas (*Paris*), Dean Michener (*Menelaus*), Portia Nelson (*Minerva*), Shannon Bolin (*Mrs. Juniper*).

The legend of Ulysses, relocated to the state of Washington between 1900 and 1910, is set in both Angel's Roost, near Mt. Olympus, and the seaport of Rhododendron. After a salesman named Paris carries off Helen, the all-too-willing wife of Menelaus, stalwart Ulysses, who has just returned from the Spanish-American War, goes off to bring her back. It takes him 10 years, during which he resists temptations, beats Paris in a bare-knuckle fight, and again returns home to his long-neglected wife, Penelope. The musical first played off-Bway, but its initial success prompted producers Alfred de Liagre and Roger Stevens to resettle it at the Alvin Theatre slightly over a month following the opening. There was very little dialogue in the production, with the story told through an almost continuous series of musical numbers. A 1962 off-Bway revival ran for 112 performances. In the cast were Jan McArt (*Penelope*), Stan Page (*Ulysses*), Swen Swenson (*Hector*), Jane Connell (*Lovey Mars*).

"Golden Days." Music by Sigmund Romberg; lyric by Dorothy Donnelly. Evocative song of youth sung by Howard Marsh, as the prince, and Greek Evans, as his tutor, as they prepare to leave for the university in *The Student Prince in Heidelberg* (NY 1924). In London production (1925) it was offered by Allan Prior and Herbert Waterous.

"Gonna Build a Mountain." Music & lyric by Anthony Newley & Leslie Bricusse. Song of unlimited optimism sung by Anthony Newley in *Stop the World—I Want to Get Off*, both in London (1961) and in NY (1962).

"Good Morning Starshine." Music by Galt MacDermot; lyric by Gerome Ragni & James Rado. "Early morning singing song" introduced by Jill O'Hara and cast in *Hair* (NY 1967); in London transplant (1968), sung by Annabel Leventon and cast.

Good News! (1927). Music by Ray Henderson; lyrics by B. G. DeSylva & Lew Brown; book by DeSylva & Laurence Schwab.

SONGS: "Flaming Youth," "Just Imagine," "He's a Ladies' Man," "The Best Things in Life Are Free," "The Varsity Drag," "Lucky in Love," "Good News."

NEW YORK: Sept. 6, 1927
46TH ST. THEATRE; 557 p.

Presented by Laurence Schwab & Frank Mandel; directed by Edgar MacGregor; choreographed by Bobby Connolly; settings, Donald Oenslager; costumes, Kiviette; music director, Al Goodman.

CAST: Mary Lawlor (*Connie Lane*); Gus Shy (*Bobby Randall*), Inez Courtney (*Babe O'Day*), John Price Jones (*Tom Marlowe*), John Sheehan (*Pooch Kearney*), Shirley Vernon (*Patricia Bingham*), Zelma O'Neal (*Flo*), Ruth Mayon (*Millie*), Don Tomkins (*Sylvester*), John Grant (*Beef Saunders*), Wally Coyle (*Windy*), George Olsen Orch.

LONDON: Aug. 15, 1928
CARLTON THEATRE; 132 p.

Presented by Herbert Clayton & Jack Waller; directed by William Mollison; choreographed by Claude Watts.

CAST: Evelyn Hoey (*Connie Lane*), Bobby Jarvis (*Bobby Randall*), Goodee Montgomery (*Babe O'Day*), Neil Collins (*Tom Marlowe*), Arthur West (*Pooch Kearney*), Amy Revere (*Patricia Bingham*), Zelma O'Neal (*Flo*), Julie Johnston (*Millie*), Michael Tripp (*Sylvester*), Edward Gargan (*Beef Saunders*), George Murphy (*Windy*).

The first book musical by DeSylva, Brown and Henderson inaugurated a series of animated John Held cartoon musicals dealing with some of the happier aspects of modern living (the others: *Hold Everything!*, *Follow Thru*, *Flying High*). Youth was unquenchably flaming in *Good News!*, a collegiate caper concerned with the issue of whether Tom Marlowe, the star football player at Tait, will be allowed to play in the big game against Colton despite his failing grade in astronomy. Since college spirit easily counts more than grades, he plays and wins. The show was replete with appropriately high-kicking routines and modern slang; it also offered the sight of George Olsen's Band, before the overture, filing down the aisles in college sweaters and giving out with a resounding football cheer.

A revised version, sponsored by Harry Rigby and starring Alice Faye and John Payne, began its pre-Bway tour in the fall of 1973 and reached NY the end of 1974. By that time Michael Kidd had succeeded Abe Burrows as director and Donald Saddler as choreographer, Garry Marshall had succeeded Burrows as librettist, and Gene Nelson had succeeded John Payne. It lasted two weeks.

Other Bway musicals dealing with college football were *Leave It to Jane* (1917), *Too Many Girls* (1939), *Toplitzky of Notre Dame* (1946), *All American* (1962).

FILM VERSIONS: Mary Lawlor and Stanley Smith (MGM 1930, Nick Grinde and Edgar MacGregor dirs.); June Allyson and Peter Lawford (MGM 1947, Charles Walters dir.).

"Good News." Music by Ray Henderson; lyric by B. G. DeSylva & Lew Brown. In *Good News!* (NY 1927), after seeing a lucky star, a new moon, a milk-white horse, and a load of hay, Zelma O'Neal has a spirited welcome all set for the expected glad tidings. Miss O'Neal also did the welcoming in the London company (1928).

"Good Old Bad Old Days, The." Music & lyric by Leslie Bricusse & Anthony Newley. Spirited salute to our mixed-up world sung by Anthony Newley in the musical of the same name (L 1973).

"Good-bye Broadway, Hello France!" Music by Billy Baskette; lyric by C. Francis Reisner & Benny Davis. Patriotic finale of the Bway revue *The Passing Show of 1917*, sung by the company.

"Goodnight, My Someone." Music & lyric by Meredith Willson. With no sweetheart to say goodnight to on the evening star, Marian Paroo (Barbara Cook) in *The Music Man* (NY 1957) sings her heart out to an indefinite "someone." The melody of this waltz is the same as that of the march "Seventy-Six Trombones," sung by Harold Hill (Robert Preston) because Willson wanted to suggest that these seemingly dissimilar people have more in common than is apparent. At the end of the play the songs are joined when Hill, about to skip out of town, hears Marian's voice and knows he's in love. In London company (1961), the parts were played by Patricia Lambert and Van Johnson.

Gordon, Max (né Mechel Salpeter), producer; b. New York, June 28, 1892. Gordon sponsored some of the most distinctive productions on the Bway musical stage of the 30s (incl. *Three's a Crowd, The Band Wagon, The Cat and the Fiddle, Roberta, The Great Waltz*). Arthur Schwartz and Howard Dietz wrote four scores for Gordon, Jerome Kern wrote three (two with Otto Harbach). The producer also offered many nonmusical plays, incl. *The Women, My Sister Eileen, Born Yesterday*. Bib: *Max Gordon Presents*

by Gordon & Lewis Funke (Geis, NY 1963). (*D. NY, Nov. 2, 1978.*)

- 1930 Three's a Crowd
- 1931 The Band Wagon
         The Cat and the Fiddle
- 1932 Flying Colors
- 1933 Roberta
- 1934 The Great Waltz
- 1935 Jubilee
- 1938 Sing Out the News
- 1939 Very Warm for May
- 1945 The Firebrand of Florence
         Hollywood Pinafore
- 1946 Park Avenue

"Got a Date with an Angel." Music by Joseph Tunbridge & Jack Waller; lyric by Clifford Grey. Bobby Howes preparing for a big night in *For the Love of Mike* (L 1931).

Gould, Elliott (né Elliott Goldstein), actor; b. Brooklyn, NY, Aug. 29, 1938. Lanky actor who made success in films (incl. *M.A.S.H.*), and was once married to Barbra Streisand.

- 1957 Rumple (chorus)
- 1958 Say, Darling (*Earl Jorgeson*)
- 1960 Irma la Douce (*usher, priest, warder*)
- 1962 I Can Get It for You Wholesale (*Harry Bogen*)
- 1963 On the Town (L) (*Ozzie*)
- 1965 Drat! The Cat! (*Bob Purefoy*)

Goulet, Robert, actor, singer; b. Lawrence, Mass., Nov. 26, 1933. Square-jawed strong-voiced baritone who introduced "If Ever I Would Leave You" in *Camelot*. Goulet has appeared in films, nightclubs, makes records, and is married to actress Carol Lawrence.

- 1960 Camelot (*Sir Lancelot*)
- 1968 The Happy Time (*Jacques Bonnard*)

Graham, Harry (Joscelyn Clive), lyricist, librettist; b. London, Dec. 23, 1874; d. London, Oct. 30, 1936. Graham's biggest London hit was *The*

Maid of the Mountains ("Love Will Find a Way"); other West End successes include *White Horse Inn, The Lady of the Rose, Katja the Dancer, Mme. Pompadour.* He turned to writing for the stage after a career as an officer in the Coldstream Guards. Among his collaborators: Jean Gilbert, Haydn Wood, Victor Jacobi, Harold Fraser Simson, Emmerich Kalman, Robert Stolz, Leo Fall, Ivor Novello, Oscar Straus, Franz Lehar, Vivian Ellis, Albert Sirmay, Noel Gay ("The King's Horses"), Ralph Benatzky, Paul Abraham, Johann Strauss.

Asterisk indicates Mr. Graham was also librettist:

1914   The Cinema Star (Gilbert)
1915   Tina * (Wood)
1916   Sybil * (NY) (Jacobi)
1917   The Maid of the Mountains (Simson)
1920   A Southern Maid * (Simson)
        The Little Dutch Girl * (Kalman)
1922   The Lady of the Rose (Gilbert)
        Whirled into Happiness * (Stolz)
1923   Head Over Heels (Simson)
        Mme. Pompadour * (Fall)
1924   Our Nell (Novello, Simson)
1925   Katja the Dancer * (Gilbert)
        Sky High * (Stolz)
        Cleopatra (Straus)
        Clo-Clo * (Lehar)
        Betty in Mayfair (Simson)
1926   My Son John (Ellis, Straus)
1927   The Blue Mazurka (Lehar)
1928   Lady Mary (Sirmay)
1931   White Horse Inn * (Benatzky, Stolz)
        Land of Smiles * (Lehar)
        Viktoria and Her Hussar * (Abraham)
1932   Casanova * (Straus)
1936   Rise and Shine * (Stolz)

Grant, Cary (né Alexander Archibald Leach), actor, singer; b. Bristol, Eng., Jan. 18, 1904. Grant, who was known on Bway as Archie Leach, made his debut with Bob Pender's acrobatic troupe, then became leading man until beginning his durable film career in 1932.

1920   Good Times
1927   Golden Dawn (*Anzac*)
1929   Boom Boom (*Reggie Phipps*)
        A Wonderful Night (*Max Grunewald*)
1931   Nikki (*Cary Lockwood*)

Gray, Dolores, actress, singer; b. Chicago, Ill., June 7, 1924. Junoesque blonde song belter who made biggest hit of her career in London production of *Annie Get Your Gun.* On Bway she introduced "If You Hadn't but You Did" (*Two on the Aisle*), "Here's That Rainy Day" (*Carnival in Flanders*), "Anyone Would Love You" (*Destry Rides Again*).

1944   Seven Lively Arts
1945   Are You with It? (*Bunny LaFleur*)
1947   Annie Get Your Gun (L) (*Annie Oakley*)
1951   Two on the Aisle
1953   Carnival in Flanders (*Cornelia*)
1959   Destry Rides Again (*Frenchie*)
1967   Sherry! (*Lorraine Sheldon*)
1973   Gypsy (L) (*Rose*, repl.)

Grease (1972). Music, lyrics & book by Jim Jacobs & Warren Casey.

SONGS: "Freddy, My Love," "Greased Lightnin'," "Look at Me, I'm Sandra Dee," "It's Raining on Prom Night," "Shakin' at the High School Hop," "Alone at a Drive-In Movie," "We Go Together."

NEW YORK: Feb. 14, 1972
EDEN THEATRE

Presented by Kenneth Weissman & Maxine Fox; directed by Tom Moore; choreographed by Patricia Birch; settings, Douglas Schmidt; costumes, Carrie Robbins; lighting, Karl Eigsti; music director, Louis St. Louis; orchestrations, Michael Leonard.

CAST: Carole Demas (*Sandy Dumbrowski*), Barry Bostwick (*Danny Zuko*), Adrienne Barbeau (*Betty*

Rizzo), Walter Bobbie (*Roger*), James Canning (*Doody*).

LONDON: June 26, 1973
NEW LONDON THEATRE; 236 p.
Presented by Paul Elliott & Duncan Weldon, with Donald Langdon; directed by Tom Moore; choreographed by Patricia Birch; settings, Douglas Schmidt; costumes, Carrie Robbins; lighting, Robert Ornbo; music director, Barry Booth; orchestrations, Michael Leonard.
CAST: Stacey Gregg (*Sandy Dumbrowski*), Richard Gere (*Danny Zuko*), Jacquie-Ann Carr (*Betty Rizzo*), Stephen Bent (*Roger*), Derek James (*Doody*).
"A New '50s Rock 'n Roll Musical," *Grease* takes a nostalgic, somewhat free-form look at the manners, morals, and mores of the James Dean–Sandra Dee generation. In June 1972 the original production moved from its off-Bway home to the Broadhurst Theatre. A US road company began its travels in January 1973, and continued for two years.

"**Great Day!**" Music by Vincent Youmans; lyric by Edward Eliscu & William (Billy) Rose. Thumping revival number sung by baritone Lois Deppe and Russell Wooding's Jubilee Singers in *Great Day!* (NY 1929).

Green, Adolph, lyricist, librettist; b. New York, Dec. 2, 1915. Green and his partner, Betty Comden, have been together longer than any writing team in the history of the Bway musical theatre. Their librettos and/or lyrics have shown special affinity for the varied faces of NY, particularly in such musicals as *On the Town* ("New York, New York," "Lucky to Be Me"), *Wonderful Town* ("Ohio," "A Quiet Girl," "It's Love"), *Bells Are Ringing* ("Just in Time," "The Party's Over"),

Do Re Mi ("Make Someone Happy"), *Subways Are for Sleeping* ("Comes Once in a Lifetime"), *Applause*. Their most frequent composer collaborator has been Jule Styne, with whom they wrote eight scores plus additional songs for *Lorelei*. Others: Leonard Bernstein and Morton Gould. Bert Lahr, Dolores Gray, Rosalind Russell, Mary Martin, Cyril Ritchard, Judy Holliday, Phil Silvers, Carol Burnett, Lauren Bacall have all appeared in Comden and Green musicals. The team has also written film scripts, incl. *Singin' in the Rain*.

Unless otherwise noted, Comden and Green wrote librettos and lyrics for following:
1944 On the Town (Bernstein) (also *Ozzie*)
1945 Billion Dollar Baby (Gould)
1951 Two on the Aisle (Styne)
1953 Wonderful Town (lyr. only) (Bernstein)
1954 Peter Pan (lyr. only) (Styne)
1956 Bells Are Ringing (Styne)
1958 Say, Darling (lyr. only) (Styne)
1960 Do Re Mi (lyr. only) (Styne)
1961 Subways Are for Sleeping (Styne)
1964 Fade Out—Fade In (Styne)
1967 Hallelujah, Baby! (lyr. only) (Styne)
1970 Applause (lib. only)
1978 On the 20th Century (Coleman)

Greenbank, Percy, lyricist; b. London, Jan. 24, 1878; d. Rickmansworth, Eng., Dec. 8, 1968. Eleven Greenbank musicals ran over 400 performances in London, with six going over 500: *The Toreador, A Country Girl, The Orchid, Our Miss Gibbs, The Quaker Girl, The Boy*. His most frequent composer collaborators were Lionel Monckton, Ivan Caryll, Paul Rubens, and Howard Talbot; others with whom he wrote include Sidney Jones, André Messager, Leo Fall, Emmerich Kalman, Herman Finck, Max Darewski, Franz Lehar, H. Fraser

Simson, Jean Gilbert. Greenbank was a brother of lyricist Harry Greenbank.

1900 The Messenger Boy (Caryll, Monckton)
1901 The Toreador (Caryll, Monckton)
1902 A Country Girl (Monckton)
1903 My Lady Molly (Jones)
      The Orchid (Caryll, Monckton)
      The Earl and the Girl (Caryll)
1904 The Cingalee (Monckton)
      Veronique (Messager)
      Lady Madcap (Rubens)
1905 The Little Michus (Messager)
      The Spring Chicken (Caryll, Monckton)
      The Blue Moon (Talbot)
1906 The New Aladdin (Caryll, Monckton)
1907 Three Kisses (Talbot) (also lib.)
1908 The Belle of Britanny (Talbot)
1909 Our Miss Gibbs (Caryll, Monckton)
      A Persian Princess (Jones)
1910 The Quaker Girl (Monckton)
1911 The Mousmé (Monckton, Talbot)
1912 Princess Caprice (Fall)
      Autumn Maneouvers (Kalman)
      The Dancing Mistress (Monckton)
1913 The Girl from Utah (Jones)
1914 After the Girl (Rubens)
1915 Tonight's the Night (Rubens)
      Tina (Rubens)
1916 Half-Past Eight (Rubens)
      Vanity Fair (Finck, Darewski)
      Houp-la! (Talbot)
1917 The Boy (Monckton, Talbot)
1919 The Girl for the Boy (Carr, Holt)
      The Kiss Call (Caryll)
1921 My Nieces (Talbot) (also lib.)
1923 The Merry Widow (r) (Lehar)
1924 The Street Singer (Simson)
1926 Yvonne (Gilbert) (also lib.)

"**Green-Up Time.**" Music by Kurt Weill; lyric by Alan Jay Lerner. Nanette Fabray happily announces the arrival of spring in *Love Life.* (NY 1948).

Greenwich Village Follies, The (1919). Music by A. Baldwin Sloane; lyrics by Arthur Swanstrom & John Murray Anderson; sketches by Anderson & Philip Bartholomae.

SONGS: "My Little Javanese," "Red as the Rose," "My Marionette," "I Want a Daddy who Will Rock Me to Sleep," "Message of the Cameo," "I'm Ashamed to Look the Moon in the Face," "I'll See You in C-U-B-A" (Irving Berlin) (added).

NEW YORK: July 15, 1919
GREENWICH VILLAGE THEATRE; 232 p.

Presented by The Bohemians Inc.; directed by John Murray Anderson; settings, Charles B. Falls; costumes, Shirley Barker; music director, Hilding Anderson; orchestrations, Anderson.

CAST: Bessie McCoy Davis, Ted Lewis Orch., James Watts, Rex Story, Bobby Edwards, Harry Delf, Charles Derickson, Irene Olsen, Cecil Cunningham.

Director John Murray Anderson made his Bway debut with this first *Greenwich Village Follies.* He was in charge of six of the eight editions, and is credited with adding scenic beauty and innovative stagecraft to the revue field. In artistic quality, these revues —originally called *Greenwich Village Nights*—were generally considered the only rivals to the *Ziegfeld Follies.* The substitution of *"Follies"* for *"Nights"* much annoyed Ziegfeld, especially when the revue moved uptown to the Nora Bayes Theatre. Under the overall description of "A Revusical Comedy of New York's Latin Quarter," the show kidded such Greenwich Village topics as ballet, free love, prohibition, and the arts in general. Staple items of most editions were female impersonators and extended "ballet ballads" based on literary works, incl. "The Nightingale and the Rose," "The Raven," and "The Happy Prince."

All *Follies* were presented by The Bohemians Inc. (Al Jones and Morris Green). Though the first two originated in the Village, all were shown on Bway—at the Shubert (1920–1922, 1924), Winter Garden (1923, 1928), 46th St. (1925). The two other directors for the series were Hassard Short (1925) and J. C. Huffman (1928). The first edition had the longest run, with the second and fourth also running over 200 performances.

Among performers on the series: Savoy and Brennan, Frank Crumit, Howard Marsh, Irene Franklin, Joe E. Brown, John Hazzard, Carl Randall, Irene Delroy, Tom Howard, Dolly Sisters, Moran and Mack, Blossom Seeley, and Benny Fields. Though the *Follies* were not celebrated for their songs, the 1924 edition had most of its numbers (incl. "I'm in Love Again") by Cole Porter.

Greenwood, (Frances) Charlotte, actress, dancer; b. Philadelphia, Pa., June 25, 1893. Long-legged, blonde comedienne, famed for her flat-footed high kicks. Miss Greenwood began her career in vaudeville, later became Hollywood film actress. Husband was composer Martin Broones. Bib: *Never Too Tall* by Miss Greenwood (1947).

1905   The White Cat (dancer)
1907   Rogers Brothers in Panama (*Lola*)
1908   Nearly a Hero (*Pussy Foote*, repl.)
1912   The Passing Show
1913   The Man with Three Wives (*Sidonie*)
       The Passing Show
1914   Pretty Mrs. Smith (*Letitia Proudfoot*)
1915   Town Topics
1916   So Long, Letty (*Letty Robbins*)
1919   Linger Longer, Letty (*Letty Larkin*)
1922   Letty Pepper (*Letty Pepper*)
       Music Box Revue
1924   Ritz Revue
1927   Rufus LeMaire's Affairs
1932   Wild Violets (L) (*Augusta*)

1934   Three Sisters (L) (*Tiny Barbour*)
1935   Gay Deceivers (L) (*Isabel Ferris*)
1950   Out of This World (*Juno*)

Grenfell, Joyce (née Joyce Irene Phipps), actress, singer; b. London, Feb. 10, 1910. Bright-eyed toothy monologuist specializing in shopgirls, spinsters, teachers. Since 1954, has appeared in one-woman shows, both in London and NY. Miss Grenfell has also acted in many British films.

1939   The Little Revue
1942   Light and Shade
1945   Sigh No More
1947   Tuppence Coloured
1951   Penny Plain

Grey, Clifford, lyricist, librettist; b. Birmingham, Eng., Jan. 5, 1887; d. Ipswich, Eng., Sept. 25, 1941. Grey was associated with long-running hits both in London (*Theodore & Co., Mr. Cinders*) and NY (*Sally, Hit the Deck, The Three Musketeers*). Among his best-known songs: "If You Were the Only Girl in the World," "Wild Rose," "Valencia," "Hallelujah!," "March of the Musketeers," "Spread a Little Happiness," "Got a Date with an Angel," "Oceans of Time." Grey wrote seven scores with composer Nat Ayer, six with J. Fred Coots, four with Maurice Rubens, Jack Waller, and Joseph Tunbridge, three with Ivor Novello; among others: Herman Finck, Charles Cuvillier, Willie Redstone, Armand Vecsey, Jerome Kern, Howard Talbot, Ivan Caryll, Werner Janssen, George Gershwin, Herbert Stothart, Stephen Jones, Edward Kunneke, Alfred Goodman, Sigmund Romberg, Vivian Ellis, Vincent Youmans, Melville Gideon, Jean Schwartz, Rudolf Friml, Lewis Gensler, Richard Myers, Oscar Levant, Johnny Green, Noel Gay, Edmond Samuels, Paul Sheron.

Asterisk indicates Mr. Grey was also librettist or co-librettist:

1916 The Bing Boys Are Here (Ayer)
 Pell-Mell (Ayer)
 Theodore & Co. (Novello, Kern)
1917 The Bing Girls Are There (Ayer)
 The Other Bing Boys (Ayer)
 Arlette (Lefeuvre, Novello)
 Yes, Uncle! (Ayer)
1918 The Bing Boys on Broadway
 (Ayer)
 Hullo, America! (Finck)
1919 Who's Hooper? (Novello, Talbot)
1920 Johnny Jones (Cuvillier)
 A Night Out (Redstone)
 Sally (NY) (Kern)
1922 The Hotel Mouse (NY) (Vecsey,
 Caryll)
 Phi-Phi (Christine)
 The Smith Family * (Ayer)
1923 Lady Butterfly * (NY) (Janssen)
 The Rainbow (Gershwin)
1924 Vogues of 1924 (NY) (Stothart)
 Marjorie (NY) (Romberg, Stothart,
 Jones)
 Artists and Models (NY) (Romberg, Coots)
 Annie Dear (NY) (Romberg)
1925 Artists and Models (NY) (Goodman, Coots, Rubens)
 June Days (NY) (Coots)
 Gay Paree (NY) (Goodman, Coots)
 Mayflowers * (NY) (Kunneke)
1926 A Night in Paris (NY) (Coots,
 Rubens)
 The Great Temptations (NY) (Rubens)
 The Merry World (NY) (Coots)
1927 Hit the Deck (NY) (Youmans)
1928 The Optimists (NY) (Gideon)
 The Madcap (NY) (Rubens)
 Sunny Days * (NY) (Schwartz)
 The Three Musketeers * (NY)
 (Friml)
 Ups-a-Daisy * (NY) (Gensler)
1929 Mr. Cinders * (Ellis, Myers)
1930 Smiles (NY) (Youmans)
1931 For the Love of Mike * (Waller,
 Tunbridge)
1932 Out of the Bottle (Ellis, Levant)
1933 The One Girl * (Smiles)
 Command Performance * (Waller,
 Tunbridge)
1934 Mr. Whittington * (Waller, Tunbridge, Green)
1935 Jack o' Diamonds * (Gay)

 Love Laughs—! * (Gay)
1936 At the Silver Swan * (Samuels)
1937 Oh, You Letty * (Sheron)
1938 Bobby Get Your Gun (Waller,
 Tunbridge)

Grey, Joel (né Joel Katz), actor, singer, dancer; b. Cleveland, Ohio, April 11, 1932. A slight, wiry song-and-dance man, Grey achieved his greatest Bway success in *Cabaret* (introducing "Willkommen") and *George M!* (his first starring part). The son of comic Mickey Katz, he has also appeared in nightclubs.
1956 The Littlest Revue
1963 Stop the World—I Want to Get
 Off (US tour) (*Littlechap*)
 Stop the World—I Want to Get
 Off (*Littlechap*, repl.)
1965 Half a Sixpence (*Arthur Kipps*,
 repl.)
1966 Cabaret (*Master of Ceremonies*)
1968 George M! (*George M. Cohan*)
1975 Goodtime Charley (*Charley*)
1979 The Grand Tour (*Jacobowski*)

Griffith, Robert E., producer; b. Methuen, Mass., 1907; d. Port Chester, NY, June 7, 1961. Bway producer who formed partnership with Harold Prince in 1953 which lasted until his death. Griffith began career as actor, then became stage manager for George Abbott in 1935.
1950 Touch and Go (L)
1954 The Pajama Game
1955 Damn Yankees
1957 New Girl in Town
 West Side Story
1958 West Side Story (L)
1959 Fiorello!
1960 Tenderloin

Grimes, Tammy, actress, singer; b. Lynn, Mass., Jan. 30, 1934. Blonde, buzz-saw-voiced actress who has appeared in dramas as well as musicals. Biggest Bway success: *The Unsinka-*

ble Molly Brown (in which she sang "I Ain't Down Yet").

1956 The Littlest Revue
1960 The Unsinkable Molly Brown
(*Molly Brown*)
1964 High Spirits (*Elvira*)

Groody, Louise, actress, singer, dancer; b. Waco, Texas, March 26, 1897; d. Canadensis, Pa., Sept. 16, 1961. Buoyant performer who began as a cabaret dancer and rose to Bway fame in *No, No, Nanette* (singing "No, No, Nanette," "I Want to Be Happy," "Tea for Two") and *Hit the Deck* ("Sometimes I'm Happy").

1915 Around the Map (dancer)
1918 Toot-Toot! (*Mrs. Walter Colt*)
Fiddlers Three (*Gilda Varelli*)
1920 The Night Boat (*Barbara*)
1921 Good Morning Dearie (*Rose-Marie*)
1923 One Kiss (*Eva*)
1925 No, No, Nanette (*Nanette*)
1927 Hit the Deck (*Loulou*)

Grossmith, George, actor, librettist, lyricist, director, producer; b. London, May 11, 1874; d. London, June 6, 1935. The multitalented Grossmith, son of the D'Oyly Carte's George Grossmith, introduced the "dude" character in London musicals. He was usually either top-hatted and monocled or uniformed and monocled, and enjoyed his greatest successes in *The Shop Girl, The Toreador, The Orchid, Our Miss Gibbs* (singing "Yip-I-Addy"), *Tonight's the Night, Theodore & Co., Kissing Time, No, No, Nanette.* Grossmith also produced musicals, first with Edward Laurillard (1914–1921), then with J. A. E. Malone (1921–1926). As lyricist, he wrote songs with composer Jerome Kern. Bib: "*GG*" by Grossmith (Hutchinson, L 1933).

Asterisk indicates Mr. Grossmith was also sketch writer, librettist, or co-librettist; dagger indicates he was also co-producer and/or director:

1893 Morocco Bound (*Lord Percy Pimpleton*)
1894 Go-Bang (*Hon. Augustus Fitzpoop*)
A Gaiety Girl (r) (*Major Barclay*)
The Shop Girl (*Bertie Boyd*)
1895 The Shop Girl (NY) (*Bertie Boyd*)
1900 The Gay Pretenders * (*Prince Harry*)
1901 The Toreador (*Sir Archibald Hackett*)
1903 The Orchid (*Hon. Guy Scrymgeour*)
1904 The Love Birds (lib. only)
The School Girl (NY) (*Sir Ormsby St. Leger*)
1905 The Spring Chicken * (*Gustave Babori*)
Rogues and Vagabonds (sk. only)
1906 The New Aladdin (*Genie*)
1907 The Girls of Gottenberg * (*Otto*)
1908 A Waltz Dream (*Count Lothar*)
Havana (co-lib. only)
Fluffy Ruffles (NY) (*Hon. Augustus Traddles*)
1909 Our Miss Gibbs (*Hon. Hughie Pierrepoint*)
The Dollar Princess (NY) (lib. only)
1910 Hullo, London! (sk. only)
1911 Peggy * (*Auberon Blow*)
By George! (sk. only)
1912 Everybody's Doin' It! (sk. only)
The Sunshine Girl (*Lord Bingo Bicester*)
Kill that Fly! (sk., dir. only)
1913 The Girl on the Film (*Max Daly*)
Eightpence a Mile (sk. only)
The Girl on the Film (NY) (*Max Daly*)
1914 Not Likely! * †
Tonight's the Night † (NY) (*Hon. Dudley Mitten*)
1915 Tonight's the Night † (*Hon. Dudley Mitten*)
The Only Girl (co-prod. only)
1916 Mr. Manhattan (co-prod. only)
The Bing Boys Are Here (co-lib., co-prod. only)
Theodore & Co.* † (*Lord Theodore Wragge*)
1917 The Bing Girls Are There (co-lib. only)
The Other Bing Boys (co-lib. only)

Arlette (co-prod. only)
Yes, Uncle! (co-prod. only)
1918 The Bing Boys on Broadway (co-lib. only)
1919 Oh, Joy! (co-prod. only)
Kissing Time † (*Max Touquet*)
Baby Bunting (co-prod. only)
1920 A Night Out (co-lib., co-prod. only)
The Naughty Princess † (*Ladislas Brandiski*)
1921 Faust on Toast (dir., co-prod. only)
Sally † (*Otis Hooper*)
1922 The Cabaret Girl * † (*Mr. Gripps*)
1923 The Beauty Prize * † (*Flutey Warboy*) (also co-lyr.) (Kern)
1924 Tonight's the Night (r) † (*Hon. Dudley Mitten*)
Primrose (co-lib., dir., co-prod. only)
1925 No, No, Nanette (*Billy Early*)
Tell Me More (co-prod. only)
1926 Kid Boots (co-prod. only)
Princess Charming (*King Christian*)
1927 Up with the Lark (dir. only)
1928 Lady Mary (*Hatpin Pinge*)
1929 The Five o'Clock Girl (*Huggins*)
1930 Princess Charming (NY) (*King Christian*)
Meet My Sister (NY) (*Marquis de Chatelard*)
1931 My Sister and I (Meet My Sister) † (*Marquis de Chatelard*)

"Guards' Brigade, The." Music by Herman Darewski; lyric by Arthur Wimperis. Roistering march added to score of *The Shop Girl* for its revised version (L 1920), in which it was performed by Evelyn Laye, dressed as a drum majorette, leading a 60-piece marching band of real Guardsmen. According to Miss Laye, there were eight encores opening night.

"Guess Who I Saw Today." Music by Murray Grand; lyric by Elisse Boyd. In one of the few musical-comedy songs about infidelity, a wife reveals to her husband that she has just seen him with another woman. June Carroll introduced the narrative ballad in *New Faces of 1952* (NY).

Guys and Dolls (1950). Music & lyrics by Frank Loesser; book by Abe Burrows & Jo Swerling, based on Damon Runyon's short story "The Idyll of Miss Sarah Brown."

SONGS: "Fugue for Tinhorns," "The Oldest Established," "I'll Know," "A Bushel and a Peck," "Adelaide's Lament," "Guys and Dolls," "If I Were a Bell," "My Time of Day," "I've Never Been in Love Before," "Take Back Your Mink," "More I Cannot Wish You," "Luck Be a Lady," "Sue Me," "Sit Down, You're Rockin' the Boat."

NEW YORK: Nov. 24, 1950
46TH ST. THEATRE; 1,200 p.

Presented by Cy Feuer & Ernest Martin; directed by George S. Kaufman; choreographed by Michael Kidd; settings & lighting, Jo Mielziner; costumes, Alvin Colt; music director, Irving Actman; orchestrations, George Bassman, Ted Royal.

CAST: Robert Alda (*Sky Masterson*), Vivian Blaine (*Miss Adelaide*), Sam Levene (*Nathan Detroit*), Isabel Bigley (*Miss Sarah Brown*), Pat Rooney, Sr. (*Arvide Abernathy*), B. S. Pully (*Big Jule*), Stubby Kaye (*Nicely-Nicely Johnson*), Tom Pedi (*Harry the Horse*), Johnny Silver (*Benny Southstreet*), Peter Gennaro (dancer), Onna White (dancer).

LONDON: May 28, 1953
COLISEUM; 555 p.

Presented by Prince Littler & Arthur Lewis; directed by George S. Kaufman; choreographed by Michael Kidd; settings & lighting, Jo Mielziner; costumes, Alvin Colt; music director, Philip Green, orchestrations, George Bassman, Ted Royal.

CAST: Jerry Wayne (*Sky Masterson*), Vivian Blaine (*Miss Adelaide*),

Sam Levene (*Nathan Detroit*), Lizbeth Webb (*Miss Sarah Brown*), Ernest Butcher (*Arvide Abernathy*), Lew Herbert (*Big Jule*), Stubby Kaye (*Nicely-Nicely Johnson*), Tom Pedi (*Harry the Horse*), Johnny Silver (*Benny Southstreet*), Lou Jacobi (*Liver Lips Louie*).

In its hard-shelled but soft-centered look at the guys and dolls of Damon Runyon's Bway world, this "Musical Fable" relates the tale of how Miss Sarah Brown of the Save-a-Soul Mission saves the souls of assorted Times Square riffraff, while in the process losing her heart to gambler Sky Masterson. A second romance involves Nathan Detroit, the organizer of the oldest established permanent floating crap game in New York, and Miss Adelaide, the featured attraction at the Hot Box nightclub, to whom he has been engaged for 14 years. The idea for the musical originated with producers Feuer and Martin. Their initial librettist was Robert Carson, who was succeeded by Jo Swerling, and finally Abe Burrows (but Swerling is always credited as co-author). Because Loesser wrote his songs to fit the Swerling libretto, Burrows had to write *his* libretto to fit the songs. Among actors originally sought for the leads were Ethel Merman, Tony Martin, and Frank Sinatra.

During Bway run, Robert Alda was succeeded by Norwood Smith (9-52); Vivian Blaine by Iva Withers (2-53); Sam Levene by Julie Oshins (1-53); Isabel Bigley by Susan Hight (3-53). The US touring company, which began in June 1951, continued for two years, four months. The cast was headed by Allan Jones (*Sky*), Pamela Britton (*Adelaide*), Julie Oshins (*Nathan*), Jan Clayton (*Sarah*), Maxie Rosenbloom (*Julie*). In London, Jerry Wayne was succeeded by Edmund Hockridge.

Other Bway musicals with Salvation Army heroines: *The Belle of New York* (1898) and *Smiles* (1930).

FILM VERSION: Marlon Brando, Frank Sinatra, Jean Simmons, Vivian Blaine (Goldwyn 1955, Joseph Mankiewicz dir.).

"Guys and Dolls." Music & lyric by Frank Loesser. Whenever a guy starts acting crazy, such as spending more money than he can afford, "you can bet that he's doing it for some doll." The sentiment was lustily belted out in the musical of the same name by Stubby Kaye and Johnny Silver both in NY (1950) and London (1953).

Gypsy (1959). Music by Jule Styne; lyrics by Stephen Sondheim; book by Arthur Laurents, based on Gypsy Rose Lee's autobiography.

SONGS: "Let Me Entertain You," "Some People," "Small World," "Mr. Goldstone, I Love You," "Little Lamb," "You'll Never Get Away from Me," "If Mamma Was Married," "All I Need Is the Girl," "Everything's Coming Up Roses," "Together Wherever We Go," "You Gotta Have a Gimmick," "Rose's Turn."

NEW YORK: May 21, 1959
BROADWAY THEATRE; 702 p.

Presented by David Merrick & Leland Hayward; directed & choreographed by Jerome Robbins; settings & lighting, Jo Mielziner; costumes, Raoul Pène du Bois; music director, Milton Rosenstock; orchestrations, Sid Ramin, Robert Ginzler.

CAST: Ethel Merman (*Rose*), Jack Klugman (*Herbie*), Sandra Church (*Louise*), Maria Karnilova (*Tessie Tura*), Paul Wallace (*Tulsa*), Mort Marshall (*Uncle Jocko*), Lane Bradbury (*June*), Jacqueline Mayro (*Baby June*), Joe Silver (*Weber*), Peg Murray (*Miss Cratchitt*), Michael Parks (*LA*).

LONDON: May 29, 1973
PICCADILLY THEATRE; 300 p.

Presented by Barry M. Brown & Fritz Holt, with Edgar Lansbury, Joseph Beruh & H. M. Tennent Ltd.; directed by Arthur Laurents; dances reproduced by Robert Tucker; settings, Robert Randolph; costumes, Raoul Pène du Bois; lighting, Joe Davis; music director, Richard Leonard.

CAST: Angela Lansbury (*Rose*), Barrie Ingham (*Herbie*), Zan Charisse (*Louise*), Valerie Walsh (*Tessie Tura*), Andrew Norman (*Tulsa*), Debbie Bowen (*June*), Bonnie Langford (*Baby June*), George Moon (*Uncle Jocko*).

The autobiography of stripper Gypsy Rose Lee so intrigued producer Merrick that he bought the stage rights after having read only one chapter. Originally, Betty Comden and Adolph Green were to have been both librettists and lyricists, but they withdrew in favor of Messrs. Laurents and Sondheim. Sondheim, in fact, was also to have provided the music as well as the lyrics, but Miss Merman, concerned about giving the assignment to one with so little experience, wanted a better-known composer and they went to Jule Styne. In the story, the emphasis is on the ruthless character of Rose, the ambitious mother of Gypsy Rose Lee. To escape from her humdrum life, Rose does everything possible to further the stage career of her daughter June; after June runs away to get married, she focuses her attention on daughter Louise. Eventually Louise evolves into Gypsy Rose Lee, and though mama is relegated to the background and suffers an emotional breakdown, she ends by finding some fulfillment in her daughter's success.

Except for composer Styne, the other creators of *Gypsy* had all worked on *West Side Story:* librettist Laurents, lyricist Sondheim, and director-choreographer Robbins. As Rose, Ethel Merman had the most dramatically impressive role of her career. Following the Bway run, she headed the road company, which, after opening March 1961, toured for eight months. In the cast were Julienne Marie (*Louise*), Alfred Sandor (*Herbie*), and Alice Playton (*Baby Louise*). In London version, Angela Lansbury made a notable West End debut and was succeeded in Dec. 1973 by Dolores Gray. This production opened in NY on Sept. 23, 1974, with cast replacements including Rex Robbins as Herbie, and Mary Louise Wilson as Tessie. It ran 120 performances.

FILM VERSION: Rosalind Russell, Natalie Wood, Karl Malden (Warner 1962, Mervyn LeRoy dir.).

"Gypsy Love Song." Music by Victor Herbert; lyric by Harry B. Smith. A comforting lullaby, Herbert's first song hit, sung by Eugene Cowles in *The Fortune Teller* (NY 1898).

⚘ H ⚘

Hague, Albert, composer; b. Berlin, Germany, Oct. 13, 1920. Hague's biggest Bway hits were *Plain and Fancy* ("Young and Foolish") and *Redhead* ("Merely Marvelous"). He has written with lyricists Arnold Horwitt, Dorothy Fields, Marty Brill, Allan Sherman.

1955 Plain and Fancy (Horwitt)
1959 Redhead (Fields)
1964 Café Crown (Brill)
1969 The Fig Leaves Are Falling (Sherman)

Hair (1967). Music by Galt MacDermot; lyrics & book by Gerome Ragni & James Rado.

SONGS: "Aquarius," "Ain't Got No," "Frank Mills," "Hare Krishna," "Where Do I Go?," "Easy to Be Hard," "Good Morning, Starshine," "Let the Sunshine In."

NEW YORK: Oct. 29, 1967
PUBLIC THEATRE; 94 p.

Presented by Joseph Papp; directed by Gerald Freedman; settings, Ming Cho Lee; costumes, Theoni Aldredge; lighting, Martin Aronstein; music director, John Morris.

CAST: Walker Daniels (*Claude*), Gerome Ragni (*Berger*), Jill O'Hara (*Sheila*), Steve Dean (*Woof*), Sally Eaton (*Jeannie*), Jonelle Allen (*Dionne*), Shelley Plimpton (*Crissy*), Arnold Wilkerson (*Hud*).

NEW YORK: April 29, 1968
BILTMORE THEATRE; 1,742 p.

Presented by Michael Butler; directed by Tom O'Horgan; choreographed by Julie Arenal; settings, Robin Wagner; costumes, Nancy Potts; lighting, Jules Fisher; music director, Galt MacDermot.

CAST: James Rado (*Claude*), Gerome Ragni (*Berger*), Lynn Kellogg (*Sheila*), Steve Curry (*Woof*), Sally Eaton (*Jeannie*), Melba Moore (*Dionne*), Shelley Plimpton (*Crissy*), Diane Keaton (*Waitress*), Lamont Washington (*Hud*).

LONDON: Sept. 27, 1968
SHAFTESBURY THEATRE; 1,998 p.

Presented by Robert Stigwood, David Conyers, John Nasht; directed by Tom O'Horgan; choreographed by Julie Arenal; settings, Robin Wagner; costumes, Nancy Potts; lighting, Jules Fisher; music director, Derek Wadsworth.

CAST: Paul Nicholas (*Claude*), Oliver Tobias (*Berger*), Annabel Leventon (*Sheila*), Michael Feast (*Woof*), Linda Kendrick (*Jeannie*), Marsha Hunt (*Dionne*), Liz White (*Crissy*), Peter Straker (*Hud*).

The "American Tribal Love-Rock Musical" was a milestone in Bway musical history. A look at the styleless life style of assorted East Village hippies, it celebrated the uninhibited world of social dropouts and their opposition to the draft and the Vietnam war. For about half its original run, *Hair* was presented at a Bway nightclub named Cheetah. The redirected, redesigned, and recast Bway version achieved a breakthrough of sorts by having the cast totally nude at the first-act finale. During Bway run, Lynn Kellogg was succeeded by Diane Keaton (7-68), Heather MacRae (1-69), Melba Moore (10-69). For a time, seven road companies were playing throughout the US. The London run was forced to terminate when the roof of the Shaftesbury Theatre collapsed in July 1973. It reopened June 1974 at the Queen's Theatre and ran 111 performances. Bib: *Letting My Hair Down* by Lorrie Davis (Fields, NY 1972).

Hale, Binnie (née Beatrice Mary Hale-Monro), actress, singer, dancer; b. Liverpool, Eng., May 22, 1899. Blonde, vivacious Binnie Hale was one of London's most popular stars during the 20s and 30s. Her hits included *No, No, Nanette* (singing "No, No, Nanette," "I've Confessed to the Breeze," "I Want to Be Happy," "Tea for Two"), *Sunny,* and *Mr. Cinders* ("Spread a Little Happiness," "I'm a One-Man Girl"). Other song successes: "You're Blasé" (*Bow Bells*),

"London Pride" (*Up and Doing*). She is the daughter of actor Robert Hale and the sister of actor Sonnie Hale.

1916 Follow the Crowd
We're All in It
Houp-la! (*Annette*)
1917 150 Pound Revue
1919 The Kiss Call (*Charlotte Chapman*)
1920 Just Fancy
Jumble Sale
1921 My Nieces (*Betty Culverwell*)
1923 Katinka (*Helen Hopper*)
1924 Puppets
The Odd Spot
1925 No, No, Nanette (*Nanette*)
1926 Sunny (*Sunny Peters*)
1929 Mr. Cinders (*Jill Kemp*)
1930 Nippy (*Nippy Grey*)
1932 Bow Bells
The DuBarry (UK tour) (*Jeanne*)
1933 Give Me a Ring (*Peggy*, repl.)
1934 Yes, Madame? (*Sally Ganthony*)
1936 Rise and Shine (*Anne*)
1937 Home and Beauty
1939 Magyar Melody (*Roszi Belvary*)
1940 Up and Doing
1941 Flying Colours
1947 One, Two, Three! (also co-prod.)
1948 Four, Five, Six!
1950 Out of This World
1955 The Punch Revue

Hale, Sonnie (né John Robert Hale-Munro), actor, singer, director; b. London, May 1, 1902; d. London, June 9, 1959. Bland, blond Sonnie was the son of actor Robert Hale, the brother of Binnie Hale, and the husband of both Evelyn Laye and Jessie Matthews. He appeared with Miss Matthews in six London musicals (1927–1940), introducing "A Room with a View" and "Dance, Little Lady" (both in *This Year of Grace!*) and "Dancing on the Ceiling" (*Ever Green*). Hale also acted in and directed British films.

1921 The Fun of the Fayre
1923 Little Nellie Kelly (*Sidney Potter*)
1924 The Punch Bowl
1925 Mercenary Mary (*Jerry Warner*)

1926 Queen High (*Richard Johns*)
1927 One Dam Thing After Another
1928 This Year of Grace!
1929 Wake Up and Dream!
1930 Ever Green (*Tommy Thompson*)
1931 Hold My Hand (*Pop Curry*)
1940 Come Out to Play (also dir.)
1943 The Knight Was Bold (*Sir Guy de Vere*)
1947 One, Two, Three! (also dir., co-prod.)
1948 Four, Five, Six! (dir. only)

Haley, (John) Jack, actor, singer; b. Boston, Mass, Aug. 10, 1899. Usually playing the innocent hick, eye-rolling Jack Haley scored successes in *Follow Thru* (introducing "Button Up Your Overcoat"), *Take a Chance* ("You're an Old Smoothie"), and *Inside USA*. A member of vaudeville team of Crofts and Haley before making Bway debut, he also appeared in Hollywood films (*D. Los Angeles, June 6, 1979.*)

1924 Round the Town
1925 Gay Paree
1926 Gay Paree
1929 Follow Thru (*Jack Martin*)
1931 Free for All (*Steve Potter*)
1932 Take a Chance (*Duke Stanley*)
1940 Higher and Higher (*Zachary Ash*)
1948 Inside USA

Half a Sixpence (1963). Music & lyrics by David Heneker; book by Douglas Cross, based on H. G. Wells's novel *Kipps*.

SONGS: "All in the Cause of Economy," "Half a Sixpence," "Money to Burn," "She's Too Far Above Me," "If the Rain's Got to Fall," "Flash! Bang! Wallop!," "I Know What I Am."

LONDON: March 21, 1963
CAMBRIDGE THEATRE; 677 p.

Presented by Harold Fielding; directed by John Dexter; choreographed by Edmund Balin; settings & costumes, Loudon Sainthill; lighting, Richard Pilbrow; music director, Kenneth Alwyn.

CAST: Tommy Steele (*Arthur Kipps*), Marti Webb (*Ann Pornick*), James Grout (*Harry Chitterlow*), Anna Barry (*Helen Walsingham*), Jessica James (*Mrs. Walsingham*), Anthony Valentine (*Pearce*), John Bull (*Sid Pornick*), Colin Farrell (*Buggins*).

NEW YORK: April 25, 1965
BROADHURST THEATRE; 512 p.

Presented by Allen-Hodgdon, Stevens Productions, Harold Fielding, Harry Rigby; directed by Gene Sacks; choreographed by Onna White; settings & costumes, Loudon Sainthill; lighting, Jules Fisher; music director, Stanley Lebowsky; orchestrations, Jim Tyler.

CAST: Tommy Steele (*Arthur Kipps*), Polly James (*Ann Pornick*), James Grout (*Harry Chitterlow*), Carrie Nye (*Helen Walsingham*), Ann Shoemaker (*Mrs. Walsingham*), Grover Dale (*Pearce*), Will Mackenzie (*Sid Pornick*), Norman Allen (*Buggins*).

Written specifically for Tommy Steele, the musical followed the career of orphan Arthur Kipps, a draper's apprentice in Folkestone, England, at the turn of the century. Arthur loves and loses rich Helen Walsingham, inherits and loses a fortune, but finds eventual happiness with faithful Ann Pornick. The NY production placed greater emphasis on dancing than the London original and there were changes in the David Heneker score. During Bway run, Steele was succeeded by Tony Tanner and Joel Grey. The US tour, headed by Dick Kallman and Anne Rogers, began in July 1966, and lasted 11 months.

FILM VERSION: Tommy Steele and Cyril Ritchard (Par. 1967, George Sidney dir.).

"Half a Sixpence." Music & lyric by David Heneker. In *Half a Sixpence* (L 1963), Tommy Steele gave Marti Webb half a sixpence as a love token and kept the other half. In NY version, Steele shared the keepsake with Polly James (1965).

"Half-Caste Woman." Music & lyric by Noël Coward. The bitter dreams of a Eurasian working in a waterfront dive were revealed by Ada May in *Cochran's 1931 Revue* (L 1931) and by Helen Morgan in *Ziegfeld Follies* (NY 1931). The heroine of the piece is apparently a half-caste sister of the taxi dancer in Rodgers and Hart's "Ten Cents a Dance" and the streetwalker in Cole Porter's "Love for Sale."

Hall, Adelaide (Louise), actress, singer; b. Brooklyn, NY, Oct. 20, 1895. Strong-voiced singer who scored a hit in Bway revue *Blackbirds of 1928* (singing "Diga Diga Doo," "I Can't Give You Anything but Love," and "I Must Have That Man"). Miss Hall has also had a career as nightclub entertainer in US and England.

1921	Shuffle Along (chorus)
1923	Runnin' Wild (*Adalade*)
1928	Blackbirds of 1928
1930	Brown Buddies (*Betty Lou Johnson*)
1951	Kiss Me, Kate (L) (*Hattie*)
1952	Love from Judy (L) (*Butterfly*)
1957	Jamaica (*Grandma Obeah*)

Hall, Bettina, actress, singer; b. North Easton, Mass., 1906; Miss Hall's biggest Bway success was scored in *The Cat and the Fiddle* (in which she sang "She Didn't Say 'Yes'"). She is the sister of Natalie Hall.

1929	The Little Show
1930	Three Little Girls (*Marie, Mme Morrossoni*)
	Meet My Sister (*Dolly Molinar*)
1931	The Cat and the Fiddle (*Shirley Sheridan*)
1934	Anything Goes (*Hope Harcourt*)

Hall, Juanita (née Juanita Long), actress, singer; b. Keysport, NJ, Nov. 6, 1901; d. Bay Shore, NY, Feb. 28, 1968. Miss Hall was a short, heavy-set actress best remembered for singing "Bali Ha'i" and "Happy Talk" in *South Pacific*.

1944	Sing Out, Sweet Land (chorus)
1946	Show Boat (chorus)
	St. Louis Woman (*Leah*)
1947	Street Scene (chorus)
1949	South Pacific (*Bloody Mary*)
1954	House of Flowers (*Madame Tango*)
1958	Flower Drum Song (*Madam Liang*)

Hall, Natalie, actress, singer; b. Providence, RI, Sept. 23, 1904. Miss Hall's biggest Bway success was scored in *Music in the Air* (in which she sang "The Song Is You"). She also introduced "Through the Years" in musical of the same name. Miss Hall is the sister of Bettina Hall.

1930	Three Little Girls (*Beate*)
1932	Through the Years (*Kathleen, Moonyeen*)
	Music in the Air (*Frieda Hatzfeld*)
1933	Ball at the Savoy (L) (*Madeleine*)
1934	Music Hath Charms (*Marchese Maria, Maria Sovrani*)

Hall, Owen (né James Davis), librettist; b. Dublin, Ireland, 1853; d. Harrowgate, Eng., April 9, 1907. Hall's best-known musical, both in London and NY, was *Florodora*. Other long-run London hits: *A Gaiety Girl, An Artist's Model, The Geisha, The Girl from Kay's*. He also wrote lyrics with composer Ivan Caryll.

1893	A Gaiety Girl
1895	An Artist's Model
1896	The Geisha
1898	A Greek Slave
1899	Florodora
1901	The Silver Slipper
1902	The Girl from Kay's
1903	The Medal and the Maid
1904	Sergeant Brue

1906	The Little Cherub (also lyr.) (Caryll)

"Hallelujah!" Music by Vincent Youmans; lyric by Leo Robin. Revivalistic number belted out by Stella Mayhew, in blackface, and chorus in *Hit the Deck* (NY 1927). In London production (1927) it was sung by Alice Morley, also in blackface. The music for the song, the first Youmans had ever written, was composed during World War I at the Great Lakes Naval Training Station. Red Carney, the bandmaster there, encouraged the young composer—though the song was not performed until 10 years later.

Halliday, Robert, actor, singer; b. Loch Lomond, Scotland. On Bway, Halliday was the hero of *The Desert Song* (singing "The Desert Song," "One Alone") and *The New Moon* ("Stouthearted Men," "Wanting You," "Lover, Come Back to Me"). He married Evelyn Herbert, his co-star in three productions.

1921	The Rose Girl (chorus)
1922	The Springtime of Youth (chorus)
1923	Dew Drop Inn (*Bobby Smith*)
1924	Paradise Alley (*Jack Harriman*, repl.)
	Topsy and Eva (*George Shelby*)
1925	Holka Polka (*Karel Boleslav*)
	Tip-Toes (*Rollo Metcalf*)
1926	The Desert Song (*Pierre Birabeau*)
1928	The New Moon (*Robert Misson*)
1930	Princess Charming (*Capt. Torrelli*)
1931	Waltzes from Vienna (L) (*Johann Strauss Jr.*)
1934	Music Hath Charms (*Charles Parker, Duke of Orsano*)
1936	White Horse Inn (*Donald Hutton*)
1952	Three Wishes for Jamie (*Tim Shanahan*)

Hamilton, Nancy, lyricist, sketch writer, actress, singer; b. Sewickley, Pa., July 27, 1908. Bway writer-actress, best remembered for her series of "One-Two-Three" revues, originally conceived as something of a right-wing answer to the left-wing *Pins and Needles*. Miss Hamilton wrote all the sketches and, with composer Morgan Lewis, all the songs (incl. "How High the Moon" and "The Old Soft Shoe"). Among actors who appeared in her revues: Brenda Forbes (3); Alfred Drake, Keenan Wynn, and William Archibald (2 each); plus Gene Kelly, Eve Arden, Ray Bolger, Arthur Godfrey, Harold Lang, and Gordon MacRae.

> Unless otherwise noted, Miss Hamilton wrote sketches and lyrics for following:
> 1934   New Faces (also actress)
> 1939   One for the Money (also actress)
> 1940   Two for the Show
> 1942   Count Me In (co-lib. only)
> 1946   Three to Make Ready

Hammerstein, Arthur, producer; b. New York, Dec. 21, 1872; d. Palm Beach, Fla., Oct. 12, 1955. The son of opera impressario Oscar Hammerstein, he was mostly a producer of Bway operettas, with 10 by composer Rudolf Friml (incl. *The Firefly, Rose-Marie*), eight of them written with librettist-lyricist Otto Harbach, of which two found Harbach also collaborating with Oscar Hammerstein II (Arthur's nephew). The team of Harbach and Hammerstein was also responsible for six other musicals produced by Arthur Hammerstein (incl. *Wildflower*, music by Vincent Youmans).

> 1912   The Firefly
> 1913   High Jinks
> 1915   Katinka
> 1917   You're in Love
>   Furs and Frills
> 1918   Sometime
>   Somebody's Sweetheart
> 1919   Tumble In
> 1920   Always You
>   Tickle Me

>   Jimmie
> 1922   The Blue Kitten
>   Daffy Dill
> 1923   Wildflower
>   Hammerstein's 9 o'Clock Revue
>   Mary Jane McKane
> 1924   Rose-Marie
> 1925   Song of the Flame
> 1926   The Wild Rose
> 1927   Golden Dawn
> 1928   Good Boy
> 1929   Polly
>   Sweet Adeline
> 1930   Luana
>   Ballyhoo

Hammerstein, Oscar, producer, composer, lyricist, librettist; b. Berlin, Germany, May 8, 1847; d. New York, Aug. 1, 1919. Primarily an opera impressario, Hammerstein built and managed the Manhattan Opera House (1906–1910), plus others incl. the London Opera House. He also presented vaudeville at the Victoria Theatre, NY. His most notable Bway musical was *Naughty Marietta*. Hammerstein was the father of producer Arthur Hammerstein and the grandfather of librettist-lyricist Oscar Hammerstein II. Bib: *Oscar Hammerstein I* by Vincent Sheean (S&S, NY 1956).

> Asterisk indicates Mr. Hammerstein was also composer, lyricist, librettist:
> 1896   Santa Maria *
> 1897   In Greater New York *
>   The Isle of Gold
>   La Poupée
> 1898   War Bubbles *
> 1901   Sweet Marie
> 1903   Punch, Judy & Co.
> 1910   Hans the Flute Player
>   Naughty Marietta

Hammerstein, Oscar (Greeley Clendenning) II, lyricist, librettist, director, producer; b. New York, July 12, 1895; d. Doylestown, Pa., Aug, 23, 1960. Hammerstein was a creator of poetic, idiomatic, painstakingly crafted lyrics that reflected his love for simple, rural pleasures. In the 20s, with composers Rudolf Friml and Sigmund Romberg and co-librettist-lyricist Otto Harbach, he was an exponent of Bway-styled swashbuckling operetta; in the late 20s and early 30s, with composer Jerome Kern, he developed the first modern musical plays; in the 40s and 50s, with composer Richard Rodgers, he made his most durable contribution with a series of musicals noted for the strength of their librettos and the skill with which they were integrated with song and dance.

Hammerstein's earliest successes were *Wildflower* ("Bambalina"), *Rose-Marie* ("Rose-Marie," "The Mounties," "Indian Love Call"), *Sunny* ("Sunny," "Who?"), *The Desert Song* ("The Riff Song," "The Desert Song," "One Alone"), *Show Boat* ("Make Believe," "Ol' Man River," "Why Do I Love You?," "You Are Love," "Can't Help Lovin' Dat Man," and "Bill," written with P. G. Wodehouse), *The New Moon* ("Softly, as in a Morning Sunrise," "Lover, Come Back to Me," "Stouthearted Men," "One Kiss"), *Sweet Adeline* ("Why Was I Born?," "Don't Ever Leave Me"), *Music in the Air* ("I've Told Ev'ry Little Star," "The Song Is You"). He also wrote "All the Things You Are" for *Very Warm for May*, and adapted Bizet's *Carmen* into *Carmen Jones* ("Dat's Love," "Beat Out Dat Rhythm on a Drum," "My Joe"). Among other composer collaborators: Herbert Stothart, Lewis Gensler, Dudley Wilkinson, Vincent Youmans, George Gershwin, Emmerich Kalman, Richard Whiting, Paul Abraham. He also wrote with lyricist William Cary Duncan.

With Rodgers, Hammerstein wrote the landmark musical *Oklahoma!* ("People Will Say We're in Love," "Oh, What a Beautiful Mornin'," "The Surrey with the Fringe on Top," "Oklahoma," "I Cain't Say No"), *Carousel* ("If I Loved You," "Soliloquy," "June Is Bustin' Out All Over," "You'll Never Walk Alone"), *South Pacific* ("Some Enchanted Evening," "There Is Nothin' Like a Dame," "Bali Ha'i," "I'm Gonna Wash That Man Right Outa My Hair," "A Wonderful Guy," "Younger than Springtime"), *The King and I* ("I Whistle a Happy Tune," "Hello, Young Lovers," "Getting to Know You," "Something Wonderful," "Shall We Dance?"), *The Sound of Music* ("The Sound of Music," "Do-Re-Mi," "My Favorite Things," "Maria," "Climb Ev'ry Mountain"). Other Rodgers and Hammerstein songs: "A Fellow Needs a Girl," "You Are Never Away," "The Gentleman Is a Dope" (*Allegro*); "No Other Love" (*Me and Juliet*); "I Enjoy Being a Girl," "Love, Look Away" (*Flower Drum Song*). Among singers associated with Rodgers and Hammerstein works were Alfred Drake, Celeste Holm, John Raitt, Mary Martin, Ezio Pinza, Gertrude Lawrence. Hammerstein was the grandson of impressario Oscar Hammerstein and the nephew of producer Arthur Hammerstein. Bib: *Lyrics* by Hammerstein (S&S, NY 1949); *Some Enchanted Evenings* by Deems Taylor (Harper, NY 1952); *The Rodgers and Hammerstein Song Book* (S&S, NY 1958); *The Rodgers and Hammerstein Story* by Stanley Green (Day, NY 1963).

Unless otherwise noted, Mr. Hammerstein was lyricist-librettist or co-lyricist-librettist of following; one asterisk indicates collaboration with Mr. Harbach, two indicate collaboration with Mr. Rodgers; one dagger indicates he was also director, two indicate he was also co-producer:

1920 Always You (Stothart)
      Tickle Me * (Stothart)
      Jimmie * (Stothart)
1922 Daffy Dill (Stothart)

Queen o' Hearts (Gensler, Wilkinson)
1923 Wildflower * (Youmans, Stothart)
Mary Jane McKane (Youmans, Stothart-Duncan)
1924 Rose-Marie * (Friml, Stothart)
1925 Sunny * (Kern)
Song of the Flame * (Gershwin, Stothart)
1926 The Wild Rose * (Friml)
The Desert Song * (Romberg)
1927 Golden Dawn * (Kalman, Stothart)
Show Boat † (Kern)
1928 Good Boy * (co-lib. only)
The New Moon † (Romberg)
Rainbow † (Youmans)
1929 Sweet Adeline (Kern)
1931 The Gang's All Here (co-lib. only)
Free for All † (Whiting)
East Wind † (Romberg)
1932 Music in the Air † (Kern)
1933 Ball at the Savoy † (L) (Abraham)
1934 Three Sisters † (L) (Kern)
1935 May Wine (lyr. only) (Romberg)
1939 Very Warm for May † (Kern)
1941 Sunny River † (Romberg)
1943 Oklahoma! **
Carmen Jones (Bizet)
1945 Carousel **
1946 Show Boat †† (r) (Kern)
Annie Get Your Gun (co-prod. only)
1947 Allegro **
1949 South Pacific **††
1951 The King and I **††
1953 Me and Juliet **††
1955 Pipe Dream **††
1958 Flower Drum Song **††
1959 The Sound of Music **†† (lyr. only)

Haney, Carol, actress, dancer, choreographer; b. New Bedford, Mass., Dec. 24, 1924; d. New York, May 10, 1964. Gamin-like dancer who scored hit in *The Pajama Game* (in which she introduced "Hernando's Hideaway"), then became choreographer. She was married to and divorced from actor Larry Blyden.

Unless otherwise noted, Miss Haney was choreographer of following:
1954 The Pajama Game (*Gladys* only)
1958 Flower Drum Song
1962 Bravo Giovanni!
1963 She Loves Me
Jennie
1964 Funny Girl

Hanley, James F(rederick), composer; b. Rensselaer, Ind., Feb. 17, 1892; d. Douglaston, NY, Feb. 8, 1942. Hanley's best-known Bway songs were "Rose of Washington Square" (*Ziegfeld 9 o'Clock Frolic* and *Ziegfeld Follies 1934*); "Second Hand Rose" (*Ziegfeld Follies 1921*); "The Little White House" (*Honeymoon Lane*); and "Zing! Went the Strings of My Heart!" (*Thumbs Up!*), for which he also wrote the lyric. Other lyric-writing partners: Harry Cort, George Stoddard, Ballard Macdonald, Irving Ceasar, James Stanley, McElbert Moore, B. G. DeSylva, Gene Buck, Eddie Dowling. He also wrote with composer Joseph Meyer.
1920 Jim Jam Jems (Cort, Stoddard)
1922 Pins and Needles (Macdonald, Caesar)
Spice of 1922 (Stanley, Moore)
1925 Big Boy (DeSylva-Meyer)
1926 No Foolin' (Buck)
Honeymoon Lane (Dowling)
1927 Sidewalks of New York (Dowling)

"Happiness." Music & lyric by Clark Gesner. Enumerated bliss (finding a pencil, sleeping in moonlight, telling the time) sung by the company as the finale of *You're a Good Man, Charlie Brown* (NY 1967, L 1968).

"Happy in Love." Music by Sammy Fain; lyric by Jack Yellen. Bubbly proclamation announced by Ella Logan in *Sons o' Fun* (NY 1941).

"**Happy Talk.**" Music by Richard Rodgers; lyric by Oscar Hammerstein II. In *South Pacific* (NY 1949), Bloody Mary (Juanita Hall), a Polynesian, wants an American lieutenant (William Tabbert) to marry her daughter Liat (Betta St. John). "Talk about beautiful things," she says, "and make love all day long. You like? You buy?" Then to a singsong melody, accompanied by Liat's pantomime gestures, she urges him to talk about such happy things as a moon, a bird, a star—and a girl and a boy. Muriel Smith was Bloody Mary in the London company (1951).

"**Happy Time, The.**" Music by John Kander; lyric by Fred Ebb. Scenes of a happy childhood remembered by Robert Goulet in *The Happy Time* (NY 1968).

Harbach, Otto (né Otto Abels Hauerbach), librettist, lyricist; b. Salt Lake City, Utah, Aug. 18, 1873; d. New York, Jan. 24, 1963. A protean writer, identified with both operetta and musical comedy, Harbach had two early successes with *Three Twins* ("Cuddle Up a Little Closer, Lovey Mine") and *Madame Sherry* ("Every Little Movement"), both in collaboration with composer Karl Hoschna. Other Bway hits followed: *The Firefly* ("Giannina Mia," "Sympathy"), *Going Up* ("The Tickle Toe"), *Mary* ("The Love Nest"), *Wildflower* ("Bambalina"), *Rose-Marie* ("Rose-Marie," "The Mounties," "Indian Love Call"), *No, No, Nanette* ("No, No, Nanette," "I've Confessed to the Breeze"), *Sunny* ("Sunny," "Who?"), *The Desert Song* ("The Riff Song," "The Desert Song," "One Alone"), *The Cat and the Fiddle* ("She Didn't Say 'Yes,' " "The Night Was Made for Love"), *Roberta* ("Smoke Gets in Your Eyes," "Yesterdays," "The Touch of Your Hand"). Harbach was also co-librettist of *Kid Boots*.

In 1920 Harbach formed a partnership with lyricist-librettist Oscar Hammerstein II, which resulted in 10 productions. His most frequent composer partner was Rudolf Friml (10 scores); he also wrote with Aladar Renyi, Herbert Stothart, Louis Hirsch, Vincent Youmans, Alfred Newman, William Daly, Con Conrad, Sigmund Romberg, Jerome Kern, Emmerich Kalman, George Gershwin, Harry Ruby, and lyricists-librettists Anne Caldwell and Bert Kalmar.

Unless otherwise noted, Mr. Harbach was librettist-lyricist or co-librettist-lyricist of following; asterisk indicates collaboration with Mr. Hammerstein:

1908	Three Twins (lyr. only) (Hoschna)
1910	Bright Eyes (lyr. only) (Hoschna)
	Madame Sherry (Hoschna)
1911	Dr. Deluxe (Hoschna)
	The Girl of My Dreams (Hoschna)
	The Fascinating Widow (Hoschna)
1912	The Firefly (Friml)
1913	High Jinks (Friml)
1914	The Crinoline Girl (lib. only)
	Suzi (Renyi)
1915	Katinka (Friml)
1917	You're in Love (Friml)
	Kitty Darlin' (Friml)
	Going Up (Hirsch)
1919	Tumble In (Friml)
	The Little Whopper (Friml)
1920	Tickle Me * (Stothart)
	Mary (Hirsch)
	Jimmie * (Stothart)
1921	June Love (co-lib. only)
	The O'Brien Girl (Hirsch)
1922	The Blue Kitten (Friml)
	Molly Darling (co-lib. only)
1923	Wildflower * (Youmans, Stothart)
	Jack and Jill (Newman, Daly)
	Kid Boots (co-lib. only)
1924	Rose-Marie * (Friml, Stothart)
	Betty Lee (Hirsch, Conrad)
1925	No, No, Nanette (Youmans)

Sunny * (Kern)
Song of the Flame * (Gershwin, Stothart)
1926 Kitty's Kisses (co-lib. only)
      Criss-Cross (Kern-Caldwell)
      The Wild Rose * (Friml)
      The Desert Song * (Romberg)
      Oh, Please! (co-lib. only)
1927 Lucky (Ruby-Kalmar)
      Golden Dawn * (Kalman, Stothart)
1928 Good Boy * (co-lib. only)
1930 Nina Rosa (lib. only)
1931 The Cat and the Fiddle (Kern)
1932 Roberta (Kern)
1936 Forbidden Melody (Romberg)

Harburg, E. Y. ("Yip"), lyricist, librettist; b. New York, April 8, 1898. A socially conscious lyricist with an antic, puckish sense of humor, Harburg scored his biggest Bway hits with *Bloomer Girl* ("Right as the Rain," "Evelina"), music by Harold Arlen, and *Finian's Rainbow* ("How Are Things in Glocca Morra?," "Look to the Rainbow," "Old Devil Moon," "If This Isn't Love," "When I'm Not Near the Girl I Love"), music by Burton Lane. Other songs with Arlen include "Let's Take a Walk Around the Block" (lyric with Ira Gershwin) for *Life Begins at 8:40;* "Moanin' in the Mornin'" and "Down with Love" for *Hooray for What!;* "Cocoanut Sweet" for *Jamaica.* Other songs with Lane: "Don't Let It Get You Down" and "The World Is in My Arms" for *Hold on to Your Hats.* Harburg wrote his first Bway songs for the *Earl Carroll Sketch Book* (1929), music by Jay Gorney, with whom he also wrote "Brother, Can You Spare a Dime?" for *New Americana.* His lyrics have also been mated to the music of Lewis Gensler, Vernon Duke ("April in Paris," "I Like the Likes of You"), Sammy Fain ("Here's to Your Illusions," "He's Only Wonderful," "The World Is Your Balloon," "The Spring-time Cometh"), Jacques Offenbach, Jule Styne. *The Wizard of Oz* is Harburg's best-known film score.

1929 Earl Carroll Sketch Book (Gorney)
1930 Earl Carroll Vanities (Gorney)
1932 Ballyhoo of 1932 (Gensler)
      New Americana (misc.)
      Walk a Little Faster (Duke)
1934 Ziegfeld Follies (Duke)
      Life Begins at 8:40 (Arlen, Gershwin)
1937 Hooray for What! (Arlen)
1940 Hold on to Your Hats (Lane)
1946 Bloomer Girl (Arlen)
1947 Finian's Rainbow (Lane) (also co-lib.)
1951 Flahooley (Fain) (also co-lib., dir.)
1957 Jamaica (Arlen) (also co-lib.)
1961 The Happiest Girl in the World (Offenbach)
1968 Darling of the Day (Styne)

"Harlem on My Mind." Music & lyric by Irving Berlin. In the topical revue *As Thousands Cheer* (NY 1933), Ethel Waters, as Josephine Baker, is bored with her luxurious Parisian surroundings and longs to return to her old hi-de-ho haunts.

Harnick, Sheldon (Mayer), lyricist; b. Chicago, Ill., Dec. 27, 1924. With composer Jerry Bock, Harnick has created Bway scores that are noted for capturing the locale and color of their subjects, ranging from NY of the 20s and 30s in *Fiorello!* ("Little Tin Box") to Mitteleuropa of the 30s in *She Loves Me* ("Will He Like Me?," "She Loves Me") to a Jewish village in czarist Russia in his biggest hit, *Fiddler on the Roof* ("Matchmaker, Matchmaker," "If I Were a Rich Man," "Sunrise, Sunset," "Miracle of Miracles"). Harnick, who has also collaborated with composer David Baker, wrote songs for revues before teaming with Bock (incl. "The Boston Beguine" in *New Faces of 1952*). He is married to actress Margery Gray.

Unless otherwise noted, following were written with Mr. Bock:

1958 The Body Beautiful
1959 Fiorello!
1960 Tenderloin
1961 Smiling the Boy Fell Dead (Baker)
1963 She Loves Me
1964 Fiddler on the Roof
1966 The Apple Tree
1970 The Rothschilds

"Harrigan." Music & lyric by George M. Cohan. Sung by James C. Marlowe in *Fifty Miles from Boston* (NY 1908). Though this orthographic song is a self-description of a proud and apparently beloved Irish character in the play, it was also written as a tribute to Edward Harrigan, the writer-actor best known for his pioneering *Mulligan Guards* musicals. The number was also sung by Joel Grey in *George M!* (NY 1968).

Harrigan, Edward ("Ned"), actor, librettist, lyricist, director, producer; b. New York, Oct. 26, 1844; d. New York, June 6, 1911. Harrigan wrote and directed a series of "knockdown and slapbang" farces with music in which he appeared with his partner, Tony Hart. These shows, mostly about the Mulligan Guards, were the first to deal with recent Irish, German, Italian, and Jewish immigrants, and included topical songs written by Harrigan and composer David Braham. Harrigan was the father-in-law of director Joshua Logan. Bib: *The Merry Partners* by E. J. Kahn (Random, NY 1955).

Asterisk indicates appearance with Mr. Hart:

1878 Old Lavender * (*George Coggswell*)
     The Mulligan Guards' Picnic * (*Dan Mulligan*)
1879 The Mulligan Guards' Ball * (*Dan Mulligan*)
     The Mulligan Guards' Chowder * (*Dan Mulligan*)
     The Mulligan Guards' Christmas * (*Dan Mulligan*)
1880 The Mulligan Guards' Surprise * (*Dan Mulligan*)
     The Mulligan Guards' Nominee * (*Dan Mulligan*)
     The Mulligans' Silver Wedding * (*Dan Mulligan*)
1881 The Major * (*Major Gilfeather*)
1882 Squatter Sovereignty * (*Felix McIntyre*)
     Mordecai Lyons * (*Mordecai*)
     McSorley's Inflation * (*Peter McSorley*)
1883 The Muddy Day * (*Roger McNab*)
     Cordelia's Aspirations * (*Dan Mulligan*)
1884 Dan's Tribulations * (*Dan Mulligan*)
     Investigation * (*DeArcy Flynn*)
1885 McAllister's Legacy * (*Dr. McAllister*)
     The Grip (*Patrick Reilly*)
1886 The Leather Patch (*Jeremiah McCarthy*)
     The O'Reagans (*Bernard O'Reagan*)
1887 McNooney's Visit (*Martin McNooney*)
     Pete (*Pete*)
1888 Waddy Googan (*Waddy Googan*)
1889 The Lorgaire (*Lorgaire*)
1890 Reilly and the Four Hundred (*Wily Reilly*)
1891 The Last of the Hogans (*Dominick McKeever*)
1893 The Woolen Stocking (*Larry McLarney*)

Harris, Barbara, actress, singer; b. Evanston, Ill., 1937. Round-faced, sandpaper-voiced actress specializing in "kookie" characters.

1965 On a Clear Day You Can See Forever (*Daisy Gamble*)
1966 The Apple Tree (*Eve; Barbára; Ella*)
1970 Mahagonny (r) (*Jenny*)

Harris, Sam H., producer; b. New York, Feb. 3, 1872; d. New York, July

3, 1941. Between 1904 and 1920 Harris and George M. Cohan were associated with 18 Bway musicals, of which 15 were by Cohan, who also appeared in seven of them. Harris produced seven shows by songwriter Irving Berlin (incl. four *Music Box Revues*, *As Thousands Cheer*), plus others by George ·and Ira Gershwin (*Of Thee I Sing*), Cole Porter (*Jubilee*), Rodgers and Hart (*I'd Rather Be Right*), Kurt Weill and Ira Gershwin (*Lady in the Dark*). Among actors who appeared in Harris productions: Victor Moore (3), William Gaxton (3), Marx Brothers (2), Clark and McCullough (2); also Raymond Hitchcock, Fanny Brice, Clifton Webb, Marilyn Miller, Ethel Waters, Gertrude Lawrence.

Asterisk indicates Cohan and Harris production:

1904 Little Johnny Jones
1906 George Washington, Jr.
1907 The Honeymooners
The Talk of New York *
1908 Fifty Miles from Boston *
The Yankee Prince *
The American Idea *
1909 The Man Who Owns Broadway *
1911 The Little Millionaire *
The Red Widow *
1912 Forty-Five Minutes from Broadway * (r)
1914 The Beauty Shop
Hello, Broadway *
1916 The Cohan Revue *
1917 Going Up *
The Cohan Revue *
1918 The Voice of McConnell *
1919 The Royal Vagabond *
1920 Honey Girl
1921 Music Box Revue
1922 Music Box Revue
1923 Music Box Revue
1924 Music Box Revue
1925 The Cocoanuts
1928 Animal Crackers
1931 Of Thee I Sing
Face the Music
1933 As Thousands Cheer
Let 'Em Eat Cake
1935 Jubilee

1937 I'd Rather Be Right
1941 Lady in the Dark

Harrison, (Reginald Carey) Rex, actor; b. Huyton, Eng., March 5, 1908. Dramatic actor who has appeared on both London and Bway stages (*Design for Living, Anne of a Thousand Days*) and in films. He introduced songs "The Rain in Spain" and "I've Grown Accustomed to Her Face" in his only musical, *My Fair Lady*. Bib: *Rex* by Harrison (Morrow, NY 1974).

1956 My Fair Lady (NY) (*Henry Higgins*)
1958 My Fair Lady (L) (*Henry Higgins*)

Hart, Lorenz (Milton), lyricist, librettist; b. New York, May 2, 1895; d. New York, Nov. 22, 1943. With composer Richard Rodgers, his only Bway collaborator, Hart was responsible for many varied, innovative musicals. As a lyricist, he was noted for his originality of themes, his talent for multisyllabic rhyming, and his bittersweet wit.

Rodgers and Hart teamed up in 1919 and first won notice with their score for *The Garrick Gaieties* (incl. "Manhattan"). They continued on Bway (and occasionally London) through 1931, contributing scores for *Dearest Enemy* ("Here in My Arms"), *Peggy-Ann* ("Where's That Rainbow?"), *A Connecticut Yankee* ("My Heart Stood Still," "Thou Swell"), and *Ever Green* ("Dancing on the Ceiling"). After a period writing for Hollywood films (incl. *Love Me Tonight*), they resumed their Bway career with *Jumbo* ("The Most Beautiful Girl in the World," "My Romance," "Little Girl Blue"), *On Your Toes* ("There's a Small Hotel," "Glad to Be Unhappy," "Slaughter on Tenth Avenue"), *Babes in Arms* ("My Funny Valentine," "Johnny One Note," "The Lady Is a Tramp," "Where or When"),

I'd Rather Be Right ("Have You Met Miss Jones?"), I Married an Angel ("I Married an Angel," "Spring Is Here"), The Boys from Syracuse ("Falling in Love with Love," "This Can't Be Love"), Pal Joey ("Bewitched," "I Could Write a Book"). Other songs included "The Blue Room" (The Girl Friend), "Mountain Greenery" (second Garrick Gaieties), "You Took Advantage of Me" (Present Arms), "With a Song in My Heart" (Spring Is Here), "A Ship Without a Sail" (Heads Up), "Ten Cents a Dance" (Simple Simon), "I Didn't Know What Time It Was" (Too Many Girls), "Wait Till You See Her" (By Jupiter), "To Keep My Love Alive" (revised Connecticut Yankee). Helen Ford, Ray Bolger, and Vivienne Segal were each in three Rodgers and Hart musicals, Jessie Matthews was in two. Bib: The Rodgers and Hart Song Book (S&S, NY 1951); Musical Stages by Richard Rodgers (Random, NY 1975).

1920	Poor Little Ritz Girl
1925	The Garrick Gaieties
	Dearest Enemy
1926	The Girl Friend
	The Garrick Gaieties
	Lido Lady (L)
	Peggy-Ann
	Betsy
1927	One Dam Thing After Another (L)
	A Connecticut Yankee
1928	She's My Baby
	Present Arms
	Chee-Chee
1929	Spring Is Here
	Heads Up!
1930	Simple Simon
	Ever Green (L)
1931	America's Sweetheart
1935	Jumbo
1936	On Your Toes (also co-lib.)
1937	Babes in Arms (also co-lib.)
	I'd Rather Be Right
1938	I Married an Angel (also co-lib.)
	The Boys from Syracuse
1939	Too Many Girls
1940	Higher and Higher
	Pal Joey
1941	By Jupiter
1943	A Connecticut Yankee (r)

Hart, Moss, librettist, director; b. New York, Oct. 24, 1904; d. Palm Springs, Cal., Dec. 20, 1961. Hart won greatest musical-comedy acclaim on Bway as sketch writer of As Thousands Cheer, librettist of Lady in the Dark, and director of My Fair Lady. With George S. Kaufman he wrote three musicals and five nonmusicals (incl. Once in a Lifetime, You Can't Take It with You, The Man Who Came to Dinner). Hart, who also contributed sketches to revues (The Show Is On, Inside USA), was associated with composer Irving Berlin on three productions, with Lerner and Loewe on two. He was married to actress Kitty Carlisle. Bib: Act One by Hart (Random, NY 1959).

Unless otherwise noted, Mr. Hart was librettist, co-librettist, or sketch writer of following:

1932	Face the Music
1933	As Thousands Cheer
1934	The Great Waltz
1935	Jubilee
1937	I'd Rather Be Right
1938	Sing Out the News (also co-prod.)
1941	Lady in the Dark (also co-dir.)
1949	Miss Liberty (dir., co-prod. only)
1956	My Fair Lady (dir. only)
1960	Camelot (dir., co-prod. only)

Hart, Tony (né Anthony J. Cannon), actor, singer, producer; b. Worcester, Mass., July 25, 1855; d. Worcester, Nov. 4, 1891. With partner Edward Harrigan, Hart appeared in a series of "knockdown and slapbang" farces with music, mostly about the Mulligan Guards, which were the first to deal with recent Irish, German, Italian, and Jewish immigrants. All these shows had topical songs written by Harrigan and composer Davis Braham. Round-faced, angelic-looking

Hart usually played female roles. Bib: *The Merry Partners* by E. J. Kahn (Random, NY 1955).

All but last two shows were Harrigan and Hart productions:

1878 Old Lavender (*Dick the Warf Rat*)
      The Mulligan Guards' Picnic (*Rebecca Allup*)
1879 The Mulligan Guards' Ball (*Rebecca Allup*)
      The Mulligan Guards' Chowder (*Rebecca Allup*)
      The Mulligan Guards' Christmas (*Rebecca Allup*)
1880 The Mulligan Guards' Surprise (*Rebecca Allup*)
      The Mulligan Guards' Nominee (*Rebecca Allup*)
      The Mulligans' Silver Wedding (*Dennis Mulligan*)
1881 The Major ('*Enry 'Iggins*)
1882 Squatter Sovereignty (*Widow Nolan*)
      Mordecai Lyons (*Leon Mendoza*)
      McSorley's Inflation (*Bridget McSorley*)
1883 The Muddy Day (*Mary Ann O'Leary*)
      Cordelia's Aspirations (*Rebecca Allup*)
1884 Dan's Tribulations (*Rebecca Allup*)
      Investigation (*Bernard McKenna*)
1885 McAlliser's Legacy (*Molly McGoldrick*)
1886 The Maid and the Moonshiner (*Upton O. Dodge*)
      Donnybrook (*Con O'Grady*)

"Has Anybody Here Seen Kelly?" Music & lyric by C. W. Murphy & Will Letters; American version by William McKenna. Sung by Nora Bayes in *The Jolly Bachelors* (NY 1909). Under its original title, "Kelly from the Isle of Man," this number was popular in British music halls, but NY audiences were confused by its local references. Lyricist McKenna was then called in to write a new version, substituting "Emerald Isle" for "Isle of Man," and using the first line of the song as the title. That did it. The plaint of the Irish lass who loses her sweetheart in New York became the hit of the show and a perennial Nora Bayes favorite.

"Has Anybody Seen Our Ship?" Music & lyric by Noël Coward. Playing a third-rate music-hall team, Noël Coward and Gertrude Lawrence, in sailor suits and red wigs and carrying telescopes, bounded on stage to offer this raffish plaint of two boozy sailors whose ship has sailed off without them. The number was performed in the one-act musical *Red Peppers,* included in the collection *Tonight at 8:30* (L, NY 1936).

Hassall, Christopher, lyricist; b. London, March 24, 1912; d. London, April 25, 1963. Hassall, who began his career as an actor in London (1932–1948), supplied the lyrics for Ivor Novello's greatest hits, incl. *Glamorous Night* ("Fold Your Wings," "Glamorous Night"), *Careless Rapture, The Dancing Years* ("Waltz of My Heart," "I Can Give You the Starlight"), *King's Rhapsody* ("Someday My Heart Will Awake"). He also wrote with composers Anthony Spurgin, Michael Sayer, and Harry Parr Davies.

1932 The Oxford Blazers (Spurgin, Sayer) (also actor)
1935 Glamorous Night (Novello)
1936 Careless Rapture (Novello)
1937 Crest of the Wave (Novello)
1939 The Dancing Years (Novello)
1943 Arc de Triomphe (Novello)
1949 King's Rhapsody (Novello)
1950 Dear Miss Phoebe (Davies) (also lib.)

"Haunted Heart." Music by Arthur Schwartz; lyric by Howard Dietz. Presented in a San Francisco waterfront setting in the revue *Inside USA* (NY

1948), the suitably haunting torch ballad was sung by John Tyers and danced by Valerie Bettis, with J. C. McCord, George Reich, and Rod Alexander.

"Have You Met Miss Jones?" Music by Richard Rodgers; lyric by Lorenz Hart. Sung by Austin Marshall and Joy Hodges as a self-introduction to President Roosevelt's cabinet in *I'd Rather Be Right* (NY 1937). In London revue, *All Clear* (1939), it was sung by Bobby Howes.

Hayward, Leland, producer; b. Nebraska City, Neb., Sept. 13, 1902; d. Yorktown Hts., NY, March 18, 1971. Former publicist and talent agent who produced dramas on Bway (incl. *State of the Union, Mister Roberts*) in addition to musicals.
- 1949 South Pacific
- 1950 Call Me Madam
- 1952 Wish You Were Here
- 1959 Gypsy
  The Sound of Music
- 1962 Mr. President

Hazell, Hy (née Hyacinth Hazel O'Higgins), actress, singer; b. London, Oct. 4, 1922; d. London, May 10, 1970. Brassy actress-singer whose biggest London hits were *Lock Up Your Daughters* (in which she sang "When Does the Ravishing Begin?") and *Charlie Girl*. She also introduced "Time" in *Expresso Bongo*.
- 1937 On Your Toes (chorus)
- 1947 Here, There and Everywhere
- 1958 Expresso Bongo (*Dixie Collins*)
- 1959 Lock Up Your Daughters (*Mrs. Squeezum*)
- 1960 Innocent as Hell (*Inez Packard*)
- 1962 Lock Up Your Daughters (r) (*Mrs. Squeezum*)
- 1963 No Strings (*Mollie Plummer*)
- 1965 Charlie Girl (*Kay Connor*)
- 1968 The Beggar's Opera (r) (*Mrs. Peachum*)

- 1969 Ann Veronica (*Miss Miniver*)
  Fiddler on the Roof (*Golde*, repl.)

"He Loves and She Loves." Music by George Gershwin; lyric by Ira Gershwin. Romantic desire delicately expressed by Adele Astaire and Allen Kearns in *Funny Face* (NY 1927) and also sung by Miss Astaire and Bernard Clifton in London version (1928). The song, which replaced "How Long Has This Been Going On?" during the tryout, was developed from four bars ("I love and you love and he loves and she loves") in the previously written "Something About Love," lyric by Lou Paley.

"He Wears a Pair of Silver Wings." Music by Michael Carr; lyric by Eric Maschwitz. Love ballad written as a tribute to the British Air Force and sung by Frances Day in London revue *Black Vanities* (1941).

"Heart." Music and lyric by Richard Adler & Jerry Ross. A comically exaggerated inspirational song sung by a baseball-playing foursome (Russ Brown, Jimmie Komack, Nathaniel Frey, Albert Linville) in *Damn Yankees* (NY 1955). In London version (1957), it was sung by Donald Stewart, Robin Hunter, Edward Devereaux, Robert Crane.

"Heat Wave." Music & lyric by Irving Berlin. Ethel Waters as the syncopated weather report ("Heat Wave Hits New York") in the newspaper revue *As Thousands Cheer* (NY 1933). Also in the number were dancers Letitia Ide, José Limon, and the Charles Weidman Dancers. For a time radio censors forced the substitution of the word "feet" for "seat" in the line, "She started the heat wave by making her seat wave."

"Heather on the Hill, The." Music by Frederick Loewe; lyric by Alan Jay Lerner. Mist-shrouded ballad sung by David Brooks and Marion Bell in *Brigadoon* (NY 1947), and by Philip Hanna and Patricia Hughes in London version (1949).

"Heaven Will Protect the Working Girl." Music by A. Baldwin Sloane; lyric by Edgar Smith. Tongue-in-cheek number, sung by Marie Dressler in *Tillie's Nightmare* (NY 1909), which satirized heartrending ballads of the late 19th century. Sloane had based his melody on the verse to the 1898 tearjerker "She Was Bred in Old Kentucky."

Helburn, Theresa, producer; b. New York, Jan. 12, 1887; d. Weston, Conn., Aug. 18, 1959. Bib: *A Wayward Quest* by Miss Helburn (1960). See **Theatre Guild, The.**

Held, Anna, actress, singer; b. Warsaw, Poland, March 18, 1873; d. New York, Aug. 13, 1918. With her wide eyes, hour-glass figure, and flashing hand mirror, coquettish Anna Held became one of the earliest French entertainers to capture Bway. Though raised in Paris, she made her singing debut in London music halls, then became a cabaret attraction in Paris and Berlin. Producer Florenz Ziegfeld brought her to NY, married her, starred her in all but her second and last Bway appearances, and divorced her. Among songs identified with Miss Held: "Won't You Come and Play with Me?," "I Just Can't Make My Eyes Behave," "It's Delightful to Be Married."

1896   A Parlor Match (r) (*Lucille*)
1897   La Poupée (*Alesia*)
1899   Papa's Wife (*Anna*)
1901   The Little Duchess (*Niniche*)
1903   Mam'selle Napoleon (*Mlle. Mars*)
1904   Higgledy Piggledy (*Mimi de Chartreuse*)
1906   The Parisian Model (*Anna*)
1908   Miss Innocence (*Anna*)
1916   Follow Me (*Claire LaTour*)

Hello, Dolly! (1964). Music & lyrics by Jerry Herman; book by Michael Stewart, based on Thornton Wilder's play *The Matchmaker*, adapted from his previous play *The Merchant of Yonkers*, founded on Johann Nestroy's Viennese play *Einen Jux Will Er Sich Machen*, which stemmed from John Oxenford's English play *A Day Well Spent*.

SONGS: "It Takes a Woman," "Put on Your Sunday Clothes," "Ribbons Down My Back," "Before the Parade Passes By" (music & lyric with Charles Strouse & Lee Adams), "Elegance," "Dancing," "Motherhood," "Hello, Dolly!," "It Only Takes a Moment," "So Long, Dearie."

NEW YORK: Jan. 16, 1964
ST. JAMES THEATRE; 2,844 p.

Presented by David Merrick; directed & choreographed by Gower Champion; settings, Oliver Smith; costumes, Freddy Wittop; lighting, Jean Rosenthal; music director, Shepard Coleman; orchestrations, Philip J. Lang.

CAST: Carol Channing (*Dolly Gallagher Levi*), David Burns (*Horace Vandergelder*), Eileen Brennan (*Irene Molloy*), Sondra Lee (*Minnie Fay*), Charles Nelson Reilly (*Cornelius Hackl*), Jerry Dodge (*Barnaby Tucker*), Gordon Connell (*Judge*), Alice Playten (*Ermengarde*), Barbara Sharma (dancer).

LONDON: Dec. 2, 1965
DRURY LANE THEATRE; 794 p.

Presented by H. M. Tennent Ltd.; directed & choreographed by Gower Champion; settings, Oliver Smith; costumes, Freddy Wittop; lighting,

Joe Davis; music director, Alyn Ainsworth; orchestrations, Philip J. Lang.

CAST: Mary Martin (*Dolly Gallagher Levi*), Loring Smith (*Horace Vandergelder*), Marilynn Lovell (*Irene Molloy*), Coco Ramirez (*Minnie Fay*), Garrett Lewis (*Cornelius Hackl*), Johnny Beecher (*Barnaby Tucker*)

Though it had a shaky pre-Bway tryout, requiring the help of new writers, the changing of the first-act finale, and the addition of four songs, *Hello, Dolly!* went on to set the record for the longest-running Bway musical (it's since been overtaken by *Fiddler on the Roof*). Originally intended for but rejected by Ethel Merman, the musical was initially announced as *Dolly: A Damned Exasperating Woman*, a title that was changed to *Call on Dolly*, and eventually *Hello, Dolly!* Opening night reviews were full of praise for Carol Channing and particularly director Gower Champion. In the story, Dolly Gallagher Levi, a NY matchmaker of the 1890s, succeeds not only in helping three young couples but also manages to snare a rich Yonkers merchant, Horace Vandergelder, for herself. Dolly's big moment—as well as the musical's—occurs in the second scene of Act II when the lady makes a grand reappearance at the Harmonia Gardens Restaurant. Despite the multiplicity of credited plot derivations, *Hello, Dolly!* also claims kinship with the turn-of-the-century musical *A Trip to Chinatown*. In both productions, young couples, aided by a widow, spend a frantic evening at a gala restaurant trying to avoid detection by a wealthy gentleman. Both shows end with the gentleman stuck with the bills and unable to pay because his wallet is missing.

During NY run, Miss Channing was succeeded by Ginger Rogers (8-65), Martha Raye (2-67), Betty Grable (6-67), Bibi Osterwald (11-67), Pearl Bailey (heading an all-Negro cast beginning 11-67, and frequently spelled by Thelma Carpenter), Phyllis Diller (12-69), and Ethel Merman (3-70). David Brooks was succeeded by Max Showalter (3-67), Cab Calloway (11-67), Richard Deacon (12-69), and Jack Goode (3-70). Russell Nype played Cornelius during Miss Merman's tenure.

A touring company, headed by Mary Martin and Loring Smith, opened in April 1965 and performed in 11 US cities, plus Tokyo, South Vietnam, Korea, and Okinawa, before beginning a run in London. In May 1966 Dora Bryan became Dolly and Bernard Spear was Horace. A second US touring company, headed by Miss Channing and Horace MacMahon, began its travels Sept. 1965. During its two-year, nine-month journey, Eve Arden replaced ·Miss Channing for four months, and in Nov. 1967 Dorothy Lamour took over. A third road company, headed by Betty Grable—and later by both Ginger Rogers and Dorothy Lamour—toured for two years, four months.

FILM VERSION: Barbra Streisand, Walter Matthau, Michael Crawford (20th Cent. 1969, Gene Kelly dir.).

"Hello, Dolly!" Music & lyric by Jerry Herman. A turn-of-the-century-type song for Carol Channing and waiters in *Hello, Dolly!* (NY 1964). The number, performed at the Harmonia Gardens in the second scene of Act II, spotlights an elegantly dolled-up Dolly making her entrance down a flight of stairs. The reappearance of the lady at a once-favored haunt so energizes the waiters that they race through a split .second whirlwind galop, manipulating trays, food, and shish-kebab skewers, and end by strutting with Dolly across a runway in front of the orchestra pit. In London version (1965), Mary Martin led the celebration. Songwriter Herman was sued by writer Mack David, who claimed that the song's main four-bar theme was the same as his 1948 song, "Sunflower." The case was settled out of court and David was awarded $250,000. Other high-stepping serenades in Jerry Herman's musicals were "Mame" (*Mame*) and "When Mabel Comes in the Room" (*Mack & Mabel*).

"Hello, Frisco." Music by Louis Hirsch; lyric by Gene Buck. Ina Claire and Bernard Granville introduced the number in the *Ziegfeld Follies of 1915*. One story has it that Ziegfeld, trying to make a long-distance call to San Francisco, impatiently asked, "Hello—Frisco? Hello?" Gene Buck, the producer's assistant, overheard him, and got the idea for the lyric.

"Hello, Young Lovers." Music by Richard Rodgers; lyric by Oscar Hammerstein II. Gertrude Lawrence introduced this song in *The King and I* (NY 1951) as she thinks of her dead husband and counsels young lovers to be "brave and faithful and true." In London production (1953), it was sung by Valerie Hobson.

Hellzapoppin (1938). Music by Sammy Fain, etc.; lyrics by Charles Tobias, etc.; sketches by Ole Olsen & Chic Johnson.
SONGS: "Fuddle Dee Duddle," "Abe Lincoln" (music & lyric, Earl Robinson & Alfred Hayes), "Strolling thru the Park," "Shaganola," "It's Time to Say Aloha," "Boomps-a-Daisy" (music & lyric, Annette Mills).

NEW YORK: Sept. 22, 1938
46TH ST. THEATRE; 1,404 p.
Presented by the Messrs. Shubert (uncredited) & Olsen & Johnson; directed by Edward Duryea Dowling; costumes, Veronica, Mahieu; music director, Harold Stern.
CAST: Ole Olsen & Chick Johnson, Dewey Barto & George Mann, The Radio Rogues, Hal Sherman, Ray Kinney & Aloha Maids, Walter Nilsson, The Charioteers, Bettymae & Beverly Crane, Theo Hardeen.

A raucous, rowdy show, more vaudeville than revue, *Hellzapoppin* was based on a madcap act Olsen and Johnson had been touring in for some 14 years. Within two months after its Bway opening the production was transferred to the Winter Garden, where it remained for the rest of its run. Despite largely negative reviews, the show caught on and became the longest-running musical in Bway history, a position it held until overtaken by *Oklahoma!* Audiences enjoyed its knockabout action, pellmell pace, and all kinds of audience-participation gimmicks, including dancing in the aisles. A memorable running gag was that of a man walking throughout the theatre with a growing plant intended for Mrs. Jones. In June 1940, Olsen and Johnson were succeeded by Happy Felton and J. C. Flippen. The show set the pattern for three subsequent Olsen and Johnson revues: *Sons o' Fun* opened in 1941 with Carmen Miranda and Ella Logan, and ran for 742 performances; *Laffing Room Only* in 1944 ran for 233; *Pardon Our French* in 1950 ran for 100.
FILM VERSION: Olsen & Johnson, Martha Raye (with story and new songs) (Univ. 1941, H. C. Potter dir.).

Henderson, Florence, actress, singer; b. Dale, Indiana, Feb. 14, 1934. Angelic-looking actress-singer who

Reid Shelton (Daddy Warbucks), Andrea McArdle (Annie) and Sandy Faison (Warbuck's secretary) as they appeared in the long-run comic-strip musical, *Annie.* (Photo by Martha Swope.)

Annie Get Your Gun brought together **Ethel Merman**, co-producer **Richard Rodgers** and composer-lyricist **Irving Berlin.**

Bold face names indicate entries in book

In a sketch from the "newspaper revue," *As Thousands Cheer,* four hotel employees – **Ethel Waters, Marilyn Miller, Helen Broderick,** and **Clifton Webb** – fall under the influence of recent guest Noël Coward. (Photo by Vandamm.)

Fred and **Adele Astaire** at the time of *Smiles*.

Ray Bolger teaches his students "The Three B's" in an early scene from the pioneering ballet musical, *On Your Toes.* (Courtesy Lynn Farnol Group.)

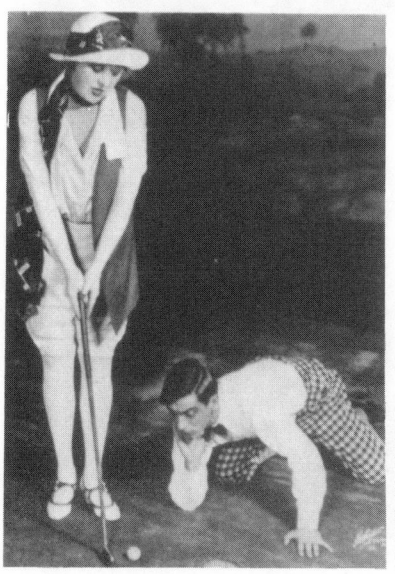

Caddy **Eddie Cantor** distracts Jobyna Howland in *Kid Boots*, the first "book" musical he appeared in on Broadway. (N.Y. Public Library.)

Bobby Clark, here chosen the *"Amigo Americano"* in *Mexican Hayride,* was one of the main reasons theatregoers lined up to see this wartime hit. (Courtesy Chappell Music.)

Yankee-Doodle-Boy
George M. Cohan.

In *Company,* Dean Jones is seen with the company he keeps – including the kneeling **Elaine Stritch.** (Photo by Martha Swope.)

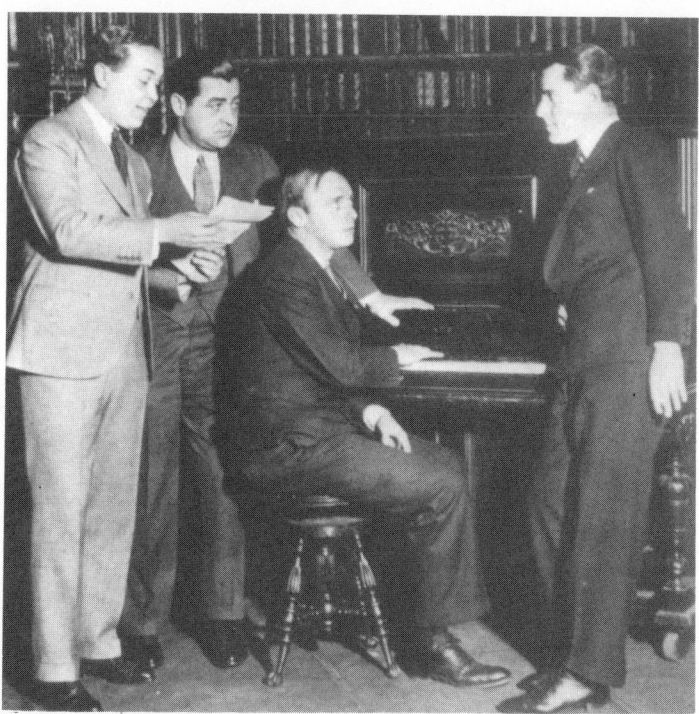

The **"Den of Iniquity"** scene in *Pal Joey* with patroness **Vivienne Segal** and hoofer **Gene Kelly.** (N.Y. Public Library.)

Songwriters **B.G. DeSylva, Lew Brown** and **Ray Henderson** audition a number for **George White**, impressario of the *George White's Scandals.* (Photo by N.Y. Daily News.)

Before joining her husband in Siberia in *Fiddler on the Roof*, Julia Migenes bids **Zero Mostel** a sad farewell. (Photo by Friedman-Abeles.)

George and **Ira Gershwin** at the time they were writing *Porgy and Bess*. (N.Y. Public Library.)

In *Hello, Dolly!*, **Carol Channing** is so thrilled to be back at the
Harmonia Gardens that she breaks into the title song.

A big advertising campaign in *How to Succeed in Business Without Really Trying* involves **Rudy Vallee**, Virginia Martin and **Robert Morse**. (Photo by Friedman-Abeles.)

"I'm Gonna Wash that Man Right Outa My Hair," sings **Mary Martin** in her great Broadway triumph, *South Pacific*. (Courtesy Lynn Farnol Group.)

Jerome Kern, the father of the modern musical theatre.

Knickerbocker Holiday was the musical in which **Walter Huston,** as Gov. Pieter Stuyvesant, sang his **"September Song"** to Jeanne Madden.

In 1977, a highly successful revival of *The King and I* brought back **Yul Brynner,** here indicating the twin status of two of his children during the "**March of the Siamese Children**" number. (Photo by Ernst Haas.)

The epitome of theatrical glamour — **Gertrude Lawrence** and **Noël Coward** strike a pose as they sing the title song from the one-act play, "We Were Dancing," part of Coward's *Tonight at 8:30* collection. (N.Y. Public Library.)

Queen **Bea Lillie** surrounded by co-star **Jack Haley**, lyricist **Howard Dietz** and composer **Arthur Schwartz** as they go through the numbers for *Inside U.S.A.* (Photo by Eileen Darby.)

A scene in *Man of La Mancha* in which Don Quixote (**Richard Kiley**), to the irritation of Sancho Panza (Irving Jacobson), mistakes a trollop (Gerrianne Raphael) for an innocent maid. (Photo by Arthur Cantor.)

The winning-ticket in *Of Thee I Sing* – John P. Wintergreen and Alexander Throttlebottom, also known as **William Gaxton** and **Victor Moore.** (N.Y. Public Library.)

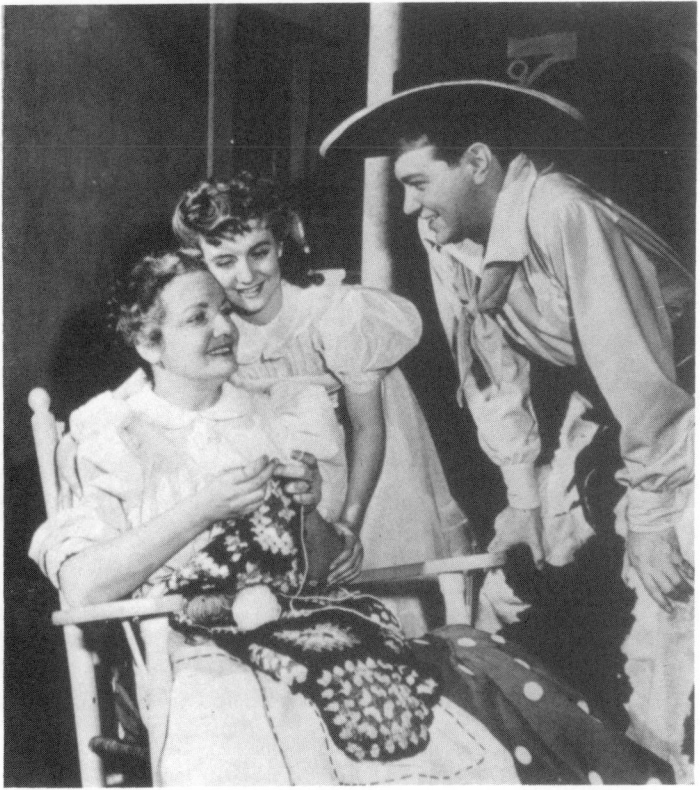

The first scene of the legendary *Oklahoma!* with Betty Garde, Joan Roberts and **Alfred Drake.** (Courtesy Lynn Farnol Group.)

In the cast of the original production of *Porgy and Bess* were J. Rosamond Johnson, Todd Duncan and Anne Brown. (N.Y. Public Library.)

Broadway's elegant **Cole Porter.**

The magical **"Rain in Spain"** sequence in *My Fair Lady* with Robert Coote, **Julie Andrews** and **Rex Harrison.** (Photo by Friedman-Abeles.)

Richard Rodgers (at the piano) with his first collaborator, **Lorenz Hart,** during a rehearsal of *Pal Joey.* (Courtesy Lynn Farnol Group.)

Richard Rodgers (with hand forward) with his second collaborator, **Oscar Hammerstein II** (hand on face) and director **Joshua Logan** during a rehearsal of *South Pacific* (Courtesy Lynn Farnol Group.)

The saga of **"Seventy-Six Trombones"** as recounted in *The Music Man* by **Robert Preston** to Marilyn Siegel.

Show Boat, Broadway's outstanding musical of the 20s, was successfully revived in 1946 with Ralph Dumke as Cap'n Andy and **Carol Bruce** as Julie. (Photo by Eileen Darby.)

Barbra Streisand, as Fanny Brice, is wooed by **Sydney Chaplin** in *Funny Girl.*

In West Side Story, star-crossed lovers **Larry Kert** and **Carol Lawrence** are obviously smitten, despite **Chita Rivera's** sceptical look. (Photo by Fred Fehl.)

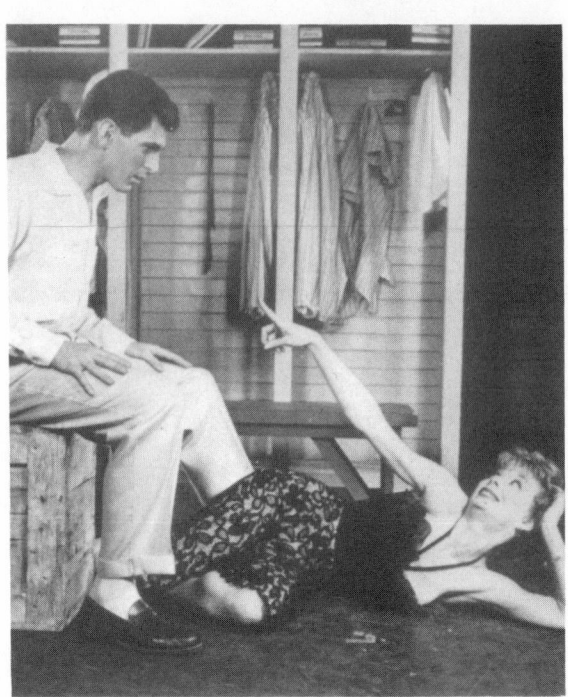

"Whatever Lola Wants" she obviously seems to be getting in this scene from *Damn Yankees* with baseball player Stephen Douglass and temptress **Gwen Verdon.** (Photo by Talbot.)

Great Glorifier **Florenz Ziegfeld.** (N.Y. Public Library.)

has also appeared on tv and in night-clubs.

1952 Wish You Were Here (*New Girl*)
      Oklahoma! (US tour) (*Laurey
      Williams*, repl.)
1954 Fanny (*Fanny*)
1961 The Sound of Music (US tour)
      (*Maria Rainer*)
1963 The Girl Who Came to Supper
      (*Mary Morgan*)

Henderson, Ray (né Raymond Brost), composer; b. Buffalo, NY, Dec. 1, 1896; d. Greenwich, Conn., Dec. 31, 1970. With co-lyricists B. G. DeSylva and Lew Brown, Henderson wrote scores for Bway musicals that reflected the youthful, carefree spirit of the Flapper Age. The trio's first song was "It All Depends on You" for *Big Boy,* and their first score was for *George White's Scandals* of 1925. For the next year's edition, they had two hits: "Lucky Day" and "The Birth of the Blues." Their biggest stage successes were *Good News!* ("The Best Things in Life Are Free," "Lucky in Love," "The Varsity Drag"), *Hold Everything!*("You're the Cream in My Coffee"), *Follow Thru* ("Button Up Your Overcoat"), *Flying High* ("Thank Your Father"). After DeSylva left the team, Brown and Henderson created songs for the 1931 *Scandals* ("Life Is Just a Bowl of Cherries," "This Is the Missus," "The Thrill Is Gone," "My Song"). Henderson also wrote with lyricists Ted Koehler, Jack Yellen, Irving Caesar. Willie and Eugene Howard and Bert Lahr were each in four Henderson musicals, Harry Richman was in three, Rudy Vallee and Ann Pennington were in two each.

Unless otherwise noted, the following were written with Messrs. Brown and DeSylva or with Mr. Brown alone; asterisk indicates Mr. Henderson was also co-producer:

1925 George White's Scandals
1926 George White's Scandals
1927 Good News!
      Manhattan Mary
1928 George White's Scandals
      Hold Everything!
1929 Follow Thru
1930 Flying High
1931 George White's Scandals
1932 Hot-Cha! (also co-lib.)
1933 Strike Me Pink * (also co-dir.)
1934 Say When * (Koehler)
1935 George White's Scandals (Yellen)
1936 Transatlantic Rhythm (L) (Caesar)
1943 Ziegfeld Follies (Yellen)

Heneker, David, composer, lyricist; b. Southsea, Eng., March 31, 1906. Heneker's biggest London hits were *Irma la Douce* ("Our Language of Love"), *Half a Sixpence* ("Half a Sixpence"), *Charlie Girl* ("Charlie Girl"). Before devoting full time to writing, he was a regular army officer, 1925–1948. His collaborators have been Julian More, Monty Norman, Marguerite Monnot, John Taylor, Percy French.

Unless otherwise noted, Mr. Heneker was composer-lyricist or co-composer–co-lyricist of following:

1958 Expresso Bongo (More, Norman)
      Irma la Douce (lyr. only w. More,
      Norman) (Monnot)
1959 Make Me an Offer (Norman)
1960 The Art of Living (More, Norman)
1963 Half a Sixpence
1965 Charlie Girl (Taylor)
1966 Jorrocks
1969 Phil the Fluter (French)
1972 Popkiss

Henson, Leslie, actor, director, producer; b. London, Aug. 3, 1891; d. Harrow Weald, Eng., Dec. 2, 1957. Frog-faced, frog-voiced Leslie Henson was one of London's leading stage clowns from his very first musical, *Tonight's the Night,* right through his entire career. From 1914 to 1926 he was associated with George Grossmith, with whom he appeared in six musicals; from 1929 to 1942, with producer Firth Shephard. Bib: *My Laugh*

Story (1926), *Yours Faithfully* (1948), both by Henson.

Asterisk indicated Mr. Henson was also co-producer and/or director:

1914   Tonight's the Night (NY) (*Henry*)
1915   Tonight's the Night (*Henry*)
1916   Theodore & Co. (*Pony Twitchin*)
1917   Yes, Uncle! (*Bobby Summers*)
1919   Kissing Time (*Bibi St. Pol*)
1920   A Night Out (*Joseph Pinglet*)
1921   Sally (*Connie*).
1923   The Cabaret Girl (*Mr. Gravvins,* repl.)
        The Beauty Prize (*Odo Philpotts*)
1924   Tonight's the Night (r) (*Henry*)
        Primrose (*Toby Mopham*)
1925   Tell Me More (*Monte Sipkin*)
1926   Kid Boots (*Kid Boots*)
1927   Lady Luck * (*Wyndham Bleugh*)
1928   So This Is Love (dir. only)
        Funny Face (*Dugsie Gibbs*)
1929   Follow Through * (*Jack Martin*)
1930   The Co-Optimists (dir. only)
1933   Nice Goings On * (*Olaf Henscuttle*)
1934   Lucky Break * (*Tommy Turtle*)
1935   Seeing Stars * (*Jimmy Swing*)
1936   Swing Along * (*Maxie Mumm*)
1937   On Your Toes (dir. only)
        Going Greek * (*Alexandros Saggappopolous*)
1938   Running Riot * (*Cornelius Crumpet*)
1940   Up and Doing *
1942   Fine and Dandy *
1945   The Gaieties *
1948   Bob's Your Uncle * (*Bob Popejoy*)
1951   And So to Bed (*Samuel Pepys*)

Hepburn, Katharine (Houghton), actress; b. Hartford, Conn., Nov. 9, 1909. Equine, flamboyant actress of Bway stage and films.

1969   Coco (*Coco Chanel*)

Herbert, A(lan) P(atrick), lyricist, librettist; b. Elstead, Eng., Sept. 24, 1870; d. London, Nov. 11, 1971. Knighted 1945. One of Britain's leading writers of light verse, Sir Alan was Independent member of Parliament, 1935–1950. He wrote five scores with Vivian Ellis (incl. songs "Other People's Babes," "This Is My Lovely Day," "Ma Belle Marguerite"); others with Frederick Austen, Alfred Reynolds, Thomas Dunhill, Jacques Offenbach, Oscar Straus, Nicholas Brodszky, Henry Sullivan, Franz Lehar. Bib:*A.P.H.—His Life and Times* by Herbert (1970).

1926   Riverside Nights (Austen, Reynolds)
1931   Tantivy Towers (Dunhill)
1932   Helen! (Offenbach)
        Derby Day (Reynolds)
1933   Mother of Pearl (Straus)
1934   Streamline (Ellis)
1937   Home and Beauty (Brodszky, Sullivan)
        Paganini (Lehar)
1946   Big Ben (Ellis)
1947   Bless the Bride (Ellis)
1949   Tough at the Top (Ellis)
1955   The Water Gipsies (Ellis)

Herbert, Evelyn (née Evelyn Houstellier), actress, singer; b. Philadelphia, Pa., 1898. Miss Herbert, who had an operatic career in Chicago and NY before Bway debut, won her greatest fame introducing "One Kiss," "Wanting You," and "Lover, Come Back to Me" in *The New Moon*. She is the wife of Robert Halliday, who played opposite her in three operettas.

1923.   Stepping Stones (*Lupina*)
1925   The Love Song (*Herminie*)
        Princess Flavia (*Princess Flavia*)
1926   The Merry World
1927   My Maryland (*Barbara Frietchie*)
1928   The New Moon (*Marianne Beaunoir*)
1930   Princess Charming (*Princess Elaine*)
1931   Waltzes from Vienna (L) (*Resi Ebeseder*)
1933   Melody (*Andrée de Nemours*)

Herbert, Victor, composer; b. Dublin, Ireland, Feb. 1, 1859; d. New York,

May 26, 1924. Herbert was the dominant composer for the Bway musical stage during the first two decades of the century. Trained in Germany, he helped maintain the tradition of Viennese operetta with a series of romantic scores, full of soaring ballads, lilting waltzes, and stirring marches.

After settling in NY, Herbert was first employed by the Metropolitan Opera as cellist. He later became director of the Pittsburgh Symphony (1898 – 1904), and was a leader in the formation of ASCAP (US performing rights society). Herbert's first Bway success was *The Serenade*. Other major works: *The Fortune Teller* ("Gypsy Love Song"), *Babes in Toyland* ("March of the Toys," "Toyland"), *Mlle. Modiste* ("Kiss Me Again," "I Want What I Want When I Want It"), *The Red Mill* ("When You're Pretty and the World Is Fair," "Moonbeams," "Every Day Is Ladies' Day with Me," "The Streets of New York"), *Naughty Marietta* ("Tramp! Tramp! Tramp!," "Italian Street Song," "Ah! Sweet Mystery of Life," "'Neath the Southern Moon," "I'm Falling in Love with Someone"), *Sweethearts* ("Sweethearts," "Every Lover Must Meet His Fate"), *The Only Girl* ("When You're Away"). He also composed "Thine Alone" (*Eileen*), "I Might Be Your Once-in-a-While" (*Angel Face*), "A Kiss in the Dark" (*Orange Blossoms*).

Herbert's most frequent lyric-writing partner was Harry B. Smith (13 scores). He also wrote with Henry Blossom (8), Glen MacDonough (5), Robert B. Smith (3), George V. Hobart (2), Rida Johnson Young (2), plus one score each with Francis Neilson, Frederic Ranken and Kirke La Shelle, Edgar Smith, Joseph Herbert, James O'Dea, David Stevens and Justin Huntly McCarthy, P. G. Wodehouse, William Le Baron, Frederic Kummer, B. G. DeSylva. Fritzi Scheff starred in four Herbert musicals, Alice Nielsen and Lew Fields in three each. Bib: *Victor Herbert: America's Greatest Romantic Composer* by Joseph Kaye (Watt, NY 1931); *Victor Herbert: American Music-Master* by Claire Lee Purdy (Messner, NY 1944); *Victor Herbert: A Life in Music* by Edward Waters (Macmillan, NY 1955).

1894	Prince Ananias (Neilson)
1895	The Wizard of the Nile (H. B. Smith)
1896	The Gold Bug (MacDonough)
1897	The Serenade (H. B. Smith)
	The Idol's Eye (H. B. Smith)
1898	The Fortune Teller (H. B. Smith)
1899	Cyrano de Bergerac (H. B. Smith)
	The Singing Girl (H. B. Smith)
	The Ameer (Ranken, La Shelle)
1900	The Viceroy (H. B. Smith)
1903	Babes in Toyland (MacDonough)
	Babette (H. B. Smith)
1904	It Happened in Nordland (MacDonough)
1905	Miss Dolly Dollars (H. B. Smith)
	Wonderland (MacDonough)
	Mlle. Modiste (Blossom)
1906	The Red Mill (Blossom)
	Dream City and the Magic Knight (E. Smith)
1907	The Tattooed Man (H. B. Smith)
1908	Algeria (MacDonough)
	Little Nemo (H. B. Smith)
	The Prima Donna (Blossom)
1909	Old Dutch (Hobart)
1910	Naughty Marietta (Young)
1911	When Sweet Sixteen (Hobart)
	The Duchess (J. Herbert, H. B. Smith)
	The Enchantress (H. B. Smith)
1912	The Lady of the Slipper (O'Dea)
1913	Sweethearts (R. B. Smith)
	The Madcap Duchess (Stevens, McCarthy)
1914	The Only Girl (Blossom)
	The Débutante (R. B. Smith)
1915	The Princess Pat (Blossom)
1916	The Century Girl (Blossom)
1917	Eileen (Blossom)
	Miss 1917 (Wodehouse)
	Her Regiment (Le Baron)
1919	The Velvet Lady (Blossom)
	Angel Face (R. B. Smith)

1920 My Golden Girl (Kummer)
The Girl in the Spotlight (R. B. Smith)
1922 Orange Blossoms (DeSylva)
1924 The Dream Girl (Young)

"Here and Now." Music & lyric by Noël Coward. Lilting ballad of unrestrained exuberance caused by falling in love. Introduced in *The Girl who Came to Supper* (NY 1963) by Florence Henderson.

"Here I'll Stay." Music by Kurt Weill; lyric by Alan Jay Lerner. Despite lure of fields of gold or isles of clover, Ray Middleton and Nanette Fabray affirmed their decision in *Love Life* (NY 1948) to remain where they were.

"Here in My Arms." Music by Richard Rodgers; lyric by Lorenz Hart. The main romantic duet in the Revolutionary War musical *Dearest Enemy* (NY 1925), sung by Helen Ford, as the American maid, and Charles Purcell, as the British officer. Phyllis Dare and Jack Hulbert sang it in London in *Lido Lady* (1926).

"Here's That Rainy Day." Music by James Van Heusen; lyric by Johnny Burke. Torch ballad ("Maybe I should have saved those left-over dreams") introduced by Dolores Gray in *Carnival in Flanders* (NY 1953).

"Here's to Your Illusions." Music by Sammy Fain; lyric by E. Y. Harburg. Two lovers delight in each other's hopes, dreams, and "sweet confusions." Barbara Cook and Jerome Courtland introduced the ballad in *Flahooley* (NY 1951).

Herman, (Gerald) Jerry, composer, lyricist; b. New York, July 10, 1932. After beginning with off-Bway musicals, Herman had a spectacular success with *Hello, Dolly!* ("Hello, Dolly!," "So Long, Dearie," "Before the Parade Passes By"), then followed it with another long-run hit, *Mame* ("Mame," "It's Today," "If He Walked into My Life").

1954 I Feel Wonderful
1960 Parade (also dir.)
1961 Milk and Honey
Madame Aphrodite
1964 Hello, Dolly!
1966 Mame
1969 Dear World
1974 Mack & Mabel
1979 The Grand Tour

"Hernando's Hideaway." Music & lyric by Richard Adler & Jerry Ross. Slinky comic tango sung in *The Pajama Game* (NY 1954) by Carol Haney, and danced by Miss Haney, John Raitt, and company (incl., in the chorus, Shirley MacLaine). In London production (1955) it was sung by Elizabeth Seal.

"He's Only Wonderful." Music by Sammy Fain; lyric by E. Y. Harburg. Unqualified adoration expressed by Barbara Cook—then reprised by Jerome Courtland (singing "She's Only Wonderful") and Miss Cook—in *Flahooley* (NY 1951).

"Hey, Look Me Over." Music by Cy Coleman; lyric by Carolyn Leigh. Introduced by Lucille Ball and Paula Stewart in *Wildcat* (NY 1960). Since this was to be the first song in the show sung by Miss Ball in her Broadway debut, the writers knew that it had to make an impression. At first they tried sophisticated, Broadway-type numbers, but they all sounded as if they had been written for Ethel Merman. After two weeks Miss Leigh said to her partner, "Cy, if you didn't care at all, if it wasn't the opening number and it wasn't for Lucille Ball, what kind of song would you write for the character and the scene?" Coleman answered, "Well, if this number weren't so important, I suppose I'd just write something as corny and simple as this. . . ." And he played the main theme of "Hey, Look Me Over."

"Hey, There." Music & lyric by Richard Adler & Jerry Ross. Sung by John Raitt in *The Pajama Game* (NY 1954) in the form of a memo he sends to himself via dictaphone. When he hears the playback, he interrupts it with his own comments, and ends by singing a duet with himself. In London version (1955) it was sung by Edmund Hockridge.

Hickman, Charles, director; b. Snaresbrook, Essex, Eng., Jan. 18, 1905. Formerly an actor, Hickman became a director in 1939. His most successful London musicals: *Sweet and Low* (three editions), *Song of Norway, Annie Get Your Gun, Zip Goes a Million, Love from Judy, Wedding in Paris.* He has also directed in Australia, So. Africa.

1942	Big Top (actor only)
1943	Sweet and Low
1944	Sweeter and Lower
	Keep Going
1946	Song of Norway
	Sweetest and Lowest
1947	The Red Mill (r)
	Annie Get Your Gun
1948	Cage Me a Peacock
	Slings and Arrows (also sk.)
1950	Dear Miss Phoebe
1951	Zip Goes a Million
1952	Love from Judy
1954	Wedding in Paris
1955	The Water Gipsies
1956	Summer Song
1963	All Square

Hicks, (Edward) Seymour, actor, singer, librettist, director; b. St. Helier's, Jersey, Jan. 30, 1871; d. Hampshire, Eng., April 6, 1949. Knighted 1935. Hicks was a slight, bland, foppish actor-writer of the early London musical stage whose most successful works included *The Shop Girl, The Circus Girl, A Runaway Girl, Bluebell in Fairyland, The Catch of the Season.* After making his acting debut at 16, he toured the provinces and appeared on Bway (1889–1891). He was leading man for George Edwardes for three years, then became associated with producer Charles Frohman, who built the Aldwych and Hicks Theatres for him. He was married to actress Ellaline Terriss, with whom he appeared in nine productions and whom he replaced in one (*The Dashing Little Duke*). Bib: *24 Years of an Actor's Life* (Rivers, L 1910), *Between Ourselves* (L 1930), *Me and My Missus* (Cassell, L 1939), all by Hicks.

Asterisk indicates appearance with Miss Terriss; dagger indicates Mr. Hicks was also librettist and/or director:

1893	Under the Clock †
1894	Little Jack Sheppard (*Jonathan Wild*)
	The Shop Girl * (*Charley Appleby*)
1895	Papa's Wife † (*Gerald Singleton*)
	The Shop Girl (NY) (*Charley Appleby*)
1896	The Circus Girl * (*Dick Capel*)
1897	The Yashmak (co-lib. only)
1898	A Runaway Girl (co-lib. only)
1901	Bluebell in Fairyland * † (*Dicky*)
1903	The Cherry Girl * † (*Moonshine, Happy Joe*)
1904	The Catch of the Season * † (*Duke of St. Jermyns*)
1906	The Beauty of Bath * † (*Lt. Richard Alington*)
1907	My Darling (lib., dir. only)
	The Gay Gordons * † (*Angus Graeme*)
1909	The Dashing Little Duke † (*Duc de Richelieu,* repl.)
1910	Captain Kidd * † (*Viscount Albany*)
1913	All the Winners
1916	The Happy Day (lib. only)
1917	Cash on Delivery * † (*Face Bell*)
1918	Jolly Jack Tar (lib. only)

1920 The Shop Girl (r) (dir., co-prod. only)
A Little Dutch Girl (co-lib. only)
1923 Head Over Heels (lib. only)

High Button Shoes (1947). Music by Jule Styne; lyrics by Sammy Cahn; book by George Abbott & Phil Silvers (uncredited), based on Stephen Longstreet's novel *The Sisters Liked Them Handsome.*

SONGS: "Can't You Just See Yourself?," "There's Nothing Like a Model T," "You're My Girl," "Papa, Won't You Dance with Me?," "On a Sunday by the Sea," "I Still Get Jealous," "Nobody Ever Died for Dear Old Rutgers."

NEW YORK: Oct. 9, 1947
NEW CENTURY THEATRE; 727 p.

Presented by Monte Proser & Joseph Kipness; directed by George Abbott; choreographed by Jerome Robbins; settings, Oliver Smith; costumes, Miles White; music director, Milton Rosenstock; orchestrations, Philip J. Lang.

CAST: Phil Silvers (*Harrison Floy*), Nanette Fabray (*Sara Longstreet*), Jack McCauley (*Henry Longstreet*), Mark Dawson (*Oggle Ogglethorpe*), Joey Faye (*Mr. Pontdue*), Lois Lee (*Fran*), Helen Gallagher (*Nancy*), Paul Godkin (*Uncle Willie*), Johnny Stewart (*Stevie Longstreet*), Nathaniel Frey (*Elmer Simpkins*), Sondra Lee (dancer).

LONDON: Dec. 22, 1948
HIPPODROME; 291 p.

Presented by Jack Hylton; directed by Robert Nesbitt & Archie Thomson; dances reproduced by Fred Hearn; settings, Alick Johnstone; costumes, Alec Shanks, Slade Lucas; music director, Freddie Bretherton.

CAST: Lew Parker (*Harrison Floy*), Kay Kimber (*Sara Longstreet*), Sidney James (*Henry Longstreet*), Jack Coo-

per (*Oggle Ogglethorpe*), Tommy Godfrey (*Mr. Pontdue*), Hermene French (*Fran*), Joan Heal (*Nancy*), Peter Felgate (*Uncle Willie*), Michael Nicholls (*Stevie Longstreet*), James Ramsey (*Elmer Simpkins*).

Phil Silvers' first starring role was in a musical adaptation of Stephen Longstreet's semi-autobiographical account of his family and its encounter with a con artist. Set in New Brunswick, NJ, in 1913, the story relates how Harrison Floy tries to help the Longstreets by selling off some swamp property they own. He escapes to Atlantic City with the proceeds but the money is stolen; once it is recovered, he loses it again by betting on the Princeton football team over Rutgers. After failing at other money-making schemes, Floy makes his final getaway. The musical, which marked the first Bway score by Jule Styne and Sammy Cahn, also helped establish the careers of Nanette Fabray and choreographer Jerome Robbins, whose Mack Sennett Keystone Kops chase was a memorably hilarious ballet. During Bway run, Miss Fabray was succeeded by Joan Roberts and Carol Stone; Paul Godkin by Donald Saddler; Phil Silvers by Joey Faye (5-49); Faye by Jack Albertson (5-49). The musical toured with Eddie Foy Jr. as Floy.

"High Hat." Music by George Gershwin; lyric by Ira Gershwin. In which gentlemen are informed that the quickest way to make girls "come around" is to treat 'em high hat. Fred Astaire introduced the brisk number in *Funny Face* (NY 1927, L 1928), in which, for the first time, he appeared with a line of top-hatted chorus boys.

Hines, Elizabeth, actress, singer, dancer; b. Albany, NY, 1894; d. Lake

Forest, Ill., Feb. 19, 1971. Leading lady of early 20s best remembered as heroine of *Little Nellie Kelly.*

1916 Molly O' (chorus)
1917 Oh, Boy! (US tour) (dancer)
1919 See-Saw (*Helen*)
1921 Love Birds (*Allene Charteris*)
     The O'Brien Girl (*Alice O'Brien*)
1922 Little Nellie Kelly (*Nellie Kelly*)
1924 Marjorie (*Marjorie Daw*)
1925 June Days (*Elise Benedotti*)
1926 Cochran's Revue of 1926 (L)

Hirsch, Louis A(chille), composer; b. New York, Nov. 28, 1887; d. New York, May 13, 1924. Hirsch's chief Bway songs were "The Tickle Toe" (*Going Up*) and "The Love Nest" (*Mary*). After beginning his career writing for Lew Dockstader's Minstrels, he became a staff composer for the Shubert brothers, 1910–1912. Lyricists he worked with include Edward Madden, Harold Atteridge, Arthur George, Gene Buck, Channing Pollock, Rennold Wolf, Otto Harbach, P. G. Wodehouse, Earl Derr Biggers, John Murray Anderson, Irving Caesar.

1910 He Came from Milwaukee (Madden)
1911 The Revue of Revues (Atteridge)
     Vera Violetta (Atteridge)
1912 The Whirl of Society (Atteridge)
     The Passing Show (Atteridge)
     Hullo, Ragtime! (L) (George)
1913 Hullo, Tango! (L) (George)
1914 Honeymoon Express (L) (George)
     Dora's Doze (L) (George)
1915 Ziegfeld Follies (Buck, Pollock, Wolf)
1916 Ziegfeld Follies (Buck)
1917 The Grass Widow (Pollock, Wolf)
     Going Up (Harbach)
1918 The Rainbow Girl (Wolf)
     Ziegfeld Follies (Buck)
     Oh, My Dear! (Wodehouse)
1919 See-Saw (Biggers)
1920 Mary (Harbach)
1921 The O'Brien Girl (Harbach)
1922 Greenwich Village Follies (Anderson, Caesar)
1923 Greenwich Village Follies (Anderson, Caesar)
1924 Betty Lee (Harbach, Caesar)

Hit the Deck (1927). Music by Vincent Youmans; lyrics by Clifford Grey & Leo Robin; book by Herbert Fields, based on Hubert Osborne's play *Shore Leave.*

SONGS: "Join the Navy," "What's a Kiss Among Friends?," "Harbor of My Heart," "Lucky Bird," "Why, Oh Why," "Sometimes I'm Happy" (lyric, Irving Caesar), "Hallelujah!," "Loo-Loo."

NEW YORK: April 25, 1927
BELASCO THEATRE; 352 p.

Presented by Lew Fields & Vincent Youmans; directed by Alexander Leftwich; choreographed by Seymour Felix; settings, John Wenger; costumes, Mark Mooring; music director, Paul Lannin.

CAST: Louise Groody (*Loulou Martin*), Charles King (*Bilge Smith*), Stella Mayhew (*Lavinia*), Madeline Cameron (*Charlotte Payne*), Brian Donlevy (*Donkey*), Franker Woods (*Battling Smith*), John McCauley (*Capt. Clark*), Roger Gray (*Matt Barlow*), Bobbie Perkins (*Toddy Gaie*).

LONDON: Nov. 3, 1927
HIPPODROME; 277 p.

Presented by Moss's Empires Ltd., Herbert Clayton & Jack Waller; directed by William Mollison; choreographed by Max Scheck; settings, F. L. Lyndhurst; costumes, Reville; music director, Joseph Tunbridge; book adapted by Bert Lee & R. P. Weston.

CAST: Ivy Tresmand (*Loulou Martin*), Stanley Holloway (*Bill Smith*), Alice Morley (*Magnolia*), Mamie Watson (*Charlotte Payne*), Reginald Sheridan (*Donkey*), Sydney Howard (*Battling Smith*), Gerald Nodin (*Lt. Clark*), Dick Francis (*Matt Barlow*).

Vincent Youmans' second most memorable musical (after *No, No, Nanette*) had the first libretto written by Herbert Fields that was not mated to a score by Rodgers and Hart. In the story, Loulou, a coffeehouse owner, meets and falls in love with sailor Bilge Smith. She loves him so much, in fact, that she salvages a ship for him and follows him all the way to China. Bilge is too proud to accept the gift, but eventually a way is found for him to keep both pride and ship. During tryout, Charles King replaced Donald Brian as Bilge, and John McCauley replaced Franklyn Baur as the captain. During Bway run, Miss Groody was succeeded by Queenie Smith. In London adaptation, Newport, RI, was changed to Plymouth, Eng., and the USS *Nebraska* became the HMS *Inscrutable*.

FILM VERSIONS: Jack Oakie and Polly Walker (RKO 1930, Luther Reed dir.); Fred Astaire and Ginger Rogers (called *Follow the Fleet* with altered story, new songs) (RKO 1937, Mark Sandrich dir.); Jane Powell, Tony Martin, Debbie Reynolds (new story) (MGM 1955, Roy Rowland dir.).

Hitchcock, Raymond, actor, producer; b. Auburn, NY, Oct. 22, 1865; d. Beverly Hills, Cal., Nov. 24, 1929. Hitchcock was a lanky, raspy-voiced comic with sharp features and straw-colored hair that he brushed across his forehead. He became a professional actor in 1890 and also appeared in comedies without music. His first starring role was in *The Yankee Consul* (in which he sang "Ain't It Funny What a Difference Just a Few Hours Make?"). Hitchcock was married to Flora Zabelle, who appeared in many of his productions.

1899 Three Little Lambs (*David Tooke*)

1900 The Belle of Bridgeport (*Bokhara Skitboliski*)
The Burgomaster (*E. Booth Tarkington*)
1901 Vienna Life (*Rudolph Kaegler*)
1902 King Dodo (*King Dodo*)
1904 The Yankee Consul (*Abijah Booze*)
1906 The Student King (*Rudolph*)
1907 A Yankee Tourist (*Copeland Schuyler*)
1908 The Merry-Go-Round
1909 La Mascotte (*Laurent XVII*)
The Man Who Owns Broadway (*Sid Lyons*)
1911 The Red Widow (*Cicero Hannibal Butts*)
1914 The Beauty Shop (*Arbustus Budd*)
1916 Mr. Manhattan (L) (*Mr. Manhattan*)
Betty (*Lord D'Arcy Playne*)
1917 Hitchy-Koo (also co-prod.)
Words and Music (sk., co-prod. only)
1918 Follow the Girl (co-prod. only)
Hitchy-Koo (also prod.)
Hullo, America! (L)
1919 Hitchy-Koo (also prod.)
1920 Hitchy-Koo (also prod.)
1921 Ziegfeld Follies (also sk.)
1922 Raymond Hitchcock's Pinwheel
1924 Ritz Revue
1927 Just Fancy (*Charley Van Bibber*)

Hold Everything! (1928). Music by Ray Henderson; lyrics by B. G. DeSylva & Lew Brown; book by DeSylva & John McGowan.

SONGS: "Don't Hold Everything," "You're the Cream in My Coffee," "To Know You Is to Love You," "Too True to Be Good," "When I Love I Love," "Oh, Gosh."

NEW YORK: Oct. 10, 1928
BROADHURST THEATRE; 413 p.

Presented by Alex A. Aarons & Vinton Freedley; director uncredited; choreographed by Sam Rose & Jack Haskell; settings, Henry Dreyfuss;

costumes, Kiviette; music director, Oscar Radin.

CAST: Jack Whiting (*Sonny Jim Brooks*), Ona Munson (*Sue Burke*), Bert Lahr (*Gink Schiner*), Victor Moore (*Nosey Bartlett*), Betty Compton (*Norine Lloyd*), Alice Boulden (*Betty Dunn*), Nina Olivette (*Toots*).

LONDON: June 12, 1929
PALACE THEATRE: 173 p.

Presented by Herbert Clayton & Jack Waller; directed by William Mollison; choreographed by Ralph Reader; book adapted by R. P. Weston & Bert Lee.

CAST: Owen Nares (*Jim Brooks*), Mamie Watson (*Sue O'Keefe*), George Gee (*Spike Skinner*), John Kirby (*Chubby Bartlett*), Pamela Carne (*Norine Lloyd*), Sunny Jarmann (*Toots*).

Though comic Victor Moore was also in the cast, *Hold Everything!* focused most of its comic attention on Bert Lahr in his first role in a book musical. Despite a title that would indicate a plot dealing with wrestling, the show is concerned with the career of welterweight boxing champ Sonny Jim Brooks, who successfully defends both his championship and the honor of his beloved, Sue Burke. The action takes place at a training camp on Long Island and at Madison Square Garden, NY. This was the second of DeSylva, Brown and Henderson's four breezy musical comedies concerned with modern sports and fads (the others: *Good News!*, *Follow Thru*, *Flying High*). In London, Miss Watson succeeded by Dorothy Dickson, Nares by Arthur Margetson (both 7–29).

Holliday, Judy (née Judith Tuvim), actress, singer; b. New York, June 21, 1921; d. New York, June 7, 1965. Baby-voiced blonde actress who won stardom in first Bway play, *Born Yes-*terday*, and who scored even bigger hit in *Bells Are Ringing* (introducing "Just in Time," "The Party's Over"). Miss Holliday also appeared in Hollywood films.

1956 Bells Are Ringing (*Ella Peterson*)
1963 Hot Spot (*Sally Hopwinder*)

Holloway, Stanley (Augustus), actor, singer; b. London, Oct. 1, 1890. An effusive, man-of-the people comic, Holloway was primarily identified in London with *The Co-Optimists* revues before his impressive appearance in *My Fair Lady* (singing "Get Me to the Church on Time" and "With a Little Bit of Luck"). He has also appeared in concert parties, in variety, and in films. Bib: *Wiv a Little Bit o' Luck* by Holloway (Stein & Day, NY 1967).

1919 Kissing Time (*Capt. Wentworth*)
1920 A Night Out (*René*)
1921 The Co-Optimists
1922 The Co-Optimists
1923 The Co-Optimists
1924 The Co-Optimists
1925 The Co-Optimists
1926 The Co-Optimists
1927 Hit the Deck (*Bill Smith*)
1928 Song of the Sea (*Lt. Richard Manners*)
1929 Coo-ee
      The Co-Optimists
1930 The Co-Optimists
1932 Savoy Follies
1934 Three Sisters (*Eustace Titherley*)
1936 All Wave
1938 London Rhapsody
1940 Up and Doing
1942 Fine and Dandy
1956 My Fair Lady (NY) (*Alfred P. Doolittle*)
1958 My Fair Lady (*Alfred P. Doolittle*)

Holm, Celeste, actress, singer; b. New York, April 29, 1919. Wide-eyed, blonde actress appearing in dramatic roles as well as musicals. Miss Holm, who made Bway debut in 1938, achieved fame in *Oklahoma!*, in which she introduced "I Cain't Say No" and "All er Nothin'." She was starred for the first time in *Bloomer Girl* ("Evelina," "Right as the Rain").

1943 Oklahoma! (*Ado Annie Carnes*)
1944 Bloomer Girl (*Evelina*)
1952 The King and I (*Anna Leono-wens*, temp. repl.)
1967 Mame (US tour) (*Mame Dennis*)

Holm, Hanya (née Johanna Eckert), choreographer; b. Worms-am-Rhine, Germany. Miss Holm is particularly noted for her dance creations for *Kiss Me, Kate* and *My Fair Lady*. She founded her own dance school and has appeared in concert throughout the US.

1948 Kiss Me, Kate
1950 The Liar
Out of This World
1951 Kiss Me, Kate (L)
1952 My Darlin' Aida
1954 The Golden Apple
1956 My Fair Lady
1958 Where's Charley? (L)
My Fair Lady (L)
1960 Christine
Camelot
1965 Anya

Holman, Libby (née Elizabeth Holtzman), actress, singer; b. Cincinnati, Ohio, May 23, 1906; d. Stamford, Conn., June 18, 1971. Dark-haired, dark-voiced Libby Holman was the personification of the torch singer of the 20s and 30s. Her greatest Bway successes: *The Little Show* (singing "Moanin' Low"), *Three's a Crowd* ("Body and Soul," "Something to Remember You By"). She also introduced "You and the Night and the Music" in *Revenge with Music*. Miss Holman made records and, in later years, gave concerts in program, *Blues, Ballads and Sin Songs*.

1925 The Garrick Gaieties
1926 Greenwich Village Follies (added)

1927 Merry-Go-Round
Americana (US tour)
1928 Rainbow (*Lotta*)
1929 Ned Wayburn's Gambols
The Little Show
1930 Three's a Crowd
1934 Revenge with Music (*Maria*)
1938 You Never Know (*Jeanne Montaigne*)

Holtz, Lou, actor; b. San Francisco, Cal., April 11, 1898. Yiddish-accented comedian and raconteur who appeared mostly in revues.

1919 George White's Scandals
1920 George White's Scandals
1921 George White's Scandals
1923 The Dancing Girl
1925 Tell Me More (*Monty Sipkin*)
1927 Manhattan Mary (*Sam Katz*)
1931 You Said It (*Pinky Pincus*) (also co-prod.)
1934 Calling All Stars
1936 Transatlantic Rhythm (L)
Laughter Over London (L)

"Homework." Music & lyric by Irving Berlin. Plaintive desire for domesticity revealed by Mary McCarty in *Miss Liberty* (NY 1949).

"Honey Bun." Music by Richard Rodgers; lyric by Oscar Hammerstein II. In *South Pacific*, the Seabees and nurses put on a Thanksgiving Day show during which Nellie Forbush, as "Bosun Butch," appears on stage in a white sailor suit many sizes too large and sings of the charms of his Honey Bun. The object of affection turns out to be Luther Billis as "The Siren of the Coral Sea," wearing a straw-colored wig, exaggerated makeup, a bra made of two cocoanut shells, and a grass skirt. Mary Martin introduced the number both in NY (1949) and in London (1951), and the "Siren" was, respectively, Myron McCormick and Ray Walston.

Hood, Basil, librettist, lyricist; b. April 5, 1864; d. London, Aug. 7, 1917. Hood's specialty was adapting Viennese operettas into English, among them the outstanding London hit, Franz Lehar's *The Merry Widow*. Other successes: Leo Fall's *The Dollar Princess*, Lehar's *The Count of Luxembourg* and *Gipsy Love*. He also collaborated with composers Walter Slaughter, Arthur Sullivan, Edward German, Hugo Felix, Howard Talbot. Before devoting full time to the theatre, Hood served with the Yorkshire Regiment (1883–1898), rising to the rank of captain.

Unless otherwise noted, Capt. Hood was librettist-lyricist of following:

1897	The French Maid (Slaughter)
	Dandy Dan (Slaughter)
1898	Orlando Dando (Slaughter)
	Her Royal Highness (Slaughter)
1899	The Rose of Persia (Sullivan)
1901	The Emerald Isle (Sullivan, German)
1902	Merrie England (German)
1903	A Princess of Kensington (German)
1906	The Merveilleuses (Felix)
1907	The Merry Widow (lib. only)
1908	A Waltz Dream (lib. only)
1909	The Dollar Princess (lib. only)
1911	The Count of Luxembourg (Lehar)
1912	Gipsy Love (lib. only)
1913	The Pearl Girl (Felix, Talbot)

Hooker, Brian, librettist, lyricist; b. New York, Nov. 2, 1880; d. New London, Conn., Dec. 28, 1946. Hooker is best remembered for *The Vagabond King*, whose score, written with composer Rudolf Friml, included "Only a Rose," "Some Day," "The Song of the Vagabonds." He also collaborated with Hugo Felix, George Gershwin, William Daly, Franklin Hauser.

Unless otherwise noted, Mr. Hooker was co-librettist-lyricist of following:

1921	June Love (lyr. only) (Friml)
1922	Marjolaine (lyr. only) (Felix)
	Our Nell (Gershwin, Daly)
1925	The Vagabond King (Friml)
1927	The White Eagle (Friml)
1932	Through the Years (lib. only)
1934	The O'Flynn (Hauser)

"Hoops." Music by Arthur Schwartz; lyric by Howard Dietz. In a scene in *The Band Wagon* (NY 1931), Fred and Adele Astaire played two naughty French children who gossiped about their parents and—as the revolving stage went round—made life miserable for everyone else in Paris' Parc Monceau.

"Hooray for Captain Spalding." Music by Harry Ruby; lyric by Bert Kalmar. Groucho Marx as Capt. Spalding, the African explorer ("Did someone call me schnorer?") is welcomed by Robert Greig, Zeppo Marx, and Margaret Dumont in *Animal Crackers* (NY 1928).

Hope, (Leslie Townes) Bob, actor, singer; b. Eltham, Eng., May 26, 1903. Self-assured, wise-cracking Bob Hope first attracted notice on Bway in *Roberta;* later he scored successes in *Ziegfeld Follies* (singing "I Can't Get Started") and in *Red, Hot and Blue!* ("It's De-Lovely"). His first film, *The Big Broadcast of 1938,* launched his durable screen career. Hope has also been seen on tv and has made many trips to entertain US servicemen abroad. Bib: *Have Tux Will Travel* by Hope (S&S, NY 1954); *The Amazing Careers of Bob Hope* by Joe Morelli, Edward Epstein, Eleanor Clarke (Arlington, NY 1973).

1926	The Ramblers (chorus)
1927	Sidewalks of New York (*Monk*)
1928	Ups-a-Daisy (*Screeves*)
1930	Smiles (chorus)
1932	Ballyhoo of 1932
1933	Roberta (*Huck Haines*)

1934 Say When (*Jimmy Blake*)
1936 Ziegfeld Follies
Red, Hot and Blue! (*Bob Hale*)

Hopper, (William) De Wolf, actor, singer, producer; b. New York, March 30, 1858; d. Kansas City, Mo. Sept. 23, 1935. Tall, broad-shouldered comic actor with booming basso who scored greatest Bway hits in *Castles in the Air, Wang,* and *El Capitan.* Hopper also appeared in Gilbert and Sullivan operettas and was celebrated for reciting "Casey at the Bat" as a curtain speech. Actress Edna Wallace Hopper and actress-turned-writer Hedda Hopper were the third and fifth of Hopper's six wives. Bib: *Once a Clown Always a Clown* by Hopper (Little, Brown, Boston 1927).

1885 The Black Hussar (*Theophil Hackenback*)
The Beggar Student (*Gen. Ollendorf*)
1887 The Begum (*How ja-Dhu*)
Lorraine (*Gaspard*)
1888 The Lady or the Tiger (*Pausanias*)
Boccaccio (r) (*Lambertuccio*)
1889 The May Queen (*Lord Middleditch*)
1890 Castles in the Air (*Filacoudre*)
1891 Wang (*Wang*)
1893 Panjandrum (*Pedro*)
1894 Dr. Syntax (*Dr. Syntax*)
1896 El Capitan (*Don Errico Madigna*)
1898 The Charlatan (*Demidoff*)
1899 El Capitan (L) (*Don Errico Madigna*)
The Mystical Miss (The Charlatan) (L) (*Demidoff*)
1900 Fiddle-Dee-Dee (*Hoffman Barr*)
1901 Hoity Toity (*Gen. Steele*)
1903 Mr. Pickwick (*Pickwick*)
1905 Happyland (*King Ecstaticus*)
1908 The Pied Piper (*Pied Piper*)
1910 A Matinee Idol (*Medford Griffin*)
1913 Lieber Augustin (*Bogumil*)
Hop o' My Thumb (*King of Mnemonica*)
1917 The Passing Show
1918 Everything

1919 The Better 'Ole (US tour) (*Bill*)
1921 Erminie (r) (*Ravennes*)
Snapshots
1922 Some Party
1927 The Student Prince (*Lutz,* repl.)
1928 White Lilacs (*Debusson*)

Horne, Lena, singer, actress; b. Brooklyn, NY, June 30, 1917. Sultry, elegant song stylist whose career began as a dancer in Harlem's Cotton Club, then featured vocalist with Charlie Barnet orchestra. Made great success in nightclubs, Hollywood films, concerts, and on records. On Bway, introduced "Cocoanut Sweet" in *Jamaica,* her only starring musical. Bib: *In Person—Lena Horne* (Greenberg, NY 1950), *Lena* (Doubleday, NY 1965), both by Miss Horne.

1939 Blackbirds of 1939
1957 Jamaica (*Savannah*)

Horwitt, Arnold B., lyricist; b. Richmond, Ind., July 21, 1918. Horwitt's most successful Bway musicals were *Make Mine Manhattan* and *Plain and Fancy* ("Young and Foolish"). Composers he has worked with include Harry Revel, Richard Lewine, Albert Hague. He also wrote revue sketches for *Call Me Mister, Inside USA.*

1945 Are You with It? (Revel)
1948 Make Mine Manhattan (Lewine) (also sk.)
1955 Plain and Fancy (Hague)
1959 The Girls Against the Boys (Lewine) (also sk.)

Hoschna, Karl, composer; b. Kuschwarda, Bohemia, Aug. 16, 1877; d. New York, Dec. 22, 1911. Hoschna's two biggest Bway hits were *Three Twins* ("Cuddle Up a Little Closer, Lovey Mine") and *Madame Sherry* ("Every Little Movement"), both with lyricist Otto Harbach. Other collaborators: Richard Carle, Sidney Rosenfeld, Benjamin Hapgood Burt.

1908 Three Twins (Harbach)

1910 Bright Eyes (Harbach)
Madame Sherry (Harbach)
1911 Jumping Jupiter (Carle, Rosenfeld)
Dr. Deluxe (Harbach)
The Girl of My Dreams (Harbach)
The Fascinating Widow (Harbach)
1912 The Wall Street Girl (Burt)

"How Are Things in Glocca Morra?" Music by Burton Lane; lyric by E. Y. Harburg. Wistful ballad of homesickness sung by Ella Logan in *Finian's Rainbow* (NY 1947) as she recalled a pastoral Ireland. In London version (1947), it was sung by Beryl Seton. Harburg got the idea for the lyric after dreaming up the name "Glocca Morra," which he felt had an authentic "Irish" sound. In the story, the song is prompted by the sound of a skylark—"the same skylark music we have back in Ireland."

"How Do You Speak to an Angel?" Music by Jule Styne; lyric by Bob Hilliard. John Howard introduced the starry-eyed love song in *Hazel Flagg* (NY 1953).

"How High the Moon." Music by Morgan Lewis; lyric by Nancy Hamilton. A ballad of longing for a distant love introduced in the revue *Two for the Show* (NY 1940). Alfred Drake and Frances Comstock sang it, and Eunice Healey, Tommy Wonder, Nadine Gae, and William Archibald danced it. In the production, the song is presented against the background of a London wartime blackout. It begins with an all-clear siren heard in Belgrave Square, with the lights going on and varied couples coming outdoors. At the end, the lights grow dim as the siren again sounds—this time to signal an air raid.

"How Long Has This Been Going On?" Music by George Gershwin; lyric by Ira Gershwin. A song of wonderment caused by a kiss, sung by Bobbie Arnst in *Rosalie* (NY 1928). Originally, the number had been intended for *Funny Face* (1927), and was introduced during the tryout—when the show was called *Smarty*—by Adele Astaire and Stanley Ridges. It was replaced in that score by "He Loves and She Loves."

"How Much of the Dream Comes True?" Music by John Barry; lyric by Trevor Peacock. Mingling romanticism with trepidation ("There will be violins playing softly, somewhere, won't there?"), a young girl anticipates her first night with a boy. Introduced by Francesca Annis in *Passion Flower Hotel* (L 1965).

"How to Handle a Woman." Music by Frederick Loewe; lyric by Alan Jay Lerner. Merlyn's advice to King Arthur: "The way to handle a woman is to love her." Richard Burton introduced the meditative piece in *Camelot* (NY 1960); Laurence Harvey sang it in London version (1964).

How to Succeed in Business Without Really Trying (1961). Music & lyrics by Frank Loesser; book by Abe Burrows, Jack Weinstein, & Willie Gilbert, based on Shepherd Mead's book.

SONGS: "Coffee Break," "The Company Way," "A Secretary Is Not a Toy," "Been a Long Day," "Grand Old Ivy," "Paris Original," "Rosemary," "Happy to Keep His Dinner Warm," "I Believe in You," "Brotherhood of Man."

NEW YORK: Oct. 14, 1961
46TH ST. THEATRE; 1,417 p.

Presented by Cy Feuer & Ernest Martin, with Frank Productions;

directed by Abe Burrows & Bob Fosse; choreographed by Hugh Lambert; settings & lighting, Robert Randolph; costumes, Robert Fletcher; music director, Elliott Lawrence; orchestrations, Robert Ginzler.

CAST: Robert Morse (*J. Pierpont Finch*), Rudy Vallée (*J. B. Biggley*), Bonnie Scott (*Rosemary*), Claudette Sutherland (*Smitty*), Charles Nelson Reilly (*Bud Frump*), Ruth Kobart (*Miss Jones*), Virginia Martin (*Hedy La Rue*), Sammy Smith (*Mr. Twimble*), Donna McKechnie (dancer).

LONDON: March 28, 1963
SHAFTESBURY THEATRE; 520 p.

Presented by Arthur Lewis; directed by Abe Burrows & Bob Fosse; choreographed by Hugh Lambert; settings & lighting, Robert Randolph; costumes, Robert Fletcher; music director, Roy Lowe; orchestrations, Robert Ginzler.

CAST: Warren Berlinger (*J. Pierpont Finch*), Billy De Wolfe (*J. B. Biggley*), David Knight (*Bud Frump*), Patricia Michael (*Rosemary*), Eileen Gourlay (*Hedy La Rue*), Josephine Blake (*Smitty*), Bernard Spear (*Mr. Twimble*), Olive Lucius (*Miss Jones*).

Unlike a Horatio Alger hero, J. Pierpont Finch rises from humble beginnings (a window cleaner) to the presidency of World Wide Wickets Co., not by hard work but by knowing how to make others work hard for him. The outlook of the musical was totally unsentimental as it satirized such institutions of modern big business as the executive washroom, the coffee break, the office party, and the board room presentation. Both librettist Abe Burrows and composer-lyricist Frank Loesser had previously been associated with producers Feuer and Martin in *Guys and Dolls;* Bob Fosse was called in during rehearsals to han-

dle the musical staging. Robert Morse rose to stardom with this production, which also marked Rudy Vallée's first Bway book musical. During run, Morse was succeeded by Darryl Hickman (10-63) and Ronnie Welsh (8-64); Bonnie Scott by Lois Leary (8-62) and Michele Lee (10-62). The US tour, which began Feb. 1963, featured Dick Kallman (*Finch*), William Waterman (*Biggley*), Dyan Cannon (*Rosemary*).

FILM VERSION: Robert Morse, Rudy Vallée, Michele Lee (UA 1967, David Swift dir.).

Howard, Sydney, actor, singer; b. Yeadon, Eng., Aug. 7, 1885; d. London, June 12, 1946. Oversized, fluttery London comedian who was starred in Firth Shephard productions during late 30s and early 40s. Also toured in revues, variety shows, and acted in movies.

1919	Box o Tricks
1927	Hit the Deck (*Battling Smith*)
1928	Funny Face (*Herbert*)
1929	The Co-Optimists
	Dear Love (*Maurice Gerrard*)
1930	Heads Up (*Skippy Dugan*)
1935	Anything Goes (*Moonface Mooney*)
1937	Oh! You Letty (*Mr. Simmons*)
1938	Wild Oats (*Samuel Cloppitt*) (also dir.)
1939	Sitting Pretty (*Mr. Tuttle*) (also dir.)
	Shephard's Pie
1941	Fun and Games
1943	The Magic Carpet

Howard, Willie (né Wilhelm Levkowitz), actor; b. Neustadt, Germany, April 13, 1886; d. New York, Jan. 12, 1949. Tousle-haired Willie Howard spent most of his Bway career with his brother, Eugene Howard (1881–1965), in an act in which he played a grimacing, mischievous, Yiddish-accented clown pitted against Eugene's domineering, pompous straight man. After beginning as a boy soprano and song plugger, Willie appeared with Eugene in vaudeville, 1903–1912 and 1922–1926.

Asterisk indicates appearance with Eugene Howard:

1901 The Little Duchess (boy soprano)
1912 The Passing Show *
1914 The Whirl of the World *
1915 The Passing Show *
1916 The Show of Wonders *
1918 The Passing Show *
1920 The Passing Show *
1922 The Passing Show *
1925 Sky High (*Jimmy*)
1926 George White's Scandals *
1928 George White's Scandals *
1929 George White's Scandals *
1930 Girl Crazy (*Gieber Goldfarb*)
1931 George White's Scandals *
1932 Ballyhoo of 1932 *
1933 George White's Music Hall Varieties * (added)
1934 Ziegfeld Follies *
1935 George White's Scandals *
1937 The Show Is On * (repl.)
1939 George White's Scandals *
1941 Crazy with the Heat
1943 My Dear Public (*Barney*)
1948 Sally (r) (*Connie*)

"How'd You Like to Spoon with Me?" Music by Jerome Kern; lyric by Edward Laska. Fetching invitation exchanged by Georgia Caine and Victor Morley in *The Earl and the Girl* (NY 1905). As Oscar Hammerstein II once described the scene: "It seems that six girls were seated on swings, and during the course of the singing they would swing out over the audience. The ropes of the swings were decked with blossoms, and the girls were dressed in fluffy organdy, and the whole thing made the audience very happy indeed." The song, which was added to the NY version of the London musical, was Kern's first hit. In 1971, the number was part of the score of the London revival of *Show Boat*, in which it was sung by Jan Hunt and Kenneth Nelson.

Howes, (Robert William) Bobby, actor, singer, dancer; b. Battersea, Eng., Aug. 4, 1895. Howes was a short, wistful comic whose London successes included *Mr. Cinders* (singing "I'm a One-Man Girl"), *Yes, Madam?*, *Please, Teacher!*, and *Paint Your Wagon* (appearing with daughter Sally Ann Howes). He began in music halls in 1909, performed in concert parties, and introduced "Got a Date with an Angel" and "She's My Lovely." (D. April 27, 1972.)

1923 The Little Revue Starts at 9
1924 The Second Little Revue
1925 The Punch Bowl (repl.)
    The Blue Kitten (*Octave*)
1926 Vaudeville Vanities
1927 The Blue Train (*Freddie Royce*)
1928 The Yellow Mask (*Sam Slider*)
1929 Mr. Cinders (*Jim*)
1930 Sons o' Guns (*Jimmy Canfield*)
1931 Song of the Drum (*Chips Wilcox*)
    For the Love of Mike (*Bob Seymour*)
1932 Tell Her the Truth (*Bobbie*)
1933 He Wanted Adventure (*Bobby Bramstone*)
1934 Yes, Madam? (*Bill Quinton*)
1935 Please, Teacher! (*Tommy Deacon*)
1937 Big Business (*Jimmy Rackstraw*)
    Hide and Seek (*Tommy, Mike*)
1938 Bobby Get Your Gun (*Bobby Lockwood*)
1939 All Clear
1941 Shephard's Pie (repl.)
    Lady Behave (*Tony Meyrick*, repl.)
1942 Let's Face It! (*Jerry Walker*)
1946 Here Come the Boys
1948 Four, Five, Six!
1949 Roundabout (*Billy Warren*)
1953 Paint Your Wagon (*Ben Rumson*)
1960 Finian's Rainbow (NY) (r) (*Finian*)

Howes, Sally Ann, actress, singer; b. London, July 20, 1930. Blonde, delicate-featured beauty who has also appeared in films and on tv. Her most successful London role was in *Paint Your Wagon*, in which she acted with her father, Bobby Howes. She also introduced "A Room Without Windows" in Bway musical *What Makes Sammy Run?* Miss Howes, the granddaughter of producer J. A. E. Malone, was married for a time to US composer Richard Adler.

1951	Fancy Free
1952	Bet Your Life (*Jane*)
1953	Paint Your Wagon (*Jennifer Rumson*)
1955	Romance in Candlelight (*Margaret*)
1956	Summer Song (*Karolka*)
1958	My Fair Lady (NY) (*Eliza Doolittle*, repl.)
1961	Kwamina (NY) (*Eve*)
1964	What Makes Sammy Run? (NY) (*Kit Sargent*)
1973	The King and I (r) (*Anna Leonowens*)

"How's Chances?" Music & lyric by Irving Berlin. Ardent entreaty used by Prince Mdivani (Clifton Webb) to woo and win heiress Barbara Hutton (Marilyn Miller) in the topical revue *As Thousands Cheer* (NY 1933). In London revue *Stop Press* (1935), based on *As Thousands Cheer*, the piece was performed by Tony Hulley and Dorothy Dickson.

Hoyt, Charles Hale, librettist, lyricist, producer; b. Concord, NH, 1860; d. New York, Nov. 20, 1900. Prolific writer of satirical farces—both with and without music—whose scripts reflected contemporary American themes. Biggest hit: *A Trip to Chinatown* ("Reuben and Cynthia," "The Bowery"). Collaborators: Edward Solomon, Percy Gaunt, Richard Stahl.

1886	The Maid and the Moonshiner (Solomon)
1891	A Trip to Chinatown (Gaunt)
1896	A Black Sheep (Stahl)
	A Parlor Match (r) (lib. only)
1898	A Day and Night in New York (Stahl)

Hubbell, Raymond, composer; b. Urbana, Ohio, June 1, 1879; d. Miami, Fla., Dec. 13, 1954. Between 1915 and 1922, Hubbell composed the songs for six Hippodrome spectacles, incl. *The Big Show*, whence came "Poor Butterfly." Six of his scores were written with R. H. Burnside; other lyricists: Addison Burkhardt, Robert B. Smith, Harry B. Smith, Glen MacDonough, E. Ray Goetz, George V. Hobart, Henry Blossom, Gene Buck, John Golden, Anne Caldwell.

1903	The Runaways (Burkhardt)
1905	Fantana (R. B. Smith)
1906	Mexicana (R. B. Smith)
	Mam'selle Sallie (H. B. Smith)
1907	A Knight for a Day (R. B. Smith)
1909	The Midnight Sons (MacDonough)
1910	The Jolly Bachelors (MacDonough)
	The Bachelor Belles (H. B. Smith)
1911	The Never Homes (Goetz)
	The Three Romeos (Burnside)
	Ziegfeld Follies (Hobart)
1912	Ziegfeld Follies (H. B. Smith)
	The Man from Cook's (Blossom)
	A Winsome Widow (H. B. Smith)
1913	Ziegfeld Follies (Hobart)
1914	Ziegfeld Follies (Buck)
1915	Fads and Fancies (MacDonough)
	Hip-Hip-Hooray! (Golden)
1916	The Big Show (Golden)
1917	Ziegfeld Follies (Hobart, Buck)
	Cheer Up (Golden)
1918	The Kiss Burglar (MacDonough)
1919	Happy Days (Burnside)
	Miss Millions (Burnside)
1920	Good Times (Burnside)
1921	Sonny (Hobart)
1922	Better Times (Burnside)
1927	Yours Truly (Caldwell)

1928 Three Cheers (Burnside, Caldwell)

Hulbert, Jack, actor, singer, dancer, librettist, director, choreographer, producer; b. Ely, Eng., April 24, 1892.
Jaunty, lantern-jawed performer who
appeared with wife, Cicely Courtneidge, in 13 London musicals. Their
first success, *By the Way,* established
them as a team, and their longest-
running attractions were *Clowns in
Clover, Under Your Hat,* and *Full
Swing.* They also acted together in
films during the 30s. Hulbert introduced "She's Such a Comfort to
Me" in *The House That Jack Built.*
He was the brother of comedian Claude
Hulbert. *(D. London, Mar. 25, 1978.)*

Mr. Hulbert was director of all productions from 1925 on; asterisk indicates appearance with Miss Courtneidge:
1913 Cheer Oh! Cambridge (*Algy Vere*)
(also lib.)
The Pearl Girl * (*Robert Jaffray*)
1914 The Cinema Star * (*Billy*)
1915 The Arcadians * (r) (*Bobby*)
1916 The Light Blues * (*Arthur Hobbs*)
(also co-lib.)
See-Saw (*Jack Lane*)
1917 Bubbly
1919 Bran-Pie
1920 A Little Dutch Girl (*Capt. Constantine Posch*)
1921 Ring Up *
Pot Luck
1923 The Little Revue Starts at 9 *
1925 By the Way * (also co-prod.)
By the Way * (NY)
1926 Lido Lady * (*Harry Bassett*) (also
co-prod.)
1927 The Blue Train (dir. only)
Clowns in Clover * (also co-prod.)
1928 Lady Mary (chor. only)
Song of the Sea (dir. only)
1929 The House that Jack Built * (also
co-prod.)
1930 Follow a Star (*Bobby Hillary*)
(also co-prod.)
1931 Folly to Be Wise (dir., co-prod.
only)

1933 On with the Show (dir., co-prod.
only)
1937 Hide and Seek (dir. only)
1938 Under Your Hat * (*Jack Millet*)
(also co-lib., chor.)
1942 Full Swing * (*Jack Millet*) (also
co-lib., chor.)
1943 Something in the Air * (*Jack
Pendleton*) (also co-lib., chor.)
1945 Sweet Yesterday (dir. only)
Under the Counter (dir., chor.
only)
1946 Here Come the Boys
1947 Under the Counter (NY) (dir.,
chor, only)
The Nightingale (dir., prod. only)
1949 Her Excellency (dir. only)
1951 Gay's the Word (dir. only)
1953 Over the Moon (dir., chor. only)

"Hundred Million Miracles, A."
Music by Richard Rodgers; lyric by
Oscar Hammerstein, II. An imitation
traditional Chinese flower drum song
about the miracles found in everyday
life. Miyoshi Umeki, accompanied by
gong and drum, sang it in *Flower
Drum Song* (NY 1958) with Juanita
Hall, Keye Luke, Conrad Yama, and
Rose Quong. In London production
(1960), it was sung by Yau Shan Tung,
with Ida Shepley, George Pastell, Zed
Zakari, and Mei Juan Chang.

Huston, Walter (né Walter Hough-
ston), actor; b. Toronto, Canada, April
6, 1884; d. Beverly Hills, Cal., April 7,
1950. Gruff-voiced actor specializing
in he-man, realistic roles (*Desire
Under the Elms, Dodsworth*), who appeared in one Bway musical (in which
he introduced "September Song").
Huston made his professional bow
in 1905, appeared in vaudeville
1909–1924, acted in Hollywood films
1929–1950.
1938 Knickerbocker Holiday (*Pieter
Stuyvesant*)

Hylton, Jack, producer; b. Bolton, Eng., July 2, 1892; d. London, Jan. 29, 1965. Popular British bandleader who became successful London producer. Among long-running attractions: seven Crazy Gang shows, *Salad Days*, *Annie Get Your Gun* (one of 10 Bway musicals he imported).

1925	London Revue (bandleader only)
1927	Shake Your Feet (bandleader only)
1941	Lady Behave
1943	The Merry Widow (r)
	Hi-De-Hi
	The Love Racket
1944	The Lilac Domino (r)
1945	For Crying Out Loud
	Follow the Girls
1946	Can-Can
1947	Romany Love
	Together Again
	Annie Get Your Gun
1948	High Button Shoes
1950	Take It from Here
	Knights of Madness
	Take It from Us
1951	Kiss Me, Kate
1952	Bet Your Life
	Call Me Madam
	London Laughs
	Ring Out the Bells
1953	Paint Your Wagon
	Wish You Were Here
1954	You'll Be Lucky
	Pal Joey
	Salad Days
	The Talk of the Town
	Jokers Wild
1955	Wonderful Town
	Such Is Life
1956	Summer Song
	United Notions
	These Foolish Kings
1959	Clown Jewels
	When in Rome
1960	Young in Heart
1961	King Kong
1964	Camelot

"Hymn to Him, A." Music by Frederick Loewe; lyric by Alan Jay Lerner. Panegyric to male superiority passionately expressed by Rex Harrison to Robert Coote in *My Fair Lady* (NY 1956, L 1958). The song is familiarly known as "Why Can't a Woman Be More Like a Man?"

I

"I Ain't Down Yet." Music & lyric by Meredith Willson. Thumping march proclaiming heroine Tammy Grimes's dauntless determination to rise to the top in *The Unsinkable Molly Brown* (NY 1960).

"I Am Loved." Music & lyric by Cole Porter. In *Out of This World* (NY 1950), Patricia Gillette radiantly revealed what a wonderful and glorious thing it is to be able to say.

"I Believe in You." Music & lyric by Frank Loesser. Hymn of adoration sung by Robert Morse to Robert Morse in *How to Succeed in Business Without Really Trying* (NY 1961). In a scene depicting the executive men's room of a large corporation, J. Pierpont Finch, a young lad on his way up, expresses his belief while gazing into a mirror and accompanying himself with the buzz of an electric razor. In London production (1963), sung by Warren Berlinger to Warren Berlinger.

"I Cain't Say No." Music by Richard Rodgers; lyric by Oscar Hammerstein II. Comic song of romantically uninhibited Ado Annie in *Oklahoma!* (NY

1943), introduced by Celeste Holm. Dorothea McFarland sang it in London production (1947).

"I Can Dream, Can't I?" Music by Sammy Fain; lyric by Irving Kahal. Ballad of rejected love introduced by Tamara in *Right This Way* (NY 1938).

"I Can Give You the Starlight." Music by Ivor Novello; lyric by Christopher Hassall. In which Mary Ellis pledged her devotion to Ivor Novello in *The Dancing Years* (L 1939).

"I Can't Get Started." Music by Vernon Duke; lyric by Ira Gershwin. Catalogue song first sung by Bob Hope to break down the resistance of Eve Arden in a scene in the *Ziegfeld Follies* (NY 1936). Both formally attired, the two are on a street corner as Miss Arden vainly tries to hail a taxi following what is apparently a first date. Hope's itemized accomplishments—including flying around the world in a plane, settling revolutions in Spain, and charting the North Pole—fail to impress the lady. Then, using a more direct approach, he gives her a good, solid kiss, which does the trick. But now that she has finally succumbed, he leaves her with a jaunty "Well, that's all I wanted to know." Lyricist Gershwin set his words to a melody Duke had previously written called "Face the Music with Me."

"I Can't Give You Anything but Love." Music by Jimmy McHugh; lyric by Dorothy Fields. McHugh and Fields's first hit was written for *Harry Delmar's Revels* (NY 1927) and intended to be sung by Bert Lahr and Patsy Kelly. Although Delmar dropped the song before the revue's Bway opening, two months later he reinstated it for singer Lew Mann. The number's "official" Bway debut was in *Blackbirds of 1928*, in which the sentiments of an impecunious lover were sung by Aida Ward, Willard McLean, and Adelaide Hall.

"I Could Be Happy with You." Music & lyric by Sandy Wilson. Inverted-phrase-type love duet—"I could be happy with you if you could be happy with me"—purposely reminiscent of lyrics of the 20s. Introduced by Anne Rogers and Anthony Hayes in *The Boy Friend* (L 1954), then repeated by Julie Andrews and John Hewer in NY version (also 1954).

"I Could Have Danced All Night." Music by Frederick Loewe; lyric by Alan Jay Lerner. Song of breathless self-satisfaction following Julie Andrews' discovery in *My Fair Lady* (NY 1956, L 1958) that she could at last speak proper English. The song also offers the first indication that our heroine has fallen in love with her speech teacher.

"I Could Write a Book." Music by Richard Rodgers; lyric by Lorenz Hart. The nearest thing to a romantic expression in *Pal Joey* (NY 1940) was presented as little more than a musical put-on to impress a dumb chorus girl. Gene Kelly, in the title role, sang it to Leila Ernst in front of a pet-shop window. In London production (1954), Harold Lang sang it to Sally Bazely.

"I Didn't Know What Time It Was." Music by Richard Rodgers; lyric by Lorenz Hart. Romantic naivety admitted by Marcy Westcott and Richard Kollmar in *Too Many Girls* (NY 1939).

"I Enjoy Being a Girl." Music by Richard Rodgers; lyric by Oscar Hammerstein II. Buoyant expression of feminine self-appreciation sung in

Flower Drum Song by Pat Suzuki (NY 1958) and by Yama Saki (1960).

"I Feel at Home with You." Music by Richard Rodgers; lyric by Lorenz Hart. Duet for illiterates introduced by Jack Thompson and June Cochrane in *A Connecticut Yankee* (NY 1927); also sung by Billy Holland and Gladys Cruickshank in London version, called *A Yankee at the Court of King Arthur* (1929).

"I Feel Pretty." Music by Leonard Bernstein; lyric by Stephen Sondheim. Buoyant self-esteem prompted by a girl's anticipation of getting married. Introduced by Carol Lawrence in *West Side Story* (NY 1957), with deflating comments by Marilyn Cooper and Reri Grist; in London facsimile (1958) sung by Marlys Watters, with Francesca Bell. Stephen Sondheim has related that when fellow lyricist Sheldon Harnick first heard the piece he felt that the interior rhymes (i.e. "It's alarming how charming I feel") were too sophisticated for an uneducated Puerto Rican girl. Though Sondheim then wrote a simpler version of the lyric, everyone else connected with the musical insisted that the original words be retained.

"I Feel Sorry for the Girl." Music & lyric by Glenn Paxton, Robert Goldman, & George Weiss. In *First Impressions* (NY 1959), Donald Madden and Phyllis Newman gaily expressed sympathy for any girl who doesn't have a beau, " 'specially in the springtime."

"I Found a Million Dollar Baby (in a Five and Ten Cent Store)." Music by Harry Warren; lyric by Mort Dixon & Billy Rose. Sung by Ted Healy, Phil Baker, Fanny Brice (wearing top hat and tails), and Lew Brice in Billy Rose's *Crazy Quilt* revue (NY 1931).

"I Get a Kick Out of You." Music & lyric by Cole Porter. Bored by such stimulants as champagne, cocaine, and a plane ride, Ethel Merman ruefully admitted in *Anything Goes* (NY 1934) that the only thing that gave her a kick was the sight of William Gaxton's "fabulous face." In London production (1935), Jeanne Aubert sang it about Jack Whiting. For a while censorship forced the line "I get no kick from cocaine" to be changed to "Some like the perfume from Spain" whenever the song was performed over the air.

"I Got Lost in His Arms." Music & lyric by Irving Berlin. Blissful feeling recalled in *Annie Get Your Gun* by Ethel Merman in NY (1946) and by Dolores Gray in London (1947).

"I Got Love." Music by Gary Geld; lyric by Paul Udell. Melba Moore made this blazing declaration a showstopper in *Purlie* (NY 1970).

"I Got Plenty o' Nuttin'." Music by George Gershwin; lyric by Ira Gershwin & DuBose Heyward. Joyous expression of a man content with his meager lot, sung in *Porgy and Bess* by Todd Duncan (NY 1935), then in London production by William Warfield (1952).

"I Got Rhythm." Music by George Gershwin; lyric by Ira Gershwin. Irrefutable announcement trumpeted by Ethel Merman in *Girl Crazy* (NY 1930). The show was Miss Merman's Bway debut and the song was the single most important factor in making her a star. As the singer has recalled: "On the second chorus I just held the 'I' . . . one long note . . . while the orchestra played the tune. The audience started clapping after about four bars, clapping, clapping, clapping, and they didn't stop till I'd done I don't know how many encores. It was like electricity." Note that in the refrain, lyricist Ira allowed himself only two rhymes: "more" and "door" and "mind him" and "find him." Even more unusual, as Gershwin has pointed out, "is that the phrase 'Who could ask for anything more?' occurs four times—which, ordinarily and unquestionably, should make that phrase the title. Somehow the first line of the refrain sounded more arresting and provocative. Therefore, 'I Got Rhythm.' "

"I Got the Sun in the Morning." Music & lyric by Irving Berlin. Ethel Merman sang this zesty appreciation of life's simple pleasures in *Annie Get Your Gun* (NY 1946); Dolores Gray sang it in London version (1947).

"I Gotta Right to Sing the Blues." Music by Harold Arlen; lyric by Ted Koehler. Torchy confession introduced in *Earl Carroll Vanities* (NY 1932) by Lillian Shade.

"I Guess I'll Have to Change My Plan." Music by Arthur Schwartz; lyric by Howard Dietz. Once known as "The Blue Pajama Song," this casual acceptance of the termination of a love affair—because of an unsuspected husband—was introduced by Clifton Webb in *The Little Show* (NY 1929). (In second chorus, however, the frustrated lover changes his mind and decides that it would be more fun wooing one who's wed.) The melody dated from 1924, when, as counselors in a summer camp, composer Schwartz and lyricist Lorenz Hart had written a song called "I Love to Lie Awake in Bed":

I love to lie awake in bed
Right after taps
I pull the flaps
     above my head.
I let the stars shine on my pillow,
Oh, what a light the moonbeams shed.
I feel so happy I could cry
And tears are born
Within the corn-
     er of my eye.
To be at home with ma was never like this.
I could live forever like this.
I love to lie awake awhile
And go to bed with a smile.

"I Had Myself a True Love." Music by Harold Arlen; lyric by Johnny Mercer. Lament of a woman whose man has "gone an' left her for good." Introduced by June Hawkins in *St. Louis Woman* (NY 1946).

"I Happen to Like New York." Music & lyric by Cole Porter. Insistent affirmation of civic pride added to score of *The New Yorkers* (NY 1930) during run and sung by Oscar Ragland.

"I Hate Men." Music & lyric by Cole Porter. Banging a pewter mug on a table, Patricia Morison—as Katherine in a scene from *The Taming of the Shrew*—excoriated the species in *Kiss Me, Kate* (NY 1948, L 1951).

"I Have Dreamed." Music by Richard Rodgers; lyric by Oscar Hammerstein II. Ardent duet of dreams turning to reality sung in *The King and I* by Larry Douglas and Doretta Morrow in NY (1951), and Jan Mazarus and Doreen Duke in London (1953).

"I Just Can't Make My Eyes Behave." Music by Gus Edwards; lyric by Will D. Cobb. With body rigidly erect, Anna Held sang—and demonstrated —this coquettish number in *The Parisian Model* (NY 1907).

"I Know Now." Music by Ron Grainer; lyric by Ronald Millar. Impassioned duet for June Bronhill and Keith Michell in *Robert and Elizabeth* (L 1964).

"I Know That You Know." Music by Vincent Youmans; lyric by Anne Caldwell. Beatrice Lillie and Charles Purcell introduced this staccato romantic duet in *Oh, Please!* (NY 1926).

"I Left My Heart at the Stage Door Canteen." Music & lyric by Irving Berlin. Ballad of a fleeting love introduced by Earl Oxford in the all-soldier revue *This Is the Army* (NY 1942, L 1943). During World War II, the Stage Door Canteen, located in the basement of the 44th St. Theatre, was operated by the American Theatre Wing exclusively for US and allied servicemen. In the revue, it served as the setting in which performers impersonated some of the actors who worked and entertained at the canteen.

"I Lift Up My Finger and Say Tweet-Tweet." Music & lyric by Leslie Sarony. Stanley Lupino's trade-mark number—in which audiences dutifully joined by raising fingers and saying, "Tweet-tweet, shush-shush, now-now, come-come"—was introduced in *Love Lies* (L 1929).

"I Like the Likes of You." Music by Vernon Duke; lyric by E. Y. Harburg. Bubbly, befuddled song of affection sung in *Ziegfeld Follies* (NY 1934) by Judith Barron and Brice Hutchins (Robert Cummings) and danced by Vilma and Buddy Ebsen.

"I Like to Recognize the Tune." Music by Richard Rodgers; lyric by Lorenz Hart. Opposition to swing-band distortions voiced in *Too Many*

Girls (NY 1939) by Eddie Bracken, Marcy Westcott, Mary Jane Walsh, Richard Kollmar, and Hal LeRoy.

"I Love a Piano." Music & lyric by Irving Berlin. "I know a fine way to treat a Steinway," sang Harry Fox and chorus in revue *Stop! Look! Listen!* (NY 1915). In London, Ethel Levey showed her affection in *Follow the Crowd* (1916).

"I Love Louisa." Music by Arthur Schwartz; lyric by Howard Dietz. Teutonic avowal—part of the lyric is in German—sung by Fred and Adele Astaire and company in the first-act finale of the revue *The Band Wagon* (NY 1931). The scene featured a gaily bedecked merry-go-round on a revolving stage. The song was written as a tribute to a chambermaid at the St. Moritz Hotel, NY, where most of the show's score was written.

"I Love Paris." Music & lyric by Cole Porter. In *Can-Can* (NY 1953), Lilo offered this minor-key evocation of Paris before a huge panoramic backdrop of the city. The London production (1954) featured Irene Hilda.

"I Love You." Music by Harry Archer; lyric by Harlan Thompson. Straightforward declaration sung by Ann Sands and Jay Velie in *Little Jessie James* (NY 1923).

"I Love You." Music & lyric by Cole Porter. Sung by Wilbur Evans in *Mexican Hayride* (NY 1944). Porter wrote the song as a result of a wager he made with his friend Monty Woolley. Woolley was convinced that the composer was incapable of writing a song with such a trite title as "I Love You"—with words to match—and end up with a success. Porter accepted the challenge, wrote the song, and won the bet—though he always maintained that the song's popularity was due more to the melody than to the lyric.

"I Love You So." Music by Franz Lehar; lyric by Adrian Ross. "The Merry Widow Waltz," first sung in English in London production of *The Merry Widow* (1907) by Lily Elsie and Joseph Coyne, and in NY production (also 1907) by Ethel Jackson and Donald Brian. The waltz occurs at the end of Act I during a ball at the Marsovian Embassy in Paris and is the means through which hero and heroine reveal their love. The operetta, originally titled *Die Lustige Witwe*, with libretto by Victor Léon and Leo Stein, was initially presented in Vienna (1905).

"I Loves You, Porgy." Music by George Gershwin; lyric by DuBose Heyward & Ira Gershwin. Anne Brown and Todd Duncan introduced this impassioned pledge in *Porgy and Bess* (NY 1935). The London production (1952) featured Leontyne Price and William Warfield.

I Married an Angel (1938). Music by Richard Rodgers; lyrics by Lorenz Hart; book by Rodgers & Hart, based on Hungarian play by Janos Vaszary.

SONGS: "Did You Ever Get Stung?," "I Married an Angel," "I'll Tell the Man in the Street," "How to Win Friends and Influence People," "Spring Is Here," "A Twinkle in Your Eye," "At the Roxy Music Hall."

NEW YORK: May 11, 1938
SHUBERT THEATRE; 338 p.

Presented by Dwight Deere Wiman; directed by Joshua Logan; choreographed by George Balanchine; settings, Jo Mielziner; costumes, John Hambleton; music director, Gene Salzer; orchestrations, Hans Spialek.

CAST: Dennis King (*Willy Palaffi*), Vera Zorina (*Angel*), Vivienne Segal (*Peggy Palaffi*), Walter Slezak (*Harry Szigetti*), Charles Walters (*Peter Mueller*), Audrey Christie (*Anna Murphy*), Charles Laskey (dancer).

In Hollywood in 1933, Rodgers and Hart with nonrelative Moss Hart wrote a screen adaptation for MGM of a Hungarian play called *I Married an Angel*, but the studio scratched the production (though eventually they did make it). The songwriters then took the story to producer Wiman, who secured the rights, and it became one of Bway's major attractions of the 30s. It was also the first musical to be directed by Joshua Logan and the first in NY with Vera Zorina. The play is a satirical fantasy in which a disillusioned Budapest banker, Count Willy Palaffi, vows that the only girl he'll marry is an angel. And he does, though the girl's heavenly honesty almost wrecks their marriage. The musical began its road tour in Feb. 1939, and continued for 11 months (during travels Karen Van Ryn succeeded Zorina, Dan Dailey took over from Charles Walters).

FILM VERSION: Jeanette MacDonald and Nelson Eddy (MGM 1942, W.S. Van Dyke dir.).

"I Married an Angel." Music by Richard Rodgers; lyric by Lorenz Hart. Overawed proclamation in *I Married an Angel* (NY 1938) after hero Dennis King has actually achieved the distinction of marrying a real live angel.

"I May Be Wrong, but I Think You're Wonderful." Music Henry Sullivan; lyric by Harry Ruskin. Self-doubting confession sung by Trixie Friganza and Jimmy Savo in Bway revue *John Murray Anderson's Almanac* (1929). Because Anderson believed that the best songs are created under pressure, he locked Sullivan in a room with a piano and threatened to keep him there until he came up with a potential hit. When finally liberated, the composer had written the most successful number in the show.

"I Might Be Your Once-in-a-While." Music by Victor Herbert; lyric by Robert B. Smith. Lilting love duet in *Angel Face* (NY 1919) sung by John E. Young and Emilie Lea.

"I Must Have That Man." Music by Jimmy McHugh; lyric by Dorothy Fields. Near-hysterical romantic acquisitiveness ("I'm half alive and it's driving me mad") expressed by Adelaide Hall in *Blackbirds of 1928* (NY 1928).

"I Never Has Seen Snow." Music by Harold Arlen; lyric by Truman Capote & Arlen. Aglow with love, Diahann Carroll in *House of Flowers* (NY 1954) radiantly asserts that nothing in the world could possibly be as beautiful as "that near-to-me boy with the faraway look."

"I See Your Face Before Me." Music by Arthur Schwartz; lyric by Howard Dietz. A beloved's persistent image first haunted Evelyn Laye in *Between the Devil* (NY 1937), then Adele Dixon and Jack Buchanan.

"I Still Get Jealous." Music by Jule Styne; lyric by Sammy Cahn. Old-fashioned song, dance, and patter number introduced by Nanette Fabray and Jack McCauley in *High Button Shoes* (NY 1947). In London version (1948) it was performed by Kay Kimber and Sidney James.

"I Still See Elisa." Music by Frederick Loewe; lyric by Alan Jay Lerner. James Barton's tender remembrance of his dead wife in *Paint Your Wagon* (NY 1951). Bobby Howes sang it in London version (1953).

"I Talk to the Trees." Music by Frederick Loewe; lyric by Alan Jay Lerner. A young Mexican gold prospector in *Paint Your Wagon* (NY 1951) meets a girl in a California mining town who listens to him, and suddenly he's sure his dreams will come true. After he leaves, the girl conveys her feelings by repeating his words. Tony Bavaar and Olga San Juan sang the song in NY (1951), Ken Cantril and Sally Ann Howes sang it in London (1953).

"I Wanna Be Loved By You." Music by Harry Ruby & Herbert Stothart; lyric by Bert Kalmar. Helen Kane squeaked and boop-boop-a-dooped her way through this piece—in a duet with Dan Healy—in *Good Boy* (NY 1928).

"I Wanna Get Married." Music by Phil Charig; lyric by Milton Pascal & Dan Shapiro. Gertrude Niesen's throaty proclamation—with its numerous encores—became the show-stopper of *Follow the Girls* (NY 1944). In London version (1945), it was sung by Evelyn Dall.

"I Want to Be Happy." Music by Vincent Youmans; lyric by Irving Caesar. Sung by Binnie Hale and Joseph Coyne in *No, No, Nanette* (L 1925), and by Louise Groody and Charles Winninger in NY production (also 1925). Youmans and Caesar added the song during the show's pre-Bway tryout tour to replace "Santa Claus," by Youmans and Otto Harbach, which had a similar theme of achieving happiness through making others happy.

"I Want to Be With You." Music by Charles Strouse; lyric by Lee Adams.

Sammy Davis and Paula Wayne introduced this emotional avowal of dependency in *Golden Boy* (NY 1964). Davis also sang it in London production (1968), joined by Gloria De Haven.

"I Want What I Want When I Want It." Music by Victor Herbert; lyric by Henry Blossom. Crotchety credo introduced by William Pruette in *Mlle. Modiste* (NY 1905).

"I Was Born in Virginia." Music & lyric by George M. Cohan. Tribute to the Old Dominion State sung by Ethel Levey in *George Washington, Jr.* (NY 1906). Jamie Donnelly also sang it in *George M!* (NY 1968). Miss Levey became so closely identified with the number that it was also known as "Ethel Levey's Virginia Song."

"I Went to a Marvellous Party." Music & lyric by Noël Coward. Increasingly hysterical description of an utterly mad bash on the Riviera which was written specially for Beatrice Lillie. She sang it in both *Set to Music* (NY 1939) and *All Clear* (L 1939) wearing slacks, a fisherman's shirt, several ropes of pearls, dark glasses, and a huge sun hat. The creation of the song, which is also known as "I've Been to a Marvellous Party," was prompted by a real event presided over by Elsa Maxwell, who had tried to get Coward and Miss Lillie to provide free entertainment.

"I Whistle a Happy Tune." Music by Richard Rodgers; lyric by Oscar Hammerstein II. Whistling as an antidote to fear, first prescribed by Gertrude Lawrence in *The King and I* (NY 1951), later by Valerie Hobson in London version (1953).

"I Wish I Were in Love Again." Music by Richard Rodgers; lyric by Lorenz Hart. Breezy confession maintaining that, despite never-ending squabbles, being in love is better than not being in love. Grace McDonald and Rolly Pickert introduced the number in *Babes in Arms* (NY 1937).

"I Wonder What Became of Me." Music by Harold Arlen; lyric by Johnny Mercer. June Hawkins' torchy lament in *St. Louis Woman* (NY 1946) was deleted after opening night.

"Ice Cream." Music by Jerry Bock; lyric by Sheldon Harnick. Writing to an unknown correspondent, the heroine of *She Loves Me* becomes distracted when she realizes how a gift of vanilla ice cream and a friendly visit have changed her opinion about a man she thought she despised. Barbara Cook had the change of heart in NY (1963), Anne Rogers in London (1964).

"I'd Do Anything." Music & lyric by Lionel Bart. Demonstrations of friendship spiritedly pledged by Martin Horsey, Georgia Brown, Keith Hamshere, and cast in *Oliver!* (L 1960). In NY company (1963), pledged by David Jones, Miss Brown, Bruce Prochnik, and cast.

I'd Rather Be Right (1937). Music by Richard Rodgers; lyrics by Lorenz Hart; book by George S. Kaufman & Moss Hart.
    SONGS: "A Homogeneous Cabinet," "Have You Met Miss Jones?," "A Little Bit of Constitutional Fun," "Sweet Sixty-Five," "We're Going to Balance the Budget," "I'd Rather Be Right," "Off the Record."

NEW YORK: Nov. 2, 1937
ALVIN THEATRE; 290 p.

Presented by Sam H. Harris; directed by George S. Kaufman; choreographed by Charles Weidman, Ned McGurn; settings, Donald Oenslager; costumes, Irene Sharaff, John Hambleton; music director, Harry Levant; orchestrations, Hans Spialek.

CAST: George M. Cohan (*Franklin D. Roosevelt*), Taylor Holmes (*Secretary Morgenthau*), Joy Hodges (*Peggy Jones*), Austin Marshall (*Phil Barker*), Paul Parks (*Postmaster General Farley*), Marion Green (*Secretary Hull*), Mary Jane Walsh (*Judge's Girl*), Georgie Tapps (*messenger*).

The idea of devising a satirical musical with the President of the US as chief target was considered so daring that the show was probably the most eagerly awaited theatrical event of the 30s. Adding to its importance was the fact that Franklin D. Roosevelt would be played by George M. Cohan, returning to the musical stage after an absence of 10 years. It was also the only stage musical Cohan ever appeared in that he did not write himself. The musical was almost as much of a revue as a book show, as it told how Peggy and Phil, while sitting in NY's Central Park, fall asleep and dream that they meet President Roosevelt. FDR tries to help them by thinking of ways to balance the budget, but none of his schemes works. At the end Peggy and Phil decide to get married anyway. Among the entertainment's targets: the Cabinet, the WPA, the Supreme Court, fireside chats, Alf Landon, press conferences. The President's mother was depicted but not wife Eleanor, and though the barbs were never really too sharp, the mere fact that such a musical could be presented at all was considered proof of the freedom enjoyed in the US, particularly when compared to other countries. Beginning Oct. 1938, the show toured five months.

I'd Rather Be Right still remains the only Bway book musical with a real President as leading character. Revue sketches, however, have shown such chief executives as Wilson (**Walter Catlett in the** *Ziegfeld Follies of 1917*), Coolidge (John McGovern in *The Garrick Gaieties*, 1925) and Hoover (Leslie Adams in *As Thousands Cheer*, 1933). In 1950, Irving Fisher, as Harry S. Truman, took a nightly curtain call in *Call Me Madam*. Fictitious presidents have been portrayed in *Of Thee I Sing* (1931) and its sequel, *Let 'Em Eat Cake* (1933) (both played by William Gaxton), and in *Mr. President* (1962) (played by Robert Ryan). In *As the Girls Go* (1948), Bobby Clark appeared as the husband of the first woman President (Irene Rich).

"If Ever I Would Leave You." Music by Frederick Loewe; lyric by Alan Jay Lerner. A song of love's constancy during all four seasons introduced by Robert Goulet in *Camelot* (NY 1960). In London version (1964), it was sung by Barry Kent.

"If He Walked Into My Life." Music & lyric by Jerry Herman. Affecting ruminations of a woman who wonders where she went wrong in bringing up an adopted nephew. Sung in *Mame* by Angela Lansbury in NY (1966) and Ginger Rogers in London (1969).

"If I Ever Fall in Love Again." Music by Peter Greenwell; lyric by Peter Wildeblood. In *The Crooked Mile* (L 1959) Elisabeth Welch thinks she may have found a new romance.

"If I Gave You." Music & lyric by Hugh Martin & Timothy Gray. In

High Spirits (NY 1964), Edward Woodward and Louise Troy recall a love poem and sing it as a gentle madrigal. The singers in the London company (1964) were Denis Quilley and Jan Waters.

"If I Love Again." Music by Ben Oakland; lyric by J. P. Murray. Ballad of a tenacious love sung by Rex Weber in *Hold Your Horses* (NY 1933).

"If I Loved You." Music by Richard Rodgers; lyric by Oscar Hammerstein II. The main romantic duet in *Carousel* (NY 1945), sung by Jan Clayton and John Raitt; in London version (1950), by Iva Withers and Stephen Douglass. Hammerstein's lyric was prompted by dialogue in Ferenc Molnar's play *Liliom*, from which *Carousel* was adapted. In the scene, Liliom asks the shy Julie, "But you wouldn't marry a rough guy like me—that is—eh—if you loved me?" And Julie answers, "Yes, I would—if I loved you, Mr. Liliom."

"If I Ruled the World." Music by Cyril Ornadel; lyric by Leslie Bricusse. Sung by Harry Secombe in the title role in *Pickwick*, both in London (1964) and NY (1965). In the story, Pickwick is mistaken for a candidate standing for Parliament and sings the song as a thumping campaign speech.

"If I Were a Bell." Music & lyric by Frank Loesser. True love revealed in *Guys and Dolls* (NY 1950) by heroine Isabel Bigley when, a bit tipsy, she likens her feeling to a ringing bell, a lighted lamp, a waving banner, a swinging gate, a watch popping its spring, a burning bridge, a quacking duck, a cooked goose, and a salad splashing its dressing. In London production (1953), the part was played by Lizbeth Webb.

"If I Were a Rich Man." Music by Jerry Bock; lyric by Sheldon Harnick. In *Fiddler on the Roof* (NY 1964), poor Tevye the milkman, played by Zero Mostel, sings—with many a cabalistic gurgle and grunt—about the advantages of wealth. In London version (1967), the piece was sung by Topol.

"If Love Were All." Music & lyric by Noël Coward. Ivy St. Helier introduced the song during a rehearsal scene at Schlick's Café in Vienna in *Bitter Sweet* (L 1929), and Mireille sang it in the NY production (1929). In this credo of a "humble diseuse," the singer reveals that while she occasionally yearns for an all-consuming romance, she realistically accepts the fact that "the most I've had is just a talent to amuse." The song's rhyming pattern contains no rhymes within the three sections of the main theme. Instead, the first three lines of the first section rhyme with the first three lines of the other two: "can . . . must . . . choose," "man . . . trust . . . lose," and "began . . . just . . . amuse."

"If My Friends Could See Me Now." Music by Cy Coleman; lyric by Dorothy Fields. Finding herself in a movie star's apartment, the heroine of *Sweet Charity* (NY 1966) asks the actor for "some article of personal apparel" to prove to her friends she was really with him. He provides her with a top hat and cane and she provides the audience with an exultant song-and-dance number to express her amazement at being where she is. Gwen Verdon was the original Charity; Juliet Prowse played the part in London (1967).

"If the Rain's Got to Fall." Music & lyric by David Heneker. In *Half a*

Sixpence (L 1963, NY 1965), Tommy Steele sang of his hope for a rain-free Sunday (" 'cause that's when I'm meetin' my girl").

"If There Is Someone Lovelier Than You." Music by Arthur Schwartz; lyric by Howard Dietz. Ardent serenade introduced by Georges Metaxa in *Revenge with Music* (NY 1934).

"If This Isn't Love." Music by Burton Lane; lyric by E. Y. Harburg. Buoyant affirmation that it's the real thing. Donald Richards and Ella Logan introduced the number in *Finian's Rainbow* (NY 1947); Alan Gilbert and Beryl Seton sang it in London version (1947).

"If You Could Care." Music by Herman Darewski; lyric by Arthur Wimperis. The main aria in *As You Were*, sung by Alice Delysia in London (1918) and by Irene Bordoni in NY (1920).

"If You Hadn't but You Did." Music by Jule Styne; lyric by Betty Comden & Adolph Green. Explosive catalogue of reasons why Dolores Gray, in *Two on the Aisle* (NY 1951), just bumped off her husband.

"If You Knew Susie Like I Know Susie." Music by Joseph Meyer; lyric by B. G. De Sylva. Though sung by Al Jolson in *Big Boy* (NY 1925), the bubbly song has since become associated with Eddie Cantor.

"If You Were the Only Girl in the World." Music by Nat D. Ayer; lyric by Clifford Grey. Duet of solitary bliss introduced by Violet Loraine and George Robey in *The Bing Boys Are Here* (L 1916). It was revived in *Funny Side Up* (L 1940), in which it was sung by Florence Desmond (as Miss Loraine) to Stanley Lupino (as Robey). The song did not become popular in the US until 1929, when its rhythm was changed to a waltz.

"I'll Be Seeing You." Music by Sammy Fain; lyric by Irving Kahal. Rueful torch ballad sung by Tamara in *Right This Way* (NY 1938). The piece became popular during World War II when the lyric was made to apply to a girl waiting for the return of a soldier.

"I'll Build a Stairway to Paradise." Music by George Gershwin; lyric by Arthur Francis (Ira Gershwin) & B. G. DeSylva. Revivalistic number introduced in the first-act finale ("The Patent Leather Forest") of *George White's Scandals* (NY 1922). It was sung and danced by Winnie Lightner, Pearl Regay, Colette Ryan, Olive Vaughn, George White, Jack McGowan, Richard Bold, Newton Alexander, and chorus, accompanied by Paul Whiteman's orchestra. In London (1923), the song was added to the score of *Stop Flirting* (known as *For Goodness Sake* on Bway), sung by Marjorie Gordon, Jack Melford, Mimi Crawford, and Henry Kendall, danced by Fred and Adele Astaire. Describing its presentation in the *Scandals*, George Gershwin wrote: "Two circular staircases surrounded the orchestra on the stage, leading high up into theatrical Paradise, or the flies, which in everday language means the ceiling. Mr. White had draped 50 of his most beautiful girls in a black patent leather material which brilliantly reflected the spotlights." The number evolved out of a song George had written with Ira called "New Step Every Day," which concluded with the lines "I'll build a staircase to Paradise/ With a new step every day." Lyricist DeSylva thought these lines indicated a production routine and asked the brothers to collaborate with him on a song built around them—except that the "staircase" became a "stairway."

"I'll Buy You a Star." Music by Arthur Schwartz; lyric by Dorothy Fields. At the end of Act I of *A Tree Grows in Brooklyn* (NY 1951), shiftless Johnny Nolan (Johnny Johnston) tries desperately to convince his wife, Katie (Marcia Van Dyke), that they'll soon be living in luxury.

"I'll Follow My Secret Heart." Music & lyric by Noël Coward. Yvonne Printemps sang this tender waltz in *Conversation Piece* both in London (1934) and NY (1934). Coward had had such a problem in creating this song that at one point he considered postponing the entire production for at least six months. In the depths of creative despair, as the composer has recounted, "I poured myself a large whisky and soda, dined in grey solitude, poured myself another, even larger whisky and soda, and sat gloomily envisaging everybody's disappointment and facing the fact that my talent had withered and that I should never write any more music until the day I died. The whisky did little to banish my gloom, but there was no more work to be done and I didn't care if I became fried as a coot, so I gave myself another drink and decided to go to bed. I switched off the lights at the door and noticed that there was one lamp left on by the piano. I walked automatically to turn it off, sat down and played 'I'll Follow My Secret Heart,' straight through in G flat, a key I had never played in before."

"I'll Know." Music & lyric by Frank Loesser. In *Guys and Dolls*, the missionary heroine tells the gambler hero exactly the kind of noble person she will fall in love with; he, in turn, tells the girl he'll leave romance to chance and chemistry. Isabel Bigley and Robert Alda introduced the conversational ballad in NY (1950); Lizbeth Webb and Jerry Wayne sang it in London (1953).

"I'll Never Fall in Love Again." Music by Burt Bacharach; lyric by Hal David. Song of disillusionment introduced by Jill O'Hara, accompanying herself on the guitar, in *Promises, Promises* (NY 1968). In London version (1969), it was sung by Betty Buckley.

"I'll See You Again." Music & lyric by Noël Coward. The recurring waltz theme from *Bitter Sweet*, sung by Peggy Wood and Georges Metaxa (L 1929), and Evelyn Laye and Gerald Nodin (NY 1929). This piece, which Coward claimed "just dropped into my head, whole and complete," during a NY taxi ride, was first presented in the operetta as a musical exercise for the pupil heroine and the music-teacher hero.

"I'll Tell the Man in the Street." Music by Richard Rodgers; lyric by Lorenz Hart. Rather than confiding their romantic feelings to the red, red rose or the babbling brook, Vivienne Segal and Walter Slezak in *I Married an Angel* (NY 1938) happily revealed their plans to tell the whole world.

"I'm a Brass Band." Music by Cy Coleman; lyric by Dorothy Fields. Being loved causes a deliriously happy girl to feel like everything from the Philadelphia Orchestra and the Modern Jazz Quartet to a Count Basie blast and the bells of St. Peter's in Rome. Sung and danced in *Sweet Charity* by Gwen Verdon in NY

(1966) and Juliet Prowse in London (1967).

"I'm a Little Bit Fonder of You." Music & lyric by Irving Caesar. Hit duet of *Mercenary Mary* (L 1925), sung by Peggy O'Neil and A. W. Baskcomb. Also in *Ripples* (NY 1930), sung by Janet Martin and Andrew Tombes.

"I'm a Little Blackbird Looking for a Bluebird." Music by George W. Meyer & Arthur Johnston; lyric by Grant Clarke & Roy Turk. Florence Mills's poignant ballad, which she sang in both *Dixie to Broadway* (NY 1924) and *Blackbirds* (L 1926).

"I'm a One-Man Girl." Music by Richard Myers; lyric by Leo Robin. Gentle song-and-dance duet for Bobby Howes and Binnie Hale in *Mr. Cinders* (L 1929). The number dated back to 1926 when it was sung by Jeanette MacDonald and Cecil Lean in *Bubbling Over*, a Bway-bound musical that never reached its destination.

"I'm All Smiles." Music by Michael Leonard; lyric by Herbert Martin. How it feels to be in love with "Someone to fly to the sun, moon and sky for." Carmen Alvarez introduced this waltzing ballad in *The Yearling* (NY 1965).

"I'm Always Chasing Rainbows." Music by Harry Carroll; lyric by Joseph McCarthy. Sung by Harry Fox in *Oh, Look!* (NY 1918), and by Phyllis Titmuss in *Bran Pie* (L 1919). In 1974, during Bway run of *Irene*, the song was added to the score and sung by Jane Powell. The melody was adapted by the composer from the middle sections of Chopin's *Fantaisie Impromptu* in C-sharp minor. A follow-up number, "I'm Forever Blowing Bubbles," was another confession of a self-indulgent daydreamer.

"I'm an Ordinary Man." Music by Frederick Loewe; lyric by Alan Jay Lerner. Professor Higgins' outburst about what would happen to his tranquillity if he ever let a woman in his life. Sung in *My Fair Lady* by Rex Harrison (NY 1956, L 1958).

"I'm Bringing a Red, Red Rose." Music by Walter Donaldson; lyric by Gus Kahn. Love token proffered by Paul Gregory to Frances Upton in *Whoopee* (NY 1928).

"I'm Building Up to an Awful Let-Down." Music by Fred Astaire; lyric by Johnny Mercer. Binnie Hale and Jack Whiting voiced romantic doubts in this interpolated number in *Rise and Shine* (L 1936).

"I'm Falling in Love with Someone." Music by Victor Herbert; lyric by Rida Johnson Young. The symptoms of falling in love revealed by Orville Harrold (who gave four encores opening night) in *Naughty Marietta* (NY 1910).

"I'm Flying." Music by Mark Charlap; lyric by Carolyn Leigh. Levitational feat proclaimed by Mary Martin, Kathy Nolan, Robert Harrington, and Joseph Stafford in *Peter Pan* (NY 1954) while on their way to Never Never Land.

"I'm Gonna Wash That Man Right Outa My Hair." Music by Richard Rodgers; lyric by Oscar Hammerstein II. Mary Martin expresses her determination to forget about the man she loves in *South Pacific* (NY 1949, L 1951). The idea for the song had its beginning when Miss Martin told director Joshua Logan that because her hair dries very fast after it's been shampooed, she thought it would be a good idea to wash her hair on stage during the play. This gave Hammerstein the idea for a song lyric that, with Rodgers' spirited melody, was originally intended to be sung in time to the washing. During the pre-Bway tryout, however, audiences were more interested in the shampooing than the song, and Logan quickly restaged the scene so that Miss Martin would sing first and shampoo after.

"I'm in a Dancing Mood." Music by Al Hoffman; lyric by Al Goodhart & Maurice Sigler. Jack Buchanan and Elsie Randolph sang and danced this light-footed piece in *This'll Make You Whistle* (L 1936).

"I'm Just Wild About Harry." Music by Eubie Blake; lyric by Noble Sissle. High-stepping cakewalk in praise of a mayoral candidate in *Shuffle Along* (NY 1921), introduced by Lottie Gee. Though originally written as a waltz— and almost dropped from the show before the NY opening—the melody was changed to a one-step because Miss Gee feared white audiences would not accept a waltz in an all-black musical. Florence Mills sang the number in London revue *Dover Street to Dixie* (1923).

"I'm Like a New Broom." Music by Arthur Schwartz; lyric by Dorothy Fields. In which Johnny Nolan (Johnny Johnston) in *A Tree Grows in Brooklyn* (NY 1951) vows to make something of himself now that he's going to be married.

"I'm on a See-Saw." Music by Vivian Ellis; lyric by Desmond Carter. Love's highs and lows recounted in a musical dialogue by Louise Browne

and John Mills in *Jill Darling* (L 1934).

"I'm Still Here." Music & lyric by Stephen Sondheim. Show-stopping number celebrating personal durability belted out by Yvonne De Carlo in *Follies* (NY 1971). The song was written on the road before the Bway opening to replace "Can That Boy Fox Trot."

"Impossible Dream, The." Music by Mitch Leigh; lyric by Joe Darion. Man's indomitable will as expressed by Richard Kiley, as Don Quixote, in *Man of La Mancha* (NY 1965). The hymnlike song, also known as "The Quest," was sung in London production by Keith Michell (1968).

"In a Little While." Music by Mary Rodgers; lyric by Marshall Barer. In which Anne Jones and Allen Case blissfully look forward to the birth of their illegitimate child in *Once Upon a Mattress* (NY 1959). In London company (1960), the parts were played by Bill Newman and Patricia Lambert.

"In Egern on the Tegern See." Music by Jerome Kern; lyric by Oscar Hammerstein II. In *Music in the Air* (NY 1932), Ivy Scott, as a former prima donna of the Munich Opera House, is coaxed into singing the tender title song of her most famous operetta. In London production (1933), it was sung by Muriel George. The piece was spoofed in Rick Besoyan's "In Izzenschnooken on the Lovely Essenzook Zee" in *Little Mary Sunshine* (NY 1962).

"In the Heart of the Dark." Music by Jerome Kern; lyric by Oscar Hammerstein II. Romantic nocturnal reverie introduced in *Very Warm for May* (NY 1939) by Hollace Shaw and reprised by Frances Mercer. The song is similar in theme to Cole Porter's "All Through the Night."

"Indian Love Call." Music by Rudolf Friml; lyric by Otto Harbach & Oscar Hammerstein II. Echoey mating call for Mary Ellis and Dennis King in *Rose-Marie* (NY 1924), and for Edith Day and Derek Oldham in London version (1925).

Irene (1919). Music by Harry Tierney; lyrics by Joseph McCarthy; book by James Montgomery, based on his play *Irene O'Dare.*

SONGS: "Alice Blue Gown," "The Talk of the Town," "To Be Worthy of You," "Castle of Dreams," "Irene," "Sky Rocket," "The Last Part of Every Party."

NEW YORK: Nov. 18, 1919
VANDERBILT THEATRE; 670 p.

Presented by Carle Carlton; directed by Edward Royce; settings, Robert Law; costumes, Lucile, Finchley; music director, Gus Salzer.

CAST: Edith Day (*Irene O'Dare*), Walter Regan (*Donald Marshall*), Bobbie Watson (*Mme. Lucy*), Dorothy Walters (*Mrs. O'Dare*), John B. Litel (*Lawrence Hadley*), Hobart Cavanaugh (*Robert Harrison*), Arthur Burckly (*J. P. Bowden*), Bernice McCabe (*Eleanor Worth*), Eva Puck (*Helen Cheston*), Florence Mills (*Mrs. Marshall*).

LONDON: April 7, 1920
EMPIRE THEATRE; 399 p.

Presented by J. L. Sacks, with Alfred Butt; directed by Tom Reynolds; settings, Alfred Terraine, E. H. Ryan, Raphael; costumes, Stein & Blaine; music director, Sydney Ffoulkes.

CAST: Edith Day (*Irene O'Dare*), Robert Hale (*Mme. Lucy*), Pat Somer-

set (*Donald Marshall*), Helen Kinnaird (*Mrs. O'Dare*), Hubert Neville (*Lawrence Hadley*), Robert Blythe (*Robert Harrison*), Robert Michaelis (*J. P. Beaudon*), Daisy Hancox (*Eleanor Worth*), Margaret Campbell (*Helen Cheston*), Bertha Belmore (*Mrs. Cheston*), Maidie Hope (*Mrs. Marshall*).

NEW YORK: March 13, 1973
MINSKOFF THEATRE; 605 p.

Presented by Harry Rigby, Albert Selden, & Jerome Minskoff; directed by Gower Champion; choreographed by Peter Gennaro; settings & costumes, Raoul Pène du Bois; Miss Reynolds' costumes, Irene Sharaff; lighting, David Segal; music director, Jack Lee; orchestrations, Ralph Burns; book revised by Joseph Stein, Hugh Wheeler, & Harry Rigby; added songs by Charles Gaynor & Otis Clements.

CAST: Debbie Reynolds (*Irene O'Dare*), Patsy Kelly (*Mrs. O'Dare*), Monte Markham (*Donald Marshall*), George S. Irving (*Mme. Lucy*), Ruth Warrick (*Mrs. Marshall*), Janie Sell (*Jane Burke*), Carmen Alvarez (*Helen McFudd*).

Irene was Bway's longest-running musical for 18 years before it was overtaken by *Pins and Needles.* Created as a vehicle for Edith Day, it marked the first Bway score written by composer Harry Tierney, recently teamed with lyricist Joseph McCarthy. Soon after the opening, Miss Day married producer Carle Carlton, who was also her manager, and in April 1920 left the cast to star in the London version. Because of a romance with Pat Somerset, her leading man, Miss Day and Carlton were subsequently divorced and the actress then married Somerset (that union didn't last long, either). On Bway, Miss Day was succeeded by Adele Rowland and Patti Harrold (daughter of Orville Harrold, hero of *Naughty Marietta*), and Bernice McCabe was succeeded by Jeanette MacDonald. During US tour, Busby Berkeley played Mme. Lucy, John Litel was Donald.

The libretto of *Irene* tells a Cinderella tale of poor Irene O'Dare, from NY's Ninth Avenue, who works for an upholsterer and is sent to mend some cushions at the Long Island home of wealthy Donald Marshall. Donald is attracted to the talkative girl and gets her a job—along with two of her friends—to model the creations of a male fashion designer named Mme. Lucy. Since the modeling involves passing herself off as a member of society, Irene is wooed by social-climbing J. P. Bowden, but he is aghast when her humble origins are revealed. Donald, however, loves her the way she is.

In 1973, in the wake of the *No, No, Nanette* revival, *Irene* was re-created on Bway with almost equal box-office approval, thanks largely to the appeal of Debbie Reynolds in her Bway debut. Sir John Gielgud, the original director, withdrew on the road and was succeeded by Gower Champion. In Feb. 1974, however, when Champion refused to work with Miss Reynolds' successor, Jane Powell, the director was denied program credit. During run, Monte Markham was succeeded by Ron Husmann (6-73), George S. Irving by Hans Conried (6-74). For this version the heroine's occupation was changed to a piano tuner and the character of J. P. Bowden was dropped. Among interpolated songs were "You Made Me Love You" (music, James Monaco) and, for Miss Powell, "I'm Always Chasing Rainbows" (music, Harry Carroll, based on Chopin). The revival was the first production at the Minskoff Theatre.

FILM VERSION: Anna Neagle and Ray Milland (RKO 1940, Herbert Wilcox dir.).

"Irene." Music by Harry Tierney; lyric by Joseph McCarthy. Sung by Edith Day in the title role in both NY (1919) and London (1920) productions of *Irene*. It was introduced in a scene in which Irene's prospective mother-in-law, anxious to prove that the poor shopgirl is of royal Irish lineage, shows her a diagram of her supposed family tree.

Irma La Douce (1958). Music by Marguerite Monnot; lyrics & book by Julian More, Monty Norman, David Heneker, based on French book & lyrics by Alexandre Breffort.

SONGS: "Valse Milieu," "The Bridge at Coulaincourt," "Our Language of Love," "She's Got the Lot," "Dis-Donc," "Le Grisbi Is le Root of le Evil in Men," "There Is Only One Paris for That."

LONDON: July 17, 1958
LYRIC THEATRE; 1,512 p.
Presented by Donald Albery, H. M. Tennent Ltd., Two Arts Ltd.; directed by Peter Brook; choreographed by John Heawood; settings & costumes, Rolf Gerard; lighting, Joe Davis; music director, Alexander Faris; orchestrations, André Popp.
CAST: Elizabeth Seal (*Irma-la-Douce*), Keith Michell (*Nestor-le-Fripe*), Clive Revill (*Bob-le-Hontu*), John East (*Polyte-le-Mou*), Julian Orchard (*Police Inspector*), Gary Raymond (*Frangipane*).

NEW YORK: Sept. 29, 1960
PLYMOUTH THEATRE; 524 p.
Presented by David Merrick, with Donald Albery & H. M. Tennent Ltd.; directed by Peter Brook; choreographed by Onna White; settings & costumes, Rolf Gerard; lighting, Joe Davis; music director, Stanley Le-

bowsky; orchestrations, André Popp, Robert Ginzler.

CAST: Elizabeth Seal (*Irma-la-Douce*), Keith Michell (*Nestor-le-Fripe*), Clive Revill (*Bob-le-Hontu*), Fred Gwynne (*Polyte-le-Mou*), George S. Irving (*Police Inspector*), Stuart Damon (*Frangipane*), Elliott Gould (*Usher, Priest, Warder*).

The British writer's adapted *Irma la Douce* from a Parisian success starring Colette Renard, and turned it into an even bigger West End hit. Elizabeth Seal, the only female member of the cast, was acclaimed for her performance in both London and NY. Set in a dingy quarter of Paris, the plot revolves around a pure-at-heart prostitute who loves a poor student named Nestor. To have Irma all to himself, Nestor disguises himself as Oscar, a man rich enough to be her only provider. But Nestor grows jealous of Oscar, "kills" him, and is sent to Devil's Island for his "crime." Eventually he escapes, proves his innocence, and has a Christmas reunion with Irma. A US touring company, headed by Taina Elg (*Irma*) and Denis Quilley (*Nestor*), began its journey in Jan. 1962.

FILM VERSION: Shirley MacLaine and Jack Lemmon (no songs) (UA 1963, Billy Wilder dir.).

"Island in the West Indies." Music by Vernon Duke; lyric by Ira Gershwin. Calypso-ish ode to a tropical haven ("Away from Reuben's and from Lindy's") introduced in *Ziegfeld Follies* (NY 1936) by Gertrude Niesen and danced by Josephine Baker.

"Isn't It a Pity?" Music by George Gershwin; lyric by Ira Gershwin. Tender regret at the years wasted ("You reading Heine, I somewhere in China") because the lovers had never met before. Josephine Huston and George Givot introduced the song in *Pardon My English* (NY 1933).

"It Ain't Necessarily So." Music by George Gershwin; lyric by Ira Gershwin. Sceptical view of such biblical tales as David and Goliath, Jonah in the whale, Moses being fished from a stream, Methuselah living 900 years, Daniel in the lion's den, and Solomon having 600 wives. Performed with relish by the character of Sportin' Life in the Kittiwake Island picnic scene in *Porgy and Bess*. John W. Bubbles did the part originally (1935), Cab Calloway played it in London (1952).

"It All Depends on You." Music by Ray Henderson; lyric by B. G. DeSylva & Lew Brown. This ballad of romantic dependency was the first piece written together by the songwriting trio. It was added to the score of *Big Boy* (NY 1925), in which it was introduced by Al Jolson. The following year Phyllis Dare sang it in London in *Lido Lady*.

"It Never Entered My Mind." Music by Richard Rodgers; lyric by Lorenz Hart. Rueful reflections on the end of a romance sung by Shirley Ross in *Higher and Higher* (NY 1940).

"It Never Was You." Music by Kurt Weill; lyric by Maxwell Anderson. In *Knickerbocker Holiday* (NY 1938), this search for love and its ultimate discovery was rendered by Richard Kollmar and Jeanne Madden.

"Italian Street Song." Music by Victor Herbert; lyric by Rida Johnson Young. Emma Trentini gave it the old "Zing-zing, zing-a-zing-a-zing!" in *Naughty Marietta* (NY 1910), while recalling her youth in Naples.

"It's a Big Wide Wonderful World." Music & lyric by John Rox. Rollicking confession of the exaggerated, outlandish ways one feels when one's in love. Introduced in *All in Fun* (NY 1940) by Wynn Murray, Walter Cassel, Marie Nash, and Bill Johnson, and danced by Rosita Moreno, Anita Alvarez, and William Archibald.

"It's a Lovely Day Today." Music & lyric by Irving Berlin. Sprightly duet extolling the pleasures of companionship in *Call Me Madam*. Russell Nype and Galina Talva sang it in NY (1950); Jeff Warren and Shani Wallis in London (1952).

"It's a Lovely Day Tomorrow." Music & lyric by Irving Berlin. Sung by Irene Bordoni as a bit of optimistic philosophy to perk up the spirits of heroine Vera Zorina in *Louisiana Purchase* (NY 1940).

"It's a Musical World." Music & lyric by Leslie Bricusse & Anthony Newley. Joyous tribute to the miracles of melody that abound around us, sung by Anthony Newley in *The Good Old Bad Old Days!* (L 1972).

"It's All Right With Me." Music & lyric by Cole Porter. In *Can-Can* (NY 1953), Peter Cookson, after a temporary row with his beloved, contemplates a dalliance with Gwen Verdon. The London version (1954) found Edmund Hockridge doing the contemplating.

"It's Delightful to Be Married." Music by Vincent Scotto; lyric by Anna Held. Miss Held adapted a French song, *"La Petite Tonkinoise,"* and sang it in *The Parisian Model* (NY 1906) while coquettishly flashing a hand mirror in the faces of the gentlemen in the audience. Part of the song's appeal was the stammered word "be" preceding "married" in the second line of the song.

"It's De-Lovely." Music & lyric by Cole Porter. Sung by Ethel Merman and Bob Hope in *Red, Hot and Blue!* (NY 1935); in London, by Frances Day in *The Fleet's Lit Up* (1938). The number relates, via a self-kidding verse and four choruses, the blissful saga of a boy and girl from the night they fall in love, through their marriage and honeymoon, and right up to the arrival of their firstborn. Another extended matrimonial story—though with a less happy conclusion—was the Donaldson-Kahn "Makin' Whoopee" in *Whoopee* (1928).

"It's Good to Be Alive." Music & lyric by Bob Merrill. Going out to sea on her father's barge gives Anna Christie an optimistic feeling about life. Introduced by Gwen Verdon in *New Girl in Town* (NY 1957), later reprised by George Wallace.

"It's Got to Be Love." Music by Richard Rodgers; lyric by Lorenz Hart. Ruling out tonsilitis, neuritis, indigestion, and a hangover, the buoyant sentiment asserts that the fatally unnerving symptoms can only mean love. Doris Carson and Ray Bolger performed the song-and-dance number in *On Your Toes* (NY 1936); Gina Malo and Jack Whiting did it in the London production (1937).

"It's Love." Music by Leonard Bernstein; lyric by Betty Comden & Adolph Green. Joyous discovery made by George Gaynes in *Wonderful Town* (NY 1953), and by Dennis Bowen in London version (1955).

"It's Never Too Late to Fall in Love." Music & lyric by Sandy Wilson. In which aging roué and squealing flapper—with many a boop-a-doop, whack-a-do and vodeo—gaily affirm that "a jolly old flame has lots of sparks." It was sung in *The Boy Friend* by John Rutland and Maria Charles in London (1954) and by Geoffrey Hibbert and Dilys Lay in NY (1954).

"It's the Going Home Together." Music by Jerome Moross; lyric by John Latouche. In *The Golden Apple* (NY 1954), Ulysses (Stephen Douglass), just back from the Spanish-American War, and his wife, Penelope (Priscilla Gillette), sing lovingly of what it means to be together again.

"It's Today." Music & lyric by Jerry Herman. This credo of making every day a celebration was radiantly proclaimed by bugle-tooting Angela Lansbury, in gold pajamas, as she greeted party guests from the top of a staircase in *Mame* (NY 1966). Later in the same scene Miss Lansbury sang a slower, more intimate version to her 10-year-old nephew. In London production (1969), Ginger Rogers did the proclaiming. Composer Herman had previously used the same melody for a number called "There's No Tune Like a Show Tune" in the off-Bway revue *Parade* (1954).

"I've Come to Wive It Wealthily in Padua." Music & lyric by Cole Porter. During a performance of *The Taming of the Shrew* in *Kiss Me, Kate*, Petruchio reveals his reason for coming to Padua. Alfred Drake sang it in NY (1948), Bill Johnson in London (1951). The lyric was based on the concluding lines of Petruchio's speech in the original Shakespeare play:

> . . . were she as rough
> As are the swelling Adriatic seas;
> I come to wive it wealthily in Padua;
> If wealthily then happily in Padua.

"I've Confessed to the Breeze." Music by Vincent Youmans; lyric by Otto Harbach. Lilting confession of timid twosome who, after telling of their love to the breeze, the birds and the bees, "ev'ry star above you," and the red rose, finally reveal their feelings to each other. (The song's sentiment is somewhat similar to Kern and Hammerstein's "I've Told Ev'ry Little Star.") Though the number was in the original score of *No, No, Nanette*, it was dropped before the 1925 Bway production. It was, however, sung in the London version (also 1925), in which the couple was played by Seymour Beard and Binnie Hale. In 1970 Bway revival, Roger Rathburn and Susan Watson sang the duet.

"I've Got a Crush on You." Music by George Gershwin; lyric by Ira Gershwin. Lively number of mutual affection sung and danced by Mary Hay and Clifton Webb in *Treasure Girl* (NY 1928), and also by Doris Carson and Gordon Smith in *Strike Up the Band* (NY 1930). This is the only example of a Gershwin song being used in two Bway musicals.

"I've Got Five Dollars." Music by Richard Rodgers; lyric by Lorenz Hart. Inventory-type love duet sung by Jack Whiting and Harriette Lake (Ann Sothern) in *America's Sweetheart* (NY 1930).

"I've Got Rings on My Fingers." Music by Maurice Scott; lyric by J. F. Barnes & R. P. Weston. Subtitled "Mumbo Jumbo Jijiboo J. O'Shea," the number was sung by Blanche Ring in both *The Midnight Sons* (NY

1909) and *The Yankee Girl* (NY 1910), and was long identified with the singer. It was also sung in *Hullo, London!* (L 1910). The number's comic appeal is in its bizarre account of an Irish girl being married to an Oriental nabob on St. Patrick's Day.

"I've Got to Be Me." Music & lyric by Walter Marks. Declaration of independence asserted by Steve Lawrence in *Golden Rainbow* (NY 1968).

"I've Got You on My Mind." Music & lyric by Cole Porter. Despite each other's failings, Fred Astaire and Claire Luce revealed their mutual attraction in *Gay Divorce* (NY 1932, L 1933).

"I've Got Your Number." Music by Cy Coleman; lyric by Carolyn Leigh. In which Swen Swenson in *Little Me* (NY 1962) propositioned Virginia Martin and then stopped the show with a stomping, sinewy dance. In London version (1964), Swenson sized up Eileen Gourlay.

"I've Gotta Crow." Music by Mark Charlap; lyric by Carolyn Leigh. Sung by a self-satisfied Mary Martin—complete with crowing—in the title role of *Peter Pan* (NY 1954).

"I've Grown Accustomed to Her Face." Music by Frederick Loewe; lyric by Alan Jay Lerner. Rex Harrison's final number in *My Fair Lady* (NY 1956, L 1958), in which—without saying it—Henry Higgins reveals his love for Eliza Doolittle.

"I've Never Been in Love Before." Music & lyric by Frank Loesser. Robert Alda and Isabel Bigley discovered love for the first time in *Guys and Dolls* (NY 1950). In London production (1953), Lizbeth Webb and Jerry Wayne did the discovering.

"I've Told Ev'ry Little Star." Music by Jerome Kern; lyric by Oscar Hammerstein II. Love song of a timid suitor introduced by Walter Slezak as part of a choral society recital in *Music in the Air* (NY 1932). It was later reprised by Slezak and Katherine Carrington as an audition for a music publisher. In London production (1933), it was sung by Bruce Carfax and Eve Lister. The composer claimed to have first heard the basic melody in the song of a New England swallow. Vincent Youmans and Otto Harbach dealt with a similar theme in "I've Confessed to the Breeze," in *No, No, Nanette*.

J

Janis, Elsie (née Elsie Bierbower), actress, singer, lyricist, producer; b. Columbus, Ohio, March 16, 1889; d. Los Angeles, Cal., Feb. 26, 1956. A slender, energetic singer and mimic, Miss Janis began her career as a child actress known in vaudeville as Little Elsie. Her activities entertaining US troops in World War I won her the title "The Sweetheart of the AEF." As lyricist, Miss Janis collaborated with Jerome Kern. Bib: *So Far So Good* by Miss Janis (Dutton, NY 1932).

Asterisk indicates Miss Janis was also sketch writer and/or producer:
1905 When We Were Forty-One
1906 The Vanderbilt Cup (*Dorothy Willetts*)

1907 The Hoyden (*Joan Talbot*)
1909 The Fair Coed (*Cynthia Bright*)
1911 The Slim Princess (*Princess Kalora*)
1912 The Lady of the Slipper (*Cinderella*)
1914 The Passing Show (L)
1915 The Passing Show (L)
     Miss Information (*Dot*) (also lyr.) (Kern)
1916 The Century Girl
1917 Miss 1917
1918 Hullo, America! (L)
1919 Elsie Janis and Her Gang *
1920 It's All Wrong * (L)
1922 Elsie Janis and Her Gang *
1925 Puzzles of 1925 * (also dir.)
1927 Oh, Kay! (US tour) (*Kay*)
1928 Clowns in Clover (L) (added)

     Helen of Troy, New York (co-prod. only)
1930 Sweet and Low
1941 High Kickers (*George M. Krause*) (also co-lib., co-prod.)

"Jenny." Music by Kurt Weill; lyric by Ira Gershwin. Gertrude Lawrence's show-stopper—also known as "The Saga of Jenny"—in *Lady in the Dark* (NY 1941). Unlike the musical's indecisive heroine, the heroine of the song gets into all kinds of trouble just because "she *would* make up her mind." Miss Lawrence, in a circus dream sequence, socked across the number with many a burlesque bump and grind. The piece was added to the score just before the Boston tryout because it was felt that as the star, Miss Lawrence needed something to top Danny Kaye's specialty, "Tschaikowsky," which immediately preceded it.

Jessel, George (Albert), actor, singer; b. New York, April 3, 1898. Jessel was a rambling raconteur in Bway revues whose trademark routine was a telephone call to his mother. He made his first vaudeville appearance in 1907, and scored his biggest nonmusical hit in *The Jazz Singer*. Bib: *So Help Me* by Jessel (1943).
1919 Shubert Gaieties
1923 The Passing Show

Jesus Christ Superstar (1971). Music by Andrew Lloyd Webber; lyrics by Tim Rice; book by Tom O'Horgan, based on the New Testament.

SONGS: "What's the Buzz?," "Everything's All Right," "This Jesus Must Die," "I Don't Know How to Love Him," "Damned for All Time," "The Last Supper," "King Herod's Song," "Superstar."

NEW YORK: Oct. 12, 1971
MARK HELLINGER THEATRE; 711 p.

Presented by Robert Stigwood, with MCA Inc.; directed by Tom O'Horgan; settings, Robin Wagner; costumes, Randy Barcelo; lighting, Jules Fisher; music director, Marc Pressel; orchestrations, Andrew Lloyd Webber.

CAST: Jeff Fenholt (*Jesus*), Yvonne Elliman (*Mary Magdalene*), Ben Vereen (*Judas*), Barry Dennen (*Pontius Pilate*).

LONDON: Aug. 9, 1972
PALACE THEATRE

Presented by Robert Stigwood, with MCA Inc.; directed by Jim Sherman; settings, Brian Thomson; costumes, Gabriella Falk; lighting, Jules Fisher; music director, Anthony Bowles; orchestrations, Andrew Lloyd Webber.

CAST: Paul Nicholas (*Jesus*), Dana Gillespie (*Mary Magdalene*), Stephen Tate (*Judas*), John Parker (*Pontius Pilate*).

A so-called rock opera, the musical had its roots in the song "Superstar," which the British song writers then expanded into a score that was recorded by Decca. The album's success triggered a series of concert tours that eventually evolved into the Bway production. While this approach to the last seven days of Christ was opposed by various religious denominations, the flamboyantly staged musical had a successful run, though the more simply mounted London version has become an even greater hit. During Bway run, Ben Vereen was succeeded by Patrick Jude (7-72), Jeff Fenholt by Denis Cooley (4-73). The story covered the same basic theme as *Godspell*, which opened off-Bway five months earlier. Bib: *Rock Opera* by Ellis Nassour & Richard Broderick (Hawthorn, NY 1973).

FILM VERSION: Ted Neeley and Carl Anderson (Univ. 1973, Norman Jewison dir.).

"Joey, Joey, Joey." Music & lyric by Frank Loesser. A ranch hand's wanderlust revealed by Art Lund in *The Most Happy Fella* both in NY (1956) and London (1960).

"Johnny One Note." Music by Richard Rodgers; lyric by Lorenz Hart. The account of a vocal phenomenon rendered by Wynn Murray in *Babes in Arms* (NY 1937). In the scene—part of a makeshift revue called *Lee Calhoun's Follies*—the song is performed in an Egyptian setting with the actors clad in such household items as towels, coat hooks, bathmats, brooms, etc. Also in the number were Douglas Perry, Alfred Drake, Eleanor Tennis, the Nicholas Brothers, Bobby Lane, and dancers Mitzi Green and Duke McHale.

"Johnny's Song." Music by Kurt Weill; lyric by Paul Green. The theme-melody of *Johnny Johnson* (NY 1936), in which Johnny (Russell Collins) proclaims his innocent faith in man's goodness. The piece was later given a commercial lyric by Edward Heyman and called "To Love You and to Lose You."

Johnson, Bill, actor, singer; b. Baltimore, Md., March 22, 1918; d. Flemington, NJ, March 6, 1957. One of Bway's stalwart leading men, Johnson introduced "It's a Big, Wide Wonderful World" (*All in Fun*) and "All at Once You Love Her" (*Pipe Dream*). He was married to actress Shirl Conway. Actor was known as William Johnson beginning 1955.

1940	Two for the Show
	All in Fun
1941	Banjo Eyes (*Charlie*)
1943	Something for the Boys (*Rocky Fulton*)
1945	The Day Before Spring (*Alex*)
1947	Annie Get Your Gun (L) (*Frank Butler*)
1951	Kiss Me, Kate (L) (*Fred Graham*)
1955	Kismet (US tour) (*Hajj*)
	Pipe Dream (*Doc*)

Johnson, Chick. See **Olsen and Johnson.**

"Joker, The." Music & lyric by Leslie Bricusse & Anthony Newley. *Pagliacci*-type plaint of Anthony Newley in *The Roar of the Greasepaint—The Smell of the Crowd* (NY 1964).

Jolson, Al (né Asa Yoelson), actor, singer; b. St. Petersburg, Russia, March 26, 1886; d. San Francisco, Cal., Oct. 23, 1950. Exuberant Al Jolson was one of the most dynamic performers to appear on the Bway stage. He was celebrated for his blackface characterizations, which always gave him the chance to get down on one knee and sing his "Mammy" songs. The man who billed himself "The World's Greatest Entertainer" first appeared on stage with Lew Dockstader's Minstrels and made his Bway debut in 1899. His biggest hits, *Sin-*

bad and *Bombo,* included interpolated songs "Avalon," "Rockabye Your Baby with a Dixie Melody," "Swanee," "My Mammy," "April Showers," "California, Here I Come," and "Toot, Toot, Tootsie! Goo'bye." He appeared in Hollywood films, incl. *The Jazz Singer,* the first talkie. Jolson was married to and divorced from Ruby Keeler. Bib: *The Immortal Jolson* by Pearl Seiben (Fell, NY 1962); *Jolson* by Michael Freedland (Stein & Day, NY 1972).

1911	La Belle Paree (*Erastus Sparkler*)
	Vera Violetta (*Claude*)
1912	The Whirl of Society (*Gus*)
1913	The Honeymoon Express (*Gus*)
1914	Dancing Around (*Gus*)
1916	Robinson Crusoe, Jr. (*Gus Jackson*)
1918	Sinbad (*Gus, Inbad*)
1921	Bombo (*Bombo*)
1925	Big Boy (*Gus*)
1926	Artists and Models (added)
1927	A Night in Spain (US tour)
1931	The Wonder Bar (*Al*)
1940	Hold on to Your Hats (*Lone Rider*) (also co-prod.)

Jones, Sidney, composer; b. Leeds, Eng., June 17, 1869; d. London, Jan. 29, 1946. Earliest successful London theatre composer whose hits included *A Gaiety Girl, An Artist's Model, The Geisha,* and *San Toy,* all produced by George Edwardes. Lyric-writing partners: Harry Greenbank, Adrian Ross, George Jessup, Charles Taylor, Percy Greenbank.

1893	A Gaiety Girl (H. Greenbank)
1895	An Artist's Model (H. Greenbank)
1896	The Geisha (H. Greenbank)
1898	A Greek Slave (H. Greenbank, Ross)
1899	San Toy (H. Greenbank, Ross)
1903	My Lady Molly (Jessup)
	The Medal and the Maid (Taylor)
1906	See-See (Ross)
1908	The King of Cadonia (Ross)
1909	A Persian Princess (P. Greenbank)
1913	The Girl from Utah (Ross, P. Greenbank)
1916	The Happy Day (Ross)

Jones, Tom, lyricist, librettist; b. Littlefield, Texas, Feb. 17, 1928. Jones and his partner, composer Harvey Schmidt, were responsible for off-Bway's eternally running phenomenon *The Fantasticks* ("Soon It's Gonna Rain," "Try to Remember"). On Bway, their hits were "Simple Little Things" in *110 in the Shade* and "My Cup Runneth Over" in *I Do! I Do!* Since 1967 the team has been working on intimate experimental musicals at their own studio, and in 1975 they presented four (including *Philemon*) for limited runs.

1960	The Fantasticks
1963	110 in the Shade
1966	I Do! I Do!
1969	Celebration (also dir.)

"Jubilation T. Cornpone." Music by Gene de Paul; lyric by Johnny Mercer. Panegyric honoring the Southland's most inept general, introduced by Stubby Kaye and the citizens of Dogpatch, USA, in *Li'l Abner* (NY 1956).

Jubilee (1935). Music & lyrics by Cole Porter; book by Moss Hart.

SONGS: "Why Shouldn't I?," "The Kling-Kling Bird on the Divi-Divi Tree," "When Love Comes Your Way," "Me and Marie," "Just One of Those Things," "A Picture of Me Without You," "Begin the Beguine," "Mr. and Mrs. Smith."

NEW YORK: Oct. 12, 1935
IMPERIAL THEATRE; 169 p.

Presented by Sam H. Harris & Max Gordon; directed & lighted by Hassard Short; choreographed by Albertina Rasch; settings, Jo Mielziner; costumes, Irene Sharaff, Connie De Pinna; music director, Frank Tours;

orchestrations, Robert Russell Bennett.

CAST: Mary Boland (*The Queen*), June Knight (*Karen O'Kane*), Melville Cooper (*The King*), Derek Williams (*Eric Dare*), May Boley (*Eve Standing*), Charles Walters (*Prince James*), Margaret Adams (*Princess Diana*), Mark Plant (*Charles Rausmiller*), Montgomery Clift (*Prince Peter*).

Cole Porter and Moss Hart wrote most of the musical while on a four-and-a-half-month, round-the-world trip on the SS *Franconia*. The title occurred to them on the night of King George V's Silver Jubilee Celebration, and the story itself was concerned with an unspecified but Anglified king and queen. Bored with matters of state, the members of the royal family pose as commoners and set off on a variety of adventures. Along the way they meet up with prototypes of Noel Coward (called Eric Dare), Elsa Maxwell (Eve Standing), and Johnny Weissmuller (Charles Rausmiller). Though well received, the musical had a relatively brief run because star Mary Boland elected to return to Hollywood and replacement Laura Hope Crews was unable to attract the customers.

Jumbo (1935). Music by Richard Rodgers; lyrics by Lorenz Hart; book by Ben Hecht & Charles MacArthur.

SONGS: "Over and Over Again," "The Circus Is on Parade," "The Most Beautiful Girl in the World," "My Romance," "Little Girl Blue," "The Song of the Roustabouts."

NEW YORK: Nov. 16, 1935
HIPPODROME; 233 p.

Presented by Billy Rose; directed by John Murray Anderson & George Abbott; choreographed by Allan K. Foster; settings, Albert Johnson; costumes, Raoul Pène du Bois; music director, Adolph Deutsch; orchestrations, Deutsch, Hans Spialek, Conrad Salinger.

CAST: Jimmy Durante (*Claudius B. Bowers*), Paul Whiteman Orchestra, Gloria Grafton (*Mickey Considine*), Donald Novis (*Matt Mulligan Jr.*), Poodles Hanneford (*Poodles*), Arthur Sinclair (*John Considine*), Bob Lawrence (singer).

Producer Billy Rose spent over $340,000 (a record at the time) of his own and mostly John Hay Whitney's money on this elaborate combination of musical comedy and circus, which was presented at the newly reconstructed Hippodrome. Although the premiere was set for Labor Day, difficulties in coordinating all the elements in the production—story, dances, circus acts, songs—caused an 11-week postponement. Reviews were enthusiastic, but the high cost of the production prevented it from remaining longer than five months on Bway. The story dreamed up by playwrights Hecht and MacArthur (their only musical as a team) was something of a tanbark *Romeo and Juliet*, as it told of the rivalry between two circus families and the way they are brought together by the daughter and son of the feuding owners. During rehearsals (there was no out-of-town tryout) Gloria Grafton replaced Ella Logan as the romantic lead and the role played by Blanche Ring was eliminated.

FILM VERSION: Doris Day, Jimmy Durante, Stephen Boyd, Martha Raye (MGM 1962, Charles Walters, Busby Berkeley dirs.).

June (née June Howard Tripp), actress, dancer, singer; b. Blackpool, Eng., June 11, 1901. Former ballet dancer who became leading musical-comedy actress in such London hits as *Mercenary Mary* and *Clowns in Clo-*

ver. Bib: *The Glass Ladder* by June (Heinemann, L 1960).

1914	The Passing Show (dancer)
1915	Watch Your Step (dancer)
1918	Buzz-Buzz (dancer)
1920	London, Paris and New York (dancer)
1921	The Fun of the Fayre
1922	Phi-Phi (*Aspasia*)
1923	Little Nellie Kelly (*Nellie Kelly*)
1924	Toni (*Princess Stephanie*)
1925	Boodle (*Daphne Drew*)
	Mercenary Mary (*June Somers*)
1926	Happy-Go-Lucky (*June Willard*)
1927	Clowns in Clover
1929	Polly (NY) (*Polly Shannon*)
1932	Fanfare
	Over the Page (Fanfare)
1934	Here's How! (*Mimi Lorraine*, repl.)
	Hi-Diddle-Diddle
1935	Shall We Reverse?
1936	The Town Talks

"June Is Bustin' Out All Over." Music by Richard Rodgers; lyric by Oscar Hammerstein II. Propulsive announcement of the arrival of summer proclaimed in *Carousel* (NY 1945) by Christine Johnson, Jean Darling, and chorus; danced by Pearl Lang and chorus. In London version (1950), the principals were Marion Ross, Margot Moser and Mavis Ray.

"Just a Little Joint with a Jukebox." Music and lyric by Hugh Martin & Ralph Blane. Song in praise of a local watering hole, sung by Nancy Walker and Kenneth Bowers in *Best Foot Forward* (NY 1941).

"Just for Today." Music & lyric by Ervin Drake. Gentle desire to return to the innocence of childhood voiced by Leslie Uggams (as Cleopatra) in *Her First Roman* (NY 1968), a musical version of Shaw's *Caesar and Cleopatra*.

"Just in Time." Music by Jule Styne; lyric by Betty Comden & Adolph Green. Propitious discovery made by Sydney Chaplin and Judy Holliday in *Bells Are Ringing* (NY 1956). The London version (1957) featured Janet Blair and George Gaynes. In the story, the song is performed as a vaudeville song-and-dance routine in Central Park to entertain passers-by.

"Just Once Around the Clock." Music by Sigmund Romberg; lyric by Oscar Hammerstein II. Fond goodbye to a fleeting love sung by Vera Van, Walter Woolf King, and Leo G. Carroll in *May Wine* (NY 1935).

"Just One of Those Things." Music & lyric by Cole Porter. Fatalistic acceptance of the end of a love affair sung by June Knight and Charles Walters in *Jubilee* (NY 1935). The piece was written just before rehearsals were to begin at the suggestion of librettist Moss Hart, who felt that the show's second act was in need of a major song. Hart and Porter were then spending the weekend at a friend's farm in Ohio, and the following morning, according to Hart, "Cole placed a scribbled sheet of paper on the music rack of the piano and then played and sang the verse and chorus of 'Just One of Those Things.' No word of either verse or chorus was ever altered. It has been played and sung through the years exactly as I heard it on that Sunday morning in Ohio, a song written overnight." A previous song called "Just One of Those Things" was also written by Porter but it had an entirely different melody and lyric. It was sung in *The New Yorkers* (NY 1930) but apparently cut after the opening.

"Just One Way to Say I Love You." Music & lyric by Irving Berlin. Romantic duet for Eddie Albert and Allyn McLerie in *Miss Liberty* (NY 1949).

⚓ K ⚓

Kahn, Gus, lyricist; b. Coblenz, Germany, Nov. 6, 1886; d. Beverly Hills, Cal., Oct. 8, 1941. Primarily a pop song lyricist, Kahn wrote "Makin' Whoopee" and "I'm Bringing a Red, Red Rose" (*Whoopee*) with Walter Donaldson, and "Liza" (*Show Girl*) with George and Ira Gershwin. Other composers he worked with: Will Ortman, Con Conrad.

1925	Holka Polka (Ortman)
1926	Kitty's Kisses (Conrad)
1928	Whoopee (Donaldson)
1929	Show Girl (Gershwins)

Kalmar, Bert, lyricist, librettist; b. New York, Feb. 16, 1884; d. Los Angeles, Cal., Sept. 18, 1947. The most popular Bway musicals written by Kalmar and his partner, composer-librettist Harry Ruby, were *The Ramblers* ("All Alone Monday"), *The Five o'Clock Girl* ("Thinking of You"), *Good Boy* ("I Wanna Be Loved by You"), and *Animal Crackers* ("Hooray for Captain Spalding"). Kalmar began his career as a child magician in tent shows, then appeared in vaudeville. During the 30s he and Ruby wrote films in Hollywood. The team also wrote with composers Jerome Kern and Herbert Stothart.

Unless otherwise noted, Mr. Kalmar was lyricist of following:

1923	Helen of Troy, New York
1924	No Other Girl
1925	Holka Polka (co-lib. only)
1926	The Ramblers (also co-lib.)
1927	Lucky (Kern) (also co-lib.)
	The Five o'Clock Girl
1928	She's My Baby (co-lib. only)
	Good Boy (Stothart)
	Animal Crackers
1929	Top Speed (also co-prod.)
1941	High Kickers (also co-lib.)

"Ka-lu-a." Music by Jerome Kern; lyric by Anne Caldwell. Romantic memories of a Hawaiian moonlit night sung by Oscar Shaw in *Good Morning Dearie* (NY 1921). Fred Fisher brought a law suit against Kern claiming that the bass figures—not the melody—of "Ka-lu-a" were an infringement on the ones in his song "Dardanella." Judge Learned Hand awarded the plaintiff the minimum damages of $250. The song was also in *The Cabaret Girl* (L 1922), sung by Dorothy Dickson.

Kander, John (Harold), composer; b. Kansas City, Mo., March 18, 1927. Kander and his partner, lyricist Fred Ebb, wrote three Bway scores for producer Harold Prince, incl. their biggest hit, *Cabaret* ("Willkomen," "Tomorrow Belongs to Me," "Married," "Cabaret"). The composer has also collaborated with James and William Goldman.

Unless otherwise noted, following written with Mr. Ebb:

1962	A Family Affair (Goldmans)
1965	Flora, the Red Menace
1966	Cabaret
1968	The Happy Time
	Zorbá
1971	70, Girls, 70
1975	Chicago
1977	The Act

Kane, Helen (née Helen Schroeder), actress, singer; b. New York, Aug. 4, 1904; d. New York, Sept. 26, 1966. The roundfaced, Boob-Boop-a-Doop girl with the squeaky baby voice was a vauderville headliner and sang "I Wanna Be Loved by You" in *Good Boy*.

1927	A Night in Spain

1928 Good Boy (*Pansy McManus*)
1933 Shady Lady (*Millie Mack*)

"Kansas City." Music by Richard Rodgers; lyric by Oscar Hammerstein II. Rollicking tribute to the city where everything's up to date. Introduced by Lee Dixon and male dancing chorus in *Oklahoma!* (NY 1943); also sung and danced by Walter Donahue and male chorus in London company (1947).

Karnilova, Maria (née Maria Karnilovich Dovgolenko), actress, dancer, singer; b. Hartford, Conn., Aug. 3, 1920. Former soloist with Ballet Theatre and Metropolitan Opera, Miss Karnilova sang "You Gotta Have a Gimmick" in *Gypsy* and created the role of Golde in *Fiddler on the Roof.* She is the wife of actor George S. Irving.

1938 Stars in Your Eyes (dancer)
1945 Hollywood Pinafore (dancer)
1946 Call Me Mister
1948 High Button Shoes (dancer, repl.)
1949 Miss Liberty (*Ruby*)
1950 Out of This World (dancer)
1952 Two's Company
1957 Kaleidoscope
1959 Gypsy (*Tessie Tura*)
1962 Bravo, Giovanni (*Signora Pandolfi*)
1964 Fiddler on the Roof (*Golde*)
1968 Zorbá (*Hortense*)
1973 Gigi (*Inez Alvarez*)

"Katie Went to Haiti." Music & lyric by Cole Porter. The escapades of a lady of easy virtue as related by Ethel Merman in a nightclub floor show in *DuBarry Was a Lady* (NY 1939). In London version (1942), it was sung by Frances Day. The song provided the germ of an idea for the next Cole Porter–Ethel Merman musical, *Panama Hattie* (NY 1940).

Kaufman, George S., librettist, director; b. Pittsburgh, Pa., Nov. 14, 1889;

d. New York, June 2, 1961. Kaufman won his greatest musical-comedy acclaim on Bway as sketch writer of *The Band Wagon*, co-librettist of *Of Thee I Sing*, and director of *Guys and Dolls.* With Moss Hart he wrote three musicals and five nonmusicals (incl. *Once in a Lifetime, You Can't Take It with You, The Man Who Came to Dinner*). Kaufman, who also contributed sketches to revues (*The Little Show*), was associated with George and Ira Gershwin on three productions. As lyricist, he wrote words to the music of Lewis Gensler, Milton Schwarzwald, Sir Arthur Sullivan. Kaufman was married for a while to actress-librettist Leueen McGrath. Bib: *George S. Kaufman* by Howard Teichmann (Atheneum, NY 1971); *George S. Kaufman and His Friends* by Scott Meredith (Doubleday, NY 1974).

Unless otherwise noted, Mr. Kaufman was librettist, co-librettist, or sketch writer of following; asterisk indicates he was also director:

1923 Helen of Troy, New York
1924 Be Yourself! (also lyr.) (Gensler, Schwarzwald)
1925 The Cocoanuts
1928 Animal Crackers
1930 Strike Up the Band
1931 The Band Wagon
      Of Thee I Sing *
1932 Face the Music (dir. only)
1933 Let 'Em Eat Cake *
1937 I'd Rather Be Right *
1938 Sing Out the News (also co-prod.)
1945 Hollywood Pinafore * (also lyr.) (Sullivan)
1946 Park Avenue *
1950 Guys and Dolls (dir. only)
1952 Of Thee I Sing * (r)
1955 Silk Stockings

Kaye, Danny (né David Daniel Kominsky), actor, singer; b. Brooklyn, NY, Jan. 18, 1913. Slim, graceful comic who first won notice with his rapid-fire routines. Kaye sang "Tschaikowsky" in *Lady in the Dark*, which led to his being starred in *Let's Face It!* He has appeared in many Hollywood films (incl. *Up in Arms*) and has had his own tv series. Bib: *The Danny Kaye Story* by Kurt Singer (Nelson, NY 1958).

1939 The Straw Hat Revue
1941 Lady in the Dark (*Russell Paxton*)
       Let's Face It! (*Jerry Walker*)
1970 Two by Two (*Noah*)

Kearns, Allen, actor, singer; b. Ontario, Canada, 1893; d. Albany, NY, April 20, 1956. Durable Bway leading man, hero of three Gershwin musicals: *Tip-Toes* (introducing "That Certain Feeling"), *Funny Face* ("He Loves and She Loves," "'S Wonderful"), *Girl Crazy* ("Embraceable You").

1910 Tillie's Nightmare (chorus)
1912 The Red Petticoat (*Miner*)
1914 Miss Daisy (*Fred*)
1919 Come Along (*Pvt. Peanuts Barker*)
       Good Morning, Judge (*Hughie Cavanagh*, repl.)
1920 What's in a Name
       Tickle Me (*Jack Barton*)
1921 Tangerine (*Lee Loring*, repl.)
1923 Lady Butterfly (*Billy Browning*)
       Little Jessie James (*Tommy Tinker*)
1925 Mercenary Mary (*Jerry*)
       Tip-Toes (*Steve Burton*)
1926 Tip-Toes (L) (*Steve Burton*)
       Betsy (*Archie*)
1927 Castles in the Air (L) (*Monty Blair*)
       Up with the Lark (L) (*Freddy Van Bozer*)
       Funny Face (*Peter Thurston*)
1928 Here's Howe (*Billy Howe*)
       Hello, Daddy (*Lawrence Tucker*)
1930 Girl Crazy (*Danny Churchill*)
1935 Love Laughs—! (L) (*Tony Thornton*)

Keel, (Harold Clifford) Howard, actor, singer; b. Gillespie, Ind., April 13, 1919. Oak-sturdy baritone who ap-

peared in MGM film musicals, 1950–55. Through 1947, he was known as Harold Keel.

1945 Carousel (*Billy Bigelow*, repl.)
       Oklahoma! (*Curly McLain*, repl.)
1947 Oklahoma! (L) (*Curly McLain*)
1959 Saratoga (*Clint Maroon*)
1963 No Strings (*David Jordan*, repl.)
1971 Ambassador (L) (*Lambert Strether*)
1972 Ambassador (*Lambert Strether*)

Keeler, (Ethel Hilda) Ruby, actress, dancer; b. Halifax, Nova Scotia, Aug. 25, 1909. A blank-faced buck-and-wing dancer, Miss Keeler tapped to the song "Liza" in *Show Girl*, and won greatest Bway acclaim in revival of *No, No, Nanette*. Best known for series of Warner Bros. screen musicals, 1933–1937. Miss Keeler's first husband was Al Jolson.

1923 The Rise of Rosie O'Reilly (chorus)
1927 Bye, Bye, Bonnie (*Ruby*)
       Lucky (*Mazie Maxwell*)
       Sidewalks of New York (*Mamie*)
1929 Show Girl (*Dixie Dugan*)
1971 No, No, Nanette (r) (*Sue Smith*)

Kelly, (Eugene Curran) Gene, actor, dancer, singer, director; b. Pittsburgh, Pa., Aug. 23, 1912. After rising to Bway fame as the conniving hero of *Pal Joey* (in which he introduced "I Could Write a Book"), Kelly became a Hollywood film star in a series of notable musicals (*Cover Girl, An American in Paris*, etc.) and later turned to directing.

1938 Leave It to Me! (dancer)
1939 One for the Money
1940 Pal Joey (*Joey Evans*)
1941 Best Foot Forward (chor. only)
1958 Flower Drum Song (dir. only)

Kelly, (Sarah Veronica Rose) Patsy, actress; b. Brooklyn, NY, Jan. 12, 1910. Down-to-earth, wisecracking, laundry-bag–shaped comedienne who made comeback in Bway revivals of *No, No, Nanette* and *Irene*. Miss Kelly also appeared in Hollywood films.

1927 Harry Delmar's Revels
1928 Three Cheers *(Bobbie Bird)*
1929 Earl Carroll Sketch Book
1930 Earl Carroll Vanities
The Wonder Bar *(Electra Pivonka)*
1932 Flying Colors
1971 No, No, Nanette (r) *(Pauline)*
1973 Irene (r) *(Mrs. O'Dare)*

Kerker, Gustave, composer; b. Westphalia, Germany, Feb. 28, 1857; d. New York, June 29, 1923. Kerker's *The Belle of New York* was the first Bway musical to win success in London. The composer settled in NY in 1870, and began career as music director of the Casino Theatre. Among lyricists he worked with: Charles Alfred Byrne, Richard Carroll, C. M. S. McLellan, Harry B. Smith, Frederick Ranken, Joseph Herbert, R. H. Burnside, Paul West, George Broadhurst, Arthur Anderson, Harold Atteridge.

1888 Pearl of Pekin (Byrne)
1890 Castles in the Air (Byrne)
1894 Prince Kam (Byrne)
1895 Kismet (Carroll)
1896 In Gay New York (McLellan)
The Lady Slavey (McLellan)
An American Beauty (McLellan)
1897 The Whirl of the Town (McLellan)
The Belle of New York (McLellan)
1898 Yankee Doodle Dandy (McLellan)
The Telephone Girl (McLellan)
1901 The Girl from Up There (McLellan)
1902 The Billionaire (Smith)
1903 The Blonde in Black (Smith)
Winsome Winnie (Ranken)
1906 The Social Whirl (Herbert)
The Tourists (Burnside)
1907 The White Hen (West)
Fascinating Flora (Burnside)

The Lady from Lane's (Broadhurst)
1912 Two Little Brides (Anderson, Atteridge)
The Grass Widows (L) (Anderson)

Kern, Jerome (David), composer; b. New York, Jan. 27, 1885; d. New York, Nov. 11, 1945. Kern was the recognized father of the modern musical theatre, whose work greatly influenced George Gershwin, Vincent Youmans, and Richard Rodgers. Between 1915 and 1918 he pioneered the intimate, integrated musicals with his productions at the Princess Theatre, mostly written with Guy Bolton and P. G. Wodehouse. These include *Very Good Eddie*, *Oh, Boy!* ("Till the Clouds Roll By"), and *Oh, Lady! Lady!!*, plus *Leave It to Jane* ("Leave It to Jane," "The Siren's Song").

In the 20s, Kern wrote the scores for two Marilyn Miller hits, *Sally* ("Look for the Silver Lining," "Wild Rose") and *Sunny* ("Sunny," "Who?"), the latter written with Otto Harbach and Oscar Hammerstein II. His major work of the decade was *Show Boat*, the first modern musical play, which he wrote with Hammerstein ("Make Believe," "Why Do I Love You?," "Ol' Man River," "Bill," "Can't Help Lovin' Dat Man"). The 30s found Kern creating a modern, more intimate form of operetta with *The Cat and the Fiddle* ("The Night Was Made for Love," "She Didn't Say 'Yes' ") and *Music in the Air* ("The Song Is You," "I've Told Ev'ry Little Star"). He also had a long-running hit with *Roberta* ("Smoke Gets in Your Eyes," "The Touch of Your Hand").

Other Kern songs: "They Didn't Believe Me" *(The Girl from Utah)*; "Kalu-a" *(Good Morning Dearie)*; "Why Was I Born?" and "Don't Ever Leave Me" *(Sweet Adeline)*; "All the Things You Are" *(Very Warm for May)*.

Among Kern collaborators: Harry B. Smith, Elsie Janis, Schuyler Greene, Adrian Ross, Anne Caldwell, B. G. DeSylva, Clifford Grey, George Grossmith, Howard Dietz, Bert Kalmar, Graham John. Oscar Shaw appeared in four Kern musicals, Louise Groody and Dorothy Dickson in three; others included George Grossmith, Clifton Webb, Helen Morgan, Fred Stone. The composer also wrote Hollywood film scores (incl. *Swing Time*). Bib: *The Jerome Kern Song Book* (S&S, NY 1955); *The World of Jerome Kern* by David Ewen (Holt).

1912 The Red Petticoat (West)
1913 Oh, I Say! (Smith)
1915 90 in the Shade (Smith)
 Rosy Rapture (L) (Mark)
 Nobody Home (Greene)
 Miss Information (Janis)
 Very Good Eddie (Greene)
1916 Theodore & Co. (L) (Ross, Grey)
1917 Have a Heart (Wodehouse)
 Love o' Mike (Smith)
 Oh, Boy! (Wodehouse)
 Leave It to Jane (Wodehouse)
 Miss 1917 (Wodehouse)
1918 Oh, Lady! Lady!! (Wodehouse)
 Toot-Toot! (Braley)
 Rock-a-bye Baby (Reynolds)
 Head Over Heels (Woolf)
1919 She's a Good Fellow (Caldwell)
1920 The Night Boat (Caldwell)
 Hitchy-Koo (Caldwell)
 Sally (Grey, etc.)
1921 Good Morning Dearie (Caldwell)
1922 The Cabaret Girl (L) (Wodehouse)
 The Bunch and Judy (Caldwell)
1923 The Beauty Prize (L) (Wodehouse, Grossmith)
 Stepping Stones (Caldwell)
1924 Sitting Pretty (Wodehouse)
 Dear Sir (Dietz)
1925 Sunny (Harbach, Hammerstein)
 The City Chap (Caldwell)
1926 Criss-Cross (Caldwell, Harbach)
1927 Lucky (Kalmar)
 Show Boat (Hammerstein)
1928 Blue Eyes (L) (John)
1929 Sweet Adeline (Hammerstein)

1931 The Cat and the Fiddle (Harbach)
1932 Music in the Air (Hammerstein)
1933 Roberta (Harbach)
1934 Three Sisters (L) (Hammerstein)
1939 Very Warm for May (Hammerstein)

Kert, (Frederick Lawrence) Larry, actor, singer, dancer; b. Los Angeles, Cal., Dec. 5, 1930. Kert's most memorable Bway appearance was in *West Side Story*, in which he introduced "Something's Coming," "Tonight," and "Maria." He also scored in *Company*, though he took over the role after the musical had opened.

1950 Tickets Please (chorus)
1953 John Murray Anderson's Almanac (chorus)
1956 Mr. Wonderful (*Stage Manager*, repl.)
1957 West Side Story (*Tony*)
1962 A Family Affair (*Gerry Seigel*)
 I Can Get It for You Wholesale (*Harry Bogen*, repl.)
1968 Cabaret (*Clifford Bradshaw*, repl.)
1969 La Strada (*Mario*)
1970 Company (*Robert*, repl.)
1972 Company (L) (*Robert*)
1973 Two Gentlemen of Verona (US tour) (*Proteus*)

Keys, Nelson ("Bunch"), actor, singer, dancer; b. London, Aug. 7, 1886; d. London, April 26, 1939. Diminutive London comic known for variety of revue characterizations. Bib: *Bunch* by John Paddy Carstairs (his son) (Hurst, L 1941).

1909 The Arcadians (*Bobby*)
1911 The Mousmé (*Lt. Makei*)
1912 Princess Caprice (*Ensign Pips*)
 Oh, Molly! (*Jimmy Cann*)
1913 The Girl in the Taxi (*Hubert*)
 Love and Laughter (*Lt. Skrydloff*)
1914 The Passing Show
1915 The Passing Show
 Bric-a-brac
1916 Vanity Fair

1917	Round the Map
1918	Very Good Eddie (*Eddie Kettle*) Buzz-Buzz
1920	London, Paris and New York
1922	The Curate's Egg (also prod.)
1924	Ziegfeld Follies (NY) (repl.) André Charlot's Revue (NY) (repl.)
1926	Rose-Marie (*Hard-Boiled Herman*, repl.)
1931	Folly to Be Wise
1932	Bow Bells
1933	After Dark
1934	Why Not Tonight?
1936	Spread It Abroad
1937	Home and Beauty

Kidd, Michael (né Milton Greenwald), choreographer, director; b. New York, Aug. 12, 1919. A former soloist with the Ballet Theatre (1942–1947), Kidd won recognition on Bway as choreographer of *Finian's Rainbow, Guys and Dolls, Can-Can,* and *Li'l Abner* (which he also directed). He has also choreographed and appeared in Hollywood films.

Asterisk indicates Mr. Kidd was also director:

1947	Finian's Rainbow
1948	Hold It
1949	Love Life
1950	Arms and the Girl Guys and Dolls
1953	Can-Can
1956	Li'l Abner * (also co-prod.)
1959	Destry Rides Again *
1960	Wildcat * (also co-prod.)
1961	Subways Are for Sleeping *
1963	Here's Love
1964	Ben Franklin in Paris *
1965	Skyscraper
1970	The Rothschilds *
1973	Cyrano *
1974	Good News * (r)

"Kids." Music by Charles Strouse; lyric by Lee Adams. "Why can't they be like we were, perfect in every way?" bemoans Paul Lynde as a distraught father in *Bye Bye Birdie* (NY

1960). Robert Nichols played the part in London production (1961).

Kiley, Richard (Paul), actor, singer; b. Chicago, Ill., March 31, 1922. A tall, commanding actor, Kiley has appeared in Bway dramas as well as musicals, and scored his greatest success in *Man of La Mancha* (introducing "The Impossible Dream"). Other notable roles were in *Kismet* ("Stranger in Paradise," "And This Is My Beloved"), *Redhead,* and *No Strings* ("The Sweetest Sounds").

1953	Kismet (*Caliph*)
1959	Redhead (*Tom Baxter*)
1962	No Strings (*David Jordan*)
1964	Here's Love (*Fred Gaily,* repl.) I Had a Ball (*Stan the Spieler*)
1965	Man of La Mancha (*Don Quixote*)
1968	Her First Roman (*Julius Caesar*)
1969	Man of La Mancha (L) (*Don Quixote*)
1977	Man of La Mancha (r)

King and I, The (1951). Music by Richard Rodgers; lyrics & book by Oscar Hammerstein II, based on Margaret Landon's novel *Anna and the King of Siam,* and Talbot Jennings & Sally Benson's screen adaptation, both taken from Anna Leonowens' diaries, *The English Governess at the Siamese Court.*

SONGS: "I Whistle a Happy Tune," "My Lord and Master," "Hello, Young Lovers," "March of the Siamese Children," "A Puzzlement," "Getting to Know You," "We Kiss in a Shadow," "Something Wonderful," "I Have Dreamed," "Shall We Dance?"

NEW YORK: March 29, 1951
ST. JAMES THEATRE; 1,246 p.

Presented by Richard Rodgers & Oscar Hammerstein II; directed by John Van Druten; choreographed by Jerome Robbins; settings & lighting, Jo Mielziner; costumes, Irene Sharaff; music director, Frederick Dvonch; orchestrations, Robert Russell Bennett.

CAST: Gertrude Lawrence (*Anna Leonowens*), Yul Brynner (*The King*), Dorothy Sarnoff (*Lady Thiang*), Doretta Morrow (*Tuptim*), Larry Douglas (*Lun Tha*), Johnny Stewart (*Prince Chulalongkorn*), John Juliano (*The Kralahome*).

LONDON: Oct. 8, 1953
DRURY LANE THEATRE; 926 p.

Presented by Williamson Music Ltd.; restaged by Jerome Whyte; dances reproduced by June Graham; settings & lighting, Jo Mielziner; costumes, Irene Sharaff; music director, Reginald Burston; orchestrations, Robert Russell Bennett.

CAST: Valerie Hobson (*Anna Leonowens*), Herbert Lom (*The King*), Muriel Smith (*Lady Thiang*), Doreen Duke (*Tuptim*), Jan Mazarus (*Lun Tha*), Timothy Brooking (*Prince Chulalongkorn*), Martin Benson (*The Kralahome*).

LONDON: Oct. 10, 1973
ADELPHI THEATRE; 260 p.

Presented by Harold Fielding, with Triumph Theatre Prod. & Hemdale; directed by Roger Redfarn; choreographed by Sheila O'Neill; settings, Terry Parsons; lighting, Barry Griffiths; music director, Reg Cole; orchestrations, Keith Amos.

CAST: Sally Ann Howes (*Anna Leonowens*), Peter Wyngarde (*The King*), Moyna Cope (*Lady Thiang*), Pauline Antony (*Tuptim*), Valentine Palmer (*Lun Tha*), David Morris (*Prince Chulalongkorn*), David Davenport (*The Kralahome*).

Gertrude Lawrence first conceived the idea of a musical treatment of the story of the English governess in Siam, though initially she wanted Cole Porter to write the songs and her husband, Richard Aldrich, to produce. When Aldrich demurred, Miss Lawrence then approached Rodgers and Hammerstein. Set in Bangkok in the early 1860s, the play's central theme is the importance of mutual understanding between people of differing ethnic and cultural backgrounds. Anna, who has accepted the post of teacher to the Siamese king's children, soon exerts great influence on the king, who is torn between his semibarbaric background and his desire to help his people. When the monarch dies late in the play, Anna, who has decided to leave, changes her mind and remains with the children at court. One of the memorable sequences in the lavishly mounted production was Jerome Robbins' ballet "The Small House of Uncle Thomas," an oriental version of *Uncle Tom's Cabin*.

Though Rex Harrison and Alfred Drake were originally considered for the part of the king, the role went to the relatively inexperienced Yul Brynner. Drake, however, replaced Brynner for three months in 1952, and that summer Celeste Holm spelled Miss Lawrence. In Sept. 1952, after Miss Lawrence's death, her role was taken by Constance Carpenter, who was succeeded by Annamary Dickey (1-54) and Patricia Morison (2-54). Beginning March 1954, *The King and I* toured for one year, nine months. During first London run, Valerie Hobson was succeeded by Eve Lister, and Herbert Lom by George Pastell, both in May 1955.

Film version: Deborah Kerr and Yul Brynner (20th Cent. 1956, Walter Lang dir.).

King, Charles, actor, singer; b. New York, Oct. 31, 1889; d. London, Jan. 11, 1944. Breezy, round-faced song-and-dance man who scored his biggest Bway hits in *Little Nellie Kelly* (singing "Nellie Kelly, I Love You") and *Hit the Deck* ("Sometimes

I'm Happy"). Originally a vaudeville and Bway partner of singer Elizabeth Brice, King also introduced "Play a Simple Melody" in *Watch Your Step.* In 1929 he appeared in the first original film musical, *The Broadway Melody.*

1908	The Yankee Prince (chorus)
	The Mimic World
1911	The Slim Princess (*Ted Norcross*)
1912	A Winsome Widow (*Wilder Daly*)
1913	The Geisha (r) (*Dick Cunningham*)
	The Passing Show
1914	Watch Your Step (*Algy Cuffs*)
1917	Miss 1917
1919	Good Morning, Judge (*Hughie Cavanagh*)
1920	Buddies (US tour) (*Sonny*)
1921	It's Up to You (*Ned Spencer*)
	George White's Scandals
1922	Little Nellie Kelly (*Jerry Conroy*)
1924	Keep Kool
1926	No Foolin'
1927	Hit the Deck (*Bilge Smith*)
1928	Present Arms (*Chick Evans*)
1930	The New Yorkers (*Al Spanish*)
1937	Sea Legs (*Capt. Nordstrom*)

King, Dennis (né Dennis Pratt), actor, singer; b. Coventry, Eng., Nov. 2, 1897; d. New York, May 21, 1971. A classically trained romantic singing actor, King was equally at home in the plays of Shakespeare, Ibsen, and Chekhov as he was in the musicals of Friml (*Rose-Marie, The Vagabond King, The Three Musketeers*), Kern and Hammerstein (*Show Boat, Music in the Air*), and Rodgers and Hart (*I Married an Angel*). He settled in the US in 1921, and also appeared in Hollywood films. His robust baritone introduced such impassioned pieces as "Indian Love Call," "Rose-Marie," "Song of the Vagabonds," "Only a Rose," "March of the Musketeers," "I Married an Angel."

| 1919 | Monsieur Beaucaire (L) (*Townbrake*) |
| 1924 | Rose-Marie (*Jim Kenyon*) |

1925	The Vagabond King (*François Villon*)
1928	The Three Musketeers (*D'Artagnan*)
1930	The Three Musketeers (L) (*D'Artagnan*)
1932	Show Boat (r) (*Gaylord Ravenal*)
1933	Command Performance (L) (*Peter Mali*)
1937	Frederika (*Goethe*)
1938	I Married an Angel (*Count Willi Palaffi*)
1951	Music in the Air (r) (*Bruno Mahler*)
1956	Shangri-la (*Hugh Conway*)

"King's Horses (and the King's Men), The." Music by Noel Gay; lyric by Harry Graham. Perky description of the royal guards sung by Cicely Courtneidge in *Folly to Be Wise* (L 1931) and *Over the Moon* (L 1953).

King's Rhapsody (1949). Music & book by Ivor Novello; lyrics by Christopher Hassall.

SONGS: "Some Day My Heart Will Awake," "Fly Home, Little Heart," "If This Were Love," "A Violin Began to Play," "The Gates of Paradise," "Muranian Rhapsody."

LONDON: Sept. 15, 1949
PALACE THEATRE; 839 p.

Presented by Tom Arnold; directed by Murray MacDonald; choreographed by Pauline Grant; settings, Edward Delaney; costumes, Frederick Dawson; music director, Harry Acres; orchestrations, Acres.

CAST: Ivor Novello (*King Nikki*), Zena Dare (*Queen Elena*), Phyllis Dare (*Marta Karillos*), Olive Gilbert (*Countess Vera Lemainken*), Vanessa Lee (*Queen Christiane*), Denis Martin (*Count Egon Stanieff*), Victor Bogetti (*King Peter*), Robert Andrews (*Vanescu*).

Prompted by the celebrated romance between King Carol of Rumania and actress Magda Lupescu—as well as the abdication of King Edward VIII—Ivor Novello's final (and favorite) operetta dealt with the romance between King Nikki of Murania and actress Marta Karillos. Nikki, who had been exiled to Paris because of his scandalous behavior, must return to his homeland to succeed his dead father and to marry Princess Christiane of Norseland. He also brings along Marta, which makes things a bit sticky. Eventually Nikki abdicates when his democratic reform bill is turned down by the assembly and he returns to Paris with Marta. Christiane serves as regent until her son—and Nikki's—is old enough to ascend the throne. Novello died three hours after the performance of March 5, 1951; his role was then assumed by Jack Buchanan. A prior Novello musical, *Glamorous Night* (1935), was also based—though even more loosely—on the Carol-Lupescu affair. In 1936, the Bway musical *Forbidden Melody* was suggested by an early indiscretion of King Carol.

FILM VERSION: Anna Neagle and Errol Flynn (Brit. Lion 1956, Herbert Wilcox dir.).

Kirk, Lisa, actress, singer; b. Roscoe, Pa. Statuesque song-belter who introduced "The Gentleman Is a Dope" in *Allegro* and "Always True to You in My Fashion" in *Kiss Me, Kate*. Miss Kirk has also scored as a nightclub entertainer.

1947   Allegro (*Emily*)
1948   Kiss Me, Kate (*Lois Lane*)
1964   Here's Love (*Doris Walker*, repl.)
1974   Mack & Mabel (*Lottie Ames*)

Kismet (1953). Music & lyrics by Robert Wright & George Forrest, themes adapted from Aleksandr Borodin; book by Charles Lederer & Luther Davis, based on play by Edward Knoblock.

SONGS: "Rhymes Have I," "Fate" (Symphony No. 2 in B-minor), "Not Since Nineveh" ("Polovtsian Dances"), "Baubles, Bangles and Beads" (String Quartet in D), "Stranger in Paradise" ("Polovtsian Dances"), "He's in Love" ("Polovtsian Dances"), "Night of My Nights" ("Serenade"), "And This Is My Beloved" (String Quartet in D), "Sands of Time" ("In the Steppes of Central Asia").

NEW YORK: Dec. 3, 1953
ZIEGFELD THEATRE; 583 p.

Presented by Charles Lederer; directed by Albert Marre; choreographed by Jack Cole; settings & costumes, Lemuel Ayers; lighting, Peggy Clark; music director, Louis Adrian; orchestrations, Arthur Kay.

CAST: Alfred Drake (*Hajj*), Doretta Morrow (*Marsinah*), Joan Diener (*Lalume*), Richard Kiley (*Caliph*), Henry Calvin (*Wazir*), Philip Coolidge (*Omar Khayyam*), Beatrice Kraft (*Princess Samaris*), Steve Reeves (*Guard*).

LONDON: April 20, 1955
STOLL THEATRE; 648 p.

Presented by Jack Hylton; directed by Albert Marre; choreographed by Jack Cole; settings & costumes, Lemuel Ayers; lighting, Peggy Clark, Alec Shanks; music director, Cyril Ornadel.

CAST: Alfred Drake (*Hajj*), Doretta Morrow (*Marsinah*), Joan Diener (*Lalume*), Peter Grant (*Caliph*), Paul Whitsun-Jones (*Wazir*), Donald Eccles (*Omar Khayyam*), Juliet Prowse (*Princess Samaris*).

This "Musical Arabian Night" was first unveiled by producer Edwin Lester for the Los Angeles and San Francisco Light Opera Co. The action occurs within a dawn-to-dawn period in and around ancient Baghdad. A public poet takes the place of Hajj, a beggar, and soon finds himself involved with the wicked Wazir of Police and the Wazir's seductive wife, Lalume. By the end of the day he's tricked the Wazir into drowning and goes off into the desert with Lalume. A second theme involves the poet's daughter, Marsinah, and the Caliph, who fall in love and marry within the day. With Alfred Drake making a dashing appearance as the wily hero, the production achieved its success despite the lack of newspaper reviews caused by a strike. During Bway run, Richard Kiley was succeeded by Richard Oneto. Beginning April 1955, the US tour was headed by William Johnson (*Hajj*), Elaine Malbin (*Marsinah*), Julie Wilson (*Lalume*), and Oneto. Prior to *Kismet,* the most successful musical set in Baghdad was *Chu Chin Chow* (L 1916). (For other Bway musicals with scores based on the classics, see *Blossom Time.*)

FILM VERSION: Howard Keel, Ann Blyth, Dolores Gray (MGM 1955, Vincente Minnelli dir.).

"Kiss in the Dark, A." Music by Victor Herbert; lyric by B. G. DeSylva. Sung by Edith Day in *Orange Blossoms* (NY 1922). In the story, the heroine sings the song to her godfather (played by Pat Somerset) as she recalls a kiss in the dark from a stranger while on vacation in Deauville.

"Kiss Me Again." Music by Victor Herbert; lyric by Henry Blossom. Sung by Fritzi Scheff in *Mlle. Modiste* (NY 1905). In a routine called "If I Were on the Stage," Miss Scheff, as a stagestruck French girl, offered three types of songs to display her versatility. As a country girl she sang a gavotte, as a lady of history a polonaise, and as a romantic heroine a waltz, "Kiss Me Again." At first Miss Scheff refused to sing the piece, insisting that it was too low for her voice. Lyricist Blossom agreed with her, but composer Herbert was adamant and the song remained in the operetta—to become the diva's greatest success.

Kiss Me, Kate (1948). Music & lyrics by Cole Porter; book by Bella & Sam Spewack, based, in part, on Shakespeare's *Taming of the Shrew.*

SONGS: "Another Op'nin', Another Show," "Why Can't You Behave?," "Wunderbar," "So in Love," "We Open in Venice," "Tom, Dick or Harry," "I've Come to Wive It Wealthily in Padua," "I Hate Men," "Were Thine That Special Face," "Too Darn Hot," "Where Is the Life That Late I Led?," "Always True to You in My Fashion," "Bianca," "Brush Up Your Shakespeare."

NEW YORK: Dec. 30, 1948
NEW CENTURY THEATRE; 1,077 p.

Presented by Saint Subber & Lemuel Ayers; directed by John C. Wilson; choreographed by Hanya Holm; settings & costumes, Ayers; music director, Pembroke Davenport; orchestrations, Robert Russell Bennett.

CAST: Alfred Drake (*Fred Graham*), Patricia Morison (*Lilli Vanessi*), Harold Lang (*Bill Calhoun*), Lisa Kirk (*Lois Lane*), Harry Clark (*Gangster*), Jack Diamond (*Gangster*), Lorenzo Fuller (*Paul*), Annabelle Hill (*Hattie*), Marc Breaux (dancer).

LONDON: March 8, 1951
COLISEUM; 501 p.

Presented by Jack Hylton; restaged by Sam Spewack; choreographed by Hanya Holm; settings & costumes, Lemuel Ayers; music director, Freddie Bretherton; orchestrations, Robert Russell Bennett.

CAST: Bill Johnson (*Fred Graham*), Patricia Morison (*Lilli Vanessi*), Julie Wilson (*Lois Lane*), Walter Long (*Bill Calhoun*), Danny Green (*Gangster*),

Sidney James (*Gangster*), Adelaide Hall (*Hattie*), Archie Savage (*Paul*).

The genesis for Cole Porter's most successful musical began in 1935 when producer Saint Subber, then a stagehand for the Theatre Guild's production of *The Taming of the Shrew*, became aware that stars Alfred Lunt and Lynn Fontanne quarreled almost as much off stage as they did in the play. Years later he took his idea of a musical version of the battling couple to librettist Bella Spewack, who insisted that Cole Porter write the score (their previous effort together had been *Leave It to Me!*). Because Porter had not had a recent success and Mrs. Spewack had had little experience in the musical theatre, the neophyte producers experienced difficulties raising the money for the production. Alfred Drake was sought for the male lead from the start, but Patricia Morison won the female lead only after it had been turned down by Jarmila Novotna, Mary Martin, Lily Pons, and Jeanette MacDonald. Sam Spewack joined his wife as co-librettist during the pre-Bway tour.

The entire action of *Kiss Me, Kate* occurs in and around Ford's Theatre, Baltimore, during a tryout of a musical version of *The Taming of the Shrew*. The time span is 5 P.M., following a run-through, to midnight of the same day after the first performance. The main story involves Fred Graham, the producer-director, who is co-starring in the production with his ex-wife, Lilli Vanessi. Despite their off-stage brawls, which echo their on-stage roles, their enduring affection for each other—as with Petruchio and Kate—becomes increasingly apparent. A secondary romance deals with actress Lois Lane, who has a weakness for actor Bill Calhoun, who has a weakness for gambling. During Bway run, Drake was succeeded by Keith

Andes (6-50), Ted Scott (7-50), Robert Wright (6-51); Miss Morison by Anne Jeffreys (6-50), Holly Harris (7-51). The US road company, which began touring in July 1949, was headed by Andes (succeeded by Wright), Miss Jeffreys (by Frances McCann), Julie Wilson, and Marc Platt. It continued for one year, 11 months. In London, Miss Morison was followed by Helena Bliss (12-51), Miss Wilson by Valerie Tandy (8-51). A 1970 London revival, with Emile Belcourt and Ann Howard, had a brief run. (For other musicals based on Shakespeare's plays, see *The Boys from Syracuse*.)

FILM VERSION: Howard Keel, Kathryn Grayson, Ann Miller (MGM 1953, George Sidney dir.).

Knickerbocker Holiday (1938). Music by Kurt Weill; lyrics & book by Maxwell Anderson.

SONGS: "There's Nowhere to Go but Up," "How Can You Tell an American?," "September Song," "It Never Was You," "The Scars," "Dirge for a Soldier."

NEW YORK: Oct. 19, 1938
ETHEL BARRYMORE THEATRE; 168 p.

Presented by The Playwrights Co.; directed by Joshua Logan; choreographed by Carl Randall, Edwin Denby; settings, Jo Mielziner; costumes, Frank Bevan; music director, Maurice de Abravanel; orchestrations, Kurt Weill.

CAST: Walter Huston (*Gov. Pieter Stuyvesant*), Ray Middleton (*Washington Irving*), Jeanne Madden (*Tina Tienhoven*), Richard Kollmar (*Brom Broeck*), Mark Smith (*Tienhoven*), Robert Rounseville (chorus).

In one of the first musicals to use historic subjects to make comments on current issues, Maxwell Anderson tackled the broad theme of democracy vs. totalitarianism in a retelling of the reign of Gov. Stuyvesant in New Amsterdam, 1647. Pitted against the autocratic governor is Brom Broeck, the freedom-loving "first American," who wins the argument and steals the Governor's intended bride. As Stuyvesant, Walter Huston (in his only Bway musical) gave such a winning performance—especially when he .sang "September Song"—that audience sympathies were somewhat confused. The production also marked the first of two collaborations between playwright Anderson and composer Weill (the second was *Lost in the Stars*).

In 1900, Henry E. Dixey played the role of Gov. Stuyvesant in a Bway musical called *The Burgomaster*.

FILM VERSION: Nelson Eddy and Charles Coburn (UA 1944, Harry Joe Brown dir.).

Knight, June (née Margaret Rose Valliquietto), actress, singer, dancer; b. Hollywood, Cal., Jan. 22, 1911. Platinum blonde, pencil-eyebrowed dancer-singer who introduced "Begin the Beguine" and "Just One of Those Things" in *Jubilee*.
1929 Fifty Million Frenchmen (chorus)
1932 Hot-Cha! (*Dorothy Maxwell*)
      Take a Chance (*Toni Ray*)
1935 Jubilee (*Karen O'Kane*)
1936 Going Places (L) (*Jeanne LaPorte*)
1937 And on We Go (L)
1947 Sweethearts (r) (*Liane*)

L

"Ladies Who Lunch, The." Music & lyric by Stephen Sondheim. Cynical toast to affluent modern women—"the dinosaurs surviving the crunch"—proposed by Elaine Stritch in *Company* (NY 1970, L 1972).

Lady, Be Good! (1924). Music by George Gershwin; lyrics by Ira Gershwin; book by Guy Bolton & Fred Thompson.
SONGS: "Hang on to Me," "So Am I," "Fascinating Rhythm," "Oh, Lady Be Good!," "The Half of It, Dearie, Blues," "Juanita," "Little Jazz Bird," "Swiss Miss."

NEW YORK: Dec. 1, 1924
LIBERTY THEATRE; 330 p.
Presented by Alex A. Aarons & Vinton Freedley; directed by Felix Edwardes; choreographed by Sammy Lee; settings, Norman Bel Geddes; costumes, Jenkins, Kiviette, Iverson, & Henneage; music director, Paul Lannon; orchestrations, Stephen Jones.

CAST: Fred Astaire (*Dick Trevor*), Adele Astaire (*Susie Trevor*), Walter Catlett (*J. Watterson Watkins*), Cliff Edwards (*Jeff*), Alan Edwards (*Jack Robinson*), Gerald Oliver Smith (*Bertie Bassett*); Phil Ohman and Vic Arden (duo-pianos).

LONDON: April 14, 1926
EMPIRE THEATRE; 326 p.
Presented by Alfred Butt, with Aarons & Freedley; directed by Felix Edwardes; choreographed by Max Scheck; settings, Joseph & Phil Harker; costumes, Idare, Jenny, Morris Angel, Mary Fisher; music director, Jacques Heuvel.

CAST: Fred Astaire (*Dick Trevor*), Adele Astaire (*Susie Trevor*), William Kent (*J. Watterson Watkins*), George Vollaire (*Jack Robinson*), Buddy Lee (*Jeff*), Ewart Scott (*Bertie Bassett*).

The Gershwin brothers' most successful musical of the 20s was also their first Bway collaboration and their first of two scores for Fred and Adele Astaire. Primarily a vehicle for the dancers, the story (originally called *Black-Eyed Susan*) relates the adventures of Dick and Susie, brother and sister, who, when dispossessed, continue their singing and dancing at the homes of well-heeled friends. They eventually come into money when Susie, somehow, passes herself off as a Spanish heiress. One casualty of the road was "The Man I Love," which was dropped before the Bway opening. The original London run was terminated only because the theatre had to be torn down. A 1968 London revival, with Lionel Blair and Aimi Macdonald, ran 156 performances.

FILM VERSION: Eleanor Powell, Ann Sothern, Robert Young, Red Skelton (new story, added songs) (MGM 1941, Norman Z. McLeod dir.).

Lady in the Dark (1941). Music by Kurt Weill; lyrics by Ira Gershwin; book by Moss Hart.

SONGS: "Oh, Fabulous One," "One Life to Live," "Girl of the Moment," "This Is New," "The Princess of Pure Delight," "My Ship," "Jenny," "Tschaikowsky."

NEW YORK: Jan. 23, 1941
ALVIN THEATRE; 467 p.

Presented by Sam H. Harris; directed by Hassard Short & Moss Hart; choreographed by Albertina Rasch; settings, Harry Horner; costumes, Irene Sharaff, Hattie Carnegie; music director, Maurice Abravanel; orchestrations, Kurt Weill.

CAST: Gertrude Lawrence (*Liza Elliott*), Bert Lytell (*Kendall Nesbitt*), Macdonald Carey (*Charley Johnson*), Victor Mature (*Randy Curtis*), Danny Kaye (*Russell Paxton*), Donald Randolph (*Dr. Brooks*), Evelyn Wyckoff (*Miss Foster*), Natalie Schafer (*Alison Dubois*).

Moss Hart's experience in psychoanalysis led to his writing a play on that subject (originally called *I Am Listening*) for Katharine Cornell in the leading role; as the work progressed, however, it began taking the form of a musical, which meant replacing Miss Cornell. Gertrude Lawrence, the first choice, delayed her approval until Hart's threat of signing Irene Dunne made her give him a definite yes. The musical, which was Ira Gershwin's first following the death of his brother, was also the first of two collaborations between him and Kurt Weill (the other: *The Firebrand of Florence*).

In the story, Liza Elliott, a fashion-magazine editor, tries psychoanalysis to help break down her feeling of insecurity. The mistress of publisher Kendall Nesbitt, she is briefly attracted to movie star Randy Curtis, but at the play's end she has fallen in love with Charley Johnson, the magazine's acerbic advertising manager. The musical was so constructed that, with the exception of "My Ship," all the numbers are sung only during the dream sequences Liza describes to her doctor.

Lady in the Dark helped give career boosts to Victor Mature, Macdonald Carey, and, in the role of an effeminate photographer, Danny Kaye. The musical closed in June for a 10-week vacation and reopened in Sept. with the following cast changes: Paul McGrath (*Kendall*), Walter Coy (*Charley*), Willard Parker (*Randy*), Eric Brotherson (*Russell*).

FILM VERSION: Ginger Rogers, Ray Milland, Warner Baxter (Par. 1944, Mitchell Leisen dir.).

"Lady Is a Tramp, The." Music by Richard Rodgers; lyric by Lorenz

Hart. Regular gal's bold assertion that anyone who resists phony "social" conventions (i.e., dinner at eight, arriving late to theatre, shooting craps with nobility) and enjoys simple pleasures (Coney Island beach, rowing on Central Park Lake) is branded a tramp. Proudly proclaimed by Mitzi Green in *Babes in Arms* (NY 1937).

"Lady of the Evening." Music & lyric by Irving Berlin. Serenade to the night sung by John Steel in the *Music Box Revue* (NY 1922) in front of a simple rooftop setting.

Lahr, Bert (né Irving Lahrheim), actor; b. New York, Aug. 13, 1895; d. New York, Dec. 4, 1967. Raucous, rubber-faced Bert Lahr was one of Bway's most popular clowns from the late 20s through the 30s. Originally an uninhibited buffoon—with his trademarks "Gnong-gnong" and "Some fun, eh, kid?"—he later turned to a more satirical approach, specializing in ridiculing the upper crust. Lahr, who began his career in vaudeville and burlesque, enjoyed Bway successes in *Hold Everything!*, *Flying High*, *The Show Is On* (singing "The Song of the Woodman"), and *DuBarry Was a Lady* ("Friendship" with Ethel Merman). The comedian also appeared in Hollywood films (incl. *The Wizard of Oz*), and in his later years appeared in nonmusical plays. Bib: *Notes on a Cowardly Lion* by John Lahr (his son) (Knopf, NY 1969).

1927　Harry Delmar's Revels
1928　Hold Everything! (*Gink Schiner*)
1930　Flying High (*Rusty Krause*)
1932　Hot-Cha! (*Alky Schmidt*)
　　　George White's Music Hall Varieties
1934　Life Begins at 8:40
1935　George White's Scandals
1936　The Show Is On
1939　DuBarry Was a Lady (*Louis Blore*)

1944　Seven Lively Arts
1948　Make Mine Manhattan (US tour)
1951　Two on the Aisle
1959　The Boys Against the Girls
1964　Foxy (*Foxy*)

"Lambeth Walk, The." Music by Noel Gay; lyric by Douglas Furber. This strutting song-and-dance celebration of London's Cockney area was introduced by Lupino Lane, Teddie St. Denis, and chorus as the first-act finale of *Me and My Girl* (L 1937). During the number, the members of the cast—and also the audience—joined in by slapping their knees, cocking their thumbs, and shouting, "Oi!" in the approved Cockney manner. The song's success was responsible for turning the show into a long-run hit.

Lane, Burton (né Burton Levy), composer; b. New York, Feb. 2, 1912. Lane's most notable Bway score was *Finian's Rainbow*, lyrics by E. Y. Harburg, which included "How Are Things in Glocca Morra?," "Look to the Rainbow," "Old Devil Moon," "If This Isn't Love," "When I'm Not Near the Girl I Love." With Harburg, Lane also wrote "Don't Let It Get You Down," "The World Is in My Arms." He was his own lyricist (in collaboration with Al Dubin) on "Feudin' and Fightin'," and with Alan Jay Lerner he wrote "On a Clear Day" and "Come Back to Me." Lane's first Bway songs were sung in *Three's a Crowd* (1930), lyrics by Howard Dietz. He also wrote with Harold Adamson before going to Hollywood.

1931　Earl Carroll Vanities (Adamson)
1940　Hold on to Your Hats (Harburg)
1944　Laffing Room Only (also lyr.)
1947　Finian's Rainbow (Harburg)
1965　On a Clear Day You Can See Forever (Lerner).
1979　Carmelina (Lerner)

Lane, Lupino (né Henry George Lupino), actor, singer, dancer, choreographer, director, librettist, producer; b. London, June 16, 1892; d. London, Nov. 10, 1959. A comic and acrobatic dancer specializing in Cockney littleman roles, Lane enjoyed his biggest London hit in *Me and My Girl* (in which he introduced "The Lambeth Walk"). A cousin of actor Stanley Lupino, he also appeared in and directed films. Active in London to 1949.

Asterisk indicates Mr. Lane was also producer-director:

1915 Watch Your Step (*Clarence De-Vere*)
1916 Follow the Crowd
We're All in It
Extra Special
1919 Afgar (*Coucourli*)
1920 Afgar (NY) (*Coucourli*)
1921 League of Notions (added)
Puss-Puss (chor. only)
1923 Brighter London
1924 Ziegfeld Follies (NY)
1926 Turned Up (*George Medway*)
Hearts and Diamonds (*Jefferson*)
1930 Silver Wings (*Jerry Wimpole*)
1933 The One Girl (*Freddy Stone*)
Please
1934 The Golden Toy (*Barber*)
1935 Twenty to One * (*Bill Snibson*)
1937 Me and My Girl * (*Bill Snibson*)
1943 La-De-Da-De-Da * (*Bill Stubb*)
1944 Meet Me Victoria * (*Bill Fish*)
(also co-lib.)
1946 Sweetheart Mine * (*Harry Hawkins*) (also co-lib.)

Lang, Harold (Richard) actor, dancer, singer; b. Daly City, Cal., Dec. 21, 1923. A slight, athletic dancing actor, Lang won notice on Bway in *Kiss Me, Kate* and had the title role in the hit revival of *Pal Joey*. He has also toured with ballet companies.

1945 Mr. Strauss Goes to Boston (dancer)
1946 Three to Make Ready
1948 Look, Ma, I'm Dancin' (*Eddie Winkler*)
Kiss Me, Kate (*Bill Calhoun*)

1951 Make a Wish (*Ricky*)
1952 Pal Joey (r) (*Joey Evans*)
1954 Pal Joey (L) (*Joey Evans*)
1956 Shangri-la (*Robert Henderson*)
1957 Ziegfeld Follies
1959 On the Town (r) (*Gabey*)
1960 Once Upon a Mattress (US tour) (*Jester*)
1962 I Can Get It for You Wholesale (*Teddy Asch*)

Langner, Lawrence, producer; b. Swansea, S. Wales, May 30, 1890; d. New York, Dec. 26, 1962. Bib: *The Magic Curtain* by Langner (Dutton, NY 1951). See **Theatre Guild, The.**

Lansbury, Angela (Brigid), actress, singer; b. London, Oct. 16, 1925. After a Hollywood career that began in 1944, the abundantly versatile Miss Lansbury won Bway acclaim in *Mame* (singing "If He Walked into My Life" and "It's Today"), then scored again in London—and later NY—in *Gypsy*. The actress, who is the sister of producer Edgar Lansbury, has also appeared in nonmusical plays, incl. *A Taste of Honey*.

1964 Anyone Can Whistle (*Cora Hoover Hoople*)
1966 Mame (*Mame Dennis Burnside*)
1969 Dear World (*Countess Aurelia*)
1973 Gypsy (L) (*Rose*)
1974 Gypsy (r) (*Rose*)
1979 Sweeney Todd (*Mrs. Lovett*)

"Last Roundup, The." Music & lyric by Billy Hill. A loping threnody interpolated in the *Ziegfeld Follies* (NY 1934), in which it was sung by Don Ross (serious) and Willie and Eugene Howard (comic).

"Later Than Spring." Music & lyric by Noël Coward. Romance in maturity was the theme of this entreaty sung in *Sail Away* by James Hurst (NY 1961) and David Holliday (L 1962).

Latouche, John (Treville), lyricist, librettist; b. Richmond, Va., Nov. 13,

1917; d. Calais, Vt., Aug. 7, 1956. Inventive Bway lyricist who worked with composer Vernon Duke on *Cabin in the Sky* ("Cabin in the Sky," "Taking a Chance on Love") and with Jerome Moross on *The Golden Apple* ("It's the Going Home Together," "Lazy Afternoon"). He also joined Earl Robinson to write "Ballad of Uncle Sam" (later "Ballad for Americans"), which was sung in revue *Sing for Your Supper*. Other lyrics were mated to the music of Fritz Kreisler, Frederic Chopin, Duke Ellington, and James Mundy.

Asterisk indicates Mr. Latouche was also librettist:
1939 From Vienna (misc.)
1940 Cabin in the Sky (Duke)
1941 Banjo Eyes (Duke)
     The Lady Comes Across (Duke)
1944 Rhapsody (Kreisler)
1945 Polonaise (Chopin)
1946 Beggar's Holiday * (Ellington)
1948 Ballet Ballads (Moross)
1954 The Golden Apple * (Moross)
1955 The Vamp * (Mundy)

Laurents, Arthur, librettist, director; b. New York, July 14, 1918. Bway playwright (*Home of the Brave, Time of the Cuckoo*) who wrote highly praised librettos for *West Side Story* and *Gypsy*. Laurents has worked with lyricist Stephen Sondheim on four shows.

Unless otherwise noted, Mr. Laurents was librettist of following:
1957 West Side Story
1959 Gypsy
1962 I Can Get It for You Wholesale (dir. only)
1964 Anyone Can Whistle (also dir.)
1965 Do I Hear a Waltz?
1967 Hallelujah, Baby!
1973 Gypsy (L) (also dir.)
1974 Gypsy (r) (also dir.)

Lawrence, Carol (née Carol Maria Laraia), actress, singer, dancer; b. Melrose Park, Ill., Sept. 5, 1932. Miss Lawrence won fame as the heroine of *West Side Story* (singing "Tonight" and "I Feel Pretty"). She has also sung in nightclubs and on tv, and is married to actor Robert Goulet.
1952 New Faces of 1952
1954 Me and Juliet (US tour) (dancer)
1955 Plain and Fancy (dancer, repl.)
1956 Shangri-la (*Arana*)
1957 Ziegfeld Follies
     West Side Story (*Maria*)
1959 Saratoga (*Cleo Dulaine*)
1961 Subways Are for Sleeping (*Angela McKay*)
1967 I Do! I Do! (*Agnes*, repl.)

Lawrence, Gertrude (née Gertrud Alexandra Dagmar Lawrence Klasen), actress, singer, dancer; b. London, July 4, 1898; d. New York, Sept 6., 1952. Lustrous performer whose gossamer grace and plaintive voice made her one of the most acclaimed British stars ever to appear on Bway. In London, her major appearances were in Noël Coward's *London Calling!* (introducing "Parisian Pierrot"), *Nymph Errant* ("Experiment"), and Coward's *Tonight at 8:30* (a collection of nine one-act plays, incl. three musicals *Red Peppers, Shadow Play*, and *Family Album*). In NY, she made her bow with Beatrice Lillie and Jack Buchanan in *André Charlot's Revue of 1924* (singing "Limehouse Blues"), and starred in *Oh, Kay!* ("Someone to Watch Over Me," "Do Do Do"), *Lady in the Dark* ("This Is New," "My Ship," "Jenny"), and *The King and I* ("I Whistle a Happy Tune," "Getting to Know You," "Hello, Young Lovers," "Shall We Dance?"). Miss Lawrence also introduced "A Cup of Coffee, a Sandwich and You" (*Charlot Revue 1926*) and "Exactly Like You" (*International Revue*). She appeared with Noël Coward in three productions incl. his play *Private Lives*.

Raised in poverty, Miss Lawrence

became a professional dancer at 12, Beatrice Lillie's understudy at 18. Her first nonmusical role was in *Candle-Light* (NY 1929). She also sang in nightclubs and acted in films. Bib: *A Star Danced* by Miss Lawrence (Doubleday, NY 1945); *Gertrude Lawrence as Mrs. A.* by Richard Aldrich (her husband) (Greystone, NY 1954).

1916 Some (dancer)
1917 Cheep (repl.)
1918 Tabs
      Buzz-Buzz
1921 A to Z
1922 Dé-Dé (*Denise*)
1923 Rats
      London Calling!
1924 André Charlot's Revue (NY)
1925 Charlot's Revue (added)
      The Charlot Revue of 1926 (NY)
1926 Oh, Kay! (NY) (*Kay*)
1927 Oh, Kay! (*Kay*)
1928 Treasure Girl (NY) (*Ann Wainwright*)
1930 International Revue (NY)
1933 Nymph Errant (*Evangeline Edwards*)
1936 Tonight at 8:30 (*Lily Pepper, Victoria Gayforth, Jane Featherways*)
      Tonight at 8:30 (NY) (*Lily Pepper, Victoria Gayforth, Jane Featherways*)
1941 Lady in the Dark (NY) (*Liza Elliott*)
1948 Tonight at 8:30 (NY) (r) (*Lily Pepper, Victoria Gayforth, Jane Featherways*)
1951 The King and I (NY) (*Anna Leonowens*)

Lawrence, Jerome, librettist; b. Cleveland, Ohio, July 14, 1915. Lawrence and his co-librettist, Robert E. Lee, enjoyed their biggest Bway hit with *Mame*, based on their play *Auntie Mame*. They also wrote the play *Inherit the Wind*. As lyricists, the team collaborated with composer Harry Warren.

1948 Look, Ma, I'm Dancin'

1956 Shangri-la (also lyr.) (Warren)
1966 Mame
1968 Dear World

Lawrence, Steve (né Sidney Liebowitz), actor, singer; b. Brooklyn, NY, July 8, 1935. Primarily a nightclub belter, Lawrence introduced "A Room Without Windows" in *What Makes Sammy Run?* and "I've Gotta Be Me" in *Golden Rainbow* (in which he appeared with his wife, Eydie Gormé).

1964 What Makes Sammy Run? (*Sammy Glick*)
1968 Golden Rainbow (*Larry Davis*)

Laye, Evelyn, actress, singer; b. London, July 10, 1900. During the 20s, Miss Laye was the supremely Dresden star of British operetta. Her biggest successes were the revised *Shop Girl* (singing "The Guard's Brigade"), the revived *Merry Widow*, plus *Madame Pompadour, Blue Eyes,* and *Wedding in Paris*. On Bway, she won acclaimed in *Bitter Sweet* and introduced "I See Your Face Before Me" in *Between the Devil*. Her first husband was musical-comedy actor Sonnie Hale. Bib: *Boo, to My Friends* by Miss Laye (Hurst, L 1958).

1918 The Beauty Spot (*Leonie Bramble*, repl.)
      Going Up (*Madeline Manners*)
1919 The Kiss Call (*Dollis Prym*)
1920 The Shop Girl (r) (*Bessie Brent*)
1921 Mary (*Mary Howells*)
      League of Notions (repl.)
      The Fun of the Fayre
1922 Phi-Phi (*Helen*)
1923 The Merry Widow (r) (*Sonia*)
      Madame Pompadour (*Madame Pompadour*)
1925 Cleopatra (*Cleopatra*)
      Betty in Mayfair (*Betty Head*)
1926 Merely Molly (*Molly*)
1927 Princess Charming (*Princess Elaine*, repl.)
      Lilac Time (r) (*Lili*)
1928 Blue Eyes (*George Ann Bellamy*)

1929 The New Moon (*Marianne Beaunoir*)
     Bitter Sweet (NY) (*Sarah Millick*)
1930 Bitter Sweet (*Sarah Millick,* repl.)
1932 Helen! (*Helen*)
1933 Give Me a Ring (*Peggy*)
1937 Paganini (*Princess Anne*)
     Between the Devil (NY) (*Natalie*)
1940 Lights Up
1942 The Belle of New York (r) (*Violet Gray*)
1943 Sunny River (*Marie Sauvinet*)
1945 Three Waltzes (*Katherine*)
1954 Wedding in Paris (*Marcelle Thibault*)
1966 Strike a Light (*Annie Besant*)
1969 Charley Girl (*Lady Hadwell,* repl.)
     Phil the Fluter (*Mrs. Fitzmaurice*)

Layton, Joe (né Joseph Lichtman), director, choreographer; b. Brooklyn, NY, May 3, 1931. Dancer who became choreographer, then director with *No Strings* and *George M!*

Unless otherwise noted, Mr. Layton was choreographer of following; asterisk indicates he was also director:

1947 Oklahoma! (repl. dancer only)
1948 High Button Shoes (US tour) (dancer only)
1950 Miss Liberty (dancer only)
1953 Wonderful Town (dancer only)
1959 On the Town (r)
     Once Upon a Mattress
     The Sound of Music
1960 Greenwillow
     Tenderloin
1961 The Sound of Music (L)
     Sail Away
1962 No Strings *
     Sail Away (L)
1963 On the Town * (L)
     The Girl Who Came to Supper *
1965 Drat! The Cat! *
1967 Sherry! *
1968 George M! *
1969 Dear World *
1970 Two by Two *
1972 Gone with the Wind * (L)
1978 Platinum *

"Lazy Afternoon." Music by Jerome Moross; lyric by John Latouche. Languid ode to a summer day sung by Kaye Ballard in *The Golden Apple* (NY 1954).

Leave It to Jane (1917). Music by Jerome Kern; lyrics by P. G. Wodehouse; book by Guy Bolton & Wodehouse, based on George Ade's play *The College Widow.*

SONGS: "Just You Watch My Step," "Leave It to Jane," "The Siren's Song," "Cleopatterer," "The Crickets Are Calling," "The Sun Shines Brighter," "Sir Galahad," "Wait 'Til Tomorrow," "I'm Going to Find a Girl."

NEW YORK: Aug. 28, 1917
LONGACRE THEATRE; 167 p.

Presented by William Elliott, F. Ray Comstock, Morris Gest; directed by Edward Royce; settings, Aitken; costumes, Collins, Finchley; music director, John McGhie; orchestrations, Robert Russell Bennett.

CAST: Edith Hallor (*Jane Witherspoon*), Georgia O'Ramey (*Flora Wiggins*), Oscar Shaw (*Stub Talmadge*), Ann Orr (*Bessie Tanner*), Robert Pitkin (*Billy Bolton*), Olin Howland (*Bub Hicks*), Ruloff Cutten (*Ollie Mitchell*).

NEW YORK: May 25, 1959
SHERIDAN SQUARE THEATRE; 928 p.

Presented by Joseph Beruh & Peter Kent; directed by Lawrence Carra; choreographed by Mary Jane Doerr; settings, Lloyd Burlingham; costumes, Al Lehman; lighting, George Corrin; music director, Joseph Stecko; orchestrations, Stecko & Robert Hess.

CAST: Kathleen Murray (*Jane Witherspoon*), Dorothy Greener (*Flora Wiggins*), Angelo Mango (*Stub Talmadge*), Jeanne Allen (*Bessie Tanner*), Art Matthews (*Billy Bolton*), Ray Tudor (*Bub Hicks*), George Segal (*Ollie Mitchell*).

Though *Leave It to Jane* was a Bolton-Wodehouse-Kern musical written for the Princess Theatre management, it was not a Princess Theatre musical because it never played that theatre. Yet in its style and construction it conveyed the same general flavor as those bona fide Princess attractions—*Oh, Boy!* and *Oh, Lady! Lady!!*—which preceded and followed it. The musical, set in Atwater College, deals with the efforts of Jane, the college widow, to get Billy Bolton, star player of Atwater's football rival, Bingham, to play for Atwater under an assumed name. The show marked the first occasion that members of the chorus were billed as "Ladies and Gentlemen of the Ensemble." The 1959 production is still the longest-running off-Bway revival.

Other Bway musicals dealing with college football were *Good News!* (1927), *Too Many Girls* (1939), *Toplitzky of Notre Dame* (1946), *All American* (1962).

"Leave It to Jane." Music by Jerome Kern; lyric by P. G. Wodehouse. Self-appreciative advice offered by Edith Hallor and chorus in *Leave It to Jane* (NY 1917).

Leave It to Me! (1938). Music & lyrics by Cole Porter; book by Bella & Sam Spewack, based on their play *Clear All Wires.*

SONGS: "Get Out of Town," "Most Gentlemen Don't Like Love," "From Now On," "My Heart Belongs to Daddy," "I Want to Go Home," "Tomorrow," "Far, Far Away."

NEW YORK: Nov. 9, 1938
IMPERIAL THEATRE; 291 p.

Presented by Vinton Freedley; directed by Sam Spewack; choreographed by Robert Alton; settings, Albert Johnson; costumes, Raoul Pène du Bois; music director, Max Meth; orchestrations, Don Walker.

CAST: William Gaxton (*Buckley Joyce Thomas*), Victor Moore (*Alonzo P. Goodhue*), Sophie Tucker (*Mrs. Goodhue*), Tamara (*Colette*), Mary Martin (*Dolly Winslow*), George Tobias (*Alexander Tomofsky*), Gene Kelly (dancer).

A satire on communism and US diplomacy, *Leave It to Me!* provided a field day for Victor Moore, as an unwilling ambassador, and also gave NY audiences their first chance to appreciate the charms of Mary Martin. Moore played "Stinky" Goodhue, whose ambitious wife contributed the money to FDR's campaign that resulted in her husband's being named ambassador to the USSR. Goodhue does everything he can to be recalled, but succeeds only when he comes up with a plan, concocted with the aid of foreign correspondent Buckley Joyce Thomas, to ensure peace in the world. Two of the show's highlights: Moore kicking the Nazi ambassador in the belly and the first-act finale with Stalin dancing a jig while the band plays the "Internationale." During road tour, because of the Stalin-Hitler nonaggression pact, the role of the Russian dictator was eliminated.

Lederer, George W., producer, director; b. Wilkes Barre, Pa., 1861; d. Jackson Hts., NY, Oct. 8, 1938. Bway theatre manager who formed partnership with Thomas Canary (1893–97), and sponsored first revue, *The Passing Show* (title later used by Shuberts). Lederer's *The Belle of New York* became the first American hit in London.

1893 The Princess Nicotine
1894 Prince Kam
      About Town
      The Passing Show
1895 The 20th Century Girl
      The Merry World
1896 The Lady Slavey

In Gay New York
The Gold Bug
An American Beauty
1897 The Whirl of the Town
The Belle of New York
The Telephone Girl
1898 The Belle of New York (L)
Yankee Doodle Dandy
A Dangerous Maid
The Jolly Musketeer
1899 In Gay Paree
The Man in the Moon
The Rounders
1900 The Princess Chic
The Casino Girl
The Casino Girl (L)
The Belle of Bohemia
1901 The Strollers
The New Yorkers
1902 The Wild Rose
Sally in Our Alley
1903 The Jewel of Asia
The Blonde in Black
The Jersey Lily
1904 The Southerners
1910 Madame Sherry
1911 The Happiest Night of His Life
Jumping Jupiter
1912 The Charity Girl
Mama's Baby Boy
1919 Angel Face
1920 The Girl in the Spotlight

Lee, Gypsy Rose (née Rose Louise Hovick), actress, dancer; b. Seattle, Wash., Jan. 9, 1914; d. Los Angeles, Cal., April 26, 1970. Miss Lee is best remembered as the world's foremost strip-tease artist. She and her sister, June Havoc, began their careers in vaudeville. Bib: *Gypsy* by Miss Lee (1957), the basis for the 1959 musical.
1932 Hot-Cha! (chorus)
1933 Melody (*Claire Lolive*)
1936 Ziegfeld Follies
1940 DuBarry Was a Lady (*May Daly*, repl.)
1942 Star and Garter

Lee, Robert E(dwin), librettist; b. Elyria, Ohio, Oct. 15, 1918. Lee and his co-librettist, Jerome Lawrence, en-

joyed their biggest Bway hit with *Mame,* based on their play *Auntie Mame.* They also wrote the play *Inherit the Wind.* As lyricists, the team collaborated with composer Harry Warren.
1948 Look, Ma, I'm Dancin'
1956 Shangri-la (also lyr.) (Warren)
1966 Mame
1968 Dear World

Lee, Sammy (né Samuel Levy), choreographer, dancer; b. New York, 1890; d. Woodland Hills, Cal., March 30, 1968. Lee directed the dances for four musicals produced by Ziegfeld, four by Aarons and Freedley, four by Laurence Schwab. He became a Hollywood choreographer in the mid-30s.
1912 The Firefly (also *Pietro*)
1914 The Belle of Bond Street (L) (also *Jack Richley*)
1920 Little Miss Charity
1922 The Gingham Girl
1923 Earl Carroll Vanities
Music Box Revue
Mary Jane McKane
1924 Sweet Little Devil
Earl Carroll Vanities
Lady, Be Good!
1925 Tell Me More
Captain Jinks
No, No, Nanette
The Cocoanuts
Tip-Toes
1926 Tip-Toes (L)
Queen High
The Ramblers
Oh, Kay!
Betsy
1927 Rio Rita
Talk About Girls
Ziegfeld Follies
Yes, Yes, Yvette
Show Boat
1928 Here's Howe
Cross My Heart (also prod., dir.)
1929 Lady Fingers
1931 Crazy Quilt

Leftwich, Alexander, director; b. Baltimore, Md., 1884; d. Hollywood, Cal.,

Jan. 13, 1947. Leftwich's best-known Bway musicals were *Hit the Deck, A Connecticut Yankee, Rain or Shine, The Little Show, Strike Up the Band, Girl Crazy.*

1923	Fashions of 1923
1924	Vogues of 1924
1925	Big Boy
	Sky High
	Artists and Models
1926	A Night in Paris
1927	Hit the Deck
	Take to the Air
	A Connecticut Yankee
1928	Rain or Shine
	Present Arms
	Chee-Chee
	Hello, Daddy
1929	Spring Is Here
	The Little Show
1930	Strike Up the Band
	9:15 Revue
	Girl Crazy
	Sweet and Low
1931	The Third Little Show
1932	Hey Nonny Nonny
1937	Orchids Preferred

"Legalize My Name." Music by Harold Arlen; lyric by Johnny Mercer. Impatient marital plea that Pearl Bailey turned into a show-stopper in *St. Louis Woman* (NY 1946).

Leigh, Carolyn, lyricist; b. New York, Aug. 21, 1926. Miss Leigh's lyrics have been mated to the music of Mark Charlap ("I've Gotta Crow," "I'm Flying"), Cy Coleman ("Hey, Look Me Over," "Real Live Girl," "I've Got Your Number"), and Elmer Bernstein ("Step to the Rear").

1954	Peter Pan (Charlap)
1960	Wildcat (Coleman)
1962	Little Me (Coleman)
1967	How Now, Dow Jones (Bernstein)

Leigh, Mitch (né Irwin Mitchnick), composer; b. Brooklyn, NY, Jan. 30, 1928. With lyricist Joe Darion, Leigh made an impressive Bway debut with the score for *Man of La Mancha* ("The Impossible Dream," "To Each His Dulcinea"). He has also written with William Alfred and Phyllis Robinson. Leigh's primary work has been as composer of commercial jingles.

1965	Man of La Mancha (Darion)
1970	Cry for Us All (Alfred, Robinson)
1975	Home Sweet Homer (Burr, Brown)
1979	Saravá (Nash)

Leigh, Vivien (née Vivian Mary Hartley), actress; b. Darjeeling, India, Nov. 5, 1913; d. London, July 8, 1967. Minxlike stage and screen actress who appeared in one Bway musical and is best remembered as Hollywood's Scarlett O'Hara in *Gone with the Wind.* Miss Leigh was married to and divorced from actor Laurence Olivier.

1963	Tovarich (*Tatiana*)

Lenya, Lotte (née Karoline Blamauer), actress, singer; b. Vienna, Austria, Oct. 18, 1900. Miss Lenya's steel-file voice is most closely identified with songs by her late husband, composer Kurt Weill. She appeared in four of Weill's Berlin musicals (incl. *Die Dreigroschenoper, Mahagonny*), and was in Marc Blitzstein's off-Bway adaptation, *The Threepenny Opera* (singing "Pirate Jenny"). Settling in the US in 1935, she also acted in *Cabaret*, has given concerts and made records of Weill's songs.

1945	The Firebrand of Florence (*Duchess*)
1954	The Threepenny Opera (r) (*Jenny*)
1966	Cabaret (*Fraulein Schneider*)

"Lemon in the Garden of Love, A." Music by Richard Carle; lyric by M. E. Rourke. Comic number of romantic misjudgment sung by Mr. Carle in *The Spring Chicken* (NY 1906).

Lerner, Alan Jay, lyricist, librettist; b. New York, Aug. 31, 1918. With composer Frederick Loewe, with whom he collaborated on seven Bway scores, Lerner was identified primarily with a musical theatre that captured the romance and fantasy of a bygone age. The team's greatest success was *My Fair Lady*, whence came such songs as "On the Street Where You Live," "I Could Have Danced All Night," "Get Me to the Church on Time," "The Rain in Spain," and "I've Grown Accustomed to Her Face." Other stage hits were *Brigadoon* ("Almost Like Being in Love," "The Heather on the Hill"), *Paint Your Wagon* ("I Still See Elisa," "I Talk to the Trees"), and *Camelot* ("If Ever I Would Leave You," "Camelot"). Lerner has also written with composers Kurt Weill ("Here I'll Stay," "Green-Up Time"), Burton Lane ("On a Clear Day," "Come Back to Me"), and André Previn. Lerner, who has worked in films (incl. *Gigi*), was once married to singer Marion Bell. Bib: *The Lerner and Loewe Song Book* (S&S, NY 1962).

Asterisk indicates Mr. Lerner was also producer:
1943 What's Up (Loewe)
1945 The Day Before Spring (Loewe)
1947 Brigadoon (Loewe)
1948 Love Life (Weill)
1951 Paint Your Wagon (Loewe)
1956 My Fair Lady (Loewe)
1960 Camelot * (Loewe)
1965 On a Clear Day You Can See Forever * (Lane)
1969 Coco (Previn)
1973 Gigi (Loewe)

LeRoy, Hal (né John LeRoy Schotte), dancer, actor; b. Cincinnati, Ohio, 1913. Boyish-looking, nonstop tap dancer whose machine-gun routines won particular favor in the *Ziegfeld Follies* of 1931. LeRoy also appeared in vaudeville, nightclubs, and films.
1931 The Gang's All Here (*Hal LeRoy*)
     Ziegfeld Follies

1933 Strike Me Pink
1934 Thumbs Up!
1939 Too Many Girls (*Al Terwilliger*)
1942 Count Me In (*Alvin York Brandywine*)
1966 Autumn's Here (dir., chor. only)

Leslie, Lew (né Lewis Lessinsky), producer, director; b. 1886; d. Orangeburg, NY, March 10, 1963. Leslie was primarily associated with all-black revues, both in NY and London. Florence Mills appeared in four, Bill Robinson and Ethel Waters in two each. The producer was married to singer Belle Baker.
1922 Plantation Revue
1923 Dover Street to Dixie (L) (Plantation Revue)
1924 Dixie to Broadway
1926 Blackbirds (L)
1927 Whitebirds (L)
1928 Blackbirds of 1928
1930 International Revue
     Blackbirds
1931 Rhapsody in Black
1933 Blackbirds
1934 Blackbirds of 1934 (L)
1936 Blackbirds of 1936 (L)
1939 Blackbirds of 1939

"Let Me Entertain You." Music by Jule Styne; lyric by Stephen Sondheim. Used as a show-business theme in *Gypsy* (NY 1959), the number was offered in three different settings and styles: first, as "May We Entertain You?," it was done plaintively by two children auditioning for a kiddies' show; later it became a more aggressive signature for a vaudeville act; finally it was the slinky, blaring accompaniment to a strip tease. In NY it was sung by Jacqueline Mayro and Karen Moore (children), then by Lane Bradbury and Sandra Church (children grown up); in London production (1973), by Bonnie Langford and Helen Raye, then by Debbie Bowen and Zan Charisse.

"Let's Be Buddies." Music & lyric by Cole Porter. Ethel Merman's show-stopper in *Panama Hattie* (NY 1940), through which flashy Hattie Maloney ingratiates herself with eight-year-old Joan Carroll, playing the daughter of the divorced man Hattie plans to marry. Because of child labor laws, Miss Carroll was forbidden to sing, thus requiring Porter to write a spoken recitation for her. In London revue *Black Vanities* (1941), it was performed by Bud Flanagan and Chesney Allen; two years later Bebe Daniels sang it to Betty Blackler in London version of *Panama Hattie*.

"Let's Do It." Music & lyric by Cole Porter. Zoological mating habits catalogued by Irene Bordoni in *Paris* (NY 1928), which replaced number in similar vein called "Let's Misbehave." It was also sung by Jessie Matthews and Sonnie Hale in *Wake Up and Dream!* (L 1929).

Let's Face It! (1941). Music & lyrics by Cole Porter; book by Herbert & Dorothy Fields, based on play *The Cradle Snatchers* by Russell Medcraft & Norma Mitchell.

SONGS: "Let's Face It," "Farming," "Everything I Love," "Ace in the Hole," "You Irritate Me So," "Let's Not Talk About Love," "A Little Rumba Numba," "I Hate You, Darling," "Melody in 4F" (Sylvia Fine–Max Liebman).

NEW YORK: Oct. 29, 1941
IMPERIAL THEATRE; 547 p.

Presented by Vinton Freedley; directed by Edgar MacGregor; choreographed by Charles Walters; settings, Harry Horner; costumes, John Harkrider; music director, Max Meth; orchestrations, Hans Spialek, Donald Walker, Ted Royal.

CAST: Danny Kaye (*Jerry Walker*), Eve Arden (*Maggie Watson*), Benny Baker (*Frankie Burns*), Mary Jane Walsh (*Winnie Potter*), Edith Meiser (*Cornelia Abigail Pigeon*), Vivian Vance (*Nancy Collister*), Mary Parker & Billy Daniel (featured dancers), Jack Williams (*Eddie Hilliard*), Nanette Fabray (*Jean Blanchard*), Joseph Macaulay (*Julian Watson*).

LONDON: Nov. 19, 1942
HIPPODROME; 348 p.

Presented by Jack Waller & Tom Arnold; directed by Richard Bird; choreographed by Joan Davis; settings, Clifford Pember; music director, George Windeatt.

CAST: Bobby Howes (*Jerry Walker*), Joyce Barbour (*Maggie Watson*), Jack Stamford (*Frankie Burns*), Pat Kirkwood (*Winnie Potter*), Babette O'Deal (*Cornelia Abigail Pigeon*), Noele Gordon (*Nancy Collister*), Leigh Stafford (*Eddie Hilliard*), Pat Leonard (*Jean Blanchard*), Debroy Somers Orch.

In his first leading role on Bway, Danny Kaye was elevated to stardom within a week after the opening of *Let's Face It!* The idea for the musical began when producer Freedley read a newspaper account about a number of patriotic ladies who, anxious to improve the morale of recently inducted selectees, had written to army camps for permission to entertain soldiers at their homes. In the Herbert and Dorothy Fields script (the first libretto they wrote together), three Southampton matrons, having grown suspicious of their husbands' numerous hunting trips, hire three rookies from a nearby army camp as gigolos. Comic complications arise when both the husband and the soldiers' neglected girl friends show up. After Milton Berle and Martha Raye turned down the leading roles, Freedley secured Kaye (who had recently scored a hit in *Lady in the Dark*) and Eve Arden. Kaye's biggest applause-catcher was the interpolated "Melody in 4F," in which, in 90 seconds of double-talk and gestures, he recounted a draftee's career from the time he receives his notice to his winning a medal on maneuvers. The show marked the fifth collaboration between Cole Porter and Herbert Fields and it was the first with choreography by Charles Walters (after Robert Alton proved unavailable). The US touring company was headed by Benny Rubin, Mary Jane Walsh, Cynda Glenn, Brenda Forbes, and Jacqueline Susann.

FILM VERSION: Bob Hope, Betty Hutton, Eve Arden (Par. 1943, Sidney Lanfield dir.).

"Let's Have Another Cup o' Coffee." Music & lyric by Irving Berlin. Optimism in the face of the Depression, expressed through a satirical compilation of chins-up clichés. It was sung by Katherine Carrington and J. Harold Murray in *Face the Music* (NY 1932) as they dined at the Automat.

"Let's Kiss and Make Up." Music by George Gershwin; lyric by Ira Gershwin. Fred and Adele Astaire sang and danced this breezy song of reconciliation in *Funny Face* (NY 1927, L 1928).

"Let's Take a Walk Around the Block." Music by Harold Arlen; lyric by Ira Gershwin & E. Y. Harburg. Jaunty itinerary of a delayed adventure itemized by Earl Oxford and Dixie Dunbar in *Life Begins at 8:40* (NY 1934).

"Let's Take an Old-Fashioned Walk." Music & lyric by Irving Berlin. Eddie Albert proffered this perambulatory invitation to Allyn McLerie in *Miss Liberty* (NY 1949). The song had originally been intended for the film *Easter Parade* (1948).

Levene, Sam (né Samuel Levine), actor; b. New York, Aug. 28, 1905. Sour-faced comic actor whose biggest Bway musical success was *Guys and Dolls* (in which he sang "Sue Me"). Levene, who made his Bway debut in 1927, has also appeared in such non-musicals as *Three Men on a Horse* and *Room Service*.

1950 Guys and Dolls (*Nathan Detroit*)
1953 Guys and Dolls (L) (*Nathan Detroit*)
1961 Let It Ride (*Patsy*)
1964 Café Crown (*Hymie*)

Levey, Ethel (née Ethelia Fowler), actress, singer, dancer; b. San Francisco, Cal., Nov. 22, 1881; d. New York, Feb. 27, 1955. Slim, deep-voiced, high-kicking Ethel Levey appeared with her first husband, George M. Cohan, in four of his Bway musicals. Beginning with such hits as *Hullo, Ragtime!* and *Hullo, Tango!* she then spent almost 10 years as a star of London revues and British music halls.

1901 The Governor's Son (NY) (*Emerald Green*)
1903 Running for Office (NY) (*Gertie Gayland*)
1904 Little Johnny Jones (NY) (*Goldie Gates*)
1906 George Washington, Jr. (NY) (*Dolly Johnson*)
1908 Nearly a Hero (NY) (*Angeline de Vere*)
1912 Hullo, Ragtime!
1913 Hullo, Tango!
1914 Watch Your Step (*Stella Sparkes*)
1916 Follow the Crowd
      Look Who's Here
      Three Cheers
1917 Here and There
1920 Oh, Julie! (*Julie*)
1922 Go Easy, Mabel (NY) (*Mabel Montmorency*)
1923 Yes!

1925 The Blue Kitten (*Totoche*)
1941 Sunny River (NY) (*Lolita*)
1945 Marinka (NY) (*Mme. Sacher*)

Levin, Herman, producer; b. Philadelphia, Pa., Dec. 1, 1907. Levin's most celebrated Bway offering was Lerner and Loewe's *My Fair Lady;* other successes were *Call Me Mister* and *Gentlemen Prefer Blondes.*

1946 Call Me Mister
1949 Gentlemen Prefer Blondes
1950 Bless You All
1956 My Fair Lady
1963 The Girl Who Came to Supper
1970 Lovely Ladies, Kind Gentlemen
1973 Tricks
1976 My Fair Lady (r)

Lewine, Richard, composer; b. New York, July 28, 1910. Lewine wrote scores for off-Bway musical melodramas with Ted Fetter and Bway revues with Arnold Horwitt (their biggest hit: *Make Mine Manhattan*). He has also been a tv producer.

1937 Naughty-Naught ('00) (Fetter)
      The Fireman's Flame (Fetter)
1938 The Girl from Wyoming (Fetter)
1948 Make Mine Manhattan (Horwitt)
1959 The Girls Against the Boys (Horwitt)
1970 Look to the Lilies (co-prod. only)

Lewis, (William) Morgan ("Buddy"), composer; b. Rockville, Conn., Dec. 26, 1906; d. New York, Dec. 8, 1968. With lyricist Nancy Hamilton, Lewis wrote the scores for three Bway revues, incl. songs "How High the Moon" and "The Old Soft Shoe." He also contributed numbers for other revues and composed film scores.

1939 One for the Money
1940 Two for the Show
1946 Three to Make Ready

Lewis, Robert, director; b. New York, March 16, 1909. A former actor, Lewis has directed dramas and films as well as such Bway musical hits as *Brigadoon* and *Jamaica.*

1947 Brigadoon
1949 Regina
1957 Jamaica
1959 Candide (L)
1961 Kwamina
1964 Foxy
1965 On a Clear Day You Can See Forever

"Life Is Just a Bowl of Cherries." Music by Ray Henderson; lyric by Lew Brown. Lighthearted, philosophical view expressed by Ethel Merman in *George White's Scandals* (NY 1931).

"Life Upon the Wicked Stage." Music by Jerome Kern; lyric by Oscar Hammerstein II. Comic put-down of the glamorous world of the theatre sung and danced by Eva Puck and Sammy White in *Show Boat* (NY 1927). In London version (1928), it was performed by Dorothy Lena and Leslie Sarony.

Lightner, Winnie (née Winifred Hanson), actress, singer, dancer; b. Greenport, NY, Sept. 17, 1901; d. Sherman Oaks, Cal., March 5, 1971. Energetic blonde remembered for three *George White's Scandals* in which she introduced "I'll Build a Stairway to Paradise" (1922) and "Somebody Loves Me" (1924). Also appeared in vaudeville (1919–1922) films (1929–1933).

1922 George White's Scandals
1923 George White's Scandals
1924 George White's Scandals
1925 Gay Paree
1926 Gay Paree
1927 Harry Delmar's Revels

Li'l Abner (1956). Music by Gene de Paul; lyrics by Johnny Mercer; book by Norman Panama & Melvin Frank, based on comic strip by Al Capp.

SONGS: "If I Had My Druthers," "Jubilation T. Cornpone," "Namely You," "Unnecessary Town," "The

Country's in the Very Best of Hands," "Oh, Happy Day," "Past My Prime," "Love in a Home," "Progress Is the Root of All Evil," "Put 'Em Back."

NEW YORK: Nov. 15, 1956
ST. JAMES THEATRE; 693 p.

Presented by Norman Panama, Melvin Frank, Michael Kidd; directed & choreographed by Michael Kidd; settings & lighting, William & Jean Eckart; costumes, Alvin Colt; music director, Lehman Engel; orchestrations, Philip J. Lang.

CAST: Edith Adams (*Daisy Mae*) Peter Palmer (*Abner Yokum*), Howard St. John (*Gen. Bullmoose*), Stubby Kaye (*Marryin' Sam*), Charlotte Rae (*Mammy Yokum*), Tina Louise (*Appassionata von Climax*), Julie Newmar (*Stupifyin' Jones*), Marc Breaux (*Romeo Scragg*), James Hurst (*Clem Scragg*), Carmen Alvarez (*Moonbeam McSwine*), Tom Panko (dancer), Grover Dale (dancer).

Originally a project of Alan Jay Lerner, first with composer Arthur Schwartz, then with Burton Lane, *Li'l Abner* re-created the comic-strip world of Dogpatch USA. There the simple hill folk become involved with the US government, which wants to use the town for atom bomb tests. The chief choreographic scene was the chase on Sadie Hawkins Day, in which the girl who catches the man she wants is entitled to marry him. Other NY musicals based on comic strips: *Buster Brown* (1905), *Little Nemo* (1908), *Bringing Up Father* (1925), *You're a Good Man, Charlie Brown* (1967), *Annie* (1977).

FILM VERSION: Peter Palmer and Leslie Parrish (Par. 1959, Norman Panama and Melvin Frank dirs.).

Lilac Time (1922). Music by Franz Schubert, adapted by Heinrich Berté & G. H. Clutsam; lyrics & book by Adrian Ross, based on Viennese operetta *Das Dreimäderlhaus*, by A. M. Willner & Heinz Reichert, adapted from novel *Schwammerl*, by Dr. R. H. Bartsch.

SONGS: "Hark, Hark! The Lark," "Under the Lilac Bough," "The Golden Song," "Serenade," "My Sweetest Song of All," "When the Lilac Bloom Uncloses."

LONDON: Dec. 22, 1922
LYRIC THEATRE; 626 p.

Presented by Chappell & Co. Ltd.; directed by Dion Boucicault; choreographed by Carlotta Mossetti; settings, E. H. Ryan; costumes, Comelli; music director, Clarence Reybould.

CAST: Courtice Pounds (*Franz Schubert*), Clara Butterworth (*Lili Veit*), Percy Heming (*Baron von Schober*), Edmund Gwenn (*Veit*).

The first English-language adaptation of the 1916 Viennese operetta was *Blossom Time* (NY 1921) with the Schubert melodies arranged by Sigmund Romberg. The London version, *Lilac Time*, used both the original Berté arrangements plus new ones by G. H. Clutsam. Set in Vienna, the story is concerned with Schubert's unrequited love for Lili. Being timid, the composer has his friend Von Schober sing his songs to Lili, with the result that Von Schober and Lili fall in love. The operetta was revived in London in 1925, 1927, 1928, 1930, 1932, 1933, 1936, and 1949. In 1942, a musical called *Blossom Time*, though not the Romberg version, was presented in London with Richard Tauber as Schubert. Rodney Acklund was responsible for the adaptation.

Other composers whose works were adapted as scores for London musicals include Tschaikowsky (*Catherine*, 1923); Chopin (*The Damask Rose*, 1930); Johann Strauss Jr. and Sr. (*Waltzes from Vienna*, 1931); Strauss

Jr. (*Casanova*, 1932); Schumann (*The Golden Toy*, 1934); Mozart, Scarlatti, etc. (*An Elephant in Arcady*, 1938); Chopin (*Waltz Without End*, 1942); Strauss Jr. and Sr. and Oscar Straus (*Three Waltzes*, 1945); Offenbach (*Can-Can*, 1946); Offenbach (*Music at Midnight*, 1950); Dvorak (*Summer Song*, 1956).

Lillie, Beatrice (Gladys), actress, singer; b. Toronto, Canada, May 29, 1894. The British Empire's most regal lady clown needed no more than the raise of an eyebrow or the curl of a lip to start her audiences laughing. Always a mistress of the surprise, out-of-character prank—roller-skating in an evening dress or swinging a lengthy strand of pearls around her neck—she was universally acclaimed the Funniest Woman in the World. Miss Lillie began her career in London revues, then triumphed in NY in *André Charlot's Revue* (singing "March with Me!"), with Gertrude Lawrence and Jack Buchanan. Other Bway successes: *At Home Abroad* ("Paree," "Get Yourself a Geisha"), *The Show Is On, Inside USA*. She also introduced "I Know That You Know" in *Oh, Please!*, "Mad Dogs and Englishmen" in *The Third Little Show*, "I Went to a Marvellous Party" in *Set to Music*. Bib: *Every Other Inch a Lady* by Miss Lillie (Doubleday, NY 1972).

1914	Not Likely!
1915	5064 Gerrard
	Now's the Time
1916	Samples (repl.)
	Some
1917	Cheep
1918	Tabs
1919	Oh, Joy! (*Jackie Sampson*)
	Bran-Pie
1921	Now and Then
	Pot Luck
1922	The Nine o'Clock Revue
1924	André Charlot's Revue (NY)

1925	Charlot's Revue (added)
	The Charlot Revue of 1926 (NY)
1926	Oh, Please! (NY) (*Lily Valli*)
1928	She's My Baby (NY) (*Tilly*)
	This Year of Grace (NY)
1930	Charlot's Masquerade
1931	The Third Little Show (NY)
1932	Walk a Little Faster (NY)
1933	Please
1935	At Home Abroad (NY)
1936	The Show Is On (NY)
1938	Happy Returns
1939	Set to Music (NY)
	All Clear
1942	Big Top
1944	Seven Lively Arts (NY)
1946	Better Late
1948	Inside USA (NY)
1957	Ziegfeld Follies (NY)
1964	High Spirits (NY) (*Mme. Arcati*)

"Limehouse Blues." Music by Philip Braham; lyric by Douglas Furber. Atmospheric song of London's Chinatown, which was added to the revue *A to Z* (L 1921) during its run. It was sung by Teddie Gerard, as a Chinese tart, to Gerald Kirby, as a sailor. Gertrude Lawrence, who was also in the revue, reintroduced the song in NY when she appeared in *André Charlot's Revue of 1924*, and was thereafter identified with it.

Linden, Hal (né Harold Lipshitz), actor, singer; b. New York, March 20, 1931. Versatile singing actor who scored personal success in *The Rothschilds*. Appeared in tv series as Barney Miller.

1958	Bells Are Ringing (*Jeff Moss*, repl.)
1961	Wildcat (*Matt*)
1962	Anything Goes (r) (*Billy Crocker*)
1964	Something More (*Dick*)
1967	Illya Darling (*No Face*)
1968	The Education of H*Y*M*A*N K*A*P*L*A*N (*Yissel Fishbein*)
1970	The Rothschilds (*Mayer Rothschild*)
1973	The Pajama Game (r) (*Sid Sorokin*)

Lindsay, Howard, librettist, director; b. Waterford, NY, March 29, 1888; d. New York, Feb. 11, 1968. Lindsay joined Russel Crouse in 1934 as a writing team, and together they wrote seven musicals, including their biggest hit, *The Sound of Music.* Lindsay and Crouse wrote four librettos for Ethel Merman, and were associated with composers Cole Porter and Irving Berlin on two shows each. The partners were also responsible for eight nonmusical plays, among them *Life with Father* (in which Lindsay appeared with his wife, Dorothy Stickney) and *State of the Union.* Lindsay began his professional career as an actor in 1909, became a director in 1921.

> Asterisk indicates production written with Mr. Crouse:
>
> 1922 The 49ers (actor, dir.)
> 1932 Gay Divorce (dir.)
> 1934 Anything Goes * (also dir.)
> 1936 Red, Hot and Blue! * (also dir.)
> 1937 Hooray for What! * (also. dir.)
> 1950 Call Me Madam *
> 1956 Happy Hunting *
> 1959 The Sound of Music *
> 1962 Mr. President *

"Little Fish in a Big Pond." Music & lyric by Irving Berlin. In which little fish Eddie Albert, in *Miss Liberty* (NY 1949), confesses his desire to return to the little pond back home. His girl, Mary McCarty, however, urges him to stay in the big pond and grow.

"Little Girl Blue." Music by Richard Rodgers; lyric by Lorenz Hart. Tender plaint of a lonely heroine sung by Gloria Grafton in *Jumbo* (NY 1935). In the blue-tinted scene, the first-act finale, the girl dreams she is a child again entertained by circus clowns, jugglers, and aerialists, plus Henderson's Singing Razorbacks.

"Little Girl from Little Rock, A." Music by Jule Styne; lyric by Leo Robin. Carol Channing's happy tale in *Gentlemen Prefer Blondes* (NY 1949) of the way she done right after being done wrong. In London version (1962), Dora Bryan was the little girl; in revised version, *Lorelei* (NY 1974), it was again Miss Channing.

Little Johnny Jones (1904). Music, lyrics, & book by George M. Cohan.

SONGS: "The Yankee Doodle Dandy," "Give My Regards to Broadway," "Life's a Funny Proposition After All," "If Mr. Boston Lawson Got His Way," "I'm Mighty Glad I'm Living and That's All."

NEW YORK: Nov. 7, 1904
LIBERTY THEATRE; 52 p.

Presented by Sam H. Harris; directed by George M. Cohan; settings, W. F. Hamilton; music director, Charles Gebest.

CAST: George M. Cohan (*Johnny Jones*), Jerry Cohan (*Anthony Anstey*), Helen Cohan (*Mrs. Kenworth*), Donald Brian (*Genry Hapgood*), Ethel Levey (*Goldie Gates*), Tom Lewis (*Whitney Wilson*).

Cohan's first success starred him as an American jockey in England—his horse is called Yankee Doodle—who is accused of throwing a race but eventually clears his name. Cohan got the idea for the musical, which marked his first association with Sam H. Harris, when he read a newspaper account of the career of jockey Tod Sloan. Though the production's Bway run lasted only six weeks, Cohan toured in it successfully and brought it back to NY twice during 1905 for a total of 20 weeks.

FILM VERSION: Eddie Buzzell and Alice Day (Warner 1930, Mervyn Le Roy dir.).

Little Mary Sunshine (1959). Music, lyrics & book by Rick Besoyan.

SONGS: "Look for a Sky of Blue," "In Izzenschnooken on the Lovely Ezzenzook Zee," "Playing Croquet," "Tell a Handsome Stranger," "Once in a Blue Moon," "Colorado Love Call," "Every Little Nothing," **"Naughty Naughty Nancy," "Do You Ever Dream of Vienna?"**

NEW YORK: Nov. 18, 1959
ORPHEUM THEATRE; 1,143 p.

Presented by Howard Barker, Cynthia Baer, Robert Chambers; directed by Ray Harrison & Rick Besoyan; choreographed by Harrison; settings & costumes, Barker; lighting, Jim Gore; music director, Jack Holmes.

CAST: Eileen Brennan (*Mary Potts*), William Graham (*Capt. Big Jim Warington*), Elmarie Wendel (*Nancy Twinkle*), John McMartin (*Cpl. Billy Jester*), Mario Siletti (*Gen. Oscar Fairfax*), Elizabeth Parrish (*Mme. Ernestine Von Liebedich*), John Aniston (*Chief Brown Bear*).

LONDON: May 17, 1962
COMEDY THEATRE; 44 p.

Presented by Migdal Productions Ltd.; directed & choreographed by Paddy Stone; settings & costumes, Kenneth Mellor; lighting, Richard Pilbrow; music director, Philip Martel; orchestrations, Arnold Goland.

CAST: Patricia Routledge (*Mary Potts*), Terence Cooper (*Capt. Big Jim Warington*), Joyce Blair (*Nancy Twinkle*), Bernard Cribbins (*Cpl. Billy Jester*), Erik Chitty (*Gen. Oscar Fairfax*), Gita Denise (*Mme. Ernestine Von Liebedich*), Edward Bishop (*Chief Brown Bear*).

This "New Musical About an Old Operetta" was a spoof of the *Naughty Marietta–Rose Marie* school and succeeded so well that it is currently the fourth-longest-running off-Bway musical. Originally presented in abbreviated form in a nightclub some three years before the full-length production, *Little Mary Sunshine* is set high in the Colorado Rockies and is concerned with the romance between the titular heroine and Capt. Big Jim Warington of the Forest Rangers. Big Jim spends most of his time in pursuit of the treacherous Indian, Yellow Feather, whose designs on Mary are thwarted at the last minute by the hero's reappearance singing the "Colorado Love Call." During run, Eileen Brennan was succeeded by Marian Mercer (8-61), John McMartin by Dom DeLuise, Elizabeth Parrish by Janice Mars. A previous operetta spoof, *The Rose of Arizona*, written by Rodgers and Hart and Herbert Fields, served as the first-act finale of the 1926 *Garrick Gaieties*.

Little Night Music, A (1973). Music & lyrics by Stephen Sondheim; book by Hugh Wheeler, based on Ingmar Bergman's film *Smiles of a Summer Night*.

SONGS: "Night Waltz," "Now," "Later," "Soon," "The Glamorous Life," "Remember?," "Liaisons," "Every Day a Little Death," "A Weekend in the Country," "Send in the Clowns," "The Miller's Son."

NEW YORK: Feb. 25, 1973
SHUBERT THEATRE; 601 p.

Presented by Harold Prince, with Ruth Mitchell; directed by Prince; choreographed by Patricia Birch; settings, Boris Aronson; costumes, Florence Klotz; lighting, Tharon Musser; music director, Harold Hastings; orchestrations, Jonathan Tunick.

CAST: Glynis Johns (*Desirée Armfeldt*), Len Cariou (*Fredrik Egerman*), Hermione Gingold (*Mme. Armfeldt*),

Victoria Mallory (*Anne Egerman*), Laurence Guittard (*Count Carl-Magnus Malcolm*), Patricia Elliott (*Countess Charlotte Malcolm*), Mark Lambert (*Henrik Egerman*), Judy Kahan (*Fredrika Armfeldt*), D. Jamin-Bartlett (*Petra*), George Lee Andrews (*Frid*).

LONDON: April 15, 1975
ADELPHI THEATRE; 406 p.

Presented by Ruth Mitchell, Frank Milton, Eddie Kulukundis, & Richard Pilbrow, with Bernard Delfont; directed by Harold Prince; choreographed by Patricia Birch; settings, Boris Aronson; costumes, Florence Klotz; lighting, Tharon Musser; music director, Ray Cook; orchestrations, Jonathan Tunick.

CAST: Jean Simmons (*Desirée Armfeldt*), Hermione Gingold (*Mme. Armfeldt*), Joss Ackland (*Fredrik Egerman*), Maria Aitken (*Countess Charlotte Malcolm*), Veronica Page (*Anne Egerman*), Diane Langton (*Petra*), Christine McKenna (*Fredrika Armfeldt*), David Kernan (*Count Carl-Magnus Malcolm*), Terry Mitchell (*Henrik Egerman*), Michael Harbour (*Frid*).

Love as viewed from the perspectives of age and social position was the theme of the third collaboration between composer-lyricist Stephen Sondheim and producer-director Harold Prince (the others: *Company* and *Follies*). Adapted from an Ingmar Bergman film, the story, set in Sweden at the turn of the century, involves middle-aged lawyer Fredrik Egerman, his virginal child-bride Anne, and his former mistress, the actress Desirée Armfeldt, now the mistress of self-centered Count Carl-Magnus. All four show up for a weekend at the country home of Desirée's mother, where the proper partners are sorted out. Among the musical innova-

tions: the score was written entirely in three-quarter time or multiples thereof, and the overture is sung by a vocal quartet.

The US tour began Feb. 1974, with Jean Simmons (*Desirée*), Margaret Hamilton (*Mme. Armfeldt*), and George Lee Andrews (*Fredrik*). It lasted a year. Production delays in London forced the substitution of Miss Simmons for Glynis Johns and Hermione Gingold for Margaret Leighton. During West End run Miss Gingold was succeeded by Angela Baddeley (9-75).

"Little Old Lady." Music by Hoagy Carmichael; lyric by Stanley Adams. Perky serenade sung and danced by Mitzi Mayfair and Charles Walters in *The Show Is On* (NY 1936).

Little Show, The (1929). Music by Arthur Schwartz, etc.; lyrics by Howard Dietz, etc.; sketches by Dietz, Newman Levy, George S. Kaufman, etc.

SONGS: "I Guess I'll Have to Change My Plan," "I've Made a Habit of You," "Or What Have You?" (Morris Hamilton–Grace Henry), "Moanin' Low" (music, Ralph Rainger), "Hammacher-Schlemmer, I Love You," "Can't We Be Friends?" (Kay Swift–Paul James), "A Little Hut in Hoboken" (Herman Hupfeld).

NEW YORK: April 20, 1929
MUSIC BOX THEATRE; 331 p.

Presented by William A. Brady Jr. & Dwight Deere Wiman, with Tom Weatherly; directed by Alexander Leftwich & Wiman; choreographed by Danny Dare; settings, Jo Mielziner; costumes, Ruth Brenner; music director, Ralph Rainger.

CAST: Clifton Webb, Fred Allen, Libby Holman, Romney Brent, Portland Hoffa, Bettina Hall, Harold Moffet, Helen Lynd, John McCauley, Joan Carter-Waddell, Peggy Conklin (chorus), Constance Cummings (chorus)

The Little Show grew out of a series of Sunday-evening variety shows that Tom Weatherly had co-produced at the Selwyn Theatre. It inaugurated a succession of smart, intimate, imaginative revues that first combined the talents of composer Schwartz with lyricist Dietz. It was also the first show to give major assignments to Fred Allen and Libby Holman, who, with veteran Clifton Webb, became something of an American counterpart to Britain's Gertrude Lawrence, Beatrice Lillie and Jack Buchanan in *André Charlot's Revue of 1924*. Honors in musical humor went to "Hammacher-Schlemmer, I Love You," and in sketches to George S. Kaufman's classic account "The Still Alarm," about well-mannered indifference to an incendiary holocaust. During run, Bettina Hall was succeeded by Lucy Monroe (8-29), and Katherine Carrington was added to the cast (1-30).

There were two subsequent *Little Shows* on Bway (thus making the first *Little Show* popularly known as *The First Little Show*). Because the producers feared that casting Webb, Holman, and Allen in *The Second Little Show* would make audiences think of it as something of a déjà-vu revue, they secured the services of Al Trahan, Ruth Tester (who won out over Ethel Merman), and Jay C. Flippen. (Webb, Holman, and Allen then went into Max Gordon's first revue, *Three's a Crowd.*) *The Second Little Show* opened Sept. 2, 1930, at the Royale Theatre, with Schwartz and Dietz again supplying the songs, though the hit turned out to be Herman Hupfeld's "Sing Something Simple." It lasted 63 performances.

The Third Little Show, co-starring Beatrice Lillie and Ernest Truex, was considered an improvement over *Little Show* No. 2 though still no match for *Little Show* No. 1. It opened at the Music Box June 1, 1931, and ran 136 performances. "Mad Dogs and Englishmen" (Noël Coward), "When Yuba Plays the Rumba on the Tuba" (Hupfeld), and "There Are Fairies at the Bottom of My Garden" (Liza Lehmann–Rose Fyleman) were sung in this edition.

"Little Things You Do Together, The." Music & lyric by Stephen Sondheim. Catalogue of the little things that keep marriages intact ("It's people that you hate together, bait together, date together") sung in *Company* by Elaine Stritch and company (NY 1970, L 1972).

"Little Tin Box." Music by Jerry Bock; lyric by Sheldon Harnick. Sung by Howard Da Sylva, Ron Husmann, Stanley Simmonds, Julian Patrick, with Del Horstmann, Michael Quinn, David London in *Fiorello!* (NY 1959). In the scene, a Republican clubhouse in NY, a group of political hacks react to the Seabury investigation of Tammany Hall by reenacting the courtroom questioning. The song (written just two weeks before the show's Bway opening) relates how politicos, found with their hands in the till, innocently detail the way they saved their money by giving up smoking, returning empty bottles to the grocer, and going without lunch for a week. In London version (1962), it was sung by Peter Reeves and Bryan Blackburn.

Part of the song's melody was taken from a discarded song dealing with the rivalry between airmen and soldiers during World War I:

Airmen:
Oh, a rare sort of bird is the flyer,
One of nature's uncrowned kings.
With the valor of an eagle
And the vision of a hawk
And a condor's enormous wings . . .
Soldiers:
Oh, a rare sort of bird is the flyer,
Would to God that he'd fly south.
With the valor of a chicken
And the vision of a bat
And a parrot's enormous mouth . . .

"Little White House (at the End of Honeymoon Lane), The." Music by James F. Hanley; lyric by Eddie Dowling. Marital proposal made by Eddie Dowling in *Honeymoon Lane* (NY 1926).

Littler, Emile, producer; b. Ramsgate, Eng., Sept. 9, 1903. After working as stage manager, Littler became assistant producer in NY (1927–1931), then producer in London. His biggest hit was *Annie Get Your Gun;* others: *The Night and the Music, Song of Norway, Blue for a Boy, Zip Goes a Million, Love from Judy.* He was a brother of producer Prince Littler.

1942	The Maid of the Mountains (r)
1943	The Knight was Bold
	Sunny River
	Flying Colours
	Panama Hattie
1945	The Night and the Music
	The Quaker Girl (r)
1946	Song of Norway
	The Night and the Laughter
1947	Annie Get Your Gun
	Finian's Rainbow
1950	Dear Miss Phoebe
	Blue for a Boy
1951	Zip Goes a Million
1952	Excitement
	Love from Judy
1959	Fine Fettle
1967	110 in the Shade

Littler, Prince, producer; b. Ramsgate, Eng., July 25, 1901; d. Sussex, Eng., Sept. 13, 1973. Littler was director of the largest group of theatres in England, incl. Stoll Theatre Corp., Moss' Empires, Associated Theatre Properties; also chairman, managing dir., Drury Lane Theatre, 1945–1973. His biggest London hits were *Brigadoon, Carousel, Guys and Dolls, The Pajama Game.* He was a brother of producer Emile Littler.

1934	The Bing Boys Are Here (r)
1940	White Horse Inn (r)
1943	It's Foolish but It's Fun
	Show Boat (r)
1946	Pacific 1860
1949	Brigadoon
1950	Carousel
1951	Rainbow Square
1953	Guys and Dolls
1954	Can-Can
1955	The Pajama Game
1956	Plain and Fancy

"Liza (All the Clouds'll Roll Away)." Music by George Gershwin; lyric by Ira Gershwin & Gus Kahn. Minstrel number sung by Nick Lucas and danced by Ruby Keeler and chorus in *Show Girl* (NY 1929). The musical received much publicity because of an incident during the opening night in Boston involving Al Jolson, who had recently married Miss Keeler. As the dancer has recalled, "There was this tremendous *Ziegfeld Follies* number, 'Liza.' I was to come down a flight of steps dancing. Mr. Jolson was in the first or second row. As I started down the steps he got up from the audience and sang, right from the beginning of the song. He just wanted to be a part of the show, I think. I thought that was marvelous."

"Lizzie Borden." Music & lyric by Michael Brown. First performed in *New Faces of 1952*, this narrative ballad takes a merry look at the Fall River spinster who allegedly killed her father and stepmother with an ax ("They said 'Lizzie cut it out,'/And that's exactly what she did"). The number was sung and danced by Rosemary O'Reilly, Carol Lawrence, Virginia de Luce, Carol Nelson, Virginia Bosler, Allen Conroy, Jimmy Russell, Michael Dominico (as *Townspeople*); Bill Mullikin (*Man*); Paul Lynde (*Judge*); Patricia Hammerlee (*Lizzie*); and Joe Lautner (*DA*).

Lock Up Your Daughters (1959). Music by Laurie Johnson; lyrics by Lionel Bart; book by Bernard Miles, based on Henry Fielding's novel *Rape Upon Rape*.

SONGS: "A Proper Man," "It Must Be True," "Red Wine and a Wench," "On the Side," "When Does the Ravishing Begin?," "Lovely Lover," "Lock Up Your Daughters," "Kind Fate," "Sunny Sunday Morning."

LONDON: May 28, 1959
MERMAID THEATRE; 328 p.

Presented by the Mermaid Theatre; directed by Peter Coe; choreographed by Gilbert Vernon; settings & costumes, Sean Kenny; music director, Laurie Johnson.

CAST: Stephanie Voss (*Hilaret Politic*), Hy Hazell (*Mrs. Squeezum*), Terence Cooper (*Capt. Constant*), Frederick Jaeger (*Ramble*), John Sharp (*Politic*), Brendan Barry (*Dabble*), Richard Wordsworth (*Squeezum*), Keith Marsh (*Sotmore*).

LONDON: May 17, 1962
MERMAID THEATRE; 664 p.

Presented by the Mermaid Theatre; directed by Richard Wordsworth; choreographed by Denys Palmer; settings, David Myerscough Jones.

CAST: Sally Smith (*Hilaret Politic*), Hy Hazell (*Mrs. Squeezum*), Laurie Payne (*Capt. Constant*), Peter Gilmore (*Ramble*), Richard Goolden (*Politic*), William Stephens (*Dabble*), Bernard Miles (*Squeezum*), Joss Ackland (*Sotmore*).

This bawdy romp, the inaugural production at the Mermaid Theatre, ran twice as long when it was revived three years later, first at the Mermaid and subsequently at Her Majesty's. The story, set in London in 1730, is concerned with Hilaret's charge of rape against the roguish rake Ramble, her experience fending off the advances of Justice Squeezum, Squeezum's wife's gambol with Ramble, and Hilaret's eventual reunion with her constant Capt. Constant. Though a Bway version was scheduled in 1960, it closed in Boston before reaching NY. With Alfred Drake directing, the cast included Nancy Dussault, John Michael King, and George S. Irving, in addition to original cast members Hy Hazell, Frederick Jaeger, and Brendan Barry. In 1969 a third Mermaid production was unveiled with Veronica Clifford and Russell Hunter.

FILM VERSION: Christopher Plummer, Susannah York, Glynis Johns, Jim Dale (Col. 1969, Peter Coe dir.).

"Lock Up Your Daughters." Music by Laurie Johnson; lyric by Lionel Bart. Rollicking warning to fathers to protect their daughters against rakish young men. Introduced in *Lock Up Your Daughters* (L 1959) by Keith Marsh, Frederick Jaeger, and Terence Cooper.

Loesser, Frank (Henry), composer, lyricist, producer; b. New York, June 29, 1910; d. New York, July 26, 1969. Loesser was an eclectic composer-lyricist whose Bway scores ranged from period musical comedy (*Where's Charley?*) to Damon Runyon fable (*Guys and Dolls*) to Italianate opera (*The Most Happy Fella*) to big-business satire (*How to Succeed in Business Without Really Trying*). Among his best-known songs: "My Darling, My Darling," "Once in Love with Amy," "Make a Miracle," "If I Were a Bell," "Luck Be a Lady," "Sue Me," "Sit Down, You're Rockin' the Boat," "Standing on the Corner," "Big 'D'," "Summertime Love," "I Believe in You." He began career as a Hollywood lyricist, then became a composer in 1942. His second wife was singer Jo Sullivan. Bib: *Frank Loesser Song Book* (S&S, NY 1972).

Asterisk indicates Mr. Loesser was also co-producer:
- 1936 The Illustrators' Show (lyrics only) (Actman)
- 1944 Skirts (L)
- 1948 Where's Charley?
- 1950 Guys and Dolls
- 1956 The Most Happy Fella (also lib.)
- 1960 Greenwillow * (also co-lib.)
- 1961 How to Succeed in Business Without Really Trying *

Loewe, Frederick, composer; b. Berlin, Germany, June 10, 1904 (Austrian parents). With lyricist-librettist Alan Jay Lerner, with whom he collaborated on seven Bway scores, Loewe is primarily identified with a musical theatre that captured the romance and fantasy of a bygone age. The team's greatest success was *My Fair Lady*, whence came such songs as "On the Street Where You Live," "I Could Have Danced All Night," "Get Me to the Church on Time," "The Rain in Spain," and "I've Grown Accustomed to Her Face." Other stage hits were *Brigadoon* ("Almost Like Being in Love," "The Heather on the Hill"), *Paint Your Wagon* ("I Still See Elisa," "I Talk to the Trees"), and *Camelot* ("If Ever I Would Leave You," "Camelot"). Loewe, who settled in the US in 1924, also wrote with lyricist Earle Crooker. He and Lerner have also written for films, incl. *Gigi*. Bib: *The Lerner and Loewe Song Book* (S&S, NY 1962).

Unless otherwise noted, following written with Mr. Lerner:
- 1938 Great Lady (Crooker)
- 1943 What's Up
- 1945 The Day Before Spring
- 1947 Brigadoon
- 1951 Paint Your Wagon
- 1956 My Fair Lady
- 1960 Camelot (also co-prod.)
- 1973 Gigi

Logan, Ella, actress, singer; b. Glasgow, Scotland, March 6, 1913; d. Burlingame, Cal., May 1, 1969. Miss Logan, who settled in the US in 1932, is most fondly remembered for creating the leading role in *Finian's Rainbow*, in which she introduced "How Are Things in Glocca Morra?," "Look to the Rainbow," "Something Sort of Grandish," "When the Idle Poor Become the Idle Rich," "Old Devil Moon," and "If This Isn't Love." She also sang in nightclubs and films.
- 1930 Darling! I Love You (L) (*Bebe Van Stuyvesant*)
- 1934 Calling All Stars
- 1939 George White's Scandals
- 1941 Sons o' Fun
- 1947 Finian's Rainbow (*Sharon McLonergan*)

Logan, Joshua (Lockwood), director, librettist; b. Texarkana, Texas, Oct. 5, 1908. Protean director and occasional librettist whose Bway successes include *I Married an Angel, By Jupiter, Annie Get Your Gun, South Pacific, Wish You Were Here, Fanny*. Logan has done four shows with Richard Rodgers (three with Hart, one with Hammerstein) and two each with Irving Berlin and Harold Rome. He has also written and directed nonmusicals, incl. *Mister Roberts*. Logan is the son-in-law of actor-librettist Edward Harrigan.

Asterisk indicates Mr. Logan was also librettist or co-librettist:
- 1938 I Married an Angel
  Knickerbocker Holiday
- 1939 Stars in Your Eyes

1940 Two for the Show
      Higher and Higher *
1942 By Jupiter
      This Is the Army
1946 Annie Get Your Gun
1949 South Pacific * (also co-prod.)
1951 South Pacific * (L)
1952 Wish You Were Here * (also co-prod.)
1954 Fanny * (also co-prod.)
1962 All American
      Mr. President
1970 Look to the Lilies

"London Pride." Music & lyric by Noël Coward. Though not written for the theatre, the song was added to the score of the second edition of *Up and Doing* (L 1941), in which it was sung by Binnie Hale. For his lyric, Coward symbolically used the flower London Pride to affirm his affection for the city and its people during World War II; for his melody he went back to a traditional lavender-seller's song, "Won't You Buy My Sweet Blooming Lavender?" As the composer has noted, "This age-old melody was appropriated by the Germans and used as a foundation for 'Deutschland über Alles,' and I considered that the time had come for us to have it back in London where it belonged."

"Lonely Town." Music by Leonard Bernstein; lyric by Betty Comden & Adolph Green. Any town is a lonely town without love. John Battles sang the lament in *On the Town* (NY 1944); Don McKay sang it in the London production (1963).

"Long Before I Knew You." Music by Jule Styne; lyric by Betty Comden & Adolph Green. In *Bells Are Ringing* (NY 1956), Sydney Chaplin and Judy Holliday confessed that, even before meeting, they knew they would fall in love. The couple in the London version (1957) were George Gaynes and Janet Blair.

"Look for the Silver Lining." Music by Jerome Kern; lyric by B. G. DeSylva. To lift a poor girl's spirits, young millionaire Irving Fisher gave this advice to dishwashing drudge Marilyn Miller in *Sally* (NY 1920). In London production (1921), it was sung by Gregory Stroud and Dorothy Dickson.

"Look to the Rainbow." Music by Burton Lane; lyric by E. Y. Harburg. In *Finian's Rainbow* (NY 1947), Irish immigrant Sharon McLonergan (Ella Logan) tells labor organizer Woody Mahoney (Donald Richards): "In Glocca Morra, where we come from, there's an old legend—'You'll never grow old and you'll never grow poor, if you look to the rainbow beyond the next moor.'" "Lovely legend," says Woody. "I wonder who thought it up." "My father," says Sharon—who proceeds to sing about it. In the musical's London production (1947), Beryl Seton played Sharon.

"Look Who's Dancing." Music by Arthur Schwartz; lyric by Dorothy Fields. Breezy expression of uncontrolled bliss sung by Marcia Van Dyke and Shirley Booth—and danced by Miss Van Dyke, Miss Booth, and Johnny Johnston—in *A Tree Grows in Brooklyn* (NY 1951).

"Looking for a Boy." Music by George Gershwin; lyric by Ira Gershwin. Poignant quest undertaken in *Tip-Toes* by Queenie Smith in NY (1925) and by Dorothy Dickson in London (1926).

Lorraine, Lillian (née Eulallean de Jacques), actress, singer; b. San Francisco, Cal., Jan. 1, 1892; d. New York, April 17, 1955. Serenely beautiful actress who was a special favorite of producer Florenz Ziegfeld. She sang

"My Pony Boy" in *Miss Innocence,* "By the Light of the Silvery Moon" in the *Follies of 1909,* "Row, Row, Row" in the *Ziegfeld Follies* (1912).

1906	The Tourists (chorus)
1907	The Gay White Way
1908	Miss Innocence (*Angele*)
1909	Follies of 1909
1910	Follies of 1910
1911	Ziegfeld Follies
1912	Over the River (*Myrtle Billtopper*)
	Ziegfeld Follies
1914	The Whirl of the World
1917	Odds and Ends
1918	Ziegfeld Follies
1919	The Little Blue Devil (*Paulette Divine*)
1922	The Blue Kitten (*Totoche*)

Losch, (Ottilie Ethel) Tilly, dancer, actress, choreographer; b. Vienna, Austria, Nov. 15, 1902. After appearing at the Royal Opera House, Vienna, Miss Losch joined Max Reinhardt's company as featured dancer in *A Midsummer Night's Dream.* She was brought to London by producer Charles Cochran; in NY she is best remembered for her appearance in *The Band Wagon.* (*D.* Dec. 24, 1975.)

Asterisk indicates production that Miss Losch choreographed but in which she did not appear:

1928	This Year of Grace! (L)
	This Year of Grace! * (NY)
1929	Wake Up and Dream! (L)
	Bitter Sweet * (L)
	Wake Up and Dream! (NY)
1931	The Gang's All Here * (NY)
	The Band Wagon (NY)
1934	Streamline (L)

"Losing My Mind." Music & lyric by Stephen Sondheim. In *Follies* (NY 1971), Dorothy Collins sang of a love that torments her from sun-up to sleepless nights. The torch ballad was performed by Miss Collins wearing a clinging, beaded silver gown, as part of an imaginary *Follies* production intended to expose the psychological hangups of the musical's leading characters. Though intentionally written to suggest the style of a Gershwin song with a Dorothy Fields lyric, the music also recalls Jack Strachey ("These Foolish Things") and André Previn ("You're Gonna Hear from Me").

Lost in the Stars (1949). Music by Kurt Weill; lyrics by Maxwell Anderson & Alan Paton; book by Anderson, based on Paton's novel *Cry, the Beloved Country.*

SONGS: "The Hills of Ixipo," "Thousands of Miles," "Train to Johannesburg," "The Little Grey House," "Trouble Man," "Lost in the Stars," "Stay Well," "Cry, the Beloved Country," "Big Mole," "A Bird of Passage."

NEW YORK : Oct. 30, 1949
MUSIC BOX THEATRE; 273 p.

Presented by the Playwrights Co.; directed by Rouben Mamoulian; settings, George Jenkins; costumes, Anna Hill Johnstone; music director, Maurice Levine; orchestrations, Kurt Weill.

CAST: Todd Duncan (*Stephen Kumalo*), Leslie Banks (*James Jarvis*), Julian Mayfield (*Absalom Kumalo*), Inez Matthews (*Irena*), Herbert Coleman (*Alex*), Warren Coleman (*John Kumalo*), Sheila Guyse (*Linda*).

Weill's last Bway score (his second with Maxwell Anderson) was written to convey "a message of hope that people, through a personal approach, will solve whatever racial problems exist." In the story, set in and around Johannesburg, South Africa, Absalom Kumalo, the erring son of Stephen Kumalo, an *umfundisi,* accidentally kills a white man in a robbery attempt and is condemned to hang. Through the tragedy, however, a tentative bond is formed between Stephen and James Jarvis, the dead man's racist father, which offers some optimism for the future.

In 1972 the musical was revived by the Kennedy Center under the direction of Gene Frankel. It was brought to NY with Brock Peters (*Stephen*), Jack Gwillim (*Jarvis*), Gilbert Price (*Absalom*), and Margaret Cowie (*Irena*), and ran 39 performances.

FILM VERSION: Brock Peters and Melba Moore (AFT 1974, Daniel Mann dir.).

"**Lost in the Stars.**" Music by Kurt Weill; lyric by Maxwell Anderson. At the end of Act I in *Lost in the Stars* (NY 1949), a South African *umfundisi* (Todd Duncan), tormented because his son has killed a white man in a robbery attempt, sings of his fear that God has become indifferent to stars and to people.

"**Lot of Livin' to Do, A.**" Music by Charles Strouse; lyric by Lee Adams. Assertive ode to living life to the fullest sung by Presley-type rock-and-roll singer Conrad Birdie (Dick Gautier) and Sweet Apple Kids in *Bye Bye Birdie* (NY 1960). Marty Wilde played Conrad in London production (1961).

"**Louisiana Hayride.**" Music by Arthur Schwartz; lyric by Howard Dietz. Jubilant first-act finale of the revue *Flying Colors* (NY 1932) performed by the entire company, including, for the first time, both white and black choruses. In the number, the huge hayride wagon was backed by a motion-picture projection of a shady country road, giving the impression that the wagon was moving.

Louisiana Purchase (1940). Music & lyrics by Irving Berlin; book by Morrie Ryskind, based on story by B. G. DeSylva.

SONGS: "Louisiana Purchase," "It's a Lovely Day Tomorrow," "Outside of That I Love You," "You're Lonely and I'm Lonely," "Latins Know How," "The Lord Done Fixed Up My Soul," "Fools Fall in Love," "You Can't Brush Me Off," "What Chance Have I?"

NEW YORK: May 28, 1940
IMPERIAL THEATRE; 444 p.

Presented by B. G. DeSylva; directed by Edgar MacGregor; choreographed by George Balanchine, Carl Randall; settings & costumes, Tom Lee; music director, Robert Emmett Dolan; orchestrations, Robert Russell Bennett.

CAST: William Gaxton (*Jim Taylor*), Vera Zorina (*Marina Van Linden*), Victor Moore (*Sen. Oliver P. Loganberry*), Irene Bordoni (*Mme. Bordelaise*), Carol Bruce (*Beatrice*), Nick Long, Jr. (*Lee Davis*), Hugh Martin (singer), Ralph Blane (singer).

Prompted by recent political scandals involving Huey Long in Louisiana, Morrie Ryskind devised a libretto in which Sen. Oliver P. Loganberry goes to New Orleans to investigate. Attempting to block the probe, local lawyer Jim Taylor tries framing the incorruptible senator with such attractions as the seductive Marina, the coquettish Mme. Bordelaise, and the flashy Beatrice. But Loganberry wiggles out of the trap by marrying the madam, and Jim, somehow uninvolved in misdeeds, is free to face the future with Marina. The show was hailed for its production, songs, and performances, particularly those of comic Victor Moore (his fifth appearance with William Gaxton), dancer Vera Zorina, and new songbelter Carol Bruce.

FILM VERSION: Bob Hope, Vera

Zorina, Victor Moore, Irene Bordoni (Par. 1941, Irving Cummings dir.).

"Love for Sale." Music and lyric by Cole Porter. A prostitute's weary invitation proffered in *The New Yorkers* (NY 1930) by Kathryn Crawford and The Three Girl Friends (June Shafer, Ida Pearson, Stella Friend). The song was banned from the air for many years. The theme was similar to a song by Rudolf Friml and Brian Hooker in *The Vagabond King*, also called "Love for Sale" ("Love for sale, love for sale,/Ready for any who'll buy").

"Love Is a Dancing Thing." Music by Arthur Schwartz; lyric by Howard Dietz. Love in a delicate musical mood offered by singer Woods Miller and dancers Paul Haakon and Nina Whitney in *At Home Abroad* (NY 1935). In London revue *Follow the Sun* (1936), the piece was performed by Irene Eisinger.

"Love Is a Simple Thing." Music by Arthur Siegel; lyric by June Carroll. Series of definitions enumerated in Bway revue *New Faces of 1952*, by Rosemary O'Reilly, Robert Clary, Eartha Kitt, and June Carroll, and danced by Virginia Bosler and Allen Conroy, Carol Nelson and Jimmy Russell, and Carol Lawrence and Michael Dominico. A special "Charles Addams" version was also sung by Miss Carroll.

"Love Is Sweeping the Country." Music by George Gershwin; lyric by Ira Gershwin. Sung and danced by George Murphy, June O'Dea, and chorus in *Of Thee I Sing* (NY 1931), just before the big political rally at Madison Square Garden, NY. The patter music for the song was the same as the opening number of *Ming Toy*, the

Gershwins' unproduced musical based on play *East Is West*.

"Love Is the Reason." Music by Arthur Schwartz; lyric by Dorothy Fields. Catalogue song in which love's symptoms are found in everything from "the gleam in poppa's eye" to "a toothache in your heart." Shirley Booth sang it in *A Tree Grows in Brooklyn* (NY 1951).

"Love, Look Away." Music by Richard Rodgers; lyric by Oscar Hammerstein II. Lament for a lost love sung in *Flower Drum Song* by Arabella Hong in NY (1958) and by Joan Pethers in London (1960).

"Love Makes the World Go 'Round." Music & lyric by Bob Merrill. Also known as "Theme from *Carnival*," the song was performed by Anna Maria Alberghetti and puppets at the end of Act I of *Carnival* (NY 1961). In London production (1963), it was sung by Sally Logan. The piece was intended to convey much the same spirit as "Hi Lili, Hi Lo" in the film *Lili*, the basis for *Carnival*.

"Love Me or Leave Me." Music by Walter Donaldson; lyric by Gus Kahn. All-or-nothing proposition introduced by Ruth Etting in *Whoopee* (NY 1928). The song was also added to the score of *Simple Simon* (NY 1930) during run, and was again sung by Miss Etting.

"Love Nest." Music by Louis Hirsch; lyric by Otto Harbach. Ballad of marital contentment sung by Janet Velie and Jack McGowan in *Mary* (NY 1920). Also offered in London production (1921) by Alec Regan and Evelyn Laye.

"Love Never Went to College." Music by Richard Rodgers; lyric by Lorenz Hart. Love's power, despite lack of education, was attested to by Marcy Westcott and Richard Kollmar in *Too Many Girls* (NY 1939).

"Love Will Find a Way." Music by Eubie Blake; lyric by Noble Sissle. Duet of romantic optimism sung by Lottie Gee and Roger Matthews in *Shuffle Along* (NY 1921).

"Love Will Find a Way." Music by Harold Fraser-Simson; lyric by Harry Graham. The hit song of *The Maid of the Mountains* (L 1917), in which it was introduced by José Collins. In NY version (1918) it was sung by Sidonie Espero. The melody of the first four bars of the waltz is actually the same as that of the first two bars of "The Merry Widow Waltz," with each note played twice.

"Love Will Find Out the Way." Music & lyric by Glenn Paxton, Robert Goldman, & George Weiss. A supposedly old English ballad performed at the spinet by Polly Bergen as Elisabeth Bennet in *First Impressions* (NY 1959), the musical version of *Pride and Prejudice*. The piece delicately upholds the conviction that the road of love—though as winding and wand'ring as the one from Uxbridge to Tunbridge to Selsey by the Sea—is sure to find out the way.

"Lovelier Than Ever." Music & lyric by Frank Loesser. Sweeping ode to eternal springtime sung in *Where's Charley?* by Paul England and Jane Lawrence in NY (1948), and by Jerry Desmonde and Marion Grimaldi in London (1958).

"Lover, Come Back to Me." Music by Sigmund Romberg; lyric by Oscar Hammerstein II. Ardent plea—eventually, of course, answered—sung by Evelyn Herbert on the deck of the good ship *New Moon* in the musical of that name (NY 1928). Entreaty also made by Evelyn Laye in London version (1929). Romberg, who wrote the song at the request of Miss Herbert, based the release on the opening theme of Tschaikowsky's piano piece "June Barcarolle."

Luce, Claire, actress, dancer, singer; b. Syracuse, NY, Oct. 15, 1903. Blonde dancer-turned-actress, Miss Luce is best known as Fred Astaire's partner in *Gay Divorce*, in which the couple introduced "Night and Day." As dramatic actress, Miss Luce appeared in *Of Mice and Men* on Bway and played Shakespearean roles both in US and UK.

1923	Little Jessie James
1924	Dear Sir (*Clair*)
	Music Box Revue
1926	No Foolin'
1927	Ziegfeld Follies
1932	Gay Divorce (*Mimi*)
1933	Gay Divorce (L) (*Mimi*)
1935	Gay Deceivers (L) (*Maricousa*)
1936	Follow the Sun (L)

"Luck Be a Lady." Music & lyric by Frank Loesser. Robert Alda introduced this galvanic plea in *Guys and Dolls* (NY 1950) as he implored Lady Luck to be on his side in a crucial dice game. In London version (1953), it was sung by Jerry Wayne.

"Lucky Day." Music by Ray Henderson; lyric by B. G. DeSylva & Lew Brown. Harry Richman introduced this exuberant number (in which "horseshoe" rhymes with "of course you") in *George White's Scandals* (NY 1926). In the scene, the singer was surrounded by young ladies representing such symbols of luck as a Wishbone, a Horseshoe, a Four-Leaf

Clover, a Star, a New Moon, and a Haystack (presumably with a needle). In London, the song was interpreted by Billy Milton in the revue *Shake Your Feet* (1927).

"Lucky in Love." Music by Ray Henderson; lyric by B. G. DeSylva & Lew Brown. In which being lucky in love has it all over being lucky at gambling. John Price Jones and Mary Lawlor introduced the jaunty piece in *Good News!* (NY 1927); Neil Collins and Evelyn Hoey sang it in the London company (1928).

"Lucky to Be Me." Music by Leonard Bernstein; lyric by Betty Comden & Adolph Green. A boy's bursting self-congratulations at discovering that the girl he loves loves him. Sung in *On the Town* by John Battles (NY 1944) and by Don McKay (L 1963).

Luders, Gustav, composer; b. Bremen, Germany, Dec. 13, 1865; d. New York, Jan. 24, 1913. Luders, who settled in the US in 1888, achieved his greatest Bway success with *The Prince of Pilsen,* with librettist Frank Pixley. Other collaborators: Harry B. Smith, Joseph Herbert, George Ade, Avery Hopwood.

1899 Little Robinson Crusoe (Smith)
1900 The Burgomaster (Pixley)
1902 King Dodo (Pixley)
1903 The Prince of Pilsen (Pixley)
      Mam'selle Napoleon (Herbert)
1904 The Sho-Gun (Ade)
      Woodland (Pixley)
1907 The Grand Mogul (Pixley)
1908 Marcelle (Pixley)
1909 The Fair Co-ed (Ade)
1910 The Old Town (Ade)
1912 The Gypsy (Pixley)
1913 Somewhere Else (Hopwood)

Lupino, Stanley, actor, dancer, singer, librettist, director, producer; b. London, May 15, 1894; d. London, June 10, 1942. Breezy, agile dancing comic and member of theatrical Lupino family (brother of actor Barry Lupino, cousin of Lupino Lane, father of Ida Lupino). Lupino began career as acrobat, and made London debut in 1913. Between 1928 and 1936 he was associated with actor-producer Laddie Cliff. Best-known number: "I Lift Up My Finger" in *Love Lies.* Bib: *From the Stocks to the Stars* by Lupino (1934).

Asterisk indicates Mr. Lupino was also librettist, director:

1913 All the Winners (added)
1916 Girl Wanted
1917 Suzette (*Tibbs*)
      Arlette (*Rono*)
1918 Hullo, America!
1919 The Kiss Call (*Dr. Thomas Pym*)
1920 Jig-Saw
      It's All Wrong
1921 The Peep Show
1922 His Girl (*James Hicks*)
      Phi-Phi (*Mercury*)
1923 Dover Street to Dixie
1924 Puppets
1925 Better Days
1926 Turned Up (co-lib. only)
      Naughty Riquette (NY) (*Theophile Michu*)
1927 The Nightingale (NY) (*Mr. Carp*)
1928 So This Is Love * (*Potiphar Griggs*)
1929 Love Lies * (*Jerry Walker*)
1930 The Love Race * (*Reggie Powley*)
1931 Hold My Hand * (*Eddy Marston*)
1934 Sporting Love * (*Percy Brace*)
1936 Over She Goes * (*Tommy Teacher*)
1937 Crazy Days * (*Bertie Barnes*)
1938 The Fleet's Lit Up (*Horatio Roper*)
1940 Funny Side Up *
1941 Lady Behave * (*Tony Meyrick*)
1943 La-De-Da-De-Da (lib. only)

Lynde, Paul (Edward), actor; b. Mt. Vernon, Ohio, June 13, 1926. Giggly, waspish comic who introduced "Kids" in *Bye Bye Birdie*. Later became well known on tv.

1952	New Faces of 1952
1956	New Faces of 1956 (sk., dir. only)
1960	Bye Bye Birdie (*Mr. McAfee*)

⚘ M ⚘

"Ma Belle Marguerite." Music by Vivian Ellis; lyric by A. P. Herbert. Georges Guétary performed this effervescent number as a supposedly traditional French song in *Bless the Bride* (L 1947). Herbert's original lyric to the melody had been about a donkey, then he wrote one about a soldier, and eventually about beautiful grape-picking, grape-treading, wine-drinking Marguerite. Though Guétary at first thought the piece unsuitable, it turned out to be his show-stopper in the musical.

"Ma Blushin' Rosie (Ma Posie Sweet)." Music by John Stromberg; lyric by Edgar Smith. Negro dialect song—also known by its first line, "Rosie, You Are Ma Posie"—introduced by Fay Templeton and polka-dot-costumed chorus in Weber and Fields' *Fiddle-Dee-Dee* (NY 1900). The song, which became the most popular to emanate from a Weber and Fields show, stemmed from a dance number the composer had written for Bessie Clayton. Because she didn't like it, Smith added the lyric and the number was given to Miss Templeton.

MacDermot, Galt, composer; b. Montreal, Canada, Dec. 18, 1928. MacDermot made a great impact on the Bway scene with rock score for *Hair* (incl. "Aquarius," "Good Morning Starshine," "Easy to Be Hard," "Let the Sunshine In," "Where Do I Go?"). Collaborators: Gerome Ragni, James Rado, John Guare, William Dumaresq, Christopher Gore.

1967	Hair (Ragni, Rado)
1968	Hair (revised) (Ragni, Rado)
1970	Isabel's a Jezebel (L) (Dumaresq)
1971	Two Gentlemen of Verona (Guare)
1972	Dude (Ragni)
	Via Galectica (Gore)

MacDonald, Christie, actress, singer; b. Pictou, Nova Scotia, Feb. 28, 1875; d. Westport, Conn., July 25, 1962. Miss MacDonald was a properly demure operetta heroine, who is best remembered for her Bway appearances in *The Spring Maid* (singing "Day Dreams") and *Sweethearts* ("Sweethearts").

1894	The Devil's Deputy (*Bob*)
1895	The Sphinx (*Shafra*)
	The Chieftain (*Dolly Grigg*)
1896	Half a King (*Lucinda*)
1898	The Bride-Elect (*Minutezza*)
1899	The Man in the Moon (*Diana*)
	In Gay Paree
1900	The Princess Chic (*Chic*)
	The Cadet Girl (*Antoinette*)
	Hodge, Podge and Co.
1902	The Toreador (*Nancy Staunton*)
1904	An English Daisy (*Daisy Maitland*)
	The Sho-Gun (*Princess Hunni-Bun*)
1906	Mexicana (*Tita*)
	The Belle of Mayfair (*Julia Caldicott*)
1907	Miss Hook of Holland (*Sally Hook*)
1910	The Prince of Bohemia (*Angela Tritton*)
	The Spring Maid (*Princess Bozena*)

1913 Sweethearts (*Sylvia*)
1920 Florodora (r) (*Lady Holyrood*)

MacDonald, Jeanette (Anna), actress, singer; b. Philadelphia, Pa., June 18, 1901; d. Houston, Texas, Jan. 14, 1965. Slim, blonde, delicate-looking soprano who was a Bway ingenue before beginning her film career in 1929.

1920 The Night Boat (chorus)
      Irene (*Eleanor Worth*, repl.)
1921 Tangerine (*Kate Allen*, repl.)
1922 Fantastic Fricassee
1923 The Magic Ring (*Iris Bellamy*)
1925 Tip-Toes (*Sylvia Metcalf*)
1927 Yes, Yes, Yvette (*Yvette Ralston*)
1928 Sunny Days (*Ginette Bertin*)
      Angela (*Princess Angela*)
1929 Boom Boom (*Jean*)

MacDonough, Glen, librettist, lyricist; b. Brooklyn, NY, Nov. 12, 1870; d. Stamford, Conn., March 30, 1924. MacDonough's biggest Bway hit was *Babes in Toyland* ("Toyland"), written with Victor Herbert. Other composers with whom he was associated: John Philip Sousa, Johann Strauss, Raymond Hubbell, A. Baldwin Sloane, Franz Lehar, Jean Gilbert.

1896 The Gold Bug (Herbert)
1900 Chris and the Wonderful Lamp (Sousa)
      The Belle of Bridgeport (lib. only)
1901 Vienna Life (Strauss)
      The New Yorkers (lib. only)
1903 Babes in Toyland (Herbert)
1904 It Happened in Nordland (Herbert)
1905 Wonderland (Herbert)
1908 Algeria (Herbert)
1909 The Midnight Sons (Hubbell)
      The Rose of Algeria (Algeria) (Herbert)
1910 The Jolly Bachelors (Hubbell)
      The Summer Widowers (Sloane)
1911 The Hen Pecks (lib. only)
      The Never Homes (lib. only)
1912 The Count of Luxembourg (lib. only)
      Eva (Lehar)

1914 The Queen of the Movies (Gilbert)
1915 Fads and Fancies (Hubbell)
1917 Hitchy-Koo (sk. only)
1918 The Kiss Burglar (Hubbell)
      Hitchy-Koo (Hubbell)
1920 As You Were (lib. only)
      Hitchy-Koo (sk. only)

MacGregor, Edgar, director; b. Rochester, NY, 1879; d. New York, April 3, 1957. MacGregor's biggest Bway successes: *The Gingham Girl, Queen High, Honeymoon Lane, The Desert Song, Good News!, Funny Face, The New Moon, Follow Thru, Take a Chance, DuBarry Was a Lady, Louisiana Purchase, Panama Hattie, Let's Face It!*

1918 The Kiss Burglar
      The Girl Behind the Gun
1919 The Velvet Lady (also lib.)
      George White's Scandals
1920 The Sweetheart Shop
      Jim Jam Jems
1921 The Love Birds
1922 The Gingham Girl (also lib.)
      Our Nell
1923 Elsie (also lib.)
      Adrienne
1924 Sweet Little Devil
      Keep Kool
1925 Nadja
      Captain Jinks
1926 Queen High (also co-lib.)
      Honeymoon Lane
      The Desert Song
1927 Bye, Bye, Bonnie
      Lady Do
      Good News!
      Sidewalks of New York
      Funny Face
1928 Earl Carroll Vanities
      The New Moon
      Ups a Daisy
1929 Fioretta
      Follow Thru
      Lady Fingers
      Earl Carroll Sketch Book
1931 Earl Carroll Vanities
1932 Through the Years
      Hot-Cha!

Earl Carroll Vanities
Take a Chance
1939 DuBarry Was a Lady
1940 Louisiana Purchase
Hold on to Your Hats
Panama Hattie
1941 Let's Face It!
1943 My Dear Public
1946 Nellie Bly
1947 Louisiana Lady

"Mack the Knife." Music by Kurt Weill; lyric by Marc Blitzstein. Blitzstein's English-language version of the original Bert Brecht German text was sung by Gerald Price in the off-Bway production of *The Threepenny Opera* (1954), and also by Ewen MacColl in London (1956). Originally heard in *Die Dreigroschenoper* (Berlin 1928), the song was composed the day before dress rehearsal because Weill felt something was needed to give the story a unifying theme. Overnight he and Brecht created a 64-bar piece in imitation of a ghoulish form of 17th-century ballad called a *Moritat* (literally, "murder deed"). The first English-language Bway version of the musical was written by Gifford Cochran and Jerrold Krimsky and presented on Bway in 1933. In that production, the song was called "The Legend of Mackie Messer" and was sung by George Heller.

"Mad About the Boy." Music & lyric by Noël Coward. As performed in the London revue *Words and Music* (1932), the song revealed the impression made by a male movie star on four admirers: Joyce Barbour as "The Lady," Steffi Duna as "The Street Walker," Norah Howard as "The School Girl," and Doris Hare as "The Servant." In *Set to Music* (NY 1939), it was sung by Penelope Dudley Ward, Gladys Henson, Laura Duncan, and Beatrice Lillie.

"Mad Dogs and Englishmen." Music & lyric by Noël Coward. Disdainful look at the British, who, in tropical climes, are foolhardy enough to go out in the noonday sun. Beatrice Lillie did the taking to task in *The Third Little Show* (NY 1931), and Romney Brent, as a missionary, has his turn in *Words and Music* (L 1932). Coward composed the entire song while motoring through Indo-China from Hanoi to Saigon.

"Magic Moment." Music by Arthur Schwartz; lyric by Howard Dietz. In which a girl who is ignored implores the man she loves to love her. Barbara Cook introduced it in *The Gay Life* (NY 1961).

"Magic to Do." Music & lyric by Stephen Schwartz. Introductory number in *Pippin*, setting the stage for Ben Vereen (NY 1972) and Northern J. Calloway (L 1973) to open the show's box of tricks.

Maid of the Mountains, The (1917). Music by Harold Fraser-Simson, James W. Tate; lyrics by Harry Graham, F. Clifford Harris, (Arthur) Valentine; book by Frederick Lonsdale.
SONGS: "Live for Today" (Simson-Graham), "My Life Is Love" (Tate-Harris, Valentine); "Love Will Find a Way" (Simson-Graham); "A Paradise for Two" (Tate-Harris, Valentine); "A Bachelor Gay" (Tate-Harris, Valentine).
LONDON: Feb. 10, 1917
DALY'S THEATRE; 1,352 p.
Presented by Robert Evett; directed by Oscar Asche; settings, Joseph Harker; costumes, Comelli; music director, Merlin Morgan.
CAST: José Collins (*Teresa*), Arthur Wontner (*Baldasarre*), Thorpe Bates (*Beppo*), Lauri de Frece (*Antonio*),

Mabel Sealby (*Vittoria*), Mark Lester (*Gen. Malona*).

NEW YORK: Sept. 11, 1918
CASINO THEATRE; 37 p.

Presented by William Elliott, F. Ray Comstock, Morris Gest; directed by J. A. E. Malone; choreographed by Bert French; settings, Unitt & Wicks; costumes, Dazian, Schneider-Anderson; music director, John McGhie.

CAST: Sidonie Espero (*Teresa*), William Courtenay (*Baldasarre*), Carl Gantvoort (*Beppo*), Bert Clark (*Antonio*), Miriam Doyle (*Vittoria*), William Danforth (*Gen. Malona*), John Steel (*Lt. Rugini*).

Next to *Chu Chin Chow*, *The Maid of the Mountains* was London's biggest hit of World War I. Librettist Lonsdale had written the original script some nine years before, and Fraser-Simson's score had been intended for a different story (possibly accounting for the additional songs by Tate, Harris, and Valentine). José Collins scored her greatest triumph in the show, which played to capacity during its entire run. It was, in fact, only because Miss Collins was so closely associated with the role of the Maid that the producer decided to close the production when the actress' doctor ordered her to take a rest (at the final performance she lost her voice completely). At one time there were 14 UK road companies touring in the musical.

The story opens in the mountain hideout of Baldassare and his brigands. Teresa, who loves the bandit chief, is arrested by Gen. Malona, the retiring governor of Santo, and her release has been promised on the condition that Baldassare give himself up. Baldassare, however, disguises himself as the new governor, and plans to take Teresa away with him. Things go awry, though, when the bandit becomes attracted to Malona's daughter, Angela, and Teresa, in a jealous rage, exposes her lover. Baldassare and his men are sentenced to Devil's Island, but the repentant Teresa helps them all escape. *The Maid of the Mountains* was revived in London in 1921 (with José Collins), 1930 (Anne Croft), 1942 (Sylvia Cecil), 1971 (Lynn Kennington).

In 1920, Miss Collins appeared in a London successor, *A Southern Maid*, which ran over 300 performances. It was also written by Fraser-Simson and Graham, produced by Robert Evett, and directed by Oscar Asche.

"Make a Miracle." Music & lyric by Frank Loesser. It's 1892 in *Where's Charley?* (NY 1948) and heroine Allyn McLerie, who's just read a book on what's to be expected, babbles on about such future scientific miracles as wireless telegraphy, electric lights, fountain pens, lie detectors, horseless carriages, exploding breakfast cereals, and stereopticons that move. As she sings, frustrated swain Ray Bolger keeps interrupting by pleading with the girl to make a current miracle and marry him. Pip Hinton and Norman Wisdom played the roles in the London production (1958).

"Make a Wish." Music & lyric by Hugh Martin. Spirited advice offered by Stephen Douglass and Nanette Fabray in *Make a Wish* (NY 1951).

"Make Believe." Music by Jerome Kern; lyric by Oscar Hammerstein II. Indirect expression of affection sung upon first meeting by Norma Terris and Howard Marsh in *Show Boat* (NY 1927), and by Edith Day and Howett Worster in London production (1928). According to lyricist

Hammerstein, "Jerome Kern played a melody for me and I got some words to fit the middle part. The words were 'Couldn't I? Couldn't you? Couldn't we?' At the moment, though, I had no idea what I and you and we couldn't do. It just seemed to sing. Later, of course, I wrote words up to that section and then away from it. But this is not the way to write a song." In "Till Good Luck Comes My Way," sung by the Ravenal character a bit later in *Show Boat*, the music to the lines "I let fate decide/ If I walk or ride" is the same as that of the lines in "Make Believe," "You do not offend/ We only pretend." This, of course, is to emphasize—despite his words—that Ravenal is falling in love with Magnolia.

"Make It Another Old-Fashioned, Please." Music & lyric by Cole Porter. Ethel Merman's tear-stained attempt at drowning her sorrow in *Panama Hattie* (NY 1940). Bebe Daniels was the imbiber in the London production (1943).

"Make Someone Happy." Music by Jule Styne; lyric by Betty Comden & Adolph Green. Altruistic prescription for romantic bliss offered by John Reardon and Nancy Dussault in *Do Re Mi* (NY 1960). In London version (1961), the singers were Steve Arlen and Jan Waters.

"Make the Man Love Me." Music by Arthur Schwartz; lyric by Dorothy Fields. Romantic determination expressed by Marcia Van Dyke in *A Tree Grows in Brooklyn* (NY 1951), with response by Johnny Johnston.

"Makin' Whoopee." Music by Walter Donaldson; lyric by Gus Kahn. Comic saga of marriage and near-divorce sung by Eddie Cantor in *Whoopee*

(NY 1928). Another extended piece about matrimony, but with a happier ending, was Cole Porter's "It's De-Lovely."

Mame (1966). Music & lyrics by Jerry Herman; book by Robert E. Lee & Jerome Lawrence, based on their play *Auntie Mame*, adapted from the novel by Patrick Dennis.

SONGS: "It's Today," "Open a New Window," "My Best Girl," "We Need a Little Christmas," "Mame," "Bosom Buddies," "If He Walked into My Life."

NEW YORK: May 24, 1966
WINTER GARDEN THEATRE; 1,508 p.

Presented by Robert Fryer, Lawrence Carr, & Sylvia & Joseph Harris; directed by Gene Saks; choreographed by Onna White; settings, William & Jean Eckart; costumes, Robert Mackintosh; lighting, Tharon Musser; music director, Donald Pippin; orchestrations, Philip J. Lang.

CAST: Angela Lansbury (*Mame Dennis Burnside*), Beatrice Arthur (*Vera Charles*), Jane Connell (*Agnes Gooch*), Willard Waterman (*Dwight Babcock*), Frankie Michaels (*Patrick Dennis*), Charles Braswell (*Beauregard Burnside*), Jerry Lanning (*Patrick Dennis*).

LONDON: Feb. 20, 1969
DRURY LANE THEATRE; 443 p.

Presented by Bernard Delfont & Harold Fielding; restaged by Lawrence Kasha; choreographed by Onna White; settings, William & Jean Eckart; costumes, Robert Mackintosh; lighting, Tharon Musser; music director, Ray Cook; orchestrations, Philip J. Lang.

CAST: Ginger Rogers (*Mame Dennis Burnside*), Margaret Courtenay (*Vera Charles*), Ann Beach (*Agnes Gooch*),

Guy Spaull (*Dwight Babcock*), Guy Warren (*Patrick Dennis*), Barry Kent (*Beauregard Burnside*), Tony Adams (*Patrick Dennis*).

Though *Mame* was based on the play *Auntie Mame*, its madcap heroine and Jerry Herman score made it something of a successor to *Hello, Dolly!* The story traces Mame's life—mostly in and around New York—from 1928 to 1946, and it relates how the unconventional, hedonistic lady raises a nephew, weds a courtly southerner who is killed on their honeymoon, and ends up making sure that the nephew marries the right girl. Patrick Dennis, who wrote the original book about his own aunt, is portrayed by two actors at different ages in his life (Dennis was also depicted in *Little Me*, NY 1962, again adapted from one of his books). *Mame*, which was originally announced under the title *My Best Girl*, was to have starred Mary Martin. Eventually, Angela Lansbury beat out over 40 other actresses for the title role. During Bway run, she was succeeded by Janis Paige (4-68), Jane Morgan (12-68), and Ann Miller (5-69). Beatrice Arthur was succeeded by Anne Francine (7-67) and Audrey Christie (4-68); Jane Connell by Helen Gallagher (4-68) and Marilyn Cooper (12-69). In Aug. 1967, Celeste Holm (*Mame*), Vicki Cummings (*Vera*), and Wesley Addy (*Babcock*) began a road tour that continued for 10 months. A second road company, with Miss Lansbury, Miss Francine, and Miss Connell, toured four months after opening in April 1968. A third company, headed by Susan Hayward, played Las Vegas for four months. A fourth company, which began its tour Jan. 1969, traveled for five months with Janet Blair (*Mame*) and Elaine Stritch (*Vera*).

FILM VERSION: Lucille Ball, Beatrice Arthur, Robert Preston (Warner 1974, Gene Saks dir.).

"Mame." Music & lyric by Jerry Herman. High-strutting cakewalk sung by Charles Braswell and company as they pledged devotion to Angela Lansbury in the first-act finale of *Mame* (NY 1966). Barry Kent and company sang it to Ginger Rogers in London production (1969). The number is in the same Jerry Herman spirit as "Hello, Dolly!" (*Hello, Dolly!*) and "When Mabel Comes in the Room" (*Mack & Mabel*).

Mamoulian, Rouben, director; b. Tiflis, Russia, Oct. 8, 1898. Mamoulian was responsible for directing two landmarks of the Bway musical stage: the Gershwins' *Porgy and Bess* and Rodgers and Hammerstein's *Oklahoma!* Other major works were *Carousel* and *Lost in the Stars*. He began his career as a Hollywood director in 1931 and has such musicals as *Love Me Tonight* and *High, Wide and Handsome* to his credit.

1935	Porgy and Bess
1943	Oklahoma!
1944	Sadie Thompson (also co-lib.)
1945	Carousel
1946	St. Louis Woman
1949	Lost in the Stars
1950	Arms and the Girl (also co-lib.)

Man of La Mancha (1965). Music by Mitch Leigh; lyrics by Joe Darion; book by Dale Wasserman, based on his television play *I, Don Quixote*, adapted from the novel by Miguel de Cervantes y Saavedra.

SONGS: "Man of La Mancha," "Little Bird, Little Bird," "It's All the Same," "Dulcinea," "I'm Only Thinking of Him," "I Really Like Him," "Golden Helmet of Mambrino," "To

Each His Dulcinea," "The Impossible Dream," "Aldonza."

NEW YORK: Nov. 22, 1965
ANTA WASHINGTON SQUARE THEATRE; 2,328 p.

Presented by Albert W. Selden & Hal James; directed by Albert Marre; choreographed by Jack Cole; settings & lighting, Howard Bay; costumes, Bay & Patten Campbell; music director, Neil Warner; orchestrations, Music Makers Inc.

CAST: Richard Kiley (*Don Quixote*), Joan Diener (*Aldonza*), Irving Jacobson (*Sancho Panza*), Ray Middleton (*Innkeeper*), Robert Rounseville (*Padre*), Jon Cypher (*Dr. Carrasco*), Eleanor Knapp (*Housekeeper*).

LONDON: April 24, 1968
PICCADILLY THEATRE: 253 p.

Presented by Donald Albery; directed by Albert Marre; dances reproduced by Edward Roll; settings & lighting, Howard Bay; costumes, Bay & Patten Campbell; music director, Denys Rawson; orchestrations, Music Makers Inc.

CAST: Keith Michell (*Don Quixote*), Joan Diener (*Aldonza*), Bernard Spear (*Sancho Panza*), David King (*Innkeeper*), Alan Crofoot (*Padre*), Peter Arne (*Dr. Carrasco*), Olive Gilbert (*Housekeeper*).

Man of La Mancha had a balmy old gaffer for its hero and was originally presented at a temporary theatre far from Bway. Yet its theme of man's spiritual need for illusion was presented so compellingly that it is the current fourth longest-running NY musical. Director Albert Marre was the one who first thought of turning a tv play about Cervantes and Don Quixote into a stage musical. Originally, W. H. Auden and Chester Kallman were to have collaborated on the score with composer Mitch Leigh (here writing his first musical) and the lead was slated for Michael Redgrave. The show was first tried out at the Goodspeed Opera House, East Haddam, Conn.; during its NY run it transferred to the Martin Beck Theatre early in 1968.

For his book, librettist Dale Wasserman combined two stories: one dealing with Cervantes and his imprisonment for debts during the Spanish Inquisition, the second the adventures of Don Quxiote that Cervantes tells his fellow prisoners. Most of the adventures deal with the Don's love for the servant wench Aldonza, whom he calls Dulcinea, and his battles to save her honor. At the end, as the old man lies dying, he manages to convey to the girl his belief in dreaming the impossible dream.

During run, Richard Kiley, who became closely identified with the leading role, was succeeded by José Ferrer (5-66), John Cullum (2-67), David Atkinson (7-67), Hal Holbrook (7-68), Bob Wright (9-68), Mexican actor Claudio Brook (9-69), English Keith Michell (12-69), Japanese Somegoro Ichikawa (3-70), Australian Charles West (5-70), Israeli Gideon Singer (9-70). Joan Diener was succeeded by Marion Marlowe (1-67), Maura K. Wedge (4-67), Bernice Massi (7-67), Gaylea Byrne (5-69). Beginning Sept. 1966, the touring company was on the road for three years, six months. The Don was played by José Ferrer, Richard Kiley (4-67), Keith Andes (9-67), Bob Wright (9-69); Aldonza by Maura K. Wedge, Joan Diener (4-67), Marion Marlowe (7-67), Carolyn Maye (11-67), Natalie Costa (3-68).

In June 1969, *Man of La Mancha* returned to the Piccadilly Theatre, London, with Richard Kiley and Ruth Silvestri. This engagement lasted 118 performances.

FILM VERSION: Peter O'Toole, Sophia Loren, James Coco (UA 1972, Arthur Hiller dir.).

Mandel, Frank, librettist, producer; b. San Francisco, Cal., May 31, 1884; d. Hollywood, Cal., April 20, 1958. Mandel was united with co-producer Laurence Schwab in the presentation of eight Bway musicals between 1925 and 1931, with successes in both Romberg-Hammerstein operetta (*The Desert Song, The New Moon*) and De Sylva–Brown–Henderson musical comedy (*Good News!, Follow Thru*). Mandel also wrote three librettos with Schwab, three with Otto Harbach (incl. two hits, *Mary* and *No, No, Nanette*), two with Oscar Hammerstein II, three with Harbach and Hammerstein.

Unless otherwise noted, Mr. Mandel was librettist or co-librettist of following; asterisk indicates musical presented with Mr. Schwab:

1912 Miss Princess
1920 Look Who's Here
      Tickle Me
      Mary
      Jimmie
1921 The O'Brien Girl
1922 Queen o' Hearts
1924 Sweet Little Devil
1925 Captain Jinks *
      No, No, Nanette
1926 The Desert Song *
1927 Good News! * (co-prod. only)
1928 The New Moon * (also co-dir.)
1929 Follow Thru * (co-prod. only)
1931 America's Sweetheart * (co-prod. only)
      Free for All * (co-prod. only)
      East Wind *
1935 May Wine

"Mandy." Music & lyric by Irving Berlin. Cakewalking marriage proposal sung by John Murphy in *Yip, Yip, Yaphank* (NY 1918), an all-soldier show, and by Van and Schenck as part of Act I finale, "The Follies Min-strels," in *Ziegfeld Follies* (NY 1919). In the number, Marilyn Miller played minstrel George Primrose and Ray Dooley was Mandy. The song was revived in *This Is the Army* (NY 1942, L 1943), in which it was sung by a minstrel chorus, with Richard Irving as Mandy and Fred Kelly as Her Boy Friend.

"Manhattan." Music by Richard Rodgers; lyric by Lorenz Hart. Sung in *The Garrick Gaieties* (NY 1925) by Sterling Holloway and June Cochrane as a tribute to romantic New York. Among locations and points of interest covered: the zoo, Delancey Street, the subway, Mott Street, Greenwich Village, Bowling Green, Brighton Beach, Jamaica Bay, Canarsie, Yonkers (beyond city limits but it rhymes with "true love conquers"), Child's Restaurant, Coney Island, Central Park, the play *Abie's Irish Rose*, Fifth Avenue, the Bronx Park Express, Flatbush, and Inspiration Point. The song, which was Rodgers and Hart's first hit, had been written in 1921 for an unproduced musical called *Winkle Town*.

"March of the Musketeers." Music by Rudolf Friml; lyric by Clifford Grey & P. G. Wodehouse. Self-praising march sung by Dennis King, Douglass Dumbrille, Detmar Poppen, and Joseph Macaulay in *The Three Musketeers* (NY 1928). In London version (1930), sung by King, Raymond Newell, Robert Woolard, and Jack Livesey.

"March of the Siamese Children." Music by Richard Rodgers. Stately march performed for entrance of royal children as their father the king introduces each one separately to the new teacher in *The King and I* (NY 1951, L 1953). As the children enter, one by one, they advance first to their father and prostrate themselves; then they greet their teacher by taking her two hands and pressing them to their foreheads. The aggressively martial section in the music accompanies the entrance of the crown prince.

"**March of the Toys.**" Music by Victor Herbert. Marched by toys in *Babes in Toyland* (NY 1903).

"**March with Me!**" Music by Ivor Novello; lyric by Douglas Furber. Though this spirited command ("March! March! April, May and June!") was introduced by Maisie Gay when she joined the cast of the London revue *A to Z* (1922), it won its fame through Beatrice Lillie's delivery in NY in *André Charlot's Revue of 1924*. According to Miss Lillie, the piece "is sung by a very dignified and slightly matronly Britannia, who runs into trouble with her spear, her shield, her helmet and her feet."

Margetson, Arthur, actor, singer; b. London, April 27, 1897; d. London, Aug. 13, 1951. Suave leading man whose biggest London hits were *Tell Me More* and *Music in the Air*. In NY, he introduced "Let's Do It" in *Paris*.

1918	Telling the Tale (*Capt. Laverdet*)
1919	Follies
	The Whirligig
1920	It's All Wrong
1921	The Little Girl in Red (*Hubert Faverolles*)
1922	His Girl (*Hon. Geoffrey Custance*)
	The Passing Show (NY)
1923	The Dancing Girl (NY) (*Bruce Chattfield*)
1925	Tell Me More (*Kenneth Dennison*)
	Betty in Mayfair (*Barnaby Haddon*)
1926	Kid Boots (*Tom Sterling*)
	Just a Kiss (*Kenneth Courtney*)
1927	The Blue Train (*Lord Anthony Stowe*)
1928	Paris (NY) (*Guy Pennel*)

1929	Hold Everything (*Jim Brooks,* repl.)
1930	Heads Up! (*Jack Mason*)
1932	Lovely Lady (*George Letts*)
1933	Music in the Air (*Bruno Mahler*)
1937	The Laughing Cavalier (*Laughing Cavalier*)
1939	Magyar Melody (*Count Ferenc*)
1946	Around the World (NY) (*Phileas Fogg*)
	Park Avenue (NY) (*Ogden Bennett*)

"**Maria.**" Music by Leonard Bernstein; lyric by Stephen Sondheim. Ardent revelation of love at first sight sung by Larry Kert in *West Side Story* (NY 1957). In London version (1958), sung by Don McKay.

"**Maria.**" Music by Richard Rodgers; lyric by Oscar Hammerstein II. The problems in taming the free spirit of Maria Rainer were musically discussed in *The Sound of Music* (NY 1959) by Mother Abbess Patricia Neway and nuns Muriel O'Malley, Elizabeth Howell and Karen Shepard. In London version (1961), the singers were Constance Shacklock, Olive Gilbert, Sylvia Beamish, and Lynn Kennington.

Marre, Albert (né Albert Moshinski), director; b. New York, Sept. 20, 1925. Marre, who staged his first Bway play in 1951, has directed dramas as well as such musicals as *Kismet* and *Man of La Mancha*. He is married to singer Joan Diener.

1953	Kismet
1955	Kismet (L)
1956	Shangri-la
1959	The Love Doctor (L)
1961	The Conquering Hero
	Milk and Honey
1965	Man of La Mancha
1968	Man of La Mancha (L)
1970	Cry for Us All
1975	Home Sweet Homer

"Married." Music by John Kander; lyric by Fred Ebb. Sentimental duet in *Cabaret* for Jack Gilford and Lotte Lenya in NY (1966) and for Peter Sallis and Lila Kedrova in London (1968).

Marsh, Howard (Warren), actor, singer; b. Bluffton, Ind.; d. Long Branch, NJ, Aug. 7, 1969. Marsh is best remembered as the romantic hero of *The Student Prince* (in which he sang "Golden Days," "Deep in My Heart, Dear," "Serendade") and *Show Boat* ("Make Believe," "Why Do I Love You?" "You Are Love").

   1917 The Grass Widow (*Count de Cluny*)
   1918 Maytime (*Rudolfo*, repl.)
   1920 Greenwich Village Follies
   1921 Blossom Time (*Baron Franz Schober*)
   1924 The Student Prince in Heidelberg (*Karl Franz*)
   1927 Cherry Blossoms (*Ned Hamilton*) Show Boat (*Gaylord Ravenal*)
   1930 The Well of Romance (*Poet*)

Martin, Ernest (né Ernest H. Markowitz), producer; b. Pittsburgh, Pa., Aug. 28, 1919. All of Martin's Bway musicals—incl. three with scores by Frank Loesser, two by Cole Porter—were presented in partnership with Cy Feuer.

   1948 Where's Charley?
   1950 Guys and Dolls
   1953 Can-Can
   1954 The Boy Friend
   1955 Silk Stockings
   1958 Whoop-Up
   1961 How to Succeed in Business Without Really Trying
   1962 Little Me
   1965 Skyscraper
   1966 Walking Happy
   1977 The Act

Martin, Hugh, composer, lyricist, singer; b. Birmingham, Ala., Aug. 11, 1914. Martin's most celebrated Bway score was *Best Foot Forward* ("Buckle Down, Winsocki," "Ev'ry Time," "Just a Little Joint with a Jukebox"), which he wrote with composer-lyricist Ralph Blane. He began his career as a vocal arranger, then, with Blane, organized the singing quartet called The Martins (1940–1942). The two men also wrote Hollywood film scores, incl. *Meet Me in St. Louis*. In addition to supplying his own lyrics, Martin has also worked with lyricist Timothy Gray.

Unless otherwise noted, Mr. Martin was either composer or composer-lyricist of following:

   1937 Hooray for What! (singer only)
   1939 The Streets of Paris (singer only)
   1940 Louisiana Purchase (singer only)
   1941 Best Foot Forward (Blane)
   1942 The Lady Comes Across (singer only)
   1948 Look, Ma, I'm Dancin'
   1951 Make a Wish
   1952 Love from Judy (L) (Gray)
   1964 High Spirits (Gray)

Martin, Mary (Virginia), actress, singer; b. Weatherford, Texas, Dec. 1, 1913. Miss Martin's vivacity, wholesome appeal, and clear soprano voice helped make her Bway's most dominant musical-comedy performer of the 50s. After a brief career as a nightclub singer, she made her Bway debut in *Leave It to Me!* singing "My Heart Belongs to Daddy." She became a star in *One Touch of Venus* (in which she introduced "That's Him" and "Speak Low"), then scored her greatest successes in *South Pacific* ("I'm Gonna Wash That Man Right Outa My Hair," "A Wonderful Guy") and *The Sound of Music* ("The Sound of Music," "Do-Re-Mi," "My Favorite Things"). Miss Martin also introduced "Mountain High, Valley Low" (*Lute Song*), "I've Gotta Crow" and "I'm Flying" (*Peter Pan*), and "My Cup Runneth Over" (*I Do! I Do!*). She was married to deceased producer Richard Halliday.

1938	Leave It to Me! (*Dolly Winslow*)
1943	One Touch of Venus (*Venus*)
1946	Lute Song (*Tchao-Ou-Niang*)
	Pacific 1860 (L) (*Elena Salvador*)
1947	Annie Get Your Gun (US tour)
	(*Annie Oakley*)
1949	South Pacific (*Nellie Forbush*)
1951	South Pacific (L) (*Nellie Forbush*)
1954	Peter Pan (*Peter Pan*)
1959	The Sound of Music (*Maria von Trapp*)
1963	Jennie (*Jennie Malone*)
1965	Hello, Dolly! (L) (*Dolly Levi*)
1966	I Do! I Do! (*Agnes*)

Martin, Millicent, actress, singer; b. Romford, Eng., June 8, 1934. Blonde singing actress who appeared in the London hit *Expresso Bongo* and scored personal successes in *The Crooked Mile* and *Our Man Crichton.* Miss Martin has had her own tv show and has sung in nightclubs.

1948	Lute Song (*Handmaiden*)
1954	The Boy Friend (NY) (*Nancy*)
1958	Expresso Bongo (*Maisie King*)
1959	The Crooked Mile (*Cora*)
1960	The Dancing Heiress (*Marion Laverne*)
1961	The Lord Chamberlain Regrets
1963	Round Leicester Square
1964	Our Man Crichton (*Tweenie*)
1973	The Card (*Ruth Earp*)

Marx Brothers, actors. Chico (né Leonard), b. New York, March 22, 1891; d. Hollywood, Cal., Oct. 11, 1961. Groucho (né Julius Henry), b. New York, Oct. 2, 1895. Harpo (né Adolph), b. New York, Nov. 23, 1893; d. Hollywood, Cal., Sept. 28, 1964. Zeppo (né Herbert), b. New York, Feb. 25, 1901. Zany, surrealistic clowns who began in vaudeville (1917–1924), and later became world-famous through their Hollywood films (*Monkey Business, Horse Feathers, A Night at the Opera,* etc.). In their act, Chico wore a cone-shaped hat, spoke with an Italian accent, played piano, and was thick-headed; Groucho, the acknowledged leader, was a wise-cracking con man who sported a painted-on mustache, a long cigar, and a leer, and walked in a crouch; the impish, mute Harpo wore a top hat and curly orange wig and played the harp; Zeppo was the bland juvenile and singer. Groucho was closely identified with the song "Hooray for Captain Spalding," from *Animal Crackers.* The brothers were nephews of actor Al Shean. In 1970 the Bway musical *Minnie's Boys* was based on their early lives. Bib: *The Marx Brothers* by Kyle Crichton (Doubleday, NY 1950); *Groucho and Me* by Groucho (Geis, NY 1959); *Harpo Speaks* by Harpo (Geis, NY 1961); *Groucho, Harpo, Chico and Sometimes Zeppo* by Joe Adamson (Macmillan, NY 1973); *The Marx Brothers Scrapbook* (Crown, NY 1973). (*Groucho d. Aug. 19, 1977.*)

1924	I'll Say She Is (*Poorman*, Chico; *Lawyer*, Groucho; *Beggarman*, Harpo; *Doctor*, Zeppo)
1925	The Cocoanuts (*Willie the Wop*, Chico; *Henry W. Schlemmer*, Groucho; *Silent Sam*, Harpo; *Jamison*, Zeppo)
1928	Animal Crackers (*Ravelli*, Chico; *Capt. Spalding*, Groucho; *The Professor*, Harpo; *Jamison*, Zeppo)

"Mary's a Grand Old Name." Music & lyric by George M. Cohan. Fay Templeton, as Mary Jane Jenkins, introduced this appreciation of her simple name in *Forty-Five Minutes from Broadway* (NY 1906). It was also sung by Jacqueline Alloway in *George M!* (NY 1968). Other "name" songs by Cohan were "Ring to the Name of Rose" (*The Rise of Rosie O'Reilly*) and "Billie" (*Billie*).

Maschwitz, Eric, lyricist, librettist; b. Birmingham, Eng., June 10, 1901; d.

London, Oct. 27, 1969. Maschwitz, who wrote three London musicals that ran over 500 performances (*Balalaika, Zip Goes a Million, Love from Judy*), is best known for the songs "These Foolish Things" (*Spread It Abroad*) and "A Nightingale Sang in Berkeley Square" (*New Faces*). His lyrics were mated to the music of George Posford, Bernard Grun, Jack Strachey, Manning Sherwin, George Melachrino, Hans May, plus Chopin and Dvorak. An executive of the BBC for many years, Maschwitz also wrote under the name Holt Marvell. His first wife was actress Hermione Gingold. Bib: *No Chip on My Shoulder* by Maschwitz (Jenkins, L 1957).

Unless otherwise noted, Mr. Maschwitz was librettist (or sketch writer) and lyricist of following:

1936   Balalaika (Posford, Grun) (also prod.)
1938   Paprika (Posford, Grun)
1939   Magyar Melody (Paprika) (Posford, Grun)
1940   New Faces (Strachey, Sherwin)
1942   Waltz Without End (Chopin, Grun)
1943   Flying Colours (misc.)
1946   Evangeline (lyr. only) (Posford)
1947   Starlight Roof (lyr. only) (Melachrino)
1948   Carissima (May)
1949   Belinda Fair (Strachey)
1951   Zip Goes a Million (Posford)
1952   Love from Judy (lib. only)
1955   Romance in Candlelight (lib. only)
1956   Summer Song (Dvorak, Grun)

"Matchmaker, Matchmaker." Music by Jerry Bock; lyric by Sheldon Harnick. Harmonized by Tevye's daughters—Joanna Merlin, Julia Migenes, and Tanya Everett—in anticipation of marriage in *Fiddler on the Roof* (NY 1964). In London version (1967), the girls were Rosemary

Nicols, Linda Gardner, and Caryl Little.

"Matelot." Music & lyric by Noël Coward. Haunting ballad about French sailor Jean Louis Domenic Pierre Bouchon, who sails the wide world over but always hears the voice of his true love. Graham Payn introduced it in *Sigh No More* (L 1945).

Matthews, Jessie, actress, dancer, singer; b. London, March 11, 1907. Wide-eyed, chipmunk-cheeked dancing actress whose airy grace delighted Londoners in such musicals as *One Dam Thing After Another* (in which she introduced "My Heart Stood Still"), *This Year of Grace!* ("A Room with a View"), *Wake Up and Dream!*, and *Ever Green* ("Dancing on the Ceiling"). Miss Matthews, who began her career as an understudy to Gertrude Lawrence, became Britain's most popular star of musical films (*Evergreen, It's Love Again*) in mid 30s. She appeared in six stage productions with Sonnie Hale, to whom she was once married. Bib: *Over My Shoulder* by Miss Matthews (Allen, L 1974); *Jessie Matthews* by Michael Thornton (Hart-Davis, L 1974).

1923   Music Box Revue
1924   André Charlot's Revue (NY) (chorus)
1925   Charlot's Revue (chorus)
1926   The Charlot Show
1927   Earl Carroll Vanities (NY)
        One Dam Thing After Another
1928   This Year of Grace!
1929   Wake Up and Dream!
        Wake Up and Dream! (NY)
1930   Ever Green (*Harriet Green*)
1931   Hold My Hand (*Paula Bond*)
1940   Come Out to Play
1942   Wild Rose (Sally) (*Sally Green*)
1948   Maid to Measure
1949   Sauce Tartare (repl.)

"Maxim's." Music by Franz Lehár; lyric by Adrian Ross. In *The Merry Widow* (L 1907, NY 1907), Prince Danilo describes all the delights of his favorite Parisian restaurant, where he enjoys the company of such dazzlers as Lolo, Dodo, Jou-Jou, Clo-Clo, Margot, and Frou-Frou. Joseph Coyne played the Prince in London, Donald Brian in NY. Originally titled *Die Lustige Witwe*, the operetta had a libretto by Victor Léon and Leo Stein when it was first shown in Vienna (1905).

May, Edna (née Edna May Pettie), actress, singer; b. Syracuse, NY, Sept. 2, 1878; d. Lausanne, Switzerland, Jan. 2, 1948. Classical beauty who, in *The Belle of New York*, became the first American star to conquer London. She continued to be a West End favorite in such attractions as *Three Little Maids, The School Girl*, and *The Belle of Mayfair*.

- 1896   Santa Maria (NY)
- 1897   The Belle of New York (NY) (*Violet Gray*)
- 1898   The Belle of New York (*Violet Gray*)
- 1900   An American Beauty (*Gabrielle Dalmonte*)
- 1901   The Girl from Up There (NY) (*Olga*)
         The Girl from Up There (*Olga*)
         Kitty Grey (*Baroness de Tregue*)
- 1902   Three Little Maids (*Edna Branscombe*)
- 1903   The School Girl (*Lillian Leigh*)
- 1904   The School Girl (NY) (*Lillian Leigh*)
- 1905   The Catch of the Season (NY) (*Angela Crystal*)
- 1906   The Belle of Mayfair (*Julia Caldicott*)
- 1907   Nelly Neil (*Nelly Neil*)

"Maybe." Music by George Gershwin; lyric by Ira Gershwin. Romantic duet for Gertrude Lawrence and Oscar Shaw in *Oh, Kay!* (NY 1926), and for Miss Lawrence and Harold French in London version (1927).

Maytime (1917). Music by Sigmund Romberg; lyrics & book by Rida Johnson Young, based on Viennese operetta *Wie einst im Mai.*

SONGS: "The Road to Paradise," "Jump Jim Crow," "Will You Remember?," "In Our Little Home Sweet Home," "Dancing Will Keep You Young" (lyric, Cyrus Wood), "Only One Girl for Me."

NEW YORK: Aug. 16, 1917
SHUBERT THEATRE; 492 p.

Presented by Messrs. Shubert; directed by Edward P. Temple; choreographed by Allan K. Foster; settings & costumes, Homer Conant; music director, Frank Tours.

CAST: Peggy Wood (*Ottilie Van Zandt*), Charles Purcell (*Richard Wayne*), William Norris (*Matthew Van Zandt*), Maude Odell (*Lizzie*), Ralph J. Herbert (*John Rutherford*), Gertrude Vanderbilt (*Ermintrude D'Albert*), Arthur Albro (*Rudolfo*).

Bway's biggest hit during World War I was a sentimental tale of New York's Washington Square, covering a 60-year period beginning in 1840. Rich Ottilie and poor Richard love each other but are forced to part when Ottilie's father makes her wed another. Eventually, their grandchildren meet, fall in love, and presumably find lasting happiness. *Maytime*, which was the only score Sigmund Romberg wrote with Rida Johnson Young, helped establish the composer as a major creator of romantic operetta. During Bway run, Peggy Wood was succeeded by Carolyn Thomson (6-18), Laura Arnold (8-18), Eileen

Von Biene (9-18); Charles Purcell by John Charles Thomas (6-18).

FILM VERSION: Jeanette MacDonald and Nelson Eddy (different story) (MGM 1937, Robert Z. Leonard dir.).

McCarthy, Joseph, lyricist; b. Somerville, Mass., Sept. 27, 1885; d. New York, Dec. 18, 1943. With composer Harry Tierney, McCarthy had three major Bway hits: *Irene* ("Irene," "Alice Blue Gown"), *Kid Boots,* and *Rio Rita* ("Rio Rita," "The Rangers' Song"). He also wrote "I'm Always Chasing Rainbows" (*Oh, Look!*) with Harry Carroll, and contributed songs for revues. He was the father of lyricist Joseph Allan McCarthy.

Unless otherwise noted, following were written with Mr. Tierney:
1918 Oh, Look! (Carroll)
1919 Irene
1921 The Broadway Whirl
1922 Up She Goes
     Glory
1923 Kid Boots
1927 Rio Rita
1928 Cross My Heart

McCauley, (John) Jack, actor, singer, dancer; b. New York, 1900. McCauley's best-remembered Bway appearance was in *High Button Shoes,* singing "Papa, Won't You Dance with Me?" and "I Still Get Jealous." He also introduced "Bye, Bye, Baby" in *Gentlemen Prefer Blondes.*
1923 Earl Carroll Vanities (chorus)
1925 No, No, Nanette (US tour) (*Tom Trainor*)
1927 Hit the Deck (*Capt. Clark*)
1929 The Little Show
1935 Life Begins at 8:40 (repl.)
     At Home Abroad (repl.)
1936 The Show Is On
1939 The Streets of Paris
1942 Count Me In (*Sergeant*)
1943 Ziegfeld Follies
1944 Sing Out, Sweet Land
1947 Three to Make Ready (US tour) (repl.)

High Button Shoes (*Henry Longstreet*)
1949 Gentlemen Prefer Blondes (*Gus Esmond*)

McCracken, Joan, actress, dancer, singer; b. Philadelphia, Pa., Dec. 31, 1922; d. New York, Nov. 1, 1961. Pert dancing actress who first won notice in *Oklahoma!,* and who had major roles in *Bloomer Girl* (singing "T'morra, T'morra") and *Me and Juliet* ("It's Me!"). Miss McCracken, who began her career with the American Ballet Co., was once married to director Bob Fosse.
1943 Oklahoma! (*Sylvie*)
1944 Bloomer Girl (*Daisy*)
1945 Billion Dollar Baby (*Maribelle Jones*)
1950 Dance Me a Song
1953 Me and Juliet (*Betty Loraine*)

McGuire, William Anthony, librettist, director; b. Chicago, Ill., July 9, 1885; d. Beverly Hills, Cal., Sept. 16, 1940. McGuire wrote sketches and librettos for nine Ziegfeld productions on Bway. He was also the author of the film *The Great Ziegfeld.*

Unless otherwise noted, Mr. McGuire was librettist-director of following:
1920 Frivolities of 1920 (sk. only)
1923 Kid Boots (lib. only)
1924 Ziegfeld Follies (sk. only)
1926 No Foolin' (sk. only)
     Betsy
1928 Rosalie
     The Three Musketeers
     Whoopee
1929 Show Girl
1930 Ripples
     Smiles

McHugh, (James Francis) Jimmy, composer; b. Boston, Mass., July 10, 1894; d. Beverly Hills, Cal., May 23, 1969. With lyricist Dorothy Fields, McHugh wrote the score for the longrunning Bway revue *Blackbirds of*

1928 ("I Can't Give You Anything but Love," "I Must Have That Man," "Diga Diga Doo"), and such hits as "Exactly Like You" and "On the Sunny Side of the Street" (both in the *International Revue*). Other stage successes included *The Streets of Paris* ("South American Way") and *As the Girls Go*. Among McHugh's lyricists: Al Dubin, Howard Dietz, Harold Adamson. The composer first wrote scores for Cotton Club revues, later for many Hollywood films.

1928	Blackbirds of 1928 (Fields)
	Hello, Daddy (Fields)
1930	International Revue (Fields)
1939	The Streets of Paris (Dubin)
1940	Keep Off the Grass (Dietz, Dubin)
1948	As the Girls Go (Adamson)

McLellan, C(harles) M. S., lyricist, librettist; b. Bath, Maine, 1865; d. London, Sept. 22, 1916. McLellan, who wrote under the name Hugh Morton between 1896 and 1904, collaborated with composer Gustave Kerker on eight scores incl. *The Belle of New York*, the first Bway musical to become a hit in London. His major NY success was *The Pink Lady* ("My Beautiful Lady"), written with Ivan Caryll. McLellan also wrote with composers Bernard Holt and Herman Finck.

Unless otherwise noted, Mr. McLellan was lyricist-librettist of following:

1896	In Gay New York (Kerker)
	The Lady Slavey (lyr. only) (Kerker)
	An American Beauty (Kerker)
1897	The Whirl of the Town (Kerker)
	The Belle of New York (Kerker)
1898	Yankee Doodle Dandy (Kerker)
	The Telephone Girl (Kerker)
1901	The Girl from Up There (Kerker)
1904	Glittering Gloria (Holt)
1907	Nelly Neil (L) (Caryll)
1911	Marriage à la Carte (Caryll)
	The Pink Lady (Caryll)
1912	Oh! Oh! Delphine (Caryll)
1913	The Little Café (Caryll)
1915	Around the Map (Finck)

Me and My Girl (1937). Music by Noel Gay; lyrics & book by L. Arthur Rose & Douglas Furber.

SONGS: "Me and My Girl," "A Bright Little Girl Like Me," "Once You Lose Your Heart," "The Lambeth Walk," "The Girl I Left Behind Me," "Don't Be Silly, Sally."

LONDON: Dec. 16, 1937
VICTORIA PALACE THEATRE; 1,646 p.

Presented & directed by Lupino Lane; choreographed by Fred Leslie; settings, Edward Delaney; costumes, Louis Brooks; music director, George Windeatt.

CAST: Lupino Lane (*Bill Snibson*), Teddie St. Denis (*Sally Smith*), Wallace Lupino (*Parchester*), George Graves (*Sir John Tremayne*), Doris Rogers (*Duchess*), Betty Frankiss (*Jacqueline Carston*).

London's longest-running musical of the 30s and its biggest wartime hit starred Lupino Lane as a Lambeth Cockney who turns out to be the long-lost 17th Baron and eighth Viscount of Hareford. Despite temptations of the grand life at Hareford Hall, Bill Snibson gives it all up to return to his Lambeth sweetheart, Sally Smith. Lane, who revived the musical in London in 1941 and 1945, previously played the role of Bill Snibson in *Twenty to One* (1935).

FILM VERSION: Lupino Lane, Sally Gray, Seymour Hicks (called *The Lambeth Walk*) (MGM 1939, Albert De Courville dir.).

Melville, Alan (né William Melville Caverhill), lyricist, librettist; b. Berwick-on-Tweed, Eng., April 9, 1910. Melville's biggest London hits were the revue *Sweetest and Lowest*, written with composer Charles Zwar, and

Gay's the Word ("Vitality"), with Ivor Novello. He contributed sketches and lyrics to other revues, compiled *The Déjà Revue* in 1974, and also collaborated with composer Kenneth Leslie-Smith. Bib: *Myself When Young* (1955), *Merely Melville* (1971), both by Melville.

1942 Sky High (Zwar)
1946 Sweetest and Lowest (Zwar)
1948 A la Carte (Zwar)
1951 Gay's the Word (lyr. only) (Novello)
1952 Bet Your Life (Leslie-Smith, Zwar)
1953 At the Lyric (Leslie-Smith, Zwar)
1959 Marigold (Zwar)
1963 All Square (Zwar)

"Memories of You." Music by Eubie Blake; lyric by Andy Razaf. Sung by Minto Cato in *Blackbirds*, all-black revue (NY 1930).

Mercer, (John H.) Johnny, lyricist, composer; b. Savannah, Ga., Nov. 18, 1909. Mercer's gift for idiomatic, regional lyrics was well suited to such Bway musicals as *St. Louis Woman* ("Come Rain or Come Shine"), *Texas, Li'l Darlin'*, and *Li'l Abner* ("Namely You," "Jubilation T. Cornpone"). He also contributed to revues (incl. *New Americana*) and has written for Hollywood films (incl. *Seven Brides for Seven Brothers*). Among composers with whom he has collaborated: Harold Arlen, Hoagy Carmichael, Robert Emmett Dolan, **Gene de Paul, André Previn, and himself.** *(D. Los Angeles, June 25, 1976).*

1940 Walk with Music (Carmichael)
1946 St. Louis Woman (Arlen)
1949 Texas, Li'l Darlin' (Dolan)
1951 Top Banana (also comp.)
1956 Li'l Abner (de Paul)
1959 Saratoga (Arlen)
1964 Foxy (Dolan)
1974 The Good Companions (L) (Previn)

"Merely Marvelous." Music by Albert Hague; lyric by Dorothy Fields. In *Redhead* (NY 1959), Gwen Verdon liltingly expressed how she felt after a kiss from Richard Kiley ("I look nearly beautiful/ I don't look like me").

Merman, Ethel (née Ethel Agnes Zimmermann), actress, singer; b. Astoria, NY, Jan. 16, 1909. A dynamic, clarion-throated singing actress, Ethel Merman was the epitome of the Bway musical-comedy star. Usually portraying a gutsy dame whose heart of gold is revealed through a voice of brass, she won instant fame singing "I Got Rhythm" in her first hit, *Girl Crazy.* From then on she scored in such attractions as *George White's Scandals* ("Life Is Just a Bowl of Cherries," "My Song"), *Take a Chance* ("Rise 'n Shine," "Eadie Was a Lady"), *Anything Goes* ("I Get a Kick Out of You," "You're the Top," "Blow, Gabriel, Blow"), *Red, Hot and Blue!* ("Ridin' High," "It's De-Lovely"), *DuBarry Was a Lady* ("Friendship," "Do I Love You?"), *Panama Hattie* ("Let's Be Buddies"), *Call Me Madam* ("You're Just in Love"), *Happy Hunting* ("Mutual Admiration Society"), *Gypsy* ("Some People," "Everything's Coming Up Roses," "Small World").

Miss Merman's longest-running musical was *Annie Get Your Gun,* in which she introduced "They Say It's Wonderful," "There's No Business Like Show Business," "I Got the Sun in the Morning," "You Can't Get a Man with a Gun," "Doin' What Comes Natur'lly." The singer appeared in five musicals with scores by Cole Porter, two by Irving Berlin. She has also made records and acted in Hollywood films. Bib: *Who Could Ask for Anything More?* by Miss Merman (Doubleday, NY 1955).

1930 Girl Crazy (*Kate Fothergill*)

1931 George White's Scandals
1932 Take a Chance (*Wanda Brill*)
1934 Anything Goes (*Reno Sweeney*)
1936 Red, Hot and Blue! (*Nails Duquesne*)
1939 Stars in Your Eyes (*Jeanette Adair*)
DuBarry Was a Lady (*May Daly*)
1940 Panama Hattie (*Hattie Maloney*)
1943 Something for the Boys (*Blossom Hart*)
1946 Annie Get Your Gun (*Annie Oakley*)
1950 Call Me Madam (*Sally Adams*)
1956 Happy Hunting (*Liz Livingstone*)
1959 Gypsy (*Rose*)
1966 Annie Get Your Gun (r) (*Annie Oakley*)
1970 Hello, Dolly! (*Dolly Levi*, repl.)

Merrick, David (né David Margulois), producer; b. St. Louis, Mo., Nov. 27, 1911. Merrick was Bway's most prolific sponsor of musicals during the 60s with a string of hits that included *Fanny, Jamaica, Gypsy, Irma la Douce, Do Re Mi, Carnival, Oliver!, Hello, Dolly!* (his longest running attraction), and *Promises, Promises.* Five of Merrick's shows were directed by Gower Champion and four had scores by Jule Styne. The producer has also presented many nonmusicals, incl. *Look Back in Anger, Becket.*

1954 Fanny
1957 Jamaica
1959 Destry Rides Again
Gypsy
Take Me Along
1960 Vintage '60
Irma la Douce
Do Re Mi
1961 Carnival
Subways Are for Sleeping
1962 I Can Get It for You Wholesale
Stop the World—I Want to Get Off
Oliver!
1963 110 in the Shade
1964 Hello, Dolly!
Foxy
Oh, What a Lovely War

1965 The Roar of the Greasepaint—The Smell of the Crowd
Pickwick
1966 I Do! I Do!
1967 How Now, Dow Jones
1968 The Happy Time
Promises, Promises
1972 Sugar
1974 Mack & Mabel
1975 Very Good Eddie

Merrill, Bob (né Henry Lavan), composer, lyricist; b. Atlantic City, NJ, May 17, 1921. Originally a writer of doggerel pop songs, Merrill has seen all but one of his Bway musicals run past 400 performances. His most admired achievements were as composer-lyricist of *Carnival* ("Love Makes the World Go Round," "Mira") and as lyricist of *Funny Girl* ("People," "Don't Rain on My Parade"), with music by Jule Styne.

1957 New Girl in Town
1959 Take Me Along
1961 Carnival
1964 Funny Girl (Styne)
1967 Henry, Sweet Henry
1972 Sugar (Styne)

"Merry Little Minuet." Music & lyric by Sheldon Harnick. Dainty rundown of violence throughout the world ("They're rioting in Africa . . .") and the happy prospect that it can be halted only by the atom bomb. Introduced by Orson Bean in *John Murray Anderson's Almanac* (NY 1953).

Merry Widow, The (1907). Music by Franz Lehar; lyrics by Adrian Ross; book by Basil Hood (uncredited), based on Viennese operetta *Die Lustige Witwe*, by Victor Leon & Leo Stein, adapted from Henri Meilhac's play *L'Attaché d'Ambassade.*

SONGS: "Maxim's," "Vilia," "Girls, Girls, Girls," "Love in My Heart," "Women," "A Dutiful Wife," "I Love You So" ("Merry Widow Waltz").

LONDON: June 8, 1907
DALY'S THEATRE; 778 p.

Presented by George Edwardes; directed by J. A. E. Malone; choreographed by Fred Farren; settings, Alfred Terraine, Joseph Harker; costumes, Lucile, Pascaud, Percy Anderson; music director Harold Vicars.

CAST: Lily Elsie (*Sonia Sadoya*), Joseph Coyne (*Prince Danilo*), W. H. Berry (*Nisch*), George Graves (*Baron Popoff*), Robert Evett (*Camille de Jolidon*), Elizabeth Furth (*Natalie Popoff*).

NEW YORK: Oct. 21, 1907
NEW AMSTERDAM THEATRE; 416 p.

Presented by Henry W. Savage; directed by George Marion; settings, Walter Burrage; costumes, Mme. Zimmerman, Percy Anderson, Landolff; music director, Louis Gottschalk.

CAST: Ethel Jackson (*Sonia Sadoya*), Donald Brian (*Prince Danilo*), R. E. Graham (*Baron Popoff*), William Weedon (*Camille de Jolidon*), Lois Ewell (*Natalie Popoff*), Fred Frear (*Nisch*).

LONDON: May 19, 1923
DALY'S THEATRE; 239 p.

Presented by George Graves; directed by Fred Blackman; choreographed by Alfred Majilton; settings, Alfred Terraine; costumes, Paquin, Miss Thornton; music director, Sheridan Gordon; new lyrics by Percy Greenbank.

CAST: Evelyn Laye (*Sonia Sadoya*), Carl Brisson (*Prince Danilo*), W. H. Rawlins (*Nisch*), George Graves (*Baron Popoff*), Derek Oldham (*Camille de Jolidon*), Nancie Lovat (*Natalie Popoff*), Ivy Tresmand (*Frou-Frou*).

LONDON: March 4, 1943
HIS MAJESTY'S THEATRE; 302 p.

Presented by Jack Hylton; directed by William Mollison & Cyril Ritchard.

CAST: Madge Elliott (*Sonia Sadoya*), Cyril Ritchard (*Prince Danilo*), George Graves (*Baron Popoff*), Leo Franklyn (*Nisch*), Nancy Evans (*Natalie Popoff*), Charles Dorning (*Camille de Jolidon*), Carol Raye (*Frou-Frou*), Christopher Hewett (*Khadja*).

NEW YORK: Aug. 4, 1943
MAJESTIC THEATRE; 322 p.

Presented by Yolanda Mero-Irion for the New Opera Co.; directed by Felix Brentano; choreographed by George Balanchine; settings, Howard Bay; costumes, Walter Florell; music director, Robert Stolz; orchestrations, Stolz; book revised by Sidney Sheldon & Ben Roberts; new lyrics by Robert Gilbert.

CAST: Jan Kiepura (*Prince Danilo*), Marta Eggerth (*Sonia Sadoya*), Melville Cooper (*Baron Popoff*), Ruth Matteson (*Natalie Popoff*), David Wayne (*Nisch*), Robert Field (Robert Rounseville) (*Camille de Jolidon*), Ralph Dumke (*Gen. Bardini*), Lubov Roudenko (featured dancer), Milada Mladova (featured dancer).

Among the most enduring of all operettas, *The Merry Widow* was first presented at the Theater an der Wien in 1905. In the English version (uncredited to Basil Hood to spare the feelings of the original librettist, whose work had been rejected), the Pontevedrian Embassy in Paris became the Marsovian, and the characters of Hanna Glawari, Baron Zita, Valencienne Zita, and Camille Rosillon became, respectively, Sonia Sadoya, Baron Popoff, Natalie Popoff, and Camille de Jolidon. In the story, Baron Popoff, the Marsovian ambassador to France, is anxious that Prince Danilo, a young attaché, marry wealthy widow Sonia Sadoya because the country's treasury is empty. Though he had once been in love with Sonia, Danilo is now wary of being considered a fortune-hunter and tries to resist the lady's charms. At a party in the widow's home in Paris, Sonia succeeds in arousing Danilo's jealousy. She gets him to propose marriage but only after she has teasingly led him to believe she is penniless. A secondary plot involves Popoff's flirtatious wife and a Frenchman named Camille.

In London, *The Merry Widow* was the biggest success for co-stars Lily Elsie and Joseph Coyne. Though he had agreed to conduct opening night, composer Lehar almost left because of his dissatisfaction with Coyne's singing ability. During run, Miss Elsie was succeeded by Clara Evelyn and Constance Drever, Coyne by Robert Michaelis. In NY production, Ethel Jackson and Donald Brian won renown equal to their London counterparts, though Miss Jackson remained in the part only five months. She was succeeded by Lois Ewell (3-08), Lina Abarbanell (who had played the role in Chicago) (4-08), Rosemary Glosz (6-08), Georgia Caine (8-08), Ruby Dale (9-08); Brian was succeeded by Charles Meakins (8-08). The success of both productions revived the appeal of European operetta and also had great influence on fashion, with the introduction of Merry Widow hats, gowns, and corsets. It also prompted a Joe Weber takeoff, *The Merry Widow Burlesque* (NY 1908), with Lulu Glaser (followed by Lois Ewell and Blanche Ring) and Charles J. Ross. In it, the Lehar melodies were combined with a new book and lyrics by George V. Hobart.

In addition to those listed, London saw revivals in 1924 with Carl Brisson and Nancie Lovat; 1932 with Brisson and Helen Gilliland; 1944 with Cyril Ritchard and Madge Elliott; 1958 (lyrics by Christopher Hassall) with June Bronhill and Thomas Round; 1969 with Lizbeth Webb and John Rhys Evans. Other major NY revivals were in 1909 with Frances Cameron and Donald Brian, and 1921 with Lydia Lipkowska and Reginald Pasch.

FILM VERSIONS: Mae Murray and John Gilbert (MGM 1925, Erich Von Stroheim dir.); Jeanette MacDonald and Maurice Chevalier (lyrics, Lorenz Hart) (MGM 1934, Ernst Lubitsch dir.); Lana Turner and Fernando Lamas (lyrics, Paul Francis Webster) (MGM 1952, Curtis Bernhardt dir.).

"Merry Widow Waltz, The." See "I Love You So."

Mexican Hayride (1944). Music & lyrics by Cole Porter; book by Herbert & Dorothy Fields.

SONGS: "Sing to Me, Guitar," "I Love You," "There Must Be Someone for Me," "Abracadabra," "Girls, Girls, Girls," "Count Your Blessings," "What a Crazy Way to Spend Sunday."

NEW YORK: Jan. 28, 1944
WINTER GARDEN THEATRE; 481 p.

Presented by Michael Todd; directed by Hassard Short & John Kennedy; choreographed by Paul Haakon; settings, George Jenkins; costumes, Mary Grant; music director, Harry Levant; orchestrations, Robert Russell Bennett.

CAST: Bobby Clark (*Joe Bascom*), June Havoc (*Montana*), George Givot (*Lombo Campos*), Wilbur Evans (*David Winthrop*), Luba Malina (*Dagmar Marshak*), Corinna Mura (*Lolita Cantine*), Paul Haakon (*Paul*), Edith Meiser (*Eadie Johnson*).

Though Cole Porter never liked the show, *Mexican Hayride* was one of Bway's most popular wartime musicals, thanks largely to the raucous clowning of Bobby Clark. As Joe Bascom, alias Humphrey Fish, Clark played a numbers racketeer who flees to Mexico, where he assumes various disguises. When female bullfighter Montana, after dispatching a bull, throws its ear to Joe instead of to the intended recipient, Joe finds, much to his embarrassment, that he is hailed as Mexico's honored guest of the week. This was the last of three musicals (the others: *Let's Face It!* and *Something for the Boys*) that had a Porter score and a libretto by both Herbert and Dorothy Fields.

FILM VERSION: Abbott and Costello (new songs) (Univ. 1948, Charles Barton dir.).

Meyer, Joseph, composer; b. Modesto, Cal., March 12, 1894. On Bway, Meyer's song hits included "California, Here I Come" (*Bombo*), "If You Knew Susie" (*Big Boy*), "A Cup of Coffee, a Sandwich and You" (*Charlot Revue 1926*), and "Crazy Rhythm" (*Here's Howe*). In London, with co-composer Philip Charig, he wrote the score for *That's a Good Girl* ("Fancy Our Meeting"). He also worked with composers James F. Hanley and Roger Wolfe Kahn, and collaborated with lyricists B. G. DeSylva, Leo Robin, Irving Caesar, Douglas Furber, Ira Gershwin, Edward Eliscu.

1925   Big Boy (DeSylva-Hanley)
1927   Just Fancy (Charig-Robin)
1928   Here's Howe (Kahn-Caesar)
       That's a Good Girl (L) (Charig-Furber, Gershwin)
1929   Lady Fingers (Eliscu)

Michell, Keith (Joseph), actor, singer; b. Adelaide, Australia, Dec. 1, 1928. Classically trained leading man who made his biggest musical-comedy hit in London in *Irma la Douce* (in which he sang "Our Language of Love") and *Robert and Elizabeth*. Michell has also appeared in Shakespearean plays.

1951   And So to Bed (*Charles II*)
1958   Irma la Douce (*Nestor*)
1960   Irma la Douce (NY) (*Nestor*)

1964   Robert and Elizabeth (*Robert Browning*)
1968   Man of La Mancha (*Don Quixote*)
1969   Man of La Mancha (NY) (*Don Quixote*, repl.)

Middleton, (Raymond) Ray, actor, singer; b. Chicago, Ill, Feb. 8, 1907. A robust, deep-voiced baritone, Middleton had his most impressive Bway role in *Annie Get Your Gun*, in which he sang "The Girl That I Marry," "There's No Business Like Show Business," "My Defenses Are Down," and "They Say It's Wonderful." He also introduced "Here I'll Stay" in *Love Life*.

1933   Roberta (*John Kent*)
1938   Knickerbocker Holiday (*Washington Irving*)
1939   George White's Scandals
1946   Annie Get Your Gun (*Frank Butler*)
1948   Love Life (*Samuel Cooper*)
1950   South Pacific (*Emile de Becque*, repl.)
1965   Man of La Mancha (*Innkeeper*)

"Milk and Honey." Music & lyric by Jerry Herman. Anthem to the good life in Israel introduced by Tommy Rall in *Milk and Honey* (NY 1961) with deprecating asides by Juki Arkin.

Millar, Gertie, actress, singer; b. Bradford, Eng., Feb. 21, 1879; d. Chiddingford, Eng., April 25, 1952. Miss Millar was the ideal George Edwardes heroine—cameo-faced, dainty, and flirtatious. Among her biggest London successes: *The Toreador, The Orchid, The Spring Chicken, Our Miss Gibbs* (singing "Moonstruck"), *The Quaker Girl.* All these plus six others had scores composed by Miss Millar's first husband, Lionel Monckton.

1901   The Toreador (*Cora Bellamy*)
1903   The Orchid (*Lady Violet Anstruther*)
1905   The Spring Chicken (*Rosalie*)

1906	The New Aladdin (Lally)
1907	The Girls of Gottenberg (Mitzi)
1908	A Waltz Dream (Franzi Steingruber)
	The Girls of Gottenberg (NY) (Mitzi)
1909	Our Miss Gibbs (Mary Gibbs)
1910	The Quaker Girl (Prudence Pym)
1912	Gipsy Love (Lady Babby)
	The Dancing Mistress (Nancy Joyce)
1913	The Marriage Market (Kitty Kent)
1914	A Country Girl (r) (Nan)
1915	Bric-a-brac
1916	Houp-La! (Tillie Runstead)
1917	Airs and Graces
1918	Flora (Flora Brapwick)

Miller, Marilyn (née Mary Ellen Reynolds), actress, dancer, singer; b. Evansville, Ind., Sept. 1, 1898; d. New York, April 7, 1936. No other Bway musical-comedy actress of the 20s was more adored than this sprite-like, tiny blonde dancing star. After appearing in revues for both the Shubert brothers and Ziegfeld, she won acclaim in *Sally* (in which she introduced "Look for the Silver Lining" and "Wild Rose"), *Sunny* ("Who?"), *Rosalie,* and *As Thousands Cheer* ("Easter Parade," "Not for All the Rice in China"). Miss Miller began her career in vaudeville with her mother and stepfather, then toured the world for 10 years in act known as the Five Columbians.

1914	The Passing Show
1915	The Passing Show
1916	The Show of Wonders
1917	The Passing Show
1918	Fancy Free (Betty Pestlethwaite)
	Ziegfeld Follies
1919	Ziegfeld Follies
1920	Sally (Sally Green)
1925	Sunny (Sunny Peters)
1928	Rosalie (Princess Rosalie)
1930	Smiles (Smiles)
1933	As Thousands Cheer

Mills, Florence, singer, dancer; b. Washington, DC, Jan. 25, 1895; d. New York, Nov. 1, 1927. Flashing-eyed, tiny Negro entertainer famed in both NY and London for her plaintive voice and quicksilver dancing. Miss Mills introduced "I'm a Little Black-bird Looking for a Bluebird" and "Mandy, Make Up Your Mind" in *Dixie to Broadway.*

1921	Shuffle Along (Ruth Little, repl.)
1922	Plantation Revue
1923	Greenwich Village Follies (added)
	Dover Street to Dixie (Plantation Revue) (L)
1924	Dixie to Broadway
1926	Blackbirds (L)

Mills, John, actor, singer, dancer; b. Suffolk, Eng., Feb. 22, 1908. Primarily known as a dramatic actor on both stage and screen, Mills introduced "I'm on a See-Saw" in the London musical *Jill Darling.*

1929	The Five o'Clock Girl (chorus)
1931	Cochran's 1931 Revue
1932	Words and Music
1933	Give Me a Ring (Cliff Read)
1934	Jill Darling (Bobby Jones)
1937	Floodlight
1938	Pelissier's Follies
1974	The Good Companions (Jess Oakroyd)

"Mine." Music by George Gershwin; lyric by Ira Gershwin. Sung by William Gaxton and Lois Moran in *Let 'Em Eat Cake* (NY 1932). The song, introduced at a political rally, is punctuated by a countermelody in which the chorus comments on the blissful state of the principals. In 1952 it was added to the score of the revival of *Of Thee I Sing* and sung by Jack Carson and Betty Oakes.

Minnelli, Liza (May), actress, singer; b. Los Angeles, Cal., March 12, 1946. Miss Minnelli, a nerve-tingling song stylist and actress, introduced "A Quiet Thing" in *Flora, the Red Menace.* The daughter of Judy Garland

and Vincente Minnelli, she won renown in the film *Cabaret*.

1963 Best Foot Forward (r) (*Ethel Hofflinger*)
1965 Flora, the Red Menace (*Flora*)
1975 Chicago (*Roxie Hart*, temp. repl.)

Minnelli, Vincente, director; b. Chicago, Ill, Feb. 28, 1909. Minnelli began his Bway career as a designer for the 1931 *Earl Carroll Vanities* and he continued in this capacity for all the shows he directed. In Hollywood, his credits include *Meet Me in St. Louis, An American in Paris,* and *Gigi*. He was married for a time to Judy Garland and is the father of Liza Minnelli. Bib: *I Remember It Well* by Minnelli (Doubleday, NY 1974).

1935 At Home Abroad
1936 The Show Is On
1937 Hooray for What!
1939 Very Warm for May

"Mira." Music and lyric by Bob Merrill. In *Carnival* (NY 1961), a young waif, having traveled on two buses and a train to find work, longingly recalls a hometown so tiny everybody knew her name. Anna Maria Alberghetti introduced the wistful ballad; in the show's London version (1963), it was sung by Sally Logan.

"Miracle of Miracles." Music by Jerry Bock; lyric by Sheldon Harnick. Blast of emotion in *Fiddler on the Roof* (NY 1964), in which the miracles of manliness and love are likened to such biblical miracles as Daniel in the lion's den, the walls of Jericho falling down, the parting of the Red Sea, and David's slaying of Goliath. Introduced by Austin Pendleton; also sung by Jonathan Lynn in London version (1967).

"Miss Otis Regrets." Music & lyric by Cole Porter. In the London revue *Hi-Diddle-Diddle* (1934), Douglas Byng, as a properly starched butler, conveyed over the telephone the mock-solemn reason why Miss Otis was unable to keep a luncheon appointment. Seems that the lady, having shot the lover who had led her astray the previous evening, had just been dragged from the jail and lynched.

Mitchell, Julian, director, choreographer; b. 1854; d. Long Branch, NJ, June 24, 1926. Bway's most prolific director of musicals, Mitchell began his career as a dancer at Niblo's Garden. In 1884 he became director of Charles Hoyt productions (incl. *A Trip to Chinatown*); later directed and/or choreographed Weber and Fields shows, *The Wizard of Oz, Babes in Toyland, The Pink Lady, Little Nellie Kelly,* and nine *Ziegfeld Follies*. Mitchell was married to dancer Bessie Clayton.

1886 The Maid and the Moonshiner
1891 A Trip to Chinatown
1896 A Black Sheep
1897 At Gay Coney Island
       The Glad Hand
       The Idol's Eye
       Pousse-Café
1898 The Con-Curers
       Hurly Burly
       The Fortune Teller
       Cyranose de Bric-a-Brac
1899 Catherine
       The Three Dragoons
       Helter Skelter
       An Arabian Girl
       Whirl-i-Gig
       The Singing Girl
1900 The Princess Chic
       Fiddle-Dee-Dee
1901 The Girl from Up There
       Hoity Toity
1902 Twirly Whirly
1903 The Wizard of Oz
       Babes in Toyland (also co-prod.)
1904 It Happened in Nordland (also co-prod.)

1905 Wonderland (also prod.)
1906 About Town
     The Parisian Model
1907 The White Hen
     The Tattooed Man
     Follies of 1907
     The Girl Behind the Counter
     Hip! Hip! Hooray!
1908 The Merry Widow Burlesque
     The Soul Kiss
     Follies of 1908
     Miss Innocence
1909 Follies of 1909
     The Silver Star
1910 Follies of 1910
     The Bachelor Belles
1911 The Pink Lady
     Ziegfeld Follies
1912 A Winsome Widow
     The Count of Luxembourg (chor. only)
     Ziegfeld Follies
     Eva (chor. only)
1913 Ziegfeld Follies
1914 Queen of the Movies (chor. only)
     Papa's Darling
1915 Fads and Fancies (chor. only)
     Ziegfeld Follies
     Around the Map (chor. only)
1916 Miss Springtime (chor. only)
1917 Hitchy-Koo
1918 The Rainbow Girl
     The Kiss Burglar
     The Girl Behind the Gun (chor. only)
1919 The Velvet Lady
     The Royal Vagabond
     The Midnight Whirl
1920 As You Were (chor. only)
     Mary
1921 The O'Brien Girl
     The Perfect Fool
     The Blue Kitten
1922 Daffy Dill
     Molly Darling
     The Yankee Princess
     Little Nellie Kelly
     Our Nell (chor. only)
1923 The Rise of Rosie O'Reilly
1924 Ziegfeld Follies
     The Chocolate Dandies
     The Grab Bag
1925 Sunny (chor. only)

Mlle. Modiste (1905). Music by Victor Herbert; lyrics & book by Henry Blossom.

SONGS: "Kiss Me Again," "The Time, the Place and the Girl," "When the Cat's Away," "The Nightingale and the Star," "I Want What I Want When I Want It," "The Mascot of the Troop."

NEW YORK: Dec. 25, 1905
KNICKERBOCKER THEATRE; 202 p.

Presented by Charles B. Dillingham; directed by Fred G. Latham; settings, Homer Emens; music director, John Lund; orchestrations, Victor Herbert.

CAST: Fritzi Scheff (*Fifi*), Walter Percival (*Capt. Etienne de Bouvray*), William Pruette (*Henri de Bouvray*), Claude Gillingwater (*Hiram Bent*), Josephine Bartlett (*Mme. Cécile*).

Although *Babette*, Victor Herbert's first operetta for Fritzi Scheff, had been a failure, his second, *Mlle. Modiste*, gave the prima donna her most endearing role. Set in Paris, the story is all about stagestruck Fifi, who works in Mme. Cécile's hat shop on the Rue de la Paix. With the help of rich American Hiram Bent, she becomes the toast of Paris, which also helps break down the opposition of the aristocratic uncle of her beloved Capt. Etienne. Mlle. Scheff returned to NY in the operetta in 1906 (three weeks), twice in 1907 (four weeks and three weeks), and in 1929 (six weeks).

"Moanin' in the Mornin'." Music by Harold Arlen; lyric by E. Y. Harburg. Romantic disillusionment revealed by Vivian Vance in *Hooray for What!* (NY 1937).

"Moanin' Low." Music by Ralph Rainger; lyric by Howard Dietz. Moaned by Libby Holman (in tan face) in *The*

Little Show (NY 1929). The scene in which the torch ballad was introduced was a squalid Harlem tenement flat, dominated by an iron-frame bed. After rousing her lover (Clifton Webb) from a drunken stupor, the girl brings him to his feet and they perform a dance of smoldering passion. As the climax to the scene, and to prove the song's line about the man being "mean as can be," the drug-crazed sweetback chokes his devoted paramour.

"Momma, Look Sharp." Music & lyric by Sherman Edwards. The cry of a dying soldier in the American Revolution recalled by Scott Jarvis, with William Duell and B. J. Slater in *1776* (NY 1969). In London production (1970), it was sung by David Firth, with Ritchie Stewart and Terry Mitchell.

Monckton, Lionel, composer; b. London, Dec. 18, 1861; d. London, Feb. 15, 1924. Monckton was one of producer George Edwardes' most successful composers, with three of his London musicals running over 700 performances (*A Country Girl, The Arcadians, The Boy*) and seven over 400 (*A Runaway Girl, The Messenger Boy, The Toreador, The Orchid, The Spring Chicken, Our Miss Gibbs, The Quaker Girl*). He also wrote additional music for *The Shop Girl, The Geisha, The Circus Girl,* and *San Toy.* Most of his songs were written with lyricists Adrian Ross and Percy Greenbank, Basil Hood, Arthur Wimperis, Claude Aveling, Frank Dix, George Arthurs. Monckton was the first husband of Gertie Millar, who appeared in 11 of his musicals.

1898   A Runaway Girl (Hopwood, H. Greenbank)
1900   The Messenger Boy (Ross, P. Greenbank)
1901   The Toreador (Ross, P. Greenbank)
1902   A Country Girl (Ross, P. Greenbank)
1903   The Orchid (Ross, P. Greenbank)
1904   The Cingalee (Ross, P. Greenbank)
1905   The Spring Chicken (Ross, P. Greenbank)
1906   The New Aladdin (Ross, P. Greenbank)
1907   The Girls of Gottenberg (Ross, Hood)
1909   Our Miss Gibbs (Ross, P. Greenbank)
        The Arcadians (Wimperis)
1910   The Quaker Girl (Ross, P. Greenbank)
1911   The Mousmé (Wimperis, P. Greenbank)
1912   The Dancing Mistress (Ross, P. Greenbank)
1914   The Belle of Bond Street (Ross, Aveling)
1915   Bric-a-brac (Wimperis, Hood)
1916   We're All in It (Dix, Arthurs)
1917   Airs and Graces (Ross)
        The Boy (Ross, P. Greenbank)

"Monotonous." Music by Arthur Siegel; lyric by June Carroll & Ronny Graham. In *New Faces of 1952* (NY 1952), femme fatale Eartha Kitt slinked around the stage and wailed about the boredom of a life of luxury, adventure, and the adoration of such gentlemen as Jacques Fath, Johnnie Ray, Harry Truman, T. S. Eliot, King Farouk, and Eisenhower.

Montgomery, David (Craig), actor; b. St. Joseph, Mo., April 21, 1870; d. Chicago, Ill., April 20, 1917. Montgomery teamed with Fred Stone in 1894 and played variety theatres throughout US and England. On Bway, they scored great successes in *The Wizard of Oz* and *The Red Mill* (in which they introduced "The Streets of New York").

1901   The Girl from Up There (*Solomon Scarlet*)
        The Girl from Up There (L) (*Solomon Scarlet*)

1903 The Wizard of Oz (*Tin Woodman*)
1906 The Red Mill (*Kid Connor*)
1909 The Old Town (*Archibald Hawkins*)
1912 The Lady of the Slipper (*Punks*)
1914 Chin-Chin (*Chin Hop Lo*)

Moody, Ron (né Ronald Moodnick), actor, singer; b. London, Jan. 8, 1924. Moody's greatest success on the London musical stage was scored in *Oliver!* He has also appeared in many films.

1952 Intimacy at Eight
1953 More Intimacy at Eight
1954 Intimacy at Eight-Thirty
1956 For Amusement Only
1958 For Adults Only
1959 Candide (*Gov. of Buenos Aires*)
1960 Oliver! (*Fagin*)
1966 Joey, Joey (*Joey Grimaldi*) (also comp., lyr.)

"Moonbeams." Music by Victor Herbert; lyric by Henry Blossom. Augusta Greenleaf's plaintive plea to the moonbeams to find her love was sung as part of the first-act finale of *The Red Mill* (NY 1906). Gladys Simmonds sang the piece in the London production (1919).

"Moon-Faced, Starry-Eyed." Music by Kurt Weill; lyric by Langston Hughes. Sung and danced—all over a tenement front stoop—by Sheila Bond and Danny Daniels in *Street Scene* (NY 1947).

"Moonstruck." Music & lyric by Lionel Monckton. Gertie Millar, in blue Pierrot costume, accompanied by eight similarly attired ladies, introduced this "skipping, hopping" piece ("I'm such a silly when the moon comes out/ I hardly seem to know what I'm about") in a party scene in *Our Miss Gibbs* (L 1909). In NY version (1910), it was sung by Pauline Chase.

Moore, Grace, actress, singer; b. Del Rio, Tenn., Dec. 5, 1901; d. plane crash, Denmark, Jan. 26, 1947. Blonde soprano who was with Metropolitan Opera (1928–1931) and appeared in films, notably *One Night of Love.* On Bway, Miss Moore sang "What'll I Do?," "An Orange Grove in California," and "All Alone" in the *Music Box Revues* of 1923 and 1924, and "I Give My Heart" in *The DuBarry.* Bib: *You're Only Human Once* by Miss Moore (Doubleday, NY 1944).

1920 Hitchy-Koo
1922 Up in the Clouds (*Jean Jones*)
1923 Music Box Revue
1924 Music Box Revue
1932 The DuBarry (*Jeanne*)

Moore, Victor (Frederick), actor; b. Hammonton, NJ, Feb. 24, 1876; d. East Islip, NY, July 23, 1962. During the 30s and early 40s, this potato dumpling of a man with the bleating voice and befuddled manner was the most endearing clown on the Bway musical stage. Generally cast as an innocent adrift in a sea of intrigue, he played a US vice-president (*Of Thee I Sing*), a harmless gangster (*Anything Goes*), a US ambassador (*Leave It to Me!*), and a US senator (*Louisiana Purchase*). In these and three other musicals, his personality was strikingly contrasted with the brash manner of co-star William Gaxton. Moore scored a hit in his first musical, *Forty-Five Minutes from Broadway,* in which he introduced the title song, and he also acted in nonmusical plays (incl. a revival of *On Borrowed Time*). For many years he and his first wife, Emma Littlefield, toured in vaudeville in "Change Your Act, or Back to the Woods." He also appeared in Hollywood films (incl. *Swing Time*).

Asterisk indicates appearance with Mr. Gaxton:

1906 Forty-Five Minutes from Broadway (*Kid Burns*)

1907 The Talk of New York (*Kid Burns*)
1911 The Happiest Night of His Life (*Dick Brennan*)
1926 Oh, Kay! (*Shorty McGee*)
1927 Allez-Oop!
Funny Face (*Herbert*)
1928 Hold Everything (*Nosey Bartlett*)
1929 Heads Up! (*Skippy Dugan*)
1930 Princess Charming (*Irving Huff*)
1931 Of Thee I Sing * (*Alexander Throttlebottom*)
1933 Let 'Em Eat Cake * (*Alexander Throttlebottom*)
1934 Anything Goes * ("*Moon-Face*"*Mooney*)
1938 Leave It to Me! (*Alonzo P. Goodhue*)
1940 Louisiana Purchase * (*Sen. Oliver P. Loganberry*)
1945 Hollywood Pinafore * (*Joseph W. Porter*)
1946 Nellie Bly * (*Phineas T. Fogarty*)

"**More Than You Know.**" Music by Vincent Youmans; lyric by Edward Eliscu & William (Billy) Rose. Song of slavish devotion sung by Mayo Methot in *Great Day!* (NY 1929).

Morgan, Frank (né Francis Philip Wuppermann), actor; b. New York, June 1, 1890; d. Hollywood, Cal., Sept. 18, 1949. A debonair but bumbling character comedian, Morgan scored his biggest Bway hit in *The Band Wagon*. He made his stage debut in 1914 and appeared in over 70 Hollywood films.
1918 Rock-a-bye Baby (*Alfred Hardy*)
1920 Her Family Tree (misc.)
1928 Rosalie (*King Cyril*)
1931 The Band Wagon
1932 Hey Nonny Nonny!

Morgan, Helen, actress, singer; b. Danville, Ohio, 1900; d. Chicago, Ill., Oct. 8, 1941. Torch singer with tear-stained voice who scored successes in vaudeville, Bway musicals, night-clubs. She introduced "Bill" and "Can't Help Lovin' Dat Man" in *Show Boat*, "Why Was I Born?" and "Don't Ever Leave Me" in *Sweet Adeline*. Bib: *Helen Morgan* by Gilbert Maxwell (Hawthorn, NY 1974).
1924 Sally (US tour) (chorus)
1925 George White's Scandals
1926 Americana
1927 Show Boat (*Julie La Verne*)
1929 Sweet Adeline (*Addie Schmidt*)
1931 Ziegfeld Follies
1932 Show Boat (r) (*Julie La Verne*)
1936 George White's Scandals (US tour)

Morison, Patricia, actress, singer; b. New York, March 19, 1915. Regal brunette singing actress who made her name in the Bway musical theatre as co-star of *Kiss Me, Kate*, in which she introduced "So in Love" and "Wunderbar." Miss Morison first appeared on the NY stage in 1933 and acted in Hollywood films, 1938–1944.
1938 The Two Bouquets (*Laura Rivers*)
1944 Allah Be Praised! (*Marcia Moore*)
1948 Kiss Me, Kate (*Lilli Vanessi*)
1951 Kiss Me, Kate (L) (*Lilli Vanessi*)
1954 The King and I (*Anna Leonowens*, repl.)

Moross, Jerome, composer; b. Brooklyn, NY, Aug. 1, 1913. Moross' best-known work for the Bway stage was *The Golden Apple* ("Lazy Afternoon"), lyrics by John Latouche. He also wrote with Paul Peters and George Sklar, and is the composer of concert works and film scores.
1935 Parade (Peters, Sklar)
1948 Ballet Ballads (Latouche)
1954 The Golden Apple (Latouche)

Morrow, Doretta (née Doretta Marano), actress, singer; b. Brooklyn, NY, Jan. 27, 1928; d. London, Feb. 28, 1968. Miss Morrow was a dark-haired lyric soprano who introduced "My Darling, My Darling" in *Where's*

Charley?, "I Have Dreamed" and "We Kiss in a Shadow" in *The King and I*, "Baubles, Bangles and Beads" and "And This Is My Beloved" in *Kismet*.

1946 The Red Mill (r) (*Gretchen*, repl.)
1948 Where's Charley? (*Kitty Verdun*)
1951 The King and I (*Tuptim*)
1953 Kismet (*Marsinah*)
1955 Kismet (L) (*Marsinah*)
1957 Fanny (US tour) (*Fanny*)

Morse, Robert, actor, singer; b. Newton, Mass., May 18, 1931. Peck's-Bad-Boyish-looking actor who won stardom in *How to Succeed in Business Without Really Trying* (in which he sang "I Believe in You"). Morse made his Bway debut in 1955 in nonmusical play, *The Matchmaker*.

1958 Say, Darling (*Ted Snow*)
1959 Take Me Along (*Richard Miller*)
1961 How to Succeed in Business Without Really Trying (*J. Pierpont Finch*)
1972 Sugar (*Jerry*)
1976 So Long 174 St. (*David*)

Morton, Hugh. See **McLellan, C(harles) M. S.**

"Most Beautiful Girl in the World, The." Music by Richard Rodgers; lyric by Lorenz Hart. Waltzing hyperbolic duet sung in *Jumbo* (NY 1935) by Donald Novis and Gloria Grafton.

Most Happy Fella, The (1956). Music, lyrics & book by Frank Loesser, based on Sidney Howard's play *They Knew What They Wanted*.

SONGS: "Somebody, Somewhere," "The Most Happy Fella," "Standing on the Corner," "Joey, Joey, Joey," "Rosabella," "Abbondanza," "Sposalizio," "Happy to Make Your Acquaintance," "Big D," "Warm All Over," "My Heart Is So Full of You," "How Beautiful the Days."

NEW YORK: May 3, 1956
IMPERIAL THEATRE; 676 p.

Presented by Kermit Bloomgarden & Lynn Loesser; directed by Joseph Anthony; choreographed by Dania Krupska; settings & lighting, Jo Mielziner; costumes, Motley; music director, Herbert Greene; orchestrations, Don Walker.

CAST: Robert Weede (*Tony*), Jo Sullivan (*Rosabella*), Art Lund (*Joey*), Susan Johnson (*Cleo*), Shorty Long (*Herman*), Mona Paulee (*Marie*), Zina Bethune (*Tessie*).

LONDON: April 21, 1960
COLISEUM; 288 p.

Presented by H. M. Tennent Ltd., with Frank Productions; directed by Jerome Eskow; choreographed by Ralph Beaumont; settings & costumes, Tony Walton; lighting, Joe Davis; music director, Kenneth Alwyn; orchestrations, Don Walker.

CAST: Inia Wiata (*Tony*), Helena Scott (*Rosabella*), Art Lund (*Joey*), Libi Staiger (*Cleo*), Jack De Lon (*Herman*), Nina Verushka (*Marie*).

Sidney Howard's sentimental play about an aging wine-grower in California's Napa Valley and his love for a waitress struck Frank Loesser as the perfect vehicle for him to make his debut as librettist as well as composer-lyricist. Working on the project for four years, he created a near-operatic musical with more than 30 separate numbers, including arias, duets, trios, quartets, and choral passages, plus recitative. In the story, Tony, the wine-grower, proposes to Rosabella by mail, and she accepts not knowing what he looks like. Upset to find him old and fat, Rosabella allows herself to be seduced by Joe, the foreman, on their wedding night. Once it is discovered that Rosabella is to have Joe's child, Tony throws her out, but he eventually takes her back. The musical, which marked the Bway debut of opera star Robert Weede, toured for six months, beginning Dec. 1957.

Mostel, (Samuel Joel) Zero, actor; b. Brooklyn, NY, Feb. 28, 1915. Rotund, domineering actor who made notable Bway appearances as the slave in *A Funny Thing Happened on the Way to the Forum* (introducing "Comedy Tonight" and "Free") and the dairyman in *Fiddler on the Roof* ("Sunrise, Sunset," "If I Were a Rich Man"). Mostel, who began his career in nightclubs, also acted in nonmusicals, incl. *Rhinoceros. (D. Sept. 8, 1977.)*

1946 Beggar's Holiday (*Hamilton Peachum*)
1955 Once Over Lightly
1962 A Funny Thing Happened on the Way to the Forum (*Pseudolus*)
1964 Fiddler on the Roof (*Tevye*)
1976 Fiddler on the Roof (r) (*Tevye*)

"Mountain Greenery." Music by Richard Rodgers; lyric by Lorenz Hart. Sung by Sterling Holloway and Bobbie Perkins in the second *Garrick Gaieties* (NY 1926). The number was something of a follow-up to "Manhattan," also by Rodgers and Hart, in that it put the young city couple in an equally romantic country setting. It was also sung in *The Girl Friend* (L 1927) by Louise Browne and Roy Royston. In 1947 it was added to the score of the Rodgers and Hammerstein *Allegro*, in which it served as the musical accompaniment to a college dance.

"Mountain High, Valley Low." Music by Raymond Scott; lyric by Bernard Hanighen. Tender leave-taking expressed in "Chinese" musical *Lute Song* by Mary Martin and Yul Brynner in NY (1946) and by Dolly Haas and Brynner in London (1948).

"Mounties, The." Music by Rudolf Friml & Herbert Stothart; lyric by Otto Harbach & Oscar Hammerstein II. Stirring tribute to the Canadian Northwest Mounted Police sung by Arthur Deagon and Mounties in *Rose-Marie* (NY 1924), also by John Dunsmore and Mounties in London production (1925).

"Mr. Gallagher and Mr. Shean." Music by Al Shean; lyric by Ed Gallagher, Al Shean, Bryan Foy (uncredited). Against a painted backdrop of an Egyptian desert, a tall thin man (Gallagher), wearing a pith helmet, emerges from a small tent, and a short fat man (Shean), wearing a fez, emerges from another. As they greet each other they sing a conversational, question-and-answer ditty, usually ending with the exchange "Positively, Mr. Gallagher?"—"Absolutely, Mr. Shean!" Originally the melody (the only one Shean ever wrote), with a lyric by Bryan Foy, was called "The Two Horsemen of the Eucalyptus." Gallagher and Shean changed the title and some lines and introduced the number in 1920 at the Crotona Theatre, The Bronx. It caught on immediately and was introduced on Bway in the *Ziegfeld Follies of 1922*. New lyrics were continually being added and at one time it was the most parodied song in the nation.

"Mr. Wonderful." Music by Jerry Bock; lyric by Larry Holofcener & George Weiss. In the title song from the 1956 Bway musical, Olga James revealed to Sammy Davis Jr. the way she feels when he's near.

"Much More." Music by Harvey Schmidt; lyric by Tom Jones. "Please, God," pleads the innocent heroine of *The Fantasticks*, "Don't let me be normal!"—and thereupon rapturously itemizes all the daring things she'd like to do "just once before I'm old." Rita Gardner was the first to sing the piece in NY (1960); Stephanie Voss was her London counterpart (1961).

Murray, J. Harold, actor, singer; b. South Berwick, Me., Feb. 17, 1891; d. Killingsworth, Conn., Dec. 11, 1940. Sandy-haired, strong-featured baritone who introduced "Rio Rita" and "The Rangers' Song" in *Rio Rita,* "Let's Have Another Cup o' Coffee" and "Soft Lights and Sweet Music" in *Face the Music,* "Autumn in New York" in *Thumbs Up!*

    1920 The Passing Show
    1921 The Whirl of New York (*Harry Bronson*)
    1922 Make It Snappy
          The Springtime of Youth (*Richard Stokes*)
    1923 Caroline (*Capt. Robert Langdon*)
    1924 Vogues of 1924
          China Rose (*Prince Cha-Ming*)
    1925 Captain Jinks (*Capt. Robert Jinks*)
    1926 Castles in the Air (*John Brown*)
    1927 Rio Rita (*Capt. James Stewart*)
    1931 East Wind (*Capt. Paul Beauvais*)
    1932 Face the Music (*Pat Mason*)
    1934 Thumbs Up!

Music Box Revue (1921). Music & lyrics by Irving Berlin; sketches by Frances Nordstrom, William Collier, Thomas Gray, George V. Hobart.

SONGS: "Everybody Step," "Say It with Music," "The Schoolhouse Blues," "In a Cozy Kitchenette Apartment," "My Ben Ali Haggin Girl," "They Call It Dancing," "The Legend of the Pearls."

NEW YORK: Sept. 22, 1921
MUSIC BOX THEATRE; 440 p.

Presented by Sam H. Harris; directed by Hassard Short & William Collier; choreographed by Bert French, I. Tarasoff; settings, Clark Robinson; costumes, Ralph Mulligan, Cora MacGeachey, Alice O'Neill; music director, Frank Tours; orchestrations, Tours, Maurice De Packh, Stephen Jones, Harry Akst.

CAST: William Collier, Wilda Bennett, Paul Frawley, Sam Bernard, Ivy Sawyer, Joseph Santley, Florence Moore, Brox Sisters, Rose Rolando, Emma Haig, Hugh Cameron, Margaret Irving, Rene Riano, Chester Hale, Irving Berlin, Miriam Hopkins (chorus).

LONDON: May 15, 1923
PALACE THEATRE; 119 p.

Presented by Charles B. Cochran; directed by Hassard Short & Frank Collins; choreographed by Bert French, Chester Hale, Irving Carpenter; settings, Clark Robinson; costumes, Ralph Mulligan, Cora MacGeachey; music director, J. B. Hastings.

CAST: Ivy Sawyer, Joseph Santley, Fred Duprez, Solly Ward, Ethelind Terry, Brox Sisters, Maggie Dickinson, Sid Culver, Doris Patston, Gregory Stroud, Albertine Vitack, Chester Hale, Jessie Matthews.

One day during World War I, Irving Berlin suggested to producer Sam Harris that the Music Box would be a great name for a theatre built solely for musicals. Harris and Berlin eventually built the Music Box, which became the only theatre ever designed as a showplace for the songs of one composer. The first attraction, the *Music Box Revue,* was lavish and elegant and benefited from the imaginative stagecraft of Hassard Short and the comedy of William Collier and Sam Bernard. Just as "A Pretty Girl Is Like a Melody" had become the theme of the *Ziegfeld Follies,* so another Berlin song, "Say It with Music," was the theme of the *Music Box Revue.* In the show, the songs covered a variety of subjects from dancing to dining (the girls paraded as musical dinner courses in one scene). During run, Sam Bernard was succeeded by Solly Ward (2-22), Wilda Bennett by Ethelind Terry (6-22).

There were four annual editions in the series, with the first one also repeated in London. Though all were popular, each successive revue on Bway had a shorter run than the previous edition—440 in 1921, 330 in 1922, 273 in 1923, 184 in 1924. Hassard Short directed the first three; John Murray Anderson took over for the fourth (when Short replaced him at the *Greenwich Village Follies*). Among performers in various editions: Charlotte Greenwood, Grace La Rue, William Gaxton, Clark and McCullough, Frank Tinney, John Steel, Grace Moore, Robert Benchley (doing his "Treasurer's Report"), Fanny Brice, Oscar Shaw. Among songs: "Crinoline Days" (1922), "Lady of the Evening" (1922), "Pack Up Your Sins and Go to the Devil" (1922), "An Orange Grove in California" (1923), "What'll I Do?" (1923), "All Alone" (1924), "Tell Her in the Springtime" (1924).

Music in the Air (1932). Music by Jerome Kern; lyrics & book by Oscar Hammerstein II.

SONGS: "There's a Hill Beyond a Hill," "I've Told Ev'ry Little Star," "I Am So Eager," "When the Spring Is in the Air," "And Love Was Born," "One More Dance," "In Egern on the Tegern See," "I'm Alone," "The Song Is You," "We Belong Together."

NEW YORK: Nov. 8, 1932
ALVIN THEATRE; 342 p.

Presented by Peggy Fears; directed by Kern & Hammerstein; settings, Joseph Urban; costumes, Joseph Harkrider; music director, Victor Baravalle;

orchestrations, Robert Russell Bennett.

CAST: Reinhold Werrenrath (*Cornelius*), Natalie Hall (*Frieda Hatzfeld*), Tullio Carminati (*Bruno Mahler*), Katherine Carrington (*Sieglinde Lessing*), Al Shean (*Dr. Walther Lessing*), Walter Slezak (*Karl Reder*), Nicholas Joy (*Ernst Weber*), Ivy Scott (*Lili Kirschner*), Marjorie Main (*Anna*), Vivian Vance (chorus).

LONDON: May 19, 1933
HIS MAJESTY'S THEATRE; 275 p.

Presented by Charles B. Cochran; directed by Kern & Hammerstein; settings & costumes, G. E. Calthrop; music director, Hyam Greenbaum; orchestrations, Robert Russell Bennett.

CAST: Mary Ellis (*Frieda Hatzfeld*), Arthur Margetson (*Bruno Mahler*), Eve Lister (*Sieglinde Lessing*), Horace Hodges (*Dr. Walther Lessing*), Bruce Carfax (*Karl Reder*), Herbert Ross (*Ernst Weber*), Muriel George (*Lili Kirschner*), Lance Fairfax (*Cornelius*).

The Kern and Hammerstein musical was something of a successor to the previous year's Kern and Harbach *Cat and the Fiddle*. Again the locale was modern Europe, again the tale dealt with the preparation of a musical production, and again the score was created as a closely integrated part of the story. In this "Musical Adventure," innocent Sieglinde and Karl join their local walking club on a hike from Edendorf, Bavaria, to Munich. There they meet prima donna Frieda Hatzfeld and her lover, librettist Bruno Mahler, and soon Frieda is flirting with Karl and Bruno is flirting with Sieglinde. After a row, Frieda refuses to star in Bruno's next operetta, *Tingle Tangle*, and Sieglinde is given the chance to take over. The untrained girl, however, proves inadequate, Frieda returns to Bruno, and

Sieglinde and Karl return to their mountain village. In July 1933 Natalie Hall was succeeded by Desirée Tabor, Tullio Carminati by Donald Brian. After Bway run, the company toured three months.

In 1951 Oscar Hammerstein directed a Bway revival with a cast incl. Jane Pickens (*Frieda*), Dennis King (*Bruno*), Charles Winninger (*Dr. Lessing*), Conrad Nagel (*Weber*), Mitchell Gregg (*Karl*), Lillian Murphy (*Sieglinde*), and Muriel O'Malley (*Lili Kirschner*). The run lasted 56 performances. For this production, the locale was changed to Switzerland and the role of Cornelius (played by William Wilderman) was eliminated during tryout.

FILM VERSION: Gloria Swanson, John Boles, Al Shean (Fox 1934, Erich Pommer dir.).

Music Man, The (1957). Music, lyrics & book by Meredith Willson, from a story by Willson & Franklin Lacey.

SONGS: "Rock Island," "Trouble," "Goodnight, My Someone," "Seventy-Six Trombones," "Marian the Librarian," "My White Knight," "Wells Fargo Wagon," "Shipoopi," "Lida Rose," "Gary, Indiana," "Till There Was You."

NEW YORK: Dec. 19, 1957
MAJESTIC THEATRE; 1,375 p.

Presented by Kermit Bloomgarden, with Herbert Greene & Frank Productions; directed by Morton Da Costa; choreographed by Onna White; settings & lighting, Howard Bay; costumes, Raoul Pène du Bois; music director, Herbert Greene; orchestrations, Don Walker.

CAST: Robert Preston (*Harold Hill*), Barbara Cook (*Marian Paroo*), David Burns (*Mayor Shinn*), Pert Kelton (*Mrs. Paroo*), Iggie Wolfington (*Marcellus Washburn*), The Buffalo Bills (singing quartet), Helen Raymond (*Eulalie Shinn*), Eddie Hodges (*Winthrop Paroo*), Barbara Williams (chorus), Tom Panko (dancer).

LONDON: March 16, 1961
ADELPHI THEATRE; 395 p.

Presented by Harold Fielding, with Kermit Bloomgarden; restaged by Robert Merriman; dances reproduced by James Barron; settings, Howard Bay; costumes, Raoul Pène du Bois; lighting, Michael Northen; music director, Gareth Davies; orchestrations, Don Walker.

CAST: Van Johnson (*Harold Hill*), Patricia Lambert (*Marian Paroo*), C. Denier Warren (*Mayor Shinn*), Ruth Kettlewell (*Mrs. Paroo*), Bernard Spear (*Marcellus Washburn*), The Iowa Four (singing quartet), Nan Munro (*Eulalie Shinn*), Denis Waterman (*Winthrop Paroo*).

Fast-moving, George M. Cohan-type musical (its opening scene even takes place on the Fourth of July), *The Music Man* re-created the innocent world of middle America in 1912. Harold Hill, a traveling salesman of musical instruments, invades River City, Iowa, and fleeces the citizens into believing that he can teach their children how to play in a marching band. But the love of a good woman, Marian the Librarian, makes Harold repent, and the play ends with the children—miraculously—being able to play the instruments. The idea for the show was first suggested to Meredith Willson in 1949 by composer Frank Loesser, who enjoyed hearing Willson's stories of his Iowa boyhood. Originally, under the title *The Silver Triangle*, the musical was to have been presented by Cy Feuer and Ernest Martin with, hopefully, Danny Kaye in the lead (among others considered: Dan Dailey, Gene Kelly, Ray Bolger, Jason Robards, Art Carney,

Bert Parks). Willson wrote over 30 drafts and over 40 songs before Kermit Bloomgarden put the show into production with Robert Preston making his auspicious musical-comedy debut.

During Bway run, Preston was succeeded by Eddie Albert (1-60) and Bert Parks (6-60); David Burns by Paul Ford (6-59) and Mort Marshall (12-59); Barbara, Cook by Arlyne Frank (6-59) and Barbara Williams (6-60). Beginning Aug. 1958, *The Music Man* toured three years, seven months, with Forrest Tucker (*Harold*), Joan Weldon (*Marian*), Cliff Hall (*Shinn*), and Benny Baker (*Marcellus*). Bib: *But He Doesn't Know the Territory* by Willson (Putnam, NY 1957).

FILM VERSION: Robert Preston, Shirley Jones, Hermione Gingold (Warner 1962, Morton DaCosta dir.).

"Mutual Admiration Society." Music by Harold Karr; lyric by Matt Dubey. Bouncy mother-daughter duet for Ethel Merman and Virginia Gibson in *Happy Hunting* (NY 1956).

"My Beautiful Lady." Music by Ivan Caryll; lyric by C. M. S. McLellan. Waltzing serenade in *The Pink Lady* (NY 1911), sung by Pink Lady Hazel Dawn (accompanying herself on the violin) and Alice Dovey as they imagine what they'd sing if they could be the violinist at the Café de Paris. Earlier in the musical, Miss Dawn sang "The Kiss Waltz," which had the same music but a different lyric. Both Misses Dawn and Dovey repeated their roles in the London production (1912).

"My Cup Runneth Over." Music by Harvey Schmidt; lyric by Tom Jones. Tender admission of marital bliss sung in *I Do! I Do!* (NY 1966) by its entire cast, Mary Martin and Robert Preston. In London version (1968) the couple was played by Anne Rogers and Ian Carmichael. Though the song has become the most popular from the show, it was dropped from the score during rehearsals because Miss Martin and Preston had difficulty sustaining the long final note (on the word "love"). Once everyone agreed to shorten it, the number was reinstated for the Boston tryout.

"My Darling, My Darling." Music & lyric by Frank Loesser. Sung by Byron Palmer and Doretta Morrow in *Where's Charley?* (NY 1948), and by Terence Cooper and Pamela Gale in London version (1958). In the first scene of *Charley's Aunt*, the play from which *Where's Charley?* was adapted, Jack Chesney, a love-smitten Oxford student, attempts various salutations for a letter to his beloved. Though he rejects "My darling" as too strong, it seemed just right for composer-lyricist Loesser, who even repeated the phrase and made it the title of the musical's romantic duet.

"My Defenses Are Down." Music & lyric by Irving Berlin. In *Annie Get Your Gun* (NY 1946), Frank Butler (Ray Middleton) finds his resistance is broken and that he's falling for hillbilly sharpshooter Annie Oakley. Bill Johnson played Frank in the London production (1947).

My Fair Lady (1956). Music by Frederick Loewe; lyrics & book by Alan Jay Lerner, based on Bernard Shaw's play *Pygmalion*.

SONGS: "Wouldn't It Be Loverly?," "With a Little Bit of Luck," "I'm an Ordinary Man," "Just You Wait," "The Rain in Spain," "I Could Have Danced All Night," "Ascot Gavotte," "On the Street Where You Live," "Show Me," "Get Me to the Church on Time," "A Hymn to Him," "Without You," "I've Grown Accustomed to Her Face."

NEW YORK: March 15, 1956
MARK HELLINGER THEATRE; 2,717 p.

Presented by Herman Levin; directed by Moss Hart; choreographed by Hanya Holm; settings, Oliver Smith; costumes, Cecil Beaton; lighting, Feder; music director, Franz Allers; orchestrations, Robert Russell Bennett, Philip J. Lang.

CAST: Rex Harrison (*Henry Higgins*), Julie Andrews (*Eliza Doolittle*), Stanley Holloway (*Alfred P. Doolittle*), Robert Coote (*Col. Pickering*), Cathleen Nesbitt (*Mrs. Higgins*), Michael King (*Freddy Eynsford-Hill*), Christopher Hewett (*Zoltan Karpathy*).

LONDON: April 30, 1958
DRURY LANE THEATRE; 2,281 p.

Presented by H. M. Tennent Ltd.; directed by Moss Hart; choreographed by Hanya Holm; settings, Oliver Smith; costumes, Cecil Beaton; music director, Cyril Ornadel; orchestrations, Robert Russell Bennett, Philip J. Lang.

CAST: Rex Harrison (*Henry Higgins*), Julie Andrews (*Eliza Doolittle*), Stanley Holloway (*Alfred P. Doolittle*), Robert Coote (*Col. Pickering*), Zena Dare (*Mrs. Higgins*), Leonard Wier (*Freddy Eynsford-Hill*), Max Oldaker (*Zoltan Karpathy*).

One of the most highly esteemed musicals of all time was the brainchild of Hungarian film producer Gabriel Pascal, who approached Alan Jay Lerner to write the adaptation of *Pygmalion* in 1952 (after being turned down by Noël Coward, Cole Porter, E. Y. Harburg, Howard Dietz and Arthur Schwartz, and Rodgers and Hammerstein). Pascal died in 1954 at about the time Lerner and composer Frederick Loewe first became convinced that the adaptation could be done. Lerner then took the script to Herman Levin, who was to have produced *Li'l Abner*, a musical that the librettist had abandoned. At first considering Dolores Gray or Mary Martin for the role of Eliza, they turned to Julie Andrews, whose only previous major role had been in *The Boy Friend*. Rex Harrison had been the choice for Higgins from the start.

In writing the adaptation, originally announced as *My Lady Liza*, Lerner used most of Shaw's original dialogue, while expanding the action to include scenes in Tottenham Court Road, the Ascot Races, the street outside Higgins' home, and the Embassy Ball, in addition to those in Covent Garden, Higgins' study, and Mrs. Higgins' home, which were in *Pygmalion*. The main change was at the end—the scenes in which Higgins sings "I've Grown Accustomed to Her Face" and Eliza returns to Higgins' study. (Shaw, in an epilogue to the play, insisted that Eliza ends up married to her simpering suitor, Freddy Eynsford-Hill.)

During Bway run, Harrison was succeeded by Edward Mulhare (11-57) and Michael Allinson (2-60); Miss Andrews by Sally Ann Howes (2-58), Pamela Charles (2-59), and Margot Moser (2-61); Stanley Holloway by Ronald Radd (12-57) and Gordon Dilworth (12-61); Robert Coote by Reginald Denny (11-57) and Melville Cooper (7-59). The US tour began in March 1957, and continued for six years, nine months. The cast was headed by Brian Aherne (succeeded by Michael Evans, Ronald Drake, Louis Hayward) and Anne Rogers (by Diane Todd, Caroline Dixon, Gaylea Byrne). In London, Harrison was succeeded by Alec Clunes (3-59) and Charles Stapley (3-61); Miss Andrews by Anne Rogers (8-59), Tonia Lee (1961), and Jean Scott (1962); Holloway by James Hayter (10-59). The UK tour began Oct. 1963 and lasted six months.

For nine years, until overtaken by *Hello, Dolly!* in 1971, *My Fair Lady* held the record as Bway's longest-running musical. It is currently in third place. In London, it's the fourth longest-running, though it still holds the record at the Drury Lane.

Other plays by Bernard Shaw adapted as musicals: *Arms and the Man* (*The Chocolate Soldier*, NY 1909) and *Caesar and Cleopatra* (*Her First Roman*, NY 1968).

FILM VERSION: Rex Harrison, Audrey Hepburn, Stanley Holloway (Warner 1964, George Cukor dir.).

"My Favorite Things." Music by Richard Rodgers; lyric by Oscar Hammerstein II. Catalogue song of simple pleasures sung by Mary Martin and Patricia Neway in *The Sound of Music* (NY 1959) and in London production (1961) by Jean Bayless and Constance Shacklock.

"My Funny Valentine." Music by Richard Rodgers; lyric by Lorenz Hart. Song of affection despite—or because of—physical imperfections sung by Mitzi Green about Ray Heatherton (who played the part of "Val") in *Babes in Arms* (NY 1937). A similar theme was covered in the Gershwins' "Funny Face."

"My Heart Belongs to Daddy." Music & lyric by Cole Porter. Sung by Mary Martin in *Leave It to Me!* (NY 1938), accompanied by dancers Gene Kelly, Maurice Kelly, Roy Ross, Jack Seymour, Jack Stanton, and Walter Long Jr. Miss Martin, who made her debut in the musical and scored a personal success in this number, pledged her devotion to her affluent "daddy" while stranded on a freezing Siberian railway station, and then proceeded to warm up the natives by doing an innocent strip tease. In London revue *Black Velvet* (1939) the song was performed by Pat Kirkwood, Roberta Huby, Carole Lynne, and Norma Dawn.

"My Heart Stood Still." Music by Richard Rodgers; lyric by Lorenz Hart. Sung by Jessie Matthews and Richard Dolman in London revue *One Dam Thing After Another* (1927), then by William Gaxton and Constance Carpenter in *A Connecticut Yankee* (NY 1927). The idea for the song originated from a near traffic accident while Rodgers and Hart were in a taxi with two girls in Paris. One of the girls exclaimed, "Oh, my heart stood still!" Hart said it was a good song title, and Rodgers jotted it down in a notebook. When the writers returned to London, where they were working on the songs for *One Dam Thing After Another*, the composer wrote the melody and the lyricist supplied the words to go with the title. Note that except for "single," "spoken," "unfelt," "never," "until," and "moment," the refrain is made up solely of one-syllable words.

"My Hero." Music by Oscar Straus; lyric by Stanislaus Stange. Waltzing paean to a military hero first sung in English by Ida Brooks Hunt in *The Chocolate Soldier* (NY 1909). In London version (1910), sung by Constance Drever. Original operetta, *Der Tapfere Soldat*, with text by Rudolf Bernauer and Leopold Jacobson, was initially presented in Vienna (1908). The song was then known as *"Komm, Komm! Held Meiner Träume."*

"My Mammy." Music by Walter Donaldson; lyric by Sam Lewis & Joe Young. Al Jolson added this song of maternal devotion to the score of *Sin-*

bad (NY 1918) after the show had opened. It became so closely identified with Jolson that he was thenceforth known as a "Mammy singer."

"My Man." Music by Maurice Yvain; lyric by Channing Pollock. Sung by Fanny Brice in both *Ziegfeld 9 o'Clock Frolic* (NY 1920) and *Ziegfeld Follies* (NY 1921). Yvain's lachrymose ballad was originally a French song, *"Mon Homme,"* with lyric by Albert Willemetz and Jacques-Charles, sung by Mistinguett in Parisian revue *Paris qui jazz* (1920), but it became closely associated with Miss Brice. At the time she introduced the English version, the singer was married to Nick Arnstein, a gambler recently indicted for receiving stolen securities. Pollock deliberately based his lyric on the Brice-Arnstein romance, and Fanny insisted that Ziegfeld let her sing it even though she had previously been identified as a comedienne. The producer, however, took strong exception to Miss Brice's garish costume and red wig, and made her sing the piece leaning against a lamppost wearing a tattered dress with a shawl draped over her head. Years later, in a newspaper article, Arnstein blamed the song for ruining his marriage. The original French version was introduced in NY by Yvonne George in the *Greenwich Village Follies* of 1922.

"My Man's Gone Now." Music by George Gershwin; lyric by DuBose Heyward. Serena's wailing threnody in *Porgy and Bess* after her man has been killed in a fight. Sung by Ruby Elzy in NY (1935) and by Helen Thigpen in London (1952).

"My Motter." Music by Howard Talbot; lyric by Arthur Wimperis. Comic

show-stopper in *The Arcadians*, sung by Alfred Lester (L 1909), then by Percival Knight (NY 1910).

"My One and Only." Music by George Gershwin; lyric by Ira Gershwin. Rhythmic love song in *Funny Face*, sung and tap-danced by Fred Astaire, Gertrude McDonald, and Betty Compton in NY (1927), and by Astaire and Eileen Hatton in London (1928).

"My Own Morning." Music by Jule Styne; lyric by Betty Comden & Adolph Green. A poor black girl (Leslie Uggams) in `Hallelujah, Baby!* (NY 1967) expresses her determination to have her own possessions.

"My Romance." Music by Richard Rodgers; lyric by Lorenz Hart. Duet describing a love so strong it has no need of customary romantic settings or accompaniments. Pridefully sung by Gloria Grafton and Donald Novis in *Jumbo* (NY 1935).

"My Ship." Music by Kurt Weill; lyric by Ira Gershwin. Introduced by Gertrude Lawrence in *Lady in the Dark* (NY 1941). The melody serves as a recurring motif within the story since it is a song the heroine has learned as a child but cannot finish. When hero Macdonald Carey does finish it at the end of the play, heroine knows he is for her. A similar use was made of the song "Ah! Sweet Mystery of Life" in *Naughty Marietta*.

"My Song." Music by Ray Henderson; lyric by Lew Brown. Rudy Vallée and Ethel Merman revealed their musical creativity in *George White's Scandals* (NY 1931). During the pre-

Bway tryout, the number was presented more elaborately with Everett Marshall, as Franz Schubert, interpolating the "Serenade," and Willie Howard, as Irving Berlin, singing "Always."

"My Time of Day." Music & lyric by Frank Loesser. Sky Masterson's affinity for the wee small hours in *Guys and Dolls*. In NY (1950), sung by Robert Alda; in London (1953) by Jerry Wayne.

❧ N ☙

"Namely You." Music by Gene de Paul; lyric by Johnny Mercer. Boy-girl duet in *Li'l Abner* (NY 1956) sung by Peter Palmer and Edith Adams.

Nash, (Frederick) Ogden, lyricist, librettist; b. Rye, NY, Aug. 19, 1902; d. Rye, May 19, 1971. Nash was a preeminent creator of light verse whose Bway collaborators were Kurt Weill ("That's Him," "Speak Low") and Vernon Duke ("Out of the Clear Blue Sky," "Roundabout").

    1943   One Touch of Venus (Weill) (also co-lib.)
    1952   Two's Company (Duke)
    1956   The Littlest Revue (Duke)

Naughty Marietta (1910). Music by Victor Herbert; lyrics & book by Rida Johnson Young.
    Songs: "Tramp! Tramp! Tramp!," "Naughty Marietta," " 'Neath the Southern Moon," "Italian Street Song," "I'm Falling in Love with Someone," "Ah! Sweet Mystery of Life."

New York: Nov. 7, 1910
New York Theatre; 136 p.
    Presented by Oscar Hammerstein; directed by Jacques Coini; choreographed by Pauline Verhoeven; settings, Theodore Reisig, Julius Dowe; costumes, Will Barnes; music director, Gaetano Merola; orchestrations, Victor Herbert.

Cast: Emma Trentini (*Marietta d'Altena*), Orville Harrold (*Capt. Dick Warrington*), Edward Martindel (*Etienne Grandet*), Marie Duchene (*Adah*), Peggy Wood (chorus).
    From time to time mounting debts forced opera impressario Oscar Hammerstein to abandon grand opera for comic opera. For *Naughty Marietta,* his most celebrated offering in the field, he teamed Victor Herbert and Rida Johnson Young for their first of two collaborations and co-starred his leading attractions of the Manhattan Opera House, Emma Trentini and Orville Harrold. Originally titled *Little Paris,* the operetta tells of the adventures of Marietta d'Altena, who, to avoid an unhappy marriage in her native Naples, joins a boatload of French casquette girls who have come to New Orleans in search of husbands. Marietta is first attracted to Etienne, the son of the lieutenant governor, but she eventually finds true love in the arms of stalwart Capt. Dick Warrington—but only after he has completed the fragment of a melody that had come to her in a dream.
    Though the story clearly places New Orleans under French control, in the period in which it was set—1780—the city was actually owned by Spain. (The same general period and locale are also found in *The New Moon,* whose authors made the same error.) During a return engagement of

Naughty Marietta in 1912, while Herbert was conducting, Miss Trentini would not sing an encore of the "Italian Street Song." This so enraged the composer that he refused to write the score for her next operetta, *The Firefly*, and the assignment went to Rudolf Friml.

FILM VERSION: Jeanette MacDonald and Nelson Eddy (MGM 1935, W. S. Van Dyke dir.).

Neagle, Anna (née Florence Marjorie Robertson), actress, dancer, singer; b. London, Oct. 20, 1904. Dame of British Empire 1970. Miss Neagle, who is best known for her screen portrayals of historical women, was Marjorie Robertson until scoring her first London stage success in *Stand Up and Sing* (in which she introduced "There's Always Tomorrow"). In 1965 she appeared in her biggest hit, *Charlie Girl.*

1925	Charlot's Revue (chorus)
	Tricks (chorus)
1926	Rose-Marie (chorus)
	The Charlot Show (chorus)
1927	The Desert Song (chorus)
1928	This Year of Grace! (chorus)
1929	Wake Up and Dream! (dancer)
	Wake Up and Dream! (NY) (dancer)
1931	Stand Up and Sing (*Mary Clyde-Burkin*)
1953	The Glorious Days (*Carol Beaumont*, etc.)
1965	Charlie Girl (*Lady Hadwell*)
1973	No, No. Nanette (r) (*Sue Smith*)
1977	Maggie (*Comtesse*)

"Nellie Kelly, I Love You." Music & lyric by George M. Cohan. Nellie Kelly, the daughter of Officer Kelly, lives in The Bronx and has hundreds of beaux who are forever pledging their love and sending her "flowers all dripping with dew." Charles King introduced the waltz in *Little Nellie Kelly* (NY 1922).

Nesbitt, Robert, director, lyricist, sketch writer; b. London, Jan. 11, 1906. Primarily a director of lavish revues, Nesbitt had 10 London shows running over 500 performances, of which seven went over 600 (*Black Velvet, Get a Load of This, Strike a New Note, Happy and Glorious, The Night and the Music, Starlight Roof, Plaisirs de Paris*). He also directed pantomimes and nightclub revues, and wrote songs with composer William Walker.

1932	Ballyhoo (also lyr.) (Walker)
1934	Here's How (also lyr.) (Walker)
	Hi-Diddle-Diddle (also lyr.) (Walker)
1935	Charlot's Char-a-Bang!
	Shall We Reverse?
	Stop . . . Go!
1936	The Town Talks
1937	And On We Go
1938	Pelissier's Follies
	Maritza (r)
1939	Black and Blue
	The Little Dog Laughed
	Black Velvet
1940	Up and Doing
	Top of the World
1941	Black Vanities
	Get a Load of This
	Gangway
1942	Happidrome
	Blossom Time
	Fine and Dandy
	Wild Rose (Sally)
	Best Bib and Tucker
1943	Strike a New Note
	The Magic Carpet
1944	Happy and Glorious
1945	The Night and the Music
	Fine Feathers
1946	High Time
	The Night and the Laughter
1947	Here, There and Everywhere
	Starlight Roof
1948	High Button Shoes
1949	Latin Quarter
1950	Latin Quarter 1950
1951	Rainbow Square
1952	Excitement
1953	The Glorious Days
	Three Cheers

1956 Rocking the Town
1957 Plaisirs de Paris
     We're Having a Ball
1958 Large as Life
1959 Startime
     Swinging Down the Lane
1960 The Music Box Show
     Stars in Your Eyes
1961 Let Yourself Go
1962 Every Night at the Palladium
1963 Swing Along
     The Man in the Moon
1966 London Laughs

"Never Again." Music & lyric by Noël Coward. The end of an affair brings an avowal to forgo forever love's strange unthinking joy and pain. Eva Ortega and Hugh French introduced the piece in Set to Music (NY 1938); Graham Payn sang it in Sigh No More (L 1945).

"Never Never Land." Music by Jule Styne; lyric by Betty Comden & Adolph Green. In Peter Pan (NY 1954) Peter (Mary Martin) tells the Darling children all about the place he came from.

"Never Will I Marry." Music & lyric by Frank Loesser. Because of a family curse that he was "born to wander solitary," the hero of Greenwillow (NY 1960), played by Anthony Perkins, fiercely resists his longing for marriage.

New Faces of 1952 (1952). Music & lyrics by Ronny Graham, Arthur Siegel, June Carroll, Sheldon Harnick, Michael Brown, etc.; sketches by Ronny Graham, Melvin Brooks, etc.
    SONGS: "Lucky Pierre" (Graham), "Guess Who I Saw Today" (Murray Grand–Elisse Boyd), "Love Is a Simple Thing" (Siegel–Carroll), "Boston Beguine" (Harnick), "Lizzie Borden" (Brown), "I'm in Love with Miss Logan" (Graham), "Penny Candy" (Siegel-Carroll), "Monotonous" (Siegel-Carroll).

NEW YORK: May 16, 1952
ROYALE THEATRE; 365 p.
    Presented by Leonard Sillman; directed by John Murray Anderson & John Beal; choreographed by Richard Barstow; settings, Raoul Pène du Bois; costumes, Thomas Becher; music director, Anton Coppola; orchestrations, Ted Royal.
    CAST: Ronny Graham, Eartha Kitt, Robert Clary, Virginia Bosler, June Carroll, Virginia de Luce, Alice Ghostley, Patricia Hammerlee, Carol Lawrence, Paul Lynde, Bill Millikin.
    New Faces of 1952 was the most successful of all six of Leonard Sillman's tyro talent shows. As with the others, the production was intimate and the view mostly satirical. Among highlights: Ronny Graham as a pouting Truman Capote in a hammock ("Oedipus Goes South"), Eartha Kitt being bored by fawning notables in "Monotonous," Robert Clary offering his admission of a schoolboy crush in "I'm in Love with Miss Logan," June Carroll (Sillman's sister) in the rueful ballad of infidelity, "Guess Who I Saw Today," Alice Ghostley's revelation of improper love in a proper setting ("Boston Beguine"), Paul Lynde, swathed in bandages, cheerfully recounting his African misadventures in "Trip of the Month." Next to the French import La Plume de Ma Tante, New Faces of 1952 had the longest Bway run of any revue of the decade.
    The first New Faces, in 1934, was a revised version of Sillman's revue Low and Behold, which had played the Pasadena Playhouse the previous year. The California cast included Charles Walters, Tyrone Power, Eve

Arden (then Eunice Quedens), and Sillman. On Bway, the cast included Imogene Coca, Nancy Hamilton, Walters, James Shelton, Henry Fonda, and Sillman. Charles Dillingham was the nominal producer (Elsie Janis and Mary Pickford were the main backers), and the show ran 149 performances at the Fulton Theatre. In 1936, at the Vanderbilt, Miss Coca was again among the *New Faces*, along with Helen Craig, Nancy Noland, Ralph Blane, Van Johnson, and Marion Martin (later the more familiar faces of the Duncan Sisters were added). This edition lasted 193 performances.

The 1942 *New Faces*, which introduced John Lund, Irwin Corey, Alice Pearce, and Doris Dowling, was seen at the Ritz for 94 performances. Following the 1952 edition, Sillman offered one in 1956, which played 220 times at the Ethel Barrymore. In the cast were T. C. Jones, Virginia Martin, Inga Swenson, Maggie Smith, John Reardon, Jane Connell, and Bill McCutcheon. More *New Faces* showed up at the Booth in 1968, with the best remembered being those of Robert Klein and Madeline Kahn. It lasted 52 performances.

Sillman's 1938 revue, *Who's Who*, was essentially another *New Faces* with a change in title to please its sponsor, Elsa Maxwell. Imogene Coca, Rags Ragland, and Sonny Tufts were in the cast.

In London, a non-Sillman *New Faces* opened at the Comedy Theatre April 11, 1940, and ran 257 performances. The cast was headed by Charles Hawtrey and Judy Campbell (who sang "A Nightingale Sang in Berkeley Square").

FILM VERSIONS: Joe Penner, Milton Berle, Harriet Hilliard (with plot) (RKO 1937, Leigh Jason dir.); Ronny Graham, Eartha Kitt, Alice Ghostley,

Paul Lynde (with slight plot) (20th Cent. 1954, Harry Horner dir.).

New Moon, The (1928). Music by Sigmund Romberg; lyrics by Oscar Hammerstein II; book by Hammerstein, Frank Mandel & Laurence Schwab.

SONGS: "Marianne," "The Girl on the Prow," "Softly, as in a Morning Sunrise," "Stouthearted Men," "One Kiss," "Wanting You," "Lover, Come Back to Me," "Love Is Quite a Simple Thing."

NEW YORK: Sept. 19, 1928
IMPERIAL THEATRE; 509 p.

Presented by Laurence Schwab & Frank Mandel; directed by Hammerstein, Schwab & Mandel (uncredited); choreographed by Bobby Connolly; settings, Donald Oenslager; costumes, Charles Le Maire; music director, Alfred Goodman; orchestrations, Goodman, Emil Gerstenberger.

CAST: Evelyn Herbert (*Marianne Beaunoir*), Robert Halliday (*Robert Misson*), Gus Shy (*Alexander*), William O'Neal (*Philippe*), Marie Callahan (*Julie*).

LONDON: April 4, 1929
DRURY LANE THEATRE; 148 p.

Presented by Alfred Butt; directed by Felix Edwardes; choreographed by Bobby Connolly; settings, Prince Galitzine, Joseph & Phil Harker; costumes, Irene Segalla; music director, Herman Finck.

CAST: Evelyn Laye (*Marianne Beaunoir*), Howett Worster (*Robert Misson*), Gene Gerrard (*Alexander*), Ben Williams (*Philippe*), Dolores Farris (*Julie*).

The New Moon was the successor to *The Desert Song*, with the same kind of romantic and improbable story, soaring melodies, and sumptuous mounting. It also had the same composer, lyricist, librettists, producers, choreographer, and male lead.

Though it ran longer than its predecessor, the operetta had rough going before the NY opening, and had to shut down for major repairs following its Philadelphia tryout early in 1928. Eight months later the new *New Moon* reopened on the road with a new book, new songs, a new leading lady, and a new comic. The story was still based on the same historic incident involving one Robert Misson, who, late in the 18th century, set up an independent government on an island off North America. In the operetta, Robert works as a bondservant in New Orleans in 1792 to avoid detection that he is really a French nobleman wanted for murder. He is captured and shipped back to France on *The New Moon*, whose passenger list also includes his beloved, Marianne Beaunoir. After Robert is rescued by his followers, he takes Marianne with him to establish a colony of freemen on the Isle of Pines. One year later, after the French Revolution has overthrown the monarchy, Robert is appointed governor of the island. (Actually, at the time both New Orleans and the Isle of Pines were under Spanish rule. The historical error was also made in *Naughty Marietta*, set in New Orleans at about the same period.) Following its run the NY company went on a five-month tour. The road company, headed by Charlotte Lansing and George Houston, began its travels in Aug. 1929, and toured nine months.

In London, the operetta was the fourth Hammerstein musical in a row to play Drury Lane Theatre, though it turned out to be the least successful. During run, Howett Worster was succeeded by Harry Welchman.

FILM VERSIONS: Lawrence Tibbett and Grace Moore (different story) (MGM 1930, Jack Conway dir.); Jea-nette MacDonald and Nelson Eddy (MGM 1940, Robert Z. Leonard dir.).

"New Sun in the Sky." Music by Arthur Schwartz; lyric by Howard Dietz. Effulgent expression of new-found bliss sung and danced by Fred Astaire in *The Band Wagon* (NY 1931) while donning top hat, white tie, and tails in front of a mirror.

"New York, New York." Music by Leonard Bernstein; lyric by Betty Comden & Adolph Green. Bustling celebration of a bustling city introduced in *On the Town* (NY 1944) by John Battles, Adolph Green, and Cris Alexander, as three sailors on shore leave. In London production (1963), the sailors were Don McKay, Elliott Gould, and Franklin Kiser.

Newley, Anthony, actor, singer, composer, lyricist, librettist, director; b. London, Sept. 24, 1931. Stylized performer whose "morality" musicals—all written with Leslie Bricusse—cast him as little man bucking the system. Best-known songs: "What Kind of Fool Am I?," "Gonna Build a Mountain," "Once in a Lifetime" (all from *Stop the World—I Want to Get Off*); "A Wonderful Day Like Today," "Who Can I Turn To?," "Nothing Can Stop Me Now" (*The Roar of the Greasepaint—The Smell of the Crowd*); and title song from *The Good Old Bad Old Days!* Newley has also appeared in, written for, and directed films.

Unless otherwise noted, Mr. Newley was director and co-composer-lyricist-librettist with Mr. Bricusse of following:
1955 Cranks (L) (actor only)
1956 Cranks (NY) (actor only)
1961 Stop the World—I Want to Get Off (L) (also *Littlechap*)
1962 Stop the World—I Want to Get Off (NY) (also *Littlechap*)

1965 The Roar of the Greasepaint—
The Smell of the Crowd (NY)
(also *Cocky*)

1972 The Good Old Bad Old Days! (L)
(also *Bubba*)

"Night and Day." Music & lyric by Cole Porter. Love's constancy in contrasting times and climes revealed by Fred Astaire in *Gay Divorce* (NY 1932, L 1933), and danced by Astaire and Claire Luce all over the furniture of a resort hotel. Porter claimed the melody was suggested by a Mohammedan call to worship he had heard in Morocco and that the lyric first began to germinate when he heard Mrs. Vincent Astor complain of a leaky faucet, "That drip, drip, drip is driving me mad!"

"Night Letter." Music by Galt Mac-Dermot; lyric by John Guare. In *Two Gentlemen of Verona* (NY 1971), Silvia (Jonelle Allen), unhappy about marrying her father's choice, Thurio, bids professional letter writer Valentine (Clifton Davis) send a message to her secret lover, Eglamour. But by the time the girl finishes singing the rocking praises of a "hot night letter," she and Valentine are in each other's arms. Now she appeals to her new love, who offers to rescue her by means of a "long night ladder." In London version (1973), the parts were played by B. J. Arnau and Samuel E. Wright.

"Night Was Made for Love, The." Music by Jerome Kern; lyric by Otto Harbach. Introduced by George Meader as a recurring theme in *The Cat and the Fiddle* (NY 1931). In London production (1932), sung by Henri Leoni. This so-called *canzonetta* (Italian for "little song") had a French lyric by Robert Russell Bennett.

"Nightingale Sang in Berkeley Square, A." Music by Manning Sherwin; lyric by Eric Maschwitz. Wartime London takes heart from the song of a bird. Sung by Judy Campbell in *New Faces* (L 1940).

"Nina." Music & lyric by Noël Coward. Set to a rumba beat, the piece traced the saga of Señorita Nina from Argentina who disliked dancing so much she not only "declined to begin the 'Beguine' tho' they besought her to," she even cursed Cole Porter too! Introduced in *Sigh No More* (L 1945) by Cyril Ritchard, with Tom Linden as a Gigolo and Gail Kendal as Nina.

"No Harm Done." Music & lyric by Sandy Wilson. In the spoof of 30s musicals, *Divorce Me, Darling!* (L 1965), a Riviera hotel terrace (which had a convenient piano) provided the setting for this suave, civilized view of an innocent flirtation. The participants were Cy Young and Patricia Michael, who sipped champagne and did a tap dance.

No, No, Nanette (1925). Music by Vincent Youmans; lyrics by Irving Caesar & Otto Harbach; book by Harbach & Frank Mandel, based on play *My Lady Friends* by Mandel & Emile Nyitray, adapted from novel *Oh James!* by May Edgington.

SONGS: "The Call of the Sea" (Caesar), "Too Many Rings Around Rosie" (Caesar), "I Want to Be Happy" (Caesar), "No, No, Nanette" (Harbach), "Peach on the Beach" (Harbach), "Tea for Two" (Caesar), "You Can Dance with Any Girl at All" (Caesar), "I Want to Be Happy" (Caesar), "Telephone Girlie" (Harbach), "'Where Has My Hubby Gone?' Blues" (Caesar), "I've Confessed to the Breeze" (Harbach; London & revivals only), "Take a Little One Step" (lyric, Zelda Sears; London & revivals only).

LONDON: March 11, 1925
PALACE THEATRE; 665 p.

Presented by Herbert Clayton & Jack Waller; directed by William Mollison; choreographed by Patrick Leonard; settings, F. L. Lyndhurst; costumes, Idare, Peron; music director, Percival Mackey.

CAST: Binnie Hale (*Nanette*), Joseph Coyne (*Jimmy Smith*), Irene Browne (*Lucille Early*), George Grossmith (*Billy Early*), Seymour Beard (*Tom Trainor*), Marie Hemingway (*Sue Smith*), Gracie Leigh (*Pauline*).

NEW YORK: Sept. 16, 1925
GLOBE THEATRE; 321 p.

Presented & directed by H. H. Frazee; choreographed by Sammy Lee; settings, P. Dodd Ackerman; costumes, Schneider-Anderson, Milgrim, Frances; music director, Niclas Kempner.

CAST: Louise Groody (*Nanette*), Charles Winninger (*Jimmy Smith*), Josephine Whittell (*Lucille Early*), Wellington Cross (*Billy Early*), Eleanor Dawn (*Sue Smith*), Jack Barker (*Tom Trainor*), Georgia O'Ramey (*Pauline*).

NEW YORK: Jan. 19, 1971
46TH ST. THEATRE; 861 p.

Presented by Pyxidium Ltd.; directed & adapted by Burt Shevelove; choreographed by Donald Saddler; supervisor, Busby Berkeley; settings & costumes, Raoul Pène du Bois; lighting, Jules Fisher; music director, Buster Davis; orchestrations, Ralph Burns.

CAST: Ruby Keeler (*Sue Smith*), Jack Gilford (*Jimmy Smith*), Bobby Van (*Billy Early*), Helen Gallagher (*Lucille Early*), Patsy Kelly (*Pauline*),

Susan Watson (*Nanette*), Roger Rathburn (*Tom Trainor*), K. C. Townsend (*Flora Latham*), Loni Zoe Ackerman (*Betty Brown*), Pat Lysinger (*Winnie Winslow*).

LONDON: May 16, 1973
DRURY LANE THEATRE; 277 p.

Presented by H. M. Tennent Ltd.; directed & adapted by Burt Shevelove; choreographed by Donald Saddler; settings & costumes, Raoul Pène du Bois; lighting, Joe Davis; music director, Grant Hossack; orchestrations, Ralph Burns.

CAST: Anna Neagle (*Sue Smith*), Anne Rogers (*Lucille Early*), Thora Hird (*Pauline*), Tony Britton (*Jimmy Smith*), Teddy Green (*Billy Early*), Barbara Brown (*Nanette*), Peter Gale (*Tom Trainor*), Anita Graham (*Flora Latham*), Elaine Holland (*Betty Brown*), Jenny Wren (*Winnie Winslow*).

Although it would win a universally positive reception, *No, No, Nanette* appeared to be a decidedly negative undertaking when it began its pre-Bway tryout in April 1924. Then directed by Edward Royce, the original cast included Phyllis Cleveland (*Nanette*), Skeets Gallagher (*Jimmy*), Francis X. Donegan (*Billy*), Anna Wheaton (*Lucille*), and Juliette Day (*Sue*). It looked so unpromising that producer Frazee took over the direction himself, replaced five songs (with, among others, "Tea for Two" and "I Want to Be Happy"), and substituted Louise Groody and Charles Winninger for Miss Cleveland and Gallagher. During year-long Chicago run, Donegan was succeeded by Bernard Granville and Wellington Cross, Miss Wheaton by Blanche Ring and Josephine Whittell.

By the time the musical opened in NY, a second company had been touring since Jan. 1925. The cast was headed by Ona Munson (*Nanette*), Cecil Lean (*Jimmy*), Donald Brian (*Billy*), Cleo Mayfield (*Lucille*), Jack McCauley (*Tom*). During tour, Lean and Mayfield alternated with Frank Crumit and Julia Sanderson. The London version, which preceded the one in NY, became the third longest-running West End musical of the 20s. During NY run, Miss Groody was succeeded by Miss Munson (5-26); during NY company road tour, Winninger was succeeded by Hal Skelly. *No, No, Nanette* was revived in London at the Hippodrome in 1936, and ran 115 performances. The cast was headed by Barbara Vernon (*Nanette*), Shaun Glenville (*Jimmy*), Phyllis Monkman (*Lucille*), and Clifford Mollison (*Billy*).

The revised 1971 version ran into pre-Bway problems similar to those of the original production. Both Hiram Sherman (*Jimmy*) and Carole Demas (*Nanette*) were replaced on the road, Busby Berkeley was replaced as director by Burt Shevelove, and co-producer Harry Rigby, who had conceived the idea of the revival, was bought out by Cyma Rubin. During Bway run, Ruby Keeler, who returned to Bway to play the expanded role of Sue Smith, was succeeded by Ruth Maitland (11-72) and Joy Hodges (11-72); Jack Gilford by Benny Baker (1-72); Patsy Kelly by Lillian Hayman (10-72) and Martha Raye (11-72); Susan Watson by Barbara Heuman (12-71). Two road companies toured the US, both for 10 months each. The first, which began Dec. 1971, was headed by June Allyson (*Sue*), Dennis Day (*Jimmy*), Jerry Antes (*Billy*), Sandra Deel (*Lucille*), Judy Canova (*Pauline*), Dana Swenson (*Nanette*). During tour, Miss Allyson was replaced by Virginia Mayo, Day by Elliott Reid. The second company, which began its journey Oct. 1972, was

headed by Evelyn Keyes (*Sue*), Don Ameche (*Jimmy*), Swen Swenson (*Billy*), Lainie Nelson (*Lucille*), Ruth Donnelly (*Pauline*), Darlene Anders (*Nanette*).

The story of *No, No, Nanette* relates how Jimmy Smith, a married NY Bible manufacturer and Nanette's guardian, innocently helps the careers of three girls in three different cities. Complications arise when they all show up in Jimmy's Chickadee Cottage in Atlantic City at the same time. (The original London production changed the locales to London and the Riviera). The unsuccessful successor to the original *No, No, Nanette* was *Yes, Yes, Yvette* (NY 1927), which was produced by Frazee, had lyrics by Caesar, and a cast headed by Charles Winninger, Jeanette MacDonald, and Jack Whiting. The 1971 Bway production sparked the revivals of *Irene* (1973) and *Good News* (1974). Bib: *The Making of "No, No, Nanette"* by Don Dunn (Citadel, NJ 1972).

FILM VERSIONS: Alexander Gray, Bernice Claire, ZaSu Pitts (misc. songs) (Warner 1930, Clarence Badger dir.); Anna Neagle, Victor Mature, ZaSu Pitts (RKO 1940, Herbert Wilcox dir.).

"No, No, Nanette." Music by Vincent Youmans; lyric by Otto Harbach. Breezy admonitory number sung in *No, No, Nanette* by Binnie Hale (L 1925) and Louise Groody (NY 1925). The melody of the refrain, which was the same as Youmans' previous "My Boy and I" (though that was a waltz), may also be detected in Romberg's later "One Kiss."

"No Other Love." Music by Richard Rodgers; lyric by Oscar Hammerstein II. Romantic faithfulness pledged by Bill Hayes and Isabel Bigley in *Me and Juliet* (NY 1953). As presented in the play the song is first used in a rehearsal scene in which assistant stage manager Hayes coaches aspiring actress Bigley how to sing in a theatre. The melody of the song was based on the tango theme "Beneath the Southern Cross," which Rodgers had written for an episode in the tv series *Victory at Sea* (1952).

No Strings (1962). Music & lyrics by Richard Rodgers; book by Samuel Taylor.

SONGS: "The Sweetest Sounds," "How Sad," "Loads of Love," "You Don't Tell Me," "Love Makes the World Go," "Nobody Told Me," "Look No Further," "An Orthodox Fool," "Maine," "No Strings."

NEW YORK: March 15, 1962
54TH ST. THEATRE; 580 p.

Presented by Richard Rodgers, with Samuel Taylor; directed & choreographed by Joe Layton; settings & lighting, David Hays; costumes, Fred Voelpel, Donald Brooks; music director, Peter Matz; orchestrations, Ralph Burns.

CAST: Diahann Carroll (*Barbara Woodruff*), Richard Kiley (*David Jordan*), Noelle Adam (*Jeanette Valmy*), Bernice Massi (*Comfort O'Connell*), Don Chastain (*Mike Robinson*), Alvin Epstein (*Luc Delbert*), Mitchell Gregg (*Louis de Pourtal*), Polly Rowles (*Mollie Plummer*).

LONDON: Dec. 30, 1963
HER MAJESTY'S THEATRE; 135 p.

Presented by Williamson Music Ltd.; restaged & dances reproduced by Wakefield Poole; settings & lighting, David Hays; costumes, Fred Voelpel, Donald Brooks; music director, Johnnie Spence; orchestrations, Ralph Burns; supervisor, Jerome Whyte.

CAST: Art Lund (*David Jordan*), Beverly Todd (*Barbara Woodruff*),

Hy Hazell (*Mollie Plummer*), Ferdy Mayne (*Louis de Pourtal*), David Holliday (*Mike Robinson*), Erica Rogers (*Jeanette Valmy*), Geoffrey Hutchings (*Luc Delbert*).

Richard Rodgers' first production for which he also served as lyricist included such innovations as placing the orchestra backstage, featuring instrumentalists on stage from time to time, having the principals and chorus move scenery and props, and, to conform to the play's title, eliminating a string section from the orchestra. The musical also offered Bway's first interracial romance since *Show Boat* as it told of a love affair between a black fashion model in Paris and a former Pulitzer Prize-winning novelist now a "Europe bum." At the end, the lovers must part so that David can be free to resume his career back home in Maine. In addition to Paris, the locales included Monte Carlo, Honfleur, Deauville, and St. Tropez. In June 1963, Diahann Carroll, for whom Rodgers conceived the musical, was succeeded by Barbara McNair, Richard Kiley by Howard Keel. The US tour, which began Aug. 1963, lasted five months.

"No Time at All." Music & lyric by Stephen Schwartz. Vaudeville turn—complete with "follow-the-bouncing-ball" singalong—about the importance of living life to the fullest. Sung in *Pippin* (NY 1972, L 1973) by, respectively, Irene Ryan and the Boys and Elisabeth Welch and the Boys.

"Nobody." Music by Bert Williams; lyric by Alex Rogers. Williams' trademark saga of a chronic loser was first sung in vaudeville, then in just about every *Ziegfeld Follies* in which the black comedian appeared (nine beginning in 1910).

"**Nobody Else but Me.**" Music by Jerome Kern; lyric by Oscar Hammerstein II. Lively song of self-contentment (she has "a lover who likes me the way I am") introduced in final scene of 1946 Bway revival of *Show Boat* by Jan Clayton (as Magnolia's daughter, Kim). The number, performed as a 1927 show tune, took the place of Norma Terris' impersonations in the original production. For the 1971 London revival, the song was taken at a slower tempo for Cleo Laine (as Julie) to sing in a St. Louis bar. This was the last music Kern wrote for Bway.

"**Nobody Makes a Pass at Me.**" Music & lyric by Harold Rome. In the ILGWU revue *Pins and Needles* (NY 1937), Millie Weitz (Local 22, Dressmakers) revealed the plight of a girl who has tried all the beauty products advertised on radio but still finds herself ignored by the boys.

"**Nobody's Heart.**" Music by Richard Rodgers; lyric by Lorenz Hart. A song of feigned amatory indifference sung by Constance Moore and reprised by Ray Bolger in *By Jupiter* (NY 1942).

Norworth, Jack, actor, singer, composer; b. Philadelphia, Pa., Jan. 5, 1879; d. Laguna Beach, Cal., Sept. 1, 1959. Began in US vaudeville as blackface comic; later won fame with tongue-twisting numbers. Second of three wives was Nora Bayes, with whom he appeared on Bway 1908–1912 and introduced their own song, "Shine On, Harvest Moon," in Ziegfeld's *Follies of 1908*.

  1906   About Town
  1908   Follies of 1908
  1909   Follies of 1909
  1910   The Jolly Bachelors (*Howson Lot*)
  1911   Little Miss Fix-It (*Buddy Arnold*) (also co-comp., lyr.)
  1912   Roly-Poly (*Percy Fitzsimmons*)

  1914   Hullo, Tango! (L)
  1915   Rosy Rapture (L) (*Lord Lil Languor*)
           Looking Around (L) (also comp.)
           Oh! La-La! (L) (Looking Around)
  1917   Odds and Ends (also co-prod.)

"**Not for All the Rice in China.**" Music & lyric by Irving Berlin. Sung by Marilyn Miller and Clifton Webb in finale of the revue *As Thousands Cheer* (NY 1933). In the show, a Supreme Court ruling held that the customary use of reprised songs as part of the finale has been forbidden. Therefore, the two principals break tradition by introducing a new song that had not been previously heard in the revue.

"**Nothing Can Stop Me Now.**" Music & lyric by Leslie Bricusse & Anthony Newley. Anthony Newley socked across this propulsive number in *The Roar of the Greasepaint—The Smell of the Crowd* (NY 1965).

Novello, Ivor (né David Ivor Davies), composer, librettist, lyricist, actor; b. Cardiff, Wales, Jan. 15, 1893; d. London, March 6, 1951. From 1935 until his death, Novello created a series of seven highly popular British operettas, noted for their lush music, bittersweet stories, and romantic settings. Christopher Hassall was lyricist for six of them, and Novello, who did not sing, appeared in six. The first of these productions was *Glamorous Night* ("Fold Your Wings," "Glamorous Night"). The three biggest hits: *The Dancing Years* ("Waltz of My Heart," "My Life Belongs to You"), *Perchance to Dream* ("We'll Gather Lilacs"), *King's Rhapsody* ("Someday My Heart Will Awake"). In his final work, *Gay's the Word* ("Vitality"), lyrics by Alan Melville, Novello kidded his own flamboyant style.

After beginning his career as a composer, Novello won international fame as a silent film star. He made his London stage debut in 1921 and wrote the first of his 22 plays in 1925. Among his revue songs were "And Her Mother Came Too" and "March with Me!" Novello's lyric-writing collaborators include Adrian Ross, Clifford Grey, Ronald Jeans, P. G. Wodehouse, Dion Titheradge, Harry Graham, Douglas Furber, Donovan Parsons, and himself. Bib: *Ivor Novello: Man of the Theatre* by Peter Noble (Falcon, L 1951); *Ivor* by W. Macqueen-Pope (Hutchinson, L 1952).

Asterisk indicates Mr. Novello was also librettist:

1916 Theodore & Co. (Ross, Grey)
1917 Arlette (Ross, Grey)
1918 Tabs (Jeans)
1919 Who's Hooper? (Grey)
1921 The Golden Moth (Wodehouse)
1924 Puppets (Titheradge)
     Our Nell (Graham)
1929 The House That Jack Built (Parsons)
1935 Glamorous Night * (Hassall) (also *Anthony Allen*)
1936 Careless Rapture * (Hassall) (also *Michael*)
1937 Crest of the Wave * (Hassall) (also *Don Gantry*)
1939 The Dancing Years * (Hassall) (also *Rudi Kleber*)
1942 The Dancing Years * (r) (also *Rudi Kleber*)
1943 Arc de Triomphe * (Hassall)
1945 Perchance to Dream * (also lyr.) (also *Sir Graham Rodney, Valentine Fayre, Bay*)
1949 King's Rhapsody * (Hassall) (also *Nikki*)
1951 Gay's the Word * (Melville)

"Now." Music by Vernon Duke; lyric by Ted Fetter. Gossamer plea to avoid romantic delay. Introduced by Gracie Barrie and Robert Shafer in *The Show Is On* (NY 1936), and danced by Paul Haakon and Evelyn Thawl.

"Now!" Music & lyric by Robert Wright & George Forrest, adapted from Grieg's Waltz (op. 12, no. 2) and his Violin Sonata No. 2 in G. The aria, an assertive demand for immediate gratification, was sung in *Song of Norway* by Irra Petina (NY 1944) and Janet Hamilton-Smith (L 1946).

Nymph Errant (1933). Music & lyrics by Cole Porter; book by Romney Brent, based on novel by James Laver.

Songs: "Experiment," "It's Bad for Me," "How Could We Be Wrong?," "Nymph Errant," "The Physician," "Solomon," "If You Like Les Belles Poitrines."

London: Oct. 6, 1933
Adelphi Theatre; 154 p.

Presented by Charles B. Cochran; directed by Romney Brent; choreographed by Agnes de Mille; settings & costumes, Doris Zinkeisen; music director, Hyam Greenbaum; orchestrations, Robert Russell Bennett.

Cast: Gertrude Lawrence (*Evangeline Edwards*), Elisabeth Welch (*Haidee Robinson*), Moya Nugent (*Miss Pratt*), David Burns (*Constantine*), Norah Howard (*Joyce*), Austin Trevor (*André de Croissant*), Walter Crisham (*Ben Winthrop*), Morton Selten (*Count Hohenadelborn-Mantalini*), Iris Ashley (*Madeleine*), Alexander Ivo (*Alexei*).

With its spectacular and varied scenes used to set off the adventures of a young girl, *Nymph Errant* was the successor to *Ever Green*, which Charles Cochran had also produced at the same theatre. And just as Jessie Matthews had scored a success in the previous musical with songs by Rodgers and Hart, so Gertrude Lawrence was acclaimed for singing the songs of another American, Cole Porter. In the story, she played a girl fresh from a Swiss finishing school, who decides to experiment with life before settling down in England. This puts her in contact with a variety of people in such locales as Neauville-sur-Mer, Venice, Athens, Smyrna, and the stage of the Folies de Paris. With each romance ending in frustration, she returns home to North Oxford still longing to experiment. This was the first musical with choreography credited to Agnes de Mille.

In 1946, a new version of *Nymph Errant*, called *Evangeline*, was mounted in London. Romney Brent again did the adaptation, but it had a new score by composers George Posford and Harry Jacobson and lyricist Eric Maschwitz. The musical, which was unsuccessful, starred Frances Day, with Sebastian Cabot and Guy Rolfe also in the cast.

"Nymph Errant." Music & lyric by Cole Porter. Staccato expression of a free spirit sung by Gertrude Lawrence in London musical of the same name (1933).

Nype, Russell (Harold), actor, singer; b. Zion, Ill., April 26, 1924. Slim, bespectacled actor who first attracted notice on Bway singing "You're Just in Love" with Ethel Merman in *Call Me Madam*.

1949   Regina (*Leo Hubbard*)
1950   Great to Be Alive (*Freddy*)
         Call Me Madam (*Kenneth Gibson*)
1958   Goldilocks (*George Randolph Brown*)
1970   Hello, Dolly! (*Cornelius Hackl*, repl.)
1972   Lady Audley's Secret (*Capt. Robert Audley*)

O

"Oceans of Time." Music by John Green; lyrics by Douglas Furber, Clifford Grey, & Greatrex Newman. Jack Buchanan and Elsie Randolph—never too busy to find time for each other—performed this jaunty song-and-dance number in *Mr. Whittington* (L 1934).

Of Thee I Sing (1931). Music by George Gershwin; lyrics by Ira Gershwin; book by George S. Kaufman & Morrie Ryskind.

SONGS: "Wintergreen for President," "Because, Because," "Of Thee I Sing, (Baby)," "Who Cares?," "Love Is Sweeping the Country," "Hello, Good Morning," "The Illegitimate Daughter," "I'm About to Be a Mother."

NEW YORK: Dec. 26, 1931
MUSIC BOX THEATRE; 441 p.
Presented by Sam H. Harris; directed by George S. Kaufman; choreographed by George Hale; settings, Jo Mielziner; costumes, Charles Le Maire; music director, Charles Previn; orchestrations, Robert Russell Bennett, William Daly.

CAST: William Gaxton (*John P. Wintergreen*), Lois Moran (*Mary Turner Wintergreen*), Victor Moore (*Alexander Throttlebottom*), George Murphy (*Sam Jenkins*), Florenz Ames (*French Ambassador*), Grace Brinkley (*Diana Devereaux*), June O'Dea (*Emily Benson*), Dudley Clements (*Matthew Arnold Fulton*), Ralph Riggs (*Chief Justice*), Edward H. Robbins (*Sen. Carver Jones*).

Of Thee I Sing, which had the longest run of any Bway book musical of the 30s, took a satirical look at a variety of political and cultural institutions, such as presidential campaigns, the Miss America pageant, the Supreme Court, the role of the vice-president, congressional debate, foreign affairs, marriage, and motherhood. In the story, the ticket of Wintergreen and Throttlebottom—with the romantic help of Mary Turner—runs on a platform of Love, wins the election, but then runs afoul of the law: Wintergreen is to be impeached because he jilted the beauty-contest winner he had promised to marry. But all ends happily when the President's wife gives birth to twins, an event that somehow calls off the impeachment. The musical, which was more in the spirit of Gilbert and Sullivan comic opera than of Bway musical comedy, was an extension of the satirical approach the same writers had previously displayed in *Strike Up the Band* (NY 1930). Victor Moore, as the befuddled Throttlebottom, was warmly praised, as was the Jimmy Walkerish William Gaxton as Wintergreen. The US touring company was headed by Oscar Shaw (*Wintergreen*), Harriette Lake (Ann Sothern) (*Mary*), and Donald Meek (*Throttlebottom*).

A sequel to *Of Thee I Sing,* called *Let 'Em Eat Cake,* opened on Bway in 1933. Again written by the Gershwin brothers and George S. Kaufman and Morrie Ryskind, it starred Gaxton, Moore, and Lois Moran in the same roles they had played in *Of Thee I Sing.* The story, which dealt with a revolution that overthrows the President, was considered too bitter and the show ran only 90 performances.

In 1952 a revival of *Of Thee I Sing* was to have co-starred Jack Carson and Victor Moore, but Moore withdrew before the opening and his role was taken by Paul Hartman. Others in the cast were Jack Whiting, Betty Oakes, Loring Smith, and Jonathan Lucas. George S. Kaufman directed, and the production lasted 72 performances.

"Of Thee I Sing, Baby." Music by George Gershwin; lyric by Ira Gershwin. Rousing campaign song of presidential candidate William Gaxton and bride-to-be Lois Moran in *Of Thee I Sing* (NY 1931). Though director George S. Kaufman objected to the word "baby" following the phrase taken from "My Country 'Tis of Thee," audience enthusiasm kept the song the way it was written.

Oh, Boy! (1917). Music by Jerome Kern; lyrics by P. G. Wodehouse; book by Guy Bolton & Wodehouse.

SONGS: "Till the Clouds Roll By," "An Old-Fashioned Wife," "You Never Knew About Me," "Nesting Time in Flatbush," "A Pal Like You," "A Package of Seeds," "Rolled into One," "Words Are Not Needed."

NEW YORK: Feb. 20, 1917
PRINCESS THEATRE; 463 p.

Presented by William Elliott & F. Ray Comstock; directed by Edward Royce & Robert Milton; settings, Clifford Pember; costumes, Harry Collins; music director, Max Hirschfeld; orchestrations, Frank Sadler.

CAST: Anna Wheaton (*Jackie Sampson*), Tom Powers (*George Budd*), Marie Carroll (*Lou Ellen Carter*), Hal Forde (*Jim Marvin*), Edna May Oliver (*Penelope Budd*), Marion Davies (*Jane Packard*), Justine Johnstone (*Polly Andrus*), Dorothy Dickson and Carl Hyson (dancers).

LONDON: Jan. 27, 1919
KINGSWAY THEATRE; 167 p.

Presented by George Grossmith & Edward Laurillard; directed by Austen Hurgon; choreographed by Harry French, Hylda Lewis; settings, J. A. Fraser; costumes, St. Martin, Hockley; music director, Leonard Hornsey; retitled *Oh, Joy!*

CAST: Beatrice Lillie (*Jackie Sampson*), Tom Powers (*George Budd*), Dot Temple (*Lou Ellen Carter*), Billy Leonard (*Jim Marvin*), Helen Rous (*Penelope Budd*), Isabel Jeans (*Jane Packard*), Judith Nelmes (*Polly Andrus*).

Oh, Boy! was the most successful production of the seven so-called Princess Theatre musicals, and the first at the theatre written by the trio of Bolton, Wodehouse and Kern. With a deliberate attempt to make the humor evolve from situations rather than being interjected as set routines by the comics, the musical told a funny yet believable tale of modern marital misunderstanding. Attending a party while his fiancée, Lou Ellen, is away, George Budd finds himself confronted with the problem of hiding Jackie, one of the guests, in his apartment. Lou Ellen's sudden return makes things pretty sticky until George's innocence is proved. The London version gave Beatrice Lillie her first part in a book musical.

"Oh, How I Hate to Get Up in the Morning." Music & lyric by Irving Berlin. The most popular comic number to come out of World War I was sung by Irving Berlin and soldier chorus in *Yip, Yip, Yaphank* (NY 1918). Berlin also sang it in *This Is the Army* (NY 1942, L 1943), accompanied by his *Yip, Yip, Yaphank* buddies.

Oh, Kay! (1926). Music by George Gershwin; lyrics by Ira Gershwin; book by Guy Bolton & P. G. Wodehouse.

SONGS: "Dear Little Girl," "Maybe," "Clap Yo' Hands," "Someone to Watch Over Me," "Fidgety Feet," "Oh, Kay!" (lyric, Howard **Dietz**), **"Heaven on Earth"** (lyric, Dietz), "Do Do Do."

NEW YORK: Nov. 8, 1926
IMPERIAL THEATRE; 256 p.

Presented by Alex A. Aarons & Vinton Freedley; directed by John Harwood; choreographed by Sammy Lee; settings, John Wenger; costumes, Hattie Carnegie, Brooks; music director, William Daly; orchestrations, Daly.

CAST: Gertrude Lawrence (*Kay*), Oscar Shaw (*Jimmy Winter*), Victor Moore (*Shorty McGee*), Harland Dixon (*Larry Potter*), Marion & Madeleine Fairbanks (*Phil & Dolly Ruxton*), Gerald Oliver Smith (*Duke*), Sascha Beaumont (*Constance Appleton*), Harry T. Shannon (*Revenue Officer*), Betty Compton (*Molly Morse*), Constance Carpenter (*Mae*); Phil Ohman & Vic Arden (duo-pianos).

LONDON: Sept. 21, 1927
HIS MAJESTY'S THEATRE; 214 p.

Presented by Musical Plays Ltd., with Aarons & Freedley; directed by William Ritter; dances reproduced by Elsie Neal; settings, Phil Harker; costumes, Idare, Guy de Gerald; music director, Arthur Wood.

CAST: Gertrude Lawrence (*Kay*), Harold French (*Jimmy Winter*), John Kirby (*Shorty McGee*), Claude Hulbert (*Duke of Datchet*), Beth & Betty Dodge (*Phil & Dolly Ruxton*), Eric Coxon (*Larry Potter*), April Harmon (*Constance Appleton*), Percy Parsons (*Revenue Officer*), Rita McLean (*Molly Morse*).

Gertrude Lawrence, in her first

book musical, became the first English actress to originate a role on Bway before playing it in London. As Kay, she appeared as the sister of a titled English bootlegger. They come ashore in the US at Beachampton, LI, where Kay gets a job as a maid to be near playboy Jimmy Winter, and where the Duke hides the hooch. Despite the entanglement of two previous marriages, Jimmy finally is free to wed Kay. The musical, which was at various times during its preparation called *Mayfair, Miss Mayfair,* and *Cheerio!,* was the first of two (the other was the unsuccessful *Treasure Girl*) that the Gershwins wrote for Miss Lawrence.

Oh, Kay! was revived off-Bway in 1960, with Marti Stevens (*Kay*) David Daniels (*Jimmy*), Bernie West (*McGee*), Murray Matheson (*Earl of Blandings*), and, in minor roles, Linda Lavin and Penny Fuller. It ran 89 performances. In 1974 the musical was presented in London with Amanda Barrie and Royce Mills. It ran 228 performances.

"Oh, Lady Be Good!" Music by George Gershwin; lyric by Ira Gershwin. Sung by Walter Catlett in *Lady, Be Good!* (NY 1924) and by William Kent in London version (1926). Though the musical was originally called *Black-Eyed Susan,* the pre-Bway popularity of this song dictated the change in title.

Oh, Lady! Lady!! (1918). Music by Jerome Kern; lyrics by P. G. Wodehouse; book by Guy Bolton & Wodehouse.

SONGS: "Not Yet," "When the Ships Come Home," "You Found Me and I Found You," "Moon Song," "Do Look at Him," "Before I Met You," "Greenwich Village," "It's a Hard, Hard World."

NEW YORK: Feb. 1, 1918
PRINCESS THEATRE; 219 p.

Presented by F. Ray Comstock & William Elliott; directed by Robert Milton & Edward Royce; settings, Clifford Pember; costumes, Harry Collins; music director, Max Hirschfeld; orchestrations, Frank Sadler.

CAST: Vivienne Segal (*Mollie Farringdon*), Carl Randall (*Willoughby "Bill" Finch*), Harry C. Browne (*Hale Underwood*), Reginald J. Mason (*Cyril Twombley*), Carroll McComas (*May Barber*), Edward Abeles (*Spike Hudgins*), Florence Shirley (*Fanny Welch*), Margaret Dale (*Mrs. Farringdon*), Constance Binney (*Parker*), Charles Columbus (*C. Ollie Flower*).

The exclamatory successor to *Oh, Boy!* was the second and final musical comedy written by Bolton, Wodehouse and Kern to be presented at the Princess Theatre, and it adhered to the prescribed format of intimacy, modernity, and musical integration. The complications arise when May Barber, Bill Finch's old flame from Gilead, Ohio, shows up unexpectedly at the Long Island home of Bill's fiancée, Mollie Farringdon, just before the wedding. Though May is there only as a dressmaker, this causes enough problems for the Farringdon-Finch nuptials to be called off. Things, however, are straightened out at a Greenwich Village party where the disappointed guests have all repaired. During the show's tryout, Vivienne Segal sang "Bill" (later in *Show Boat*), which proved inappropriate and was replaced by "Do Look at Him."

"Oh, Look at Me, I'm Dancing!" Music by Julian Slade; lyric by Dorothy Reynolds & Slade. A magical piano in *Salad Days* (L 1954) makes a young couple, Eleanor Drew and John Warner, kick up their heels all over a London park. Presently they are joined by other similarly afflicted citizens. Barbara Franklin and Richard Easton sang and danced to the frisky number in the NY version (1958).

"Oh, Promise Me!" Music by Reginald De Koven; lyric by Clement Scott. Sung by contralto Jessie Bartlett Davis, as Alan-a-Dale, in *Robin Hood* (NY 1891). The song was not part of the score when the operetta gave its first performance in Chicago, June 9, 1890. After the opening, Miss Davis threatened to walk out if she did not get a more suitable aria than the one she had been given. Since there was no time to create anything new, De Koven gave her a ballad, "Oh, Promise Me!," which he had written some years earlier. Miss Davis sang it as a marriage proposal on the second performance; since then it not only became the hit of the show, it also won a place as the most popular American wedding-day anthem. The piece was also sung in 1892 London version of *Robin Hood* (called *Maid Marian*) by Violet Cameron.

"Oh So Nice." Music by George Gershwin; lyric by Ira Gershwin. Mutual attraction expressed by Gertrude Lawrence and Paul Frawley in *Treasure Girl* (NY 1928). The song was cut during Bway run.

Oh, What a Beautiful Mornin'." Music by Richard Rodgers; lyric by Oscar Hammerstein, II. The lazy, arm-stretching waltz that opened *Oklahoma!* (NY 1943) was introduced by Alfred Drake. In London version (1947), it was sung by Harold (Howard) Keel. The idea for the lyric was found in the stage directions written by Lynn Riggs to set the scene of his play *Green Grow the Lilacs,* on which

Oklahoma! was based. As Hammerstein once wrote, "My indebtedness to Mr. Riggs' description is obvious. The cattle and the corn and the golden haze on the meadow are all there. I added some observations of my own based on my experience with beautiful mornings, and I brought the words down to the more primitive poetic level of Curly's character. He is, after all, just a cowboy and not a playwright." This was the first collaboration between Rodgers and Hammerstein.

O'Hara, Jill, actress, singer; b. Warren, Pa., Aug. 23, 1947. Miss O'Hara introduced "Good Morning Starshine" in *Hair* and "I'll Never Fall in Love Again" in *Promises, Promises.*
  1967 Hair (*Sheila*)
  1968 George M! (*Agnes Nolan*)
          Promises, Promises (*Fran Kubelik*)

"Ohio." Music by Leonard Bernstein; lyric by Betty Comden & Adolph Green. Duet of homesickness harmonized by Rosalind Russell and Edith Adams in *Wonderful Town* (NY 1953). In London version (1955), by Pat Kirkwood and Shani Wallis.

O'Horgan, Tom, director; b. Chicago, Ill., 1928. O'Horgan's frenetic theatricality helped turn *Hair* and *Jesus Christ Superstar* into long-running Bway hits.
  1968 Hair
          Hair (L)
  1971 Jesus Christ Superstar
          Inner City
  1972 Dude

Oklahoma! (1943). Music by Richard Rodgers; lyrics & book by Oscar Hammerstein II, based on Lynn Riggs's play *Green Grow the Lilacs.*
  SONGS: "Oh, What a Beautiful Mornin'," "The Surrey with the Fringe on

Top," "People Will Say We're in Love," "Kansas City," "I Cain't Say No," "Pore Jud Is Daid," "Out of My Dreams," "The Farmer and the Cowman," "All er Nothin'," "Oklahoma."

NEW YORK: March 31, 1943
ST. JAMES THEATRE; 2,212 p.

Presented by the Theatre Guild; directed by Rouben Mamoulian; choreographed by Agnes de Mille; settings, Lemuel Ayers; costumes, Miles White; music director, Jacob Schwartzdorf (Jay S. Blackton); orchestrations, Robert Russell Bennett.

CAST: Betty Garde (*Eller Murphy*), Alfred Drake (*Curly McLain*), Joan Roberts (*Laurey Williams*), Howard Da Silva (*Jud Fry*), Joseph Buloff (*Ali Hakim*), Celeste Holm (*Ado Annie Carnes*), Lee Dixon (*Will Parker*), Ralph Riggs (*Andrew Carnes*), George Church (*Jess*), Katherine Sergava (*Ellen*), Joan McCracken (*Sylvie*), Bambi Linn (*Aggie*), George S. Irving (*Joe*), Marc Platt (*Chambers*), Diana Adams (dancer).

LONDON: April 29, 1947
DRURY LANE THEATRE; 1,548 p.

Presented by H. M. Tennent Ltd.; restaged by Jerome Whyte; dances reproduced by Gemze DeLappe; settings, Lemuel Ayers; costumes, Miles White; music director, Salvatore Dell'Isola; orchestrations, Robert Russell Bennett.

CAST: Mary Marlo (*Eller Murphy*), Harold (Howard) Keel (*Curly McLain*), Betty Jane Watson (*Laurey Williams*), Henry Clarke (*Jud Fry*), Marek Windheim (*Ali Hakim*), Dorothea MacFarland (*Ado Annie Carnes*), Walter Donahue (*Will Parker*), William S. McCarthy (*Andrew Carnes*), Remington Olmstead, Jr. (*Jess*), Suzanne Lloyd (*Ellen*), Beatrice Lynn (*Sylvie*), Margaret Auld Nelson (*Aggie*), Erik Kristen (*Chambers*), Isa-

bel Bigley (*Armina*), Gemze DeLappe (*Terry*).

For 15 years, from July 1946 to July 1961, *Oklahoma!* held the record as the longest-running musical in Bway history. Currently it's in fifth place. Because of its close interweaving of story, song, and dance, it is a recognized landmark in the development of the musical stage and was the most influential musical of the postwar years. The idea for the production originated with Theresa Helburn of the Theatre Guild, who proposed to Rodgers and Hart that they adapt the play *Green Grow the Lilacs* as a musical. Because Hart was uninterested, Rodgers then formed a partnership with Oscar Hammerstein II. (Hammerstein had earlier wanted to do an adaptation of the play with Jerome Kern.) The Guild experienced difficulty raising the money for the production and out-of-town reports gave little indication of its eventual overwhelming success.

The story is set just after the turn of the century in Indian Territory. Curly and Jud Fry, both ranch hands working for Eller Murphy, are rivals for the affection of Eller's niece, Laurey. Laurey spites Curly by letting Jud escort her to a dance, where Curly proves his love by bidding all he owns for Laurey's food basket. They marry, but Jud, who is enraged with jealousy, has a fight with Curly and is accidentally killed by his own knife. Curly is tried for murder but is quickly acquitted—just in time to celebrate the admittance of Oklahoma as a state.

During NY run, Alfred Drake was succeeded by Harry Stockwell (6-44), Bob Kennedy (6-45), Harold Keel (9-45), Jack Kilty (6-46), and Wilton Clary (7-47); Joan Roberts by Evelyn Wyckoff (7-44), Iva Withers (9-45), Betty Jane Watson (10-45), Ann Crowley (2-46), Mary Hatcher (12-46), Gloria Hamilton (8-47), and Carolyn Tanner (1-48); Celeste Holm by Edna Skinner (6-44), Bonnie Primrose (10-45), Dorothea MacFarland (12-46), Vivienne Allen (4-47), and Shelley Winters (9-47); Joseph Buloff by David Burns (8-46). Following Bway run, NY company toured for one year, beginning May 1948. The regular touring company opened in Oct. 1943 and traveled almost continuously for 10½ years. The cast was headed by Harry Stockwell (*Curly*), Evelyn Wyckoff (*Laurie*), Mary Marlo (*Eller*), David Burns (*Ali*), Lou Polan (*Jud*), Pamela Britton (*Ado Annie*), Walter Donahue (*Will*), Dania Krupska (*Ellen*), Charles Laskey (*Chambers*), Gemze DeLappe (*Aggie*). During tour, Stockwell was succeeded by John Raitt (6-44), James Alexander (4-45), Ridge Bond (11-47), and Ralph Lowe (8-52); Miss Wyckoff by Betty Jane Watson (7-44), Mary Hatcher (8-45), Peggy Engel (8-46), Ann Crowley (10-47), Marilyn Landers (2-48), Carolyn Adair (10-48), Patricia Northrop (8-49), Patricia Johnson (9-51), and Florence Henderson (8-52); Miss Britton by Dorothea MacFarland (3-45) and Barbara Cook (8-53). In London, Harold Keel was succeeded by Chris Robinson; Betty Jane Watson by Ann Crowley and Isabel Bigley.

FILM VERSION: Gordon MacRae, Shirley Jones, Charlotte Greenwood, Rod Steiger, Eddie Albert, Gene Nelson (Magna 1955; Fred Zinnemann dir.).

"Oklahoma." Music by Richard Rodgers; lyric by Oscar Hammerstein II. Wind-swept final number in the musical of the same name (NY 1943), sung by Alfred Drake, Joan Roberts, and company, and by Harold (Howard) Keel, Betty Jane Watson, and company in London production (1947). This celebration of the state carved out of Indian Territory is now Oklahoma's official state song.

"Ol' Man River." Music by Jerome Kern; lyric by Oscar Hammerstein II. Though intended for Paul Robeson, the song was introduced in *Show Boat* (NY 1927) by Jules Bledsoe when Robeson was unable to appear in the production. He did, however, sing it in the London version (1928) and in the NY revival (1932). In an interview, Hammerstein once said, "Edna Ferber had written a sprawling kind of novel in *Show Boat*. It didn't have the tightness that a play requires. I wanted to keep the spirit of Edna's book and the one focal influence I could find was the Mississippi River, because she had quite consciously brought the river into every important turn in the story. So I decided to write a theme, a river theme. I put the song into the throat of a character who is a rugged and untutored philosopher. It's a song of resignation with an implied protest. . . . There are no rhymes at all for a long part of the song's refrain, and when you imagine the refrain with rhymes you realize how much weaker it might be."

"Old Devil Moon." Music by Burton Lane; lyric by E. Y. Harburg. Sung by the bewitched Donald Richards and Ella Logan in *Finian's Rainbow* (NY 1947), and by Alan Gilbert and Beryl Seton in London version (1947). In the play the boy leads into the song by telling the girl: "That's the valley legend—'They who meet on an April night are forever lost in love/ If there is moonlight all about and there's no moon above.'" "I wonder who thought it up," says the girl. "I did," says the boy. The song's melody had been previously written for a movie but never used.

"Old Soft Shoe, The." Music by Morgan Lewis; lyric by Nancy Hamilton. Ray Bolger's trademark number from *Three to Make Ready* (NY 1946), which found the performer—in straw hat, striped blazer, white flannels, and cane—recalling the dance that always got the biggest hand at the Palace.

Oliver! (1960). Music, lyrics & book by Lionel Bart, based on Charles Dickens' novel *Oliver Twist*.

SONGS: "Food, Glorious Food," "Oliver!," "Boy for Sale," "That's Your Funeral," "Where Is Love?," "Consider Yourself," "You've Got to Pick a Pocket or Two," "It's a Fine Life," "I'd Do Anything," "Oom-Pah-Pah," "As Long as He Needs Me," "Who Will Buy?," "Reviewing the Situation."

LONDON: June 30, 1960
NEW THEATRE; 2,618 p.

Presented by Donald Albery; directed by Peter Coe; settings & costumes, Sean Kenny; lighting, John Wyckham; music director, Marcus Dods; orchestrations, Eric Rogers.

CAST: Ron Moody (*Fagin*), Georgia Brown (*Nancy*), Keith Hamshere (*Oliver Twist*), Paul Whitsun-Jones (*Mr. Bumble*), Hope Jackman (*Mrs. Corney*), Danny Sewell (*Bill Sikes*), George Bishop (*Mr. Brownlow*), Martin Horsey (*The Artful Dodger*), Barry Humphries (*Sowerberry*).

NEW YORK: Jan. 6, 1963
IMPERIAL THEATRE; 744 p.

Presented by David Merrick & Donald Albery; directed by Peter Coe; settings & costumes, Sean Kenny; lighting, John Wyckham; music director, Donald Pippin; orchestrations, Eric Rogers.

CAST: Clive Revill (*Fagin*), Georgia Brown (*Nancy*), Bruce Prochnick (*Oliver Twist*), Willoughby Goddard (*Mr. Bumble*), Hope Jackman (*Mrs. Corney*), Danny Sewell (*Bill Sikes*), Geoffrey Lumb (*Mr. Brownlow*), David Jones (*The Artful Dodger*), Barry Humphries (*Sowerberry*).

LONDON: April 26, 1967
PICCADILLY THEATRE; 331 p.

Presented by Donald Albery; restaged by David Phethean; settings & costumes, Sean Kenny; lighting, John Wyckham; music director, Michael Moores; orchestrations, Eric Rogers.

CAST: Barry Humphries (*Fagin*), Marti Webb (*Nancy*), Paul Bartlett (*Oliver Twist*), Tom De Ville (*Mr. Bumble*), Pamela Pitchford (*Mrs. Corney*), Martin Dell (*Bill Sikes*), Gavin Gordon (*Mr. Brownlow*), Leslie Stone (*The Artful Dodger*).

Dickens' novel about the orphan Oliver Twist and his adventures as one of Fagin's pickpocketing crew became, for twelve years, the longest-running musical in the history of the London stage. It also holds the distinction of having the longest run of any British musical ever presented in NY. Before London, however, the production received mixed notices and there was talk of closing it on the road. With his third musical and first as composer-lyricist-librettist, Lionel Bart established himself as Britain's outstanding musical-theatre talent of the 60s. The performance of Ron Moody and the sets and costumes of Sean Kenny were also highly praised. During original London run, four actors played Fagin (the last was Aubrey Woods), four actresses played Nancy (the last, Nicolette Roeg), and 12 boys played Oliver. In NY, Clive Revill was succeeded as Fagin by Robin Ramsey (6-64), Georgia Brown by Maura K. Wedge (6-64) and Judy

Bruce (7-64). Beginning Nov. 1964, the company toured eight months.

Other Dickens novels adapted as musicals: *The Posthumous Papers of the Pickwick Club* (*Mr. Pickwick*, NY 1903, and *Pickwick*, L 1963); *A Tale of Two Cities* (*Two Cities*, L 1969).

FILM VERSION: Ron Moody, Harry Secombe, Shani Wallis (Col. 1968, Carol Reed dir.).

Olsen and Johnson, actors, producers. (John Siguard) Ole Olsen, b. Peru, Ind., Nov. 6, 1892; d. Albuquerque, N. Mex., Jan. 26, 1963. (Harold) Chick Johnson, b. Chicago, Ill., March 5, 1891; d. Las Vegas, Nev., Feb. 25, 1962. Raucous, raffish comedy team that toured vaudeville circuits, 1914–1937, until scoring resounding Bway hit in *Hellzapoppin*.

Asterisk indicates team was also co-producer:

1933 Take a Chance (*Duke Stanley; Louis Webb,* repl.)
1938 Hellzapoppin *
1939 Streets of Paris (co-prod. only)
1941 Sons o' Fun *
1942 Count Me In (co-prod. only)
1944 Laffing Room Only *
1950 Pardon Our French *

"On a Clear Day (You Can See Forever)." Music by Burton Lane; lyric by Alan Jay Lerner. In *On a Clear Day You Can See Forever* (NY 1965), psychiatrist John Cullum urges a patient with extrasensory perception (Barbara Harris) to appreciate her own worth.

"On the Amazon." Music by Vivian Ellis; lyric by Clifford Grey & Greatrex Newman. In *Mr. Cinders* (L 1929) Bobby Howes recounted his adventures in the South American jungles where hypodermics howl, prophylactics prowl, pax vobiscum bite, and epiglottis fight, and where he was surrounded by snarling equinox, wild velocipedes, frenzied adenoids, and deadly stethoscopes.

"On the Street Where You Live." Music by Frederick Loewe; lyric by Alan Jay Lerner. The only romantic ballad in *My Fair Lady* (NY 1956) was sung by the tenacious Michael King as he paced up and down Wimpole Street just to get a glimpse of his beloved. In London version (1958), it was sung by Peter Gilmore.

"On the Sunny Side of the Street." Music by Jimmy McHugh; lyric by Dorothy Fields. Antidepression Depression song sung by Harry Richman in Lew Leslie's *International Revue* (NY 1930).

On the Town (1944). Music by Leonard Bernstein; lyrics & book by Betty Comden & Adolph Green, from idea by Jerome Robbins.

SONGS: "New York, New York," "Come Up to My Place," "Carried Away," "Lonely Town," "I Can Cook, Too" (lyric with Bernstein), "Lucky to Be Me," "Ya Got Me," "Some Other Time."

NEW YORK: Dec. 28, 1944
ADELPHI THEATRE; 463 p.

Presented by Oliver Smith & Paul Feigay; directed by George Abbott; choreographed by Jerome Robbins; settings, Oliver Smith; costumes, Alvin Colt; lighting, Peggy Clark; music director, Max Goberman; orchestrations, Bernstein, Hershy Kay, Don Walker, Ted Royal.

CAST: Sono Osato (*Ivy Smith*), Nancy Walker (*Brunhilde Esterhazy*), Betty Comden (*Claire de Loon*), Adolph Green (*Ozzie*), John Battles (*Gabey*), Robert Chisholm (*Judge Pitkin W. Bridgework*), Cris Alexander (*Chip Offenbloch*), Alice Pearce (*Lucy*

Schmeeler), Ray Harrison (*Great Lover*), Allyn Ann McLerie (*Doll Girl*), Ben Piazza (*Boy*).

LONDON: May 30, 1963
PRINCE OF WALES THEATRE; 53 p.
Presented by H. M. Tennent Ltd., with Roger Stevens & Oliver Smith; directed & choreographed by Joe Layton; settings, Olivet Smith; costumes, Cynthia Tingey; lighting, Joe Davis; music director, Lawrence Leonard.

CAST: Andrea Jaffe (*Ivy Smith*), Carol Arthur (*Hildegarde Esterhazy*), Gillian Lewis (*Claire deLoon*), Elliott Gould (*Ozzie*), Don McKay (*Gabey*), Franklin Kiser (*Chip Offenbloch*), John Humphrey (*Judge Pitkin W. Bridgework*), Rosamund Greenwood (*Lucy Schmeeler*).

During World War II, *On the Town* was the urban counterpart to the rural *Oklahoma!*, celebrating the wonders of big-city life just as the previous musical had sung of the glories of the American Southwest. Its plot was slight: three sailors, Gabey, Chip, and Ozzie, on 24-hour shore leave in NY, meet three girls, Ivy, Claire, and Hildy, and discover such landmarks as the subway, the Museum of Natural History, Central Park, Times Square, assorted nightclubs, and Coney Island. Once their leave is up, the boys go back to their ship—and another trio of bounding sailors go on the town. What conflict there was had to do with Gabey's mistaking Ivy, a struggling ballet dancer, for a celebrity because she was chosen "Miss Turnstiles" in a subway competition.

The musical stemmed from the Robbins-Bernstein ballet *Fancy Free*, about three sailors trying to pick up girls, which Smith and Feigay wanted to expand as a musical comedy for their first producing venture. At one time the lyricist was supposed to be John Latouche, but Bernstein brought in Betty Comden and Adolph Green. Because all six involved with the show were making their Bway debuts, they signed the experienced George Abbott as director. During Bway run, Miss Comden was succeeded by Ruth Webb, Green by Joshua Shelley, Miss Osato by Allyn Ann McLerie.

The first NY revival was an off-Bway production in 1959, which lasted 70 performances. The cast included Harold Lang (*Gabey*), Pat Carroll (*Hildy*), Evelyn Russell (*Claire*), Wisa D'Orso (*Ivy*), Joe Bova (*Ozzie*), and William Hickey (*Chip*). It marked Joe Layton's professional debut as choreographer.

The second NY revival was an on-Bway production in 1971, which lasted 73 performances. The cast included Phyllis Newman (*Claire*), Bernadette Peters (*Hildy*), Ron Husmann (*Gabey*), Donna McKechnie (*Ivy*), Jess Richards (*Chip*), and Remak Ramsay (*Ozzie*). It was directed and choreographed by Ron Field.

FILM VERSION: Frank Sinatra, Gene Kelly, Vera-Ellen, Betty Garrett (mostly new songs) (MGM 1949, Kelly and Stanley Donen dirs.).

On Your Toes (1936). Music by Richard Rodgers; lyrics by Lorenz Hart; book by Rodgers, Hart & George Abbott.

SONGS: "The Three B's," "It's Got to Be Love," "Too Good for the Average Man," "There's a Small Hotel," "The Heart Is Quicker than the Eye," "Quiet Night," "Glad to Be Unhappy," "On Your Toes," "Slaughter on Tenth Avenue."

NEW YORK: Nov. 29, 1936
IMPERIAL THEATRE; 315 p.
Presented by Dwight Deere Wiman; directed by Worthington Miner; choreographed by George Balanchine; settings, Jo Mielziner; cos-

tumes, Irene Sharaff; music director, Gene Salzer; orchestrations, Hans Spialek.

CAST: Ray Bolger (*Junior Dolan*), Tamara Geva (*Vera Barnova*), Luella Gear (*Peggy Porterfield*), Monty Woolley (*Sergei Alexandrovitch*), Doris Carson (*Frankie Frayne*), David Morris (*Sidney Cohen*), Robert Sidney (*Vassilli*), Demetrios Vilan (*Konstantine Morrosine*), George Church (dancer), Edgar Fairchild & Adam Carroll (duo-pianos).

LONDON: Feb. 5, 1937
PALACE THEATRE; 123 p.

Presented by Lee Ephraim & Dwight Deere Wiman; directed by Leslie Henson; dances reproduced by Andy Anderson; settings, Joseph & Phil Harker; costumes, Betty Boor; music director, Lew Stone; orchestrations, Hans Spialek.

CAST: Jack Whiting (*Junior Dolan*), Vera Zorina (*Vera Barnova*), Olive Blakeney (*Peggy Porterfield*), Vernon Kelso (*Sergei Alexandrovitch*), Gina Malo (*Frankie Frayne*), Dick Taylor (*Vassilli*), Eddie Pola (*Sidney Cohen*), Jack Donohue (*Konstantine Morrosine*), Hyacinth Hazell (chorus), Bruce Merryl & Harry Foster (duo-pianos).

On Your Toes was a major theatrical breakthrough because of its use of ballet as an integral part of the plot of a musical. In the story, Junior Dolan, an ex-vaudeville hoofer now a NY music teacher, persuades a Russian ballet company to perform a modern ballet, "Slaughter on Tenth Avenue," with himself in the lead. During the performance Junior is mistaken for another dancer who owes a gambling debt and is forced to keep dancing after the ballet is over in order to avoid being shot by two thugs in the theatre. The musical marked Ray Bolger's first major role and George Balanchine's first

major choreography on Bway. Monty Woolley made his acting debut in it as a Diaghilev-type impressario (a part originally earmarked for Gregory Ratoff). One of the comic highlights was the finale of Act I in which Bolger, a last-minute substitute as a nubian slave in "La Princesse Zenobia" ballet, forgets to blacken his body below the neck.

Initially, Rodgers and Hart had conceived the idea of the musical as a screen vehicle for Fred Astaire, but Astaire turned it down because it gave him no chance to wear top hat, white tie, and tails. George Abbott, the book's co-author, was to have been the director but delays forced him to withdraw; he did, however, help restage the show during its Boston tryout. Vera Zorina had her first musical-comedy role in the London production.

Spurred by the success of the 1952 revival of *Pal Joey*, Abbott produced and staged a revival of *On Your Toes* in 1954. Zorina, Bobby Van (*Junior*), Elaine Stritch (*Peggy*), Kay Coulter (*Frankie*), Joshua Shelley (*Sidney*), and Nathaniel Frey (*thug*) were in the cast. The run lasted 64 performances.

FILM VERSION: Vera Zorina and Eddie Albert (no songs) (Warner 1939, Ray Enright dir.).

"On Your Toes." Music by Richard Rodgers; lyric by Lorenz Hart. The importance of scaling the heights—whether it's to pick apples, live in luxury, or win the pretty lady. Doris Carson, Ray Bolger, and David Morris offered the advice in *On Your Toes* (NY 1936); Gina Malo, Jack Whiting, and Eddie Pola did it in the London version (1937).

"Once in a Blue Moon." Music by Jerome Kern; lyric by Anne Caldwell.

Philosophical observation on the un-likelihood of finding true love introduced in *Stepping Stones* (NY 1923) by Roy Hoyer, Evelyn Herbert, John Lambert, and Lilyan and Ruth White.

"Once in a Lifetime." Music & lyric by Leslie Bricusse & Anthony Newley. Emotional number of unbounded self-assurance sung by Anthony Newley in *Stop the World—I Want to Get Off* (L 1961, NY 1962).

"Once in Love with Amy." Music & lyric by Frank Loesser. Ray Bolger's show-stopper in *Where's Charley?* (NY 1948), in which the singer not only expressed his own affection but also had the entire audience singing Amy's praises. In London version (1958) the lover was played by Norman Wisdom. Loesser had originally written the piece during World War II as "Once in Love with Mary" to show his fondness for Mary Healy, the wife of close friend Peter Lind Hayes.

"Once Upon a Time." Music by Charles Strouse; lyric by Lee Adams. In *All American* (NY 1962), Ray Bolger and Eileen Herlie gently tell each other about the loves they had "very long ago."

"One Alone." Music by Sigmund Romberg; lyric by Otto Harbach & Oscar Hammerstein II. Vow of romantic fidelity taken by Robert Halliday in *The Desert Song* (NY 1926) and by Harry Welchman in London version (1927). The song was presented as the third number in a musical debate entitled "Eastern and Western Love." Upholding the "Eastern" view, a desert chieftain, in "Let Love Go," advocates brief, uninvolved flings, and a Riff lieutenant, in "If One

Flower Grows Alone in Your Garden," proposes a harem. The Red Shadow then rejects both philosophies by revealing the "Western" attitude—"One alone, to be my own."

"One Big Union for Two." Music & lyric by Harold Rome. Romantic devotion expressed through the language of collective bargaining ("We'll have no lockouts to make us frown,/ No scabbing when I'm out of town"). Introduced by the chorus in *Pins and Needles* (NY 1937).

"One Boy." Music by Charles Strouse; lyric by Lee Adams. Girlish pleasure at going steady harmonized by Susan Watson, Jessica Albright, and Sharon Lerit in *Bye Bye Birdie* (NY 1960), then reprised (as "One Guy") by Chita Rivera. Singers in the London company (1961) were Sylvia Tysick, Paula Hendrix, Alexandria Jelec, and Miss Rivera.

"One I'm Looking For, The." Music by Philip Charig & Joseph Meyer; lyric by Ira Gershwin & Douglas Furber. In a frequently encored scene in *That's a Good Girl* (L 1928), Elsie Randolph, as a detective disguised as a sniffing German girl in pigtails, expressed her desire for the blandly dissuading Jack Buchanan.

"One Kiss." Music by Sigmund Romberg; lyric by Oscar Hammerstein II. Love duet in *The New Moon*, sung by Robert Halliday and Evelyn Herbert (NY 1928), and by Howett Worster and Evelyn Laye (L 1929). The main theme of the refrain is actually a waltzing version of Vincent Youmans' "No, No, Nanette," which, in turn, had been based on Youmans' waltzing "My Boy and I."

One Touch of Venus (1943). Music by Kurt Weill; lyrics by Ogden Nash; book by S. J. Perelman & Ogden Nash, based on *The Tinted Venus* by F. Anstey.

SONGS: "One Touch of Venus," "How Much I Love You," "I'm a Stranger Here Myself," "Speak Low," "West Wind," "Foolish Heart," "The Trouble with Women," "That's Him," "Wooden Wedding."

NEW YORK: Oct. 7, 1943
IMPERIAL THEATRE; 567 p.

Presented by Cheryl Crawford & John Wildberg; directed by Elia Kazan; choreographed by Agnes de Mille; settings, Howard Bay; costumes, Paul DuPont, Kermit Love, Main Bocher; music director, Maurice Abravanel; orchestrations, Kurt Weill.

CAST: Mary Martin (*Venus*), Kenny Baker (*Rodney Hatch*), John Boles (*Whitelaw Savory*), Paula Laurence (*Molly Grant*), Teddy Hart (*Taxi Black*), Sono Osato (dance soloist), Harry Clark (*Stanley*), Allyn Ann McLerie (dancer).

Kurt Weill's longest-running Bway musical was a fantasy in the *I Married an Angel* vein about a statue of Venus—in the *Adonis* or *Pygmalion* vein—which comes to life and falls in love with a barber named Rodney Hatch. Venus is, in turn, beloved by Whitelaw Savory, head of the Whitelaw Savory Foundation of Modern Art. When, in the ballet "Venus in Ozone Heights," our heroine dreams of life with Rodney, she realizes it is not for her and back to marble she turns. Then, miraculously, Rodney finds a girl who looks just like her. The musical, originally intended for Marlene Dietrich, was Mary Martin's first starring role on Bway. During run, Kenny Baker was succeeded by Ben Cutler.

FILM VERSION: Ava Gardner, Robert Walker, Dick Haymes (Univ. 1948, William A. Seiter dir.).

O'Neal, Zelma (née Zelma Schroeder), actress, singer, dancer; b. Rock Falls, Ind., May 29, 1907. High-spirited blonde comedienne who scored biggest Bway successes in two DeSylva–Brown–Henderson shows: *Good News!* (singing "The Varsity Drag") and *Follow Thru* ("Button Up Your Overcoat").

1927 Good News! (*Flo*)
1928 Good News! (L) (*Flo*)
1929 Follow Thru (*Angie Howard*)
1931 The Gang's All Here (*Willy Wilson*)
1933 Nice Goings On (L) (*Tutti*)
1935 Jack o' Diamonds (L) (*Peggy Turner*)
1936 Swing Along (L) (*Miami*)

"Only a Rose." Music by Rudolf Friml; lyric by Brian Hooker. Carolyn Thomson's keepsake gift to Dennis King in *The Vagabond King* (NY 1925) prompted this romantic duet. In London production (1927), it was sung by Winnie Melville and Derek Oldham.

"Orange Grove in California, An." Music & lyric by Irving Berlin. Idyllic locale depicted in *Music Box Revue of 1923* (NY) and described by Grace Moore and John Steel. During the number the audience was sprayed with orange-scented perfume as orange-colored lights illuminated the scene.

Orbach, (Jerome) Jerry, actor, singer; b. New York, Oct. 20, 1935. Actor in dramas and musicals whose off- and on-Bway hits were *The Fantasticks* (introducing "Try to Remember"), *Carnival*, and *Promises, Promises*.

1958	The Threepenny Opera (r) (*Macheath*, repl.)
1960	The Fantasticks (*El Gallo*)
1961	Carnival (*Paul*)
1964	The Cradle Will Rock (r) (*Larry Foreman*)
1966	Annie Get Your Gun (r) (*Charlie Davenport*)
1969	Promises, Promises (*Chuck Baxter*)
1975	Chicago (*Billy Flynn*)

"**Other People's Babies.**" Music by Vivian Ellis; lyric by A. P. Herbert. Nanny's lament sung by Norah Howard in *Streamline* (L 1934).

"**Other Side of the Tracks, The.**" Music by Cy Coleman; lyric by Carolyn Leigh. Young Belle Poitrine's determination to better herself in *Little Me*. Virginia Martin sang it in NY (1962), Eileen Gourlay in London (1964).

"**Our Language of Love.**" Music by Marguerite Monnot; lyric by Julian More, David Heneker & Monty Norman. No words are needed for Keith Michell and Elizabeth Seal to express their love in *Irma la Douce* (L 1958, NY 1960).

Our Miss Gibbs (1909). Music by Ivan Caryll & Lionel Monckton; lyrics by Adrian Ross & Percy Greenbank; book by "Cryptos" (Caryll, Monckton, Ross, Greenbank), "constructed" by James T. Tanner.

SONGS: "Yorkshire" (Monckton-Ralph Roberts), "Mary" (Monckton-Ross), "Moonstruck" (Monckton-Monckton), "Yip-I-Addy-I-Ay!" (John Flynn-Will Cobb-George Grossmith), "My Yorkshire Lassie" (Caryll-Greenbank), "Not That Sort of Person" (Monckton-Grossmith).

LONDON: Jan. 23, 1909
GAIETY THEATRE; 636 p.

Presented by George Edwardes; directed by Edwardes & Edward Royce; settings, Joseph Harker; costumes, Comelli; music director, Ivan Caryll.

CAST: Gertie Millar (*Mary Gibbs*), George Grossmith, Jr. (*Hon. Hughie Pierrepoint*), Robert Hale (*Slithers*), J. Edward Fraser (*Lord Eynsford*), Edmund Payne (*Timothy Gibbs*), Denise Orme (*Lady Elizabeth Thanet*), Maisie Gay (*Mrs. Farquhar*).

NEW YORK: Aug. 29, 1910
KNICKERBOCKER THEATRE; 64 p.

Presented by Charles Frohman; directed by Thomas Reynolds; music director, William T. Francis; added songs by Jerome Kern.

CAST: Pauline Chase (*Mary Gibbs*), Ernest Lambart (*Hon. Hughie Pierrepoint*), Bert Leslie (*Slithers*), Craufurd Kent (*Lord Eynsford*), Fred Wright, Jr. (*Timothy Gibbs*), Julia James (*Lady Elizabeth Thanet*), Mollie Lowell (*Mrs. Farquhar*).

The musical stage's concern with the fortunes of a shop girl, begun with *The Shop Girl* in 1894, continued with *Our Miss Gibbs*. In this musical, Mary Gibbs, a Yorkshire lass, works in the flower department of Garrod's Department Stores. Her heart belongs to Lord Eynsford, masquerading as bank clerk Harry Lancaster, but Eynsford is engaged to Lady Elizabeth Thanet, who much prefers Hughie Pierrepoint, an amateur criminal. When Mary learns of Eynsford's deception, she quits her job and goes off to the Franco-British Exhibition, at White City, Shepherd's Bush. There, once Eynsford proves his honorable intentions, the lovers are reconciled. Gertie Millar scored a great hit in the title role, particularly in her singing of

"Moonstruck," written by her husband, Lionel Monckton.

"Out of My Dreams." Music by Richard Rodgers; lyric by Oscar Hammerstein II. Waltzing desire to exchange romantic dreams for reality introduced by Joan Roberts and girls in *Oklahoma!* (NY 1943). The song leads directly into the "Laurie Makes Up Her Mind" ballet, which ends Act I. Betty

Jane Watson sang the ballad in the London company (1947).

"Out of the Clear Blue Sky." Music by Vernon Duke; lyric by Ogden Nash. An accidental meeting with a stranger and it's love. Peter Kelley and Sue Hight sang it and Maria Karnilova and Robert Pagent danced it in *Two's Company* (NY 1952).

❧ P ❧

"Pack Up Your Sins and Go to the Devil." Music & lyric by Irving Berlin. Syncopated invitation to join the "thousands of Joneses, Browns, O'Hoolihans, Cohens, and Bradys" who are enjoying a hot time in Hades. The number, presented as the first-act finale of *Music Box Revue of 1922*, was sung by the McCarthy Sisters in a scene depicting Satan's Palace with Charlotte Greenwood as the underworld ruler. In London revue, *On With the Dance* (1925), it was sung by Alice Delysia.

Paige, Janis (née Donna Mae Jaden), actress, singer; b. Tacoma, Wash., Sept. 16, 1922. Statuesque blonde who had career in Hollywood films and nightclubs before making Bway bow in 1951. Miss Paige introduced "There Once Was a Man" in *The Pajama Game.*

    1954   The Pajama Game (*Babe Williams*)
    1963   Here's Love (*Doris Walker*)
    1968   Mame (*Mame Dennis,* repl.)

Pajama Game, The (1954). Music & lyrics by Richard Adler & Jerry Ross; book by George Abbott & Richard

Bissell, based on Bissell's novel *7½ Cents.*

SONGS: "I'm Not at All in Love," "I'll Never Be Jealous Again," "Hey, There," "Her Is," "Once a Year Day," "Small Talk," "There Once Was a Man," "Steam Heat," "Hernando's Hideaway," "7½ Cents."

NEW YORK: May 13, 1954
ST. JAMES THEATRE; 1,063 p.

    Presented by Frederick Brisson, Robert E. Griffith & Harold S. Prince; directed by George Abbott & Jerome Robbins; choreographed by Bob Fosse; settings & costumes, Lemuel Ayers; music director, Harold Hastings; orchestrations, Don Walker.

    CAST: John Raitt (*Sid Sorokin*), Janis Paige (*Babe Williams*), Eddie Foy Jr. (*Hines*), Carol Haney (*Gladys*), Reta Shaw (*Mabel*), Stanley Prager (*Prez*), Peter Gennaro (*Worker*), Rae Allen (chorus), Virginia Martin (chorus), Shirley MacLaine (dancer), Carmen Alvarez (dancer).

LONDON: Oct. 13, 1955
COLISEUM; 588 p.

    Presented by Williamson Music Ltd. & Prince Littler; restaged by Robert E. Griffith; dances reproduced by Zoya Leporska; settings & costumes, Lemuel Ayers; music director, Robert Lowe; orchestrations, Don Walker.

CAST: Max Wall (*Hines*), Joy Nichols (*Babe Williams*), Edmund Hockridge (*Sid Sorokin*), Elizabeth Seal (*Gladys*), Joan Emney (*Mabel*), Frank Lawless (*Prez*).

The unlikely musical-comedy subject of a threatened strike in a pajama factory was turned into one of Bway's biggest hits of the 50s. It provided songwriters Richard Adler and Jerry Ross with their first book musical, it was the first production sponsored by Brisson, Griffith and Prince, and it marked Bob Fosse's debut as a choreographer. In the story, Sid, the new superintendent of the Sleep Tite Pajama factory in Cedar Rapids, Iowa, falls in love with Babe, the leader of the workers' grievance committee. Management and labor end up singing in tune once the workers are given a 7½-cent raise. (The factory was modeled after the H. B. Glover Co., of Dubuque, Iowa, where author Bissell's father had worked.)

Carol Haney won notice in her only Bway appearance as a dancer (so did her understudy, Shirley MacLaine, when she substituted for a few performances). During Bway run, John Raitt was succeeded by George Wallace (10-56); Janis Paige by Pat Marshall (6-55) and Julie Wilson (1-56); Eddie Foy Jr. by Jack Goode (9-56); Miss Haney by Helen Gallagher (6-55). The US tour, which opened in Jan. 1955 and continued for two years, featured Larry Douglas (*Sid*), Fran Warren (*Babe*), Buster West (*Hines*), Pat Stanley (*Gladys*). In London facsimile, Elizabeth Seal scored a hit in her first featured role.

In 1973 composer Adler co-produced a revival of *The Pajama Game*, which George Abbott staged. It contained an interracial romance between black Barbara McNair (*Babe*) and white Hal Linden (*Sid*). Cab Calloway (*Hines*), Sharron Miller (*Gladys*), and Mary Jo Catlett (*Mabel*) were also in it. The show ran 65 performances.

Bissell wrote a novel, *Say, Darling*, about his experience with *The Pajama Game*, which, with his wife, he then adapted into a "comedy about a musical." Produced on Bway in 1958, it had David Wayne as the Bissell character, Johnny Desmond as a combination of Adler and Ross, Robert Morse suggesting Harold Prince, and Jerome Cowan in the Abbott part. Vivian Blaine, as an unidentifiable actress, was also in the cast, and the score was by Jule Styne, Betty Comden and Adolph Green. Abe Burrows directed. The run lasted 332 performances.

FILM VERSION: Doris Day, John Raitt, Eddie Foy Jr. (Warner 1957, George Abbott, Stanley Donen dirs.).

Pal Joey (1940). Music by Richard Rodgers; lyrics by Lorenz Hart; book by John O'Hara, based on his short stories.

SONGS: "You Mustn't Kick It Around," "I Could Write a Book," "Chicago," "That Terrific Rainbow," "Happy Hunting Horn," "Bewitched," "Pal Joey," "The Flower Garden of My Heart," "Zip," "Den of Iniquity," "Take Him," "Do It the Hard Way."

NEW YORK: Dec. 25, 1940
ETHEL BARRYMORE THEATRE; 374 p.

Presented & directed by George Abbott; choreographed by Robert Alton; settings & lighting, Jo Mielziner; costumes, John Koenig; music director, Harry Levant; orchestrations, Hans Spialek.

CAST: Vivienne Segal (*Vera Simpson*), Gene Kelly (*Joey Evans*), June

Havoc (*Gladys Bumps*), Leila Ernst (*Linda English*), Jack Durant (*Ludlow Lowell*), Jean Casto (*Melba Snyder*), Van Johnson (*Victor*), Stanley Donen (*Albert Doane*), Sondra Barrett (*The Kid*), Jerome Whyte (*Stagehand*).

NEW YORK: Jan. 3, 1952
BROADHURST THEATRE; 542 p.

Presented by Jule Styne & Leonard Key, with Anthony Brady Farrell; directed by David Alexander & Robert Alton; choreographed by Alton; settings, Oliver Smith; costumes, Miles White; lighting, Peggy Clark; music director, Max Meth; orchestrations, Don Walker, Hans Spialek.

CAST: Vivienne Segal (*Vera Simpson*), Harold Lang (*Joey Evans*), Helen Gallagher (*Gladys Bumps*), Patricia Northrop (*Linda English*), Lionel Stander (*Ludlow Lowell*), Elaine Stritch (*Melba Snyder*), Robert Fortier (*Victor*), Helen Wood (*The Kid*).

LONDON: March 31, 1954
PRINCES THEATRE; 245 p.

Presented by Jack Hylton; directed by Neil Hartley; dances reproduced by George Martin; settings, Oliver Smith; costumes, Miles White; music director, Cyril Ornadel; orchestrations, Don Walker, Hans Spialek.

CAST: Carol Bruce (*Vera Simpson*), Harold Lang (*Joey Evans*), Jean Brampton (*Gladys Bumps*), Sally Bazely (*Linda English*), Lou Jacobi (*Ludlow Lowell*), Olga Lowe (*Melba Snyder*), Malcolm Goddard (*Victor*), Maureen Creigh (*The Kid*).

The John O'Hara *New Yorker* short stories, written as a series of letters from "Your Pal Joey" to a bandleader friend, were adapted into a sharp, adult Bway musical that was considered daring because of its anti-hero hero. (A previous, though unsuccessful, example was found in the Cole Porter–Herbert Fields *The New York-*

ers, presented 10 years earlier.) Joey is an mc-entertainer at Mike's nightspot in Chicago, where he meets innocent Linda but drops her in favor of wealthy Vera. Vera builds a nightclub for her paramour—the Chez Joey—but she soon tires of him and, at the end, Joey is still scheming new schemes. *Pal Joey*, which gave Gene Kelly his first leading role, was also the only musical authored by John O'Hara. During original Bway run, Kelly was succeeded by Georgie Tapps (9-41), Jack Durant by David Burns (8-41). In the more appreciated 1952 revival, Vivienne Segal repeated her original role, and Bob Fosse was Harold Lang's understudy. During run, Helen Gallagher was succeeded by Nancy Walker (12-52). For tour, which lasted seven months, Miss Segal was succeeded by Carol Bruce, Lionel Stander by Harry Clark.

FILM VERSION: Frank Sinatra, Rita Hayworth, Kim Novak (Col. 1957, George Sidney dir.).

Panama Hattie (1940). Music & lyrics by Cole Porter; book by Herbert Fields & B. G. DeSylva.

SONGS: "Visit Panama," "My Mother Would Love You," "I've Still Got My Health," "Fresh as a Daisy," "Let's Be Buddies," "Make It Another Old Fashioned, Please," "I'm Throwing a Ball Tonight," "All I've Got to Get Now Is My Man."

NEW YORK: Oct. 30, 1940
46TH ST. THEATRE; 501 p.

Presented by B. G. DeSylva; directed by Edgar MacGregor; choreographed by Robert Alton; settings & costumes, Raoul Pène du Bois; music director, Gene Salzer; orchestrations, Robert Russell Bennett, Hans Spialek, Don Walker.

CAST: Ethel Merman (*Hattie Maloney*), Arthur Treacher (*Vivian*

Budd), Betty Hutton (*Florrie*), James Dunn (*Nick Bullett*), Phyllis Brooks (*Leila Tree*), Joan Carroll (*Geraldine Bullett*), Rags Ragland (*Woozy Hogan*), Pat Harrington (*Skat Briggs*), Frankie Hyers (*Windy Deegan*), Carmen D'Antonio (featured dancer), Nadine Gae (*Chiquita*), June Allyson (dancer), Betsy Blair (dancer), Lucille Bremer (dancer), Vera-Ellen (dancer), Constance Dowling (dancer), Doris Dowling (dancer).

LONDON: Nov. 4, 1943
PICCADILLY THEATRE; 308 p.

Presented by Emile Littler, Lee Ephraim, Tom Arnold; directed by William Mollison; choreographed by Wendy Toye; settings, Clifford Pember; costumes, Norman Hartnell; music director, Harold Collins.

CAST: Bebe Daniels (*Hattie Maloney*), Max Wall (*Eddy Brown*), Ivan Brandt (*Nick Bullett*), Claude Hulbert (*Vivian Budd*), Richard Hearne (*Loopy Smith*), Frances Marsden (*Florrie*), Jack Stanford (*Joe Briggs*), Georgia MacKinnon (*Leila Tree*), Betty Blackler (*Elizabeth Bullett*), Marian Pola (*Chiquita*).

Ethel Merman's penultimate Bway musical with songs by Cole Porter was the first to give her solo star billing. It was also the biggest hit singer and songwriter had together. The idea of the musical was vaguely suggested by "Katie Went to Haiti," a song in *DuBarry Was a Lady*, which was also written by Fields, DeSylva, and Porter for Ethel Merman. In Panama City, flashy nightclub owner Hattie Maloney is engaged to marry blueblood divorcé Nick Bullett. Nick's eight-year-old daughter must pass on her future stepmother, which makes for some tense moments before the two finally become buddies. June Allyson, Betty Hutton's understudy, took over the Hutton role for one performance. During run, Phyllis Brooks was succeeded by Virginia Field.

FILM VERSION: Ann Sothern and Red Skelton (MGM 1942, Norman Z. McLeod dir.).

"Papa, Won't You Dance with Me?" Music by Jule Styne; lyric by Sammy Cahn. Turn-of-the-century song-and-dance polka introduced—with nightly encores—by Nanette Fabray and Jack McCauley in *High Button Shoes* (NY 1947). In London production (1948) it was performed by Kay Kimber and Sidney James.

Papp, Joseph (né Joseph Papirofsky), producer; b. Brooklyn, NY, June 22, 1921. From 1956, Papp has headed the NY Shakespeare Festival, which since 1962 has given free performances in Central Park. In 1967 he founded the Public Theatre, where *Hair* was first performed, and from 1973-77 he was head of the Lincoln Center play series. Bib: *Enter Joseph Papp* by Stuart Little (Coward McCann, NY 1974).

1967 Hair
1969 Stomp
     Sambo
1970 Mod-Donna (also dir.)
1971 Two Gentlemen of Verona
1973 More than You Deserve
1975 A Chorus Line

"Parade in Town, A." Music & lyric by Stephen Sondheim. In *Anyone Can Whistle* (NY 1964), Angela Lansbury, as the mayor of the town, sadly but defiantly watches the parade pass her by.

"Paree." Music by Arthur Schwartz; lyric by Howard Dietz. The charms of Paris extolled by an enraptured Beatrice Lillie in *At Home Abroad* (NY 1935). Miss Lillie delivered the accolade while perched halfway up a

Moulin Rouge backdrop wearing an elaborately plumed black hat, gold satin evening gown, black stockings and arm-length gloves, and holding a cigarette in a foot-long holder.

"Paris Loves Lovers." Music & lyric by Cole Porter. In *Silk Stockings* (NY 1955) a smitten Don Ameche tried to convince a doubting Hildegarde Neff of the city's power to aid romance.

"Parisian Pierrot." Music & lyric by Noël Coward. Delicate ballad of sad Pierrot's transient reign sung by Gertrude Lawrence as Pierrot (with Eileen Molyneux as Harlequin and Jill Williams as Columbine) in *London Calling!* (L 1923). In *André Charlot's Revue of 1924* (NY 1924), Miss Lawrence again sang it (with Barbara Roberts and Miss Williams). Coward claimed the idea came to him at a Berlin nightclub while watching a frowsy blonde do an act with a rag Pierrot doll dressed in black velvet. He immediately thought of the title and began composing the piece in the taxi on the way back to his hotel. It became Coward's first popular song success.

"Party's Over, The." Music by Jule Styne; lyric by Betty Comden & Adolph Green. Introduced by Judy Holliday in *Bells Are Ringing* (NY 1956) as she leaves a glittering penthouse party realizing that her romance is over. Janet Blair sang it in London version (1957).

"Party's Over Now, The." Music and lyric by Noël Coward. A description of the end of an all-night party that served as the finale of the revue *Words and Music* (L 1932). It was sung by the company, including John Mills, Joyce Barbour, Steffi Duna,

Romney Brent, and Ivy St. Helier. It was also sung by Penelope Dudley-Ward and Hugh French in Bway revue *Set to Music* (1939). Considered by Mr. Coward "a pleasant little tune without being startlingly original," the song was also the composer's sign-off number during his nightclub appearances.

Payn, Graham, actor, singer; b. Pietermaritzburg, So. Africa, April 25, 1918. Payn appeared in four London musicals by Noël Coward and played Coward's roles in *Tonight at 8:30* during US tour. He also introduced "Matelot" in *Sigh No More.*

1939	Sitting Pretty
1940	Up and Doing
1942	Fine and Dandy
1943	The Magic Carpet
1944	The Lilac Domino (r)
	(*Elliston Deyne*)
1945	The Gaieties
	Sigh No More
1946	Pacific 1860 (*Kerry Sterling*)
1948	Tonight at 8:30 (NY) (r) (*George Pepper, Simon Gayforth, Jasper Featherways*)
1950	Ace of Clubs (*Harry Hornby*)
1951	The Lyric Revue
	The Globe Revue
1954	After the Ball (*Mr. Hopper*)
1964	High Spirits (co-dir. only)

Pearl, Jack, actor; b. New York, Oct. 29, 1895. German-dialect comedian, noted for story-telling Baron Munchausen character, who began career in Gus Edwards' *School Days* in vaudeville. Had successful radio series ("Vas you dere, Sharly?") in 30s.

1920	Hitchy-Koo
1921	The Whirl of New York (US tour) (*U. Cheatham*)
1923	The Dancing Girl
	Topics of 1923
1926	A Night in Paris
1927	Artists and Models
1930	International Revue

1931 Ziegfeld Follies
1933 Pardon My English (*Comm. Bauer*).

"Pedro the Fisherman." Music by Harry Parr-Davies; lyric by Harold Purcell. Perky narrative song introduced by fishermen and their families (Vincent Tildsley's Mastersingers) during Festival of Blessing the Nets in *The Lisbon Story* (L 1943). The lyric relates how Pedro, the whistling fisherman, leaves his beloved Nina to go off to sea, but returns just in time to keep her from marrying Miguel, the rich wine-grower.

Peggy-Ann (1926). Music by Richard Rodgers; lyrics by Lorenz Hart; book by Herbert Fields, based on Bway musical *Tillie's Nightmare,* by Edgar Smith & A. Baldwin Sloane.

SONGS: "A Tree in the Park," "A Little Birdie Told Me So," "Where's That Rainbow?," "Maybe It's Me," "Chuck It," "In His Arms," "Havana."

NEW YORK: Dec. 27, 1926
VANDERBILT THEATRE; 333 p.

Presented by Lew Fields & Lyle D. Andrews; directed by Robert Milton & Fields; choreographed by Seymour Felix; settings, Clark Robinson; costumes, Mark Mooring; music director, Roy Webb; orchestrations, Webb.

CAST: Helen Ford (*Peggy-Ann Barnes*), Lester Cole (*Guy Pendleton*), Lulu McConnell (*Mrs. Frost*), Betty Starbuck (*Alice Frost*), Edith Meiser (*Dolores Barnes*), Jack Thompson (*Freddie Shawn*), Margaret Breen (*Patricia Seymour*).

LONDON: July 29, 1927
DALY'S THEATRE; 130 p.

Presented by Alfred Butt; directed by Lew Fields; choreographed by Seymour Felix.

CAST: Dorothy Dickson (*Peggy-Ann Barnes*), Oliver McLennon (*Guy Pendleton*), Maisie Gay (*Mrs. Frost*), Elsie Randolph (*Alice Frost*), Sylvia Leslie (*Dolores Barnes*), Basil Howes (*Freddie Shawn*), Lalla Collins (*Patricia Seymour*).

Rodgers and Hart's fourth (out of five) musicals produced in 1926 was a daring concept in many ways: there was no opening chorus and no songs for about 15 minutes, the first and last scenes were played in almost total darkness, and scenery and costumes were changed in full view of the audience. Most important, the story was largely a surrealistic, Freudian dream as it told of the subconscious adventures of Peggy-Ann, which took her to New York's Fifth Avenue, a yachting trip (where there was a mutiny and where she got married in her underwear), and the racetrack in Havana. During Bway run, Jack Thompson was succeeded by Georgie Hale; for four-month tour, Helen Ford replaced by Betty Starbuck. In London, the locale of the boarding house where Peggy-Ann does her dreaming was changed from Glens Falls, NY, to Hants, England.

Pennington, Ann, actress, dancer; b. Camden, NJ, Dec. 23, 1894; d. New York, Nov. 4, 1971. Tiny (4'11½"), vivacious dancer with flashing legs and dimpled knees who introduced "Black Bottom" in *George White's Scandals* of 1926.

1913 Ziegfeld Follies
1914 Ziegfeld Follies
1915 Ziegfeld Follies
1916 Ziegfeld Follies
1917 Miss 1917
1918 Ziegfeld Follies
1919 George White's Scandals
1920 George White's Scandals
1921 George White's Scandals
1923 Jack and Jill (*Gloria Wayne*)
     Ziegfeld Follies (added)
1924 Ziegfeld Follies

1926 George White's Scandals
1928 George White's Scandals
1930 The New Yorkers (*Lola McGee*)
1931 Everybody's Welcome (*Louella May Carroll*)

"People." Music by Jule Styne; lyric by Bob Merrill. People's need for people was the theme of Barbra Streisand's most popular song in *Funny Girl* (NY 1964), which she sang to Sydney Chaplin. In London production (1966), she sang it to Michael Craig.

"People Will Say We're in Love." Music by Richard Rodgers; lyric by Oscar Hammerstein II. The love duet of *Oklahoma!* (NY 1943), sung by Alfred Drake and Joan Roberts. In London version (1947), it was sung by Harold (Howard) Keel and Betty Jane Watson. While the lyric offers advice to keep people from thinking that the two are in love, the purpose of the song, of course, is to show that they really are.

Perchance to Dream (1945). Music, lyrics & book by Ivor Novello.
SONGS: "Love Is My Reason," "When I Curtsied to the King," "Highwayman Love," "A Woman's Heart," "We'll Gather Lilacs," "The Glo-Glo."

LONDON: April 21, 1945
HIPPODROME; 1,022 p.
Presented by Tom Arnold; directed by Jack Minster; choreographed by Frank Staff, Keith Lester; settings, Joseph Carl; costumes, Frederick Dawson; lighting, Stanley Earnshaw; music director, Harry Acres; orchestrations, Acres.
CAST: Ivor Novello (*Sir Graham Rodney, Valentine Fayre, Bay Fayre*), Muriel Barron (*Lydia Lyddington, Veronica Lyddington, Iris*), Roma Beaumont (*Melinda Fayre, Melanie, Melody Fayre*), Olive Gilbert (*Ernestine Flavelle, Mrs. Bridport*), Margaret Rutherford (*Lady Charlotte Fayre*), Robert Andrews (*William Fayre*).

Perchance to Dream had the longest consecutive run of any Ivor Novello musical and was the only one for which the composer-librettist wrote his own lyrics (Christopher Hassall, his regular lyricist, was then in the army). Its story is set in Huntersmoon, an imposing Georgian stately home, wherein dwell three generations of an English family. In the first act, Sir Graham Rodney, Regency rake and highwayman, falls in love with his cousin, Melinda Fayre, much to the chagrin of his mistress, Lydia Lyddington. During Melinda's 21st birthday party, Sir Graham staggers in suffering from gunshot wounds caused in a holdup, and dies professing his love for Melinda. The second act, set in 1843, concerns composer-choirmaster Valentine Fayre, now the master of Huntersmoon, who marries Veronica Lyddington, the daughter of Lydia and Sir Graham. Three years later, Valentine finds himself drawn to Melanie, Sir Graham's niece, but their plans to elope are dashed when Veronica becomes pregnant. As a result Melanie commits suicide. In the final scene, which occurs in the present, Valentine's grandson, Bay, finds happiness with his new bride, Melody, the reincarnation of Melinda and Melanie. During run, Miss Barron was succeeded by Sylvia Cecil and Hilary Allen, Miss Rutherford by Zena Dare.
Multiple-generation musical romances—in which the same actors played two or three pairs of lovers—include *Maytime* (NY 1917), *Three Little Girls* (NY 1930), *Through the Years* (NY 1932), *Melody* (NY 1933), *Music Hath Charms* (NY 1934), *Three Waltzes* (NY 1937, L 1945).

Peters, Bernadette (née Bernadette Lazzara), actress, singer; b. Ozone Park, NY, Feb. 28, 1948. Miss Peters' waiflike personality and baby voice first attracted notice in the Hollywood spoof *Dames at Sea*.

1966	The Penny Friend (*Cinderella*)
1967	Curly McDimple (*Alice*)
1968	George M! (*Josie Cohan*)
	Dames at Sea (*Ruby*)
1969	La Strada (*Gelsomina*)
1971	On the Town (r) (*Hildy Esterhazy*)
1974	Mack & Mabel (*Mabel Normand*)

"Physician, The." Music & lyric by Cole Porter. Compilatory account of a young lady enamored with a doctor so devoted to his work that "he loved ev'ry part of me and yet not me as a whole." In *Nymph Errant* (L 1933), Gertrude Lawrence was the lass with the entrancing bronchial tubes, lovable larynx, darling epidermis, ravishing esophagus, brilliant cerebellum, marvelous maxillaries, stunning sternum, and perfect pancreas.

Pickens, Jane, actress, singer; b. Macon, Ga., Aug. 10. In early 30s, Miss Pickens was member of vocal trio with sisters Patti and Helen and appeared with them in her first Bway musical. She has also sung in concerts and nightclubs and on radio.

1934	Thumbs Up!
1936	Ziegfeld Follies (added)
1940	Boys and Girls Together
1949	Regina (*Regina Hubbard*)
1951	Music in the Air (r) (*Frieda Hatzfeld*)

"Picture of Me Without You, A." Music & lyric by Cole Porter. In the "You're the Top" laundry-list tradition, the piece conjures up such unlikely separations as Henry Ford without a car, Kreisler without a fiddle, Philadelphia without a Biddle, Lord minus Taylor, Ogden Nash without a rhyme, Bulova without the time, Staten Island without a ferry, George Washington without a cherry, Barbara Hutton without a nickel, and Heinz without a pickle. June Knight and Charles Walters sang and danced it in *Jubilee* (NY 1935).

Pins and Needles (1937). Music & lyrics by Harold J. Rome; sketches by Charles Friedman, Arthur Arent, Marc Blitzstein, etc.

SONGS: "Sing Me a Song with Social Significance," "Sunday in the Park," "Nobody Makes a Pass at Me," "Chain Store Daisy," "One Big Union for Two," "Four Little Angels of Peace," "The Red Mikado" (added May 1939), "Mene Mene Tekel" (added July 1939), "It's Better with a Union Man" (added Nov. 1939).

NEW YORK: Nov. 27, 1937
LABOR STAGE; 1,108 p.

Presented by Labor Stage Inc.; directed by Charles Friedman; choreographed by Benjamin Zemach, Gluck Sandor; settings by (Sointu) Syrjala; pianos, Baldwin Bergersen & Harold Rome.

CAST: ILGWU players Millie Weitz, Ruth Rubinstein, Al Levy, Lynne Jaffee, Nettie Harary, Al Eben.

Until it was overtaken by *Hellzapoppin*, *Pins and Needles* held the long-run record for Bway musicals. What was unusual was that it initially had an amateur cast composed of members of the International Garment Workers Union, which sponsored the satiric revue. The idea for the show began with the union's Louis Schaffer, who hired Harold Rome to write his first Bway score and also to serve as half of a two-piano team. Though the show's targets were militarists, reactionaries, bigots, the Federal Theatre, Prime Minister Neville Chamberlain, Nazis, Fascists, Communists, and the DAR, the tone was generally lighthearted, with songs and sketches even kidding the unions themselves. During the show's run, constant changes were made to keep up with the headlines. There were also changes in credits: beginning May 1938, Robert Gordon was billed as director, with Adele Jerome as choreographer. In April 1939 dances were credited to Felicia Sorel, and in Nov. 1939 all sketches were by Joseph Schrank. Between March and Dec. 1938 the original company went on tour and was replaced by a second company. In April 1939 the revue's title was changed to *Pins and Needles 1939*, five months later to *Pins and Needles 1940*, two months later to *New Pins and Needles*. In June 1939 the show moved from the Labor Stage (formerly the Princess Theatre) to the Windsor.

Pinza, (Fortunato) Ezio, singer, actor; b. Rome, Italy, May 18, 1892; d. Stamford, Conn., May 9, 1957. After a highly successful career as an opera basso, Pinza made his Bway debut opposite Mary Martin in Rodgers and Hammerstein's *South Pacific* (in which he introduced "Some Enchanted Evening," "This Nearly Was Mine"). Bib: *Ezio Pinza: An Autobiography* (Rinehart, NY 1959)

    1949   South Pacific (*Emile de Becque*)
    1954   Fanny (*César*)

Pippin (1972). Music & lyrics by Stephen Schwartz; book by Roger O. Hirson.
SONGS: "Magic to Do," "Corner of the Sky," "Simple Joys," "No Time at All," "Morning Glow," "On the Right Track," "Extraordinary," "Love Song."

NEW YORK: Oct. 23, 1972
IMPERIAL THEATRE; 1,944 p.
Presented by Stuart Ostrow; directed & choreographed by Bob Fosse; settings, Tony Walton; costumes, Patricia Zipprodt; lighting, Jules Fisher; music director, Stanley Lebowsky; orchestrations, Ralph Burns.
CAST: Eric Berry (*Charles*), Jill Clayburgh (*Catherine*), Leland Palmer (*Fastrada*), Irene Ryan (*Berthe*), Ben Vereen (*Leading Player*), John Rubinstein (*Pippin*).

LONDON: Oct. 30, 1973
HER MAJESTY'S THEATRE; 85 p.
Presented by Robert Stigwood; directed & choreographed by Bob Fosse; settings, Tony Walton; costumes Patricia Zipprodt; lighting, Jules Fisher; music director, Ray Cook; orchestrations, Ralph Burns.
CAST: John Turner (*Charles*), Patricia Hodge (*Catherine*), Diane Langdon (*Fastrada*), Elisabeth Welch (*Berthe*), Northern J. Calloway (*Leading Player*), Paul Jones (*Pippin*).

Though his name does not appear as *Pippin's* co-librettist, Bob Fosse rewrote much of the original material so that it became a personal statement on the subjects of war and the family. He also opened up what was initially a small-scale work by adding the commedia dell'arte concept and the character of the Leading Player (loosely based on the Master of Ceremonies in *Cabaret*, whose film version Fosse directed). The story is a modern, freewheeling account of the life of Charlemagne's son, Pippin (actually Pepin), who, yearning for glory, becomes involved with war, women, and social causes. Eventually, after rejecting the final glory of self-immolation, he settles down to an ordinary life with his wife, Catherine. In a role combining God and the Devil, Ben Vereen scored a notable hit. Irene Ryan, who died during the Bway run, was succeeded by Dorothy Stickney (6–73). The US touring company set out Nov. 1974 and travelled for five months.

"Pirate Jenny." Music by Kurt Weill; lyric by Marc Blitzstein. Jenny, a prostitute, dreams of the pirate ship, the *Black Freighter*, which will someday come to her rescue. The song, whose original German lyric was by Bertolt Brecht, was sung by Lotte Lenya in *The Threepenny Opera* (NY 1954). In London, the part was played by Maria Remusat (1956).

Pixley, Frank, librettist, lyricist; b. Richfield, Ohio, Nov. 21, 1867; d. San Diego, Cal., Dec. 30, 1919. After revising the book of *Florodora*, Pixley had his biggest Bway success with *The Prince of Pilsen*, music by his only composer partner, Gustav Luders.

    1900   Florodora (lib. only)
            The Burgomaster
    1902   King Dodo
    1903   The Prince of Pilsen
    1904   Woodland
    1907   The Grand Mogul
    1908   Marcelle
    1912   The Gypsy

"Play a Simple Melody." Music & lyric by Irving Berlin. Berlin's first contrapuntal song—in which the simple melody is contrasted with a syncopated melody—was sung by Sallie Fisher and Charles King in *Watch Your Step* (NY 1914); in London version (1915), by Ethel Levey and Blanche Tomlin. In all, Berlin wrote seven songs in counterpoint. The other six: "When I Get Back to the USA" (*Stop! Look! Listen!*), "Pack Up Your Sins and Go to the Devil" (*Music Box Revue*, 1922), "Climbing Up the Scale" (*Music Box Revue*, 1924), "You're Just in Love" (*Call Me Madam*), "Empty Pockets Full of Love" (*Mr. President*), "An Old-Fashioned Wedding" (*Annie Get Your Gun*, 1966 revival).

"Play, Gypsies—Dance, Gypsies." Music by Emmerich Kalman; lyric by Harry B. Smith. Spirited invitation—followed by a czardas—first sung in English by Walter Woolf in *Countess Maritza* (NY 1926). In London version (1938), called *Maritza*, the song was known as "Come, Gypsy, Come," lyric by Arthur Stanley, and sung by John Garrick. The operetta, originally titled *Gräfin Maritza*, was performed in Vienna (1924) with a libretto by Julius Brammer and Alfred Grünwald. In that production the song was called *"Komm Zigány!"*

"Play, Orchestra, Play." Music & lyric by Noël Coward. Brisk command for "something light and sweet and gay" introduced by Noël Coward and Gertrude Lawrence in *Shadow Play*, a one-act musical contained in the collection *Tonight at 8:30* (L 1936, NY 1936).

Playfair, Nigel, producer, director, sketch writer, actor; b. London, 1874, d. London, Aug. 19, 1934. Knighted 1928. Began as actor in London; best known as manager-director of the Lyric Theatre, Hammersmith (1918–1932), where his productions included the long-running revival of *The Beggar's Opera* and revue *Riverside Nights*. Bib: *Hammersmith Hoy* by Playfair (Faber, L 1930).

    Unless otherwise noted, Sir Nigel was
    producer-director of following:
    1903   Madame Sherry (*Mac Sherry*
            only)
    1916   Pell-Mell (actor only)
    1920   The Beggar's Opera (r) (also lib.)
    1922   Polly (r)
    1926   Riverside Nights (also actor, sk.)

1929 La Vie Parisienne
1930 Marriage à la Mode
1931 Tantivy Towers
1932 Derby Day
1933 Beau Brummell

"Politics and Poker." Music by Jerry Bock; lyric by Sheldon Harnick. Similarities between both games rollickingly itemized in *Fiorello!* (NY 1959) by politician Howard Da Silva and hacks Stanley Simmonds, Del Horstmann, Michael Quinn, Ron Husmann, and David London. In London version (1962), performed by Peter Reeves, Bryon O'Leary, Colin Kemball, Peter Dalton, and John Rickard.

"Poor Butterfly." Music by Raymond Hubbell; lyric by John Golden. In writing the score for the 1916 NY Hippodrome spectacle *The Big Show*, lyricist Golden mistakenly thought that one of the singers in it would be the Japanese opera star Tamaka Miura, who was identified with the role of *Madama Butterfly*. This gave Golden the idea of writing a lyric about the Puccini heroine, though he set it to a melody the composer did not feel was appropriate for a "Japanese" song. As it turned out, the Oriental singer engaged for the show was Haru Onuki, though Miss Onuki (whom Golden, perhaps incorrectly, claimed to be Chinese-American) was soon replaced by Sophye Bernard. Within two months, according to the lyricist, "the entire country was 'Butterfly' mad."

"Poor Little Rich Girl." Music & lyric by Noël Coward. Sung by Alice Delysia in *On with the Dance* (L 1925) and by Gertrude Lawrence in *The Charlot Revue of 1926* (NY). According to Coward, as first presented "it was led up to by a sophisticated little scene played by Hermione Baddeley, who stood about in evening dress looking drained and far from healthy, while Delysia, as her French governess, lectured her in a worldly manner about the debauched life she was all too obviously leading. . . . Gertie sang it dressed as a tart with a white fox fur. Constance Carpenter was the Poor Little Rich Girl in question and stood about in evening dress, looking drained and far from healthy."

"Pore Jud." Music by Richard Rodgers; lyric by Oscar Hammerstein II. Mock threnody sung by Alfred Drake and Howard Da Silva in *Oklahoma!* (NY 1943), and by Harold (Howard) Keel and Henry Clarke in London company (1947).

"Porgy." Music by Jimmy McHugh; lyric by Dorothy Fields. Romantic fidelity expressed by Aida Ward and Hall Johnson Choir in *Blackbirds of 1928* (NY 1928). The song was presented in a capsule musical version of the 1927 play *Porgy*, by Dorothy and DuBose Heyward, thus anticipating the Gershwin *Porgy and Bess* by over six years.

Porgy and Bess (1935). Music by George Gershwin; lyrics by DuBose Heyward & Ira Gershwin; book by Heyward, based on his & Dorothy Heyward's play *Porgy*, adapted from Heyward's novel.

SONGS: "Summertime" (Heyward), "A Woman Is a Sometime Thing" (Heyward), "My Man's Gone Now" (Heyward), "I Got Plenty o' Nothin'," "Bess, You Is My Woman Now," "It Ain't Necessarily So" (Gershwin), "I Loves You, Porgy," "There's a Boat Dat's Leavin' Soon for New York" (Gershwin), "Oh, Bess, Where's My Bess?" (Gershwin), "I'm on My Way" (Heyward).

NEW YORK: Oct. 10, 1935
ALVIN THEATRE; 124 p.

Presented by the Theatre Guild; directed by Rouben Mamoulian; settings, Sergei Soudeikine; costumes, Theatre Guild Workroom; music director, Alexander Smallens; orchestrations, George Gershwin.

CAST: Todd Duncan (*Porgy*), Anne Brown (*Bess*), Warren Coleman (*Crown*), John W. Bubbles (*Sportin' Life*), Abbie Mitchell (*Clara*), Edward Matthews (*Jake*), Ford L. Buck (*Mingo*), Georgette Harvey (*Maria*), Helen Dowdy (*Lily*), Ruby Elzy (*Serena*), J. Rosamond Johnson (*Frazier*).

NEW YORK: Jan. 22, 1942
MAJESTIC THEATRE; 286 p.

Presented by Cheryl Crawford, with John Wildberg; directed by Robert Ross; settings, Herbert Andrews; costumes, Paul DuPont; music director, Alexander Smallens; orchestrations, George Gershwin.

CAST: Todd Duncan (*Porgy*), Anne Brown (*Bess*), Warren Coleman (*Crown*), Avon Long (*Sportin' Life*), Harriett Jackson (*Clara*), Edward Matthews (*Jake*), Jimmy Waters (*Mingo*), Georgette Harvey (*Maria*), Helen Dowdy (*Lily*), Ruby Elzy (*Serena*), J. Rosamond Johnson (*Frazier*).

LONDON: Oct. 9, 1952
STOLL THEATRE; 142 p.
NEW YORK: March 10, 1953
ZIEGFELD THEATRE; 305 p.

Presented by Blevins Davis & Robert Breen; directed by Breen; settings, Wolfgang Roth; costumes, Jed Mace; music director, Alexander Smallens; orchestrations, George Gershwin.

CAST: William Warfield (London only), Le Vern Hutcherson, Leslie Scott or Irving Barnes (*Porgy*), Leontyne Price or Urylee Leonardos (*Bess*), Cab Calloway (*Sportin' Life*), John McCurry (*Crown*), Helen Thigpen (*Serena*), Helen Colbert (*Clara*), Joseph James (*Jake*), Jerry Laws (*Mingo*), Georgia Burke (*Maria*), Helen Dowdy (*Lily*), Moses La Marr (*Frazier*).

Porgy and Bess has long had the widest appeal of any opera by an American composer. Gershwin had planned to make an opera of Heyward's novel *Porgy* as early as 1926, even before the author and his wife, Dorothy, adapted it into the play produced by the Theatre Guild in 1927. That production included many spirituals and work songs. The following year a capsule musical version of the play was included in the revue *Blackbirds of 1928*, which featured the song "Porgy," written by Jimmy McHugh and Dorothy Fields. In 1932 the composer wrote Heyward of his continued interest, though other commitments forced further delays. At about that time the Guild even contemplated a version of *Porgy* starring Al Jolson to be written by Jerome Kern and Oscar Hammerstein. Heyward, however, preferred to wait for Gershwin. Collaboration began in Nov. 1933, with the composer in NY and the librettist in South Carolina; a few months later Ira Gershwin joined the project as co-lyricist. It took the composer 11 months to complete the score, nine more to orchestrate it.

The story is concerned with the inhabitants of Catfish Row (based on the actual Cabbage Row) in Charleston, SC. The character of Porgy was taken from that of Samuel Smalls, a crippled goat-cart beggar in the city, though the incidents in the story were not biographical. In the plot, Porgy and Bess, who is the brutal Crown's woman, fall in love after Crown has had to flee because he has killed a man. Following a picnic on Kittiwah Island, Bess succumbs to Crown; later when Crown comes to take her away, Porgy kills him in self-defense. Fearing that Porgy will never get out of jail, Bess agrees to run away to NY with Sportin' Life. The play ends with the freed Porgy, on his goat cart, setting out to find his Bess.

The ambitious nature of the work prompted some of the larger dailies to send both drama and music critics to cover it. *Porgy and Bess*, however, was not a financial success and it lost its entire investment. In 1942 producer Cheryl Crawford mounted a second Bway production, though it had a smaller company and orchestra than the original and all the recitative was removed. This version enjoyed the longest run of any Bway revival up to that time. It toured a year and a half, with Todd Duncan succeeded by William Franklin and Anne Brown by Etta Moten.

In June 1952, an international touring company began its travels in Dallas, Texas. It went abroad in Sept., playing Vienna, Berlin, London, and Paris. Following Bway run in 1953, *Porgy and Bess* toured the US and Canada, Dec. 1953–Sept. 1954; Europe and the Middle East, Sept. 1954–June 1955; Latin America, July–Oct. 1955; Europe again, incl. the USSR, Nov. 1955–June 1956.

Bib: *DuBose Heyward, the Man Who Wrote "Porgy"* by Frank Durham (U. So. Car. Press, SC 1954); *The Muses Are Heard* by Truman Capote (Random, NY 1956).

FILM VERSION: Sidney Poitier, Dorothy Dandridge, Sammy Davis Jr., Pearl Bailey (Goldwyn 1959, Otto Preminger dir.).

Porter, Cole (Albert), composer, lyricist; b. Peru, Ind., June 9, 1891; d. Santa Monica, Cal., Oct. 15, 1964. Porter's music and lyrics represented the Bway musical theatre at its most ele-

gant and carefree, with his throbbing, Latin-flavored minor-key ballads contrasting with his bright, intricately rhymed comic songs. Born into wealth, Porter spent most of the 20s in Europe, and did not pursue a steady writing career until the end of the decade, when he wrote *Fifty Million Frenchmen* ("You've Got That Thing," "You Do Something to Me"). The 30s and 40s found him involved in many long-run musicals: *Gay Divorce* ("Night and Day"), *Anything Goes* ("I Get a Kick Out of You," "You're the Top," "Blow, Gabriel, Blow," "Anything Goes"), *Leave It to Me!* ("Get Out of Town," "My Heart Belongs to Daddy"), *DuBarry Was a Lady* ("Do I Love You?," "Friendship"), *Panama Hattie* ("Let's Be Buddies"), *Let's Face It!* ("Everything I Love"), *Mexican Hayride* ("I Love You").

Porter's recognized classic was *Kiss Me, Kate*, incl. "Another Op'nin', Another Show," "Wunderbar," "So in Love," "Always True to You in My Fashion." During the 50s he had two popular attractions: *Can-Can* ("I Love Paris," "It's All Right with Me") and *Silk Stockings* ("All of You," "Paris Loves Lovers"). Other Porter songs: "Let's Do It" (*Paris*); "What Is This Thing Called Love?" (*Wake Up and Dream!*); "Love for Sale" (*The New Yorkers*); "Experiment" (*Nymph Errant*); "Why Shouldn't I?," "Begin the Beguine," "Just One of Those Things" (*Jubilee*); "It's De-Lovely" and "Ridin' High" (*Red, Hot and Blue!*); "At Long Last Love" (*You Never Know*); "Ev'rytime We Say Goodbye" (*Seven Lively Arts*).

Porter worked with librettists Herbert Fields on eight shows (three of them with Dorothy Fields as co-librettist), Sam and Bella Spewack on two, Abe Burrows on two. Ethel Merman starred in five of the composer's musicals; others who introduced his songs were Irene Bordoni, Fred Astaire, Gertrude Lawrence, Bob Hope, Mary Martin, William Gaxton, Beatrice Lillie, Danny Kaye, Alfred Drake. Porter also wrote scores for Hollywood films (incl. *Born to Dance, Broadway Melody of 1940*). His only collaborator was lyricist T. Lawrason Riggs. Bib: *103 Lyrics of Cole Porter*, Fred Lounsberry, ed. (Random, NY 1954); *The Cole Porter Song Book* (S&S, NY 1959); *The Cole Porter Story* by Porter & Richard Hubler (World, Cleveland 1965); *Cole Porter: The Life That Late He Led* by George Eells (Putnam, NY 1967); *Cole* by Robert Kimball & Brendan Gill (Holt, NY 1971).

1916 See America First (Riggs)
1919 Hitchy-Koo
1924 Greenwich Village Follies
1928 Paris
1929 Wake Up and Dream! (L)
     Fifty Million Frenchmen
1930 The New Yorkers
1932 Gay Divorce
1933 Nymph Errant (L)
1934 Anything Goes
1935 Jubilee
1936 Red, Hot and Blue!
1938 You Never Know
     Leave It to Me!
1939 DuBarry Was a Lady
1940 Panama Hattie
1941 Let's Face It!
1943 Something for the Boys
1944 Mexican Hayride
     Seven Lively Arts
1946 Around the World in 80 Days
1948 Kiss Me, Kate
1950 Out of This World
1953 Can-Can
1955 Silk Stockings

Powell, Eleanor (Torrey), actress, dancer; b. Springfield, Mass., Nov. 21, 1910. Miss Powell's machine-gun tapping won notice on the Bway stage, but it was not until she went to Hollywood in the mid-30s that she achieved stardom in such films as *Broadway Melody of 1936* and *Born to Dance*.

1928 The Optimists
1929 Follow Thru (*Molly*)
1930 Fine and Dandy (*Miss Hunter*)
1932 Hot-Cha! (dancer)
     George White's Music Hall Varieties
     Crazy Quilt (US tour)
1935 At Home Abroad

Preston, Robert (né Robert Preston Meservey), actor, singer; b. Newton Highlands, Mass., June 8, 1918. Rugged, light-footed actor who made a memorable musical-comedy debut on Bway in *The Music Man* (introducing "Seventy-Six Trombones" and "Till There Was You"). He also sang "My Cup Runneth Over" in *I Do! I Do!* Preston, who began his career in Hollywood films, has also appeared in nonsinging roles (notably *The Lion in Winter*).

1957 The Music Man (*Harold Hill*)
1964 Ben Franklin in Paris (*Ben Franklin*)
1966 I Do! I Do! (*Michael*)
1974 Mack & Mabel (*Mack Sennett*)

"Pretty Baby." Music by Egbert Van Alstyne; lyric by Gus Kahn. Though the Shubert brothers had inaugurated their annual *Passing Show* revues on Bway in 1912, it wasn't until the 1916 edition that the first song hit—the interpolated "Pretty Baby"—emerged. It was baby-talked by Dolly Brackett and a row of chorus dolls. In London, it was sung by Gertie Millar in *Houp-La!* (1916).

"Pretty Girl Is Like a Melody, A." Music & lyric by Irving Berlin. John Steel introduced this tribute to feminine beauty in the *Ziegfeld Follies* (NY 1919), accompanied by Mary Washburn. As part of the number, interpolated melodies, personified by pretty girls, were introduced: Dvorak's "Humoresque" (Maurisette), Mendelssohn's "Spring Song" (Hazel Washburn), Massenet's "Elegy" (Martha Pierre), Offenbach's "Barcarolle" (Jessie Reed), Schubert's "Serenade" (Alta King), and Schumann's "Traümerei" (Margaret Irving). The song became the unofficial anthem of all subsequent *Follies*.

Prince, Harold (Smith), producer, director; b. New York, Jan. 30, 1928. Since 1963, when he began directing his own productions, Prince has been recognized as one of the most creative and influential forces in the Bway musical theatre, eager to try original themes and bold methods of stagecraft. Following his apprenticeship as stage manager for George Abbott, in 1953 he formed a producing partnership with Robert Griffith which lasted until Griffith's death in 1961. Subsequent productions have usually been "in association" with Ruth Mitchell and others. Stephen Sondheim has written five scores for Prince, Jerry Bock and Sheldon Harnick four, John Kander and Fred Ebb three and Richard Adler and Jerry Ross two. Directors who have worked with Prince include George Abbott on seven shows, Jerome Robbins on two. Bib: *Contradictions* by Prince (Dodd, Mead, NY 1974).

Unless otherwise noted, Mr. Prince was producer or co-producer of following; asterisk indicates he was also director:

1954 The Pajama Game
1955 Damn Yankees
1957 New Girl in Town
      West Side Story
1958 West Side Story (L)
1959 Fiorello!
1960 Tenderloin
1962 A Family Affair (dir. only)
      A Funny Thing Happened on the Way to the Forum
1963 She Loves Me *

      A Funny Thing Happened on the Way to the Forum (L)
1964 She Loves Me * (L)
      Fiddler on the Roof
      Baker Street (dir. only)
1965 Flora, the Red Menace *
1966 It's a Bird It's a Plane It's Superman *
      Cabaret *
1967 Fiddler on the Roof (L)
1968 Cabaret * (L)
      The Beggar's Opera (L) (r)
1969 Zorbá *
1970 Company *
1971 Follies *
1972 Company * (L)
1973 A Little Night Music *
1974 Candide *
1975 A Little Night Music * (L)
1976 Pacific Overtures *

Princess Theatre Musicals. The Princess Theatre was a 299-seat house located at 39th St. and Sixth Ave., NY (now part of the site of the Millikan Bldg.). It was celebrated as the birthplace of the Jerome Kern–P. G. Wodehouse–Guy Bolton musicals, generally regarded as the first attempts to offer modern, cohesive, funny, intimate stories, with songs—more or less—fitting the characters and situations. The idea for the series was credited to Elisabeth Marbury, Bolton's literary agent, who joined F. Ray Comstock, the theatre's owner, in presenting the first two productions, both by Kern and Bolton with lyricist Schuyler Greene. Though the third Princess musical had a score by John Golden and Anne Caldwell, the next two, cosponsored by Comstock and William Elliott, united Kern and Bolton with Wodehouse. (Another 1917 musical by the trio, *Leave It to Jane*, while not shown at the Princess, was created in a similar style and was produced by Comstock and Elliott.) Bolton and Wodehouse wrote the penultimate Princess show with composer Louis Hirsch; the final offering was a revue presented by Will Morissey, with a score by Richard Whiting and Ray Egan. In 1936, the ILGWU took over the playhouse, renamed it Labor Stage, and, one year later, produced the revue *Pins and Needles.*

1915 Nobody Home (Kern-Greene-Bolton)
 Very Good Eddie (Kern-Greene-Bolton)
1916 Go to It (Golden-Caldwell)
1917 Oh, Boy! (Kern-Wodehouse-Bolton)
1918 Oh, Lady! Lady!! (Kern-Wodehouse-Bolton)
 Oh, My Dear! (Hirsch-Wodehouse-Bolton)
1919 Toot Sweet (Whiting-Egan)

Printemps, Yvonne, actress, singer; b. Ermont, France, July 25, 1895. Lydian-voiced actress who made her debut in Paris in 1908 and who sang her only English-language role in Noël Coward's *Conversation Piece* (introducing "I'll Follow My Secret Heart"). *(D. Paris, Jan. 18, 1977.)*

1934 Conversation Piece (L) *(Melanie)*
 Conversation Piece (NY) *(Melanie)*

"Promise Me a Rose." Music & lyric by Bob Merrill. Sentiments of an imaginative, incurably romantic woman, introduced by Eileen Herlie in *Take Me Along* (NY 1959).

Promises, Promises (1968). Music by Burt Bacharach; lyrics by Hal David; book by Neil Simon, based on film *The Apartment,* by Billy Wilder & I. A. L. Diamond.

SONGS: "Upstairs," "You'll Think of Something," "Our Little Secret," "She Likes Basketball," "Knowing When to Leave," "Wanting Things," "Whoever You Are," "I'll Never Fall in Love Again," "Promises, Promises."

NEW YORK: Dec. 1, 1968
SHUBERT THEATRE; 1,281 p.

Presented by David Merrick; directed by Robert Moore; choreographed by Michael Bennett; settings, Robin Wagner; costumes, Donald Brooks; lighting, Martin Aronstein; music director, Harold Hastings; orchestrations, Jonathan Tunick.

CAST: Jerry Orbach (*Chuck Baxter*), Jill O'Hara (*Fran Kubelik*), Edward Winter (*J. D. Sheldrake*), A. Larry Haines (*Dr. Dreyfuss*), Marian Mercer (*Marge MacDougall*), Paul Reed (*Dobitch*), Dick O'Neill (*Jesse Vanderhoff*), Norman Shelly (*Kirkeby*), Vince O'Brien (*Eichelberger*), Millie Slavin (*Peggy Olson*), Adrienne Angel (*Sylvia Gilhooley*), Donna McKechnie (*Vivien Della Hoya*), Ken Howard (*Karl Kubelik*), Margo Sappington (*Miss Polansky*).

LONDON: Oct. 2, 1969
PRINCE OF WALES THEATRE; 560 p.

Presented by David Merrick & H. M. Tennent Ltd; restaged by Charles Blackwell; choreographed by Michael Bennett; settings, Robin Wagner; costumes, Donald Brooks; lighting, Joe Davis; music director, Ian Macpherson; orchestrations, Jonathan Tunick.

CAST: Anthony Roberts (*Chuck Baxter*), Betty Buckley (*Fran Kubelik*), James Congdon (*J. D. Sheldrake*), Jack Kruschen (*Dr. Dreyfuss*), Kelly Britt (*Marge MacDougall*), Don Fellows (*Jesse Vanderhoff*), Ronn Carroll (*Dobitch*), Ivor Dean (*Eichelberger*), Jay Denyer (*Kirkeby*), Donna McKechnie (*Vivien Della Hoya*).

Like other Bway hits *Carnival, Sweet Charity, Applause,* and *A Little Night Music, Promises, Promises* was adapted from a successful movie. Its story was concerned with one path up the corporate ladder not covered in *How to Succeed in Business Without*

Really Trying: prompted by the promises, promises of advancement, Chuck Baxter lends his apartment to various executives at Consolidated Life to be used for their extramarital dalliances. One of these involves Fran Kubelik and J. D. Sheldrake, but eventually the girl comes to realize that Chuck, nonentity that he may be, is the better man. The production was the first with a score by Burt Bacharach and Hal David, and the first to be directed by Robert Moore. During Bway run Jerry Orbach was succeeded by Tony (né Anthony) Roberts (10-70), Gene Rupert (4-71), and Bill Gerber (11-71); Jill O'Hara by Jenny O'Hara (her sister) (12-70) and Lorna Luft (10-71). The US touring company began its travels in May 1970, with Anthony Roberts and Melissa Hart in the leads. It continued for one year, two months.

Purcell, Charles, actor, singer; b. Chattanooga, Tenn., 1883; d. New York, March 20, 1962. Purcell's most successful Bway appearances were in *Maytime* (in which he introduced "Will You Remember?," "The Road to Paradise"), and *Dearest Enemy* ("Here in My Arms"). He also sang "I Know That You Know" in *Oh, Please!*, and toured in *The Chocolate Soldier.*

1908	The Golden Butterfly (*Count Androssy*)
1914	Pretty Mrs. Smith (*Forest Smith*)
1915	Ziegfeld Follies (repl.)
1916	Flora Bella (*Prince Nicholas*)
1917	My Lady's Glove (*Capt. Poildeau*)
	Maytime (*Richard Wayne*)
1918	The Melting of Molly (*John Moore*)
1919	Monte Cristo, Jr. (*Dantes*)
	The Magic Melody (*Beppo Corsini, Arthur Stanley*)
1920	Poor Little Ritz Girl (*Billy Pemberton*)
1921	The Rose Girl (*Victor*)
	The Right Girl (*Tony Stanton*, repl.)
1925	Sky High (*Horace Deveridge*, repl.)
	Dearest Enemy (*Capt. Sir John Copeland*)
1926	Oh, Please! (*Robert Vandeleur*)
1927	Judy (*Jack Lethbridge*)
1933	Shady Lady (*Richard Brandt*)
1946	Park Avenue (*Reggie Fox*)

"Put on a Happy Face." Music by Charles Strouse; lyric by Lee Adams. Sung by Dick Van Dyke in *Bye Bye Birdie* (NY 1960) to cheer up a little girl (Karin Wolfe) who is upset because her rock-and-roll idol has been drafted. In London version (1961), it was sung by Peter Marshall.

Quaker Girl, The (1910). Music by Lionel Monckton; lyrics by Adrian Ross, Percy Greenbank; book by James T. Tanner.

SONGS: "A Bad Boy and a Good Girl," "The Quaker Girl" (Ross), "Take a Step" (Ross), "Tony from America" (lyric, Monckton), "Come to the Ball" (Ross).

LONDON: Nov. 5, 1910
ADELPHI THEATRE; 536 p.

Presented by George Edwardes; directed by J. A. E. Malone; choreographed by Willie Warde; settings, Joseph Harker, Alfred Terraine, Paquereau; costumes, Percy Anderson, Alexandra; music director, Carl Keifert.

CAST: Gertie Millar (*Prudence Pym*), Joseph Coyne (*Tony Chute*), C. Hayden Coffin (*Capt. Charteris*), Gracie Leigh (*Phoebe*), James Blakeley (*Jeremiah*), George Carvey (*Prince Carlo*), Mlle. Caumont (*Mme. Blum*), Phyllis Monkman (dancer).

NEW YORK: Oct. 23, 1911
PARK THEATRE; 240 p.

Presented by Henry B. Harris; directed by J. A. E. Malone; settings, H. H. Robert Law; costumes, Maison Blum, Lucile; music director, Augustus Barratt.

CAST: Ina Claire (*Prudence Pym*), Clifton Crawford (*Tony Chute*), Pope Stamper (*Capt. Charteris*), May Vokes (*Phoebe*), Percival Knight (*Jeremiah*), Lawrence Rea (*Prince Carlo*), Maisie Gay (*Mme. Blum*).

The Quaker Girl was the first musical to play London's Adelphi Theatre, and the first in which Gertie Millar appeared that had a complete score by her husband, composer Lionel Monckton. In an English village, Prudence, a Quaker, meets Tony, an American attaché with the US embassy in Paris, who has come to attend the wedding of his friend Capt. Charteris. Disobeying her parents, Prudence goes to the wedding reception and is caught sipping champagne. In defiance, she takes off to Paris, where she becomes a mannequin in Mme. Blum's salon. The smitten rogue Prince Carlo invites Prudence to his ball at the Pré Catalan in the Bois de Boulogne, thereby heightening Tony's jealousy and hastening his marriage proposal. During Bway run, Ina Claire was succeeded by Katherine Murray. *The Quaker Girl* was revived in London in 1934, 1944, and 1945.

"Quiet Girl, A." Music by Leonard Bernstein; lyric by Betty Comden & Adolph Green. In *Wonderful Town* (NY 1953), George Gaynes pictured the kind of quiet, gentle, tender, soft-as-snow girl he'd love to find. Dennis Bowen sang it in London version (1955).

"Quiet Thing, A." Music by John Kander; lyric by Fred Ebb. Surprised revelation that happiness comes on tiptoes, unaccompanied by drums, trumpets, or bells. Liza Minnelli introduced the song in *Flora, the Red Menace* (NY 1965).

❧ R ❧

Rado, James, lyricist, librettist, actor; b. Los Angeles, Cal., Jan. 23, 1939. Rado and co-lyricist-librettist Gerome Ragni and composer Galt MacDermot made a great impact on the Bway scene with their rock musical *Hair* (incl. "Aquarius," "Good Morning, Starshine," "Easy to Be Hard," "Let the Sunshine In," "Where Do I Go?").

1967 Hair (Ragni, MacDermot)
1968 Hair (revised) (Ragni, MacDermot) (also *Claude*)
1972 Rainbow (also comp., co-prod.)

"Raggedy Ann." Music by Jerome Kern; lyric by Anne Caldwell. Raggedy Andy's contrapuntal invitation to Raggedy Ann to hop into his flivver sedan and "rattle off to find a ragtime cabaret." Fred Stone and daughter Dorothy Stone, appropriately costumed, sang and danced the number in *Stepping Stones* (NY 1923), accompanied by John Lambert and the John Tiller Sunshine Girls.

Ragni, Gerome, lyricist, librettist, actor; b. Pittsburgh, Pa., Sept. 11, 1942. Ragni and co-lyricist-librettist James Rado and composer Galt MacDermot made a great impact on the Bway scene with their rock musical *Hair* (incl. "Aquarius," "Good Morning, Starshine," "Easy to Be Hard," "Let the Sunshine In," "Where Do I Go?").

1967	Hair (Rado, MacDermot) (also *Berger*)
1968	Hair (revised) (Rado, MacDermot) (also *Berger*)
1972	Dude (MacDermot)

"Rain in Spain, The." Music by Frederick Loewe; lyric by Alan Jay Lerner. The ecstatic moment in *My Fair Lady* (NY 1956, L 1958) when Julie Andrews, Rex Harrison, and Robert Coote celebrate Julie's sudden ability to pronounce the phrase "The rain in Spain stays mainly in the plain," without a Cockney accent. Though the musical was based on Bernard Shaw's play *Pygmalion*, the line came from Shaw's script for the film version.

Raitt, John (Emmet), actor, singer; b. Santa Ana, Cal., Jan. 19, 1917. Muscular baritone who won fame in *Carousel*, in which he introduced "Soliloquy" and "If I Loved You." Raitt's other major Bway hit was *The Pajama Game* ("Hey, There," "There Once Was a Man").

1944	Oklahoma! (US tour) (*Curly McLain,* repl.)
1945	Carousel (*Billy Bigelow*)
1948	Magdalena (*Pedro*)
1952	Three Wishes for Jamie (*Jamie McRuin*)
1953	Carnival in Flanders (*The Duke*)

1954	The Pajama Game (*Sid Sorokin*)
1960	Destry Rides Again (US tour) (*Destry,* repl.)
1966	A Joyful Noise (*Shade Motley*)

Randolph, Elsie, actress, singer, dancer; b. London, Dec. 9, 1904. Dark-haired, round-faced Elsie Randolph was Jack Buchanan's singing and dancing partner in nine London musicals, introducing such songs as "The One I'm Looking For," "Fancy Our Meeting," and "Oceans of Time." Asterisk indicates appearance with Mr. Buchanan:

1919	The Girl for the Boy (*model*)
1920	The Naughty Princess (*Bibi*)
1921	My Nieces (*schoolgirl*)
1922	His Girl (*guest*)
1923	Battling Butler * (*Flapper*)
1924	Toni * (*Folly*)
	Madame Pompadour (*Madeleine*)
1925	Boodle * (*Clematis Drew*)
1926	Sunny * (*Weenie Winters*)
1927	Peggy-Ann (*Alice Frost*)
1928	That's a Good Girl * (*Joy Dean*)
1929	Follow Through (*Ruth Vanning*)
1930	The Co-Optimists
	The Wonder Bar (*Inez*)
1931	Stand Up and Sing * (*Ena*)
1934	Mr. Whittington * (*Betty Trotter*)
1935	Charlot's Char-a-Bang
1936	This'll Make You Whistle * (*Bobbie Rivers*)
1942	The Maid of the Mountains (r) (*Vittoria*)
1943	It's Time to Dance * (*Marian Kane*)

"Rangers' Song, The." Music by Harry Tierney; lyric by Joseph McCarthy. Robust march in honor of the Texas Rangers boomed by J. Harold Murray and Rangers chorus in *Rio Rita* (NY 1927), and by Geoffrey Gwyther and chorus in London production (1930).

Rasch, Albertina, choreographer; b. Vienna, Austria, 1896; d. Woodland Hills, Cal., Oct. 2, 1967. Miss Rasch brought ballet to Bway in such popular offerings as *Rio Rita, The Three Musketeers, Sons o' Guns, Three's a Crowd, The Cat and the Fiddle, The Great Waltz, Lady in the Dark.* She was married to composer Dmitri Tiomkin.

1910 The International Cup (dancer only)
1911 The Revue of Revues (dancer only)
1925 George White's Scandals
1927 Rio Rita
Lucky
Rufus Le Maire's Affairs
Ziegfeld Follies
My Princess
1928 The Three Musketeers
1929 Show Girl
Sons o' Guns
1930 Princess Charming
Three's a Crowd
1931 The Wonder Bar
Ziegfeld Follies
Everybody's Welcome
The Cat and the Fiddle
The Laugh Parade
1932 A Little Racketeer
Face the Music
Flying Colors
Walk a Little Faster
1933 Wild Violets (L)
1934 The Great Waltz
1935 Jubilee
1939 Very Warm for May
1940 Boys and Girls Together
1941 Lady in the Dark
1945 Marinka

Raye, Martha (née Margaret Theresa Yvonne Reed), actress, singer; b. Butte, Montana, Aug. 27, 1916. Boisterous, wide-mouthed comedienne-singer who became popular in films following 1936 debut in *Rhythm on the Range.*

1934 Calling All Stars
1940 Hold on to Your Hats (*Mamie*)
1967 Hello, Dolly! (*Dolly Levi*, repl.)
1972 No, No, Nanette (*Pauline*, repl.)

"Real Live Girl." Music by Cy Coleman; lyric by Carolyn Leigh. A song of romantic innocence sung by Sid Caesar in *Little Me* (NY 1962), later reprised as an ethereal song-and-dance for World War I doughboys in the trenches. Bruce Forsythe sang it in London version (1964).

Red Mill, The (1906). Music by Victor Herbert; lyrics & book by Henry Blossom.

SONGS: "The Isle of Our Dreams," "When You're Pretty and the World Is Fair," "Every Day Is Ladies' Day with Me," "The Streets of New York," "Because You're You," "Moonbeams."

NEW YORK: Sept. 24, 1906
KNICKERBOCKER THEATRE; 274 p.

Presented by Charles B. Dillingham; directed by Fred Latham; settings, Gates & Morange, Homer Emens; costumes, Wilhelm, Lord & Taylor; music director, Max Hirschfeld; orchestrations, Victor Herbert.

CAST: David Montgomery (*Kid Conner*), Fred Stone (*Con Kidder*), Augusta Greenleaf (*Gretchen*), Joseph M. Ratliff (*Capt. Doris Van Damm*), Ethel Johnson (*Tina*), Allene Crater (*Bertha*), Neal McCay (*Governor*), Edward Begley (*Burgomaster Jan Van Borkem*), Charles Dox (*Franz*).

LONDON: Dec. 26, 1919
EMPIRE THEATRE; 64 p.
Presented by Alfred Butt.

CAST: Little Tich (*Kid Conner*), Ray Kay (*Con Kidder*), Ivy Tresmand (*Tina*), Amy Augarde (*Bertha*), Gladys Simmonds (*Gretchen*), John Luxton (*Capt. Boris Van Damm*), Gus Sharland (*Governor*), Rube Welch (*Burgomaster Jan Van Borkem*), Lily Alaine (*Countess de la Fere*).

NEW YORK: Oct. 16, 1945
ZIEGFELD THEATRE; 531 p.

Presented by Paula Stone & Hunt Stromberg Jr.; directed by Billy Gilbert; choreographed by Aida Broadbent; settings & lighting, Adrian Awan; costumes, Walter Israel; music director, Edward Ward; orchestrations, Ward; additional lyrics, Forman Brown.

CAST: Eddie Foy Jr. (*Kid Conner*), Michael O'Shea (*Con Kidder*), Dorothy Stone (*Tina*), Odette Myrtil (*Mme. La Fleur*), Charles Collins (*Gaston*), Edward Dew (*Governor*), Lorna Byron (*Juliana*), Ann Andre (*Gretchen*), Robert Hughes (*Capt. Hendrik Van Damm*), Frank Jaquet (*Burgomaster*), George Meader (*Franz*).

Herbert and Blossom wrote *The Red Mill* expressly for knockabout comics Montgomery and Stone. More musical farce than operetta, the production enjoyed the longest Bway run of any Herbert work and also had the most successful revival. In the story, which takes place in the Dutch seaport of Katwyk-aan-Zee, two impoverished Americans, Kid Conner and Con Kidder, attempt to get enough money to return to NY. In their quest, they don many disguises (including Sherlock Holmes and Dr. Watson) and also help lovers Gretchen and Doris (sic), despite the opposition of Gretchen's father, the burgomaster. Stone made a memorable entrance falling down an 18-foot ladder, later managed a heroic escape from a windmill by perching on one of the wings with a girl in his arm. *The Red Mill* was also celebrated for having the first moving electric sign on Bway. In the London version, the two stranded Americans became two Englishmen.

The popular 1945 revival, which ran longer than the original production, was co-produced by Fred Stone's daughter Paula, and featured his daughter Dorothy. During run, Michael O'Shea was succeeded by Jack Whiting, Ann Andre by Doretta Morrow. Eddie Foy's success as chief comic prompted two other revivals, both with notable clowns: *Sweethearts* (1947) with Bobby Clark and *Sally* (1948) with Willie Howard. *The Red Mill* was revived in London in 1947 with Jimmy Jewel and Ben Warriss.

Reeve, Ada, actress, singer; b. London, March 3, 1874; d. London, Sept. 25, 1966. Tiny, wide-eyed Ada Reeve was the heroine of *The Shop Girl*, the first musical comedy to play London's Gaiety Theatre. Other hits were *Florodora* and *San Toy*. Bib: *Take It for a Fact* by Miss Reeve (1954).

1894	The Shop Girl (*Bessie Brent*)
1895	All Aboard (*Mme. Montesque*)
1896	The Gay Parisienne (*Julie Bonbon*)
1898	Milord Sir Smith (*Mme. Celeste*)
1899	Great Caesar (*Cleopatra*)
	Florodora (*Lady Holyrood*)
1901	San Toy (*San Toy*, repl.)
	Kitty Grey (*Kitty Grey*, repl.)
1902	Three Little Maids (*Ada Branscombe*)
1903	The Medal and the Maid (*Miss Ventnor*)
1908	Butterflies (*Rhodanthe*)
1936	Follow the Sun
1940	Black Velvet (added)
1947	The DuBarry (r) (*Mme. Sauterelle*)

"**Remember.**" Music & lyric by Irving Berlin. Though this poignant recollection of a fleeting love was not specifically written for the theatre, it was sung by Alice Delysia to Nigel Bruce in revue *Still Dancing!* (L 1925).

"**Reuben and Cynthia.**" Music and lyric by Percy Gaunt. Also known as "Reuben, Reuben," the song was sung in *A Trip to Chinatown* (NY 1891) by Harry Conor.

Revill, Clive (Selsby), actor, singer; b. Wellington, New Zealand, April 18, 1930. Character actor who first appeared on Bway in 1952, and scored success in NY in *Oliver!*

1958 Irma la Douce (L) (*Bob Le Hotu*)
1960 Irma la Douce (*Bob Le Hotu*)
1963 Oliver! (*Fagin*)
1967 Sherry (*Sheridan Whiteside*)

Reynolds, (Mary Frances) Debbie, actress, singer, dancer; b. El Paso, Texas, April 1, 1932. Hoydenish, cute-as-pie Debbie Reynolds enjoyed a Hollywood film career before making a highly successful Bway bow.

1973 Irene (r) (*Irene O'Dare*)

"Ribbons Down My Back." Music & lyric by Jerry Herman. What to wear in summer to make a boy take notice. Eileen Brennan introduced the willowy ballad in *Hello, Dolly!* (NY 1964); Marilynn Lovell sang it in the London version (1965).

Rice, Edward E., composer, producer, director; b. Brighton, Mass., 1849; d. New York, Nov. 16, 1924. Rice was a leading creator of musical burlesques whose biggest hits were *Evangeline* (written with J. Cheever Goodwin) and *Adonis* (William Gill and Henry E. Dixey). Dixey, Lillian Russell, and Fay Templeton all made their professional debuts in Rice productions.

Asterisk indicates Mr. Rice was producer-director only:

1874 Evangeline (Goodwin)
1880 Hiawatha (Childs)
1881 Billee Taylor *
1883 Pop
1884 Adonis (Gill, Dixey)
1887 Conrad the Corsair *
1888 Pearl of Pekin *
1889 The Seven Ages
1893 1492 (Barnett)
1894 Little Christopher Columbus *
1895 Excelsior, Jr. (Barnett)
1896 The Girl from Paris *
1897 The French Maid *
      The Ballet Girl *
1898 Monte Carlo *

1902 The Show Girl *
     King Highball *
1904 Mr. Wix of Wickham *

Richman, Harry (né Harry Reichman), actor, singer; b. Cincinnati, Ohio, Aug. 10, 1895; d. Hollywood, Cal., Nov. 3, 1972. An ebullient, dapper entertainer, Richman had a full-throated, uninhibited vocal style, at first modeled after Al Jolson. His trademarks were a top hat (or straw boater), a twirling cane, a strutting dance step or two, and a slight lisp. His greatest Bway success was in *George White's Scandals* of 1926, in which he introduced "Lucky Day" and "The Birth of the Blues." He also sang "On the Sunny Side of the Street" and "Exactly Like You" in the *International Revue*. Richman, who began his career as a vaudeville pianist for Mae West, the Dolly Sisters, and Nora Bayes, spent most of his career as a nightclub singer. Bib: *A Hell of a Life* by Richman (Duell, Sloan, NY 1966).

1922 Queen o' Hearts (*Henry Rivers*)
1926 George White's Scandals
1928 George White's Scandals
1930 International Revue
     Sons o' Guns (US tour) (*Jimmy Canfield*)
1931 Ziegfeld Follies
1932 George White's Music Hall Varieties
1934 Say When (*Bob Breese*)

"Ridin' High." Music & lyric by Cole Porter. Ecstatic proclamation announced by Ethel Merman in *Red, Hot and Blue!* (NY 1936) upon finding herself a man. To emphasize her total self-satisfaction, the lady further revealed—via two patter sections—her indifference to such enviable possessions as Mrs. Harrison Williams' wardrobe, Barbara Hutton's Rolls Royces, Wallis Simpson's king, Katie Hepburn's nose, "Legs" Dietrich's pegs, Dorothy Parker's brain, Eleanor

Holm Jarrett's aquatic surroundings, Eleanor Roosevelt's writing fees, Tallulah's jewels, and Mae West's curves.

"Riff Song, The." Music by Sigmund Romberg; lyric by Otto Harbach & Oscar Hammerstein II. Also known as "Ho!," this call to battle was sung by Robert Halliday, William O'Neal, and their band of Riffians in *The Desert Song* (NY 1926). In London version (1927) it was sung by Harry Welchman, Sidney Pointer, and Riffs.

Rigby, Harry, producer; b. Haverford, Pa. Though Rigby was to have been the co-producer of the *No, No, Nanette* revival, his name was removed by the time the show reached Bway. He did better two years later with *Irene*.

1951	Make a Wish
1953	John Murray Anderson's Almanac
1963	Half a Sixpence
1967	Hallelujah, Baby!
1973	Irene (r) (also co-lib.)
1974	Good News (r)

"Right as the Rain." Music by Harold Arlen; lyric by E. Y. Harburg. *Bloomer Girl* (NY 1944) duet in which David Brooks and Celeste Holm affirmed the rightness of their love.

Ring, Blanche, actress, singer; b. Boston, Mass, April 24, 1871; d. Santa Monica, Cal., Jan. 13, 1961. Lively, diminutive singer who introduced "In the Good Old Summertime," "I've Got Rings on My Fingers," "Yip-I-Addy-I-Ay!," and "Bedelia." Miss Ring appeared in stock and vaudeville before NY debut. Her fourth husband was Charles Winninger from whom she was divorced.

1902	The Defender (*Millie Canvass*)
	Tommy Rot (*Innocence Demure*)
	Fad and Folly (Tommy Rot) (*Innocence Demure*)
1903	The Jewel of Asia (*Zaidee*)

	The Blonde in Black (*Flossie Featherley*)
	The Jersey Lily (*Lilliandra*)
1904	The Love Birds (L) (*Effie Doublehurst*)
1905	Sergeant Brue (*Lady Bickenhall*)
	It Happened in Nordland (*Katherine Peepfogle*, repl.)
1906	His Majesty (*Mrs. Brown*)
	His Honor the Mayor (*Katrinka*)
	Miss Dolly Dollars (*Dolly Dollars*)
	About Town
1907	The Gay White Way (*Mrs. Dane*)
1908	The Merry Widow Burlesque (*Sonia*, repl.)
1909	The Midnight Sons (*Carrie Margin*)
1910	The Yankee Girl (*Jessie Gordon*)
1912	The Wall Street Girl (*Jemima Greene*)
1914	When Claudia Smiles (*Claudia*)
1919	The Passing Show
1921	The Broadway Whirl
1928	The Houseboat on the Styx (*Queen Elizabeth*)
1930	Strike Up the Band (*Grace Draper*)
1938	Right This Way (*Josie Huggins*)

Rio Rita (1927). Music by Harry Tierney; lyrics by Joseph McCarthy; book by Guy Bolton & Fred Thompson.

SONGS: "Rio Rita," "The Rangers' Song," "The Kinkajou," "If You're in Love You'll Waltz," "Following the Sun Around."

NEW YORK: Feb. 2, 1927
ZIEGFELD THEATRE; 494 p.

Presented by Florenz Ziegfeld; directed by John Harwood; choreographed by Sammy Lee, Albertina Rasch; settings, Joseph Urban; costumes, John Harkrider; music director, Oscar Bradley; orchestrations, Frank Barry.

CAST: Ethelind Terry (*Rita Ferguson*), J. Harold Murray (*Capt. James Stewart*), Bert Wheeler (*Chick Beam*), Robert Woolsey (*Ed Lovett*), Ada May (*Dolly*), Vincent Serrano (*Gen. Ro-*

mero Joselito Esteban), Gladys Glad (*Raquel*).

LONDON: April 3, 1930
PRINCE EDWARD THEATRE; 59 p.

Presented by Lee Ephraim; directed by John Harwood; choreographed by Edward Royce Jr., Alexander Oumansky; settings uncredited; costumes, Idare; music director, John Heuvel.

CAST: Edith Day (*Rita Ferguson*), Geoffrey Gwyther (*Capt. James Stewart*), Leslie Sarony (*Chick Beam*), George Gee (*Ed Lovett*), Rita Page (*Dolly*), Bernard Nedell (*Gen. Romero Joselito Esteban*).

Because his original choice, *Show Boat*, was not ready in time, producer Florenz Ziegfeld opened his Ziegfeld Theatre with an elaborate spectacle of old Mexico called *Rio Rita*. The colorful tale relates the adventures of Capt. Jim of the Texas Rangers, who crosses the border to Santa Luca to apprehend a bank robber and finds true love in the arms of tempestuous Rita Ferguson. The musical marked the first joint appearance of comedians Bert Wheeler and Robert Woolsey (succeeded during run by Walter Catlett). The London version, which opened after the film version was released, reunited Edith Day with the song writers who had written her first hit, *Irene*. It was the first production at the Prince Edward Theatre (now the London Casino).

FILM VERSIONS: Bebe Daniels, John Boles, Wheeler & Woolsey (RKO 1929, Luther Reed dir.); Abbott & Costello, Kathryn Grayson (MGM 1942, S. Sylvan Simon dir.).

"**Rio Rita.**" Music by Harry Tierney; lyric by Joseph McCarthy. The chief romantic duet in *Rio Rita* (NY 1927), sung by J. Harold Murray and Ethelind Terry. In London version (1930) it was sung by Geoffrey Gwyther and Edith Day.

"**Rise 'n Shine.**" Music by Vincent Youmans; lyric by B. G. De Sylva. A chins-up exhortation of the Depression delivered by Ethel Merman in *Take a Chance* (NY 1932). In London, Jack Whiting and company sang it as the first-act finale of *Rise and Shine* (1936).

Ritchard, Cyril (Trimnell-), actor, singer, dancer, director; b. Sydney, Australia, Dec. 1, 1897. Dandified comic actor known for his gurgling giggle, who also played classical comedy roles both in London and NY. Ritchard and his wife, Madge Elliott, acted together in 10 West End musicals. One of his most memorable roles was that of Capt. Hook in NY production of *Peter Pan. (D. Dec. 18, 1977.)*

1925 Puzzles of 1925 (NY)
      Bubbly (r)
      Charlot's Revue (added)
1926 RSVP
1927 Lady Luck (*Tommy Lester*)
1928 So This Is Love (*Hon. Peter Malden*)
1929 Love Lies (*Jack Stanton*)
1930 The Co-Optimists
      The Love Race (*Harry Drake*)
1931 The Millionaire Kid (*Hon. Aubrey Forsythe*)
1936 Spread It Abroad (added)
      To and Fro
1938 Nine Sharp
1939 The Little Revue (also dir.)
1940 Up and Doing
1941 New Ambassador Revue (dir. only)
1942 Big Top
1943 The Merry Widow (r) (*Prince Danilo*)
1945 Gay Rosalinda (*Gabriel von Eisenstein*)
      Sigh No More
1953 High Spirits
      John Murray Anderson's Almanac (NY) (dir. only)

1954 Peter Pan (NY) (*Capt. Hook*)
1961 The Happiest Girl in the World (NY) (*Pluto*) (also dir.)
1965 The Roar of the Greasepaint— The Smell of the Crowd (NY) (*Sir*)
1972 Sugar (NY) (*Osgood Fielding Jr.*)

Rivera, Chita (née Dolores Conchita Figueroa del Rivero), actress, dancer, singer; b. Washington, DC, Jan. 23, 1933. Spirited, dark-haired dancing actress who scored Bway hits in *West Side Story* and *Bye Bye Birdie*.

1952 Call Me Madam (chorus, repl.)
1953 Guys and Dolls (chorus, repl.)
1954 Can-Can (chorus, repl.)
1955 Shoestring Revue
      Seventh Heaven (*Fifi*)
1956 Mr. Wonderful (*Rita Romano*)
1957 West Side Story (*Anita*)
1958 West Side Story (L) (*Anita*)
1960 Bye Bye Birdie (*Rose Grant*)
1961 Bye Bye Birdie (L) (*Rose Grant*)
1964 Bajour (*Anyanka*)
1967 Sweet Charity (US tour) (*Charity*)
1975 Chicago (*Velma Kelly*)

"Road to Paradise, The." Music by Sigmund Romberg; lyric by Rida Johnson Young. Ardent journey for Peggy Wood and Charles Purcell in *Maytime* (NY 1917).

Robbins, Jerome (né Jerome Rabinowitz), director, choreographer, dancer; b. New York, Oct. 11, 1918. Robbins began his career as dancer and choreographer for the Ballet Theatre. On Bway, he won praise for dances for *On the Town, High Button Shoes*, and *The King and I*, then became director as well as choreographer with *The Pajama Game*. After the successful *Bells Are Ringing*, he created his three major achievements: *West Side Story, Gypsy*, and *Fiddler on the Roof*. Robbins has also choreographed ballets for the Ballet Russe, NYC Ballet, and his own Ballet: USA.

Unless otherwise noted, Mr. Robbins was choreographer of following; asterisk indicates he was also director:

1938 Great Lady (dancer only)
1939 Stars in Your Eyes (dancer only)
      The Straw Hat Revue (dancer only)
1944 On the Town
1945 Billion Dollar Baby
1947 High Button Shoes
1948 Look, Ma, I'm Dancin'
1949 Miss Liberty
1950 Call Me Madam
1951 The King and I
1952 Two's Company
1954 The Pajama Game *
      Peter Pan *
1956 Bells Are Ringing *
1957 West Side Story *
1959 Gypsy *
1962 A Funny Thing Happened on the Way to the Forum *
1964 Funny Girl *
      Fiddler on the Roof *
1966 Funny Girl * (L)
1967 Fiddler on the Roof * (L)

Robert and Elizabeth (1964). Music by Ron Grainer; lyrics & book by Ronald Millar, based on unproduced musical *The Third Kiss* by Fred G. Moritt, adapted from play *The Barretts of Wimpole Street* by Rudolph Besier.

SONGS: "The World Outside," "The Moon in My Pocket," "I Said Love," "The Real Thing," "You Only to Love Me," "In a Simple Way," "I Know Now," "Escape Me Never" (lyric, Robert Browning), "The Girls That Boys Dream About," "Woman and Man."

LONDON: Oct. 20, 1964
LYRIC THEATRE; 948 p.

Presented by Martin Landau; directed by Wendy Toye; settings & costumes, Malcolm Pride; lighting, John Wyckham; music director, Alexander Faris; orchestrations, Faris.

CAST: John Clements (*Edward*

Moulton-Barrett), June Bronhill (*Elizabeth Barrett*), Keith Michell (*Robert Browning*), Angela Richards (*Henrietta*), Jeremy Lloyd (*Capt. Surtees Cook*).

The romance between poet Robert Browning and poet Elizabeth Barrett provided the subject for a lushly romantic operetta that transported London theatregoers back to the bittersweet dancing years of Coward and Novello. In the strict Victorian household of Edward Moulton-Barrett in the year 1845, ailing daughter Elizabeth falls in love with Robert, much to the disapproval of papa. Ultimately, the two elope to Italy. A projected Bway version was unable to be mounted because of legal action taken by Bklyn Judge Fred G. Moritt, whose script formed the basis of the musical.

Roberta (1933). Music by Jerome Kern; lyrics & book by Otto Harbach, based on Alice Duer Miller's novel *Gowns by Roberta*.

SONGS: "You're Devastating," "Yesterdays," "The Touch of Your Hand," "Smoke Gets in Your Eyes," "Let's Begin," "I'll Be Hard to Handle" (lyric, Bernard Dougall), "Something Had to Happen."

NEW YORK: Nov. 18, 1933
NEW AMSTERDAM THEATRE; 295 p.

Presented by Max Gordon; directed by Hassard Short (uncredited); choreographed by José Limon, John Lonergan; settings, Clark Robinson; costumes, Kiviette; music director, Victor Baravalle; orchestrations, Robert Russell Bennett.

CAST: Lyda Roberti (*Clementina Scharwenka*), Bob Hope (*Huckleberry Haines*), Fay Templeton (*Aunt Minnie*), Tamara (*Stephanie*), George Murphy (*Billy Boyden*), Sydney Greenstreet (*Lord Henry Delves*), Raymond Middleton (*John Kent*),

Helen Gray (*Sophie Teale*), William Hain (*Ladislaw*), Fred MacMurray (saxophonist in California Collegians Band).

Though the reviews were unfavorable, *Roberta* had a successful run, thanks largely to the elegant mounting (incl. a fashion show) and the popularity of "Smoke Gets in Your Eyes." The musical brought Fay Templeton back to Bway for her final performance, and also marked the first major appearance of Bob Hope. The libretto concerned itself with the romance between All-American fullback John Kent and Russian Princess Stephanie set in the Paris dress salon owned by John's Aunt Minnie, known as Roberta. At first Kern and Hammerstein directed the production—originally tried out under the name *Gowns by Roberta*—but Hassard Short was eventually called in during the break-in tour. In July 1934 Hope was succeeded by Marty May, Lyda Roberti by Odette Myrtil.

FILM VERSIONS: Irene Dunne, Fred Astaire, Ginger Rogers (RKO 1935 William A. Seiter dir.); Kathryn Grayson, Howard Keel, Red Skelton, Marge & Gower Champion (called *Lovely to Look At*) (MGM 1952, Mervyn LeRoy dir.).

Roberts, Rachel, actress, singer; b. Llanelly, Wales, Sept. 20, 1927. A dramatic actress of stage and screen best known for portrayals of middleclass women, Miss Roberts starred in longrunning London musical, *Maggie May*. She was once married to Rex Harrison.

1953   At the Lyric
1954   Going to Town (At the Lyric)
1957   Oh! My Papa! (*Iduna*)
1958   Keep Your Hair On (*Mabel Gibbs*)
1964   Maggie May (*Maggie May*)

Robertson, Guy, actor, singer; b. Denver, Col., Jan. 26, 1892. Wavy-haired, square-jawed Bway operetta hero who appeared in *Wildflower* (singing "Wildflower") and *The Great Waltz.* He was once married to actress Audrey Christie.

1919	See-Saw (*Billy Meyrick*)
1921	The Perfect Fool
1922	Daffy Dill (*Kenneth Hobson*)
1923	Wildflower (*Guido*)
1925	Rose-Marie (US tour) (*Jim Kenyon*)
	Song of the Flame (*Prince Volodyn*)
1927	The Circus Princess (*Prince Alexis*)
	Lovely Lady (*Paul de Morlaix*)
1928	White Lilacs (*Frederic Chopin*)
1929	The Street Singer (*George*)
1930	Nina Rosa (*Jack Haines*)
1932	Marching By (*Lt. Franz Almasy*)
1934	All the King's Horses (*Don McArthur*)
	The Great Waltz (*Johann Strauss Jr.*)
1938	Right This Way (*Jeff Doane*)
1939	Very Warm for May (*Johnny Graham,* repl.)

Robeson, Paul, actor, singer; b. Princeton, NJ, April 9, 1898. One of the theatre's most overpowering actors, Robeson made his Bway debut in 1921, scoring successes in dramas *All God's Chillun Got Wings, The Emperor Jones,* and *Othello.* Though identified with song "Ol' Man River" in *Show Boat,* Robeson was not in original cast. He was also a concert and recording artist and appeared in many films. Bib: *Paul Robeson, Citizen of the World* by Shirley Graham (Messner, NY 1946); *Paul Robeson: The American Othello* by Edwin Hoyt (Cleve. 1967). (*D. Jan. 23, 1976.*)

1921	Shuffle Along (singer, repl.)
1922	The Plantation Revue (chorus)
1928	Show Boat (L) (*Joe*)
1932	Show Boat (r) (*Joe*)

Robey, George (né George Edward Wade), actor; b. London, Sept. 20, 1869; d. Saltdean, Eng., Nov. 29, 1954. Knighted 1954. Dubbed "The Prime Minister of Mirth," Robey was a round-faced, bushy-browed, red-nosed clown who usually wore a baggy black clerical costume, a shallow derby, and carried a small cane. He was a headliner in music halls before winning fame in two *Bing Boys* musicals in London (introducing "If You Were the Only Girl in the World" in *The Bing Boys Are Here*). Bib: *Looking Back on Life* by Robey (Constable, L 1940); *Prime Minister of Mirth* by A. E. Wilson (Oldhams, L 1956); *George Robey* by Peter Cotes (Cassell, L 1972).

1916	The Bing Boys Are Here (*Lucifer Bing*)
1917	Zig-Zag!
1918	The Bing Boys on Broadway (*Lucifer Bing*)
1919	Joy Bells
1920	Johnny Jones (*Johnny Jones*)
1921	Robey en Casserole
1922	Round in Fifty
1923	You'd Be Surprised
1924	Leap Year
1925	Sky High
1927	Bits and Pieces (also prod.)
1928	In Other Words (also prod.)
1932	Helen! (*Menelaus*)
1933	Jolly Roger (*Bold Ben Blister*)
1934	Here's How! (*Lord Ullage*)
	The Bing Boys Are Here (r) (*Lucifer Bing*)
1936	Certainly, Sir! (*Hepplewhite*)
	Laughter Over London

Robin Hood (1891). Music by Reginald De Koven; lyrics & book by Harry B. Smith, based on the English legend.

SONGS: "Brown October Ale," "Oh, Promise Me" (lyric, Clement Scott), "Tinkers' Chorus," "Armorers' Song," "Ah, I Do Love Thee," "Sweetheart,

My Own Sweetheart," "Ho Ho Then for Jollity," "Ye Birds in Azure Winging," "Now We Never More Will Part."

NEW YORK: Sept. 28, 1891
STANDARD THEATRE

Presented by the Bostonians; directed by Harry Dixon; settings, Ernest Gros; costumes, Mme. Freisinger. Music director, Samuel Studley.

CAST: Tom Karl (Robin Hood), Eugene Cowles (Will Scarlet), Caroline Hamilton (Maid Marian), Jessie Bartlett Davis (Alan-a-Dale), W. H. MacDonald (Little John), Henry Clay Barnabee (Sheriff of Nottingham), Peter Lang (Sir Guy of Gisborne), George B. Frothingham (Friar Tuck).

LONDON: Feb. 5, 1892
PRINCE OF WALES' THEATRE; 6 weeks

Presented by Horace Sedger; directed by Charles Harris; settings, W. Telbin, E. Emden, W. Perkins; costumes, Percy Anderson; music director, John Crook: retitled Maid Marian.

CAST: C. Hayden Coffin (Robert, Earl of Huntingdon), Egbert Roberts (Will Scarlet), Marian Manola (Maid Marian), Violet Cameron (Alan-a-Dale), Leonard Russell (Little John), Harry Monkhouse (Sheriff of Nottingham), John Le Hay (Sir Guy of Gisborne), Harry Parker (Friar Tuck).

The saga of Robin Hood was turned into the most celebrated operetta offered in the US up to the early 1900s. Set in the days of King Richard the Lion-Hearted, the tale covers the exploits of Robin and his band of merry outlaws in Sherwood Forest. To save the fair Maid Marian, they do battle against such villains as the Sheriff of Nottingham and Sir Guy of Gisborne, and Robin ends with the Maid all to himself. **Robin Hood was first presented as part of the repertory of a** touring opera company called The Bostonians (managed by Henry Clay Barnabee, Tom Karl, and W. H. MacDonald). It opened at the Chicago Opera House, June 9, 1890, with Edwin Hoff as Robin and Marie Stone as Marian. Because the company had so little confidence in the work, costumes from other operas were used and the entire production cost $109.50. The show did, however, become a great favorite on tour and new costumes and scenery were designed for the successful NY engagement (terminated after a month only because of a previously scheduled booking). Though Tom Karl played the title role opening night, Hoff alternated the part, and during run Flora Finlayson replaced Jessie Bartlett Davis as Alan-a-Dale. The production returned to NY for a longer run in May 1892, at the Garden Theatre, with Camille D'Arville as Marian. Other NY revivals were presented in 1893, 1894, 1900, 1902, and 1912.

In 1902, Reginald DeKoven and Harry B. Smith wrote a sequel, Maid Marian (the same title had been used for the 1892 London version of Robin Hood). The cast included Frank Rushworth (Robin), Grace Van Studdiford (Marian), Adele Rafter (Alan), and Henry Clay Barnabee and W. H. MacDonald in their familiar roles of Sheriff and Little John. The Bostonians offered it on Bway for 64 performances.

An updated version of the tale, Twang!!, by Lionel Bart, played in London in 1965. It ran 46 performances, with James Booth and Barbara Windsor in the leads.

Robin, Leo, lyricist; b. Pittsburgh, Pa., April 6, 1900. Robin's biggest Bway hits: Hit the Deck ("Hallelujah! ") and Gentlemen Prefer Blondes ("Just a Little Girl from Little Rock," "Diamonds Are a Girl's Best Friend").

Among composers he collaborated with: Charles Rosoff, Vincent Youmans, Phil Charig, Richard Myers, Joseph Meyer, Jule Styne, Sigmund Romberg. He also wrote many Hollywood film scores.

1927   Judy (Rosoff)
         Hit the Deck (Youmans)
         Allez-Oop (Charig, Myers)
         Just Fancy (Meyer, Charig)
1928   Hello Yourself!!! (Meyer)
1949   Gentlemen Prefer Blondes (Styne)
1954   The Girl in Pink Tights (Romberg)

Robinson, Bill ("Bojangles"), actor, dancer; b. Richmond, Va., May 25, 1878; d. New York, Nov. 25, 1949. Robinson's casual, effortless tap dancing and warm personality made him a headliner in vaudeville and nightclubs. On Bway, his major productions were *Blackbirds of 1928* and *The Hot Mikado.* He also acted in Hollywood films, 1933–1939.

1928   Blackbirds of 1928
1930   Brown Buddies (*Sam Wilson*)
1933   Blackbirds
1939   The Hot Mikado (*Mikado*)
1940   All in Fun
1945   Memphis Bound (*Pilot Meriweather*)

"Rock-a-Bye Your Baby with a Dixie Melody." Music by Jean Schwartz; lyric by Sam Lewis & Joe Young. "Mammy"-styled lullaby sung by Al Jolson as an interpolation in *Sinbad* (NY 1918).

Rodgers, Mary, composer; b. New York, Jan. 11, 1931. Miss Rodgers' major score was for the off-Bway *Once Upon a Mattress* ("Shy," "In a Little While"). The daughter of composer Richard Rodgers and the wife of producer Henry Guettel, she has also written for tv, concerts, and children's records. Her collaborators have been Marshall Barer and Martin Charnin.

1959   Once Upon a Mattress (Barer)
1963   Hot Spot (Charnin)
1966   The Mad Show (Barer)

Rodgers, Richard (Charles), composer, producer, librettist; b. New York, June 28, 1902. Rodgers' career has been the most durable of any composer's in the history of the Bway musical theatre. Apart from the melodic appeal of his music, he has been associated with many works that have been influential in broadening the scope of both subject matter and stage technique. His career has also been distinguished by the fact that for the first 40 years he had only two lyric-writing collaborators: Lorenz Hart and Oscar Hammerstein II.

Rodgers and Hart teamed up in 1919 and initially won notice with their songs for *The Garrick Gaieties* (incl. "Manhattan"). They continued on Bway (and occasionally London) through 1931, contributing scores for *Dearest Enemy* ("Here in My Arms"), *Peggy-Ann* ("Where's That Rainbow?"), *A Connecticut Yankee* ("My Heart Stood Still," "Thou Swell"), and *Ever Green* ("Dancing on the Ceiling"). After a period writing for Hollywood films (incl. *Love Me Tonight*), they resumed their Bway career, creating a series of highly varied, innovative musicals: *Jumbo* ("The Most Beautiful Girl in the World," "My Romance," "Little Girl Blue"), *On Your Toes* ("There's a Small Hotel," "Glad to Be Unhappy," "Slaughter on Tenth Avenue"), *Babes in Arms* ("My Funny Valentine," "Johnny One Note," "The Lady Is a Tramp," "Where or When"), *I'd Rather Be Right* ("Have You Met Miss Jones?"), *I Married an Angel* ("I Married an Angel," "Spring Is Here"), *The Boys from Syracuse* ("Falling in

Love with Love," "This Can't Be Love"), *Pal Joey* ("Bewitched," "I Could Write a Book"). Other songs included "The Blue Room" (*The Girl Friend*), "Mountain Greenery" (second *Garrick Gaieties*), "You Took Advantage of Me" (*Present Arms*), "With a Song in My Heart" (*Spring Is Here*), "A Ship Without a Sail" (*Heads Up*), "Ten Cents a Dance" (*Simple Simon*), "I Didn't Know What Time It Was" (*Too Many Girls*), "Wait Till You See Her" (*By Jupiter*), "To Keep My Love Alive" (revised *Connecticut Yankee*). Helen Ford, Ray Bolger, and Vivienne Segal were each in three Rodgers and Hart musicals, Jessie Matthews was in two.

In 1942 Rodgers joined with Hammerstein in a succession of musicals that helped set the standards for the 40s and 50s: the landmark *Oklahoma!* ("People Will Say We're in Love," "Oh, What a Beautiful Mornin'," "The Surrey with the Fringe on Top," "Oklahoma," "I Cain't Say No"), *Carousel* ("If I Loved You," "Soliloquy," "June Is Bustin' Out All Over," "You'll Never Walk Alone"), *South Pacific* ("Some Enchanted Evening," "There Is Nothin' Like a Dame," "Bali Ha'i," "I'm Gonna Wash That Man Right Outa My Hair," "A Wonderful Guy," "Younger than Springtime"), *The King and I* ("I Whistle a Happy Tune," "Hello, Young Lovers," "Getting to Know You," "Something Wonderful," "Shall We Dance?"), *The Sound of Music* ("The Sound of Music," "Do-Re-Mi," "My Favorite Things," "Maria," "Climb Ev'ry Mountain"). Other Rodgers and Hammerstein songs: "A Fellow Needs a Girl," "You Are Never Away," "The Gentleman Is a Dope" (*Allegro*); "No Other Love" (*Me and Juliet*); "I Enjoy Being a Girl," "Love, Look Away" (*Flower Drum Song*). Among singers associated with Rodgers and Hammerstein productions were Alfred Drake, Celeste Holm, John Raitt, Mary Martin, Ezio Pinza, Gertrude Lawrence.

Since Hammerstein's death, Rodgers has written his own lyrics for *No Strings* ("The Sweetest Sounds"), and has collaborated with Stephen Sondheim ("Do I Hear a Waltz?") and Martin Charnin. Bib: *The Rodgers and Hart Song Book* (S&S, NY 1951); *Some Enchanted Evenings* by Deems Taylor (Harper, NY 1952); *Richard Rodgers* by David Ewen (Holt, NY 1957); *The Rodgers and Hammerstein Song Book* (S&S, NY 1958); *The Rodgers and Hammerstein Story* by Stanley Green (Day, NY 1963); *Musical Stages* by Rodgers (Random, NY 1975). (*D. N.Y., Dec. 30, 1979.*)

Unless otherwise noted, following were written with Mr. Hart; asterisk indicates musical written with Mr. Hammerstein; dagger indicates musical also produced or co-produced by Mr. Rodgers:

1920	Poor Little Ritz Girl
1925	The Garrick Gaieties
	Dearest Enemy
1926	The Girl Friend
	The Garrick Gaieties
	Lido Lady (L)
	Peggy-Ann
	Betsy
1927	One Dam Thing After Another (L)
	A Connecticut Yankee
1928	She's My Baby
	Present Arms
	Chee-Chee
1929	Spring Is Here
	Heads Up!
1930	Simple Simon
	Ever Green (L)
1931	America's Sweetheart
1935	Jumbo
1936	On Your Toes (also co-lib.)
1937	Babes in Arms (also co-lib.)
	I'd Rather Be Right
1938	I Married an Angel (also co-lib.)
	The Boys from Syracuse
1939	Too Many Girls
1940	Higher and Higher
	Pal Joey

1941 Best Foot Forward (co-prod. only)
1942 By Jupiter † (also co-lib.)
Beat the Band (co-prod. only)
1943 Oklahoma! *
A Connecticut Yankee † (r)
1945 Carousel *
1946 Annie Get Your Gun (co-prod. only)
1947 Allegro *
1948 Show Boat (US tour) (co-prod. only)
1949 South Pacific * †
1951 The King and I * †
1953 Me and Juliet * †
1954 On Your Toes † (r)
1955 Pipe Dream * †
1958 Flower Drum Song * †
1959 The Sound of Music * †
1962 No Strings † (also lyr.)
1965 Do I Hear a Waltz? † (Sondheim)
1970 Two by Two † (Charnin)

Rogers, Anne, actress, singer, dancer; b. Liverpool, Eng., July 29, 1933. Miss Rogers made her London debut in *The Boy Friend,* in which she introduced "I Could Be Happy with You" and "A Room in Bloomsbury."

1954 The Boy Friend (*Polly Browne*)
1957 My Fair Lady (US tour) (*Eliza Doolittle*)
1959 My Fair Lady (*Eliza Doolittle,* repl.)
1964 She Loves Me (*Amalia Balash*)
1966 Half a Sixpence (US tour) (*Ann Pornick*)
1967 Walking Happy (NY) (*Maggie Hobson,* repl.)
1968 I Do! I Do! (*Agnes*)
1973 No, No, Nanette (r) (*Lucille Early*)

Rogers, Ginger (née Virginia Katherine McMath), actress, singer, dancer; b. Independence, Mo., July 16, 1911. Vivacious blonde former Charleston dancer and band singer who introduced "Embraceable You" and "But Not for Me" in *Girl Crazy* on Bway. Became Hollywood film star in musicals (10 with Fred Astaire) and comedies. Bib: *Ginger Rogers* by

Dick Richards (Clifton, L 1969).

1929 Top Speed (*Babs Green*)
1930 Girl Crazy (*Molly Gray*)
1965 Hello, Dolly! (*Dolly Levi,* repl.)
1969 Mame (L) (*Mame Dennis*)

Rogers, (William Penn Adair) Will, actor; b. Olagah, Indian Terr., Nov. 4, 1879; d. plane crash, Point Barrow, Alaska, Aug. 15, 1935. Rope-twirling homespun philosopher-humorist who made comments on news events and prefaced his remarks with the line "All I know is what I read in the papers." Rogers began vaudeville career in 1905, entered films in 1918, and is best remembered on Bway in the incongruous surroundings of the *Ziegfeld Follies.* Bib: *Autobiography of Will Rogers* (Houghton Mifflin, Boston 1949); *Our Will Rogers* by Homer Croy (Duell, Sloan, NY 1953); *Will Rogers* by Donald Day (McKay, NY 1962); *Will Rogers: His Life and Times* by Richard Ketchum (Amer. Heritage, NY 1973).

1912 The Wall Street Girl
1915 Hands Up (*Cowboy Will*)
Town Topics
1916 Ziegfeld Follies
1917 The Passing Show (added)
Ziegfeld Follies
1918 Ziegfeld Follies
1922 Ziegfeld Follies
1924 Ziegfeld Follies
1926 Cochran's Revue of 1926 (L) (added)
1928 Three Cheers (*King Pampanola*)

Romberg, Sigmund, composer; b. Nagy Kaniza, Hungary, July 29, 1887; d. New York, Nov. 10, 1951. Romberg was the most prolific successor to Victor Herbert in perpetuating an American form of European operetta. After settling in NY in 1909, he was hired by producer J. J. Shubert as staff composer, chiefly for revues and musical comedies, though he did write two successful operettas: *The Blue Paradise* ("Auf Wiedersehn") and *May-*

time ("The Road to Paradise," "Will You Remember?"). Romberg's fame as a result of *Blossom Time* ("Song of Love") and *The Student Prince in Heidelberg* ("Golden Days," "Drinking Song," "Deep in My Heart, Dear," "Serenade") enabled him to devote himself exclusively to productions in the same musical vein: *The Desert Song* ("The Riff Song," "The Desert Song," "One Alone"), *My Maryland* ("Your Land and My Land"), *The New Moon* ("Softly, as in a Morning Sunrise," "Stouthearted Men," "One Kiss," "Lover, Come Back to Me"), *Up in Central Park* ("Close as Pages in a Book").

Though Romberg wrote 20 scores with Harold Atteridge, his most durable work was created with lyricists Rida Johnson Young, Dorothy Donnelly, Otto Harbach, Oscar Hammerstein II, and Dorothy Fields. Others with whom he collaborated: E. Ray Goetz, Herbert Reynolds, Matthew Woodward, Robert B. Smith, Edward Paulton, Cyrus Wood, Frederic Kummer, Alex Gerber, Ballard Macdonald, Sam Coslow, Clifford Grey, Arthur Wimperis, Harry B. Smith, P. G. Wodehouse, Irving Caesar, Rowland Leigh, Leo Robin. Romberg also wrote for Hollywood films and conducted his own concert orchestra. Bib: *Deep in My Heart* by Elliott Arnold (Duell, Sloan, NY 1949).

1914 The Whirl of the World (Atteridge)
The Passing Show (Atteridge)
Dancing Around (Atteridge)
1915 Maid in America (Atteridge)
Hands Up (Goetz)
The Blue Paradise (Reynolds)
A World of Pleasure (Atteridge)
1916 Robinson Crusoe, Jr. (Atteridge)
The Passing Show (Atteridge)
The Girl from Brazil (Woodward)
The Show of Wonders (Atteridge)
Follow Me (R. B. Smith)
Her Soldier Boy (Young)

1917 The Passing Show (Atteridge)
My Lady's Glove (Paulton)
Maytime (Young)
Doing Our Bit (Atteridge)
Over the Top (Manning, Woodward)
1918 Sinbad (Atteridge)
The Passing Show (Atteridge)
The Melting of Molly (Wood)
1919 Monte Cristo, Jr. (Atteridge)
The Passing Show (Atteridge)
The Magic Melody (Kummer) (also co-prod.)
1920 Poor Little Ritz Girl (Gerber)
1921 Love Birds (Macdonald) (also co-prod.)
Blossom Time (Donnelly)
Bombo (Atteridge)
1922 The Blushing Bride (Wood)
The Rose of Stamboul (Atteridge)
Springtime of Youth (Wood)
1923 The Dancing Girl (Atteridge)
The Passing Show (Atteridge)
1924 Innocent Eyes (Atteridge)
Marjorie (Grey)
The Passing Show (Atteridge)
Artists and Models (Coslow, Grey)
Annie Dear (Grey)
The Student Prince in Heidelberg (Donnelly)
1925 Louie the 14th (Wimperis)
Princess Flavia (H. B. Smith)
1926 The Desert Song (Harbach, Hammerstein)
1927 Cherry Blossoms (H. B. Smith)
My Maryland (Donnelly)
My Princess (Donnelly)
The Love Call (H. B. Smith)
1928 Rosalie (Wodehouse)
The New Moon (Hammerstein)
1930 Nina Rosa (Caesar)
1931 East Wind (Hammerstein)
1933 Melody (Caesar)
1935 May Wine (Hammerstein)
1936 Forbidden Melody (Harbach)
1941 Sunny River (Hammerstein)
1945 Up in Central Park (Fields)
1948 My Romance (Leigh)
1954 The Girl in Pink Tights (Robin)

Rome, Harold (Jacob), composer, lyricist; b. Hartford, Conn., May 27, 1908.

Rome has been particularly adept at capturing the emotions of urban working people in such Bway musicals as *Pins and Needles* ("Sing Me a Song with Social Significance," "Sunday in the Park"), *Wish You Were Here* ("Wish You Were Here," "Where Did the Night Go?"), and *Fanny* ("Fanny"). Other songs include "FDR Jones" (*Sing Out the News*), "South America, Take It Away" (*Call Me Mister*), "Anyone Would Love You" (*Destry Rides Again*). *Gone with the Wind* was originally performed by a Japanese cast in Tokyo under the title *Scarlett* (1970). Bib: *The Scarlett Letters* by Florence Rome (his wife) (Random, NY 1971).

1937	Pins and Needles
1938	Sing Out the News
1942	Let Freedom Sing
1946	Call Me Mister
1950	Bless You All
1952	Wish You Were Here
1954	Fanny
1959	Destry Rides Again
1962	I Can Get It for You Wholesale
1965	The Zulu and the Zayda
1972	Gone with the Wind (L)

"Room in Bloomsbury, A." Music & lyric by Sandy Wilson. "In our attic we'll be ecstatic" cooed Anthony Hayes and Anne Rogers in *The Boy Friend* (L 1954) as they envisaged the bliss of living together in a single room on the top floor of a walkup. The NY lovers were John Hewer and Julie Andrews (1954).

"Room with a View, A." Music & lyric by Noël Coward. Song of domestic tranquillity sung by Jessie Matthews and Sonnie Hale looking out of a window in *This Year of Grace!* (L 1928). In NY version (1928), sung by Coward and Madeline Gibson. NY theatre critic Alexander Woollcott disliked the song, taking particularly strong ex-

ception to the lines "Maybe a stork will bring/ This, that and t'other thing to/ Our room with a view." One evening he showed up at the theatre with a group of companions, including Harpo Marx, and sat in a box. As Coward began the song, they all opened newspapers and made a showy display of ignoring the singer. Coward countered by singing the last couplet in baby-talk, which sent Woollcott screaming out of the theatre. Coward, however, agreed with his detractors because he told Charles Cochran, the show's producer, that he couldn't continue singing "those terrible slushy words. It's more than I can bear, and more than one should expect of the audience." The song was then given to Billy Milton.

"Room Without Windows, A." Music & lyric by Ervin Drake. Romantic duet in praise of solitary confinement sung by Steve Lawrence and Sally Ann Howes in *What Makes Sammy Run?* (NY 1964).

Rose, Billy (né William Samuel Rosenberg), producer, lyricist; b. New York, Sept. 6, 1899; d. Jamaica, WI, Feb. 10, 1966. Rose began his career as a lyricist, contributing songs to revues (incl. "A Cup of Coffee, a Sandwich and You" in the *Charlot Revue of 1926*) and writing the score for *Great Day!* ("More than You Know," "Great Day!," "Without a Song") with Edward Eliscu and Vincent Youmans. His first Bway productions were revues, *Sweet and Low* ("Would You Like to Take a Walk?") and *Crazy Quilt* ("I Found a Million Dollar Baby"), and his longest-running shows were *Jumbo* and *Carmen Jones*. He also produced expositions and Aquacades, owned nightclubs and theatres. Rose's first wife was comedienne Fanny Brice. Bib: *Billy Rose: Manhattan Primitive* by Earl Conrad (World, Cleve. 1968); *The Nine Lives of Billy Rose* by Pearl Rose Gottlieb (his sister) (Crown, NY 1968).

Unless otherwise noted, Mr. Rose was producer of following:

1927 Padlocks of 1927 (lyr. only) (misc. comps.)
Harry Delmar's Revels (lyr. only) (misc. comps.)
1929 Great Day! (lyr. only) (Eliscu, Youmans)
1930 Sweet and Low (also lyr.) (misc. comps.)
1931 Crazy Quilt (also lyr.) (misc. comps.)
1935 Jumbo
1943 Carmen Jones
1944 Seven Lively Arts

Rose-Marie (1924). Music by Rudolf Friml & Herbert Stothart; lyrics & book by Oscar Hammerstein II & Otto Harbach.

SONGS: "Hard-Boiled Herman" (Stothart), "Rose-Marie" (Friml), "The Mounties" (Friml-Stothart), "Indian Love Call" (Friml), "Totem Tom-Tom" (Friml-Stothart), "The Door of Her Dreams" (Friml), "Pretty Things" (Friml), "Only a Kiss" (Stothart).

NEW YORK: Sept. 2, 1924
IMPERIAL THEATRE; 557 p.

Presented by Arthur Hammerstein; directed by Paul Dickey; choreographed by David Bennett; settings, Gates & Morange; costumes, Charles Le Maire; music director, Herbert Stothart; orchestrations, Robert Russell Bennett.

CAST: Mary Ellis (*Rose-Marie La Flamme*), Dennis King (*Jim Kenyon*), William Kent (*Hard-Boiled Herman*), Dorothy Mackaye (*Lady Jane*), Arthur Deagon (*Sgt. Malone*), Edward Ciannelli (*Emile La Flamme*), Pearl Regay (*Wanda*).

LONDON: March 20, 1925
DRURY LANE THEATRE; 851 p.

Presented by Alfred Butt; directed by Felix Edwardes; choreographed by J. Kathryn Scott; settings, Joseph & Phil Harker; costumes, Comelli; music director, Herman Finck.

CAST: Edith Day (*Rose-Marie La Flamme*), Derek Oldham (*Jim Kenyon*), Billy Merson (*Hard-Boiled Herman*), Clarice Hardwicke (*Lady Jane*), John Dunsmure (*Sgt. Malone*), Michael Cole (*Emile La Flamme*), Ruby Morriss (*Wanda*).

Producer Arthur Hammerstein got the idea for the musical when he read about an ice carnival in Canada. He sent nephew Oscar Hammerstein and Otto Harbach to research it as background for an operetta with a Canadian locale, but they were unable to find the carnival. Nothing daunted, the librettists dreamed up a Canadian saga about singer Rose-Marie and fur trapper Jim. Though Jim is mistakenly thought to have committed a murder, the Mounties get their man—who turns out to be a woman. The locales were Saskatchewan, the Kootenay Pass in the Canadian Rockies, and the Chateau Frontenac in Quebec. Apart from its setting, the musical was considered daring because it had a murder as an important part of the plot. It was also so conscientious about its song and story integration that the program carried a note explaining that, except for five songs that "stand out, independent of their dramatic association," no individual numbers were being listed.

During Bway run, Mary Ellis was succeeded by Desirée Ellinger (6-25) and Madeleine Massey (1-26); Dennis King by Sam Ash (6-25) and Allan Rogers (10-25). Beginning 12-25, Beatrice Kay played Lady Jane. There were two major road companies. The first began its travels Jan. 1925 and toured one year, five months with Myrtle Schaaf and Louis Templeman. The second opened Feb. 1925 and continued for four years, one month. Irene Pavloska and Guy Robertson were the original leads.

In London, where it inaugurated the policy at Drury Lane of large-scale Bway imports, *Rose-Marie* became the longest-running musical of the decade. It was revived at Drury Lane in 1929 with Edith Day repeating the starring role. Other London revivals: 1942 (Marjorie Brown and Raymond Newell); 1960 (Stephanie Voss and David Whitfield).

FILM VERSIONS: Joan Crawford and James Murray (MGM 1928, Lucian Hubbard dir.); Jeanette MacDonald and Nelson Eddy (new story) (MGM 1936, W. S. Van Dyke dir.); Ann Blyth and Howard Keel (new story, added songs) (MGM 1954, Mervyn LeRoy dir.).

"Rose-Marie." Music by Rudolf Friml; lyric by Otto Harbach and Oscar Hammerstein II. Title song from the 1924 NY musical, adoringly sung by Dennis King and Arthur Deagon. Derek Oldham and John Dunsmure sang it in London version (1925).

"Rose of Washington Square." Music by James F. Hanley; lyric by Ballard Macdonald. Sung by Fanny Brice in *Ziegfeld Nine o'Clock Frolic* (NY 1920), in *Ziegfeld Midnight Frolic* (1920), and in *Ziegfeld Follies* (1934). The saga of "Rose, in second-hand clothes," which was written for Miss Brice, provided the model for composer Hanley's later "Second Hand Rose."

"Rose's Turn." Music by Jule Styne; lyric by Stephen Sondheim. Shattering concluding number in *Gypsy* (NY 1959) in which Rose, alone on a bare stage, gives vent to her frustrations at having remained in the background while pushing the theatrical careers of her two daughters. Part of the piece contains a variation on the lyric in "Mama's Talkin' Soft," a song discarded before NY, while other parts use musical themes from "Some People" and "Everything's Coming Up Roses." Ethel Merman bared her soul in the original production; Angela Lansbury had her turn in the 1973 London revival.

Ross, Adrian (né Arthur Reed Ropes), lyricist, librettist; b. Lewisham, Eng., Dec. 23, 1859; d. London, Sept. 10, 1933. Ross's most durable work was his English-language adaptation of the lyrics to Franz Lehar's *Merry Widow* ("Vilia," "Maxim's," "Merry Widow Waltz"). Sixteen of his London musicals had runs of over 400 performances; seven ran over 600: *San Toy, The Toreador, A Country Girl, The Merry Widow, Our Miss Gibbs, The Boy, Lilac Time.* Ross wrote 13 scores with Lionel Monckton, eight with Ivan Caryll, six each with F. Osmond Carr and Sidney Jones. Other composers with whom he was associated: André Messager, Jacques Offenbach, Howard Talbot, Hugo Felix, Oscar Straus, Leslie Stuart, Leo Fall, Paul Lincke, Walter Kollo, Albert Sirmay, Victor Jacobi, Paul Rubens, Ivor Novello, Jerome Kern, Herman Darewski, Herman Finck, Willie Redstone, H. Fraser-Simson, Charles Cuvillier, Franz Schubert, and Heinrich Berté.

1891 Joan of Arc (Carr)
1892 In Town (Carr)

1893 Don Juan (Lutz)
      Morocco Bound (Carr)
1894 Go—Bang (Carr)
      Mirette (Messager)
1896 My Girl (Carr)
      The Circus Girl (Caryll)
1897 The Grand Duchess (Offenbach)
      The Ballet Girl (NY) (Kiefert)
1898 A Greek Slave (Jones)
1899 San Toy (Jones)
1900 The Messenger Boy (Caryll,
      Monckton)
1901 The Toreador (Caryll, Monckton)
      Kitty Grey (Talbot, Monckton)
1902 A Country Girl (Monckton)
      The Girl from Kay's (Cook,
      Caryll)
1903 The Orchid (Caryll, Monckton)
      Madame Sherry (Felix)
1904 The Cingalee (Monckton)
1905 The Spring Chicken (Caryll,
      Monckton)
1906 See-See (Jones)
      The Merveilleuses (Felix)
1907 The Girls of Gottenberg (Caryll,
      Monckton)
      The Merry Widow (Lehar)
1908 A Waltz Dream (Straus)
      Havana (Stuart)
      The King of Cadonia (Jones)
      The Antelope (Felix) (also lib.)
1909 Our Miss Gibbs (Caryll, Monck-
      ton)
      The Dashing Little Duke (Tours)
      The Dollar Princess (NY) (Fall)
1910 Captain Kidd (Stuart)
      The Girl in the Train (Fall)
      The Quaker Girl (Monckton)
1911 Castles in the Air (Lincke)
      The Count of Luxembourg
      (Lehar)
1912 Gipsy Love (Lehar)
      Tantalizing Tommy (NY) (Felix)
      The Dancing Mistress (Monck-
      ton)
1913 The Girl on the Film (Kollo, Sir-
      may)
      The Marriage Market (Jacobi)
      The Girl from Utah (Jones)
1915 Betty (Rubens)
1916 The Happy Day (Jones)
      The Light Blues (Talbot, Finck)
      Theodore & Co. (Novello, Kern)
      Three Cheers (Darewski)

1917 Airs and Graces (Monckton,
      Finck)
      Arlette (Lefeuvre, Novello)
      The Boy (Monckton, Talbot)
1919 Monsieur Beaucaire (Messager)
      The Kiss Call (Caryll)
      Maggie (Lattes)
1920 A Southern Maid (Fraser-Simson)
      The Naughty Princess (Cuvillier)
1921 Faust-on-Toast (Redstone)
1922 Love's Awakening (Kunneke)
      (also lib.)
      Lilac Time (Schubert, Berté) (also
      lib.)
1923 The Cousin from Nowhere (Kun-
      neke)
      Head over Heels (Fraser-Simson)
1925 Sky High (Chappelle)
1927 The Beloved Vagabond (Glass)
      (also lib.)
1930 Frederica (lib. only)

Ross, Jerry (né Jerold Rosenberg),
composer, lyricist; b. The Bronx, NY,
March 9, 1926; d. New York, Nov. 11,
1955. Ross and his writing partner,
Richard Adler, had two major Bway
successes in *The Pajama Game*
("Hey, There," "Hernando's Hideaway," "There Once Was a Man") and
Damn Yankees ("Heart," "Whatever
Lola Wants"). The writers, who were
protégés of composer-lyricist Frank
Loesser, began their Bway career with
songs for *John Murray Anderson's Almanac* (1953).
    1954 The Pajama Game
    1955 Damn Yankees

"Roundabout." Music by Vernon
Duke; lyric by Ogden Nash. Love as a
never-ending childhood game described by Ellen Hanley and danced
by Nora Kaye (with others) in *Two's
Company* (NY 1952).

Rounseville, Robert (Field), actor,
singer; b. Attleboro, Mass., March 25,
1914; d. New York, Aug. 6, 1974. Robust operatic tenor who introduced
"To Each His Dulcinea" in *Man of La*

Mancha. Rounseville, who used the name Robert Field between 1943 and 1945, also sang in opera and nightclubs.

1937 Babes in Arms (*Bob*)
1938 The Two Bouquets (chorus)
      Knickerbocker Holiday (chorus)
1940 Higher and Higher (chorus)
1943 The Merry Widow (r) (*Jolidon*)
1945 Up in Central Park (*Andrew Munroe*)
1956 Candide (*Candide*)
1965 Man of La Mancha (*The Padre*)

Routledge, Patricia, actress, singer; b. Birkenhead, Eng., Feb. 17, 1929. Versatile actress with well-trained contralto voice who has also appeared in London in many nonmusical roles. In 1972 she appeared in Noël Coward revue *Cowardy Custard.*

1957 Zuleika (*Aunt Mabel*)
1959 The Love Doctor (*Heinrietta Argan*)
1960 Follow That Girl (*Mrs. Gilchrist*)
1961 Out of My Mind
1962 Little Mary Sunshine (*Mary Sunshine*)
1963 Virtue in Danger (*Berinthia*)
1968 Darling of the Day (NY) (*Alice Challice*)
1976 1600 Pennsylvania Ave. (NY)

"Row, Row, Row." Music by James V. Monaco; lyric by William Jerome. Romantic doings in a rowboat coyly confided by Lillian Lorraine in the *Ziegfeld Follies* (NY 1912).

Royce, Edward, director, choreographer; b. Bath, Eng., Dec. 14, 1870; d. London, June 15, 1964. Beginning as choreographer, Royce became one of the musical theatre's top directors both in London (*Our Miss Gibbs, The Dollar Princess, The Marriage Market*) and in NY (*Oh, Boy!, Leave It to Jane, Irene, Sally, Kid Boots*). He did 10 shows for George Edwardes, eight each for Charles Dillingham and Florenz Ziegfeld (incl. two *Follies*), and five for Charles Frohman, who was responsible for bringing Royce to NY.

Asterisk•indicates Mr. Royce was choreographer only:

1903 The Earl and the Girl * (L)
1904 The Catch of the Season * (L)
1905 The Talk of the Town * (L)
1906 The Beauty of Bath * (L)
1907 My Darling * (L)
1908 Havana * (L)
1909 Our Miss Gibbs (L)
      The Dollar Princess (L)
1910 The Girl in the Train (L)
1911 A Waltz Dream (L)
      Peggy * (L)
      The Count of Luxembourg (L)
1912 Gipsy Love (L)
1913 The Marriage Market (L)
      The Doll Girl *
      The Marriage Market
1914 The Laughing Husband
1915 Bric-a-brac (L)
1916 Betty
      The Century Girl
1917 Have a Heart
      Oh, Boy!
      Leave It to Jane
      Kitty Darlin'
      Going Up
1918 Oh, Lady! Lady!!
      Rockabye Baby
      The Canary
      Oh, My Dear
1919 Come Along
      She's a Good Fellow
      Apple Blossoms
      Irene
1920 Lassie
      Ziegfeld Follies
      Kissing Time
      Sally
1921 Ziegfeld Follies
      The Love Letter
      Good Morning Dearie
1922 Orange Blossoms (also prod.)
1923 Cinders (also prod.)
      Kid Boots
1924 Annie Dear
1925 Louie the 14th
1927 The Merry Malones
1928 She's My Baby
      Billie
1934 A Waltz Dream (L) (r)
1935 Fritzi (L) (also co-prod.)

Rubens, Paul A(lfred), composer, lyricist, librettist; b. London, April 29, 1875; d. Falmouth, Eng., Feb. 25, 1917. Rubens' longest-running London hits were *Florodora* (music by Leslie Stuart), *The Toreador, Miss Hook of Holland, Tonight's the Night,* and *Betty*. He was also co-lyricist with Percy Greenbank, Arthur Wimperis, Adrian Ross.

Unless otherwise noted, Mr. Rubens was composer-lyricist of following; asterisk indicates he was also librettist:

1899 Great Caesar
     Florodora (lyr. only) (Stuart)
1901 The Toreador
1902 Three Little Maids *
1904 Lady Madcap * (also Greenbank)
1905 The Blue Moon
     Mr. Popple (of Ippleton) *
1906 The Dairymaids (also Wimperis)
1907 Miss Hook of Holland *
1908 My Mimosa Maid *
1909 Dear Little Denmark *
1910 The Balkan Princess (also Wimperis)
1912 The Sunshine Girl * (also Wimperis)
1913 The Girl from Utah * (also Greenbank)
1914 After the Girl * (also Greenbank)
     Tonight's the Night (NY) (also Greenbank)
1915 Betty (also Ross)
     Tina *
1916 Half-Past Eight (also Greenbank)
     The Happy Day
     The Miller's Daughters * (Three Little Maids)

Ruby, Harry (né Harry Rubinstein), composer, librettist; b. New York, Jan. 27, 1895; d. Los Angeles, Cal., Feb. 23, 1974. The most popular Bway musicals written by Ruby and his partner, lyricist-librettist Bert Kalmar, were *The Ramblers* ("All Alone Monday"), *The Five o'Clock Girl* ("Thinking of You"), *Good Boy* ("I Wanna Be Loved by You"), and *Animal Crackers* ("Hooray for Captain Spalding").

Ruby, who began his career as a pianist in vaudeville, wrote Hollywood films with Kalmar during the 30s. The team also wrote with composers Jerome Kern and Herbert Stothart.

Unless otherwise noted, Mr. Ruby was composer of following:

1923 Helen of Troy, New York
1924 No Other Girl
1925 Holka-Polka (co-lib. only)
1926 The Ramblers (also co-lib.)
1927 Lucky (Kern) (also co-lib.)
     The Five o'Clock Girl
1928 She's My Baby (co-lib. only)
     Good Boy (Stothart)
     Animal Crackers
1929 Top Speed (also co-prod.)
1941 High Kickers (also co-lib.)

Russell, Lillian (née Helen Louise Leonard), actress, singer; b. Clinton, Iowa, Dec. 4, 1861; d. Pittsburgh, Pa., June 5, 1922. Well-proportioned beauty who was the acknowledged queen of comic opera before the turn of the century. Miss Russell first won notice at Tony Pastor's Music Hall, NY, in 1883, and was later featured in Weber and Fields burlesques (she introduced "Come Down, Ma Evenin' Star" in *Twirly Whirly*) and also starred in her own Opera Comique Co. Her first two (out of four) husbands were composers Harry Braham and Edward Solomon. Bib: *Lillian Russell* by Parker Morell (1940); *Duet in Diamonds* by John Burke (Putnam, NY 1972).

1879 The Sorcerer (*Olive*)
1883 Billee Taylor (r) (*Phoebe*)
     The Princess of Trebizonde (*Prince Raphael*)
1884 Polly (L) (*Polly Pluckrose*)
     Pocahontas (L) (*Pocahontas*)
1885 Polly (*Polly Pluckrose*)
1886 Pepita (*Pepita*)
     The Maid and the Moonshiner (*Virginia*)
1887 Dorothy (*Dorothy*)
1888 The Queen's Mate (*Inez*)
     Anita (*Anita*)

1889 Nadjy (*Princess Etelka*)
The Brigands (*Fiorella*)
The Grand Duchess (*Grand Duchess*)
1890 Poor Jonathan (*Harriet*)
1891 Apollo (*Pythia*)
La Cigale (*Marton*)
The Mountebanks (*Theresa*)
Girofle-Girofla (r) (twins)
1893 Princess Nicotine (*Rosa*)
1894 The Queen of Brilliants (L) (*Betta*)
The Queen of Brilliants (*Betta*)
1895 La Périchole (*La Périchole*)
The Tzigane (*Vera*)
The Little Duke (r) (*Duke*)
1896 The Goddess of Truth (*Goddess*)
An American Beauty (*Gabrielle*)
1897 The Wedding Day (*Lucille*)
1899 La Belle Hélène (r) (*Hélène*)
Erminie (r) (*Erminie*)
Whirl-i-Gig (*Mlle. Fifi Coocoo*)
1900 Fiddle-Dee-Dee (*Mrs. Waldorf Meadowbrook*)
1901 Hoity Toity (*Lady Grafter*)
1902 Twirly Whirly (*Mrs. Stockson Bonds*)
1903 Whoop-Dee-Doo (*Countess de Quartierlatin*)
1904 Lady Teazle (*Lady Teazle*)
1912 Hokey Pokey (*Mrs. Wallingford Grafter*)

Russell, Rosalind, actress; b. Waterbury, Conn., June 4, 1912. Tall, angular performer who had successful screen career between her two appearances in Bway musicals. Miss Russell was married to producer Frederick Brisson, and was the daughter-in-law of singer Carl Brisson. (*D. Nov. 28, 1976*)

1930 The Garrick Gaieties (added)
1953 Wonderful Town (*Ruth Sherwood*)

Ryskind, Morrie, librettist; b. New York, Oct. 20, 1895. Ryskind's best-known Bway musicals were *Strike Up the Band, Of Thee I Sing,* and *Louisiana Purchase.* He was co-author with George S. Kaufman of four shows, and wrote lyrics to music by Arthur Samuels, Henry Souvaine, Jay Gorney, Walter Samuels.

Unless otherwise noted, Mr. Ryskind was co-librettist of following:

1922 The 49ers (lyr. only) (A. Samuels)
1927 Merry-Go-Round (also lyr.) (Souvaine, Gorney)
1928 Animal Crackers
1929 Ned Wayburn's Gambols (also lyr.) (W. Samuels)
1930 Strike Up the Band
1931 The Gang's All Here
Of Thee I Sing
1933 Let 'Em Eat Cake
1940 Louisiana Purchase
1942 The Lady Comes Across (dir. only)

S

" 'S Wonderful." Music by George Gershwin; lyric by Ira Gershwin. Sibilant love duet, sung in *Funny Face* by Adele Astaire and Allen Kearns in NY (1927), and by Miss Astaire and Bernard Clifton in London (1928).

Saddler, Donald (Edward), choreographer; b. Van Nuys, Cal., Jan. 24, 1920. Soloist with American Ballet Co. and associate director, Harkness Ballet, before becoming Bway dancer and choreographer. Saddler is best known for his period dances in the revival of *No, No, Nanette.*

Unless otherwise noted, Mr. Saddler was choreographer of following:

1948 High Button Shoes (*Uncle Willie,* repl., only)
1950 Dance Me a Song (dancer only)
Bless You All (dancer only)

1953	Wonderful Town
	John Murray Anderson's Almanac
1956	Shangri-la
1959	When in Rome (L)
1961	Milk and Honey
1963	Sophie
	Morning Sun
1971	No, No, Nanette
1973	Tricks

Saidy, (Fareed Milhelm) Fred, librettist; b. Los Angeles, Cal., Feb. 11, 1907. Saidy was the co-librettist of two classics of the Bway musical theatre: *Bloomer Girl* and *Finian's Rainbow.*

1944	Bloomer Girl
1947	Finian's Rainbow
1951	Flahooley
1957	Jamaica
1961	The Happiest Girl in the World

"Sail Away." Music & lyric by Noël Coward. Graham Payn introduced this buoyant prescription for getting away from life's problems in *Ace of Clubs* (L 1950). It was also sung in *Sail Away* by James Hurst (NY 1961) and David Holliday (L 1962).

Salad Days (1954). Music by Julian Slade; lyrics & book by Dorothy Reynolds & Slade.

SONGS: "We Said We Wouldn't Look Back," "I Sit in the Sun," "Oh, Look at Me, I'm Dancing!," "It's Easy to Sing," "We're Looking for a Piano," "The Time of Your Life," "The Saucer Song."

LONDON: Aug. 5, 1954
VAUDEVILLE THEATRE; 2,283 p.

Presented by Linnit & Dunfee Ltd. & Jack Hylton; directed by Denis Carey; choreographed by Elizabeth West; settings, Patrick Robertson; costumes, Alvary Williams; piano, Julian Slade.

CAST: Eleanor Drew (*Jane*), John Warner (*Timothy Dawes*), Dorothy Reynolds (*Timothy's Mother*), Newton Blick (*Tramp*), James Cairncross (*Uncle Clam*), Michael Meacham (*Nigel Danvers*), Christine Finn (*Fiona Thompson*).

NEW YORK: Nov. 10, 1958
BARBIZON PLAZA; 80 p.

Presented by Nicholas Benton & Stanley Flink; directed by Barry Morse; choreographed by Alan & Blanche Lund; settings, Murray Laufer; costumes, Clare Jeffrey; music director, Gordon Kushner; arrangements, Kushner, Bruce Snell, John Fenwick.

CAST: Barbara Franklin (*Jane*), Richard Easton (*Timothy Dawes*), Mary Savidge (*Timothy's Mother*), Powys Thomas (*Tramp*), Jack Creley (*Uncle Clam*), Tom Kneebone (*Nigel Danvers*), June Sampson (*Fiona Thompson*).

In this whimsical tale, Jane and Timothy, a young married couple, meet a tramp in a London park who gets them to mind his piano for a month. As soon as they have it, it suddenly begins to play and miraculously makes everyone dance. Because the grim Minister of Pleasures and Pastimes frowns on such gaiety, he tries to have the merry-making suppressed—with the result that the tramp must steal back his piano to save it. The musical was first presented for three weeks as part of the regular summer program of the Bristol Old Vic, and was specifically written so that all 12 members of the company would have parts. The show proved so popular that its run at the 650-seat Vaudeville Theatre is currently the third longest in London music theatre history. The company that played NY originated at the Crest Theatre,

Toronto. In 1961, *Salad Days* was revived in London at the Prince's Theatre.

Sally (1920). Music by Jerome Kern; lyrics by Clifford Grey, etc.; book by Guy Bolton, based on his & P. G. Wodehouse's unproduced musical *The Little Thing;* ballet music by Victor Herbert.

SONGS: "On with the Dance," "You Can't Keep a Good Girl Down" (lyric, P. G. Wodehouse), "Look for the Silver Lining" (lyric, B. G. DeSylva), "Sally," "Wild Rose," "The Schnitza Kommiska," "Whip-Poor-Will," "The Lorelei" (lyric, Anne Caldwell), "The Church 'Round the Corner" (lyric, Wodehouse).

NEW YORK: Dec. 21, 1920
NEW AMSTERDAM THEATRE; 570 p.
Presented by Florenz Ziegfeld Jr.; directed & choreographed by Edward Royce; settings, Joseph Urban; costumes, Alice O'Neill, Lucile, Lady Duff Gordon, Baron de Meyer, Pascaud; music director, Gus Salzer.
CAST: Marilynn Miller (*Sally Green*), Leon Errol (*Connie*), Walter Catlett (*Otis Hooper*), Irving Fisher (*Blair Farquar*), Mary Hay (*Rosalind Rafferty*), Dolores (*Mrs. Ten Broeck*), Stanley Ridges (*Jimmy Spelvin*).

LONDON: Sept. 10, 1921
WINTER GARDEN; 387 p.
Presented by George Grossmith & J. A. E. Malone; directed by Grossmith; choreographed by Jack Haskell; settings, Joseph & Phil Harker; costumes, Idare, Lucile, Alias; music director, John Ansell.
CAST: George Grossmith (*Otis Hooper*), Dorothy Dickson (*Sally Green*), Leslie Henson (*Connie*), Gregory Stroud (*Blair Farquar*), Heather Thatcher (*Rosalind Rafferty*), Molly Ramsden (*Mrs. Ten Broeck*), Seymour Beard (*Jimmy Spelvin*).

LONDON: Aug. 6, 1942
PRINCE'S THEATRE; 205 p.
Presented by Firth Shephard; directed by Robert Nesbitt; choreographed by Robert Helpmann, Ann Coventry; settings, Ernest Stern; costumes, Frederick Dawson; music director, Reginald Burston; orchestrations, Val Phillips; book revised by Frank Eyton & Richard Hearne; retitled *Wild Rose*.
CAST: Jessie Matthews (*Sally*), Richard Hearne (*Maxie*), André Randall (*Gaston de Frey*), Frank Leighton (*Tom Blair*), Elsie Percival (*Rosie Roxie*), Jack Morrison (*Diamond Jim Brady*), Linda Grey (*Lillian Russell*).

Ziegfeld commissioned P. G. Wodehouse and Guy Bolton to provide a proper vehicle in which to show off the talents of Marilynn Miller in her first starring role. Their basis, an unproduced musical called *The Little Thing*, which had been intended for the Princess Theatre, was concerned with a foundling named Sally who washes the dishes at a Greenwich Village boarding house and dreams of becoming a famous dancer. Early in the preparation, Wodehouse withdrew and Ziegfeld had Bolton refashion the book so that Sally begins as a dishwasher at the Alley Inn, passes herself off at an elegant party as a world-famous ballerina, and ends as the star of the *Ziegfeld Follies*. Once the libretto was completed, Bolton added a comic role—the exiled Grand Duke of Czechogovinia—for co-star Leon Errol. *Sally*, which began its tryout tour as *Sally of the Alley*, became the fourth longest-running musical of the 20s, even though many found similarities between its story and another current Cinderella tale, the popular

Irene. It also marked the last time Miss Miller would spell her first name with two "n's."

In London, Dorothy Dickson, in her first major role, scored almost as impressively as did Miss Miller. The 1942 London version used the same score but set the story back to NY at the turn of the century, with the second act party hosted by Diamond Jim Brady. In 1948, Bway saw a revival of *Sally* with Willie Howard (*Connie*), Bambi Linn (*Sally*), and Jack Goode (*Otis*). Howard interpolated some of his own routines in the production, which lasted 36 performances.

Film version: Marilyn Miller, Joe E. Brown, Lawrence Gray (Warner 1929, John Francis Dillon dir.).

"Sam and Delilah." Music by George Gershwin; lyric by Ira Gershwin. Bluesy narrative ballad about what happened to a floozy and her straying buckaroo. Ethel Merman introduced it in a western saloon in *Girl Crazy* (NY 1930).

"Same Sort of Girl." Music by Jerome Kern; lyric by Harry B. Smith. Though he's had his fancies, Donald Brian admitted to Julia Sanderson in *The Girl from Utah* (NY 1914), "I thought the old game was one that I knew/ But it's so different with you." The song bears a musical similarity to another Kern-Smith song, "You're Here and I'm Here."

Sanderson, Julia (née Julia Sackett), actress, singer; b. Springfield, Mass., Aug. 20, 1887; d. Springfield, Jan. 27, 1975. Petite Bway heroine who introduced "They Didn't Believe Me" in *The Girl from Utah*, and scored her biggest hit in *Tangerine.* Miss Sanderson's third husband was actor Frank Crumit, with whom she appeared in five musicals and with whom she teamed on radio, 1929–1943.

1902	A Chinese Honeymoon (chorus)
1903	Winsome Winnie (chorus; *Winnie,* repl.)
1904	Wang (r) (*Mataya*)
1905	Fantana (*Elsie Sturtevant*)
1906	The Tourists (*Dora*)
1907	The Dairymaids (*Peggy*)
1908	The Hon'ble Phil (L) (*Suzanne*)
1909	Kitty Grey (*Kitty Grey*)
	The Dashing Little Duke (L) (*Cesarine De Noce*)
1910	The Arcadians (*Eileen Cavanagh*)
1911	The Siren (*Lolotte*)
1913	The Sunshine Girl (*Delia Dale*)
1914	The Girl from Utah (*Una Trance*)
1916	Sybil (*Sybil Renaud*)
1917	Rambler Rose (*Rosamond Lee*)
1918	The Canary (*Julie*)
1920	Hitchy-Koo
1921	Tangerine (*Shirley Dalton*)
1924	Moonlight (*Betty Duncan,* repl.)
1925	No, No, Nanette (US tour) (*Lucille Early*)
1927	Oh, Kay! (US tour) (*Kay*)
	Queen High (US tour) (*Florence Cole*)

Santley, Joseph (né Joseph Mansfield), actor, singer; b. Salt Lake City, Utah, Jan. 10, 1889; d. West Los Angeles, Cal., Aug. 8, 1971. Clean-cut Bway leading man who was seen in 11 musicals with wife, Ivy Sawyer.

Asterisk indicates appearance with Miss Sawyer:

1910	A Matinee Idol (*Dick Allen*)
	Judy Forgot (*Dixie Stole*)
1911	The Never Homes (*Webster Choate*)
1912	The Woman Haters (*Camillo*)
1913	When Dreams Come True (*Kean Hedges*)
1915	Stop! Look! Listen!
1916	Betty * (*Earl of Beverley*)
1917	Oh, Boy! * (US tour) (*George Budd*)
1918	Oh, My Dear * (*Bruce Allenby*)
1919	She's a Good Fellow * (*Robert McLane*)
1920	The Half Moon * (*Charlie Hobson*)

1921 Music Box Revue *
1923 Music Box Revue * (L)
      Music Box Revue *
1925 Mayflowers * (Billy Ballard) (also
      dir.)
1926 The Wild Rose (Monte Travers)
1927 Lucky * (Jack Mansfield)
      Just Fancy * (Ed Chester) (also
      co-lib., dir.)
1933 Gay Divorce (Guy Holden, repl.)

Savage, Henry W(ilson), producer; b. New Durham, NH, March 21, 1859; d. Boston, Mass., Nov. 29, 1927. Savage's biggest Bway hit was *The Merry Widow.* Other successes: *The Prince of Pilsen, Sari.*

1902 King Dodo
      The Sultan of Sulu
1903 The Prince of Pilsen
      Peggy from Paris
1904 The Yankee Consul
      The Sho-Gun
      Woodlands
1906 The Man from Now
      The Student King
1907 A Yankee Tourist
      The Merry Widow
      Tom Jones
1909 The Gay Hussars
      The Love Cure
1911 Little Boy Blue
1913 Somewhere Else
1914 Sari
      The Maid of Athens
1916 Pom-Pom
1917 Have a Heart
1918 Toot-Toot
      Head Over Heels
1919 See-Saw
1920 Lady Billy
1922 The Clinging Vine
1923 The Magic Ring
1924 Lollipop

Savo, Jimmy, actor; b. New York, 1895; d. ʃerni, Italy, Sept. 6, 1960. Childlike pantomimist usually clad in battered derby and baggy clothes who appeared in vaudeville as well as Bway musicals (incl. *The Boys from Syracuse*). Bib: *I Bow to the Stones* by Savo (Frisch, NY 1963).

1924 Vogues of 1924
      Ritz Revue
1929 John Murray Anderson's Almanac
1930 Earl Carroll Vanities
1935 Parade
1938 The Boys from Syracuse (Dromio
      of Syracuse)
1943 What's Up (Rawa of Tanglinia)

Sawyer, Ivy, actress, singer; b. London, 1896. Regal-looking leading lady who acted in 11 Bway musicals with her husband, Joseph Santley. Miss Sawyer made London debut in 1906, settled in US in 1916.

Asterisk indicates appearance with Mr. Santley:

1907 My Darling (L)
1916 Betty * (Betty)
1917 Oh, Boy! * (US tour) (Mrs. Budd)
1918 Oh, My Dear * (Hilda Rockett)
1919 She's a Good Fellow * (Jacque-
      line Fay)
1920 The Half Moon * (Grace Bolton)
1921 Music Box Revue *
1923 Music Box Revue * (L)
      Music Box Revue *
1925 Mayflowers * (Elsie Dover)
1927 Lucky * (Grace Mansfield)
      Just Fancy * (Linda Lee Stafford)

"Say It with Music." Music & lyric by Irving Berlin. The theme song of the four annual *Music Box Revues* was introduced in the first edition by Wilda Bennett and Paul Frawley (NY 1921). Before the song's official debut, Berlin had given it to the bandleader at a nightclub to play just once. The customers, however, kept demanding it over and over again so that it was well known even before the revue's premiere. The song was also used as the first-act finale of the London revue *Mayfair and Montmartre* (1922), in which it was sung by Alice Delysia.

Scheff, (Friederike) Fritzi, actress, singer; b. Vienna, Austria, Aug. 30,

1879; d. New York, April 8, 1954. Fritzi Scheff was a petite prima donna with an hourglass figure who scored her greatest Bway success in Victor Herbert's *Mlle. Modiste* (in which she introduced "Kiss Me Again"). Before Bway debut, she was with the Metropolitan Opera, 1900–1903.

  1903   Babette (*Babette*)
  1904   The Two Roses'(*Rose de Courcelles*)
  1905   Mlle. Modiste (*Fifi*)
  1908   The Prima Donna (*Mlle. Athenée*)
  1911   The Duchess (*Rose*)
  1914   Pretty Mrs. Smith (*Drucilla Smith*)

Schmidt, Harvey (Lester), composer; b. Dallas, Texas, Sept. 12, 1929. Schmidt and his partner, lyricist-librettist Tom Jones, were responsible for off-Bway's eternally running phenomenon *The Fantasticks* ("Soon It's Gonna Rain," "Try to Remember"). On Bway, their hits were "Simple Little Things" in *110 in the Shade* and "My Cup Runneth Over" in *I Do! I Do!* Since 1967 the team has been working on intimate experimental musicals at their own studio, and in 1975 they presented four (including *Philemon*) for limited runs.

  1960   The Fantasticks
  1963   110 in the Shade
  1966   I Do! I Do!
  1969   Celebration

Schwab, Laurence, producer, librettist; b. Boston, Mass., Dec. 17, 1893; d. Southampton, NY, May 29, 1951. Schwab was united with co-producer Frank Mandel in the presentation of eight Bway musicals between 1925 and 1931, with successes in both Romberg-Hammerstein operetta (*The Desert Song, The New Moon*) and DeSylva–Brown–Henderson musical comedy (*Good News, Follow Thru*). Schwab and Mandel also collaborated on three librettos, and Schwab wrote four with B. G. DeSylva (incl. *Take a Chance*).

Unless otherwise noted, Mr. Schwab was producer–co-librettist of following; asterisk indicates production presented with Mr. Mandel:

  1922   The Gingham Girl (prod. only)
  1924   Sweet Little Devil
  1925   Captain Jinks *
  1926   Queen High
         The Desert Song * (co-prod. only)
  1927   Good News. *
  1928   The New Moon * (also co-dir.)
  1929   Follow Thru *
  1931   America's Sweetheart * (co-prod. only)
         Free for All *
         East Wind * (co-prod. only)
  1932   Take a Chance
  1935   May Wine (prod. only)

Schwartz, Arthur, composer; b. Brooklyn, NY, Nov. 25, 1900. The brooding ballads and bright rhythm numbers of Arthur Schwartz, mated to the lyrics of Howard Dietz, were heard in some of the most acclaimed Bway revues of the 30s. Among the team's songs: "I Guess I'll Have to Change My Plan" (*The Little Show*); "Something to Remember You By" (*Three's a Crowd*); "Dancing in the Dark," "I Love Louisa," "New Sun in the Sky" (*The Band Wagon*); "A Shine on Your Shoes," "Alone Together," "Louisiana Hayride" (*Flying Colors*); "You and the Night and the Music," "If There Is Someone Lovelier than You" (*Revenge with Music*); "Paree," "Get Yourself a Geisha" (*At Home Abroad*); "I See Your Face Before Me," "By Myself" (*Between the Devil*); "Haunted Heart" (*Inside USA*). Schwartz has also written with lyricists Agnes Morgan, Desmond Carter, Greatrex Newman, Arthur Swanstrom, Douglas Furber, Frank Eyton, Al Stillman, Laurence Stallings, Dorothy Fields ("Look Who's Dancing" and "I'll Buy You a Star" in *A Tree Grows* *in Brooklyn*), Ira Gershwin. Libby Holman and Clifton Webb both appeared in three Schwartz musicals, Beatrice Lillie and Shirley Booth were in two each. The composer has also written film scores. His first wife was singer Katherine Carrington.

Unless otherwise noted, following were written with Mr. Dietz:

1929 The Little Show
     The Grand Street Follies (Morgan)
1930 Here Comes the Bride (L) (also Carter)
     The Co-Optimists (L) (Newman)
     The Second Little Show
     Princess Charming (Swanstrom)
     Three's a Crowd
1931 The Band Wagon
1932 Flying Colors
1933 Nice Goings On (L) (Furber, Eyton)
1934 Revenge with Music
1935 At Home Abroad
1936 Follow the Sun (L) (Carter)
1937 Virginia (Stillman, Stallings)
     Between the Devil
1939 Stars in Yours Eyes (Fields)
1946 Park Avenue (Gershwin)
1948 Inside USA (also prod.)
1951 A Tree Grows in Brooklyn (Fields)
1954 By the Beautiful Sea (Fields)
1961 The Gay Life
1963 Jennie

Schwartz, Jean, composer; b. Budapest, Hungary, Nov. 4, 1878; d. Sherman Oaks, Cal., Nov. 30, 1956. Schwartz's most popular songs in Bway shows were "Bedelia" (*The Jersey Lily*), "Chinatown, My Chinatown" (*Up and Down Broadway*), "Rock-a-bye Your Baby with a Dixie Melody" (*Sinbad*). He wrote 12 scores with lyricist Harold Atteridge, eight with William Jerome, six with Alfred Bryan. Other collaborators: Anne Caldwell, Tot Seymour, Clifford Grey, William Cary Duncan. The composer

was married to and divorced from dancer Rosie Dolly.

1904 Piff! Paff!! Pouf!!! (Jerome)
1905 A Yankee Circus on Mars (Williams)
     Lifting the Lid (Jerome)
     The Ham Tree (Jerome)
     Fritz in Tammany Hall (Jerome)
     The White Cat (Jerome)
1907 Lola from Berlin (Jerome)
1909 In Hayti (Jerome)
1910 Up and Down Broadway (Jerome)
1913 The Honeymoon Express (Atteridge)
     The Passing Show (Atteridge)
1914 When Claudia Smiles (Caldwell)
1918 The Passing Show (Atteridge)
1919 Monte Cristo Jr. (Atteridge)
     Hello, Alexander (The Ham Tree) (Bryan)
     Shubert Gaieties (Bryan)
     The Passing Show (Atteridge)
1920 The Century Revue (Bryan)
     The Passing Show (Atteridge)
1922 Make It Snappy (Atteridge)
1923 The Passing Show (Atteridge)
     Topics of 1923 (Atteridge)
     Artists and Models (Atteridge)
1924 Innocent Eyes (Atteridge, Seymour)
     The Passing Show (Atteridge)
1927 A Night in Spain (Bryan)
1928 Sunny Days (Grey, Duncan)

Schwartz, Stephen, composer, lyricist; b. New York, March 6, 1948. Schwartz's best-known songs from his three rock-inspired Bway scores are "Day By Day," "Magic to Do," and "Corner of the Sky."

1971 Godspell
1972 Pippin
1974 The Magic Show
1978 Working (also dir.)

Scofield, (David) Paul, actor; b. Hurtspierpoint, Eng., Jan. 21, 1922. Dramatic actor of stage and screen (*A Man for All Seasons*) who appeared in one London musical.

1958 Expresso Bongo (*Johnnie*)

Seal, Elizabeth (Anne), actress, dancer, singer; b. Genoa, Italy, Aug. 28, 1933. Dark-haired, dynamic dancing actress who scored her greatest musical-comedy success in *Irma la Douce* (in which she introduced "Our Language of Love"), first in London, then in NY. Miss Seal has also acted in many nonmusical plays.

1951 Gay's the Word (dancer)
1954 Cockles and Champagne
1955 The Pajama Game (*Gladys*)
1957 Damn Yankees (*Lola,* repl.)
1958 Irma la Douce (*Irma*)
1960 Irma la Douce (NY) (*Irma*)

Secombe, Harry, actor, singer; b. Swansea, Wales, Sept. 8, 1921. Rotund high tenor who first acted on the London stage in 1946 and who introduced "If I Ruled the World" in *Pickwick.* He also appeared on the "Goon Shows" on BBC radio.

1956 Rocking the Town
1958 Large as Life
1961 Let Yourself Go
1963 Pickwick (*Pickwick*)
1965 Pickwick (NY) (*Pickwick*)
1966 London Laughs
1967 The Four Musketeers! (*D'Artagnan*)

"Second Hand Rose." Music by James F. Hanley; lyric by Grant Clarke. A successor to "Rose of Washington Square" (same composer), the song tells the funny-sad tale of a girl from Second Avenue whose life is a series of hand-me-downs. It was written for and sung by Fanny Brice in the *Ziegfeld Follies* (NY 1921).

Segal, Vivienne (Sonia), actress, singer; b. Philadelphia, Pa., April 19, 1897. From the starry-eyed romantic heroine of operetta (*The Desert Song, The Three Musketeers*) Miss Segal became the worldly comedienne of musical comedy (*I Married an Angel, Pal Joey*). Among songs she introduced:

"Auf Wiedersehn," "Romance," "The Desert Song," "Bewitched," "To Keep My Love Alive."

1915 The Blue Paradise (*Mizzy, Gaby*)
1917 My Lady's Glove (*Elly*)
     Miss 1917
1918 Oh, Lady! Lady!! (*Molly Farrington*)
1919 The Little Whopper (*Kitty Wentworth*)
1922 The Yankee Princess (*Odette Darimonde*)
1923 Adrienne (*Adrienne Grey*)
1924 Ziegfeld Follies
1925 Florida Girl (*Daphne*)
1926 Castles in the Air (*Evelyn Devine*)
     The Desert Song (*Margot Bonvalet*)
1928 The Three Musketeers (*Constance Bonacieux*)
1938 I Married an Angel (*Peggy Palaffi*)
1940 Pal Joey (*Vera Simpson*)
1943 A Connecticut Yankee (r) (*Morgan Le Fay*)
1947 Music in My Heart (*Tatiana Kerskaya*)
1950 Great to Be Alive (*Leslie Butterfield*)
1952 Pal Joey (r) (*Vera Simpson*)

"Send for Me." Music by Richard Rodgers; lyric by Lorenz Hart. Romantic pledge of dependability ("Sunrise, noon or sundown/ I'll be glad to run down") vowed by Doree Leslie and Alan Edwards in *Simple Simon* (NY 1930). The same melody, with a different lyric, was called "I Must Love You" when it was introduced in *Chee-Chee* (NY 1928) by Helen Ford and William Williams.

"Send in the Clowns." Music & lyric by Stephen Sondheim. Rueful, self-mocking ballad of missed romantic opportunities sung by Glynis Johns in *A Little Night Music* (NY 1973). In London (1975) sung by Jean Simmons.

"**Sentimental Me.**" Music by Richard Rodgers; lyric by Lorenz Hart. Romantic expression of young love in which Hart kidded the excessively ardent sentiments usually found in this type song ("I sit and sigh, you sigh and sit upon my knee"). Introduced by June Cochrane, James Norris, Edith Meiser, and Sterling Holloway in *The Garrick Gaieties* (NY 1925); also sung by Cyril Ritchard, Mimi Crawford, J. H. Roberts, and Joyce Barbour in London revue, *RSVP* (1926).

"**September Song.**" Music by Kurt Weill; lyric by Maxwell Anderson. Sung by Walter Huston to Jeanne Madden in *Knickerbocker Holiday* (NY 1938). As presented in the musical, Gov. Pieter Stuyvesant, fearful of growing old, reveals his anxieties in song to a young girl he hopes to marry. Weill and Anderson wrote the piece specifically for Huston's limited vocal range after hearing the actor sing over the radio. Though the song was written in the traditional 32-bar form, note that the first eight-bar theme is never repeated exactly the same. Also note that sections one and two use the same rhyme scheme but that in the first the rhyme is feminine ("December" and "September") and in the second it's masculine ("flame" and "game"). Except for "September" returning in the release to rhyme with "November," the song has no further rhymes.

"**Serenade.**" Music by Sigmund Romberg; lyric by Dorothy Donnelly. "Overhead the moon is beaming" begins the ardent ballad sung by Howard Marsh, Raymond Marlowe, Paul Kleeman, and Frederic Wolf in *The Student Prince in Heidelberg* (NY 1924). In London version, Allan Prior, Raymond Marlowe, Paul Clemon (né

Kleeman), and Olaf Olson did the serenading. Before the operetta's opening, producer J. J. Shubert took strong exception to the song and demanded that it be cut from the score. Romberg, however, was adament, and it became one of the musical's best-received numbers.

1776 (1969). Music & lyrics by Sherman Edwards; book by Peter Stone, based on concept by Edwards.

SONGS: "Piddle, Twiddle and Resolve," "Till Then," "The Lees of Old Virginia," "But, Mr. Adams," "He Plays the Violin," "Yours, Yours, Yours," "Cool, Cool Considerate Men," "Momma, Look Sharp," "The Egg," "Molasses to Rum," "Is Anybody There?"

NEW YORK: March 16, 1969
46TH ST. THEATRE; 1,217 p.
Presented by Stuart Ostrow; directed by Peter Hunt; choreographed by Onna White; settings & lighting, Jo Mielziner; costumes, Patricia Zipprodt; music director, Peter Howard; orchestrations, Eddie Sauter.
CAST: William Daniels (*John Adams*), Howard Da Silva (*Benjamin Franklin*), Paul Hecht (*John Dickinson*), Clifford David (*Edward Rutledge*), Roy Poole (*Stephen Hopkins*), Ronald Holgate (*Richard Henry Lee*), Ken Howard (*Thomas Jefferson*), Virginia Vestoff (*Abigail Adams*), Betty Buckley (*Martha Jefferson*).

LONDON: June 16, 1970
NEW THEATRE; 168 p.
Presented by Alexander Cohen Ltd.; directed by Peter Hunt; choreographed by Onna White; settings & lighting, Jo Mielziner; costumes, Patricia Zipprodt; music director, Ray Cook; orchestrations, Eddie Sauter.
CAST: Lewis Fiander (*John Adams*), Ronald Radd (*Benjamin Franklin*), Bernard Lloyd (*John Dickinson*),

David Kernan (*Edward Rutledge*), Tony Steedman (*Stephen Hopkins*), David Morton (*Richard Henry Lee*), John Quentin (*Thomas Jefferson*), Vivienne Ross (*Abigail Adams*), Cheryl Kennedy (*Martha Jefferson*).

1776 was a dramatic retelling of the events leading up to the signing of the Declaration of Independence by the Continental Congress meeting in Philadelphia. The story focused on the efforts of John Adams to break down the opposition to independence, revolving primarily around the issue of free states vs. slave states. Composer-lyricist Edwards, here making his Bway debut, devoted seven years to the project. During Bway run, William Daniels was succeeded by John Cunningham (5-71), Howard Da Silva by Jay Garner (7-71). The US tour began in April 1970 and lasted two years, two months. The company was headed by Patrick Bedford (*Adams*), Rex Everhart (*Franklin*), George Hearn (*Dickinson*), Gary Oakes (*Lee*), Jon Cypher (*Jefferson*), Jack Blackton (*Rutledge*).

For previous Bway musicals concerned with the American Revolution, see *Dearest Enemy*.

FILM VERSION: William Daniels, Howard Da Silva, Donald Madden (Col. 1972, Peter Hunt dir.).

"Seventy-Six Trombones." Music & lyric by Meredith Willson. Sung by Robert Preston in *The Music Man* (NY 1957) as a brassy tribute to the historic occasion when the marching bands of Patrick Gilmore, Liberatti, Patrick Conway, Giuseppe Creatore, W. C. Handy, and John Philip Sousa all came to town on the same day. In London production it was sung by Van Johnson (1961). The song intentionally had the same melody as "Goodnight, My Someone," also in

The Music Man, except that the tempos were different.

"Shady Lady Bird." Music and lyric by Hugh Martin & Ralph Blane. In *Best Foot Forward* (NY 1941), demure Maureen Cannon revealed her plans to become a femme fatale to win back her boyfriend.

"Shaking the Blues Away." Music & lyric by Irving Berlin. Ruth Etting and chorus "do as the voodoos do" in this revivalistic exhortation in *Ziegfeld Follies* (NY 1927).

"Shall We Dance?" Music by Richard Rodgers; lyric by Oscar Hammerstein II. Gertrude Lawrence's polka invitation to King Yul Brynner in *The King and I* (NY 1951). Valerie Hobson sang it to Herbert Lom in London version (1953).

"Shape of Things, The." Music & lyric by Sheldon Harnick. Offered by Charlotte Rae as an English madrigal in *The Littlest Revue* (NY 1956), the piece uses four shapes—round, square, rectangular, and triangular—as references on which to base the tearful tale of a wronged woman who kills her errant lover and is left with "a prize I had no wish to win."

Shaw, Oscar (né Oscar Schwartz), actor, singer; b. Philadelphia, Pa., 1889; d. Little Neck, NY, March 6, 1967. Shaw's slick black hair, clean-cut good looks, and straightforward singing style made him a familiar Bway leading man during the 1910s and 20s. Among songs he introduced: "Ka-lu-a" (*Good Morning Dearie*), "Maybe" and "Do, Do, Do" (*Oh, Kay!*), "Thinking of You" (*The Five*

o'Clock Girl), "Thank Your Father"
(Flying High).

1908 The Mimic World (chorus)
1909 The Girl and the Wizard (Max Andressen)
1910 Up and Down Broadway
1911 The Kiss Waltz (Albert)
1912 Two Little Brides (M. Deschamps)
      The Passing Show
      Kill That Fly! (L)
1913 Come Over Here (L) (Billy Horringer)
1914 Honeymoon Express (L)
      Dora's Doze (L)
1915 5064 Gerrard (L)
      Very Good Eddie (Dick Rivers)
1917 Leave It to Jane (Stub Talmadge)
1919 The Rose of China (Tommy Tilford)
1920 The Half Moon (Bradford Adams)
      Two Little Girls in Blue (Robert Barker)
      Good Morning Dearie (Billy Van Cortlandt)
1923 One Kiss (Bastien)
1924 Dear Sir (Laddie Munn)
      Music Box Revue
1926 Oh, Kay! (Jimmy Winters)
1927 The Five o'Clock Girl (Gerald Brooks)
1930 Flying High (Tom Addison)
1931 Everybody's Welcome (Steve Herrick)
1932 Of Thee I Sing (US tour) (John P. Wintergreen)

"She Didn't Say 'Yes.'" Music by Jerome Kern; lyric by Otto Harbach. "Ballad of Indecision"—as its original sheet music called it—sung in The Cat and the Fiddle by Bettina Hall in NY (1931) and by Peggy Wood in London (1932).

"She Is the Belle of New York." Music by Gustave Kerker; lyric by Hugh Morton (C. M. S. McLellan). Song in praise of the titular heroine of The Belle of New York ("She makes the old Bowery fragrant and flowery"). Introduced in NY (1897) by William Cameron and in London version (1898) by Frank Lawton.

She Loves Me (1963). Music by Jerry Bock; lyrics by Sheldon Harnick; book by Joe Masteroff, based on Hungarian play Parfumerie, by Miklos Laszlo.

SONGS: "Good Morning, Good Day," "Days Gone By," "Three Letters," "Tonight at Eight," "Will He Like Me?," "Ilona," "I Resolve," "A Romantic Atmosphere," "Tango Tragique," "Dear Friend," "Try Me," "Ice Cream," "She Loves Me," "A Trip to the Library," "Grand Knowing You," "Twelve Days to Christmas."

NEW YORK: April 23, 1963
EUGENE O'NEILL THEATRE; 302 p.

Presented by Harold Prince with Lawrence Kasha & Philip McKenna; directed by Prince; choreographed by Carol Haney; settings & lighting, William & Jean Eckart; costumes, Patricia Zipprodt; music director, Harold Hastings; orchestrations, Don Walker.

CAST: Barbara Cook (Amalia Balash), Daniel Massey (Georg Nowack), Barbara Baxley (Ilona Ritter), Jack Cassidy (Steven Kodaly), Ludwig Donath (Zoltan Maraczek), Nathaniel Frey (Ladislav Sipos), Ralph Williams (Arpad Laszlo).

LONDON: April 29, 1964
LYRIC THEATRE; 189 p.

Presented by Harold Prince, Tony Walton, & Richard Pilbrow; directed by Prince; choreographed by Carol Haney; settings, William & Jean Eckart; costumes, Patricia Zipprodt; lighting, Pilbrow; music director, Alyn Ainsworth; orchestrations, Don Walker.

CAST: Anne Rogers (Amalia Balash), Gary Raymond (Georg Nowack), Rita Moreno (Ilona Ritter), Gary Miller (Steven Kodaly), Karel Stepanek (Zoltan Maraczek), Peter Sallis

(*Ladislav Sipos*), Gregory Phillips (*Arpad Laszlo*).

The first musical directed as well as produced by Harold Prince was an intimate, gentle, closely integrated work containing 23 musical numbers. Based on a Hungarian play that had already been turned into two films, *The Shop Around the Corner* and *In the Good Old Summertime*, it was set in an unspecified mid-European city in the 30s and took place mostly in and outside Maraczek's Parfumerie. Amalia and Georg, who work in the store and loathe each other, are also, coincidentally, anonymous correspondents known to the other only as "Dear Friend." When they finally arrange a meeting at the Café Imperiale, Georg, realizing his pen pal is Amalia, does not reveal his identity, and the girl thinks she has been stood up. Presently they find themselves falling in love, an emotion that is heightened when, on the day before Christmas, Georg confesses to the correspondence by quoting from one of Amalia's letters.

The idea for the musical began with producer Lawrence Kasha, who brought the three writers together; because of Prince's interest in directing the project, he also took over the major production chores. Before Barbara Cook was given the lead, Julie Andrews had agreed to play the part but only if the show could be delayed six months. Other actresses considered were Julie Harris and Dorothy Collins. Rita Moreno got the part of Ilona in the London version because Nyree Dawn Porter, who had been signed for the role, became ill.

"She Loves Me." Music by Jerry Bock; lyric by Sheldon Harnick. Daniel Massey revealed this exuberant amatory discovery in *She Loves Me* (NY 1963). In London version (1964), sung by Gary Raymond.

"She Touched Me." Music by Milton Schafer; lyric by Ira Levin. Elliott Gould's ecstatic revelation in *Drat! The Cat!* (NY 1965); later reprised by Gould and Lesley Ann Warren (who sang it as "He Touched Me").

Shean, Al (né Albert Schönberg), actor; b. Dornum, Germany, May 12, 1868; d. New York, Aug. 12, 1949. German-accented comedian who won fame with vaudeville partner Ed Gallagher singing "Mr. Gallagher and Mr. Shean," which they interpolated in *Ziegfeld Follies* of 1922. Shean was an uncle of the Marx Brothers.

1903	The Fisher Maiden (*Dulovitch*)
1912	The Rose Maid (*Schmuke*)
1915	The Princess Pat (*Anthony Schmalz*)
1922	Ziegfeld Follies
1926	Betsy (*Stonewall Moskowitz*)
1932	Music in the Air (*Dr. Walther Lessing*)

Sherman, Hiram, actor; b. Boston, Mass., Feb. 11, 1908. Bland, chubby, diffident comic actor who has also appeared in Bway nonmusicals.

1937	The Cradle Will Rock (*Junior Mister, Rev. Salvation*)
1938	Sing Out the News
1939	Very Warm for May (*Ogden Quiller*)
1949	Brigadoon (L) (*Jeff*)
1952	Two's Company
1955	Three for Tonight
1960	The Art of Living (L)
1967	How Now, Dow Jones (*Wingate*)
1969	Anne of Green Gables (L) (*Matthew Hubbard*)

Sherwin, Manning, composer; b. Philadelphia, Pa., Jan. 4, 1902; d. Hollywood, Cal., July 26, 1974. After writing songs for NY revues and nightclubs, Sherwin settled in London in 1938. His longest-running shows were *Get a Load of This* and *Under the Counter*, and his biggest song hit was "A Nightingale Sang in Berkeley Square" in *New Faces* (1940). Among his collaborators: Arthur Herzog, Douglas Furber, Desmond Carter, Val Guest, Robert Nesbitt, Greatrex Newman, Harold Purcell, Max Kester, Barbara Gordon, Basil Thomas.

1926	Bad Habits of 1926 (NY) (Herzog)
1939	Sitting Pretty (Furber)
	Shephard's Pie (Furber)
1940	Up and Doing (Furber)
1941	Rise Above It (Carter)
	Fun and Games (Furber)
	Get a Load of This (Guest)
1942	Fine and Dandy (Nesbitt, Newman)
1943	The Magic Carpet (Guest)
	Something in the Air (Purcell, Kester)
1945	Under the Counter (Purcell)
1946	Here Come the Boys (Purcell, Kester)
1948	The Kid from Stratford (Gordon, Thomas)
1949	Her Excellency (Kester)

"She's My Lovely." Music & lyric by Vivian Ellis. Song of adoration in which the lovely is likened to Venus (rhymes with "serene as"), Mona Lisa, the sunset hour, and a singing thrush. This was one of Bobby Howes's most famous numbers, which he first sang in *Hide and Seek* (L 1937).

"She's Such a Comfort to Me." Music by Arthur Schwartz; lyric by Douglas Furber & Donovan Parsons. Bouncy tribute to a shy, unobtrusive, wealthy but none-too-bright girl by her calculating and none-too-faithful boy friend. Introduced by Jack Hulbert in *The House That Jack Built* (L 1929); also sung by Jack Buchanan in *Wake Up and Dream!* (NY 1929).

Shevelove, (Burton George) Burt, librettist, lyricist, director; b. Newark, NJ, Sept. 19, 1915. On Bway Shevelove's major work as librettist was *A Funny Thing Happened on the Way to the Forum;* as director it was *No, No, Nanette.* He also wrote songs with composer Albert Selden.

Unless otherwise noted, Mr. Shevelove was director of following:

1948	Small Wonder (also lyr.) (Selden)
1962	A Funny Thing Happened on the Way to the Forum (co-lib. only)
1965	Twang!! (L)
1967	Hallelujah, Baby!
1971	No, No, Nanette (r) (also lib.)
1976	So Long 174th Street

"Shine on, Harvest Moon." Music & lyric by Nora Bayes & Jack Norworth. Introduced on Bway by Bayes and Norworth in Ziegfeld's *Follies of 1908.* Also added to score of *Miss Innocence* (NY 1909), in which it was sung by Lillian Lorraine. Successfully revived by Ruth Etting in *Ziegfeld Follies,* 1931. In London, sung in revue *Hullo, London!* (1910).

"Shine on Your Shoes, A." Music by Arthur Schwartz; lyric by Howard Dietz. Rhythmic advice on the importance of a shoeshine to make you feel your best. In the revue *Flying Colors* (NY 1932), Monette Moore sang it, bootblack Buddy Ebsen and customer Vilma Ebsen danced it, and street musician Larry Adler played it on his harmonica.

"Ship Without a Sail, A." Music by Richard Rodgers; lyric by Lorenz Hart. Self-pitying ballad sung by Jack Whiting in *Heads Up!* (NY 1929) and by Arthur Margetson in London version (1930). The idea for the lyric came to lyricist Hart because he thought the melody suggested a barcarolle.

Shop Girl, The (1894). Music by Ivan Caryll; lyrics & book by H. J. W. Dam; added songs by Lionel Monckton & Adrian Ross.

SONGS: "The Charity Bazaar," "Beautiful Bountiful Bertie," "Foundlings Are We," "The Naughty Little Twinkle in Her Eye," "Her Golden Hair."

LONDON: Nov. 24, 1894
GAIETY THEATRE; 546 p.

Presented by George Edwardes; directed by James T. Tanner; choreographed by Willie Warde; settings, W. Johnstone, Walter Hann; costumes, Wilhelm, Morris Angel, Vanite; music director, Ivan Caryll.

CAST: Ada Reeve (*Bessie Brent*), Seymour Hicks (*Charlie Appleby*), George Grossmith (*Bertie Boyd*), Edmund Payne (*Mr. Miggles*), Arthur Williams (*Mr. Hooley*), Willie Warde (*Mr. Tweets*), Robert Nainby (*Count St. Vaurien*), Fanny Ward (*Eva Tudor*), Lillie Belmore (*Ada Smith*).

NEW YORK: Oct. 28, 1895
PALMER'S THEATRE; 72 p.

Presented by Al Hayman & Charles Frohman; directed by A. E. Dodson; settings, Ernest Gros; costumes, Wilhelm, Morris Angel, Vanite; music director, Barter Johns.

CAST: Ethel Sydney (*Bessie Brent*), Seymour Hicks (*Charlie Appleby*), George Grossmith (*Bertie Boyd*), Bertie Wright (*Mr. Miggles*), W. H. Rawlins (*Mr. Hooley*), Alfred Asher (*Mr. Tweets*), J. Gaillard (*Count St. Vaurien*), Violet Dene (*Eva Tudor*), Connie Ediss (*Ada Smith*).

LONDON: March 25, 1920
GAIETY THEATRE; 327 p.

Presented by Alfred Butt & Seymour Hicks; directed by Hicks; choreographed by Willie Warde, Fred Farren; settings, Marc Henri & Conrad Tritschler; music director, Arthur Wood; book revised & new lyrics by Arthur Wimperis; new music by Herman Darewski.

CAST: Alfred Lester (*Mr. Miggles*), Evelyn Laye (*Bessie Brent*), Thorpe Bates (*Hon. Bobbie Blake*), Roy Royston (*Charlie Appleby*), Fred Hearne (*Bertie Boyd*), John Danvers (*Mr. Hooley*), Ewart Scott (*Mr. Tweets*), Robert Nainby (*Count St. Vaurien*), Nancie Lovat (*Lady Dodo Hazlemere*).

The Shop Girl was the first full-length musical comedy—or "musical farce," as it was called—to play the Gaiety Theatre, London's leading musical-comedy playhouse (within months, though, it transferred to Daly's). Because of Ellaline Terriss' illness, the title role went to Ada Reeve, who was later succeeded by Miss Terriss. The tale revolved around the search for a missing American heiress who is discovered to be Bessie Brent, a shop girl at the Royal Store in London, who now has enough money and social prestige to marry Charlie Appleby, a poor but high-born medical student. The production was the first to offer a chorus line of the celebrated Gaiety Girls (a musical called *A Gaiety Girl* had previously played the Prince of Wales). The successful revised production in 1920 was noted for the Darewski-Wimperis song "The Guard's Brigade," which Evelyn Laye sang accompanied by a 60-piece marching band of real Guardsmen.

The 1896 London musical *My Girl* was the successor to *The Shop Girl*; the 1909 *Our Miss Gibbs* was also about a shop girl.

Short, (Hubert) Hassard, director, designer; b. Edington, Eng., Oct. 15, 1877; d. Nice, France, Oct. 9, 1956. Primarily identified with opulent, stylish musicals, Short was an innovative force through his imaginative treatment of action, decor, and lighting. His most notable Bway productions included three *Music Box Revues* (plus one in London), *Sunny*, *Three's a Crowd*, *The Band Wagon*, *As Thousands Cheer*, *Roberta*, *The Great Waltz*, *Jubilee*, *Lady in the Dark*, *Carmen Jones*, *Show Boat* (revival). He directed six shows for producer Sam H. Harris, five for Max Gordon (plus one for Harris and Gordon together), five for Michael Todd. Short began his career as an actor in London (1895–1901) and NY (1901–1919).

1911	Betsy (*Teddy Bacon* only)
1920	Honeydew
	Her Family Tree
1921	The Rose Girl
	Music Box Revue
1922	Music Box Revue
1923	Music Box Revue (L)
	Music Box Revue
1924	Peg o' My Dreams
	Ritz Revue (also prod.)
	The Magnolia Lady
1925	Sunny
	Greenwich Village Follies
1926	Oh, Please!
1927	Lucky
1928	Sunny Days (also prod.)
1930	Three's a Crowd
1931	The Band Wagon
	Waltzes from Vienna (L)
1932	Face the Music
	Wild Violets (L) (also co-lib.)
1933	As Thousands Cheer
	Roberta
1934	The Great Waltz (Waltzes from Vienna)
1935	Stop Press (As Thousands Cheer) (L)
	Jubilee
1937	Frederika
	Between the Devil
	Three Waltzes
1939	The Hot Mikado
	Very Warm for May
1941	Lady in the Dark
	Banjo Eyes
1942	Star and Garter
1943	Something for the Boys
	Carmen Jones
1944	Mexican Hayride
	Seven Lively Arts
1945	Marinka
1946	Show Boat (r)
1947	Music in My Heart
1948	Make Mine Manhattan
1950	Michael Todd's Peep Show
1951	Seventeen
1952	My Darlin' Aida

"Shortest Day of the Year, The." Music by Richard Rodgers; lyric by Lorenz Hart. Love as a measurement of time was the theme of Ronald Graham's ardent ballad in *The Boys from Syracuse* (NY 1938). Denis Quilley sang it in London version (1963).

Show Boat (1927). Music by Jerome Kern; lyrics & book by Oscar Hammerstein II, based on Edna Ferber's novel.

SONGS: "Cotton Blossom," "Make Believe," "Ol' Man River," "Can't Help Lovin' Dat Man," "Life Upon the Wicked Stage," "Till Good Luck Comes My Way," "You Are Love," "Why Do I Love You?," "I Might Fall Back on You," "Bill" (lyric with P. G. Wodehouse), "After the Ball" (Charles K. Harris), "Dance Away the Night" (London only).

NEW YORK: Dec. 27, 1927
ZIEGFELD THEATRE; 572 p.

Presented by Florenz Ziegfeld; directed by Oscar Hammerstein II (uncredited), Zeke Colvan; choreographed by Sammy Lee; settings, Joseph Urban; costumes, John Harkrider; music director, Victor Baravalle; orchestrations, Robert Russell Bennett.

CAST: Norma Terris (*Magnolia Hawks Ravenal*), Howard Marsh (*Gaylord Ravenal*), Charles Winninger (*Cap'n Andy Hawks*), Helen Morgan (*Julie La Verne*), Jules Bledsoe (*Joe*), Edna May Oliver (*Parthy*

Ann Hawks), Tess Gardella (*Queenie*), Eva Puck (*Ellie May Chipley*), Sammy White (*Frank Schultz*), Charles Ellis (*Steve Baker*).

LONDON: May 3, 1928
DRURY LANE THEATRE; 350 p.

Presented by Alfred Butt; directed by Felix Edwardes; choreographed by Max Scheck; settings, Joseph & Phil Harker; costumes, Irene Segalla; music director, Herman Finck.

CAST: Edith Day (*Magnolia Hawks Ravenal*), Howett Worster (*Gaylord Ravenal*), Cedric Hardwicke (*Cap'n Andy Hawks*), Marie Burke (*Julie La Verne*), Paul Robeson (*Joe*), Viola Compton (*Parthy Ann Hawks*), Alberta Hunter (*Queenie*), Dorothy Lena (*Ellie May Chipley*), Leslie Sarony (*Frank Schultz*), Colin Clive (*Steve Baker*).

NEW YORK: Jan. 5, 1946
ZIEGFELD THEATRE; 418 p.

Presented by Jerome Kern & Oscar Hammerstein II; directed by Hassard Short & Hammerstein; choreographed by Helen Tamiris; settings, Howard Bay; costumes, Lucinda Ballard; music director, Edwin McArthur; orchestrations, Robert Russell Bennett.

CAST: Jan Clayton (*Magnolia Hawks Ravenal*), Ralph Dumke (*Cap'n Andy Hawks*), Carol Bruce (*Julie La Verne*), Charles Fredericks (*Gaylord Ravenal*), Buddy Ebsen (*Frank Schultz*), Colette Lyons (*Ellie May Chipley*), Ethel Owen (*Parthy Ann Hawks*), Kenneth Spencer (*Joe*), Pearl Primus (*Dahomey Queen*), Robert Allen (*Steve Baker*), Helen Dowdy (*Queenie*), Max Showalter (*Jake*), Talley Beatty (dancer).

LONDON: July 29, 1971
ADELPHI THEATRE; 910 p.

Presented by Harold Fielding; directed & choreographed by Wendy Toye; settings & costumes, Tim Good-child; lighting, Richard Pilbrow; music director, Ray Cook; orchestrations, Keith Amos.

CAST: André Jobin (*Gaylord Ravenal*), Cleo Laine (*Julie La Verne*), Thomas Carey (*Joe*), Lorna Dallas (*Magnolia Hawks Ravenal*), Kenneth Nelson (*Frank Schultz*), Derek Royle (*Cap'n Andy Hawks*), Pearl Hackney (*Parthy Ann Hawks*), Jan Hunt (*Ellie May Chipley*), Ena Cabayo (*Queenie*), John Larsen (*Steve Baker*).

Show Boat was not only the third longest-running Bway musical of the 1920s, it was the most durable and influential, leading the way to the creation of a form of musical play that was distinct from fast-moving musical comedy on one hand and flamboyant operetta on the other. Though Oscar Hammerstein had previously worked with Jerome Kern on *Sunny*, their new offering was a distinct breakthrough because of its well-drawn characters and locales, the strength of its story, and the firmness with which the songs were wedded to the panoramic tale.

Originally intended as the premiere attraction at the Ziegfeld Theatre, *Show Boat* was delayed so often that it lost the honor to *Rio Rita*. It also lost the three main actors who had been signed to appear in it: Elizabeth Hines (*Magnolia*), Guy Robertson (*Ravenal*), Paul Robeson (*Joe*). After the musical's opening, a second company—headed by Raymond Hitchcock (*Andy*), Libby Holman (*Julie*), and Paul Robeson (*Joe*)—was planned to play concurrently in NY and then tour, but the project was abandoned. Following the Bway run, *Show Boat* toured for 10 months, with Irene Dunne replacing Norma Terris and Kathryn Manners replacing Helen Morgan.

The saga traces the fortunes of Magnolia Hawks and Gaylord Ravenal from their first meeting on the Natchez levee in the mid-1880s to their reunion aboard the *Cotton Blossom* in 1927. In between, they fall in love, act in showboat productions, marry, move to Chicago in 1893, where they take in the World's Fair, lose their money because of Ravenal's gambling debts, and separate. Magnolia then becomes a musical-comedy star on Bway, as does her daughter, Kim. A second romance, between mulatto Julie and showboat leading man Steve, was the first to deal with miscegenation on the musical stage. The story also touches on the harsh life of Negro dockworkers as expressed through the philosophy of Joe's song about the indifference and durability of the Mississippi River.

Just three years after the original engagement, Ziegfeld brought *Show Boat* back to NY, where it remained for 180 performances at the Casino Theatre. The cast was basically the same as in 1927, with major replacements being Dennis King for Howard Marsh and Paul Robeson for Jules Bledsoe. During run, Edna May Oliver was succeeded by Bertha Belmore (6-32), Charles Winninger by William Kent (10-32). This company toured almost five months, with Bledsoe replacing Robeson.

A second London production opened in 1943 and ran 264 performances. Gwyneth Lascelles (*Magnolia*), Bruce Carfax (*Ravenal*), Mark Daly (*Andy*), and Mr. Jetsam (*Joe*) headed the cast.

Though Kern was listed as co-producer of the 1946 Bway revival, he died before the opening. During run, Jan Clayton was succeeded by Nancy Kenyon (4-46), Charles Fredericks by Joe (Brian) Sullivan (11-46). A touring company, sponsored by Rodgers and Hammerstein, opened Oct. 1947, and continued for a year and a half. The cast was headed by Pamela Caveness (*Magnolia*), Norwood Smith (*Ravenal*), Billy House (*Andy*), Sammy White (*Frank*), William C. Smith (*Joe*), Martha King (*Julie*).

During run of the third London production—the longest of all—Cleo Laine was succeeded by Wilma Reading, Thomas Carey by Valentine Pringle.

FILM VERSIONS: Laura La Plante, Joseph Schildkraut, Alma Rubens, Stepin Fetchit (Univ. 1929, Harry Pollard dir.); Irene Dunne, Allan Jones, Charles Winninger, Helen Morgan, Paul Robeson (Univ. 1936, James Whale dir.); Kathryn Grayson, Howard Keel, Ava Gardner, Marge and Gower Champion, Joe E. Brown, William Warfield (MGM 1951, George Sidney dir.).

Shubert Brothers, producers. J. J. (né Jacob Szemanski), b. Shervient, Lithuania, Aug. 15, 1878; d. New York, Dec. 26, 1963. Lee (né Levi Szemanski), b. Shervient, Lithuania, March 15, 1873; d. New York, Dec. 25, 1953. Sam S. (né Samuel Szemanski), b. Shervient, Lithuania, 1876; d. train crash, Pennsylvania, May 11, 1905. Between 1900 and 1945 the Shubert brothers produced or co-produced over 500 plays and musicals, mostly under the collective name "The Messrs. Shubert," thus making them the most prolific purveyors of theatrical entertainment who ever lived. As managers, they owned 31 theatres in NY, 63 in other US cities, and had interest in five in London. Among their most memorable presentations: *Maytime, Blossom Time, Sally, Irene and Mary, The Student Prince, Countess Maritza, My Maryland, Ziegfeld Follies* (1934, 1936), *The Show Is On, Hellzapoppin.* Willie and Eugene Howard appeared in 14 Shubert musicals; Al Jolson in 11;

Marilyn Miller, Eddie Foy, Lew Fields, and Ed Wynn in four each; Fanny Brice, Clifton Webb, and Olsen and Johnson in three each. Sigmund Romberg wrote 34 scores for the brothers. Bib: *The Brothers Shubert* by Jerry Stagg (Random, NY 1968).

1902   A Chinese Honeymoon
        The Emerald Isle
1903   The Runaways
        Winsome Winnie
        The Girl from Dixie
1904   Lady Teazle
1905   Fantana
        Happyland
        The Earl and the Girl
        The Babes and the Baron
1906   Mexicana
        The Social Whirl
        The Tourists
        My Lady's Maid
        The Blue Moon
        Pioneer Days
1907   The Belle of London Town
        The Orchid
        The Girl Behind the Counter
        The Gay White Way
        The Girls of Holland
        The Auto Race
1908   Nearly a Hero
        The Mimic World
        Sporting Days
        Mlle. Mischief
        Marcelle
        The Pied Piper
        Mr. Hamlet of Broadway
1909   Havana
        The Girl and the Wizard
        The Belle of Brittany
        Old Dutch
1910   The King of Cadonia
        Up and Down Broadway
        The International Cup
        He Came from Milwaukee
        Madame Troubadour
        The Girl and the Kaiser
1911   The Balkan Princess
        La Belle Paree
        Around the World
        The Kiss Waltz
        The Revue of Revues
        The Duchess

        Vera Violetta
        The Wedding Trip
1912   The Whirl of Society
        The Little Brides
        The Passing Show
        The Merry Countess
        Under Many Flags
        The Red Petticoat
        Broadway to Paris
        All for the Ladies
1913   The Man with Three Wives
        The Honeymoon Express
        The Passing Show
        Lieber Augustin
        Oh, I Say!
        The Pleasure Seekers
        The Girl on the Film
1914   The Midnight Girl
        The Belle of Bond Street
        The Passing Show
        The Dancing Duchess
        The Wars of the World
        Dancing Around
        Tonight's the Night
        Lady Luxury
1915   Maid in America
        The Peasant Girl
        The Passing Show
        Hands Up
        The Blue Paradise
        Alone at Last
        A World of Pleasure
1916   Robinson Crusoe, Jr.
        Step This Way
        The Passing Show
        The Girl from Brazil
        The Show of Wonders
        Follow Me
        Her Soldier Boy
1917   Love o' Mike
        The Passing Show
        My Lady's Glove
        Maytime
        Doing Our Bit
        The Star Gazer
        Over the Top
1918   Girl o' Mine
        Sinbad
        Fancy Free
        The Passing Show
        Little Simplicity
        The Melting of Molly
1919   Good Morning, Judge

Monte Cristo, Jr.
A Lonely Romeo
Shubert Gaieties
Oh, What a Girl!
Hello, Alexander
The Passing Show
1920 Cinderella on Broadway
The Century Revue
The Passing Show
1921 Phoebe of Quality Street
The Last Waltz
The Whirl of New York
The Mimic World
Blossom Time
Bombo
1922 The Blushing Bride
The Rose of Stamboul
The Hotel Mouse
Make It Snappy
Red Pepper
Sally, Irene and Mary
The Passing Show
The Lady in Ermine
The Springtime of Youth
1923 The Dancing Girl
Caroline
Dew Drop Inn
The Passing Show
Artists and Models
Topics of 1923
1924 Vogues of 1924
Innocent Eyes
The Dream Girl
The Passing Show
Artists and Models
The Student Prince in Heidelberg
1925 Big Boy
The Love Song
Sky High
Artists and Models
June Days
Gay Paree
Princess Flavia
Mayflowers
1926 A Night in Paris
Hello, Lola
The Student Prince in Heidelberg (L)
The Great Temptations
The Merry World
Naughty Riquette
Countess Maritza

Katja
Gay Paree
1927 The Nightingale
Cherry Blossoms
The Circus Princess
A Night in Spain
My Maryland
The Love Call
Artists and Models
Lovely Lady
1928 The Madcap
Greenwich Village Follies
White Lilacs
Luckee Girl
Angela
1929 Boom-Boom
Pleasure Bound
Music in May
A Night in Venice
Broadway Nights
A Wonderful Night
1930 Three Little Girls
Artists and Models
Nina Rosa
Hello, Paris
Meet My Sister
1931 The Wonder Bar
Everybody's Welcome
1932 A Little Racketeer
Marching By
Smiling Faces
Americana
1933 Hold Your Horses
1934 Ziegfeld Follies
Life Begins at 8:40
Music Hath Charms
1935 At Home Abroad
1936 Ziegfeld Follies
The Show Is On
1937 Frederika
Hooray for What!
Between the Devil
The Three Waltzes
1938 You Never Know
Hellzapoppin
1939 The Streets of Paris
The Straw Hat Revue
1940 Keep Off the Grass
1941 Night of Love
Sons o' Fun
1942 Count Me In
1943 Ziegfeld Follies
1944 Laffing Room Only

1945 A Lady Says Yes
1948 My Romance

Shuffle Along (1921). Music & lyrics by Noble Sissle & Eubie Blake; book by Flournoy Miller & Aubrey Lyles.

SONGS: "I'm Just Wild About Harry," "Love Will Find a Way," "Bandana Days," "Shuffle Along," "The Baltimore Buzz," "Gypsy Blues," "I'm Craving for That Kind of Love," "If You've Never Been Vamped by a Brownskin."

NEW YORK: May 23, 1921
63RD ST. MUSIC HALL; 504 p.

Presented by Nikko Productions; directed by Walter Brooks; choreographed by Lawrence Deas; music director, Eubie Blake; orchestrations, Will Vodery.

CAST: Flournoy Miller (*Steve Jenkins*), Aubrey Lyles (*Sam Peck*), Noble Sissle (*Tom Sharper*), Gertrude Saunders (*Ruth Little*), Lottie Gee (*Jessie Williams*), Roger Matthews (*Harry Walton*), Charles Davis (*Uncle Tom*), Lawrence Deas (*Jack Penrose*), Eubie Blake (pianist).

Shuffle Along was the longest-running book musical produced, directed, written, and acted by Negroes. Developed from Miller and Lyles's vaudeville skit "The Mayor of Dixie," it was presented north of the Bway theatre district in a run-down lecture hall. Though the sponsors had little money for scenery or costumes, the show caught on with white theatregoers, who enjoyed the earthy humor, catchy songs, and spirited dancing, which included every current step but the waltz. The tenuous plot concerned a three-way race for the mayor of Jimtown, Dixieland, between crooked Steve Jenkins and Sam Peck and virtuous Harry Walton. Steve wins, appoints Sam police chief, but Harry—about whom everyone is just wild—eventually has them both thrown out of office. During run, Gertrude Saunders was succeeded by Florence Mills, then Edith Spencer, and Paul Robeson appeared briefly in singing quartet. In Aug. 1922, Josephine Baker joined the road company as a chorus girl. The original pit orchestra included Hall Johnson (viola) and William Grant Still (oboe).

The first all-black musical in NY was *A Trip to Coontown*, which lasted a week in 1898. *In Dahomey*, in 1903, later played London the same year to become the first black show on the West End. Prior to *Shuffle Along* the last all-black musical was *Mr. Lode of Koal* in 1909.

There were three titular successors to *Shuffle Along*. *Keep Shufflin'* (1928) co-starred Miller and Lyles and ran for 104 performances. *Shuffle Along of 1933* (1932), with a score by Sissle and Blake and a cast headed by Miller and Sissle, remained for 17. *Shuffle Along* (1952), again offering the trio of Miller, Sissle, and Blake, lasted four. In 1923, Miller and Lyles also played Steve Jenkins and Sam Peck in *Runnin' Wild*.

"Shy." Music by Mary Rodgers; lyric by Marshall Barer. Though maintaining throughout how demure, meek, and timid she is, the singer reveals her true character as soon as she takes the seven-note leap to trumpet the word "SHYYYYY!" Carol Burnett introduced the number in *Once Upon a Mattress* (NY 1959); Jane Connell sang it in the London version (1960).

Sillman, Leonard (Dexter), producer, director; b. Detroit, Mich., May 9, 1908. Sillman is known for his series of *New Faces* revues on Bway, which introduced Nancy Hamilton, Henry Fonda, Charles Walters, Eartha Kitt, Paul Lynde, Ronny Graham, Alice

Ghostley, Inga Swenson, Maggie Smith. The producer began his career in vaudeville act with Imogene Coca (1926–1927), who appeared in five of his productions. He is the brother of singer-lyricist June Carroll. Bib: *Here Lies Leonard Sillman* (Citadel, NY 1959).

Unless otherwise noted, Mr. Sillman was producer of following; asterisk indicates he was also director:
1926　Lady, Be Good! (US tour) (*Dick Trevor* only)
1927　Greenwich Village Follies (US tour) (actor only)
　　　Merry-Go-Round (actor only)
1934　New Faces * (also actor)
　　　Fools Rush In * (also actor)
1936　New Faces of 1936 *
1938　Who's Who *
1940　All in Fun *
1942　New Faces of 1943 * (also actor)
1946　If the Shoe Fits *
1950　Happy as Larry
1952　New Faces of 1952
1956　New Faces of 1956
1957　Mask and Gown *
1962　New Faces of 1962 *
1968　New Faces of 1968 * (also actor)

Silvers, Phil (né Philip Silver), actor; b. Brooklyn, NY, May 11, 1911. Brash, bespectacled comic who bungles through one gaucherie after another without ever being cowed or deterred. Silvers has also appeared in Hollywood films and has had his own tv series, *Sergeant Bilko*. Bib: *This Laugh Is on Me* by Silvers (Prentice-Hall, NJ 1973).
1939　Yokel Boy (*Punko Parks*)
1947　High Button Shoes (*Harrison Floy*)
1951　Top Banana (*Jerry Biffle*)
1960　Do Re Mi (*Hubie Cram*)
1972　A Funny Thing Happened on the Way to the Forum (r) (*Pseudolus*)

Simon, (Marvin) Neil, librettist; b. New York, July 4, 1927. Major Bway playwright (*The Odd Couple, Plaza Suite*), who began career as comedy writer for tv and sketch writer for revues.
1955　Catch a Star!
1962　Little Me
1966　Sweet Charity
1969　Promises, Promises
1979　They're Playing Our Song

"Simple Little Things." Music by Harvey Schmidt; lyric by Tom Jones. A plain girl dreams only the dreams that can come true. Tenderly expressed in *110 in the Shade* by Inga Swenson in NY (1963) and in London (1967).

"Sing for Your Supper." Music by Richard Rodgers; lyric by Lorenz Hart. Show-stopping harmonizing number sung by Muriel Angelus, Marcy Westcott, and Wynn Murray in *The Boys from Syracuse* (NY 1938), in which it was danced by Betty Bruce. In London revival (1963), it was sung by Lynn Kennington, Paula Hendrix, and Maggie Fitzgibbon, danced by Pat Turner.

"Sing Me a Song with Social Significance." Music & lyric by Harold Rome. Self-kidding theme of *Pins and Needles* (NY 1937), sung with mock determination by the chorus. The show was sponsored by the International Ladies Garment Workers Union.

"Sing Something Simple." Music & lyric by Herman Hupfeld. Simply sung by Ruth Tester, with Arline Judge and Fay Brady in *The Second Little Show* (NY 1930), and by Nelson Keys in *Folly to Be Wise* (L 1931).

"Sing to Me, Guitar." Music & lyric by Cole Porter. Corinna Mura's brooding request to recall a romantic evening and to summon a lover's return.

First sung in *Mexican Hayride* (NY 1944).

"Siren's Song, The." Music by Jerome Kern; lyric by P. G. Wodehouse. Song of enticement based on the legend of the Lorelei, the Rhine maiden whose siren call lured fishermen to their destruction. Edith Hallor spun the tale in *Leave It to Jane* (NY 1917). The same theme also cropped up in three other songs, all called "Lorelei": Kern and Anne Caldwell's in *Sally* (NY 1920), Noël Coward's in *This Year of Grace!* (L 1928), the Gershwin brothers' in *Pardon My English* (NY 1933).

Sissle, Noble, lyricist, actor; b. Indianapolis, Ind., July 10, 1889. Sissle teamed with his only collaborator, composer Eubie Blake, to write the score for *Shuffle Along* ("I'm Just Wild About Harry," "Love Will Find the Way"), Bway's first long-run all-Negro musical. With Blake he also wrote "You Were Meant for Me" for *London Calling!* (L 1923). Bib: *Reminiscing with Sissle and Blake* by William Bolcom & Robert Kimball (Viking, NY 1973). (*D. Dec. 17, 1975.*)

1921 Shuffle Along (also *Tom Sharper*)
1923 Elsie
1924 Chocolate Dandies (also *Dobbie Hicks*)
1932 Shuffle Along of 1933 (also *Tom Sharper*)
1952 Shuffle Along (also singer)

"Sit Down, You're Rockin' the Boat." Music & lyric by Frank Loesser. A frightening dream causes a sinner to repent. Introduced by Stubby Kaye in *Guys and Dolls* (NY 1950; L 1953) during the meeting at the Save-a-Soul Mission.

Slade, Julian, composer, lyricist, librettist; b. London, May 28, 1930.

Slade's biggest London hit was the long-running *Salad Days*, which he wrote with co-lyricist, co-librettist Dorothy Reynolds. He began his career as an actor, then became music director for the Bristol Old Vic (1953). Slade has also written with Robin Miller.

Asterisk indicates following written with Miss Reynolds:

1954 Salad Days *
1957 Free as Air *
1960 Follow that Girl *
     Hooray for Daisy! *
1961 Wildest Dreams *
1962 Vanity Fair (Miller)
1972 Trelawney

"Slaughter on Tenth Avenue." Music by Richard Rodgers. A "modern" ballet presented by a classical ballet company in *On Your Toes* (NY 1936). In the dance, a Hoofer (Ray Bolger) and a Stripper (Tamara Geva) in a sleazy dive find themselves in love and menaced by the Boss (George Church). Trying to kill the Hoofer, the Boss accidentally shoots the Stripper; Hoofer then shoots the Boss and proceeds to dance around the dead bodies. The ballet was also important to the play's story in that it served as a climx to the plot. Toward the end of the dance, the character Bolger played discovers two gunmen seated in the audience who, mistaking him for another dancer, are there to rub him out. To avoid being a target and to give the police enough time to make the arrest, he continues dancing until he drops from exhaustion. In London version (1937), the number was danced by Jack Whiting and Vera Zorina.

"Sleepin' Bee, A." Music by Harold Arlen; lyric by Truman Capote & Arlen. Delicate recounting of Haitian superstition that if a girl catches a bee and it doesn't sting her, then it's a sure sign that she will find her true love. The song was introduced by Diahann Carroll in *House of Flowers* (NY 1954).

Slezak, Walter (Leo), actor, singer; b. Vienna, Austria, May 3, 1902. Rotund character comedian who began career on Bway in romantic parts (he sang "I've Told Ev'ry Little Star" in *Music in the Air*), and has also played dramatic roles. Slezak appeared in many Hollywood films.

1930	Meet My Sister (*Eric Molinar*)
1932	Music in the Air (*Karl Reder*)
1935	May Wine (*Prof. Johann Volk*)
1938	I Married an Angel (*Harry Szigetti*)
1954	Fanny (*Panisse*)

Sloane, A. Baldwin, composer; b. Baltimore, Md., Aug. 28, 1872; d. Red Bank, NJ, Feb. 21, 1925. Sloane's biggest Bway success was *The Wizard of Oz*, with lyrics by L. Frank Baum; his best-known song, "Heaven Will Protect the Working Girl," lyric by Edgar Smith, in *Tillie's Nightmare.* Lyricist George V. Hobart was Sloane's most frequent collaborator (seven scores); others included Sydney Rosenfeld, R. H. Burnside, Glen MacDonough, E. Ray Goetz, Harry B. Smith, John Murray Anderson, Arthur Swanstrom, Harry Cort and George Stoddard.

1896	Jack and the Beanstalk (Barnett)
1900	Broadway to Tokyo (Hobart)
	Aunt Hannah (Greene)
	A Million Dollars (Hobart)
	The Giddy Throng (Hobart)
1901	The King's Carnival (Hobart)
1902	The Hall of Fame (Hobart)
	The Belle of Broadway (Hobart)
	The Mocking Bird (Rosenfeld)
1903	The Wizard of Oz (Baum)
1904	Sergeant Kitty (Burnside)
	Lady Teazle (Bangs)
1905	The Gingerbread Man (Ranken)
1906	Comin' Through the Rye (Hobart)

	Seeing New York (Hart, Crawford)
1907	The Mimic and the Maid (Lowe)
1910	Tillie's Nightmare (E. Smith)
	The Summer Widowers (MacDonough)
	The Prince of Bohemia (Goetz)
1911	The Hen-Pecks (Goetz)
1912	Hokey Pokey (Goetz)
	Hanky Panky (Goetz)
	Roly Poly (Goetz)
	The Sun Dodgers (Goetz)
1918	Ladies First (H. B. Smith)
1919	Greenwich Village Follies (Anderson, Swanstrom)
1920	Greenwich Village Follies (Anderson, Swanstrom)
1925	China Rose (Cort, Stoddard)

"Small World." Music by Jule Styne; lyric by Stephen Sondheim. Tender discovery of mutual interests and attitudes sung by Ethel Merman and Jack Klugman in *Gypsy* (NY 1959). In London version (1973), by Angela Lansbury and Barrie Ingham.

"Smiles." Music by Lee S. Roberts; lyric by J. Will Callahan. A popular wartime morale booster, with nary a reference to war, it was interpolated on Bway by Nell Carrington in *The Passing Show of 1918.*

Smith, Edgar, librettist, lyricist; b. Brooklyn, NY, Dec. 9, 1857; d. Bayside, NY, March 8, 1938. Smith wrote sketches and lyrics for Weber and Fields burlesques 1897–1903, incl. "Ma Blushin' Rosie," music by John Stromberg. He also wrote "Heaven Will Protect the Working Girl," music by A. Baldwin Sloane, sung in *Tillie's Nightmare.* Among other collaborators: Ludwig Englander, Maurice Levi, Victor Herbert, Gus Edwards, Robert Hood Bowers, Leo Fall, Oscar Straus, Gustave Kerker, Alfred Goodman.

Unless composer's name is listed, Mr. Smith wrote only sketches or libretto:

1895 The Grand Vizier (Gagel)
The Merry World (Biddle)
1897 Pousse-Café (Stromberg)
1898 The Con-Curers (Stromberg)
Hurly Burly (Stromberg)
Hotel Topsy-Turvy (Rogers)
Cyranose de Bric-a-Brac (Stromberg)
The Little Host (Francis)
1899 Catherine (Stromberg)
Helter Skelter
Mother Goose (Gagel)
Whirl-i-Gig
1900 Fiddle-Dee-Dee (Stromberg)
Sweet Anne Page (Neidlinger)
1901 Hoity Toity (Stromberg)
1902 Twirly Whirly (Stromberg, Francis)
1903 Whoop-Dee-Doo (Francis)
1904 An English Daisy
Higgledy Piggledy (Levi)
1906 Twiddle Twaddle (Levi)
Dream City and the Magic Knight (Herbert)
1907 The Girl Behind the Counter
Hip! Hip! Hooray! (Edwards)
1908 The Merry-Go-Round
The Mimic World
Mr. Hamlet of Broadway
1909 Philopoena (L) (Levi)
Old Dutch
1910 Tillie's Nightmare (Sloane)
Up and Down Broadway
1911 La Belle Paree
A Certain Party (Bowers)
The Kiss Waltz
The Revue of Revues
1912 Hokey Pokey
Hanky Panky
Roly Poly
The Sun Dodgers
1913 Lieber Augustin (Fall)
The Pleasure Seekers
1915 The Peasant Girl
Hands Up
The Blue Paradise
Alone at Last
1916 Robinson Crusoe, Jr.
Step This Way (The Girl Behind the Counter)
The Girl from Brazil
1917 My Lady's Glove (Straus)

1918 Fancy Free
The Melting of Molly
1919 Shubert Gaieties
Oh, What a Girl (Jules, Presberg)
Hello, Alexander
1921 The Whirl of New York (Kerker, Goodman)
1922 Red Pepper
1929 Broadway Nights
The Street Singer
1930 Hello, Paris

Smith, Harry B(ache), lyricist, librettist; b. Buffalo, NY, Dec. 28, 1860; d. Atlantic City, NJ, Jan. 2, 1936. Smith's 123 Bway musicals made him the most prolific librettist of all time. His biggest hits: *Robin Hood, The Rich Mr. Hoggenheimer, The Spring Maid, Sweethearts, The Girl from Utah, Watch Your Step, Countess Maritza* ("Play, Gypsies—Dance, Gypsies"). He also wrote "Gypsy Love Song" (*The Serenade*), "The Sheik of Araby" (*Make It Snappy*), and "Yours Is My Heart Alone" (*Yours Is My Heart*). Smith wrote 17 shows with composer Reginald De Koven, 16 with Ludwig Englander, 13 with Victor Herbert. Among others with whom he collaborated: Julian Edwards, John Stromberg, Aimee Lauchaume, John Bratton, Alfred Aarons, Max Hoffman, Gustave Kerker, John Philip Sousa, Maurice Levi, Raymond Hubbell, Robert Hood Bowers, Gus Edwards, Leo Fall, Franz Lehar, Jean Gilbert, Heinrich Reinhardt, Robert Planquette, Oscar Straus, Jerome Kern, Ivan Caryll, A. Baldwin Sloane, Sigmund Romberg, Walter Kollo, Jacques Offenbach, Karl Hajos, Emmerich Kalman, Victor Jacobi. Smith was the brother of librettist Robert B. Smith and the husband of actress Irene Bentley. Bib: *First Nights and First Editions* by Smith (Little, Brown, Boston 1931).

Unless otherwise noted, Mr. Smith was librettist-lyricist of following:

1887 The Begum (DeKoven)
1889 Don Quixote (DeKoven)
1891 Robin Hood (DeKoven)
    The Tar and the Tartar (Itzel)
1892 The Knickerbockers (DeKoven)
    Jupiter (J. Edwards)
1893 The Algerian (DeKoven)
    The Fencing Master (DeKoven)
1894 Rob Roy (DeKoven)
1895 The Tzigane (DeKoven)
    The Wizard of the Nile (Herbert)
1896 The Caliph (Englander)
    Half a King (Englander)
    The Mandarin (DeKoven)
1897 The Serenade (Herbert)
    Gayest Manhattan (Englander)
    The Idol's Eye (Herbert)
    The Highwayman (DeKoven)
1898 Hurly Burly (Stromberg)
    The Little Corporal (Englander)
    The Fortune Teller (Herbert)
    Cyranose de Bric-a-Brac (Stromberg)
1899 Catherine (Stromberg)
    The Three Dragoons (DeKoven)
    Helter Skelter (lyr. only) (Stromberg)
    The Rounders (Englander)
    Cyrano de Bergerac (lyr. only) (Herbert)
    Whirl-i-Gig (lyr. only) (Stromberg)
    The Singing Girl (Herbert)
    Papa's Wife (DeKoven)
1900 The Casino Girl (Englander)
    The Viceroy (Herbert)
    The Cadet Girl (Englander)
    The Belle of Bohemia (Englander)
    Foxy Quiller (DeKoven)
1901 The Prima Donna (Lauchaume)
    The Strollers (Englander)
    Rogers Brothers in Washington (lyr. only) (Levi)
    The Liberty Belles (Bratton)
    The Little Duchess (DeKoven)
1902 The Toreador (lib. only)
    Maid Marian (DeKoven)
    The Wild Rose (Englander)
    The Billionaire (Kerker)
1903 The Jewel of Asia (Englander)
    The Blonde in Black (Kerker)
    The Office Boy (Englander)
    Babette (Herbert)

The Girl from Dixie (misc.)
1904 The Madcap Princess (Englander)
    A China Doll (Aarons)
1905 Miss Dolly Dollars (Herbert)
    The White Cat (Englander)
1906 The Free Lance (Sousa)
    The Rich Mr. Hoggenheimer (Englander)
    The Parisian Model (Hoffman)
    The Belle of Mayfair (lib. only)
1907 The Tattooed Man (Herbert)
    Ziegfeld Follies (misc.)
1908 The Soul Kiss (Levi)
    Nearly a Hero (lib. only)
    Ziegfeld Follies (Levi)
    The Golden Butterfly (DeKoven)
    Little Nemo (Herbert)
    Miss Innocence (Englander)
1909 Ziegfeld Follies (Levi)
    The Silver Star (Bowers)
1910 Ziegfeld Follies (G. Edwards)
    The Girl on the Train (Fall)
    The Bachelor Belles (Hubbell)
    The Spring Maid (Reinhardt)
1911 The Paradise of Mohamet (Planquette)
    Little Miss Fix-It (co-lib. only)
    Gaby (co-lib. only)
    The Red Rose (Bowers)
    The Siren (Fall)
    The Duchess (lyr. only) (Herbert)
    Gypsy Love (Lehar)
    The Enchantress (Herbert)
    The Wedding Trip (DeKoven)
1912 Modest Suzanne (Gilbert)
    A Winsome Widow (Hubbell)
    The Rose Maid (lib. only)
    The Girl from Montmartre (Bereny)
    Ziegfeld Follies (Hubbell)
1913 The Sunshine Girl (lib. only)
    My Little Friend (Straus)
    The Doll Girl (Fall)
    Sweethearts (co-lib. only)
    Oh, I Say! (lyr. only) (Kern)
1914 The Girl from Utah (Kern)
    The Lilac Domino (lib. only)
    Papa's Darling (Caryll)
    The Débutante (lib. only)
    Watch Your Step (lib. only)
1915 90 in the Shade (lyr. only) (Kern)
    Town Topics (Orlob)
    Stop! Look! Listen! (lib. only)
1916 Sybil (Jacobi)

Molly O' (Woess)
1917   Love o' Mike (lyr. only) (Kern)
Rambler Rose (Jacobi)
1918   Ladies First (Sloane)
1919   A Lonely Romeo (co-lib. only)
Angel Face (lib. only)
1920   Betty Be Good (Reisenfeld)
1922   The Springtime of Youth (lyr. only) (Romberg, Kollo)
1923   Caroline (Rideamus)
Fashions of 1924 (lyr. only) (Snyder)
1925   The Love Song (Offenbach)
Nadja (Hajos)
Princess Flavia (Romberg)
1926   Sweetheart Time (lib. only)
Naughty Riquette (Straus)
Countess Maritza (Kalman)
1927   Cherry Blossoms (Romberg)
The Circus Princess (Kalman)
Half a Widow (Camp)
The Love Call (Romberg)
1928   White Lilacs (Hajos)
The Red Robe (Gilbert)
1930   Three Little Girls (lyr. only) (Kollo)
1932   Marching By (Gilbert)

Smith, Maggie, actress, singer; b. Ilford, Eng. Stage and screen dramatic actress who appeared in two revues.
1956   New Faces of 1956 (NY)
1957   Share My Lettuce (L)

Smith, Queenie, actress, dancer, singer; b. New York, Sept. 8, 1902. Energetic, round-faced performer whose biggest Bway hits were *Helen of Troy, New York,* and *Tip-Toes* (in which she sang "Looking for a Boy," "That Certain Feeling," and "These Charming People"). Miss Smith began her career as dancer with the Metropolitan Opera, 1916.
1919   Roly Boly Eyes (*Ida Loring*)
1922   Just Because (*Syringa*)
Orange Blossoms (*Tillie*)
1923   Cinders (*Tillie Olsen*)
Helen of Troy, New York (*Maribel*)
1924   Sitting Pretty (*Dixie*)
Be Yourself (*Tony Robinson*)

1925   Tip-Toes (*Tip-Toes Kaye*)
1927   Judy (*Judy Drummond*)
Hit the Deck (*Loulou,* repl.)
1929   The Street Singer (*Suzette*)
1932   A Little Racketeer (*Dixie*)

Smith, Robert B(ache), lyricist, librettist; b. Chicago, Ill., June 4. 1875; d. New York, Nov. 6, 1951. Smith's most successful Bway musicals were *The Spring Maid* ("Day Dreams"), music by Heinrich Reinhardt, and *Sweethearts* ("Sweethearts," "Every Lover Must Meet His Fate"), music by Victor Herbert. Other song hits: "Come Down, Ma Evenin' Star" (*Twirly Whirly*), "I Might Be Your Once-in-a-While" (*Angel Face*). Other collaborators: Raymond Hubbell, John Stromberg, Alfred Aarons, Gus Edwards, Julian Edwards, Robert Planquette, Franz Lehar, Jean Gilbert, Bruno Granichstaedten, Henri Bereny, Robert Hood Bowers, Oscar Straus, Charles Cuvillier, Harold Orlob. Smith was a brother of lyricist-librettist Harry B. Smith.
Asterisk indicates Mr. Smith was also librettist or co-librettist:
1902   Twirly Whirly (Stromberg, Francis)
1904   A China Doll * (Aarons)
1905   Fantana * (Hubbell)
When We Were Forty-One * (G. Edwards)
The Babes and the Baron (Haines)
1906   Mexicana (Hubbell)
Mam'selle Sallie * (Hubbell)
1907   Knight for a Day * (Hubbell)
1909   The Girl and the Wizard (J. Edwards)
1910   The Spring Maid * (Reinhardt)
1911   The Paradise of Mohamet * (Planquette)
Gaby (co-lib. only)
The Red Rose * (Bowers)
Gypsy Love * (Lehar)
1912   Modest Suzanne * (Gilbert)
The Rose Maid (Granichstaedten)

The Girl from Montmartre *
(Bereny)
1913　My Little Friend * (Straus)
Sweethearts (Herbert)
1914　The Lilac Domino (Cuvillier)
The Débutante (Herbert)
1915　Town Topics * (Orlob)
1916　Molly O' * (Woess)
Follow Me (Romberg)
1919　A Lonely Romeo (Franklin)
Angel Face (Herbert)
1920　The Girl in the Spotlight * (Herbert)

"Smoke Gets in Your Eyes." Music by Jerome Kern; lyric by Otto Harbach. Wearing a simple dress with her head covered by a babushka, Tamara sang the torch ballad in *Roberta* (NY 1933), accompanying herself on a guitar while seated on a bare stage. More than anything else, this reflection on a love that went up in smoke was responsible for the musical's success. As producer Max Gordon recalled, "Originally, Kern had written the melody as a signature for a radio series that never materialized. When it was decided that a song was needed for Stephanie (Tamara's role) in the second act, Kern offered it to Harbach to write the lyric. In its original straight march rhythm it appealed to none of us. Kern was ready to give up on the melody when he was seized by inspiration. He tried it in the more leisurely tempo and sentimental style that gave it immortality."

"So in Love." Music & lyric by Cole Porter. The main love ballad—though not a duet—in *Kiss Me, Kate* (NY 1948), sung by Patricia Morison, then Alfred Drake. Miss Morison also sang it in London production (1951), in which it was reprised by Bill Johnson. Note that though the 71-bar song was ostensibly written in the "AABA" form, Porter enhanced the emotion by raising the notes one tone on the 10th bar of the second and fourth stanzas (on the words "darling why" and "till I die").

"So Long, Dearie." Music & lyric by Jerry Herman. In *Hello, Dolly!*, Dolly bids Horace Vandergelder a breezy—but not to be taken seriously—goodbye. Carol Channing sang it in NY (1964), Mary Martin in London (1965).

"So Long, Mary." Music & lyric by George M. Cohan. Jaunty song of farewell first sung by Fay Templeton and chorus in *Forty-Five Minutes from Broadway* (NY 1906) at a New Rochelle railroad station. In *George M!* (NY 1968) it was performed by Joel Grey, Harvey Evans, Loni Ackerman, and Angela Martin.

"Soft Lights and Sweet Music." Music & lyric by Irving Berlin. Music's value as an adjunct to romance was appreciated by Katherine Carrington and J. Harold Murray in *Face the Music* (NY 1932).

"Softly, as in a Morning Sunrise." Music by Sigmund Romberg; lyric by Oscar Hammerstein II. Woman's faithlessness was the subject of this impassioned ballad, sung in *The New Moon* by William O'Neal (NY 1928) and Ben Williams (L 1929). In the scene, a New Orleans waterfront tavern, the song is preceded by the singer's observation, "A woman's friendship glitters like a false gem and endures as long." Language purists, however, have been more concerned about the redundancy of the titular phrase "morning sunrise."

"Soliloquy." Music by Richard Rodgers; lyric by Oscar Hammerstein II. A lengthy musical monologue, sung by John Raitt in *Carousel* (NY 1945), in which the ne'er-do-well hero ruminates about his impending father-hood. In the beginning, imagining his child-to-be as a boy, he is full of pride dreaming of how he and his son Bill will have fun together. Then suddenly he realizes that the boy might be a girl, and that he will have to be a real father. Because his little girl will grow hungry if he continues his shiftless life, he vows to do anything to get enough money to make sure she will be brought up properly. In London version (1950), Stephen Douglass sang the piece. The lyric, which occupies four pages in the printed text, took Hammerstein two weeks to write; Rodgers composed the melody in less than two hours.

"**Some Day.**" Music by Rudolf Friml; lyric by Brian Hooker. Sung by a love-lorn Carolyn Thomson in *The Vaga-bond King* (NY 1925), and by Winnie Melville in London version (1927).

"**Some Day My Heart Will Awake.**" Music by Ivor Novello; lyric by Chris-topher Hassall. Vanessa Lee, as an 18-year-old princess in *King's Rhapsody* (L 1949), dreams of the day she will fall in love.

"**Some Enchanted Evening.**" Music by Richard Rodgers; lyric by Oscar Hammerstein II. Ezio Pinza boomed this impassioned aria early in *South Pacific* (NY 1949) on discovering he had fallen in love at first sight with Mary Martin (who reprised it in sec-ond act). In London version (1951), the singers were Wilbur Evans and Miss Martin.

"**Some of Us Belong to the Stars.**" Music by John Barry; lyric by Don Black. Michael Crawford proclaims his destiny as the daydreaming hero of *Billy* (L 1974).

"**Some People.**" Music by Jule Styne; lyric by Stephen Sondheim. The song that first reveals the driving determi-nation of Gypsy Rose Lee's mother in *Gypsy*. Ethel Merman sang it in NY (1959), Angela Lansbury in London (1973).

"**Some Sort of Somebody.**" Music by Jerome Kern; lyric by Elsie Janis. Elsie Janis introduced this fickle-hearted confession in *Miss Informa-tion* (NY 1915). It was also sung by Ann Orr and Oscar Shaw in *Very Good Eddie* later the same year, and by Regine Flory and Nelson Keys in *Vanity Fair* (L 1916).

"**Somebody Loves Me.**" Music by George Gershwin; lyric by B. G. De-Sylva & Ballard Macdonald. A song of romantic conviction—despite lack of evidence—sung by Winnie Lightner, Tom Patricola, and chorus in Bway revue *George White's Scandals* (1924).

"**Somebody, Somewhere.**" Music & lyric by Frank Loesser. In *The Most Happy Fella* (NY 1956), a lonely waitress (Jo Sullivan) is all aglow at discovering that "somebody, some-where, wants me and needs me." He-lena Scott played the role in the Lon-don version (1960).

"**Somehow I Never Could Believe.**" Music by Kurt Weill; lyric by Lang-ston Hughes. Anguished aria in-troduced by Polyna Stoska in *Street Scene* (NY 1947). In this outpouring of a woman living in a NY tenement, the singer recalls the misery of her youth, reveals the coldness of her marriage and the indifference of her children, and ends by expressing her hope for happiness and her belief in a brighter day.

"Someone to Watch Over Me." Music by George Gershwin; lyric by Ira Gershwin. Plaintive expression of romantic longing introduced by Gertrude Lawrence, clutching a rag doll, in *Oh, Kay!* (NY 1926, L 1927). Originally the tune was fast and jazzy, but after the composer played it at a slower tempo both he and his brother realized that it sounded better that way. The title was suggested by Howard Dietz, who had been called in to help Ira because of the lyricist's confinement in a hospital.

"Something I Dreamed Last Night." Music by Sammy Fain; lyric by Herb Magidson & Jack Yellen. In *George White's Scandals* (NY 1939) Ella Logan could not believe it's really the end of the affair.

"Something Sort of Grandish." Music by Burton Lane; lyric by E. Y. Harburg. Dainty piece in *Finian's Rainbow* (NY 1947) in which Og, the leprechaun, explains to Sharon, another Irish immigrant, just how he feels when he's near this "amorish, glamorish dish." Introduced by David Wayne and Ella Logan; in London version (1947), sung by Alfie Bass and Beryl Seton.

"Something to Remember You By." Music by Arthur Schwartz; lyric by Howard Dietz. In Bway revue *Three's a Crowd* (1930), Libby Holman, as a French girl, sang this tender goodbye to matelot Fred MacMurray. Originally, the same melody, but at a faster clip, was called "I Have No Words" when it was introduced the previous year in the London musical *Little Tommy Tucker* (lyric by Desmond Carter):

I have no words to say how much I love
   you
That's my excuse, I have no words.

I've got a cottage and a room with a view
And H & C, but I've no words.
I would beg for you
Break a leg for you
Lay an egg for you
Like the birds up in the treetop.
I wrote a song to say how much I love you
I've got the tune but I've no words.

When Schwartz played the music for Dietz, who was expected to provide a new lyric, the lyricist thought of the title, "Something to Remember You By," with the "something" referring to a kick in the pants. It was only when, at Dietz's urging, the composer played the tune at a dreamier tempo that Schwartz realized it sounded better as a ballad.

"Something Very Strange." Music & lyric by Noël Coward. Radiant revelation of how everything looks and sounds "on this romantic day." Elaine Stritch sang it in *Sail Away*, both in NY (1961) and London (1962).

"Something Wonderful." Music by Richard Rodgers; lyric by Oscar Hammerstein II. In *The King and I* (NY 1951), Anna Leonowens (Gertrude Lawrence) is determined to leave Bangkok after a fight with the king. To make her change her mind, Lady Thiang (Dorothy Sarnoff) sings of the king's potential for doing good and her belief that, with Anna's love, he can do wonderful things. Muriel Smith sang the entreaty in the London company (1953).

"Something's Coming." Music by Leonard Bernstein; lyric by Stephen Sondheim. Nervously agitated piece in *West Side Story* (NY 1957) sung by Larry Kert in anticipation of something miraculous that he knows will be happening soon. The singer in the London version (1958) was Don McKay.

"Sometimes I'm Happy." Music by Vincent Youmans; lyric by Irving Caesar. Ballad of dispositional dependency introduced by Louise Groody and Charles King in *Hit the Deck* (NY 1927); also sung by Ivy Tresmand and Stanley Holloway in London production (1927). The melody of the song—but taken at a snappier tempo—had originally been written in 1923, when it was known as "Come on and Pet Me" ("Why don't you get me to let you pet me?"). William Cary Duncan and Oscar Hammerstein II were co-lyricists, and the song was intended for *Mary Jane McKane* but cut before Bway opening. Three years later, Caesar rewrote the words with its present title, and the song was included in the score of *A Night Out,* which closed in Philadelphia before reaching NY. It then became the hit of *Hit the Deck.*

Sondheim, Stephen (Joshua), composer, lyricist; b. New York, March 22, 1930. After writing lyrics to Leonard Bernstein's music for *West Side Story* ("Something's Coming," "Maria," "Tonight") and to Jule Styne's music for *Gypsy* ("Let Me Entertain You," "Some People," "Everything's Coming Up Roses," "Small World"), Sondheim became a Bway composer with his score for *A Funny Thing Happened on the Way to the Forum* ("Comedy Tonight"). With *Company* ("Another Hundred People," "The Ladies Who Lunch"), *Follies* ("Losing My Mind," "I'm Still Here") and *A Little Night Music* ("Send in the Clowns"), all produced and directed by Harold Prince, he won further recognition as a major innovative force in the musical theatre. Sondheim also teamed with composer Richard Rodgers ("Do I Hear a Waltz?") and wrote additional lyrics for new version of Bernstein's *Candide* (1974).

Bib: *Sondheim & Co.* by Craig Zadan (Macmillan, NY 1974).

1957	West Side Story (Bernstein)
1959	Gypsy (Styne)
1962	A Funny Thing Happened on the Way to the Forum
1964	Anyone Can Whistle
1965	Do I Hear a Waltz? (Rodgers)
1970	Company
1971	Follies
1973	A Little Night Music
1976	Pacific Overtures
1979	Sweeney Todd

"Song Is You, The." Music by Jerome Kern; lyric by Oscar Hammerstein II. Ardent aria introduced by Tullio Carminati in *Music in the Air* (NY 1932), and reprised by Carminati and Natalie Hall. In London version (1933), sung by Arthur Margetson and Mary Ellis.

"Song of Love." Music by Sigmund Romberg, adapted from the second theme of Schubert's "Unfinished" Symphony; lyric by Dorothy Donnelly. Waltzing duet sung by Olga Cook and Bertram Peacock in *Blossom Time* (NY 1921).

Song of Norway (1944). Music & lyrics by Robert Wright & George Forrest, adapted from melodies by Edvard Grieg; book by Milton Lazarus, based on play by Homer Curran.

Songs: "The Legend" (A-Minor Piano Concerto), "Hill of Dreams" (A-Minor Piano Concerto), "Freddy and His Fiddle" ("Norwegian Dance"), "Now" (Waltz, op. 12, no. 2, & Violin Sonata in G), "Strange Music" (Nocturne & "Wedding in Troldhaugen"), "Midsummer's Eve" (" 'Twas on a Lovely Eve in June" & Scherzo), "Three Loves" ('Albumblatt" & "Poème Erotique"), "I Love You" ("Ich Liebe Dich"), Piano Concerto in A Minor.

NEW YORK: Aug. 21, 1944
IMPERIAL THEATRE; 860 p.

Presented by Edwin Lester; directed by Lester & Charles K. Freeman; choreographed by George Balanchine; settings, Lemuel Ayers; costumes, Robert Davison; lighting, Howard Bay; music director, Arthur Kay; orchestrations, Kay.

CAST: Irra Petina (*Louisa Giovanni*), Lawrence Brooks (*Edvard Grieg*), Robert Shafer (*Rikard Nordraak*), Helena Bliss (*Nina Hagerup*), Sig Arno (*Count Peppi Le Loup*), Ivy Scott (*Mrs. Grieg*), Walter Kingsford (*Grieg*), Frederic Franklin (*Freddy*), Alexandra Danilova (*Adelina*), also dancers Maria Tallchief, Ruthanna Boris, Mary Ellen Moylan, Nicholas Magallenes.

LONDON: March 7, 1946
PALACE THEATRE; 526 p.

Presented by Emile Littler; directed by Charles Hickman; choreographed by Robert Helpmann, Pauline Grant; settings, Joan Jefferson Farjeon; costumes, Frederic Dawson, Sophie Fedorovitch; music director, Gideon Fagan.

CAST: Janet Hamilton-Smith (*Louisa Giovanni*), John Hargreaves (*Edvard Grieg*), Arthur Servent (*Rikard Nordraak*), Halina Victoria (*Nina Hagerup*), Bernard Ansell (*Count Peppi Le Loup*), Olive Sturgess (*Mrs. Grieg*), Colin Cunningham (*Grieg*), Jan Lawski (*Freddy*), Moyra Fraser (*Adelina*), John Pygram (*Tito*).

Song of Norway was presented in July 1944 as the first original work offered by Edwin Lester's Los Angeles and San Francisco Civic Light Opera Co. Its success prompted the transfer to Bway with the same principals except for the replacement of Walter Cassel by Lawrence Brooks. The story is set in 1860 in Troldhaugen, near

Bergen, Norway, and in Copenhagen and Rome. Composer Edvard Grieg and poet Rikard Nordraak are determined to bring new artistic stature to Norway but flirtatious Italian prima donna Louisa Giovanni engages Edvard as her accompanist and whisks him away from both his homeland and his wife, Nina. At Rikard's death, however, the composer returns home and, inspired by his friends poem "Song of Norway," composes the A-Minor Piano Concerto. The production featured members of the Ballet Russe de Monte Carlo, who performed the fantasy ballet that ends the operetta.

Other composers depicted in NY and London musicals include Franz Schubert by Bertram Peacock in *Blossom Time* (NY 1921), Courtice Pounds in *Lilac Time* (L 1922), and Richard Tauber in *Blossom Time* (L 1942); Jacques Offenbach by Allan Prior in *The Love Song* (NY 1925) and Andrew Osborn in *Music at Midnight* (L 1950); Johann Strauss Jr. by Robert Halliday in *Waltzes from Vienna* (L 1931), Guy Robertson in *The Great Waltz* (NY 1934) and George Rigaud in *Mr. Strauss Goes to Boston* (NY 1945); Frederic Chopin by Guy Robertson in *White Lilacs* (NY 1928) and Ivor Sheridan in *Waltz Without End* (L 1942).

FILM VERSION: Florence Henderson, Toralv Maurstad, Edward G. Robinson (Cinerama 1970, Andrew Stone dir.).

"Song of the Vagabonds." Music by Rudolf Friml; lyric by Brian Hooker. Dennis King led his "rabble of low degree" in this stirring call to arms in *The Vagabond King* (NY 1925). Derek Oldham led them in London version (1927).

"Song of the Woodman." Music by Harold Arlen; lyric by E. Y. Harburg. One of Bert Lahr's most celebrated numbers, the song catalogues all the varied wonders to be made from wood, incl. "seats all shapes and classes,/For little lads and little lasses." It was introduced in *The Show Is On* (NY 1936).

"Soon." Music by George Gershwin; lyric by Ira Gershwin. Romantic duet sung by Jerry Goff and Margaret Schilling in *Strike Up the Band* (NY 1930). The melody was developed from a four-bar section of the first-act finale of the musical's original 1927 production, which failed to reach Bway.

"Soon It's Gonna Rain." Music by Harvey Schmidt; lyric by Tom Jones. Fragile duet for lovers planning an equally fragile rain shelter in *The Fantasticks*. Rita Gardner and Kenneth Nelson sang it in NY (1960), Stephanie Voss and Peter Gilmore sang it in London (1961).

Sothern, Ann (née Harriette Lake), actress, singer; b. Valley City, N. Dak., Jan. 22, 1909. As Harriette Lake, this tiny blonde actress introduced "I've Got Five Dollars" in *America's Sweetheart*. In Hollywood, she appeared regularly in films between 1934 and 1950.

    1931 America's Sweetheart (*Geraldine March*)
              Everybody's Welcome (*Ann Cathway*)
    1932 Of Thee I Sing (US tour) (*Mary Turner*)

Sound of Music, The (1959). Music by Richard Rodgers; lyrics by Oscar Hammerstein II; book by Howard Lindsay & Russel Crouse, based on Maria Von Trapp's book, *The Trapp Family Singers,* & its German film version.

SONGS: "The Sound of Music," "Maria," "My Favorite Things," "Do-Re-Mi," "Sixteen Going on Seventeen," "The Lonely Goatherd," "How Can Love Survive?," "So Long, Farewell," "Climb Ev'ry Mountain," "Edelweiss."

NEW YORK: Nov. 16, 1959
LUNT-FONTANNE THEATRE; 1,443 p.

Presented by Leland Hayward, Richard Halliday, Richard Rodgers & Oscar Hammerstein II; directed by Vincent J. Donehue; musical numbers staged by Joe Layton; settings, Oliver Smith; costumes, Lucinda Ballard, Mainbocher; lighting, Jean Rosenthal; music director, Frederick Dvonch; orchestrations, Robert Russell Bennett.

CAST: Mary Martin (*Maria Rainer Von Trapp*), Theodore Bikel (*Capt. Georg Von Trapp*), Marion Marlowe (*Elsa Schraeder*), Kurt Kasznar (*Max Detweiler*), Patricia Neway (*Mother Abbess*), Lauri Peters (*Liesl Von Trapp*), Brian Davies (*Rolf Gruber*), Muriel O'Malley (*Sister Margaretta*), Joey Heatherton (singer).

LONDON: May 18, 1961
PALACE THEATRE; 2,385 p.

Presented by Williamson Music Ltd; restaged by Jerome Whyte; musical numbers staged by Joe Layton; settings, Oliver Smith; costumes, Lucinda Ballard; lighting, George Wright; music director, Robert Lowe; orchestrations, Robert Russell Bennett.

CAST: Jean Bayless (*Maria Rainer Von Trapp*), Roger Dann (*Capt. Georg Von Trapp*), Eunice Gayson (*Elsa Schraeder*), Harold Kasket (*Max Detweiler*), Constance Shacklock (*Mother Abbess*), Barbara Brown (*Liesl Von Trapp*), Nicholas Bennett (*Rolf Gruber*), Olive Gilbert (*Sister Margaretta*).

Rodgers and Hammerstein's last musical collaboration was their third longest-running production. The genesis began when director Vincent Donehue saw a German-language film based on the life of the Trapp Family Singers. He convinced Mary Martin that it would make a perfect stage vehicle for her, and she, in turn, got her husband, Richard Halliday, to co-produce it with Leland Hayward. After a lengthy time securing permission from all the members of the far-flung Trapp family, Lindsay and Crouse were signed to write the libretto. Originally, the plan was to use authentic songs of the Trapp repertory, with one additional song by Rodgers and Hammerstein. Because the song writers felt that this would not work, the producers agreed to wait until they were free to create the entire score.

The story, set in Austria in 1938, is concerned with Maria Rainer, a postulant at Nonnberg Abbey, who takes a position as governess of the seven children of widowed Capt. Georg Von Trapp. Maria and the captain fall in love and marry. Their happiness ends, however, with the invasion of the Germans, which forces the family to flee over the Alps to Switzerland. During Bway run, Miss Martin was succeeded by Martha Wright (10-61), Jeannie Carson (7-62), Nancy Dussault (9-62); Theodore Bikel by Donald Scott (10-61); Brian Davies by Jon Voight (10-61); Marion Marlowe by Lois Hunt (10-61); Kurt Kasznar by Paul Lipson (7-62). The US touring company, headed by Florence Henderson (then Barbara Meister) and John Myhers, opened in Feb. 1961, and continued for two years, nine months. The London production was the longest-running US import and the second longest-running musical in West End history.

A previous musical, Ivor Novello's *The Dancing Years* (L 1939), also dealt with the German invasion of Austria.

FILM VERSION: Julie Andrews, Christopher Plummer, Peggy Wood (20th Cent. 1965, Robert Wise dir.).

"Sound of Music, The." Music by Richard Rodgers; lyric by Oscar Hammerstein II. The closeness of music and nature exultantly revealed in *The Sound of Music* (NY 1959) by Mary Martin. In London production (1961), it was sung by Jean Bayless.

Sousa, John Philip, composer, lyricist; b. Washington, DC, Nov. 6, 1854; d. Reading, Pa., March 6, 1932. Except for *El Capitan*, Sousa was better known for his marches than for his musicals. He led the USMC Band, 1880–1892, then organized own band for worldwide tours. Some of his early operettas were not performed in NY. Sousa's lyric-writing collaborators included Tom Frost, Glen MacDonough, Harry B. Smith, and himself. Bib: *Marching Along* by Sousa (Hale Cushman, Boston 1928).

1896	El Capitan (lyr. with Frost)
1898	The Bride-Elect (also lyr., lib.)
	The Charlatan (also lyr.)
1900	Chris and the Wonderful Lamp (MacDonough)
1906	The Free Lance (Smith)
1913	The American Maid (The Glass Blowers) (Liebling)
1915	Hip-Hip-Hooray! (band leader)

"South America, Take It Away." Music & lyric by Harold Rome. Though written two years before its presentation in *Call Me Mister* (NY 1946) and somewhat out of character with the revue's theme (soldiers becoming civilians), this disenchanted look at the rumba-samba invasion of the US became the hit song in the show. Betty Garrett—accompanied by

Harry Clark, Chandler Cowles, George Hall, and Alan Manson—introduced it in a servicemen's canteen scene. It was also sung in London by Pat Kirkwood in *Starlight Roof* (1947).

"**South American Way.**" Music by Jimmy McHugh; lyric by Al Dubin. Rhythmic tribute incongruously sung as first-act finale in Bway revue *The Streets of Paris* (1939), by Carmen Miranda in fruited headdress and six-inch heels.

South Pacific (1949). Music by Richard Rodgers; lyrics by Oscar Hammerstein II; book by Hammerstein & Joshua Logan, based on stories in James Michener's book *Tales of the South Pacific*.

SONGS: "A Cockeyed Optimist," "Some Enchanted Evening," "Bloody Mary," "There Is Nothin' Like a Dame," "Bali Ha'i," "I'm Gonna Wash That Man Right Outa My Hair," "A Wonderful Guy," "Younger than Springtime," "Happy Talk," "Honey Bun," "You've Got to Be Carefully Taught," "This Nearly Was Mine."

NEW YORK: April 7, 1949
MAJESTIC THEATRE; 1,925 p.

Presented by Richard Rodgers & Oscar Hammerstein II, with Leland Hayward & Joshua Logan; directed by Logan; settings & lighting, Jo Mielziner; costumes, Motley; music director, Salvatore Dell'Isola; orchestrations, Robert Russell Bennett.

CAST: Mary Martin (*Nellie Forbush*), Ezio Pinza (*Emile de Becque*), Myron McCormick (*Luther Billis*), William Tabbert (*Lt. Joe Cable*), Juanita Hall (*Bloody Mary*), Betta St. John (*Liat*), Martin Wolfson (*Capt. George Brackett*), Harvey Stephens (*Comdr. William Harbison*), Dickinson Eastham (*Seabee Richard West*), Biff

McGuire (*Bob McCaffrey*), Sandra Deel (*Ens. Janet MacGregor*).

LONDON: Nov. 1, 1951
DRURY LANE THEATRE; 802 p.

Presented by Williamson Music Ltd.; directed by Joshua Logan; settings & lighting, Jo Mielziner; costumes, Motley; music director, Reginald Burston; orchestrations, Robert Russell Bennett; supervisor, Jerome Whyte.

CAST: Mary Martin (*Nellie Forbush*), Wilbur Evans (*Emile de Becque*), Ray Walston (*Luther Billis*), Muriel Smith (*Bloody Mary*), Peter Grant (*Lt. Joe Cable*), Betta St. John (*Liat*), Hartley Power (*Capt. George Brackett*), John McLaren (*Comdr. William Harbison*), Ivor Emmanuel (*Sgt. Johnson*).

South Pacific continued the Rodgers and Hammerstein school of musical theatre by combining a sturdy libretto with music and lyrics that were used integrally within the plot. It was the team's second longest-running Bway production and, to date, the sixth longest-running musical in Bway history. Joshua Logan first got Rodgers interested in the project when he urged him to read a short story, "Fo' Dolla," included in James Michener's World War II collection, *Tales of the South Pacific*. Rodgers and Hammerstein, however, felt that the story—about US Capt. Joe Cable's romance with a Polynesian girl—was too *Madama Butterfly* to sustain an entire evening, and they decided to combine the plot with that of another story, "Our Heroine." This dealt with the unlikely love between Emile de Becque, a worldly French planter, and "Knucklehead Nellie" Forbush, a naive Navy nurse from Little Rock. Both stories shared a common theme in showing the power of love to break down racial barriers. The musical, which had no formal choreography, was the fourth with a score by Rodgers directed by Logan.

During Bway run, Mary Martin was succeeded by Martha Wright (6-51), who was replaced for three weeks in 1952 by Cloris Leachman. Ezio Pinza was succeeded by Ray Middleton (8-50), Roger Rico (7-51), and George Britton (1-52); Juanita Hall by Diosa Costello (6-51) and Odette Myrtil (6-52). In Feb. 1953, Shirley Jones and Virginia Martin joined the cast as nurses. The US touring company began its travels in April 1950, and continued for four years, 11 months. The cast was headed by Janet Blair (*Nellie*), Richard (né Dickinson) Eastham (*de Becque*), Ray Walston (*Luther*), Diosa Costello (*Bloody Mary*), Robert Whitlow (*Cable*), Alan Baxter (*Harbison*). Miss Blair was followed by Jeanne Bal and Iva Withers; Eastham by Webb Tilton and Alan Gerard; Miss Costello by Irene Bordoni; Walston by David Burns and Benny Baker. In London production, Miss Martin was succeeded by Julie Wilson (11-52), Ray Walston by Fredd Wayne (4-52).

FILM VERSION: Mitzi Gaynor, Rossano Brazzi, John Kerr, Juanita Hall (20th Cent. 1958, Joshua Logan dir.).

"**Speak Low.**" Music by Kurt Weill; lyric by Ogden Nash. Love duet in *One Touch of Venus* (NY 1943), sung by Mary Martin and Kenny Baker. Nash based his theme on the line "Speak low, if you speak love," in Shakespeare's *Much Ado About Nothing*.

Spewack, Bella and Sam, librettists. Bella: b. Bucharest, Rumania, March 25, 1899. Sam: b. Bachmut, Russia, Sept. 16, 1899; d. New York, Oct. 14, 1971. Plays included *Clear All Wires* (which became the Bway musical *Leave It to Me!*) and *Boy Meets Girl*. Their bigger musical-comedy hit was *Kiss Me, Kate*.

   1938 Leave It to Me! (Sam also dir.)
   1948 Kiss Me, Kate

"**Spread a Little Happiness.**" Music by Vivian Ellis; lyric by Clifford Grey. Chins-up piece ("Maybe Monday or next Tuesday—Your golden-shoes day") which Binnie Hale turned into the hit song of *Mr. Cinders* (L 1929).

"**Spring Is Here.**" Music by Richard Rodgers; lyric by Lorenz Hart. Song of indifference to the usually welcomed season sung by the romantically disillusioned Dennis King and Vivienne Segal in *I Married an Angel* (NY 1938). Rodgers and Hart had previously written a different song with the same title for a 1929 Bway musical, also called *Spring Is Here*.

"**Springtime Cometh, The.**" Music by Sammy Fain; lyric by E. Y. Harburg. After having the leprechaun in *Finian's Rainbow* express himself with "ish" rhymes in "Something Sort of Grandish," lyricist Harburg had the genie (Irwin Corey) in *Flahooley* (NY 1951) express himself with "eth" rhymes as he trippingly welcomed the arrival of spring. The number was danced by Elizabeth Logue as the Flahooley doll.

"**Standing on the Corner.**" Music & lyric by Frank Loesser. Girl-watchers' anthem harmonized in *The Most Happy Fella* (NY 1956) by Shorty Long, Alan Gilbert, John Henson, and Roy Lazarus. In London production (1960), by Jack De Lon, John Lloyd Parry, Peter Rhodes, and Alan Thomas.

Stange, Stanislaus, librettist, lyricist; b. Liverpool, Eng.; d. Jan. 2, 1917. Stange settled in US in 1881 and began career as an actor. His biggest Bway hit was *The Chocolate Soldier* ("My Hero"), music by Oscar Straus. He wrote 10 scores with composer Julian Edwards, others with Ludwig Englander, Gustave Kerker, Reginald De Koven, Jean Gilbert.

1893	Friend Fritz (Edwards)
1895	Madeleine (Edwards)
1896	The Goddess of Truth (Edwards)
	Brian Boru (Edwards)
1897	The Wedding Day (Edwards)
1898	The Jolly Musketeer (Edwards)
1899	The Singing Girl (lib. only)
1902	Dolly Varden (Edwards)
	When Johnny Comes Marching Home (Edwards)
1904	Piff! Paff!! Pouf!!! (lib. only)
	Love's Lottery (Edwards)
1905	The Two Roses (Englander, Kerker)
1906	The Student King (DeKoven)
1907	The Belle of London (Edwards)
	The Girls of Holland (De Koven).
1909	The Chocolate Soldier (Straus) (also dir.)
1910	The Girl in the Taxi (Gilbert)

"Stately Homes of England, The." Music & lyric by Noël Coward. Show-stopping tour of Britain's haunted historical mansions conducted in *Operette* (L 1938) by Lord Elderley (Hugh French), Lord Borrowmere (Ross Landon), Lord Sickert (John Gatrell), and Lord Camp (Kenneth Carten). In Bway revue *Set to Music* (1939), the cicerones were French, Angus Menzies, Antony Pelissier, and Carten.

"Steam Heat." Music & lyric by Richard Adler & Jerry Ross. Song-and-dance number performed at a party in *The Pajama Game* (NY 1954) by Carol Haney, Buzz Miller, and Peter Gennaro, wearing matching black suits, bow ties, and derbies. In London company (1955), it was performed by Elizabeth Seal, Franklyn Fox, and Ivor Meggido. The song had been intended for *John Murray Anderson's Almanac* (1953) but was rejected.

Steel, John, singer; b. 1900; d. New York, June 25, 1971. Bway tenor who introduced following songs by Irving Berlin: "A Pretty Girl Is Like a Melody," "Tell Me Little Gypsy," "Lady of the Evening," "What'll I Do?"

1918	The Maid of the Mountains (*Lt. Rugini*)
1919	Ziegfeld Follies
1920	Ziegfeld Follies
1921	Ziegfeld Follies (repl.)
1922	Music Box Revue
1923	Music Box Revue
1927	Castles in the Air (L)

Steele, Tommy (né Thomas Hicks), actor, singer; b. London, Dec. 17, 1936. Toothy, ebullient Tommy Steele was a pop singing star before scoring success in his first role on the London stage (in which he introduced "Half a Sixpence" and "If the Rain's Got to Fall"). He also appeared in films.

1963	Half a Sixpence (*Arthur Kipps*)
1965	Half a Sixpence (NY) (*Arthur Kipps*)
1974	Hans Andersen (*Hans Andersen*)

Stein, Joseph, librettist; b. New York, May 30, 1912. Stein, whose biggest Bway hit was *Fiddler on the Roof,* was also the author of the nonmusical play *Enter Laughing.* His first three musicals were written in collaboration with Will Glickman.

1955	Plain and Fancy
1956	Mr. Wonderful
1958	The Body Beautiful
1959	Juno
	Take Me Along
1964	Fiddler on the Roof
1968	Zorbá
1973	Irene (r)

"Step to the Rear." Music by Elmer Bernstein; lyric by Carolyn Leigh. In

How Now, Dow Jones (NY 1968), the members of a widows' investment club are charmed by their boyish, insecure stock broker and convince him he's a winner. Principals in this triumphal march were Charlotte Jones, Francesca Smith, Sally De May, Lucie Lancaster, and Anthony Roberts (as the broker).

Stewart, Michael (né Michael Stewart Rubin), librettist; b. New York, Aug. 1, 1929. Stewart's first four Bway musicals had runs of over 400 performances, with *Hello, Dolly!* the second longest-running musical of all time. The writer began his career contributing sketches for revues.

1951 Razzle Dazzle (also lyr.) (misc. comps.)
1960 Bye Bye Birdie
1961 Carnival
1964 Hello, Dolly!
1968 George M!
1974 Mack & Mabel
1977 I Love My Wife (Coleman)
1979 The Grand Tour

Stone, (Val) Fred, actor, dancer; b. Valmont, Col., Aug. 19, 1873; d. Hollywood, Cal., March 6, 1959. An acrobatic comic and dancer, Stone, with his partner David Montgomery, scored great successes on Bway in *The Wizard of Oz* and *The Red Mill* (in which the team introduced "The Streets of New York"). Following Montgomery's death in 1917, Stone continued alone as a top stage attraction during the 20s. He also appeared in nonmusical plays (incl. *Lightnin'*) and films. He was the husband of actress Allene Crater and the father of actresses Paula Stone and Dorothy Stone. Bib: *Rolling Stone* by Stone (Whittlesey, NY 1945).

Asterisk indicates appearance with Mr. Montgomery:

1901 The Girl from Up There * (*Christopher Grunt*)
The Girl from Up There * (L) (*Christopher Grunt*)
1903 The Wizard of Oz * (*Scarecrow*)
1906 The Red Mill * (*Con Kidder*)
1910 The Old Town * (*Henry Clay Baxter*)
1912 The Lady of the Slipper * (*Spooks*)
1914 Chin-Chin * (*Chin Hop Hi*)
1917 Jack o' Lantern (*Jack o' Lantern*)
1920 Tip Top
1923 Stepping Stones (*Peter Plug*)
1926 Criss-Cross (*Christopher Cross*)
1930 Ripples (*Rip*)
1932 Smiling Faces (*Monument Spleen*)

Stone, Peter (Hess), librettist; b. Los Angeles, Cal., Feb. 27, 1930. Stone, whose biggest Bway musical hit was *1776*, has also written plays and screenplays.

1961 Kean
1965 Skyscraper
1969 1776
1970 Two by Two
1972 Sugar

Stop the World—I Want to Get Off (1961). Music, lyrics, & book by Leslie Bricusse & Anthony Newley.

SONGS: "I Want to Be Rich," "Typically English," "Lumbered," "Gonna Build a Mountain," "Once in a Lifetime," "Mumbo Jumbo," "Someone Nice Like You," "What Kind of Fool Am I?"

LONDON: July 20, 1961
QUEEN'S THEATRE; 485 p.

Presented by Bernard Delfont, with H. M. Tennent Ltd. & Marigold Music Ltd.; directed by Anthony Newley; choreographed by John Broome; settings & lighting, Sean Kenny; costumes, Kiki Byrne; music director, Ian Fraser; orchestrations, Fraser.

CAST: Anthony Newley (*Littlechap*), Anna Quayle (*Evie Littlechap*), Jennifer Baker (*Jane Littlechap*), Susan Baker (*Susan Littlechap*).

NEW YORK: Oct. 3, 1962
SHUBERT THEATRE; 555 p.

Presented by David Merrick, with Bernard Delfont; directed by Anthony Newley; choreography reproduced by Virginia Mason; settings & lighting, Sean Kenny; costumes, Kiki Byrne; music director, Milton Rosenstock; orchestrations, Ian Fraser.

CAST: Anthony Newley (*Littlechap*), Anna Quayle (*Evie Littlechap*), Jennifer Baker (*Jane Littlechap*), Susan Baker (*Susan Littlechap*).

An allegorical musical staged in a circus-tent setting, with Anthony Newley as a clownlike Everyman—named Littlechap—who marries the boss's daughter (Anna Quayle), rises in business and politics, does a bit of cheating with girls of other nationalities (all played by Miss Quayle), and ends his life reflecting on the shallowness of his ambitions. At first Newley conceived of the show to be played on a bare stage inside a huge gossamer egg with a sack for a costume. Designer Kenny, however, proposed the circus-tent setting, which led to the white-face clown concept and the use of pantomime. The show also used a seven-member all-girl Greek chorus to comment on and take part in the action. When Newley took the musical to Bway, he was succeeded in London by Tony Tanner. A US touring company, headed by Joel Grey (followed by Kenneth Nelson) and Julie Newmar (followed by Joan Eastman), opened in March 1963. It played eight months. Grey succeeded Newley on Bway in Nov. 1963.

A previous musical that also dealt with a man's rise and disillustionment (and which also had a Greek chorus) was Rodgers and Hammerstein's *Allegro* (NY 1947).

FILM VERSION: Tony Tanner and Millicent Martin (Warner 1966, Philip Saville dir.).

Stothart, Herbert, composer; b. Milwaukee, Wis., Sept. 11, 1885; d. Los Angeles, Cal., Feb. 1, 1949. Stothart, who was also a music director, teamed with co-lyricists Otto Harbach and Oscar Hammerstein II to write the scores for six Bway musicals, incl. *Wildflower* (Vincent Youmans was co-composer) and *Rose-Marie* ("The Mounties" and "Totem Tom-Tom," both with co-composer Rudolf Friml). He also wrote "I Wanna Be Loved by You" with Bert Kalmar and Harry Ruby. In the 30s Stothart became a composer, music director and arranger at MGM. Other collaborators: lyricists William Cary Duncan and Clifford Grey, composers George Gershwin and Emmerich Kalman.

One asterisk indicates lyrics by Mr. Hammerstein; two asterisks indicate lyrics by Harbach and Hammerstein:

1920	Always You *
	Tickle Me **
	Jimmie **
1922	Daffy Dill *
1923	Wildflower **
	Mary Jane McKane * (Duncan)
1924	Vogues of 1924 (Grey)
	Marjorie (Grey)
	Rose-Marie **
1925	Song of the Flame ** (Gershwin)
1927	Golden Dawn ** (Kalman)
1928	Good Boy (Kalmar, Ruby)

"Stouthearted Men." Music by Sigmund Romberg; lyric by Oscar Hammerstein II. Recruiting song for idealistic revolutionaries first performed by Robert Halliday and a chorus of male bondservants in *The New Moon* (NY 1928). In London production (1929), Howett Worster led the men.

"Strange Music." Music & lyric by Robert Wright & George Forrest, adapted from Grieg's "Nocturne" and "Wedding Day in Troldhaugen." The main romantic duet in *Song of Nor-*

way, sung in NY (1944) by Lawrence Brooks and Helena Bliss, in London (1946) by John Hargreaves and Janet Hamilton-Smith.

"Strangely Attractive." Music by Ron Grainer; lyric by Ronald Millar. Strangely haunting piece in which Angela Richards and Gary Bond revealed their sudden mutual love in *On the Level* (L 1966).

"Stranger in Paradise." Music & lyric by Robert Wright & George Forrest, adapted from Borodin's "Polovtsian Dances" in the opera *Prince Igor*. Love-at-first-sight duet for Doretta Morrow and Richard Kiley in *Kismet* (NY 1953). In London version (1955), it was sung by Miss Morrow and Peter Grant.

"Streets of New York, The." Music by Victor Herbert; lyric by Henry Blossom. Also known as "In Old New York," this waltzing tribute to the metropolis was sung in *The Red Mill* (NY 1906) by Dave Montgomery and Fred Stone.

Streisand, Barbra, actress, singer; b. Bklyn, NY, April 24, 1942. After her comic number "Miss Marmelstein" in *I Can Get It for You Wholesale*, Miss Streisand triumphed playing Fanny Brice in *Funny Girl* ("People," "Don't Rain on My Parade"). She has been a leading recording artist and has made many films (incl. *Funny Girl*). Miss Streisand was once married to actor Elliott Gould.

1961 Another Evening with Harry Stoones
1962 I Can Get It for You Wholesale (*Miss Marmelstein*)
1964 Funny Girl (*Fanny Brice*)
1966 Funny Girl (L) (*Fanny Brice*)

Strike Up the Band (1930). Music by George Gershwin; lyrics by Ira Gershwin; book by Morrie Ryskind, based on book by George S. Kaufman.

SONGS: "I Mean to Say," "A Typical Self-Made American," "If I Became the President," "Soon," "Hangin' Around with You," "Strike Up the Band!," "Mademoiselle in New Rochelle," "I've Got a Crush on You."

NEW YORK: Jan. 14, 1930
TIMES SQUARE THEATRE; 191 p.

Presented by Edgar Selwyn; directed by Alexander Leftwich; choreographed by George Hale; settings, Raymond Sovey; costumes, Charles Le Maire; music director, Hilding Anderson.

CAST: Bobby Clark (*Col. Holmes*), Paul McCullough (*Gideon*), Blanche Ring (*Grace Draper*), Jerry Goff (*Jim Townsend*), Doris Carson (*Anne Draper*), Dudley Clements (*Horace J. Fletcher*), Gordon Smith (*Timothy Harper*), Margaret Schilling (*Joan Fletcher*), Red Nichols Band (incl. Benny Goodman, Gene Krupa, Glenn Miller, Jimmy Dorsey, Jack Teagarden).

Strike Up the Band inaugurated the politically conscious satirical musicals of the 30s incl. *Of Thee I Sing, Face the Music, Let 'Em Eat Cake, I'd Rather Be Right, Leave It to Me!* Set mostly in a dream, it dealt with a war between the US and Switzerland over the issue of tariffs on imported chocolate. It also spoofed President Wilson's adviser, Col. House, in the character of Col. Holmes, played by Bobby Clark. The musical was to have been seen in NY in 1927 but its libretto by George S. Kaufman was deemed too acerbic (there was no dream and at the end the US was preparing for war with the USSR) and it closed on the road. The cast then included Lew Hearn, Jimmy Savo,

Edna May Oliver, Roger Pryor, and Morton Downey.

"Strike Up the Band!" Music by George Gershwin; lyric by Ira Gershwin. Satirical, militaristic first-act finale. of *Strike Up the Band* (NY 1930), sung by Jerry Goff and company, backed by Red Nichols' Band with Benny Goodman, Gene Krupa, Glenn Miller, Jimmy Dorsey, and Jack Teagarden. The song had first been written for the original 1927 version of the musical, which never reached NY.

Stritch, Elaine, actress, singer; b. Detroit, Mich., Feb. 2, 1925. Gritty-voiced blonde actress who usually plays cynical dames. She introduced "Civilization" (*Angel in the Wings*), "Why Do the Wrong People Travel?" (*Sail Away*), "The Ladies Who Lunch" (*Company*).

1947　Angel in the Wings
1952　Pal Joey (r) (*Melba*)
　　　Call Me Madam (US tour) (*Sally Adams*)
1954　On Your Toes (r) (*Peggy Porterfield*)
1958　Goldilocks (*Maggie Harris*)
1961　Sail Away (*Mimi Paragon*)
1962　Sail Away (L) (*Mimi Paragon*)
1969　Mame (US tour) (*Vera Charles*)
1970　Company (*Joanne*)
1972　Company (L) (*Joanne*)

Strouse, Charles, composer; b. New York, June 7, 1928. With lyricist Lee Adams, Strouse has written scores for Bway successes *Bye Bye Birdie* ("A Lot of Livin' to Do," "One Boy," "Put on a Happy Face"), *Golden Boy* ("I Want to Be with You"), *Applause* ("Applause"). The team's "Once Upon a Time" was sung in *All American*.

Unless otherwise noted, the following were written with Mr. Adams:

1960　Bye Bye Birdie
1962　All American
1964　Golden Boy
1966　It's a Bird　It's a Plane　It's Superman
1970　Applause
1971　Six (also lyr., lib.)
1972　I and Albert (L)
1977　Annie (Charnin)
1978　A Broadway Musical

Stuart, Leslie (né Thomas Augustine Barrett), composer, lyricist; b. Southport, Eng., March 15, 1864; d. Richmond, Eng., March 27, 1928. Stuart is best remembered as the composer of the London hit *Florodora*, lyrics by Ernest Boyd-Jones, Paul Rubens, and himself ("Tell Me, Pretty Maiden"). He also wrote songs not associated with the theatre and appeared on the variety stage in both England and the US. Other lyric-writing collaborators: W. H. Risque, Charles Taylor, Cosmo Hamilton, Adrian Ross, Henry Blossom, C. H. Bovill.

1899　Florodora (Boyd-Jones, Rubens, Stuart)
1901　The Silver Slipper (Risque)
1903　The School Girl (Taylor)
1906　The Belle of Mayfair (Hamilton)
1908　Havana (Ross)
1910　Captain Kidd (Ross)
1911　The Slim Princess (NY) (Blossom)
　　　Peggy (Bovill)

Student Prince in Heidelberg, The (1924). Music by Sigmund Romberg; lyrics & book by Dorothy Donnelly, based on play *Old Heidelberg,* by Rudolf Bleichman, adapted from German play *Alt Heidelberg,* which Wilhelm Meyer-Forster founded on his own story "Karl Heinrich."

SONGS: "Golden Days," "To the Inn We're Marching," "Come, Boys, Let's All Be Gay, Boys," "Drinking Song," "Deep in My Heart, Dear," "Serenade," "Just We Two," "Gaudeamus Igitur" (traditional).

NEW YORK: Dec. 2, 1924
AL JOLSON THEATRE; 608 p.
Presented by Messrs. Shubert; directed by J. C. Huffman; choreographed by Max Scheck; settings, Watson Barratt; costumes, Waldy, Vanity Fair, Erté; music director, Oscar Bradley.
CAST: Howard Marsh (*Karl Franz*), Ilse Marvenga (*Kathie*), Greek Evans (*Dr. Engel*), George Hassell (*Lutz*), Roberta Beatty (*Princess Margaret*), John Coast (*Capt. Tarnitz*), Raymond Marlowe (*Detlef*).

LONDON: Feb. 3, 1926
HIS MAJESTY'S THEATRE; 96 p.
Presented by Messrs. Shubert; directed by J. C. Huffman; choreographed by Edward Scanlan; settings, Watson Barratt; costumes, Waldy, Vanity Fair, Erté; music director, Oscar Bradley.
CAST: Allan Prior (*Karl Franz*), Ilse Marvenga (*Kathie*), Herbert Waterous (*Dr. Engel*), Oscar Figman (*Lutz*), Lucyenne Herval (*Princess Margaret*), John Coast (*Capt. Tarnitz*), Raymond Marlowe (*Detlef*).
Augmented by traditional student songs, the play *Old Heidelberg* had been a successful Richard Mansfield vehicle produced by the brothers Shubert at the turn of the century. Milan had even seen an opera version—*Eidelberga mia!*—in 1908, before the Shuberts decided to team Sigmund Romberg and Dorothy Donnelly to create the operetta. Originally called *In Heidelberg* (the location was retained as part of the title throughout the original Bway run), the musical had the longest run of any Romberg operetta and was also the longest-running musical of the 20s. Its sentimental tale, set in 1860, concerns Student Prince Karl Franz's fleeting romance with waitress Kathie, who works at the Inn of the Three Golden

Apples, in Heidelberg. Though Karl Franz must leave romantic and cultural pursuits to become king, he returns two years later to the inn—only to find that youth cannot be recaptured.

During Bway run, George Hassell was succeeded by Sydney Greenstreet (8-25), Howard Marsh by Roy Cropper (5-26), Ilse Marvenga by Helen Nord (5-26). Touring companies throughout the US appeared in the operetta between 1925 and 1933. The relatively brief London run was attributed to the lack of English actors in the leading roles, and also to the fact that London audiences were not yet ready to accept this *Kinder-Kirche-Küche* view of German life so soon after the war. An all-English touring company, however, with Harry Welchman and Rose Hignall, was well received. In 1968 *The Student Prince* was revived in London with John Hanson and Barbara Strathdee.

FILM VERSIONS: Ramon Novarro and Norma Shearer (MGM 1927, Ernst Lubitsch dir.); Edmund Purdom (Mario Lanza's singing voice) and Ann Blyth (MGM 1954, Richard Thorpe dir.).

Styne, Jule (né Julius Kerwin Stein), composer, producer; b. London, Dec. 31, 1905. Styne, who came to the US when he was eight, abandoned a career as a concert pianist to become a bandleader, then Hollywood vocal coach and composer. On Bway he has shown marked affinity for the flair and flavor of show business, best exemplified by the scores for his two major works: *Gypsy* ("Let Me Entertain You," "Some People," "Small World," "Everything's Coming Up Roses") and *Funny Girl* ("People," "Don't Rain on My Parade"). Other long-running musicals—all over 400 performances—were *High Button Shoes* ("Papa, Won't You Dance with Me?," "I Still Get Jealous"), *Gentlemen Prefer Blondes* ("A Little Girl from Little Rock," "Diamonds Are a Girl's Best Friend"), *Bells Are Ringing* ("Just in Time," "The Party's Over"), *Do Re Mi* ("Make Someone Happy"), *Sugar* ("Sugar"). Among performers who have introduced Styne songs: Phil Silvers, Nanette Fabray, Carol Channing, Dolores Gray, Mary Martin, Cyril Ritchard, Judy Holliday, Ethel Merman, Barbra Streisand, Robert Morse. Styne has collaborated with co-lyricists Betty Comden and Adolph Green on eight scores plus added songs for *Lorelei* (1974), and he has also worked with Sammy Cahn, Leo Robin, Bob Hilliard ("How Do You Speak to an Angel?"), Stephen Sondheim, Bob Merrill, E. Y. Harburg.

1947	High Button Shoes (Cahn)
1949	Gentlemen Prefer Blondes (Robin)
1951	Make a Wish (co-prod. only)
	Two on the Aisle (Comden, Green)
1952	Pal Joey (r) (co-prod. only)
1953	Hazel Flagg (Hilliard)
1954	Peter Pan (Comden, Green)
1956	Mr. Wonderful (co-prod. only)
	Bells Are Ringing (Comden, Green)
1958	Say, Darling (Comden, Green)
1959	First Impressions (co-prod. only)
	Gypsy (Sondheim)
1960	Do Re Mi (Comden, Green)
1961	Subways Are for Sleeping (Comden, Green)
1964	Funny Girl (Merrill)
	Fade Out—Fade In (Comden, Green)
	Something More! (dir. only)
1967	Hallelujah, Baby! (Comden, Green)
1968	Darling of the Day (Harburg)
1970	Look to the Lilies (Cahn)
1972	Sugar (Merrill)
1978	Bar Mitzvah Boy (L) (Blacl)

"Sue Me." Music & lyric by Frank Loesser. Vivian Blaine, unhappily unmarried, hurls her frustrations at the stone wall of Sam Levene's unnerving acquiescence in *Guys and Dolls* (NY 1950, L 1953).

"Summertime." Music by George Gershwin; lyric by DuBose Heyward. Mood-setting lullaby sung by Abbie Mitchell early in *Porgy and Bess* (NY 1935). Helen Colbert sang it in London in 1952 production.

"Summertime Love." Music & lyric by Frank Loesser. Romantic fidelity, despite seasonal changes, pledged by Anthony Perkins in *Greenwillow* (NY 1960).

"Sunday in Cicero Falls." Music by Harold Arlen; lyric by E. Y. Harburg. Stately, satirical ballet in *Bloomer Girl* (NY 1944) depicting the citizens of a small NY state community in 1861 on a day—as Celeste Holm observed—when "even the rabbits inhibit their habits."

"Sunday in the Park." Music & lyric by Harold Rome. Song in praise of Central Park, NY, as the workingman's retreat, sung by the company as the first-act finale of *Pins and Needles* (NY 1937). The revue was sponsored by the International Ladies Garment Workers Union. In London revue *Happy Returns* (1938), the number was sung by Patricia Burke and company (including Beatrice Lillie and Flanagan and Allen).

Sunny (1925). Music by Jerome Kern; lyrics & book by Otto Harbach & Oscar Hammerstein II.
SONGS: "Sunny," "Who?," "D'Ye Love Me?," "Two Little Bluebirds," "Let's Say Goodnight Till It's Morning," "I Might Grow Fond of You."

NEW YORK: Sept. 22, 1925
NEW AMSTERDAM THEATRE; 517 p.
Presented by Charles B. Dillingham; directed by Hassard Short; choreographed by Julian Mitchell, David Bennett, Alexis Kosloff, John Tiller, Fred Astaire; settings & costumes, James Reynolds; music director, Gus Salzer; orchestrations, Robert Russell Bennett.
CAST: Marilyn Miller (*Sunny Peters*), Jack Donahue (*Jim Deming*), Clifton Webb (*Harold Harcourt Wendell-Wendell*), Mary Hay (*Weenie Winters*), Joseph Cawthorn (*Siegfried Peters*), Paul Frawley (*Tom Warren*), Cliff Edwards (*Sam*), Pert Kelton (*Magnolia*), Esther Howard (*Sue Warren*), Marjorie Moss & Georges Fontana (dancers), George Olsen Orch.

LONDON: Oct. 7, 1926
HIPPODROME; 363 p.
Presented by Moss's Empires Ltd., with Lee Ephraim & Jack Buchanan; directed by Charles Mast; choreographed by Buchanan; settings, Joseph & Phil Harker; costumes, Idare; music director, Philip Braham.
CAST: Binnie Hale (*Sunny Peters*), Jack Buchanan (*Jim Deming*), Claude Hulbert (*Harold Harcourt Wendell-Wendell*), Elsie Randolph (*Weenie Winters*), Nicholas Adams (*Siegfried Peters*), Jack Hobbs (*Tom Warren*), Sam Macrae (*Sam*), Maidie Hope (*Sue Warren*), Ula Sharon (dancer), Alfred & Prince's Band.
Sunny, the first Kern-Hammerstein collaboration, was the apparent successor to *Sally*, Kern's previous musical for Marilyn Miller. It told another rags-to-riches variation in its story about the spirited circus bareback rider in England who, to avoid marrying circus owner Harold, stows aboard a ship sailing for NY. In order to be allowed to land, Sunny marries rich Jim, though her heart belongs to Tom.

After getting a divorce, Sunny realizes it's Jim she loves and they plan to remarry. During Bway run, Borrah Minevitch replaced Cliff Edwards for nine months.
FILM VERSIONS: Marilyn Miller, Joe Donahue, Lawrence Gray (Warner, 1939, William A. Seiter dir.); Anna Neagle, Ray Bolger, John Carroll (RKO 1941, Herbert Wilcox dir.)

"Sunny." Music by Jerome Kern; lyric by Otto Harbach & Oscar Hammerstein II. Title song, sung by Paul Frawley, describing the irresistibly hoydenish heroine of the 1925 Bway musical. In London version (1926), it was sung by Jack Hobbs.

"Sunny Disposish." Music by Phil Charig; lyric by Ira Gershwin. Spirited advice that "life can be delish with a sunny disposish." Arline and Edgar Gardiner introduced it in *Americana* (NY 1926).

"Sunrise, Sunset." Music by Jerry Bock; lyric by Sheldon Harnick. Zero Mostel ruminated on the swiftness of time in *Fiddler on the Roof* (NY 1964). In London version (1967), it was sung by Topol.

"Superstar." Music by Andrew Lloyd Webber; lyric by Tim Rice. Originally a best-selling song, this rocking ode to Jesus was the inspiration for the musical *Jesus Christ Superstar*. It was sung by Ben Vereen and company in NY (1971), and by Stephen Tate and company in London (1972).

"Supper Time." Music & lyric by Irving Berlin. Preceded by headline "Unknown Negro Lynched by Frenzied Mob," this threnody was sung by Ethel Waters in the "newspaper" revue, *As Thousands Cheer* (NY

1933). Miss Waters once wrote, "If one song could tell the whole tragic story of my people, that was the song." Because of the serious nature of the piece, Berlin was urged to cut the number from the show, but, as he put it, "I was convinced that a musical dealing with headline news needed at least one serious piece, and I knew that Ethel Waters had the quality to sing something really dramatic."

"Surrey with the Fringe on Top, The." Music by Richard Rodgers; lyric by Oscar Hammerstein II. Imaginary vehicle described by Alfred Drake to Joan Roberts in *Oklahoma!* (NY 1943), and by Harold (Howard) Keel to Betty Jane Watson in London production (1947). Rodgers purposely used repeated notes in the refrain to indicate a ride on a long, flat road.

Sweet and Low (1943). Music by Geoffrey Wright, Leslie Julian Jones, Robert Gordon, Marc Anthony, Jack Strachey, George Posford, etc.; lyrics by Nicholas Phipps, Alan Melville, John Jowett, Nina Warner Hooke, Harold Purcell, etc.; sketches by Leslie Julian Jones, Hermione Gingold, etc.

SONGS: "The Borgias Are Having an Orgy" (Gordon-Jowett), "Boy and Girl Number" (Anthony-Melville), "Miss Gingold's Friend" (Wright-Melville), "Valhalla" (Strachey-Hooke), "Biking in Bloomers" (Posford-Purcell).

LONDON: June 10, 1943
AMBASSADORS THEATRE; 264 p.
Presented by J. W. Pemberton & A. A. Dubens; directed by Charles Hickman; choreographed by Andrée Howard; settings & costumes, Berkeley Sutcliffe; pianos, Clarry Ashton & Pearl Caro.
CAST: Hermione Gingold, Walter Crisham, Bonar Colleano, Ilena Sylva,

Edna Wood, Brenda Bruce, Graham Penley, Yvonne Jacques.

London's most popular wartime revue series were intimate, satirical shows aiming darts primarily at the world of British show business. In the first edition Hermione Gingold won acclaim for such numbers as "Miss Gingold's Friend" ("I do miss Hermione badly"), "The Borgias Are Having an Orgy," and "Valhalla" (wearing a helmet and carrying a spear), and also her takeoffs on Carmen Miranda and Lillian Braithwaite.

A second edition, *Sweeter and Lower*, opened Feb. 17, 1944, and ran 870 performances. Henry Kendall replaced Walter Crisham, with Ilena Sylva, Bonar Colleano, Edna Wood, and Yvonne Jacques retained from the first show. Though some items remained, there were such new pieces as "Thanks Yanks" (Wright-Melville), Charles Gaynor's "Mabel" ("The horse with the hansom behind") and Miss Gingold's spoof of Robert Helpmann as Hamlet. On May 9, 1946, a third edition, *Sweetest and Lowest*, again starred Miss Gingold and Kendall. Gretchen Franklin, Richard Curnock, and George Carden, who had been in *Sweeter and Lower*, were also in the new revue. The show played 791 performances, with most of the material written by Alan Melville and composer Charles Zwar.

"Sweet and Low-Down." Music by George Gershwin; lyric by Ira Gershwin. A Palm Beach party in *Tip-Toes* (NY 1925) was the setting for this energetic salute to a jazz cabaret. Accompanied by kazoos and trombones, it was introduced by Andrew Tombes, Lovey Lee, Gertrude McDonald, and Amy Revere; in London version (1926) it was a duet for Laddie Cliff and Roberta Beatty.

Sweet Charity (1966). Music by Cy Coleman; lyrics by Dorothy Fields; book by Neil Simon, based on film *Nights of Cabiria*, by Federico Fellini, Tullio Pinelli, Ennio Flaiano.

SONGS: "You Should See Yourself," "Big Spender," "If My Friends Could See Me Now," "Too Many Tomorrows," "There's Gotta Be Something Better than This," "I'm the Bravest Individual," "Baby, Dream Your Dreams," "Rhythm of Life," "Sweet Charity," "Where Am I Going?," "I'm a Brass Band."

NEW YORK: Jan. 29, 1966
PALACE THEATRE; 608 p.
Presented by Robert Fryer, Lawrence Carr, Sylvia & Joseph Harris; directed & choreographed by Bob Fosse; settings & lighting, Robert Randolph; costumes, Irene Sharaff; music director, Fred Werner; orchestrations, Ralph Burns.
CAST: Gwen Verdon (*Charity Hope Valentine*), John McMartin (*Oscar Lindquist*), Helen Gallagher (*Nickie*), Thelma Oliver (*Helene*), James Luisi (*Vittorio Vidal*), Arnold Soboloff (*Johann Sebastian Brubeck*), Ruth Buzzi (*Good Fairy*), Barbara Sharma (*Rosie*).

LONDON: Oct. 11, 1967
PRINCE OF WALES THEATRE; 476 p.
Presented by Bernard Delfont & Harold Fielding; restaged by Lawrence Carr; dances reproduced by Robert Linden; settings & lighting, Robert Randolph; costumes, Irene Sharaff; music director, Alyn Ainsworth; orchestrations, Ralph Burns.
CAST: Juliet Prowse (*Charity Hope Valentine*), Rod McLennan (*Oscar Lindquist*), Josephine Blake (*Nickie*), Paula Kelly (*Helene*), John Keston (*Vittorio Vidal*), Fred Evans (*Johann Sebastian Brubeck*), Joyanne Delancey (*Good Fairy*).
The initial concept of the musical was as a one-act play with the second half of the evening devoted to a new work by Elaine May. Eventually director Bob Fosse abandoned the second one-act musical in favor of expanding the first one into a two-act production. Initially Fosse himself did the adaptation of the Fellini film, then Neil Simon was called in. The musical version changed the Roman prostitute to a NY dime-a-dance hostess at the Fan-Dango Ballroom. Charity's romantic, trusting nature gets her involved with an Italian screen star and a square named Oscar whom she meets in a stuck elevator at the 92nd St. "Y." Later they also get stuck on a Coney Island ferris wheel. Though Oscar promises to marry Charity, he backs down and our heroine must return to living "hopefully ever after." In 1973, Coleman and Fields also wrote the score for *Seesaw*, which offered another mismatched romance in NY between a too-trusting kook and her too-conventional beau.

During the Bway run of *Sweet Charity*, Gwen Verdon—who was acclaimed in the title role—was succeeded by Helen Gallagher (6-67). The US touring company set out in Sept. 1967, with Chita Rivera (*Charity*), Helen Gallagher (*Nickie*), Lee Goodman (*Oscar*), Thelma Oliver (*Helene*), Ben Vereen (*Brubeck*). It continued for four months. In London, Juliet Prowse was succeeded after seven months by Gretchen Wyler.
FILM VERSION: Shirley MacLaine, John McMartin, Ricardo Montalban, Chita Rivera, Sammy Davis Jr. (Univ. 1969; Bob Fosse dir.).

"Sweet Lady." Music by David Zoob & Frank Crumit; lyric by Howard Johnson. Love duet from *Tangerine* (NY 1921) sung by Julia Sanderson and Frank Crumit.

"Sweet So-and-So." Music by Joseph Meyer & Philip Charig; lyric by Ira Gershwin & Douglas Furber. Strutting compilation of pet names introduced by Jack Buchanan in *That's a Good Girl* (L 1928), and sung by Hannah Williams and Jerry Norris in *Sweet and Low* (NY 1930).

"Sweetest Sounds, The." Music & lyric by Richard Rodgers. The theme of *No Strings* (NY 1962), sung as a prologue first by Diahann Carroll, then by Richard Kiley, then together—though neither is aware of the other. In London version (1963), it was sung by Beverley Todd and Art Lund. The lyric owes something to Keats' "Ode on a Grecian Urn" ("Heard melodies are sweet, but those unheard/ Are sweeter").

Sweethearts (1913). Music by Victor Herbert; lyrics by Robert B. Smith; book by Harry B. Smith & Fred De Gressac.

SONGS: "Sweethearts," "Angelus," "Every Lover Must Meet His Fate," "Pretty as a Picture," "Jeannette and Her Little Wooden Shoes," "The Cricket on the Hearth."

NEW YORK: Sept. 8, 1913
NEW AMSTERDAM THEATRE; 136 p.

Presented by Louis Werba & Mark Luescher; directed by Fred Latham; choreographed by Charles Morgan Jr.; settings, Dodge & Castle; costumes, William Adler, Max & Mahieu; music director, John McGhie; orchestrations, Victor Herbert.

CAST: Christie MacDonald (*Princess Sylvia*), Thomas Conkey (*Prince Franz*), Edwin Wilson (*Lt. Karl*), Frank Belcher (*Petrus Von Trump*), Tom McNaughton (*Mikel Mikeloviz*), Ethel Du Fre Houston (*Dame Paula*), Hazel Kirke (*Liane*).

NEW YORK: Jan. 21, 1947
SHUBERT THEATRE; 288 p.

Presented by Paula Stone & Michael Sloane; directed by John Kennedy; choreographed by Catherine Littlefield, Theodore Adolphus; settings, Peter Wolf; costumes, Michael Lucyck; music director, Edwin McArthur; orchestrations, Robert Russell Bennett; book revised by John Cecil Holm.

CAST: Bobby Clark (*Mikel Mikeloviz*), Marjorie Gateson (*Dame Lucy*), June Knight (*Liane*), Gloria Story (*Princess Sylvia*), Mark Dawson (*Prince Franz*), Robert Shackleton (*Lt. Karl*), Paul Best (*Petrus Von Trump*), Cornell MacNeil (*Footman*).

In 1910 the Smith brothers, Harry Bache and Robert Bache, wrote a musical success for Christie MacDonald called *The Spring Maid*. Three years later, producers Werba and Luescher followed up with more of the same with *Sweethearts*, another syrupy Smith brothers formula for Miss MacDonald. This time, however, they were joined by co-librettist Fred (née Frederique) De Gressac and composer Victor Herbert. Though the story was supposed to have been based on the true adventures of a 15th-century Neapolitan princess, it dealt with the traditional dream world of operetta. To protect her from harm during a war, the infant Princess Sylvia of Zilania is taken to Bruges, where she is brought up by Dame Paula, the owner of the Laundry of the Wild Geese, as her own daughter. Traveling incognito, Prince Franz meets Sylvia, they fall in love, and, once their identities are revealed, are crowned co-rulers of Zilania. The 1947 revival was rewritten to fit the comic talents of Bobby Clark.

FILM VERSION: Jeanette MacDonald and Nelson Eddy (new story) (MGM 1938, W. S. Van Dyke dir.).

"Sweethearts." Music by Victor Herbert; lyric by Robert B. Smith. The title waltz of the 1913 NY operetta sung by Christie MacDonald, not as a personal declaration, but as a description of a highly romanticized couple. The melody, first sketched by the composer seven years before the production, should not be confused with the Sigmund Romberg waltz "Will You Remember?," which begins, "Sweetheart, sweetheart, sweetheart."

Swenson, Inga, actress, singer; b. Omaha, Neb., Dec. 29, 1932. Stratuesque blonde leading lady who made notable Bway appearances in *110 in the Shade* (introducing "Simple Little Things") and *Baker Street* ("I'm in London Again," "Finding Words for Spring").
1956   New Faces of 1956

1963   110 in the Shade (*Lizzie*)
1965   Baker Street (*Irene Adler*)
1967   110 in the Shade (L) (*Lizzie*)

Swift, Kay, composer; b. New York, April 19, 1905. Miss Swift's score for *Fine and Dandy* (incl. "Fine and Dandy") was written with lyricist Paul James, pen name of James P. Warburg, her husband at the time. She also contributed to *The Little Show* ("Can't We Be Friends?") and other Bway revues, and wrote songs for Cornelia Otis Skinner's one-woman *Paris '90*.
1930   Fine and Dandy (James)

"Sympathy." Music by Rudolf Friml; lyric by Otto Hauerbach (Harbach). Romantic waltz of *The Firefly* (NY 1912), sung by Audrey Maple and Melville Stewart.

T

Tabbert, William (Henry), actor, singer; b. Chicago, Ill., Oct. 5, 1921; d. New York, Oct. 19, 1974. Strong-voiced juvenile who sang "Younger than Springtime" in *South Pacific* and "Fanny" in *Fanny*. Tabbert began career with Chicago Civic Light Opera Co.
1943   What's Up (*Sgt. Dick Benham*)
1944   Follow the Girls (*sailor*)
       Seven Lively Arts
1945   Billion Dollar Baby (*Rocky Barton*)
1947   Three to Make Ready (US tour)
1949   South Pacific (*Lt. Joe Cable*)
1954   Fanny (*Marius*)

"Take Back Your Mink." Music & lyric by Frank Loesser. Satirical number sung in mock innocence upon receiving an indecent proposal.

Squealed by Vivian Blaine and Hot Box Girls in *Guys and Dolls* (NY 1950, L 1953).

"Taking a Chance on Love." Music by Vernon Duke; lyric by John Latouche & Ted Fetter. The song was added to the score of *Cabin in the Sky* (NY 1940) three days before the Bway opening because it was felt that Ethel Waters, as a long-suffering wife, needed to express her conviction that her shiftless husband was about to mend his ways. The music and lyric are the same as that of a previous song Duke had written with lyricist Fetter, except that the title was then "Fooling Around with Love." Lyricist Latouche, who wrote the lyrics to all the other songs in *Cabin in the Sky*, changed this line to "Taking a chance on love," and contributed the words for the song's encores.

Talbot, Howard (né Howard Munkittrick), composer; b. New York, March 9, 1865; d. London, Sept. 12, 1928. Talbot was educated in London and remained there as composer and conductor. Three of his musicals—*A Chinese Honeymoon, The Arcadians, The Boy*—ran over 800 performances. Among his lyric-writing partners: Harry Greenbank, George Dance, W. H. Risque, Percy Greenbank, Arthur Anderson, Arthur Wimperis, Basil Hood, C. H. Bovill, Adrian Ross, Clifford Grey.

    1894 Wapping Old Stairs (Robertson)
    1896 Monte Carlo (H. Greenbank)
    1901 A Chinese Honeymoon (Dance)
    1905 Miss Wingrove (Risque)
          The White Chrysanthemum (Anderson)
    1906 The Girl Behind the Counter (Anderson)
    1907 Three Kisses (P. Greenbank)
    1908 The Belle of Brittany (P. Greenbank)
    1909 The Arcadians (Wimperis)
    1911 The Mousmé (Wimperis, P. Greenbank)
    1913 The Pearl Girl (Hood)
    1914 A Mixed Grill (Risque)
    1916 My Lady Frayle (Wimperis)
          Mr. Manhattan (Bovill)
          The Light Blues (Ross)
    1917 The Boy (Ross, P. Greenbank)
    1919 Who's Hooper? (Grey)
    1921 My Nieces (P. Greenbank)

Tamara (née Tamara Drasin), actress, singer; b. Poltava, Russia, Oct. 13, 1907; d. plane crash, Lisbon, Portugal, Feb. 22, 1943. Dark-haired, throaty contralto who introduced "Smoke Gets in Your Eyes" in *Roberta*. She also sang "The Touch of Your Hand" in the same show, "I'll Be Seeing You" and "I Can Dream, Can't I?" in *Right This Way*, "Get Out of Town"

and "From Now On" in *Leave It to Me!*

    1927 The New Yorkers
    1931 Crazy Quilt
          Free for All (*Marishka Tarasov*)
    1932 New Americana
    1933 Roberta (*Stephanie*)
    1938 Right This Way (*Mimi Chester*)
          Leave It to Me! (*Colette*)

Tamiris, Helen (née Helen Becker), choreographer; b. New York, April 24, 1905; d. New York, Aug. 4, 1966. Miss Tamiris began her career as ballet dancer with the Metropolitan Opera, NY, was co-founder of Dance Repertory Theatre, and was head of the School of American Dance for 12 years. His biggest Bway successes were *Show Boat, Annie Get Your Gun,* and *Fanny*.

    1945 Up in Central Park
    1946 Show Boat (r)
          Annie Get Your Gun
          Park Avenue
    1947 Annie Get Your Gun (L)
    1948 Inside USA
    1950 Great to Be Alive
          Bless You All
          Flahooley
    1953 Carnival in Flanders
    1954 By the Beautiful Sea
          Fanny
    1955 Plain and Fancy

Tauber, Richard (né Ernst Seifert), actor, singer; b. Linz, Austria, May 16, 1892; d. London, Jan. 8, 1948. Lyric tenor who won London acclaim in *The Land of Smiles* ("You Are My Heart's Delight").

    1931 The Land of Smiles (*Sou Chong*)
    1937 Paganini (*Paganini*)
    1942 Blossom Time (*Franz Schubert*)
    1943 Old Chelsea (*Jacob Bray*) (also comp.)
    1946 Yours Is My Heat (The Land of Smiles) (NY) (*Sou Chong*)

"Tea for Two." Music by Vincent Youmans; lyric by Irving Caesar. Sung by Binnie Hale and Seymour Beard in

London version of *No, No, Nanette* (1925), then by Louise Groody and John Barker in NY (also 1925). According to lyricist Caesar, "One day I took a late nap in my apartment. Youmans came by to wake me to take me to a party. As I was dressing, he said, 'Something came to me this morning,' and he sat down to play it. Youmans asked me for a lyric but I reminded him of the party. Still he insisted. I said, 'I'll write a dummy lyric and do the real one in the morning.' In a little more than five minutes the words came to me. That lyric, even though it was supposed to be only temporary, was never changed." This is possibly why, even though the song is called "Tea for Two," the reference to tea-drinking occurs only at the beginning, with the rest of the lyric devoted to marital bliss in a hideaway barred to all visitors. The song was not part of the musical's original score but was added early in the pre-Bway Chicago run.

"Tell Her in the Springtime." Music & lyric by Irving Berlin. Grace Moore's willowy recommendation of the most congenial season for romance was first heard in the *Music Box Revue* (NY 1924).

"Tell Me Little Gypsy." Music & lyric by Irving Berlin. In the 1920 *Ziegfeld Follies*, John Steel asked a fortune teller if he'd ever find his love.

"Tell Me Pretty Maiden." Music & lyric by Leslie Stuart. Coquettish, show-stopping number performed by a double sextette in *Florodora*, first in London (1899), then in NY (1900). As staged, six girls, all of the same height (5'4") and weight (130 pounds), wearing black ostrich-plume hats and pink dresses and twirling parasols, enter from left side of the stage while six boys, in matching gray top hats and frock coats, enter from the right. The boys ask, "Tell me, pretty maiden, are there any more at home like you?" To which the girls respond, "There are a few, kind sir, and pretty maids and proper, too." The number, which was originally conceived as a duet, elevated the six young ladies to prominence as the Florodora Sextette and made them the most sought-after charmers in the theatre (in NY, they all married millionaires). The original London Sextette: Nancy Girling, Lydia West, Lily McIntyre, Fanny Dango, Blanche Carlow, Beatrice Grenville. The original on Bway: Marie L. Wilson, Agnes Wayburn, Marjorie Relyea, Vaughn Texsmith, Daisy Green, Margaret Walker.

Tempest, Marie (née Marie Susan Etherington), actress, singer; b. London, July 15, 1864; d. London, Oct. 15, 1942. Dame of British Empire 1937. Miss Tempest spent the first 15 years of her career in comic opera, then left the London musical stage to play sharp-tongued *grande dames* in drawing-room comedies. Her biggest hits: *Dorothy, The Geisha* and *San Toy*. Bib: *Marie Tempest* by Hector Bolitho (Cobden Sanderson, L 1936).

1885	Boccaccio (*Fiametta*)
	The Fay o' Fire (*Lady Blanche*)
	Erminie (*Erminie*)
1886	Frivoli (*Rosella*)
	La Bernaise (*Countess Bianca*)
1887	Dorothy (*Dorothy*, repl.)
1889	Doris (*Doris*)
	The Red Hussar (*Kitty Carroll*)
1890	The Red Hussar (NY) (*Kitty Carroll*)
1891	The Tyrolean (*Adam; Christel*)
1892	The Fencing Master (*Francesca*)
1895	An Artist's Model (*Adele*)
1896	The Geisha (*O Mimosa San*)
1898	A Greek Slave (*Maia*)
1899	San Toy (*San Toy*)

Templeton, Fay, actress, singer; b. Little Rock, Ark., Dec. 25, 1865; d. San Francisco, Cal., Oct. 3, 1939. Exuberant, throaty-voiced singer who was leading soubrette for Weber and Fields (introducing "Ma Blushin' Rosie" in *Fiddle-Dee-Dee*), starred in *Forty-Five Minutes from Broadway* ("Mary's a Grand Old Name," "So Long, Mary"), and returned to Bway to sing "Yesterdays" in *Roberta*. Miss Templeton, who began her career at three singing between acts of her father's opera company, made her NY debut in 1873.

1881 The Mascot (r) (*Bettina*)
1883 Billee Taylor (r) (*Billee Taylor*)
1885 Evangeline (r) (*Gabriel*)
1886 Monte Cristo, Jr. (L) (*Fernand*)
1890 Hendrik Hudson (*Hendrik Hudson*)
1893 Madame Favart (*Madame Favart*)
1895 Excelsior, Jr. (*H. W. Excelsior Jr.*)
1898 Hurly Burly (*Cleopatra*)
1899 Catherine (*Catherine Villun*)
1900 Broadway to Tokio (*Cleopatra*)
     Fiddle-Dee-Dee (*La Belle* Zara)
1901 Hoity Toity (*Cho Cho San*)
1902 Twirly Whirly (*Signorita Calvemelba*)
1903 The Runaways (*Josey May*, repl.)
1904 A Little Bit of Everything (*Aurora Dawn Knight*)
     In Newport (*Mme. Fleurette*)
1905 Lifting the Lid (*Mathilde Macartini*)
1906 Forty-Five Minutes from Broadway (*Mary Jane Jenkins*)
1912 Hokey Pokey (*Peaches Mullen*)
1933 Roberta (*Aunt Minnie*)

"Ten Cents a Dance." Music by Richard Rodgers; lyric by Lorenz Hart. Sung by Ruth Etting atop a portable upright piano pedaled on a bicycle by Ed Wynn in *Simple Simon* (NY 1930). Rodgers and Hart wrote the song during the Boston tryout but Lee Morse, the girl for whom it was intended, had had too much to drink and was unable to get through it. She was replaced by Miss Etting, who sang the piece for the first time during the opening-night performance on Bway. The song is a teary lament of a girl who must earn her living as a hostess in a dime-a-dance ballroom.

Tennent, Ltd., H. M., producing firm. Founded by Harry M. Tennent in 1936, the company has become Britain's major production and management organization. Upon Tennent's death in 1941, Hugh ("Binkie") Beaumont became managing director; upon Beaumont's death in 1973, Arthur Cantor, an American producer, succeeded him. The company's longest-running London musicals have been *My Fair Lady, Irma la Douce, West Side Story, Hello, Dolly!, Promises, Promises, Where's Charley?, Godspell,* and *Billy.*

1945 Sigh No More
1947 Tuppence Coloured
1948 Oranges and Lemons
1951 The Lyric Revue
1952 The Globe Revue
1953 At the Lyric
1954 Going to Town (At the Lyric)
     After the Ball
1955 The Buccaneer
1958 Where's Charley?
     My Fair Lady
     Living for Pleasure
     Irma la Douce
     West Side Story
1960 The Most Happy Fella
     Joie de Vivre
1961 Bye Bye Birdie
     On the Avenue
     Do Re Mi
1963 Carnival
     Virtue in Danger
     On the Town
1965 Hello, Dolly!
1968 I Do! I Do!
1969 Your Own Thing
     Promises, Promises
1971 Godspell
1973 No, No, Nanette (r)
1974 Billy

Terris, Norma (née Norma Allison), actress, singer; b. Columbus, Kan., Nov. 13, 1904. Miss Terris' greatest Bway success was scored in *Show Boat*, in which she introduced "Make Believe," "You Are Love," and "Why Do I Love You?" She also appeared in vaudeville with first husband Max Hoffman, Jr.

1922 Queen o' Hearts (*Grace*)
1923 Little Nellie Kelly (US tour) (*Nellie Kelly*)
1924 Be Yourself (US tour) (*Toni Robinson*)
1926 A Night in Paris
1927 A Night in Spain (added)
 Show Boat (*Magnolia Hawks*)
1930 The Well of Romance (*The Princess*)
1932 Show Boat (r) (*Magnolia Hawks*)
1938 Great Lady (*Eliza Bowen*)

Terriss, Ellaline (née Ellaline Lewin), actress, singer; b. Stanley, Falkland Islands, April 13, 1871; d. London, June 16, 1971. Flaxen-haired, cameo-faced leading lady who was seen on the London musical stage with her husband, Seymour Hicks, in nine productions and was replaced by him in one (*The Dashing Little Duke*). Miss Terriss' major hits were *The Circus Girl, A Runaway Girl, Bluebell in Fairyland, The Catch of the Season*. The actress made her London bow in 1888 and also appeared in music halls and nonmusicals. Bib: *Ellaline Terriss* by Herself (Hutchinson, L 1928); *Me and My Missus* by Seymour Hicks (Cassell, L 1939); *A Little Bit of String* by Miss Terriss (Hutchinson, L 1955).

Asterisk indicates appearance with Mr. Hicks:

1895 The Shop Girl * (*Bessie Brent*, repl.)
1896 My Girl (*May*)
 The Circus Girl * (*Dora Wemyss*)
1898 A Runaway Girl (*Winifred Gray*)
1901 Bluebell in Fairyland * (*Bluebell*)
1903 The Cherry Girl * (*The Queen*)
1905 The Catch of the Season * (*Angela*, repl.)
1906 The Beauty of Bath * (*Hon. Betty Silverthorne*)
1907 The Gay Gordons * (*Peggy Quainton*)
1909 The Dashing Little Duke (*Duc de Richelieu*)
1910 Captain Kidd * (*Lucy Sheridan*)
1917 Cash on Delivery * (*Peggy Goode*)

Terry, Ethelind, actress, singer; b. Philadelphis, Pa., Aug. 14, 1900. As the heroine of *Rio Rita*, Miss Terry introduced the title song and "If You're in Love You'll Waltz."

1920 Florodora (r) (*Dolores*, repl.)
 Honeydew (*Muriel*)
1922 Music Box Revue (repl.)
1923 Music Box Revue
 Kid Boots (*Carmen Mendoza*)
1927 Rio Rita (*Rita Ferguson*)
1930 Nina Rosa (*Nina Rosa*)
1931 Nina Rosa (L) (*Nina Rosa*)
 Sons o' Guns (US tour) (*Yvonne*)

Teyte, Maggie (née Margaret Tate), actress, singer; b. Wolverhampton, Eng., April 17, 1889. Dame of British Empire 1958. Miss Teyte played leading operatic roles, 1907–19, in Paris, London, New York, before appearing on the London musical stage. She is the sister of composer James W. Tate.

1919 Monsieur Beaucaire (*Lady Mary Carlyle*)
1920 A Little Dutch Girl (*Princess Julia*)
1934 By Appointment (*Mrs. Fitzherbert*)
1935 Tantivy Towers (*Lady Ann Gallop*)

"Thank Your Father." Music by Ray Henderson; lyric by B. G. DeSylva & Lew Brown. Duet celebrating a girl's apparently illegitimate birth, first sung by Oscar Shaw and Grace Brinkley in *Flying High* (NY 1930).

"That Certain Feeling." Music by George Gershwin; lyric by Ira Gershwin. Rhythmic revelation of love at first sight introduced by Queenie Smith and Allen Kearns in *Tip-Toes* (NY 1925); also sung by Dorothy Dickson and Kearns in London production (1926).

"That Great Come-and-Get-It Day." Music by Burton Lane; lyric by E. Y. Harburg. In the first-act finale of *Finian's Rainbow* (NY 1947, L 1947), after the mail-order house of Shears and Robust has agreed to grant the citizens of Rainbow Valley unlimited credit, everyone bursts out in revivalistic fervor enumerating all the things that will soon be theirs.

"That Lucky Fellow." Music by Jerome Kern; lyric by Oscar Hammerstein II. Indirect marriage proposal offered by Robert Shackleton in *Very Warm for May* (NY 1939), then reprised by Grace McDonald (as "That Lucky Lady").

"That's Him." Music by Kurt Weill; lyric by Ogden Nash. Song of praise in which that special "him" is likened to the way a girl feels about the good things in life—autumn in the air, the smell of bread baking, the *Rhapsody in Blue*, fireflies glimmering, et al. Mary Martin introduced it in *One Touch of Venus* (NY 1943) sitting alone on the stage leaning over the back of a wooden chair. Lest anyone think him grammatically illiterate, lyricist Nash made sure to include the lines "Identification comes easily to me/ Because—that's he."

"That's Why Darkies Were Born." Music by Ray Henderson; lyric by Lew Brown. Philosophical acceptance of racial subservience. Everett Marshall, in blackface, boomed the number in *George White's Scandals* (NY 1931) accompanied by a host of showgirl angels.

Theatre Guild, The. Founded in 1919, the Theatre Guild has offered its subscribers carefully mounted classics plus modern works by the likes of Bernard Shaw, Sidney Howard, Ferenc Molnar, Eugene O'Neill, Robert E. Sherwood, William Saroyan. Lawrence Langner, a founder and director, and Theresa Helburn, the executive director, supervised most Theatre Guild productions. Rodgers and Hart were associated with the Guild for their two *Garrick Gaieties*, and Rodgers and Hammerstein were represented by three musicals (*Oklahoma!, Carousel, Allegro*). Other memorable productions: *Porgy and Bess, Bells Are Ringing.*

1925	The Garrick Gaieties
1926	The Garrick Gaieties
1930	The Garrick Gaieties
1935	Parade
	Porgy and Bess
1943	Oklahoma!
1944	Sing Out, Sweet Land
1945	Carousel
1947	Allegro
1950	Arms and the Girl
1956	Bells Are Ringing
1960	The Unsinkable Molly Brown
1968	Darling of the Day

"There Is Nothin' Like a Dame." Music by Richard Rodgers; lyric by Oscar Hammerstein II. The lonely sailors in *South Pacific* (NY 1949), led by Myron McCormick, expressed their admiration and desire for the opposite sex. Ray Walston led the group in the London version (1951).

"There Once Was a Man." Music & lyric by Richard Adler & Jerry Ross. In this crackling western-style duet in *The Pajama Game* (NY 1954), John Raitt and Janis Paige maintained that their love for each other was greater than any love that ever was. The couple in the London company (1955) was Edmund Hockridge and Joy Nichols.

"There's a Boat Dat's Leavin' Soon for New York." Music by George Gershwin; lyric by Ira Gershwin. Sportin' Life's song in *Porgy and Bess* tempting Bess to go with him to the big city. Introduced by John W. Bubbles (NY 1935), later sung by Cab Calloway (L 1952). The lyric was taken from the following lines in Dorothy and DuBose Heyward's play *Porgy:* "Dere's a boat to Noo Yo'k tomorroh an' I'm goin'. Why yo' such a fool, Bess? What yo' goin' to do a whole yeah heah by yo' self?"

"There's a Man in My Life." Music by Thomas "Fats" Waller; lyric by George Marion Jr. Paean to the one and only, first sung by Muriel Angelus in *Early to Bed* (NY 1943).

"There's a Small Hotel." Music by Richard Rodgers; lyric by Lorenz Hart. Blissful honeymoon at a simple country hotel envisaged by Ray Bolger and Doris Carson in *On Your Toes* (NY 1936), and by Jack Whiting and Gina Malo in London version (1937). Originally intended for *Jumbo* (NY 1935), the melody then had a lyric that began, "I love you today/ More than yesterday,/ A love that will go on forever . . ."

"There's Always Tomorrow." Music & lyric by Philip Charig. Debonair acceptance of a postponed romance sung and soft-shoed by Jack Buchanan and Anna Neagle in *Stand Up and Sing* (L 1931). This was the first song Miss Neagle introduced on the London stage.

"There's No Business Like Show Business." Music & lyric by Irving Berlin. The unofficial anthem of the theatre, first sung in *Annie Get Your Gun* (NY 1946) by Ray Middleton, William O'Neal, and Marty May to convince Ethel Merman of the excitement that will be hers once she joins their wild-west show. Miss Merman's acceptance of the offer was revealed when she added her voice to theirs. In London version (1947), it was sung by Bill Johnson, Ellis Irving, Hal Bryan, and Dolores Gray.

"These Foolish Things (Remind Me of You)." Music by Jack Strachey; lyric by Eric Maschwitz. Bittersweet compilation enumerated by Dorothy Dickson in *Spread It Abroad* (L 1936). Maschwitz, who wrote it under the pseudonym Holt Marvell, claimed that Cole Porter's "You're the Top" gave him the idea of creating a catalogue-type lyric made up of "small, fleeting memories of young love."

"They Call the Wind Maria." Music by Frederick Loewe; lyric by Alan Jay Lerner. A lonely gold prospector in California thinks of his wife and pleads with the wind to "blow my love to me." Rufus Smith introduced the emotional outburst in *Paint Your Wagon* (NY 1951), and James Mitchell led the dancing miners. In London version (1953), Joseph Leader was the singer and Veit Bethke the lead dancer.

"They Didn't Believe Me." Music by Jerome Kern; lyric by Herbert Reynolds (M. E. Rourke). When the London musical *The Girl from Utah* was brought to NY in 1914, this enduring song was added to the score. It was introduced by Julia Sanderson and Donald Brian. The following year it was sung in London by George Grossmith and Haidee de Rance in *Tonight's the Night*. In the ballad, heroine and hero remain firm in their determination to marry despite their inability to convince friends how wonderful and beautiful the other one is.

"They Like Ike.". Music & lyric by Irving Berlin. The speculation that Gen. Eisenhower might run against President Truman in 1952 sparked this three-way political discussion in *Call Me Madam* (1950). Playing US solons in NY were Pat Harrington, Jay Velie, and Ralph Chambers; in London version (1952), they were Sidney Keith, Arthur Lowe, and Launce Maraschal. By changing the title's pronoun to first person singular, the number became both a campaign song and a slogan.

"They Say It's Wonderful." Music & lyric by Irving Berlin. In *Annie Get Your Gun* (NY 1946) Ethel Merman and Ray Middleton contemplated how wonderful it would be to fall in love. Dolores Gray and Bill Johnson had their turn in the London production (1947).

"Thine Alone." Music by Victor Herbert; lyric by Henry Blossom. Fervent duet in *Eileen* (NY 1917), sung by Walter Scanlon and Grace Breen.

"Thinking of You." Music by Harry Ruby; lyric by Bert Kalmar. Airy ballad of unalterable concentration sung in *The Five o'Clock Girl* by Mary Eaton and Oscar Shaw in NY (1927) and by Jean Colin and Ernest Truex in London (1929).

"This Can't Be Love." Music by Richard Rodgers; lyric by Lorenz Hart. Love revealed through denial, first sung by Marcy Westcott and Eddie Albert in *The Boys from Syracuse* (NY 1938). In London, Graham Payn and Patricia Burke sang it in revue *Up and Doing* (1940).

"This Is a Changing World." Music & lyric by Noël Coward. A warning that love, like everything else, cannot endure forever in a changing world. Sylvia Cecil sang the swooping waltz in *Pacific 1860* (L 1946).

"This Is It." Music by Arthur Schwartz; lyric by Dorothy Fields. Ethel Merman's clarion announcement—accompanied by a string of ecstatic "Oh!"s—was first heard in *Stars in Your Eyes* (NY 1939).

"This Is My Holiday." Music by Frederick Loewe; lyric by Alan Jay Lerner. In which a newly freed spirit ecstatically looks forward to an unfettered world. Irene Manning introduced the waltzing ballad in *The Day Before Spring* (NY 1945).

"This Is My Lovely Day." Music by Vivian Ellis; lyric by A. P. Herbert. Romantic duet in *Bless the Bride* (L 1947) introduced by Georges Guétary and Lizbeth Webb. The composer wrote the melody after the title had been suggested by his publisher; the release was the same as the main theme of a discarded song, "I Shall Remember This."

"This Is New." Music by Kurt Weill; lyric by Ira Gershwin. Sung by Gertrude Lawrence upon meeting movie star Victor Mature in the second dream sequence in *Lady in the Dark* (NY 1941). Originally the ballad was to have been a duet, but Mature's singing voice proved inadequate.

This Is the Army (1942)). Music & lyrics by Irving Berlin.

SONGS: "This Is the Army, Mr. Jones," "I'm Getting Tired So I Can Sleep," "I Left My Heart at the Stage Door Canteen," "Mandy," "The Army's Made a Man Out of Me," "How About a Cheer for the Navy?," "American Eagles," "With My Head in the Clouds", "Oh, How I Hate to Get Up in the Morning," "This Time."

NEW YORK: July 4, 1942
BROADWAY THEATRE; 113 p.

Presented by Uncle Sam; directed by Ezra Stone & Joshua Logan; choreographed by Robert Sidney & Nelson Barclift; settings & costumes, John Koenig; music director, Milton Rosenstock.

CAST: Gary Merrill, Chester O'Brien, Alan Manson, Zinn Arthur, Pinkie Mitchell, James MacColl, Philip Truex, Earl Oxford, Ross Elliot, Ezra Stone, Julie Oshins, William Horne, Fred Kelly, Hank Henry, Burl Ives, Nelson Barclift, Anthony Ross, Joe Cook Jr., Robert Sidney, Robert Shanley, Stuart Churchill, Irving Berlin.

Conceived and produced as a benefit for the Army Emergency Relief Fund, this all-male all-soldier revue featured a virtual nonstop succession of Irving Berlin songs as it offered a view of Army life as seen through the eyes of selectees. Among its scenes were a military minstrel show and the Stage Door Canteen (incl. impersonations of theatrical personalities), and there were musical salutes to the Air Corps and the Navy. Originally scheduled for a four-week Bway run, *This Is the Army* remained for 12, then toured the US, England (it opened at the Palladium, London, Nov. 10, 1943) and military bases throughout the world.

The revue was a successor to Irving Berlin's previous all-soldier wartime show, *Yip, Yip, Yaphank* (NY 1918). In 1946 the Bway revue *Call Me Mister*, with songs by Harold Rome, had a cast of former servicemen and women and dealt with their adjustment to civilian life.

FILM VERSION: George Murphy, Joan Leslie, Ronald Reagan, Irving Berlin (with plot) (Warner 1943, Michael Curtiz dir.).

"This Is the Army, Mr. Jones." Music & lyric by Irving Berlin. Lighthearted introduction to the military life sung by Selectees and Minstrel Men in the first scene ("A Military Minstrel Show") of *This Is the Army* (NY 1942, L 1943).

"This Is the Missus." Music by Ray Henderson; lyric by Lew Brown. Rudy Vallée's prideful marital introduction (with Alice Faye as one of the bridesmaids) in *George White's Scandals* (NY 1931).

"This Is What I Call Love." Music by Harold Karr; lyric by Matt Dubey. "Look at me, I've got that proverbial glow!" commanded Ethel Merman in *Happy Hunting* (NY 1956), as she triumphantly trumpeted her discovery.

"This Nearly Was Mine." Music by Richard Rodgers; lyric by Oscar Hammerstein II. A love that might have been. Ezio Pinza gave vent to his feelings in *South Pacific* (NY 1949); so did Wilbur Evans in London production (1951).

This Year of Grace! (1928). Music, lyrics & sketches by Noël Coward.

SONGS: "Mary Make Believe," "Lorelei," "A Room with a View," "Teach Me to Dance Like Grandma,"

"Dance, Little Lady," "Try to Learn to Love," "Caballero," "World Weary" (added in NY).

LONDON: March 22, 1928
LONDON PAVILION; 316 p.
Presented by Charles B. Cochran; directed by Frank Collins; choreographed by Max Rivers, Tilly Losch; settings, Marc Henri & Laverdet, Oliver Messel, G. E. Calthrop; costumes, Ada Peacock, Doris Zinkeisen, Messel, Calthrop, Idare; music director, Ernest Irving; pianist, Leslie Hutchinson.
CAST: Jessie Matthews, Sonnie Hale, Douglas Byng, Tilly Losch, Maisie Gay, Moya Nugent, Lance Lister, Adrienne Brune, Sheila Graham, Jean Barry, Jack Holland, Lauri Devine, Marjorie Robertson (Anna Neagle) (chorus).

NEW YORK: Nov. 7, 1928
SELWYN THEATRE; 158 p.
Presented by Arch Selwyn, with Charles B. Cochran; directed by Frank Collins; choreographed by Max Rivers, Tilly Losch; settings, Marc Henri & Laverdet, Oliver Messel, G. E. Calthrop; costumes, Idare, Norman Hartnell, Christabel Russell, Messel, Calthrop; music director, Frank Tours.
CAST: Beatrice Lillie, Noël Coward, Florence Desmond, Dick Francis, Madeline Gibson, Queenie Leonard, Marjorie Moss & Georges Fontana, Billy Milton, G. P. Huntley Jr., Tommy Hayes, Phyllis Harding.
This Year of Grace!—also billed in London as *Charles B. Cochran's 1928 Revue*—was the first revue for which Noël Coward created all the music, lyrics, and sketches. Its musical highlights were "A Room with a View" and "Dance, Little Lady." Its funniest sketches were "The English Lido Beach" (Maisie Gay as a woman who

weekly swims the English Channel), "The Bus Stop" (Miss Gay pantomiming a harried housewife), and a lampoon of the current West End season, "The Theatre Guide" (incl. "Any Noël Coward Play").
For Bway version, Beatrice Lillie took over Maisie Gay's material and Coward appeared in most of the Sonnie Hale numbers.

Thompson, Fred, librettist; b. London, Jan. 24, 1884; d. London, April 10, 1949. Thompson collaborated with Guy Bolton on the librettos of 10 musicals in London, five in NY (incl. *Lady, Be Good!, Tip-Toes, Rio Rita, The Five o'Clock Girl, Follow the Girls*). In London he also wrote *Tonight's the Night, The Bing Boys Are Here, The Boy;* in NY, *Funny Face, Sons o' Guns.*
Asterisk indicates libretto written with Mr. Bolton:

1913	Eightpence a Mile
	Alice-Up-to-Date
1914	The Merry-Go-Round
1915	Tonight's the Night
	The Only Girl
1916	Mr. Manhattan
	The Bing Boys Are Here
	Pell-Mell
	Look Who's Here
	Houp-La!
1917	The Bing Girls Are There
	The Other Bing Boys
	The Boy
1918	The Bing Boys on Broadway
1919	Who's Hooper?
	Afgar
	Baby Bunting
	The Kiss Call
	Maggie
	The Eclipse
1921	The Golden Moth
1922	Phi-Phi
1923	The Cousin from Nowhere
1924	Vogues of 1924 (NY)
	Marjorie (NY)
	Lady, Be Good! * (NY)

1925 Tell Me More! (NY)
      Tip-Toes * (NY)
1927 Rio Rita * (NY)
      The Five o'Clock Girl * (NY)
      Funny Face (NY)
1928 Here's Howe (NY)
      Treasure Girl (NY)
1929 Sons o' Guns (NY)
1931 Song of the Drum *
1932 Out of the Bottle
1935 Seeing Stars *
1936 Swing Along *
      This'll Make You Whistle *
      Going Places *
1937 Going Greek *
      Hide and Seek *
1938 The Fleet's Lit Up *
      Bobby Get Your Gun *
1939 Magyar Melody *
1940 Present Arms
1942 The Lady Comes Across (NY)
1944 Follow the Girls * (NY)

"Thou Swell." Music by Richard Rodgers; lyric by Lorenz Hart. Arthurian speech and modern slang were combined in this jaunty duet for William Gaxton and Constance Carpenter in A Connecticut Yankee (NY 1927). In 1929 London version (called A Yankee at the Court of King Arthur), it was sung by Harry Fox and Miss Carpenter. During the musical's pre-Bway tryout the producers wanted the number cut, and it was only at Rodgers' insistence that it was retained.

Three Musketeers, The (1928). Music by Rudolf Friml; lyrics by Clifford Grey; book by William Anthony McGuire, based on Dumas's novel adapted from The Memoirs of M. d'Artagnan.

SONGS: "March of the Musketeers" (lyric, P. G. Wodehouse), "He For Me," "Ma Belle," "Your Eyes" (Wodehouse), "My Sword and I," "Gascony," "Queen of My Heart."

NEW YORK: March 13, 1928
LYRIC THEATRE; 319 p.
Presented by Florenz Ziegfeld; directed by William Anthony McGuire & Richard Boleslawsky; choreographed by Albertina Rasch; settings, Joseph Urban; costumes, John Harkrider; music director, Gus Salzer; orchestrations, Hans Spialek.

CAST: Dennis King (d'Artagnan), Vivienne Segal (Constance Bonacieux), Lester Allen (Planchet), Vivienne Osborne (Lady De Winter), Yvonne D'Arle (Queen Anne), John Clarke (Duke of Buckingham), Reginald Owen (Cardinal Richelieu), Joseph Macaulay (Aramis), Harriet Hoctor (featured dancer), Detmar Poppen (Porthos), Douglass Dumbrille (Athos), Louis Hector (De Rochefort), Clarence Derwent (Louis XIII), Naomi Johnson (Zoë).

LONDON: March 28, 1930
DRURY LANE THEATRE; 240 p.
Presented by Alfred Butt; directed by Felix Edwardes; choreographed by Anatole Bourman, Vladimir Domansky; settings, Joseph Urban; costumes, John Harkrider; music director, Herman Finck.

CAST: Dennis King (d'Artagnan), Adrienne Brune (Constance Bonacieux), Jerry Verno (Planchet), Marie Ney (Lady De Winter), Lilian Davies (Queen Anne), Webster Booth (Duke of Buckingham), Arthur Wontner (Cardinal Richelieu), Raymond Newell (Aramis), Ula Sharon (featured dancer), Robert Woolard (Porthos), Jack Livesey (Athos), Louis Hector (De Rochefort), George Bishop (Louis XIII), Moya Nugent (Zoë).

Dumas's saga provided the story for the third association between composer Rudolf Friml and star Dennis King—and their third success. The story covers d'Artagnan's first meeting with the Three Musketeers, his romantic involvement with Constance, and his efforts to protect the Queen, whom the King—rightly—suspects of infidelity. This was Dennis King's only Bway musical in which he also starred in London.

In 1967, composer Laurie Johnson, lyricist Harold Kretzmer, and librettist Michael Pertwee wrote a new musical version of the Dumas tale and called it *The Four Musketeers!* This so-called "comedy musical" was presented at London's Drury Lane with Harry Secombe (*d'Artagnan*), Stephanie Voss (*Constance*), Elizabeth Larner (*Milady*). It had a run of 462 performances.

"Three O'Clock in the Morning." Music by Julian Robledo; lyric by Dorothy Terriss. The closing number in the Bway revue *Greenwich Village Follies of 1921*, it was sung by Rosalind Fuller and Richard Bold, with Margaret Petit and Valodia Vestoff as dancing chime-ringers. The waltz was first published as an instrumental composition in 1919.

"Three White Feathers." Music & lyric by Noël Coward. Narrative piece of an actress who has progressed from living above her father's pawnshop in Ealing to being presented at court ("Today it may be three white feathers/ But yesterday it was three brass balls"). The number is performed while the heroine and her escort are seated in a limousine on its way to Buckingham Palace, and is preceded by the lady's confession of her nervousness to her escort. In *Words and Music* (L 1932), the scene was played by Doris Hare and Edward Underdown; in *Set to Music* (NY 1939), by Beatrice Lillie and Hugh French.

Threepenny Opera, The (1954). Music by Kurt Weill; lyrics & book by Marc Blitzstein, based on Bertolt Brecht's German text, *Die Dreigroschenoper*, adapted from John Gay's English ballad-opera *The Beggar's Opera*.

SONGS: "Ballad of Mack the Knife," "Wedding Song," "Pirate Jenny," "Army Song," "Love Song," "Ballad of the Easy Life," "Barbara Song," "Jealousy Duet," "Solomon Song," "Useless Song."

NEW YORK: March 10, 1954
THEATRE DE LYS; 95 p.
REOPENED Sept. 20, 1955
THEATRE DE LYS; 2,611 p.

Presented by Carmen Capalbo & Stanley Chase; directed by Capalbo; settings, William Pitkin; costumes, Bolasni; music director, Samuel Matlowsky; orchestrations, Kurt Weill.

CAST: Lotte Lenya (*Jenny*), Scott Merrill (*Macheath*), Leon Lishner (*J. J. Peachum*), Jo Sullivan (*Polly Peachum*), Charlotte Rae (*Mrs. Peachum*), Gerald Price (*Streetsinger*), Beatrice Arthur (*Lucy Brown*), John Astin (*Readymoney Matt*), Joseph Beruh (*Crookfinger Jake*), Marcella Markham (*Betty*), George Tyne (*Tiger Brown*).

LONDON: Feb. 9, 1956
ROYAL COURT THEATRE; 140 p.

Presented by Oscar Lewenstein; directed by Sam Wanamaker; settings based on Caspar Neher; music director, Berthold Goldschmidt; orchestrations, Kurt Weill.

CAST: Bill Owen (*Macheath*), Eric Pohlmann (*J. J. Peachum*), Daphne Anderson (*Polly Peachum*), Lisa Lee (*Mrs. Peachum*), Maria Ramusat (*Jenny Diver*), Georgia Brown (*Lucy Brown*), Ewen MacColl (*Streetsinger*), Warren Mitchell (*Crookfinger Jake*), George Cooper (*Tiger Brown*).

The Kurt Weill–Bertolt Brecht musical was first presented in Berlin in 1928, the 200th anniversary of *The Beggar's Opera*, from which it was adapted. Its raffish, sardonic view of rampant corruption quickly became a hit throughout Europe, and in 1933 it received its first English-language production in NY. The adaptors were Gifford Cochran and Jerrold Krimsky, and the cast was headed by Robert Chisholm (*Macheath*), Steffi Duna (*Polly*), Rex Weber (*Peachum*), Evelyn Beresford (*Mrs. Peachum*), Josephine Huston (*Lucy*), Rex Evans (*Brown*), Burgess Meredith (*Crookfinger Jake*). Harshly received by the critics, it lasted 12 performances.

The Marc Blitzstein adaptation was first presented in concert form at Brandeis Univ., June 1952. Leonard Bernstein conducted. Its initial run at the Theatre de Lys was terminated by a previous booking, but it reopened because of critical and popular demand. Currently, it is the second longest-running off-Bway musical. Lotte Lenya, Weill's widow, who had appeared in the original Berlin production, was succeeded during the run by Valerie Bettis (10-55), Grete Mosheim (4-56), Katherine Sergava (6-56), Dolly Haas (12-56), Christiane Felsmann (2-58), and Marian Brash (12-59); Scott Merrill by James Mitchell (12-56), Gerald Price (4-57), Jerry Orbach (3-58), David Atkinson (2-61), and Charles Rydell (11-61); Leon Lishner by Martin Wolfson (5-54); Jo Sullivan by Gerrianne Raphael (4-54), Paula Stewart (2-57), Jo Wilder (12-57), and Annette Warren (9-58); Charlotte Rae by Mildred (Carole) Cook (5-54), Jane Connell (9-55), Jenny Lou Law (2-57), Pert Kelton (7-57), Nina Dova (8-57), and Nancy Andrews (12-59); Gerald Price by Tige Andrews (9-55) and Jerry Orbach (2-57); Beatrice Arthur by Jean Arnold (2-57), Georgia Brown (9-57), and Joanne Spiller (8-58); Joseph Beruh by Eddie Lawrence (9-55). In 1957, Edward Asner played Peachum; in 1960, Estelle Parsons played Coaxer.

In all, over 700 actors acted in 22 roles during this engagement.

The story of *The Threepenny Opera*, set in Victorian London, relates the escapades of Macheath, an outlaw known as Mack the Knife. After marrying Polly, the daughter of the leader of Soho's underworld, Mack is betrayed by his new parents-in-law and is sent to Newgate Prison. There another flame, Lucy, the daughter of the police commissioner, frees him, but he is soon recaptured. Sentenced to hang, Mack receives a last-minute pardon from Queen Victoria, who provides a mock-heroic ending by awarding the robber a title, a pension, and a castle.

The original production of *The Beggar's Opera* opened Jan. 29, 1728, at Lincoln's Inn Field, London, with a book by John Gay and a score made up of popular ballads arranged and conducted by John Christopher Pepusch. The intent was to satirize Prime Minister Robert Walpole as Macheath and also to ridicule conventions of Italianate opera. The work had its first NY production Dec. 3, 1750. In 1920, a new version by Frederick Austin was staged by Nigel Playfair at the Lyric, Hammersmith, and remained for 1,469 performances. Playfair revived the show five times. In 1963, the Royal Shakespeare Co. production was presented in London with Derek Godfrey (*Macheath*), Ronald Radd (*Peachum*), Dorothy Tutin (*Polly*). Five years later, the Edinburgh Festival production came to London with a cast headed by Peter Gilmore (*Macheath*), Hy Hazell (*Mrs. Peachum*), James Cossins (*Peachum*), Jan Waters (*Polly*), Frances Cuka (*Lucy*). In NY, *The Beggar's Opera* was revived in 1972 by the Chelsea Theatre, first at the Bklyn Academy of Music, then off-Bway. The leading roles were played by Stephen D.

Newman (*Macheath*), Gordon Connell (*Peachum*), and Kathleen Widdoes (*Polly*). The run lasted 253 performances.

A modern-dress musical version of *The Beggar's Opera*, called *Beggar's Holiday*, was presented in NY in 1946. It was written by Duke Ellington and John Latouche, and featured Alfred Drake (*Macheath*), Zero Mostel (*Peachum*), Jet MacDonald (*Polly*), Mildred Smith (*Lucy*), Bernice Parks (*Jenny*). In 1972, Hugh MacDiarmid's adaptation of the Weill-Brecht musical, also called *The Threepenny Opera*, was presented in London with Vanessa Redgrave (*Polly*), Joe Melia (*Macheath*), Ronald Radd (*Peachum*) Annie Ross (*Jenny*), Barbara Windsor (*Lucy*), Hermione Baddeley (*Mrs. Peachum*).

Polly, a sequel to *The Beggar's Opera*, was first presented in London in 1777, and was revived by Nigel Playfair at the Lyric, Hammersmith, in 1922. It was presented in NY in 1925 at the Cherry Lane Theatre; 50 years later the Chelsea Theatre revived it at the Bklyn Academy of Music.

FILM VERSION: Curt Jurgens, Hildegarde Neff, June Ritchie (Embassy 1964, Wolfgang Staudte dir.).

"Thrill Is Gone, The." Music by Ray Henderson; lyric by Lew Brown. "This is the end, so why pretend?" asks the sorrowing lover. In *George White's Scandals* (NY 1931), the threnody was sung by Everett Marshall, with Rudy Vallée and Ross McLean, and danced by Dorothy and Harry Dixon.

"Through the Years." Music by Vincent Youmans; lyric by Edward Heyman. Natalie Hall sang this hymnlike song of courage in *Through the Years* (NY 1932).

Tierney, Harry (Austin), composer; b. Perth Amboy, NJ, May 21, 1890; d. New York, March 22, 1965. With lyricist Joseph McCarthy, Tierney had three major Bway hits: *Irene* ("Irene," "Alice Blue Gown"), *Kid Boots*, *Rio Rita* ("Rio Rita," "The Rangers' Song"). Tierney also wrote with lyricist Hugh Wright.

Unless otherwise noted, following were written with Mr. McCarthy:

1913 Keep Smiling (L) (Wright)
1919 Irene
1921 The Broadway Whirl
1922 Up She Goes
     Glory
1923 Kid Boots
1927 Rio Rita
1928 Cross My Heart

"Till the Clouds Roll By." Music by Jerome Kern; lyric by P. G. Wodehouse. Romantic duet inspired by a rainy day, introduced in *Oh, Boy!* (NY 1917) by Anna Wheaton and Tom Powers. In London version, called *Oh, Joy!* (1919), it was sung by Beatrice Lillie and Powers.

"Till There Was You." Music & lyric by Meredith Willson. In *The Music Man* (NY 1957) Barbara Cook and Robert Preston expressed their love by admitting how unfeeling they had been before meeting each other. In London version (1961) Patricia Lambert and Van Johnson were the lovers.

"Time." Music by David Heneker & Monty Norman; lyric by Julian More, Heneker & Norman. Though September is in the air, a middle-aged woman is sure spring will return with a new love. Hy Hazell introduced the throbbing ballad in *Expresso Bongo* (L 1958).

"Time on My Hands." Music by Vincent Youmans; lyric by Mack Gordon & Harold Adamson. Ardent expression sung by guardian Paul Gregory to Marilyn Miller in *Smiles* (NY 1930). Miss Miller, however, sang the number with a different lyric, written by Ring Lardner, and called "What Can I Say?":

> What can I say
> Is there a way
> I can get gay with you?
> It's just too bad
> You are my dad
> Flirting would never do.
> Daughters can't bother
> Fooling with father
> But I will tell you true
> That you've been a pal
> To this grateful gal.
> What more can I do,
> Pa, for you?

Tip-Toes (1925). Music by George Gershwin; lyrics by Ira Gershwin; book by Guy Bolton & Fred Thompson.

SONGS: "Looking for a Boy," "When Do We Dance?," "These Charming People," "That Certain Feeling," "Sweet and Low-Down," "Nightie Night," "Nice Baby."

NEW YORK: Dec. 28, 1925
LIBERTY THEATRE; 194 p.
Presented by Alex A. Aarons & Vinton Freedley; directed by John Harwood; choreographed by Sammy Lee; settings, John Wenger; costumes, Kiviette, Claire; music director, William Daly; duo-pianists, Phil Ohman & Vic Arden.
CAST: Queenie Smith (*Tip-Toes Kaye*), Allen Kearns (*Steve Burton*), Andrew Tombes (*Al Kaye*), Harry

Watson Jr. (*Hen Kaye*), Jeanette MacDonald (*Sylvia Metcalf*), Robert Halliday (*Rollo Metcalf*), Amy Revere (*Peggy*), Gertrude McDonald (*Bunnie*).

LONDON: Aug. 31, 1926
WINTER GARDEN; 182 p.
Presented by Musical Plays; directed by William Ritter; choreographed by Sammy Lee; settings, Joseph & Phil Harker; costumes, Gordon Conway, Eileen Idare; music director, I. A. de Orellana; duo-pianists, Jack Clarke & George Myddleton.
CAST: Dorothy Dickson (*Tip-Toes Kaye*), Laddie Cliff (*Al Kaye*), Allen Kearns (*Steve Burton*), John Kirby (*Hen Kaye*), Vera Bryer (*Sylvia Metcalf*), Evan Thomas (*Rollo Metcalf*), Eileen Stack (*Peggy*), Peggy Beatty (*Bunnie*).

Tip-Toes, which followed *Lady, Be Good!* by about a year, had the same composer, lyricist, librettists, producers, choreographer, and duo-piano team, and played in the same Bway theatre. Though Ira Gershwin felt the score was an improvement over the previous show's, the musical was not as successful. Its story is concerned with the adventures of Tip-Toes Kaye, a vaudeville dancer stranded in Palm Beach with her two uncles. She tries to snare millionaire glue king Steve Burton by posing as a member of society, but true love is revealed when she stays by him even after he admits—just to test her, of course—that he is penniless. In London version, Allen Kearns was succeeded by Charles Lawrence soon after opening.

In 1940, co-librettist Guy Bolton was co-author of *Walk with Music*, a Bway musical that also dealt with gold diggers (this time three girls) in Palm Beach.

FILM VERSION: Dorothy Gish, Will Rogers, Nelson Keys (Brit. Natl. 1928, Herbert Wilcox dir.).

"To Each His Dulcinea." Music by Mitch Leigh; lyric by Joe Darion. In *Man of La Mancha* (NY 1965), the Padre (Robert Rounseville), thinking of Don Quixote's hallucinations, acknowledges the need for every man to "find the haunting face to light his secret flame." In London (1968), the part was played by Alan Crofoot.

"To Keep My Love Alive." Music by Richard Rodgers; lyric by Lorenz Hart. Comic threnody done as a madrigal, itemizing various ways Queen Morgan Le Fay (Vivienne Segal) bumped off her husbands in *A Connecticut Yankee* (NY revival 1943). Among the gentlemen and the way they met their fate: Sir Paul (appendectomy), Sir Thomas (arsenic), Sir Roger (crowned with harp), Sir George (method undisclosed), Sir Charles (poisoned drink), Sir Percy (tossed off balcony), Sir Jonathan (stabbed), Sir James (throttled), Sir Frank (took mickey), Sir Alfred (sent on hunting trip), Sir Peter (undisclosed), Sir Ethelbert (undisclosed), Sir Curtis (poisoned fish), Sir Marmaduke (beheaded), Sir Mark (undisclosed). Note that in reference to Sir James, lyricist Hart used the line, "His heart stood still."

Todd, Michael (né Avrom Goldbogen), producer; b. Minneapolis, Minn., June 22, 1907; d. plane crash, Grants, New Mexico, March 22, 1958. Flamboyant showman who got his start at the Chicago World's Fair, 1933. With exception of his first and last Bway musicals, all Todd productions ran over 400 performances. Bib: *The Nine Lives of Michael Todd* by Art Cohn (Random, NY 1958).

1939	The Hot Mikado
1942	Star and Garter
1943	Something for the Boys
1944	Mexican Hayride
1945	Up in Central Park
1948	As the Girls Go
1950	Michael Todd's Peep Show

"Together Wherever We Go." Music by Jule Styne; lyric by Stephen Sondheim. Song of mutual dependency sung in *Gypsy* by Ethel Merman, Sandra Church, and Jack Klugman in NY (1959) and by Angela Lansbury, Zan Charisse, and Barrie Ingham in London (1973).

"Tonight." Music by Leonard Bernstein; lyric by Stephen Sondheim. Impassioned duet for Larry Kert and Carol Lawrence in *West Side Story* (NY 1957), and Don McKay and Marlys Watters in London company (1958).

"Too Close for Comfort." Music by Jerry Bock; lyric by Larry Holofcener & George David Weiss. How propinquity breaks down one's resistance, as confessed by Sammy Davis Jr. in *Mr. Wonderful* (NY 1956).

"Too Good for the Average Man." Music by Richard Rodgers; lyric by Lorenz Hart. Comic number enumerating some of the finer things of life that are "too good for the average man": smoky supper clubs, adultery, alcoholism, plastic surgery, neurasthenia, anti-Communism, birth control, and homosexuality. Luella Gear and Monty Woolley introduced the song in *On Your Toes* (NY 1936); Olive Blakeney and Vernon Kelso sang it in London version (1937).

"Too Long at the Fair." Music & lyric by Billy Barnes. Sung by Joyce Jameson in *Billy Barnes Revue* (NY 1958, L

1960). A variation on "Oh Dear, What Can the Matter Be?," the ballad expresses the loneliness of a successful career girl in New York and her yearning to return home.

Too Many Girls (1939). Music by Richard Rodgers; lyrics by Lorenz Hart; book by George Marion Jr.

SONGS: "Pottawatomie," " 'Cause We Got Cake," "Love Never Went to College," "Spic and Spanish," "I Like to Recognize the Tune," "Look Out," "She Could Shake the Maracas," "I Didn't Know What Time It Was," "Too Many Girls," "Give It Back to the Indians."

NEW YORK: Oct. 18, 1939
IMPERIAL THEATRE; 249 p.

Presented & directed by George Abbott; choreographed by Robert Alton; settings & lighting, Jo Mielziner; costumes, Raoul Pène du Bois; music director, Harry Levant; orchestrations, Hans Spialek.

CAST: Marcy Westcott (*Consuelo Casey*), Hal LeRoy (*Al Terwilliger*), Mary Jane Walsh (*Eileen Eilers*), Richard Kollmar (*Clint Kelley*), Diosa Costello (*Pepe*), Desi Arnaz (*Manuelito*), Eddie Bracken (*Jojo Jordan*), Ivy Scott (*Mrs. Tewksbury*), Clyde Fillmore (*Harvey Casey*), Leila Ernst (*Tallulah Lou*), James MacColl (*Beverley Waverley*), Van Johnson (*Student*).

To protect his heiress daughter Consuelo from predatory suitors, millionaire Harvey Casey hires football All-Americans Terwilliger, Kelley, Manuelito, and Jordan as bodyguards when Consuelo enrolls in Pottawatomie College, Stop Gap, New Mexico. Consuelo falls in love with Clint Kelley, which provides enough complications to keep everyone singing and dancing until the finale. The funniest scene occurred when Eddie Bracken, looking for girlfriend Leila Ernst, finds not only her beanie (symbolizing chastity) in the muzzle of a cannon but also her stockings, panties, and bra. *Too Many Girls* was the fourth (out of five) Rodgers and Hart musicals directed by George Abbott. In April 1940 Richard Kollmar was succeeded by Van Johnson.

Other Bway musicals dealing with college football: *Leave It to Jane* (1917), *Good News* (1927), *Toplitzky of Notre Dame* (1946), *All American* (1962).

FILM VERSION: Lucille Ball, Richard Carlson, Ann Miller, Eddie Bracken, Desi Arnaz (RKO 1940, George Abbott dir.).

"Too Many Rings Around Rosie." Music by Vincent Youmans; lyric by Irving Caesar. In which a flirtatious flapper is warned that having too many beaux "will never get Rosie a ring." Irene Browne gave the spirited admonishment in *No, No, Nanette* in London (1925), and Josephine Whittell followed in NY (1925).

"Toot, Toot, Tootsie! (Goo'bye)." Music by Ernie Erdman, Ted Fiorito, Robert A. King, Dan Russo; lyric by Gus Kahn. Al Jolson interpolated this exuberant farewell in *Bombo* (NY 1921).

"Totem Tom-Tom." Music by Rudolf Friml & Herbert Stothart; lyric by Otto Harbach & Oscar Hammerstein II. Pearl Regay and chorus performed this pseudo-Canadian Indian dance in *Rose-Marie* (NY 1924); Ruby Morriss and chorus did it in London production (1925).

"Touch of Your Hand, The." Music by Jerome Kern; lyric by Otto Harbach. Emotional good-byes exchanged by Tamara and William Hain in *Roberta* (NY 1933).

Toye, Wendy, choreographer, director, dancer, actress; b. London, May 1, 1917. As director-choreographer, Miss Toye had her biggest London hits with *Bless the Bride, Robert and Elizabeth*, and *Show Boat*. She began career as ballet dancer with Ninette de Valois's Vic-Wells Ballet Co., 1930; also toured with other companies, incl. Anton Dolin. In 1948 she formed company, Ballet-Hoo de Wendy Toye.

Unless otherwise noted, Miss Toye was choreographer of following; asterisk indicates she was also director:

1933 Ballerina (dancer only)
1934 The Golden Toy (dancer only)
1935 Tulip Time (*Varel Naryshkinsky* only)
1938 These Foolish Things
1939 Black and Blue
The Little Dog Laughed
Black Velvet (also dancer)
Who's Taking Liberty?
1941 Black Vanities
Gangway
1942 It's About Time
Best Bib and Tucker
1943 Hi-De-Hi
Strike a New Note
The Lisbon Story
Panama Hattie
1944 Jenny Jones
Strike It Again (also dancer)
1945 Gay Rosalinda
Follow the Girls (also *Betty*)
1946 Big Ben *
The Shephard Show *
1947 Bless the Bride *
Annie Get Your Gun (*Winnie Tate* only)
1949 Tough at the Top *
1950 Peter Pan (NY)
1951 And So to Bed *
1955 Wild Thyme *
1958 Lady at the Wheel *
1963 Virtue in Danger *
1964 Robert and Elizabeth *
1966 On the Level *
1970 The Great Waltz (r) (dir. only)

1971 Show Boat * (r)
1972 Stand and Deliver *

"Toyland." Music by Victor Herbert; lyric by Glen MacDonough. Childlike theme of *Babes in Toyland* (NY 1903), sung by Bessie Wynn and chorus.

"Tramp! Tramp! Tramp!" Music by Victor Herbert; lyric by Rida Johnson Young. Vigorous march for Captain Orville Harrold and his Rangers—made up of Planters and Canucks, Virginians and Kaintucks—in *Naughty Marietta* (NY 1910).

"Tree in the Park, A." Music by Richard Rodgers; lyric by Lorenz Hart. Idyllic rendezvous discovered in *Peggy-Ann* by Helen Ford and Lester Cole in NY (1926), and by Dorothy Dickson and Oliver McLennon in London (1927).

Trentini, Emma, actress, singer; b. Milan, Italy, 1885; d. Milan, April 12, 1959. Tiny, temperamental prima donna who was brought to US by Oscar Hammerstein to sing in the impressario's Manhattan Opera House. Miss Trentini's Bway successes, *Naughty Marietta* (in which she sang "Italian Street Song" and "Ah! Sweet Mystery of Life") and *The Firefly* ("Giannina Mia"), were written specially for her.

1910 Naughty Marietta (*Marietta d'Altena*)
1912 The Firefly (*Nina*)
1915 The Peasant Girl (*Helena*)
1919 The Whirligig (L)

Trip to Chinatown, A (1891). Music by Percy Gaunt; lyrics & book by Charles H. Hoyt.

SONGS: "The Pretty Widow," "Push Dem Clouds Away" (lyric, Gaunt); "Reuben and Cynthia," "The Bowery," "After the Ball" (music & lyric, Charles K. Harris) (added).

NEW YORK: Nov. 9, 1891
MADISON SQUARE THEATRE; 657 p.
Presented by Charles H. Hoyt; directed by Hoyt & Julian Mitchell (uncredited); settings, Arthur Voegtlin; music director, Percy Gaunt.
CAST: Anna Boyd (*Mrs. Guyer*), Lloyd Wilson (*Rashleigh Gay*), George A. Beane Jr. (*Ben Gay*), Lillian Barr (*Tony Gay*), Harry Conor (*Welland Strong*), Blanche Arkwright (*Willie Grow*), Anthony Pacie (*Norman Blood*).

LONDON: Sept. 29, 1894
TOOLE'S THEATRE; 125 p.
Presented by H. Tripp Edgar; directed by William Terriss; choreographed by Georgie Wright; settings, Joseph Harker, Bruce Smith; costumes, Mrs. S. May, Morris Angel; music director, William Robins.
CAST: Edith Bruce (*Mrs. Guyer*), Edgar Stevens (*Rashleigh Gay*), H. De Lange (*Ben Gay*), Audrey Ford (*Tony Gay*), R. G. Knowles (*Welland Strong*), Clara Jecks (*Willie Grow*), Harry Hilliard (*Norman Blood*).
A Trip to Chinatown, billed as "A Musical Trifle," toured the US for over a year before settling down on Bway, where it bested the long-run record set by *Adonis* (eventually it was overtaken by *Irene*). The story, which is strikingly similar to that of *Hello, Dolly!*, concerns itself with an invitation sent by Widow Guyer to Rashleigh Gay and his sister Tony to join her at the Riche Restaurant in San Francisco. Unfortunately, through error, the invitiation is received by Rashleigh and Tony's wealthy uncle, Ben Gay, who meets the widow at the restaurant. Though forbidden to go to such a place, the young Gays also show up and spend the rest of the evening trying to avoid detection by

their uncle. Ben ends up getting the bill for the two dinners, but he's unable to pay because he's forgotten his wallet.
In Feb. 1892 Loie Fuller was added to the cast to perform her butterfly dance (*Hello, Dolly!* had one too, but it was cut after opening night). She was succeeded by Bessie Clayton (10-92). Other cast changes: Queenie Vassar for Blanche Arkwright (12-91); J. Aldrich Libbey for Lloyd Wilson (7-93); Julius Witmark for Anthony Pacie (7-93).
A revised version of *A Trip to Chinatown*—called *A Winsome Widow*—was presented by Florenz Ziegfeld Jr. in 1912. Raymond Hubbell and Harry B. Smith wrote the new score, and the cast included Emmy Wehlan (*Mrs. Guyer*), Earl Benham (*Rashleigh*), Leon Errol (*Ben Gay*), Ida Adams (*Tony*), Harry Conor (*Welland*), Elizabeth Brice (*Isabel*), Frank Tinney (*Noah*), Harry Kelly (*Slavin*), Charles King (*Wilder Daly*), Mae West (*La Petite Daffy*), and the Dolly Sisters. It ran 172 performances.

"Triplets." Music by Arthur Schwartz; lyric by Howard Dietz. The miseries of going through life as a trio first revealed by the Tune Twisters in *Between the Devil* (NY 1937). In London revue *Better Late* (1946), it was sung by Beatrice Lillie, Virginia Winter, and Prudence Hyman.

"Trouble." Music & lyric by Meredith Willson. Galvanic number through which Robert Preston, as a bogus salesman of musical instruments, convinces the small-town citizens in *The Music Man* (NY 1957) that the best way to keep their kids out of trouble is to have them play in a marching band. Van Johnson roused the citizens in the London version (1961).

"Trouble Man." Music by Kurt Weill; lyric by Maxwell Anderson. The torment of loving the wrong kind of man expressed by Inez Matthews in *Lost in the Stars* (NY 1949).

Truex, Ernest, actor, singer; b. Rich Hill, Mo., Sept. 19, 1889; d. Fallbrook, Cal., June 27, 1973. Truex was a short, sandpaper-voiced comic actor who appeared in many nonmusical plays and films. His best-remembered musical-comedy role on Bway was in *Very Good Eddie*.

1910	Girlies (*Billy Murray*)
1911	Dr. De Luxe (*Dennis*)
1915	Very Good Eddie (*Eddie Kettle*)
1920	Pitter Patter (*Dick Crawford*, rep.)
1924	Annie Dear (*George Wimbledon*)
1929	The Five o'Clock Girl (L) (*Gerald Brooks*)
1931	The Third Little Show
1937	Frederika (*Lenz*)
1944	Helen Goes to Troy (*Menelaus*)
1951	Flahooley (*B. J. Bigelow*)

"Try to Forget." Music by Jerome Kern; lyric by Otto Harbach. Ardent farewell introduced in *The Cat and the Fiddle* (NY 1931) by Bettina Hall, Eddie Foy Jr., and Doris Carson. In London version (1932), sung by Peggy Wood, Fred Conyngham, and Gina Malo.

"Try to Remember." Music by Harvey Schmidt; lyric by Tom Jones. December recalling September—or age revitalized by youth—was the song's message, transmitted by Jerry Orbach at the beginning and end of *The Fantasticks* (NY 1960). In London production, it was sung by Terence Cooper.

"Tschaikowsky." Music by Kurt Weill; lyric by Ira Gershwin. Danny Kaye's rapid-fire show-stopper in the circus dream sequence in *Lady in the Dark* (NY 1941). The lyric, which contained the names of 49 Russian composers that were rattled off in 39 seconds, was based on a humorous poem, "The Music Hour," which Gershwin had written under the pen name of "Arthur Francis." It was published in the June 12, 1924, issue of *Life* magazine.

Tucker, Sophie (née Sonia Kalish), actress, singer; b. Russia, Jan. 13, 1884; d. New York, Feb. 9, 1966. Big, blonde, brassy Sophie Tucker, the self-proclaimed "Last of the Red-Hot Mamas," became a vaudeville headliner in 1906 and remained a nightclub headliner up to her death. The 1963 Bway musical *Sophie* was based on her life. Bib: *Some of These Days* by Miss Tucker (Doubleday, NY 1945).

1909	Follies of 1909
1919	Shubert Gaieties (repl.)
	Hello, Alexander (*Aunt Kitty*)
1922	Round in Fifty (L)
1924	Earl Carroll Vanities
1927	Gay Paree (added)
1930	Follow a Star (L) (*Georgia Madison*)
1938	Leave It to Me! (*Mrs. Goodhue*)
1941	High Kickers (*Sophie Tucker*)

Two Gentlemen of Verona (1971). Music by Galt MacDermot; lyrics by John Guare; book by Guare & Mel Shapiro, based on Shakespeare's *The Two Gentlemen of Verona*.

SONGS: "Love in Bloom" (Ralph Rainger–Leo Robin), "Summer, Summer," "I Love My Father," "That's a Very Interesting Question," "Symphony," "Love, Is That You?," "Night Letter," "Calla Lily Lady," "Who Is Silvia?" (lyric, Shakespeare), "Bring All the Boys Back Home," "Eglamour."

New York: Dec. 1, 1971
St. James Theatre; 627 p.
Presented by NY Shakespeare Festival (Joseph Papp prod.); directed by Mel Shapiro; choreographed by Jean Erdman; settings, Ming Cho Lee; costumes, Theoni V. Aldredge; lighting, Lawrence Metzler; music supervisor, Harold Wheeler.
Cast: Jonelle Allen (*Silvia*), Diana Davila (*Julia*) Clifton Davis (*Valentine*), Rául Julia (*Proteus*), Alix Elias (*Lucetta*), John Bottoms (*Launce*), Frank O'Brien (*Thurio*), Norman Matlock (*Duke of Milan*), Alvin Lum (*Eglamour*).

London: April 26, 1973
Phoenix Theatre; 237 p.
Presented by Michael White, with Robert Stigwood; directed by Mel Shapiro; choreographed by Dennis Nahat; settings, Ming Cho Lee; costumes, Theoni V. Aldredge; lighting, David Hersey; music director, Ian MacPherson.
Cast: B. J. Arnau (*Silvia*), Ray C. Davis (*Proteus*), Jean Gilbert (*Julia*), Samuel E. Wright (*Valentine*), Veronica Clifford (*Lucetta*), Benny Lee (*Launce*), Derek Griffiths (*Thurio*), Keefe West (*Duke of Milan*), Minoo Golvala (*Eglamour*).

Producer Joseph Papp originally scheduled the Bard's play as part of the NY Shakespeare Festival series of free productions at the Delacorte Theatre, Central Park, NY, for the summer of 1971. He also planned to tour it throughout the five boroughs, sponsored by the NY Shakespeare Mobile Theatre. Director Mel Shapiro, however, felt that those attending street-theatre productions would find little relevance in a story about the romantic rivalry of two close friends set in Renaissance Italy. Composer Galt MacDermot and lyricist John Guare were then enlisted to provide contemporary songs. Nine were written when the show went into rehearsal; by the time it opened there were 35. The dialogue combined Shakespeare's lines with modern colloquialisms, the cast was racially integrated, and Verona was made to appear as San Juan and Milan as New York. Over 3,000 attended each free performance between late July and early September.

The major cast changes for Bway were Diana Davila for Carla Pinza and John Bottoms for Jerry Stiller. The touring company began its travels Jan. 1973 with Jonelle Allen, Edith Diaz (succeeded by Stockard Channing), Clifton Davis, and Larry Kert. It continued for 10 months. In London, Jean Gilbert replaced Cleo Sylvestre before the opening.

For other musicals based on Shakespeare, see *The Boys from Syracuse.*

"Two Ladies in de Shade of de Banana Tree." Music by Harold Arlen; lyric by Truman Capote & Arlen. Pulsating Calypso-ish number in *House of Flowers* (NY 1954) in which Ada Moore and Enid Mosier proclaimed "How de-lec-ta-ble de-sir-ous they can be." The music was then used for a dance by Carmen de Lavallade, Dolores Harper, and chorus.

"Two Lost Souls." Music & lyric by Richard Adler & Jerry Ross. Loping ballad of mutual consolation offered in *Damn Yankees* by Gwen Verdon and Stephen Douglass (NY 1955), then by Belita and Ivor Emmanuel (L 1957).

⚜ U ⚜

Uggams, Leslie, actress, singer; b. New York, May 25, 1943. Bright-eyed song-belter who scored Bway success in *Hallelujah, Baby!* (singing "My Own Morning"), and who introduced "Just for Today" in *Her First Roman.* Miss Uggams first became popular via tv musical series, has appeared in nightclubs, and has made records.

1967 Hallelujah, Baby! (*Georgina*)
1968 Her First Roman (*Cleopatra*)

"Under the Bamboo Tree." Music & lyric by Bob Cole & J. Rosamond John-son. An African marriage proposal, interpolated by Marie Cahill in *Sally in Our Alley* (NY 1902) and in *Nancy Brown* (NY 1903). The song, which was originally titled "If You Lak-a Me," was written by Cole and Johnson when they were a vaudeville team. Cole wanted to use the spiritual "Nobody Knows de Trouble I See" in the act, but Johnson objected and they compromised by simply inverting the melody and writing new words.

⚜ V ⚜

Vagabond King, The (1925). Music by Rudolf Friml; lyrics by Brian Hooker; book by Hooker, Russell Janney, & W. H. Post, based on play *If I Were King* by Justin Huntly McCarthy, adapted from novel by R. H. Russell.

SONGS: "Song of the Vagabonds," "Some Day," "Only a Rose," "Huguette Waltz," "Love Me To-night," "Nocturne," "Love for Sale."

NEW YORK: Sept. 21, 1925
CASINO THEATRE; 511 p.

Presented by Russell Janney; directed by Max Figman; choreographed by Julian Alfred; settings & costumes, James Reynolds; music director, Anton Heindl.

CAST: Dennis King (*François Villon*), Herbert Corthell (*Guy Taborie*), Carolyn Thomson (*Katherine de Vaucelles*), Max Figman (*Louis XI*), Jane Carroll (*Huguette du Hamel*), Olga Treskoff (*Lady Mary*).

LONDON: April 19, 1927
WINTER GARDEN; 480 p.

Presented by Russell Janney; directed by Richard Boleslawsky; choreographed by Royal Cutter, Helen Grenelle; settings, James Reynolds, Joseph & Phil Harker; costumes, Reynolds; music director, Jacques Heuvel.

CAST: Derek Oldham (*François Villon*), Mark Lester (*Guy Taborie*), Winnie Melville (*Katherine de Vaucelles*), H. A. Saintsbury (*Louis XI*), Norah Blaney (*Huguette du Hamel*), Betty Eley (*Lady Mary*).

Producer Russell Janney had wanted to produce a musical version of *If I Were King* ever since seeing a school production starring Dorothy Fields with a score by Rodgers and Hart. With a score by Friml and Hooker, the operetta became one of the most successful swashbuckling romances of the 1920s. Set in Paris at the time of Louis XI, it spins a fanciful tale of how poet-vagabond François Villon saves his neck by being allowed to be king of France for a day. He also saves Paris from the Duke of Burgundy's forces, and ends up in the arms of aristocratic Katherine de Vaucelles. During Bway run, Dennis King was succeeded by Alec Fraser (7-26), James R. Liddy (11-26), Robert Craik (11-26). In 1928, composer Friml and actor King were reunited for *The Three Musketeers,* which also dealt with intrigue at the French court.

FILM VERSIONS: Dennis King, Jeanette MacDonald, Lillian Roth (Par. 1930, Ludwig Berger dir.); Oreste and Kathryn Grayson (Par. 1956, Michael Curtiz dir.).

"Valencia." Music by José Padilla; lyric by Clifford Grey. Originally a French song, lyric by Lucien Jean Boyer and Jacques-Charles, sung by Mistinguett in Paris nightclub revue *Revue Mistinguett* (1925). In NY, sung in English by Hazel Dawn, Halfred Young, and Charlotte Woodruff as first-act finale of revue *The Great Temptations* (1926). In the scene, chorus girls wearing brightly colored shawls were perched on a staircase that reached up to the proscenium and back to, apparently, the rear wall of the theatre.

Vallée, (Hubert Prior) Rudy, actor, singer; b. Island Pond, Vt., July 28, 1901. Saxophone-playing, megaphone-wielding bandleader and singer who became crooning idol of late 20s and early 30s. Vallée introduced "My Song" and "This Is the Missus" in *George White's Scandals* of 1931. Bib: *Vagabond Dreams Come True* (Dutton, NY 1930), *My Time Is Your Time* (Obolensky, NY 1962), both by Vallée.

1931 George White's Scandals

1935 George White's Scandals
1961 How to Succeed in Business Without Really Trying (*J. B. Biggley*)

Van, Bobby (né Robert Van Stein), actor, dancer, singer; b. The Bronx, NY, Dec. 6, 1930. A graceful highstepper who scored hit in Bway revival of *No, No, Nanette,* Van has also appeared in Hollywood films and nightclubs.

1950 Alive and Kicking
1954 On Your Toes (r) (*Junior Dolan*)
1971 No, No, Nanette (r) (*Billy Early*)
1975 Doctor Jazz (*Steve Anderson*)

"Varsity Drag, The." Music by Ray Henderson; lyric by B. G. DeSylva & Lew Brown. A down-on-the-heels, up-on-the-toes Charleston in *Good News!* (NY 1927), taught by Zelma O'Neal, Ruth Mayon, Don Tomkins, and Wally Coyle, and demonstrated by everybody. In London production (1928), it was sung by Miss O'Neal, Julie Johnston, Michael Tripp, and George Murphy. The song cue in the musical occurred when Miss O'Neal, playing a coed at Tait College, tells the other students, "Let the professors worry about their dusty old books, we'll make Tait famous for the Varsity Drag!"

Verdon, (Gwyneth Evelyn) Gwen, actress, dancer, singer; b. Culver City, Cal., Jan. 13, 1926. Redheaded dancing actress who rose to fame in the 50s starring in Bway hits *Damn Yankees* (singing "Whatever Lola Wants"), *New Girl in Town* ("It's Good to Be Alive"), *Redhead,* and *Sweet Charity* ("Where Am I Going?," "There's Gotta Be Something Better than This," "If My Friends Could See Me Now"). As a performer, Miss Verdon was usually given roles that projected both sexuality and vulnerability. She is separated from Bob Fosse, who choreographed and/or directed all her shows since 1955.

1948   Magdalena (asst. chor. only)
1950   Alive and Kicking
1953   Can-Can (*Claudine*)
1955   Damn Yankees (*Lola*)
1957   New Girl in Town (*Anna Christie*)
1959   Redhead (*Essie Whimple*)
1966   Sweet Charity (*Charity Hope Valentine*)
1975   Chicago (*Roxie Hart*)

Vereen, Ben, actor, singer, dancer; b. Miami, Fla., Oct. 10, 1946. Catlike performer who scored impressively on Bway in *Jesus Christ Superstar* (singing "Superstar") and *Pippin* ("Magic to Do").

1967   Sweet Charity (US tour) (*Daddy Brubeck*)
1968   Golden Boy (L) (*Fight Announcer*)
1969   Hair (*Hud*, repl.)
1971   Jesus Christ Superstar (*Judas*)
1972   Pippin (*Leading Player*)

Very Good Eddie (1915). Music by Jerome Kern; lyrics by Schuyler Greene; book by Guy Bolton, based on play *Over-Night* by Philip Bartholomae.

SONGS: "Some Sort of Somebody" (lyric, Elsie Janis), "Isn't It Great to Be Married?," "On the Shore at Le Lei Wi (music with Henry Kailimai, lyric, Herbert Reynolds), "Thirteen Collar," "Babes in the Wood" (lyric, Kern & Greene), "Nodding Roses" (lyric, Greene & Reynolds).

NEW YORK: Dec. 23, 1915
PRINCESS THEATRE; 341 p.
Presented by Elisabeth Marbury & F. Ray Comstock; directed by Frank McCormack; choreographed by David Bennett; settings, Elsie De Wolfe; costumes, Melville Ellis; music director, Max Hirschfeld.
CAST: Ernest Truex (*Eddie Kettle*),

Oscar Shaw (*Dick Rivers*), Helen Raymond (*Georgina Kettle*), Alice Dovey (*Elsie Darling*), John E. Hazzard (*Al Cleveland*), Ada Lewis (*Mme. Matroppo*), John Willard (*Percy Darling*).

LONDON: May 18, 1918
PALACE THEATRE; 46 p.
Presented by André Charlot; directed by Guy Bragdon; choreographed by George Surley.
CAST: Nelson Keys (*Eddie Kettle*), Walter Williams (*Dick Rivers*), Helen Temple (*Georgina Kettle*), Nellie Briarcliffe (*Elsie Darling*), Ralph Lynn (*Al Cleveland*), Veronica Brady (*Mme. Matroppo*), Stanley Turnbull (*Percy Darling*).

Very Good Eddie was the second Princess Theatre musical for Jerome Kern and Guy Bolton and their first hit. Most important—even though P. G. Wodehouse had not yet joined the team—the show set the style for the intimate musicals presented in the small playhouse. In the story, a honeymooning couple, Eddie and Georgina, meet another couple, Percy and Elsie, as they are about to embark from NY on the Hudson river boat *Catskill*. Somehow the couples become separated and Eddie and Elsie make the trip alone. After some embarrassing situations, the proper couples are paired off at the Rip Van Winkle Inn. The show moved to the Casino Theatre after five months, then to the 39th St. Theatre, and back to the Princess. During NY run, Ernest Truex was succeeded by Georgie Mack (8-16), Oscar Shaw by Tyler Brooke (8-16) and Earl Benham (9-16). Marion Davies joined the cast in Sept. 1916. Musical was revived in 1975.

"Vilia." Music by Franz Lehar; lyric by Adrian Ross. At the opening of Act II in *The Merry Widow*, the widow entertains friends at her home by singing a supposed Marsovian folk song about a hunter's love for Vilia, the witch of the wood. Lily Elsie sang it in London (1907), Ethel Jackson sang it in NY (1907).

"Vitality." Music by Ivor Novello; lyric by Alan Melville. Staccato pep talk on the importance of vitality in the theatre given by acting coach Cicely Courtneidge to her pupils in *Gay's the Word* (L 1951). The showstopping number, which became closely identified with the singer, includes references to past headliners ("Lily Elsie as the Widow, José Collins as the Maid") who possessed the essential vigor and drive.

❦ W ❧

"Wagon Wheels." Music by Peter De Rose; lyric by Billy Hill. Loping song of homecoming which Everett Marshall sang (in blackface) in *Ziegfeld Follies* (NY 1934).

"Wait Till the Cows Come Home." Music by Ivan Caryll; lyric by Anne Caldwell. In *Jack o' Lantern* (NY 1917), Helen Falconer and Douglas Stevenson sang of the milkmaid who makes a romantically aggressive city chap "wait, wait, wait by the old red gate" until she has finished her chores.

"Wait Till You See Her." Music by Richard Rodgers; lyric by Lorenz Hart. An unbelievable girl ardently limned by Ronald Graham in *By Jupiter* (NY 1942). Though the waltz eventually became the best known in the score, it was dropped soon after the opening because it was felt the show needed tightening.

Walker, Nancy (née Anna Myrtle Swoyer), actress, singer; b. Philadelphia, Pa., May 10, 1921. Pint-sized, slack-jawed comedienne and singer who made impression on Bway in *Best Foot Forward* (introducing "The Three B's," "Just a Little Joint with a Jukebox," "Shady Lady Bird"), and *On the Town* ("I Can Cook Too"). Miss Walker has also appeared in dramas and on tv.

1941	Best Foot Forward (*Blind Date*)
1944	On the Town (*Brunhilde Esterhazy*)
1947	Barefoot Boy with Cheek (*Yetta Samovar*)
1948	Look, Ma, I'm Dancin' (*Lily Malloy*)
1949	Along Fifth Avenue
1952	Pal Joey (r) (*Gladys Bumps*, repl.)
1955	Phoenix '55
1957	Copper and Brass (*Katy O'Shea*)
1959	The Girls Against the Boys
1960	Do Re Mi (*Kay Cram*)

"Walking Away Whistling." Music & lyric by Frank Loesser. Sadly heroine Ellen McCown of *Greenwillow* (NY 1960) admits that she is powerless to hold the wandering man she loves.

Walters, Charles ("Chuck"), actor, dancer, singer, choreographer; b. Pasadena, Cal., Nov. 17, 1911. On Bway Walters introduced "Just One of Those Things" and danced to "Begin the Beguine" in *Jubilee*. He became a choreographer in 1938, later a Hollywood director (*Easter Parade, Lili*, etc.).

Asterisk indicates Mr. Walters was choreographer of following:

1934 New Faces
      Fools Rush In
1935 Parade
      Jubilee (*Prince James*)
1936 Transatlantic Rhythm (L)
      The Show Is On
1937 Between the Devil (*Freddie Hill*)
1938 I Married an Angel (*Peter Mueller*)
      Sing Out the News *
1939 DuBarry Was a Lady (*Harry Norton*)
1941 Let's Face It! *
      Banjo Eyes *
1946 St. Louis Woman *

"Waltz of My Heart." Music by Ivor Novello; lyric by Christopher Hassall. Early in *The Dancing Years* (L 1939) Mary Ellis as a Viennese prima donna buys this spiraling waltz from poor composer Ivor Novello and, to his accompaniment, sings it to him.

"Wanting You." Music by Sigmund Romberg; lyric by Oscar Hammerstein II. Surging romantic duet for Evelyn Herbert and Robert Halliday in *The New Moon* (NY 1928), and for Evelyn Laye and Howett Worster in London version (1929).

Wasserman, Dale, librettist; b. Rhinelander, Wis., Nov. 2, 1917. Bway and tv playwright who had long-run success with *Man of La Mancha.*
1957 Livin' the Life
1965 Man of La Mancha

Watch Your Step (1914). Music & lyrics by Irving Berlin; book by Harry B. Smith, based on Augustin Daly's play *Round the Clock,* adapted from French farce.
SONGS: "Play a Simple Melody," "Settle Down in a One-Horse Town," "The Syncopated Walk," "When I Discovered You," "Ragtime Opera Medley," "They Always Follow Me Around," "Show Us How to Do the Fox Trot."

NEW YORK: Dec. 8, 1914
NEW AMSTERDAM THEATRE; 175 p.
Presented by Charles B. Dillingham; directed by R. H. Burnside; settings, Helen Dryden; costumes, Dryden, Lucile Lady Duff Gordon; music director, DeWitt Coolman.
CAST: Vernon Castle (*Joseph Lilyburn*), Irene Castle (*Mrs. Vernon Castle*), Frank Tinney (*Pullman Porter*), Charles King (*Algy Cuffs*), Elizabeth Brice (*Stella Spark*), Elizabeth Murray (*Birdie O'Brien*), Harry Kelly (*Ebenezer Hardacre*), Sallie Fisher (*Ernestine Hardacre*), Justine Johnstone (*Estelle*), Max Scheck (*Old Chappy*), W. M. Holbrook (*Howe Strange*).

LONDON: May 4, 1915
EMPIRE THEATRE; 275 p.
Presented by Alfred Butt; directed by R. H. Burnside; settings, R. C. McCleery, Philip Howden, John Bull, Bruce Smith; costumes, Helen Dryden; music director, Jacques Heuvel; English book by Harry Grattan.
CAST: George Graves (*Ebenezer Hardacre*), Ethel Levey (*Stella Sparkes*), Joseph Coyne (*Joseph Lilyburn*), Dorothy Minto (*Iona Ford*), Lupino Lane (*Clarence De Vere*), Blanche Tomlin (*Ernesta Hardacre*), June Howard-Tripp (dancer).
This "Syncopated Musical Show Made in America" was Irving Berlin's first complete Bway score and the first on Bway written mostly in ragtime. It also marked the final professional appearance together of Vernon and Irene Castle (when Vernon left the post-NY tour to join the Canadian Air Force he was succeeded in the sketches by Bernard Granville and in the dances by W. M. Holbrook). Its slight story ("Plot, if any, by Harry B. Smith" was the way the program put

it) had something to do with a curious will that leaves $2 million to anyone who has never been in love. It was abandoned in the second act in favor of a floor show at a Fifth Avenue nightclub. One of the highlights was a syncopated version of the *Rigoletto* Quartet, performed at the Metropolitan despite the protests of Verdi's ghost. W. C. Fields appeared in the show before its Bway opening.

In the London version, Act I was set in NY, Act II in London, with the last scene taking place at the Palais de Fox Trot. A special feature was a Bioscope film of Lord Kitchener's visit to the French army. Lupino Lane made his stage debut in this production.

Waters, Ethel, actress, singer; b. Chester, Pa., Oct. 31, 1896. Equally distinctive as an interpreter of blues and rhythm numbers, Miss Waters became the first Negro to star on Bway in a racially mixed cast (*At Home Abroad*). Among the theatre songs she introduced were "I'm Coming Virginia" (*Africana*); "Till the Real Thing Comes Along" (*Rhapsody in Black*); "Heat Wave" and "Suppertime" (*As Thousands Cheer*); "Cabin in the Sky" and "Taking a Chance on Love" (*Cabin in the Sky*). Her first appearance in vaudeville was in 1917; she has also appeared in Hollywood films, nightclub revues, concerts, and in nonmusical plays (*The Member of the Wedding*). Bib: *His Eye Is on the Sparrow* by Miss Waters (Doubleday, NY 1951). *(D. Sept. 1, 1977.)*

1927	Africana
1930	Blackbirds
1931	Rhapsody in Black
1933	As Thousands Cheer
1935	At Home Abroad
1940	Cabin in the Sky (*Petunia Jackson*)

Watson, Susan (Elizabeth), actress, singer; b. Tulsa, Okla., Dec. 17, 1938.

Round-faced Miss Watson has specialized in roles calling for wholesome innocence, as in *Bye Bye Birdie* (in which she sang "One Boy") and *No, No, Nanette.*

1958	West Side Story (L) (*Velma*)
1959	Lend an Ear (r)
1960	The Follies of 1910
	Bye Bye Birdie (*Kim MacAfee*)
1962	Carnival (*Lili,* repl.)
1964	Ben Franklin in Paris (*Janine Nicolet*)
1966	A Joyful Noise (*Jenny Lee*)
1969	Celebration (*Angel*)
1971	No, No, Nanette (r) (*Nanette*)

Wayburn, (Edward Claudius) Ned, director, choreographer; b. Pittsburgh, Pa., March 30, 1874; d. New York, Sept. 2, 1942. Wayburn directed 14 Bway musicals for producers Klaw and Erlanger, 13 for Lew Fields (incl. *The Midnight Sons*), 10 for Ziegfeld (incl. six *Follies*), nine for the Shuberts, and four long-running London revues for Albert De Courville. He founded the Studio of Stage Dancing in 1905. Bib: *The Art of Stage Dancing* by Wayburn (Wayburn, NY 1925).

1899	By the Sad Sea Waves (*Gen. Smiles* only)
1901	The Night of the Fourth
	The Governor's Son (asst. dir.)
1902	The Hall of Fame
	The Belle of Broadway
	The Billionaire
1903	Mr. Bluebeard
	Rogers Brothers in London
	Mother Goose
1904	A Little Bit of Everything
	Rogers Brothers in Paris
	Humpty-Dumpty
	In Newport
1905	Lifting the Lid
	The Pearl and the Pumpkin
	The Ham Tree
	Rogers Brothers in Ireland
	Fritz in Tammany Hall
	The White Cat
1907	The Time, the Place and the Girl
1908	The Mimic World
	School Days

Mlle. Mischief
Mr. Hamlet of Broadway
1909 Havana
The Midnight Sons
The Rose of Algeria
The Girl and the Wizard
Old Dutch
The Goddess of Liberty
1910 The Jolly Bachelors
The Prince of Bohemia
The Yankee Girl
Tillie's Nightmare
The Summer Widowers
1911 The Hen Pecks
The Never Homes
The Wife Hunters
Peggy
1912 The Passing Show
Broadway to Paris
The Sun Dodgers
1913 The Honeymoon Express
The Passing Show
Hullo, Tango! (L)
1914 The Honeymoon Express (L)
Dora's Doze (L)
1915 Town Topics (also prod.)
1916 Ziegfeld Follies
The Century Girl
1917 Zig-Zag (L)
Ziegfeld Follies
Miss 1917
1918 Box o' Tricks (L)
Ziegfeld Follies
1919 Joy Bells (L)
Ziegfeld Follies
1920 The Night Boat
Ed Wynn's Carnival
Poor Little Ritz Girl
Hitchy-Koo
1921 Two Little Girls in Blue
1922 Ziegfeld Follies
1923 Lady Butterfly
Ziegfeld Follies
1929 Ned Wayburn's Gambols (also prod.)
1930 Smiles

Wayne, David (né Wayne Mc-Meekan), actor, singer; b. Traverse City, Mich., Jan. 30, 1914. A versatile character comedian whose greatest Bway musical success was *Finian's Rainbow* (in which he introduced "Something Sort of Grandish" and "When I'm Not Near the Girl I Love"), Wayne also appeared in non-musicals (incl. *Mister Roberts*) and in films.

1943 The Merry Widow (r) (*Nish*)
1946 Park Avenue (*Mr. Meacham*)
1947 Finian's Rainbow (*Og*)
1958 Say, Darling (*Jack Jordan*)
1965 The Yearling (*Ezra Baxter*)
1968 The Happy Time (*Grandpère Bonnard*)

"We Kiss in a Shadow." Music by Richard Rodgers; lyric by Oscar Hammerstein II. Furtive love duet sung by Doretta Morrow and Larry Douglas in *The King and I* (NY 1951), and by Doreen Duke and Jan Mazarus in London production (1953).

Webb, Clifton (né Webb Parmalee Hollenbeck), actor, dancer, singer; b. Indianapolis, Ind., Nov. 19, 1891; d. Beverly Hills, Cal., Oct. 13, 1966. A slim, elegant Bway dancer and leading man, Webb appeared in such hits as *Sunny* (singing "Two Little Blue-birds"), *The Little Show* ("I Guess I'll Have to Change My Plan"), *Three's a Crowd*, *As Thousand Cheer* ("Easter Parade," "Not for All the Rice in China"). He also introduced "I've Got a Crush on You" in *Treasure Girl*, "Alone Together" in *Flying Colors*, "At Long Last Love" in *You Never Know*. After quitting the stage, Webb acted in 20 Hollywood films.

1913 The Purple Road (*Bosco*)
1914 Dancing Around
1915 Town Topics
1916 See America First (*Percy*)
1917 Love o' Mike (*Alonzo Bird*)
1918 Listen Lester (*Jack Griffin*)
1920 As You Were (*Kiki, Louis, Mark Antony*)
1921 The Fun of the Fayre (L)
1922 Phi-Phi (L) (*Phideas*)
1923 Jack and Jill (*Jimmy Eustace*)
1925 Sunny (*Harold Wendell-Wendell*)
1928 She's My Baby (*Clyde Parker*)

Treasure Girl (*Nat McNally*)
1929 The Little Show
1930 Three's a Crowd
1932 Flying Colors
1933 As Thousands Cheer
1938 You Never Know (*Gaston*)

Weber, (Morris) Joe, actor, producer, director; b. New York, Aug. 11, 1867; d. Los Angeles, Cal., May 10, 1942. Weber won his greatest fame with his partner, Lew Fields, as "Dutch" comics in a series of musical burlesques they presented for eight years at the Weber and Fields Broadway Music Hall. In the act, both men usually wore chin whiskers, tiny derbies, and garishly checkered suits, with the diminutive, well-padded Weber constantly at odds with his domineering partner. The act broke up in 1904, but, beginning in 1912, the men were reunited occasionally. Weber produced four musicals with scores by Victor Herbert (incl. *The Only Girl, Eileen*). Lillian Russell appeared in six Weber productions, Fay Templeton in five, Marie Dressler in four. Bib: *Weber and Fields* by Felix Isman (Boni & Liveright, NY 1924).

Unless otherwise noted, Mr. Weber was producer or co-producer of following; asterisk indicates appearances and/or productions with Mr. Fields:
1896 The Art of Maryland *
        The Geezer *
1897 Under the Red Globe *
        The Glad Hand * (*Mike Koffupski*)
        Pousse-Café * (*Herr Weinschoppen*)
1898 The Con-Curers *
        Hurly Burly * (*Herr Weinschoppen*)
        Cyranose de Bricabrac *
1899 Helter Skelter *
        Catherine * (*Paul*)
        Whirl-i-gig * (*Herman Dillpickle*)
1900 Fiddle-Dee-Dee * (*Michael Krautnuckle*)
1901 Hoity Toity * (*Philip Sauerbraten*)

1902 Twirly Whirly * (*Michael Schaatz*)
1903 Whoop-Dee-Doo * (*Michael Suppegreentz*)
1904 An English Daisy *
        Higgledy Piggledy (also *Adolph Schnitz*)
1906 Twiddle Twaddle (also *Philip Grabfelder*)
        Dream City (also *Wilhelm Dinglebender*)
1907 Hip! Hip! Hooray! (also *Julius Grienbacher*)
1908 The Merry Widow Burlesque (also *Disch*)
1910 Alma, Where Do You Live?
1912 Hokey Pokey * (*Michael Dillpickle*)
        Roly Poly * (*Michael Schmaltz*)
1913 Marie Dressler's All-Star Gambol *
1914 The Only Girl
1917 Eileen
        Her Regiment
1919 The Little Blue Devil
1920 Honeydew

Weede, Robert, actor, singer; b. Baltimore, Md., Feb. 22, 1903; d. Walnut Creek, Cal., July 9, 1972. Weede had an operatic career before making Bway debut in *The Most Happy Fella*.
1956 The Most Happy Fella (*Tony*)
1961 Milk and Honey (*Phil Arkin*)
1970 Cry for Us All (*Edward Quinn*)

"Weep No More, My Baby." Music by John Green; lyric by Edward Heyman. Tender vow of fidelity introduced by Una Vallon and Billy House in *Murder at the Vanities* (NY 1933), but popularized by Jack Buchanan in *Mr. Whittington* (L 1934).

Weidman, Jerome, librettist; b. New York, April 4, 1913. Primarily a novelist, Weidman achieved notable success with his first Bway musical, *Fiorello!*
1959 Fiorello!
1960 Tenderloin

1962 I Can Get It for You Wholesale
1966 Pousse-Café

Weill, Kurt, composer; b. Dessau, Germany, March 2, 1900; d. New York, April 3, 1950. Weill was a successful Berlin theatre composer (*Die Dreigroschenoper, Mahagonny*) who emigrated to the US in 1935 and quickly became a leading figure in the Bway musical theatre. Greatly concerned with widening the scope of the musical stage, he was responsible for recruiting playwrights Paul Green (*Johnny Johnson*), Maxwell Anderson (*Knickerbocker Holiday, Lost in the Stars*), and Elmer Rice (*Street Scene*), plus poets Ogden Nash (*One Touch of Venus*) and Langston Hughes (*Street Scene*), to work in the field. Though Weill's early music was characterized by its harsh, sardonic quality, his themes became more lyrical once he began working in NY. Among his best-known Bway songs: "September Song," "It Never Was You" (*Knickerbocker Holiday*); "This Is New," "Jenny," "My Ship" (*Lady in the Dark*); "Speak Low," "That's Him" (*One Touch of Venus*); "Moon-Faced, Starry-Eyed" (*Street Scene*); "Green-Up Time," "Here I'll Stay" (*Love Life*); "Lost in the Stars" (*Lost in the Stars*). Marc Blitzstein successfully adapted Weill's *Dreigroschenoper* as *The Threepenny Opera* (1954) whence came "Mack the Knife" and "Pirate Jenny." Others who either adapted his works or wrote with the composer were Gifford Cochran and Jerrold Krimsky, Desmond Carter, Ira Gershwin, Alan Jay Lerner. Walter Huston, Gertrude Lawrence, and Mary Martin starred in Weill musicals, as did his wife, Lotte Lenya.

1933 The Threepenny Opera (Cochran, Krimsky)
1935 A Kingdom for a Cow (L) (Carter)
1936 Johnny Johnson (Green)
1938 Knickerbocker Holiday (Anderson)
1941 Lady in the Dark (Gershwin)
1943 One Touch of Venus (Nash)
1945 The Firebrand of Florence (Gershwin)
1947 Street Scene (Hughes)
1948 Love Life (Lerner)
1949 Lost in the Stars (Anderson)

Welch, Elisabeth, singer, actress; b. New York, Feb. 27, 1908. Deep-voiced Negro singer who introduced "Charleston" in *Runnin' Wild.* Miss Welch settled in London in 1933, appearing in two Ivor Novello musicals and many revues.

1923 Runnin' Wild (NY) (*Ruth Little*)
1924 The Chocolate Dandies (NY) (*Jessie Johnson*)
1928 Blackbirds of 1928 (NY)
1931 The New Yorkers (NY) (*May*, repl.)
1933 Dark Doings
       Nymph Errant (*Haidee Robinson*)
1935 Glamorous Night (*Cleo Wellington*)
1936 Let's Raise the Curtain
1937 It's in the Bag
1942 Sky High
1943 Arc de Triomphe (*Josie*)
1944 Happy and Glorious
1947 Tuppence Coloured
1949 Oranges and Lemons
1951 Penny Plain
1954 Pay the Piper
1959 The Crooked Mile (*Sweet Ginger*)
1973 Pippin (*Berthe*)

Welchman, Harry, actor, singer; b. Barnstaple, Eng., Feb. 24, 1886; d. London, Jan. 3, 1966. Welchman was the jut-jawed hero of many London operettas in which he also toured the provinces.

1907 Tom Jones (*Officer; Tom Jones*, repl.)
1909 The Arcadians (*Jack Meadows*)
1911 The Mousmé (*Capt. Fujiwara*)
1912 Princess Caprice (*Augustin Hofer*)

1913	Oh! Oh!! Delphine!!! (*Victor Joli-beau*)
	The Pearl Girl (*Duke of Trent*)
1914	The Cinema Star (*Victor de Brett*)
1919	Afgar (*Don Juan Jr.*)
1920	Oh, Julie! (*Leoni*)
1921	Sybil (*Grand Duke Constantine*)
1922	The Lady of the Rose (*Col. Belo-var*)
1924	The Street Singer (*Bonni*)
1925	Love's Prisoner (*Gaston De Sen-lis*) (also prod.)
	The Bamboula (*Jimmy Roberts*)
	Princess Flavia (NY) (*Rudolf Ras-sendyl*)
1926	The Student Prince (UK tour) (*Karl Franz*)
1927	The Desert Song (*Pierre Bira-beau*)
1929	The White Camelia (*Lt. Paul Car-ret*) (also prod.)
	The New Moon (*Robert Misson,* repl.)
1930	Silver Wings (*Pablo Santos*)
1931	Nina Rosa (UK tour) (*Jack Haines*)
	Viktoria and Her Hussar (*John Carling*)
1933	Beau Brummell (*George Brian Brummell*)

"Well Did You Evah!" Music & lyric by Cole Porter. High society's casual attitude toward disastrous news was revealed by Betty Grable and Charles Walters in *DuBarry Was a Lady* (NY 1939), and repeated by Frances Marsden and Teddy Beaumont in London version (1941).

"We'll Gather Lilacs." Music & lyric by Ivor Novello. Sung by Olive Gilbert and Muriel Barron as an audition piece in the Victorian sequence in *Perchance to Dream* (L 1945). With its theme of hoped-for reunion, the song took on special poignancy during World War II. Novello claimed the idea came to him after Alfred Lunt and Lynn Fontanne had admired the lilac trees in his garden.

Welles, (George) Orson, actor, librettist, director, producer; b. Kenosha, Wis., May 6, 1915. Before making his name in films, Welles was co-founder of NY's Mercury Theatre.

Mr. Welles was director-producer of following:

1937	The Cradle Will Rock
1946	Around the World (also *Dick Fix*; lib.)

"Were Thine That Special Face." Music & lyric by Cole Porter. In the production of *The Taming of the Shrew* performed in *Kiss Me, Kate* (NY 1948), Petruchio (Alfred Drake) serenades Katherine (Patricia Morison) by wistfully describing the perfect woman that she, as yet, is not. Bill Johnson sang the piece in the London version (1951). Porter found the idea for the song in Bianca's lines in the original play:

Believe me, sister, of all the men alive,
I never yet beheld that special face
Which I could fancy more than any other.

West Side Story (1957). Music by Leonard Bernstein; lyrics by Stephen Sondheim; book by Arthur Laurents, based on idea by Jerome Robbins & Shakespeare's *Romeo and Juliet*.

SONGS: "Jet Song," "Something's Coming," "Tonight," "Maria," "America," "Cool," "One Hand, One Heart," "I Feel Pretty," "Somewhere," "Gee, Officer Krupke!," "I Have a Love."

NEW YORK: Sept. 26, 1957
WINTER GARDEN; 734 p.

Presented by Robert E. Griffith & Harold S. Prince; directed & choreographed by Jerome Robbins; co-choreographer, Peter Gennaro; settings, Oliver Smith; costumes, Irene Sharaff; lighting, Jean Rosenthal; music director, Max Goberman; orchestrations, Leonard Bernstein, Sid Ramin, Irwin Kostal.

CAST: Carol Lawrence (*Maria*), Larry Kert (*Tony*), Chita Rivera (*Anita*), Art Smith (*Doc*), Mickey Calin (*Riff*), Ken LeRoy (*Bernardo*), Grover Dale (*Snowboy*), Martin Charnin (*Big Deal*), Lee Becker (*Anybodys*), Reri Grist (*Consuelo*), Marilyn Cooper (*Rosalia*).

LONDON: Dec. 12, 1958
HER MAJESTY'S THEATRE; 1,039 p.
Presented by H. M. Tennent Ltd.; directed & choreographed by Jerome Robbins; co-choreographer, Peter Gennaro; settings, Oliver Smith; costumes, Irene Sharaff; lighting, Joe Davis; music director, Lawrence Leonard; orchestrations, Leonard Bernstein, Sid Ramin, Irwin Kostal.

CAST: Marlys Watters (*Maria*), Don McKay (*Tony*), Chita Rivera (*Anita*), Ken LeRoy (*Bernardo*), George Chakiris (*Riff*), Sylvia Tysick (*Anybodys*), Susan Watson (*Velma*), David Bauer (*Doc*), Francesca Bell (*Rosalia*).

Bway was jolted by this effective combination of dynamic choreography and exciting music mated to a contemporary theme created out of the tensions inherent in modern big-city living. The story, based on *Romeo and Juliet*, was reset in New York City with the conflict now concerning antagonisms between native-born whites and recently arrived Puerto Ricans. Tony, who falls in love with Puerto Rican Maria, tries to keep peace between the Jets and the Sharks, rival street gangs, only to end up being killed when he attempts to break up a rumble. The idea was first conceived in 1949 by choreographer Jerome Robbins as a project for composer Leonard Bernstein (who was to write his own lyrics) and librettist Arthur Laurents (writing his first musical). The original story—called *East Side Story*—involved a Jewish boy and an Italian Catholic girl. Work had to be halted because of conflicting schedules; when it was resumed six years later the locale and ethnic backgrounds were changed because they now seemed dated. It was also at this time that newcomer Stephen Sondheim succeeded Bernstein as lyricist. Delays were caused by the problem of finding singers who could dance and dancers who could sing.

The show could have remained on Bway longer than its initial run, but it chose to close and go on tour for 10 months. It returned to the Winter Garden April 27, 1960, for an additional run of 249 performances. For tour, Carol Lawrence was succeeded by Sonya Wilde (6-59) and Leila Martin (10-59), but she returned to the cast for the Bway reopening. Larry Kert was succeeded by Don Grilley (9-60); Chita Rivera by Carmen Alvarez (3-58), Muriel Bentley (7-58), Devra Korwin (3-59), and Allyn Ann McLerie (2-60). Patricia Birch played Anybodys during return engagement. In London, *West Side Story* had longer run than in NY. It was revived there at the Shaftesbury Theatre in 1974, with Tony Kenny and Christine Matthews in the leads.

FILM VERSION: Natalie Wood, Richard Beymer, Rita Moreno (UA 1961, Robert Wise, Jerome Robbins dirs.).

Westcott, Marcy, actress, singer; b. Chicago, Ill. Lovely blonde Marcy Westcott is remembered as the heroine of two Rodgers and Hart musicals: *The Boys from Syracuse* (in which she sang "This Can't Be Love" and "Sing for Your Supper") and *Too Many Girls* ("Love Never Went to College" and "I Didn't Know What Time It Was").

1938   The Two Bouquets (*Kate Gill*)
       The Boys from Syracuse (*Luciana*)
1939   Too Many Girls (*Consuelo Casey*)

"What Do the Simple Folk Do?" Music by Frederick Loewe; lyric by Alan Jay Lerner. Royalty envies such simple pleasures as whistling, singing, and dancing. Sung in *Camelot* in NY by Julie Andrews and Richard Burton (1960), and in London by Elizabeth Larner and Laurence Harvey (1964).

"What Good Would the Moon Be?" Music by Kurt Weill; lyric by Langston Hughes. The moon holds no appeal without the right one to share its beams. Anne Jeffreys introduced the poignant aria in *Street Scene* (NY 1947) after having been offered a life of luxury by a Bway racketeer.

"What Is There to Say." Music by Vernon Duke; lyric by E. Y. Harburg. Though slightly speechless, Jane Froman and Everett Marshall managed to convey their mutual ardor ("My heart's in a deadlock,/ I'd even face wedlock") in *Ziegfeld Follies* (NY 1934).

"What Is This Thing Called Love?" Music & lyric by Cole Porter. Smoky torch ballad introduced in *Wake Up and Dream!* (L 1929) by Elsie Carlisle, and danced by Tilly Losch, Toni Birkmayer, Alanova, and William Cavanagh. In NY production (1929), sung by Frances Shelley and danced by Miss Losch and Birkmayer.

"What Kind of Fool Am I?" Music & lyric by Anthony Newley & Leslie Bricusse. Self-deprecating piece sung by Newley in *Stop the World—I Want to Get Off*, both in London (1961) and NY (1962).

"Whatever Lola Wants (Lola Gets)." Music & lyric by Richard Adler & Jerry Ross. Satan's emissary, Gwen

Verdon, sang this siren song to baseball player Stephen Douglass in *Damn Yankees* (NY 1955). In London production (1957), Belita sang it to Ivor Emmanuel.

"What'll I Do?" Music & lyric by Irving Berlin. Waltz ballad of anticipated loneliness added to score of the *Music Box Revue of 1923* during NY run, and sung by Grace Moore and John Steel. In London, Norah Blaney sang it in revue *The Punch Bowl* (1924).

"What's the Use of Wond'rin'?" Music by Richard Rodgers; lyric by Oscar Hammerstein II. Gentle ballad concerned with the impossibility of viewing love rationally. First sung by Jan Clayton in *Carousel* (NY 1945), then by Iva Withers in London production (1950). Hammerstein felt that the song could have achieved even greater popularity had he concluded the lyric with an open vowel rather than the harsh—and hard to hold—"k" sound that ends the line "And all the rest is talk." For example, he thought the phrase "That's all you need to know" would have said the same thing and made it easier for the singer.

"When I'm Not Near the Girl I Love." Music by Burton Lane; lyric by E. Y. Harburg. A leprechaun's romantic fickleness sung in *Finian's Rainbow* by David Wayne in NY (1947) and by Alfie Bass in London (1947).

"When Mabel Comes in the Room." Music & lyric by Jerry Herman. In *Mack & Mabel* (NY 1974), long-absent silent screen star Mabel Normand (played by Bernadette Peters) is welcomed back to the movie set by the night watchman (Stanley Simmonds) and the crew, who then hoist her aloft on a boom and strut about singing her praises. In sentiment and staging, the number was intended as a successor to Herman's previous high-steppers, "Hello, Dolly!" and "Mame."

"When My Baby Smiles at Me." Music by Billy Munro; lyric by Andrew Sterling. Introduced by Ted Lewis and his orchestra in *The Greenwich Village Follies* (NY 1919), the song soon became the bandleader's theme.

"When the Idle Poor Become the Idle Rich." Music by Burton Lane; lyric by E. Y. Harburg. At the beginning of Act II in *Finian's Rainbow* (NY 1947), the citizens of Rainbow Valley, Missitucky, all decked out in finery from Shears and Robust, are led by Ella Logan in this lighthearted tribute to wealth as the great destroyer of class prejudice. Beryl Seton was the songleader in the musical's London production (1947).

"When You're Away." Music by Victor Herbert; lyric by Henry Blossom. Waltzing song of loneliness, sung by Wilda Bennett in *The Only Girl* (NY 1914). Fay Compton sang it in London version (1915).

"When Yuba Plays the Rumba on the Tuba." Music & lyric by Herman Hupfeld. Comic tale of the tuba player who introduced the oompah-oompah-oompah down in Cuba. Sung by Walter O'Keefe in *The Third Little Show* (NY 1931).

"Where Am I Going?" Music by Cy Coleman; lyric by Dorothy Fields. Though determined to end her life as a taxi dancer, the distraught heroine of *Sweet Charity* (NY 1966) is in an emotional turmoil when she tries to decide what path to take next. Gwen

Verdon was the original Charity; Juliet Prowse played the part in the London company (1967).

"Where Are the Songs We Sung?" Music & lyric by Noël Coward. In this waltz in *Operette* (L 1938), Peggy Wood fondly recalls her first romance "when love in our hearts was young." Coward once wrote that he considered the piece "melodic but depressing."

"Where Did the Night Go?" Music & lyric by Harold Rome. The swiftness of nocturnal pleasures lamented by lovers Patricia Marand and Jack Cassidy in *Wish You Were Here* (NY 1952).

"Where Do I Go?" Music by Galt MacDermot; lyric by Gerome Ragni & James Rado. After the draft-card-burning ceremony in *Hair* (NY 1967), Walker Daniels and The Tribe end the first act by trying to find the answer to the meaning of life. In London production (1968), the piece was sung by Paul Nicolas.

"Where Is the Life That Late I Led?" Music & lyric by Cole Porter. In *Kiss Me, Kate* (NY 1948), a show-within-a-show production of Shakespeare's *The Taming of the Shrew* finds the recently wedded Petruchio (Alfred Drake) recalling the romantic conquests of his bachelor days. In London production (1951), they were recalled by Bill Johnson. Cole Porter's inspiration for the song was the title line that Shakespeare had Petruchio sing in Act IV, Scene 1, of the original play.

"Where, Oh Where?" Music & lyric by Cole Porter. In which romance and finance are liltingly combined in a quest for a boy who is both a "cute knight in armor" and also a millionaire. Barbara Ashley was the designing lady in *Out of This World* (NY 1950).

"Where or When." Music by Richard Rodgers; lyric by Lorenz Hart. Sung by Mitzi Green and Ray Heatherton in *Babes in Arms* (NY 1937). The song deals with the odd psychic phenomenon of feeling that an experience or an emotion, even though it is happening for the first time, is being repeated.

Where's Charley? (1948). Music & lyrics by Frank Loesser; book by George Abbott, based on play *Charley's Aunt* by Brandon Thomas.

SONGS: "Better Get Out of Here," "The New Ashmoleon Marching Society and Student Conservatory Band," "My Darling, My Darling," "Make a Miracle," "Lovelier than Ever," "Pernambuco," "Where's Charley?," "Once in Love with Amy," "At the Red Rose Cotillion."

NEW YORK: Oct. 11, 1948
ST. JAMES THEATRE; 792 p.

Presented by Cy Feuer & Ernest Martin, with Gwen Rickard; directed by George Abbott; choreographed by George Balanchine; settings & costumes, David Ffolkes; music director, Max Goberman; orchestrations, Ted Royal, Hans Spialek, Philip J. Lang.

CAST: Ray Bolger (*Charley Wykeham*), Allyn McLerie (*Amy Spettigue*), Byron Palmer (*Jack Chesney*), Doretta Morrow (*Kitty Verdun*), Paul England (*Sir Francis Chesney*), Horace Cooper (*Mr. Spettigue*), Cornell MacNeil (chorus).

LONDON: Feb. 20, 1958
PALACE THEATRE; 404 p.

Presented by H. M. Tennent Ltd. & Bernard Delfont Ltd.; directed by William Chappell; choreographed by Hanya Holm; settings & costumes,

Peter Rice; music director, Michael Collins.

CAST: Norman Wisdom (*Charley Wykeham*), Pip Hinton (*Amy Spettigue*), Terence Cooper (*Jack Chesney*), Pamela Gale (*Kitty Verdun*), Jerry Desmonde (*Sir Francis Chesney*), Felix Felton (*Mr. Spettigue*).

The durable farce *Charley's Aunt* became a durable musical thanks largely to the appeal of Ray Bolger. This was the first production presented by Feuer and Martin and the first to have both music and words by Frank Loesser. The story deals with transvestite misunderstanding: Charley and Jack, undergradutes at Oxford in the year 1892, wish to entertain their lady friends, Amy and Kitty, but to do so Charley must play chaperon by disguising himself as his own aunt. Further complications arise when the girls' guardian, Mr. Spettigue, proposes marriage to the "aunt," and when the real aunt eventually shows up. The main difference between the original story and the musical version was that in the play a third character, Lord Fancourt-Babberly, was dragged in to impersonate the aunt. The London production marked Norman Wisdom's debut in a book musical.

FILM VERSION: Ray Bolger and Allyn McLerie (Warner 1952, David Butler dir.).

"Where's That Rainbow?" Music by Richard Rodgers; lyric by Lorenz Hart. Poignant search for happiness expressed by Helen Ford in *Peggy-Ann* (NY 1926). In London version (1927), it was sung by Dorothy Dickson.

"Whip-Poor-Will." Music by Jerome Kern; lyric by B. G. DeSylva. Airy recollection of a singing bird introduced by Marilyn Miller and Irving Fisher in *Sally* (NY 1920). In London company (1921) it was sung by Dorothy Dickson and Gregory Stroud. The song was originally written for an unproduced musical based on *Brewster's Millions.*

White, George (né George Weitz), producer, director, sketch writer, dancer, actor; b. New York, 1890; d. Hollywood, Cal., Oct. 11, 1968. White's fast-packed annual *Scandals* revues put the accent on music, dancing, and comedy, and were the major rivals to the annual *Ziegfeld Follies.* Willie and Eugene Howard were in six editions, Ann Pennington was in five, Lou Holtz, Winnie Lightner, and Frances Williams in three each, Harry Richman and Rudy Vallée in two each. George Gershwin composed five *Scandals* scores, as did Ray Henderson (the first three with B. G. DeSylva and Lew Brown, the fourth with Brown alone). White also produced nightclub revues and Hollywood films. As lyricist, he wrote with composer Cliff Friend.

Unless otherwise noted, Mr. White was producer, director, sketch writer, or librettist of following; asterisk indicates he also appeared in production:

1910 The Echo (*Don Ferris* only)
1911 Ziegfeld Follies (dancer only)
1912 The Whirl of Society (dancer only)
1913 The Pleasure Seekers (*Jack Hemingway*) only)
1914 The Midnight Girl (*François* only)
1915 Ziegfeld Follies (dancer only)
1917 Miss 1917 (dancer only)
1919 George White's Scandals *
1920 George White's Scandals *
1921 George White's Scandals *
1922 George White's Scandals *
1923 George White's Scandals
       Runnin' Wild (prod., dir. only)
1924 George White's Scandals
1925 George White's Scandals
1926 George White's Scandals
1927 Manhattan Mary * (*George White*)
1928 George White's Scandals
1929 George White's Scandals * (also lyr.) (Friend)
1930 Flying High (prod. dir. only)
1931 George White's Scandals
1932 George White's Music Hall Varieties
1933 Melody (prod., dir. only)
1935 George White's Scandals
1939 George White's Scandals

White, Onna, choreographer, dancer; b. Nova Scotia, Canada. Miss White first attracted notice for her choreography for *The Music Man;* her other successes: *Irma la Douce, Half a Sixpence, Billy.* She is married to singer Larry Douglas.

1947 Finian's Rainbow (dancer only)
       Finian's Rainbow (L) (asst. chor.)
1949 Regina (dancer only)
1950 Arms and the Girl (dancer only)
       Guys and Dolls (dancer only)
1953 Guys and Dolls (L) (asst. chor.)
1955 Silk Stockings (dancer only)
1956 Fanny (L)
1957 The Music Man
1958 Whoop-Up!
1959 Take Me Along
1960 Irma la Douce
1961 Let It Ride
1964 I Had a Ball
1965 Half a Sixpence
1966 Mame
1967 Illya Darling
1969 Mame (L)
       1776
1970 Gantry (also dir.)
       1776 (L)
1971 70, Girls, 70
1973 Gigi
1974 Billy (L)
1975 Goodtime Charley

Whiting, Jack, actor, singer, dancer; b. Philadelphia, Pa., June 22, 1901; d. New York, Feb. 15, 1961. Blondhaired, sharp-featured, eternally smiling Jack Whiting was the most perennial of all Bway juveniles. Among the songs he introduced: "All Alone Monday" (*The Ramblers*), "You're the

Cream in My Coffee" (*Hold Everything*), "A Ship Without a Sail" (*Heads Up!*), "I've Got Five Dollars" (*America's Sweetheart*), "Down with Love" (*Hooray for What!*), "All in Fun" (*Very Warm for May*), "Don't Let It Get You Down" (*Hold on to Your Hats*), "Ev'ry Street's a Boulevard in Old New York" (*Hazel Flagg*).

1922	Ziegfeld Follies
	Orange Blossoms (*Frank Curran*)
1923	Cinders (*Bruce*)
	Stepping Stones (*Captain Paul*)
1924	Annie Dear (*Alfred Weatherby*)
1925	When You Smile (*Larry Patton*)
1926	Rainbow Rose (*Tommy Lansing*)
	The Ramblers (*Billy Shannon*)
1927	Yes, Yes, Yvette (*Robert Bennett*)
1928	She's My Baby (*Bob Martin*)
	Hold Everything (*Sonny Jim Brooks*)
1929	Heads Up! (*Jack Mason*)
1931	America's Sweetheart (*Michael Perry*)
1932	Take a Chance (*Kenneth Raleigh*)
1934	Calling All Stars
1935	Anything Goes (L) (*Billy Crocker*)
1936	Rise and Shine (L) (*Jack Harding*)
1937	On Your Toes (L) (*Phil Dolan III*)
	Hooray for What! (*Breezy Cunningham*)
1939	Very Warm for May (*Johnny Graham*)
1940	Walk with Music (*Wing D'Hautville*)
	Hold on to Your Hats (*Pete*)
1942	Beat the Band (*Damon Dillingham*)
1946	The Red Mill (r) (*Con Kidder*, repl.)
1947	High Button Shoes (US tour) (*Henry Longstreet*)
1952	Of Thee I Sing (r) (*Chief Justice*)
1953	Hazel Flagg (*Mayor of New York*)
1954	The Golden Apple (*Hector Charybdis*)

"**Who?**" Music by Jerome Kern; lyric by Otto Harbach & Oscar Hammerstein II. Breezy love duet sung by Marilyn Miller and Paul Frawley in *Sunny* (NY 1925), and by Binnie Hale and Jack Buchanan in London version (1926).

"**Who Can I Turn To?**" Music & lyric by Leslie Bricusse & Anthony Newley. Lonely wail of downtrodden Anthony Newley at the end of Act I of *The Roar of the Greasepaint—The Smell of the Crowd* (NY 1965). Because of a popular recording the song was a hit before the show opened.

"**Who Cares?**" Music by George Gershwin; lyric by Ira Gershwin. William Gaxton and Lois Moran showed their indifference to everything but love in *Of Thee I Sing* (NY 1931). A previous song to use the "Yonkers-conquers" rhyme was Rodgers and Hart's "Manhattan."

"**Who Will Buy?**" Music & lyric by Lionel Bart. Refulgent celebration of a glorious day. Keith Hamshere led the celebrants in *Oliver!* (L 1960); Bruce Prochnik led them in the NY production (1963).

"**Whoever You Are.**" Music by Burt Bacharach; lyric by Hal David. Heroine Jill O'Hara in *Promises, Promises* (NY 1968) ardently reveals her confusion at the ambivalent behavior of the man she loves. Betty Buckley sang the ballad in the London company (1969).

Whoopee (1928). Music by Walter Donaldson; lyrics by Gus Kahn; book by William Anthony McGuire, based on play *The Nervous Wreck*, by Owen Davis.

SONGS: "I'm Bringing a Red Red Rose," "Makin' Whoopee," "Come West, Little Girl, Come West," "Love Me or Leave Me," "Until You Get Somebody Else."

NEW YORK: Dec. 4, 1928
NEW AMSTERDAM THEATRE; 407 p.

Presented by Florenz Ziegfeld; directed by William Anthony McGuire; choreographed by Seymour Felix & Tamara Geva; settings, Joseph Urban; costumes, John Harkrider; music director, Gus Salzer.

CAST: Eddie Cantor (*Henry Williams*), Ruth Etting (*Leslie Daw*), Ethel Shutta (*Mary Custer*), Paul Gregory (*Wanenis*), Tamara Geva (*Yolandi*), Frances Upton (*Sally Morgan*), Jack Rutherford (*Sheriff Bob Wells*), Mary Jane (*Harriet*), George Olsen Orchestra, Buddy Ebsen (dancer).

Eddie Cantor's most celebrated Bway vehicle was a lavish Ziegfeld production, set in a California ranch and in a Spanish mission, where hypochondriac Henry Williams has been sent for his health. To get away from unloved fiancé Sheriff Bob, Sally runs off with Henry to an Indian camp. They also discover that Wanenis, Sally's true love, is not the halfbreed everyone supposes. Apart from Cantor's comedy and the opulence of the production, one of the main attraction was the sight of five Indian Godivas on horseback. Recently married to Al Jolson, Ruby Keeler left the show before the NY opening to be with her husband, and was succeeded by Mary Jane. During Bway run, Paul Whiteman's Orchestra spelled Mr. Olsen's for two months in 1929.

FILM VERSION: Eddie Cantor and Ethel Shutta (Goldwyn 1930, Thornton Freeland dir.).

"Why?" Music by J. Fred Coots; lyric by Benny Davis & Arthur Swanstrom. A first cousin to "Who?," the song was introduced by Jack Donahue and Lily Damita in *Sons o' Guns* (NY 1929). In London company (1930), it was sung by Bobby Howes and Mireille Perrey.

"Why Can't I?" Music by Richard Rodgers; lyric by Lorenz Hart. Lament of the lonely ("Only my book in bed/ Knows how I look in bed") harmonized by Lillian Taiz and Inez Courtney in *Spring Is Here* (NY 1929).

"Why Can't You Behave?" Music & lyric by Cole Porter. Wistful plea of Lisa Kirk to her gambling boyfriend Harold Lang in *Kiss Me, Kate* (NY 1948). The London version (1951) found Julie Wilson pleading with Walter Long.

"Why Did I Choose You?" Music by Michael Leonard; lyric by Herbert E. Martin. Tender duet in *The Yearling* (NY 1965) in which the questions of a self-doubting wife (Dolores Wilson) are answered by her reassuring husband (David Wayne).

"Why Do I Love You?" Music by Jerome Kern; lyric by Oscar Hammerstein II. Blissful love duet in *Show Boat*, sung by Norma Terris and Howard Marsh, Edna May Oliver and Charles Winninger (NY 1927), and by Edith Day and Howett Worster, Viola Compton and Cedric Hardwicke (L 1928). Because Kern hated the word "cupid," Hammerstein, after he had completed the lyric, jokingly read him the following lines before handing over the real words:

Cupid knows the way
He's the naked boy
Who can make you sway
To love's own joy.
When he shoots his little arrow
He can thrill you to the marrow.

"Why Do the Wrong People Travel?" Music & lyric by Noël Coward. An ocean liner's social director privately expresses her disdain for the tourist trade. Elaine Stritch sang it in *Sail Away* (NY 1961, L 1962).

"**Why Shouldn't I?**" Music & lyric by Cole Porter. In *Jubilee* (NY 1935), the princess, played by Margaret Adams, contemplates falling in love.

"**Why Was I Born?**" Music by Jerome Kern; lyric by Oscar Hammerstein II. Helen Morgan's torchy admission of slavish devotion in *Sweet Adeline* (NY 1929).

"**Wild Rose.**" Music by Jerome Kern; lyric by Clifford Grey. Breathless self-description of a free spirit first sung by Marilyn Miller in *Sally* (NY 1920), then by Dorothy Dickson in London version (1921).

"**Wildflower.**" Music by Vincent Youmans; lyric by Otto Harbach & Oscar Hammerstein II. Romantic serenade in *Wildflower*, sung by Guy Robertson in NY (1923) and Howett Worster in London (1926).

"**Will He Like Me?**" Music by Jerry Bock; lyric by Sheldon Harnick. Consumed by self-doubts, Barbara Cook in *She Loves Me* (NY 1963) contemplates her first meeting with a letter-writing correspondent. Anne Rogers sang the ballad in the London version (1964).

"**Will You Remember?**" Music by Sigmund Romberg; lyric by Rida Johnson Young. Romantic duet from *Maytime* (NY 1917), sung by Peggy Wood and Charles Purcell. Because of the opening line in the refrain—"Sweetheart, sweetheart, sweetheart"—the song is often confused with another waltz, Victor Herbert's "Sweethearts."

Williams, (Egbert Austin) Bert, actor, singer, composer; b. Antigua, WI, Nov. 12, 1874; d. New York, March 4, 1922. Shuffling Bert Williams in his top hat, shabby dress suit, and oversized shoes was the first black entertainer to become a major Bway attraction. His ambling trademark song, which he sang in almost every stage appearance, was "Nobody" (music by Williams). He also sang "The Darktown Poker Club" in the *Ziegfeld Follies* (1917). Williams began his career in vaudeville with partner George W. Walker, with whom he appeared until 1909. Bib: *Nobody: The Story of Bert Williams* by Ann Charters (Macmillan, NY 1970).

1896	The Gold Bug
1903	In Dahomey (*Shylock Homestead*)
1906	Abyssinia (*Jasmine Jenkins*)
1908	Bandanna Land (*Skunkton Bowser*)
1909	Mr. Lode of Koal (*Chester A. Lode*)
1910	Follies of 1910
1911	Ziegfeld Follies
1912	Ziegfeld Follies
1914	Ziegfeld Follies
1915	Ziegfeld Follies
1916	Ziegfeld Follies
1917	Ziegfeld Follies
1919	Ziegfeld Follies
1920	Broadway Brevities

Williams, Frances (née Frances Jellinek), actress, singer; b. St. Paul, Minn., 1903; d. New York, Jan. 27, 1959. Slim, platinum-blonde singer who introduced "Fun to Be Fooled" in *Life Begins at 8:40* and "As Time Goes By" in *Everybody's Welcome*. She also appeared in nightclubs and vaudeville.

1920	Mary (chorus)
1924	Innocent Eyes
1925	Artists and Models
	The Cocoanuts (*Frances Williams*)
1926	George White's Scandals
1928	George White's Scandals
1929	George White's Scandals
1930	International Revue (repl.)
	The New Yorkers (*Mona Low*)

1931 Everybody's Welcome (*Polly Bascom*)
1934 Life Begins at 8:40
1940 Walk with Music (*Polly Van Zile*)
DuBarry Was a Lady (*May Daly*, repl.)
1941 Panama Hattie (*Hattie Maloney*, repl.)

"Willkommen." Music by John Kander; lyric by Fred Ebb. Opening number of *Cabaret* in which the oily, German-accented Master of Ceremonies welcomes one and all to Berlin's Kit Kat Klub. First sung on an empty stage, the song soon brings on an all-girl band and the bare-thighed, black stockinged chorus as the cabaret itself comes into view all around the performers. Joel Grey created the MC role in NY (1966), Barry Dennen played it in London (1968).

Willson, Meredith (né Robert Meredith Reiniger), composer, lyricist, librettist; b. Mason City, Iowa, May 18, 1902. Willson made a notable Bway debut with *The Music Man* ("Trouble," "76 Trombones," "Till There Was You"), following a career as music director. "I Ain't Down Yet" was sung in *The Unsinkable Molly Brown* and "It's Beginning to Look a Lot Like Christmas" in *Here's Love*.
1957 The Music Man (also lib.)
1960 The Unsinkable Molly Brown
1963 Here's Love (also lib.)

Wilson, John C., producer, director; b. Trenton, NJ, Aug. 19, 1899; d. New York, Oct. 29, 1961. Wilson was long associated with Noël Coward, presenting three of his musicals. As producer, his most successful Bway offering was *Bloomer Girl;* as director, his biggest hits were *Kiss Me, Kate* and *Gentlemen Prefer Blondes*.

One asterisk indicates Mr. Wilson was producer only; two indicate he was director only:

1936 Tonight at 8:30 * (L)
Tonight at 8:30 *
1938 Set to Music *
Operette * (L)
1943 A Connecticut Yankee ** (r)
1944 Bloomer Girl *
1945 The Day Before Spring (prod.-dir.)
1948 Kiss Me, Kate **
1949 Gentlemen Prefer Blondes **
1950 Bless You All **
1951 Make a Wish **
1955 Seventh Heaven **

Wilson, (Alexander Galbraith) Sandy, composer, lyricist, librettist; b. Sale, Eng., May 19, 1924. Wilson's greatest London hit was *The Boy Friend,* his spoof of 20s musicals, which included "I Could Be Happy with You" and "A Room in Bloomsbury." He also contributed songs for revues *Slings and Arrows, Oranges and Lemons, Pieces of Eight.*
1954 The Boy Friend
1955 The Buccaneer
1958 Valmouth
1964 Divorce Me, Darling!
1969 As Dorothy Parker Once Said (comp. only)
1971 His Monkey Wife

Wiman, Dwight Deere, producer; b. Moline, Ill., Aug. 8, 1895; d. Hudson, NY, Jan. 20, 1951. Wiman sponsored five Rodgers and Hart musicals, incl. *On Your Toes, Babes in Arms, I Married an Angel, By Jupiter.* Other Bway successes: *The Little Show, Gay Divorce.* He became a producer in 1925, initially in partnership with William A. Brady, Jr, and presented a total of 40 nonmusicals.
1929 The Little Show
1930 The Second Little Show
1931 The Third Little Show
1932 Gay Divorce
1933 Champagne, Sec
1936 On Your Toes
1937 Babes in Arms

1938 I Married an Angel
     Great Lady
1939 Stars in Your Eyes
1940 Higher and Higher
1942 By Jupiter
1947 Street Scene
1950 Dance Me a Song

"Wind in the Willows, The." Music by Vivian Ellis; lyric by Desmond Carter. Roy Royston, in *Cochran's 1930 Revue* (L 1930), hears the sighing wind and recalls a vanished love. The dance that followed, featuring Mr. Cochran's Young Ladies, was choreographed by George Balanchine.

Winninger, (Karl) Charles, actor; b. Athens, Wis., May 26, 1884; d. Palm Springs, Cal., Jan. 19, 1969. Winninger was a plump, blustery comic actor whose memorable Bway roles included *No, No, Nanette* (in which he sang "I Want to Be Happy") and *Show Boat* (in which he first shouted his trademark line, "HAPPP-ee New Year!"). His first wife was actress Blanche Ring. Winninger also appeared in many films.

1910 The Yankee Girl (*Rudolph Schnitzel*)
1912 The Wall Street Girl (*John Chester*)
1914 When Claudia Smiles (*Charles Hoffman*)
1916 The Cohan Revue
1918 The Cohan Revue
1919 The Passing Show
1920 Ziegfeld Follies
1921 The Broadway Whirl
1925 No, No, Nanette (*Jimmy Smith*)
1926 Oh, Please (*Nicodemus Bliss*)
1927 Yes, Yes, Yvette (*S. M. Ralston*)
     Show Boat (*Cap'n Andy Hawks*)
1932 Through the Years (*Owen*)
     Show Boat (r) (*Cap'n Andy Hawks*)
1934 Revenge with Music (*Don Emilio*)
1951 Music in the Air (r) (*Dr. Walther Lessing*)

"Wintergreen For President." Music by George Gershwin; lyric by Ira Gershwin. Blaring opening chorus of *Of Thee I Sing* (NY 1931) proclaiming the presidential candidacy of John P. Wintergreen. The song was also used in *Let 'Em Eat Cake* (NY 1932), the musical's sequel. Including the repeat of the title line, there are only 18 words in the entire lyric. The song is interrupted by musical references to "The Sidewalks of New York" ("East Side, West Side"), "Tammany," "Hail, Hail, the Gang's All Here," and "A Hot Time in the Old Town Tonight."

Wisdom, Norman, actor, singer; b. London, Feb. 4, 1920. Prankish variety comic who scored in London edition of *Where's Charley?* Wisdom has also appeared in British films and on tv.

1950 Sauce Piquante
1952 Paris to Piccadilly
1955 Painting the Town
1958 Where's Charley? (*Charley Wykeham*)
1966 Walking Happy (NY) (*Will Mossop*)

"Wish You Were Here." Music & lyric by Harold Rome. The hero's longing for the heroine, expressed by Jack Cassidy in *Wish You Were Here* (NY 1952). In London version (1953), it was sung by Bruce Trent.

"With a Little Bit of Luck." Music by Frederick Loewe; lyric by Alan Jay Lerner. Accompanied by Gordon Dilworth and Rod McLennan, Stanley Holloway in *My Fair Lady* (NY 1956) put his faith in a little bit of luck to help him skip work, give in to temptation, avoid marriage, snub a neighbor in need, and go philandering. In London version (1958), Holloway performed this hopping music-hall turn with Alan Dudley and Bob Chisholm.

"With a Song in My Heart." Music by Richard Rodgers; lyric by Lorenz Hart. Because Glenn Hunter, the star of *Spring Is Here* (NY 1929), was not a singer, the musical's love duet was given to the star's rival (John Hundley) to sing with the lady they both adore (Lillian Taiz). In London, it was sung by Eric Marshall, Gunda Mordhorst, Roy Royston, and Ada May in *Cochran's 1930 Revue.*

"Without a Song." Music by Vincent Youmans; lyric by Edward Eliscu & William (Billy) Rose. Emotional testament to the power of music sung in *Great Day!* (NY 1929) by baritone Lois Deppe and Russell Wooding's Jubilee Singers.

Wizard of Oz, The (1903). Music by Paul Tietjens & A. Baldwin Sloane; lyrics & book by L. Frank Baum, based on his book *The Wonderful Wizard of Oz.*

SONGS: "In Michigan" (Sloane-lyric, Glen MacDonough), "Niccolo's Piccolo" (Sloane-MacDonough), "Alas for a Man Without Brains" (Tietjens-Baum), "When You Love Love Love" (Tietjens-Baum), "Sammy" (Edward Hutchison-James O'Dea) (added), "Hurrah for Baffins Bay" (Theodore Morse–Vincent Bryan) (added).

NEW YORK: Jan. 21, 1903
MAJESTIC THEATRE; 293 p.

Presented by Fred R. Hamlin; directed by Julian Mitchell; settings, John Young; costumes, Mrs. Edward Siedle, W. W. Denslow; music director, Charles Zimmerman.

CAST: David C. Montgomery (*Tin Woodman*), Fred A. Stone (*Scarecrow*), Anna Laughlin (*Dorothy Gale*), Arthur Hill (*Cowardly Lion*), Bessie Wynn (*Sir Dashemoff Daily*), Grace Kimball (*Tryxie Tryfle*), Ida Doerge (*Tom Piper*), Joseph Schrode (*Imo-*

gene the Cow), Owen Westford (*Pastoria II*).

The first musical to play the Majestic Theatre on Columbus Circle, NY, *The Wizard of Oz* was a showpiece for the antics of Montgomery and Stone, making their Bway debuts. In the story, Dorothy and her pet cow, Imogene, both of Kansas, are blown by a cyclone to the Country of the Munchkins. There they meet the Tin Woodman, the Scarecrow, and the Cowardly Lion, and after many adventures eventually have an audience with the fearsome Wizard. The production was highly spectacular, with the cyclone scene shown through stereopticon effects and the rainstorm on a gauze screen. During run, Grace Kimball was succeeded by Lotta Faust, Ida Doerge by Anna Fitzhugh.

The success of *The Wizard of Oz* prompted producer Hamlin and director Mitchell to commission Victor Herbert and Glen MacDonough to write another children's fantasy, *Babes in Toyland.*

In 1975 an all-black version, called *The Wiz,* opened on Bway with a new book (by William F. Brown) and score (by Charlie Smalls). Directed by Geoffrey Holder, the cast included Stephanie Mills (*Dorothy*), Hinton Battle (*Scarecrow*), Tiger Haynes (*Tinman*), Ted Ross (*Lion*), DeeDee Bridgewater (*Glinda*), André De Shields (*Wiz*).

FILM VERSION: Judy Garland, Ray Bolger, Bert Lahr, Jack Haley, Frank Morgan (new score) (MGM 1938, Victor Fleming dir.).

Wodehouse, P(elham) G(renville), lyricist, librettist; b. Guildford, Eng., Oct. 15, 1881; d. Southampton, NY, Feb. 14, 1975. Knighted 1975. Though best known for his humorous novels, Wodehouse was one of Bway's major lyricists before the 20s and greatly influenced such writers as Ira Gershwin and Lorenz Hart. He achieved his first successes with the Princess Theatre musicals (*Oh, Boy!, Oh, Lady! Lady!!*) and also *Leave It to Jane*, written with co-librettists Guy Bolton and composer Jerome Kern. Other hits: *Kissing Time* and *The Cabaret Girl* (both London); *Oh, Kay! Rosalie, The Three Musketeers, Anything Goes* (all NY). His most popular songs: "Till the Clouds Roll By," "Leave It to Jane," "The Siren's Song," "Bill," "March of the Musketeers." Among Wodehouse's collaborators: Emmerich Kalman, Victor Herbert, Rudolf Friml, Ivan Caryll, Louis Hirsch, Armand Vecsey , Ivor Novello, Sigmund Romberg. Bib: *Bring on the Girls!* by Wodehouse and Bolton (S&S, NY 1953).

Unless otherwise noted, Mr. Wodehouse was co-librettist and lyricist of following; asterisk indicates libretto written with Mr. Bolton:

1916 Miss Springtime (lyr. only) (Kalman)
1917 Have a Heart * (Kern)
Oh, Boy! * (Kern)
Leave It to Jane * (Kern)
The Riviera Girl * (Kalman)
Miss 1917 * (Kern, Herbert)
Kitty Darlin' (lyr. only) (Friml)
1918 Oh, Lady! Lady!! * (Kern)
The Girl Behind the Gun * (Caryll)
The Canary (lyr. only) (Caryll)
Oh, My Dear! * (Hirsch)
1919 Kissing Time (L) (The Girl Behind the Gun) (Caryll)
The Rose of China * (Vecsey)
1921 The Golden Moth (L) (Novello)
1922 The Cabaret Girl (L) (Kern)
1923 The Beauty Prize (L) (Kern)
1924 Sitting Pretty * (Kern)
1926 Hearts and Diamonds (L) (co-lib. only)
Oh, Kay! * (co-lib. only)
1927 The Nightingale * (Vecsey)
1928 Rosalie (lyr. only) (Romberg)
1934 Anything Goes * (co-lib. only)

"Woman Is a Sometime Thing, A." Music by George Gershwin; lyric by Du Bose Heyward. Cynical appraisal of female unpredictability introduced in *Porgy and Bess* (NY 1935) by Edward Matthews. In London production (1952), it was sung by Joseph James.

"Wonderful Day Like Today, A." Music & lyric by Leslie Bricusse & Anthony Newley. Boundless optimism conveyed by Cyril Ritchard in *The Roar of the Greasepaint—The Smell of the Crowd* (NY 1965).

"Wonderful Guy, A." Music by Richard Rodgers; lyric by Oscar Hammerstein II. Mary Martin's exultant announcement at finding herself in love, sung in *South Pacific* both in NY (1949) and London (1951).

Wonderful Town (1953). Music by Leonard Bernstein; lyrics by Betty Comden & Adolph Green; book by Joseph Fields & Jerome Chodorov, based on their play, *My Sister Eileen*, adapted from stories by Ruth McKinney.

SONGS: "Christopher Street," "Ohio," "What a Waste," "A Quiet Girl," "A Little Bit in Love," "Conversation Piece," "Conga!," "Pass That Football," "Swing," "It's Love," "Wrong Note Rag."

NEW YORK: Feb. 25, 1952
WINTER GARDEN; 559 p.

Presented by Robert Fryer; directed by George Abbott; choreographed by Donald Saddler; settings & costumes, Raoul Pène du Bois; Miss Russell's costumes, Main Bocher; lighting, Peggy Clark; music director, Lehman Engel; orchestrations, Donald Walker.

CAST: Rosalind Russell (*Ruth Sherwood*), George Gaynes (*Robert Baker*), Edith Adams (*Eileen Sher-*

wood), Henry Lascoe (Appopolous), Dort Clark (Chick Clark), Jordan Bentley (Wreck), Cris Alexander (Frank Lippencott), Ted Beniades (Speedy Valente), Nathaniel Frey (Chef), Dody Goodman (Violet), Joe Layton (dancer).

LONDON: Feb. 23, 1955
PRINCE'S THEATRE; 207 p.

Presented by Jack Hylton; directed by Richard Bird; dances reproduced by Edmund Balin; settings & costumes, Raoul Pène du Bois; music director, Cyril Ornadel.

CAST: Pat Kirkwood (Ruth Sherwood), Dennis Bowen (Robert Baker), Shani Wallis (Eileen Sherwood), David Hurst (Appopolous), Christopher Taylor (Frank Lippencott), Colin Croft (Chick Clark), Sidney James (Wreck), Stanley Robinson (Speedy Valente).

The Greenwich Village adventures of writer Ruth McKinney, which she turned into short stories that were then adapted as a Bway play, provided the plot for Rosalind Russell's only starring appearance in a musical. Set in the 30s, the story was concerned with the problems faced by the Sherwood sisters from Ohio, primarily Ruth's attempt to launch a literary career and Eileen's difficulties in warding off admirers. After some overamorous Brazilian naval officers cause a near-riot, Ruth ends up in jail but also with the man she loves. Initially the musical's score was to have been written by composer Leroy Anderson and lyricist Arnold Horwitt, but, because of differences with the librettists, they left five weeks before rehearsals. Comden and Green agreed to take over the assignment but only on the condition that their On the Town collaborator, Leonard Bernstein, supply the music. During Bway run, Miss Russell was succeeded by

Carol Channing, who also toured in the show. In London, though the locale remained the same, almost the entire cast was English.

"Won't You Charleston With Me?" Music & lyric by Sandy Wilson. Larry Drew and Denise Hirst quickly accepted each other's invitation in The Boy Friend (L 1954). In NY company (1954), the high-steppers were Bob Scheerer and Ann Wakefield.

Wood, (Margaret) Peggy, actress, singer; b. Brooklyn, NY, Feb. 9, 1892. Miss Wood's most memorable operetta roles were in Maytime (in which she sang "Will You Remember?" and "The Road to Paradise") and Bitter Sweet ("I'll See You Again" and "Zigeuner"). She also appeared in many dramatic roles on Bway, including Candida. Bib: How Young You Look by Miss Wood (Farrar, NY 1943).

1910 Naughty Marietta (chorus)
1911 The Three Romeos (Vera Steinway)
1912 Over the River (Sarah Parke, repl.)
     The Lady of the Slipper (Valerie)
1913 Mlle. Modiste (r) (Franchette)
     The Madcap Duchess (Gillette)
1914 The Madcap Duchess (US tour) (Adele)
     Hello, Broadway!
1917 Love o' Mike (Peggy)
     Maytime (Ottilie Van Zandt)
1919 Buddies (Julie)
1922 Marjolaine (Marjolaine Leschesnais)
     The Clinging Vine (Antoinette Allen)
1929 Bitter Sweet (L) (Sarah Millick)
1932 The Cat and the Fiddle (L) (Shirley Sheridan)
1933 Champagne, Sec (Rosalinde)
1938 Operette (L) (Rozanne Gray)

Woolley, (Edgar Montillion) Monty, director, actor; b. New York, Aug. 17,

1888; d. Saratoga Springs, NY, May 6, 1963. Before becoming the waspish Man Who Came to Dinner, bearded Monty Woolley had been a Yale Univ. drama professor, Bway director and actor in one musical.

Unless otherwise noted, Mr. Woolley was director of following:

1929 Fifty Million Frenchmen
1930 The New Yorkers
     The Second Little Show
1933 Champagne, Sec
1935 Jubilee
1936 On Your Toes (*Sergei Alexandrovitch* only)

"World Is Your Balloon, The." Music by Sammy Fain; lyric by E. Y. Harburg. That's what happens when you're in love. The sprightly piece was sung in *Flahooley* (NY 1951) by Barbara Cook, Jerome Courtland, and singing puppets.

"World Weary." Music & lyric by Noël Coward. In which the bustling life of the big city made Beatrice Lillie—in *This Year of Grace!* (NY 1928)—yearn "to get right back to nature and relax." In the scene, Miss Lillie was dressed as an office boy and sang the song while sitting on a high stool munching an apple.

"Would You Like to Take a Walk?" Music by Harry Warren; lyric by Mort Dixon & Billy Rose. Perambulatory invitation mutually proffered by Hannah Williams and Hal Thompson in revue *Sweet and Low* (NY 1930), then by Ethel Norris and Tom Monroe in *Crazy Quilt* (NY 1931).

"Wouldn't It Be Loverly?" Music by Frederick Loewe; lyric by Alan Jay Lerner. In *My Fair Lady* (NY 1956; L 1958), flower seller Julie Andrews dreams of a warm, comfortable room where she could spend the time "sittin' absobloominlutely still."

Wright, Robert, lyricist, composer; b. Daytona Beach, Fla., Sept. 25, 1914. Wright has worked exclusively with George Forrest, primarily in the field of adapting classics into Bway scores. They also combined the scores of Victor Herbert's *The Fortune Teller* and *The Serenade* to create *Gypsy Lady*. The team's biggest hits: *Song of Norway* ("Strange Music," "I Love You"), *Kismet* ("Baubles, Bangles and Beads," "And This Is My Beloved," "Stranger in Paradise").

1944 Song of Norway (Grieg)
1946 Gypsy Lady (Herbert)
1948 Magdalena (Villa-Lobos)
1953 Kismet (Borodin)
1959 The Love Doctor (L) (also co-lib.)
1961 Kean
1965 Anya (Rachmaninoff)
1970 The Great Waltz (L) (r) (Strauss)

"Wunderbar." Music & lyric by Cole Porter. A take-off on the exaggerated sentiments of Viennese waltzes, the piece was first sung by Alfred Drake and Patricia Morison in *Kiss Me, Kate* (NY 1948), as they reminisce about their first appearance together in an operetta called *Wunderbar*. Bill Johnson and Miss Morison did the reminiscing in London version (1951). The song's satirical approach is revealed in the first line of the verse—"Gazing down on the Jungfrau"—since the Jungfrau is the highest peak in Europe.

Wynn, Ed (né Edwin Leopold), actor; b. Philadelphia, Pa., Nov. 9, 1886; d. Beverly Hills, Cal., June 19, 1966. With his lisp, giggle, fluttering hands, zany inventions, outlandish costumes, and outrageous puns, Wynn was—as he billed himself—"The Perfect Fool." After a career in vaudeville

(1901–1914), he won Bway stardom in *Sometime*, then scored his two greatest hits in *The Perfect Fool* and *The Laugh Parade*. Wynn was on radio in the 30s and appeared in films. He was the father of actor Keenan Wynn.

Asterisk indicates Mr. Wynn was also sketch writer, director, producer:

1910 The Deacon and the Lady (*Jupiter Slick*)
1914 Ziegfeld Follies
1915 Ziegfeld Follies
1916 The Passing Show
1917 Doing Our Bit
Over the Top (repl.)
1918 Sometime (*Loney Bright*)
1920 Ed Wynn Carnival * (also comp., lyr.)
1921 The Perfect Fool * (also comp., lyr.)
1924 The Grab Bab * (also comp., lyr.)
1927 Manhattan Mary (*Crickets*)
1930 Simple Simon (*Simon*) (also co-lib.)
1931 The Laugh Parade *
1937 Hooray for What! (*Chuckles*)
1940 Boys and Girls Together *
1942 Laugh, Town, Laugh *

"Yama Yama Man, The." Music by Karl Hoschna; lyric by Collin Davis. Bessie McCoy interpolated the comic spooky number in *Three Twins* (NY 1908) wearing a satin clown costume and a cone-shaped hat. From then on, she became known as the "Yama Yama Girl."

"Yankee Doodle Boy, The." Music & lyric by George M. Cohan. Jaunty patriotic air, later retitled "Yankee Doodle Dandy," which was Cohan's entrance number in *Little Johnny Jones* (NY 1904). The song was also the actor's autobiographical trademark, since he was not only a self-proclaimed real-live nephew of his Uncle Sam, he was also born on the Fourth of July. In Bway musical *George M!* (1968), the number was sung by Joel Grey.

"Yesterdays." Music by Jerome Kern; lyric by Otto Harbach. Tender memories recalled by Fay Templeton in *Roberta* (NY 1933).

"Yesterday's World." Music by David Lee; lyric by Herbert Kretzmer. On an island after a shipwreck in *Our Man Crichton* (L 1964), a titled English lady (Patricia Lambert) longs for the order and grace of a world gone by.

"Yip-I-Addy-I-Ay!" Music by John H. Flynn; lyric by Will Cobb. Blanche Ring introduced the rollicking novelty number in *The Merry Widow Burlesque* (NY 1908) after she had taken over the leading role. In London musical *Our Miss Gibbs* (1909), George Grossmith, who revised the lyric, sang of "Herman Von Bellow, a musical fellow, who played a big 'cello each night," and so won the heart of "sweet Sally Frampton, who lives down at Hampton." It was Grossmith's biggest song hit.

"You and the Night and the Music." Music by Arthur Schwartz; lyric by Howard Dietz. Georges Metaxa and Libby Holman's smoldering duet in *Revenge with Music* (NY 1934) was also introduced to London in revue *Stop Press* (1935) by Eve Beck and Gordon Little. Originally the same melody, but in waltz time, had a lyric by Desmond Carter and was called

"To-night." It was sung by Anna Neagle in the film *The Queen's Affair* (1934).

"You Are Beautiful." Music by Richard Rodgers; lyric by Oscar Hammerstein II. Ardent ballad sung by Ed Kenney in *Flower Drum Song* (NY 1958) and by Kevin Scott in London version (1960). As presented in the musical, the song is supposedly a Chinese poem—about exchanging glances with a girl on a flower boat along the Hwang Ho Valley—which the young man has memorized to sing to his sweetheart.

"You Are Love." Music by Jerome Kern; lyric by Oscar Hammerstein II. Soaring love duet in *Show Boat* sung by Norma Terris and Howard Marsh in NY (1927) and Edith Day and Howett Worster in London (1928).

"You Are My Heart's Delight." Music by Franz Lehar; lyric by Harry Graham. Though it later became Richard Tauber's most celebrated aria, this piece was originally sung in 1923 in the Viennese operetta *Die Gelbe Jacke*, but in fragments. As *"Dein Ist Mein Ganzes Herz,"* with a Ludwig Herzer and Fritz Löhner lyric, Tauber first sang it in a revised version of the operetta, *Das Land des Lächelns*, when it was successfully performed in Berlin in 1929. Two years later, the tenor starred in London in an English-language version called *The Land of Smiles*, and the aria became "You Are My Heart's Delight." In 1946 a second English-language adaptation, known as *Yours Is My Heart*, was presented on Bway with Tauber again in the lead. It was in this production that he sang the same song retitled "Yours Is My Heart Alone," with a lyric by Harry B. Smith.

"You Are Never Away." Music by Richard Rodgers; lyric by Oscar Hammerstein II. Romantic reassurance ardently expressed by John Battles to Roberta Jonay in *Allegro* (NY 1947).

"You Can Have Him." Music & lyric by Irving Berlin. Mary McCarty and Allyn McLerie shared this song of renunciation in *Miss Liberty* (NY 1949).

"You Can't Get a Man With a Gun." Music and lyric by Irving Berlin. Practical advice offered by Ethel Merman in *Annie Get Your Gun* (NY 1946). In London production (1947), it was sung by Dolores Gray.

"You Do Something to Me." Music & lyric by Cole Porter. Love's hypnotic power (*"Do* do that *voo*doo that *you* do so well"*) revealed by William Gaxton and Genevieve Tobin in *Fifty Million Frenchmen* (NY 1929).

"You Have Cast Your Shadow on the Sea." Music by Richard Rodgers; lyric by Lorenz Hart. Shimmering ballad of farewell sung by Marcy Westcott and Eddie Albert in *The Boys from Syracuse* (NY 1938), and by Paula Hendrix and Bob Monkhouse in London version (1963).

"You Naughty, Naughty Men." Music by G. Bicknell; lyric by T. Kennick. The most popular number in *The Black Crook* (NY 1866), sung by Milly Cavendish. The lyric sees through masculine deception and accuses men of, among other things, marrying for money and constantly flirting.

"You Never Knew About Me." Music by Jerome Kern; lyric by P. G. Wodehouse. Young lovers coyly imagine the fun they could have had—such as making mud pies and feeding rabbits—had they known each other when they were children. In *Oh, Boy!* (NY 1917), the singers were Tom Powers and Marie Carroll; in *Oh, Joy!* (L 1919), Powers and Dot Temple.

"You Took Advantage of Me." Music by Richard Rodgers; lyric by Lorenz Hart. A far-from-regretful accusation, first made by Joyce Barbour and Busby Berkeley in *Present Arms* (NY 1928). It was later interpolated by Elaine Stritch in the 1954 Bway revival of *On Your Toes*.

"You Were Meant For Me." Music by Eubie Blake; lyric by Noble Sissle. Romantic inevitability expressed in *London Calling!* (L 1923) by Gertrude Lawrence and Noël Coward, who then performed a dance devised by Fred Astaire. This was the only song in the revue written by Americans. In NY, the piece was offered by Miss Lawrence and Jack Buchanan in *André Charlot's Revue of 1924*.

"You Were There." Music & lyric by Noël Coward. A memory of "that first enchanted meeting." Introduced by Noël Coward and Gertrude Lawrence in *Shadow Play*, one-act musical included in collection *Tonight at 8:30* (L 1936, NY 1936).

"You'd Be Surprised." Music & lyric by Irving Berlin. A girl's teasing invitation to a little necking as related by Eddie Cantor in the Bway revue *Ziegfeld Follies*, 1919. In London musical *Afgar* (1919) it was sung by Alice Delysia.

"You'd Better Love Me." Music & lyric by Hugh Martin & Timothy Gray. In *High Spirits*, the ghost of a gentleman's first wife, finding that she and her former husband are still in love, urges him to take advantage of her temporary reappearance. The blithe spirit in NY (1964) was Tammy Grimes; in London (1964) it was Marti Stevens.

"You'll Never Get Away from Me." Music by Jule Styne; lyric by Stephen Sondheim. Lilting expression of romantic tenacity sung by Ethel Merman to Jack Klugman in *Gypsy* (NY 1959). In London version (1973), Angela Lansbury sang it to Barrie Ingham. The melody dates back to 1954, when it was called "Why Did I Have to Wait So Long?" (lyric by Sammy Cahn) and intended for an unproduced film. In 1957, with a lyric by Leo Robin, it was known as "I'm in Pursuit of Happiness" when sung in the tv musical *Ruggles of Red Gap*.

"You'll Never Walk Alone." Music by Richard Rodgers; lyric by Oscar Hammerstein II. Inspirational song introduced by Christine Johnson in *Carousel* (NY 1945) to give courage to heroine Jan Clayton after the death of her husband. In the final scene of the musical, it is reprised by the company at the high school graduation. Marion Ross sang it in London production (1950).

Youmans, Vincent (Millie), composer; b. New York, Sept. 27, 1898; d. Denver, Col., April 5, 1946. Along with George Gershwin (who was born the day before), Youmans was one of the two major composers to emerge early in the 20s who dominated the entire decade on Bway. Though he was less prolific than most contemporaries, three of his musicals (*Wildflower, No, No, Nanette, Hit the Deck*) were among the biggest hits of the period. Youmans' best-known songs were "Bambalina," "No, No, Nanette," "I Want to Be Happy," "Tea for Two,"

"I Know That You Know," "Sometimes I'm Happy," "Hallelujah," "Great Day," "More than You Know," "Without a Song," "Time on My Hands," "Through the Years," "Drums in My Heart," and "Rise 'n Shine." His lyricists included Ira Gershwin, Otto Harbach, Oscar Hammerstein II, William Cary Duncan, Zelda Sears, Irving Caesar, Anne Caldwell, Clifford Grey, Leo Robin, Edward Eliscu, Billy Rose, Harold Adamson, Ring Lardner, and Edward Heyman.

1921 Two Little Girls in Blue (Gershwin)
1923 Wildflower (Harbach, Hammerstein
       Mary Jane McKane (Duncan, Hammerstein)
1924 Lollipop (Sears)
1925 No, No, Nanette (Caesar, Harbach)
1926 Oh, Please (Caldwell)
1927 Hit the Deck (Grey, Robin) (also co-prod.)
1928 Rainbow (Hammerstein)
1929 Great Day! (Eliscu, Rose) (also prod.)
1930 Smiles (Adamson, Grey, Lardner)
1932 Through the Years (Heyman) (also prod.)
       Take a Chance (DeSylva)

"Young and Foolish." Music by Albert Hague; lyric by Arnold Horwitt. Ballad of remembrance, sung by David Daniels to Gloria Marlowe in *Plain and Fancy* (NY 1955), then reprised as duet. Jack Drummond and Grace O'Connor recalled their youth in London version (1956).

"Young Man's Fancy, A." Music by Milton Ager; lyric by Jack Yellen & John Murray Anderson. Tripping revelation of spring's effect on man's romantic inclination introduced by Rosalind Fuller in *What's in a Name?* (NY 1920). In London revue, *League of Notions* (1921), it was sung by Josephine Trix.

Young, Rida Johnson, lyricist, librettist; b. Baltimore, Md., Feb. 28, 1869; d. Stamford, Conn., May 8, 1926. Mrs. Young scored her biggest Bway hits with *Naughty Marietta* ("Ah! Sweet Mystery of Life," " 'Neath the Southern Moon," "I'm Falling in Love with Someone," "Tramp! Tramp! Tramp!," "Italian Street Song") and *Maytime* ("Will You Remember?," "The Road to Paradise"). Before her writing career, she was an actress with E. H. Sothern's company, then with the Viola Allen Co. Among her collaborators: Victor Herbert, William Schroeder, Sigmund Romberg, Rudolf Friml, Augustus Barratt.

1910 Naughty Marietta (Herbert)
1912 The Red Petticoat (lib. only)
1914 Lady Luxury (Schroeder)
1916 Her Soldier Boy (Romberg)
1917 His Little Widows (Schroeder)
       Maytime (Romberg)
1918 Sometime (Friml)
       Little Simplicity (Barratt)
1924 The Dream Girl (Herbert)

"Younger Than Springtime." Music by Richard Rodgers; lyric by Oscar Hammerstein II. Surging expression of innocent young love sung by William Tabbert to Betta St. John in *South Pacific* (NY 1949), and by Peter Grant to Miss St. John in London version (1951). The melody had been written some years before Rodgers began composing the score for the musical. Though he soon forgot about it, his daughter, Mary, remembered it and suggested it be used for the scene between Lt. Joe Cable and Liat.

"Your Land and My Land." Music by Sigmund Romberg; lyric by Dorothy Donnelly. Stirring affirmation of a post-Civil War united America sung in *My Maryland* (NY 1927) by Nathaniel Wagner and chorus.

"You're a Builder-Upper." Music by Harold Arlen; lyric by Ira Gershwin & E. Y. Harburg. Inconsistency of behavior turns out to be no bar to romance. Sung and tapped by Ray Bolger and Dixie Dunbar in *Life Begins at 8:40* (NY 1934).

You're a Good Man, Charlie Brown (1967). Music & lyrics by Clark Gesner; book by John Gordon (Clark Gesner), based on comic strip *Peanuts*, by Charles Schulz.
SONGS: "You're a Good Man, Charlie Brown," "My Blanket and Me," "Book Report," "T.E.A.M.," "Suppertime," "Happiness."

NEW YORK: March 7, 1967
THEATRE 80 ST. MARKS; 1,597 p.
Presented by Arthur Whitelaw & Gene Persson; directed by Joseph Hardy; musical staging by Patricia Birch; settings & costumes, Alan Kimmel; lighting, Jules Fisher; music director, Joseph Raposo; orchestrations, Raposo.
CAST: Gary Burghoff (*Charlie Brown*), Reva Rose (*Lucy*), Bill Hinnant (*Snoopy*), Bob Balaban (*Linus*), Skip Hinnant (*Schroeder*), Karen Johnson (*Patty*).

LONDON: Feb. 1, 1968
FORTUNE THEATRE; 116 p.
Presented by Bernard Delfont & Harold Fielding, with Louis I. Michaels; directed by Joseph Hardy; musical staging by Patricia Birch; settings & costumes, Alan Kimmel; music director, Peter Martin.
CAST: David-Rhys Anderson (*Charlie Brown*), Boni Enten (*Lucy*), Don Potter (*Snoopy*), Gene Kidwell (*Linus*), Gene Scandur (*Schroeder*), Courtney Lane (*Patty*).
Off-Bway's fourth longest-running

musical began as a record project, with the album released before the stage adaptation had even begun. The musical dealt, in revue fashion, with events that take place in an "average day in the life of Charlie Brown"— i.e., flying a kite, writing a book report, playing baseball. Among other comic-strip characters depicted were the piano-playing Schroeder, the bossy Lucy, the blanket-loving Linus, and the goggled canine Snoopy, who imagines he's the Red Baron. During run, Gary Burghoff was succeeded by Sean Simpson (3-68), Bob Lydiard (8-68), and Alfred Mazza (2-69); Reva Rose by Boni Enten (6-68) and Ann Gibbs (12-69); Bill Hinnant by Don Potter (12-69). From 1967 to 1971, six road companies toured the US.

Previous musicals based on American comic strips: *Buster Brown* (1905), *Little Nemo* (1908), *Bringing Up Father* (1925), *Li'l Abner* (1956).

"You're a Grand Old Flag." Music & lyric by George M. Cohan. Cohan performed this strutting salute to the stars and stripes in *George Washington, Jr.* (NY 1906). The song emanated from a meeting the actor-composer had with a Civil War veteran who told Cohan that he had fought to save his tattered flag, which he called "a grand old rag." Cohan, suitably inspired, wrote a song using that phrase and called it "You're a Grand Old Rag." He then wrote the musical comedy to go with it. Because of protests in the press, however, Cohan was forced to alter the word "rag" to "flag," thereby diluting the original sentiment.

"You're an Old Smoothie." Music by Richard A. Whiting & Nacio Herb Brown; lyric by B. G. DeSylva. Lighthearted, affectionate duet introduced by Ethel Merman and Jack Haley in *Take a Chance* (NY 1932). In London musical, *Nice Goings On* (1933), it was sung by Leslie Henson and Zelma O'Neal.

"You're Blasé." Music by Ord Hamilton; lyric by Bruce Sievier. An oh-so-sophisticated love song introduced by Binnie Hale in *Bow Bells* (L 1932).

"You're Devastating." Music by Jerome Kern; lyric by Otto Harbach. Excessively idolatrous aria ("You were destined for purple-hued throne rooms") introduced by Bob Hope in *Roberta* (NY 1933). In the 1928 London musical *Blue Eyes*, the same melody had been used for a song called "Do I Do Wrong?" (lyric by Graham John), which was sung by Evelyn Laye and Geoffrey Gwyther.

"You're Here and I'm Here." Music by Jerome Kern; lyric by Harry B. Smith. According to Smith, this syncopated duet of cozy contentment was composed during the Rochester tryout of *The Laughing Husband* (NY 1914) because the producer thought the show needed a catchy tune. It was sung and danced by Venita Fitzhugh and Nigel Barrie. Though sheet music also credits it with having been sung by Donald Brian in *The Marriage Market* (NY 1913), no NY programs list the song and it was probably added during tour. The number, which is musically similar to Kern's "Same Sort of Girl," was performed in London (1914) by Elsie Janis and Basil Hallam in *The Passing Show*.

"You're Just in Love." Music & lyric by Irving Berlin. Contrapuntal duet in which Ethel Merman offered down-to-earth advice to moonstruck Russell Nype in *Call Me Madam* (NY 1950). Billie Worth and Jeff Warren sang it in London production (1952). According to George Abbott, the director of the show, "During the tryout of *Call Me Madam* we discovered that we needed a new song to fill a certain spot in Act II. I had been very much taken with one old song of Berlin's called 'Play a Simple Melody,' which was done in counterpoint and which had a revival of popularity at this time. When I urged him to contrive something along those lines for this spot, Irving went back to the hotel and disappeared for the day." Two days later he produced "You're Just in Love."

"You're Lonely and I'm Lonely." Music & lyric by Irving Berlin. Two lonely hearts—Vera Zorina and Victor Moore—take mutual comfort in *Louisiana Purchase* (NY 1940).

"You're My Everything." Music by Harry Warren; lyric by Mort Dixon & Joe Young. Pledge of total devotion sung by Jeanne Aubert and Lawrence Grey in revue *The Laugh Parade* (NY 1931).

"You're My Girl." Music by Jule Styne; lyric by Sammy Cahn. Duet of romantic possessiveness introduced by Mark Dawson and Lois Lee in *High Button Shoes* (NY 1947), and repeated by Jack Cooper and Hermene French in London production (1948).

"You're the Cream in My Coffee." Music by Ray Henderson; lyric by B. G. DeSylva & Lew Brown. A compilatory love duet in which the object of affection is likened to those necessities that add savor and flavor to life. It was sung in *Hold Everything* by Ona Munson and Jack Whiting (NY 1928) and by Mamie Watson and Owen Nares (L 1929).

"You're the Top." Music & lyric by Cole Porter. The classic "laundry-list" song, itemized by Ethel Merman and William Gaxton singing each other's praises in *Anything Goes* (NY 1934). In the number, virtues are likened to such rhymed superlatives as Colosseum and Louvre Museum, Mahatma Gandhi and Napoleon Brandy, Arrow collar and Coolidge dollar, Fred Astaire and Camembert, *Inferno's* Dante and Great Durante. For London version (1935), in which duet was sung by Jack Whiting and Jeanne Aubert, P. G. Wodehouse substituted local references incl. Ascot bonnet, young Novello and Cochran chorus. This sort of number was a Porter trademark and the composer repeated the format in "A Picture of Me Without You" (*Jubilee*, NY 1935), "From Alpha to Omega" (*You Never Know*, NY 1938), and "Cherry Pies Ought to Be You" (*Out of This World*, NY 1950).

"Yours Is My Heart Alone." See "You Are My Heart's Delight."

"You've Got Possibilities." Music by Charles Strouse; lyric by Lee Adams. A love song of encouragement to a shy inamorato, first sung by Linda Lavin to Bob Holiday (as mild-mannered Clark Kent) in *It's a Bird It's a Plane It's Superman* (NY 1966).

"You've Got That Thing." Music & lyric by Cole Porter. Jack Thompson and Betty Compton traded romantic compliments in *Fifty Million Frenchmen* (NY 1929).

"You've Got to Be Carefully Taught." Music by Richard Rodgers; lyric by Oscar Hammerstein II. The young US naval lieutenant in *South Pacific*, who has fallen in love with a Polynesian girl, realizes that prejudice is learned, not inherited. Sung by William Tabbert in NY (1949), Peter Grant in London (1951).

Z

Ziegfeld, Florenz (Jr.), producer; b. Chicago, Ill., March 15, 1867; d. New York, July 22, 1932. Ziegfeld was the most celebrated producer in Bway history. His opulent series of *Follies* ("Glorifying the American Girl") established his reputation, which was further enhanced by such productions as *Sally, Rio Rita, Show Boat, Rosalie, The Three Musketeers*, and *Whoopee*. Bert Williams was in eight *Follies;* Fanny Brice, W. C. Fields, and Ann Pennington were in seven; Lillian Lorraine, Leon Errol, Will Rogers, Eddie Cantor, and Ray Dooley were in five; Nora Bayes was in three; Marilyn Miller was in two (plus three book musicals). Ziegfeld was first mar-

ried to actress Anna Held (she was in seven Ziegfeld productions), whom he divorced to marry actress Billie Burke. Bib: *Ziegfeld, the Great Glorifier* by Eddie Cantor & David Freedman (King, NY 1934); *The Ziegfelds' Girl* by Patricia Ziegfeld (Little, Brown, Boston 1964); *Ziegfeld* by Charles Higham (Regnery, Chi. 1972); *The World of Flo Ziegfeld* by Randolph Carter (Elek, L 1974).

1896	A Parlor Match (r)
1899	Papa's Wife
1901	The Little Duchess
1903	The Red Feather
	Mam'selle Napoleon
1904	Higgledy Piggledy
1906	The Parisian Model
1907	Follies of 1907

1908	The Soul Kiss
	Follies of 1908
	Miss Innocence
1909	Follies of 1909
1910	Follies of 1910
1911	Ziegfeld Follies
1912	Over the River
	A Winsome Widow
	Ziegfeld Follies
1913	Ziegfeld Follies
1914	Ziegfeld Follies
1915	Ziegfeld Follies
1916	Ziegfeld Follies
	The Century Girl
1917	Ziegfeld Follies
	Miss 1917
1918	Ziegfeld Follies
1919	Ziegfeld Follies
1920	Ziegfeld Follies
	Sally
1921	Ziegfeld Follies
1922	Ziegfeld Follies
1923	Ziegfeld Follies
	Kid Boots
1924	Ziegfeld Follies
	Annie Dear
1925	Louie the 14th
	Ziegfeld Follies
1926	No Foolin'
	Betsy
1927	Rio Rita
	Show Boat
	Ziegfeld Follies
1928	Rosalie
	The Three Musketeers
	Whoopee
1929	Show Girl
	Bitter Sweet
1930	Simple Simon
	Smiles
1931	Ziegfeld Follies
1932	Show Boat (r)
	Hot-Cha!

Ziegfeld Follies (1919). Music by Dave Stamper, Harry Tierney, Irving Berlin, Victor Herbert, Albert Von Tilzer; lyrics by Berlin, Gene Buck, Joseph McCarthy, Lew Brown; sketches by Rennold Wolf, Buck, George Lemaire, Eddie Cantor.

SONGS: "My Baby's Arms" (Tierney-McCarthy), "Tulip Time" (Stamper-Buck), "Mandy" (Berlin), "A Pretty Girl Is Like a Melody" (Berlin), "You Cannot Make Your Shimmy Shake on Tea" (Berlin-Wolf), "You'd Be Surprised" (Berlin).

NEW YORK: June 16, 1919
NEW AMSTERDAM THEATRE; 171 p.

Presented by Florenz Ziegfeld Jr.; directed & choreographed by Ned Wayburn; settings, Joseph Urban; costumes, Lady Duff Gordon, Ben Ali Haggin; music director, Frank Darling.

CAST: Eddie Dowling, Eddie Cantor, Mary Hay, Marilyn Miller, Ray Dooley, Johnny Dooley, Bert Williams, Delyle Alda, Fairbanks Twins, Gus Van & Joe Schenck, George Lemaire, John Steel, Hazel Washburn, Addison Young.

The *Ziegfeld Follies* of 1919—the 13th annual edition—was resplendent in song, stars, and visual display. In "A Pretty Girl Is Like a Melody," it even gave a theme to the entire series. Its production numbers featured showgirls representing salads and classical music, and there were Ben Ali Haggin tableaux depicting "The 13th Folly" and mediaeval "Melody, Fantasy and Folly." The first act ended with a minstrel show in which Eddie Cantor was Tambo, Bert Williams was Bones, and Marilyn Miller was interlocutor George Primrose. The grand finale was a salute to the Salvation Army. The main topical number, Irving Berlin's "Prohibition," found the stage full of Mourners, Liquor Lovers, Bartenders, Chorus Girls, and Veterans in a scene depicting "A Saloon of the Future," with girls parading as Coca-Cola, Sarsaparilla, Grape Juice, Lemonade, Bevo, and Lady Alcohol.

The idea for a variety-style musical production first occurred to Ziegfeld in Paris in 1906 when his wife, Anna Held, suggested he adopt the then popular French cabaret revue-style show in NY. Producers Klaw and Erlanger hired Ziegfeld to stage one on the roof of the New York Theatre, which was renamed the Jardin de Paris. The first production opened July 8, 1907. Sketch writer Harry B. Smith, who had once written a newspaper column called "Follies of the Day," suggested the title *Follies of the Year*. Ziegfeld, however, insisted on 13 letters in the title and it became *Follies of 1907*, subtitled "The Ziegfeld Musical Revue." The first cast included Grace La Rue, Emma Carus, Mlle. Dazie, Tempest and Sunshine, George Bickel, Harry Watson, Nora Bayes (added during run), with the chorus known as the Anna Held Girls. The show underwent weekly changes in cast and material and continued for 70 performances. Its success on the road encouraged Ziegfeld to present a second edition the following year.

Between 1907 and 1910, the revue was presented annually as the *Follies of . . .* , with the proper year added to the name; from 1911 on, it was known as *Ziegfeld Follies*, except for 1926. That year, because of a legal fight with producer Erlanger, Ziegfeld was forbidden to use the title and he called the revue *No Foolin'*, then changed it to *Ziegfeld American Revue of 1926*, but it reverted to *Ziegfeld Follies* for the road tour. The phrase "A National Institution" was first used in 1920; two years later it was expanded to "A National Institution Glorifying the American Girl." The number of editions of the *Follies* is difficult to determine because the one in 1922 had a "Summer Edition" the following June, and the one in 1924 had "Fall," "Spring," and "Summer" editions. Including *No Foolin'*, there were at least 21 separate *Follies*. Be-

cause of its two editions, the 1922 entry, with 541 performances, had the longest run of any during Ziegfeld's life. The 1943 *Follies*, however, achieved 553.

After Ziegfeld's death in 1932, the rights to the title were bought by the Shubert brothers, who presented two editions, in 1934 and 1936, with Billie Burke, Ziegfeld's widow, as titular sponsor. A third Shubert *Follies* was the one in 1943. In 1956, a *Ziegfeld Follies*, starring Tallulah Bankhead, closed on the road before opening in NY; the following year a revised version of the same revue, starring Beatrice Lillie, did make it to Bway for a brief run.

Between 1907 and 1912, the *Follies* were presented at the Jardin de Paris (whose name was changed to Moulin Rouge in 1912). Between 1913 and 1927—except for 1921 and 1926, when it was shown at the Globe Theatre— all editions were offered at the New Amsterdam. In 1931 it played the Ziegfeld and the last four editions were at the Winter Garden.

Though the producer maintained close control of each edition, the actual direction and choreography were by Herbert Gresham (1907–1909), Julian Mitchell (1907–1913, 1915, 1924), Leon Errol (1914–1915), Ned Wayburn (1916–1923, 1926), Edward Royce (1920–1921, 1926), Zeke Colvan (1927), Albertina Rasch (1927, 1931), Gene Buck (1931). The post-Ziegfeld *Follies* were directed and choreographed by John Murray Anderson (1934, 1936, 1943), Bobby Connolly (1934), Robert Alton (1936, 1943), George Balanchine (1936), John Kennedy and Frank Wagner (1957).

Each *Follies* score was usually by a number of song writers. Those whose works were closely identified with the revue were Harry Smith,

Maurice Levi, Gus Edwards, Dave Stamper and Gene Buck (he began in 1913 and became Ziegfeld's assistant), George V. Hobart, Irving Berlin (the 1927 edition was all his), Harry Tierney and Joseph McCarthy, Raymond Hubbell, Louis Hirsch, Victor Herbert, and Rudolf Friml. After Ziegfeld's death, Vernon Duke, E. Y. Harburg, Ira Gershwin, Ray Henderson, and Jack Yellen wrote the scores. Some of the hits to emerge from the *Follies:* "Shine on, Harvest Moon" (1908, 1931), "By the Light of the Silvery Moon" (1909), "Row, Row, Row" (1912), "The Darktown Poker Club" (1914), "Hello, Frisco" (1915), "Second Hand Rose" (1921), "My Man" (1921), "Mr. Gallagher and Mr. Shean" (1922), "Shaking the Blues Away" (1927), "The Last Roundup" (1934), "Wagon Wheels" (1934), "I Can't Get Started" (1936).

The spectacular scenic effects—in which girls paraded up and down flights of stairs as anything from birds to battleships—were created by Joseph Urban for all Ziegfeld-sponsored editions beginning in 1915. Costumer James Reynolds was with the *Follies* from 1921 to 1924. The *tableaux vivants*, a *Follies* specialty, were created by Ben Ali Haggin from 1917 to 1925.

Including those productions presented after Ziegfeld's death, the following performers appeared in more than one edition (but no name was ever "starred" above the title): Fanny Brice (9), Bert Williams (8), Ann Pennington (7), W. C. Fields (7), Will Rogers (5), Ray Dooley (5), Lillian Lorraine (5), Leon Errol (5), Eddie Cantor (5), Nora Bayes (3), Van and Schenck (3), John Steel (3), Mary Eaton (3), Jack Norworth (2), Ed Wynn (2), Ina Claire (2), Marilyn Miller (2), Ruth Etting (2), Eddie Dowling (2).

As an offshoot of the *Follies*, Ziegfeld also offered a series of late-night cabaret-style revues on the New Amsterdam Roof. Called *Ziegfeld Midnight Frolic*, these shows were presented from 1915 to 1921. The roof was also the site of the *Ziegfeld 9 o'Clock Revue* (or *Frolic*) offered in 1918, 1920 (two editions, the second called *Ziegfeld Girls of 1920*), and 1921. In 1920 Ziegfeld's book musical *Sally* ended with star Marilyn Miller becoming a success in the *Follies*, and in 1929, Act II of *Show Girl* dealt with Ruby Keeler's debut in the revue. *Funny Girl* (1964) recreated production numbers from *Ziegfeld Follies*. The 1971 Harold Prince book musical *Follies* took place at a reunion of former *Follies* girls, with the Ziegfeld-type character called Dimitri Weismann.

Though the *Ziegfeld Follies* was not the first revue—that was *The Passing Show* in 1894—its successful annual editions spawned a series of similar attractions. The most durable were *George White's Scandals, Earl Carroll Vanities*, the Shuberts' *Passing Shows*, and *The Greenwich Village Follies*. Bib: *The Ziegfeld Follies* by Marjorie Farnsworth (Putnam, NY 1956); also see titles under **Ziegfeld, Florenz (Jr.)**.

FILM VERSION: Fred Astaire, Judy Garland, Gene Kelly, Fanny Brice, etc. (new and old material) (MGM 1946, Vincente Minnelli dir.).

"Zigeuner." Music & lyric by Noël Coward. Sung by Peggy Wood in *Bitter Sweet* (L 1929), then by Evelyn Laye in NY production (1929). It was presented in the story as a piece written by the heroine's husband when he was 16. On a trip to Germany his imagination was so fired by forests, castles, and gypsy encampments that he wrote this song of a flaxen-haired

German princess who fell in love with a gypsy.

"Zing! Went the Strings of My Heart!" Music & lyric by James F. Hanley. Zingy number sung and danced by Hal LeRoy and Eunice Healey in revue *Thumbs Up!* (NY 1934).

"Zip." Music by Richard Rodgers; lyric by Lorenz Hart. Stripper Gypsy Rose Lee's intellectual interests prompted this show-stopping number in *Pal Joey* (NY 1940). In it Jean Casto, as a reporter, revealed that Miss Lee's thoughts, while disrobing, were about such topics as the writings of Walter Lippmann, William Saroyan, and Schopenhauer, the paintings of Salvador Dali, the conducting of Toscanini, and the philosophy of Confucius. Olga Lowe sang it in London production (1954).

Zorina, Vera (né Brigitta Hartwig), actress, dancer; b. Berlin, Germany, Jan. 2, 1917 (Norwegian parents). Zorina's sylphlike grace graced such Bway musicals as *I Married an Angel* and *Louisiana Purchase* (in which she sang "You're Lonely and I'm Lonely"). She began her career as a ballet dancer in Norway, later joined the Ballet Russe de Monte Carlo (1934–1936). She has also appeared in films. Miss Zorina, whose first husband was George Balanchine, is the wife of record executive Goddard Lieberson.

1937 On Your Toes (L) (*Vera Barnova*)
1938 I Married an Angel (*Angel*)
1940 Louisiana Purchase (*Marina Van Linden*)
1944 Dream with Music (*Dina, Scheherezade*)
1954 On Your Toes (r) (*Vera Barnova*)

Zwar, Charles, composer; b. Bradford, Australia, April 10, 1914. Settled in London in 1937 to become music director and contributor of revue songs, most with lyrics by Alan Melville (incl. score for long-running *Sweetest and Lowest*). Also collaborated with Diane Morgan and Robert MacDermot.

Unless otherwise noted, following scores written with Mr. Melville:
1940 Swinging the Gate (Morgan, MacDermot)
1942 Sky High
1946 Sweetest and Lowest
1947 A la Carte
1952 Bet Your Life
1953 At the Lyric
1959 Marigold
1963 All Square

AWARDS AND PRIZES

Competitive "nominees" vying against one another for votes may seem more suited to the political than the artistic arena, but the following lists are part of the theatrical record and, as such, deserve to be included in this book. It should, however, always be borne in mind that awards for a particular season are, of course, dependent upon the competition for that season, rules governing eligibility, and the emotional makeup of those doing the voting. In this regard, note, for example, that neither *West Side Story* nor *Gypsy* was ever anointed "Best Musical" by either the NY Drama Critics Circle or the Tony Awards. It might also be a bit perplexing to read that, in 1974, the Tony Awards for best libretto and direction were for *Candide* (though the show itself was ineligible because it was a "revival") and the best score was for *Gigi* (though most of it had been written for a 1958 movie). Discrepancies between dates for the same productions on the Critics Circle and Tony lists result from differing rules concerning the duration of theatrical seasons.

Pulitzer Prize for Drama

1932 *Of Thee I Sing*
1944 *Oklahoma!* (special award)
1950 *South Pacific*
1960 *Fiorello!*
1962 *How to Succeed in Business Without Really Trying*
1976 *A Chorus Line*

NY Drama Critics Circle Award for Musical

1946 *Carousel*
1947 *Brigadoon*
1949 *South Pacific*
1950 *The Consul*
1951 *Guys and Dolls*
1952 *Pal Joey*
1953 *Wonderful Town*
1954 *The Golden Apple*
1955 *The Saint of Bleecker Street*
1956 *My Fair Lady*
1957 *The Most Happy Fella*
1958 *The Music Man*

1959 *La Plume de Ma Tante*
1960 *Fiorello!*
1961 *Carnival*
1962 *How to Succeed in Business Without Really Trying*
1964 *Hello, Dolly!*
1965 *Fiddler on the Roof*
1966 *Man of La Mancha*
1967 *Cabaret*
1968 *Your Own Thing*
1969 *1776*
1970 *Company*
1971 *Follies*
1972 *Two Gentlemen of Verona*
1973 *A Little Night Music*
1974 *Candide*
1975 *A Chorus Line*

Tony Awards

(sponsored first by American Theatre Wing, then by League of NY Theatres; named in honor of Antoinette Perry)

MUSICAL

1949 *Kiss Me, Kate*
1950 *South Pacific*
1951 *Guys and Dolls*
1952 *The King and I*
1953 *Wonderful Town*
1954 *Kismet*
1955 *The Pajama Game*
1956 *Damn Yankees*
1957 *My Fair Lady*
1958 *The Music Man*
1959 *Redhead*
1960 *Fiorello!* (tie)
      The Sound of Music (tie)
1961 *Bye Bye Birdie*
1962 *How to Succeed in Business Without Really Trying*
1963 *A Funny Thing Happened on the Way to the Forum*
1964 *Hello, Dolly!*
1965 *Fiddler on the Roof*
1966 *Man of La Mancha*
1967 *Cabaret*
1968 *Hallelujah, Baby!*
1969 *1776*
1970 *Applause*
1971 *Company*

467

1972 *Two Gentlemen of Verona*
1973 *A Little Night Music*
1974 *Raisin*
1975 *The Wiz*

Actress in a Musical

1948 Grace Hartman, *Angel in the Wings*
1949 Nanette Fabray, *Love Life*
1950 Mary Martin, *South Pacific*
1951 Ethel Merman, *Call Me Madam*
1952 Gertrude Lawrence, *The King and I*
1953 Rosalind Russell, *Wonderful Town*
1954 Dolores Gray, *Carnival in Flanders*
1955 Mary Martin, *Peter Pan*
1956 Gwen Verdon, *Damn Yankees*
1957 Judy Holliday, *Bells Are Ringing*
1958 Gwen Verdon, *New Girl in Town* (tie)
      Thelma Ritter, *New Girl in Town* (tie)
1959 Gwen Verdon, *Redhead*
1960 Mary Martin, *The Sound of Music*
1961 Elizabeth Seal, *Irma la Douce*
1962 Anna Maria Alberghetti, *Carnival* (tie)
      Diahann Carroll, *No Strings* (tie)
1963 Vivien Leigh, *Tovarich*
1964 Carol Channing, *Hello, Dolly!*
1965 Liza Minnelli, *Flora, the Red Menace*
1966 Angela Lansbury, *Mame*
1967 Barbara Harris, *The Apple Tree*
1968 Patricia Routledge, *Darling of the Day* (tie)
      Leslie Uggams, *Hallelujah, Baby!* (tie)
1969 Angela Lansbury, *Dear World*
1970 Lauren Bacall, *Applause*
1971 Helen Gallagher, *No, No, Nanette*
1972 Alexis Smith, *Follies*
1973 Glynis Johns, *A Little Night Music*
1974 Virginia Capers, *Raisin*
1975 Angela Lansbury, *Gypsy*

Actor in a Musical

1948 Paul Hartman, *Angel in the Wings*
1949 Ray Bolger, *Where's Charley?*
1950 Ezio Pinza, *South Pacific*
1951 Robert Alda, *Guys and Dolls*
1952 Phil Silvers, *Top Banana*
1953 Thomas Mitchell, *Hazel Flagg*
1954 Alfred Drake, *Kismet*
1955 Walter Slezak, *Fanny*
1956 Ray Walston, *Damn Yankees*

1957 Rex Harrison, *My Fair Lady*
1958 Robert Preston, *The Music Man*
1959 Richard Kiley, *Redhead*
1960 Jackie Gleason, *Take Me Along*
1961 Richard Burton, *Camelot*
1962 Robert Morse, *How to Succeed in Business Without Really Trying*
1963 Zero Mostel, *A Funny Thing Happened on the Way to the Forum*
1964 Bert Lahr, *Foxy*
1965 Zero Mostel, *Fiddler on the Roof*
1966 Richard Kiley, *Man of La Mancha*
1967 Robert Preston, *I Do! I Do!*
1968 Robert Goulet, *The Happy Time*
1969 Jerry Orbach, *Promises, Promises*
1970 Cleavon Little, *Purlie*
1971 Hal Linden, *The Rothschilds*
1972 Phil Silvers, *A Funny Thing Happened on the Way to the Forum*
1973 Ben Vereen, *Pippin*
1974 Christopher Plummer, *Cyrano*
1975 John Cullum, *Shenandoah*

Composer
(separate category for lyricist began in 1962)

1949 Cole Porter, *Kiss Me, Kate*
1950 Richard Rodgers, *South Pacific*
1951 Frank Loesser, *Guys and Dolls*
1952 Richard Rodgers, *The King and I*
1953 Leonard Bernstein, *Wonderful Town*
1954 Aleksandr Borodin, *Kismet*
1955 Richard Adler & Jerry Ross, *The Pajama Game*
1956 Richard Adler & Jerry Ross, *Damn Yankees*
1957 Frederick Loewe, *My Fair Lady*
1958 Meredith Willson, *The Music Man*
1959 Albert Hague, *Redhead*
1960 Jerry Bock, *Fiorello!* (tie)
      Richard Rodgers, *The Sound of Music* (tie)
1962 Richard Rodgers (music), *No Strings*
      Frank Loesser (lyrics), *How to Succeed in Business Without Really Trying*
1963 Lionel Bart, *Oliver!*
1964 Jerry Herman, *Hello, Dolly!*
1965 Jerry Bock & Sheldon Harnick, *Fiddler on the Roof*
1966 Mitch Leigh & Joe Darion, *Man of La Mancha*

1967 John Kander & Fred Ebb, *Cabaret*
1968 Jule Styne, Betty Comden & Adolph Green, *Hallelujah, Baby!*
1969 Sherman Edwards, *1776*
1970 Charles Strouse & Lee Adams, *Applause*
1971 Stephen Sondheim, *Company*
1972 Stephen Sondheim, *Follies*
1973 Stephen Sondheim, *A Little Night Music*
1974 Frederick Loewe & Alan Jay Lerner, *Gigi*
1975 Charlie Smalls, *The Wiz*

LIBRETTIST

1949 Bella & Sam Spewack, *Kiss Me, Kate*
1950 Oscar Hammerstein 2nd & Joshua Logan, *South Pacific*
1951 Jo Swerling & Abe Burrows, *Guys and Dolls*
1952 Oscar Hammerstein 2nd, *The King and I*
1953 Joseph Fields & Jerome Chodorov, *Wonderful Town*
1954 Charles Lederer & Luther Davis, *Kismet*
1955 George Abbott & Richard Bissell, *The Pajama Game*
1956 George Abbott & Douglass Wallop, *Damn Yankees*
1957 Alan Jay Lerner, *My Fair Lady*
1958 Meredith Willson & Franklin Lacey, *The Music Man*
1959 Herbert Fields, Dorothy Fields, Sidney Sheldon, David Shaw, *Redhead*
1960 Jerome Weidman & George Abbott, *Fiorello!* (tie)
Howard Lindsay & Russel Crouse, *The Sound of Music* (tie)
1961 Michael Stewart, *Bye Bye Birdie*
1962 Abe Burrows, Jack Weinstock, Willie Gilbert, *How to Succeed in Business Without Really Trying*
1963 Burt Shevelove & Larry Gelbart, *A Funny Thing Happened on the Way to the Forum*
1964 Michael Stewart, *Hello, Dolly!*
1965 Joseph Stein, *Fiddler on the Roof*
1966 Dale Wasserman, *Man of La Mancha*
1967 Joe Masteroff, *Cabaret*
1968 Arthur Laurents, *Hallelujah, Baby!*

1969 Peter Stone, *1776*
1970 Betty Comden & Adolph Green, *Applause*
1971 George Furth, *Company*
1972 John Guare & Mel Shapiro, *Two Gentlemen of Verona*
1973 Hugh Wheeler, *A Little Night Music*
1974 Hugh Wheeler, *Candide*
1975 James Lee Barrett, Peter Udell & Philip Rose, *Shenandoah*

DIRECTOR
(separate category for musicals began in 1960)

1950 Joshua Logan, *South Pacific*
1951 George S. Kaufman, *Guys and Dolls*
1957 Moss Hart, *My Fair Lady*
1960 George Abbott, *Fiorello!*
1961 Gower Champion, *Bye Bye Birdie*
1962 Abe Burrows, *How to Succeed in Business Without Really Trying*
1963 George Abbott, *A Funny Thing Happened on the Way to the Forum*
1964 Gower Champion, *Hello, Dolly!*
1965 Jerome Robbins, *Fiddler on the Roof*
1966 Albert Marre, *Man of La Mancha*
1967 Harold Prince, *Cabaret*
1968 Gower Champion, *The Happy Time*
1969 Peter Hunt, *1776*
1970 Ron Field, *Applause*
1971 Harold Prince, *Company*
1972 Harold Prince & Michael Bennett, *Follies*
1973 Bob Fosse, *Pippin*
1974 Harold Prince, *Candide*
1975 Geoffrey Holder, *The Wiz*

CHOREOGRAPHER

1947 Agnes de Mille, *Brigadoon* (tie)
Michael Kidd, *Finian's Rainbow* (tie)
1948 Jerome Robbins, *High Button Shoes*
1949 Gower Champion, *Lend an Ear*
1950 Helen Tamiris, *Touch and Go*
1951 Michael Kidd, *Guys and Dolls*
1952 Robert Alton, *Pal Joey*
1953 Donald Saddler, *Wonderful Town*
1954 Michael Kidd, *Can-Can*
1955 Bob Fosse, *The Pajama Game*
1956 Bob Fosse, *Damn Yankees*
1957 Michael Kidd, *Li'l Abner*
1958 Jerome Robbins, *West Side Story*

1959 Bob Fosse, *Redhead*
1960 Michael Kidd, *Destry Rides Again*
1961 Gower Champion, *Bye Bye Birdie*
1962 Agnes de Mille, *Kwamina* (tie)
Joe Layton, *No Strings* (tie)
1963 Bob Fosse, *Little Me*
1964 Gower Champion, *Hello, Dolly!*
1965 Jerome Robbins, *Fiddler on the Roof*
1966 Bob Fosse, *Sweet Charity*
1967 Ronald Field, *Cabaret*
1968 Gower Champion, *The Happy Time*
1969 Joe Layton, *George M!*
1970 Ron Field, *Applause*
1971 Donald Saddler, *No, No, Nanette*
1972 Michael Bennett, *Follies*
1973 Bob Fosse, *Pippin*
1974 Michael Bennett, *Seesaw*
1975 George Faison, *The Wiz*

London "*Evening Standard*" Award for Musical
1955 *The Pajama Game*
Salad Days
1956 *Cranks*
1958 *West Side Story*
1959 *Make Me an Offer*
1960 *Fings Ain't Wot They Used t'Be*
1961 *Beyond the Fringe*

1963 *Oh What a Lovely War*
1964 *Little Me*
1966 *Funny Girl*
1967 *Sweet Charity*
1968 *Cabaret*
1969 *Promises, Promises*
1972 *Applause*
1973 *The Rocky Horror Show*
1974 *John, Paul, George, Ringo . . . and Bert*
1975 *A Little Night Music*

"Plays and Players" London Theatre Critics Award for Musical
1965 *Hello, Dolly!*
1966 *Jorrocks*
1967 *Fiddler on the Roof*
1968 *Cabaret*
1969 *Anne of Green Gables*
1970 *1776*
1971 *Catch My Soul*
1972 *Company*
1973 *The Rocky Horror Show*
1974 *John, Paul, George, Ringo . . . and Bert*
1975 *A Little Night Music*
Note: In 1973, Angela Lansbury won the "Best Actress" Award for the musical *Gypsy*.

LONG RUNS

The following tables list all musicals in New York and London that achieved a run of over 1,000 performances. The number in parentheses following the NY run is for the London run, and vice versa. Note that nine Bway-originated musicals ran over 1,000 performances in London (the longest-running London-originated musical on Bway was *Oliver!*, which ran 774 performances). Asterisk indicates production still running Jan. 1, 1976.

New York

Fiddler on the Roof (1964)	3,242	(2,030)
Hello, Dolly! (1964)	2.844	(794)
My Fair Lady (1956)	2,717	(2,281)
Man of La Mancha (1966)	2,328	(253)
Oklahoma! (1943)	2,212	(1,543)
South Pacific (1949)	1,925	(792)
Hair (1968)	1,742	(1,998)
Grease (1972)	*	(236)
Mame (1966)	1,508	(443)
The Sound of Music (1959)	1,443	(2,386)
How to Succeed in Business Without Really Trying (1961)	1,417	(520)
Hellzapoppin (1938)	1,404	
The Music Man (1957)	1,375	(395)
Funny Girl (1964)	1,348	(112)
Pippin (1972)	*	(85)
Promises, Promises (1968)	1,281	(570)
The King and I (1951)	1,246	(926)
1776 (1969)	1,217	(168)
Guys and Dolls (1950)	1,200	(555)
Cabaret (1966)	1,165	(336)
Annie Get Your Gun (1946)	1,147	(1,304)
Pins and Needles (1937)	1,108	
Kiss Me, Kate (1948)	1,070	(501)
Don't Bother Me, I Can't Cope (1972)	1,065	

NOTE:

Grease (1972), which was still playing in New York in 1979, has become the longest running musical in Broadway history. Others that have completed their runs:

Pippin (1972)	1,944
The Magic Show (1974)	1,920
The Wiz (1975)	1,672
Shenandoah (1975)	1,050
Godspell (Off Broadway 1971)	2,124

The Pajama Game (1954)	1,063	(578)
Damn Yankees (1955)	1,019	(861)

New York Off-Bway

The Fantasticks (1960)	*	(44)
The Threepenny Opera (1955)	2,611	(140)
Godspell (1971)	*	(1,128)
You're a Good Man, Charlie Brown (1967)	1,597	(116)
Little Mary Sunshine (1959)	1,143	(44)

London

Oliver! (1960)	2,618	(774)
The Sound of Music (1961)	2,386	(1,443)
Salad Days (1954)	2,283	(80)
My Fair Lady (1958)	2,281	(2,717)
Chu Chin Chow (1916)	2,238	(208)
Charlie Girl (1965)	2,202	
The Boy Friend (1954)	2,084	(485)
Canterbury Tales (1968)	2,082	(121)
Fiddler on the Roof (1967)	2,030	(3,242)
Hair (1968)	1,998	(1,742)
Me and My Girl (1937)	1,646	
Together Again (1947)	1,566	
Oklahoma! (1947)	1,543	(2,212)
Irma la Douce (1958)	1,512	(524)
Jesus Christ Superstar (1972)	*	(711)
Knights of Madness (1950)	1,361	
The Maid of the Mountains (1917)	1,352	(37)
Annie Get Your Gun (1947)	1,304	(1,147)
Godspell (1971)	1,128	*
London Laughs (1952)	1,113	
A Chinese Honeymoon (1901)	1,075	(376)
West Side Story (1958)	1,040	(732)
Perchance to Dream (1945)	1,022	

In London, *Jesus Christ Superstar* (1972), which was still playing in 1979, has become the longest running musical in West End history. Others still playing that went over 1,000 performances: *The Rocky Horror Show* (1974); *Ipi Tombi* (1975).

BIBLIOGRAPHY

Asterisk denotes "acting edition."

Librettos & Lyrics

Ace of Clubs, Coward (incl. *Play Parade, Vol. 6,* Heinemann, L 1962).

Airs on a Shoestring, Flanders (French,* L 1955).

All American, Brooks, Adams (Dramatic Pub.,* Chi. 1972).

Allegro, Hammerstein (incl. *6 Plays by Rodgers & Hammerstein;* Random, NY 1955).

Amorous Flea, The, Devine, Montgomery (Dramatists Play,* NY 1964).

Anne of Green Gables, Harron, Campbell (French,* NY 1972).

Anyone Can Whistle, Laurents, Sondheim (Random, NY 1965).

Applause, Comden, Green, Adams (Random, NY 1971).

Apple Tree, The, Harnick, Coopersmith (Random, NY 1966).

Baker Street, Coopersmith, Grudeff, Jessel (Doubleday, NY 1961).

Barefoot Boy with Cheek, Schulman, Dee (Dramatic Pub.,* Chi. 1943).

Beggar's Opera, The, Gay (O'Connor, L 1922; Dover, NY 1973).

Belle of New York, The, Morton (French,* L 1927).

Bells Are Ringing, Comden, Green (Random, NY 1957).

Ben Franklin in Paris, Michaels (Random, NY 1965).

Best of Broadway, The, Rogers (ed.) (Dramatic Pub.,* Chi. 1961).

Bitter Sweet, Coward (incl. *Play Parade,* Vol. 1, Heinemann, L 1934).

Black Crook, The, Barras (Dutton, NY 1967).

Bless the Bride, Herbert (French,* L 1948).

Body Beautiful, The, Stein, Glickman, Harnick (French,* NY 1957).

Boy Friend, The, Wilson (Dutton, NY 1954).

Brigadoon, Lerner (incl. *10 Great Musicals,* Chilton, Phila. 1973).

By Hex, Rengier, Blankman (Dramatists Play,* NY 1953).

Bye Bye Birdie, Stewart, Adams (DBS, NY 1968).

Cabaret, Masteroff, Ebb (Random, NY 1967).

Call Me Madam, Lindsay, Crouse, Berlin (Berlin,* L 1956).

Camelot, Lerner (Random, NY 1961).

Candide, Hellman, Wilbur (Random, NY 1957).

———, Wheeler, Wilbur, Bernstein (Macmillan, NY 1976).

Carmen Jones, Hammerstein (Knopf, NY 1945).

Carnival, Stewart, Merrill (DBS, NY 1968).

Carousel, Hammerstein (incl. *6 Plays by Rodgers & Hammerstein;* Random, NY 1955).

Celebration, Jones (DBS, NY 1974).

Charlie Girl, Williams, Heneker, Taylor (Chappell,* L 1972).

Company, Furth, Sondheim (Random, NY 1970; incl. *10 Great Musicals,* Chilton, Phila. 1973).

Conversation Piece, Coward (incl. *Play Parade,* Vol. 2, Heinemann, L 1950).

Cradle Will Rock, The, Blitzstein (Random, NY 1938).

Curley McDimple, Dahdah, Boylan (French,* NY 1967).

Dames at Sea, Haimsohn, Miller (French,* NY 1968).

Damn Yankees, Abbott, Wallop, Adler, Ross (Random, NY 1956).

Desert Song, The, Harbach, Hammerstein, Mandel (French,* NY 1959).

Do I Hear a Waltz?, Laurents, Sondheim (Random, NY 1966).

*Education of H*Y*M*A*N K*A*P*L*A*N, The,* Zavin, Nassau, Brand (Dramatic Pub.,* Chi. 1968).

England, Our England, Waterhouse, Hall (Evans,* L 1956).

Fade Out—Fade In, Comden, Green (Random, NY 1965).

Fanny, Behrman, Logan, Rome (Random, NY 1955).

Fantasticks, The, Jones (DBS, NY 1974).

Fiddler on the Roof, Stein, Harnick (Crown, NY 1964; incl. *10 Great Musicals,* Chilton, Phila. 1973).

Fings Ain't Wot They Used t'Be, Norman, Bart (Secker & Warburg, L 1960).

Finian's Rainbow, Harburg, Saidy (Berkley, NY 1968).

Fiorello!, Weidman, Abbott, Harnick (Random, NY 1960).

Fireman's Flame, The, Van Antwerp, Fetter (French,* NY 1938).

First Impressions, Burrows, Goldman, Weiss (French,* NY 1962).

Flower Drum Song, Hammerstein, Fields (Farrar Straus, NY 1959).

Follies, Goldman, Sondheim (Random, NY 1971).

Follow That Girl, Slade, Reynolds (French,* L 1967).

Funny Girl, Lennart, Merrill (Random, NY 1964).

Funny Thing Happened on the Way to the Forum, A, Shevelove, Gelbart, Sondheim (Dodd Mead, NY 1963).

Golden Apple, The, Latouche (Random, NY 1954).

Golden Boy, Odets, Gibson, Adams (Atheneum, NY 1965).

Golden Screw, The, Sankey (incl. *The New Underground Theatre*, Bantam, NY 1968).

Goldilocks, Kerr, Kerr, Ford (Doubleday, NY 1959).

Good News, Schwab, DeSylva, Brown (French,* NY 1932).

Grass Harp, The, Elmslie (French,* NY 1971).

Grease, Jacobs, Casey (Pocket, NY 1972).

Guys and Dolls, Swerling, Burrows, Loesser (incl. *From the American Drama*, Vol. 4, Doubleday, NY 1956).

Gypsy, Laurents, Sondheim (Random, NY 1959; incl. *10 Great Musicals*, Chilton, Phila. 1973).

Hair, Ragni, Rado (Pocket, NY 1969).

Half a Sixpence, Cross, Heneker (Dramatic Pub.,* Chi. 1967).

Happy Hunting, Lindsay, Crouse, Dubey (Random, NY 1957).

Happy Time, The, Nash, Ebb (Dramatic Pub.,* Chi. 1969).

Hello, Dolly!, Stewart, Herman (DBS, NY 1968).

Henry, Sweet Henry, Johnson, Merrill (French,* NY 1969).

House of Flowers, Capote, Arlen (Random, NY 1968).

How Now, Dow Jones, Schulman, Leigh (French,* NY 1968).

How to Succeed in Business Without Really Trying, Burrows, Weinstock, Gilbert, Loesser (Frank Music,* L 1963).

I Can Get It for You Wholesale, Weidman, Rome (Random, NY 1962).

I'd Rather Be Right, Kaufman, Hart, Hart (Random, NY 1937).

Johnny Johnson, Green (incl. *5 Plays of the South*, Mermaid, NY 1963).

Jorrocks, Cross, Heneker (Chappell,* L 1966).

King and I, The, Hammerstein (incl. *6 Plays by Rodgers & Hammerstein*, Random, NY 1955).

King Kong, Bloom, Williams (Fontana, L 1961).

Kismet, Lederer, Davis, Wright, Forrest (Random, NY 1953).

Kiss Me, Kate, Spewack, Porter (Knopf, NY 1953; incl. *10 Great Musicals*, Chilton, Phila. 1973).

Knickerbocker Holiday, Anderson (Anderson, Wash. 1938).

Lady in the Dark, Hart, Gershwin (Random, NY 1941).

Lend an Ear, Gaynor (French,* NY 1971).

Let 'Em Eat Cake, Kaufman, Ryskind, Gershwin (Knopf, NY 1933).

Little Mary Sunshine, Besoyan (French,* NY 1960).

Little Night Music, A, Wheeler, Sondheim (Dodd Mead, NY 1974).

Living for Pleasure, McRae (French,* L 1960).

Lock Up Your Daughters, Miles, Bart (French,* L 1967).

Lovely Ladies, Kind Gentlemen, Patrick, Freeman, Underwood (French,* NY 1971).

Lute Song, Irwin, Hanighen (Dramatic Pub.,* Chi. 1956).

Lyric Revue, The, McRae (French,* L 1953).

Mad Show, The, Siegel, Hart, Barer (French,* NY 1973).

Maggie Flynn, Peretti, Creatore, Weiss (French,* NY 1968).

Mame, Lawrence, Lee, Herman (Random, NY 1967).

Man of LaMancha, Wasserman, Darion (Random, NY 1966).

Me and Juliet, Hammerstein (incl. *6 Plays*

by Rodgers & Hammerstein, Random, NY 1955).

Me and My Girl, Rose, Furber (French,* L 1954).

Music in the Air, Hammerstein (Chappell,* L 1936).

Music Man, The, Willson (Putnam, NY 1958).

My Fair Lady, Lerner (Putnam, NY 1956).

Naughty Marietta, Young, Park (Weinberger,* L 1959).

Naughty-Naught, Van Antwerp, Fetter (French,* NY 1941).

New Girl in Town, Abbott, Merrill (Random, NY 1958).

New Moon, The, Hammerstein, Mandel, Schwab (Chappell,* L 1935).

No Strings, Taylor, Rodgers (Random, NY 1962).

Now Is the Time for All Good Men, Cryer (French,* NY 1967).

Of Thee I Sing, Kaufman, Ryskind, Gershwin (Knopf, NY 1932; French,* NY 1935; incl. *10 Great Musicals*, Chilton, Phila. 1973).

Oh, What a Lovely War, Chilton (Methuen, L 1965).

Oklahoma!, Hammerstein (incl. *6 Plays by Rodgers & Hammerstein*, Random, NY 1955).

Oldest Trick in the World, The, Thompson (French,* NY 1961).

On a Clear Day You Can See Forever, Lerner (Random, NY 1966).

One Touch of Venus, Perelman, Nash (Little Brown, Boston 1944; incl. *10 Great Musicals*, Chilton, Phila. 1973).

Operette, Coward (incl. *Play Parade*, Vol. 2, Heinemann, L 1950).

Our Man Crichton, Kretzmer (Hodder-Stoughton, L 1965).

Pacific 1860, Coward (incl. *Play Parade*, Vol. 5, Heinemann, L 1958).

Paint Your Wagon, Lerner (Coward McCann, NY 1952).

Pajama Game, The, Abbott, Bissell, Adler, Ross (Random, NY 1954).

Pal Joey, O'Hara, Hart (Duel Sloane, NY 1941; Random, NY 1952).

Phoenix '55, Wallach (French,* NY 1957).

Pipe Dream, Hammerstein (Viking, NY 1955).

Pippin, Hirson, Schwartz (DBS, NY 1975).

Plain and Fancy, Stein, Glickman, Horwitt (Random, NY 1955).

Porgy and Bess, Heyward, Gershwin (incl. *10 Great Musicals*, Chilton, Phila. 1973).

Promises, Promises, Simon, David (Random, NY 1969).

Purlie, Davis, Rose, Udell (French,* NY 1971).

Regina, Blitzstein (Chappell,* NY 1953).

Riverside Nights, Herbert, Playfair (Unwin, L 1926).

Robert and Elizabeth, Millar (French,* L 1967).

Rose-Marie, Harbach, Hammerstein (French,* L 1931).

Salad Days, Reynolds, Slade (French,* L 1961).

Say, Darling, Bissell, Burrows, Comden, Green (Little Brown, Boston 1958).

Secret Life of Walter Mitty, The, Manchester, Shuman (French,* NY 1968).

Seesaw, Bennett, Fields (French,* NY 1975).

Seventeen, Benson, Gannon (French,* NY 1954).

1776, Stone, Edwards (Viking, NY 1970; incl. *10 Great Musicals*, Chilton, Phila. 1973).

She Loves Me, Masteroff, Harnick (Dodd Mead, NY 1964).

Show Me Where the Good Times Are, Thuna, Roberts (French,* NY 1970).

Show Boat, Hammerstein (Chappell,* L 1934).

Sing Out, Sweet Land, Kerr (Baker,* Boston 1949).

Skyscraper, Stone, Cahn (French,* NY 1967).

Song of Norway, Lazarus, Wright, Forrest (Chappell,* L 1951).

Sound of Music, The, Lindsay, Crouse, Hammerstein (Random, NY 1960).

South Pacific, Hammerstein, Logan (incl. *6 Plays by Rodgers & Hammerstein*, Random, NY 1955).

Streets of New York, The, Grael (French,* NY 1965).

Sunny, Harbach, Hammerstein (Chappell,* L).

Sweet Charity, Simon, Fields (Random, NY 1966).

Tenderloin, Abbott, Weidman, Harnick (Random, NY 1961).

This Year of Grace, Coward (incl. *Play Parade*, Vol. 2, Heinemann, L 1950).

Three Musketeers, The, McGuire, Grey (Chappell,* L 1938).

Three to One, Hamilton etc. (French,* NY 1952).

Tom Jones, Thompson, Courtneidge, Taylor (Chappell,* L).

Tonight at 8:30, Coward (incl. *Play Parade*, Vol. 4, Heinemann, L 1954).

Tree Grows in Brooklyn, A, Abbott, Smith, Fields (Harper, NY 1951).

Tricks, Burstein, Jory (French,* NY 1971).

Two Gentlemen of Verona, Shapiro, Guare, MacDermot (Holt, NY 1973).

Unsinkable Molly Brown, The, Morris, Willson (Putnam, NY 1961).

Vagabond King, The, Janney, Post, Hooker (French,* NY 1929).

Walking Happy, Hirson, Frings, Cahn (French,* NY 1967).

West Side Story, Laurents, Sondheim (Random, NY 1958; incl. *10 Great Musicals*, Chilton, Phila. 1973).

What Makes Sammy Run?, Schulberg, Drake (Random, NY 1965).

Where's Charley?, Abbott, Loesser (French,* L 1948).

White Horse Inn, Graham (French,* L 1957).

Wonderful Town, Fields, Chodorov, Comden, Green (Random, NY 1953).

Words and Music, Coward (incl. *Play Parade*, Vol. 2, Heinemann, L 1950).

Yearling, The, Martin, Noto (Dramatic Pub.,* Chi. 1973).

Your Own Thing, Driver, Hester, Apolinar (Dell, NY 1970).

You're a Good Man, Charlie Brown, Gesner (Fawcett Crest, NY 1970).

Zorbá, Stein, Ebb (Random, NY 1969).

Zulu and the Zayda, The, DaSilva, Leon, Rome (Dramatists Play,* NY 1966).

Reference

Agate, James: *Immoment Toys* (Cape, L 1945). "A Survey of Light Entertainment on the London Stage, 1920–1943."

Atkinson, Brooks: *Broadway* (Macmillan, NY 1970). History of the Bway stage, 1900–1970.

Baral, Robert: *Revue* (Fleet, NY 1962). "A Nostalgic Reprise of the Great Broadway Period."

Blum, Daniel: *Great Stars of the American Stage* (Grosset & Dunlap, NY 1954). Pictorial survey of over 150 stars of the Bway stage.

———: *A Pictorial History of the American Theatre 1860–1960* (Chilton, Phila. 1960).

Churchill, Allen: *The Great White Way* (Dutton, NY 1962). Bway theatre 1900–1919.

Cochran, Charles B. (ed.): *Review of Revues* (Cape, L 1930).

Curtis, Anthony (ed.): *The Rise and Fall of the Matinée Idol* (Weidenfeld, L 1974). "Past deities of stage and screen."

Drinkrow, John: *Vintage Operetta Book* (Osprey, L 1972). Plot outlines of 50 works.

Engel, Lehman: *Planning and Producing the Musical Show* (Crown, NY 1966). Handbook for amateur productions.

———: *The American Musical Theatre* (CBS Legacy, NY 1967). Illustrated history and "consideration."

———: *This Bright Day* (Macmillan, NY 1974). An autobiography.

———: *Words with Music* (Macmillan, NY 1972). Analysis of the musical theatre.

———: *Their Words Are Music* (Crown, NY 1975). "The Great Theatre Lyricists and Their Lyrics."

Ewen, David, *American Popular Songs* (Random, NY 1966). "From the Revolutionary War to the Present."

Fuld, James J.: *The Book of World-Famous Music* (Crown, NY 1966). Information regarding publications of songs, incl. first lines of music & lyric.

Geller, James J.: *Famous Songs and Their Stories* (Garden City, NY 1940). From 1870 to turn of the century.

Green, Stanley: *The World of Musical Comedy* (Barnes, NJ 1974). "The Story of the American Musical Stage as Told Through the Careers of Its Foremost Composers and Lyricists."

———: *Ring Bells! Sing Songs!* (Arlington, NY 1971). "Broadway Musicals in the Thirties."

Guernsey, Otis, Jr. (ed.): *Playwrights, Composers and Lyricists on Theatre*

(Dodd Mead, NY 1974). Articles from *The Dramatists Review*.

Hughes, Langston, & Milton Meltzer: *Black Magic* (Prentice-Hall, NJ 1967). "A Pictorial History of the Negro in American Entertainment."

Kinkle, Roger D.: *The Complete Encyclopedia of Popular Music and Jazz, 1900–1950* (Arlington, NY 1974). 4 volumes.

Laufe, Abe: *Broadway's Greatest Musicals* (Funk & Wagnall, NY 1969). Emphasis on productions running over 500 performances.

Lewine, Richard, & Alfred Simon: *Songs of the American Theatre* (Dodd Mead, NY 1973). Listing of all songs & Bway musicals, 1925–1970.

Lewis, Emory: *Stages* (Prentice-Hall, NJ 1969). "The 50-Year Childhood of the American Theatre."

Lubbock, Mark: *The Complete Book of Light Opera* (Putnam, L 1962). Plot outlines of major works since 1850.

Lynn Farnol Group: *ASCAP Biographical Dictionary* (Schirmer, NY 1966). Over 5,200 entries.

Macqueen-Pope, W.: *Theatre Royal, Drury Lane* (Allen, L 1945).

———: *Carriages at Eleven* (Hutchinson, L 1947). "The Story of the Edwardian Theatre."

———: *The Gaiety, Theatre of Enchantment* (Allen, L 1949).

———: *The Footlight Flickered* (Jenkins, L 1959). The London stage in the 1920s.

Mander, Raymond & Joe Mitchenson: *Musical Comedy* (Davies, L 1969). Pictorial history of London musicals, 1892–1968.

———: *Revue* (Davies, L 1971). Pictorial history of London revues, 1831–1970.

Marks, Edward B.: *They All Had Glamour* (Messner, NY 1944). "From the Swedish Nightingale to the Naked Lady."

———: *They All Sang* (Viking, NY 1934). "From Tony Pastor to Rudy Vallée."

Mates, Julian: *The American Musical Stage Before 1800* (Rutgers, NJ 1962). Focusing on *The Archers*, 1796.

Mattfeld, Julius: *Variety Musical Cavalcade* (Prentice-Hall, NJ 1962). Song titles & historical survey, 1620–1961.

Morehouse, Ward: *Matinee Tomorrow*

(Whittlesey, NY 1949). "Fifty Years of Our Theatre."

Morris, Lloyd: *Curtain Time* (Random, NY 1953). Illustrated history of Bway stage, 1820–1951.

Odell, George C. D.: *Annals of the New York Stage* (Columbia U., NY 1927–1949). 15-volume history up to 1894.

Oppenheimer, George (ed.): *The Passionate Playgoer* (Viking, NY 1958). Articles on the theatre.

Rigdon, Walter (ed.): *Biographical Encyclopedia and Who's Who of the American Theatre* (Heineman, NY 1966).

Rust, Brian: *London Musical Shows on Records 1894–1954.* (Brit. Inst. Recorded Sound, L 1958). Alphabetical listing of original-cast recordings, with supplement.

———: *The Complete Entertainment Discography* (Arlington, NY 1974). "From the mid-1890s to 1942."

Shapiro, Nat: *Popular Music* (Adrian, NY 1964–73). 6-volume "Annotated Index of American Popular Songs," 1920–1969.

Short, Ernest: *Sixty Years of Theatre* (Eyre & Spottiswoode, L 1951).

Smith, Cecil: *Musical Comedy in America* (Theatre Arts, NY 1950). Critical history, 1864–1950.

Spaeth, Sigmund: *A History of Popular Music in America* (Random, NY 1948).

Sobel, Bernard: *The New Theatre Handbook and Digest of Plays* (Crown, NY 1959).

Taubman, Howard: *The Making of the American Theatre* (Coward McCann, NY 1967). A history from the colonial times.

Trewin, JC: *The Gay Twenties* (Macdonald, L 1958). Illustrated year-by-year history of the London stage.

———: *The Turbulent Thirties* (Macdonald L 1960). Illustrated year-by-year history of the London stage.

Wilder, Alex, & James T. Maher: *American Popular Song* (Oxford, NY 1972). Analyses of the works of "The Great Innovators, 1900–1950."

Wilk, Max: *They're Playing Our Song* (Atheneum, NY 1973). Interviews with 22 songwriters.

Witmark, Isidore, & Isaac Goldberg: *From Ragtime to Swingtime* (Furman, NY

1939). "The Story of the House of Witmark."

ASCAP Hit Tunes. (1892–1970). Year-by-year listing.

The Best Plays (1894–1975). 59 editions. Editors: Garrison Sherwood & John Chapman (1894–1919); Burns Mantle (1919–1947); John Chapman (1947–1952); Louis Kronenberger (1952–1961); Henry Hewes (1961–1964); Otis Guernsey Jr. (1964–1975). (Dodd Mead, NY). Annual illustrated Bway theatre yearbooks and condensed versions of editors' choices of 10 best plays of each season.

The Cast (1900–1950). Weekly listings of casts of NY productions.

New York Dramatic Mirror (1879–1922). Weekly periodical.

The Play Pictorial (1902–1939). London periodical.

Plays and Players (1953–   ). London periodical.

The Stage Yearbook (1908–1929, 1948–1969). 38 editions. Editors: Lionel Carson, Frank Comerford, Anthony Merryn. (Carson & Comerford, L). London theatre yearbooks.

The Stage (1925–1935, 1940–1941). NY periodical.

The Theatre (1900–1931). NY periodical.

Theatre Arts (1916–1964). NY periodical.

Theatre World (1944–1975). 31 editions. Editors: Daniel Blum (1944–1964); John Willis (1964–1975). (Greenberg, NY 1944–1957; Chilton, Phila. 1957–1964; Crown, NY 1964–1975). Annual pictorial Bway theatre yearbooks.

Theatre World (1927–1952). London periodical.

Theatre World Annual (1949–1966). 16 editions. Editor: Frances Stephens. (Rockliffe, L 1949–1962; Iliffe, L 1964–1966). Annual pictorial London yearbooks.

Who's Who in the Theatre (1912–1972). 15 editions. Editors: John Parker (1912–1957), Freda Gaye (1961, 1967). (Pittman, L). "A Biographical Record of the Contemporary Stage."

Soft-Cover Song Collections

The Great Songs of Harold Arlen (Morris/Harwin)

Noël Coward: His Words and Music (Chappell)

The Best of DeSylva, Brown & Henderson (Chappell)

The Best of George Gershwin (Chappell)

The Songs of Oscar Hammerstein II (Williamson/TB Harms)

The Jerry Herman Songbook (Morris)

Jerome Kern: The Man and His Music (TB Harms)

The Best of Burton Lane (Chappell)

Music & Lyrics by Cole Porter (Chappell/Random) (2 volumes)

The Songs of Richard Rodgers (Williamson/Random)

The Best of Rodgers & Hart (Chappell)

The Best of Jule Styne (Chappell)

The Genius of Kurt Weill (Chappell)

Kurt Weill in America (Chappell)

Show Songs from "The Black Crook" to "The Red Mill' (Dover)

DISCOGRAPHY

Abbreviations: AF (Audio Fidelity); M-E (Monmouth-Evergreen); MFP (Music for Pleasure); PS (Painted Smiles); RD (Reader's Digest); UA (United Artists); WRC (World Record Club).

Productions

In recordings of original or substantially original casts, the city (NY or L) and year follow the record labels. Asterisk indicates RIAA Gold Record winner for sales of over $1 million.

Ace of Clubs (Coward). WRC, M-E (L 1950).

After the Ball (Coward). Philips (L 1954).

Ain't Supposed to Die a Natural Death (Van Peebles). A&M (NY 1971).

All American (Strouse-Adams). Columbia (NY 1962).

All in Love (Urbont-Geller). Mercury (NY 1961).

Allegro (Rodgers-Hammerstein). RCA (NY 1947).

Ambassador (Gohman-Hackaday). RCA (L 1971).

Ankles Aweigh (Fain-Shapiro). Decca (NY 1955).

Ann Veronica (Ornadel-Croft). CBS (L 1969).

Anne of Green Gables (Campbell-Harron). CBS (L 1969).

Annie Get Your Gun (Berlin). Decca (NY 1946); Stanyan (L 1947); RCA (NY 1966); London.

Anya (Rachmaninoff-Wright-Forrest). UA (NY 1965).

Anyone Can Whistle (Sondheim). Columbia (NY 1964).

Anything Goes (Porter). M-E (L 1935); Epic (NY 1962).

Applause (Strouse-Adams). ABC (NY 1970).

Apple Tree, The (Bock-Harnick). Columbia (NY 1966).

Arc de Triomphe (Novello-Hassall). WRC (L 1943).

Arcadians, The (Monckton-Talbot-Wimperis). EMI-Columbia.

Arms and the Girl (Gould-Fields). Decca 10" (NY 1950).

Athenian Touch, The (Straight-Eddy). Bway East (NY 1964).

Babes in Arms (Rodgers-Hart). Columbia.

Babes in Toyland (Herbert-MacDonough). Decca; RD.

Bajour (Marks). Columbia (NY 1964).

Baker Street (Grudeff-Jessel). MGM (NY 1965).

Ballad for Bimshire (Burgie). London (NY 1963).

Band Wagon, The (Schwartz-Dietz). RCA (NY 1931).

Belle (Norman). Decca (L 1961).

Bells Are Ringing (Styne-Comden, Green). Columbia (NY 1956).

Ben Franklin in Paris (Sandrich-Michaels). Capitol (NY 1964).

Best Foot Forward (Martin-Blane). Cadence (NY 1963).

Billy (Barry-Black). CBS (L 1974).

Billy Barnes Revue, The (Barnes). Decca (NY 1959).

Bitter Sweet (Coward). WRC, M-E (L 1929); Angel; MFP.

Blackbirds of 1928 (McHugh-Fields). Columbia (NY 1928).

Blitz! (Bart). HMV (L 1962).

Bloomer Girl (Arlen-Harburg). Decca (NY 1944).

Blossom Time (Schubert-Romberg-Donnelly). RD.

Boy Friend, The (Wilson). MFP, Stanyan (L 1954); RCA (NY 1954); Parlophone (L 1967); Decca (NY 1970).

Boys from Syracuse, The (Rodgers-Hart). Columbia; Capitol (NY 1963).

Bravo Giovanni (Schafer-Graham). Columbia (NY 1962).

Brigadoon (Loewe-Lerner). RCA (NY 1947); Columbia.

By Jupiter (Rodgers-Hart). RCA (NY 1967).

By the Beautiful Sea (Schwartz-Fields). Capitol (NY 1954).

Bye Bye Birdie (Strouse-Adams). Columbia (NY 1960); Mercury (L 1961).

Cabaret (Kander-Ebb). Columbia (NY 1966); CBS (L 1968).

Cabin in the Sky (Duke-Latouche). Capitol (NY 1964).

Call Me Madam (Berlin). RCA (NY 1950); Decca (NY 1950); M-E (L 1952).

Call Me Mister (Rome). Decca 10" (NY 1946).

Cambridge Circus (Oddie). Odeon (L 1963).

Camelot (Loewe-Lerner). Columbia * (NY 1960); CBS (L 1964).

Can-Can (Porter). Capitol (NY 1953); M-E (L 1954).

Candide (Bernstein-Wilbur). Columbia (NY 1956); Columbia (2) (NY 1974).

Canterbury Tales (Hill, Hawkins-Coghill). Decca (L 1968); Capitol (NY 1969).

Card, The (Trent-Hatch). Pye (L 1973).

Careless Rapture (Novello-Hassall). EMI-Columbia; WRC (L 1936).

Carmen Jones (Bizet-Hammerstein). Decca (NY 1943).

Carnival (Merrill). MGM (NY 1961); Odeon (L 1963).

Carousel (Rodgers-Hammerstein). Decca (NY 1945); Command; RCA.

Cat and the Fiddle, The (Kern-Hammerstein). Epic.

Catch My Soul (Pohlman-Zoghby-Good). Polydor (L 1970).

Celebration (Schmidt-Jones). Capitol (NY 1969).

Charlie Girl (Heneker-Taylor). CBS (L 1965).

Chicago (Kander-Ebb). Arista (NY 1975).

Chocolate Soldier, The (Straus-Stange). RCA (2).

Chorus Line, A (Hamlisch-Kleban). Columbia (NY 1975).

Christine (Fain-Webster). Columbia (NY 1960).

Chrysanthemum (Stewart-Phillips, Chancellor). Pye (L 1958).

Chu Chin Chow (Norton-Asche). MFP.

Cindy (Brandon). ABC (NY 1964).

Coco (Previn-Lerner). Paramount (NY 1969).

Come Spy with Me (Blackburn). Decca (L 1966).

Company (Sondheim). Columbia (NY 1970); CBS (L 1972).

Conversation Piece (Coward). WRC, M-E (L 1934); Columbia (2).

Cradle Will Rock, The (Blitzstein). Amer. Legacy (NY 1937); MGM (2) (NY 1964).

Cranks (Addison-Cranko). HMV (L 1960).

Crest of the Wave (Novello-Hassall). WRC (L 1937).

Crooked Mile, The (Greenwell-Wildeblood). HMV (L 1959).

Cry for Us All (Leigh-Alfred, Robinson). Project 3 (NY 1970).

Cyrano (Lewis-Burgess). A&M (2) (NY 1973).

Dames at Sea (Wise-Haimsohn, Miller). Columbia (NY 1968).

Damn Yankees (Adler-Ross). RCA (NY 1955).

Dancing Years, The (Novello-Hassall). WRC (L 1939); RCA (L 1968).

Darling of the Day (Styne-Harburg). RCA (NY 1968).

Dear World (Herman). Columbia (NY 1969).

Desert Song, The (Romberg-Harbach, Hammerstein). M-E (L 1927); Columbia; Angel; RCA; RD.

Destry Rides Again (Rome). Decca (NY 1959).

Divorce Me, Darling! (Wilson). Decca (L 1965).

Do I Hear a Waltz? (Rodgers-Sondheim). Columbia (NY 1965).

Do Re Mi (Styne-Comden, Green). RCA (NY 1960).

Donnybrook! (Burke). Kapp (NY 1961).

Dont Bother Me, I Cant Cope (Grant). Polydor (NY 1972).

Dude (MacDermot-Ragni). Kilmarnock (NY 1972).

Eileen (Herbert-Blossom). Camden.

Ernest in Love (Pockriss-Croswell). Columbia (NY 1960).

Ever Green (Rodgers-Hart). M-E (L 1930).

Expresso Bongo (Heneker-Norman-More). Nixa (L 1958).

Fade Out—Fade In (Styne-Comden, Green). ABC (NY 1964).

Family Affair, A (Kander-Goldman, Goldman). UA (NY 1962).

Fanny (Rome). RCA (NY 1954).

Fantasticks, The (Schmidt-Jones). MGM (NY 1960).

Fiddler on the Roof (Bock-Harnick). RCA * (NY 1964); CBS (L 1967).

Fings Ain't Wot They Used t'Be (Bart). Decca (L 1960).

Finian's Rainbow (Lane-Harburg). Columbia (NY 1947), RCA (NY 1960).

Fiorello! (Bock-Harnick). Capitol (NY 1959).

First Impressions (Paxton-Goldman-Weiss). Columbia (NY 1959).

Flahooley (Fain-Harburg). Capitol (NY 1951).

Flora, the Red Menace (Kander-Ebb). RCA (NY 1965).

Flower Drum Song (Rodgers-Hammerstein). Columbia * (NY 1958); Angel (L 1960).

Fly Blackbird (Jackson-Hatch). Mercury (NY 1962).

Follies (Sondheim). Capitol (NY 1971).

Follow that Girl (Slade-Reynolds). HMV (L 1960).

Four Musketeers!, The (Johnson-Kretzmer). Philips (L 1967).

Free as Air (Slade-Reynolds). Oriole (L 1957).

Funny Face (Gershwin-Gershwin). WRC, M-E (L 1928).

Funny Girl (Styne-Merrill). Capitol * (NY 1964).

Funny Thing Happened on the Way to the Forum, A (Sondheim). Capitol (NY 1962).

Gay Life, The (Schwartz-Dietz). Capitol (NY 1961).

Gay's the Word (Novello-Melville). WRC (L 1951).

Gentlemen Prefer Blondes (Styne-Robin). Columbia (NY 1949); Odeon (L 1962).

George M! (Cohan). Columbia (NY 1968).

Girl Crazy (Gershwin-Gershwin). Columbia.

Girl in Pink Tights, The (Romberg-Robin). Columbia (NY 1954).

Girl Who Came to Supper, The (Coward). Columbia (NY 1963).

Glamorous Night (Novello-Hassall). WRC (L 1935).

Godspell (Schwartz). Bell * (NY 1971).

Golden Apple, The (Moross-Latouche). Elektra (NY 1954).

Golden Boy (Strouse-Adams). Capitol (NY 1964).

Golden Rainbow (Marks). Calendar (NY 1968).

Goldilocks (Anderson-Ford, Kerr, Kerr). Columbia (NY 1958).

Gone with the Wind (Rome). EMI-Columbia (L 1972).

Good Companions, The (Previn-Mercer). EMI (L 1974).

Good Old Bad Old Days, The (Newley-Bricusse). EMI (L 1972).

Goodtime Charley (Grossman-Hackaday). RCA (NY 1975).

Grab Me a Gondola (Gilbert-More). HMV (L 1956).

Grass Harp, The (Richardson-Elmslie). PS (NY 1971).

Grease (Jacobs-Casey). MGM (NY 1972).

Greenwich Village USA (Bargy-Gehrecke-Corey). 20th Fox (2) (NY 1960).

Greenwillow (Loesser). RCA (NY 1960).

Guys and Dolls (Loesser). Decca (NY 1950).

Gypsy (Styne-Sondheim). Columbia (NY 1959); RCA (L 1973).

Hair (MacDermot-Ragni, Rado). RCA * (NY 1967); RCA (NY 1968); Atco (L 1968); Polydor (L 1968).

Half a Sixpence (Heneker). Decca (L 1963); RCA (NY 1965).

Half-Past Wednesday (Colby-Jonas). Columbia (NY 1962).

Hallelujah, Baby! (Styne–Comden, Green). Columbia (NY 1967).

Hans Andersen (Loesser). Pye (L 1974).

Happiest Girl in the World, The (Offenbach-Harburg). Columbia (NY 1961).

Happy Hunting (Karr-Dubey). RCA (NY 1956).

Happy Time, The (Kander-Ebb). RCA (NY 1968).

Hazel Flagg (Styne-Hilliard). RCA (NY 1953).

Hello, Dolly! (Herman). RCA * (NY 1964); RCA (L 1965); RCA (NY 1967).

Henry, Sweet Henry (Merrill). ABC (NY 1967).

Here's Love (Willson). Columbia (NY 1963).

High Button Shoes (Styne-Cahn). Camden (NY 1947).

High Spirits (Martin-Gray). ABC (NY 1964); Pye (L 1964).

His Monkey Wife (Wilson). President (L 1971).

Hit the Deck (Youmans-Robin, Grey). WRC, Stanyan (L 1927); Epic.

House of Flowers (Arlen-Capote). Columbia (NY 1954); UA (NY 1968).

How Now, Dow Jones (Bernstein-Leigh). RCA (NY 1967).

How to Steal an Election (Brand). RCA (NY 1968).

How to Succeed in Business Without Really Trying (Loesser). RCA (NY 1961).

I Can Get It for You Wholesale (Rome). Columbia (NY 1962).

I Do! I Do! (Schmidt-Jones). RCA (NY 1966); RCA (L 1968).

I Had a Ball (Freeman-Lawrence). Mercury (NY 1964).

Illya Darling (Hadjidakis-Darion). UA (NY 1967).

Inner City (Miller-Merriam). RCA (NY 1971).

Instant Marriage (Holloway-Grant). Oriole (L 1964).

Irene (Tierney-McCarthy). M-E (L 1920); Columbia (NY 1973).

Irma la Douce (Monnot-More, Heneker, Norman). Philips (L 1958); Columbia (NY 1960).

Isabel's a Jezebel (MacDermot-Dumaresq). UA (L 1970).

It's a Bird It's a Plane It's Superman (Strouse-Adams). Columbia (NY 1966).

Jamaica (Arlen-Harburg). RCA (NY 1957).

Jeeves (Webber-Ayckbourne). MCA (L 1975).

Jennie (Schwartz-Dietz). RCA (NY 1963).

Jesus Christ Superstar (Webber-Rice). Decca * (NY 1971); Decca (L 1972).

Jimmy (Jacob-Jacob). RCA (NY 1969).

Johnny Johnson (Weill-Green). Heliodor.

Johnny the Priest (Hopkins-Powell). Decca (L 1960).

Jorrocks (Heneker). HMV (L 1966).

Joseph and the Amazing Technicolor Dreamcoat (Webber-Rice). Scepter (L 1973).

Juno (Blitzstein). Columbia (NY 1959).

Kean (Wright-Forrest). Columbia (NY 1961).

King and I, The (Rodgers-Hammerstein). Decca (NY 1951); Philips (L 1953); RCA (NY 1964); Columbia.

King Kong (Matshikiza-Williams). Decca (L 1961).

King's Rhapsody (Novello-Hassall). WRC (L 1949); EMI-Columbia.

Kismet (Borodin-Wright-Forrest). Columbia (NY 1953); RCA (NY 1965).

Kiss Me, Kate (Porter). Columbia, Capitol (NY 1948); WRC (L 1951).

Kwamina (Adler). Capitol (NY 1961).

Lady, Be Good! (Gershwin-Gershwin). WRC, M-E (L 1926).

Lady in the Dark (Weill-Gershwin). RCA (NY 1941); Columbia.

Last Sweet Days of Isaac, The (Ford-Cryer). RCA (NY 1970).

Leave It to Jane (Kern-Wodehouse). Strand (NY 1959).

Let It Ride! (Livingston-Evans). RCA (NY 1961).

Li'l Abner (de Paul-Mercer). Columbia (NY 1956).

Lilac Time (Schubert, Berté, Clutsam-Ross). Angel.

Little Mary Sunshine (Besoyan). Capitol (NY 1959).

Little Me (Coleman-Leigh). RCA (NY 1962); WRC (L 1964).

Little Night Music, A (Sondheim). Columbia (NY 1973); RCA (L 1975).

Littlest Revue, The (Duke-Nash). PS (NY 1956).

Lock Up Your Daughters (Johnson-Bart). Decca, London (L 1959).

Look, Ma, I'm Dancin' (Martin). Decca 10" (NY 1948).

Look Who's Here (Dicks). HMV (L 1960).

Lord Chamberlain Regrets, The (Cass-Myers). Pye (L 1961).

Lorelei (Styne-Robin, Comden, Green). MGM (NY 1974).

Lost in the Stars (Weill-Anderson). Decca (NY 1949).

Lute Song (Scott-Hanighen). Decca (NY 1946).

Mack & Mabel (Herman). ABC (NY 1974).

Mad Show, The (Rodgers-Barer). Columbia (NY 1966).

Maggie Flynn (Peretti-Creatore-Weiss). RCA (NY 1968).

Maggie May (Bart). Decca (L 1964).

Magic Show, The (Schwartz). Bell (NY 1974).

Maid of the Mountains, The (Fraser Simson-Graham). WRC (L 1917).

Make a Wish (Martin). RCA (NY 1951).

Make Me an Offer (Heneker-Norman). HMV (L 1959).

Mame (Herman). Columbia * (NY 1966).

Man of La Mancha (Leigh-Darion). Kapp * (NY 1965); Decca (2) (L 1968).

Man of Magic (Wylam-Morley, Cash). CBS (L 1966).

Match Girls, The (Russell-Owen). Pye (L 1966).

Me and Juliet (Rodgers-Hammerstein). RCA (NY 1953).

Me Nobody Knows, The (Friedman-Holt). Atlantic (NY 1970).

Merry Widow, The (Lehár-Ross). Columbia; Angel; Decca.

Mexican Hayride (Porter). Decca 10" (NY 1944).

Milk and Honey (Herman). RCA (NY 1961).

Minnie's Boys (Grossman-Hackaday). Project 3 (NY 1970).

Miss Liberty (Berlin). Columbia (NY 1949).

Mlle. Modiste (Herbert-Blossom). RD.

Most Happy Fella, The (Loesser). Columbia (3) (NY 1956); Angel (L 1960).

Mr. and Mrs. (Taylor). CBS (L 1968).

Mr. President (Berlin). Columbia (NY 1962); RCA.

Mr. Wonderful (Bock-Weiss, Holofcener). Decca (NY 1956).

Music in the Air (Kern-Hammerstein). RCA.

Music Man, The (Willson). Capitol * (NY 1957); Odeon, Stanyan (L 1961).

My Fair Lady (Loewe-Lerner). Columbia * (NY 1956); Columbia (L 1958).

Naughty Marietta (Herbert-Young). Capitol; RD.

Nervous Set, The (Wolf-Landesman). Columbia (NY 1959).

New Faces of 1952 (misc.). RCA (NY 1952).

New Faces of 1956 (misc.). RCA (NY 1956).

New Faces of 1968 (misc.). Warner (NY 1968).

New Girl in Town (Merrill). RCA (NY 1957).

New Moon, The (Romberg-Hammerstein). M-E (L 1929); Capitol; RD.

No, No, Nanette (Youmans-Caesar-Harbach). WRC, Stanyan (L 1925); Columbia (NY 1971); CBS (L 1973).

No Strings (Rodgers). Capitol (NY 1962); Atlantic.

Now Is the Time for All Good Men (Ford-Cryer). Columbia (NY 1967).

Nymph Errant (Porter). MFP, M-E, WRC (L 1933).

Of Thee I Sing (Gershwin-Gershwin). Capitol (NY 1952).

Oh Captain! (Livingston-Evans). Columbia (NY 1958).

Oh, Kay! (Gershwin-Gershwin). Columbia; 20th Fox (NY 1960).

Oh What a Lovely War (misc.). Decca (L 1963); London (NY 1964).

Oklahoma! (Rodgers-Hammerstein). Decca (NY 1943); Stanyan (L 1947); Columbia.

Oliver! (Bart). Decca (L 1960); RCA * (NY 1963).

On a Clear Day You Can See Forever (Lane-Lerner). Columbia (NY 1965).

On the Brighter Side (misc.). London (L 1961).

On the Level (Grainer-Millar). CBS (L 1966).

On the Town (Bernstein-Comden, Green). Decca (NY 1944); Columbia (NY 1944); CBS (L 1963).

On Your Toes (Rodgers-Hart). Columbia; Decca (NY 1954).

Once Upon a Mattress (Rodgers-Barer). Kapp (NY 1959); HMV (L 1960).

110 in the Shade (Schmidt-Jones). RCA (NY 1963).

One Over the Eight (Mulcahey-Law). London (L 1961).

One Touch of Venus (Weill-Nash). Decca (NY 1943).

Operette (Coward). WRC, M-E (L 1938).

Our Man Crichton (Lee-Kretzmer). Polyphone (L 1964).

Out of This World (Porter). Columbia (NY 1950).

Over Here (Sherman-Sherman). Columbia (NY 1974).

Paint Your Wagon (Loewe-Lerner). RCA (NY 1951).

Pacific Overtures (Sondheim). RCA (NY 1976).

Pajama Game, The (Adler-Ross). Columbia (NY 1954); HMV (L 1955).

Pal Joey (Rodgers-Hart). Columbia (NY 1940); Capitol (NY 1952).

Parade (Herman). Kapp (NY 1960).

Passion Flower Hotel (Barry-Peacock). CBS (L 1965).

Perchance to Dream (Novello). EMI-Columbia.

Peter Pan (Styne-Comden, Green; Charlap-Leigh). RCA (NY 1954).

Peter Pan (Bernstein). Columbia (NY 1950).

Phil the Fluter (French-Heneker). Philips (L 1969).

Pickwick (Ornadel-Bricusse). Philips (L 1963).

Pieces of Eight (Wilson; Johnson-Mulcahey-Law). Decca (L 1959).

Pins and Needles (Rome). Columbia.

Pipe Dream (Rodgers-Hammerstein). RCA (NY 1955).

Plain and Fancy (Hague-Horwitt). Capitol (NY 1955); Dot (L 1956).

Polonaise (Chopin-Kaper-Latouche). Camden.

Porgy and Bess (Gershwin-Heyward-Gershwin). Mark 56 (NY 1935); Camden; Decca (NY 1942); RCA (L 1952); Odyssey (3).

Primrose (Gershwin-Carter). WRC; M-E (L 1924).

Promenade (Carmines-Fornes). RCA (NY 1969).

Promises, Promises (Bacharach-David). UA (NY 1968); UA (L 1969).

Purlie (Geld-Udell). Ampex (NY 1970).

Raisin (Woldin-Brittan). Columbia (NY 1973).

Red Mill, The (Herbert-Blossom). Decca; Capitol; RD.

Redhead (Hague-Fields). RCA (NY 1959).

Regina (Blitzstein). Columbia (NY 1949).

Rio Rita (Tierney-McCarthy). M-E (L 1930).

Riverwind (Jennings). London (NY 1962).

Roar of the Greasepaint—The Smell of the Crowd, The (Bricusse-Newley). RCA (NY 1965).

Robert and Elizabeth (Grainer-Millar). HMV (L 1964).

Roberta (Kern-Harbach). Columbia; Decca; Capitol; RD.

Rocky Horror Show, The (O'Brien). UK (L 1973).

Rose-Marie (Friml-Harbach, Hammerstein). RCA.

Rothschilds, The (Bock-Harnick). Columbia (NY 1970).

Sail Away (Coward). Capitol (NY 1961); HMV, Stanyan (L 1962).

St. Louis Woman (Arlen-Mercer). Capitol (NY 1946).

Salad Days (Slade-Reynolds). Oriole (L 1954).

Sally (Kern-Grey). M-E (L 1921).

Salvation (Link-Courtney). Capitol (NY 1969).

Sandhog (Robinson-Salt). Vanguard (NY 1954).

Saratoga (Arlen-Mercer). RCA (NY 1959).

Say, Darling (Styne-Comden, Green). RCA (NY 1958).

Secret Life of Walter Mitty, The (Carr-Shuman). Columbia (NY 1964).

Seesaw (Coleman-Fields). Buddah (NY 1973).

Set to Music (Coward). JJC (NY 1939).

Seventeen (Kent-Gannon), RCA (NY 1951).

1776 (Edwards). Columbia (NY 1969); Columbia (L 1970).

Seventh Heaven (Young-Unger). Decca (NY 1955).

70, Girls, 70 (Kander-Ebb). Columbia (NY 1971).

Share My Lettuce (Statham-Gowers-Gascoigne). Pye (L 1957).

She Loves Me (Bock-Harnick). MGM (2) (NY 1963).

Shenandoah (Geld-Udell). RCA (NY 1975).

Shoestring '57 (misc.). PS (NY 1957).

Shoestring Revue (misc.). PS (NY 1955).

Show Boat (Kern-Hammerstein). Columbia (NY 1932); Columbia (NY 1946); RCA (NY 1966); EMI, Stanyan (2) (L 1971).

Show Girl (Gaynor). Roulette (NY 1961).

Silk Stockings (Porter). RCA (NY 1955).

Simply Heavenly (Martin-Hughes). Columbia (NY 1957).

Sing a Rude Song (Grainer-Brahms-Sherrin). Polydor (L 1970).

Skyscraper (Van Heusen-Cahn). Capitol (NY 1965).

Song of Norway (Grieg-Wright-Forrest). Decca (NY 1944); Columbia (NY 1959); Angel; RD.

Sound of Music, The (Rodgers-Hammerstein). Columbia * (NY 1959); HMV (L 1961).

South Pacific (Rodgers-Hammerstein). Columbia * (NY 1949); Columbia (NY 1967).

Stop the World—I Want to Get Off (Bricusse-Newley). Decca (L 1961); London (NY 1962).

Street Scene (Weill-Hughes). Columbia (NY 1947).

Student Prince in Heidelberg, The (Romberg-Donnelly). M-E (L 1926); Columbia; Capitol; Decca; RD.

Subways Are for Sleeping (Styne-Comden, Green). Columbia (NY 1961).

Sugar (Styne-Merrill). UA (NY 1972).

Summer Song (Dvorak-Grun-Maschwitz). Philips (L 1956).

Sunny (Kern-Harbach, Hammerstein). Stanyan (L 1926).

Sweet Charity (Coleman-Fields). Columbia (NY 1966); CBS (L 1967).

Sweethearts (Herbert-Smith). Camden.

Take Me Along (Merrill). RCA (NY 1959).

Tenderloin (Bock-Harnick). Capitol (NY 1960).

Texas, Li'l Darlin' (Dolan-Mercer). Decca 10″ (NY 1949).

This Is the Army (Berlin). Decca 10″ (NY 1942).

Three Musketeers, The (Friml-Grey). M-E (L 1930).

Three Wishes for Jamie (Blane). Capitol (NY 1952).

Threepenny Opera, The (Weill-Blitzstein). MGM (NY 1954).

Time for Singing, A (Morris-Freedman). Warner (NY 1966).

Tip-Toes (Gershwin-Gershwin). M-E (L 1926).

Tom Brown's Schooldays (Andrews-Maitland, Maitland). Decca (L 1972).

Tonight at 8:30 (Coward). M-E (L 1936).

Top Banana (Mercer). Capitol (NY 1951).

Touch (Long-Crozier). Ampex (NY 1970).

Tovarich (Pokriss-Croswell). Capitol (NY 1963).

Tree Grows in Brooklyn, A (Schwartz-Fields). Columbia (NY 1951).

Trelawney (Slade). Decca (L 1972).

Twang!! (Bart). UA (L 1965).

Two by Two (Rodgers-Charnin). Columbia (NY 1970).

Two Cities (Wayne-Wayne). Columbia (L 1969).

Two Gentlemen of Verona (MacDermot-Guare). ABC (2) (NY 1971); RSO (L 1973).

Two on the Aisle (Styne-Comden, Green). Decca (NY 1951).

Two's Company (Duke-Nash). RCA (NY 1952).

Unsinkable Molly Brown, The (Willson). Capitol (NY 1960).

Up in Central Park (Romberg-Fields). Decca (NY 1945).

Vagabond King, The (Friml-Hooker). Capitol; Decca; RCA; RD.

Valmouth (Wilson) Pye (L 1958).

Virtue in Danger (Bernard-Dehn). Decca (L 1963).

Wait a Minim! (misc.). London (NY 1966).

Walking Happy (Van Heusen-Cahn). Capitol (NY 1966).

Water Gipsies, The (Ellis-Herbert). Dot (L 1956).

Wayward Way, The (Huycke-Howe). EMI (L 1964).

West Side Story (Bernstein-Sondheim). Columbia * (NY 1957).

What Makes Sammy Run? (Drake). Columbia (NY 1964).

Where's Charley? (Loesser). Columbia, M-E (L 1958).

White Horse Inn (Benatzky-Stolz-Graham). Angel.

Whoop-Up! (Charlap-Gimbel). MGM (NY 1958).

Wildcat (Coleman-Leigh). RCA (NY 1960).

Wildflower (Youmans-Harbach, Hammerstein). M-E (L 1926).

Wish You Were Here (Rome). RCA (NY 1952).

Wiz, The (Smalls). Atlantic (NY 1975).

Wonderful Town (Bernstein-Comden, Green). Decca (NY 1953).

Young Visiters, The (Kellam-Ashton). RCA (L 1968).

Your Own Thing (Hester-Apolinar). RCA (NY 1968).

You're a Good Man, Charlie Brown (Gesner). MGM (NY 1967).

Ziegfeld Follies (misc.). Veritas; Pelican.

Zorbá (Kander-Ebb). Capitol (NY 1968).

Zulu and the Zayda, The (Rome). Columbia (NY 1965).

Performers

For writers featured in their own works, see *Composers & Lyricists.*

Andrews, Julie
  Broadway's Fair Julie, Columbia
  Sings, RCA
Astaire, Fred
  The Astaire Story, Clef (4)
  Three Evenings, Choreo
  Fred Astaire, Vik
Baddeley, Hermione
  A Taste of Hermione Baddeley, Prestige
Bailey, Pearl
  Applause, Command
  Songs by Harold Arlen, Roulette
Ballard, Kaye
  Fanny Brice Story in Song, MGM
Bernardi, Herschel
  Broadway's Greatest Hits, Harmony
Bigley, Isabel, & Stephen Douglass
  Rodgers & Hammerstein, Design
Blaine, Vivian
  Broadway's All Time Hits, Mercury
Brice, Fanny
  Songs She Made Famous, AF
  Fanny Brice—Helen Morgan, RCA
Bruce, Carol
  The Fabulous Carol Bruce, Tops
Buchanan, Jack
  The Debonair Jack Buchanan, MFP
  Jack Buchanan, WRC
Burnett, Carol
  How They Stopped the Show, Decca
Cantor, Eddie
  A Date with Eddie Cantor, AF
  The Best of Eddie Cantor, Vik

Carroll, Diahann
Best Beat Forward, Vik
Sings Harold Arlen, RCA
Channing, Carol
Carol Channing, Vanguard
Show Girl, Roulette
Comden, Betty
Remember These, Ava
Cook, Barbara
At Carnegie Hall, Columbia
From the Heart, Urania
Courtneidge, Cicely, & Jack Hulbert
Cicely Courtneidge & Jack Hulbert, WRC
Davis, Sammy
Forget-Me-Nots for First Nighters, Decca
Belts the Best of Broadway, Reprise
If I Ruled the World, Reprise
Day, Edith
Edith Day, WRC
Delysia, Alice
Alice Delysia, WRC
Engel, Lehman
Ballet on Broadway, PS
Curtain Going Up, Columbia
Etting, Ruth
Original Recordings, Columbia
Gingold, Hermione
La Gingold, Dolphin
Goulet, Robert
In Person, Columbia
Gray, Dolores
Warm Brandy, Capitol
Grenfell, Joyce
Requests the Pleasure, Philips
At Home, HMV
Presenting Joyce Grenfell, Elektra
Grey, Joel
Only the Beginning, Columbia
Live, Columbia
Grimes, Tammy
Tammy Grimes, Off-Bway
Tammy Grimes, Columbia
Hale, Binnie
Spread a Little Happiness, WRC
Holliday, Judy
Trouble Is a Man, Columbia
Holman, Libby
The Legendary Libby Holman, M-E
Horne, Lena
Give the Lady What She Wants, RCA
At the Sands, RCA
Howes, Bobby
She's My Lovely, WRC

Husmann, Ron
Double Take, Capitol
Jolson, Al
Best of Al Jolson, Decca (2)
Jones, Shirley, & Jack Cassidy
Love Songs, Columbia
Kaye, Danny
Entertains, Columbia 10″
Best of Danny Kaye, Decca
Kert, Larry
Sings Leonard Bernstein, Epic
Kiley, Richard
Rodgers & Hammerstein Songbook, Camden (2)
Lawrence, Carol
Tonight at 8:30, Chancellor
Lawrence, Gertrude
The Incomparable Gertrude Lawrence, Ace of Clubs
A Remembrance, Decca
The Star Herself, MFP
Noël & Gertie, Parlophone
Noël & Gertie & Bea, Parlophone
Laye, Evelyn
The Entrancing Evelyn Laye, MFP
Lee, Michele
A Taste of the Fantastic, Columbia
Lenya, Lotte
Kurt Weill American Theatre Songs, Columbia
Lillie, Beatrice
Sings, JJC
30 Minutes with Beatrice Lillie, Liberty 10″
An Evening with Beatrice Lillie, London
Auntie Bea, London
Noël & Gertie & Bea, Parlophone
Martin, Mary
Sings for You, Columbia 10″
Anything Goes/ The Band Wagon, Columbia
Sings—Richard Rodgers Plays, RCA
Matthews, Jessie
Charlie Girl, MFP
Looking Over My Shoulder, MFP
McNair, Barbara
Front Row Center, Coral
Merman, Ethel
A Musical Autobiography, Decca (3)
Merman—Roberti—West, Columbia
Sings Cole Porter, JJC
Her Greatest, Reprise
Sings Merman, London
Ethel's Ridin' High, London

Michell, Keith
  Sings Broadway, Spark
Millar, Gertie
  Our Miss Gibbs, etc., WRC
Minnelli, Liza
  Liza! Liza!, Capitol
  Liza with a Z, Columbia
Morgan, Helen
  Helen Morgan, AF
  Fanny Brice—Helen Morgan, RCA
Morse, Robert, & Charles Nelson Reilly
  Jolly Theatrical Season, Capitol
Newley, Anthony
  Who Can I Turn To?, RCA
Orbach, Jerry
  Off-Broadway, MGM
Powell, Jane
  Can't We Be Friends?, Verve
  Sings, MGM
Richman, Harry
  His Broadway and Hers, M-E
Ritchard, Cyril
  Odd Songs and a Poem, Dolphin 10"
Roberts, Joan
  Joan Roberts, Quality
Rogers, Ginger
  Hello, Ginger, Citel
Roth, Lillian
  I'll Cry Tomorrow, Epic
Secombe, Harry
  Phenomenal Voice of Harry Secombe, Philips
Sothern, Ann
  Sothern Exposure, Zenith
Steele, Tommy
  Sixpenny Millionaire, Liberty
Streisand, Barbra
  My Name Is Barbra Two, Columbia
  People, Columbia
  Color Me Barbra, Columbia
Stritch, Elaine
  Elaine Stritch, Dolphin
Suzuki, Pat
  Broadway '59, RCA
Swenson, Inga
  I'm Old Fashioned, Liberty
Tucker, Sophie
  His Broadway and Hers, M-E
Van Dyke, Dick
  Songs I Like, Command
Verdon, Gwen
  The Girl I Left Home For, RCA
Walker, Nancy
  I Can Cook, Too, Dolphin
  I Hate Men, Camden
Waters, Ethel
  On Stage & Screen, Columbia
  Miss Ethel Waters, M-E
Wright, Martha
  Censored, Jubilee
Wyler, Gretchen
  Wild, Wyler, Wildest, Jubilee

Composers & Lyricists

Asterisk indicates composer &/or lyricist is featured on the recording.

Arlen, Harold
  Arlen & His Songs,* Capitol
  Harold Sings Arlen,* Columbia
  Music of Harold Arlen,* Columbia
  Music of Harold Arlen,* Walden (2)
  Harold Arlen Sings,* Mark 56 (2)
  Pearl Bailey: Songs by Harold Arlen, Roulette
  Diahann Carroll Sings, RCA
  Lee Wiley Sings, M-E
  Arlen Revisited, PS
Berlin, Irving
  Jay Blackton: Let Me Sing & I'm Happy, Epic
  Max Morath: The Ragtime Years, Vanguard
  All by Myself, M-E (3)
  Berlin Revisited, PS
Bernstein, Leonard
  Drake & Peters: Music of Bernstein, Command
  Larry Kert Sings, Epic
Blake, Eubie
  86 Years of Eubie Blake,* Columbia (2)
Blitzstein, Marc
  Theatre Compositions,* Westminster
Caesar, Irving
  And Then I Wrote,* Coral
Cahn, Sammy
  Words and Music,* RCA
Cohan, George M.
  Mickey Rooney Sings, RCA
Comden, Betty & Adolph Green
  A Party,* Capitol
  Perform Their Own Songs,* Heritage
  Blossom Dearie Sings, Verve
Coward, Noël
  Sail Away,* Capitol
  Noël Coward Album,* Columbia (2)
  Noël Coward's Theatre,* Eclipse
  We Were Dancing,* M-E
  The Master Sings,* MFP
  A Talent to Amuse,* Parlophone
  Noël and Gertie,* Parlophone
  Noël and Gertie and Bea,* Parlophone

*1899–1973,** Stanyan
Carmen McRae: Mad About the Man, Decca
Bobby Short Is Mad About Noël Coward, Atlantic (2)
Joan Sutherland Sings, London
Oh Coward!, Bell (2)
Cowardy Custard, RCA (2)
Coward Revisited, PS
Coleman, Cy
*Sings Cy Coleman,** Columbia
DeSylva, Brown, & Henderson
Gordon MacRae: Best Things in Life Are Free, Capitol
DeSylva, Brown, & Henderson Revisited, PS
Duke, Vernon
Vernon Duke Revisited, PS
Friml, Rudolf
*Indian Love Call,** Westminster
Nathaniel Shilkret: Music of Friml, Camden
Gershwin, George
George Bassman: The Gershwin Years, Decca (3)
Frances Gershwin: For George & Ira, M-E
*Gershwin Plays Gershwin & Kern,** Klavier
*Gershwin by Gershwin,** Mark 56 (2)
*Gershwin Conducts Porgy & Bess,** Mark 56
*From Tin Pan Alley to Broadway,** Mark 56
*At the Piano,** 20th-Fox
Bobby Short Is K-ra-zy for Gershwin, Atlantic (2)
Whyte & Hudson: We Like a Gershwin Tune, M-E
Lee Wiley Sings, M-E
'S Wonderful 'S Marvelous 'S Gershwin, Daybreak
Gershwin Revisited, PS
Gershwin Rarities, Walden (2)
Gershwin in London, WRC
Gershwin, Ira
Mitzi Gaynor Sings, Verve
Ira Gershwin Revisited, PS
Lyrics by Ira Gershwin, Walden
Hammerstein, Oscar II
*Recorded Portrait,** MGM
Hart, Moss
*Moss Hart,** Westminster
Herbert, Victor
Richard Crooks: Music of Herbert, Camden

Robert Shaw: Immortal Herbert, RCA
Herman, Jerry
*Hello, Jerry,** UA
Kern, Jerome
George Byron: Premiere Performance, Atlantic
Leonard Joy: Music of Kern, Camden
Wrightson & Hunt: A Night with Kern, Columbia
Kern Revisited, PS
All the Things You Are, M-E
Kern in London, WRC, M-E
Melodies of Kern, Walden (2)
Lerner, Alan Jay
*Performs His Own Songs,** Heritage
Lerner Revisited, PS
An Evening with Lerner & Loewe, RCA (2)
MacDermot, Galt
*Disin-Hair-ited,** RCA
*Hair Cuts,** Kilmarnock
Novello, Ivor
Hilda Gueden: My Secret Heart, London
Porter, Cole
Carlyle & Shaver: Cole Porter Songs, Walden
Mabel Mercer Sings, Atlantic
Ethel Merman Sings, JJC
*Cole,** Columbia
Bobby Short Loves Porter, Atlantic (2)
Cesare Siepi: Easy to Love, London
Jeri Southern Meets Porter, Capitol
Lee Wiley Sings, M-E
Decline of the Entire World, Columbia
Porter Revisited, PS
Unpublished Cole Porter, PS
Cole Porter in London, WRC
Rodgers, Richard
Bigley & Douglass: Rodgers & Hammerstein, Design
Carlyle & Shaver: Rodgers & Hart, Walden
Barbara Cook: From the Heart, Urania
Matt Dennis: She Dances Overhead, RCA
Sergio Franchi: Songs of Richard Rodgers, RCA
Richard Kiley: Rodgers & Hammerstein Songbook, Camden (2)
*Mary Martin Sings—Rodgers Plays,** RCA
*Rodgers Conducts NY Philharmonic,** Columbia
*Recorded Portrait,** MGM
Bobby Short Celebrates Rodgers & Hart, Atlantic (2)

Whyte & Hudson: It's Smooth It's Smart It's Rodgers It's Hart, M-E
Lee Wiley Sings, M-E
Rodgers & Hart Revisited, PS (2)
Rodgers & Hart in London, WRC
Romberg, Sigmund
*Dinner Music,** RCA
*Gems of Sigmund Romberg,** RCA 10" (4)
Nathaniel Shilkret: Music of Romberg, Camden
Wrightson & Hunt: A Night with Romberg, Columbia
Rome, Harold
*And Then I Wrote,** Coral
*Fanny,** Heritage 10"
*Harold Sings Rome,** Heritage
*Rome-antics,** Heritage
Schwartz, Arthur & Howard Dietz
Lynn Taylor: I See Your Face Before Me, Grand Award
Mel Tormé: My Kind of Music, Verve
Alone Together, M-E (2)
Schwartz Revisited, PS
Songs by Arthur Schwartz, Walden
Sondheim, Stephen
*A Tribute,** Warner (2)
Styne, Jule
*My Name Is Jule,** UA
Swift, Kay
*Fine & Dandy,** Mark 56 (2)
Weill, Kurt
Georgia Brown Sings, London
Morton Gould: 2 Worlds of Kurt Weill, RCA
Holt & Schlamme: Kurt Weill Cabaret, MGM
Lotte Lenya: American Theatre Songs, Columbia
Felicia Sanders: Songs of Kurt Weill, Time
*Tryout,** Heritage
From Berlin to Broadway, Paramount (2)
Willson, Meredith
*The Music Man,** Capitol
Youmans, Vincent
Through the Years, M-E (2)
Youmans Revisited, PS

Collections

Ace of Clubs
Great Stars of Musical Comedy

Lawrence, Hale, Lorraine, Dickson, Collins, Day, Delysia.
Audio Rarities
Curtain Calls of Yesteryear
Cantor, Brice, Lawrence, Cohan, Morgan, etc.
They Stopped the Show
Cohan, Russell, Dressler, Montgomery & Stone, Weber & Fields, Janis, Ring, Bayes, etc.
Camden
Great Personalities of Broadway
Cohan, Lillie, Morgan, Brice, Merman, Pinza, Vallée.
CBS Legacy
The American Musical Theatre (2)
From *Show Boat* to *Fiddler on the Roof.*
Columbia (EMI)
Theatreland Showstoppers (3)
Original London casts, 1943–1968
Theatreland Showstoppers (2)
Original London casts, 1926–1939.
Decca
They Stopped the Show
Bolger, Drake, Garrett, Gray, Huston, Lawrence, Martin, Raitt, Niesen, Russell, etc.
Discourses
Musical Comedy's Golden Days (1896–1918)
Gower, Boyd, Corrie.
Epic
Great Moments in Show Business
Houston, Robinson, Cantor, Jolson, Durante, etc.
Parlophone
Revue 1912–1918
Millar, Hale, Janis, Compton, Levey, Robey, Lawrence, etc.
Revue 1919–1929
Buchanan, Lillie, Matthews, June, Metaxa, Courtneidge, etc.
Revue 1930–1940
Hale, Mills, Day, Laye, Grenfell, Ritchard, Buck & Bubbles, etc.
RCA
Originals—Musical Comedy (1909–1935)
Cantor, Day, Gallagher & Shean, Groody & King, Holman, Janis, Jolson, Lillie, Morgan, Porter, Powell, Ring, Sissle & Blake.
Show Biz

ADDENDA

NOTE: Wherever possible, additions have been made under entries in the body of the book.

≝ A ≝

Adler, Richard, composer.
  1976 Rex (co-prod. only)
        Music Is (Holt) (also co-prod.)

Annie (1977). Music by Charles Strouse; lyrics by Martin Charnin; book by Thomas Meehan.

NEW YORK: April 21, 1977
ALVIN THEATRE
  Presented by Mike Nichols; directed by Charnin; choreography by Peter Gennaro.
  CAST: Reid Shelton, Andrea McArdle, Dorothy Loudon, Sandy Faison.

LONDON: May 13, 1978
VICTORIA PALACE
  Presented by Michael White; directed by Charnin; choreography by Peter Gennaro.
  CAST: Stratford Johns, Andrea McArdle, Sheila Hancock, Judith Paris.

≝ B ≝

Birch, Patricia, choreographer.
  1976 Music Is
  1977 Happy End
        Hot Grog
  1979 They're Playing Our Song
        Zoot Suit

Bricusse, Leslie, lyricist.
  1978 Kings and Clowns (L) (also comp.)
        Beyond the Rainbow (L) (Trovaioli)

≝ C ≝

Champion, Gower, director, choreographer.
  1976 Rockabye Hamlet
  1977 The Act
  1978 A Broadway Musical

Chorus Line, A.
LONDON: July 22, 1976
DRURY LANE THEATRE; 901 p.
  Presented by Michael White; directed & choreographed by Michael Bennett.
  CAST: Christine Barker, Jane Summerhays, Mitzi Hamilton, Jeff Hyslop, T. Michael Reed, Jean Fraser, Jennifer Ann Lee, Loida Iglesias, Eivind Harum, Sandy Roveta, Steve Baumann, Tommy Aguilar.

Coleman, Cy, composer.
  1977 I Love My Wife (Stewart)
  1978 On the 20th Century
        (Comden, Green)

≝ D ≝

Delfont, Bernard, producer.
  1976 Mardi Gras
  1978 Beyond the Rainbow

Delysia, Alice, actress; d. Brighton, Eng., Feb. 9, 1979.

≝ E ≝

Evita (1978). Music by Andrew Lloyd Webber; lyrics by Tim Rice.

LONDON: June 21, 1978
PRINCE EDWARD THEATRE
  Presented by Robert Stigwood; di-

489

rected by Harold Prince; choreography by Larry Fuller.
CAST: Elaine Paige, Joss Ackland, David Essex.

NEW YORK: Sept. 25, 1979
BROADWAY THEATRE:
CAST: Patti LuPone, Bob Gunton, Mandy Patinkin

❧ F ❧

Feuer, Cy, producer.
1977   The Act
1979   I Remember Mama (dir. only)

Fielding, Harold, producer.
1976   Irene (r)
1977   I Love My Wife
1978   Beyond the Rainbow

Fryer, Robert, producer.
1978   On the 20th Century
1979   Sweeney Todd

❧ G ❧

Gennaro, Peter, choreographer.
1977   Annie
1978   Annie (L)
       Bar Mitzvah Boy (L)
1979   Carmelina

Greenwood, Charlotte, actress; d. Beverly Hills, Cal., Jan. 18, 1978.

Grenfell, Joyce, actress; d. London, Nov. 30, 1979.

❧ H ❧

Harnick, Sheldon, lyricist.
1976   Rex (Rodgers)
1979   Umbrellas of Cherbourg (Legrand)

Horwitt, Arnold B., lyricist; d. Santa Monica, Cal., Oct. 20, 1977.

❧ I ❧

Irene.
LONDON: June 15, 1976
ADELPHI THEATRE; 978 p.
Presented by Harold Fielding; directed by Freddie Carpenter.
CAST: Julie Anthony, Jessie Evans, Eric Flynn, Jon Pertwee, Helen Christie, Janet Mahoney, Jenny Logan.

❧ L ❧

Lerner, Alan Jay, lyricist, librettist.
1976   1600 Pennsylvania Ave. (Bernstein)
1979   Carmelina (Lane)

❧ M ❧

Marre, Albert, director.
1977   Man of LaMancha (r)
1978   Kismet (L) (r)

Marx, Zeppo, actor; d. Palm Springs, Cal., Nov. 30, 1979.

❧ P ❧

Papp, Joseph, producer.
1976   Apple Pie (also dir.)
       The 3-Penny Opera (r)
1977   On the Lock-In
       The Misanthrope
1978   Runaways
       I'm Getting My Act Together and Taking It on the Road
1979   Sancocho
       Dispatches

Prince, Harold, director.
1978 On the 20th Century
        Evita (L)
1979 Sweeney Todd
        Evita

⚜ R ⚜

Ritchard, Cyril, actor; d. Chicago, Dec. 18, 1977.

Rodgers, Richard, composer.
1976 Rex (Harnick)
1979 I Remember Mama (Charnin)

⚜ S ⚜

Smith, Queenie, actress; d. Burbank, Cal., Aug. 5, 1978.

Stein, Joseph, librettist.
1976 So Long 174 Street
1978 King of Hearts
1979 Carmelina

Sweeney Todd (1979). Music & lyrics by Stephen Sondheim; book by Hugh Wheeler.

New York: March 1, 1979
Uris Theatre
Presented by Barr, Woodward, Fryer, Johnson, Richards; directed by Harold Prince; choreography by Larry Fuller.
Cast: Angela Lansbury, Len Cariou, Merle Louise, Sarah Rice, Victor Garber, Ken Jennings.

⚜ T ⚜

Teyte, Maggie, actress, singer; d. London, May 26, 1976.

⚜ W ⚜

White, Onna, choreographer.
1977 I Love My Wife
        I Love My Wife (L)
1978 Working

Wood, Peggy, actress; d. Stamford, Conn., March 18, 1978.

AWARDS AND PRIZES

NY Drama Critics Circle Award for Musical
1976 Pacific Overtures
1977 Annie
1978 Ain't Misbehavin'
1979 Sweeney Todd

Tony Awards
  Musical
1976 A Chorus Line
1977 Annie
1978 Ain't Misbehavin'
1979 Sweeney Todd

Actress in a Musical
1976 Donna McKechnie, *A Chorus Line*
1977 Dorothy Loudon, *Annie*
1978 Liza Minnelli, *The Act*
1979 Angela Lansbury, *Sweeney Todd*

Actor in a Musical
1976 George Rose, *My Fair Lady*
1977 Barry Bostwick, *The Robber Bridegroom*
1978 John Cullum, *On the 20th Century*
1979 Len Cariou, *Sweeney Todd*

AWARDS AND PRIZES

COMPOSER & LYRICIST
1976 Marvin Hamlisch & Edward Kleban, *A Chorus Line*
1977 Charles Strouse & Martin Charnin, *Annie*
1978 Cy Coleman, Betty Comden & Adolph Green, *On the 20th Century*
1979 Stephen Sondheim, *Sweeney Todd*

LIBRETTIST
1976 James Kirkwood & Nicholas Dante, *A Chorus Line*
1977 Thomas Meehan, *Annie*
1978 Betty Comden & Adolph Green, *On the 20th Century*
1979 Hugh Wheeler, *Sweeney Todd*

DIRECTOR
1976 Michael Bennett, *A Chorus Line*
1977 Gene Saks, *I Love My Wife*
1978 Richard Maltby Jr., *Ain't Misbehavin'*
1979 Harold Prince, *Sweeney Todd*

CHOREOGRAPHER
1976 Michael Bennett & Bob Avian, *A Chorus Line*
1977 Peter Gennaro, *Annie*
1978 Bob Fosse, *Dancin'*
1979 Michael Bennett & Bob Avian, *Ballroom*

London "Evening Standard" Award for Musical
1976 A Chorus Line
1977 Elvis
1978 Annie

Society of West End Theatres Award (Wedgie) for Musical
1976 A Chorus Line
1977 The Comedy of Errors
1978 Evita
1979 Songbook

Other DA CAPO titles of interest